# The Compendium of
# CHESTER GOLD & SILVER MARKS
## 1570 to 1962
### From the Chester Assay Office Registers

Chester Assay Office, 13-15 Goss Street, Chester (Courtesy of *Cheshire Life*)

Title Page: (opposite) Arms of the Chester Goldsmiths' Company from the demolished Assay Office (Courtesy of Chester Goldsmiths' Company)

# The Compendium of CHESTER GOLD & SILVER MARKS

## 1570 to 1962

**From the Chester Assay Office Registers**

MAURICE H RIDGWAY, BA, FSA

and

PHILIP T PRIESTLEY, BSc, FSA

## DEDICATION

Dedicated to all goldsmiths and silversmiths, masters, journeymen and apprentices, throughout the British Isles and the Commonwealth, whose work passed through the Chester Assay Office. Also dedicated to the members of the Chester Goldsmiths' Company and the staff who worked at the Chester Assay Office over the centuries.



ISBN 1 85149 447 2

First published in 2004



British Library Cataloguing-in-Publication Data
A catalogue record for this book is available from the British Library

Published in England by the Antique Collectors' Club Ltd
Woodbridge, Suffolk, IP12 4SD

## COMPENDIUM OF CHESTER GOLD & SILVER MARKS

**Contents** **Page**


| | | |
|---|---|---|
| Key to abbreviations | | vi |
| Acknowledgements | | vii |
| Foreword | | viii |
| Introduction | | ix |
| Overview of Chester Plates and Records | | xiv |
| Illustrations | – First copper plate | xvii |
| | – Second copper plate | xviii |
| | – Third copper plate | xix |
| | – Last copper plate of makers' marks | xx |
| | – Last copper plate of assay office marks | xxi |
| | – Assay office punches | xxi |
| | – Page from small punch book | xxii |
| | – Last page in last register | xxii |

**PART 1 ASSAY OFFICE and STANDARD MARKS 1686 to 1962**

| | |
|---|---|
| Date letters 1687 to 1697 and pre-1720 sterling silver marks | 1 |
| Date letters 1701 to 1962 | 2 |
| The Chester City mark | 7 |
| Britannia and post-1720 sterling silver marks | 8 |
| The Leopard's head mark | 9 |
| The Duty mark 1784 to 1890 | 10 |
| Gold marks | 11 |
| Import marks for gold and silver | 13 |

**PART 2 MAKERS' MARKS 1570 to 1962**

| | |
|---|---|
| How to use the makers' marks tables | 17 |
| Pictograms | 19 |
| Tables of Makers' marks | 20 |
| Monograms and cryptic marks | 484 |

| | |
|---|---|
| **Appendices** | 491 |
| Date profile of makers' registrations and assayed silverware | 492 |
| Volume of gold and silver wares assayed at Chester | 493 |
| Assay office expenses and staff salaries | 494 |
| Charges for assays | 496 |
| Liverpool watchcase makers | 497 |
| Thimble makers | 500 |
| Addenda to previous Ridgway publications | 501 |
| Addenda to previous Priestley publication | 502 |
| **Bibliography** | 503 |
| **Subject Index** | 504 |
| **Makers' Names and Marks Index** | 505 |

# KEY TO ABBREVIATIONS

| | | |
|---|---|---|
| * | = | Indicates existence of biography in *Culme* |
| ? | = | Maker's name attribution not well proven |
| B | = | Baillie, *Clockmakers of the World* |
| BAO | = | Birmingham Assay Office |
| BAO### | = | Mark registration reference at BAO |
| *c.* | = | Circa (about) |
| CAO | = | Chester Assay Office |
| cm | = | Centimetre |
| CMC/1 | = | Page 1 of *Clockmakers of Cheshire* by K Appleby |
| Cripps/1 | = | Page 1 of *Old English Plate* by W J Cripps |
| CWCE/1 | = | Page 1 of *Clockmakers & Watchmakers of Central England,* J McKenna, 2002 |
| CWMP | = | Coventry Watch Museum Project Computer Database of all Coventry Makers and Dates Working |
| d | = | Penny (1/240 of a pound sterling) |
| dwt | = | Pennyweight (1/20th of a troy ounce or 1.55g) |
| g | = | Gram |
| (G) | = | Indicates existence of biography in *Grimwade* |
| GMCS/1 | = | Item 1 of *Grosvenor Museum Catalogue of Silver* by P Boughton |
| grn | = | Grain (1/24 part of a troy pennyweight or 0.0648g) |
| GSJW/1 | = | Page 1 of *1861 Directory of Goldsmiths, Silversmiths, Jewellers, Watchmakers, Opticians and Cutlers* |
| GTD | = | *Gore's Trade Directory* |
| in | = | Inch |
| IR1 | = | Inland Revenue Apprenticeship Indenture Tax Records, Kew, London |
| J1 | = | *English Goldsmiths & their Marks*, 1st edition, 1905, by C J Jackson |
| J3 | = | *Jackson's Silver & Gold Marks*, 3rd edition by Ian Pickford, 1989 (Chester chapter by M H Ridgway) |
| KOC/1 | = | Page 1 of *Clock & Watch Trademark Index of European Origin* by K Kochmann, 2nd edition, 1988 |
| LAO | = | London Assay Office |
| LAO## | = | Mark registration reference at LAO |
| LGM | = | London Goldsmiths' Company Minutes |
| LGSJ | = | Entered in *Liverpool 1825 Gazetteer of Goldsmiths, Silversmiths & Jewellers* |
| LLCC | = | Brian Loomes, *Lancashire Clocks & Clockmakers*, David & Charles, 1972 |
| LMS | = | Brian Loomes, *Watch Makers and Clockmakers of the World, Volume 2* |
| LPB/1 | = | Page 1 of Chester Large Punch Book |
| LSD | = | Liverpool Street Directory |
| LTB | = | Liverpool Town Freedom Book |
| MDGC | = | Morris *Directory & Gazetteer of Coventry 1866* |
| MG/1 | = | Page 1 of Margaret A V Gill, *Directory of Newcastle Goldsmiths,* 1980 |
| MR1/1 | = | Page 1 of M H Ridgway Book 1 *Chester Goldsmiths from early times to 1726* |
| MR2/1 | = | Page 1 of M H Ridgway Book 2 *Chester Silver 1727 to 1837* |
| MR3/1 | = | Page 1 of M H Ridgway Book 3 *Chester Silver 1837 to 1962* |
| NAO | = | Newcastle Assay Office |
| oz | = | Ounce Troy (31.1g) |
| P1/1/x2 | = | Plate 1 Square 1, and so on (x2 indicates two similar marks) |
| P2/A/x2 | = | Plate 2 Square A, and so on (x2 indicates two similar marks) |
| P3/A/x2 | = | Plate 3 Square A, and so on (x2 indicates two similar marks) |
| P5/A/# | = | Plate 5 Square A with mark register cross-reference number |
| P9/A/# | = | Plate 9 Square A with mark register cross-reference number |
| P13/A/# | = | Plate 13 Square A with mark register cross-reference number |
| P15/A/# | = | Plate 15 Square A with mark register cross-reference number |
| P21/A/# | = | Plate 21 Square A with mark register cross-reference number |
| PCR-1773 | = | Parliamentary Committee Report of 1773 on State of Assay Offices |
| PDB | = | Chester Plate Duty Books |
| PMR | = | Prescot Museum Records- Watch and Clock Trade |
| PP1/1 | = | Page 1 of P T Priestley, *Watchcase Makers of England 1720 to 1920*, NAWCC Bulletin Supplement #20, 1994 |
| PP2/1 | = | Page 1 of D S Moore and P T Priestley. *Some Account of Liverpool Watchcase Makers 1785-98,* Antiquarian Horology, Summer 1997 |
| PP3/1 | = | Page 1 of P T Priestley, *Early Watchcase Makers of England 1631 to 1720*, NAWCC Special Order Supplement #3, 2000 |
| PTD | = | *Pigot's Trade Directory* |
| R1/1 | = | Page 1 of 1st marks register of Chester |
| R2/1 | = | Page 1 of 2nd marks register of Chester |
| R3/1 | = | Page 1 of 3rd marks register of Chester |
| s | = | Shilling (1/20 pound sterling) |
| § | = | Maker's mark shown less than sixteen times life size |
| SIL/1 | = | Page 1 of *Catalogue of Silver on Exhibition at the Grosvenor Museum, Chester,* 1973 |
| SOT/1 | = | Page 1 of *Chester Silver Exhibition at Sotheby's in conjunction with the Grosvenor Museum, Chester,* 1984 |
| SAO | = | Sheffield Assay Office |
| SAO## | = | Mark registration reference at SAO |
| SGP | = | St George's Parish, Liverpool |
| SNP | = | St Nicholas Parish, Liverpool |
| SP24-33 | = | Small Plates 24 to 33 |
| SPB/1 | = | Page 1 of Chester Small Punch Book |
| SPP | = | St Paul's Parish, Liverpool |
| SPT | = | St Peter's Parish, Liverpool |
| WCI | = | *Watch & Clockmakers of Ireland*, J Stuart and D A Boles, 2000 |
| WCM | = | Watchcase maker |

# ACKNOWLEDGEMENTS

The main *raison d'être* for this Compendium of all known Chester marks lies with the Birmingham Assay Office who became custodians of the Chester Assay Office archives following the Chester Closure Act of 1962. As a result, they field most of the queries from the public on Chester marks and have encouraged the production of this Compendium. They have been particularly generous and hospitable during many visits to the Birmingham Assay Office to research and photograph records through the good offices of the Assay Master, Michael Allchin and his predecessor Bernard Ward. In particular, Phyllis Benedikz, Librarian, has been extremely helpful in finding Birmingham attributions for marks entered at Chester during the period from 1886 to 1894 where Chester registration details no longer exist. Fortunately, it transpires that many silversmiths registered the same mark at Birmingham and Chester. Ruth Moore, Punch Mark clerk and now retired, has also been of enormous assistance checking plates and registers over the years for both authors. Her successor, Linda Moran, must also be thanked for her assistance in handling queries during the final stage of the project.

The authors would also like to express their grateful thanks to Cathlyn and Simon Davidson who toiled diligently over the original drafts making corrections, suggesting modifications and completing the numerous cross-references to the authors' works. We are also deeply indebted to Michael Sherratt who read the script and suggested improvements. The authors would also like to thank John Culme, author of the definitive tome *London Gold & Silversmiths 1838-1914*, who has commented on the Compendium and who has provided extremely helpful advice on handling large numbers of small photographs and layout of the marks. His sequence of incuse and cameo font styles has been followed in this work. Furthermore, his book has helped in the identification of those Chester marks without written records which were also registered at London. The authors are also deeply indebted to Winslow Schrank, a personal friend (of Priestley) and medieval spoon specialist, who carried out the onerous task of cross-referencing thousands of Compendium names to entries in Culme's Biographical Directory.

We must also thank David Beasley, Librarian of the Goldsmiths' Hall, and Ian Pickford, author and broadcaster, for their review of the manuscript and helpful suggestions regarding layout. Peter Boughton, Keeper of Fine Art and Silver at the Grosvenor Museum, Chester, must also be thanked for his generous assistance with regard to photographing the first Chester copper plate which is on exhibition there in the Ridgway Silver Gallery. In particular, we are grateful for his extremely helpful suggestion that each mark or entry without a mark should be given an individual reference number. Grahame Jones, one of the last employees at the Chester Assay Office, is thanked for his first-hand knowledge of assaying and his contribution regarding platinum. The authors are also deeply indebted to Anthony Dove of the Silver Society who kindly provided advice and information regarding gold marks and duty marks.

Dennis Moore, visiting researcher and John Griffiths, Curator of the Prescot Clock Museum are also thanked for their valuable contribution on Liverpool watchcase makers. Thanks are also due Mary Montes of Coventry for her specialist knowledge and help with details of craftsmen in Coventry and its suburbs, Earlsdon and Chapel Fields. The authors are also deeply indebted to Jean Priestley for her assistance with extracting information at Birmingham Assay Office and Birmingham Central Library, and for her substantial contribution to the typing and proof-reading of this Compendium.

Finally, we should like to acknowledge the following who helped to make this publication financially viable:

| | | |
|---|---|---|
| Birmingham Assay Office | Penny Anne and Jeremy Griffin | Lowe & Sons (Chester) |
| Claude Blair | Historic Society of Lancashire and Cheshire | Manifold Trust |
| H L Brown & Son Ltd | Jewellery Society of GB | David Orfeur |
| Helen and Sandy Campbell | Peter Jones | Silver Society of GB |
| Chester Archaeological Society | Leverhulme Trust | South Square Trust |
| Chester Goldsmiths' Company | London Goldsmiths' Company | Dolf Sweerts |
| Cathlyn and Simon Davidson | Joyce Lowe | Alan G Walton |

Reproductions of the marks are based upon small sections of photographs taken by Philip Priestley on Ilford FP2 and Fuji 400-ASA 35-mm film, developed using Kodak C41 colour processing system and printed on Kodak black and white paper by Chalfont Photographic Services, Chalfont St Peter, Buckinghamshire.

In conclusion, the authors would be most grateful for any additional information from readers regarding makers' marks attributions.

# FOREWORD

The publication of this Compendium has been long overdue with the increased interest by a discerning public who naturally, on acquisition of a piece of silver or gold assayed in Chester, would like to know who made the piece. This is particularly so since the sheer volume of gold and silver assayed in Chester, especially in the nineteenth century, made it one of the major centres in the British Isles.

This Compendium documents all goldsmiths and silversmiths who sent their wares for quality assay in Chester from the mid-sixteenth century up to the closure of the Assay Office in August 1962. It will be an important source of reference for collectors and dealers, and indeed for further academic research. It also brings new information, not previously published anywhere else, of makers' marks of many Birmingham designers and manufacturers of gold and silver. In addition, for the first time, there is a comprehensive review of all Chester gold and silver marks.

It is the result of some fifty years of painstaking research by Maurice Ridgway, the author of three previous books on specific periods of Chester silver and numerous articles. We have personally been acquainted with his research for over thirty years, particularly concerning the Richardson family of Chester silversmiths. Sadly Maurice died before the publication of this book, but he had seen the proofs of the text and marks and could see the final shape of the publication.

His co-author Philip Priestley, is well known for his two books on watchcase makers in Britain. During his twenty years of research into makers' marks, he rediscovered the Chester Plate Duty Books of 1784-1840, lost amongst the Birmingham Assay Office archives. His skilled photography and detective work in matching the marks recorded in Chester in the nineteenth century by goldsmiths and silversmiths from Chester, Birmingham and elsewhere makes it possible to ascribe a name to most of the wares assayed in Chester. This in turn will allow future researchers to review the style and designs of individual goldsmiths and silversmiths of the nineteenth century.

This book now brings together in one volume all that is known about the goldsmiths and silversmiths who worked in Chester or who worked elsewhere and brought their goods to Chester for assay, and sheds new light from whence they came and the periods in which they worked.

Cathlyn and Simon Davidson
London

## INTRODUCTION

It may not have been by accident that the Romans laid the foundations of Chester within easy reach of the lead ore deposits of North Wales in the territory of the Deceangli, later to become the County of Flint. Lead played an important part in the Roman scene for building water pipes and other items, but it is clear that their main interest lay in its chief by-product, silver. Lead was worked as an imperial monopoly either under direct control or by private lessees. Chester had no official mint for coining money in Roman times.

The Saxon invasion heralded six centuries of unsettlement, but the later Saxons, working in the comparative safety of the walled city, stamped their coins with LEGE, short for the name they gave the City, Legeceastre, and other abbreviations. To this Saxon period belongs a small clay pot containing 520 coins, jewellery and bullion weighing fifteen thousand grains (2.24 pounds avoirdupois or 1.017 kilograms) of silver. There were also fragments of brooches, parts of a silver bracelet and ingots. The hoard was found in Castle Esplanade and had been the property of a jeweller who was also interested in the manufacture of silver wares. It introduces us to the first moneyers working in Chester. Their names and those of other Saxon moneyers working in Chester are stamped on the coins they made; Abba, Boiga, Sigeferth and Oslac, are examples amongst the hundred known moneyers. They were still minting coins at Chester until the time of Henry II. The moneyer was a specialist, but it is likely that he may have made other artefacts.

In about 1200, Randle the independent Earl of Chester, confirmed by charter the establishment of the Guild Merchant which gave official approval to an already long established practice. Within this guild would be found the workers in gold and silver, but their work has not survived. Nicholas, called the Great Goldsmith, was at Chester when Edward I held his court there for the invasion of Wales at the close of the thirteenth century.

Many silversmiths and goldsmiths continued to work at Chester throughout the medieval period. John, a goldsmith, was Sheriff of Chester with Hugh Frere who died in office in 1463 and John Dedwode, a goldsmith, was Sheriff in 1481, an office which William Mutton was to hold almost a century later and who played such an interesting part in the city life. His goldsmith's mark was a rebus on his name, a sheep's head, the earliest known mark of a Chester goldsmith seen on silver and dating from *c.*1570.

Over the years, the City had evolved into having Trade Companies and Guilds. When an attempt was made in the sixteenth century to save the navigation of the River Dee, the City appealed to the various Companies for assistance. In the first half of the sixteenth century there were twenty-six, of which the Goldsmiths were ranked tenth. A manuscript book in the Chester archives states that the goldsmiths gave towards the haven £2 quarterly! However, the Dee silted up quicker than the money came in.

The Reformation upheaval was now taking place and it had a challenging effect on everyone. They saw much of the work of previous goldsmiths destroyed, pilfered or used by bankers as currency or security. Among the changes came the directive from the Archbishop of York to change massing chalices into larger laity communion cups. For the goldsmiths in Chester the year which stands out was 1573 when it became the turn of the local dioceses of St Asaph and Bangor to obey the directive. It was also the year in which the Wardens of the London Goldsmiths' Company came into Cheshire and called at Nantwich in the newly formed Diocese of Chester. They had taken care to follow in the wake of the Episcopal directions, and staggered their visits to the Dioceses so that they would not be overwhelmed with orders for new wares. There were at least a hundred and forty goldsmiths in London, and their ancient Company wished to expand their power and authority.

The Chester Company had always preserved its independence and based it upon the wording of the rulings of Edward I and Edward IV. So when the London Goldsmiths' Company threatened their rights, independence and trade they stood firm and in this they had the backing of other Cestrians, citizens of Chester. They were not indifferent to this threat and took steps to put their own house in order. The earliest book of the Chester Company dates from the time of William Mutton, *c.*1555, and on the 16th May 1585 on St Dunstan's Day (the patron saint of goldsmiths) they listed the names of their ten members. William Mutton had died the year before but his contemporaries, brothers John and Joseph Lingley, John's son (also John) with Griffith Edwardes and his son (also Griffith) continued until the beginning of the seventeenth century.

When the Civil War started the Company and its records were in danger of being destroyed, but Gerrard Jones and Peter Edwardes kept the ancient books and they survived the vicious siege of the City and the Commonwealth period. With the return of Charles II in 1660 they had established a strong band of apprentices and goldsmiths and by about 1664 they became known as the Company of Goldsmiths and Watchmakers, recognising the close association of the crafts for items such as watchcases. In 1680 they had produced new rules concerning admission and working of the Company. Shortly afterwards due to a desire to put the Company in a position beyond criticism they drew up a statement on 1st February 1687 which again referred to their independence, and agreed among other things the following:

*The Wardens' marks shall be the coat and crest of the City of Chester on two puncons [punches] with a letter for the year in addition to the maker's mark. Furthermore, the wardens should seek out and destroy silver of sub-standard quality.*

The statement was signed by the new Alderman, Peter Edwardes the Master, Ralph Walley and Peter Edwardes junior, the Wardens and by the rest of the Company, Thomas Chapman, Nathaniel Bullen, Peter Pemberton, Joseph Clarke and Thomas Robinson.

With the new punches came the introduction of the first series of Chester date letters. Curiously, the *lion passant guardant* mark associated with sterling silver at London, Norwich and Exeter was not immediately introduced at Chester and the local goldsmiths used personal cameo marks based upon various combinations of the word "sterling", and it was not until 1720 that the traditional mark was used.

The Company's attempts to regulate the trade were frustrated when a Statute of 25th March 1697 decreed that no goldsmith in the country was permitted to work in silver less than 11 ounce 10 pennyweight in every pound Troy, also that the maker's mark was to consist of the first two letters of their surname. On silver the lion passant was to be replaced by the figure of a woman commonly called Britannia, a lion's head erased instead of the leopard's head and a new style of annual date letter. The Act was primarily introduced to prevent melting of coinage for plate, but possibly due to poor drafting of the edict, it implied that all provincial assay offices were to close leaving the London Goldsmiths' Hall with country-wide responsibilities and power. Chester Goldsmiths' Company reacted to this order by ceasing to use a date letter after "G" (1697) and for a short time continued to use their own personal sterling marks without any date letter or city reference.

The consequence was that enormous amounts of silver from all over the country now awaited assay in London. This forced Parliament to bring in another Act in 1701 which authorised certain cities where there had been mints to open assay offices under the same conditions as applied to London. Curiously, the only reason why Chester was granted powers by the compilers of the Act was because there had been a mint at Chester in the time of William III, albeit open for only eighteen months, and there were a few local craftsmen who understood silver. However, there was no reference to the Chester Goldsmiths' Company although Thomas Robinson had been a Company member and attached to the Chester mint.

Before the Act of 1697, London goldsmiths had exercised their rights to monitor or police the provincial craftsmen and on occasion had fined them for sub-standard wares. Once the new assay office was incorporated it embraced the control of standards in the local area. From time to time they castigated goldsmiths for sub-standard wares. For example, Peter Hopwood of Preston in Lancashire was convicted in 1730 of selling two large silver spoons below the standard required by the Act of 1697 and, in 1785, several Liverpool watchcase makers were admonished for sending cases without joints or mouldings. On 10th May 1820 they issued a memorandum to prevent substitution of inferior parts to articles after they had been marked. It seems that the practice of transferring pieces of silver with early hallmarks to a more modern piece, common in London, was not seen in the Chester area. If the records show that some goldsmiths stretched the bounds of good practice, the events of 1840 make them pale into insignificance. A most spectacular offence was committed by the controlling body when the incumbent assay master, John Walker, who had been in the post thirty-one years, and his son, Arthur Davies Walker the assistant assayer, were found guilty at Chester City Sessions of frauds against Her Majesty's Commissioners of Stamps. The Goldsmiths' Company revoked their appointments and directed them to transfer to the new assay master, George Lowe, all books, papers, stamps, dies, punches, scales, weights and other implements upon pain of litigation. It is unclear from the records if duty payments were being siphoned off or sub-standard wares being passed and marked. Joseph Duke was sworn in as assistant assay master. In view of the long tenure of the disgraced John Walker, it is likely that offences took place over a substantial period of time.

The transfer of responsibility in 1701 to the new authority from the Company was not acceptable to many of its members with the result that some of the best goldsmiths no longer made silverware, including Alexander Pulford, Peter Edwardes and Ralph Walley. Others were grouped together around Thomas Robinson, but the Company itself was not allowed to assay as they had done before 1696. It became a time when the Company and the parliamentary assay authority had to work together, but it led to times of friction. This curious relationship between each body has never been satisfactorily resolved, nor fully explained.

Those who continued in the Company and attracted others as Freemen of the City and were prepared to accept and follow the new rules included Thomas Robinson, Peter Pemberton, Nathaniel Bullen, Benjamin Pemberton and Thomas Maddock. Among the new rules was the provision of a copper plate on which the new goldsmiths, silversmiths and watchcase makers registered their marks, many of whom came from a distance and had nothing to do with the life of the City of Chester.

From now on and for 262 years Company and Parliament worked together. The close connection between those who made gold and silver watchcases and the traditional workers had been recognised since the end of the seventeenth century, but now their numerous marks smothered the first copper plate which the Company had probably intended to reserve for the marks of their own Company craftsmen.

Attempts in the 1770s to bring some sort of order in the registering failed, and the plate was not renewed until 1841 by which time many of the original marks had been partially overstruck. The makers' marks plates were renewed several times and in different ways until the office closed in 1962.

Throughout the eighteenth century the family of Richardson dominated the scene. The first was Richard Richardson I who came from Worcester when the 1697 Act began to operate and he worked outside the Company before being apprenticed to Ralph Walley. Since Walley would not follow the new arrangements he completed his apprenticeship before being admitted a Freeman and member of the Company. Richard Richardson had already proved himself a fine silversmith and had produced communion cups for churches in Anglesey and Flintshire as an independent silversmith. With William his brother and Richard his son, together with other members of the family, they established an important centre for their work in Eastgate Street.

The Birmingham and Sheffield assay offices opened in 1773 and all workers within the initial mandatory 20-mile radius catchment area had to use their local assay offices. The area was extended to 30 miles around Birmingham and Sheffield in 1824 when the right to assay gold at Birmingham was introduced (incidentally, Sheffield had to wait until 1904 for similar gold assaying rights). The initial impact on Chester must have been quite serious as all Coventry and Birmingham goldsmiths had to use their local assay office. To make matters worse, four high-volume Liverpool watchcase makers temporarily transferred their assay work from Chester to Birmingham during the 1790s. On the other hand, the plate duty books show William Pugh of Birmingham submitting three gold boxes for assay in each of the years 1810, 1813 and 1814, most probably because Birmingham was not allowed to assay gold at that time.

The existence of three duty books, introduced in 1784 by the Plate Duty Act, is so important for the assigning of attributions in the period before 1863 when extant registration books start. Curiously, several items by goldsmiths in Liverpool and Chester have been seen with duty and assay marks, but they are not mentioned in the duty books. It is possible the clerk forgot to enter the items or entered the wrong item. Another possibility, and much more serious because it potentially deprived the Government of taxes, is that there was fraud on the part of the clerk who stamped the duty mark, pocketed the duty or shared it with the silversmith and did not enter the record in the book. Another conundrum is that the plate duty books contain the names of a dozen or so goldsmiths, but to date their marks have not been identified on copper plates or silverware. Curiously, there are another fifty examples of correctly assayed and marked silverware, including the famous Richardson family and Boulton & Fothergill, with maker's marks not recorded on extant copper plates. A "missing" copper plate or fraud on the part of the officials might explain this. Some artefacts only have a maker's mark, often struck several times to simulate a full set of assay marks. A pair of spoons *c.*1779-91 by Richard Richardson IV have four RR marks without assay marks. As manager of the Richardson family business, he might have been expected to set a good example, unless they were for family use and not retail where assaying was not required, but four strikings seems illogical unless it was an attempt to deceive.

When the Act of 1854 introduced lower grades of 15, 12 and 9 carat gold throughout the country, it also removed the 30-mile boundary limitations around Birmingham and Sheffield thereby allowing a great influx of craftsmen from the Midlands who preferred to have the Chester mark, particularly the watchcase makers of Coventry. When Liverpool began to copy Birmingham and agitate for its own assay office, those who were advocating the idea quickly changed their minds when they learned the trade preferred the Chester mark and so dropped the matter. On two occasions during the nineteenth century the popularity of Chester prompted others to ask for closure of its office, but due to the energies of John Lowe I, the attempts were defeated. Throughout 1845 and until March 1846 there was considerable activity involving the Board of Trade. There had been other attempts to close the Chester assay office because it was thought they were passing sub-standard silverware. The Company was faced with litigation in this matter and being doubtful whether their funds would meet the cost of the trial they agreed on the 19th February 1846 that 10% of the officers' salary should be withheld until the expenses of the trial and all other expenses and arrears of the Company had been paid. At the same meeting it was resolved that more commodious premises be obtained for the use of the assay office. They rented new premises in Goss Street for £10 a year until 1853 when it was purchased for the sum of £393. The assay office remained there until closure in 1962. It was later demolished, but the coat of arms of the Goldsmiths' Company once on the wall of the building was saved and is now in the Grosvenor Museum, Chester, following storage in Southport.

A report made by the Inspector General of Stamps and Taxes in 1851 mentions that there were only four Chester-based goldsmiths. Two were appointed as Prime Warden, John Lowe, and assistant Warden, John Garner. The assay master was Thomas Lowe, brother of John Lowe but "not of the trade" and an assistant, Mr Green. The assay days were Thursday and Friday, though more days were available should the demand increase. At this time, twelve Liverpool silversmiths, George Ward of Manchester plus the four from Chester mentioned above were sending in wares for assay at Chester.

Recognising that both Liverpool and Chester could be the losers in any battle, both parties acted together. The opposition of Liverpool watchcase maker Ralph Samuel who employed 100 men and boys to any closure of the Chester assay office became a forceful argument in retaining the status quo.

The London Goldsmiths' Company was still trying to establish that both Liverpool silversmiths and the Chester assay office were at fault, and that if it were proved it should lead to the closure of the Chester office. The following letter from the London Goldsmiths' Hall to James Wilson MP, dated 21st June 1855 does not reflect favourably upon either the Chester assay office or upon Mr Samuel.

*I have had more difficulty in procuring wares recently marked at Chester where very little gold or silver is marked excepting watchcases and these are not kept in shops but are sent chiefly from Liverpool by manufacturers there and immediately after they are marked are despatched to the watch movement makers at Coventry and elsewhere. I sent a person to Coventry and he succeeded in buying some gold watches the cases of which have been marked exactly. They bear the mark of this year. I sent for reports of Assays of four cases manufactured by Ralph Samuel of Liverpool all of which are worse than standard, some of them viz. item 21456 being upward of one carat worse than the 18 carat grade for which it is marked.*

Mr Wilson and the Chancellor of the Exchequer introduced a Bill to close not only the assay office at Chester, but also those at Exeter, Newcastle upon Tyne and York, leaving just London, Birmingham and Sheffield as places of assay in England. A special meeting of the Chester Company was convened on 11th June 1855 to oppose the Bill. The support of Lord Robert Grosvenor was sought, and John Lowe was sent to London to present the Chester case in April 1856 with the help of Mr Roberts (who sent a bill to Thomas Lowe with nineteen pages of itemised expenses for £172-6-2). The evidence was set out before the Select Committee on gold and silver wares appointed by the House of Commons. The minutes and proceedings of the Committee were printed and made available in May 1856, and it is from this report that the following information is gleaned.

There had been a suggestion, doubtless fostered by the London, Sheffield and Birmingham goldsmiths that ideally provincial offices like Chester should be closed down so that assaying might be centred at these offices. The Liverpool silversmiths joined with the Chester Goldsmiths to oppose any such suggestion and signed a petition to prevent this. When Mr Samuel was reminded that about 1840 he and many others signed a petition to establish an assay office at Liverpool, independent of Chester, he replied that since then they, and especially he, had changed their opinion and wished to support the claim of Chester being retained as their trade there had doubled during the past ten years. The outcome of these discussions confirmed the importance of the Chester assay office, and did not recommend that Liverpool should either take its place, or establish a separate assay office. The Liverpool watchcase makers were perfectly satisfied with the result even though some fifteen years earlier they had petitioned for an office to be established there. It seems the Chester mark had become a status symbol with a high reputation among overseas customers, and was referred to as the "Liverpool" mark, indeed, there were some at Liverpool who acted as though Liverpool had in fact such an office.

As evidence of this, one Alfred Lutschaunig, who describes himself as Manager of the Liverpool assay office, produced a book in 1872, which is a manual of English assay marks and a reference source for gold and silversmiths, and includes tables for the proper mixing of alloys of gold and silver to make them of standard fineness. A second edition was published in 1878. The Liverpool Trade Directory of 1872 shows Lutschaunig and Company as gold and silver refiners and analytical chemists at 50b Lord Street, Liverpool with the assay office at Melville Chambers, 39 Cable Street, Liverpool. In spite of their claims, they could not have had any legal or official status and were probably bullion dealers carrying on a commercial assay of gold and silver.

By the end of the nineteenth century, Chester saw the end of the Richardson era and other families had taken over, among them the Walkers and Lowes, both working in Chester. The century witnessed a great expansion of the assay office embracing silversmiths, watchcase makers and minor jewellers from all over the country. The watchcase makers especially welcomed Chester for their swiftness in dealing with the assaying; it was close to the port of Liverpool and was easy for the export of their goods to America and Australia. In the twentieth century, Chester established agencies in Liverpool and Birmingham in order to attract assay work from companies in those towns who may have preferred to have the Chester mark on their wares or took advantage of using Chester when their local office was overloaded. Indeed, several makers registered identical marks at Birmingham, London and Sheffield. Grahame Jones, who worked at the Chester office during the 1950s remembers unpacking the hamper received daily by train from their agent J. Heavan (trading as S E Cooke) in Birmingham.

The two world wars had a devastating impact upon the work of the men who staffed the assay office. Men were called up and trade declined, but when peace was declared, it revived and by 1956 about 1½ million ounces of silver and 20,000 ounces of gold were being assayed yearly at Chester. The fate of the assay office there was already being considered but the office could have been saved from closure if there had been support from the Company members, and had the assay master and others not been tempted by a substantial pension. A few years later Sir Leonard Stone was put in charge of a report on the running of all assay offices in England, but by the time the report reached Parliament, Chester was singled out for action. There was a lone voice of opposition from John ffoulkes Lowe who was a member of the Company but not connected with the assay office. He was a direct descendant of George Lowe, the founding member of the Chester Lowe goldsmiths, but to no avail; the assay office closed on 24th August 1962.

It had been suggested that the Chester Goldsmiths' Company should also be disbanded at the same time but in the House of Lords the Bishop of Chester, Gerald Ellison, put forward a strong case for its retention. His request was granted although Chester never regained its individual right to assay silver as established by the 1701 Act. Following a suggestion from Maurice Ridgway, and after many years of campaigning, the right to have a City of Origin mark on gold, silver and platinum wares made in Chester was finally granted in 1988 by the Committee of Assay Offices of Great Britain. Such pieces are first assayed and marked at Birmingham, Edinburgh, London or Sheffield with their usual punches and then returned to Chester to be struck with the special, additional, Chester punch. This special punch and a record of wares marked with it are under the control of the Chester Goldsmiths' Company.

## Assay Masters

The following persons have held the post of Assay Master at Chester from the seventeenth century:

| | |
|---|---|
| Peter Edwardes I | Appointed 1st February 1687, and 1693 to 25th March 1697. |
| Nathaniel Bullen | Appointed 1692 or 1693. Re-appointed 29th September 1701 to 1713. |
| Richard Richardson I | Appointed 1713, died January 1730. |
| Thomas Maddock | Appointed 2nd February 1729, resigned 20th July 1761, died 19th December 1761. |
| Richard Richardson II | Appointed 20th July 1761, died in office September 1769. |
| John Scasebrick | Appointed 21st October 1769, died in office 1st December 1784. |
| Richard Richardson IV | Appointed 28th January 1785, resigned 19th March 1791. |
| George Walker I | Appointed 19th March 1791, died in office 1809. |
| John Walker | Appointed 16th March 1809, sworn-in 7th September 1819, dismissed 1st April 1840. |
| George Lowe I | Appointed 1st April 1840, died in office 28th December 1841. |
| Thomas Lowe | Appointed 30th December 1841, resigned 27th October 1864. |
| James Foulkes Lowe | Appointed 27th October 1864, died in office 27th March 1911. |
| Richard Edward Tatler | Appointed 4th April 1911, resigned 1915. |
| William Foulkes Lowe | Appointed 1st July 1915, died in office November 1931. |
| Frank Ernest Clark | Appointed 19th November 1931, resigned November 1954. |
| Arthur Vincent Ward | Appointed 30th December 1954, resigned 24th August 1962 on closure of CAO. |

## Early Chester Goldsmiths

The following early goldsmiths from the 13th century to the mid 18th century are extracted from Chester Records, Deeds, and related papers, and are conveniently seen in Jackson. The list excludes those goldsmiths with marks shown in Part 2 of the Compendium.

| Name of Goldsmith | Earliest mention | Latest mention | Freedom and details |
|---|---|---|---|
| John the Goldsmith | 1225 | | |
| Bartholomew the Goldsmith | 1265 | | |
| Nicholas the Great Goldsmith | 1271 | 1292 | |
| Mathew the Goldsmith | 1282 | 1293 | |
| Bertram the Goldsmith | 1292 | | |
| Walter the Goldsmith | 1292 | | |
| John the Goldsmith | 1297 | 1304 | |
| Nicholas the Goldsmith | 1309 | 1315 | |
| Thomas (de Cotes?) | 1312 | | |
| John de Paris | 1337 | | |
| David ap Wyn ap Wylor | 1340 | These four listed as fugitives and goldsmiths in the trial of David ap Blethin | |
| David ap Wyn Voil | 1340 | | |
| Yerran ap Gurgen | 1340 | | |
| David Edenowen | 1340 | | |
| William the Goldsmith | 1393 | | |
| Walter (or Will'm) de Radford | 1401 | | |
| Richard Pratt | 1402 | | |
| Richard de Horsley | 1406/7 | | |
| Roger the Goldsmith | 1406 | | |
| John Herteshorne | 1412 | | |
| John Haddoc | 1429 | | |
| John Goldsmith | 1462 | | Sheriff |
| Thomas Coke | 1474 | | |
| John Werine | 1474 | | |
| James Wermincham | 1481 | | |
| Stephen Wermyncham | 1481 | | |
| John Dedwode | 1485 | | Sheriff |
| William | 1487/8 | | |
| Ralph Pole | 1488 | 1499 | |
| John Maseyn | 1490 | 1492 | |
| Peter Assheton | 1493/4 | | |
| Robert Bellyn | 1495 | | |
| Hugh Johnson | 1499 | | |
| John ap Lle(wellyn?) | 1499 | | |
| Christopher Wermynsham I | 1501 | | |
| John Hatton | 1531 | | |
| John Trevour | 1531 | | |

| Name of Goldsmith | Earliest mention | Latest mention | Freedom and details |
|---|---|---|---|
| Richard Woodwarde | 1533 | | |
| Sir Lawrence Smith | 1540 | 1585 | Myr 1540 |
| Christopher Wermynsham II | 1542/3 | | |
| Richard Bexwick | 1545 | | 1546 |
| Peter Mutton? | 1550 | | |
| Richard Trevor | 1553/4 | | |
| Ralph Trevor | 1555 | | |
| John Trevis | 1560 | | |
| Thomas Trevis | 1560 | | |
| Robert Smyth | 1573 | 1615 | |
| Christopher Conway | 1577 | 1603 | 1583 |
| Thomas Price (Pryce) | 1585 | d1635 | 1607 |
| Sylvanus Glegg | 1631 | | 1631 |
| Gerrard Jones | 1632 | 1674 | Mayor 1638 |
| William Chritchley | 1634 | | |
| Dutton Bunbury | 1636 | d1652 | 1636 |
| Thomas Chapman | 1661 | 1702 | 1661 |
| Thomas Wright | 1664 | 1676 | Sheriff 1675 |
| John Buck | 1664 | 1677 | 1664 |
| William Warmenshaw | 1666 | 1670 | 1666 |
| Joseph Billington | | | 1669 |
| Puleston Partington | 1673 | Shrf 1686 | Mayor 1706 |
| Robert Drew | 1675 | d1680 | 1675 |
| Symon Wynne | 1676 | | 1676 |
| George Oulton | 1678 | | |
| Charles Ashton | | | 1682 |
| Joseph Clarke | 1685 | 1686 | |
| John Deane | | | 1695 |
| John Wrench | 1696 | 1725 | 1696 |
| Benjamin Critchley | 1717 | 1752 | |
| Robert Downes | | | 1720 |
| John Sharman | 1723 | 1726 | |
| Charles Brother | | | 1731 |
| George Crookes | | | 1731 |
| Samuel Pemberton | 1732 | 1752 | |
| John Eccles | 1733 | 1796 | 1733 |

## OVERVIEW OF CHESTER PLATES AND RECORDS

### Metal Plates of Makers' Marks and Assay Office Marks

The Chester registers and metal plates are located at Birmingham Assay Office with the exception of the earliest plate 1 which is on loan to the Ridgway Silver Gallery of Chester Grosvenor Museum. The daybooks and miscellaneous records are archived in Birmingham Central Library. The plates are made of copper with the exception of plate 4 and ten small plates numbered 24 to 33 which are of tin. Plates 1, 2 and 3 have a top border area containing assay office marks while the remainder of the plate is divided into squares for the makers' marks. Plates 5, 9, 13, 15, 21 and the small plates have solely makers' marks. Plate 5 has a single series of reference numbers (1-999) covering the whole plate, while the others have a separate series for each alphabetic square. The other plates contain assay office marks (see table below).

Plate 1 has 32 numbered squares that from 1701 to 1726 were allocated to individual Chester makers. Unfortunately, until a new plate 2 was introduced in 1841 it was covered with hundreds of countrywide marks in a haphazard manner; indeed, some are so badly struck or over-struck that they are difficult to decipher. Squares 21, 22 and 23 are engraved 1785, 1786 and 1787 respectively, indicating an attempt to date the squares perhaps as a result of the Duty Act of 1784, but there is no proof that all the marks in these squares can be so dated. The squares on the other plates have alphabetic annotations in which individual maker's marks are assigned on a surname initial basis. On occasion the assay office clerk punched the mark in the wrong square and sometimes even on an earlier plate.

The marks registers for plates 1 and 2 no longer exist and the only extant contemporary documents are lists of names in the Chester Goldsmiths' Company records and the Plate Duty Books of 1784 to 1840. It is conjectured that Jackson also saw later duty books since he published information on makers working up to 1893. Analysis of the marks on these first two copper plates shows that 585 individual maker's marks were struck in the first 160 years, indicating an average of 37 mark entries per decade. The earliest extant register of marks, the Small Punch Book, dates from 1863, some three years after the introduction of plate 3. Further registers provide details of makers in an unbroken run until 1962 apart for the period 1886 to 1894 where the register is missing.

The following table shows approximate plate sizes (width first) and chronological assignment to extant records – note that the small plates vary in size. Note also that the assay office on occasion issued to the trade a cardboard sample of current assay marks for gold and silver, including import marks.

| PLATE | | | ASSAY OFFICE MARKS | MAKERS' MARKS | ASSAY OFFICE and COMPANY RECORDS |
|---|---|---|---|---|---|
| Number | size inch | size cm | | | |
| 1 | 5 x 8 | 13 x 20 | 1701 - 1841 | | Goldsmiths' Company Records |
| 2 | 6 x 8 | 14 x 20 | 1841 - 60 | | Plate Duty Books 1784 - 1840 |
| 3 | 6 x 8 | 14 x 21 | 1860 - 83 | | Small Punch Book 1863 - 77 |
| 4 | 8 x 10 | 20 x 26 | 1881 - 88 | | |
| 5 | 8 x 12 | 21 x 31 | | 1883 - 98 | Large Punch Book 1877 - 86 |
| 24-33 | 2-3 x 2-5 | 5-8 x 5-14 | | 1883 - 86 | |
| 6 | 12 x 18 | 30 x 46 | 1888 - 1901 | | ("Missing" Register 1886 - 94) |
| 7 | 2 x 3 | 5 x 8 | 1896 - 97 | | |
| 8 | 2 x 5 | 5 x 13 | 1897 | | |
| 9 | 12 x 18 | 31 x 46 | | 1898 - 1907 | Makers' Marks Register #1 |
| 10 | 4 x 11 | 9 x 29 | 1898 - 1906 | | 1894 - 1905 |
| 11 | 9 x 14 | 23 x 35 | 1902 | | |
| 12 | 12 x 18 | 30 x 46 | 1902 - 12 | | |
| 13 | 12 x 19 | 30 x 48 | | 1907 - 12 | Makers' Marks Register #2 |
| 14 | 3 x 12 | 8 x 31 | 1906 - 14 | | 1905 - 21 |
| 15 | 12 x 19 | 30 x 48 | | 1912 - 36 | |
| 16 | 12 x 19 | 30 x 48 | 1912 - 22 | | |
| 17 | 3 x 12 | 8 x 31 | 1915 - 22 | | |
| 18 | 7 x 19 | 18 x 49 | 1923 - 34 | | Makers' Marks Register #3 |
| 19 | 17 x 4 | 42 x 10 | 1923 - 39 | | 1921 - 62 |
| 20 | 12 x 20 | 30 x 51 | 1934 - 53 | | |
| 21 | 12 x 19 | 31 x 49 | | 1936 - 62 | |
| 22 | 19 x 4 | 49 x 10 | 1942 - 62 | | |
| 23 | 12 x 20 | 31 x 51 | 1954 - 62 | | |

**Chester Goldsmiths' Company Records**

The following Chester Goldsmiths' Company records are located in the Records Department of Chester City Town Hall. None of the records shows makers' marks, but as practising goldsmiths had to register with the Company or the Chester assay office, these records do allow tentative attributions to be made.

- A mid-sixteenth century book containing the names of those admitted to the Company, the Oath of the master, steward and assay master, and the minutes of the Company up to 1703.
- Minute book containing orders, election of officers, admissions, etc., for 1703 to 1803.
- Minute book 1808 to 1882.
- Minute book including admissions 1882 (kept by the Chester Goldsmiths' Company).
- Account book 1663 to 1803.
- A small red Morocco bound book dating from *c.*1840 (in private ownership) measuring 5½ by 3½ inches (14 by 9 cm) containing a catalogue of plate held by the Company. The contents, amended over the years as plate was added, lost or sold, are recorded in *Chester Silver 1837-1962,* page 37. The nineteen remaining items are displayed in the Ridgway Silver Gallery of Chester Grosvenor Museum.

**Plate Duty Books (PDB)**

Three very important documents, initiated as a result of the 1784 Plate Duty Act, covering the periods 1784-1809, 1809-37 and 1838-40, were rediscovered in the Archive Department of Birmingham Central Library during 1994. They are effectively day-books showing the number, type and weight of items being submitted for assay, together with maker's name, gross duty payable to the State and duty allowance to cover finishing and polishing. Although individual maker's marks are not annotated, the existence of an entry is proof of the goldsmith being registered with a mark although, curiously, ten of the entries are for makers whose marks are not on Plate 1 nor have been seen on silverware. It is possible the assay master knew the individuals and turned a blind eye or shared the duty. However, we cannot rule out the prior existence of a further copper plate, now lost, which contained these marks and those of some fifty makers, including the prestigious silversmiths Matthew Boulton of Birmingham and the Richardsons of Chester, seen on eighteenth-century silverware with assay marks, but which are not struck on Plate 1.

Most of the PDB names have been matched to marks struck on Plate 1, but without extant corresponding registers of names and marks, the attributions are of varying accuracy. It is of interest to note that the Chester data in the 1905 edition of Jackson shows earliest and latest working dates which correspond to entries in the PDB so it is certain that Jackson used this important source of information. It is highly probable that he also had sight of later duty books, now missing, since his first edition lists the working dates of other goldsmiths in the period 1840 up to 1893, three years after the abolition of duty.

**Small Punch Book (SPB)**

The Small Punch Book (SPB) covering the period 16th October 1863 to 21st June 1877, contains maker's name, mark and address, but lacks trade details. There are 147 registration entries during the 13⅔ years, that is an average of 10.7 per annum. This heavy book is unique in having 24 pages made of lead metal partly covered by strips of parchment. The marks are punched on the metal with the written details scribed on the parchment alongside. The left-hand pages have the maker's mark while the accompanying text sprawls across both left and right sides. The corresponding marks are also struck on Chester Plate 3 with the exception of some that seem to be erroneously punched on Plate 2. The marks were entered in chronological order but the assay office allowed the book to be used for three passes instead of introducing a new book when most of the metal and paper had been covered. The second pass starts in 1869 and the third in early 1877. The writing on the parchment is beginning to deteriorate possibly from contact with the lead which itself is showing signs of chemical decomposition. A photographic copy and computerised record of this book has been established (by Priestley) and lodged with the BAO.

**Large Punch Book (LPB) and The Small Plates (SP)**

The Large Punch Book (LPB) covering the period 17th October 1877 to 4th January 1886, contains maker's mark, names and address, but lacks trade details. It is similar in construction to the SPB, but larger and with pages made of tin metal. There are 513 registration entries during the 8¼ years representing an average of 62 registrations per annum. Marks for the first six years are also struck on copper Plate 3 while those entered in the last two years are to be found on copper Plate 5. The book was started chronologically but part way through switches to alphabetical sequence with much haphazard entering of the marks. The pages are numbered and it appears that some early records may be missing. This book is also showing signs of age deterioration. The BAO has held a photographic copy of this book for some years, and a computerised archive record has been established (by Priestley) and lodged with the office.

The mark records in the LPB are incomplete as the metal sheets filled up faster than the paper sheets leading, in August 1883, to a second pass through the book in order to make use of the blank sheets. Since there was no metal surface left, the office introduced a series of small sheets of tin metal for the later maker's mark, one for each surname initial, known as Chester Small Plates (SP). Curiously, only small plates for surnames beginning with the letters D, E, F, G, J, M, N, S, T and V survive and it is possible that other small plates covering the remainder of the alphabet existed at one time. A chronological sequence of mark punching on the small plates and Plate 5 entries in the LPB has been assumed in order to match marks to maker's details. Plate 3 started three years before the SPB was introduced, and there are some 40 marks without corresponding names and addresses. Fortunately, some of these marks were also registered at Birmingham while others were identified from entries in an 1861 *Directory of Goldsmiths and Silversmiths.*

### Three Registers of Makers' Marks, Details and Trade (R1, R2 and R3)

These three important registers show trade for the first time as well as maker's name, initials of the mark, business and home address, and name of person/company making the entry. There used to be four registers but the earliest one covering the period 1886 to 1894 is missing, thought to have been lost during the Blitz. This is here referred to as the "missing register" (see below). The first register (R1) covering 1894 to 1905 contains 1185 entries or 108 per annum. The first mark number entry is #553 but curiously is located on page 80, while #554 is on page 85 and #555 on page 1. One theory is that the clerk was going to use the first 80 pages for transcribing the missing register, but with only 5 rows per page, that would give 400 spaces which does not jibe with 552 marks thought to be in the missing register. Another curiosity of R1 is that mark #901 follows #800 but later the clerk realised his mistake and started to re-use the "800" series. The second register (R2) covering 1905 to 1921 also contains 1185 entries or 74 per annum. The third (R3) covering 1921 to 1962, contains 930 entries or 23 per annum. Against each entry is a 1 to 3 digit number which is also struck alongside the maker's mark on the relevant copper plate.

The registers contain entries with addresses from around the British Isles, the largest number being from Birmingham with over 2,000 entries. There are nearly 2,000 entries for *Jewellers* of all descriptions and nearly 800 entries for the *Watch and Clock* trade.

### Missing Register (Old Book) 1886 to 1894

Although no longer extant, its prior existence is confirmed on page 58 of Large Register 1 where the entry for Augustus Dreyfus dated 12th February 1898 refers to his previous mark number "228" entered in the *Old Book* on 30th August 1890. As the lowest mark number in R1 is "553" it is assumed the *missing register* held at least 552 entries with all the associated marks located on Plate 5 with cross-reference numbers. Although it is unlikely that the 552 marks were entered evenly over the eight years, a linear rate of entry of 66 per annum has been assumed in order to estimate approximate year of registration to assist in making attributions. Curiously, some of the Plate 5 numbers are used more than once, and it is possible that a single mark number was used for all the entries on a given day. Most of these *missing register* marks have been allocated maker's names by comparing with contemporary entries at Birmingham, Chester, London and Sheffield Assay Offices or through the use of trade directories.

### Miscellaneous Records

The following ledgers are in the Archive Department of Birmingham Central Library:-

Day Ledger - Salaries, etc. 1856 to 1882.
Foreign and English Wares Assayed - Weights, 1913 to 1962.
Watch Cases - Quantity, weight, value, 1934 to 1962.
Work Record Book - Quantity, weight, value, 1937 to 1962.
Silverware - Maker, type, quantity, 1934 to 1947.
Day Book Goldware - Maker, type, quantity, 1960 to 1962.
Day Book Silverware - Maker, type, quantity, 1947 to 1962.
Day Book Goldware - Maker, type, quantity, 1934 to 1940.
Day Book Goldware - Maker, type, quantity, 1940 to 1954.
Day Book Goldware - Maker, type, quantity, 1954 to 1959.

### Registers of Chester Assay Office Punches

Three registers of Chester assay office punches covering the periods 1899 to 1922, 1922 to 1934 and 1935 to 1962 are located at the Birmingham assay office.

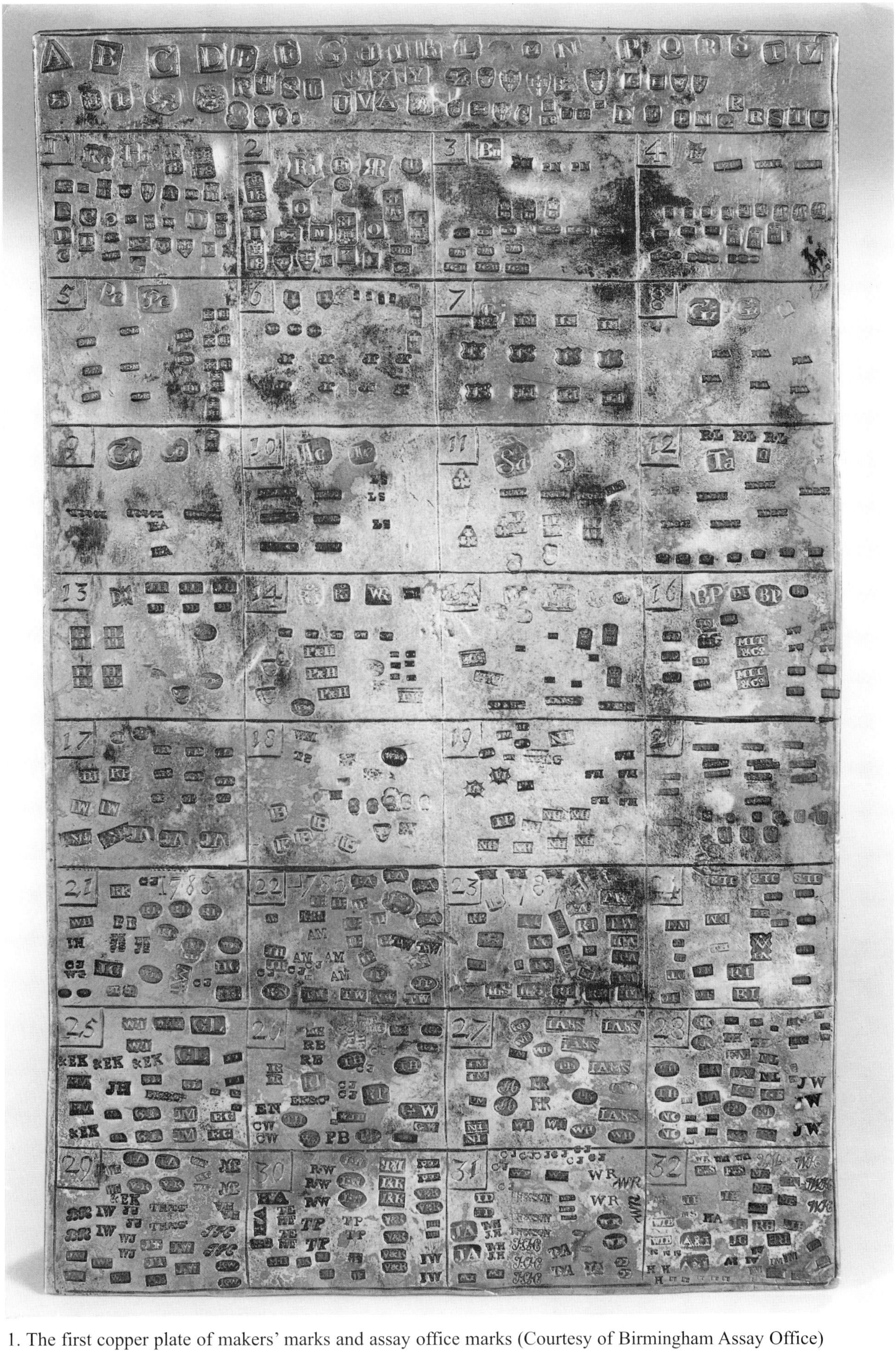

1. The first copper plate of makers' marks and assay office marks (Courtesy of Birmingham Assay Office)

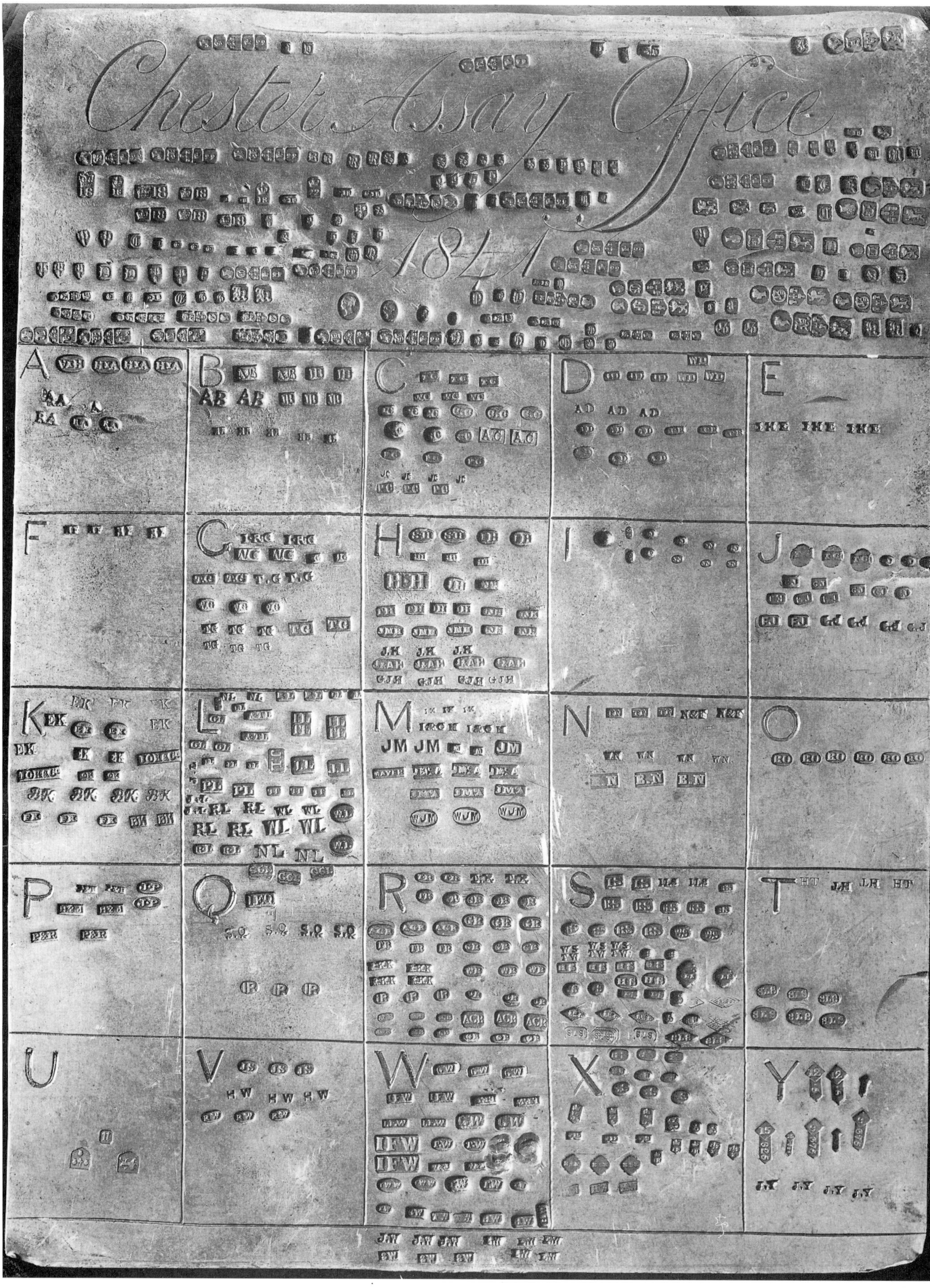


2. The second copper plate of markers' marks and assay office marks (Courtesy of Birmingham Assay Office)

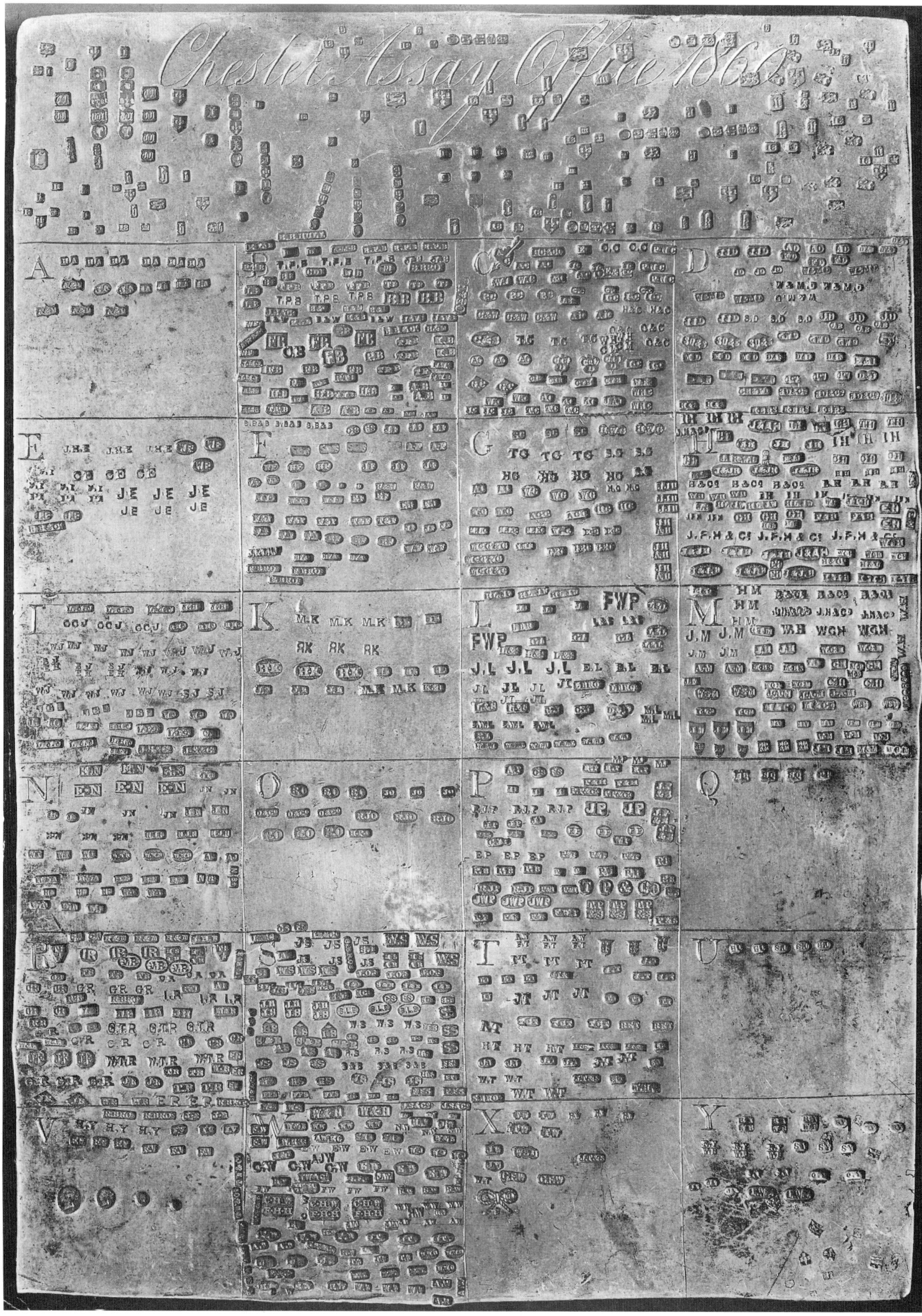


3. The third copper plate of makers' marks and assay office marks (Courtesy of Birmingham Assay Office)

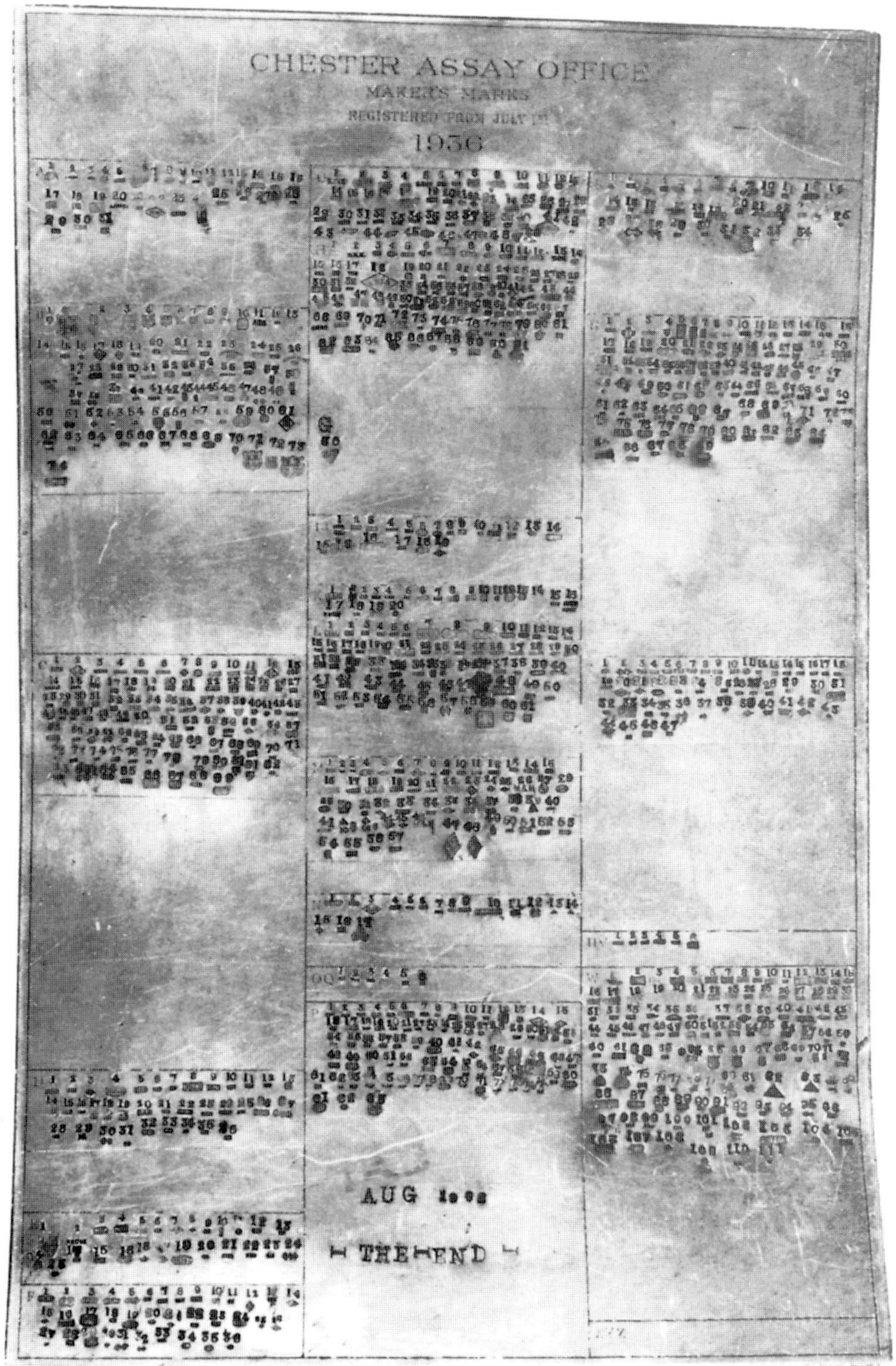


4. The last copper plate of makers' marks (Courtesy of Birmingham Assay Office)

5. The last copper plate of assay office marks (Courtesy of Birmingham Assay Office)

6. Chester City mark punch and three makers' punches
(Courtesy of National Museums & Galleries on Merseyside, Liverpool)

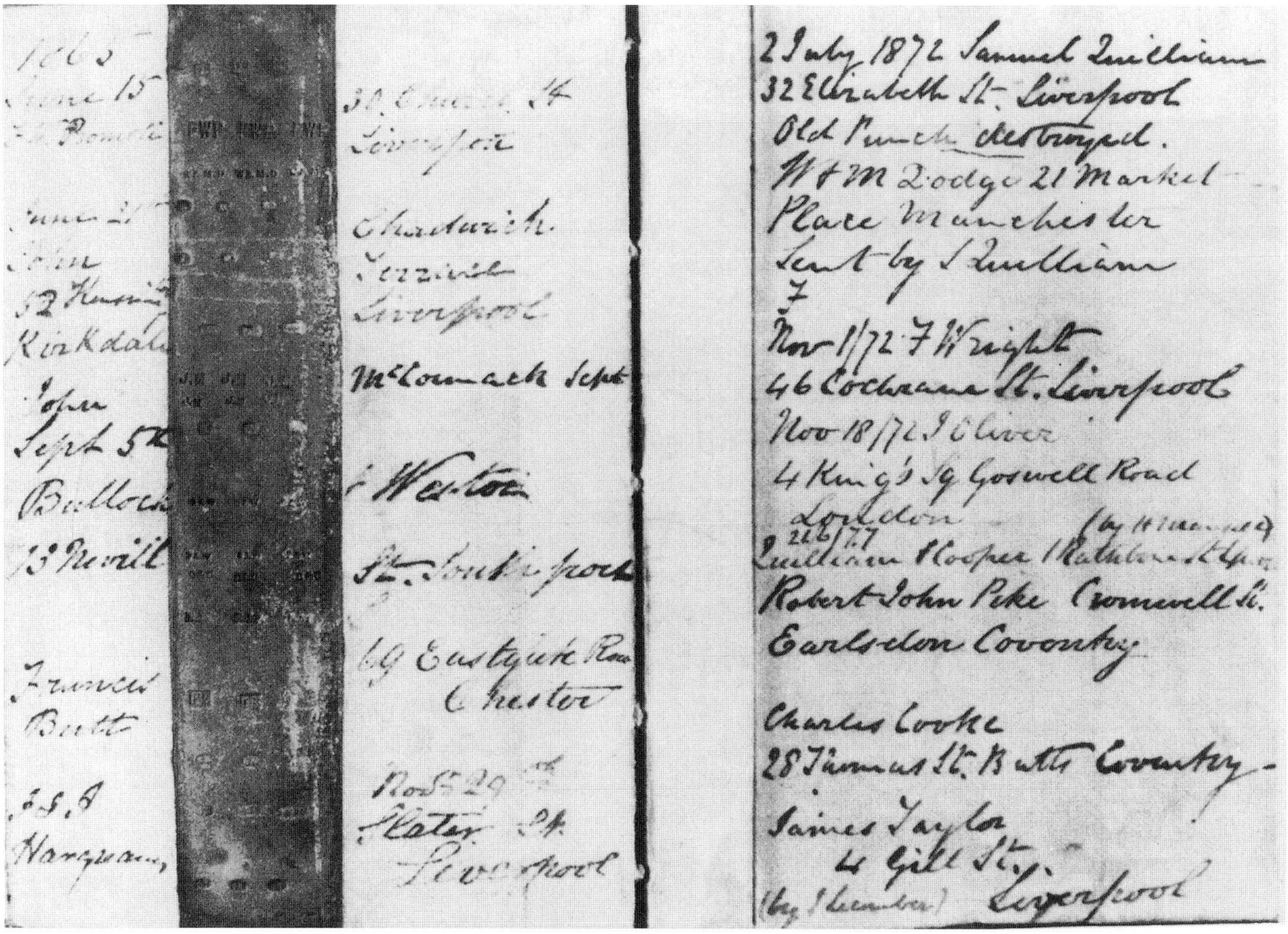
2 July 1872 Samuel Quilliam
32 Elizabeth St. Liverpool
Old Punch destroyed.
W & M Dodge 21 Market
Place Manchester
Sent by S Quilliam
Nov 1/72 F Wright
46 Cochrane St. Liverpool
Nov 18/72 J Oliver
4 King's Sq Goswell Road
London
Robert John Peke Cromwell St.
Earlsdon Coventry
Charles Cooke
James Taylor
4 Gill St.
Liverpool

7. Sample page of assay office small punch book (Courtesy of Birmingham Assay office)

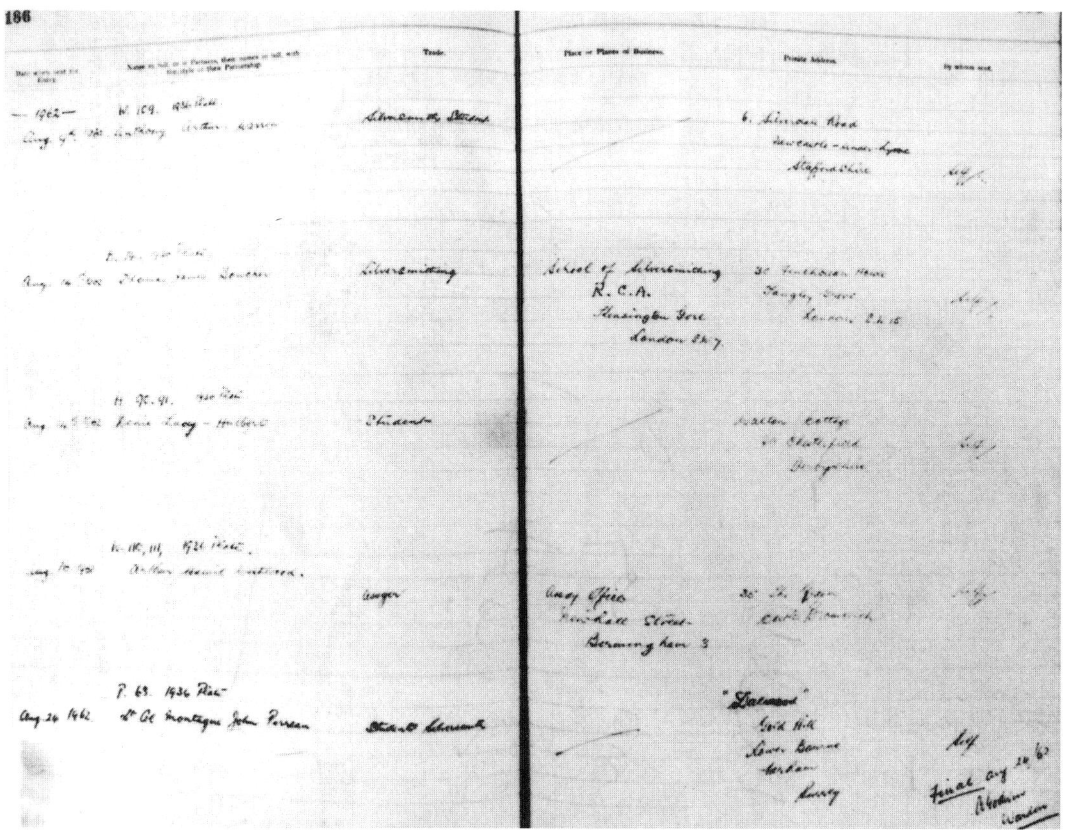

8. Last page of last register of makers' marks (Courtesy of Birmingham Assay Office)

# PART 1

# ASSAY OFFICE
# and
# STANDARD MARKS
# 1687 to 1962

**Date Letters 1687 to 1697 and Pre-1720 sterling silver marks**
**Date Letters 1701 to 1962**
**The Chester City marks**
**Britannia silver and Post-1720 sterling silver marks**
**The Leopard's Head mark**
**The Duty mark 1784 to 1890**
**Gold marks**
**Import marks for gold and silver**

## DATE LETTERS 1686 TO 1697 AND PRE-1720 STERLING SILVER MARKS

By 1544, the London Goldsmiths' Company was using three assay marks: a *date letter* to identify the assay master in the event of fraud, a *lion passant* to denote sterling silver (and gold until 1844) and a *leopard's head* to indicate that a satisfactory assay had been carried out. None of these was used at Chester until 1687 which makes the identification of early Chester silver difficult and entirely dependent on the *maker's mark*. However, on the 1st February 1687 (modern calendar) the Chester Goldsmiths' Company introduced three assay marks in an attempt to regulate the trade; a series of *date letters, a City Coat of Arms* and a *City Crest* as shown in Table I. Curiously, they did not introduce the *lion passant* or *leopard's head* marks. This short series of date letters ran until 1697 when the Britannia Silver Act closed down all provincial assay offices. When a new Chester Assay Office was established by the Act of 1701, the regulation of the craft was transferred to an Assay Master and two Wardens, and a new series of *date letters* was started. (See tables II-XIII from *Jackson* – Antique Collectors' Club edition, and printed with their permission.)

The *date letter* was usually changed on the 9th July at the annual meeting, later the 20th July with the new calendar. Between 1796 and 1808 the date varied but then settled down to the 5th July. After a meeting held on the 5th August 1839, the change over date moved to 5th August each year. On 3rd August 1889, the date was changed for the last time to 1st July with some minor exceptions. In all, thirteen series of date letters were used up to 1962. The *date letters* for 1697, 1714, 1720, 1745, 1770, 1808, 1830 and 1831 are neither on copper plates nor seen on wares, and are conjectured.

Instead of a *lion passant* to assure quality, local goldsmiths used personal sterling silver marks based upon the word sterling (see below). When the new arrangements started in 1701, some of the old guild declined to register while others refused to use the new Britannia standard and continued with sterling silver and their unofficial marks. Others abided by the new regulations. The unofficial sterling marks continued until the Act of 1720 re-introduced the sterling silver standard alongside the Britannia standard.

TABLE I

| DATE | CITY ARMS | CITY CREST | DATE LETTER |
|---|---|---|---|
| 1 Feb. 1687 -2 June 1690 |  |  |  |
| 2 June 1690-92 | " | " |  |
| 1692-93 or 1694 | " | " |  |
| 1693 or 1694 | " | " |  |
| 1695 | " | " |  |
| 1696 | " | " |  |
| Until 25 March 1697* | " | " |  |

Used only by Ralph Walley, perhaps as early as 1683. He used no other form.

Used by Peter Pemberton with mark type 1 1677 to 1687, type 2 1687 and perhaps with mark type 1a in 1692/3.

Used by Peter Pemberton with mark type 2 1687 and type 3 1697 to 1701. Also used by Timothy Gardner *c*.1686.

Used by Nathaniel Bullen with mark type 1 *c*.1692. He used no other form.

Found once on a spoon in association with an ED cameo mark *c*.1698 previously attributed to Samuel Edwardes but now thought to be Ellen Dare of Taunton.

Used by Thomas Robinson *c*.1720 with his re-use of mark type 1 after the re-introduction of the Sterling standard in 1720. May also have used a mark similar to the second one above.

Used by Richard Richardson I *c*.1719 on the Caernarfon maces when the sterling standard was re-introduced. This mark has not been associated with any other goldsmith.

Used by Benjamin Brancker of Liverpool in association with the BB and bird mark *c*.1715-20. A distinctive feature is the rounded top right-hand corner of the frame.

Used *c*.1699 by a goldsmith having the script initials TM, possibly for Mr Marsh of Chester.

Seen in conjunction with the SH mark attributed to Robert Shields of Liverpool *c*.1710. A distinctive feature is the sharp angled top right hand corner of the frame.

Found in association with the script TH mark *c*.1700 attributed provisionally to Thomas Howell mentioned in the list of Chester freemen.

# DATE LETTERS 1701 to 1751

TABLE II

| | BRIT-ANNIA | LION'S HEAD ERASED | CITY ARMS | DATE LETTER |
|---|---|---|---|---|
| 29 Sept. 1701 |  |  |  | A |
| 1702-7 April 1703 | " | " | " | B |
| 7 April 1703-4 | " | " | " | C |
| 1704-5 | " | " | " | D |
| 1705-6 | " | " | " | E |
| 1706-7 | " | " | " | F |
| 1707-8 | " | " | " | G |
| 1708-9 | " | " | " | H |
| 1709-10 | " | " | " | I |
| 1710-11 | " | " | " | K |
| 9 July 1711-9 July 1712 | " | " | " | L |
| 1712-13 | " | " | " | M |
| 1713-14 |  | " | " | N |
| 1714-15 | " | " | " | O |
| 1715-16 | " | " | " | P |
| 1716-17 | " | " | " | Q |
| 1717-18 | " | " | " | R |
| 1718-19 | " | " | " | S |
| 1719-1 June 1720 | " | " | " | T |
| 2 June 1720-9 July 1720 | LION PASSANT  | LEOPARD'S HEAD  |  | T |
| 9 July 1720-21 | " | " | " | U |
| 1721-22 | " | " | " | V |
| 1722-23 | " | " | " | W |
| 1723-24 | " | " | " | X |
| 9 July 1724-25* | " | " | " | Y |
| 1725-26* | " | " |  | Z |

TABLE III

| | LION PASSANT | LEOPARD'S HEAD | CITY ARMS | DATE LETTER |
|---|---|---|---|---|
| 9 July 1726-* † 10 July 1727 |  |  |  | A |
| 10 July 1727-* † 9 July 1728 | " | " | " | B |
| 9 July 1728-* † 9 July 1729 | " | " | " | C |
| 9 July 1729- † 9 July 1730 |  | " | " | D |
| 9 July 1730- † 9 July 1731 |  | " | " | E |
| 9 July 1731-10 July 1732 | " |  | " | F |
| 10 July 1732-9 July 1733 | " | " | " | G |
| 9 July 1733-9 July 1734 | " | " | " | H |
| 9 July 1734-9 July 1735 | " | " | " | I |
| 9 July 1735 9 July 1736 | " |  | " | K |
| 9 July 1736-9 July 1737 | " | " | " | L |
| 9 July 1737-10 July 1738 | " | " | " | M |
| 10 July 1738-9 July 1739 | " | " | " | N |
| 9 July 1739-9 July 1740 | " | " | " | O |
| 9 July 1740-§ 9 July 1741 | " | " | " | P |
| 9 July 1741 - 9 July 1742 | " | " | " | Q |
| 9 July 1742-‡ 9 July 1743 | " | " | " | R |
| 9 July 1743-9 July 1744 | " | " | " | S |
| 9 July 1744-9 July 1745 | " | " | " | T |
| 9 July 1745-9 July 1746 | " | " | " | U |
| 9 July 1746-9 July 1747 | " | " | " | V |
| 9 July 1747-9 July 1748 | " | " | " | W |
| 9 July 1748-10 July 1749 | " | " | " | X |
| 10 July 1749-9 July 1750 | " | " | " | Y |
| 9 July 1750-9 July 1751 | " | " | " | Z |

* Alternative lion passant 1724-29 

† Alternative leopard's head 1726-31 

§ Alternative City Arms used in 1741 

‡ A short bodied lion with unclipped corners to the punch may be found in 1742.

# DATE LETTERS 1751 to 1797

TABLE IV

| | LION PASSANT | LEOPARD'S HEAD* | CITY ARMS | DATE LETTER |
|---|---|---|---|---|
| 9 July 1751-<br>9 July 1752 |  |  |  | a |
| 9 July 1752-<br>20 July 1753 | " | " | " | b |
| 20 July 1753-<br>20 July 1754 | " | " | " | c |
| 20 July 1754-<br>21 July 1755 | " | " | " | d |
| 21 July 1755<br>21 July 1756 | " | " | " | e |
| 21 July 1756-<br>20 July 1757 | " | " | " | f |
| 20 July 1757§<br>20 July 1758 | " | " | " | g |
| 20 July 1758-<br>20 July 1759 | " | " | " | h |
| 20 July 1759-<br>20 July 1760 | " | " | " | i |
| 20 July 1760-<br>20 July 1761 | " | " |  | k |
| 20 July 1761-<br>20 July 1762 | " | " | " | l |
| 20 July 1762-<br>20 July 1763 |  | " | " | m |
| 20 July 1763-<br>20 July 1764 | " | " | " | n |
| 20 July 1764-<br>20 July 1765 | " | " | " | o |
| 20 July 1765-<br>20 July 1766 | " | " | " | p |
| 20 July 1766-<br>20 July 1767 | " | " | " | q |
| 20 July 1767-<br>20 July 1768 | " | " | " | R |
| 20 July 1768-<br>20 July 1769 | " | " | " | S |
| 20 July 1769-<br>20 July 1770 | " | " | " | T |
| 20 July 1770-<br>20 July 1771 | " | " | " | U |
| 20 July 1771-<br>20 July 1772 | " | " | " | V |
| 20 July 1772-<br>20 July 1773 | " | " | " | W |
| 20 July 1773-<br>20 July 1774 | " | " | " | X |
| 20 July 1774-<br>20 July 1775 | " | " | " | Y |
| 20 July 1775-<br>20 July 1776 | " | " | " | Z |

Seen 1773/4 X

TABLE V

| | LION PASSANT | LEOPARD'S HEAD* | CITY ARMS | DATE LETTER | DUTY MARK |
|---|---|---|---|---|---|
| 20 July 1776-<br>20 July 1777 |  |  |  | a | |
| 20 July 1777-<br>20 July 1778 | " | " | " | b | |
| 20 July 1778-<br>20 July 1779 ┼ | " |  |  | c | |
| 20 July 1779-<br>20 July 1780 ┼ | " | " | " | d | |
| 20 July 1780-<br>20 July 1781 ┼ | " | " | " | e | |
| 20 July 1781-<br>20 July 1782 ┼ |  | " | " | f | |
| 20 July 1782-<br>20 July 1783 | " |  |  | g | |
| 20 July 1783-<br>31 Nov. 1784 | " | " | " | h | |
| 1 Dec. 1784-<br>28 Jan. 1785 ‡ | " | " | " | " |  |
| 28 Jan. 1785-<br>20 July 1785 | " | " | " | i | " |
| 20 July 1785-<br>20 July 1786 | " | " | " | k | " |
| " " " | " | " | " | " |  |
| 20 July 1786-<br>20 July 1787 | " | " | " | l | " |
| 20 July 1787-<br>20 July 1788 | " | " | " | m | " |
| 20 July 1788-<br>20 July 1789 | " | " | " | n | " |
| 20 July 1789-<br>20 July 1790 | " | " | " | o | " |
| 20 July 1790<br>20 July 1791 | " | " | " | p | " |
| 20 July 1791-<br>20 July 1792 | " | " | " | q | " |
| 20 July 1792-<br>20 July 1793 | " | " | " | r | " |
| 20 July 1793-<br>20 July 1794 | " | " | " | s | " |
| 20 July 1794-<br>20 July 1795** | " |  | " | t | " |
| 20 July 1795-<br>20 July 1796** | " | " | " | u | " |
| 20 July 1796-<br>[20 July 1797] | " | " | " | v | " |

* The leopard's head punch used 1735-1778 becomes very worn during this period. 

§ Alternative City Arms used in 1757. 

┼ Alternative leopard's head 1778-82. 

‡ Duty mark incuse.

** Leopard's head as in 1782 may be found.

# DATE LETTERS 1797 to 1839

TABLE VI

| | LION PASSANT | LEOPARD'S HEAD | CITY ARMS | DATE LETTER | DUTY* MARK |
|---|---|---|---|---|---|
| [20 July 1797-1798] |  |  |  | A |  |
| [20 July 1798-20 July 1799] | " | " | " | B | " |
| [20 July 1799-20 July 1800] † |  |  | " | C | " |
| [20 July 1800-20 July 1801 † | " | " | " | D | " |
| [20 July 1801-20 July 1802] | " | " | " | E | " |
| 1802-1803 | " | " | " | F | " |
| 1803-1804 | " | " | " | G | " |
| 1804-1805 | " | " | " | H | " |
| 1805-1806 | " | " | " | I | " |
| 1806-1807 |  |  |  | K | " |
| 1807-5 July 1808 | " | " | " | L | " |
| 5 July 1808-5 July 1809 | " | " | " | M | " |
| 5 July 1809-1810 | " |  |  | N | " |
| 1810-5 July 1811 | " | " | " | O | " |
| 5 July 1811-1812 | " | " | " | P | " |
| 1812-5 July 1813 | " | " | " | Q | " |
| 5 July 1813-5 July 1814 | " | " | " | R | " |
| 5 July 1814-1815 | " | " | " | S | " |
| 1815-1816 | " | " | " | T | " |
| 1816-5 July 1817 | " | " | " | U | " |
| 5 July 1817-5 July 1818 | " | " | " | V | " |

TABLE VII

| | LION PASSANT | LEOPARD'S HEAD | CITY ARMS | DATE LETTER | DUTY* MARK |
|---|---|---|---|---|---|
| 5 July 1818-7 Sept. 1819 |  |  |  | A |  |
| 7 Sept. 1819-10 May 1820 |  |  | " | B | " |
| 10 May 1820-8 Nov. 1821 | " | " | " | C | " |
| 8 Nov. 1821-5 July 1823 ‡ | " |  | " | D | " |
| 5 July 1823 5 July 1824 | " | " |  | E | " |
| 5 July 1824-5 July 1825§ | " |  | " | F | " |
| 5 July 1825-5 July 1826§ | " | " | " | G | " |
| 5 July 1826-5 July 1827§ | " | " | " | H | " |
| 5 July 1827-5 July 1828§ | " | " | " | I | " |
| 5 July 1828-5 July 1829§ | " | " | " | K | " |
| 5 July 1829-5 July 1830§ |  | " | " | L | " |
| 5 July 1830-5 July 1831§ | " | " | " | M | " |
| 5 July 1831-5 July 1832§ | " | " | " | N | " |
| 5 July 1832-5 July 1833§ | " | " | " | O | " |
| 5 July 1833-5 July 1834 | " | " |  | P | " |
| 5 July 1834-5 July 1835 |  | " | " | Q | " |
| 5 July 1835-5 July 1836 | " | " | " | R | " |
| 5 July 1836-5 July 1837 | " | " | " | S | " |
| 5 July 1837-5 July 1838 | " | " |  | T |  |
| 5 July 1838-5 July 1839 | " | " | " | U | " |

* Other known duty marks used between 1797-1837. 

† The lion passant guardant and leopard's head as used in 1797 may still be found.

‡ Lion also appears in plain rectangular punch in 1821-23. The leopard's head may be found as in 1819. There was also a variant of the city arms.

§ Leopard's head may be found as in 1821.

# DATE LETTERS 1839 to 1901

TABLE VIII

| | LION PASSANT | CITY ARMS | DATE LETTER | DUTY MARK |
|---|---|---|---|---|
| 1839-40 |  |  | A |  |
| 1840-41 | ″ | ″ | B | ″ |
| 1841-42 | ″ | ″ | C | ″ |
| 1842-43 | ″ | ″ | D | ″ |
| 1843-44 | ″ | ″ | E | ″ |
| 1844-45 | ″ | ″ | F | ″ |
| 1845-46 | ″ | ″ | G | ″ |
| 1846-47 | ″ | ″ | H | ″ |
| 1847-48 | ″ | ″ | I | ″ |
| 1848-49 | ″ | ″ | K | ″ |
| 1849-50 | ″ | ″ | L | ″ |
| 1850-51 | ″ | ″ | M | ″ |
| 1851-52 | ″ | ″ | N | ″ |
| 1852-53 | ″ | ″ | O | ″ |
| 1853-54 | ″ | ″ | P | ″ |
| 1854-55 | ″ | ″ | Q | ″ |
| 1855-56 | ″ | ″ | R | ″ |
| 1856-57 | ″ | ″ | S | ″ |
| 1857-58 | ″ | ″ | T | ″ |
| 1858-59 | ″ | ″ | U | ″ |
| 1859-60 | ″ | ″ | V | ″ |
| 1860-61 | ″ | ″ | W | ″ |
| 1861-62 | ″ | ″ | X | ″ |
| 1862-63 | ″ | ″ | Y | ″ |
| 1863-64 | ″ | ″ | Z | ″ |

TABLE IX

| | LION PASSANT | CITY ARMS | DATE LETTER | DUTY MARK |
|---|---|---|---|---|
| 1864-65 |  |  | a |  |
| 1865-66 | ″ | ″ | b | ″ |
| 1866-67 | ″ | ″ | c | ″ |
| 1867-68 | ″ | ″ | d | ″ |
| 1868-69 | ″ | ″ | e | ″ |
| 1869-70 | ″ | ″ | f | ″ |
| 1870-71 | ″ | ″ | g | ″ |
| 1871-72 | ″ | ″ | h | ″ |
| 1872-73 | ″ | ″ | i | ″ |
| 1873-74 | ″ | ″ | k | ″ |
| 1874-75 | ″ | ″ | l | ″ |
| 1875-76 | ″ | ″ | m | ″ |
| 1876-77 | ″ | ″ | n | ″ |
| 1877-78 | ″ | ″ | o | ″ |
| 1878-79 | ″ | ″ | p | ″ |
| 1879-80 | ″ | ″ | q | ″ |
| 1880-81 | ″ | ″ | r | ″ |
| 1881-82 | ″ | ″ | s | ″ |
| 1882-83 | ″ | ″ | t | ″ |
| 1883-84 | ″ | ″ | u | ″ |

TABLE X

| | LION PASSANT | CITY ARMS | DATE LETTER | DUTY MARK |
|---|---|---|---|---|
| 1884-85 |  |  | A |  |
| 1885-86 | ″ | ″ | B | ″ |
| 1886-87 | ″ | ″ | C | ″ |
| 1887-88 | ″ | ″ | D | ″ |
| 1888-89 | ″ | ″ | E | ″ |
| 1889- 1 May 1890 | ″ | ″ | F | ″ |
| 2 May 1890 5 July 1890 | ″ | ″ | ″ | |
| 1890-91 | ″ | ″ | G | |
| 1891-92 | ″ | ″ | H | |
| 1892-93 | ″ | ″ | I | |
| 1893-94 | ″ | ″ | K | |
| 1894-95 | ″ | ″ | L | |
| 1895-96 | ″ | ″ | M | |
| 1896-97 | ″ | ″ | N | |
| 1897-98 | ″ | ″ | O | |
| 1898-99 | ″ | ″ | P | |
| 1899-1900 | ″ | ″ | Q | |
| 1900-1 | ″ | ″ | R | |

# DATE LETTERS 1901 to 1962

TABLE XI

| | LION PASSANT | CITY ARMS | DATE LETTER |
|---|---|---|---|
| EDW.VII 1901-2 |  |  | A |
| 1902-3 | " | " | B |
| 1903-4 | " | " | C |
| 1904-5 | " | " | D |
| 1905-6 | " | " | E |
| 1906-7 | " | " | F |
| 1907-8 | " | " | G |
| 1908-9 | " | " | H |
| 1909-10 | " | " | I |
| GEO.V 1910-11 | " | " | K |
| 1911-12 | " | " | L |
| 1912-13 | " | " | M |
| 1913-14 | " | " | N |
| 1914-15 | " | " | O |
| 1915-16 | " | " | P |
| 1916-17 | " | " | Q |
| 1917-18 | " | " | R |
| 1918-19 | " | " | S |
| 1919-20 | " | " | T |
| 1920-21 | " | " | U |
| 1921-22 | " | " | V |
| 1922-23 | " | " | W |
| 1923-24 | " | " | X |
| 1924-25 | " | " | Y |
| 1925-26 | " | " | Z |

TABLE XII

| | LION PASSANT | CITY ARMS | DATE LETTER |
|---|---|---|---|
| 1926-27 |  |  | A |
| 1927-28 | " | " | B |
| 1928-29 | " | " | C |
| 1929-30 | " | " | D |
| 1930-31 | " | " | E |
| 1931-32 | " | " | ff |
| 1932-33 | " | " | G |
| 1933-34 | " | " | H |
| 1934-35* | " | " | I |
| 1935-36* | " | " | K |
| EDW.VIII 1936-37 | " | " | L |
| GEO.VI 1937-38 | " | " | M |
| 1938-39 | " | " | N |
| 1939-40 | " | " | O |
| 1940-41 | " | " | P |
| 1941-42 | " | " | Q |
| 1942-43 | " | " | R |
| 1943-44 | " | " | S |
| 1944-45 | " | " | T |
| 1945-46 | " | " | U |
| 1946-47 | " | " | V |
| 1947-48 | " | " | W |
| 1948-49 | " | " | X |
| 1949-50 | " | " | Y |
| 1950-51 | " | " | Z |

TABLE XIII

| | LION PASSANT | CITY ARMS | DATE LETTER |
|---|---|---|---|
| 1951-52 |  |  | A |
| ELIZ.II 1952-53 † | " | " | B |
| 1953-54 † | " | " | C |
| 1954-55 | " | " | D |
| 1955-56 | " | " | E |
| 1956-57 | " | " | F |
| 1957-58 | " | " | G |
| 1958-59 | " | " | H |
| 1959-60 | " | " | J |
| 1960-61 | " | " | K |
| 1961-62 | " | " | L |
| 1 July- 24 Aug. 1962 | " | " | M |

* Jubilee mark optional 

† Coronation mark optional 

The Chester Assay Office closed on 24 August 1962

# THE CHESTER CITY MARK

On 1st February 1687 the Chester Goldsmiths' Company drew up a Statement ordering a series of assay office marks to be placed on silver and gold plate assayed in Chester. In addition to the *date letter* "A" punch, the Company purchased a punch depicting the *City Coat of Arms* and another showing the *City Crest*. These two punches, shown below, were used only between 1687 and 1697, and were discontinued when the Britannia Silver Act of 1697 closed down all provincial assay offices. When assay rights were restored to Chester in 1701 the *City Coat* was re-instated in a different form but the *City Crest* was not restored. It is conjectured that official Chester "hallmarking" started at this time. Strictly speaking, Chester did not have a Goldsmiths' Hall similar to the one in London so the term assay office mark may be more appropriate than "hallmark".

The earlier *City Coat* was three wheat-sheaves with a sword erect between them. This had been the accepted Chester coat of arms since the time of Elizabeth I and the use of the *garb* or *wheatsheaf* has been linked with the County Palatine and Earldom of Chester from at least the thirteenth century. In 1580, the Queen's Norroy King of Arms, William Flower, granted a new coat of arms depicting three lions (or leopards) of England dimidiating (halving) the three garbs of Chester. This new style of *Coat* was ignored by Chester goldsmiths at the time, possibly because of the independence of the Palatine before Tudor times. Indeed, Chester was not mentioned in the fifteenth-century Statute relating to assay offices, possibly because of its long standing. The old *City Coat* is to be found on brass of 1584, seventeenth-century civic plate and on Chester-minted half crowns of Charles I. Curiously, when the assay office was established in 1701, the later Norry form of *City Coat* was used as the new assay office mark for Chester.

In 1720 a new set of punches was introduced to coincide with the restoration of the Sterling standard in June of that year. The form was similar to the 1701 punch but included seven tiny pellets in the margin above the *Coat*. Forms without pellets were used sporadically until 1760 when this style became the norm until 1778. With the exception of the first four marks below, all other *City* marks are on extant copper plates.

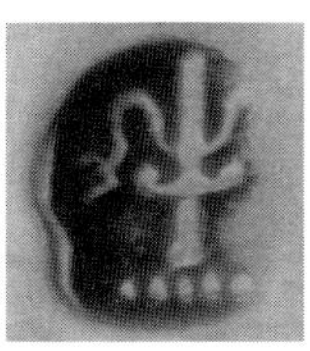

City Crest
1686/7 to 1697

Coat of Arms
1686/7 to 1697

Coat of Arms
1701 to 1720

Coat of Arms
1720 to 1760

Further minor variations in the form followed until a major change in 1778 curiously re-introduced the earlier Elizabethan style. This continued in various forms until closure of the assay office in 1962.

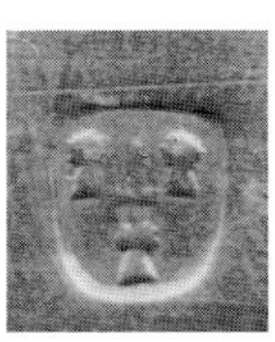

Coat of Arms
1778 to 1782

Coat of Arms
1782 to 1806

Coat of Arms
1806 to 1822

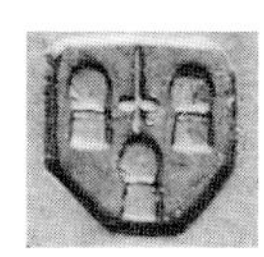

Coat of Arms
1823 to 1842

Coat of Arms
1843 to 1881

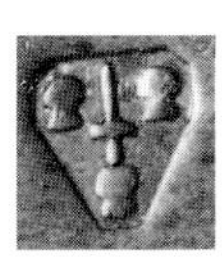

Coat of Arms
1882 to 1886

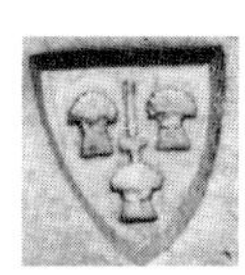

Coat of Arms
1886 to 1962

In passing, it is of interest to note that with the exception of the *Duty mark* punch produced in London, all Chester assay office punches and makers' mark punches were produced locally.

## BRITANNIA AND POST-1720 STERLING SILVER MARKS

### Britannia silver marks

The Act of 25th March 1697 introduced to protect the newly issued milled-edge sterling silver currency being melted down and coin clipping, mandated the use of the higher *Britannia* silver standard for all non-coinage silver wares. The Act raised the standard purity from 92.5% to 95.84% (23 parts pure silver in 24) which was in force until the Act of 1st June 1720 restored the old *sterling* standard alongside the new *Britannia* standard, both of which survive into the twenty-first century. By design or through inadequate wording of the Act, provincial offices were ignored in the preliminary legislation and Chester had to petition alongside other cities and await the Act of 29th September 1701 before its own right of assay was restored. Curiously, there are no *Britannia* marks struck on the extant early Chester copper plates (a similar situation exists for London), and so the examples shown below are taken from actual wares. It seems from the lack of extant wares that Britannia silver was not used in the Chester area once sterling grade was re-introduced. One has to wait over 200 years to the twentieth century before Britannia marks are struck on assay office copper plates for the first time. The early *Britannia* mark was struck in a rectangular frame, but by 1713 the corners were rounded and by 1715 a *Britannia* mark in an oval frame was in use. The Act required the lion passant guardant and leopard's head marks to be replaced by the *seated figure of Britannia* and a *lion's head erased* (cut-off).

1703

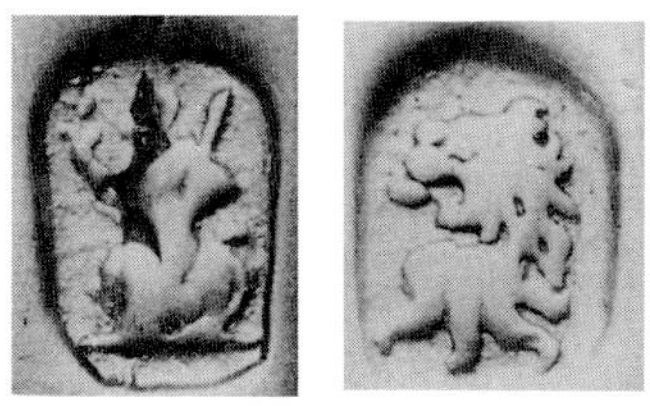

1717

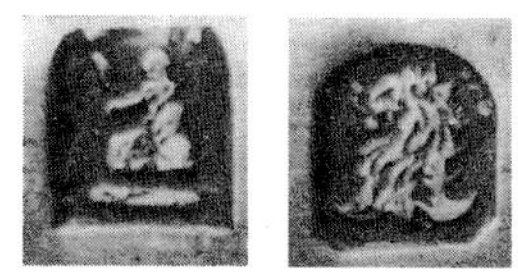

1953

### Sterling silver marks

The *lion passant* mark at Chester was always shown in *guardant* form with the head looking outwards. It was first portrayed in a rounded rectangle until 9th July 1730 when the frame became slightly less regular with sharply docked corners, a form which continued until 1762. Minor changes took place as old punches were replaced. By 1762 the docking of the corners is less severe but the overall shape continued throughout the eighteenth century. A punch with sharp corners has been noted in 1756 showing, as one might expect, that a number of punches were in use at the same time. Note that the design of the lion also changes over time. In 1799 the bottom of the frame became a pronounced double *ogee* and this lasted for five years until in 1807, the rectangle with docked corners was again introduced to accompany the letter "K". The double *ogee* on the bottom side returned in 1835 with the letter "Q", and by Victoria's reign this had become a centrally placed drop. During 1882, a new form of oblong surround was introduced alongside the centrally placed drop cameo and both were in use until closure in 1962. The mark was often stamped as part of a combination punch which included the town mark and date letter.

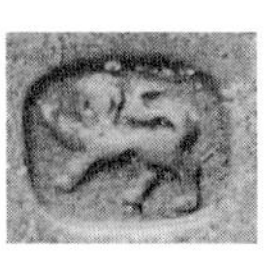

1720 to 1730

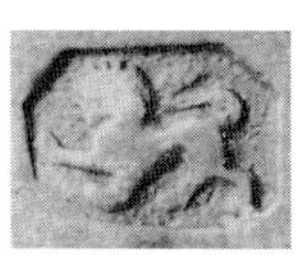

1730 to 1762

1762 to 1799

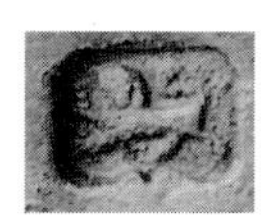

1799 to 1806

1806 to 1834

1835 to 1962

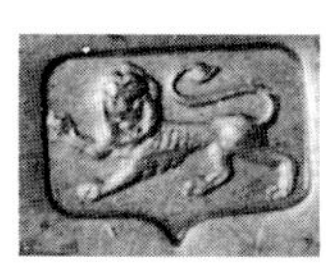

1835 to 1962

1882 to 1962

## THE LEOPARD'S HEAD MARK

### Introduction

The *leopard's head* mark is the earliest form of hallmark in the country. It was introduced in 1300 by King Edward I to counter frauds perpetrated by goldsmiths and was probably directed at the London trade. The Statute stipulated that no silver or gold wares should leave the hands of the workers unless marked with the *leopard's head.* Silver was to be of the sterling alloy (92.5% silver) and *no worse than money*, and since at this time there was no gold coinage in England, gold wares were to be *of the Touch of Paris*, a standard equivalent to 19.2 carats (or 80%). By the same order, all other assay towns were to use the new mark. The Ordinance of 1363 signed by Edward III introduced the individual *maker's* mark and made it clear that the assay office should put on the *leopard's head* mark first, and then the goldsmith his mark. The Statute of 1477 under Edward IV lowered the gold standard to 18 carats (75%) and to differentiate between old and new standards, the *leopard's head* became crowned. The Act of 1567 restored the standard to 22 carat.

### Chester

There is no evidence from records and extant goldware and silverware that the *leopard's head* mark was ever used at Chester before the restoration of the sterling silver standard in 1720. It was used in conjunction with the other hallmarks from 1720 until the accession of Queen Victoria in 1837 and then discontinued. The first Chester version appears in the top border of the first copper plate, and is struck with a broad face well executed and with a pronounced crown. The style continued with a wider clearance between the head and the cameo outline but frequent use of the same punch led to increasing wear and indistinct marks. By 1778 the mark has a rounded bottom and the face has pronounced whiskers and mane.

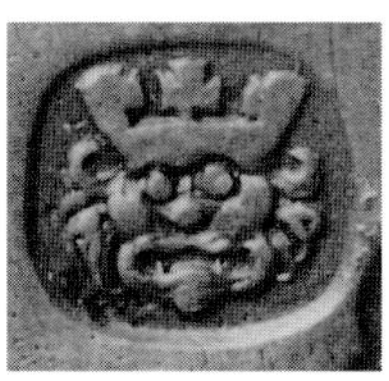

1720 to 1731

1726 to 1735

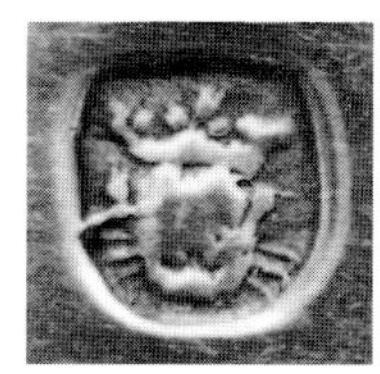

1778 to 1794

By 1794 the mark had become elongated with a narrower face, prominent ears and a larger crown. From 1799 to 1818 the form became less distinct. In 1822 the head was well made without a crown and this style continued until the mark was discontinued in 1837.

1794 to 1822

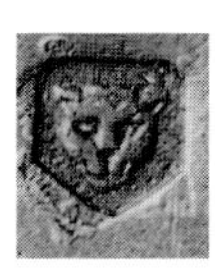

1822 to 1824

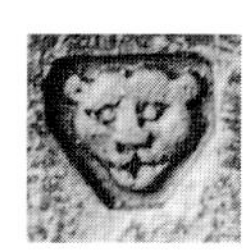

1824 to 1837

## THE DUTY MARK 1784 TO 1890

The authors are indebted to Anthony Dove for permission to refer to his comprehensive article in the magazine *Antique Collecting* (September 1984). A duty was first imposed on wrought silver plate from 1st June 1720 at the rate of 6 pence per troy ounce, but did not involve a new punch. This was replaced in 1758 by a dealers' licence of £2 per annum. On 1st December 1784 (effective starting date 2nd December) duty was re-imposed, in addition to the licence, at the rate of 6 pence per ounce on silver and, for the first time, it was imposed on gold at the rate of 8 shillings (i.e. 16 times the silver rate). This was to be placed under the management of the Commissioner of Stamps (later Inland Revenue) and resulted in the employment of special staff in London.

A new punch mark was introduced, consisting of an intaglio (incuse) head of George III facing left, in a rectangular punch with clipped corners. It was struck, apparently, before the assay was made because the Act states that *the wardens shall, previous to the touching, marking or assaying demand the sum of sixpence for every ounce of silver plate*. If the item was found on assay to be sub-standard, the duty was refunded. In London, 29th May 1786 was the start of their next annual date letter and it was decided that the duty mark be merged with the other hallmarks at the London assay office for use in a machine press. It was found impractical to mix incuse and cameo punches so the duty mark was changed to conform and became a head facing right in an oval cameo. This form was also adopted at provincial assay offices from 1st January 1787.

On 5th July 1797 the duty was doubled on both silver and gold to one shilling and 16 shillings respectively. The next change took place after 10th October 1804 when silver was increased to 1s/3d per ounce, while gold remained unchanged at 16 shillings. The final change took place from 31st August 1815 when silver was increased to 1s/6d per ounce and gold to 17 shillings. The duty mark between 1797 and 1837 appears to be made by a monarch's head cameo punch with notches filed in various places in order to indicate the duty rate changes. The final forms are various styles of the head of Queen Victoria facing left in an oval cameo. Curiously, the first three types of duty mark are not to be found on the Chester copper plates.

Incuse head
9th December 1784 to
30th December 1786

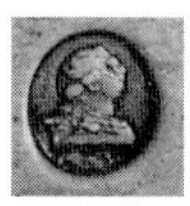

Cameo head
January 1787-97
and 1837-9

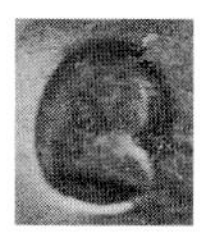

Cameo head
*c.* 1790

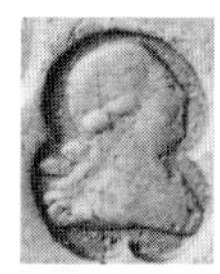

Modified cameo head
1797-1839

Cameo head 1842

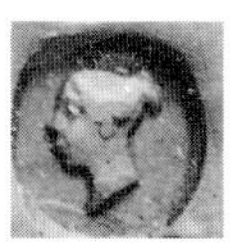

Cameo head 1848

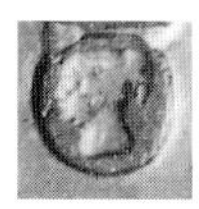

Cameo head 1860

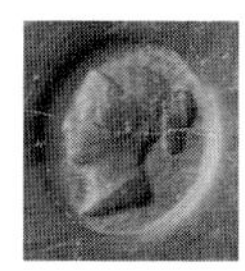

Cameo head 1888

As far as Chester is concerned, the first entry in the Plate Duty Book is dated 18th December 1784 when the Assay Master, Richard Richardson, submitted for analysis, a wine funnel, a pap boat and a caddy spoon. Around that time, 6 shillings was paid for the duty book itself, a fee of 5 shillings was paid to London for two duty punches, and 1 shilling and 4 pence for postage. The Act also made an allowance for a draw-back (or refund) of duty when plate was exported. In order to prevent the return of wares after the draw-back had been refunded, a new incuse mark was introduced, the standing figure of Britannia. In due course, eight draw-back punches in two sizes were delivered to Chester. However, the mark was to be stamped on finished goods, immediately before their export, and there were complaints of damage. The mark, but not the payment of draw-back, was revoked country-wide on 24th July 1785. This draw-back mark has not been seen on Chester wares or copper plates.

Not all the duty collected was passed on to the Treasury. From the beginning, one fifth of the duty (from 15th August 1785 reduced to one sixth) was refunded to the goldsmith in recognition that a certain amount of material would be lost in the finishing and polishing processes as wares were submitted to the assay office in semi-finished state. An accountant was employed and he charged sixpence in the pound or 2½% on all duty collected for gold and silver. The duty mark punches were provided centrally from the Commissioners of Stamps in London as the money raised by duty went straight to central government. Strictly speaking, the duty and draw-back marks were not hallmarks in the accepted sense as they were not under the control of the Assay Office although struck by them.

On 24th March 1798, duty on watchcases was abolished throughout the country and by 7th May 1798 all over-paid duty at Chester had been returned to the watchcase makers. The Plate Duty Act remained in force until 1st May 1890 for all other types of goldware and silverware. Duty payment and punching of the duty mark did not apply to grades of gold lower than 18 carat.

## GOLD MARKS

There is only written evidence that early Chester goldsmiths actually worked in gold. The London Goldsmiths' Company records indicate that Peter Edwardes of Chester was fined in February 1699 for *putting to sale gold and silver wares which were sub-standard* but the articles were not defined and one can only assume the gold was in the form of small rings. There seem to be no extant pieces of seventeenth or eighteenth century Chester assayed gold while the three surviving gold cups given as prizes at the Chester Races during the mid-eighteenth century were actually assayed at London so are not relevant.

It is possible that the earliest substantial pieces of gold were the 22-carat watchcases made by Liverpool workers during the last quarter of the eighteenth century. The plate duty books mention 24 cases submitted in 1785 by Henry Rigby and William Tarleton. In the period 1785 to 1798 when duty on watchcases was repealed, six Liverpool craftsmen submitted 84 gold cases for assay. Unfortunately, none of these items have been located in museums or private collections to confirm the marks, so it has to be assumed these watchcases followed the London practice of having the *lion passant* mark to denote 22 carat with the usual *date letter, leopard's head* and *town* marks. London introduced a special *sun in splendour* mark in 1816 for 22-carat gold, but there is no evidence it was used at Chester. By the Act of 1844, the *lion passant* for 22-carat gold was replaced throughout England by a *crown* with the *figure* 22.

22 carat
1844 to 1860

22 carat
1860 to 1888

22 carat
1902

22 carat
1955

The Act of 1798 re-introduced the ancient 18 carat gold standard alongside 22 carat. This followed requests from the London Clockmakers' Company and the London watchcase makers who actually wanted the cheaper and tougher 14 carat gold to compete fairly with similar gold-cased Swiss watch imports. The Goldsmiths' Company themselves had requested 14 carat at a reduced duty rate of 11 shillings per ounce, but the Order in Council confirmed 18 carat (at the 22 carat duty rate) and a new punch with a *crown* and the figure "18" was introduced. The new punches arrived in Chester in January 1799, and were first punched in the top border of Plate 1 and later the top borders of Plates 2 and 3.

18 carat
1799 to 1844

18 carat
1844 to 1860

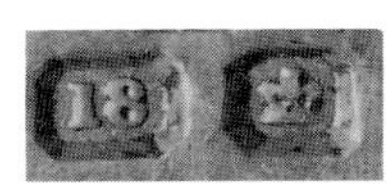
18 carat
1860 to 1888

18 carat
1955

Around 1850, the Coventry watchcase makers and the Birmingham jewellers asked the Birmingham Assay Office to obtain an Order in Council for permission to mark watchcases of 16, 14, 12 and 8 carat gold in order to compete with foreign imports. The London Goldsmiths' Company opposed the move strongly, but to no avail and the Act of 1854 allowed the manufacture of gold wares of any standard not less than one-third part pure gold (equivalent to 8 carat). The Act also removed the 30-mile radius geographic constraints on Birmingham and Sheffield goldsmiths who hitherto had been restricted to their local offices, and allowed any goldsmith in the land to use any assay office. This eventually led to an increase in business at Chester and London. The subsequent Order in Council actually introduced three lower gold standards of 15, 12 and 9 carat. The Act did not call for a crown to be incorporated in the three new marks (like 18 and 22 carat) and Chester may be unique in that on square X of Plate 2, near the date letter for 1856/7, there are lower grade marks incorporating crowns. However, there is no evidence that these marks were ever used as none have been seen.

Crowned 15 carat

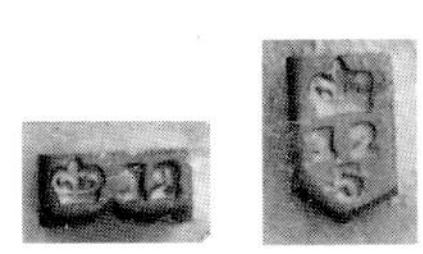
Crowned 12 carat

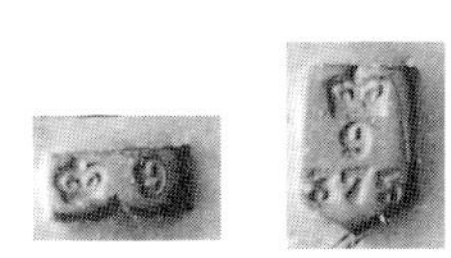
Crowned 9 carat

On square Y of Plate 2, possibly dating also for 1856/7, are the corrected versions of the punches without crowns. Examples of these latter marks are shown in an 1871 book on hallmarking by Alfred Lutschaunig of Liverpool. Curiously, there are no lower gold standard marks punched on Plate 3 (1860 to 1883) as might be expected for replacements and so the first punches lasted until new impressions on assay office plate 4 (1881).

## GOLD MARKS

The official marks for the lower grades of gold are shown below. The final change to gold standards took place in 1932 when 14 carat replaced the 15 and 12 carat standards. The 14 carat standard expressed as a decimal fraction is 0.583, but the new standard was set at 0.585 for the purpose of securing entry of the new standard into foreign markets (DeCastro).

15 carat
1854/6 to 1932

14 carat
1932 to 1962

12 carat
1854/6 to 1932

9 carat
1854/6 to 1962

After the 1932 Act, 15 carat and 12 carat could still be used, but were assayed and marked as 14 carat and 9 carat respectively. The four gold standards of 22, 18, 14 and 9 carat then continued at Chester until the assay office closed.

### Gold marks on watchcases

It seems that special multiple punches were used to stamp three or four assay marks in one operation. Indeed, in the twentieth century, the Dennison Watch Case Company of Handsworth, Birmingham supplied Birmingham Assay Office with a special foot-operated machine to prevent damage to watchcases. It is thought that similar multiple punches were used at Chester.

18 carat 1902

12 carat 1916

9 carat 1916

### Note on Platinum

In 1891, the Birmingham Trade magazine *The Jewellers and Watchmakers Trade Advertiser* reported that bracelets in fine chain made of alternate squares of gold and platinum are much in favour. Later, platinum became fashionable for ladies' watchcases, and such items were normally stamped "Plat" or "Platinum" by the maker. The assay offices were not involved at all in these endeavours although by the early twentieth century there was an unofficial country wide standard of 95% platinum with the addition of 5% iridium to improve machining properties. A similar alloy was already in widespread use as a component of thermo-couples used for measuring furnace temperatures.

There was a feeling in the trade that as platinum cost more than gold, such articles should be subject to hallmarking or at least to a minimum standard. According to Forbes, a draft Bill was prepared by the trade associations in 1924, and the London Goldsmiths' Company was asked for comments. These were favourable, but only if compulsory hallmarking was envisaged. Little progress was made on these proposals over the next 25 years, mainly because of the absence of a rapid and accurate assay technique. In the event, it took until 1973 before a new sophisticated assay technique based upon atomic adsorption was deemed successful. A new platinum mark, the "Orb", was then introduced.

According to Grahame Jones, experiments on assaying platinum were carried out at Chester during the 1950s by using the existing gold cupellation furnaces. However, the furnaces took two days to reach the desired melting temperature and were not really suitable. In the event, Chester closed down before the technical difficulties were overcome and never took delivery of punches for platinum nor saw the introduction of the new platinum standard.

## IMPORT MARKS FOR GOLD AND SILVER

The Customs Act of 1867 enacted that all gold and silver plate imported from foreign parts should be stamped with an additional mark, a letter **F** in an oval cameo. Curiously, there is little evidence that the new mark was used at Chester before 1888 which is the date of the earliest copper plate with this mark. This is surprising in view of the steady volume of imported watchcases from 1876 onwards (see Appendix 5). The **F** mark was also used in combination assay office punches from 1897 onwards as shown in the following examples. Curiously, the combination marks for 22 and 12 carat gold have not been seen on wares or copper plates.

The **F** mark

Sterling silver 1902

18 carat gold
1902

15 carat gold
1902

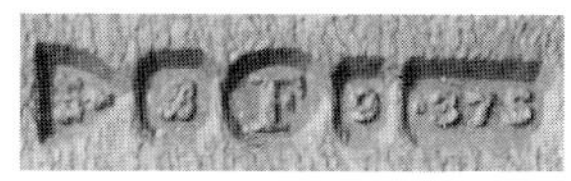

9 carat gold
1902

The Merchandise Marks Act of 1887 with its associated Order in Council introduced a special compulsory *Foreign* mark for imported watchcases. This took the form of a cross cameo for gold and an octagon for silver; it was repealed in 1907 (DeCastro). These marks appear only on copper Plate 6 and since they have not been seen on watchcases they can be considered very rare. It is possible they were never used by the assay office and certainly these very large punches would have distorted the back of a watchcase. It is difficult to explain why they were introduced at all.

18 carat watchcase 1888

Sterling silver watchcase 1887

The Act of 1904 abolished the **F** mark for foreign made wares and introduced an entirely new type of town mark, *an acorn with two leaves*, replacing the traditional Chester shield of three sheaves and a sword. This was used in conjunction with the usual standard marks and date letter. The new town mark was also used in combination punches. The new scheme for imports continued at Chester until closure of the office. According to Grahame Jones, Italy sent heavy 22-carat gold chains during the 1950s and these were struck with the mark shown below. However, this mark and the import Britannia silver mark have not been located on the extant copper plates. The following notification was sent to the trade in 1957 in the form of a thick card punched with the official marks for that year. Marks for home manufacture are shown on the left, import on the right.

| | *CHESTER* | |
|---|---|---|
|  | *22 CARAT GOLD*<br>*18 " "*<br>*14 " "*<br>*9 " "*<br>*STANDARD SILVER*<br>*BRITANNIA SILVER* |  |

## IMPORT MARKS FOR GOLD AND SILVER

The following combination punches were introduced for watchcases.

18-carat gold
watchcase
1912

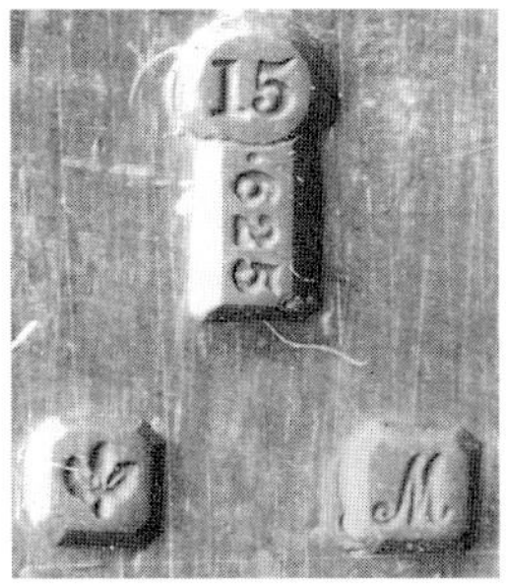


15-carat gold
watchcase
1912

12-carat gold
watchcase
1912

9-carat gold
watchcase
1933

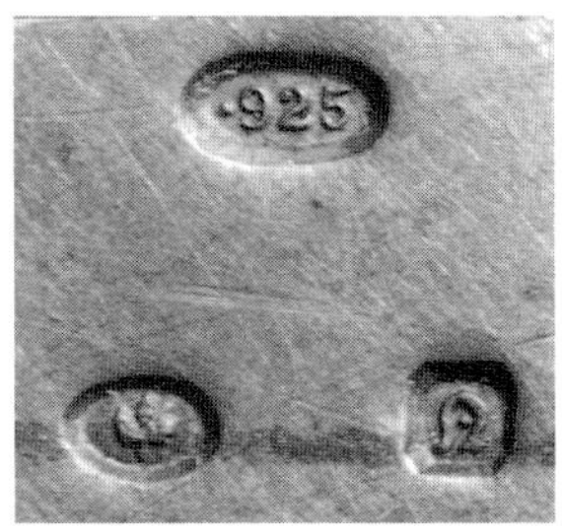


Sterling silver watchcase
1933

### Spurious marks

The literature has several examples of fraud concerning Chester gold marks. Many American-made watchcases appear at first sight to have a Chester mark, but the sword is missing; indeed the mark looks like the three castles for Newcastle. Furthermore, the 18 carat and leopard's head marks do not exactly match official ones. These items are probably made of gold of lower than 18 carat standard, possibly 14 or even 10 carat, and were intended to deceive the public. Whatever the source of these fake imports, they turn up from time to time indicating that the practice was widespread. Most of the examples of spurious marks on watchcases do not include a date letter so perhaps this is a key distinguishing aspect. Another difference is the way in which the three marks are struck in a line with the maker's mark above, as opposed to the cruciform arrangement used in Britain.

The marks shown below are from the gold case of a Liverpool-made watch by John Harrison (Baillie has him working 1824 to 1829; Kemp has 1818 to 1861 which matches better with the 1855 Select Committee Report which mentions similar frauds). Note the lack of sword in the town mark and absence of date letters – also note that the inner and outer parts of the double-backed case have different makers' marks but identical movement numbers (6428).

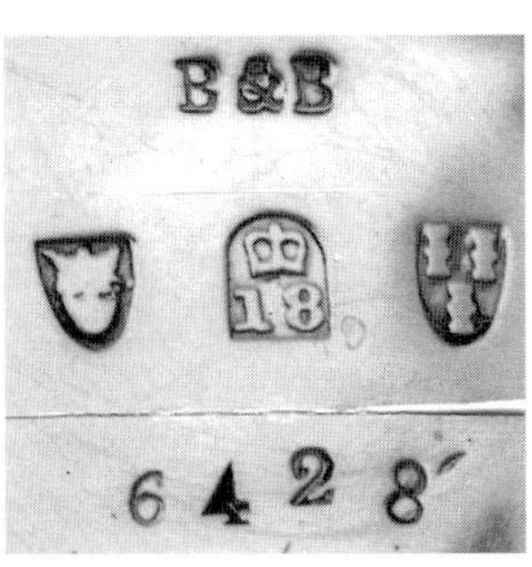


Inner gold case marks

Outer gold case marks

# PART 2

# MAKERS' MARKS

# 1570 to 1962

**How to use makers' marks tables**

**Pictograms**

**Tables of makers' marks 1570 to 1962**

**Monograms and cryptic marks**

## HOW TO USE THE MAKERS' MARKS TABLES

The makers' marks from the copper plates are reproduced approximately four times life size (or sixteen times in area), except for large marks which are shown approximately life size and annotated thus (§). Many of the marks are poorly struck and the copper plates are extremely difficult to photograph satisfactorily. Some marks taken from silverware are of varying enlargements while others are indistinct and artists' impressions have been used in the tables. The makers' marks are arranged in font style sequence starting with **plain** font letters without serifs, followed by **roman** type, ***italic*** and finally **gothic**. Within each font style, the letters are arranged alphabetically: namely, aa, aA, Aa, AA, AB, ABC, etc., with combinations containing ampersands (&) placed last within a group of similar marks. Within each alphabetic sequence, the style of the mark is further sub-divided into the categories: incuse unframed, incuse framed, single letters in individual cameos, multiple letters in oblong cameo, oval cameo and finally other cameo styles such as shield surround. Marks with letters separated by dots at the base of the letters or by pellets half way up the height of the letters are placed after those without. Where there are multiple examples of the same type, they are arranged chronologically. Where there are more than two letters to a mark they are to be read first at the top, then left to right and finally, the base as follows:

| | | | |
|---|---|---|---|
| A<br>B C | A<br>B<br>C | A B<br>C | are to be found in the position ABC of the Compendium |
| A<br>B C<br>D | A B<br>C D | A<br>B<br>C<br>D | are to be found in the position ABCD of the Compendium |

A tabular layout is used allowing convenient searching of multiple entries for a given maker. The format is loosely based upon the three extant registers of marks which contain six columns of information: Date of Entry, Business Address, Trade, Private Address of the individual/company and, finally, "By whom sent", the name of the person/company who entered the mark. In this Compendium the tables have only five columns:

**Column 1** contains registration information on register and page number, and entry date. For the period up to 1894 it also contains information and references used to make the attribution, for example the plate duty books. After 1863 it contains links to the small and large punch books and the three registers. Dates not entered by the clerk have been estimated from contiguous dated entries. Marks on plate 3 without entries in SPB or LPB are shown as *Not in SPB or LPB so struck 1860-3*. From 1877, the column also contains the name(s) and sometimes address of the person or company taken from the "By whom sent" column in the registers. They may have been "local" representatives, agents or associated partners and may even have had permission to use the mark. The page numbers for these latter names are shown in *italics* in the index. For the period 1886 to 1894 it is assumed that the mark was in the *Missing Register,* and the approximate year of entry calculated on the basis of regular registrations of the 550 marks in that register. Where the clerk has entered marks for a given person at different dates on the same register page, then these are grouped together under a single page number. The annotation *Two sizes*, etc., indicates registration of multiple sizes; each has a separate compendium number (see column 3), but only one photograph is shown. The entry BAO 16.281 indicates a mark also registered with that number at Birmingham Assay Office; similarly LAO or SAO followed by a number refers to London or Sheffield.

**Column 2** contains maker's private address. The earliest date for these in the registers is 1894. Where multiple names and private addresses are entered without clear distinction, then one can only assume that the first business name relates to the first private address and so on. For entries dated before 1894 this column may have other information relating to the maker. The entry "Kelly" indicates that trade was taken from this directory.

**Column 3** contains maker's mark, relevant copper plate number and square details. Marks on Plate 1 generally can be dated to before 1841 and those on plate 2 before 1860. However, the clerk sometimes struck the mark on an earlier plate or in the wrong square; these are shown in the Compendium as P1*sic*/34/x2 or P3/B*sic*/x1. Before 1886, the clerk did not sequence number the marks on each plate so there is no cross-matching numbers in the records. Where there are multiple strikings of the same mark these are shown as P1/23/x2 indicating two similar marks on square 23 of Plate 1. Multiple sizes of the same mark are similarly indicated. Where the clerk has given the same number to, say, an incuse and cameo version of the same letters, then these are designated P5/W/123a,b. This will allow future research on numbers of punches submitted by individual makers. After 1886 marks were given reference numbers such as P5/B/567 indicating mark number 567 in square B of plate 5. Plate 5 is unusual in having a single series of numbers in the range 1 to 999 in contrast to the later plates which have a separate sequence starting at "1" for each alphabetic letter square. Furthermore, not all the numbers are used and some are used for more than one mark on different alphabetic squares. It is possible that for Plate 5 a unique number was used for each day to cover all the marks submitted on that day.

Occasionally, some entries only indicate a change of address or company ownership and have no new marks. These latter and each individual mark have been given a Compendium number in the style of #1234. Makers' marks before 1701 have no plate details. Some fifty unregistered marks used before 1841 are annotated *Not on P1*. The tables also include conjectured initials for some unseen marks of makers mentioned in the plate duty books, Parliamentary Report of 1773 and Jackson 1st edition: shown in roman type with a "?".

The occasional annotation in the mark details column such as *type 2a* is a reference to the original naming system used by Maurice Ridgway in his three books on Chester marks. Occasionally, the clerk forgot to punch the mark on plates 3 and 5 in which case the relevant mark in the SPB or LPB is shown. Five of the earliest of makers' marks are not initials but pictograms. They are shown on the first page of the tables and are included for completeness. Unusual monograms or cryptic marks used after 1863 are shown in a separate section at the end of the tables.

**Column 4** contains maker/company details and business address. Readers are reminded that there are no extant registrations before 1863 or for the "missing register" period of 1888 to 1894, and so attributions for these periods cannot be absolutely confirmed. Much reliance for the early attributions is based upon the authors' five books and Jackson, the research for which is based upon records of goldsmiths, matching of their initials to marks seen on silver plate and on assay office copper plates, reinforced by cross-referencing to entries in the very important plate duty books. Attributions for the 1886-94 period are in the main based upon contemporary registrations at Chester and other assay offices with additional information taken from trade directories. In the interests of keeping a tidy structure the use of the query (?) sign has been kept to a minimum. An asterisk (*) behind a maker/company name indicates the existence of an associated biography in Culme's *The Directory of Gold & Silversmiths 1838 to 1914*: a (G) similarly refers to Grimwade's *London Goldsmiths 1697 to 1837.*

**Column 5** contains trade information which is shown in extant registers from 1894 onwards. For the period up to 1700 the trade is shown as *silversmith* or *goldsmith* based upon Chester Goldsmiths' Company freedom records. Between 1701 and 1894 trades have been deduced from registrations at other assay offices, trade directories, examples of actual silverware or from entries in the plate duty books running from 1784 to 1840.

Regarding trade descriptions, it should be noted that from around the 1890s, the term *Jeweller* usually implies a retailer of items with perhaps a limited repair or manufacturing capability on site. Similarly, the term *Watchmaker* or *Clockmaker* denotes a retailer of watches or clocks with perhaps a repair facility on site but hardly ever a manufacturing capability. On the other hand a *Watchcase maker* was definitely involved in making cases but they were never offered for sale directly to the general public. The term *manufacturer* implies a Manufactory (nowadays contracted to Factory) devoted to the actual making of wares for sale. The entries for *Tobacconist* probably cover the need for assaying silver ferrules on briar-wood pipes, silver shields on cigar boxes and imported fancy silver goods.

## PICTOGRAMS

| REFERENCES | ARTEFACTS | MARK DETAILS | MAKER and ADDRESS | TRADE |
|---|---|---|---|---|
| MR1/51-65<br>MR3/179<br>J3/389 SIL/9,30,34,35<br>LGM 1573<br>J1 c.1570-80<br>GMSC/1-3<br>Free 1555 so may have used the mark before 1570 | Church plate and spoons *c.*1570-80<br><br>**EARLIEST EXTANT MAKER'S MARK** | Pre-dates P1<br>#1<br> | **William MUTTON**<br>Bridge Street<br>Chester | Silversmith |
| MR1/143<br>MR3/183<br>J3 1672-91<br>J3/416<br>Bird mark, possibly an allusion to water and Liverpool, is only seen in conjunction with his EL mark | Spoons, tankard *c.*1700 | Pre-dates P1<br>#2<br> | **Edward LEWIS**<br>Water Street<br>Liverpool | Silversmith |
| This rebus of a bull's head only seen alongside his type 1 NB mark | Trifid spoons *c.*1700 and communion cup | Pre-dates P1<br>#3<br><br>type 2 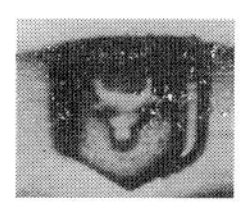 | **Nathaniel BULLEN**<br>Goss Street<br>Chester | Silversmith |
| MR1/148-57 MR3/184 SIL/30/1,45/6,48<br>J1 1677-1706 J3/389<br>Free 1676/7<br>This wheatsheaf only seen with his type 1 PP mark | Two communion cups *c.*1685 | Pre-dates P1<br>#4<br><br>type 1  | **Peter PEMBERTON I**<br>Chester | Silversmith |
| MR1/159<br>J2/381,387 | A lone striking on the reverse of the first copper plate<br><br>Possibly the coppersmith with Welsh connections who provided Plate 1<br><br>A similar mark noted by Jackson on a trifid spoon with date letter for 1686-90 with Alexander Pulford's mark – owned by the Marquess of Breadalbane | P1/reverse/x1<br>#5<br> | **Unidentified** | Silversmith<br>or<br>Coppersmith |

| REGISTRATION DETAILS | MAKER'S PRIVATE ADDRESS and DETAILS | PLATE and MARK DETAILS | MAKER/COMPANY and BUSINESS ADDRESS | MAKER'S TRADE |
|---|---|---|---|---|
| R3/97<br>4 May 1940<br>Sent by C A Horton<br>109 Spencer Street<br>Birmingham | 164 Thorpe Road<br>Norwich | P21/A/3<br>***#11***<br> | **Albert Arthur AMES**<br>8 Goat Lane<br>Norwich | Jeweller |
| LPB/14 no mark<br>6 February 1885<br>$7^{th}$ name on LPB/14<br>and $7^{th}$ mark on P5<br>Allday & Allday? | See also J A | P5/A/x1<br>***#12***<br>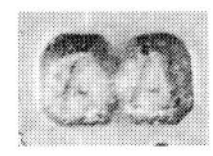 | **John ALLDAY & SON**<br>8 Warstone Lane<br>Birmingham | Manufacturing jewellers |
| R1/40<br>27 February 1897<br>Sent by E Langridge & Co | Private address same as business | P5/A/820<br>***#13***<br> | **Adolphe ARON and Albert ARON**<br>trading as **ARON BROTHERS** *<br>2 Bridewell Place<br>London EC | Fancy goods manufacturers |
| R2/65<br>29 September 1908<br>Sent by Albert Aron | 11 Clifford Street [1]<br>London W<br>22 Rue de Bondy<br>Paris | P13/A/4<br>***#14***<br>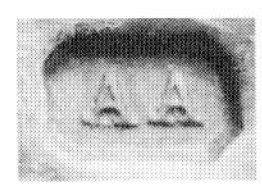 | **Albert ARON** [1]<br>**Ernest ARON** trading as<br>**ARON BROTHERS** *<br>2 Bridewell Place<br>London EC and<br>22 Rue de Bondy<br>Paris | Fancy goods dealers |
| R1/48<br>22 July 1897<br>Sent by A Ashford | A Ashford<br>Guest Street<br>Birmingham | P5/A/858<br>***#15***<br> | **Albert ASHFORD**<br>Back of 61 Graham Street<br>Birmingham | Ring maker and jeweller |
| R1/69<br>11 October 1898<br>Sent by A H Tongue | Clifton<br>222 Hithsdale Road<br>Pollokshields<br>Glasgow | P9/A/2<br>***#16***<br> | **Arthur Angus ANDERSON**<br>65 Argyle Street<br>Glasgow | Tobacco and cigar merchant |
| R1/23<br>6 March 1896<br>Sent by A H Tongue | Clifton<br>Pollokshields<br>Glasgow | P5/A/733<br>***#17***<br> | | |
| R3/93<br>24 February 1939<br>Sent by A A Kerridge | 4 Mount Road<br>West Kirby<br>Cheshire | P21/K/1<br>***#18***<br> | **Arthur Andrews** (*sic*) **KERRIDGE**<br>No business address entered | Art student |
| R1/73<br>7 September 1898<br>Sent by A Appleby Ltd | Alfred Appleby<br>Brierly, Littleton Road<br>Edgbaston, Birmingham<br>160 Bristol Road [1]<br>Edgbaston<br>Birmingham | P9/A/1<br>***#19***<br> | **Alfred APPLEBY & CO LTD**<br>J L Jacobs [1] (Managing Director)<br>124 Vyse Street<br>Birmingham | Manufacturing jewellers |
| Missing register<br>*c*.1891 | | P5/P/391<br>***#20***<br> | **Unidentified** | |
| R3/181<br>4 October 1961<br>Sent by A A Ward | Fairholme<br>Chester Road<br>Sandiway<br>Northwich<br>Cheshire | P21/W/106<br>***#21***<br> | **Miss Alice Audrey WARD**<br>No business address entered | Silversmith student |

| REGISTRATION DETAILS | MAKER'S PRIVATE ADDRESS and DETAILS | PLATE and MARK DETAILS | MAKER/COMPANY and BUSINESS ADDRESS | MAKER'S TRADE |
|---|---|---|---|---|
| R3/186<br>9 August 1962<br>Sent by A A Warren | 6 Silverdale Road<br>Newcastle-under-Lyme<br>Staffordshire | P21/W/109<br>***#22***<br> | **Anthony Arthur WARREN**<br>No business address entered | Silversmith student |
| PP1/186 | | P2/B/x2<br>***#23,4*** | **Adam BURGESS**<br>48 Prescot Street<br>Liverpool or | Watch and watchcase manufacturer |
| J1 1845-6<br>Similar mark entered<br>LAO 9 March 1846 | |  | **Adam BURGESS**<br>5 Chatham Terrace (later 29 Vine Street)<br>Liverpool or | Spoon and fork maker |
| GTD 1829<br>Perhaps worked after 1841 | | | **Alfred BENNY**<br>Liverpool | Watchcase maker |
| R2/115<br>8 July 1910<br>Sent by E Durban Co | 13 Linden Road<br>Bearwood<br>Birmingham | P13/B/79-82<br>***#25-8***<br> | **Alfred BROCKINGTON**<br>56 Albion Street<br>Birmingham | Goldsmith |
| R2/196<br>22 May 1915<br>Sent by Coley Brothers | | P15/A/60<br>***#29***<br> | | Jewellers factor |
| R2/198<br>17 August 1915<br>Sent by George F Bickerton | Bishop Road<br>Sutton Coldfield<br>32 Reddington Road<br>Moseley<br>Birmingham | P15/A/1<br>***#30***<br> | **Arthur John ABRAHALL**<br>**John William BINT** trading as<br>**ABRAHALL & BINT** *<br>22 Frederick Street<br>Birmingham | Jewellers |
| R2/155<br>2 April 1912<br>Sent by Arthur Bromage<br>temporary address<br>129 West High<br>Salford | 116 Cross Lane<br>Manchester | P13/B/131<br>***#31***<br> | **Arthur BROMAGE**<br>116 Cross Lane<br>Manchester<br>4 Hague Street (22 November 1947)<br>London Road<br>Manchester | Pipe and stick mounter |
| R2/188<br>12 June 1914<br>Sent by Alfred Barling | 60 Perryn Road<br>Acton<br>London N | P15/B/34,35<br>***#32,3***<br> | **Alfred BARLING** trading as<br>**B BARLING & SONS** *<br>9-11 Praik Street<br>Camden Street<br>London NW | Silversmiths and briar pipe manufacturers |
| R1/51<br>29 September 1897<br>Sent by W Walker | Private address same as business | P5/aboveB/873<br>***#34***<br> | **Andrew BORLAND**<br>20 Waring Street<br>Belfast<br>Ireland | Tobacconist |
| LPB/16<br>10 April 1879 | CWMP has 62 Mount Street, Coventry in 1883 and 3 Trafalgar Street, Coventry 1886-91 | P3/B/x2<br>***#35,6***<br> | **Abraham BEAL**<br>3 and 4 Derby Lane<br>Coventry | Watch pendant maker |
| R3/176<br>3 January 1961<br>Sent by Arthur Cecil Gibson | 50 Hatton Garden<br>London EC1<br>(Ed: Agents for Longines Watch Co) | P21/B/64<br>***#37***<br> | **BAUME & CO LTD** *<br>50 Hatton Garden<br>London EC1 | Watch and clock importers and distributors |

| REGISTRATION DETAILS | MAKER'S PRIVATE ADDRESS and DETAILS | PLATE and MARK DETAILS | MAKER/COMPANY and BUSINESS ADDRESS | MAKER'S TRADE |
|---|---|---|---|---|
| Missing register<br>*c.*1887 | | P5/B/71<br>***#38***  | **Unidentified** | |
| SPB/23 no name entered<br>16 September 1876<br>Sent by Frederick Francis Seeland<br>Similar mark entered LAO 19 September 1876 Four sizes | Private address same as business<br><br>Seen on silver and gold cases made for Waltham by Dennisons of Birmingham during the period 1876-1902 | P3/B/x8<br>***#39-46***  | **Alfred BEDFORD** *<br>(Ed: Manager of Waltham Watch Co UK)<br>Waltham Buildings<br>Holborn Circus<br>London | Gold watchcase maker |
| Missing register<br>*c.*1886 | | P5/B/34<br>***#47***  | | |
| SPB/23<br>16 September 1876 | | P3/B/x2<br>***#48,9***  | **Alfred BEDFORD** *<br>Waltham Buildings<br>Holborn Circus<br>London | |
| Missing register<br>*c.*1890 | | P5/B/327<br>***#50***  | | |
| R1/7<br>15 February 1895<br>Sent by Alfred Burgess | 29 Cavendish Road<br>Birmingham | P5/aboveB/639<br>***#51***  | **Alfred BURGESS**<br>58 Tenby Street North<br>Birmingham | Manufacturing jeweller |
| R1/94<br>5 March 1899<br>Sent by Broadhead & Adelman | Halliwell Lane<br>Cheetham<br>Manchester<br>Highfield Street<br>Urmston<br>Manchester | P9/A/10<br>***#52***  | **Joseph ADELMAN**<br>**Edgar BROADHEAD** trading as<br>**ADELMAN & BROADHEAD**<br>72, 72a Lancaster Avenue<br>Fennel Street<br>Manchester | Jewellers |
| R1/178<br>22 October 1902<br>Sent by R J Wakefield | Bishops Road<br>Sutton Coldfield<br>Salisbury Road<br>Moseley<br>Birmingham | P9/A/42<br>***#53***  | **Arthur John ABRAHALL**<br>**John William BINT** trading as<br>**ABRAHALL & BINT** *<br>22 Frederick Street<br>Birmingham | Jewellers |
| R1/187<br>11 March 1903<br>Sent by A Bates | 63 Moor Street<br>Earlsdon<br>Coventry | P9/B/100<br>***#54***  | **Albert Alan BATES**<br>Portland House<br>Chapel Fields<br>Coventry | Gold watch pendant maker |
| R2/70<br>16 January 1909<br>Sent by Abraham Blackman | 85 Dempsey Road<br>London E | P13/B/45<br>***#55***  | **Abraham BLACKMAN** *<br>52 Clerkenwell Road<br>London EC | Gem ring maker |
| R1/30<br>18 June 1896<br>Sent by Wigley & Hall<br>C Horner<br>E Vaughton | Maney Cottage [1]<br>Sutton Coldfield<br>Holly Green [2]<br>Church Road<br>Moseley | P5/A/778<br>***#56***  | **Arthur John ABRAHALL**[1]<br>**John William BINT** [2] trading as<br>**ABRAHALL & BINT** *<br>48 Frederick Street<br>Birmingham | Jewellers and silversmiths |
| R2/49<br>31 October 1907<br>Sent by R Parke | Bishops Road<br>Sutton Coldfield<br>Salisbury Road<br>Moseley<br>Birmingham | P9/A/91,92<br>***#57,8***  | **Arthur John ABRAHALL**<br>**John William BINT** trading as<br>**ABRAHALL & BINT** *<br>22 Frederick Street<br>Birmingham | Jewellers |

| REGISTRATION DETAILS | MAKER'S PRIVATE ADDRESS and DETAILS | PLATE and MARK DETAILS | MAKER/COMPANY and BUSINESS ADDRESS | MAKER'S TRADE |
|---|---|---|---|---|
| R3/5<br>26 November 1921<br>Sent by J & R Griffin | Blencoe<br>Honor End Road<br>London | P15/B/158<br>***#59***<br> | **A C BLOXHAM LTD** *<br>114, 115 Holborn Circus<br>London | Silversmiths and electroplaters |
| Missing register<br>*c.*1890<br>Similar mark entered BAO 21 July 1896 | | P5/B/324<br>***#60***<br> | **Alfred BUCKLEY**<br>20 Vyse Street<br>Birmingham | Jeweller |
| R1/86<br>23 November 1898<br>Sent by Abrahall & Bint | Maney Cottage [1]<br>Sutton Coldfield<br>Church Road [2]<br>Moseley<br>Birmingham | P9/A/5<br>***#61***<br> | **Arthur John ABRAHALL** [1]<br>**John William BINT** [2] trading as<br>**ABRAHALL & BINT** *<br>48 Frederick Street<br>Birmingham | Gold and silversmiths |
| WTD 1880<br>PP1/186<br>CWMP 1886-91 | | P2/B/x2<br>***#62,3***<br> | **Alexander BELL**<br>21 Fleet Street<br>Coventry | Gold watchcase maker |
| R1/105<br>30 June 1899<br>Sent by H Perkins | 52 Highbury Grove North [1]<br>London<br>7 Bury Road [2]<br>Wood Green<br>London N | P9/B/21<br>***#64***<br>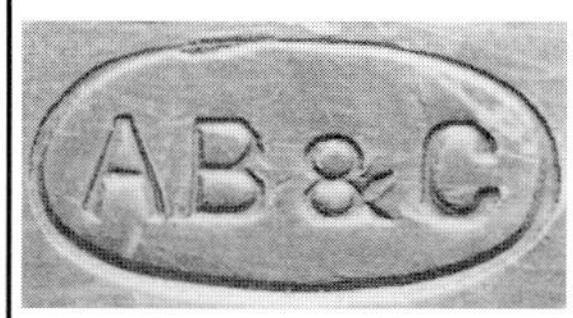 | **Albert BAKER & CO LTD** *<br>Nathaniel De Meza [1] (Director)<br>P E Cooper [2] (Secretary)<br>65 Holloway Road<br>London N | Tobacconists |
| Missing register<br>*c.*1891<br>Two sizes | | P5/B/348a,b<br>***#65,6***<br> | **A BROMET & CO** *<br>38 Jewin Street<br>London | Wholesale jewellers |
| Missing register<br>*c.*1890 | | P5/B/326<br>***#67***<br>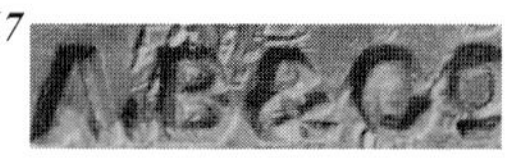 | | |
| R1/90<br>6 February 1899<br>Sent by H Griffith & Sons Ltd | Fillebrook House<br>Leytonstone<br>Essex | P9/B/12<br>***#68***<br> | **Emanuel Henry LEVI** trading as<br>**A BROMET & CO** *<br>38, 39 Jewin Street<br>London | Wholesale jewellers |
| LPB/34<br>25 May 1883<br>Sent by E Bennett<br>Similar mark entered LAO 4 June 1892 | | P3/B/x1<br>***#69***<br> | **A BROMET & CO** *<br>38 Jewin Street<br>London | Smallworkers |
| LPB/18<br>14 March 1884<br>Sent by Coley Brothers, Vyse Street Birmingham | Possibly linked to A Bromet & Co who had a Director named Cohen | P5/B/x1<br>***#70***<br> | **COHEN & CO** *<br>43 London Wall<br>London EC | Wholesale jewellers and importers |
| Missing register<br>*c.*1890 | | P5/B/345<br>***#71***<br> | | |
| Missing register<br>*c.*1894<br>Mark suggests Able surname and #P5/A/552 (#8140) was also used for Thomas Able | **PROBABLY LAST MARK IN MISSING REGISTER** | P5/A/552a<br>***#72***<br> | **Thomas ABLE**<br>56 Tenby Street North<br>Birmingham | Jeweller |

| REGISTRATION DETAILS | MAKER'S PRIVATE ADDRESS and DETAILS | PLATE and MARK DETAILS | MAKER/COMPANY and BUSINESS ADDRESS | MAKER'S TRADE |
|---|---|---|---|---|
| R3/97<br>9 April 1940<br>Sent by Joseph Smith & Sons (Birmingham) Ltd and Smith, Ewen & Stylic Ltd | 35 Portland Road [1]<br>Edgbaston<br>46 Portland Road [2]<br>Edgbaston | P21/A/2<br>*#73*<br> | **Judah ALBURY** [1]<br>**Albert ALBURY** [2] trading as<br>**ALBURY BROTHERS**<br>Century Buildings<br>Summerhill Road<br>Birmingham | Wholesale jewellers |
| 6 January 1950 | | P21/A/10<br>*#74*<br> | | |
| 24 June 1954 | | P21/A/20<br>*#75*<br> | | |
| R2/67<br>29 October 1908<br>Sent by Eaton & Wrighton | 46 Portland Road<br>Edgbaston | P13/A/5<br>*#76*<br> | **Judah AHRONSBERG**<br>**Albert AHRONSBERG**<br>**Lionel AHRONSBERG** trading as<br>**AHRONSBERG BROTHERS** *<br>Century Buildings<br>Birmingham | Manufacturing jewellers |
| R1/133<br>12 October 1900<br>Sent by Ahronsberg Brothers | 46 Portland Road [2]<br>Birmingham<br>23 Clarendon Road [1 & 3]<br>Birmingham | P9/A/18<br>*#77*<br> | **Judah AHRONSBERG** [1]<br>**Lionel AHRONSBERG** [2]<br>**Albert AHRONSBERG** [3] trading as<br>**AHRONSBERG BROTHERS** *<br>39 Albion Street<br>Birmingham | Wholesale jewellers |
| R1/27<br>18 April 1896<br>Sent by C M Wrighton<br>Authority to Wigley & Hall and S Pitt | Private address same as business | P5/A/757<br>*#78*<br> | **Judah AHRONSBERG** trading as<br>**AHRONSBERG BROTHERS** *<br>39 Albion Street<br>Birmingham | |
| R3/155<br>23 August 1955<br>Sent by W J Pellow Ltd<br>31 Hylton Street<br>Birmingham | Greenway [1]<br>Woodburn Road<br>Brooklands<br>Cheshire<br>33 Cavendish Road [2]<br>Salford 7 | P21/A/23<br>*#79*<br> | **George ABELSON** [1]<br>**Myer ABELSON** [2] trading as<br>**ABELSON BROTHERS**<br>10 Withy Grove<br>Manchester 4 | Wholesale jewellers |
| R1/169<br>30 May 1902<br>Sent by J H Wynn<br>Two sizes | 4 York Road<br>Edgbaston<br>Birmingham | P9/A/37,38<br>*#80,1*<br> | **Percy Abel ABRAHAMS** trading as<br>**ABRAHAMS BROTHERS**<br>92 Vyse Street<br>Birmingham | Wholesale jewellers |
| Missing register<br>*c.*1888<br>Similar mark BAO<br>20 February 1889 | | P5/A/169<br>*#82*<br> | **ALLEN BROTHERS**<br>183 Warstone Lane<br>Birmingham | Jewellers |
| R1/102<br>20 May 1899<br>Sent by G R Allen | 24 Hampton Road<br>Handsworth<br>231 Birchfield Road<br>Handsworth<br>Birmingham | P9/A/11,12<br>*#83,4*<br>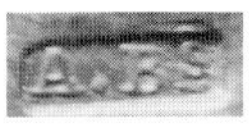 | **George Robert ALLEN**<br>**Richard Hooper ALLEN** trading as<br>**ALLEN BROTHERS**<br>35 Northampton Street<br>Birmingham | |
| R2/53<br>28 December 1907<br>Sent by Allen Brothers<br>(recut and entered 93, 94 and 95) | Hampton Road<br>Handsworth<br>39 Farm Road<br>Sparkbrook | P9/A/93-95<br>*#85-7*<br> | **George Robert ALLEN**<br>**Richard Hooper ALLEN**<br>35 Northampton Street<br>Birmingham | |

| REGISTRATION DETAILS | MAKER'S PRIVATE ADDRESS and DETAILS | PLATE and MARK DETAILS | MAKER/COMPANY and BUSINESS ADDRESS | MAKER'S TRADE |
|---|---|---|---|---|
| R1/42<br>30 March 1897<br>Sent by Stokes & Ireland | St James's Chambers<br>Albermarle Street<br>London W | P5/aboveB/828<br>*#88*<br> | **R J BARRETT, H A BARRETT**<br>**H H BARRETT, Walter BARRETT**<br>trading as **A BARRETT & SONS** *<br>63,64,158 Piccadilly<br>London | Silversmiths |
| Missing register<br>*c.*1891<br>Similar mark entered<br>LAO 24 October 1892 | | P5/B/387<br>*#89*<br> | | Brush and comb manufacturers |
| R1/223<br>3 December 1904<br>Sent by Thomas Able | Anglesey Street<br>Lozells<br>Rookery Road<br>Handsworth, Birmingham | P9/A/57<br>*#90*<br> | **Thomas ABLE**<br>**Walter James CHARNELL** trading as<br>**ABLE & CHARNELL**<br>44½ Frederick Street<br>Birmingham | Silversmiths and jewellers |
| R2/35<br>19 March 1907<br>Sent by T Able<br>Partnership dissolved<br>4 March 1913 | 47 Anglesey Street<br>Lozells<br>Haseler<br>Jockey Street<br>Sutton | P9/A/84<br>*#91*<br> | 44 Frederick Street<br>Birmingham | Jewellers |
| LPB/4<br>17 October 1877<br>Similar mark entered<br>LAO 25 August 1875 | | P3/C/x3<br>*#92-4*<br> | **Antoine CASTELBERG** *<br>58 Holborn Viaduct<br>London | Watchcase maker |
| Missing register<br>*c.*1886 Similar mark<br>LAO 25 August 1875<br>and CAO 17 October<br>1877 -Two sizes | | P5/C/2a,b<br>*#95,6*<br> | | |
| R1/53<br>1 November 1897<br>Sent by<br>W H Carrington & Son | Private address same as business | P5/C/902<br>*#97*<br> | **Richard CARTER** trading as<br>**A CARTER**<br>4 Oldham Road<br>Manchester | Tobacconist |
| LPB/22<br>31 January 1884 | | P5/C/x1<br>*#98*<br>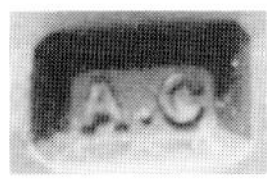 | **Alfred COOPER**<br>179 Warstone Lane<br>Birmingham | Jeweller |
| R1/189<br>31 March 1903 | Kelly 1902 directory | P9/C/82<br>*#99*<br> | **Arthur COOK**<br>6/8 Carver Street<br>Birmingham | Silversmith |
| R3/119<br>12 August 1947<br>Sent by A Clayton<br>Two sizes | Private address same as business | P21/C/37,38<br>*#100,1*<br> | **Angela CLAYTON**<br>5 Range Road<br>Whalley Range<br>Manchester 16 | Art student |
| R3/144<br>12 May 1953<br>Sent by A Coulthard | Private address same as business | P21/C/61<br>*#102*<br> | **Albert COULTHARD**<br>136 Barlow Moor Road<br>West Didsbury<br>Manchester 20 | Retired research chemist |
| Missing register<br>*c.*1889 | | P5/C/247<br>*#103*<br> | **Unidentified** | |
| Missing register<br>*c.*1890 | | P5/C/288<br>*#104*<br> | **Unidentified** | |
| LPB/20<br>8 November 1879<br>Punched on P2 in error | | P2*sic*/C/x2<br>*#105,6*<br> | **Antoine CASTELBERG** *<br>58 Holborn Viaduct<br>London | Watchcase maker |

| REGISTRATION DETAILS | MAKER'S PRIVATE ADDRESS and DETAILS | PLATE and MARK DETAILS | MAKER/COMPANY and BUSINESS ADDRESS | MAKER'S TRADE |
|---|---|---|---|---|
| Missing register<br>*c.*1888 | | P5/C/162<br>***#107***<br>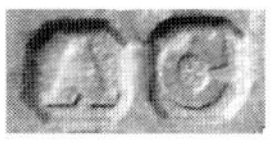 | **Unidentified** | |
| Missing register<br>*c.*1891 | | P5/C/392<br>***#108***<br>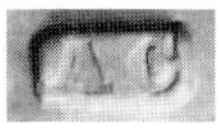 | **Unidentified** | |
| SPB/1<br>16 October 1863<br>Sent by Penlington & Hutton | 7 Mount View<br>Penton Lane<br>Tranmere | P3/C/x2<br>***#109,10***<br> | **Alexander CRUIKSHANKS**<br>18 Richmond Street<br>Liverpool | Manufacturing jeweller, electroplater and gilder |
| LPB/20<br>17 November 1880 | | P3/C/x3<br>***#111-3***<br> | **Andrew CONWAY & CO** *<br>21 Charterhouse Street<br>Holborn Circus<br>London | Watch manufacturers and importers |
| R2/193<br>26 February 1915<br>Sent by I Kirkley | 25 Gainsborough Road<br>Liverpool | P15/C/44<br>***#114***<br>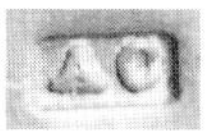 | **Isaac KIRKLEY** trading as<br>**A CRUICKSHANK & CO**<br>28, 31 Tarleton Street<br>Liverpool | Manufacturing jewellers |
| LGSJ 1825<br>GSJW/133-61<br>Not in SPB or LPB so struck 1860-3 | | P3/C/x1<br>***#115***<br> | **Asher COHEN**<br>26 Pool Lane (1825)<br>53 South Castle Street (1861)<br>Liverpool | Goldsmith |
| Missing register<br>*c.*1888<br>Similar mark entered LAO 25 April 1890 | | P5/C/199<br>***#116***<br> | **Albert CURTIS** *<br>17 Cope Street<br>Coventry | Watchcase maker |
| LPB/92<br>20 January 1882<br>No name entered | Arthur Cash at this address in 1880 | P3/C/x1<br>***#117***<br> | **Arthur CASH**<br>72 Vyse Street<br>Birmingham | Manufacturing jewellers |
| R1/121<br>22 February 1900<br>Sent by A Cameron | Glenkirk<br>Cambuslang<br>Glasgow | P9/C/34<br>***#118***<br> | **Alexander CAMERON**<br>74 Bromclowe<br>Glasgow | Pipe mounter |
| Missing register<br>*c.*1889 | | P5/A/251<br>***#119***<br>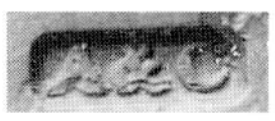 | **Unidentified** | |
| R3/92<br>3 October 1938<br>Sent by A Carter | Beechcroft<br>Hagley Road<br>Edgbaston<br>Birmingham | P21/C/8<br>***#120***<br>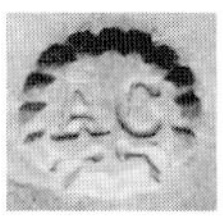 | **Albert CARTER**<br>Vicarage Works<br>40 Frederick Street<br>Birmingham | Manufacturing silversmith |
| R3/138<br>2 September 1952<br>Sent by A Creighton | 24 Belle-Vue Drive<br>Lancaster | P21/C/57<br>***#121***<br> | **Arthur CREIGHTON**<br>College of Arts and Crafts<br>Poulton Road<br>Morecambe | Teacher of jewellery and silverwork |
| R1/168<br>12 May 1902<br>Sent by Thomas Able | Anglesey Street<br>Aston<br>22 Stamford Street<br>Handsworth<br>Birmingham | P9/A/36<br>***#122***<br> | **Thomas ABLE**<br>**Walter James CHARNELL** trading as<br>**ABLE & CHARNELL**<br>44½ Frederick Street<br>Birmingham | Goldsmiths and jewellers |

| REGISTRATION DETAILS | MAKER'S PRIVATE ADDRESS and DETAILS | PLATE and MARK DETAILS | MAKER/COMPANY and BUSINESS ADDRESS | MAKER'S TRADE |
|---|---|---|---|---|
| R2/169<br>12 March 1913<br>Sent by Able & Charnell<br>Able new partner? | Jordan Road<br>Four Oaks<br>391 City Road<br>Birmingham | No new mark entered<br>*#123* | **Walter James CHARNELL**<br>**Arthur James LINE** trading as<br>**ABLE & CHARNELL**<br>44½ Frederick Street<br>Birmingham | Manufacturing jewellers |
| LPB/20<br>26 April 1881 | Also a registered trademark for jewellery, imitation metals and watchcases | P3/C/x1<br>*#124*<br>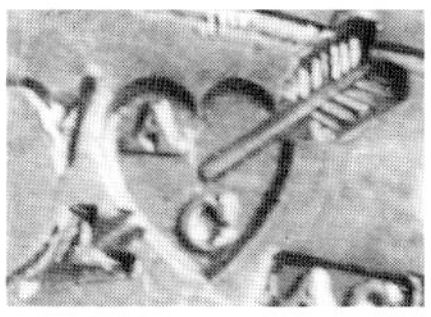 | **Andrew CONWAY & CO** *<br>21 Charterhouse Street<br>Holborn Circus<br>London | Watch manufacturers and importers |
| R1/220<br>4 October 1904<br>Sent by the company | Harborne Road<br>Edgbaston<br>Barnt Green<br>Birmingham | P9/D*sic*/215<br>*#125*<br> | **Walter Hayes RABONE**<br>**Frank RABONE** trading as<br>**ALBION CHAIN CO** *<br>39 Albion Street<br>Birmingham | Gold jewellery, chains, etc |
| R2/87<br>14 July 1909<br>Sent by Frank Rabone<br>BAO 15.595 | Dalecross Grange<br>Barnt Green<br>White Lodge<br>Four Oaks | P13/A/16<br>*#126*<br> | **Frank RABONE**<br>**Walter Hayes RABONE** trading as<br>**THE ALBION CHAIN CO** *<br>37, 38, 39 Albion Street<br>Birmingham | Chain makers |
| R2/140<br>26 July 1911<br>Sent by Frank Rabone | White Lodge<br>Four Oaks<br>Dalecross Grange<br>Barnt Green<br>Birmingham | P13/A/28-30<br>*#127-9*<br> | **Walter Hayes RABONE**<br>**Frank RABONE** trading as<br>**THE ALBION CHAIN CO** *<br>39 Albion Road<br>Birmingham | |
| R2/146<br>30 October 1911<br>Sent by Frank Rabone | White Lodge<br>Four Oaks<br>Dalecross Grange<br>Barnt Green<br>Birmingham | P13/A/35<br>*#130*<br>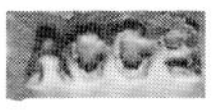 | **Walter Hayes RABONE** *<br>**Frank RABONE** *<br>49 Frederick Street and<br>39 Albion Street<br>Birmingham | Jewellers, silversmiths and chain makers |
| R3/41<br>23 June 1928<br>Sent by the company | | P15/A/45-48<br>*#131-4*<br> | **ALBION CHAIN CO** *<br>Walter Davis (Secretary)<br>Albion Street<br>Birmingham | Manufacturing jewellers |
| R3/139<br>19 September 1952<br>Sent by S Blanckensee (London) Ltd associated with Podolsky | | P21/A/16<br>*#135*<br> | **ALBION CHAIN CO** incorporated by<br>**S BLANCKENSEE & SON** * **(LONDON) LTD** and associated with<br>**PODOLSKY**<br>102-108 Clerkenwell Road<br>London EC1 | Manufacturing jewellers |
| R2/87<br>14 July 1909<br>Sent by Frank Rabone<br>BAO 15.595 | Dalecross Grange<br>Barnt Green<br>White Lodge<br>Four Oaks | P13/A/15<br>*#136*<br> | **Frank RABONE**<br>**Walter Hayes RABONE** trading as<br>**THE ALBION CHAIN CO** *<br>37, 38, 39 Albion Street<br>Birmingham | Chain makers |
| R2/146<br>30 October 1911<br>Sent by Frank Rabone | White Lodge<br>Four Oaks<br>Dalecross Grange<br>Barnt Green<br>Birmingham | P13/A/33,34<br>*#137,8*<br> | **Walter Hayes RABONE** *<br>**Frank RABONE**<br>49 Frederick Street and<br>39 Albion Street<br>Birmingham | Jewellers, silversmiths and chain makers |
| R3/69<br>16 December 1933<br>Sent by Albion Chain Co Ltd | | P15/A/51,52<br>*#139,40*<br> | **ALBION CHAIN CO** *<br>(S Blanckensee & Son Ltd Proprietors)<br>39 Albion Street<br>Birmingham | Manufacturing jewellers |

| REGISTRATION DETAILS | MAKER'S PRIVATE ADDRESS and DETAILS | PLATE and MARK DETAILS | MAKER/COMPANY and BUSINESS ADDRESS | MAKER'S TRADE |
|---|---|---|---|---|
| R1/197<br>20 July 1903<br>Sent by Frank Rabone | Harborne Road<br>Edgbaston 7<br>Barnt Green<br>Worcestershire | P9/C/94,95<br>***#141,2***<br> | **Walter Hayes RABONE**<br>**William James CROSS** trading as<br>**ALBION CHAIN CO** *<br>39 Albion Street<br>Birmingham | Gold chain manufacturers |
| R1/16<br>6 September 1895<br>Sent by E F Darnsley & Co<br>C Lyster & Sons<br>G Perkins & Sons<br>W Neale & Sons<br>F Marson<br>W Manton | | P5/aboveC/686<br>***#143***<br> | **Albert COHEN**<br>**Charles SOLOMON** trading as<br>**COHEN & CHARLES** *<br>11 Thavies Inn<br>Holborn<br>London | Jewellers and silversmiths |
| R2/146<br>15 June 1918<br>Sent by Frank Rabone<br>New impression<br>BAO 24.126 | White Lodge<br>Four Oaks<br>Dalecross Grange<br>Barnt Green<br>Birmingham | P15/A/9<br>***#144***<br> | **Walter Hayes RABONE** *<br>**Frank RABONE**<br>49 Frederick Street and<br>39 Albion Street<br>Birmingham | Jewellers, silversmiths and chain makers |
| R2/110<br>6 May 1910<br>Sent by Walter Hayes Rabone<br>BAO 16.899<br>LAO 5126 | Dalecross Grange<br>Barnt Green<br>Birmingham<br>White Lodge<br>Four Oaks | P13/A/25<br>***#145***<br> | **Frank RABONE**<br>**Walter Hayes RABONE** trading as<br>**ALBION CHAIN CO** *<br>39, 40 Albion Street<br>Birmingham<br>49 Frederick Street<br>Birmingham | Chain makers |
| R3/3<br>Entered between 24 May and 11 July 1921<br>Sent by Alexander Clark Co Ltd | | P15/A/16<br>***#146***<br> | **Alexander CLARK CO LTD** *<br>W H Candland (Secretary from 28 May 1918)<br>125, 126 Fenchurch Street<br>London and<br><br>38, 40 Mitre Street<br>Aldgate<br>London EC3 and<br><br>James Works<br>St Paul's Square<br>Birmingham and<br><br>17 Sycamore Street<br>Sheffield | Goldsmiths and silversmiths |
| R2/55<br>1 February 1908<br>Sent by Charles Horner | 137 Handsworth Road<br>Birmingham | P13/C/30<br>***#147***<br> | **Alfred CONSTANTINE**<br>219 Well Street<br>Hockley<br>Birmingham | Wholesale jewellers |
| R2/146<br>21 October 1911<br>BAO 14.529<br>Sent by R Parkes Co | The Anchorage<br>Handsworth Wood<br>Birmingham | P13/D*sic*/146<br>***#148***<br> | | Manufacturing jewellers |
| R2/155<br>30 March 1912<br>Sent by<br>G & H Bendall | 137 Handsworth Wood Road<br>Birmingham | P13/D*sic*/149<br>***#149***<br> | **Alfred CONSTANTINE**<br>**James Mackintosh SUTHERLAND**<br>**Allan CONSTANTINE** trading as<br>**Alfred CONSTANTINE**<br>219 Well Street<br>Hockley<br>Birmingham | |

| REGISTRATION DETAILS | MAKER'S PRIVATE ADDRESS and DETAILS | PLATE and MARK DETAILS | MAKER/COMPANY and BUSINESS ADDRESS | MAKER'S TRADE |
|---|---|---|---|---|
| R2/15<br>4 April 1906<br>Sent by Alexander Clark Manufacturer Co<br>Three sizes | Westwood<br>Sydenham<br>Brincliffe<br>Sheffield | P9/D*sic*/225-227<br>***#150-2***<br> | **Alexander CLARK**<br>**Robert Frederick MOSLEY** trading as<br>**ALEXANDER CLARK MANUFACTURING CO** *<br>125/126 Fenchurch Street and<br>188 Oxford Street and<br>29 Market Place<br>London and<br>Welbeck Works<br>Randall Street<br>Sheffield | Silversmiths |
| R1/189<br>1 April 1903<br>annotated *ought to have been* P9/A/47<br>Sent by W A Leather | Private address same as business | P9/A/17(47)<br>***#153***<br> | **Abraham Levi ABRAHAMS**<br>137 Hockley Hill<br>Birmingham | Jeweller |
| R1/61<br>18 February 1898<br>Mark #933 in R1 - #939 on P5<br>Sent by William Worrall | Private address same as business | P5/aboveA/939<br>***#154***<br> | **William WORRALL** trading as<br>**AKERMAN & CO** *<br>18 Shaftsbury Road<br>Hammersmith<br>London | Gold and silver mounters |
| R2/39<br>13 May 1907<br>Sent by W Neale & Son | Sherwood<br>Westgate Road<br>Beckenham<br>Kent | P9/A/88<br>***#155***<br> | **James AITCHISON** trading as<br>**AITCHISON & CO** *<br>12 Cheapside<br>London | Opticians |
| R2/41<br>11 June 1907<br>Sent by Akerman & Co | 28 Drury Road<br>Harrow | P9/A/89<br>***#156***<br> | **Edgar WORRALL** trading as<br>**AKERMAN & SON** *<br>31 High Street<br>Marylebone<br>London | Silver mounters |
| R1/233<br>17 May 1905<br>Sent by W Neale & Son | Masonette Hotel<br>28 Devon Gardens<br>London W | P9/A/60<br>***#157***<br> | **Lionel Charles ASPREY**<br>**Charles George ASPREY**<br>**George Edward ASPREY**<br>**George Kenneth ASPREY**<br>**A W HILLING** trading as<br>**ASPREY & CO** *<br>19/21 Heddon Street<br>London | Jewellers, silversmiths and leather workers |
| R2/4<br>16 October 1905<br>Sent by Lionel Charles Asprey<br>Two sizes<br>P9/A/60,75,76 cancelled<br>3 February 1910 | Gateham<br>Surrey<br>Chesterfield, Kent<br>Orchard View<br>Beckley, Kent<br>42 Avenue Road<br>London NW<br>Fairbrooke<br>Strathbone Road<br>Tooting | P9/A/74-77<br>***#158-61***<br> | **Charles George ASPREY**<br>**George Edward ASPREY**<br>**George Kenneth ASPREY**<br>**Lionel Charles ASPREY**<br>**A W HILLING** trading as<br>**ASPREY & CO** *<br>165/166 New Bond Street connecting<br>22 Albermarle Street<br>21 Heddon Street<br>London | Silversmiths |
| R3/13<br>2 December 1922<br>Sent by Stokes & Ireland<br>Two sizes | | P15/A/42,43<br>***#162,3***<br> | **George Kenneth ASPREY**<br>**Arthur William HILLING**<br>**Julian Oliver HILLING**<br>**Philip Rolls ASPREY** trading as<br>**ASPREY & CO LTD** *<br>166 New Bond Street and<br>6 Bird Street, Oxford Street and<br>Bruton Mews, Bond Street<br>London | Gold and silversmiths |

| REGISTRATION DETAILS | MAKER'S PRIVATE ADDRESS and DETAILS | PLATE and MARK DETAILS | MAKER/COMPANY and BUSINESS ADDRESS | MAKER'S TRADE |
|---|---|---|---|---|
| R3/119<br>27 August 1947<br>Sent by A C Walter<br>Two sizes | Private address same as business | P21/W/43,44<br>***#164,5***<br> | **Amy Coral WALTER**<br>Lynton Vale<br>Lynton Park Road<br>Cheadle Hulme<br>Cheshire | Silversmith |
| R1/176<br>25 September 1902<br>Sent by<br>A Detheridge | 328 New John Street West<br>Birmingham | P9/D/37<br>***#166***<br> | **Arthur DETHERIDGE**<br>77a? Vyse Street<br>Birmingham | Manufacturing jeweller |
| LPB/24<br>19 January 1881 | | P3/D/x3<br>***#167-9***<br> | **Alfred DINGLEY**<br>Harlington Buildings<br>Branston Street<br>Birmingham | Jeweller |
| | | P3/D/x3<br>***#170-2***<br> | | |
| R1/58<br>12 February 1898<br>Sent by Allen & Co<br>Annotated<br>*Old register*<br>*30 August 1890 mark 228* | 50 Parliament Hill<br>Hampstead Gate<br>London<br>**THIS ENTRY CONFIRMS EXISTENCE OF MISSING REGISTER** | P9/D/1<br>***#173***<br> | **Auguste DREYFUS** trading as<br>**A DREYFUS & CO** *<br>15, 16 Featherstone Street<br>London | Pipe manufacturers |
| Similar mark entered LAO 15 October 1885 and CAO 30 August 1890 | | P2*sic*/D/x3<br>***#174-6***<br> | **Auguste DREYFUS** *<br>15, 16 Featherstone Street<br>London | |
| Missing register<br>30 August 1890<br>Sent by Allen & Co<br>- see *#173* has mark 228 while Plate 5 has 238 | | P5/D/238(228)<br>***#177***<br> | **Auguste DREYFUS** *<br>15, 16 Featherstone Street<br>London | |
| R1/155<br>5 October 1901<br>Sent by F C Berkeley member of staff | Oak Hill<br>Handsworth Wood<br>Birmingham | P9/D/25<br>***#178***<br> | **Arthur DOWNING LTD**<br>John M Mantle (Director)<br>160 Warstone Lane<br>Birmingham | Manufacturing jewellers |
| PP1/186<br>WTD 1854<br>Similar marks entered BAO 28 December 1854 | | P2/D/x3<br>***#179-81***<br> | **Alfred DENHAM**<br>3 Digby Street<br>Birmingham | Watchcase maker |
| | | P2/D/x3<br>***#182-4***<br> | | |
| R2/28<br>3 November 1906<br>Dissolved partnership<br>13 February 1907<br>Sent by A Dalby & Co | 3 Lodge Terrace<br>Bowling Park<br>1 Park Avenue<br>Wibsey<br>Bradford | P9/D/56<br>***#185***<br> | **Arthur DALBY**<br>**George Henry BARRACLOUGH**<br>trading as **A DALBY & CO**<br>80 Sunbridge Road<br>Bradford<br>Yorkshire | Umbrella and walking stick manufacturers |
| LPB/52<br>29 April 1885 | | P5/L/x1<br>***#186***<br> | **Abraham David LOEWENSTARK** *<br>218 Strand<br>London | Silversmiths |
| R3/29<br>1 July 1925<br>Sent by Annie Eastwood | 10 Ramsgrove Road<br>Ramsgrove<br>Blackburn | P15/E/31<br>***#187***<br> | **Annie EASTWOOD**<br>City School of Art<br>Hope Street<br>Liverpool | Art teacher |

| REGISTRATION DETAILS | MAKER'S PRIVATE ADDRESS and DETAILS | PLATE and MARK DETAILS | MAKER/COMPANY and BUSINESS ADDRESS | MAKER'S TRADE |
|---|---|---|---|---|
| R3/126<br>23 October 1948<br>Sent by Annabel Evans<br>Two sizes | | P21/E/7, 8<br>***#188,9***<br> | **Annabel EVANS**<br>151 Hill Lane<br>Blackley<br>Manchester 9 | None shown |
| R1/135<br>26 October 1900<br>Sent by Jonas Brothers<br>A Everington | Private address same as business | P9/E/5<br>***#190***<br>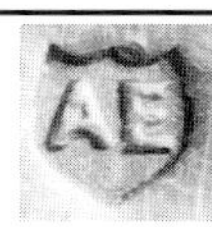 | **Alfred EVERINGTON**<br>5 Pelham Street<br>Nottingham | Goldsmith and silversmith |
| R1/47<br>15 July 1897<br>Sent by T P Hewitt<br>(Ed: Lancashire Watch Co) | Private address same as business | P5/E/856<br>***#191***<br> | **Arthur EDWARDS**<br>2 High Street<br>West Bromwich<br>Birmingham | Watch manufacturer |
| R3/73<br>8 October 1934<br>Sent by A E Brown<br><br>20 November 1940 | 119 New Spring Street<br>Birmingham | P15/G*sic*/215<br>***#192***<br><br>P21/B/11<br>***#193***<br> | **Alfred Ernest BROWN**<br>119 New Spring Street<br>Birmingham and<br>187 Lee Bank Road<br>Edgbaston<br>Birmingham | Manufacturing jeweller |
| R1/133<br>13 October 1900<br>Sent by J Hayward | Melrose<br>Rotten Park Road<br>Birmingham | P9/C/41<br>***#194***<br> | **Arthur Edward COHEN** *<br>21 Frederick Street<br>Birmingham | Jeweller |
| R1/1<br>25 October 1894<br>Sent by A E Dudley | 111 Clifton Street<br>Lozells<br>Birmingham | P5/D/614<br>***#195***<br> | **Albert E DULEY**<br>46 Northampton Street<br>Birmingham | Jeweller |
| R3/120<br>19 November 1947<br>Two sizes<br>Sent by A E Eden | Private address same as business | P21/E/5,6<br>***#196,7***<br> | **Albert Edmund EDEN**<br>167 Henrietta Street<br>Ashton-under-Lyne<br>Lancashire | Retired dental surgeon |
| R1/194<br>28 May 1903<br>Sent by A & E Evans | 207 Villa Street<br>Lozells (crossed out)<br>16 St Vestas Road<br>Handsworth | P9/E/13<br>***#198***<br> | **Albert Edward EVANS**<br>**Edward E EVANS**<br>16 Hockley Street<br>Birmingham | Manufacturing jewellers |
| R1/181<br>9 December 1902<br>Sent by A E Jenkins<br>Not in R2 as expected *c.*1900 | Oakhurst<br>Selly Oak<br>Birmingham | P9/J/35<br>***#199***<br><br>P15/J/13<br>***#200***<br> | **Albert Ernest JENKINS**<br>30 Vittoria Street<br>Birmingham | Manufacturing jewellers |
| R2/125<br>3 January 1911<br>BAO 13.362, 13.363<br>18.472<br>SAO 8101<br>LAO 5359-62<br>Sent by Albert Edward Jones<br>Four sizes | 10 Princes Road<br>Edgbaston<br>Birmingham | P13/J/42-45<br>***#201-4***<br> | **Albert Edward JONES** *<br>Windmill Street<br>Horse Fair<br>Birmingham (undated moved to)<br>111 Livery Street<br>Birmingham | Art silversmith |
| R2/205<br>2 June 1916<br>Sent by A E Magen | 5 Greenfield Street<br>Stepney<br>London | P15/M/20<br>***#205***<br> | **Abraham Emanuel MAGEN**<br>5 Greenfield Street<br>Stepney<br>London | Ring and chain maker |

| REGISTRATION DETAILS | MAKER'S PRIVATE ADDRESS and DETAILS | PLATE and MARK DETAILS | MAKER/COMPANY and BUSINESS ADDRESS | MAKER'S TRADE |
|---|---|---|---|---|
| R2/197<br>13 July 1915<br>Sent by A E Stewart<br>Two sizes | Private address same as business | P15/S/17,18<br>*#206,7*<br> | **Amy Eleanor STEWART**<br>28 The Crescent<br>Northwich | Artist |
| R3/129<br>2 June 1949<br>Sent by A E West<br>Two sizes | 25 Percy Street<br>Liverpool 8<br>Flat 15 (10 December 1952)<br>1 Princess Avenue<br>Liverpool | P21/W/53,54<br>*#208,9*<br> | **Annie Ethel WEST**<br>Business address not entered | Adviser in needlework to Liverpool Education Authority |
| R3/124<br>26 June 1948<br>Two sizes<br>Sent by Alfred Forth | Private address same as business | P21/F/10,11<br>*#210,1*<br> | **Alfred FORTH**<br>51 Liverpool Road<br>Manchester 3 | Art student |
| R3/72<br>4 September 1934<br>Sent by A Fenwick Ltd | | P15/F/40<br>*#212*<br> | **Arthur FENWICK LTD**<br>Athletic Works<br>Vyse Street<br>Birmingham | Medallists |
| Missing register<br>*c.*1889<br>Similar mark entered LAO 24 October 1882 | CWMP 1874-1901 | P5/F/258<br>*#213*<br> | **Alfred FRIDLANDER** *<br>62 Holyhead Road<br>Coventry | Watch manufacturer |
| MDGC 1866<br>PP3/83<br>CWMP1874-01<br>Similar mark entered LAO 13 October 1868 | Not in SPB or LPB so struck 1860-3 | P3/F/x3<br>*#214-6*<br> | **Alfred FRIDLANDER** *<br>62 Holyhead Road<br>Coventry | |
| R1/55<br>16 December 1897<br>Sent by A Fenwick<br>R J Wakefield | 131 Linwood Road<br>Handsworth | P5/F/913<br>*#217*<br> | **Arthur FENWICK**<br>108 Vyse Street<br>Birmingham | Medallist and die-smith |
| Missing register<br>*c.*1889<br>Similar mark entered LAO 29 September 1890 | | P5/F/252<br>*#218*<br>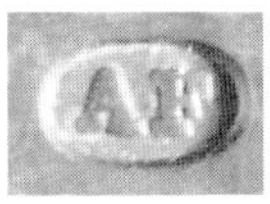 | **Arthur FENNELL** *<br>2 Mount Street (1892)<br>Chapel Fields<br>Coventry | Watchcase maker |
| R1/211<br>23 March 1904<br>Sent by<br>A Thorneywork | 70 Wilmore Road<br>Perry Barr<br>Jockey Road<br>Sutton Coldfield | P9/T/50<br>*#219*<br> | **Arthur THORNEYWORK**<br>**Fred THORNEYWORK** trading as<br>**A & F THORNEYWORK**<br>62 Great Hampton Street<br>Birmingham | Gold and silversmiths |
| R1/74<br>12 September 1898<br>Sent by E Dicken | 10 Rackley Band Road<br>Birkenhead | P9/G/3<br>*#220*<br> | **Alfred GURNEY**<br>81 Lord Street<br>46 Berry Street<br>5 St John's Lane<br>Liverpool | Tobacconist |
| R3/104<br>19 January 1943<br>Sent by Albert Gleadall | Private address same as business | P21/G/6<br>*#221*<br> | **Albert GLEADALL**<br>1 Banners Gate Road<br>Sutton Coldfield<br>Warwickshire | Jeweller |
| SPB/12<br>23 April 1875 | CWMP has 3 Mount Street Coventry in 1896 | P3/G/x2<br>*#222,3*<br> | **Alfred GURNEY** *<br>4 Conway Buildings<br>Smithfield Street<br>Coventry | Watchcase maker |

| REGISTRATION DETAILS | MAKER'S PRIVATE ADDRESS and DETAILS | PLATE and MARK DETAILS | MAKER/COMPANY and BUSINESS ADDRESS | MAKER'S TRADE |
|---|---|---|---|---|
| LPB/36 P32/5<br>5 February 1885<br>No mark alongside LPB entry | | P5/G/x1<br>***#224***<br> | **Alfred GRIMSDALE**<br>39 St John Street Road<br>Clerkenwell<br>London | Gold chain maker |
| R1/89<br>31 January 1899<br>Sent by W Walker | 10 Wolseley Road<br>Crouch End<br>London N | P9/G/7<br>***#225***<br> | **Arthur GARSTIN**<br>**Arthur George GARSTIN** trading as<br>**A GARSTIN & CO** *<br>Queens Square<br>Aldersgate Street<br>London | Leather goods manufacturers and metal workers |
| R2/43<br>12 July 1907<br>Sent by selves<br>Two sizes | 21 Upper Woburn Place<br>London | P9/G/90,91<br>***#226,7***<br> | **Arthur GRAF**<br>9 Goswell Road<br>London | Manufacturers agent and importer |
| R3/82<br>21 March 1936<br>Sent by T J Skelton<br>86 Vyse Street<br>Birmingham | 16 Harold Road [1]<br>Upton Park<br>London E13 | P15/K*sic*/227<br>***#228***<br> | **Edward Charles Victor WELLS**<br>**Dorothy Ethel CORR** [1] trading as<br>**A G CORR LTD**<br>17 Upton Gate<br>Forest Gate<br>London E7 | Silversmiths and medallists |
| LPB/30<br>30 September 1880 | | P3/G/x2<br>***#229,30***<br> | **Alfred George GRIFFITHS**<br>10½ Hylton Street<br>Birmingham | Jeweller |
| R3/89<br>17 March 1938<br>Cancelled<br>7 May 1949<br>Sent by A G Lugg, Coley Brothers, Leonardt Ltd<br>119 Vyse Street<br>Birmingham | Private address same as business | P21/L/4-6<br>***#231-3***<br> | **Albert George LUGG**<br>400 Romford Road<br>Forest Gate<br>London E7 | Wholesale jewellers |
| R3/110<br>11 November 1945<br>Cancelled<br>7 May 1949<br>Sent by Albert George Lugg | 91 Wellesley Road<br>Ilford<br>Essex | P21/L/13-18<br>***#234-9***<br> | | |
| R3/128<br>7 May 1949<br>All previous entries cancelled<br>Sent by A G Lugg & Co<br>Two sizes | Both residing at<br>17 Castle Drive<br>Ilford | P21/L/23-30<br>***#240-7***<br> | **Albert George LUGG**<br>**George Luke LUGG** trading as<br>**A G LUGG & CO**<br>400 Romford Road<br>Forest Gate<br>London E7 | |
| R1/28<br>28 April 1896<br>Sent by T P Hewitt | 10 Albion Terrace<br>Borough Road<br>Middlesborough | P5/M/762<br>***#248***<br> | **Alfred George MASCALL**<br>Linthorpe Road<br>Middlesborough | Wholesale jeweller and watch manufacturer |
| PP1/186<br>J1 1855-61 | See also S&R | P2/R/x4<br>***#249-52***<br> | **Arthur Guinness ROGERS** trading as<br>**SAMUEL & ROGERS** *<br>72 Wood Street<br>Liverpool | Watchcase makers |
| Similar mark entered LAO 17 February 1859 | | P2/D*sic*/x3 and P2/R/x1<br>***#253-6***<br> | | |

| REGISTRATION DETAILS | MAKER'S PRIVATE ADDRESS and DETAILS | PLATE and MARK DETAILS | MAKER/COMPANY and BUSINESS ADDRESS | MAKER'S TRADE |
|---|---|---|---|---|
| PP1/186<br>J1 1855-61 | See also S&R | P2/R/x6<br>***#257-62***  | **Arthur Guinness ROGERS** trading as<br>**SAMUEL & ROGERS** *<br>72 Wood Street<br>Liverpool | Watchcase makers |
| PP1/186<br>J1 1855-61 | See also S&R | P2/R/x3<br>***#263-5***  | | |
| R2/42<br>15 June 1907<br>Sent by R Pringle & Son | 17 Duckett Road<br>Harringay N | P9/R/90<br>***#266***  | **Arthur George RENDELL** *<br>40, 42 Clerkenwell Road<br>London | Silversmith |
| R2/42<br>10 July 1907<br>Sent by R Pringle & Son | | P9/R/94-99<br>***#267-72***  | | |
| R2/47<br>10 October 1907<br>Sent by R Pringle & Son | | P9/R/101-104<br>***#273-6***  | | |
| R2/64<br>5 September 1908<br>Sent by R Pringle & Son | | P13/A/19-21<br>***#277-9***  | | |
| R1/115<br>4 November 1899<br>Sent by J Deakin & Son<br>Passed to<br>Myatt & Pulligne | 17 Birchington Road<br>West Hampstead<br>London NW | P9/G/14<br>***#280***  | **Alfred Charles GOAD** trading as<br>**Alfred GOAD & SON**<br>195 High Street<br>Kensington<br>London W | Gold and silversmiths |
| R1/107<br>29 July 1899<br>Sent by W Neale & Sons | | P9/G/13<br>***#281***  | **Alfred Charles GOAD** trading as<br>**Alfred GOAD & SON** and<br>**Percy GOAD & CO**<br>87, 89 Westbourne Grove<br>London W | Gold and silversmiths and watchmakers |
| R1/120<br>10 February 1900<br>Sent by H Griffith & Sons Ltd | | P9/G/15<br>***#282***  | **Alfred Charles GOAD** trading as<br>**Alfred GOAD & SONS**<br>87, 89 Westbourne Grove<br>London W | Gold and silversmiths |
| R3/149<br>19 December 1953<br>Sent by A Hand | 33 Broadway<br>Withington<br>Manchester 20 | P21/H/67<br>***#283***  | **Arthur HAND**<br>No business address entered | Student |
| Missing register<br>*c.*1886 | | P5/H/40<br>***#284***  | **Unidentified** | |
| R1/222<br>12 November 1904<br>Sent by Arthur Hands | 63 Hall Road<br>Handsworth<br>Birmingham | P9/H/66<br>***#285***  | **Arthur HANDS**<br>27 Hylton Street<br>Birmingham | Ring maker |
| R3/119<br>28 July 1947<br>Sent by A Hopwood | Private address same as business | P21/H/38<br>***#286***  | **Arthur HOPWOOD**<br>12 Earl Road<br>Bramhall<br>Cheshire (moved to – undated)<br>29 Crichton Road<br>Carshalton Beeches<br>Surrey | Student metal worker and silversmith |

| REGISTRATION DETAILS | MAKER'S PRIVATE ADDRESS and DETAILS | PLATE and MARK DETAILS | MAKER/COMPANY and BUSINESS ADDRESS | MAKER'S TRADE |
|---|---|---|---|---|
| R3/152<br>13 April 1954<br>Sent by A Hobson | 1 Shore Road<br>Ainsdale<br>Southport | P21/H/70<br>***#287***  | **Mrs Annie HOBSON**<br>No business address entered | Art student |
| R2/12<br>6 March 1906<br>Sent by A Hewlett | 221 Grove Lane<br>Handsworth<br>Birmingham | P9/H/79<br>***#288***  | **Arthur HEWLETT**<br>126 Branston Street<br>Birmingham | Ring manufacturer |
| R2/208<br>26 September 1916<br>Sent by A Hewlett | 6 Henstock Road<br>Handsworth Wood<br>Birmingham | P15/H/36,37<br>***#289,90***  | **Arthur HEWLETT** trading as<br>**A HEWLETT LTD**<br>44 Hockley Hill<br>Birmingham | Gem and fancy ring makers |
| R3/180<br>15 August 1961<br>Sent by Frank Eakin<br>Three sizes | 46 Vale View Towers<br>Liverpool 25 | P21/H/86-88<br>***#291-3*** 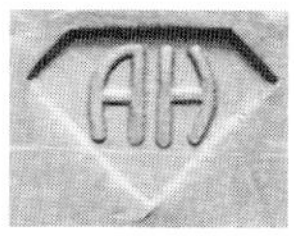 | **Frank EAKIN** trading as<br>**A HILL**<br>14 Waterloo Buildings<br>6 Wood Street<br>Liverpool 1 | Practical jeweller |
| R1/142<br>14 February 1901<br>Sent by A Hill | 18 Rawlins Street<br>Liverpool | P9/H/42<br>***#294***  | **Arthur HILL**<br>14 Waterloo Buildings<br>Wood Street<br>Liverpool | Jeweller and silversmith |
| R1/202<br>22 October 1903<br>Sent by A Hill | | P9/H/54<br>***#295***  | | |
| R1/92<br>22 February 1899<br>Sent by A Hands | 159 Albert Road<br>Aston<br>Birmingham | P9/H/9<br>***#296***  | **Arthur HANDS**<br>90 Spencer Street<br>Birmingham | Ring maker and diamond mounter |
| R1/59<br>1 February 1898<br>Sent by Benson Brothers | 7 Needham Road<br>Southport | P5/*Zsic*/926<br>***#297***  | **Alfred HIGHLAND**<br>96 Seel Street<br>Liverpool | Watchmaker |
| R1/120<br>6 February 1900<br>Sent by A Haseler | Hall Road<br>Handsworth<br>Birmingham | P9/H/24<br>***#298***  | **Herbert HASELER**<br>**Arnold HASELER**<br>**HASELER & MILNER**<br>31 Tenby Street<br>Birmingham | Manufacturing jewellers |
| R1/108<br>24 August 1899<br>Sent by A Higgison | 35 St Silas Square<br>Lozells<br>Birmingham | P9/H/18<br>***#299***  | **Alfred HIGGISON**<br>56 Branston Street<br>Birmingham | Ring maker and diamond mounter |
| Not in R3 as expected - between 18 and 27 March 1925 Similar mark entered BAO 3 October 1919 | | P15/H/88<br>***#300***  | **Abraham HARRIS**<br>470 Dudley Road<br>Birmingham | Jeweller |
| R2/178<br>25 October 1913<br>Sent by Albert Hundy | 10 Wye Cliff Road<br>Handsworth<br>Birmingham | P15/H/5<br>***#301***  | **Albert HUNDY**<br>50 Vyse Street<br>Birmingham | Gold ring manufacturer |
| R3/133<br>26 May 1950<br>Sent by<br>A H Ainsworth | Leckomby<br>Reservoir Road North<br>Prenton<br>Birkenhead | P21/A/12<br>***#302***  | **Anne Helen AINSWORTH**<br>School of Art<br>Liverpool | Student |
| R1/137<br>8 November 1900<br>Sent by A Hundy & Co | 217 Park Road<br>Hockley<br>292 Park Road<br>Hockley<br>Birmingham | P9/H/35,36<br>***#303,4***  | **Albert HUNDY**<br>**Robert WILSON** trading as<br>**A HUNDY & CO**<br>41 Hylton Street<br>Birmingham | Ring manufacturers and diamond mounters |

| REGISTRATION DETAILS | MAKER'S PRIVATE ADDRESS and DETAILS | PLATE and MARK DETAILS | MAKER/COMPANY and BUSINESS ADDRESS | MAKER'S TRADE |
|---|---|---|---|---|
| R1/166<br>17 April 1902<br>punch recut<br>Sent by A Hundy | 292 Park Road<br>Hockley | P9/H/40[7] *sic*<br>***#305***<br> | **Albert HUNDY** (Manager)<br>**Robert WILSON** trading as<br>**HUNDY & CO**<br>64 Hylton Street<br>Birmingham | Gold ring makers |
| R1/10<br>30 April 1895<br>Sent by A H Darby | 5 Richmond Road<br>Handsworth<br>Birmingham | P5/D/655<br>***#306***<br> | **Alfred Horatio DARBY**<br>51 Caroline Street<br>Birmingham | Medallist and jeweller |
| R1/6<br>15 January 1895<br>Sent by<br>A H Landless | Cunnington<br>35 Pickford Street<br>Stretford | P5/L/632<br>***#307***<br> | **Alfred Howarth LANDLESS**<br>27 Corn Exchange Chambers<br>Hanging Ditch<br>Manchester | Pipe and stick mounter |
| R2/101<br>22 January 1910<br>Sent by<br>A H Rollason | 7 Lime Avenue<br>Allens Road<br>Soho<br>Birmingham | P13/R/29<br>***#308***<br> | **Albert Henry ROLLASON**<br>169½ Hockley Hill<br>Birmingham | Fancy rings |
| Missing register<br>*c.*1890 | | P5/R/314<br>***#309***<br> | **Unidentified** | |
| Missing register<br>*c.*1894<br>Similar mark entered LAO 17 January 1883 | CWMP has watch manufacturer 1883-1901 | P5/R/545<br>***#310***<br> | **Alfred Henry READ** *<br>Hill Street<br>Coventry | Watchcase maker |
| Missing register<br>*c.*1891 - similar mark CAO 13 September 1902 and LAO 17 December 1907 | CWMP has watch manufacturer 1891-1901 | P5/R/394<br>***#311***<br> | **Alexander Henry RATCLIFF** *<br>18 Norfolk Street<br>Coventry | Gold and silver watchcase maker and watch manufacturer |
| Missing register<br>*c.*1891<br>Adjacent P5/R/394 | | P5/R/x1<br>***#312***<br>§<br> | | |
| R1/175<br>13 September 1902<br>Sent by W Sexton<br>Two sizes | The Rectory<br>Baginton | P9/R/51,52<br>***#313,4***<br> | | Watch manufacturer |
| R3/63<br>6 September 1935<br>Sent by W H & F Rabone and Albion Chain Co | 39 Albion Street<br>Birmingham | P15/I/11<br>***#315***<br> | **Alfred ISHERWOOD** trading as<br>**W H & F RABONE** * and<br>**ALBION CHAIN CO** *<br>S Blanckensee & Son Ltd, Proprietors<br>Common seal of company affixed in the presence of:-<br>S Blanckensee (Director)<br>Walter Davis (Director)<br>W Davis (Secretary)<br>14, 15 Frederick Street<br>Birmingham (Registered Office) | Manufacturing jewellers |
| R1/225<br>11 January 1905<br>Sent by F Rabone | Barnt Green<br>Harborne Green<br>Birmingham | P9/I/9<br>***#316***<br> | **Walter Hayes RABONE** *<br>**Frank RABONE** trading as<br>**A ISHERWOOD**<br>49 Frederick Street<br>Birmingham | Jewellers |

| REGISTRATION DETAILS | MAKER'S PRIVATE ADDRESS and DETAILS | PLATE and MARK DETAILS | MAKER/COMPANY and BUSINESS ADDRESS | MAKER'S TRADE |
|---|---|---|---|---|
| R1/117<br>30 November 1899<br>Sent by Frank Rabone<br>Two sizes | 151 Hamstead Road [1]<br>Handsworth<br>67 Laburnum Road [2]<br>Birmingham | P9/I/5a,b<br>***#317,8***<br> | **Frank RABONE** [1] *<br>**Alfred ISHERWOOD** [2]<br>**W Hayes RABONE** * trading as<br>**I ISHERWOOD & PARTNERS**<br>49 Frederick Street<br>Birmingham | Jewellers |
| Missing register<br>*c.*1887<br>Similar mark LAO 21 February 1889 | | P5/S*sic*/112<br>***#319***<br> | **Arthur George IRELAND** trading as<br>**STOKES & IRELAND** *<br>83/84 Great Hampton Street<br>Birmingham | Silversmiths |
| R1/25<br>19 March 1896<br>Sent by<br>W H & F Rabone | 12 Holly Road [1]<br>Handsworth<br>151 Hamstead Road [2]<br>Handsworth | P5/J/746<br>***#320***<br> | **Walter Hayes RABONE** [1] *<br>**Frank RABONE** [2] * trading as<br>**Alfred ISHERWOOD**<br>49 Frederick Street<br>Birmingham | Manufacturing jewellers |
| R1/71<br>25 October 1898<br>Sent by Frank Rabone | 151 Hamstead Road [1]<br>Handsworth<br>22 Holly Road [2]<br>Edgbaston<br>Birmingham | P9/I/1-4<br>***#321-4***<br> | **Frank RABONE** [1]<br>**Walter Hayes RABONE** [2]<br>**Alfred ISHERWOOD** trading as<br>**W H & F RABONE** *<br>49 Frederick Street<br>Birmingham | Jewellers |
| R3/63<br>30 July 1932<br>Sent by W H & F Rabone and Albion Chain Co<br>Details as per #315 | 39 Albion Street<br>Birmingham | P15/I/10<br>***#325***<br> | **Alfred ISHERWOOD** trading as<br>**W H & F RABONE** and<br>**ALBION CHAIN CO** *<br>14, 15 Frederick Street<br>Birmingham (Registered Office) | Manufacturing jewellers |
| R1/221<br>4 October 1904<br>Sent by Selves | Harborne Road<br>Barnt Green<br>Birmingham | P9/I/8<br>***#326***<br> | **Walter Hayes RABONE** *<br>**Frank RABONE** * trading as<br>**A ISHERWOOD**<br>49 Frederick Street<br>Birmingham | Gold jewellery, rings, brooches, etc |
| PDB 1812-4<br>MR3/89<br>PP1/186 | Gold rings | P1/32/x2<br>***#327,8***<br> | **ABBOTT & JONES**<br>(also **JONES & ABBOTT**)<br>Liverpool | Goldsmiths and silversmiths |
| LPB42<br>25 March 1879 | CWMP has watch manufacturer 1886-91 | P3/N*sic*/x2<br>***#329,30***<br> | **Alfred JOHNSON**<br>**Charles LOAKE** trading as<br>**JOHNSON & CO**<br>37 Hill Street<br>Coventry | Watch pendant makers |
| R3/163<br>2 April 1958<br>Sent by J D Watts | 14 Berkeley Avenue [1]<br>2 Berkeley Avenue [2]<br>Four Oaks<br>Sutton Coldfield | P21/IJ/13<br>***#331***<br> | **James Daniel WATTS** [1]<br>**Roy Joseph BROWN** [2]<br>Joint partners trading as<br>**ATTROW JEWELLERY**<br>38 Hylton Street<br>Hockley<br>Birmingham 18 | Manufacturing jewellers |
| R1/161<br>7 February 1902<br>Sent by Albert Jackson | Wellesbourne<br>Back Lane<br>Birmingham | P9/J/33<br>***#332***<br> | **Albert JACKSON**<br>57 Albion Street<br>Birmingham | Manufacturing jeweller |
| R3/157<br>22 March 1957<br>Sent by B O Bailey | 70 Coopers Road<br>Handsworth Wood<br>Birmingham 20 | P21/B/53<br>***#333***<br> | **Brian Oswald BAILEY** trading as<br>**A J BAILEY & SON**<br>53 Tenby Street North<br>Birmingham 1 | Silversmiths |

| REGISTRATION DETAILS | MAKER'S PRIVATE ADDRESS and DETAILS | PLATE and MARK DETAILS | MAKER/COMPANY and BUSINESS ADDRESS | MAKER'S TRADE |
|---|---|---|---|---|
| R2/67<br>29 October 1908<br>Sent by J Culver<br>Two sizes | 106 St John Street<br>London EC | P13/B/41,42 and<br>P13/D*sic*/4,5<br>***#334-7***   | **Alfred James BLAKE** *<br>106 St John Street<br>London EC | Working and wholesale jewellers |
| R3/157<br>14 June 1956<br>Sent by B O Bailey | 70 Coopers Road<br>Handsworth Wood<br>Birmingham 20 | P21/B/50<br>***#338***   | **Brian Oswald BAILEY** trading as<br>**A J BAILEY & SON**<br>53 Tenby Street North<br>Birmingham 1 | Silversmiths |
| Missing register<br>*c.*1890 | See next entry | P5/C/304<br>***#339*** 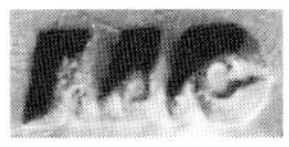 | **Alfred James CHESHIRE**<br>52 Tenby Street North<br>Birmingham | Jeweller |
| R1/77<br>20 December 1898<br>Sent by A J Cheshire<br>Three sizes | Normanbrush<br>City Road<br>Birmingham | P9/C/3-5<br>***#340-2***   | | |
| SPB/20<br>19 March 1875 | | P3/C/x2<br>***#343,4***  | **Alfred John CRAFTS** *<br>25 Gloucester Street<br>Clerkenwell<br>London | Watchcase maker |
| R3/127<br>9 November 1948<br>Sent by Eaton Wrighton Ltd<br>121 Vyse Street<br>Birmingham 18 | 55 Aytown Road [1]<br>Glasgow S1<br>27 Coverdale Street [2]<br>Glasgow S2 | P21/IJ/4<br>***#345***   | **A JACOBSON & CO**<br>Julius Jacobson[1]<br>Aaron Harry Jacobson[2]<br>54 Miller Street<br>Glasgow C1 | Wholesale jewellers |
| R1/127<br>25 May 1900<br>Sent by A Jackson | 195 Frederick Road<br>Aston Manor<br>Birmingham | P9/J/28<br>***#346***   | **Arthur JACKSON** *<br>67 Hockley Street<br>Birmingham | Manufacturing jeweller |
| R1/28<br>30 April 1896<br>Sent by C Horner | Private address same as business | P5/D/763<br>***#347***   | **Catherine Jennings DAVENPORT**<br>trading as **A J DAVENPORT & CO**<br>48 Clerkenwell Road<br>London EC | Wholesale jewellers |
| R3/39<br>23 November 1927<br>Sent by selves | Treliske [1]<br>Dunlop<br>13 Battlefield Gardens [2]<br>Longside<br>Glasgow | P15/F/33<br>***#348*** 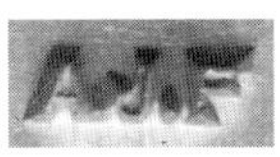  | **Angus Jeffrey FRASER** [1]<br>**Jean Agnes Gordon MACLEOD** [2]<br>trading as **A J FRASER & CO**<br>Argyll Chambers<br>30 Buchanan Street<br>Glasgow | Wholesale jewellers |
| R2/142<br>29 August 1911<br>Sent by A J Heasman | 63 Elm Road<br>Leigh-on-Sea | P13/H/79<br>***#349***   | **Alfred John HEASMAN** trading as<br>**HEASMAN & CO** *<br>39 Hatton Garden<br>London EC | Jewellery manufacturers agent |
| R1/140<br>23 January 1901<br>Sent by A J Horwitz | Private address same as business | P9/H/40<br>***#350***   | **Arthur Julius HORWITZ** *<br>58 Edgerton Road<br>Withington<br>Manchester | Jeweller |
| R1/146<br>6 May 1901<br>Sent by A J Horwitz | | P9/H/44<br>***#351***   | | |

| REGISTRATION DETAILS | MAKER'S PRIVATE ADDRESS and DETAILS | PLATE and MARK DETAILS | MAKER/COMPANY and BUSINESS ADDRESS | MAKER'S TRADE |
|---|---|---|---|---|
| R2/75<br>16 March 1909<br>This punch<br>reset and new | 170 Antrobus Road<br>Handsworth<br>Birmingham | P13/L/8<br>***#352***  | **Arthur James LAWRENCE**<br>99 Vyse Street<br>Birmingham | Jeweller and ring manufacturer |
| R2/75<br>Impression taken of<br>20 January 1912<br>Sent by A J Lawrence | | P13/L/63<br>***#353***  | | |
| Not in R3 as expected<br>*c.*1923 | | P15/L/26<br>***#354***  | | |
| R1/172<br>18 July 1902<br>Sent by J G Newbold | Lime Villa<br>Clea Avenue<br>Clapham Common<br>London SW | P9/N/13<br>***#355***  | **Alfred Jerrold NATHAN** *<br>17 Farringdon Avenue<br>London EC | Tobacconist and fancy goods agent |
| Missing register<br>*c.*1894<br>Similar mark entered<br>LAO 13 July 1882 | | P5/P/534<br>***#356*** 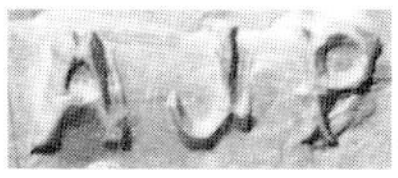 | **Alfred James PHELPS** *<br>22 Canal Road (1882)<br>Kingsland<br>London E<br>12 Cowper Road (1882)<br>Hornsey<br>London N<br>2 Woodville Road (1886)<br>Mildmay Road<br>Newington Green<br>London N | Smallworker |
| R2/206<br>24 June 1916<br>Sent by Thomas S<br>Osborne | Netherstone<br>Lichfield | P15/P/74<br>***#357*** 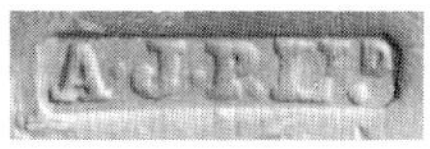 | **A J PEPPER LTD**<br>A J Pepper (Principal)<br>54 Frederick Street<br>Birmingham | Manufacturing jewellers |
| R2/63 22 May 1909<br>Sent by A J Smith<br>Cancelled 25 May<br>1909 used twice | 39 Handsworth Wood Road<br>Birmingham | P13/S/34<br>***#358***  | **Arthur Johnson SMITH**<br>Variety Works<br>46 Frederick Street<br>Birmingham | Manufacturing jeweller |
| R1/222<br>15 October 1904<br>Sent by A J Smith | | P9/S/80<br>***#359***  | | |
| R2/110<br>6 May 1910<br>BAO 17.783,17.782<br>Sent by A J Smith | | P13/S/52,53<br>***#360,1***  | | |
| R1/11<br>29 May 1895<br>Sent by A J Smith | | P5/S/663<br>***#362***  | | |
| R1/70<br>24 October 1898<br>Sent by A J Smith | | P9/S/4-6<br>***#363-5***  | **Arthur John** (*sic*) **SMITH**<br>46 Frederick Street<br>Birmingham | Jeweller |
| R1/236<br>8 July 1905<br>Sent by A J Smith | | P9/S/91<br>***#366***  | **Arthur Johnson SMITH**<br>46 Frederick Street<br>Birmingham | Manufacturing jeweller |
| R2/85<br>19 June 1909<br>Sent by A J Smith<br>BAO 16.383<br>16.384, 16.385<br>Two sizes | | P13/S/37-39<br>***#367-9***  | | |

| REGISTRATION DETAILS | MAKER'S PRIVATE ADDRESS and DETAILS | PLATE and MARK DETAILS | MAKER/COMPANY and BUSINESS ADDRESS | MAKER'S TRADE |
|---|---|---|---|---|
| R2/59<br>13 May 1908<br>Sent by A J Smith | 39 Handsworth Wood Road<br>Birmingham | P13/S/6<br>***#370***  | **Arthur Johnson SMITH**<br>Variety Works<br>46 Frederick Street<br>Birmingham | Manufacturing jeweller |
| R2/63<br>29 July 1908<br>Sent by A J Smith | | P13/S/7<br>***#371***  | | |
| 22 May 1909 | | P13/S/33<br>***#372***  | | |
| R2/217<br>26 November 1918<br>Sent by A J Smith | 13 Brougham Street<br>Hockley<br>Birmingham | P15/S/36<br>***#373***  | **Alfred John SMITH**<br>162 Hockley Hill<br>Birmingham | Diamond mounter and ring maker |
| LPB/88<br>6 November 1882 | CWMP has working 1896-1909 in Earlsdon Street | P3/W/x1<br>***#374*** 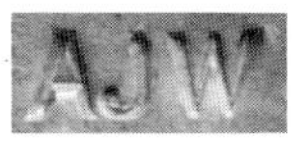 | **Arthur James WALKER** *<br>Earlsdon Street<br>Coventry | Watchcase maker |
| Missing register<br>*c.*1890 | | P5/W/324<br>***#375***  | | |
| R1/182<br>7 January 1903<br>Sent by A J Watts | 67 Mildmay Grove<br>Mildmay Park<br>London N | P9/W/85a<br>***#376***  | **Albert John WATTS** *<br>2 Upper Ashby Street<br>Goswell Road<br>London EC | Silversmith |
| | | P9/W/85b<br>***#377***  | | |
| R2/18<br>19 May 1906<br>Sent by A J Wortley | Private address same as business | P9/V*sic*/141<br>***#378***  | **A J WORTLEY**<br>36 Bowling Green Lane<br>Clerkenwell<br>London EC | Gold chain maker |
| R1/226<br>31 January 1905<br>Sent by W H Cask | 32 Claremont Road<br>Handsworth | P9/K/34<br>***#379***  | **Alfred KENT**<br>6 Tenby Street North<br>Birmingham | Jewellers |
| R1/122<br>14 March 1900<br>Sent by R J Pike | 213 Plymouth Grove<br>Manchester | P9/A/17<br>***#380***  | **Oscar KATZ** trading as<br>**ABEL & KATZ** *<br>79 Piccadilly<br>Manchester | Watch manufacturers and importers |
| Missing register<br>*c.*1891<br>Similar mark entered BAO 10 December 1900 | | P5/K/348<br>***#381*** 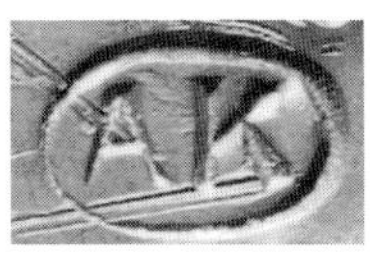 | **Aaron KUIT**<br>5a Blackfriars Street<br>Manchester | Tobacconist |
| R1/20<br>5 July 1894<br>Sent by Alfred Kent | 16 Worcester Street<br>Birmingham<br>**LOWEST MARK NUMBER IN R1** | P5/K/551x2<br>***#382,3***  | **Alfred KENT**<br>40½ Hockley Street<br>Birmingham | Jeweller |
| R3/129<br>10 May 1949<br>Sent by A M Kean<br>Two sizes | Private address same as business | P21/K/8,9<br>***#384,5***  | **Annie Macfarlane KEAN**<br>5 Wilmslow Road<br>Withington<br>Manchester 20 | Dental surgeon |

| REGISTRATION DETAILS | MAKER'S PRIVATE ADDRESS and DETAILS | PLATE and MARK DETAILS | MAKER/COMPANY and BUSINESS ADDRESS | MAKER'S TRADE |
|---|---|---|---|---|
| R1/7<br>16 February 1895<br>Sent by Adie & Lovekin | Tudor Grange<br>Solihull | P5/A/641<br>*#386*<br> | **ADIE & LOVEKIN**<br>**Alfred LOVEKIN** (Director)<br>Regent Street<br>Birmingham | Silversmiths and jewellers |
| R1/99<br>28 April 1899<br>Sent by W Walker Hollins & Jacques | | P9/L/7<br>*#387*<br> | **Alfred LEWIS** *<br>4 Moorfields<br>Fore Street<br>London EC | Tobacco pouch manufacturer |
| Missing register<br>*c.*1893 | | P5/L/515<br>*#388*<br> | **Unidentified** | |
| R1/214<br>17 May 1904<br>Sent by A Lowe | Private address same as business | P9/L/60<br>*#389*<br> | **Adrian LOWE**<br>55 Ogden Street<br>Ardwick<br>Manchester (and later, undated)<br>40 Garnett Street<br>Bradford | Stick and umbrella handle mountings |
| R2/57<br>19 March 1908<br>Sent by Adrian Lowe | 40 Garnett Street<br>Bradford | P9/L/93,94<br>*#390,1*<br> | **Adrian LOWE**<br>40 Garnett Street<br>Bradford | Umbrella and walking stick mountings |
| LPB/14<br>8 August 1883<br>No mark in LPB<br>Sent by Jackson Brothers | Mark deduced from sequence on square | P5/A/x1<br>*#392*<br> | **ADIE & LOVEKIN**<br>Regent Street<br>Birmingham | Silversmiths and jewellers |
| R1/170<br>11 June 1902<br>Sent by W Mills<br>Mark cancelled<br>1 July 1927 | Carlton House<br>Bury Old Road<br>Heaton Park | P9/L/34,35<br>*#393,4*<br> | **Arthur LOFTHOUSE**<br>32 Kilverts Building<br>Manchester | Wholesale jeweller |
| R3/39<br>3 January 1928<br>Sent by self | 8 Grosvenor Road<br>Perry Barr<br>Birmingham | P15/L/35<br>*#395*<br>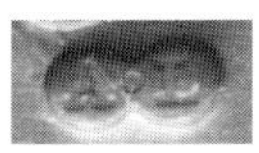 | **Alfred LAWTON**<br>87 Vyse Street<br>Birmingham | Silversmith |
| R1/52<br>22 October 1897<br>#800 entered – should have been 880 on plate 5<br>Sent by Moore Brothers, Derby | 51 Mildmay Park [1]<br>London<br>51 Pyrland Road [2]<br>London N | P5/A/800<br>*#396*<br> | **Joseph ABRAHAMS** [1]<br>**Edward LYON** [2] trading as<br>**S ABRAHAMS & SONS** *<br>36 Clerkenwell Road<br>London | Manufacturing jewellers |
| R1/52<br>22 October 1897<br>R1 entry is 801 over written 901<br>P5 has 801<br>Sent by E Vaughton | | P5/A/801<br>*#397*<br>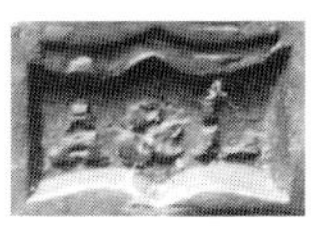 | | |
| R2/79<br>16 April 1909<br>Sent by Clark and Sewell | 35 Camphill Avenue<br>Glasgow<br>Horton Villa<br>Totley Rise<br>Glasgow | P13/L/10<br>*#398*<br> | **William ALEXANDER**<br>**George Duncan LAWSON**<br>trading as<br>**ALEXANDER & LAWSON**<br>68 Gordon Street<br>Glasgow | Silversmiths |

| REGISTRATION DETAILS | MAKER'S PRIVATE ADDRESS and DETAILS | PLATE and MARK DETAILS | MAKER/COMPANY and BUSINESS ADDRESS | MAKER'S TRADE |
|---|---|---|---|---|
| R2/145<br>18 October 1911<br>Sent by Alfred Lobel | 131 Broadhurst Gardens<br>London NW | P13/L/62<br>*#399*<br>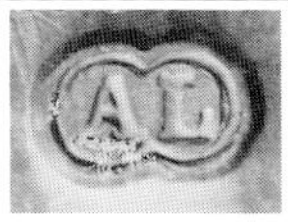 | **Alfred LOBEL**<br>Ever Ready Works<br>Hercules Place<br>London NW | Electricians |
| R2/156<br>4 May 1912<br>Sent by Agnes Lee | Private address same as business | P13/L/73<br>*#400*<br> | **Agnes LEE**<br>Bartford Lodge<br>1 Parkhill Road<br>Hampstead<br>London | Trade not entered<br><br>Worker in silver? |
| R2/8<br>19 December 1905<br>Sent by Dennison & Wigley Watch Case Co | Roxbury<br>Church Lane<br>Handsworth Wood<br>Birmingham | P9/D/49<br>*#401*<br><br>P9/D/48<br>*#402*<br> | **Franklin DENNISON** trading as<br>**DENNISON & WIGLEY** *<br>Terrace Road<br>Handsworth and<br>234 Soho Hill<br>Birmingham | Watchcase manufacturers |
| R2/15<br>3 April 1906<br>Sent by Franklin Dennison | | P9/D/54<br>*#403*<br> | **Franklin DENNISON**<br>sole proprietor trading as<br>**DENNISON WATCH CASE CO** *<br>43 Terrace Road<br>Handsworth<br>Birmingham | |
| R3/9<br>20 April 1922<br>Sent by Adolph Lionel Goldstone | 5 Wolsely Place<br>Withington<br>Manchester | P15/G/45<br>*#404*<br> | **Adolph Lionel GOLDSTONE**<br>22 Kilverts Buildings<br>Withy Grove<br>Manchester | Wholesale jeweller and watch importer |
| R3/93<br>24 February 1939<br>Sent by A L Holland | 45 Easton Road<br>New Ferry<br>Cheshire | P21/H/7<br>*#405*<br> | **Arthur Leslie HOLLAND**<br>Art School<br>Liverpool | Silversmith |
| R2/76<br>22 March 1909<br>Sent by Adie & Lovekin Ltd | Solihull [1]<br>Birmingham<br>Edgbaston [2]<br>Birmingham<br>Moseley [3]<br>Birmingham | P13/A/8<br>*#406*<br><br>P13/A/7<br>*#407*<br> | **Alfred LOVEKIN**[1]<br>**Frederick SIMMONS**[2]<br>**George DEEBY**[3] trading as<br>**ADIE & LOVEKIN**<br>Alfred Lovekin (Director)<br>Frederick Street<br>Birmingham | Manufacturing silversmiths |
| R2/102<br>3 February 1910<br>Sent by William Neale & Son | Finsbury Pavement [1]<br>London | P13/A/22<br>*#408*<br> | **ASPREY & CO** *<br>E C Smith [1] (Secretary)<br>166 New Bond Street<br>London | Goldsmiths |
| Not in R2 as expected and sent between March 1913 and March 1919 | | P15/A/10<br>*#409*<br> | **ASPREY & CO LTD** * | |
| R1/211<br>15 April 1904<br>Sent by A Moore | Private address same as business | P9/M/77<br>*#410*<br> | **Albert MOORE**<br>57 Sacheverel Street<br>Derby | Manufacturing jeweller |

| REGISTRATION DETAILS | MAKER'S PRIVATE ADDRESS and DETAILS | PLATE and MARK DETAILS | MAKER/COMPANY and BUSINESS ADDRESS | MAKER'S TRADE |
|---|---|---|---|---|
| R2/20<br>7 July 1906<br>Sent by Lawson, Ward & Gammage | 102 Cazemore Road<br>Stoke Newington | P9/M/102-104<br>***#411-3*** 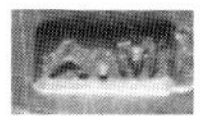 | **Arthur MEYER** *<br>76/78 Goswell Road<br>London | Diamond mounter and jeweller |
| R2/48<br>19 October 1907<br>Sent by W G Harris | | P9/M/121<br>***#414***  | | Diamond mounter |
| R3/104<br>13 January 1943<br>Sent by Alfred Mihil | Private address same as business | P21/M/15<br>***#415***  | **Alfred MIHILL**<br>176 Ninevah Road<br>Soho<br>Winson Green<br>Birmingham | Gold ring maker |
| R2/69<br>30 November 1908<br>Sent by A Marston<br>Two sizes | 61 Earlsbury Gardens<br>Birchfields<br>Birmingham | P13/M/5,6<br>***#416,7*** 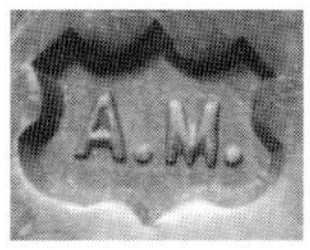 | **Alfred MARSTON**<br>263 Icknield Street<br>Birmingham | Silversmith |
| Cameo mark entered LAO 16 January 1764 | Square marked 1786 | P1/22/x4<br>***#418-21***  | **Ann MILLER** (G)<br>Bristol or | Smallworker |
| B/212 Incuse mark suggests a watch or watchcase maker | | | **Alexander MASON**<br>Liverpool (died 1792) or | Watch manufacturer |
| PMR 1738-61<br>B/218 Incuse mark suggests a watch or watchcase maker | Metcalfe may be too early | | **Augustine METCALFE**<br>Cable Street (1739)<br>Liverpool | Watchmaker |
| R1/98<br>25 April 1899<br>Sent by A Moore | Private address same as business | P9/M/11<br>***#422***  | **Alfred MOORE**<br>57 Sacheverel Street<br>Derby | Manufacturing jeweller |
| R3/50<br>14 November 1929<br>Sent by A E Moore | 68 Wilson Street<br>Derby | P15/M/74<br>***#423***  | **Alice Emma MOORE**<br>29a Grove Street<br>Derby | Manufacturing jeweller |
| Missing register<br>*c.*1887 | | P5/M/118<br>***#424***  | **Unidentified** | |
| R1/75<br>1 October 1899<br>Sent by Adelman & Broadhead | Private address same as business | P9/M/1<br>***#425***  | **Abraham MARTIN**<br>213 Great Chatham Street<br>Manchester | Jeweller |
| SPB/12<br>7 November 1876<br>Sent by J Harris<br>Manchester | GSJW/140 has business at<br>7 Holliwell Street (1861)<br>Long Milegate<br>Manchester | P3/M/x2<br>***#426,7***  | **Abraham MICHAELS**<br>36 Swan Street<br>Manchester | Wholesale watch and clock dealer |
| R2/55<br>7 February 1908<br>Sent by G E Walton Ltd | 15 Stanmore Road<br>Edgbaston<br>Birmingham | P9/M/123,124<br>***#428,9***  | **Arthur Joseph MASON**<br>52/54 Hylton Street (*sic*)<br>Birmingham | Wholesale jeweller |
| R2/153<br>20 March 1912<br>Sent by A Wilcox<br>BAO 16.572 | 88 Alexander Road<br>Acocks Green<br>Birmingham | P13/M/47<br>***#430***  | **Andrew MOODIE**<br>52/54 Hylton Street (*sic*)<br>Birmingham | Manufacturing jeweller and silversmith |

 AM–AM

| REGISTRATION DETAILS | MAKER'S PRIVATE ADDRESS and DETAILS | PLATE and MARK DETAILS | MAKER/COMPANY and BUSINESS ADDRESS | MAKER'S TRADE |
|---|---|---|---|---|
| LPB/5 SP27/3<br>21 June 1884<br>No mark in LPB just initials AM | (Ed: Partner in Allen & Martin – home address The Willows) | P5/M/x1<br>***#431***<br>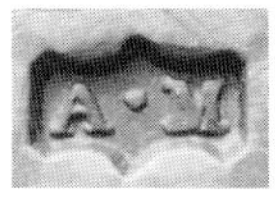 | **Alfred MARTIN**<br>Chester Road<br>Erdington<br>Birmingham | Jewellers |
| Missing register<br>*c.*1886 | | P5/M/53<br>***#432***<br>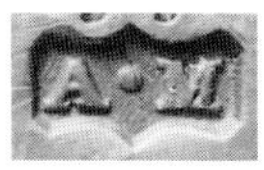 | | |
| LPB/12<br>no day May 1881<br>Sent by E Vaughton | | P3/A/x1<br>***#433***<br> | **Frederick ALLEN &**<br>**Alfred MARTIN** trading as<br>**ALLEN & MARTIN** *<br>70 Great Hampton Street<br>Birmingham | |
| LPB/12<br>22 February 1882<br>Sent by E Whitehouse | | P3/A/x1<br>***#434***<br> | | |
| LPB/62<br>13 February 1883<br>Sent by A Russell & Co | | P3/A/x2<br>***#435,6***<br> | | |
| LPB/16<br>30 April 1879<br>Sent by<br>E Vaughton | | P3/B/x2<br>***#437,8***<br> | **Abraham Meyer BLANCKENSEE** *<br>2A Summer Hill<br>Terrace Parade<br>Birmingham | Watch manufacturer and importer |
| LPB/16<br>27 October 1880 | | P3/B/x1<br>***#439***<br> | | |
| Missing register<br>*c.*1886 | | P5/B/67<br>***#440***<br> | | |
| R1/19<br>17 December 1895<br>Sent by Lucas Brothers Ltd, Candelesch & Adams and Kinsey Brothers & Patrick | 51 Beaufort Road<br>Edgbaston<br>Birmingham | P5/aboveB/714<br>***#441***<br> | **Abraham Meyer BLANCKENSEE** *<br>3 Summer Hill Terrace<br>Birmingham | Jeweller |
| R1/199<br>18 August 1903<br>Sent by A & M Cohen | Private address same as business | P9/C/97<br>***#442***<br> | **Abraham COHEN & Myer COHEN**<br>trading as **A & M COHEN**<br>63 Lime Street<br>Liverpool | Fancy goods dealers |
| R3/179<br>5 May 1961<br>Sent by A M Gunn | The Lodge<br>Madeira Walk<br>Church Stretton<br>Salop | P21/H*sic*/83<br>***#443***<br> | **Arthur Mainwaring GUNN**<br>No business address entered | Retired |
| R1/94<br>6 March 1899<br>Sent by C Widmer & Sons | 173 Brixton Road [1]<br>London SW<br>155 Acre Lane [2]<br>Brixton<br>London SW | P9/P*sic*/23<br>***#444***<br>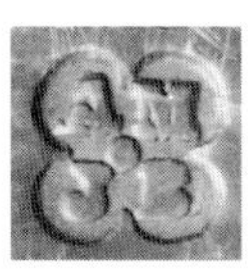 | **Alfred MANSFIELD** [1]<br>**James BRITTON** [2] trading as<br>**PEACOCK, MANSFIELD & BRITTON** *<br>18 Salisbury Square<br>Fleet Street<br>London EC | Register binders and fancy leather goods manufacturers |
| LPB/76<br>20 February 1881<br>Only the mark is shown in LPB, no name or address | This trade mark registered 22 October 1880 KOC/178 | P3/X*sic*/x1<br>***#445***<br>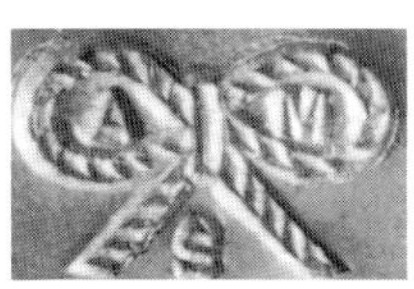 | **Albert MARCIUS** trading as<br>**SILBER & FLEMING** *<br>56 Wood Street<br>Cheapside<br>London | Manufacturer and merchant for timepieces and clocks |

| REGISTRATION DETAILS | MAKER'S PRIVATE ADDRESS and DETAILS | PLATE and MARK DETAILS | MAKER/COMPANY and BUSINESS ADDRESS | MAKER'S TRADE |
|---|---|---|---|---|
| R3/154<br>11 March 1955<br>Sent by A M West | Grangebrooke<br>51 Wilmslow Road<br>Cheadle<br>Cheshire | P21/W/75<br>***#446***  | **Ann Mavis WEST**<br>No business address entered | Student of silver work |
| R2/44<br>25 July 1907<br>Clerk entered #33 instead of #40<br>Sent by Augusta North | Private address same as business | P9/N/33<br>***#447*** 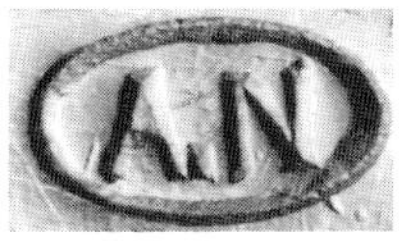 | **Augusta NORTH**<br>152 Adelphi Street<br>Preston | Pipe manufacturer |
| R3/181<br>11 November 1961<br>Sent by A Nicol | Hest Croft<br>Coastal Rise<br>Hest Bank<br>nr Lancaster | P21/N/16<br>***#448*** 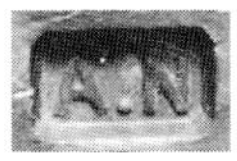 | **Andrew NICOL**<br>No business address entered | Student silversmith |
| R1/11<br>28 May 1895<br>Sent by<br>A W Newbold | 43 Mercers Road<br>Holloway<br>London N | P5/N/662<br>***#449***  | **Alfred William NEWBOLD** *<br>37 Spencer Street<br>Clerkenwell<br>London | Gold spectacle and eye glass maker |
| R1/123<br>4 April 1900<br>Sent by A Noel | 35 Ronald Road<br>Highbury<br>London | P9/N/9<br>***#450***  | **Alfred NOEL**<br>51 King Square<br>Goswell Road<br>London | Gold chain maker and jeweller |
| R1/181<br>12 December 1902<br>Sent by Augusta North | Private address same as business | P9/N/14<br>***#451***  | **Augusta NORTH**<br>152 Adelphi Street<br>Preston | Pipe manufacturer |
| R1/89<br>26 January 1899<br>Sent by W Mills | Private address same as business | P9/N/4<br>***#452***  | **Arthur NOBLE senior**<br>**Arthur NOBLE junior** trading as<br>**A NOBLE & SON**<br>Smithfield House<br>Leonard Street<br>Leek<br>Staffordshire | Wholesale jewellers |
| R3/118<br>29 May 1947<br>Sent by selves | | P21/A/5<br>***#453***  | **ANGLO-ORIENT TRADING CO LTD**<br>Sealed in the presence of:<br>J Abrahams (Director)<br>Lily Goldstein (Director)<br>D Abrahams (Secretary)<br>815 Finchley Road<br>London NW11 | Manufacturing jewellers |
| R3/26<br>6 December 1924<br>Sent by Andrea Pallis | Private address same as business | No mark entered<br>***#454*** | **Andrea Pandea PALLIS**<br>130 Princes Road<br>Liverpool 8 | Silversmith |
| R3/30<br>11 October 1925<br>Sent by Andrea Pallis | | P15/P/194<br>***#455*** 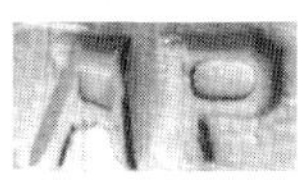 | | |
| Missing register<br>*c.*1886 | | P5/P/51<br>***#456***  | **Albert PLATNAUER** * | Jewellers |
| Missing register<br>*c.*1891 | | P5/P/344<br>***#457***  | | |
| R1/11<br>18 May 1895<br>Sent by<br>A G Griffiths | 257 Monument Road<br>Birmingham | P5/P/659<br>***#458***  | **Albert PLATNAUER**<br>**Percy L PLATNAUER** trading as<br>**Albert PLATNAUER** *<br>89 Vyse Street<br>Birmingham | |

| REGISTRATION DETAILS | MAKER'S PRIVATE ADDRESS and DETAILS | PLATE and MARK DETAILS | MAKER/COMPANY and BUSINESS ADDRESS | MAKER'S TRADE |
|---|---|---|---|---|
| R3/30<br>11 July 1929<br>Sent by Andrea Pallis | Private address same as business | P15/P/220<br>***#459***<br> | **Andrea Pandea PALLIS**<br>130 Princes Road<br>Liverpool 8 | Silversmith |
| 2 December 1931 | | P15/P/234<br>***#460***<br> | | |
| Post 1883 but not in LPB or R1 as expected | 5th mark on square-P between Pope & Phelps 31 May 1884 and Pendleton & Sons 26 March 1885 | P5/P/x1<br>***#461***<br> | **Albert PLATNAUER** *<br>89 Vyse Street<br>Birmingham | Jewellers |
| R1/29<br>4 June 1896<br>Sent by W Walker and A J Cole | Noland House<br>Hazlitt Road<br>West Kensington, London | P5/P/771<br>***#462***<br> | **Adolph POSENER** *<br>60, 60½ Mansell Street<br>Minories<br>London EC | Pipe manufacturers and importers of tobacconist goods |
| R1/152<br>5 September 1901<br>Sent by<br>J G Newbold | Noland House<br>Hazlitt Road<br>West Kensington<br>London | P9/P/118<br>***#463***<br> | **Adolph POSENER** trading as<br>**Adolph POSENER & CO** *<br>61 Mansell Street, Goodmans Field<br>London | Tobacconist and fancy goods dealers |
| R2/10<br>5 February 1906<br>Sent by<br>J G Newbold | 148 Abbey Road<br>London NW | P9/Q*sic*/231<br>***#464***<br> | | |
| R2/60<br>22 May 1908<br>Sent by J G Newbold<br>Cancelled<br>6 January 1910<br>Two sizes | 64 Fordwych Road<br>Brondesbury | P13/P/1-3<br>***#465-7***<br> | . | |
| R1/10<br>27 April 1895<br>Sent by W Walker | 38 Brownhill Road<br>Catford<br>London SE | P5/P/654<br>***#468***<br>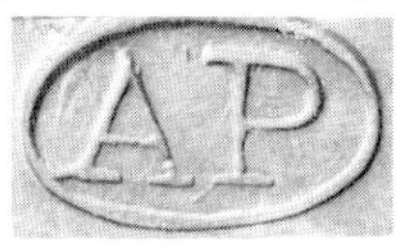 | **Alfred PARKER**<br>16 Houndsditch<br>London E | Importer of fancy goods |
| Missing register<br>*c.*1886 | | P5/P/61<br>***#469***<br> | **Unidentified** | |
| R1/173<br>15 August 1902<br>Sent by A Poyser | Private address same as business | P9/R*sic*/49<br>***#470***<br> | **Arthur W POYSER**<br>10 North Front<br>Southampton | Silversmith and stick mounter |
| LPB/64<br>8 May 1882<br>Sent by A Russell & Co<br>Liverpool | | P3/P/x1<br>***#471***<br> | **Alfred PEEL**<br>35 Warstone Lane<br>Birmingham | Jeweller |
| R2/18<br>19 May 1906<br>Sent by Rink & Dalby | Darley Street<br>Bradford | P9/U*sic*/252<br>***#472***<br> | **Arthur PICKERING** trading as<br>**Arthur PICKERING & CO**<br>Darley Street<br>Bradford and<br>3 County Arcade<br>Leeds | Umbrella and walking stick manufacturers |
| R2/101<br>6 January 1910<br>Sent by A Posener & Co<br>Two sizes | 1 Maismore Mansions<br>Caufield Gardens<br>London NW | P13/P/108,109<br>***#473,4***<br> | **Adolph POSENER** trading as<br>**A POSENER & CO** *<br>61 Mansell Street<br>Goodman Fields<br>London E | Pipe and fancy goods manufacturers |

| REGISTRATION DETAILS | MAKER'S PRIVATE ADDRESS and DETAILS | PLATE and MARK DETAILS | MAKER/COMPANY and BUSINESS ADDRESS | MAKER'S TRADE |
|---|---|---|---|---|
| Not in R2 as expected<br>Between Q/226 and Q/227 October 1904 to June 1905 | | P9/*Qsic*/0*sic*<br>***#475***  | **Unidentified** | |
| Missing register<br>*c.*1887 | | P5/P/128<br>***#476***  | **Unidentified** | |
| R1/8<br>1 March 1895<br>Sent by<br>A A Richmond | Clydesdale<br>Wheelwright Road<br>Erdington | P5/R/644<br>***#477***  | **Alfred Ernest RICHMOND**<br>112 Spencer Street<br>Birmingham | Manufacturing jeweller |
| R1/175<br>10 September 1902<br>Sent by A Rex | Private address same as business | P9/R/50<br>***#478***  | **Arthur REX**<br>25 Redditch Road<br>King's Norton<br>Birmingham | Chain manufacturer |
| LPB/72<br>2 April 1881<br>Sent by E Whitehouse | | P3/R/x1<br>***#479***  | **Arthur ROGERS** trading as<br>**SAMUEL & ROGERS** *<br>72 Wood Street<br>Liverpool | Watchcase makers |
| R2/110<br>9 May 1910<br>Sent by Saunders & Shepherd<br>MR3/137 | Iona | P13/R/31<br>***#480***  | **Alex RITCHE**<br>Iona<br>Northumberland | Iona Celtic Art |
| R1/54<br>20 November 1897<br>Sent by<br>A R Arrowsmith | 18 Waverhill Road<br>Handsworth<br>Birmingham | P5/aboveA/908<br>***#481***  | **Alfred Robert ARROWSMITH**<br>35 Warstone Lane<br>Birmingham | Jeweller |
| R3/53<br>28 April 1930<br>Sent by T J Skelton | 86 Vyse Street<br>Birmingham | P15/R/48<br>***#482***  | **A RODEN & SON**<br>55 Hatton Garden<br>London EC1 | Silversmiths |
| R1/126<br>7 May 1900<br>Sent by W H Carrington & Co | Private address same as business | P9/T/15<br>***#483***  | **Alfred Richard TAYLOR**<br>113 Bath Street<br>Ilkeston | Tobacconist |
| R1/83<br>11 November 1898<br>Sent by A H Tongue | Clifton<br>Pollokshields<br>Glasgow | P9/A/4<br>***#484*** 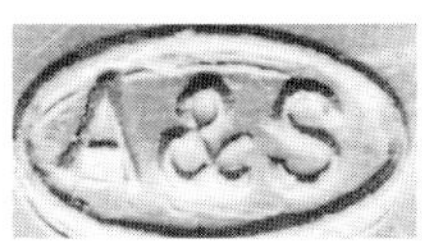 | **Andrew A ANDERSON** trading as<br>**ANDERSON & SON**<br>195 Argyle Street<br>Glasgow | Tobacco and cigar importers |
| R3/120<br>11 December 1947<br>Sent by A Simm<br>Two sizes | 35 Baistor Street<br>Preston<br>Barkside (later - undated)<br>7 Kings Drive<br>Fulwood, Lancashire | P21/S/32,33<br>***#485,6***  | **Alfred SIMM**<br>School of Art<br>Liverpool | Art student |
| Missing register<br>*c.*1890 | | P5/S/332<br>***#487***  | **Unidentified** | |
| Missing register<br>*c.*1891 | | P5/S/358<br>***#488***  | **Unidentified** | |

| REGISTRATION DETAILS | MAKER'S PRIVATE ADDRESS and DETAILS | PLATE and MARK DETAILS | MAKER/COMPANY and BUSINESS ADDRESS | MAKER'S TRADE |
|---|---|---|---|---|
| R3/25<br>22 October 1924<br>Sent by Adolph Scott | 41 Hagley Road<br>Birmingham | P15/S/63<br>***#489***<br> | **Adolph SCOTT** *<br>24, 26 Great Hampton Street<br>Birmingham | Wholesale jewellers and merchants |
| R3/45<br>25 February 1929<br>Sent by Adolph Scott | Private address same as business | P15/S/84<br>***#490***<br> | | Silversmiths |
| R3/66<br>12 May 1933<br>Sent by A Scott Ltd | | P15/S/100<br>***#491***<br> | **Adolph SCOTT LTD** *<br>Common seal of company affixed in the presence of:-<br>D McCame (Director)<br>Adolph Scott (Director)<br>23-26 Great Hampton Street<br>Birmingham | Jewellers and plate manufacturers |
| R3/10<br>2 June 1922<br>Sent by<br>Geo G Ashling | 55 Stockport Road<br>Levenshulme<br>Manchester<br>41 Sandown Street<br>Gorton<br>Manchester | P15/A/41<br>***#492***<br> | **George Gilbert ASHLING**<br>**George SHENTON**<br>10 New Street<br>Bradshaw Street<br>Manchester | Walking stick and umbrella mounters |
| R3/162<br>17 July 1957<br>Sent by A Sharples<br>Two sizes | Worrall House<br>683 Old Chester Road<br>Old Trafford<br>Manchester 16 | P21/S/71,72<br>***#493,4***<br> | **Annie SHARPLES**<br>No business address entered | Student |
| R1/90<br>3 February 1899<br>Sent by J Bray for W Walker | Clifton<br>Pollokshields<br>Glasgow | P9/A/8<br>***#495***<br> | **Andrew A ANDERSON** trading as<br>**ANDERSON & SON**<br>195 Argyle Street<br>Glasgow | Cigar importers and tobacco furnishers |
| R1/5<br>27 November 1894<br>Sent by A Schneader | 21 Norfolk Street<br>Birmingham | P5/S/626<br>***#496***<br> | **Alexander SCHNEADER**<br>21 Norfolk Street<br>Birmingham | Jeweller |
| LPB/76<br>3 October 1880<br>Sent by Myell Brothers | | P3/S/x3<br>***#497-9***<br> | **Albert SYDENHAM**<br>11 Northampton Street<br>Birmingham | Wholesale jewellers |
| Not in LPB as expected<br>*c.* 1884 | | P5/S/x1<br>***#500***<br> | **Unidentified** | |
| Missing register<br>*c.*1887 | | P5/S/78<br>***#501***<br> | **Unidentified** | |
| Missing register<br>*c.*1891 | | P5/S/383<br>***#502***<br> | **Unidentified** | |
| LPB/76<br>2 September 1882<br>Sent by Pope & Phelps | | P3/S/x1<br>***#503***<br> | **Alfred Henry SHAW**<br>238 Clifton Road<br>Aston<br>Birmingham | Jeweller (from 1881 census) |
| LPB/79 SP31/4<br>6 November 1884<br>No mark alongside entry | Position of mark on SP31 used to assign mark to name in the LPB | P5/S/x1<br>***#504***<br> | | |

| REGISTRATION DETAILS | MAKER'S PRIVATE ADDRESS and DETAILS | PLATE and MARK DETAILS | MAKER/COMPANY and BUSINESS ADDRESS | MAKER'S TRADE |
|---|---|---|---|---|
| R1/36<br>24 November 1896<br>Sent by J Hayward<br>Wigley & Hall | 46 Carlyle Road<br>Edgbaston<br>Birmingham | P5/*Osic*/807<br>***#505***  | **Adolph SCOTT** *<br>41 Vyse Street<br>Birmingham | Manufacturing jeweller and factor |
| Not in R2 as expected<br>Between October 1910 and February 1911 Similar mark entered<br>BAO 11 January 1910 | | P13/S/62<br>***#506***  | **Adolph SCOTT** *<br>41 Vyse Street<br>Birmingham | Jeweller |
| R3/62<br>18 April 1932<br>Sent by Benson Brothers<br>72 Wood Street<br>Liverpool | | P15/S/99<br>***#507***  | **Adolph SCOTT LTD** *<br>Adolph Scott (Director)<br>24/25/26 Great Hampton Street<br>Birmingham | Wholesale jewellers and merchants |
| LPB/98 SP31/7<br>11 August 1885<br>No mark alongside entry<br>Sent by W Butler | Position of mark on SP31 used to assign to name in the LPB | P5/S/x1<br>***#508***  | **Albert SYDENHAM**<br>11 Northampton Street<br>Birmingham | Wholesale jeweller |
| R3/2<br>29 April 1921<br>Sent by Adolph Scott<br>Two sizes | Private address same as business | P15/S/49,50<br>***#509,10***  | **Adolph SCOTT LTD** *<br>Adolph Scott (Director)<br>24/25/26 Great Hampton Street<br>Birmingham | Silversmiths |
| R1/33<br>1 October 1896<br>Sent by E Vaughton | 110 Murdock Road [1]<br>Handsworth<br>The Shambles [2]<br>King's Heath<br>Birmingham | P5/A/791<br>***#511***  | **Ambrose Platt AUSTIN** [1]<br>**William Henry STEELY** [2]<br>Vittoria Street<br>Birmingham | Jewellers |
| Missing register<br>*c.*1892<br>Similar mark entered<br>LAO 3 January 1903 | | P5/S/413<br>***#512***  | **Albert SLADE** *<br>55 Richmond Road<br>Dalston<br>London E | Silversmith |
| R2/64<br>18 August 1908<br>Sent by F Banks | St Bernard's Road<br>Olton | P13/S/8<br>***#513***  | **Albert SYDENHAM**<br>26 Frederick Street<br>Birmingham | Wholesale jeweller |
| Not in R1 as expected<br>Next to CSFS dated<br>1 December 1899 | | P9/S/0*sic*<br>***#514***  | | |
| R1/192<br>8 May 1903<br>Sent by W H Ashford | Olton<br>Warwickshire | P9/S/63<br>***#515***  | | |
| R2/44<br>13 August 1907<br>Sent by Albert Sydenham | | P13/S/1<br>***#516***  | | Wholesale and manufacturing jeweller |
| R2/108<br>6 April 1910<br>Sent by A S Holman | 514 Slade Road<br>Erdington<br>Birmingham | P13/H/49<br>***#517***  | **Archibald Stephen HOLMAN**<br>67 George Street<br>Lozells<br>Birmingham | Jeweller |
| R2/113<br>28 June 1910<br>Sent by A S Holman | | P13/H/53<br>***#518***  | | |
| R2/113<br>28 June 1910<br>Sent by A S Holman | | P13/H/54<br>***#519***  | | |

| REGISTRATION DETAILS | MAKER'S PRIVATE ADDRESS and DETAILS | PLATE and MARK DETAILS | MAKER/COMPANY and BUSINESS ADDRESS | MAKER'S TRADE |
|---|---|---|---|---|
| R3/48<br>17 July 1929<br>Sent by A Timmins | Private address same as business | P15/T/56<br>***#520***<br> | **Albert TIMMINS**<br>120 High Road<br>Beeston<br>Nottingham | Jeweller |
| R2/9<br>16 January 1906<br>Sent by<br>A Thorneywork | 70 Willmore Road<br>Perry Barr<br>Birmingham | P9/T/57<br>***#521***<br> | **Arthur THORNEYWORK**<br>62 Great Hampton Street<br>Birmingham | General jewellery |
| R1/219<br>18 August 1904<br>Sent by A T Oliver | 67 Endsleigh Gardens<br>Ilford | P9/O/7<br>***#522***<br> | **Albert Thomas OLIVER** *<br>31 Wynyatt Street<br>Clerkenwell<br>London EC | Watchcase maker |
| R3/32<br>15 May 1926<br>Sent by A T Oliver | 65 Herongate Road<br>London E12 | P15/O/7<br>***#523***<br> | | |
| R3/75<br>19 April 1935<br>Sent by A Taylor & Son | 13 Westland Drive [1]<br>Glasgow W4 | P15/T/78<br>***#524***<br> | **Andrew TAYLOR & SON**<br>Charles Taylor [1] (Sole partner)<br>259 Hope Street<br>Glasgow | Jewellers and silversmiths |
| R3/184<br>15 May 1962<br>Sent by A T S Mitchell | 382 Manchester Road<br>Warrington | P21/M/56,57<br>***#525,6***<br> | **Allan Thomas Smith MITCHELL**<br>c/o Imperial Tobacco Industries<br>Research Department<br>Widnes | Chemist |
| LPB/95 SP29/1<br>2 February 1884 | | P5/Z*sic*/x1<br>***#527***<br> | **Alfred VERNON** *<br>15 Sherbourne Street<br>Coventry | Watchcase maker |
| Missing register<br>*c.*1888 | | P5/V/141<br>***#528***<br> | | |
| R3/77<br>21 August 1935<br>Sent by A V Ward<br>MR3/143 | Private address same as business | P15/W/112<br>***#529***<br> | **Arthur Vincent WARD**<br>Heighfield<br>Great Langhall<br>Cheshire | Goldsmith |
| R2/39<br>1 May 1907<br>Sent by self<br>Two sizes | 9 West Lorne Street<br>Chester | P9/V*sic*/169,170<br>***#530,1***<br>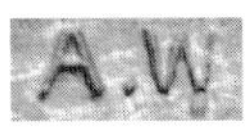 | **Albert E WARD**<br>3 Watergate Row<br>Chester | Agent and bookbinder |
| R1/194<br>4 June 1903<br>Sent by A Wright | Private address same as business | P9/W/98<br>***#532***<br> | **Arthur WRIGHT** *<br>2 Victoria Road<br>Stoke Newington<br>London N | Gold and silversmith |
| R2/196<br>29 May 1915<br>Sent by Agnes Lloyd | The Elms [1]<br>Hockley Heath<br>60 Lansdown Road<br>Birmingham<br>Kineton Road<br>Birmingham | P15/W/14<br>***#533***<br> | **Alice ANDREWS** [1]<br>**Alfred Mathew ANDREWS**<br>**Stanley ANDREWS** trading as<br>**Alfred WILCOX**<br>84 Vyse Street<br>Birmingham | Manufacturing jewellers |
| R1/81<br>9 April 1908<br>Sent by A Wilcox | 208 Hamstead Road<br>Handsworth<br>Birmingham | P9/V*sic*/172<br>***#534***<br> | **Alfred WILCOX**<br>Tenby Street North<br>Birmingham | Jeweller |

| REGISTRATION DETAILS | MAKER'S PRIVATE ADDRESS and DETAILS | PLATE and MARK DETAILS | MAKER/COMPANY and BUSINESS ADDRESS | MAKER'S TRADE |
|---|---|---|---|---|
| Not in R3 as expected - struck between June and July 1923 | Not registered at BAO | P15/W/67<br>***#535***<br> | **Unidentified** | |
| Not in R3 as expected - struck between November 1923 and January 1925<br>Two sizes | Not registered at BAO | P15/W/72-76<br>***#536-40***<br> | **Unidentified** | |
| R1/112<br>20 September 1899<br>Sent by W H Carrington & Co | West Bridgford<br>Nottinghamshire | P9/W/25<br>***#541***<br> | **Arthur WATTS**<br>Station Street<br>Greyfriars Gate and<br>Carrington Street<br>Northampton | Tobacconist |
| R3/97<br>1 May 1940<br>Sent by B H Britton & Sons | 35 Hockley Hill<br>Birmingham<br>6 Woolstone Road<br>London S E 23 | P21/W/31<br>***#542***<br> | **Arthur WITTING**<br>39 Hatton Garden<br>London EC1 | Wholesale jeweller |
| R3/147<br>21 November 1953<br>Sent by A Wright | 70 Talbot Road<br>Old Trafford<br>12 Princess Mansions<br>(from 30 November 1954)<br>Princess Parkway<br>Wythenshawe, Manchester | P21/W/68,69<br>***#543,4***<br> | **Annie WRIGHT**<br>No business address entered | Student |
| R1/191<br>25 April 1903<br>Sent by Alabaster & Wilson | Salisbury Road<br>Mosely<br>37 Westfield Road<br>Edgbaston | P9/A/48-50<br>***#545-7***<br> | **Arthur Alabaster LONGFIELD**<br>**Joshua Edward CARTWRIGHT**<br>trading as **ALABASTER & WILSON**<br>Legge Lane<br>Birmingham | Manufacturing jewellers |
| R1/90<br>10 February 1899<br>Sent by A Wheatley | 36 Church Road<br>Chorlton cum Hardy<br>Manchester | P9/W/10<br>***#548***<br> | **Amos WHEATLEY**<br>45 Hanging Ditch<br>Manchester | Pipe mounter and general engraver |
| R1/194<br>4 June 1903<br>Sent by A Wright | Private address same as business | P9/W/98<br>***#549***<br> | **Arthur WRIGHT** *<br>2 Victoria Road<br>Stoke Newington<br>London N | Gold and silversmith |
| R3/30<br>15 September 1925<br>Sent by A N Andrews<br>Five sizes | 133 Heathfield Road<br>Birmingham<br>The Nook<br>Olton | P15/W/79-85<br>***#550-6***<br> | **Alfred Nathan ANDREWS**<br>**Harry Stanley ANDREWS** trading as<br>**A WILCOX**<br>15 Nursery Road<br>Hockley<br>Birmingham | Jewellers and silversmiths |
| R3/81<br>21 February 1948<br>Sent by A Wall<br>Two sizes | 10 Bush Grove<br>Handsworth<br>Birmingham | P21/W/47,48<br>***#557,8***<br> | **Arthur WALL**<br>27 Northampton Street<br>Birmingham 18 | Manufacturing jeweller |
| SPB/19<br>28 January 1869<br>GSJW/137 1861 | CWMP has Wickes & Trahern, gold watchcase makers, at this address in 1874 | P3/W/x3<br>***#559-61***<br> | **Alfred WICKES** *<br>50 Craven Street<br>Chapel Fields<br>Coventry | Watchcase maker |

| REGISTRATION DETAILS | MAKER'S PRIVATE ADDRESS and DETAILS | PLATE and MARK DETAILS | MAKER/COMPANY and BUSINESS ADDRESS | MAKER'S TRADE |
|---|---|---|---|---|
| R1/213<br>12 May 1904<br>Sent by Salmon & Gluckstein Ltd | Private address same as business | P9/W/112<br>***#562***<br> | **Arthur WRIGHT** *<br>2 Victoria Road<br>Stoke Newington<br>London N | Silversmith |
| R1/216<br>22 June 1904<br>Sent by Imperial Tobacco Co, Salmon & Gluckstein Ltd | | P9/W/113<br>***#563***<br> | | |
| R1/216<br>13 September 1904<br>Two sizes | | P9/V*sic*/121,122<br>***#564,5***<br> | | |
| R2/7<br>18 November 1905<br>Sent by Imperial Tobacco Co | | P9/V*sic*/136,137<br>***#566,7***<br> | **Arthur WRIGHT** *<br>20 St Margaret's Mansions<br>Lillie Road<br>Fulham<br>London | Gold and silversmith |
| SPB/10<br>4 July 1873 | One George Harrison, working jeweller, at this address in 1874 | P3/W/x2<br>***#568,9***<br> | **Andrew WEDDELL**<br>101 Brook Street<br>Old Garrat Road<br>Manchester | Working jeweller? |
| LPB/92<br>29 September 1882<br>MR3/145 | | P3/W/x2<br>***#570,1***<br> | **Alfred WILCOX**<br>Spencer Street<br>Birmingham | Jeweller |
| Missing register<br>*c.*1886 | | P5/W/63<br>***#572***<br> | **Unidentified** | |
| Missing register<br>*c.*1891 | | P5/W/361<br>***#573***<br> | **Unidentified** | |
| R1/104<br>14 June 1899<br>Sent by A Wigley<br>Two sizes | 152 Hamstead Road<br>Handsworth<br>Birmingham | P9/W/18,19<br>***#574,5***<br> | **Alfred WIGLEY** *<br>Terrace Road<br>(Ed: Factory of Dennison & Wigley)<br>Birmingham | Watchcase manufacturer |
| Missing register<br>*c.*1886<br>Similar mark entered LAO 9 December 1885 | CWMP1886-1901 | P5/W/7<br>***#576***<br> | **Albert WATERFALL** *<br>15 Hertford Terrace<br>Coventry | Watchcase maker |
| R3/1<br>29 March 1921<br>Note 40 series on P15/W used twice!<br>Sent by T J Skelton | Private address same as business | P15/W/40,41<br>***#577,8***<br> | **Albert WOOD**<br>185 Green Lane<br>Rawmarsh<br>Rotherham | Wholesale jeweller |
| R3/6<br>9 January 1922<br>Sent by Alfred Ward | Private address same as business | P15/W/52<br>***#579***<br>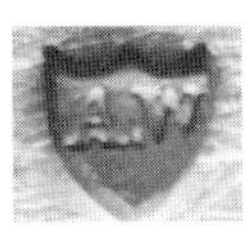 | **Alfred WARD** *<br>116 Westwood Road<br>Coventry | Watchcase maker |
| R2/218<br>22 March 1919<br>Sent by Atkins & Wigley | 2 Sycamore Street and<br>127 Johnson Road<br>Erdington<br>Birmingham | P15/A/12<br>***#580***<br>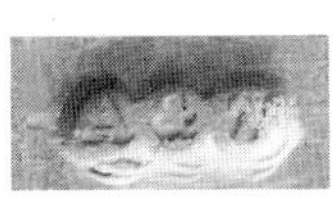 | **Charles Herbert ATKINS**<br>**Ernest WIGLEY** trading as<br>**ATKINS & WIGLEY**<br>171 Hockley Hill<br>Birmingham | Manufacturing jewellers |

| REGISTRATION DETAILS | MAKER'S PRIVATE ADDRESS and DETAILS | PLATE and MARK DETAILS | MAKER/COMPANY and BUSINESS ADDRESS | MAKER'S TRADE |
|---|---|---|---|---|
| R3/81<br>22 November 1935<br>Sent by A Wall | 10 Bush Grove<br>Handsworth<br>Birmingham | P15/W/113<br>***#581***<br> | **Arthur WALL**<br>27 Northampton Street<br>Birmingham 18 | Manufacturing jeweller |
| R1/101<br>31 May 1899<br>Sent by A W Butt<br>Replacement punch<br>7 April 1902 | Grey Friars<br>Chester<br><br>Authority to Planche? & Co | P9/B/19<br>***#582***<br> | **Alfred Wathew BUTT**<br>32 Eastgate Row<br>Chester | Silversmith |
| R3/6<br>6 February 1922<br>Sent by Handcock & Walker | Pembroke Lodge [1]<br>View Road<br>Highgate N6 | P15/B/159<br>***#583***<br> | **EVANS CONCINNUM METAL WORKS LTD**<br>A W Bishop [1]<br>85a Tollington Street<br>London SW1 | Tobacconist supplier |
| R1/23<br>7 March 1896<br>Sent by A W Butt<br>MR3/118<br>Cancelled 7 April 1902 | Grey Friars<br>Chester | P5/aboveB/734<br>***#584***<br> | **Alfred Wathew BUTT** *<br>32 Eastgate Row<br>Chester | Silversmith |
| R1/166<br>7 April 1902<br>Sent by A W Butt | | P9/B/91<br>***#585***<br> | **Alfred Wathew BUTT** *<br>32 Eastgate Street Row<br>Chester and<br>Wrexham and<br>Warrington and<br>Shrewsbury | |
| R1/227<br>11 February 1905<br>Sent by A W Butt | | P9/XYZ*sic*/130<br>***#586***<br> | **Alfred Wathew BUTT** *<br>32 Eastgate Street Row<br>Chester and<br>42 High Street<br>Wrexham | Goldsmith and silversmith |
| R1/229<br>7 March 1905<br>Sent by A W Butt | | P9/XYZ*sic*/131<br>***#587***<br> | **Alfred Wathew BUTT** *<br>32 Eastgate Street Row<br>Chester and<br>42 High Street<br>Wrexham and<br>10, 41/43 Sankey Street<br>Warrington and<br>9/10 The Square<br>Shrewsbury | |
| R1/163<br>11 March 1902<br>Sent by Loach Brothers | 79 Greenfield Road<br>Harborne | P9/C/76<br>***#588***<br> | **Arthur Walter CROSBEE** trading as<br>**A W CROSBEE & CO**<br>7 Vyse Street<br>Birmingham | Wholesale jewellers |
| R2/127<br>7 February 1911<br>BAO 18.581<br>Sent by R Parks & Co | | P13/C/88<br>***#589***<br> | **Arthur Walter CROSBEE** trading as<br>**A W CROSBEE & CO**<br>7 Vyse Street<br>Birmingham | |
| R3/32<br>6 May 1926<br>Sent by Stylic Watch Case Co Ltd | | P15/C/168<br>***#590***<br> | **A W CROSBEE & SONS LTD**<br>7 Vyse Street<br>Birmingham | Jewellers |

| REGISTRATION DETAILS | MAKER'S PRIVATE ADDRESS and DETAILS | PLATE and MARK DETAILS | MAKER/COMPANY and BUSINESS ADDRESS | MAKER'S TRADE |
|---|---|---|---|---|
| R1/150<br>5 July 1901<br>Sent by E Durban & Co | 8 Windsor Quadrant<br>Glasgow | P9/D/20-22<br>***#591-3***<br> | **Alexander Whyte DYKES**<br>(Sole partner)<br>11 Royal Exchange Square<br>Glasgow | Jeweller, silversmith and watch factor |
| LPB/90<br>27 February 1884 | | P5/W/x1<br>***#594***<br>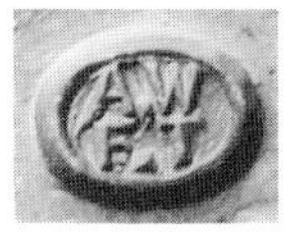 | **Alfred WICKES**<br>**Frederick TRAHERNE** trading as<br>**WICKES & TRAHERN** *<br>Clifton Villa<br>Allesley Old Road<br>Chapel Fields<br>Coventry | Watchcase makers |
| LPB/6<br>15 December 1877<br>No mark in LPB | | P3/T/x3<br>***#595-7***<br> | | |
| R1/7<br>6 February 1895<br>Sent by<br>J Gammage | 44 Canonbury Road<br>London N | P5/H/636<br>***#598***<br> | **Alfred William HUMPHREYS** *<br>46 Clerkenwell Road<br>London EC | Goldsmith and jeweller |
| R2/69<br>17 December 1908<br>Sent by Edward Lilley | | P13/H/5-9<br>***#599-603***<br> | | Jeweller |
| R2/95<br>16 October 1909<br>BAO 10.179<br>Sent by A W Jenner & Co | Alderbrook Road<br>Solihull<br>Alderbrook Road<br>Solihull<br>4 Birmingham Street<br>Dudley | P13/J/19,20<br>***#604,5***<br> | **James MANISON**<br>**W E MANISON**<br>**Leonard SMITH** trading as<br>**A W JENNER & CO**<br>30 Tenby Street<br>Birmingham | Manufacturing silversmiths |
| R3/172<br>12 May 1960 and<br>6 July 1960<br>Sent by Asher Loftus<br>Two sizes | | P21/A/26-29<br>***#606-9***<br> | **ACCURIST WATCHES LTD**<br>169 Regent Street<br>London W1 | Watch importers |
| R3/169<br>9 September 1959<br>Sent by Alterman & Watson | 112 Wilton Road [1]<br>Manchester 8<br>145 Mauldeth Road [2]<br>Manchester 20 | P21/A/25<br>***#610***<br> | **ALTERMAN & WATSON LTD**<br>Izek Alterman [1] (Director)<br>Charles Watson [2] (Director)<br>18 Corporation Street and<br>96 Deansgate (Registered Office)<br>Manchester 4 | Working jewellers |
| R3/123<br>3 April 1948<br>Sent by A W MacDonald | Private address same as business | P21/M/22<br>***#611***<br> | **Archibald William MACDONALD**<br>5 Westmorland Road<br>Southport | Designer craftsman |
| Missing register<br>*c.*1893<br>Cameo mark entered<br>BAO 2 May 1901 | Kelly 1892 | P5/P/512<br>***#612***<br> | **Arthur Willmore PENNINGTON**<br>28 Augusta Street<br>Birmingham | Manufacturing silversmith |
| R2/33<br>28 February 1907<br>Sent by J G Newbold | 73 Caeran Road<br>Newport<br>Monmouthshire | P9/U*sic*/278<br>***#613***<br> | **Arthur William PAYNE**<br>Westgate Buildings<br>Newport<br>Monmouth<br>58 High Street<br>Merthyr Tydfil | Tobacconist |

| REGISTRATION DETAILS | MAKER'S PRIVATE ADDRESS and DETAILS | PLATE and MARK DETAILS | MAKER/COMPANY and BUSINESS ADDRESS | MAKER'S TRADE |
|---|---|---|---|---|
| R2/62<br>30 June 1908<br>Sent by J G Newbold | 73 Caeran Road<br>Newport<br>Monmouthshire | P13/P/4<br>***#614***<br> | **Arthur William PAYNE**<br>Westgate Buildings<br>Newport<br>Monmouth<br>58 High Street<br>Merthyr Tydfil | Tobacconist |
| Missing register<br>*c.*1892<br>Similar mark entered<br>BAO 2 May 1901 | Kelly 1892 | P5/P/426<br>***#615***<br> | **Arthur Willmore PENNINGTON**<br>28 Augusta Street<br>Birmingham | Manufacturing silversmith |
| R1/139<br>15 December 1900<br>Sent by A W Rothery<br>Two sizes | 53 Bradshaw Street<br>Broughton<br>Manchester | P9/R/27,28<br>***#616,7***<br> | **Arthur William ROTHERY**<br>6 John Dalton Street<br>Manchester | Working jeweller and mounter |
| R2/194<br>24 April 1915<br>Sent by A W Richard | 25 Crowstone Road South<br>Westcliff-on-Sea | P15/R/6<br>***#618***<br> | **A W RICHARD**<br>24 Red Lion Street<br>Clerkenwell<br>London | Gold and silversmith |
| LPB/88<br>25 May 1881 | | P3/W/x1<br>***#619***<br> | **Albert WATERFALL**<br>**Robert GRAVENOR** trading as<br>**WATERFALL & GRAVENOR** *<br>15 Hertford Terrace<br>Coventry | Watchcase makers |
| R1/121<br>17 February 1900<br>Sent by W Andrews<br>F S Banks authority<br>W Bullock | Manager same address as business<br><br>CWMP has them at this address in 1901 | P9/A/16<br>***#620***<br> | **THE ANDREWS CORPORATED WATCH MANUFACTURING SOCIETY LTD** *<br>William Andrews (Manager)<br>9 Radford Street<br>Coventry | Watch manufacturers |
| LPB/88<br>16 June 1880<br>LPB mark shown | | Not on P3<br>***#621***<br> | **J WARD** trading as<br>**A WARD & SON**<br>7½ Warstone Lane<br>Birmingham | Jeweller |
| R1/210<br>14 March 1904<br>Sent by A W Taylor | Montserrat House<br>Highams Park<br>Essex | P9/T/49<br>***#622***<br> | **Alfred William TAYLOR** *<br>35 Hatton Garden<br>London | Manufacturing jeweller and agent |
| Missing register<br>*c.*1889<br>Similar mark entered<br>LAO 30 June 1885 | CWMP has Spon End, Coventry in 1896 | P5/Y/261<br>***#623***<br> | **Alfred YARDLEY** *<br>4 Florence Terrace<br>Barrow Lane<br>Coventry | Watchcase maker |
| R1/126<br>5 May 1900<br>Sent by T P Hewitt for Lancashire Watch Company | Private address same as business | P9/Y/2<br>***#624***<br> | **Albert YEWDALL**<br>12 Lovell Street<br>Leeds | Watch dealer |

| REGISTRATION DETAILS | MAKER'S PRIVATE ADDRESS and DETAILS | PLATE and MARK DETAILS | MAKER/COMPANY and BUSINESS ADDRESS | MAKER'S TRADE |
|---|---|---|---|---|
| R2/209<br>17 October 1916<br>Sent by B Ainsworth | Private address same as business | P15/A/8<br>***#625***<br> | **B AINSWORTH**<br>16 Bridge Street<br>Accrington | Briar pipe makers and repairers |
| Missing register<br>*c.*1894<br>1894 Kelly | | P5/aboveB/542<br>***#626***<br> | **BALL & CO**<br>**BALL BROTHERS**<br>14 Regent Parade<br>Birmingham | Manufacturing jewellers |
| R2/170<br>11 April 1913<br>Sent by<br>George Dresden<br>Pforzheim<br>Germany | Motor Club<br>Coventry Street<br>London W | P15/B/43<br>***#627***<br> | **Fritz WEISS** junior<br>**George DRESDEN** * trading as<br>**BRITISH AUTOMATIC MESH CO**<br>12 Hatton Garden<br>London | Manufacturer of machine made mesh bags |
| PDB 1809<br>MR3/78<br>Square marked 1785 | Silver knife rests | P1/21/x1<br>***#628***<br> | **BURRELL & CO**<br>Liverpool | Silversmiths |
| MR1/123<br>MR3/180,181<br>SOT/110-3<br>J1 *c.*1681-1734<br>J3/416 | Church alms plates, tea pot *c.*1705-25 - no assay marks on any of the items<br>Free 1715 - working *c.*1705-25 | Not on P1<br>***#629***<br>type 1<br> | **Benjamin BRANCKER**<br>Water Street<br>Liverpool | Silversmith |
| Bezeliel Burgess was also working in Liverpool as a silversmith *c.*1740, but may be too late | Flagon, saucepans, tankard, coffee pot, castor and marrow scoop *c.*1705-25<br>No assay office marks on any of the items | Not on P1<br>***#630***<br>type 2<br> | | |
| LPB/12<br>18 November 1882<br>See also BBHULL #659 page 58 | | P3/B/x2<br>***#631,2***<br> | **Barnie BARNETT** *<br>45 Whitefriar Gate<br>Hull | Goldsmiths, jewellers, silversmiths, watch and clockmakers |
| R1/5<br>15 December 1894<br>Sent by Benson Brothers | 31 Virginia Road [1]<br>New Brighton<br>41 Halkyn Avenue [2]<br>Liverpool | P5/aboveB/628a<br>***#633***<br> | **John BENSON** [1]<br>**William Hilton BENSON** [2] trading as<br>**BENSON BROTHERS**<br>72 Wood Street<br>Liverpool | Watchcase manufacturers |
| R1/69<br>14 October 1898<br>Sent by John Benson | 31 Virginia Road [1]<br>New Brighton<br>Cheshire | P9/B/7,8<br>***#634,5***<br> | | |
| Not in R2 as expected October 1908 to January 1909 | | P13/B/43<br>***#636***<br> | | |
| Not in R2 as expected April 1917 to November 1917 | | P15/B/74<br>***#637***<br> | | |
| Not in R2 as expected December 1911 to March 1912 | | P13/B/128<br>***#638***<br> | | |
| Not in R2 as expected May 1918 to March 1919 | | P15/B/94,95<br>***#639,40***<br> | | |

| REGISTRATION DETAILS | MAKER'S PRIVATE ADDRESS and DETAILS | PLATE and MARK DETAILS | MAKER/COMPANY and BUSINESS ADDRESS | MAKER'S TRADE |
|---|---|---|---|---|
| R1/69<br>14 October 1898<br>Sent by John Benson | 31 Virginia Road [1]<br>New Brighton<br>41 Hallyn Road [2]<br>Liverpool | P9/B/5,6<br>***#641,2***<br> | **John BENSON** [1]<br>**William Hilton BENSON** [2] trading as<br>**BENSON BROTHERS**<br>72 Wood Street<br>Liverpool | Watchcase manufacturers |
| R1/5<br>15 December 1894<br>Sent by Benson Brothers | | P5/aboveB/628b<br>***#643***<br> | | |
| SPB/10<br>28 April 1873<br>LMS 1865-78 | | P3/B/x2<br>***#644,5***<br> | **BROWN BROTHERS**<br>Bridge Street Row<br>Chester | Clockmakers |
| R1/26<br>23 March 1896<br>Sent by Barber Brothers | 7 Park Avenue<br>Soho Hill<br>Birmingham | P5/aboveB/749<br>***#646***<br> | **John Vaughan BARBER** trading as<br>**BARBER BROTHERS** *<br>44 Warstone Lane<br>Birmingham | Jewellers |
| R1/58<br>4 June 1894<br>Sent by J V Barber | Grasmere<br>Park Avenue<br>Handsworth<br>Staffordshire | P5/aboveB/563<br>***#647***<br> | **John Vaughan BARBER** trading as<br>**BARBER BROTHERS** *<br>11 Northampton Street<br>Birmingham | Manufacturing jewellers |
| LPB/68<br>6 August 1883 | | P3/B/x1<br>***#648***<br> | **BARNETT BROTHERS**<br>54 Hockley Hill<br>Birmingham | Jewellers |
| Missing register<br>*c.*1890<br>Similar mark BAO<br>18 February 1898 | | P5/B/331<br>***#649***<br>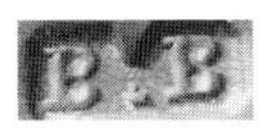 | **BARNETT BROTHERS**<br>21 Hockley Hill (1898)<br>Birmingham | |
| R2/77<br>2 April 1909<br>Sent by S Phelps | Colebrook House<br>Plympton<br>Devon | P13/B/46<br>***#650***<br> | **B BURLAND**<br>90 Old Town Street<br>Plymouth | Wholesale and retail jewellers |
| R3/65<br>18 February 1933<br>Sent by Bendall Brothers | Mark probably BB<br><br>Previous B is P15/B/209 next is P15/B/210 | Not on P15 as expected<br>***#651*** | **BENDALL BROTHERS (JEWELLERS) LTD**<br>79-81 Hockley Street<br>(previously 24 Spencer Street)<br>Birmingham | Manufacturing jewellers |
| R1/5<br>8 January 1894<br>Sent by Bacon & Bill | 124 Thornhill Road [1]<br>Handsworth<br>19 Handsworth Wood Road [2]<br>Handsworth | P5/aboveB/631<br>***#652***<br> | **Charles Walter BACON** [1]<br>**Frank BILL** trading as<br>**BACON & BILL** [2]<br>37, 39 Hylton Street<br>Birmingham | Jewellers |
| R3/101<br>4 September 1941<br>Sent by Bannister Brothers<br>Two sizes | Private address same as business | P21/B/14,15<br>***#653,4***<br> | **W H TINDLEY LTD** trading as<br>**BANNISTER BROTHERS**<br>Sealed in the presence of:-<br>C Stirk<br>William H Tindley (Director)<br>W D Tindley (Secretary)<br>169 Hockley Hill (Registered Office)<br>Birmingham | Manufacturing and wholesale jewellers |
| LPB/96<br>9 May 1882<br>Only address entered in LPB | See also next entry | P3/B/x1<br>***#655***<br> | **BROOKE, BROOKE & CO**<br>104 Vyse Street<br>Birmingham | Factors and silversmiths |
| Not in LPB<br>This mark identical to previous one | | P3/*Esic*/x1<br>***#656***<br> | | |

| REGISTRATION DETAILS | MAKER'S PRIVATE ADDRESS and DETAILS | PLATE and MARK DETAILS | MAKER/COMPANY and BUSINESS ADDRESS | MAKER'S TRADE |
|---|---|---|---|---|
| LPB/16<br>17 September 1880<br>LPB mark shown<br>Sent by Coley Brothers | | Not on P3<br>***#657***<br> | **BROOKE, BROOKE & CO**<br>(104) Vyse Street<br>Birmingham | Factors and silversmiths |
| LPB/18<br>21 June 1883<br>No mark with LPB entry | Only mark on P5 that matches entry and date | P5/B/x1<br>***#658***<br> | **BROOKE, BROOKE & CO**<br>Ruby Building, Frederick Street<br>Birmingham | |
| LPB/28<br>21 June 1883<br>Sent by R Nevill | | P3/B/x1<br>***#659***<br> | **Barney BARNETT** *<br>45 Whitefriar Gate<br>Hull | Gold and silversmith, watch and clockmaker and jeweller |
| R2/3<br>5 October 1905<br>Sent by Lawson, Ward & Gammage | Douglas House<br>Maida Hill<br>London W | P9/XYZ*sic*/137,138<br>***#660,1***<br> | **Philip BERNSTEIN** trading as<br>**BERNSTEIN BROTHERS**<br>59/61 Hatton Garden<br>London EC | Jewellers |
| LPB/84<br>3 October 1882<br>Sent by N Butler | | P3/B/x1<br>***#662***<br> | **BURGESS BROTHERS**<br>3 Victoria Street<br>6 Powell Street (1880 BAO)<br>Birmingham | Silversmiths and jewellers |
| LPB/18<br>23 September 1884<br>No mark in LPB | This P5 mark only one to reasonably match this entry | P5/B/x1<br>***#663***<br> | **BOOTH BROTHERS**<br>43 Northampton Street<br>Birmingham | Jewellers and silversmiths |
| R2/10<br>3 February 1906<br>Sent by W Pendleton & Son | Hillside<br>Hamstead Road<br>Handsworth<br>Maiden Hill<br>London<br>24 Mayfield Road<br>Handsworth<br>Birmingham | P9/XYZ*sic*/161-164<br>***#664-7***<br> | **Edward DURBAN**<br>**Philip BERNSTEIN**<br>**Ernest Thomas PENDLETON** (Director)<br>trading as<br>**BERNSTEIN BROTHERS LTD**<br>59/61 Hatton Garden<br>London | Wholesale jewellers |
| Missing register<br>*c.*1888<br>Similar mark entered BAO 4 February 1889 | | P5/B/183<br>***#668***<br> | **BOOTH BROTHERS**<br>43 Northampton Street<br>Birmingham | Jewellers and silversmiths |
| R2/112<br>11 June 1910<br>Sent by Philip James Breen | 30 Erskine Street<br>Liverpool | P13/B/78<br>***#669***<br> | **Philip James BREEN**<br>**Laurence Joseph BREEN** trading as<br>**BREEN BROTHERS**<br>30 Erskine Street<br>Liverpool | Wholesale jewellers |
| R1/204<br>19 December 1903<br>Sent by Henry Bunce | 151 North Road<br>12 North Street<br>102 Gloucester Road<br>Bristol | P9/B/113<br>***#670***<br> | **Henry BUNCE**<br>**Thomas BUNCE**<br>**John BUNCE**<br>trading as **BUNCE BROTHERS**<br>12 North Street<br>Bristol | Jewellers |
| LPB/16<br>24 July 1880<br>LPB mark shown<br>Sent by E Whitehouse | | Not on P3<br>***#671***<br> | **BROCKINGTON BROTHERS**<br>250 New John Street West<br>Birmingham | Jewellers |
| Missing register<br>*c.*1886 | | P5/B/21<br>***#672***<br> | | |

| REGISTRATION DETAILS | MAKER'S PRIVATE ADDRESS and DETAILS | PLATE and MARK DETAILS | MAKER/COMPANY and BUSINESS ADDRESS | MAKER'S TRADE |
|---|---|---|---|---|
| Missing register<br>*c.*1891 | | P5/B/342<br>***#673***<br> | **BROCKINGTON BROTHERS**<br>250 New John Street West<br>Birmingham | Jewellers |
| R1/39<br>10 February 1897<br>Sent by Loach Brothers | The Manor House<br>Wasperton<br>Warwick | P5/aboveB/813<br>***#674***<br> | **George Samuel BROCKINGTON**<br>trading as<br>**BROCKINGTON BROTHERS**<br>44 Hylton Street<br>Birmingham | Manufacturing jewellers |
| R3/86<br>1 March 1937<br>Sent by Barker Brothers Silversmiths Ltd<br>Six sizes | | P21/B/2-7<br>***#675-80***<br> | **BARKER BROTHERS SILVERSMITHS LTD** *<br>Common seal of company affixed in the presence of:-<br>Frank E Harller (Director)<br>Walter H Collins (Director)<br>Cloe J Levi (Secretary)<br>Unity Works (Registered Office)<br>16 Constitution Hill<br>Birmingham | Silver and electroplate manufacturers |
| R3/185<br>14 July 1962<br>Sent by Barker Brothers<br>Three sizes | | P21/B/71-73<br>***#681-3***<br> | **BARKER BROTHERS SILVERSMITHS LTD** *<br>16 Constitution Hill<br>Birmingham 12 | Manufacturing silversmiths |
| R1/27<br>20 April 1896<br>Sent by W Walker | West Wycombe[1]<br>Bucks<br>7 Brunswick Square[2]<br>London WC | P5/aboveB/759<br>***#684***<br> | **James BRADLEY** [1]<br>**Herman COHN** [2] trading as<br>**BRADLEY & COHN** *<br>36 Basinghall Street<br>London | Export merchants |
| R1/25<br>20 March 1896<br>Sent by A H Tongue | | P5/aboveB/747<br>***#685***<br> | | Merchants |
| Missing register<br>*c.*1886<br>Similar mark SAO 15 December 1893 and BAO 22 June 1900 | | P5/B/26<br>***#686***<br> | **BROOKES & CROOKES**<br>Atlantic Works<br>St Phillips Road<br>Sheffield | Cutlery manufacturers |
| LPB/16<br>6 December 1878<br>LPB mark shown | | Not on P3<br>***#687***<br> | **BISHTON & COHEN**<br>40 St Paul's Square<br>Birmingham | Manufacturing silversmiths |
| R3/74<br>22 February 1935<br>Sent by Smith, Ewen & Stylic Ltd<br>42 Frederick Street<br>Birmingham | 91 Oxford Road<br>Moseley | P15/G*sic*/216<br>***#688***<br> | **B C BACCHUS**<br>50 Newhall Street<br>Birmingham | Jeweller |
| R2/169<br>7 March 1913<br>Sent by selves<br>BAO 20.975 20.974<br>Two sizes | 106 Avenue<br>Acocks Green<br>Manor Hill<br>Sutton Coldfield | P15/C/26,27<br>***#689,90***<br> | **Charles Thomas COULTHARD**<br>**Walter BAYLISS**<br>60 Branston Street<br>Birmingham | Silversmiths and electroplate manufacturers |
| R1/225<br>19 January 1905<br>Sent by T C Smith<br>Two sizes | 46 Charterville Road<br>Handsworth<br>Birmingham | P9/XYZ*sic*/128,129<br>***#691,92***<br> | **Henry BUSHELL** trading as<br>**BUSHELL & CO**<br>39/40 Tenby Street North<br>Birmingham | Silversmiths |

| REGISTRATION DETAILS | MAKER'S PRIVATE ADDRESS and DETAILS | PLATE and MARK DETAILS | MAKER/COMPANY and BUSINESS ADDRESS | MAKER'S TRADE |
|---|---|---|---|---|
| R2/5<br>2 November 1905<br>Sent by J Haywood | London Rowing Club<br>Headquarters<br>Putney<br>London SW | P9/XYZ*sic*/139-141<br>***#693-5***<br> | **BULLER & CO** *<br>J N Cameron (Secretary)<br>124 Vyse Street<br>Birmingham and<br>6/8 Charterhouse Street<br>London EC | Manufacturing jewellers |
| R2/13<br>7 March 1906<br>Sent by S Barnett<br>MR3/117<br><br>Two sizes | 7 Victoria Parkway<br>Queens Park<br>Chester | P9/XYZ*sic*/169,170<br>***#696,7***<br><br>P9/XYZ*sic*/165-168<br>***#698-701***<br> | **BUTT & CO LTD**<br>Samuel Barnett (Managing Director)<br>32 Eastgate Row<br>Chester and<br>42 High Street<br>Wrexham | Jewellers and silversmiths |
| R3/62<br>10 May 1932<br>Sent by Suckling Ltd<br>Two sizes | | P15/B/208, 209<br>***#702,3***<br> | **SUCKLING LTD** trading as<br>**BEDDOES & CO**<br>Kingsway House (Registered Office)<br>Albion Street<br>Birmingham | Silversmiths |
| R1/225<br>5 January 1905<br>Sent by F O Banyard<br>Banyard & Co | 125 College Road<br>Bradford<br>9 Bingley Street<br>Bradford | P9/XYZ*sic*/127<br>***#704***<br> | **Arthur DALBY**<br>**Frank O BANYARD** trading as<br>**BANYARD & CO**<br>30 Worthington Street<br>City Road<br>Bradford | Gold and silver stick mounters |
| R2/2<br>19 September 1905<br>Sent by T C Beasley | 211 Ladywood Road<br>Birmingham | P9/XYZ*sic*/136<br>***#705***<br> | **Thomas Charles BEASLEY**<br>1 Great Hampton Street<br>Birmingham | General jeweller |
| R1/125<br>28 April 1900<br>Sent by Blow & Co<br>(Culme has ZEHETMAYR) | Bellevue Street<br>St Margarets<br>Middlesex<br>69 Christchurch Road<br>Toilen? Villa<br>London | P9/B/27,28<br>***#706,7***<br> | **Ferdinand FEKELMEYER**<br>**Francis William LLOYD** trading as<br>**BLOW & CO** *<br>85 Gracechurch Street<br>London EC | Merchants |
| R2/95<br>16 October 1909<br>Sent by Broadway & Co Ltd<br>Two sizes | Jennyson Road[1]<br>Small Heath<br>Birmingham | P13/B/68,69<br>***#708,9***<br> | **BROADWAY & CO LTD**<br>W B Broadway [1] (Director)<br>G A Richards (Secretary)<br>36 Spencer Street<br>Birmingham | Manufacturing silversmiths |
| Missing register<br>*c.*1887 | | P5/B/98<br>***#710***<br> | **Unidentified** | |
| R2/168<br>18 February 1913<br>Sent by Bertram Eaton | 37 Cromwell Grove<br>Levenshulme<br>Manchester | P13/E/28<br>***#711***<br> | **Bertram EATON**<br>17 Withy Grove<br>Manchester | Manufacturing jeweller and diamond setter |
| R3/149<br>5 January 1954<br>Sent by B Foster<br>Two sizes | 141 College Road<br>Whalley Range<br>Manchester 16 | P21/F/27,28<br>***#712,3***<br> | **Miss Barbara FOSTER**<br>No business address entered | Student |
| R3/180<br>10 August 1961<br>Sent by B Foster<br>Two sizes | 13 Belgrave Avenue<br>Flixton<br>Urmston<br>near Manchester | P21/F/35,36<br>***#714,5***<br> | **Mrs Betty FOSTER**<br>No business address entered | Student |

| REGISTRATION DETAILS | MAKER'S PRIVATE ADDRESS and DETAILS | PLATE and MARK DETAILS | MAKER/COMPANY and BUSINESS ADDRESS | MAKER'S TRADE |
|---|---|---|---|---|
| LPB/12<br>18 November 1882<br>LPB mark shown<br>Sent by Coley Brothers and Tandy & Rudge | | Not on P3<br>***#716***<br> | **BISHTON & FLETCHER**<br>7 Northampton Street<br>Birmingham | Jewellers |
| LPB/8<br>7 January 1885<br>No mark in LPB | Mark similar to one above so assumed to be Bishton & Fletcher | P5/B/x1<br>***#717***<br> | **BISHTON & FLETCHER**<br>Albion Street<br>Birmingham | |
| MR2/60-64<br>MR3/149,192<br>SOT/98-101<br>J1 1769-73<br>J3/389 | Transferred business to BAO as soon as it opened on 31 August 1773 and was its first customer | Not on P1<br>***#718***<br>type 1<br>§<br> | **Matthew BOULTON &**<br>**John FOTHERGILL**<br>Soho Works<br>Soho Hill<br>Birmingham | Silverware manufacturer |
| John Foliott (agent) | Candlesticks and mazarine seen with Chester mark for 1769 | Not on P1<br>***#719***<br>type 2<br>§<br> | | |
| R2/186<br>2 April 1914<br>Sent by Ginder & Couch | Private address same as business | P15/G/18<br>***#720***<br> | **Barnett GERBER**<br>7 Main Street<br>Gorbals<br>Glasgow | Wholesale jeweller |
| R3/112<br>25 February 1946<br>Sent by Bert Gordon<br>Two sizes | 59 Elmbridge Road<br>Perry Bar<br>Birmingham 22 | P21/G/11,12<br>***#721,22***<br> | **Bert GORDON**<br>34 Warstone Lane<br>Birmingham 18 | Manufacturing gold and silversmith |
| R1/236<br>12 July 1905<br>Sent by Bamber & Gibson | West Street<br>Stalybridge<br>151 Bradford Road<br>Manchester | P9/XYZ*sic*/134 and 0*sic*<br>***#723,4***<br> | **Wilfred BAMBER**<br>**Robert GIBSON** trading as<br>**BAMBER & GIBSON**<br>11 Todd Street<br>Manchester | Ring makers |
| R1/118<br>7 December 1899<br>Sent by Villiers & Jackson<br>C Dreyfus | 12 Cloudesdale Road<br>Balham, London SW<br>Nesslyn<br>Palmers Green<br>London N | P9/B/25<br>***#725***<br> | **Walter H BRITTON**<br>**Edward Havelock GOULD** trading as<br>**BRITTON & GOULD** *<br>83 Hatton Garden<br>London | Jewellers and silversmiths |
| R2/16<br>6 April 1906<br>Sent by J & R Griffin<br>BAO #9494 | 38 Cloudsdale Road<br>Balham<br>12 The Villas<br>Palmers Green | P9/G/73<br>***#726***<br> | **Walter Haseler BRITTON**<br>**Edward Havelock GOULD** * trading as<br>**BRITTON, GOULD & CO**<br>83 Hatton Garden<br>London | Wholesale jewellers |
| R2/108<br>7 April 1910<br>BAO 11.253, 11.254<br>Sent by Albert Whitehouse<br>Two sizes | Ardendale<br>Knowle<br>Birmingham<br>Bayscroft<br>Barnt Green<br>Birmingham | P13/B/72-75<br>***#727-30***<br> | **Edwin WHITEHOUSE**<br>**Albert WHITEHOUSE** trading as<br>**THE BIRMINGHAM GOLD AND SILVER CHAIN CO**<br>52 Vyse Street<br>Birmingham | Gold chain manufacturers |
| R3/36<br>15 June 1927<br>Sent by Bromage & Hawkins | 59 Great Cheetham Street West[1]<br>Salford<br>26 Bunyard Street[2]<br>Manchester | P15/B/186<br>***#731***<br> | **Arthur BROMAGE**[1]<br>**Joseph HAWKINS**[2] trading as<br>**BROMAGE & HAWKINS**<br>13 Swan Street<br>Manchester | Tobacco pipe mounters |
| LPB/38<br>2 August 1880<br>LPB mark shown | | Not on P3<br>***#732***<br> | **William BAKER & John HINKS**<br>44 Northampton Street<br>Birmingham | Jewellers |

| REGISTRATION DETAILS | MAKER'S PRIVATE ADDRESS and DETAILS | PLATE and MARK DETAILS | MAKER/COMPANY and BUSINESS ADDRESS | MAKER'S TRADE |
|---|---|---|---|---|
| R2/58<br>5 May 1908<br>Sent by Britton & Hewett | 5 Thorpe Street<br>York<br>16 Cromer Street<br>York | P13/B/19<br>*#733*<br> | **William HEWETT**<br>**Charles Ernest BRITTON** trading as<br>**BRITTON & HEWETT**<br>City Chambers, Clifford Street<br>York | Jewellers and engravers |
| R3/37<br>14 March 1927<br>Sent by selves | Both at<br>8 Oakroyd Villas<br>Bradford | P15/B/183<br>*#734*<br> | **Rebecca AUNSBERG**<br>**Merton AUNSBERG** trading as<br>**BARWICK & HAGGAS**<br>63 Row Street<br>Keighley | Jewellers and silversmiths |
| Similar mark entered BAO 3 October 1838 | | P1/28/x4<br>*#735a-735d*<br> | **Benjamin HUMPHRIES**<br>27 Ellis Street<br>Birmingham | Jeweller |
| R1/195<br>10 June 1903<br>Sent by T C Smith | 131 Lodge Road<br>Birmingham | P9/H/51<br>*#736*<br> | **James LLOYD** trading as<br>**Bertram HORNER**<br>35 Warstone Lane<br>London | Jeweller |
| R2/72<br>9 February 1909<br>Sent by Barnett H Abrahams | 140 Western Road<br>Brighton, Sussex<br>11 Priory Mansions<br>Priory Park Road<br>Kilburn<br>London | P13/A/6<br>*#737*<br> | **Joseph Henry ABRAHAMS**<br>**Henry Clarence ABRAHAMS** trading as<br>**BARNETT H ABRAHAMS** *<br>133/135 Houndsditch<br>London EC | Wholesale merchants |
| R2/223<br>4 September 1919<br>Sent by Lionel Smith & Co | 17 Portland Court<br>London<br>Mona, The Leas<br>Westcliff-on-Sea<br>Essex | P15/A/14,15<br>*#738,9*<br> | **Joseph Henry ABRAHAMS**<br>**Henry Clarence ABRAHAMS** trading as<br>**BARNETT H ABRAHAMS** *<br>133 to 135 Houndsditch<br>London EC | Wholesale jewellers |
| R1/18<br>30 November 1895<br>Sent by W Aitken | 104 Fordwych Road<br>Hampstead<br>London | P5/A/711<br>*#740*<br> | **Barnett Henry ABRAHAMS**<br>**Joseph Henry ABRAHAMS**<br>**Henry Clarence ABRAHAMS** trading as<br>**BARNETT H ABRAHAMS** *<br>133/135 Houndsditch<br>London EC | Jewellers |
| Not in R2 as expected – adjacent P9/A/89 – between June and July 1907 | | P9/A/0*sic*<br>*#741*<br> | | |
| R2/159<br>19 July 1912<br>Sent by W H Tandy & Son | 17 Portland Court<br>London<br>Riverdale<br>Canvey Island<br>Essex | P13/A/38<br>*#742*<br> | **Joseph Henry ABRAHAMS**<br>**Henry Clarence ABRAHAMS**<br>133 to 135 Houndsditch<br>London EC | Wholesale jewellers |
| R1/92<br>20 February 1899<br>Sent by<br>B H Abrahams | 104 Fordwych Road<br>West Hampstead<br>31 Plympton Road<br>Brondsbury | P9/A/9<br>*#743*<br>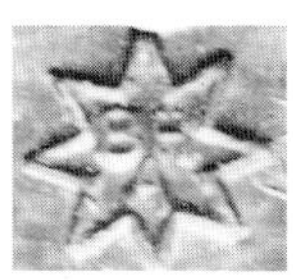 | **Barnett Henry ABRAHAMS**<br>**Joseph Henry ABRAHAMS**<br>**Henry Clarence ABRAHAMS** trading as<br>**BARNETT H ABRAHAMS** *<br>128 Houndsditch<br>London | |
| LPB/44<br>7 August 1885<br>No mark in LPB | 10th mark on P5 matches<br>10th name on LPB page 44 | P5/J/x1<br>*#744*<br> | **Barnet Henry JOSEPH** trading as<br>**B H JOSEPH & CO** *<br>20 Frederick Street<br>Birmingham | Manufacturing jewellers |

| REGISTRATION DETAILS | MAKER'S PRIVATE ADDRESS and DETAILS | PLATE and MARK DETAILS | MAKER/COMPANY and BUSINESS ADDRESS | MAKER'S TRADE |
|---|---|---|---|---|
| Missing register<br>*c.*1890 | | P5/J/326a<br>***#745***<br> | **B H JOSEPH & CO** *<br>20 Frederick Street<br>Birmingham | Manufacturing jewellers |
| LPB/44<br>9 March 1885<br>No mark in LPB<br>Sent by W H & F Rabone | 7th mark on P5 matches<br>7th name on LPB page 7 | P5/J/x1<br>***#746***<br> | | |
| R2/143<br>12 September 1911<br>Sent by Miss Ada Hadgkiss<br>Two sizes | 4 Plough & Harrow Road<br>5 Greenfield Crescent<br>4 Plough & Harrow Road<br>4 Plough & Harrow Road<br>Edgbaston | P13/J/49-55<br>***#747-53***<br> | **Joseph JOSEPH**<br>**George L JOSEPH**<br>**Percy JOSEPH**<br>**Leslie JOSEPH** trading as<br>**B H JOSEPH & CO** *<br>20 Frederick Street<br>Birmingham | Goldsmiths |
| LPB/42<br>28 August 1879<br>Sent by J B Robertson | | P3/I/x2<br>***#754,5***<br> | | Manufacturing jewellers |
| LPB/42<br>15 October 1879<br>Sent by James Rooker | | P3/I/x1<br>***#756***<br> | | |
| LPB/42<br>5 October 1882 | | P3/I/x1<br>***#757***<br> | | |
| Missing register<br>*c.*1886<br>Similar mark entered LAO 23 May 1878 | | P5/B*sic*/8<br>***#758***<br> | **B H JOSEPH & CO** *<br>20 Frederick Street<br>Birmingham | |
| R1/87<br>8 December 1898<br>Sent by B H Joseph & Co | 26 Harborne Road [1]<br>4 Plough & Harrow Road [2]<br>Edgbaston<br>Birmingham | P9/J/6-8<br>***#759-61***<br> | **Barnett Henry JOSEPH** [1]<br>**Joseph JOSEPH** [2] trading as<br>**B H JOSEPH & CO** *<br>18, 19, 20 Frederick Street<br>Birmingham | Manufacturing and wholesale jewellers |
| R1/105<br>30 June 1899 | | P9/J/17<br>***#762***<br> | | |
| R1/119<br>25 January 1900<br>Sent by B H Joseph | | P9/J/25<br>***#763***<br> | | |
| R1/219<br>10 September 1904<br>Sent by B H Joseph<br>Two sizes | 4 Plough and Harrow Road<br>Edgbaston [1 2 3]<br>26 Harborne Road [4]<br>Edgbaston<br>Birmingham | P9/J/42-50<br>***#764-72***<br> | **Joseph JOSEPH** [1]<br>**Percy Barnett JOSEPH** [2]<br>**Leslie Henry JOSEPH** [3]<br>**George Lionel JOSEPH** [4] trading as<br>**B H JOSEPH & CO** *<br>18/19/20 Frederick Street<br>Birmingham | Manufacturing jewellers |
| Missing register<br>*c.*1886 | | P5/J/45<br>***#773***<br> | | |
| Missing register<br>*c.*1893 | | P5/J/511<br>***#774***<br> | | |
| Missing register<br>*c.*1889<br>Similar mark entered LAO 13 March 1891 | | P5/J/243<br>***#775***<br> | | |

| REGISTRATION DETAILS | MAKER'S PRIVATE ADDRESS and DETAILS | PLATE and MARK DETAILS | MAKER/COMPANY and BUSINESS ADDRESS | MAKER'S TRADE |
|---|---|---|---|---|
| Missing register<br>*c.*1890<br>Similar mark entered LAO 13 March 1891 | | P5/J/326b<br>***#776***  | **B H JOSEPH & CO** *<br>20 Frederick Street<br>Birmingham | Manufacturing jewellers |
| R1/87<br>8 December 1898<br>Sent by B H Joseph & Co | | P9/J/3-5<br>***#777-9***  | | |
| R1/105<br>30 June 1899<br>Sent by B H Joseph & Co | | P9/J/16<br>***#780***  | | |
| LPB/44<br>25 July 1885<br>Only initials BHJ in LPB | 7th name on LPB page 44 and 9th mark on P5/J but only mark to match the entry | P5/J/x1<br>***#781***<br>§  | | |
| R2/163<br>6 October 1912<br>Sent by selves<br>Three sizes | 18 Gunnersbury Avenue<br>Ealing | P13/M/53-55<br>***#782-4***  | **Berthold H MULLER** *<br>187 Wardour Street<br>London W | Silversmith |
| R3/165<br>4 December 1958<br>Sent by A G Du Plat | | P21/R/29-31<br>***#785-7***  | **B H RIES LTD** *<br>Treasure House<br>Hatton Garden<br>London EC1 | Watch and clock importers |
| MR1/123 | Free 1697<br>Work seen *c.*1701 | P1/4/x1<br>***#788***  | **Charles BIRD**<br>Broxton<br>Cheshire (later moved to)<br>Chester | Silversmith |
| MR1/122<br>MR3/180 | Assumed to be Bingley's mark as he was made Free after Bird and this square is later. The *pheon* above Bi is in the recorded crest of the Bingley family. Free 1698<br>Spoon, porringer, communion cup 1702 | P1/7/x1<br>***#789***  | **John BINGLEY**<br>Chester | Silversmith |
| R2/76<br>25 March 1909<br>Sent by Bernard Inge | 7 Gordon Street<br>Aston<br>Birmingham | P13/I/2<br>***#790*** 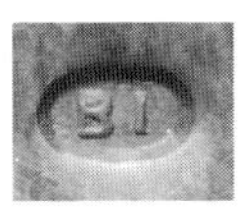 | **Bernard INGE**<br>Lines Buildings<br>Vittoria Street<br>Birmingham | Ring manufacturer |
| R2/95<br>20 October 1909<br>BAO 16.595<br>Sent by B J Keyzor | Glenheris<br>Anderton Park Road<br>Moseley<br>Birmingham | P13/K/3<br>***#791***  | **Baron Isaac KEYZOR** trading as<br>**B J KEYZOR & CO**<br>24 Spencer Street<br>Birmingham | Manufacturing silversmiths |
| PP1/159,186<br>CWMP 1830-51<br>Similar mark entered BAO 2 March 1848 | Spelt Kirby in directories | P2/K/x2<br>***#792,3***  | **Benjamin KERBY (KIRBY)**<br>Spon Street<br>Coventry | Watchcase maker |
| PP1/159,186<br>Similar mark entered LAO 12 January 1842 | May be same person as the Coventry one? | P1/29/x2<br>***#794,5***  | **Benjamin KERBY** *<br>9 Dover Place<br>Kent Street Road<br>London | Watchcase maker |
| PP1/159,186<br>Similar mark entered LAO 12 January 1842 | | P2/K/x2<br>***#796,7*** 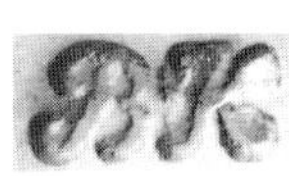 | | |

| REGISTRATION DETAILS | MAKER'S PRIVATE ADDRESS and DETAILS | PLATE and MARK DETAILS | MAKER/COMPANY and BUSINESS ADDRESS | MAKER'S TRADE |
|---|---|---|---|---|
| PP1/159,186<br>Similar mark entered LAO 12 January 1842 | | P2/K/x2<br>***#798,9***<br> | **Benjamin KERBY** *<br>9 Dover Place<br>Kent Street Road<br>London | Watchcase maker |
| LPB/86<br>10 November 1882 | No street number at BAO or CAO – Kelly has Canada Works between numbers 15_ and 17 Vittoria Street | P3/B/x1<br>***#800***<br> | **Joel BLANCKENSEE & Hymen LEVETUS**<br>Vittoria Street, Birmingham | Silversmiths |
| R1/143<br>19 February 1901<br>Sent by F Coulthurst | 66 Hawthorn Road [1]<br>Chorlton-cum-Hardy<br>Creswell Grine [2]<br>West Didsbury, Manchester | P9/B/34<br>***#801***<br> | **Frank BROADHURST** [1] and **Herbert LEE** [2] trading as **BROADHURST & LEE**<br>60 Swan Street<br>Manchester | Umbrella and walking stick manufacturers |
| R1/219<br>10 September 1904<br>Sent by C Michael & Co | 16 Newport Road [1]<br>Chorlton-cum-Hardy<br>Pine Road [2]<br>Didsbury | P9/XYZ*sic*/124<br>***#802***<br> | | |
| R1/164<br>18 March 1902 | | P9/L/27<br>***#803***<br> | **Benjamin LOFTHOUSE**<br>Bank Building,<br>Shude Hill<br>Manchester | Wholesale jeweller |
| R2/229<br>10 April 1920<br>Sent by Henry Bendall | 8 Wells Street [1]<br>Lozells<br>Birmingham | P15/B/135–146<br>***#804-15***<br> | **Gordon James BENDALL**[1]<br>**Henry BENDALL**<br>**David BENDALL**<br>24 Spencer Street<br>Birmingham | Manufacturing jewellers |
| R3/142<br>11 March 1953<br>Sent by Charles William Westwood<br>89 Fountain Road<br>Birmingham 17 | | P21/B/37<br>***#816***<br> | **BISHTONS LTD** *<br>19 Northampton Street<br>Birmingham 18 | Manufacturing silversmiths and electroplaters |
| R2/62<br>18 July 1908<br>Sent by Bennett 1907 Ltd<br>8 Hylton Street<br>Birmingham<br>Two sizes | 87 Bethune Road<br>59 Vittoria Street<br>Birmingham<br>5 Barnstaple Mansions<br>London | P13/B/24-35<br>***#817-28***<br> | **William Rabone HASELER**<br>**John Baker BENNETT**<br>**John HASELER**<br>**Henry James HULBERT** trading as<br>**BENNETT 1907 LTD** *<br>7 Charterhouse Street<br>Holborn Circus<br>London EC | Wholesale and manufacturing jewellers |
| | | P13/B/38,39<br>***#829,30***<br> | | |
| R2/41<br>4 June 1907<br>Sent by Lawson, Ward & Gammage | Fairmount<br>Sanderstead | P9/Q*sic*/208, 209<br>***#831,2***<br> | **BOWMAN LTD** *<br>68, 70 Goswell Road<br>London | Jewellers |
| R2/41<br>30 May 1909 | 5 Barnstaple Mansions<br>Roseberry Avenue<br>London | P13/B/47<br>***#833***<br> | **J B BENNETT & CO LTD** *<br>C Stanley Bennett (Director)<br>58a Hatton Garden, London EC | Wholesale jewellers |
| R1/114<br>18 October 1899<br>Sent by J Gammage | | P9/B/22<br>***#834***<br> | **BOWMAN LTD** *<br>Samuel Bowman (Secretary)<br>68, 70 Goswell Road<br>London EC | Jewellers |
| R2/148<br>7 December 1911<br>Sent by<br>W G Matthews | Fairmont [1]<br>Sanderstead<br>Surrey | P13/B/127<br>***#835***<br> | **BOWMAN LTD** *<br>Samuel Bowman[1] (Managing Director)<br>68, 70 Goswell Road, Clerkenwell<br>London EC and<br>26, 28 London Road, Croydon<br>Surrey | |

| REGISTRATION DETAILS | MAKER'S PRIVATE ADDRESS and DETAILS | PLATE and MARK DETAILS | MAKER/COMPANY and BUSINESS ADDRESS | MAKER'S TRADE |
|---|---|---|---|---|
| R2/10<br>3 February 1906<br>Sent by J & R Griffin | Limewood<br>Lyndhurst Road<br>Wallasey<br>Cheshire | P9/XYZ*sic*/160<br>***#836***  | **BUNNEY LTD**<br>Gibson Marshall (Secretary)<br>Church Street<br>Liverpool | Fancy goods dealers |
| R2/84<br>22 May 1909<br>Sent by G Marshall | | P13/B/50<br>***#837***  | **BUNNEY LTD**<br>G Marshall (Secretary)<br>1, 3, 5, Church Street<br>3, 4, Whitechapel<br>Liverpool also at<br>Llandudno | General dealers |
| R2/125<br>16 December 1910<br>Sent by J & H Taylor | 1 Tydraw Road<br>Cardiff | P13/M/39<br>***#838***  | **Bonner MORGAN**<br>101 Queen Street<br>Cardiff | Opticians |
| R3/141<br>17 February 1953<br>Sent by B Margrave | 25 Corringham Road<br>Levenshulme<br>Manchester 19 | P21/M/25<br>***#839***  | **Bessie MARGRAVE**<br>No business address entered | Student |
| R1/63<br>10 March 1898<br>MR3/136<br>Sent by B Muller<br>Two sizes | 28 Girdlers Road<br>London | P5/Z*sic*/942x2<br>***#840,1***  | **Berthold MULLER** trading as<br>**B MULLER & SON** *<br>187 Wardour Street<br>London | Silversmiths |
| LPB/96<br>11 May 1882 | No name or address in LPB | P3/B/x3<br>***#842-4***  | **BURROWS & MILLS**<br>107 Vyse Street<br>Birmingham | Jewellers and watchmakers |
| LPB/84<br>3 October 1882<br>Sent by N Butler | | P3/B/x1<br>***#845***  | | |
| LPB/18<br>13 September 1884<br>No mark in LPB | | P5/B/x1<br>***#846***  | | |
| LPB/96<br>1 March 1882<br>Similar mark entered<br>CAO 3 October 1882 | | P3/B/x1<br>***#847***  | | |
| Missing register<br>*c.*1886 | | P5/B/10<br>***#848***  | | |
| Missing register<br>*c.*1886 | | P5/B/60<br>***#849***  | | |
| Missing register<br>*c.*1886 | | P5/B/339<br>***#850***  | | |
| R3/27<br>7 November 1925<br>Sent by British Machine Chain Ltd | 194 Ewell Road<br>Surbiton<br>Surrey | P15/C/166<br>***#851***  | **BRITISH MACHINE CHAIN LTD**<br>Cyril F Ashton (Secretary)<br>145 Ewell Road<br>Surbiton<br>Surrey | Manufacturing jewellers |
| R2/36<br>26 March 1907<br>Sent by B M Landeck | 4 South Villas<br>Camden Square<br>London N | P9/L/86,87<br>***#852,3***  | **Boaz Moses LANDECK** *<br>4 South Villas, Camden Square<br>London NW (moved, undated to)<br>5 Anson Road, Tufnell Park<br>London N | Importer of foreign plate |

| REGISTRATION DETAILS | MAKER'S PRIVATE ADDRESS and DETAILS | PLATE and MARK DETAILS | MAKER/COMPANY and BUSINESS ADDRESS | MAKER'S TRADE |
|---|---|---|---|---|
| R3/149<br>30 December 1953<br>Sent by B M Wyatt | 94 Manchester Road<br>Prescot<br>Lancashire | P21/W/72<br>***#854***  | **Barbara Margaret WYATT**<br>No business address entered | Metalworker |
| LPB/58<br>22 October 1879 | | P3/N/x3<br>***#855-7***  | **Fanny NATHAN**<br>(late **Benjamin NATHAN**)<br>103 Vyse Street<br>Birmingham | Jeweller |
| R3/105<br>29 June 1943<br>Sent by Browns of Chester | | P21/B/21<br>***#858***  | **BROWNS OF CHESTER LTD**<br>Sealed in the presence of:-<br>Leonard Harris (Director)<br>R Mayers (Secretary)<br>Crypt Chambers (Registered Office)<br>Eastgate Row<br>Chester | Auctioneers and Estate Agents |
| MR1/146-8<br>MR2/120-5<br>MR3/183<br>SIL/40,44,49<br>SOT/47<br>GMSC/15-18 | Free 1723<br>Flatware, tumbler cups 1723-49 | P1/16/x1<br>***#859***<br>type 1a  | **Benjamin PEMBERTON I**<br>Eastgate Street<br>Chester | Silversmith |
| | Saucepans, mug and jug | P1/16/x1<br>***#860***<br>type 1b  | | |
| Missing register<br>*c.*1886 | | P5/B/41<br>***#861***  | **BAKER & PARKER** | Jewellers |
| R1/80<br>8 October 1894<br>Sent by Baker & Parker | 60 Heartfield Road<br>Handsworth<br>63 Albert Road<br>Aston | P5/B/597<br>***#862***  | **Henry PARKER**<br>**Eli BAKER** trading as<br>**BAKER & PARKER**<br>12 Hylton Street<br>Birmingham | |
| MR1/146-8<br>MR2/120-5<br>MR3/183<br>SIL/40,44,49 | | P1/16/x1<br>***#863***<br>type 2a 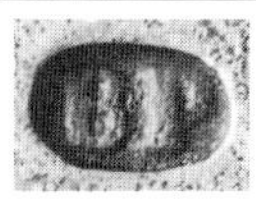 | **Benjamin PEMBERTON I**<br>Eastgate Street<br>Chester | Silversmith |
| SOT/47<br>GMSC/15-18 | | P1/16/x1<br>***#864***<br>type 2b  | | |
| R1/210<br>15 March 1904<br>Sent by Payton Pepper | 5 Patrick Road<br>West Bridgford<br>Nottingham | P9XYZ*sic*/118<br>***#865***  | **BOOTS PURE DRUG CO LTD** *<br>Albert Thompson (Director)<br>Station Street<br>Nottingham | Silversmiths |
| R2/126<br>14 January 1911<br>BAO 15.470-475<br>18.550-555<br>Sent by W J Myatt & Co<br>Two sizes | | P13/B/105-109,116<br>***#866-71***  | **BOOTS PURE DRUG CO LTD** *<br>Albert Thompson (Director)<br>Station Street<br>Nottingham | |
| R1/210<br>17 March 1904<br>Two sizes | | P9/XYZ*sic*/120,121<br>***#872,3***  | | |

| REGISTRATION DETAILS | MAKER'S PRIVATE ADDRESS and DETAILS | PLATE and MARK DETAILS | MAKER/COMPANY and BUSINESS ADDRESS | MAKER'S TRADE |
|---|---|---|---|---|
| R1/210<br>15 March 1904 | 5 Patrick Road<br>West Bridgford<br>Nottingham | P9/XYZ*sic*/119<br>***#874***<br> | **BOOTS PURE DRUG CO LTD** *<br>Albert Thompson (Director)<br>Station Street<br>Nottingham | Silversmiths |
| R2/7<br>24 November 1905<br>Sent by W J Myatt<br>Two sizes | The Pines<br>Patrick Road<br>West Bridgford<br>Nottingham | P9/XYZ*sic*/145-153<br>***#875-83***<br> | | |
| Not in R2 as expected<br>*c.* November 1905 to February 1906 | | P9/XYZ*sic*/155-159<br>***#884-8***<br>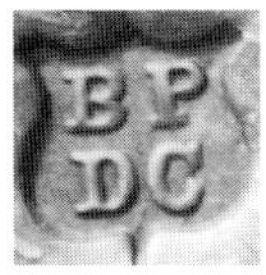 | | |
| R2/126<br>14 January 1911 | . | P13/B/110-115<br>***#889-94***<br> | | |
| R3/158<br>20 October 1956<br>Sent by B L Perry | 32 Queen's Road<br>Cheadle Hulme<br>Cheshire | P21/P/69<br>***#895***<br> | **Bernard Leslie PERRY**<br>No business address entered | Student silversmith |
| R3/155<br>26 July 1955<br>Sent by Bostock & Rayner | | P21/B/42<br>***#896***<br> | **BOSTOCK & RAYNER (LONDON) LTD**<br>Sealed in the presence of:-<br>A P Rayner (Director)<br>W A Rayner (Secretary)<br>57 Hatton Garden<br>London EC1 | Manufacturing jewellers |
| R3/181<br>15 August 1961<br>Sent by J Harrison & Sons Ltd<br>63 Warstone Lane<br>Birmingham 18<br>18 April 1962 | Calthorpe Cottage [1]<br>Welford-on-Avon<br>26 Kenilworth Road [2]<br>Leamington Spa<br>No street entered [3]<br>Bristol | P21/B/67<br>***#897***<br> | **BOLTON & REDFERN LTD**<br>Edwin Bolton [1] (Director)<br>Kathleen Edith Bolton [1] (Director)<br>Phillip Henry Redfern [2] (Director)<br>Herbert J Swain [3] (Director)<br>19 Wood Street<br>Stratford-upon-Avon<br>Warwickshire | Wholesale jewellers |
| | | P21/B/68<br>***#898***<br> | | |
| Missing register<br>*c.*1891<br>Similar mark entered SAO 21 March 1907 | | P5/R/357<br>***#899***<br>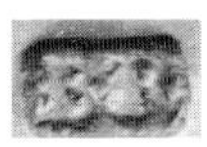 | **Bernard ROBINSON**<br>26 Ernest Road<br>Sparkhill<br>Birmingham | Silversmith |
| R2/88<br>23 July 1909<br>Sent by W G Harris | 38 London Road<br>London | P13/R/26<br>***#900***<br> | **Benjamin ROSE**<br>38 London Road<br>London | Watchmaker and jeweller |
| R2/67<br>27 October 1908<br>BAO 15.273<br>Sent by B R Simmons | 6 Harborne Road<br>Edgbaston | P13/S/11<br>***#901***<br> | **Bernard Rintel SIMMONS**<br>21 Vyse Street<br>Birmingham | Manufacturing jeweller |

| REGISTRATION DETAILS | MAKER'S PRIVATE ADDRESS and DETAILS | PLATE and MARK DETAILS | MAKER/COMPANY and BUSINESS ADDRESS | MAKER'S TRADE |
|---|---|---|---|---|
| R2/187<br>15 May 1914<br>Sent by Lawson, Ward & Gammage | Beechwood<br>Marlow<br>Buckinghamshire | P15/B/53<br>***#902***<br> | **Frank William BRAVINGTON**<br>trading as **BRAVINGTONS** *<br>296, 298 Pentonville Road and<br>71 Ludgate Hill<br>London EC | Jewellers |
| R3/2<br>29 April 1921<br>Sent by Coley Brothers | | P15/B/151-157<br>***#903-9***<br> | | Jewellers, silversmiths and cutlers |
| R3/108<br>19 June 1957<br>Sent by B H Britton & Sons Ltd | | P21/B/51<br>***#910***<br> | **B H BRITTON & SONS** *<br>35 Hockley Hill<br>Birmingham 18 | Manufacturing goldsmiths |
| R3/57<br>5 May 1931<br>Sent by B H Britton & Sons | Bracebridge Road [1]<br>Sutton Coldfield<br>2 Silver Birch Road [2]<br><br>Erdington<br>Richfield Road [3]<br>Four Oaks | P15/B/201<br>***#911***<br>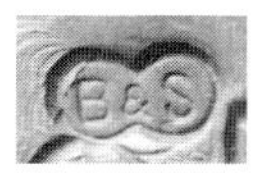 | **Charles Henry BRITTON** [1]<br>**Walter BRITTON** [2]<br>**Herbert BRITTON** [3] trading as<br>**B H BRITTON & SONS** *<br>35 Hockley Hill<br>Birmingham | |
| 23 May 1931 | | P15/B/202<br>***#912***<br> | | |
| R3/108<br>22 February 1945<br>Sent by B H Britton & Sons Ltd<br>All previous punches for G H Britton are valid | | P21/B/23<br>**#913**<br>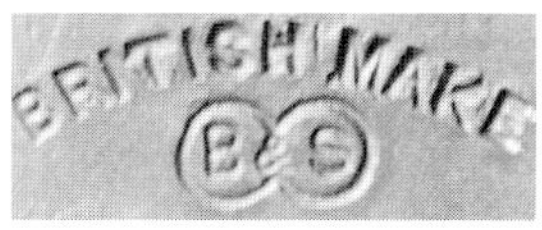 | **B H BRITTON & SONS LTD** *<br>Sealed in the presence of:-<br>Walter Britton (Director)<br>Richard A Britton (Director)<br>J W Britton (Secretary)<br>35 Hockley Hill<br>Birmingham 18 | |
| 21 August 1946 | | P21/B/26<br>***#914***<br> | | |
| 4 January 1947 | | P21/B/27<br>***#915***<br> | | |
| R2/215<br>28 February 1918<br>Sent by Benjamin Sacov | 24 St Mark's Street<br>Aldgate<br>London E | P15/S/33<br>***#916***<br>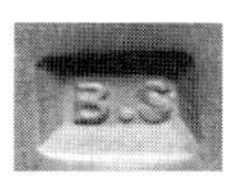 | **Benjamin SACOV** *<br>103 Hatton Gardens<br>Holborn<br>London WC | Manufacturing jeweller |
| R2/85<br>12 June 1909<br>Sent by Albert Britton<br>BAO 15.909-919 | Bracebridge Road<br>Four Oaks<br>Westward House<br>Solihull<br>Orchard Road<br>Erdington | P13/B/51-60<br>***#917-26***<br> | **Charles Henry BRITTON**<br>**Albert BRITTON**<br>**Herbert BRITTON** trading as<br>**BRITTON & SONS** *<br>left 45 Vyse Street<br>35 Hockley Hill<br>Birmingham | Gold chain manufacturers |
| R2/85<br>17 June 1909<br>Sent by Britton & Sons<br>BAO 8.114,<br>15.920, 15.914<br>Two sizes | | P13/B/61-63<br>***#927-9***<br> | | |

| REGISTRATION DETAILS | MAKER'S PRIVATE ADDRESS and DETAILS | PLATE and MARK DETAILS | MAKER/COMPANY and BUSINESS ADDRESS | MAKER'S TRADE |
|---|---|---|---|---|
| R3/20<br>29 February 1924<br>Sent by B H Britton & Sons | Bracebridge Road<br>Four Oaks<br>Silver Birch Road<br>Erdington<br>Lichfield Road<br>Four Oaks | P15/B/172<br>***#930***<br> | **Charles Henry BRITTON**<br>**Albert BRITTON**<br>**Herbert BRITTON** trading as<br>**BRITTON & SONS** *<br>left 45 Vyse Street<br>35 Hockley Hill<br>Birmingham | Manufacturing goldsmiths and silversmiths |
| 23 December 1949 | | P21/B/33<br>***#931***<br> | | |
| 9 September 1953 | | P21/B/40<br>***#932***<br> | | |
| 24 October 1959 | | P21/B/58<br>***#933***<br> | | |
| R1/31<br>22 July 1896<br>Sent by B Stapleton | 13 St John's Square<br>London EC | P5/S/782<br>***#934***<br> | **Benjamin STAPLETON** *<br>62 Red Lion Street<br>London EC | Register mounter |
| R1/177<br>10 October 1902<br>Sent by B Stein | | P9/S/51<br>***#935***<br> | **Barnett STEIN**<br>2 Livingstone Place<br>Edinburgh | Jeweller and watchmaker |
| LPB/78 SP31/1<br>5 February 1884<br>MR3/117<br>Sent by J Sharpe | | P5/S/x1<br>***#936***<br> | **BARNETT & SCOTT** *<br>45 White Friar Gate<br>Hull | Goldsmiths, jewellers, silversmiths, watch and clockmakers |
| Missing register<br>*c.*1886 | | P5/B/31<br>***#937***<br> | | |
| Missing register<br>*c.*1889 | | P5/B/216<br>***#938***<br> | | |
| Missing register<br>*c.*1886 | | P5/B/124<br>***#939***<br> | | |
| R2/161<br>10 September 1912<br>Sent by B H Britton & Sons | Bracebridge Road<br>Sutton Coldfield<br>Holly Lane<br>Erdington<br>Lichfield Road<br>Sutton Coldfield | P15/B/26-28<br>***#940-42***<br> | **Charles Henry BRITTON**<br>**Herbert BRITTON**<br>**Walter BRITTON** trading as<br>**B H BRITTON & SONS** *<br>35 Hockley Hill<br>Birmingham | Manufacturing jewellers |
| R2/225<br>7 November 1919<br>Sent by B H Britton & Sons<br>Two sizes | Bracebridge Road<br>Sutton Coldfield<br>Holly Lane<br>Erdington<br>Lichfield Road<br>Four Oaks (*sic*) | P15/B/110-133<br>***#943-66***<br> | | Gold and silver chain manufacturers |
| R3/89<br>7 April 1938<br>Sent by B H Britton & Sons | Swanston [1]<br>Bracebridge Road<br>Erdington<br>Silverbush Road [2] | P21/B/8<br>***#967***<br> | **B H BRITTON & SONS** *<br>Charles Henry Britton [1] (Partner)<br>Walter Britton [2] (Partner)<br>Herbert Britton [3] (Partner)<br>35 Hockley Hill<br>Birmingham | Manufacturing jewellers |
| 11 April 1938 | Erdington<br>7 Wyvern Road [3]<br>Sutton Coldfield | P21/B/9<br>***#968***<br> | | |

| REGISTRATION DETAILS | MAKER'S PRIVATE ADDRESS and DETAILS | PLATE and MARK DETAILS | MAKER/COMPANY and BUSINESS ADDRESS | MAKER'S TRADE |
|---|---|---|---|---|
| Missing register<br>*c.*1889<br>Similar mark BAO<br>6 December 1894 | CWMP 1891-6 | P5/B/211<br>***#969***<br> | **Benjamin Stuart CHINN**<br>37 Hill Street<br>Coventry | Silver watchcase manufacturer |
| R2/227<br>18 February 1929<br>Sent by Joseph Smith | 26 Craven Street<br>Hulme<br>Manchester<br>146 Spa Road<br>Bolton<br>117 Husband Street<br>Queens Road<br>Manchester | P15/B*sic*/134<br>***#970***<br> | **Joseph SMITH**<br>**Robert BAXENDALE**<br>**Samuel GRIMES**<br>213 Great Jackson Street<br>Hulme<br>Manchester | Pipe stick and umbrella mountings |
| R3/121<br>12 January 1948<br>Sent by Beatrice Taylor<br>Two sizes | Greenbank<br>29 Wilmslow Road<br>Withington<br>Manchester 20 | P21/T/11,12<br>***#971,2***<br> | **Beatrice TAYLOR**<br>Central School of Domestic Economy<br>231 Wilmslow Road<br>Rusholme<br>Manchester 14 | Silverwork student |
| R2/42<br>1 July 1907<br>Sent by P H Bennett | 32 Waverhill Road<br>Handsworth<br>21 Lozells Street<br>Aston Manor | P13/B/1<br>***#973***<br> | **Philip Henry BENNETT**<br>**Arthur James THOMPSON** trading as<br>**BENNETT & THOMPSON**<br>50 Northampton Street<br>Birmingham | Silversmiths |
| R1/202<br>6 November 1903<br>see also R1/213<br>Sent by J & R Griffin | Gladsmuir<br>Spenser Road<br>Harpenden<br>Herts | P9/G/53<br>***#974***<br> | **Benjamin Thomas GREENING** *<br>(Ed: trading as **J HORTON & SON**)<br>30 Hatton Garden<br>London | Wholesale jeweller |
| R2/11<br>15 February 1906<br>Sent by R Richardson | | P9/G/67-72<br>***#975-80***<br> | **Benjamin Thomas GREENING** *<br>30 Hatton Garden<br>London and<br>21 Hylton Street<br>Birmingham | Silversmith and manufacturing jeweller |
| R3/52<br>14 February 1930<br>Sent by B Gordon<br>Cancelled<br>25 February 1944 | 115 Kingstanding Road<br>Erdington<br>Birmingham | P15/B*sic*/199<br>***#981***<br> | **Bert GORDON**<br>54 Northampton Street<br>Birmingham | Manufacturing silversmith |
| MR1/124-130<br>MR3/181<br>SIL/44 | Spoons, tumbler cup and church plate 1703-12<br>Free 1669<br>See also NB | P1/3/x1<br>***#982***<br>type 4<br> | **Nathaniel BULLEN**<br>East side of Bridge Street<br>Chester | Silversmith |
| Not in R1 as expected<br>*c.* 16 April 1896 | | P5/B*sic*/755<br>***#983***<br> | **Unidentified** | |
| R2/220<br>1 June 1919<br>Sent by B Whitehouse | 41 Wellington Road<br>Handsworth Wood<br>Birmingham | P15/W/47,48<br>***#984,5***<br> | **Bernard WHITEHOUSE**<br>87 Vyse Street<br>Birmingham | Manufacturing jeweller |
| SPB/7<br>5 September 1865 | | P3/B/x3<br>***#986-8***<br> | **William BULLOCK**<br>**Joseph WESTON**<br>13 Nevill Street<br>Southport | Watchmakers and jewellers |

| REGISTRATION DETAILS | MAKER'S PRIVATE ADDRESS and DETAILS | PLATE and MARK DETAILS | MAKER/COMPANY and BUSINESS ADDRESS | MAKER'S TRADE |
|---|---|---|---|---|
| LPB/90<br>23 November 1883<br>No mark in LPB just initials BW<br>Incuse BW over EW mark entered SAO 28 August 1900 | This mark and the next punched slightly overlapping. Both assumed to be associated with Benjamin Wade. Eliza Wade possibly his widow. | P5/W/x1<br>*#989*<br> | **Eliza WADE**<br>9 Albion Street (1883)<br>38 York Place (1900)<br>Leeds | Manufacturer and importer of tobacco goods |
| | | P5/W/x1<br>*#990*<br> | | |
| R2/167<br>27 January 1913<br>Sent by B Wade | 146 Otley Road<br>Headingley<br>Leeds | P15/W/2<br>*#991*<br>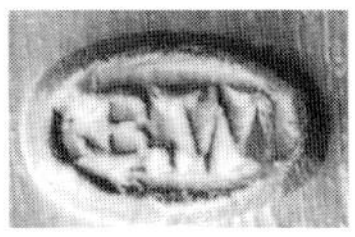 | **Eliza WADE**<br>**Edwin WADE**<br>**Herbert WADE** trading as<br>**B WADE**<br>38 York Place<br>Leeds | Pipe manufacturers |
| R2/221<br>5 June 1919<br>Sent by Handcock & Walker | Otley Road<br>Leeds<br>175 Otley Road<br>Leeds | P15/W/49<br>*#992*<br> | **Edwin WADE**<br>**Herbert WADE**<br>37, 38, 39 York Place<br>Leeds | Briar pipe manufacturers |
| R3/70<br>16 December 1933<br>Sent by Margaret Wade<br>All BW initial punches valid | 277 Otley Road<br>Headingley<br>Leeds | No new mark entered<br>*#993* | **Margaret WADE** Sole Executrix of and trading as<br>**Ben WADE**<br>37-39 York Place<br>Leeds | |
| R3/78<br>17 September 1935<br>Sent by B Wade Ltd<br>All previous punches entered for B Wade valid | | No new mark entered<br>*#994* | **Ben WADE LTD**<br>29 Clarendon Road (Registered Office)<br>Leeds 2 | |
| R3/61<br>22 January 1932<br>Sent by B Walton<br>Two sizes | 5 Selkirk Road<br>Curzon Park<br>Chester | P15/W/99,100<br>*#995,6*<br> | **Bertram WALTON**<br>45 Eastgate Street<br>Chester<br>2 Eastgate Street<br>Chester | Jeweller |
| R3/16<br>15 June 1923<br>Sent by Stylic Manufacturing Co | 158 College Road<br>Moseley<br>15 Hull Road<br>Handsworth | P15/B/167<br>*#997*<br> | **Bernard Charles BACCHUS**<br>**Eric WHITEHOUSE** trading as<br>**BACCHUS & WHITEHOUSE**<br>122 Livery Street<br>Birmingham | Wholesale jewellers |
| R3/21<br>2 April 1924<br>Sent by T J Skelton | 158 College Road<br>Moseley<br>Birmingham<br>101 Handsworth Wood Road<br>Birmingham | P15/B/173<br>*#998*<br> | **Bernard Charles BACCHUS**<br>**Eric WHITEHOUSE**<br>12 Vyse Street<br>Birmingham | |
| R3/31<br>12 January 1926<br>Sent by E Whitehouse & Son | | P15/W*sic*/88<br>*#999*<br>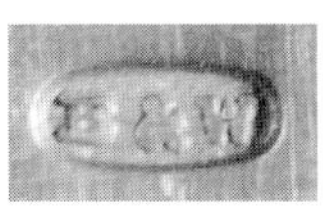 | **Bernard Charles BACCHUS**<br>**Eric WHITEHOUSE** trading as<br>**BACCHUS & WHITEHOUSE**<br>12 Vyse Street<br>Birmingham | |

| REGISTRATION DETAILS | MAKER'S PRIVATE ADDRESS and DETAILS | PLATE and MARK DETAILS | MAKER/COMPANY and BUSINESS ADDRESS | MAKER'S TRADE |
|---|---|---|---|---|
| R2/85<br>12 June 1909<br>BAO 16.281<br>Sent by C Allen | Overley<br>Station Road<br>Yardley | P13/A/14<br>***#1000***<br>  | **Charles ALLEN**<br>27 Hylton Street<br>Birmingham | Manufacturing jeweller |
| R1/8<br>27 February 1895<br>Sent by Candelent & Adams | 27 Westminster Road<br>(Ed: also noted as Candelesch & Adams) | P5/aboveC/643<br>***#1001***<br>  | **Joseph CANDELENT**<br>**George ADAMS** trading as<br>**CANDELENT & ADAMS** *<br>121 Branston Street<br>Birmingham | Jewellers |
| R2/21<br>18 July 1906<br>BAO 12.354<br>Sent by Reeves & Herzberg | 6 Cromer Road<br>Leyton<br>Essex | P9/XYZ*sic*/173<br>***#1002***<br>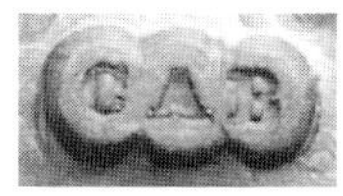  | **Charles Aloysius BRIX** *<br>3 Butler Street<br>London EC | Tobacco and pipe manufacturer |
| R3/123<br>3 April 1948<br>Sent by C A Curtis<br>Two sizes | 10 Kinnard Road<br>Withington<br>Manchester 20 | P21/C/47,48<br>***#1003,4***<br>  | **Cecil Albert CURTIS (Dr)**<br>Clayton Aniline Company Ltd<br>Manchester | Student of Arts and Crafts |
| R1/140<br>30 January 1901<br>Sent by H Griffith & Sons Ltd | Private address as for business | P9/C/47<br>***#1005***<br>  | **Charles Arthur CHIBNALL** *<br>19 Thavies Inn<br>Holborn<br>London EC | Silversmith |
| R1/50<br>1 September 1897<br>Sent by W H Carrington & Co | Edge Hill<br>Alexander Road<br>Gloucester | P5/aboveC/869<br>***#1006***<br>  | **Percy Edward CADLE**<br>6 Westgate Street<br>Gloucester | Tobacconist |
| R1/17<br>5 November 1895<br>Sent by Faraday & Davey<br>G K Leeson<br>C Drefus<br>Authority to W Neale & Sons and<br>J Horton<br>Three sizes | 61 Hilldrop Crescent<br>Campden Road<br>London<br>57 Gladmuir Road<br>Hornsey Lane<br>London N<br>5 Addington Road<br>London<br>27 Hillmorton Road<br>Campden Road<br>London | P5/F/696x3<br>***#1007-9***<br>  | **Charles Adkins FARADAY**<br>**Charles Arthur FARADAY**<br>**Warren FARADAY**<br>**Henry ROWE** trading as<br>**FARADAY & DAVEY** *<br>66 Hatton Garden<br>London | Jewellers and silversmiths |
| R2/72<br>18 February 1909<br>Sent by C A Horton | 7 Gordon Street<br>Lozells<br>Birmingham | P13/H/10<br>***#1010***<br>  | **Charles Arthur HORTON**<br>2 Lines Buildings<br>Vittoria Street<br>Birmingham | Ring manufacturer |
| R2/203<br>22 February 1916<br>BAO 23.262,23.263<br>Sent by C A Horton<br>Two sizes | 60 Aston Lane<br>Perry Bar<br>Birmingham | P15/H/29,30<br>***#1011,2***<br>  | **Charles Arthur HORTON**<br>21 Pitsford Street<br>Birmingham | Hollow and solid signet gem fancy ring manufacturer |
| R3/157<br>6 June 1956<br>Sent by C Biddulph<br>Two sizes | 33 Manley Road<br>Whalley Range<br>Manchester 16 | P21/B/48,49<br>***#1013,4***<br>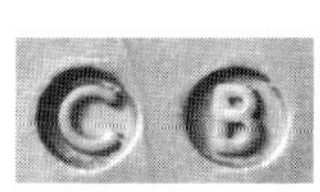  | **Constance BIDDULPH**<br>No business address entered | Student silversmith |
| R1/185<br>20 February 1903<br>Sent by<br>H Litherland | 7 Rathen Road<br>Withington<br>Manchester | P9/B/97<br>***#1015***<br>  | **Charles BROMHALL**<br>8 Newton Street<br>Manchester | Manufacturer of umbrellas |
| R1/97<br>7 April 1899<br>Sent by Cuthbert Butler | 44 Bold Street<br>Blackburn | P9/B/16<br>***#1016***<br>  | **Cuthbert BUTLER**<br>131 Warstone Lane<br>Birmingham | Watchmaker, jeweller and gem ring maker |

| REGISTRATION DETAILS | MAKER'S PRIVATE ADDRESS and DETAILS | PLATE and MARK DETAILS | MAKER/COMPANY and BUSINESS ADDRESS | MAKER'S TRADE |
|---|---|---|---|---|
| R1/196<br>30 June 1903<br>Sent by C Butler | 44 Bold Street<br>Blackburn | P9/B/107<br>***#1017***<br>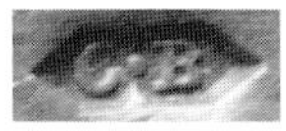 | **Cuthbert BUTLER**<br>37 Lord Street<br>Blackburn<br>Lancashire | Watchmaker and jeweller |
| R1/101<br>20 May 1899<br>Two sizes<br>Sent by C Buckton<br>Authority given to Radcliffe, Pollard & Co and B H Joseph & Co | Private address same as business | P9/B/18x2<br>***#1018,9***<br><br>P9/B/17<br>***#1020***<br> | **Christopher BUCKTON**<br>Moravian House<br>Lightcliffe<br>Halifax | Dealer in fancy jewellery |
| R2/29<br>7 November 1906<br>Sent by C Butler | 44 Bold Street<br>Blackburn | P9/XYZ*sic*/178<br>***#1021***<br> | **Cuthbert BUTLER**<br>37 Lord Street<br>Blackburn<br>Lancashire | Working jeweller |
| LPB/92<br>6 June 1882 | | P3/B/x1<br>***#1022***<br><br>P3/D*sic*/x3<br>***#1023-5***<br> | **C BRADFORD**<br>27 Augusta Street<br>Birmingham | Silversmith |
| Missing register<br>*c.*1889 Two sizes<br>Similar marks LAO 30 Dec. 1881 and BAO 27 March 1896 | CWMP 1886-91 | P5/B/255x2<br>***#1026,7***<br> | **Charles BAND** *<br>2 Portland Terrace<br>Chapel Fields<br>Coventry | Gold watchcase manufacturer |
| Missing register<br>*c.*1890<br>Two sizes | | P5/B/279x2<br>***#1028,9***<br> | **Unidentified** | |
| R2/28<br>4 December 1906<br>Sent by G E Walton | 175 Tufnell Park Road<br>London EC | P9/O*sic*/182<br>***#1030***<br> | **Charles Henry Stuart BROOKS**<br>trading as **C BROOKS LTD** *<br>Audrey House<br>Ely Place<br>London EC | Manufacturing jewellers and silversmiths |
| R2/55<br>5 February 1908<br>Sent by G E Walton Ltd<br>Two sizes | | P13/B/8-10<br>***#1031-3***<br> | **C BROOKS LTD** *<br>Charles Henry Stuart Brooks (Managing Director)<br>Audrey House<br>Ely Place<br>London EC | Wholesale jewellers |
| R2/111<br>2 June 1910<br>Sent by Cahoon Brothers Ltd<br>Two sizes | Rosedale [1 & 2]<br>Earlswood Road<br>Strandtown<br>Belfast<br>75 Belmont Road [3]<br>Belfast | P13/C/69-74<br>***#1034-9***<br>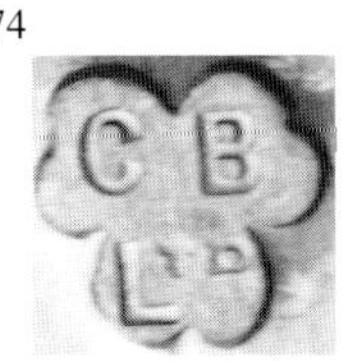 | **CAHOON BROTHERS LTD**<br>John Cahoon [1] (Director)<br>James M Cahoon [2] (Director)<br>George Herron [3] (Secretary)<br>33 Donegal Place<br>Belfast | Jewellers and silversmiths |
| R1/215<br>18 June 1904<br>Sent by Lawson, Ward & Gammage | 55 Pritchard Street<br>Johannesburg<br>69 Myddelton Square<br>London EC | P9/D*sic*/208-210<br>***#1040-2***<br> | **Sidney Napoleon Cromwell COLLINS**<br>**Ernest Albert Edward COLLINS**<br>**Louis Bonaparte COLLINS** trading as<br>**COLLINS BROTHERS**<br>H Collins as Attorney and Agent<br>55, 56 Pritchard Street<br>Johannesburg<br>South Africa | Jewellers |

| REGISTRATION DETAILS | MAKER'S PRIVATE ADDRESS and DETAILS | PLATE and MARK DETAILS | MAKER/COMPANY and BUSINESS ADDRESS | MAKER'S TRADE |
|---|---|---|---|---|
| Missing register<br>*c.*1891 | Similar mark entered<br>BAO 9 March 1905 | P5/C/335<br>***#1043***<br> | **COWDRILL BROTHERS**<br>1 Great Hampton Street<br>Birmingham | Jewellers |
| R3/64<br>21 October 1932<br>Sent by Kinsey<br>Brothers & Patrick<br>Ltd, 17 Vyse Street<br>Birmingham | The Crest (both)<br>Elm Road<br>Earley<br>near Reading | P15/K*sic*/218<br>***#1044***<br> | **Albert Edward CLARK**<br>**Frederick CLARK** trading as<br>**CLARK BROTHERS**<br>15 Charterhouse Street<br>London EC1 | Wholesale<br>jewellers |
| R3/170<br>6 October 1959<br>Sent by Charles<br>Clarke (Director)<br>Woodcote<br>Hale Road, Hale | | P21/C/82<br>***#1045***<br> | **CLARKE BROTHERS (LIVERPOOL) LTD**<br>Parke Works<br>Speke Hall Road<br>Speke<br>Liverpool 24 | Manufacturing<br>jewellers |
| Missing register<br>*c.*1888<br>Similar mark BAO<br>28 February 1888 | | P5/C/171<br>***#1046***<br> | **COX BROTHERS**<br>7 Warstone Lane<br>Birmingham | Jewellers |
| Missing register<br>*c.*1889 | | P5/C/226<br>***#1047***<br> | | |
| R2/224<br>11 October 1919<br>Sent by Charles<br>Boyton & Son Ltd | Pinner Wood House<br>Pinner, Middlesex<br>41 Mowbray Road<br>Brondesbury<br>London NW<br>46 Silbourne Road<br>Southgate<br>London N<br>Lincoln House<br>Eastern Road<br>Fortes Green<br>East Finchley | P15/B/104,105<br>***#1048,9***<br>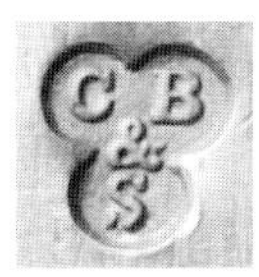 | **Charles BOYTON**<br>**R M PEMBRIDGE**<br>**Charles HORNER**<br>**Brook COSE** trading as<br>**Charles BOYTON & SON LTD** *<br>Upper Charles Street<br>Goswell Road and<br>Hall Street<br>City Road and<br>Birkbeck Road<br>Dalston<br>London | Manufacturing<br>silversmiths |
| R2/158<br>29 June 1912<br>Sent by C Perry & Co | One Ash<br>Dare<br>Sheffield<br>The Grove<br>Dare<br>Sheffield<br>One Ash<br>Dare<br>Sheffield<br>Thornsett<br>Dare, Sheffield | P13/D*sic*/152<br>***#1050***<br> | **Thomas COOPER**<br>**Joseph COOPER**<br>**Arthur COOPER**<br>**Thomas COOPER junior** trading as<br>**COOPER BROTHERS & SON LTD** *<br>Don Plate Works<br>Arundel Street<br>Sheffield and<br>54 Holborn Viaduct<br>London EC | Silversmiths |
| PDB 1815<br>MR3/78 | Gold rings | P1/31/x2<br>***#1051,2***<br>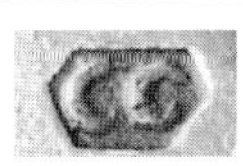 | **C CARELESS**<br>Town not entered | Goldsmith |
| R1/139<br>1 January 1901<br>Sent by T P Hewitt<br>and R J Pike | 257 Woodstock Road<br>Belfast | P9/C/43<br>***#1053***<br> | **Charles CALOM**<br>21 Albert Bridge<br>Belfast | Watchmaker |
| R3/170<br>11 December 1959<br>Sent by C Cooper<br>Two sizes | 29 Cawdor Street<br>Patricroft<br>Near Manchester | P21/C/83,84<br>***#1054,5***<br>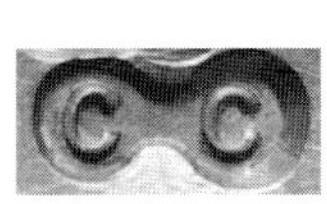 | **Charles COOPER**<br>No business address entered | Student<br>silversmith |
| LPB/28<br>7 October 1881 | CWMP 1874-86 | P3/C/x2<br>***#1056,7***<br> | **Charles COOKE** *<br>28 Thomas Street<br>The Butts<br>Coventry | Watchcase<br>maker |

| REGISTRATION DETAILS | MAKER'S PRIVATE ADDRESS and DETAILS | PLATE and MARK DETAILS | MAKER/COMPANY and BUSINESS ADDRESS | MAKER'S TRADE |
|---|---|---|---|---|
| SPB/6<br>15 January 1872<br>CWMP 1874-86 | | P3/C/x3<br>***#1058-60***<br> | **Charles COOKE** *<br>28 Thomas Street<br>The Butts<br>Coventry | Watchcase maker |
| R1/5<br>28 November 1894<br>Sent by C H Cheshire and<br>W J Spencer<br>Three sizes | 22 Soho Road<br>Handsworth<br>Birmingham | P5/aboveC/627x3<br>***#1061-3***<br>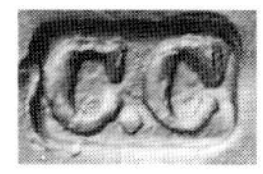 | **Colen Hewer CHESHIRE** *<br>3 Northampton Street<br>Birmingham | Silversmith |
| R1/5<br>3 July 1904<br>Should be on later P9! | | P5/aboveC/628<br>***#1064***<br>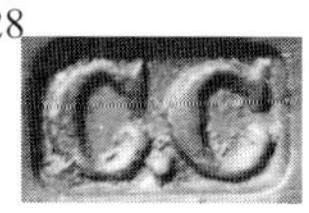 | | |
| R2/52<br>9 December 1907<br>Sent by Colen Hewer Cheshire<br>Five sizes | | P13/C/12-29<br>***#1065-82***<br> | | |
| SPB/8<br>12 February 1873<br>Should be on later P3! | CWMP 1874-86 | P2*sic*/C/x3<br>***#1083-5***<br> | **Charles COOKE** *<br>28 Thomas Street, Butts<br>66 Craven Street (1894)<br>Coventry | Watchcase maker |
| Missing register<br>*c.*1891<br>Similar mark entered BAO 13 November 1894 | | P5/C/347<br>***#1086***<br> | | |
| Missing register<br>*c.*1887<br>Similar mark BAO<br>13 November 1894 | | P5/C/102<br>***#1087***<br>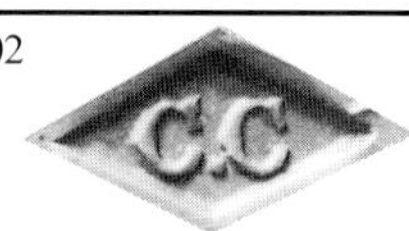 | | |
| R3/17<br>10 March 1956<br>Punch sent by<br>W J Pillar and Cohen & Charles Solomon | 72 Canfield Gardens<br>London NW6<br>36 Queens Road<br>London NW8<br>51 Aberdare Street<br>London NW6 | P21/C/73<br>***#1088***<br> | **Albert COHEN** *<br>**Charles SOLOMON** * (Culme has<br>**Isidor(e) COHEN** * Soloman)<br>12-13 Thavies Inn<br>Holborn Circus<br>London EC | Manufacturing goldsmiths and silversmiths |
| R1/16<br>6 September 1895<br>Two sizes Sent by<br>E F Darnsley & Co<br>C Lyster & Sons<br>G Perkins & Sons<br>W Neale & Sons<br>F Marson<br>W Manton | 123 Alexander Road South<br>London | P9/C/1<br>***#1089***<br>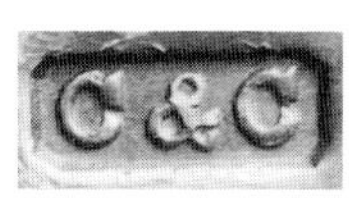 | **Albert COHEN**<br>**Charles SOLOMON** trading as<br>**COHEN & CHARLES** *<br>11 Thavies Inn<br>Holborn Circus<br>London | Jewellers & silversmiths |
| R3/17<br>26 July 1923<br>Punch sent by<br>W J Pillar and Cohen & Charles Solomon | 72 Canfield Gardens<br>London NW6<br>36 Queens Road<br>London NW8<br>51 Aberdare Street<br>London NW6 | P15/C/148,149<br>***#1090,1***<br> | **Albert COHEN** *<br>**Charles SOLOMON** *<br>**Isadore COHEN** *<br>12 and 13 Thavies Inn<br>Holborn Circus<br>London EC | Manufacturing goldsmiths and silversmiths |
| R1/148<br>13 June 1901<br>Sent by E J Trevitt & Sons,<br>J Fray<br>W Vale & Sons | 12 Carlton Hill [1]<br>123 Alexander Road [2]<br>London NW | P9/C/68<br>***#1092***<br> | **Albert COHEN** [1]<br>**Charles SOLOMON** [2] trading as<br>**COHEN & CHARLES** *<br>13 Thavies Inn<br>Holborn Circus<br>London | Silversmiths |

| REGISTRATION DETAILS | MAKER'S PRIVATE ADDRESS and DETAILS | PLATE and MARK DETAILS | MAKER/COMPANY and BUSINESS ADDRESS | MAKER'S TRADE |
|---|---|---|---|---|
| R1/155<br>17 October 1901 | 12 Carlton Hill [1]<br>123 Alexandra Road [2]<br>London NW | P9/C/72<br>***#1093***<br> | **Albert COHEN** [1] **and**<br>**Charles SOLOMON** [2] trading as<br>**COHEN & CHARLES** *<br>13 Thavies Inn<br>Holborn Circus<br>London | Silversmiths |
| R1/198<br>24 July 1903<br>Sent by R Chandler | | P9/C/96<br>***#1094***  | | Jewellers and silversmiths |
| R2/31<br>23 January 1907<br>Sent by J & R Griffin | 72 Canfield Gardens<br>London NW<br>123 Alexandra Road<br>London NW | P9/D*sic*/237<br>***#1095***  | 12-13 Thavies Inn<br>London | Manufacturing silversmiths and jewellers |
| R2/33<br>14 February 1907<br>Sent by Cohen & Charles<br>Clark & Sewill P<br>Two sizes | (P=Partner?) | P9/D*sic*/238,239<br>***#1096,7***<br> | | Silversmiths |
| R2/41<br>11 June 1907<br>Sent by Akerman & Co | | P9/E*sic*/243<br>***#1098***  | | Jewellers and silversmiths |
| R2/57<br>18 March 1908<br>Sent by<br>W Davenport | | P13/C/31<br>***#1099***  | | Goldsmiths and jewellers |
| R2/102<br>1 February 1910<br>Sent by Clark & Sewell | | P13/C/58<br>***#1100***  | | Silversmiths |
| R2/106<br>19 March 1910<br>Sent by Williams Ltd | | P13/C/60-62<br>***#1101-3***  | | |
| R2/210<br>6 June 1917<br>Sent by Clark & Sewell Ltd | 72 Canfield Gardens [2]<br>Hampstead<br>36 Queens Road [1]<br>St Johns Wood, London<br>51 Aberdare Gardens<br>London NW6 [3] | P15/C/68<br>***#1104***  | **Charles SOLOMON** [1]<br>**Albert COHEN** [2]<br>**Isadore COHEN** [3] trading as<br>**COHEN & Charles SOLOMON** *<br>12, 13 Thavies Inn, Holborn<br>London | Goldsmiths and silversmiths |
| R2/231<br>20 May 1920<br>Sent by F Field<br>57 Frederick Street<br>Birmingham | | P15/C/93<br>***#1105***  | | |
| R3/156<br>9 December 1955<br>Sent by C C Bennett | 327 Manchester Road<br>Northwich<br>Cheshire | P21/B/45,46<br>***#1106,7***  | **Clarence Courtney BENNETT**<br>No business address entered | Student silversmith |
| R3/10<br>7 July 1922<br>Sent by C C Duguid | 15 Holland Road<br>Wallasey | P15/D/65<br>***#1108***  | **Christine Catherine DUGUID**<br>City School of Art<br>Liverpool | Silversmith |
| R3/63<br>19 August 1932<br>Sent by Cottrill & Cattlow Ltd | | P15/K*sic*/215<br>***#1109***<br> | **COTTRILL & CATTLOW LTD**<br>Common seal of company affixed in the presence of:-<br>A Evenson (Director)<br>J T Cottrill (Director)<br>E Cottrill (Secretary)<br>2 Nicholas Croft (Registered Office)<br>Manchester | Manufacturing jewellers |

| REGISTRATION DETAILS | MAKER'S PRIVATE ADDRESS and DETAILS | PLATE and MARK DETAILS | MAKER/COMPANY and BUSINESS ADDRESS | MAKER'S TRADE |
|---|---|---|---|---|
| Missing register<br>*c.*1888 | | P5/C/175<br>***#1110***<br> | **George CROSS & CO LTD** | Manufacturing jewellers |
| R2/47<br>22 October 1907<br>Sent by T Nightingale | The Oaklands<br>Northfield<br>Birmingham | P13/C/3,4<br>***#1111,2***<br> | **George CROSS & CO LTD** *<br>George Cross (Managing Director)<br>14, 15 Northampton Street<br>Birmingham | |
| R2/142<br>1 September 1911<br>Sent by R Parkes & Co | | P13/D*sic*/145<br>***#1113***<br> | **George CROSS & CO LTD** *<br>Leslie Coleman Cross (Director)<br>15 Northampton Street<br>Birmingham | |
| R3/40<br>25 April 1928<br>Sent by E Smith | | P15/C/186<br>***#1114***<br> | **George CROSS & CO LTD** *<br>Leslie Coleman Cross (Director)<br>14 Northampton Street<br>Birmingham | |
| R3/55<br>9 December 1930<br>Sent by G Cross & Co | | P15/K*sic*/208<br>***#1115***<br>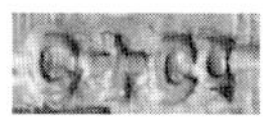 | **George CROSS & CO (1930) LTD** *<br>Common seal of company affixed in the presence of:-<br>Leslie Cross (Director) | |
| 7 May 1931<br>Cancelled<br>5 July 1947 | | P15/K*sic*/209<br>***#1116***<br>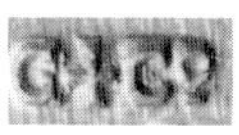 | William Weston (Secretary)<br>28 Hylton Street (Registered Office)<br>Birmingham | |
| Missing register<br>*c.*1889 | Cross sign between C and Co suggests George Cross | P5/C/253<br>***#1117***<br> | | |
| Missing register<br>*c.*1887 | | P5/C/116<br>***#1118***<br> | **Unidentified** | |
| R1/228<br>27 February 1905<br>Sent by Twine & Gilpin | 83 Aberdeen Road<br>Highbury<br>London N | P9/D*sic*/218<br>***#1119***<br> | **Edgar COOMBS** trading as<br>**COOMBS & CO**<br>14/16 Fan Street<br>Aldersgate<br>London EC | General merchants |
| R2/25<br>20 September 1906<br>Sent by W Weston | 2 Addington Road<br>Strand Green<br>London N | P9/D*sic*/233-235<br>***#1120-2***<br> | | Wholesale jewellers |
| Missing register<br>*c.*1886 | | P5/C/56<br>***#1123***<br> | **Unidentified** | |
| Missing register<br>*c.*1891 | | P5/C/342<br>***#1124***<br> | **Unidentified** | |
| R3/61<br>13 February 1932<br>Sent by Payton, Pepper & Son Ltd<br>3, 5 Vyse Street<br>Birmingham | | P15/K*sic*/213<br>***#1125***<br> | **CARRINGTON & CO LTD** *<br>Sealed in the presence of:-<br>Frank Bruford (Director)<br>William J Upton (Secretary)<br>130 Regent Street (Registered Office)<br>London W 1 | Goldsmiths and silversmiths |
| R3/185<br>25 July 1962<br>Sent by William Comyns and Sons<br>Comyns House<br>Lower Street, W2 | | P21/C/89<br>***#1126***<br>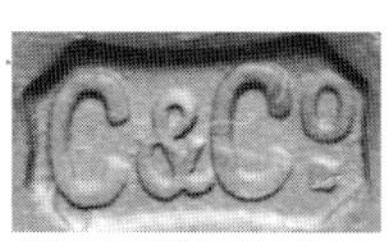 | **CARRINGTON & CO LTD** *<br>130 Regent Street<br>London W1 | Silversmiths and jewellers |

| REGISTRATION DETAILS | MAKER'S PRIVATE ADDRESS and DETAILS | PLATE and MARK DETAILS | MAKER/COMPANY and BUSINESS ADDRESS | MAKER'S TRADE |
|---|---|---|---|---|
| Missing register<br>*c.*1891 | | P5/C/338<br>***#1127***  | **Unidentified** | |
| R2/71<br>4 February 1909<br>Sent by B M Cotton<br>Wigley & Hall | 13 Percy Street [1]<br>Edgbaston<br>Birmingham | P13/C/36<br>***#1128***  | **Benjamin Marcus COTTON** [1]<br>**Ephraim Harris COTTON** trading as<br>**B M COTTON & CO**<br>62 Albion Street<br>Birmingham and Port Elizabeth (*sic*) | Merchants |
| R2/222<br>28 June 1919<br>Sent by B M Cotton | 34 Augustus Road<br>Edgbaston<br>Birmingham | P15/C/74<br>***#1129***  | **Benjamin Marcus COTTON**<br>62 Albion Street<br>Birmingham | Merchant and manufacturer |
| R3/118<br>5 July 1947<br>Previous punches cancelled<br>Sent by W Weston & Son<br>28 Hylton Street<br>Birmingham | | P21/C/36<br>***#1130***  | **George CROSS & CO (1930) LTD**<br>Common seal of company affixed in the presence of:-<br>Leslie Cross (Director)<br>William Weston (Secretary)<br>28 Hylton Street (Registered Office)<br>Birmingham | Manufacturing jewellers |
| R3/161<br>22 March 1957<br>Sent by C T Dixon | Woodthorpe<br>Warrington Road<br>Cuddington<br>Northwich<br>Cheshire | P21/D/28<br>***#1131***  | **Miss Christine Tate DIXON**<br>No business address entered | Student |
| LPB/24<br>3 February 1882<br>LPB mark shown | | Not on P3<br>***#1132*** 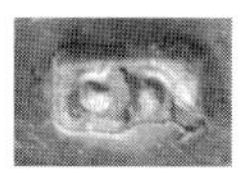 | **DIMIER BROTHERS & CO** *<br>46 Cannon Street<br>London | Watch manufacturers and importers |
| LPB/26 SP25/5<br>16 April 1885<br>No mark in LPB | | P5/D/x1<br>***#1133*** 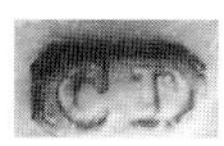 | | |
| LPB/24<br>3 February 1882<br>LPB mark shown | | Not on P3<br>***#1134***  | | |
| R1/65<br>2 May 1898<br>Sent by C Dreyfus | 19 Adamson Road<br>Swiss Cottage<br>London NW | P5/aboveD/953<br>***#1135*** 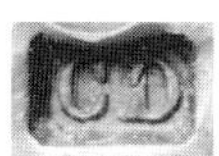 | **Charles DREYFUS**<br>111 Farringdon Road<br>London | Manufacturing jeweller |
| R1/160<br>30 January 1902<br>Sent by C Dreyfus | | P9/D/34<br>***#1136***  | | |
| R2/49<br>23 October 1907 | | P9/D/60<br>***#1137***  | | |
| | | P9/D/59<br>***#1138***  | | |
| R2/115<br>16 July 1910<br>Sent by C H Dumenil Ltd | 15 Westford Road<br>Balham<br>London S W | P13/D/31<br>***#1139***  | **Charles Henry DUMENIL** trading as<br>**C H DUMENIL LTD** *<br>16 and 17 Broad Street<br>Golden Square<br>London | Manufacturing silversmiths |
| LPB/92<br>20 January 1882 | Charles A Broughton at this address PO 1882 directory | P3/B/x1<br>***#1140***  | **C D BROUGHTON**<br>21, 22, 23 St Paul's Square<br>Birmingham | Gold and silver chain maker |

| REGISTRATION DETAILS | MAKER'S PRIVATE ADDRESS and DETAILS | PLATE and MARK DETAILS | MAKER/COMPANY and BUSINESS ADDRESS | MAKER'S TRADE |
|---|---|---|---|---|
| R3/171<br>4 February 1960<br>Sent by C De Boer | 9 The Serpentine<br>Liverpool 19 | P21/B/59<br>***#1141***<br> | **Charles DE BOER**<br>31 Rodney Street<br>Liverpool 1 and<br>14 Winrarleigh Street<br>Warrington<br>Lancashire | Consultant obstetrician and gynaecologist |
| R3/78<br>10 September 1935<br>Sent by S Blanckensee & Sons Ltd<br>Two sizes | 64 Dorset Road<br>Bexhill-on-Sea<br>Sussex | P15/E/45,46<br>***#1142,3***<br> | **Cyril EMARY**<br>65 Devonshire Road<br>Bexhill-on-Sea<br>Sussex | Jeweller and silversmith |
| R2/132<br>3 November 1919<br>Sent by Charles Elliott | 68 Kingston Street<br>Birmingham | P15/E/15<br>***#1144***<br> | **Charles ELLIOTT**<br>Back 245 King Edward Road<br>Birmingham | Manufacturing jeweller |
| R2/219<br>30 April 1919<br>Sent by David Edwards | 335 Grey Mare Lane<br>Olenshaw<br>50 St Oswalds Grove<br>Rochdale Road<br>Manchester | P15/C/73<br>***#1145***<br> | **William CARRUTHERS**<br>**David EDWARDS**<br>33 Thomas Street<br>Manchester | Walking stick and umbrella mounters |
| SPB/23<br>16 September 1876 | | P3/E/x3<br>***#1146-8***<br> | **Charles ELSTON**<br>22/24 Myddleton Street<br>Clerkenwell<br>London | Watchcase maker |
| Missing register<br>*c.*1888 | | P5/E/198<br>***#1149***<br>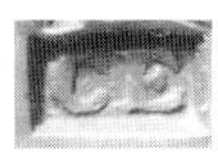 | **Unidentified** | |
| R3/165<br>11 February 1959<br>Sent by C Ellison | 136 Chester Road<br>Northwich<br>Cheshire | P21/E/12<br>***#1150***<br> | **Charles ELLISON**<br>Dental Clinic<br>Imperial Chemical Industries Ltd<br>Alkali Division, Winnington<br>Northwich<br>Cheshire | Dental surgeon |
| R2/132<br>4 April 1911<br>BAO 12.839<br>Sent by C Elliott | 103 Prescot Street<br>Birmingham | P13/E/19<br>***#1151***<br> | **Charles ELLIOTT**<br>51 Vyse Street<br>Birmingham | Jeweller and silversmith |
| R2/221<br>27 June 1919<br>Sent by C Elliott | 68 Kingston Street<br>Birmingham<br>Annotated *same punch* | No new mark<br>***#1152*** | **Charles ELLIOTT**<br>Back 245 King Edward Road<br>Birmingham | Manufacturing jeweller |
| R2/88<br>16 July 1909<br>Sent by<br>J W Cunnington | 33 Sutherland Mount<br>Leeds<br>93 St Mark's Road<br>Leeds | P13/C/44<br>***#1153***<br> | **John William CUNNINGTON**<br>**George Smith EASTWOOD**<br>trading as<br>**CUNNINGTON & EASTWOOD**<br>19 King Charles Croft<br>Leeds | Pipe mounters and repairers |
| R2/76<br>30 March 1909<br>Sent by C E Adams | 259 Icknield Street<br>Birmingham<br>Perry & Co bought business | P13/A/9<br>***#1154***<br> | **Charles E ADAMS**<br>259 Icknield Street<br>Birmingham | Jewellers and silversmiths |
| R3/133<br>13 May 1950<br>Sent by F & R Beach Ltd<br>184 Warstone Lane<br>Birmingham 18 | Richmond<br>Leamington Road<br>Kenilworth<br>Warwickshire | P21/B/35<br>***#1155***<br> | **Charles Edwin BURFORD** trading as<br>**Charles E BURFORD & CO**<br>53 Parade<br>Leamington Spa<br>Warwickshire | Watch importers and wholesale jewellers |

| REGISTRATION DETAILS | MAKER'S PRIVATE ADDRESS and DETAILS | PLATE and MARK DETAILS | MAKER/COMPANY and BUSINESS ADDRESS | MAKER'S TRADE |
|---|---|---|---|---|
| R1/195<br>6 June 1903<br>Sent by self | 16 Preston Road<br>Leytonstone<br>London | P9/C/92,93<br>***#1156,7***  | **Claude Ernest COLLINS** *<br>52 Hatton Garden<br>London EC | Manufacturing jeweller |
| R1/182<br>22 January 1903<br>Sent by Vale & Sons | 16 Preston Street<br>Leytonstone<br>London | P9/C/80<br>***#1158***  | | Wholesale jeweller |
| R3/177<br>17 February 1961<br>Sent by C E Day<br>Two sizes | 4 Stanley Villas<br>Greenway Road<br>Runcorn<br>Cheshire | P21/D/32,33<br>***#1159,60***  | **Charles Edward DAY**<br>No business address entered | Student |
| 12 September 1961 | | P21/D/35<br>***#1161***  | | |
| Missing register<br>*c.*1892 | | P5/C/418<br>***#1162***  | **CONSTANTINE & FLOYD** *<br>82 Caroline Street<br>Birmingham | Manufacturing jewellers and silversmiths |
| LPB/22<br>10 January 1885<br>Sent by Tandy & Rudge | No mark in LPB | P5/C/x1<br>***#1163***  | | |
| Missing register<br>*c.*1890 | | P5/C/292<br>***#1164***  | | |
| R1/118<br>23 December 1899<br>Sent by A Isherwood | Handsworth Wood Road<br>Nr Birmingham | P9/C/31<br>***#1165***  | **Alfred CONSTANTINE**<br>**William Henry FLOYD** trading as<br>**CONSTANTINE & FLOYD** *<br>14 Regent Place<br>Birmingham | |
| LPB/28<br>10 October 1881<br>Sent by Tandy & Rudge | LPB mark shown | Not on P3<br>***#1166***  | **CONSTANTINE & FLOYD** *<br>82 Caroline Street<br>Birmingham | |
| LPB/24<br>5 April 1882<br>Sent by Pope & Phelps | | P3/D*sic*/x1<br>***#1167***  | | |
| LPB/20<br>2 May 1882<br>Sent by Myer Brothers | LPB mark shown | Not on P3<br>***#1168***  | | |
| LPB/86<br>27 October 1882<br>Sent by Pope & Phelps | | P3/C/x1<br>***#1169***  | | |
| Missing register<br>*c.*1892 | | P5/G*sic*/422<br>***#1170***  | | |
| R2/141<br>1 August 1911<br>Sent by W J Pellow Ltd | 116 Poplar Avenue<br>Edgbaston<br>Birmingham | P13/D*sic*/144<br>***#1171***  | **CONSTANTINE & FLOYD LTD** *<br>George G Clark (Director)<br>14 Regent Place<br>Birmingham | Manufacturing jewellers |
| R1/146<br>4 May 1901<br>Sent by F Banks | 137 Handsworth Wood Road<br>Birmingham | P9/C/49<br>***#1172***  | **CONSTANTINE & FLOYD** *<br>Alfred Constantine (Managing Director)<br>14 Regent Place<br>Birmingham | Wholesale jewellers |

| REGISTRATION DETAILS | MAKER'S PRIVATE ADDRESS and DETAILS | PLATE and MARK DETAILS | MAKER/COMPANY and BUSINESS ADDRESS | MAKER'S TRADE |
|---|---|---|---|---|
| R1/165<br>21 March 1902<br>Sent by Loach Brothers<br>J & R Griffin | 137 Handsworth Wood Road<br>Birmingham | P9/C/77<br>***#1173***<br> | **CONSTANTINE & FLOYD** *<br>Alfred Constantine (Managing Director)<br>14 Regent Place<br>Birmingham | Wholesale jewellers |
| R2/171<br>18 January 1916<br>Sent by<br>Chas Horner Ltd<br>10 May 1913 | | P15/C/48<br>***#1174***<br> | **CONSTANTINE & FLOYD** *<br>George G Clark (Manager)<br>Regent Place<br>Birmingham | |
| | | P15/C/29<br>***#1175***<br> | | |
| LPB/56 SP27/8,9<br>6 June 1885<br>No mark in LPB<br>9th entry LPB/56 and 9th mark on SP27 | John Wilkinson & Son, mourning ring makers, at this address in 1875-85. Edward Charles Middleton, born 1859, shown as a Jeweller at 171 Holloway Road in 1881 Census | P5/M/x1<br>***#1176***<br> | **Charles Edward MIDDLETON**<br>8 Skinner Street<br>Clerkenwell<br>London | Jeweller |
| R1/191<br>22 April 1903<br>Sent by C E F Potter<br>Two sizes | Private address same as business | P9Q/184,185<br>***#1177,8***<br> | **Charles Edward Farquar POTTER** *<br>72 Myddleton Street<br>Clerkenwell<br>3 Green Terrace (May 1932)<br>Rosebury Avenue<br>London | Gold chain and ring maker |
| R3/20<br>12 December 1923<br>Sent by Chester Electro Plate Co<br>Three sizes | Oakland<br>Hoole<br>Chester | P15/C/151-153<br>***#1179-81***<br> | **THE CHESTER ELECTRO PLATE CO**<br>Frederick William Jones<br>Wilfred Hird Jones<br>City Road<br>Chester | Silver and electroplate manufacturers |
| 8 December 1927<br>Two sizes | | P15/C/180,181<br>***#1182,3***<br>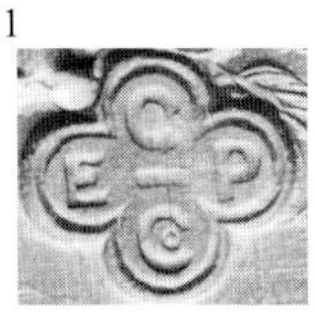 | | |
| R2/147<br>28 November 1911<br>Sent by R Parks & Co<br>BAO 14.393 | Heather Bank<br>Halifax | P13/R/44<br>***#1184***<br> | **Charles Edgar ROSE** *<br>20 and 22 Crown Street<br>Halifax | Jeweller |
| LPB/78 SP31/8<br>12 November 1885<br>No mark in LPB | 8th entry on LPB/78 and 8th mark on SP31 | P5/S/x1<br>***#1185***<br> | **Charles Edward SOLOMAN**<br>50 Vyse Street<br>Birmingham | Jeweller |
| | | P5/S/x1<br>***#1186***<br> | | |
| R2/129<br>4 March 1911<br>BAO 18113<br>Sent by C E Turner | 212 Hamstead Road<br>Handsworth<br>Birmingham | P13/T/31<br>***#1187***<br> | **Charles Edwin TURNER**<br>23 Vyse Street<br>Birmingham | Silversmith |
| R3/178<br>25 March 1961<br>Sent by<br>C E Woosnam | 11 The Laund<br>Wallasey | P21/W/100<br>***#1188***<br> | **Catherine Evelyn WOOSNAM**<br>No business address entered | Student |
| R1/234<br>2 June 1905<br>Sent by Charles E Watson | 49 Darnley Street<br>Old Trafford<br>Manchester | P9/V*sic*/133<br>***#1189***<br> | **Charles Edward WATSON**<br>68a Corporation Street<br>Manchester | Working jeweller |

| REGISTRATION DETAILS | MAKER'S PRIVATE ADDRESS and DETAILS | PLATE and MARK DETAILS | MAKER/COMPANY and BUSINESS ADDRESS | MAKER'S TRADE |
|---|---|---|---|---|
| R3/90<br>24 June 1938<br>Sent by C Fisher | 21 Pelham Road<br>Wallasey<br>Cheshire | P21/F/2<br>***#1190***<br> | **Charles FISHER**<br>Townsend Lane School<br>Anfield<br>Liverpool | Teacher of handicrafts |
| R3/135<br>24 April 1951<br>Sent by Smith, Ewen & Stylic Ltd | Followed by<br>J Smith & Sons Ltd<br>Birmingham<br>13 May 1954 | P21/C/52<br>***#1191***<br>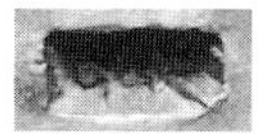 | **CROPP & FARR LTD** *<br>42 Frederick Street<br>Birmingham 1 and<br>94 Hatton Garden (Registered Office)<br>London EC1 | Manufacturing jewellers |
| R3/151<br>1 April 1954 and<br>13 May 1954<br>Sent by Smith & Pepper Ltd<br>77-78 Vyse Street<br>Birmingham 18 | | P21/C/66,70<br>***#1192,3***<br> | **CROPP & FARR LTD** *<br>94 Hatton Garden<br>London EC1 | |
| R3/159<br>23 January 1957<br>Sent by W H Collins & Co Ltd<br>Excelsior Works<br>Rookery Road<br>Handsworth, Birm<br><br>13 June 1957 | | P21/C/74<br>***#1194***<br> | | |
| | | P21/C/76<br>***#1195***<br> | | |
| R3/111<br>22 January 1946<br>Sent by Smith, Ewen & Stylic Ltd<br>42 Frederick Street<br>Birmingham 1<br><br>6 July 1946 | | P21/C/27<br>***#1196***<br> | **CROPP & FARR LTD** *<br>Sealed in the presence of:-<br>H J Cropp (Director)<br>Francis Cropp (Secretary)<br>94 Hatton Garden (Registered Office)<br>London EC1 | Manufacturing and wholesale jewellers |
| | | P21/C/32<br>***#1197***<br> | | |
| R3/122<br>18 March 1948<br>Sent by Edwin Whitehouse & Sons<br>52 Vyse Street<br>Birmingham 18 | | P21/C/46<br>***#1198***<br> | | |
| R3/151<br>29 April 1954 | | P21/C/68<br>***#1199***<br> | | |
| R3/163<br>15 October 1957<br>Sent by W J Pellow Ltd<br>31 Vyse Street<br>Birmingham 18 | | P21/C/77<br>***#1200***<br> | **CROPP & FARR LTD** *<br>Sealed in the presence of:-<br>H J Cropp (Director)<br>Francis Cropp (Director)<br>94 Hatton Garden<br>London EC1 | Manufacturing jewellers |
| Missing register<br>*c.*1887 | | P5/C/88<br>***#1201***<br> | **Unidentified** | |
| Missing register<br>*c.*1893 | | P5/C/514<br>***#1202***<br> | **Unidentified** | |

| REGISTRATION DETAILS | MAKER'S PRIVATE ADDRESS and DETAILS | PLATE and MARK DETAILS | MAKER/COMPANY and BUSINESS ADDRESS | MAKER'S TRADE |
|---|---|---|---|---|
| R3/37<br>29 March 1927<br>Sent by C Horner Ltd | 45 Mount View Road<br>Hornsey, London N<br>Rayleigh, Beechcroft Ave<br>Golders Green<br>London NW | P15/C/179<br>*#1203*<br> | **John Francis CROPP**<br>**Horace John Adams FARR**<br>trading as **CROPP & FARR** *<br>94 Hatton Garden<br>London | Goldsmiths and jewellers |
| R3/161<br>4 May 1957<br>Sent by W J Pellow Ltd<br>31 Hylton Street<br>Birmingham 18 | | P21/C/75<br>*#1204*<br> | | |
| R3/151<br>1 April 1954 and<br>13 May 1954<br>Sent by Smith & Pepper Ltd<br>77-78 Vyse Street<br>Birmingham 18 | | P21/C/67<br>*#1205*<br> | **CROPP & FARR LTD** *<br>94 Hatton Garden<br>London EC1 | Manufacturing jewellers |
| LPB/32 SP26/2<br>15 October 1883<br>No mark in LPB | | P5/F/x1<br>*#1206*<br> | **Charles Frederick FLOYD**<br>9 Hylton Street<br>Birmingham | Jeweller |
| R1/147<br>14 May 1901<br>Sent by W H Ashford | | P9/C/50<br>*#1207*<br> | **CONSTANTINE & FLOYD** *<br>**Alfred CONSTANTINE** (Managing Director)<br>14 Regent Place<br>Birmingham | Wholesale jewellers |
| R2/78<br>8 April 1909<br>Sent by E Whitehouse & Son | Handsworth Wood Road<br>Handsworth<br>Birmingham<br><br>All other punches cancelled | P13/C/38-40<br>*#1208-10*<br> | **CONSTANTINE & FLOYD** *<br>William Henry Floyd (Managing Director)<br>Regent Place<br>Birmingham | Wholesale jewellers |
| R2/200<br>5 October 1915<br>Sent by S Usher Ltd | Brodrick Road<br>Wandsworth Common<br>London | P15/F/14<br>*#1211*<br> | **Charles Edwin FRY** trading as<br>**C E FRY & SONS**<br>35 Warwick Street<br>Westminster<br>London SW | Jewellers |
| LPB/32 SP26/1<br>22 September 1883<br>Sent by E Roek | No mark in LPB only initials CFSD | P5/F/x1<br>*#1212*<br> | **Charles FARADAY and**<br>**Samuel DAVEY** *<br>37 Hatton Garden<br>London | Wholesale jewellers, silversmiths and jet manufacturers |
| Missing register<br>*c.*1891 | | P5/F/379<br>*#1213*<br> | | |
| Missing register<br>*c.*1886 | | P5/F/67<br>*#1214*<br> | | |
| R2/174<br>26 June 1913<br>Sent by E L Merle | Private address same as business | P15/G/3<br>*#1215*<br> | **Charles GOLLNER**<br>52 Queen's Road<br>Walthamstow | Briar pipe maker |
| Missing register<br>*c.*1886<br>Similar mark entered<br>LAO 10 January 1884 | | P5/G/65<br>*#1216*<br> | **Carl GLAZER** *<br>33 Poland Street<br>London W | Goldworker |
| R1/36<br>20 November 1896<br>Sent by Charles Green | Rockerley<br>Griffin Hill<br>Selly Oak<br>Birmingham | P5/G/803<br>*#1217*<br>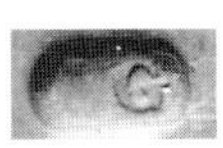 | **Charles GREEN**<br>**Charles Stevenson GREEN** trading as<br>**Charles GREEN & SON** *<br>48 Augusta Street<br>Birmingham | Manufacturing jewellers |

| REGISTRATION DETAILS | MAKER'S PRIVATE ADDRESS and DETAILS | PLATE and MARK DETAILS | MAKER/COMPANY and BUSINESS ADDRESS | MAKER'S TRADE |
|---|---|---|---|---|
| R3/82<br>6 December 1935<br>Sent by C Gaffin | Private address same as business | P15/G/60<br>***#1218***<br>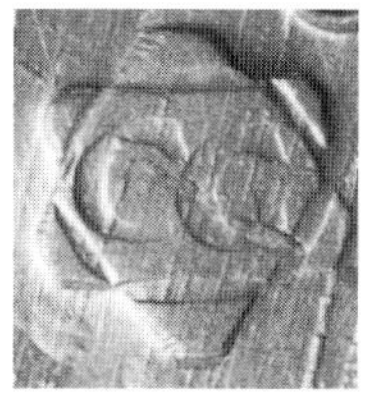 | **Charles GAFFIN**<br>10 Elizabeth Street<br>Cheetham<br>Manchester 8 | Student |
| R3/67<br>17 July 1933<br>Sent by C G Chatelain & Fils | Wildacre [1]<br>Lower Bourne<br>Farnham<br>Surrey<br>Eversleigh [2]<br>Bramley<br>Surrey | P15/K*sic*/220<br>***#1219***<br> | **C G CHATELAIN & FILS** *<br>Charles Gaston Chatelain [1] (Partner)<br>Cyril Chatelain [2] (Partner)<br>Diamond House<br>Hatton Garden<br>London EC | Watch importers |
| R1/179<br>15 November 1902<br>Sent by<br>C G Heaven | 32 Hamstead Road<br>Handsworth<br>Birmingham | P9/H/45[7] *sic*<br>***#1220***<br> | **Charles George HEAVEN** *<br>20 Vyse Street<br>Birmingham | Manufacturing jeweller |
| R2/34<br>8 March 1907<br>Sent by<br>C G Heaven | 112 Thornhill Road<br>Handsworth<br>Birmingham | P9/H/89,90<br>***#1221,2***<br> | | |
| R1/54<br>2 November 1897<br>Sent by C G Heaven | 32 Hamstead Road<br>Handsworth<br>Birmingham | P5/aboveD/906<br>***#1223***<br> | **Charles George HEAVEN** *<br>107 Vyse Street<br>Birmingham | |
| LPB/44<br>3 August 1883<br>No mark in LPB | CWMP 1886-83<br>1st name on LPB/44 and<br>1st mark on P5/J | P5/J/x1<br>***#1224***<br>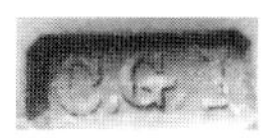 | **Charles George ILLIFFE** *<br>Percy House<br>Percy Street<br>Coventry | Watchcase maker |
| R2/61<br>6 June 1908<br>Sent by Charles Green & Son | Greenbank<br>Barat Avenue<br>Worcester<br>Bars Bush<br>Sutton Coldfield<br>Near Birmingham | P13/G/3<br>***#1225***<br> | **Lionel A GREEN**<br>**Roland GREEN** trading as<br>**Charles GREEN & SON** *<br>48 Augusta Street<br>Birmingham | Manufacturing jewellers |
| R3/48<br>14 September 1929<br>Sent by C Horner Ltd | 23 Seaview Park<br>Halifax | P15/H/107<br>***#1226***<br>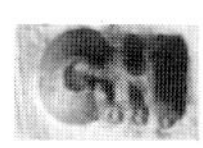 | **Charles HORNER LTD** *<br>Mile Cross<br>Halifax | Manufacturing jewellers |
| R2/151<br>2 March 1912<br>Sent by Charles Heath | Private address same as business | P13/H/82<br>***#1227***<br>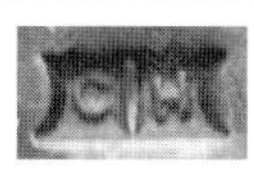 | **Charles HEATH**<br>1 Holyhead Road<br>Coventry | Jewellery and fancy goods |
| Not in R3 as expected<br>*c.* June 1921 | | P15/H/66<br>***#1228***<br>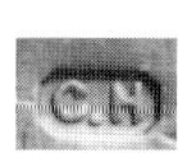 | **C HORNER LTD** * see below | |
| R3/113<br>11 March 1946<br>Sent by C Horner Ltd | 23 Seaview Park<br>Halifax | P21/H/29<br>***#1229***<br> | **Charles HORNER LTD** *<br>**Colin Stephen Horner** (Director)<br>Mile Cross<br>Halifax and<br>38 Frederick Street<br>Birmingham | Manufacturing jewellers |
| R3/113<br>3 March 1955 | | P21/H/73<br>***#1230***<br>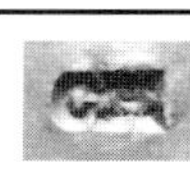 | | |
| Missing register<br>*c.*1890 | See other CH marks. This and the following mark located together on plate. | P5/H/299a<br>***#1231***<br> | **Unidentified** | |

| REGISTRATION DETAILS | MAKER'S PRIVATE ADDRESS and DETAILS | PLATE and MARK DETAILS | MAKER/COMPANY and BUSINESS ADDRESS | MAKER'S TRADE |
|---|---|---|---|---|
| Missing register<br>*c.*1890<br>Similar mark entered BAO 1903 | | P5/H/299b<br>***#1232***<br> | **Charles HORNER** *<br>21/23 Mortley Street<br>Halifax | Thimble maker, gold and silver jewellery |
| PP1/179<br>Not in SPB or LPB so struck 1860-3 | | P3/H/x3<br>***#1233-5***<br> | **Charles John HILL** *<br>1 Russell Terrace<br>Chapel Fields<br>Coventry | Watchmaker and watchcase maker |
| Missing register<br>*c.*1890<br>Similar mark entered CAO 24 July 1884 | See also Charles Harris below, similar mark entered BAO 8 September 1893 | P5/H/299<br>***#1236***<br> | **Charles HARROLD** *<br>2 and 3 St Paul's Square<br>Birmingham | Refiner |
| SPB/23<br>11 August 1869<br>Sent by Samuel & Rogers | CWMP 1883-1901 | P3/H/x3<br>***#1237-9***<br> | **Charles John HILL** *<br>1 Russell Terrace<br>Chapel Fields<br>Coventry | Watch and watchcase manufacturer |
| Not in LPB | This mark on P5/M is next to one for LPB/7 | P3/M*sic*/x2<br>***#1240,1***<br> | **Charles HARRIS** or<br>**Charles HILL** | |
| LPB/7<br>21 July 1878 CWMP 1886-1901 | Seen on pendant of silver case 1895/6 | P3/M*sic*/x2<br>***#1242,3***<br> | **Charles HARRIS** *<br>6 Norfolk Street<br>Coventry | Watchcase maker |
| LPB/40<br>2 December 1884<br>No mark in LPB<br>MR3/120 | This is the only CH on P5 without a number alongside. Could be any of the other CH attributions. | P5/H/x1<br>***#1244***<br> | **Charles HORNER** *<br>21/23 Mortley Street<br>Halifax | Thimble maker, gold and silver jewellery |
| R1/83<br>9 November 1898<br>Sent by Charles Harold & Co | 2 Finchley Road [1], Lozells, Handsworth, Staffordshire<br>Claremont [2]<br>28 Holyhead Road, Handsworth, Staffordshire<br>Brooklands [3]<br>Manor Road, Sutton Coldfield, Warwickshire | P9/H/4<br>***#1245***<br> | **Charles WESTWOOD** [1]<br>**Alfred Henry WESTWOOD** [2]<br>**Francis Herbert WESTWOOD** [3]<br>trading as **Charles HARROLD & CO** *<br>2 and 3 St Paul's Square<br>Birmingham | Bullion dealers |
| R1/204<br>3 December 1903<br>Sent by C Horner | Green Hayes<br>Halifax<br>Savile Crescent<br>Halifax | P9/H/55<br>***#1246***<br> | **James Dobson HORNER**<br>**Charles Henry HORNER** trading as<br>**C HORNER** *<br>23 Northgate<br>Halifax | Manufacturing jewellers |
| R2/101<br>1 January 1910<br>Sent by Charles Horner Ltd | Green Hayes<br>Halifax<br>11 Eversley Place<br>Halifax | No new mark entered<br>***#1247*** | **Charles HORNER LTD** *<br>James Dobson Horner (Director)<br>Arthur Halliday (Secretary)<br>Mile Cross<br>Halifax and<br>38 Frederick Street<br>Birmingham | |
| R3/23<br>31 June 1924<br>Sent by C Horner Ltd | 23 Seaview Park<br>Halifax | P15/H/80<br>***#1248***<br> | **Charles HORNER LTD** *<br>**Colin Stephen Horner** (Director)<br>Mile Cross<br>Halifax and<br>38 Frederick Street<br>Birmingham | |
| 1 March 1946 | | P21/H/25<br>***#1249***<br>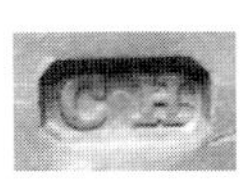 | | |

| REGISTRATION DETAILS | MAKER'S PRIVATE ADDRESS and DETAILS | PLATE and MARK DETAILS | MAKER/COMPANY and BUSINESS ADDRESS | MAKER'S TRADE |
|---|---|---|---|---|
| R3/23<br>15 March 1946<br>Sent by C Horner Ltd | 23 Seaview Park<br>Halifax | P21/H/26<br>***#1250***<br> | **Charles HORNER LTD** *<br>**Colin Stephen Horner** (Director)<br>Mile Cross<br>Halifax and<br>38 Frederick Street<br>Birmingham | Manufacturing jewellers |
| R3/113<br>11 March 1946<br>Sent by C Horner Ltd | 23 Seaview Park<br>Halifax | P21/H/27<br>***#1251***<br> | | |
| | | P21/H/28<br>***#1252***<br> | | |
| Missing register<br>*c.*1888<br>Similar mark entered<br>BAO 9 January 1889 | | P5/C/168<br>***#1253***<br>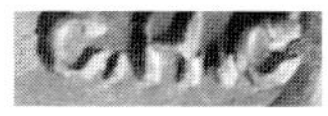 | **Charles Howard COLLINS**<br>146 Hockley Hill<br>Birmingham | Stud and link manufacturer |
| Similar mark entered<br>CAO 9 June 1899 | | P5/C/x1<br>***#1254***<br> | | |
| R1/103<br>9 June 1899<br>Sent by C H Collins | Osborn House<br>Hall Road<br>Handsworth<br>Birmingham | P9/C/24<br>***#1255***<br> | **Charles Howard COLLINS**<br>48 Hockley Hill<br>Birmingham | |
| R1/220<br>14 September 1904<br>Sent by C E Collins | Laurel Mount<br>Four Oaks<br>Warwickshire | P9/D*sic*/213,214<br>***#1256,7***<br> | **Charles Howard COLLINS**<br>**Charles Ernest COLLINS**<br>**George D COLLINS** trading as<br>**C H COLLINS & SONS**<br>48 Hockley Hill<br>Birmingham | |
| R2/151<br>28 February 1912<br>Sent by C E Collins | Ladywood Four Oaks<br>Sutton Coldfield<br>Wynstead Four Oaks<br>Sutton Coldfield<br>Fairlock, Purses Lane<br>Four Oaks<br>Sutton Coldfield | P13/D*sic*/148<br>***#1258***<br> | **Charles Howard COLLINS**<br>**Charles Ernest COLLINS**<br>**George Dawson COLLINS** trading as<br>**C H COLLINS & SON**<br>47 and 48 Hockley Hill<br>Birmingham | Manufacturing jewellers |
| Not in R3 as expected<br>Between January and<br>July 1922 | | P15/C/107<br>***#1259***<br> | **C H COLLINS & SON** | |
| R1/87<br>24 December 1898<br>Sent by J Moore<br>Errington Watch Co | Alleseley Old Road<br>Coventry | P9/E/1<br>***#1260***<br> | **Charles Huton ERRINGTON** *<br>2 Holyhead Road (1883)<br>Spon Street (1886)<br>Coventry | Engraver and watch, dial, and watchcase manufacturer |
| Missing register<br>*c.*1887 | CWMP 1883-86 | P5/E/73<br>***#1261***<br> | | |
| Missing register<br>*c.*1889 | | P5/E/264<br>***#1262***<br> | | |
| LPB/30<br>24 July 1880<br>LPB mark shown<br>Sent by Brockington<br>Brothers | | Not on P3<br>***#1263***<br> | **Charles H FERGUSON**<br>(**FARQUHARSON** in trade directory)<br>26 Low Terrace<br>Leith Street<br>Edinburgh | Working jeweller and watch maker |

| REGISTRATION DETAILS | MAKER'S PRIVATE ADDRESS and DETAILS | PLATE and MARK DETAILS | MAKER/COMPANY and BUSINESS ADDRESS | MAKER'S TRADE |
|---|---|---|---|---|
| R3/5<br>26 November 1921<br>Sent by C P Humpidge | Private address same as business | P15/H/68<br>***#1264***<br> | **Chauncey HUMPIDGE LTD**<br>C P Humpidge (Director)<br>54 Frederick Street<br>Birmingham | Manufacturing goldsmiths and silversmiths |
| | | P15/H/69<br>***#1265***<br> | | |
| R3/116<br>26 November 1946<br>Sent by C H Lander | Private address same as business | P21/L/22<br>***#1266***<br> | **Charles Herbert LANDER**<br>85 Bernards Road<br>Olton<br>Birmingham 27 | Jeweller and stone dealer |
| R2/201<br>13 November 1915<br>BAO 22.791,22.792<br>Sent by C H Powell | 11 Aylesford Road<br>Handsworth<br>Birmingham | P15/P/72,73<br>***#1267,8***<br> | **Charles Henry POWELL**<br>126 Branston Street<br>Birmingham | Gold ring maker |
| R3/47<br>25 June 1929<br>Sent by selves | Tudor Lodge<br>Llandudno | P15/W/92<br>***#1269***<br> | **Henry WARTSKI** (Partner)<br>**C H WARTSKI** (Partner) trading as<br>**C H WARTSKI**<br>31/33 Mostyn Street<br>Llandudno and<br>5 Quadrant Arcade<br>80 Regent Street<br>London | Jewellers, silversmiths and art dealers |
| R3/160<br>14 February 1957<br>Sent by<br>C H Warburton<br>Two sizes | Greylands<br>Hawkshaw<br>Nr Bury<br>Lancashire | P21/W/82,83<br>***#1270,1***<br> | **Cynthia Hazel WARBURTON**<br>No business address entered | Student |
| SPB/9 undated<br>November 1865 to<br>February 1866 | | P3/W/x3<br>***#1272-4***<br> | **C H WHITE and**<br>**F H HAWKINS**<br>95 Albion Street and<br>16 Legge Lane<br>Birmingham | Silversmiths |
| Not in R1 as expected - dated<br>20 October 1900 to<br>13 February 1901 | Could be read as GJ ? for George Jackson | P9/J/31<br>***#1275***<br>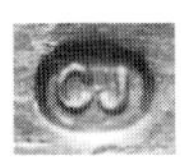 | **Leonard George JACKSON** | |
| R1/108<br>3 August 1899<br>Sent by L G Jackson | 4 Stanley Terrace<br>Coventry<br>Could be read as GJ ? for George Jackson | P9/J/19<br>***#1276***<br> | **Leonard George JACKSON**<br>4 Stanley Terrace<br>Coventry | Gold watch pendant maker |
| PDB 1825-31<br>MR2/91<br>MR3/88<br>PP1/186<br>Similar marks entered BAO 27 May 1834,<br>2 December 1836 and<br>5 January 1839<br>GTD 1843-59<br>PMR 1834-71 | Gold rings, snuff box and castor tops | P1/21/x1<br>***#1277***<br> | **Christopher JONES** *<br>13 Highfield Street (1834-7)<br>15 Highfield Street (1839-51)<br>Garston Shop (1853-58)<br>5 Highfield Street<br>Liverpool | Goldsmith, silversmith and watchcase maker |
| | Square is marked 1786 | P1/22/x1<br>***#1278***<br> | | |
| | | P1/26/x4<br>***#1279-82***<br> | | |
| | | P1/31/x9<br>***#1283-91***<br> | | |
| | | P2/J/x2<br>***#1292,3***<br>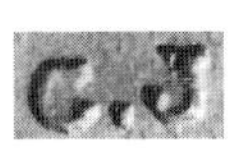 | | |

| REGISTRATION DETAILS | MAKER'S PRIVATE ADDRESS and DETAILS | PLATE and MARK DETAILS | MAKER/COMPANY and BUSINESS ADDRESS | MAKER'S TRADE |
|---|---|---|---|---|
| GTD 1843-59<br>PMR 1834-71 | | P2/J/x2<br>***#1294,5***<br> | **Christopher JONES**<br>5 Highfield Street<br>Liverpool | Goldsmith, silversmith and watchcase maker |
| | | P2/J/x3<br>***#1296-8***<br> | | |
| Similar mark entered LAO 16 February 1846 | | P2/J/x3<br>***#1299-1301***<br>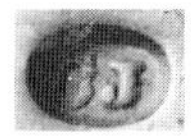 | | |
| | | P2/J/x2<br>***#1302,3***<br>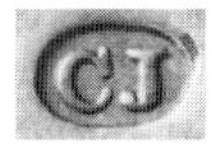 | | |
| R1/54<br>19 November 1897<br>Sent by C J Fox | The Laurels<br>Park Avenue<br>Wood Green<br>London | P5/F/907<br>***#1304***<br>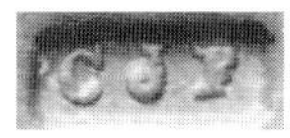 | **Charles James FOX** trading as<br>**C J FOX & CO** *<br>21, 22 Great Sutton<br>Clerkenwell, London EC1 | Silversmiths |
| R1/132<br>25 September 1900<br>Sent by C J Fox | 16 Park Terrace<br>Wood Green<br>London W | P9/F/7,8<br>***#1305,6***<br> | **Charles James FOX** (Director)<br>**Charles FOX & CO LTD** *<br>17, 18 Great Sutton Street<br>Clerkenwell<br>London EC1 | Manufacturing jewellers and silversmiths |
| R2/199<br>13 September 1915<br>Sent by<br>W Oakley Davies | 48 Parade<br>Sutton Coldfield | P15/H/25<br>***#1307***<br> | **Charles James HARMER**<br>125 Vyse Street<br>Birmingham | Manufacturing jeweller |
| R1/26<br>23 March 1896<br>Sent by C J H Marlow | 16 King Street<br>Coventry<br>CWMP 1874-1901 | P5/M/751<br>***#1308***<br> | **Charles J H MARLOW**<br>Croft House (1874)<br>Spon Street<br>15 King Street (1886-1901)<br>Coventry | Watch and watchcase manufacturer |
| R1/111<br>12 September 1899<br>Sent by W Walker<br>Two sizes | 35 Mayflower Road<br>Clapham<br>5 Alexander Road<br>Hornsey<br>3 Chatsworth Road<br>Brondesbury<br>London | P9/C*sic*/27,28<br>***#1309,10***<br> | **Joseph Crabb KERSHAW** *<br>**Frederick Francis KERSHAW**<br>**Sidney Herbert JONES**<br>(Ed: possibly trading as **COULSHAW, JONES & KERSHAW** *)<br>72 Newman Street<br>London W | Wholesale tobacconists and sundries manufacturers |
| LPB/68<br>4 January 1883 | BAO has 42 Vyse Street in 1882 | P3/P/x1<br>***#1311***<br> | **Charles John PERKS**<br>26 Vyse Street<br>Birmingham | Jeweller |
| R1/51<br>25 September 1897<br>Sent by J Gammage | 123 Camden Road<br>London NW | P5/P/872<br>***#1312***<br> | **Charles John PLUCKNETT** *<br>29 Poland Street<br>London | Jeweller |
| Not in R1 as expected<br>Similar mark entered CAO 24 November 1899 | CWMP 1886-1901 | P5/R/0*sic*,100<br>***#1313,4***<br> | **Charles James RICHARDSON**<br>Cornwall House<br>Carman Road<br>Coventry | Watch manufacturer |
| R1/116<br>24 November 1899<br>Sent by R J Pike<br>J Harris<br>J McKnight<br>T R Arnott<br>C J Richardson<br>F Wright<br>E W Linnett<br>Benson Brothers | Private address same as business | P9/R/10<br>***#1315***<br> | **Charles James RICHARDSON**<br>Cornwall House<br>Carman Road<br>Coventry | |

| REGISTRATION DETAILS | MAKER'S PRIVATE ADDRESS and DETAILS | PLATE and MARK DETAILS | MAKER/COMPANY and BUSINESS ADDRESS | MAKER'S TRADE |
|---|---|---|---|---|
| R2/212<br>11 July 1917<br>Sent by Chas J Wigley | Lonsdale<br>45 Douglas Road<br>Handsworth, Birmingham | P15/W/34,35<br>***#1316,7***<br> | **Charles J WIGLEY**<br>Late Wigley & Hall<br>87 Vyse Street<br>Birmingham | Jeweller and silversmith |
| R3/69<br>10 November 1933<br>Sent by L Wigley | 14 Welford Road<br>Sutton Coldfield | P15/W/105<br>***#1318***<br> | **Leslie WIGLEY** trading as<br>**Charles J WIGLEY & SON**<br>87 Vyse Street<br>Birmingham | Manufacturing jewellers and silversmiths |
| GTD 1829-49 P1/191<br>Seen on 1828/9 watchcase | Square marked 1785 | P1/21/x1<br>***#1319***<br>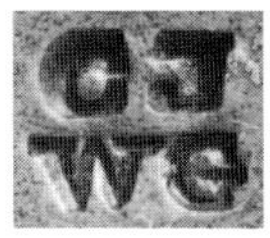 | **Christopher JONES** *<br>**William GRIFFITHS**<br>Liverpool | Watchcase makers |
| R1/237<br>27 July 1905<br>Sent by C Kirkham | 9 Baker Street<br>Lloyd Square<br>London EC | P9/K/39<br>***#1320***<br> | **Charles KIRKHAM** *<br>35 Hatton Garden<br>London EC | Manufacturing jewellers |
| Missing register<br>*c.*1892<br>Cameo C&K mark entered LAO 7 July 1902 | | P5/C/432<br>***#1321***<br>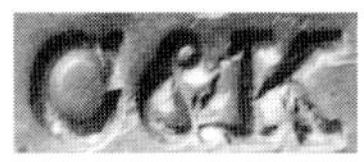 | **COOKE & KELVEY** *<br>20 Old Court House Street<br>Calcutta and<br>150 Leadenhall Street<br>London EC | Silver plate merchants |
| R2/226<br>12 January 1920<br>Sent by Charnell & Line | Jordan Road<br>Four Oaks<br>391 City Road<br>Birmingham | P15/C/75<br>***#1322***<br> | **Walter James CHARNELL**<br>**Arthur James LINE** trading as<br>**CHARNELL & LINE**<br>44 Frederick Street<br>Birmingham | Manufacturing jewellers |
| R1/213<br>27 April 1904<br>Sent by E J Trevitt & Son | 24 Mulgrave Street<br>Liverpool | P9/L/59<br>***#1323***<br> | **Constant Francis LATAICHE**<br>6 Clayton Square<br>17 and 21 Parker Street<br>19 London Road<br>Liverpool | Jeweller |
| LPB/50<br>1 April 1880 | 1881 census has Charles Lucas senior and junior as jewellers at 46 Summer Lane, Birmingham which may be home address | P3/L/x2<br>***#1324,5***<br> | **Charles LUCAS** *<br>29 Mary Street<br>Caroline Street<br>Birmingham | Ring maker |
| R2/117<br>19 August 1910<br>Sent by C Lucas | 110 Birchfield Road<br>Handsworth<br>Birmingham | P13/L/44<br>***#1326***<br> | **Charles LUCAS** *<br>115 Spencer Street<br>Birmingham | Signet and fancy ring maker |
| R2/102<br>29 January 1910<br>Sent by<br>C M Landenberger | 2 Downside Crescent<br>Hampstead<br>London NW | P13/L/33<br>***#1327***<br>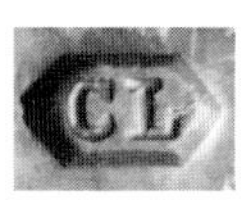 | **Christian Martin LANDENBERGER**<br>trading as<br>**LANDENBERGER & CO** *<br>91 Aldergate Street<br>London EC | Merchants and importers |
| R3/1<br>14 April 1921<br>Sent by C Lacy | 150 South Road<br>Erdington | P15/L/23<br>***#1328***<br> | **Charles LACY**<br>38 Vyse Street<br>Birmingham | Wholesale jeweller |
| R3/39<br>10 December 1927<br>Sent by selves | 11 Soho Avenue [1]<br>Handsworth<br>4 Mayfair Gardens [2]<br>Edmonton, Essex<br>Jersey Road [3]<br>Osterley<br>Middlesex<br>70 Leadenhall Street [4]<br>London | P15/C/182<br>***#1329***<br> | **Ernest LEESON** [1]<br>**Claude Ernest COLLINS** [2]<br>**Henry Herbert BEACH** [3]<br>**Herbert Henry TAYLOR** [4] trading as<br>**COLLINS & LEESON LTD** *<br>110 Vyse Street<br>Birmingham | Manufacturing jewellers |

| REGISTRATION DETAILS | MAKER'S PRIVATE ADDRESS and DETAILS | PLATE and MARK DETAILS | MAKER/COMPANY and BUSINESS ADDRESS | MAKER'S TRADE |
|---|---|---|---|---|
| R3/174<br>7 October 1960<br>Sent by<br>C L Nicholson | Tree Tops<br>25 Fieldside<br>Hawarden<br>Chester | P21/N/11<br>***#1330***<br> | **Cuthbert Laws NICHOLSON**<br>No business address entered | Silversmith |
| R3/164<br>24 June 1958<br>Previous punches cancelled<br>Sent by C Lucas & Son | 15 Crown Lane[1]<br>Four Oaks, Sutton Coldfield<br>White Swan Hotel [2]<br>Henley-in-Arden<br>81 Station Road [3]<br>Sutton Coldfield | P21/L/37<br>***#1331***<br> | **Bertram Charles Busby LUCAS** [1]<br>**Charles Walter LUCAS** [2]<br>**Norman LUCAS** [3] trading as<br>**Charles LUCAS & SON** *<br>111 Vyse Street<br>Birmingham 18 | Manufacturing jewellers |
| 29 April 1959<br>Two sizes | | P21/L/39,41<br>***#1332,3***<br> | | |
| 7 July 1959 | | P21/L/42,43<br>***#1334,5***<br> | | |
| 30 December 1959 | | P21/L/44,45<br>***#1336,7***<br> | | |
| 6 April 1960 | | P21/L/46<br>***#1338***<br> | | |
| 25 December 1960 | | P21/L/49-52<br>***#1339-42***<br> | | |
| 18 October 1961 | | P21/L/54<br>***#1343***<br>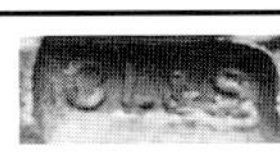 | | |
| 6 January 1962 | | P21/L/55<br>***#1344***<br> | | |
| 29 April 1959 | | P21/L/40<br>***#1345***<br>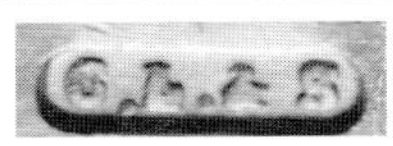 | | |
| R3/68<br>19 August 1933<br>Sent by C L Lucas & Co | 110 Birchfield Road [1]<br>Handsworth<br>Lyndhurst [2]<br>Hunton Hill<br>Erdington<br>110 Birchfield Road [3]<br>Handsworth<br>Birmingham | P15/L/42<br>***#1346***<br>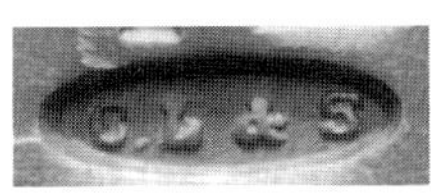 | **Charles LUCAS & CO** *<br>Charles Lucas [1] (Partner)<br>Bertram Charles Lucas [2] (Partner)<br>Charles Walter Lucas [3] (Partner)<br>115 Spencer Street<br>Hockley<br>Birmingham | Manufacturing ring makers |
| R1/100<br>11 May 1899<br>Sent by Samuel Lyster | 20 Stamford Road<br>Handsworth<br>Birmingham | P9/L/9<br>***#1347***<br> | **Samuel LYSTER** trading as<br>**Charles LYSTER & SON**<br>28 Spencer Street<br>Birmingham | Silversmiths |
| R3/74<br>10 January 1935<br>Sent by<br>T J Skelton<br>86 Vyse Street<br>Birmingham | Private address same as business | P15/K*sic*/222,223<br>***#1348,9***<br>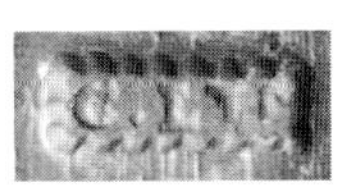 | **COLBOURNE LTD**<br>F Colbourne (Chairman)<br>T F Colbourne (Secretary)<br>15 Fore Street<br>Trowbridge<br>Wiltshire | Jewellers and silversmiths |
| R3/84<br>22 June 1936<br>Sent by<br>T J Skelton<br>86 Vyse Street<br>Birmingham | 77 Clarendon Avenue<br>Trowbridge<br>Wiltshire | P21/C/1<br>***#1350***<br> | **COLBOURNE LTD**<br>T F Colbourne<br>15 Fore Street<br>Trowbridge<br>Wiltshire | Jewellers |

| REGISTRATION DETAILS | MAKER'S PRIVATE ADDRESS and DETAILS | PLATE and MARK DETAILS | MAKER/COMPANY and BUSINESS ADDRESS | MAKER'S TRADE |
|---|---|---|---|---|
| R3/93<br>1 February 1939<br>Sent by<br>T J Skelton<br>86 Vyse Street<br>Birmingham | Both residing at<br>77 Clarendon Avenue<br>Trowbridge<br>Wiltshire | P21/C/9-11<br>***#1351-53***<br>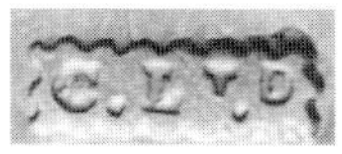 | **COLBOURNE LTD**<br>Thomas Colbourne (Director)<br>Thomas Frank Colbourne (Director and Secretary)<br>15 Fore Street<br>Trowbridge<br>Wiltshire | Jewellers and silversmiths |
| R3/114<br>22 March 1946<br>Sent by Callaways Ltd | | P21/C/29<br>***#1354***<br>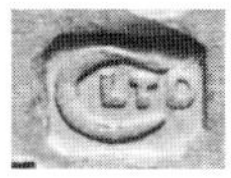 | **CALLAWAYS LTD**<br>Sealed in the presence of:-<br>Isa Crawshay (Director)<br>K J Mercer (Director)<br>Julia M Masters (Director Secretary)<br>23 High Street (Registered Office)<br>Hitchin<br>Herts | Manufacturing jewellers and silversmiths |
| 9 April 1946<br>Two sizes | | P21/C/30,31<br>***#1355,6***<br> | | |
| 18 November 1947 | | P21/C/41,42<br>***#1357,8***<br> | | |
| 28 January 1948 | | P21/C/44,45<br>***#1359,60***<br> | | |
| Missing register<br>*c.*1887<br>Similar mark LAO<br>16 June 1893 and 19 November 1888 | | P5/*Csic*/88<br>***#1361***<br>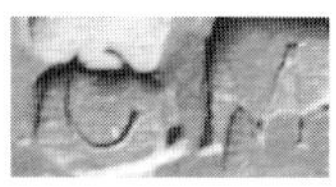 | **Charles MAAS & CO** *<br>13 Crescent Street<br>London EC | Pipe manufacturers and tobacconists |
| R2/160<br>21 August 1912<br>Sent by Charles Maas & Co | 182 Watson Lane<br>Cricklewood<br>London N W | P13/M/52<br>***#1362***<br> | **Charles MAAS** trading as<br>**Charles MAAS & CO** *<br>1a Aldermanbury Avenue<br>London | Tobacco and pipe merchants |
| R2/178<br>24 October 1913<br>Sent by Charles Maas & Co | | P13/M/61<br>***#1363***<br> | **Charles Leopold MAAS** trading as<br>**Charles MAAS & CO** *<br>Marcus Maas (Manager)<br>1a Aldermanbury<br>London E C | Tobacco pipe manufacturers and dealers |
| R2/196<br>15 May 1915<br>Sent by Edgar L Merle | Private address same as business | P15/M/16<br>***#1364***<br> | **Charles Leopold MAAS** (Governing Director) trading as<br>**Charles MAAS & CO** *<br>1 Aldermanbury Avenue<br>London E C | |
| R2/137<br>2 June 1911<br>Sent by Imperial Tobacco Co | Private address same as business | P13/M/42,43<br>***#1365,6***<br> | **Charles MARLOW**<br>3 Harbord Street<br>Fulham<br>London SW | Fancy goods dealer |
| R2/184<br>13 March 1914<br>Sent by Imperial Tobacco Co | | P15/M/8<br>***#1367***<br> | **Charles MARLOW**<br>406 Fulham Palace Road<br>Fulham<br>London SW | |

| REGISTRATION DETAILS | MAKER'S PRIVATE ADDRESS and DETAILS | PLATE and MARK DETAILS | MAKER/COMPANY and BUSINESS ADDRESS | MAKER'S TRADE |
|---|---|---|---|---|
| Missing register<br>*c.*1890<br>Similar mark entered<br>LAO 12 August 1890 | | P5/M/324<br>***#1368***<br>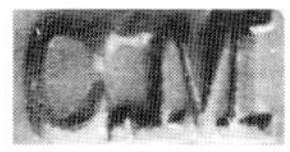  | **Charles MAAS & CO** *<br>13 Crescent Street<br>London EC | Pipe manufacturers and tobacconists |
| R2/128<br>23 February 1911<br>Sent by C Mason | The Nest<br>Moor End Lane<br>Erdington | P13/M/40<br>***#1369***<br> | **Claud MASON**<br>114 Warstone Lane<br>Birmingham | Goldsmith and jewellers |
| LPB/22<br>24 August 1883<br>No mark in LPB<br>Similar mark entered<br>BAO 1875 | | P5/C/x1<br>***#1370***<br>  | **CROZIER & MARTIN**<br>12 Brook Street<br>St Paul's Square<br>Birmingham | Watch manufacturers |
| R3/146<br>31 July 1953<br>Sent by<br>C McDonald<br>Two sizes | 28 Clayton Avenue<br>Wigshaw Lane<br>Culcheth<br>Nr Warrington | P21/D/33,34<br>***#1371,2***<br>  | **Catherine MACDONALD**<br>No business address entered | Student |
| R3/19<br>31 Novcmber 1923<br>Sent by<br>J E Weetman | 10 Onston Drive<br>Glasgow | P15/C*sic*/120<br>***#1373***<br>  | **Charles Cumming MACDONALD**<br>354 Duke Street<br>Glasgow and<br>20 Vyse Street<br>Birmingham | Wholesale jeweller and stone dealer |
| R1/202<br>23 October 1903<br>Sent by F Pickering | 7 Woodbine Street<br>88 Horton Lane<br>8 Barlow Street<br>Sheffield | P9/M/69<br>***#1374***<br>  | **Charles MICHAEL**<br>**George William PICKERING**<br>**Fred PICKERING** trading as<br>**C MICHAEL & CO**<br>7 Woodbine Street<br>Barkerend Road<br>Sheffield | Walking stick and umbrella manufacturers |
| R2/141<br>26 August 1911<br>Sent by J & R Griffin Ltd | 354 Duke Street<br>Glasgow | P13/M/46<br>***#1375***<br>  | **Charles Cumming MACDONALD**<br>trading as<br>**CUMMING MACDONALD LTD**<br>252 Duke Street<br>Glasgow and<br>20 Vyse Street<br>Birmingham | Wholesale jewellers |
| R2/103<br>16 February 1910<br>Sent by M Maas<br>Cancelled<br>21 August 1912 | 182 Watson Lane<br>Cricklewood<br>London NW<br>33 Hampstead Hill Gardens<br>London NW | P13/M/35<br>***#1376***<br>  | **Charles Leopold MAAS** trading as<br>**Charles MAAS & CO** *<br>Marcus Maas (Manager)<br>13 Jewin Crescent<br>London EC | Tobacco pipe manufacturers and dealers |
| R2/22<br>8 August 1906<br>Sent by J Reid | 9 Brook Street<br>Liverpool | P9/D*sic*/232<br>***#1377***<br>  | **James REID** trading as<br>**CROWN MOUNTING REPAIRING CO**<br>54 Cable Street<br>off Paradise Street<br>Liverpool | Pipe and stick mounters |
| Not in R3 as expected<br>*c.* Jan. to Sept. 1925<br>Similar marks entered<br>BAO 1880 to 1925 | | P15/W/78<br>***#1378***<br>  | **C M WRIGHTON ?**<br>127 Vyse Street<br>Birmingham | Jeweller |
| Missing register<br>*c.*1888 | | P5/W/164a<br>***#1379***<br>  | | |
| Missing register<br>*c.*1888 | | P5/W/164b<br>***#1380***<br> | | |

| REGISTRATION DETAILS | MAKER'S PRIVATE ADDRESS and DETAILS | PLATE and MARK DETAILS | MAKER/COMPANY and BUSINESS ADDRESS | MAKER'S TRADE |
|---|---|---|---|---|
| Missing register<br>*c.*1888 | | P5/W/176<br>***#1381***  | **C M WRIGHTON**<br>127 Vyse Street<br>Birmingham | Jeweller |
| Missing register<br>*c.*1887 | | P5/X*sic*/122<br>***#1382***  | | |
| R1/230<br>21 March 1905<br>Sent by self<br>Two sizes | Radnor Road<br>Handsworth | P9/V*sic*/125,126<br>***#1383,4***  | | |
| Missing register<br>*c.*1887 | | P5/W/122<br>***#1385***  | | |
| R1/230<br>21 March 1905<br>Sent by self | Radnor Road<br>Handsworth | P5/*Vsic*/124<br>***#1386***  | | |
| R2/128<br>11 February 1911<br>Sent by Charles Wrighton<br>P13/W/86 also used for EW&S | 31 Radnor Road<br>Handsworth<br>16 Wye Cliff Road<br>Handsworth | P13/W/86<br>***#1387***  | **Charles WRIGHTON**<br>**Frank WRIGHTON** (Director) of<br>**C M WRIGHTON LTD**<br>127 Vyse Street<br>Birmingham | Jewellers |
| R2/30<br>13 December 1906<br>Sent by C Nicholet | Glenhurst<br>Burbage Road<br>Herne Hill<br>London SE | P9/N/38,39<br>***#1388,8a***  | **Charles NICHOLET** trading as<br>**STAUFFER, SON & CO** *<br>13 Charterhouse Street<br>Holborn<br>London | Watch importers and manufacturers |
| LPB/58<br>27 October 1880<br>Sent by William Neale | | P3/I*sic*/x1<br>***#1389*** 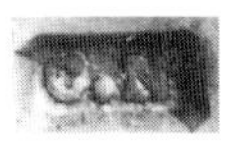 | **Charles NEVILL**<br>5 Upper Hockley Street<br>Birmingham | Jeweller |
| R1/89<br>2 February 1899<br>Sent by J Hayward | 6 Rotten Park Road<br>Birmingham<br>118 Brondesbury Villas<br>Kilburn, London | P9/C/7<br>***#1390***  | **Arthur Edward COHEN**<br>**Lionel COHEN** trading as<br>**COHEN BROTHERS** *<br>67 Vyse Street | Jewellers |
| R1/90<br>4 February 1890<br>Sent by W F Twine<br>C G Heaven | | P9/C/8<br>***#1391***  | Birmingham and<br>108 Hatton Garden<br>London | |
| R1/19<br>7 November 1895<br>Sent by C N Heeley | 57 Ravenhurst Road<br>Harborne<br>Birmingham | P5/H/713<br>***#1392***  | **Charles Norman HEELEY**<br>53 Northampton Street<br>Birmingham | Manufacturing jeweller |
| MR1/131 | Working *c.*1701<br>Jug mounts | P1/9/x1<br>***#1393*** 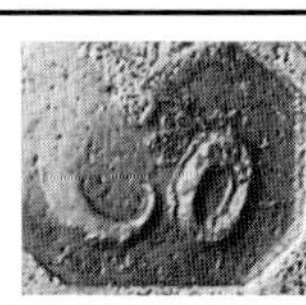 | **R COOPER**<br>Warrington | Silversmith |
| | | P1/9/x1<br>***#1394*** 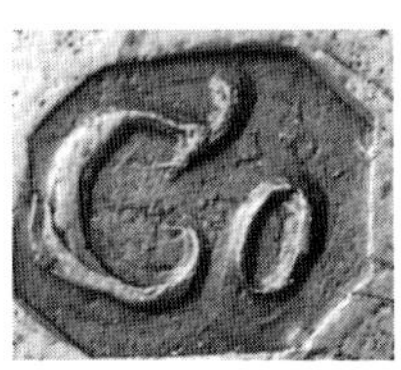 | | |
| Not in R2 as expected<br>*c.* June 1920 to September 1920 | See following entry | P15/P/159<br>***#1395*** 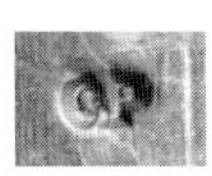 | **Charles PEACH ?**<br>30 Augusta Street<br>Birmingham | Jewellers |

| REGISTRATION DETAILS | MAKER'S PRIVATE ADDRESS and DETAILS | PLATE and MARK DETAILS | MAKER/COMPANY and BUSINESS ADDRESS | MAKER'S TRADE |
|---|---|---|---|---|
| R2/90<br>30 July 1909<br>Sent by C Peach | Lismore<br>Silverbirch Road<br>Erdington<br>Westray<br>Chester Road, Erdington | P13/P/103-106<br>***#1396-9*** 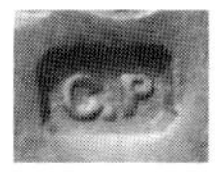 | **Charles PEACH**<br>**Aubrey Charles PEACH** trading as<br>**Charles PEACH & SON**<br>30 Augusta Street<br>Birmingham | Jewellers |
| R2/159<br>25 July 1912<br>BAO 20.344<br>Sent by C Peach & Sons | Westray<br>Chester Road<br>Erdington<br>Birmingham | P13/Q*sic*/211<br>***#1400***  | **Aubrey Charles PEACH** trading as<br>**C PEACH & SONS**<br>20 and 30 Augusta Street<br>Birmingham | |
| PDB 1815-16<br>MR3/79 | Gold rings and jug mounts | P1/32/x1<br>***#1401***  | **COMPTON & PARRY**<br>Liverpool | Goldsmiths |
| Missing register<br>*c.*1891 | | P5/P/375<br>***#1402***  | **Unidentified** | |
| R2/90<br>30 July 1909<br>Sent by C Peach | Lismore<br>Silverbirch Road<br>Erdington<br>Westray<br>Chester Road<br>Erdington | P13/P/99-102<br>***#1403-6***  | **Charles PEACH**<br>**Aubrey Charles PEACH** trading as<br>**Charles PEACH & SON**<br>30 Augusta Street<br>Birmingham | Jewellers |
| R2/173<br>6 June 1913<br>Sent by C Powell | 25 Headingley Road<br>Handsworth<br>197 Holey Road<br>Handsworth<br>Birmingham | P15/P/55,56<br>***#1407,8*** 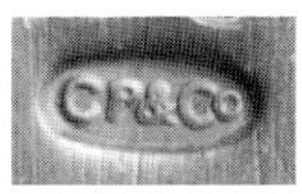 | **Charles POWELL**<br>**Thomas LORTON** trading as<br>**C POWELL & CO**<br>126 Branston Street<br>Birmingham | Gem and signet ring manufacturers |
| Not in R2 as expected<br>Two sizes | | P15/P/185,186<br>***#1409,10***  | **C PERRY & CO** | |
| R2/145<br>14 October 1911<br>BAO 19.423,19.424<br>Sent by C Perry | Wentworth Road [1]<br>Four Oaks<br>32 Oxford Road [2]<br>Acocks Green, Birmingham | P13/Q*sic*/208,209<br>***#1411,2***  | **William Arthur PERRY** [1]<br>**Annie Louse PERRY** [1]<br>**Christopher PERRY** [2] trading as<br>**C PERRY & CO**<br>259 Icknield Street<br>Birmingham | Jewellers and silversmiths |
| 12 May 1928 | | P15/P/209<br>***#1413***  | | |
| 15 May 1928 | | P15/P/210<br>***#1414***  | | |
| R3/43<br>5 September 1928<br>Two sizes<br>Sent by C Perry & Co | Wentworth Road [1]<br>Four Oaks<br>32 Oxford Road [2] | P15/P/214-217<br>***#1415-8***  | **William Arthur PERRY** [1]<br>**Annie Louise PERRY** [1]<br>**Christopher PERRY** [2] trading as<br>**C PERRY & CO**<br>259 Icknield Street<br>Birmingham | |
| 1 June 1929<br>Two sizes | Acocks Green<br>Birmingham | P15/P/218,219<br>***#1419,20***  | | |
| R1/96<br>25 March 1899<br>Sent by C P Deykin | Roslyn<br>Littleton Road<br>Edgbaston<br>Birmingham | P9/D/8<br>***#1421***  | **Charles Pemberton DEYKIN**<br>37 Warstone Lane<br>Birmingham | Ring maker and diamond mounter |
| R3/25<br>5 December 1924<br>Sent by Parsons Ltd | 107 Poplar Road<br>Smethwick | P15/R/33<br>***#1422***  | **Charles Percy REEVES**<br>37 Warstone Lane<br>Birmingham | Manufacturing jeweller |

| REGISTRATION DETAILS | MAKER'S PRIVATE ADDRESS and DETAILS | PLATE and MARK DETAILS | MAKER/COMPANY and BUSINESS ADDRESS | MAKER'S TRADE |
|---|---|---|---|---|
| R3/84<br>8 May 1936<br>Sent by CPS Jewellery Co | 17 Oakham Road [1]<br>Birmingham<br>32 Wynn Street [2]<br>Birmingham | P15/S/105<br>***#1423***<br> | **C P S JEWELLERY CO**<br>Ralph Victor Hippisley Cox [1]<br>Pesach Zwagelski [2]<br>110 Vyse Street<br>Birmingham | Mounters and ring makers |
| Missing register<br>*c.*1889 | See CR below | P5/R/235<br>***#1424***<br> | **Unidentified** | |
| Missing register<br>*c.*1890 | | P5/R/325<br>***#1425***<br> | **Unidentified** | |
| LPB/74<br>10 August 1883<br>No mark in LPB | | P5/R/x1<br>***#1426***<br> | **Charles ROWBOTHAM**<br>36 Warstone Lane<br>Birmingham | Ring maker |
| LPB/72<br>13 May 1880 | | P3/R/x2<br>***#1427,8***<br> | | |
| R3/8<br>27 March 1922<br>Sent by C Roberts | 25 Gronant Street<br>Rhyl<br>North Wales | P15/R/21<br>***#1429***<br> | **Charles ROBERTS**<br>15 Sussex Street<br>Rhyl<br>North Wales | Jobbing and manufacturing jeweller |
| GSJW/148,178<br>PP1/186<br>CWMP 1874-1900<br>Not in SPB or LPB so struck 1860-3 | | P3/R/x3<br>***#1430-2***<br> | **Charles READ** *<br>13 Hope Street<br>Liverpool and<br>Summerland Place<br>Coventry | Watch manufacturer |
| SPB/17<br>6 April 1873<br>Sent by Samuel & Rogers | | P3/R/x4<br>***#1433-6***<br> | **Charles RADGES**<br>No business address entered<br>(Liverpool?) | Watchmaker or jeweller ? |
| R1/77<br>20 December 1898<br>Sent by Charles Reeves | 131 High Street<br>Kings Heath<br>Moseley<br>Birmingham | P9/R/6<br>***#1437***<br> | **Charles REEVES**<br>83, 83a and 131 High Street<br>Kings Heath, Moseley<br>Birmingham and<br>140 Chester Road<br>Birmingham | Tobacconist |
| LPB/74<br>28 January 1884<br>Similar mark BAO<br>17 December 1883 | No mark in LPB | P5/R/x1<br>***#1438***<br> | **Charles REVELL**<br>back of 60 Great Hampton Street<br>Birmingham | Silversmith |
| Missing register<br>*c.*1886<br>Similar mark BAO<br>17 December 1883 | | P5/R/12<br>***#1439***<br> | | |
| SPB/15<br>20 August 1867<br>Sent by Samuel & Rogers | CWMP 1874 | P3/R/x2<br>***#1440,1***<br> | **Charles READ** *<br>The Butts<br>Coventry | Watch and watchcase maker |
| Missing register<br>*c.*1890<br>Near mark P5/R/319 | | P5/R/x1<br>***#1442***<br> | **Unidentified** | |
| Missing register<br>*c.*1886 | | P5/R/68<br>***#1443***<br> | **Unidentified** | |

| REGISTRATION DETAILS | MAKER'S PRIVATE ADDRESS and DETAILS | PLATE and MARK DETAILS | MAKER/COMPANY and BUSINESS ADDRESS | MAKER'S TRADE |
|---|---|---|---|---|
| LPB/74<br>7 August 1883 | | P5/R/x1<br>***#1444***<br> | **Charles REVELL**<br>206 Berness Street<br>Lozells<br>Birmingham | Silversmith |
| Missing register<br>*c.*1886 | | P5/R/68<br>***#1445***<br> | See other CR marks | |
| Not in SPB or LPB<br>Similar mark entered<br>LAO 16 July 1860 | | P2/R/x3<br>***#1446-8***<br> | **Charles READ** *<br>The Butts<br>Coventry | Watch and watchcase maker |
| SPB/23<br>28 February 1871<br>Sent by Samuel &<br>Rogers | | P3/R/x2<br>***#1449,50***<br> | | |
| R1/126<br>7 May 1900<br>Damaged in<br>September 1900<br>Sent by<br>C Rowbotham | Chaucer Villa<br>South Yardley<br>Birmingham | P9/R/14<br>***#1451***<br> | **Charles ROWBOTHAM**<br>36 Warstone Lane<br>Birmingham | Gold ring manufacturer |
| R1/126<br>19 September 1900<br>replacement for mark<br>P9/R/14 | | P9/R/20<br>***#1452***<br> | | |
| R1/141<br>5 February 1901<br>Sent by<br>C Rowbotham | Chanon Villa<br>Milton Crescent<br>South Yardley<br>Birmingham | P9/R/29<br>***#1453***<br> | | |
| R2/202<br>13 November 1915<br>BAO 23.088 to 23.093<br>Sent by C R Avery | Private address same as business | P15/A/2-7<br>***#1454-9***<br> | **Charles Robert AVERY**<br>57 Oakfield Road<br>Ilford | Jeweller |
| R2/111<br>3 June 1910<br>Sent by H Griffith &<br>Son | Melrose<br>Gilbert Road<br>Romford<br>Essex<br>50 Western Park<br>Couch End<br>London W | P13/R/32<br>***#1460***<br> | **Alfred George CLAYDON**<br>**Charles ROBIN** trading as<br>**CLAYDON, ROBIN & CO** *<br>15 New Union Street<br>London E C | Wholesale jewellers |
| R2/178<br>28 October 1913<br>Sent by M M Cohen | 83 Wilson Road<br>Handsworth<br>66 Gough Road<br>Handsworth<br>Birmingham | P15/R/2 and P15/P*sic*/0*sic*<br>***#1461,2***<br> | **Charles REVELL**<br>**M M COHEN** trading as<br>**C REVELL & CO** *<br>74 Vyse Street<br>Birmingham | Ring manufacturers |
| R3/138<br>8 April 1952<br>Sent by C R Dodson<br>Three sizes | 17 Browneville Road<br>Heaton Moor<br>Stockport<br>Cheshire | P21/D/22-24<br>***#1463-5***<br> | **Charles Robert DODSON**<br>No business address entered | Student silversmith |
| R2/64<br>18 August 1908<br>Sent by C R Engley | 88 Eccleston Square<br>London SW | P13/E/2<br>***#1466***<br> | **Charles Richard ENGLEY** *<br>88 Eccleston Square<br>London SW | Diamond and pearl merchant and jewellers agent |
| R2/44<br>7 August 1907<br>Sent by Frederick<br>Robert Charlick | Goddfin Terrace<br>Stoke<br>Devonport<br>Devon | P13/C/1 and P13/B*sic*/0*sic*<br>***#1467,8***<br>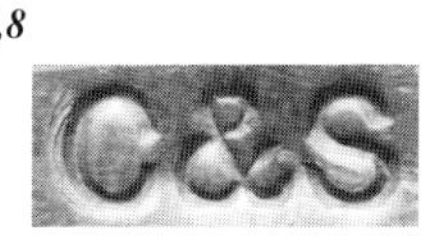 | **Frederick Robert CHARLICK**<br>trading as<br>**Charles CROYDON & SON**<br>20 Fore Street<br>Devonport<br>Devon | Watchmakers, jewellers, gold and silversmiths |

| REGISTRATION DETAILS | MAKER'S PRIVATE ADDRESS and DETAILS | PLATE and MARK DETAILS | MAKER/COMPANY and BUSINESS ADDRESS | MAKER'S TRADE |
|---|---|---|---|---|
| R1/227<br>2 February 1905<br>Sent by C Schaefer<br>Two sizes | 28 Booth Street<br>Birmingham | P9/S/81,82<br>***#1469,70*** 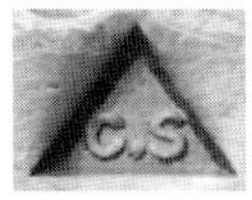 | **C SCHAEFER**<br>74 Vyse Street<br>Birmingham | Manufacturing agent |
| Not in R3 as expected<br>Between November 1921 and June 1923 | Not entered at BAO or LAO | P15/S/53<br>***#1471***  | **Unidentified** | |
| R2/75<br>16 March 1909<br>BAO 15.594<br>Sent by Charles Smallwood | 38 Davey Road<br>Moseley<br>Birmingham | P13/S/27<br>***#1472***  | **Charles SMALLWOOD**<br>79 Vyse Street<br>Birmingham | Manufacturing jeweller |
| R2/193<br>24 February 1915<br>Sent by Charles Appleton Seymour | 215 Mainwaring Road<br>Brockley<br>London SE | P15/S/15<br>***#1473*** 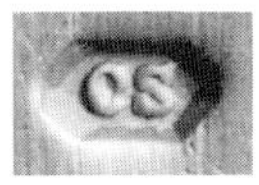 | **Charles Appleton SEYMOUR**<br>7 President Street<br>Clerkenwell<br>London EC | Manufacturing jeweller |
| R2/193<br>24 February 1915<br>Sent by Samuel Ernest Pearsall | Warnity House<br>Jerrys Lane<br>Erdington<br>93 Linwood Road<br>Handsworth<br>77 Linwood Road<br>Handsworth, Birmingham | No new marks<br>***#1474*** | **CLARK & SEWELL LTD**<br>James P Clark (Director)<br>John A Sewell (Director)<br>Samuel Ernest Pearsall (Secretary)<br>5 Legge Lane<br>Birmingham | Manufacturing goldsmiths and silversmiths |
| SPB/22<br>19 January 1876<br>LPB mark shown | | Not on P3<br>***#1475***  | **CHANCELLOR & SONS**<br>(Ed: John and Jonathan)<br>55 Lower Sackville Street<br>Dublin | Watchmakers, clockmakers and musical box dealers |
| Missing register<br>*c.*1886<br>Two sizes | | P5/C/1x2<br>***#1476,7***  | | |
| R1/28<br>25 April 1896<br>Sent by T P Hewitt<br>J McKnight | | P5/aboveC/761<br>***#1478***  | **Horatio Nelson COLLINGWOOD**<br>trading as **COLLINGWOOD & SON**<br>Linthorpe Road<br>Middlesborough | Watch manufacturer and jewellers |
| SPB/13<br>8 January 1877 | | P3/C*sic*/x1<br>***#1479*** 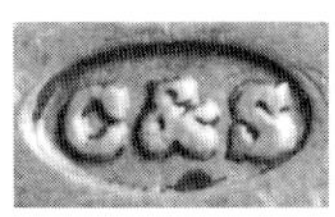 | **E L COMBERBACH & SONS**<br>48 Market Place<br>Blackburn<br>Lancashire | Watchmakers and jewellers |
| R2/15<br>4 April 1906<br>Sent by Clark & Sewell<br>Two sizes<br>BAO 3935 | 17 Halifax Road<br>Erdington<br>22 Regent Road<br>Handsworth<br>Birmingham | P9/D*sic*/228-231<br>***#1480-3***  | **James CLARK**<br>**John SEWELL** trading as<br>**CLARK & SEWELL**<br>5 Legge Lane<br>Birmingham | Silversmiths |
| R2/203<br>Undated – between 22 February and 2 April 1916<br>Sent by Clark & Sewell Ltd<br>Three sizes | 77 Linwood Road<br>Handsworth<br>Birmingham | P15/C/49–53<br>***#1484-8*** 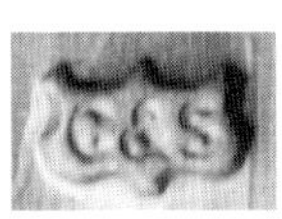 | **CLARK & SEWELL LTD**<br>S E Pearsall (Secretary)<br>4 and 5 Legge Lane<br>Birmingham | Gold and silversmiths |
| R3/44<br>10 November 1928<br>Sent by Clark & Sewell | | P15/C/201<br>***#1489***  | **CLARK & SEWELL**<br>4 and 5 Legge Lane<br>Birmingham | Manufacturing silversmiths |

| REGISTRATION DETAILS | MAKER'S PRIVATE ADDRESS and DETAILS | PLATE and MARK DETAILS | MAKER/COMPANY and BUSINESS ADDRESS | MAKER'S TRADE |
|---|---|---|---|---|
| R3/32<br>13 April 1926<br>Sent by S Blanckensee & Son<br>Birmingham | | P15/C/167<br>***#1490*** 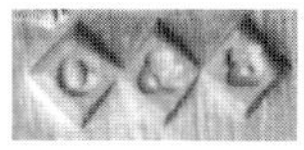 | **CONNARD & SON LTD**<br>421 Lord Street<br>Southport | Jewellers and silversmiths |
| R3/40<br>22 March 1928<br>Sent by Bendall Brothers | | P15/C/184,185<br>***#1491,2*** 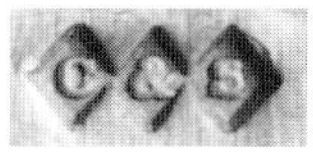 | **CONNARD & SON LTD**<br>W Connard (Managing Director)<br>421 Lord Street<br>Liverpool | Jewellers |
| R1/100<br>9 May 1899<br>Sent by C Dreyfus Hemming & Hazlewood | Private address same as business | P9/C/11<br>***#1493***  | **George Eugene CHANDLER**<br>**F CHANDLER** trading as<br>**CHANDLER & SON** *<br>12 Newman Street<br>London | Goldsmiths and jewellers |
| R3/116<br>4 March 1947<br>Sent by H T A Becker | Private address same as business | P21/C/33<br>***#1494***  | **Harry Thomas Alfred BECKER**<br>**Dorothy BECKER** trading as<br>**THE CHESHIRE SILVER CO**<br>111 Thorley Lane<br>Timperley<br>Cheshire | Antique silver and modern silverplate dealers |
| 12 April 1949 | | P21/C/50<br>***#1495***  | | |
| R1/207<br>9 February 1902<br>Sent by R Rholeder<br><br>Cancelled<br>28 July 1905 | Beaumont House<br>Chalford | P9/D*sic*/202<br>***#1496***  | **THE CHALFORD STICK CO LTD** *<br>H C Daun (Director)<br>St Mary's Mill<br>Chalford<br>Gloucestershire | Manufacturers of umbrellas and sticks |
| R2/1<br>28 July 1905<br>Sent by G B Chell | Mellor<br>near Manchester | P9/D*sic*/221<br>***#1497***  | **THE CHALFORD STICK CO LTD** *<br>George B Chell (Director)<br>St Mary's Mill<br>Chalford<br>Gloucestershire | |
| LPB/20<br>15 August 1878 | | P3/C/x3<br>***#1498-1500*** 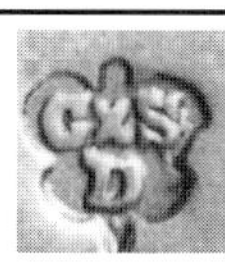 | **CHANCELLOR & SONS**<br>(Ed: John and Jonathan)<br>55 Lower Sackville Street<br>Dublin | Watchmakers, clockmakers and musical box dealers |
| LPB/76<br>8 April 1881<br>MR3/139<br>Sent by Coley Brothers | | P3/S/x1<br>***#1501***  | **Charles SAUNDERS** and<br>**Francis SHEPHERD** *<br>Bartlett's Passage Buildings<br>Holborn Circus<br>London | Manufacturing jewellers, gold and silversmiths |
| LPB/76 SP26/6<br>13 March 1883 | | P3/F*sic*/x1<br>***#1502***  | | |
| Missing register<br>*c.*1887 | | P5/S/125<br>***#1503***  | | |
| Missing register<br>*c.*1888<br>Four sizes | | P5/S/193x4<br>***#1504-7***  | | |
| Missing register<br>*c.*1894<br>Three sizes | | P5/S/536x3<br>***#1508-10***  | | |

| REGISTRATION DETAILS | MAKER'S PRIVATE ADDRESS and DETAILS | PLATE and MARK DETAILS | MAKER/COMPANY and BUSINESS ADDRESS | MAKER'S TRADE |
|---|---|---|---|---|
| R1/54<br>24 November 1897<br>Annotated imp(ressed?) 1883 in (square) O.<br>Sent by Adie & Lovekin<br>E Vaughton<br>Saunders & Shepherd<br>EJ Robinson<br>H Hyde & Son | Fern Bank [1]<br>17 Broomhouse Road, Fulham<br>The Gables [2]<br>Hampstead Heath, London<br>20 The Crescent [3]<br>Hadley Wood, Middlesex<br>37 Smitham? Road [4]<br>London NW<br>111 Marnock Road [5]<br>Brockley<br>London SE<br>91 Mitcham Lane [6]<br>Streatham | P5/O*sic*/909x2<br>***#1511,2***<br> | **James Francis Hollings SHEPHERD** [1]<br>**Cornelius Desormeaux SAUNDERS** [2]<br>**John Cooper SAUNDERS** [3]<br>**Lawrence SAUNDERS** [4]<br>**William Charles HOLLAND** [5]<br>**Arthur WHELPDALE** [6] trading as<br>**SAUNDERS & SHEPHERD** *<br>Bartlett's Passage Buildings<br>Holborn Circus<br>London | Jewellers and silversmiths |
| R1/117<br>1 December 1899<br>Sent by A Jackson<br>Saunders & Shepherd | Southeath<br>East Twickenham | P9/S/28<br>***#1513***<br>§  | **SAUNDERS & SHEPHERD LTD** *<br>William John Player (Secretary)<br>2, 3 Bartlett's Passage Buildings<br>Holborn Circus<br>London | Goldsmiths, jewellers and silversmiths |
| R1/177<br>8 October 1902<br>Sent by Saunders & Shepherd<br>C A Cheshire | | P9/S/50<br>***#1514***<br> | **SAUNDERS & SHEPHERD** *<br>William J Player (Manager)<br>2, 3 Bartlett's Passage Buildings<br>Holborn Circus<br>London EC | Manufacturing jewellers |
| R1/201<br>14 October 1903<br>Sent by C E Turner<br>Three sizes | Fortescue Lodge<br>Twickenham | P9/S/67-69<br>***#1515-7***<br> | | |
| R2/16<br>6 April 1906<br>Sent by C H Cheshire | 94 Effingham Road<br>Hornsey<br>Caers Wood<br>Alexandra Road<br>Epsom<br>Surrey | P9/S/97,98<br>***#1518,9***<br> | **SAUNDERS & SHEPHERD LTD** *<br>Arthur Whelpdale (Managing Dir)<br>Alfred Russell MacKenzie (Secretary)<br>58-61 Fetter Lane<br>Bartlett's Passage Buildings<br>Holborn Circus<br>London EC | Manufacturing goldsmiths, jewellers and silversmiths |
| R2/30<br>18 December 1906<br>Sent by C E Turner<br>Two sizes | 94 Effingham Road<br>Hornsey<br>Middlesex | P9/S/114-116<br>***#1520-2***<br> | **SAUNDERS & SHEPHERD LTD** *<br>Alfred Russell Mackenzie (Secretary)<br>58-61 Fetter Lane<br>Bartlett's Passage Buildings<br>Holborn Circus<br>London EC | |
| R2/163<br>6 October 1912<br>Sent by Clark & Sewell | 39 Belsize Avenue [1]<br>Bowes Park<br>London W | P13/S/104<br>***#1523***<br> | **SAUNDERS & SHEPHERD LTD** *<br>A R Mackenzie [1] (Secretary)<br>58-61 Fetter Lane and<br>Bartlett's Passage Buildings<br>Holborn Circus<br>London EC | |
| R2/128<br>17 February 1911<br>Sent by Saunders & Shepherd Ltd<br>BAO 16.227 | | P13/S/64<br>***#1524***<br> | | Manufacturing silversmiths |
| R3/86<br>14 January 1937<br>Sent by Saunders & Shepherd Co Ltd | | P21/S/1<br>***#1525***<br> | **SAUNDERS & SHEPHERD CO LTD** *<br>Sealed by:-<br>C P Saunders (Director)<br>William Shepherd (Director and Secy)<br>58-61 Fetter Lane (Registered Office)<br>London EC4 | Manufacturing jewellers and silversmiths |

| REGISTRATION DETAILS | MAKER'S PRIVATE ADDRESS and DETAILS | PLATE and MARK DETAILS | MAKER/COMPANY and BUSINESS ADDRESS | MAKER'S TRADE |
|---|---|---|---|---|
| R2/165<br>6 November 1912<br>Sent by Charles S Green & Co Ltd | 3 Carpenter Road<br>Edgbaston<br>Birmingham | P13/G/45-49<br>***#1526-30***<br>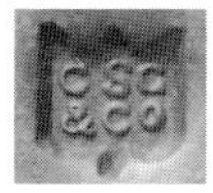 | **Charles S GREEN & CO LTD** *<br>Charles S Green (Managing Director)<br>Cogent Works<br>54 St Paul's Square<br>Birmingham | Manufacturing silversmiths |
| R3/10<br>30 June 1922<br>Two sizes Sent by C Smallwood Ltd | 30 St Andrews Place<br>Bradford | P15/S/54, 55<br>***#1531,2***<br> | **C SMALLWOOD LTD**<br>21 North Parade<br>Bradford | Jewellers and silversmiths |
| R3/180<br>27 June 1961<br>Sent by<br>C S Nicholson | 4 Demside Avenue<br>Low Fell<br>Gateshead | P21/N/15<br>***#1533***<br> | **Charles Stanley NICHOLSON**<br>No business address entered | Hobby |
| R1/122<br>5 March 1900<br>Sent by C Taylor | Private address same as business | P9/T/14<br>***#1534***<br> | **Charles TAYLOR**<br>48 Anglesea Terrace<br>Harpurhey<br>Manchester | Walking stick and umbrella mounter |
| PCR-1773<br>MR2/194 | | Not on P1<br>***#1535*** **C T ?** | **Christian THYNE**<br>Liverpool | Silversmith |
| R1/202<br>6 November 1903<br>Two sizes Sent by C T Burrows who retired from business 15 February 1907 | 13 Wells Road<br>Birmingham<br>3 The Crescent<br>South Road, Hockley<br>11 Booth Street<br>Handsworth<br>Birmingham | P9/B/110,111 and 0*sic*<br>***#1536-8***<br> | **Charles Turman BURROWS**<br>**Charles William BURROWS**<br>**F J BURROWS** trading as<br>**C T BURROWS & SONS** *<br>59 Branston Street<br>Birmingham | Watch manufacturers, silversmiths and jewellers |
| R3/98<br>17 January 1941<br>Sent by C T Kirby<br>Two sizes | Private address same as business | P21/K/3,4<br>***#1539,40***<br> | **Charles Thomas KIRBY**<br>1 Kineton Road<br>Sutton Coldfield<br>Warwickshire | Manufacturing jeweller |
| R2/144<br>12 September 1911<br>Sent by J & R Griffin & Son | Hillside<br>Birstall<br>Leicester | P13/U/5<br>***#1541***<br> | **Reuben USHER** trading as<br>**Charles USHER** *<br>2 Humberstone Gate<br>Leicester and<br>High Street<br>Kettering and<br>21 Bedford Street<br>Plymouth | Gold and silversmiths |
| R3/69<br>25 October 1933<br>Sent by selves | Portland House<br>Kirby Muxloe<br>near Leicester | P15/U/15<br>***#1542***<br> | **Reuben Percival USHER** trading as<br>**THE USHER MANUFACTURING CO** *<br>Vittoria Works<br>32/34 Vittoria Street<br>Birmingham | Manufacturing jewellers and silversmiths |
| Two sizes | | P15/U/16,17<br>***#1543,4***<br>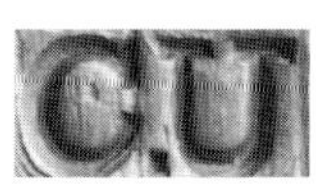 | | |
| R3/92<br>9 November 1938<br>Sent by selves | | P21/UV/2<br>***#1545***<br>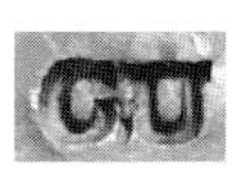 | | |
| Not in R1 as expected Adjacent mark P5/V/662 entered in R1 28 May 1895 | Henry Vale and Charles Vale dissolved their partnership in 1897 so this may be the mark of Charles Vale. Charles and Henry Vale with Rowland Sermon entered VBS mark at LAO 31 July 1890. | P5/V/661<br>***#1546***<br> | **Charles VALE, Henry VALE**<br>**Rowland SERMON** trading as<br>**VALE BROTHERS & SERMON** *<br>12 Bartletts Building<br>London EC and<br>27 Spencer Street<br>Birmingham | Silversmiths and electroplate manufacturers |

| REGISTRATION DETAILS | MAKER'S PRIVATE ADDRESS and DETAILS | PLATE and MARK DETAILS | MAKER/COMPANY and BUSINESS ADDRESS | MAKER'S TRADE |
|---|---|---|---|---|
| R1/158<br>23 December 1901<br>Sent by Charles Van Kalken | 34 Manley Road<br>Manchester | P9/K/23<br>***#1547***  | **Charles Van KALKEN**<br>92 Market Street<br>Manchester | Church decorator |
| LPB/28<br>7 June 1883 | | P3/W/x1<br>***#1548***  | **Christopher WALKER**<br>25 Naylor Street<br>William Road<br>Manchester | Pipe and stick mounter |
| R2/150<br>20 January 1912<br>BAO 6.902<br>Sent by C Weale | 100 Grove Lane<br>Handsworth<br>Birmingham | P13/W/104<br>***#1549***  | **Charles WEALE**<br>42 Hockley Street<br>Birmingham | Silversmith |
| LPB/98<br>21 October 1884 | | P5/W/x1<br>***#1550***  | **Christopher WALKER**<br>25 Naylor Street<br>William Road<br>Manchester | Pipe and stick mounter |
| Missing register<br>*c.*1887<br>Two sizes | | P5/W/126x2<br>***#1551,2***  | | |
| Missing register<br>*c.*1891<br>Next to P5/W/344 | | P5/W/x1<br>***#1553***  | | |
| Missing register<br>*c.*1890 | | P5/W/309<br>***#1554***  | | |
| Missing register<br>*c.*1890 | | P5/W/297<br>***#1555***  | | |
| Missing register<br>*c.*1890 | | P5/W/315<br>***#1556***  | | |
| R1/125<br>24 April 1900<br>Sent by C Walker<br>Annotated *Old Punch defaced* | 385 Oldham Road<br>Manchester<br><br>Note "C" looks like a "G" | P9/W/35<br>***#1557*** 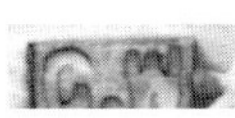 | **Amelia WALKER** trading as<br>**Christopher WALKER**<br>H Litherland (Manager)<br>12a Thorniley Brow<br>off Shude Hill<br>Manchester | |
| R2/182<br>6 January 1914<br>Sent by Herbert Litherland | Silverwood<br>Washway Road<br>Sale<br>Nr Manchester | P15/W/6<br>***#1558***  | **Herbert LITHERLAND** trading as<br>**C WALKER**<br>5 New Street<br>Bradshaw Street<br>Shudehill<br>Manchester | Stick mounter |
| R2/231<br>13 May 1920<br>Sent by<br>H Litherland | Silverwood<br>Washway Road<br>Sale | P15/W/55<br>***#1559***  | | Mounter |
| R1/177<br>24 October 1902<br>Sent by<br>H Litherland | 41 Duke Street<br>Manchester | P9/W/83<br>***#1560***  | **Amelia WALKER** trading as<br>**C WALKER**<br>4 Amber Street<br>Bradshaw Street<br>Manchester | Stick mounter |
| 16 December 1903<br>Between #102 and #103 | | P9/W/0*sic*<br>***#1561*** 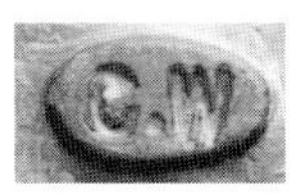 | | |

| REGISTRATION DETAILS | MAKER'S PRIVATE ADDRESS and DETAILS | PLATE and MARK DETAILS | MAKER/COMPANY and BUSINESS ADDRESS | MAKER'S TRADE |
|---|---|---|---|---|
| R3/3<br>5 May 1921<br>Sent by C Walker Litherland | Private address same as business | P15/W/42-47<br>***#1562-7***<br> | **C WALKER LITHERLAND LTD**<br>14 Angel Street<br>Rochdale Road<br>Manchester | Silversmiths |
| PDB 1837<br>MR3/18,101<br>WTD 1822<br>J1 1838-40 | Admitted to Chester GC *c.*1834 as a book-seller but expelled 22 February 1841 | P1/26/x2<br>***#1568,9***<br> | **Charles Burton WALKER**<br>Chester or | Spectacle frames |
| PP1/186 | | | **Charles WALKER**<br>Little Park Street<br>Coventry or | Watchcase maker |
| GSJW | | | **Charles WELLS**<br>103 Bold Street<br>Liverpool | Silversmith |
| SPB/1<br>26 November 1863<br>Sent by James Walker | | P3/W/x3<br>***#1570-2***<br> | **Christopher WHITTEM & CO**<br>Much Park Street<br>Coventry | Watch and chronometer manufacturers |
| R1/148<br>4 June 1901<br>Sent by C Walter | 209 Sussex Road<br>Southport | P9/W/59<br>***#1573***<br> | **Carl WALTER**<br>36 Scarisbrick Avenue<br>Southport | Pipe maker and repairer |
| R2/71<br>4 February 1909<br>Sent by C Wilkes<br>Five sizes | Lansdowne<br>Warwick Road<br>Olton | P13/W/41-43,46,47<br>***#1574-8***<br>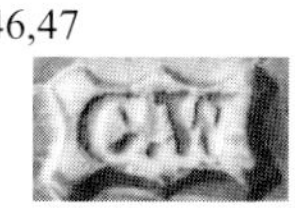 | **Charles WILKES**<br>16 Mott Street<br>Birmingham | Silversmith |
| Missing register<br>*c.*1890 | | P5/W/315<br>***#1579***<br> | **Christopher WALKER**<br>25 Naylor Street<br>William Road<br>Manchester | Pipe and stick mounter |
| SPB/16<br>22 October 1874 | Not found in directories. Collins & Osborne and Collins and Adkins, silversmiths, are listed in 1871 | P3/C/x3<br>***#1580-2***<br> | **COLLINGS & WALLACE**<br>(Street not entered)<br>Birmingham | Unidentified |
| R2/113<br>24 June 1910<br>LAO 5183<br>Sent by Clark & Ward | 53 Far Gosford Street<br>Coventry<br>55 Kensington Road<br>Coventry | P13/C/76<br>***#1583***<br> | **Thomas Samuel CLARKE**<br>**Alfred WARD** trading as<br>**CLARKE & WARD** *<br>55 Kensington Road<br>Coventry | Silver watchcase makers |
| R2/143<br>2 September 1911<br>Sent by Robert Murray | 52 Moorfield Road<br>Pendleton<br>Salford | P13/E/23<br>***#1584***<br> | **Charles William ELKINGTON**<br>Thomas Elkington—Executor for widow of C W Elkington<br>36 Grosvenor Chambers<br>16 Deansgate<br>Manchester | Silver engraver |
| R2/136<br>23 May 1911<br>SAO 2742 and 346<br>Sent by C W Fletcher & Son Ltd<br>Two sizes | 747 Ecclesall Road [1]<br>Sheffield | P13/F/25,26<br>***#1585,6***<br> | **C W FLETCHER & SON LTD** *<br>C W Fletcher [1] (Managing Director)<br>Sterling Works<br>Bramhall Lane<br>Sheffield | Manufacturing silversmiths |
| R3/34<br>1 September 1926<br>Sent by C W Fletcher & Sons Ltd | 747 Ecclesall Road<br>Sheffield | P15/F/28<br>***#1587***<br> | **C W FLETCHER & SONS LTD** *<br>Bramhall Lane<br>Sheffield<br>76 Arundel Street (Head Office)<br>Sheffield | Silversmiths |

| REGISTRATION DETAILS | MAKER'S PRIVATE ADDRESS and DETAILS | PLATE and MARK DETAILS | MAKER/COMPANY and BUSINESS ADDRESS | MAKER'S TRADE |
|---|---|---|---|---|
| R3/86<br>3 April 1937<br>Sent by C W Fletcher & Sons Ltd | | P21/F/1<br>***#1588***<br> | **C W FLETCHER & SONS LTD** *<br>Seal affixed in the presence of:<br>E Bailey (Director)<br>Harold Fletcher (Director)<br>C Walter Fletcher (Secretary)<br>Sterling Works (Registered Office)<br>Arundel Street<br>Sheffield | Silversmiths cutlers and electroplate manufacturers |
| R3/75<br>4 April 1935<br>Sent by C W Kibble | Knock<br>Oak Lane<br>Bramhall<br>Cheshire | P15/K/22<br>***#1589***<br> | **Constance Winifred KIBBLE**<br>Accountant at<br>British Sun Insurance Co Ltd<br>15 York Street<br>Manchester | Accountant |
| R2/226<br>19 January 1920<br>Sent by Cedric Harold Whitehouse<br><br>Two sizes | Bayscroft<br>Barnt Green<br>Birmingham | P15/W/52a<br>***#1590***<br> | **Cedric Harold WHITEHOUSE**<br>(Sole Director) trading as<br>**Cedric Harold WHITEHOUSE LTD**<br>(a private Limited Company) | Gold and silver chain manufacturers |
| | | P15/W/52b<br>***#1591***<br> | 58 Tenby Street North<br>Birmingham | |
| R3/100<br>21 August 1941<br>Sent by C & W Manison | W Manison<br>4 Nursery Road<br>Lozells<br>Birmingham | P21/M/12<br>***#1592***<br> | **C & W MANISON**<br>Walter Manison (Sole Proprietor)<br>16 Hockley Street<br>Birmingham | Manufacturing jewellers |
| Missing register<br>*c.*1894<br>CWMP 1891-1909 | | P5/aboveC/541a<br>***#1593***<br> | **COVENTRY WATCH MANUFACTURING SOCIETY**<br>32 Bishop Street<br>Coventry | Watch manufacturers |
| Missing register<br>*c.*1894<br>KOC/16 1889-1917 | | P5/aboveC/541b<br>***#1594***<br> | | |
| R1/139<br>12 January 1901<br>Sent by F Wright | 72 Barrington Road [1]<br>Crescent End<br>5 Felix Avenue [2]<br>Crescent End<br>London | P9/P/79<br>***#1595***<br> | **Charles William PADGETT** [1]<br>**Walter John PADGETT** [2] trading as<br>**C & W PADGETT** *<br>49 Leamington Street<br>London W | Manufacturing jewellers |
| R3/129<br>23 November 1949<br>Sent by C W Ross | Private address same as business | P21/R/7<br>***#1596***<br> | **Charles William ROSS**<br>13 Beryldene Avenue<br>Watnall<br>Nottingham | Teacher of metalworking |
| R3/146<br>12 August 1953<br>Two sizes<br>Sent by C W Ross | 13 Beryldene Avenue<br>Watnall<br>Nottingham | P21/R/18,19<br>***#1597,8***<br> | **Charles William ROSS**<br>No business address entered | Teacher |
| R3/63<br>9 June 1932<br>Sent by Cooperative Wholesale Society Ltd<br>Invincible Works<br>Redfern Road<br>Syseley<br>Birmingham | | P15/K*sic*/214<br>***#1599***<br> | **COOPERATIVE WHOLESALE SOCIETY LTD**<br>Common seal of company affixed in the presence of:-<br>R F Lancaster (Secretary)<br>1 Balloon Street (Registered Office)<br>Manchester | Manufacturing jewellers |

| REGISTRATION DETAILS | MAKER'S PRIVATE ADDRESS and DETAILS | PLATE and MARK DETAILS | MAKER/COMPANY and BUSINESS ADDRESS | MAKER'S TRADE |
|---|---|---|---|---|
| R1/176<br>3 October 1902<br>Sent by Alfred Henry Westwood<br>Two sizes | Elmshurst [1]<br>Handsworth Wood Road<br>Wetherensell [2]<br>Stowmarket, Suffolk<br>Alesbury House [3]<br>Knowle | P9/W/76-82<br>***#1600-6***<br> | **Alfred Henry WESTWOOD** [1]<br>**William Walker WESTWOOD** [2]<br>**Francis Herbert WESTWOOD** [3]<br>trading as **C WESTWOOD & SON** *<br>14 Hall Street<br>Birmingham | Bullion dealers and silversmiths |
| R3/70<br>20 February 1934<br>Sent by Kinsey Brothers & Patrick<br>17 Vyse Street<br>Birmingham | Eastwood House [1]<br>Essex<br>49 Firmoy Road [2]<br>Thorpe Bay<br>Essex | P15/W/106<br>***#1607***<br> | **Charles WALLER** [1]<br>**Frederick John WALLER** [2] trading as<br>**Charles WALLER & SON**<br>57 High Street<br>Southend-on-Sea<br>Essex | Jewellers |
| R3/1<br>12 April 1921<br>Sent by Cooperative Wholesale Society Ltd | Kings Road<br>Tysley<br>Birmingham | P15/C/95-97<br>***#1608-10***<br> | **THE COOPERATIVE WHOLESALE SOCIETY**<br>Thomas Brodrick (Secretary)<br>1 Balloon Street (Registered Office)<br>Manchester | Manufacturing jewellers |
| R3/12<br>26 October 1922<br>Sent by E Whitehouse & Son | Private address same as business | P15/C/111-113<br>P15/W*sic*/0*sic*<br>***#1611-4***<br> | **THE COOPERATIVE WHOLESALE SOCIETY**<br>Kings Road<br>Tyseley<br>Birmingham | |
| Not in R3 as expected<br>Between July and December 1923 | | P15/C/150<br>***#1615***<br> | | |
| Not in R3 as expected<br>*c.*1925 | | P15/C/162-165<br>***#1616-9***<br> | | |
| R3/11<br>22 August 1922<br>Sent by E Whitehouse & Son | Private address same as business | P15/C/109,110<br>***#1620,1***<br> | **THE COOPERATIVE WHOLESALE SOCIETY**<br>**Chas F Jenner** (Manager)<br>Kings Road<br>Tyseley | |
| R1/55<br>26 November 1897<br>Sent by Casimer Widmer | | P5/X*sic*/910<br>***#1622***<br> | **Casimer WIDMER** trading as<br>**C WIDMER & SONS** *<br>113 St John Street Road<br>Clerkenwell<br>London EC | Engravers and piercers |
| R2/229<br>10 March 1920<br>Sent by W A Coley | 33 Devonshire Road<br>Handsworth Wood<br>4 Endwood Court Road<br>Handsworth | P15/C/92<br>***#1623***<br> | **Alfred George COLEY**<br>**William Arthur COLEY** trading as<br>**COLEY BROTHERS**<br>119 Vyse Street<br>Birmingham | Gold ring manufacturers |
| R2/120<br>13 October 1910<br>Sent by William Arthur Coley | 90 Handsworth Wood<br>33 Devonshire Road<br>52 Landowne Road<br>Handsworth | P13/C/83<br>***#1624***<br> | **William Henry COLEY**<br>**Alfred George COLEY**<br>**William Arthur COLEY** trading as<br>**COLEY BROTHERS**<br>119 Vyse Street<br>Birmingham | Jewellers |

| REGISTRATION DETAILS | MAKER'S PRIVATE ADDRESS and DETAILS | PLATE and MARK DETAILS | MAKER/COMPANY and BUSINESS ADDRESS | MAKER'S TRADE |
|---|---|---|---|---|
| LPB/20<br>12 August 1880<br>Two sizes | | P3/C/x4<br>***#1625-8***<br> | **COLEY BROTHERS**<br>119 Vyse Street<br>Birmingham | Jewellers |
| R1/106<br>24 July 1899<br>Sent by Edward Brothers | Trevanglen<br>Handsworth<br>Birmingham | P9/C/25<br>***#1629***<br> | **W H COLEY** trading as<br>**COLEY BROTHERS**<br>119 Vyse Street<br>Birmingham | |
| R1/145<br>18 April 1901<br>Sent by W H Coley | 90 Handsworth Wood Road<br>Handsworth<br>Birmingham | P9/C/48<br>***#1630***<br> | **William Henry COLEY** trading as<br>**COLEY BROTHERS**<br>119 Vyse Street<br>Birmingham | |
| R1/209<br>5 March 1904<br>Sent by W H Coley | | P9/D*sic*/203<br>***#1631***<br> | | |
| R2/227<br>23 February 1920<br>Sent by W A Coley | 33 Devonshire Road<br>Handsworth Wood<br>4 Enderwood Court Road<br>Handsworth | P15/C/77,78<br>***#1632,3***<br> | **Alfred George COLEY**<br>**William Arthur COLEY** trading as<br>**COLEY BROTHERS**<br>119 Vyse Street<br>Birmingham | Gold ring manufacturers |
| R2/229<br>10 March 1920 | | P15/C/80–91<br>***#1634-45***<br> | | |
| Not in R3 as expected<br>*c.*1925 | | P15/C/155-161<br>***#1646-52***<br> | | |
| Not in R3 as expected<br>*c.*1926 | | P15/C/171-178<br>***#1653-60***<br> | | |
| R3/53<br>5 April 1930<br>Sent by Coley Brothers | | P15/N*sic*/208-213<br>***#1661-6***<br> | **COLEY BROTHERS**<br>119 Vyse Street<br>Birmingham | Goldsmiths |
| R3/71<br>11 May 1934<br>Sent by<br>Samuel Hope<br>126 Vyse Street<br>Birmingham | 4 Enderwood Court Road [1]<br>Handsworth Wood<br>Birmingham | P15/K*sic*/221<br>***#1667***<br> | **William Arthur COLEY** [1] trading as<br>**COLEY BROTHERS**<br>119 Vyse Street<br>Birmingham | Ring makers |
| Not in R3 as expected<br>ca:1941 | | P21/C/15<br>***#1668***<br> | | |
| R3/89<br>6 January 1938<br>Sent by W A Coley | 4 Enderwood Court Road<br>Handsworth Wood<br>Birmingham | P21/C/3-6<br>***#1669-72***<br> | **COLEY BROTHERS & LEONARDT LTD** *<br>Sealed in the presence of:-<br>O Leonardt (Director)<br>W A Coley (Director)<br>W A Coley (Secretary)<br>119 Vyse Street<br>Birmingham | Manufacturing jewellers |

| REGISTRATION DETAILS | MAKER'S PRIVATE ADDRESS and DETAILS | PLATE and MARK DETAILS | MAKER/COMPANY and BUSINESS ADDRESS | MAKER'S TRADE |
|---|---|---|---|---|
| R1/141<br>9 February 1901<br>Sent by E J Clewley | The Cedars [1]<br>Trinity Road<br>Birchfields<br>The Laurels [2]<br>Highfield Road<br>Edgbaston, Birmingham | P9/C/46<br>***#1673***<br> | **Edward John CLEWLEY** [1]<br>**Henry DAVIES** [2]<br>111 Vyse Street<br>Birmingham | Manufacturing jewellers |
| R2/38<br>27 April 1907<br>Sent by Edward Davies | 46 Beaufort Road<br>Edgbaston<br>Birmingham | P9/E*sic*/240<br>***#1674***<br> | **Edward DAVIES** trading as<br>**E J CLEWLEY & CO**<br>111/112 Vyse Street<br>Birmingham | |
| R3/21<br>2 April 1924<br>Sent by C J Clewley & Co | Wentworth Road<br>Four Oaks<br>St Agnes Road<br>Moseley | P15/C/154<br>***#1675***<br> | **Alfred Henry BISHTON**<br>**Herbert DAVIES**<br>(Ed: trading as **E J CLEWLEY & CO**)<br>111 Vyse Street<br>Birmingham | |

| REGISTRATION DETAILS | MAKER'S PRIVATE ADDRESS and DETAILS | PLATE and MARK DETAILS | MAKER/COMPANY and BUSINESS ADDRESS | MAKER'S TRADE |
|---|---|---|---|---|
| R3/181<br>18 November 1961<br>Sent by Miss D A M Colvin | Strathisla<br>Fleet Street<br>Horwich<br>Lancashire | P21/C/88<br>*#1676*  | **Dorothy Annette Michie COLVIN**<br>No business address entered | Student |
| PDB 1786-92<br>MR3/77<br>PP2/350 | His mark not seen. He may have used Thomas Pierrepoint's mark since he married his widow | Not on P1<br>*#1677* **D B?** | **David BEYENDORFE**<br>St John's Square<br>Liverpool | Watchcase maker |
| LPB/16<br>20 July 1880 | | P3/B/x2<br>*#1678,9*  | **David BEASLEY**<br>18 Regent Place<br>Caroline Street<br>Birmingham | Jeweller |
| R2/83<br>19 May 1909<br>Sent by D E Beasley | 16 Handsworth Wood Road<br>Handsworth<br>Birmingham | P13/B/48<br>*#1680*  | **Douglas Edward BEASLEY**<br>22 Regent Place<br>Caroline Street<br>Birmingham | Gold charm manufacturer |
| Missing register<br>*c.*1890 | Square D suggests a surname beginning with "D" with the "B" possibly Brothers | P5/D/295<br>*#1681*  | **Unidentified** | |
| R3/27<br>27 March 1925<br>Sent by Docker & Burn | | P15/D/66<br>*#1682*  | **DOCKER & BURN LTD**<br>F Docker, F J Burn and S Howard<br>Sterling Works<br>Barr Street<br>Birmingham | Silversmiths |
| Not in R3 as expected<br>*c.*1926 | | P15/D/72<br>*#1683*  | | |
| R2/11<br>6 February 1906<br>Sent by G Dresden<br>Punch returned to be altered | 58 Rue Leopold Robert [1]<br>La Chaux–de–Fonds<br>Switzerland | P9/D/0*sic*<br>*#1684*  | **Georges DIMIER**<br>**DIMIER FRERES & CO** [1]<br>trading as<br>**DIMIER BROTHERS & CO** *<br>46 Cannon Street<br>London | Watch manufacturers in Switzerland and merchants of clocks and jewellery in England |
| 14 February 1906<br>Received back correct | Sainte Clotilde<br>Longton Avenue<br>Upper Sydenham, London | P9/D/50<br>*#1685*  | | |
| R2/186<br>5 May 1914<br>Sent by Stephens & Myddleton | Oak Lea<br>532 Lordships Lane<br>East Dulwich, London | P15/D/21<br>*#1686*  | **DIMIER BROTHERS & CO** *<br>46 Cannon Street<br>London | Watch manufacturers |
| R2/151<br>21 February 1912<br>Sent by Benson Brothers | 111 Louisville Road [1]<br>Balham | P13/D/39<br>*#1687*  | **DIMIER BROTHERS** *<br>Georges Dimier [1]<br>46 Cannon Street<br>London and<br>24 Rue Leopold Robert<br>La Chaux-de-Fonds<br>Switzerland | Watch manufacturers and merchants |
| R1/221<br>12 October 1904<br>Sent by J Hawley & Son | St Clotilde<br>Longton Avenue<br>Upper Sydenham<br>London | P9/D/44<br>*#1688*  | **Georges DIMIER** trading as<br>**DIMIER BROTHERS & CO** *<br>46 Cannon Street<br>London | Watch manufacturers |
| R2/77<br>3 April 1909<br>Sent by Dingley Brothers | 161 Antrobus Road<br>Handsworth<br>104 Regent Road<br>Handsworth<br>Birmingham | P13/D/10<br>*#1689*  | **Alfred Harry DINGLEY**<br>**George Frederick DINGLEY** trading as<br>**DINGLEY BROTHERS**<br>29 St Mary's Street, St Paul's<br>Birmingham | Silversmiths and goldsmiths |

| REGISTRATION DETAILS | MAKER'S PRIVATE ADDRESS and DETAILS | PLATE and MARK DETAILS | MAKER/COMPANY and BUSINESS ADDRESS | MAKER'S TRADE |
|---|---|---|---|---|
| R2/46<br>10 September 1907<br>Sent by George Cross | 46 Parade<br>Birmingham<br>24 Sheveland Road<br>Smethwick | P9/D/57<br>***#1690***<br> | **George CROSS**<br>**Leonard PRITCHARD** trading as<br>**DAVIES BROTHERS**<br>33a Spencer Street<br>Birmingham | Manufacturing jewellers |
| R3/152<br>11 May 1954<br>Sent by D Chandler | 202 Perville Avenue<br>Mossley Hill<br>Liverpool 18 | P21/C/69<br>***#1691***<br>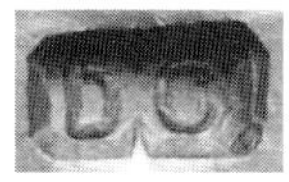 | **Dorothy CHANDLER**<br>No business address entered | Silversmith |
| R3/113<br>26 February 1946<br>Sent by Donald Collins | 480 College Road<br>Erdington<br>Birmingham | P21/C/28<br>***#1692***<br> | **Frederick Joseph COLLINS** trading as<br>**Donald Reginald COLLINS**<br>**Donald COLLINS**<br>53 Great Hampton Street<br>Birmingham | Manufacturing silversmiths |
| R3/119<br>12 August 1947<br>Two sizes<br>Sent by D C Clayton | Private address same as business | P21/C/39,40<br>***#1693,4***<br> | **Doris Claire CLAYTON**<br>5 Range Road<br>Whalley Range<br>Manchester 16 | Art student |
| Missing register<br>*c.*1891 | | P5/D/352<br>***#1695***<br> | **Unidentified** | |
| R2/189<br>28 July 1914<br>Sent by<br>W H Carrington & Co | 304 High Street<br>Wood Green<br>London N | P15/D/22–24<br>***#1696-8***<br> | **Arthur BAYMAN** trading as<br>**DAVIES & CO**<br>18 Liverpool Street<br>London EC | Tobacconists |
| R1/158<br>13 December 1901<br>Sent by selves | 160 Hamstead Road<br>Handsworth<br>Birmingham | P9/D/28- 33<br>***#1699-1704***<br> | **Edward Henry DURBAN**<br>trading as **Edward DURBAN & CO**<br>41 Frederick Street<br>Birmingham | Manufacturing jewellers |
| Missing register<br>*c.*1889 | Same style of mark as the one below suggests Durban & Co | P5/D/265<br>***#1705***<br> | | |
| R1/81<br>30 October 1898 | Kelly 1900 directory | P9/D/3<br>***#1706***<br> | **DURBAN & CO**<br>No other details listed | |
| R1/56<br>3 January 1898<br>Sent by C Widmer<br>& Co | Mederin House<br>Forest Hill<br>London SE<br><br>Culme has Jewin Street | P5/D/915<br>***#1707***<br> | **John William DEWSNAP** trading as<br>**DEWSNAP & CO** *<br>48 Jermyn Street<br>London and<br>Howard Case Works<br>(Eyre Street)<br>Sheffield | Dressing case makers |
| R1/103<br>1 June 1899<br>Sent by W Aitken<br>J W Dewsnap | Forest Hill<br>London SE | P9/D/9<br>***#1708***<br> | | Fancy goods dealers and manufacturers |
| J1 1853-62 | | Not on P1<br>***#1709*** **D D?** | **Daniel DAVIES**<br>Chester | Silversmith |

| REGISTRATION DETAILS | MAKER'S PRIVATE ADDRESS and DETAILS | PLATE and MARK DETAILS | MAKER/COMPANY and BUSINESS ADDRESS | MAKER'S TRADE |
|---|---|---|---|---|
| R2/237<br>22 February 1921<br>Sent by Emily Doris Daniel | 37 Underley Street<br>Liverpool<br>4 May 1932 | P15/D/59<br>***#1710***<br> | **Emily Doris DANIEL**<br>City School of Art<br>Liverpool | Metalwork student |
| 17 July 1935 | 37 Woodlands Road<br>Augburth<br>Liverpool | P15/D/88<br>***#1711***<br> | | |
| 4 May 1932 | | P15/D/78<br>***#1712***<br> | | |
| R3/32<br>No day May 1926<br>Sent by Dance & Duerden | 1a Colwyn Road<br>Dewsbury<br>Leeds<br>17 Park View<br>Beeston<br>Leeds | P15/D/73<br>***#1713***<br> | **DANCE & DUERDEN**<br>(Ed: Albert Dance and H Duerden)<br>84 Queens Street<br>Morley<br>Yorkshire | Jewellers and medallists |
| R3/95<br>14 June 1939<br>Sent by D D Peat | Private address same as business | P21/P/6<br>***#1714***<br> | **Duncan Dalziel PEAT**<br>28 St James's Road<br>Liverpool 1 | Teacher |
| R3/148<br>11 December 1953<br>Sent by D E Criech<br>Two sizes | 62 Boswell Street<br>Liverpool 8 | P21/C/63,64<br>***#1715,6***<br> | **Doris Evelyn CRIECH**<br>No business address entered | Art school student |
| R1/157<br>7 December 1901<br>Sent by Stokes & Ireland<br>Two sizes | 5 Grosvenor Terrace<br>Glasgow | P9/E/6,7<br>***#1717,8***<br>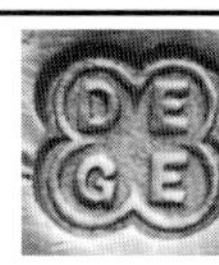 | **David EDWARD**<br>**George EDWARD** trading as<br>**EDWARD & SON** (*sic*) *<br>92 Buchanan Street<br>Glasgow | Jewellers and silversmiths |
| R2/43<br>16 July 1907<br>Sent by W Aitken<br>Three sizes | 20 Queensborough Gardens<br>13 Queens Gate<br>Kilmalcolm<br>Glasgow | P9/E/22-24<br>***#1719-21***<br> | **David Herbert EDWARD**<br>**George EDWARD**<br>**James MACINNES** trading as<br>**EDWARD & SONS** *<br>92 and 96 Buchanan Street<br>Glasgow | Goldsmiths, silversmiths and jewellers |
| R2/91<br>19 August 1909<br>Sent by Gorham Manufacturing Co<br>Two sizes | 13 Queens Gate<br>Glasgow<br>Senga<br>Helensburgh | P13/E/11,12<br>***#1722,3***<br> | **George EDWARD**<br>**David Herbert EDWARD** trading as<br>**EDWARD & SONS** *<br>92 and 96 Buchanan Street<br>Glasgow | |
| R2/112<br>10 June 1910<br>Sent by Barker Brothers | | P13/E/16<br>***#1724***<br> | 92 Buchanan Road<br>Glasgow | Silversmiths and jewellers |
| R2/192<br>18 February 1915<br>Sent by Gorham Manufacturing Co | 13 Queens Gate<br>Glasgow<br>The Fifth Avenue<br>Glasgow<br>Alipore<br>Shelworth NB | P15/E/5<br>***#1725***<br> | **George EDWARD**<br>**David Herbert EDWARD**<br>**Arthur EDWARD** trading as<br>**EDWARD & SONS** *<br>92 Buchanan Street<br>Glasgow | Goldsmiths, silversmiths and jewellers |
| R3/131<br>25 February 1950<br>Sent by D E Hamersley | 4 Scarisbrick Place<br>Hatton Hall Avenue<br>Liverpool 11 | P21/H/53<br>***#1726***<br> | **Donald Edward HAMERSLEY**<br>School of Art<br>Liverpool | Student |

| REGISTRATION DETAILS | MAKER'S PRIVATE ADDRESS and DETAILS | PLATE and MARK DETAILS | MAKER/COMPANY and BUSINESS ADDRESS | MAKER'S TRADE |
|---|---|---|---|---|
| R3/141<br>26 February 1953<br>Sent by D E Jeremiah | | P21/IJ/8<br>***#1727***<br> | **Dr Duncan Eric JEREMIAH**<br>Medical Officer with special duties<br>Salford Public Health Department<br>143 Regent Road<br>Salford 5 | Student goldsmith and silversmith |
| R3/42<br>4 September 1928<br>Sent by Donald Fraser | Glebe Terrace<br>Frodsham<br>Nr Warrington | P15/F/34<br>***#1728***<br> | **Donald FRASER**<br>Church School<br>Balfour Road<br>Runcorn | Schoolmaster |
| LPB/46<br>14 April 1883<br>Sent by C Bradford | | P3/D/x3<br>***#1729-31***<br> | **DEELY & FISHER**<br>14 Vyse Street<br>Birmingham | Jewellers |
| LPB/24<br>14 January 1882<br>Sent by Jackson & Sons | | P3/D/x1<br>***#1732***<br> | **DEAKIN & FRANCIS** *<br>29/30 Regent Place<br>Birmingham | Jewellers and silversmiths |
| LPB/24<br>26 May 1882<br>Sent by Jackson & Sons | | P3/L*sic*/x1<br>***#1733***<br> | | |
| LPB/26 SP25/3<br>12 April 1884<br>No mark in LPB | | P5/D/x1<br>***#1734***<br> | | |
| LPB/26 SP25/7<br>20 July 1885<br>No mark in LPB<br>Sent by AG Griffiths | | P5/D/x1<br>***#1735***<br>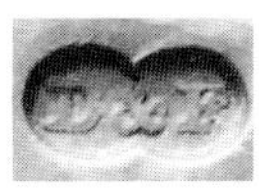 | | |
| Missing register<br>*c.*1886 | | P5/D/1<br>***#1736***<br> | **DEAKIN & FRANCIS** * | |
| R1/108<br>4 August 1899<br>Sent by T Nightingale | 283 Hagley Road<br>Birmingham<br>26 Portland Road<br>Birmingham | P9/D/11<br>***#1737***<br> | **John Horace FRANCIS**<br>**Stephen Henry DEAKIN** trading as<br>**DEAKIN & FRANCIS** *<br>17 Regent Place<br>Birmingham | |
| R2/166<br>27 November 1912<br>Clerk entered P13/D/3 in error used for WD&Co.<br>Sent by J H Francis | Weir End<br>Ross<br>Herefordshire<br>Westbourne Road<br>Edgbaston, Birmingham | P13/D/57<br>***#1738***<br>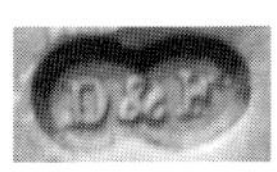 | | |
| R3/33<br>1 September 1926<br>Sent by E Page | 39 Woodstock Road<br>Moseley<br>Birmingham | P15/F/75<br>***#1739***<br>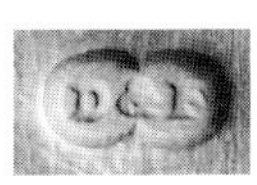 | **DEAKIN & FRANCIS LTD** *<br>17 Regent Place<br>Birmingham | |
| R3/90<br>1 June 1938<br>Sent by C M Wrighton<br>127 Vyse Street<br>Birmingham | | P21/D/2<br>***#1740***<br> | **DEAKIN & FRANCIS** *<br>James Vann (Managing Director)<br>17 Regent Place<br>Birmingham and<br>Audrey House<br>Ely Place<br>London WC1 | Manufacturing jewellers |

| REGISTRATION DETAILS | MAKER'S PRIVATE ADDRESS and DETAILS | PLATE and MARK DETAILS | MAKER/COMPANY and BUSINESS ADDRESS | MAKER'S TRADE |
|---|---|---|---|---|
| R3/100<br>31 July 1941<br>Sent by Joseph Smith & Son Ltd<br>63/65 Vittoria Street<br>Birmingham | | P21/D/6<br>*#1741*<br><br> | **DEAKIN & FRANCIS LTD** *<br>Sealed by:-<br>J R Vann (Director)<br>Regent Place (Registered Office)<br>Birmingham 1 | Manufacturing jewellers |
| R1/114<br>21 October 1899<br>Sent by R J Pike | Private address same as business (Ed: DF in mark = Dimier Frères) | P9/D/13<br>*#1742*<br><br> | **Georges DIMIER**<br>**Edward DIMIER** trading as<br>**DIMIER BROTHERS & CO** *<br>46 Cannon Street<br>London and<br>6 Rue Detilot?<br>Geneva | English and Swiss watch manufacturers |
| R3/131<br>2 March 1950<br>Sent by J Randle<br>182 Berkely Road E<br>Yardley<br>Birmingham 25 | | P21/J/5<br>*#1743*<br>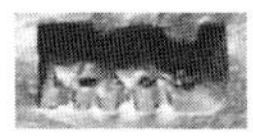 | **D F JACKSON LTD**<br>Sealed in the presence of:-<br>Walter Jackson (Director)<br>J W Jackson (Secretary)<br>35 Frederick Street<br>Birmingham 1 | Wholesale jewellers |
| R3/33<br>10 June 1926<br>Sent by J & R Griffin Ltd | Wilmington<br>Kent | P15/C/169<br>*#1744*<br><br> | **Daniel George COLLINS LTD** *<br>118 Newgate Street<br>London EC | Silversmiths |
| Missing register<br>*c.*1894<br>Similar mark entered LAO 11 June 1897 | | P5/C/548a<br>*#1745*<br><br> | **Daniel George COLLINS**<br>95, 96 Newgate Street<br>London | Silverworker and goldworker |
| Missing register<br>*c.*1894 | | P5/C/548b<br>*#1746*<br><br> | | |
| R1/49<br>17 August 1897<br>Sent by W Aitken<br>C E Soloman | The Briars<br>Grove Park<br>Kent | P5/D/865<br>*#1747*<br>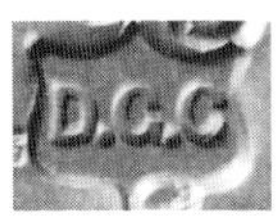<br> | **Daniel George COLLINS**<br>95, 96 Newgate Street<br>London | Silversmith |
| R3/50<br>3 January 1930<br>Sent by D Huntriss | Private address same as business | P15/H/108<br>*#1748*<br><br> | **Dorothy HUNTRISS**<br>Keldhurst<br>Horton Road<br>Willaston<br>Wirral<br>Cheshire | Maker of jewellery |
| R3/33<br>26 July 1926<br>Sent by Dorothy H Darry | Private address same as business | P15/D/74<br>*#1749*<br> | **Dorothy H DARRY**<br>26 Addington Road<br>Liverpool | Metalworker |
| R2/119<br>30 September 1910<br>Sent by E Whitehouse & Son<br>BAO 13.670 | 344 Gillost Road<br>Birmingham | P13/H/62<br>*#1750*<br><br> | **Elias Pinkus HOLLANDER**<br>proprietor of<br>**David HOLLANDER & SON**<br>33 Northampton Street<br>Birmingham | Manufacturers |
| R2/74<br>5 March 1909<br>Sent by Victor Block | 21 Portland Road<br>Edgbaston<br>Birmingham<br>32 Porchester Terrace<br>Bayswater<br>London W | P13/D/7<br>*#1751*<br><br> | **Victor BLOCK**<br>**Arthur Danziger ISAACS** trading as<br>**DANZIGER & ISAACS** *<br>9 Vyse Street<br>Birmingham and<br>84 Hatton Garden<br>London EC | Importers of Jewellers' materials |

| REGISTRATION DETAILS | MAKER'S PRIVATE ADDRESS and DETAILS | PLATE and MARK DETAILS | MAKER/COMPANY and BUSINESS ADDRESS | MAKER'S TRADE |
|---|---|---|---|---|
| R2/153<br>23 March 1912<br>Sent by Victor Block | 21 Portland Road<br>Birmingham<br>170 Piccadilly<br>London | P13/D/42<br>***#1752***<br>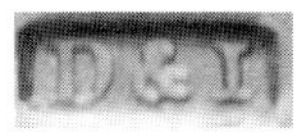 | **Victor BLOCK**<br>**Arthur Danziger ISAACS** trading as<br>**DANZIGER & ISAACS** *<br>9 Vyse Street<br>Birmingham and<br>26, 27 Hatton Garden<br>London | Jewellery importers |
| R3/164<br>7 June 1958<br>Sent by D I Hopkinson | 46 Hawaster Avenue<br>Wallasey | P21/H/77<br>***#1753***<br> | **Dorothy Irene HOPKINSON**<br>No business address entered | No trade entered<br>Student? |
| R2/17<br>28 April 1906<br>Sent by J G Newbold | 12 Wildeston Road<br>Stamford Hill<br>London N | P9/J/56<br>***#1754***<br>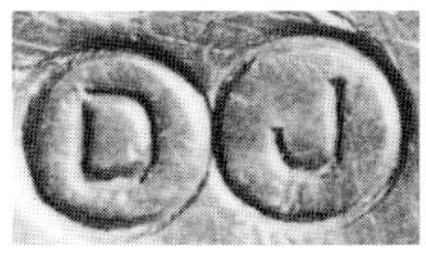 | **Daniel JACOBS**<br>68 Aldersgate Street<br>London EC | Merchant |
| MR2/50,94<br>J3/405 1727/8 | Free 5 February 1727/8 - see also gothic script mark in monogram section at end of part 2 | P1/17/x2<br>***#1755,6***<br> | **Daniel KIRKES**<br>Chester | Silversmith |
| R2/188<br>22 May 1914<br>Sent by J Griffiths<br>BAO 22.071<br>22.073, 22.083 | 47 Eastern Avenue<br>London | P15/L/3<br>***#1757***<br><br>P15/L/4,5<br>***#1758,9***<br> | **David LOEBL** trading as<br>**SCHINDLER & CO** *<br>9 Alderbury Avenue<br>London | Merchants |
| R3/182<br>14 February 1961<br>Sent by D Lampin<br>Two sizes | 31 Wellington Street East<br>Salford 7<br>Lancashire | P21/L/57,58<br>***#1760,1***<br> | **David LAMPIN**<br>No business address entered | Student of goldsmith and silversmith |
| PDB 1828-31<br>MR3/90<br>J1 1828-31 | Gold rings<br>Small DL or DK mark struck deeply and very difficult to decipher | P1/15/x1<br>***#1762***<br> | **David LLOYD**<br>Liverpool | Goldsmith |
| PDB 1828-31<br>MR3/90<br>J1 1828-31 | Gold rings<br><br>Mark very indistinct | P1/21/x1<br>***#1763***<br>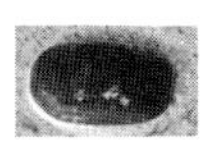 | | |
| R3/186<br>14 August 1962<br>Sent by D Lacy-Hulbert | Walton Cottage<br>near Chesterfield<br>Derbyshire | P21/H/90,91<br>***#1764,5***<br> | **Denise LACY-HULBERT**<br>No business address entered | Student |
| R1/226<br>31 January 1905<br>Sent by Lionel Smith & Co | 52 Cadogan Square<br>London SW | P9/D/45,46<br>***#1766,7***<br> | **Thomas De La RUE & CO LTD** *<br>Stuart De la Rue (Secretary/Director)<br>110 Bunhill Row<br>London EC | Wholesale stationers |
| LPB/78<br>16 July 1884<br>No mark in LPB | | P5/S/x1<br>***#1768***<br> | **David SPIERS**<br>**Lionel SPIERS** *<br>27 Hylton Street<br>Birmingham | Jewellers |
| R2/225<br>7 November 1919<br>Sent by Davis & Matthews<br>Clerk should have entered 36 | 44 Arthur Road<br>Handsworth<br>45 Selsey Road<br>Edgbaston<br>Birmingham | P15/D/56<br>***#1769***<br> | **James DAVIS**<br>**W MATTHEWS** (Ed: trading as)<br>**DAVIS & MATTHEWS**<br>40 Hockley Street<br>Birmingham | Jewellers (Lockets) |

| REGISTRATION DETAILS | MAKER'S PRIVATE ADDRESS and DETAILS | PLATE and MARK DETAILS | MAKER/COMPANY and BUSINESS ADDRESS | MAKER'S TRADE |
|---|---|---|---|---|
| R3/38<br>18 July 1927<br>Sent by self | Private address same as business | P15/M/68<br>*#1770*  | **Dorothy MACLEAN**<br>Norwood<br>Dentons Green<br>St Helens | Art student at Liverpool Art School |
| R2/75<br>17 March 1909<br>Sent by F J Davies<br>BAO 14.436 | Shackerley<br>Four Oaks<br>79 Wheeleys Road<br>Birmingham | P13/M/10<br>*#1771*  | **W Henry MOSS**<br>**Frederick Joseph DAVIES** trading as<br>**DAVIES MOSS & CO**<br>15a Harford Street<br>Birmingham | Silversmiths |
| | | P13/M/9<br>*#1772*  | | |
| | | P13/M/8<br>*#1773*  | | |
| R1/16<br>10 October 1895<br>Sent by D & M Davis<br>Two sizes | 3 Livery Street<br>Birmingham | P5/D/689a,b<br>*#1774,5* 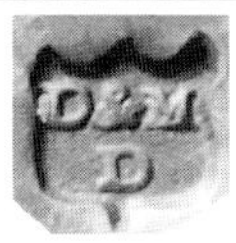 | **David DAVIS** trading as<br>**David and Maurice DAVIS** *<br>3 Livery Street<br>Birmingham | Silversmiths |
| Different style of mark | | P5/D/689c<br>*#1776*  | | |
| R3/114<br>20 March 1946<br>Sent by D M Hart<br>Three sizes | Private address same as business | P21/H/30-33<br>*#1777-80*  | **Dorothy Mary HART**<br>33 Childwall Park Avenue<br>Liverpool 16 | Amateur worker in jewellery and light metal |
| R3/3<br>14 May 1921<br>Sent by D M Posnett | The Mount<br>Runcorn<br>6 June 1921 now Mrs D M Thompson | P15/P/170<br>*#1781*  | **Doris Mary POSNETT**<br>Liverpool School of Art<br>Edgeley House (6 June 1921)<br>Whitchurch<br>Shropshire | Silverwork student |
| R3/147<br>21 November 1953<br>Sent by D M Taylor<br>Two sizes | Stanley Cottage<br>Atherton<br>Nr Manchester | P21/T/20,21<br>*#1782,3*  | **Dora Margaret TAYLOR**<br>No business address entered | Student |
| LPB/24<br>1 March 1880<br>Sent by Coley Brothers | Mark only in LPB - no name or address in LPB | P3/D/x3<br>*#1784-86*  | **DEAKIN & NEPHEW** *<br>30 Regent Place<br>Birmingham | Manufacturing jewellers and silversmiths |
| LPB/24<br>14 January 1881<br>Sent by Jackson & Sons, Albion Street Birmingham | | P3/D/x3<br>*#1787-9*  | | |
| R1/37<br>28 November 1896<br>Sent by W H Haseler C E Soloman | 33 Maxwell Drive<br>Pollokshields | P5/D/808<br>*#1790*  | **David DOW**<br>68 Argyle Street<br>Glasgow | Watchmaker and jeweller |
| R2/12<br>27 February 1906<br>Sent by W Davies | 146 Limewood Road<br>Handsworth<br>88 Wills Street<br>Lozells<br>Birmingham | P9/D/51<br>*#1791*  | **William DAVIES**<br>**George POWERS** trading as<br>**DAVIES & POWERS**<br>146½ Hockley Hill<br>Birmingham | General ring makers |

| REGISTRATION DETAILS | MAKER'S PRIVATE ADDRESS and DETAILS | PLATE and MARK DETAILS | MAKER/COMPANY and BUSINESS ADDRESS | MAKER'S TRADE |
|---|---|---|---|---|
| R2/14<br>21 March 1906<br>Two sizes<br>Cancelled<br>2 July 1906 | 146 Limewood Road<br>Handsworth<br>88 Wills Street<br>Lozells<br>Birmingham | P9/D/53x2<br>***#1792,3***<br> | **William DAVIES**<br>**George POWERS** trading as<br>**DAVIES & POWERS**<br>146½ Hockley Hill<br>Birmingham | General ring makers |
| R2/236<br>11 December 1920<br>Sent by William Thomas Entwhistle | 8 Clifford Road<br>Seacombe<br>Cheshire | P15/D/58<br>***#1794***<br> | **DAWELLS PATENT PIPE CO LTD**<br>William Thomas Entwistle (Secretary)<br>23 William Street<br>Liverpool | Tobacco pipe manufacturers and mounters |
| R3/148<br>8 December 1953<br>Sent by D Redman | 16 Dunbar Road<br>Hillside<br>Southport | P21/R/20<br>***#1795***<br> | **David REDMAN**<br>No business address entered | Amateur |
| Missing register<br>*c.*1888<br>Similar mark entered<br>LAO 26 March 1890 | | P5/R/194<br>***#1796***<br> | **David RANDLE** *<br>47 The Butts<br>Coventry | Watchcase maker |
| R3/88<br>7 July 1937<br>Sent by B H Bolton & Sons, 35 Hockley Hill, Birmingham | | P21/H/2<br>***#1797***<br> | **Dudley Russell HOWITT**<br>67, 68 Hatton Garden<br>London EC1 | Wholesale jeweller |
| R3/168<br>27 June 1959<br>Sent by D R Williams | Private address same as business | P21/W/90<br>***#1798***<br> | **Daniel Richard WILLIAMS**<br>42 Parkfield Road<br>Aigburth<br>Liverpool 17 | Goldsmith and silversmith |
| R2117<br>30 August 1910<br>Sent by Benson Brothers | 64 Clarence Drive<br>Glasgow | P13/S/57<br>***#1799***<br> | **David SPECULAND**<br>136 Irongate<br>Glasgow | Wholesale jeweller |
| R3/73<br>29 September 1934<br>Sent by Dimmer & Son | Both residing at<br>Cotteswold<br>Clarence Road<br>Devonshire Park<br>Birkenhead | P15/D/87<br>***#1800***<br>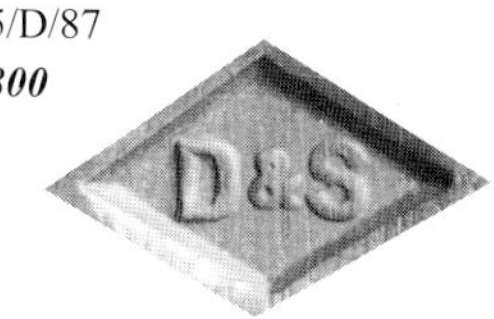 | **George DIMMER**<br>**George DIMMER junior** trading as<br>**DIMMER & SON** *<br>20 Eastgate Row<br>Chester | Retail jewellers |
| R2/144<br>22 September 1911<br>B.O 18.261<br>Sent by J & R Griffin Ltd | 376 Great Western Road<br>Glasgow | P13/D/37<br>***#1801***<br> | **George Gabriel DUNCAN**<br>trading as **DUNCAN & SCOBBIE** *<br>81 St Vincent Street<br>Glasgow | Silversmiths |
| R2/185<br>17 March 1914<br>Two sizes Sent by Clark & Sewell | | P15/D/15-17<br>***#1802-4***<br> | | |
| R2/220<br>29 May 1919<br>Sent by J & R Griffin Ltd | | P15/D/34,35<br>***#1805,6***<br> | **George G DUNCAN** (Sole Partner)<br>trading as **DUNCAN & SCOBBIE** *<br>81 St Vincent Street<br>Glasgow | |
| R1/186<br>3 March 1903<br>Sent by Nathan & Hayes<br>Two sizes | Martello Terrace<br>Holywood<br>County Down<br>Ireland | P9/N/17,18<br>***#1807,8***<br>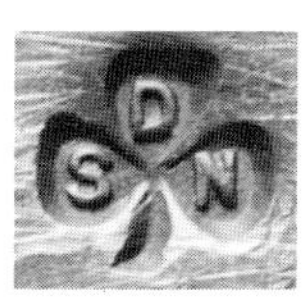 | **Sharman Dermott NEILL** *<br>12 Donegall Place<br>Belfast | Silversmith |
| R1/192<br>12 May 1903<br>Sent by J Thomason<br>Two sizes | | P9/N/23,24<br>***#1809,10***<br>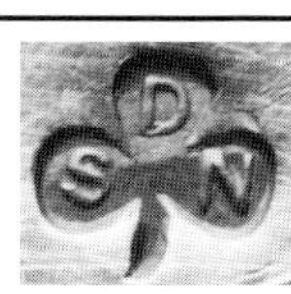 | | Silversmith and jeweller |

| REGISTRATION DETAILS | MAKER'S PRIVATE ADDRESS and DETAILS | PLATE and MARK DETAILS | MAKER/COMPANY and BUSINESS ADDRESS | MAKER'S TRADE |
|---|---|---|---|---|
| R1/211<br>30 March 1904<br>Sent by Stokes & Ireland | Martello Terrace<br>Holywood<br>County Down<br>Ireland. | P9/N/31<br>***#1811***<br> | **Sharman Dermott NEILL** *<br>12 Donegall Place<br>Belfast | Silversmith |
| R2/13<br>16 March 1906<br>Sent by Stokes & Ireland | Martello Terrace<br>Holywood<br>County Down | P9/N/35<br>***#1812***<br>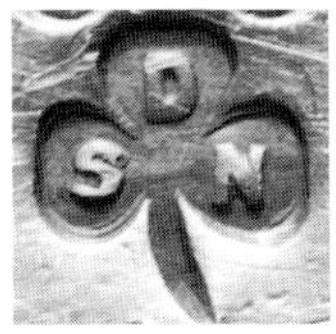 | | Silversmith and jeweller |
| R2/66<br>2 October 1908<br>Sent by Adie Brothers<br>Two sizes | Ardmoyle<br>Cultra | P13/N/5,6<br>***#1813,4***<br>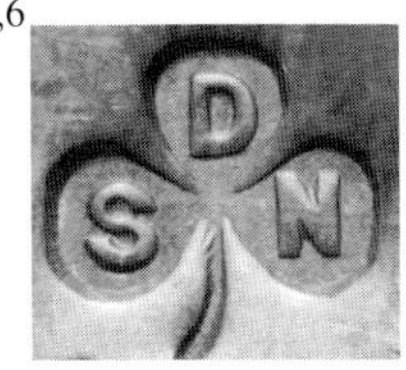 | | Silversmith |
| R2/92<br>16 September 1909<br>Sent by S Blanckensee & Son<br>Two sizes | | P13/D/7,8<br>***#1815,6***<br> | **H HAMILTON**<br>**G W SMALLWOOD**<br>**T CALDWELL**<br>Hugh Smylie (Secretary)<br>Sharman D Neill (Managing Director)<br>22 Donegal Place<br>Belfast | Silversmiths |
| R2/176<br>30 September 1913<br>Two sizes<br>Sent by S Blanckensee & Son | | P13/N/34,35<br>***#1817,8***<br> | **Sharman D NEILL LTD** *<br>H Hamilton (Director)<br>22 Donegal Place<br>Belfast | Jewellers and silversmiths |
| 12 May 1928 | | P15/N/16<br>***#1819***<br>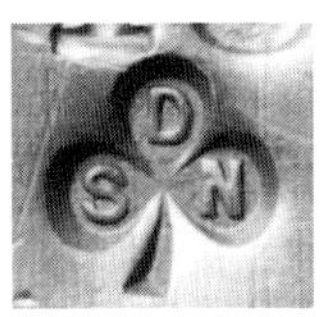 | | |
| R3/60<br>20 November 1931<br>Sent by S Blanckensee & Son Ltd<br>19–35 Regent Place<br>Birmingham | | P15/N/19<br>***#1820***<br>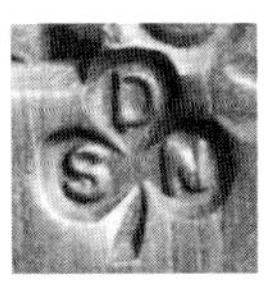 | **SHARMAN D NEILL LTD** *<br>(Incorporating Gibson & Co)<br>Common seal of company affixed in the presence of<br>J H Lunn (Director)<br>J F Gieve (Director)<br>T F Weir (Secretary)<br>22 Donegall Place (Registered Office)<br>Belfast | Goldsmiths and silversmiths |
| R3/68<br>28 October 1933<br>Sent by Payton, Pepper & Son Ltd<br>3-5 Vyse Street<br>Birmingham | | P15/N/23<br>***#1821***<br>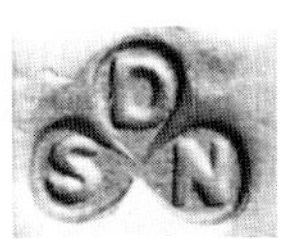 | **Sharman D NEILL LTD** *<br>22 Donegal Place<br>Belfast | |

| REGISTRATION DETAILS | MAKER'S PRIVATE ADDRESS and DETAILS | PLATE and MARK DETAILS | MAKER/COMPANY and BUSINESS ADDRESS | MAKER'S TRADE |
|---|---|---|---|---|
| R3/72<br>13 August 1934<br>Sent by S Blanckensee & Sons Ltd<br>19-35 Regent Place<br>Birmingham | | P15/N/24,25<br>***#1822,3***<br> | **Sharman D NEILL LTD** *<br>Common seal of company affixed in the presence of<br>John H Lunn (Director)<br>George T Weir (Director)<br>T F Weir (Secretary)<br>36 Donegall Place (Registered Office)<br>Belfast | Jewellers, silversmiths and opticians |
| R2/10<br>5 February 1906<br>Sent by R J Wakefield | Private address same as business | P9/T/58<br>***#1824***<br> | **David TAYLOR**<br>2 Jenner Road<br>Stoke Newington<br>London | Wholesale jeweller |
| R3/58<br>15 July 1931<br>Sent by Miss Dollie Turner | Private address same as business | P15/T/58<br>***#1825***<br> | **Dollie TURNER (Miss)**<br>9 Waverley Road<br>Sefton Park<br>Liverpool | Gold and silversmith |
| 16 January 1932 | | P15/T/68<br>***#1826***<br> | | |
| R3/173<br>16 June 1960<br>Two sizes<br>Sent by D Titterington | 14 Olive Road<br>Timperley<br>Altrincham<br>Cheshire | P21/T/42,43<br>***#1827,8***<br> | **Doris TITTERINGTON**<br>No business address entered | Student of silversmithing |
| MR1/132<br>Free 1716 | | P1/13/x1<br>***#1829***<br> | **Bartholomew DUKE**<br>Lower Bridge Street (West)<br>Chester | Silversmith |
| R3/73<br>16 October 1934<br>Sent by D Willington | Private address same as business | P15/W/108<br>***#1830***<br> | **Dorothy WILLINGTON**<br>Dalmeny<br>17 Hillside Road<br>Birkdale<br>Lancashire | No trade entered |
| R3/162<br>19 July 1957<br>Sent by D Weston | 27 Rye Bank Road<br>Old Trafford<br>Manchester 16 | P21/W/88<br>***#1831***<br> | **Miss Dorothy WESTON**<br>No business address entered | Student |
| R1/199<br>13 August 1903<br>Sent by H Mottram<br>A H Tongue | Private address same as business | P9/A/51<br>***#1832***<br> | **David William ALLMAN** trading as<br>**THE ALLMAN PIPE CO**<br>257 Wilmslow Road<br>Fallowfield<br>Manchester | Pipe manufacturer |
| LPB/90<br>13 November 1884 | | P5/W/x1<br>***#1833***<br>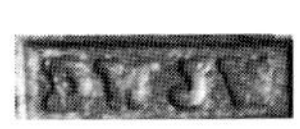 | **David and John WELLBY** *<br>18, 20 Garrick Street<br>London | Diamond merchants, jewellers and manufacturers of plate |
| Missing register<br>*c.*1886<br>Similar mark entered LAO 7 December 1887 | | P5/W/34<br>***#1834***<br> | | |

EA–EB

| REGISTRATION DETAILS | MAKER'S PRIVATE ADDRESS and DETAILS | PLATE and MARK DETAILS | MAKER/COMPANY and BUSINESS ADDRESS | MAKER'S TRADE |
|---|---|---|---|---|
| R3/87<br>20 April 1937<br>Sent by E G Anderson | 39 Caldwell Road<br>Liverpool 19 | P21/A/1<br>***#1835***<br> | **Eric Gordon ANDERSON**<br>City School of Art<br>Liverpool | Art student |
| R3/139<br>30 September 1952<br>Sent by E Almond<br>Two sizes | 6 Cleveland Avenue<br>Darlington | P21/A/17-19<br>***#1836-8***<br> | **Edward ALMOND** (Proprietor)<br>11 Duke Street<br>Darlington<br>Co Durham | General engraving, repairing, etc |
| 25 January 1955 | | P21/A/21<br>***#1839***<br> | | |
| R3/59<br>14 October 1931<br>Sent by E A C Bennett | Private address same as business | P15/B/205<br>***#1840***<br> | **Eric Arthur Coley BENNETT**<br>4 Woodlands Road<br>Aigburth<br>Liverpool | Grain salesman |
| R3/125<br>5 August 1948<br>Sent by E A Hart<br>Two sizes | 8 Cranmere Avenue<br>Levenshulme<br>Manchester 19 | P21/H/45,46<br>***#1841,2***<br> | **Ernest Albert HART**<br>No business address entered | Student silversmith |
| Missing register<br>*c.*1891<br>Similar mark entered LAO 30 March 1885 | | P5/H/374<br>***#1843***<br> | **Edward Albert HAYNES** *<br>377 Liverpool Road<br>Islington<br>London N | Tobacconist |
| R1/88<br>17 December 1898<br>Sent by E A Marsh<br>J H Wynn<br>Edwards Brothers | Whitehead Road<br>Aston<br>Birmingham | P9/M/5-8<br>***#1844-7***<br> | **Edwin Alfred MARSH**<br>Klondyke Works<br>Northampton Street<br>Birmingham | Jeweller |
| Missing register<br>*c.*1889 | | P5/M/258<br>***#1848***<br> | | |
| R2/232<br>9 June 1920<br>Sent by Benson Brothers | 38 Mansion House Road<br>Glasgow<br><br>Seen on 1920/1 watchcase | P15/M/38<br>***#1849***<br> | **E A MARSH LTD**<br>(Philip Woolfson)<br>182 Vyse Street<br>Birmingham | Manufacturing jewellers |
| Not in R1 as expected | | P5/M/822<br>***#1850***<br> | | |
| R1/23<br>13 March 1896<br>Sent by A H Tongue | 100 Aston Road<br>Birmingham | P5/X*sic*/737<br>***#1851***<br> | **Edward Albert WOOD**<br>100 Aston Road<br>Birmingham | Clay pipe manufacturer |
| R3/144<br>22 May 1953<br>Sent by E Beeson | 86 Schofield Road<br>Peel Green<br>Eccles<br>NB. #38 also used for MJB | P21/B/38<br>***#1852***<br>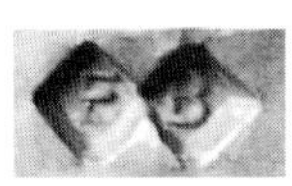 | **Edith BEESON**<br>No business address entered | Student |
| R1/181<br>15 December 1902<br>Sent by J W Caldicott<br>Two sizes | Strathmore<br>Orton<br>Birmingham | P9/A*sic*/43,44<br>***#1853,4***<br> | **John William CALDICOTT** trading as **Edward BAKER & SON** *<br>31 Augusta Street<br>Birmingham | Pencil case makers |
| Missing register<br>*c.*1886 | See other EB marks | P5/B/19<br>***#1855***<br> | **Unidentified** | |

| REGISTRATION DETAILS | MAKER'S PRIVATE ADDRESS and DETAILS | PLATE and MARK DETAILS | MAKER/COMPANY and BUSINESS ADDRESS | MAKER'S TRADE |
|---|---|---|---|---|
| R1/95<br>17 March 1899<br>Sent by Ernest Bell | Private address same as business | P9/B/13<br>***#1856***<br> | **Ernest BELL**<br>26 Gordon Road<br>Handsworth<br>Birmingham | Goldsmith and jeweller |
| R2/132<br>4 April 1911<br>Sent by Edward Bott | Private address same as business | P13/B/118<br>***#1857***<br> | **Edward BOTT**<br>57 Liversage Street<br>Derby | Jeweller |
| Missing register<br>*c.*1886<br>Similar mark BAO<br>25 September 1888 | | P5/E/61<br>***#1858***<br> | **EVANS & BROWN** *<br>Northampton Street<br>Birmingham | Jewellers |
| LPB/16<br>6 August 1879<br>LPB mark shown | | Not on P3<br>***#1859***<br> | **E BURNETT**<br>4 Moon Street<br>Crown Street<br>Liverpool | Trade not identified |
| Not in R2 as expected<br>*c.* March 1918 | | P15/B/98<br>***#1860***<br> | | |
| R1/129<br>30 June 1900<br>Sent by E Baker & Son | Southbourne<br>Acocks Green<br>Nr Birmingham | P9/B/31<br>***#1861***<br> | **J William CALDICOTT**<br>**Edward BAKER & SON** *<br>31 Augusta Street<br>Birmingham | Gold and silver pencil case makers |
| R1/181<br>15 December 1902<br>Two sizes | | P9/A*sic*/45,46<br>***#1862,3***<br>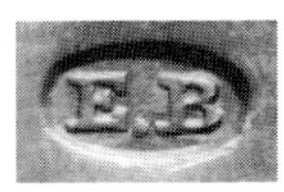 | | |
| R1/185<br>13 February 1903<br>Sent by J W Caldicott | Strathmore<br>Olton<br>Warwickshire | P9/B/96<br>***#1864***<br> | **John William CALDICOTT** *<br>31 Augusta Street<br>Birmingham | |
| R2/166<br>27 November 1912<br>Sent by E Baker & Son<br>BAO 20.740, 20.741<br>Two sizes | Stratford House<br>St Bernard Road<br>Olton | P13/B/136,137<br>***#1865,6***<br> | **John Richard MANSON** trading as<br>**Edward BAKER & SON** *<br>31 Augusta Street<br>Birmingham | Gold and silver pencil case manufacturers |
| R2/187<br>15 May 1914<br>Sent by George Wells | | P15/B/49-52<br>***#1867-70***<br> | | |
| R2/211<br>28 March 1917<br>Sent by Dorothy Roberts | | P15/B/67<br>***#1871***<br> | **E BAKER & SON** *<br>J R Manson (Proprietor)<br>30, 31 Augusta Street<br>Birmingham | |
| Not in R2 as expected<br>*c.* June 1919<br>Two sizes | | P15/B/97,100-102<br>***#1872-75***<br>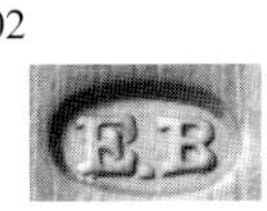 | | |
| R3/37<br>19 May 1927<br>Sent by Civic Co Ltd | | P15/B/184,185<br>***#1876,7***<br> | **Edward BOTSHALL**<br>49 Highlever Road<br>London W10 | Fancy goods dealer |
| R1/69<br>29 June 1894<br>Sent by Joseph Adelman<br>Cancelled<br>26 November 1899 | 20 Cheetham Street<br>Cheetham<br>Manchester | P5/A/569<br>***#1878***<br> | **Joseph ADELMAN** trading as<br>**Edgar BROADHEAD** * &<br>**Joseph ADELMAN** *<br>68a Lancaster Avenue<br>Fennel Street<br>Manchester | Jewellers |

| REGISTRATION DETAILS | MAKER'S PRIVATE ADDRESS and DETAILS | PLATE and MARK DETAILS | MAKER/COMPANY and BUSINESS ADDRESS | MAKER'S TRADE |
|---|---|---|---|---|
| Missing register<br>*c.*1893 | | P5/E/488<br>***#1879*** 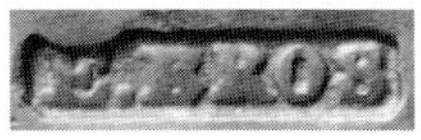 | **Unidentified** | |
| Missing register<br>*c.*1894<br>Adjacent P5/E/541 | | P5/E/x1<br>***#1880***  | **Unidentified** | |
| R3/164<br>28 August 1958<br>Sent by Lowe & Sons<br>11 Bridge Street Row<br>Chester | | P21/B/55<br>***#1881***  | **Edward BARNARD & SONS LTD** *<br>54 Hatton Garden<br>London EC1 | Silversmiths and goldsmiths |
| 11 July 1962 | | P21/B/70<br>***#1882***  | | |
| R3/136<br>30 January 1952<br>Sent by E Cordery | Private address same as business | P21/C/53<br>***#1883***  | **Elizabeth CORDERY**<br>Greendale<br>382 Walkden Road<br>Worsley<br>Lancashire | Student |
| PDB 1825-30<br>MR3/78<br>PP1/186<br>J1 1825-9 | Gold rings | P1/25/x2<br>***#1884,5***  | **Edward CHRISTIAN**<br>Liverpool | Goldsmith |
| MR2/70<br>J3/400 | Spoon 1753<br>Tentative attribution – probate 1767 – possibly too early for Edward Christian - relative? | Not on P1<br>***#1886***  | **Edmund CRESWELL**<br>Manchester | Jeweller |
| LPB/20<br>5 August 1881 | | P3/C/x1<br>***#1887***  | **Edward CULVER** *<br>Spencer Works<br>Clerkenwell Road<br>London | Wholesale manufacturer of jewellery |
| LPB/96<br>19 April 1882<br>LPB mark shown | | Not on P3<br>***#1888***  | **Edward CASTELBERG** *<br>38 Sekforde Street<br>London | Watchcase maker |
| R1/192<br>12 May 1903<br>Sent by E Culver | 9 Amhurst Park Drive<br>Stamford Hill | P9/C/84,89,90<br>***#1889-91***  | **Edward CULVER**<br>**Alfred Ernest CULVER** trading as<br>**E CULVER & SON** *<br>59/60 Myddleton Street<br>London | Gold chain makers and jewellers |
| R1/133<br>9 October 1900<br>Two sizes Sent by<br>W H Ashford | | P9/C/38,39<br>***#1892,3***  | **Edward CULVER** trading as<br>**E CULVER & SON** *<br>59/60 Myddleton Street<br>London EC | Manufacturing jewellers and chain makers |
| R1/192<br>12 May 1903<br>Sent by E Culver | | P9/C/85,86,88<br>***#1894-6***  | **Edward CULVER**<br>**Alfred Ernest CULVER** trading as<br>**E CULVER & SON** *<br>59/60 Myddleton Street<br>London | Gold chain makers and jewellers |
| Not in R2 as expected<br>*c.* February 1910 | | P13/C/57<br>***#1897***  | | |
| R1/83<br>9 November 1898<br>Sent by<br>E C Arrowsmith | 32 Tenby Street<br>Birmingham<br><br>#8 in R1 (*sic*) | P9/A/3<br>***#1898***  | **Edwin Clement ARROWSMITH**<br>32 Tenby Street<br>Birmingham | Manufacturing jeweller |

| REGISTRATION DETAILS | MAKER'S PRIVATE ADDRESS and DETAILS | PLATE and MARK DETAILS | MAKER/COMPANY and BUSINESS ADDRESS | MAKER'S TRADE |
|---|---|---|---|---|
| Missing register<br>*c.*1893 | | P5/E/513<br>***#1899***<br> | **ELLIS & CO** ? | |
| R1/43<br>1 May 1897<br>Sent by W Aitken | 37 Sterling Road<br>Birmingham | P5/E/837<br>***#1900***<br> | **Israel Sigmund GREENBERG**<br>trading as **ELLIS & CO** *<br>15½ Great Hampton Street and<br>**I S GREENBERG & CO** *<br>126 Great Hampton Street<br>Birmingham | Silversmiths |
| R1/86<br>2 December 1898<br>Sent by W Aitken | Claremont<br>Woodburn Road<br>Edgbaston<br>Birmingham | P9/E/2<br>***#1901***<br> | **Israel Sigmund GREENBERG**<br>trading as **ELLIS & CO** *<br>Empire Works<br>Great Hampton Street<br>Birmingham | Silversmiths and electro-platers |
| R2/100<br>14 January 1928<br>Sent by Elkington & Co Ltd | Kingston<br>Trinity Road<br>Handsworth | P15/E/37<br>***#1902***<br>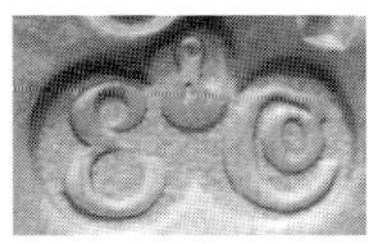 | **ELKINGTON & CO LTD** * | Goldsmiths and silversmiths |
| R2/70<br>23 December 1908<br>Sent by Elkington & Co Ltd<br>Four sizes | Kingston [1]<br>Trinity Road<br>Handsworth | P13/E/3-6<br>***#1903-6***<br> | **ELKINGTON & CO LTD** *<br>Hula G Elkington (Director)<br>T B Reid [1] (Secretary)<br>Newhall Street and<br>Brearley Street<br>Birmingham in addition to the addresses shown above. | Goldsmith silversmith and jewellers |
| R2/100<br>18 December 1909<br>Sent by Elkington & Co Ltd<br>Kingston<br>Trinity Road<br>Handsworth<br>Two sizes<br>BAO 17.292,17.293 | | P13/E/13,14<br>***#1907,8***<br>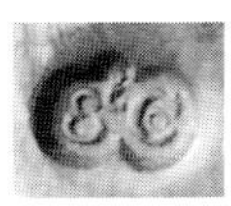 | **ELKINGTON & CO LTD**<br>also trading as<br>**WATTS & RUMBALL LTD** *<br>T B Reid (Secretary)<br>34 Buchanan Street<br>Glasgow and<br>22 Regent Street and<br>73 Cheapside<br>London and<br>Lord Street<br>Liverpool and<br>St Anne's Square<br>Manchester and<br>Northumberland Street<br>Newcastle upon Tyne | Goldsmiths and silversmiths |
| R3/96<br>24 November 1939<br>Sent by Ellis & Co | | P21/E/1<br>***#1909***<br> | **ELLIS & CO (BIRMINGHAM) LTD** *<br>Empire Works<br>3 Hall Street<br>Birmingham | Silversmiths |
| R3/176<br>3 January 1961<br>Sent by William Margulis (Director) | | P21/W/97<br>***#1910***<br> | **ELCO CLOCKS & WATCHES LTD**<br>51 Hatton Garden<br>London EC1 | Watch importers and distributors |
| Missing register<br>*c.*1886<br>Similar mark entered LAO 2 February 1885 | | P5/D/21<br>***#1911***<br> | **Edward DAVIS** *<br>125 Houndsditch<br>London E | Tobacconist |

| REGISTRATION DETAILS | MAKER'S PRIVATE ADDRESS and DETAILS | PLATE and MARK DETAILS | MAKER/COMPANY and BUSINESS ADDRESS | MAKER'S TRADE |
|---|---|---|---|---|
| Missing register<br>*c.*1890<br>Similar mark entered<br>LAO 2 February 1885 | | P5/D/273<br>***#1912***<br> | **Edward DAVIS** *<br>125 Houndsditch<br>London E | Tobacconist |
| Missing register<br>*c.*1887<br>Adjacent P5/D/681<br>E Dimier | | P5/D/81<br>***#1913***<br> | **Unidentified** | |
| R1/136<br>7 November 1900<br>Sent by W H Ashford | 64 Wills Street<br>Lozells<br>Birmingham | P9/D/19<br>***#1914***<br> | **Edgar DAVIES**<br>Lozells<br>Birmingham | Wholesale jeweller |
| Not in R1 as expected<br>Adjacent P5/D/81 see E D above<br>Similar mark entered<br>LAO 8 July 1884 | Ed: A major importer of Swiss watches – company later called Selling Agency | P5/D/681<br>***#1915***<br> | **Edward DIMIER** trading as<br>**DIMIER BROTHERS** *<br>46 Cannon Street<br>London EC | Watch importers and jewellers |
| LPB/24<br>14 October 1880<br>Sent by J Knight<br>Similar mark entered<br>BAO 12 March 1860 | | P3/D/x1<br>***#1916***<br> | **Joseph EMANUEL**<br>**Isaac DAVIS** trading as<br>**DAVIS & CO** *<br>Frederick Street<br>Birmingham | Factors |
| R3/12<br>24 August 1922<br>Sent by W H Tandy & Sons | 58 Princess Way<br>Wallasey<br>24 Kings Way<br>Wallasey<br>Cheshire | P15/P/183<br>***#1917***<br> | **William Edmund PHILLIP**<br>**John PHILLIP** trading as<br>**E DIXON PHILLIP**<br>84 Renshaw Street<br>Liverpool | Jewellers |
| R1/196<br>16 June 1903<br>Sent by A H Tongue | Mill Hill Park<br>Acton<br>London W1 | P9/D/42<br>***#1918***<br>§<br> | **E DEGUINGAND**<br>**F T DEGUINGAND**<br>**P C DEGUINGAND**<br>5 Colonial Road<br>Minories<br>London | Briar pipe manufacturers |
| LPB/94<br>31 July 1884<br>Sent by John Harrison | | P5/W/x1<br>***#1919***<br> | **Edward D WILMOT & SON** *<br>30 Hylton Street<br>Birmingham | Wholesale and manufacturing jewellers and silversmiths and factors |
| Missing register<br>*c.*1894 | | P5/E/541<br>***#1920***<br> | **Unidentified** | |
| R3/24<br>22 October 1924<br>Sent by Civic Company Ltd | Private address same as business | P15/E/27<br>***#1921***<br> | **Edgar EVERETT**<br>71 Balfour Road<br>West Ealing<br>London W13 | Fancy goods dealer |
| R3/114<br>24 May 1946<br>Sent by Eedee Manufacturing Co | 374 Boldmere Road [1]<br>Sutton Coldfield<br>Warwickshire<br>10 Victoria Terrace [2]<br>Arthur Street<br>Small Heath<br>Birmingham | P21/E/2<br>***#1922***<br> | **EEDEE MANUFACTURING CO**<br>Arthur Edwards[1]<br>Thomas Davis[2]<br>27 Northampton Street<br>Hockley<br>Birmingham 18 | Jewellers and novelties |
| R3/111<br>27 November 1945<br>Sent by E E Ward | 12 Hazel Bank<br>Kings Norton<br>Birmingham 13 | P21/W/41<br>***#1923***<br> | **Edgar Ernest WARD**<br>**WARD BROTHERS BIRMINGHAM LTD**<br>124 Branston Street<br>Birmingham | Manufacturing jewellers |

| REGISTRATION DETAILS | MAKER'S PRIVATE ADDRESS and DETAILS | PLATE and MARK DETAILS | MAKER/COMPANY and BUSINESS ADDRESS | MAKER'S TRADE |
|---|---|---|---|---|
| PDB 1821<br>MR3/82 | Gold rings | Not on P1<br>***#1924*** **E F?** | **E FOXALL**<br>Town not entered | Goldsmith |
| PDB 1819-22<br>MR3/82 | Gold rings | Not on P1<br>***#1925*** **E F?** | **Elizabeth FRANCE** (widow of<br>Manchester James France) | Goldsmith |
| Not in LPB as expected struck next to mark for Edwin Fear - see below | Mark struck post-1860<br>Fear also dealer in tools and materials<br>May also be for Edward Francis – see next entry | P3/F/x2<br>***#1926,7***  | **Edwin FEAR**<br>4 Bristol Bridge<br>Bristol | Wholesale and retail watch and clock manufacturer |
| R1/123<br>20 March 1900<br>Sent by R Gravenor | Private address same as business | P9/F/5<br>***#1928***  | **Edward FRANCIS**<br>Carno RSO<br>Montgomeryshire | Watchmaker and jeweller |
| Missing register<br>*c.*1887 | | P5/F/104<br>***#1929*** 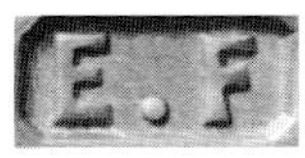 | | |
| Missing register<br>*c.*1892 | | P5/F/442<br>***#1930***  | | |
| Missing register<br>*c.*1888 | | P5/F/152<br>***#1931***  | | |
| LPB/30<br>8 November 1880 | Also dealer in tools and materials | P3/F/x2<br>***#1932,3***  | **Edwin FEAR**<br>4 Bristol Bridge<br>Bristol | Wholesale and retail watch and clock manufacturer |
| Missing register<br>*c.*1887 | | P5/F/104<br>***#1934***  | **Unidentified** | |
| LPB/30<br>CWMP 1866-86<br>*c.*1880-3<br>Sent by W Hickman<br>46 Mount Street<br>Coventry | Curiously name and date not in LPB | P3/F/x3<br>***#1935-7***  | **Edwin FLYNN**<br>Oxford Terrace (1866)<br>3 Hearsall Terrace (1874)<br>10 Russell Terrace (1886)<br>Chapel Fields<br>Coventry | Watch manufacturer |
| R3/80<br>1 November 1935<br>Sent by E Finch | Private address same as business | P15/F/42<br>***#1938*** 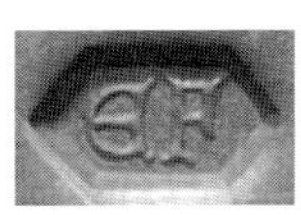 | **Eliza FINCH**<br>4 Town Lane (1935)<br>20 Everard Road (moved 1 Dec 1960)<br>Southport | Art student |
| 30 November 1960 | | P21/F/34<br>***#1939***  | | |
| R2/137<br>30 May 1911<br>Sent by Edward F Braham | 34 Clarendon Road<br>Edgbaston<br>87 Holly Road<br>Handsworth<br>Birmingham | P13/B/125,126<br>***#1940,1***  | **Edward F BRAHAM LTD**<br>E F Braham (Director)<br>F C Tinings (Director)<br>88 Vyse Street<br>Birmingham | Jewellers and silversmiths |

| REGISTRATION DETAILS | MAKER'S PRIVATE ADDRESS and DETAILS | PLATE and MARK DETAILS | MAKER/COMPANY and BUSINESS ADDRESS | MAKER'S TRADE |
|---|---|---|---|---|
| R2/162<br>1 October 1912<br>Sent by Edward F Braham Ltd | 34 Clarendon Road<br>Edgbaston | P15/B/29-31<br>***#1942-4***<br> | **Edward F BRAHAM LTD**<br>88 Vyse Street<br>Birmingham | Wholesale jewellers and silversmiths |
| R2/215<br>23 April 1918<br>Sent by E F Braham | Knowle<br>Near Birmingham | P15/B/87-92<br>***#1945-50***<br> | **Edward F BRAHAM LTD**<br>**E F BRAHAM** (Secretary and Director)<br>88 Vyse Street<br>Birmingham | |
| R1/2<br>31 October 1894<br>Sent by W Aitken<br>Hilliard & Thomason<br>A J Smith<br>Three sizes | 37 Vyse Street<br>Birmingham | P5/aboveB/619x3<br>***#1951-3***<br> | **Edward Foligne BRAHAM**<br>88 Vyse Street<br>Birmingham | |
| LPB/16<br>29 October 1880<br>Similar mark BAO 18 December 1866 | | P3/B/x3<br>***#1954-6***<br> | **Edward Foster BOOTH**<br>111 Vyse Street<br>Birmingham | Jeweller |
| Not in LPB as expected<br>*c.*1883 | | P5/B/x1<br>***#1957***<br> | | |
| Missing register<br>*c.*1889 | | P5/B/245<br>***#1958***<br>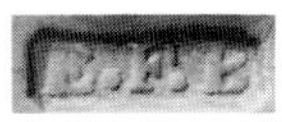 | | |
| Missing register<br>*c.*1889 | | P5/B/262<br>***#1959***<br> | | |
| Missing register<br>*c.*1891 | | P5/B/392<br>***#1960***<br> | | |
| Missing register<br>*c.*1891 | | P5/B/396<br>***#1961***<br> | | |
| Missing register<br>*c.*1893 | | P5/B/516<br>***#1962***<br> | | |
| Missing register<br>*c.*1886 | | P5/B/62<br>***#1963***<br> | | |
| R1/6<br>3 May 1894<br>Sent by Hollis & Newman | | P5/aboveB/556a<br>***#1964***<br> | **Emil BAUER and**<br>**Frank BAUER** *<br>52 Albion Street<br>Birmingham | Jewellers |
| | | P5/aboveB/556b<br>***#1965***<br> | | |
| R1/167<br>29 April 1902<br>Sent by W H Ashford | 14 Brighton Place<br>Portobello N8 and<br>6 Wellington Road<br>Handsworth Wood<br>Birmingham | P9/B/92<br>***#1966***<br> | **Emil Frederick BAUER** trading as<br>**E & F BAUER** *<br>52 Albion Street<br>Birmingham | |
| Not in R2 as expected<br>*c.* December 1915 to June 1916 | | P15/B/63<br>***#1967***<br> | | |
| R2/126<br>18 January 1911<br>Sent by Dempsey | 25 Edenhall Avenue<br>Burrage | P13/G/32<br>***#1968***<br> | **Edward GOUGH**<br>17 Thomas Street<br>Manchester | Working jeweller |

| REGISTRATION DETAILS | MAKER'S PRIVATE ADDRESS and DETAILS | PLATE and MARK DETAILS | MAKER/COMPANY and BUSINESS ADDRESS | MAKER'S TRADE |
|---|---|---|---|---|
| R3/133<br>14 June 1950<br>Sent by E E Green | Silverdale<br>18 Ashton Road<br>Newton-le-Willows<br>Lancs | P21/G/21,22<br>***#1969,70***  | **Edith Emily GREEN**<br>No business address entered | Student |
| R3/165<br>13 February 1959<br>Sent by E W Grundy<br>Three sizes | 209 Wilmslow Road<br>Rusholme<br>Manchester 14 | P21/G/42-44<br>***#1971-3***  | **Eric GRUNDY**<br>No business address entered | Student silversmith |
| LPB/34<br>26 April 1881<br>Sent by A G Griffiths | | P3/G/x2<br>***#1974,5***  | **Ephraim GOOCH**<br>9 Hylton Street<br>Birmingham | Jeweller |
| R1/12<br>20 June 1895<br>Sent by A G Griffiths | 380 Lodge Road<br>Hockley<br>Birmingham | P5/G/668<br>***#1976***  | **Ernest GRIFFITHS**<br>380 Lodge Road<br>Hockley later at<br>13 Writham Road<br>Handsworth<br>Birmingham | Jeweller and ring maker |
| R3/182<br>3 January 1962<br>Sent by selves<br>Three sizes | | P21/E/21-23<br>***#1977-9***  | **EUROPEAN & GENERAL EXPRESS CO LTD**<br>37 Upper Thames Street<br>London EC4 | Shipping agents |
| R1/71<br>14 June 1894<br>Sent by C Horner<br>Halifax, E G Parker | | P5/P/543<br>***#1980***  | **Eustace George PARKER** *<br>George Street<br>Altrincham | Jeweller |
| R1/124<br>10 April 1900<br>Sent by W Neale & Sons | Broomfield Lane<br>Hale | P9/P/66<br>***#1981***  | | Silversmith |
| R3/120<br>13 December 1952 | | P21/P/48<br>***#1982***  | **Eustace George PARKER LTD** *<br>Tower Works<br>Altrincham | Watchmakers, jewellers and silversmiths |
| R1/71<br>14 June 1894<br>Sent by C Horner<br>Halifax, E G Parker<br>Two sizes | P5/P/543 is too low for date – perhaps clerk should have entered P5/P/573 | P5/P/543x2<br>***#1983,4***  | **Eustace George PARKER** *<br>George Street<br>Altrincham | Jeweller |
| Missing register<br>*c.*1891 | | P5/P/356<br>***#1985***  | | |
| R1/89<br>18 January 1899<br>Sent by J & R Griffin for Edward Evans & Son<br>64 Northampton Street, Birm'ham | Private address same as business | P9/P/13<br>***#1986***  | **Eustace George PARKER** *<br>Broomfield Lane<br>Near Altrincham | Manufacturer, wholesale dealer and importer |
| R1/144<br>27 February 1901<br>Sent by E J Trevitt & Sons | Broomfield Lane<br>Sale<br>Cheshire | P9/P/97<br>***#1987***  | **Eustace George PARKER** *<br>Tower Works<br>Altrincham and Knutsford | Dealer In watches and jewellery |
| R3/120<br>16 October 1947<br>Sent by Brian H Parker (Manager) | | P21/P/17<br>***#1988***  | **Eustace G PARKER LTD** *<br>Sealed in the presence of:-<br>Charlotte N Diem ? (Director)<br>K Biddulph (Secretary)<br>Tower Works<br>45 Stamford New Road<br>Altrincham | Watchmakers, jewellers and silversmiths |

| REGISTRATION DETAILS | MAKER'S PRIVATE ADDRESS and DETAILS | PLATE and MARK DETAILS | MAKER/COMPANY and BUSINESS ADDRESS | MAKER'S TRADE |
|---|---|---|---|---|
| R3/103<br>6 July 1942<br>Sent by Ernest Griffith | 78 Friary Road<br>Handsworth<br>Birmingham | P21/G/5<br>***#1989***<br> | **E GRIFFITH & SONS**<br>Ernest Griffith<br>109 Vyse Street<br>Birmingham | Jewellers |
| R3/62<br>3 March 1932<br>Sent by E Gray & Son Ltd | | P15/G/57<br>***#1990***<br>  | **E GRAY & SON LTD**<br>Seal of the company affixed in the presence of :<br>Joseph Gray (Director)<br>Lionel E Morris (Secretary)<br>18 Clerkenwell Road (Registered<br>London EC1 Office) | Goldsmiths and silversmiths |
| SPB/24<br>30 March 1871<br>SPB mark shown<br>CWMP 1874 | | P3/H/x3<br>***#1991-3***<br> | **Edward HICKMAN** *<br>Old Allesley Road<br>Coventry | Watchcase maker |
| SPB/14<br>2 June 1874 | | P3/H/x3<br>***#1994-6***<br>  | **Edward HUGH**<br>14 Glover Street<br>Preston<br>Lancashire | Working jeweller |
| LPB/28<br>22 June 1883 | | P3/H/x2<br>***#1997,8***<br> | **Edwin HOPPER**<br>382 City Road, Islington<br>London | Jeweller |
| Missing register<br>*c.*1889 | | P5/H/234a<br>***#1999***<br> | **Unidentified** | |
| Missing register<br>*c.*1889<br>Similar mark entered<br>LAO 2 January 1896 | | P5/H/234b<br>***#2000***<br> | **Edwin George HARROP** *<br>1 Amwell Street<br>London | Manufacturing jeweller |
| R1/125<br>25 April 1900<br>Sent by W H & F Rabone<br>Smith & Pepper<br>E G Harrop, A Noel<br>G E Walton Ltd<br>Three sizes | Earlswood<br>Hornsey Lane<br>London N1 | P9/H/33x3<br>***#2001-3***<br> | **Edwin George HARROP** *<br>1 Amwell Street<br>London<br>Culme has 1918 E G Harrop as Director<br>*The London* Watchcase *Company*<br>*157 Farringdon Road*<br>*London, EC* | |
| R3/44<br>24 October 1928<br>Sent by Edwin Horton | 21 Newton Place<br>Soho<br>Birmingham | P15/H/105<br>***#2004***<br> | **Edwin HORTON** trading as<br>**HORTON & CO**<br>15a Harford Street<br>Birmingham | Jewellers and silversmiths |
| R2/215<br>16 March 1918<br>Sent by L Smith<br>(per F W Cole) | 29 Addison Road<br>London<br>4 Cavendish Place<br>Brighton<br>47 Park Avenue<br>London | P15/H/39<br>***#2005***<br>  | **E HART**<br>**L SMITH**<br>**F DAVIES** trading as<br>**E HART & CO**<br>6 Cherry Street<br>Birmingham and<br>20 Clerkenwell Road<br>London E C | Bullion dealers and jewellers |
| R3/3<br>30 April 1921<br>Sent by E H Pars | 16 Williams Street<br>Cheetham Hill<br>Manchester | P15/P/169<br>***#2006***<br> | **Ernest Henry PARS**<br>31, 32, 33 Withy Grove<br>Manchester | General jewellery mounting |
| R3/105<br>19 April 1943<br>Sent by Edgar Harold Smith | Private address same as business | P21/S/14<br>***#2007***<br>  | **Edgar Harold SMITH**<br>33 Barrow Street<br>Much Wenlock<br>Shropshire | Jeweller |

| REGISTRATION DETAILS | MAKER'S PRIVATE ADDRESS and DETAILS | PLATE and MARK DETAILS | MAKER/COMPANY and BUSINESS ADDRESS | MAKER'S TRADE |
|---|---|---|---|---|
| MR2/90<br>LGSJ 1825 | Seen on mustard pot 1806 | P1/24/x2<br>***#2008,9***<br> | **Ebenezar IRWIN**<br>24 John Street<br>Liverpool | Silversmith |
| PP1/187<br>J1 1839-67<br>PMR 1800-30 | | P1/28/x2<br>***#2010,1***<br> | **Edward JONES**<br>14 Lumber Street (1800-3)<br>3 Highfield Street (1805)<br>41 Prussia Street (1807-10)<br>45 Prussia Street (1813-14)<br>7 Highfield Street (1830)<br>Liverpool | Watchcase maker and jeweller |
| R3/132<br>25 April 1950<br>Sent by E I Savage | 70 Dilloway Street<br>St Helens<br>Lancashire | P21/S/44<br>***#2012***<br> | **Ethel Irene SAVAGE**<br>No business address entered<br>Liverpool School of Art? | Art student |
| R3/160<br>22 February 1957<br>Sent by E I Turton | Private address same as business | P21/T/33<br>***#2013***<br> | **Emily Irene TURTON**<br>91 Kimberley Road<br>Nuthall<br>Nr Nottingham | No trade entered |
| Missing register<br>*c.*1889 | | P5/V*sic*/262<br>***#2014***<br> | **Unidentified** | |
| | | P2/J/x3<br>***#2015-7***<br> | **Unidentified** | |
| R1/77<br>20 December 1898<br>Sent by Edward Jackson | 74 Cawder Street<br>Liverpool | P9/J/9<br>***#2018***<br> | **Edward JACKSON**<br>12a Don Chambers<br>Paradise Street<br>Liverpool | Goldsmith and diamond mounter |
| R1/99<br>29 April 1899<br>Sent by A Hands<br>Edward Jackson | | P9/J/11<br>***#2019***<br> | 12 Don Chambers<br>Paradise Street<br>Liverpool | |
| R1/216<br>28 June 1904<br>Sent by J & R Griffin | | P9/J/39,40<br>***#2020,1***<br> | **Edward JINKS & CO**<br>56 Broughton Road<br>Handsworth<br>Birmingham | Manufacturing jeweller |
| R3/32<br>10 May 1926<br>Sent by E J Evans<br>Two sizes | 21 Icknield Street<br>Birmingham | P15/E/34,35<br>***#2022,3***<br> | **E J EVANS**<br>18 Icknield Street<br>Birmingham | Silver box Maker, etc |
| R3/136<br>11 December 1951<br>Sent by E J Haysty<br>Two sizes | Private address same as business | P21/H/61,62<br>***#2024,5***<br> | **Eric John HAYSTY**<br>32 Hogarth Road<br>Eastham<br>Cheshire | Silversmith |
| LPB/38<br>11 April 1880<br>Sent by Mayell or (Mayer) Brothers | | P3/H/x1<br>***#2026***<br> | **Edward John HARDMAN**<br>64 Bull Street<br>Birmingham | Jeweller |
| R2/232<br>23 June 1920<br>Sent by Haseler & Bill<br>Three sizes | 119 Thornhill Road<br>Handsworth<br>Berwyn Cottage<br>Streetley<br>Staffs | P15/H/41-43<br>***#2027-9***<br> | **Edward John HASELER**<br>**Charles Alfred BILL** *<br>58 – 60 Villa Road<br>Handsworth, Birmingham and<br>94 Hatton Garden<br>London | Silversmiths |

| REGISTRATION DETAILS | MAKER'S PRIVATE ADDRESS and DETAILS | PLATE and MARK DETAILS | MAKER/COMPANY and BUSINESS ADDRESS | MAKER'S TRADE |
|---|---|---|---|---|
| R1/12<br>6 June 1895<br>MR3/119<br>Sent by Noble Haseler for Haseler Brothers<br>Two sizes | 77 Hall Road<br>Handsworth<br>Birmingham | P5/H/665x2<br>***#2030,1***  | **Noble HASELER**<br>**Edward John HASELER** trading as<br>**HASELER BROTHERS** *<br>53 Branston Street<br>Birmingham | Silversmiths |
| R1/188<br>24 March 1903<br>Sent by N Haseler<br>Two sizes | 199 Holly Road<br>Handsworth<br>118 Thornhill Road<br>Birmingham | P9/H/477,487 *sic*<br>***#2032,3*** 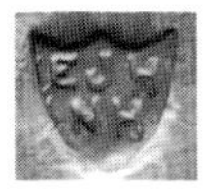 | **Noble HASELER**<br>**Edward John HASELER** *<br>53 Branston Street<br>Birmingham | Manufacturing jewellers |
| R1/224<br>8 December 1904<br>Two sizes<br>Sent by Haseler Brothers | | P9/H/67,68<br>***#2034,5***  | | Silversmiths |
| Missing register<br>*c.*1894<br>Similar mark entered LAO 17 May 1893 | | P5/O/546<br>***#2036***  | **Edward James OKLEY**<br>6 Addington Square<br>Camberwell<br>London SE | Silversmith and tobacconist |
| R2/209<br>17 November 1916<br>Sent by self | 35 Livingstone Road<br>Handsworth<br>Birmingham | P15/R/14–17<br>***#2037-40***  | **Elizabeth Jane ROOKER** trading as<br>**E J ROOKER & CO**<br>28 Pemberton Road<br>Birmingham | Manufacturing jewellers |
| | | P15/R/9–12<br>***#2041-4***  | | |
| R1/30<br>11 June 1896<br>Sent by E J Rudge<br>Edward Brothers | 719 Gordan Road<br>Heathfield Road<br>Handsworth | P5/R/777<br>***#2045***  | **Edwin James RUDGE**<br>119 Vyse Street<br>Birmingham | Ring manufacturer |
| R1/87<br>3 December 1898 | | P9/R/5<br>***#2046***  | | |
| Not in R2 as expected<br>*c.* July 1909 | | P13/R/25<br>***#2047***  | | |
| Not in R2 as expected<br>*c.* December 1919 | | P15/R/27,28<br>***#2048,9***  | | |
| Missing register<br>*c.*1886<br>Similar mark entered BAO 28 May 1880 | | P5/S/64<br>***#2050***  | **Edward John SCOTT**<br>21 Upper Hockley Street<br>Birmingham | Gold chain maker |
| LPB/44<br>5 March 1885<br>No mark in LPB<br>Sent by Jonathan Hazell | 6th name on LPB/44 and 6th mark on P5/J | P5/J/x1<br>***#2051***  | **Edward JOHNSON & SON**<br>35 Victoria Street<br>Derby | Jeweller, watch manufacturers, goldsmiths and silversmiths |
| R1/219<br>18 August 1904<br>Sent by J & R Griffin | The Rookery<br>Handsworth<br>Eskdale<br>Handsworth | P9/J/41<br>***#2052***  | **Edward Lewis JACOBS**<br>**Lewis H GODFREY** trading as<br>**E JACOBS & SON**<br>88 Vittoria Street<br>Birmingham | Manufacturing jewellers and silversmiths |

| REGISTRATION DETAILS | MAKER'S PRIVATE ADDRESS and DETAILS | PLATE and MARK DETAILS | MAKER/COMPANY and BUSINESS ADDRESS | MAKER'S TRADE |
|---|---|---|---|---|
| LPB/44<br>7 June 1884<br>No mark in LPB<br>Kelly 1884 | 4th name on LPB/44 and 4th mark on P5/J | P5/J/x1<br>***#2053***  | **E JACOBS & SON**<br>88 Vittoria Street<br>Birmingham | Wholesale jewellers |
| R1/116<br>25 November 1899<br>Through W H Ashford *#0* on P5 | | P5/J/0*sic*<br>***#2054***  | | |
| R1/116<br>25 November 1899<br>Impression taken E Jacobs & Son<br>10 February 1903<br>Sent by W H Ashford<br>Edward Brothers<br>Hemming &<br>Hazlewood | The Rookery [1]<br>Handsworth<br>Birmingham<br>Eskdale [2]<br>Rookery Road<br>Handsworth<br>Birmingham | P9/J/24<br>***#2055***  | **Edward Lewis JACOBS** [1]<br>**Lewis Henry JACOBS** [2] trading as<br>**E JACOBS & CO**<br>88 Vittoria Street<br>Birmingham and<br>15 Charterhouse Street<br>London | Manufacturing jewellers |
| Not in R1 as expected<br>Adjacent P5/J/799 | | P5/J/x1<br>***#2056***  | | |
| R2/93<br>23 September 1909<br>Sent by W H Ashford | The Rosary, Handsworth<br>Birmingham<br>The Chantry<br>Fladbury, Worcestershire | P13/J/6<br>***#2057***  | | Jewellers |
| Missing register<br>*c.*1890<br>Adjacent P5/G/272 | | P5/G*sic*/x1<br>***#2058***  | **E JACOBS & CO** or<br>**Edward JOHNSON & SON** | |
| R1/196<br>18 June 1903<br>Sent by E J Trevitt | 179 Heathfield Road<br>Birmingham | P9/T/30<br>***#2059***  | **Enoch James TREVITT** trading as<br>**G E CRAMP** *<br>121 Vyse Street<br>Birmingham | Gem ring maker |
| R3/143<br>18 April 1953<br>Sent by<br>E J Walmsby | 17 Meadow Bank<br>Chorlton-cum-Hardy<br>Manchester 21 | P21/W/64<br>***#2060***  | **Ethel Joan WALMSBY**<br>No business address entered | Student |
| Missing register<br>*c.*1888<br>Similar mark BAO<br>25 February 1881 | | P5/W/140<br>***#2061*** 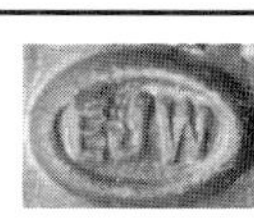 | **Edwin James WALKER ?** | |
| LPB/46<br>31 March 1882<br>CWMP 1886-1901 | | P3/W/x1<br>***#2062***  | **Edwin James WALKER** *<br>10 Earlsdon Road<br>Coventry | Gold watchcase maker |
| Missing register<br>*c.*1887<br>Similar mark entered<br>LAO 24 July 1882 | | P5/W/74<br>***#2063***  | | |
| R1/67<br>14 June 1898<br>Cancelled<br>24 February 1909<br>Sent by Edwin Kenning | 16 Walley Road<br>Accrington | P9*sic*/K/963<br>***#2064*** 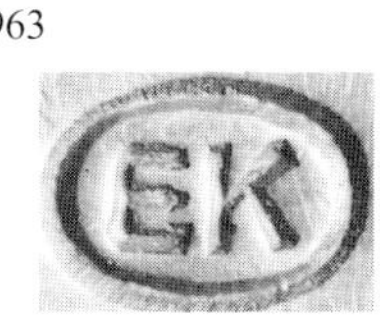 | **Edwin KENNING**<br>16 Walley Road<br>Accrington | Pipe and stick mounter and engraver |
| PP1/187 | Attributed to Edward Kirkman because of the unique initials match | P2/K/x8<br>***#2065-72***  | **Edward KIRKMAN**<br>35 Highfield Street<br>Liverpool | Watchcase maker and jeweller |

| REGISTRATION DETAILS | MAKER'S PRIVATE ADDRESS and DETAILS | PLATE and MARK DETAILS | MAKER/COMPANY and BUSINESS ADDRESS | MAKER'S TRADE |
|---|---|---|---|---|
| Missing register<br>*c.*1889<br>CWMP 1874-83<br>Similar mark BAO<br>16 December 1881 | | P5/K/226<br>***#2073***<br> | **Edward KERBY**<br>46 Spon Street (1874)<br>5 Spon Street (1886)<br>Coventry | Watchcase and watch manufacturer |
| R2/73<br>24 February 1909<br>Sent by Imperial Tobacco Co | Private address same as business | P13/K/1<br>***#2074***<br> | **Edwin KENNING**<br>53 Tabor Road<br>Hammersmith<br>London | Silversmith |
| PDB 1832-39<br>MR3/89 | Gold rings and busk<br>This mark with "&" may indicate a partnership with another company<br>This mark without "&" seen on the case of a watch by Richard Todd 1830 | P1/25/x4<br>***#2075-8***<br> | **Edward KIRKMAN**<br>35 Highfield Street<br>Liverpool | Watchcase maker and jeweller |
| | | P1/29/x1<br>***#2079***<br> | | |
| Similar mark entered BAO 25 June 1828 | | P2/K/x2<br>***#2080,1***<br> | | |
| R1/162<br>25 February 1902<br>Sent by E Korn | Private address same as business | P9/K/24<br>***#2082***<br> | **Elias KORN** *<br>4 Little Alie Street<br>Goodman Fields<br>London E | Rings, charms and bracelet manufacturer |
| PP1/187<br>GTD1827-55 | | P1/25/x1<br>***#2083***<br> | **Edward KIRKMAN & CO**<br>3 Plan Street<br>Liverpool | Watchcase maker |
| | | P1/26/x1<br>***#2084***<br> | | |
| | Square marked 1786 | P1/21/x1<br>***#2085***<br> | **Edward KIRKMAN**<br>**John STUART**<br>Liverpool | Watchcase makers |
| R1/237<br>22 July 1905<br>Sent by Edward Lilley | 76 Stanmore Road<br>Birmingham | P9/L/67<br>***#2086***<br> | **Edward LILLEY**<br>113 Warstone Lane<br>Birmingham | Gold bracelet and pendant manufacturer |
| R2/9<br>16 January 1906<br>Cancelled<br>19 February 1906<br>Sent by E A Lilley | | P9/L/71<br>***#2087***<br> | | Manufacturing jeweller |
| SPB/10<br>7 March 1873<br>CWMP 1874-83 | | P3/L/x3<br>***#2088-90***<br> | **Edwin LEE** *<br>7 Albion Street (1874)<br>Butts<br>2 Norfolk Street (1883)<br>Coventry | Watchcase maker |
| R2/181<br>20 December 1913<br>Sent by Fred Lamb | 25 Algernon Road<br>Rotten Park<br>Birmingham<br>169 Metchley Lane<br>Birmingham | P13/E/36,37<br>***#2091,2***<br> | **Fred LAMB**<br>**Bert William EVETTS**<br>(Ed: trading as **EVETTS & LAMB**)<br>58 Tenby Street N<br>Birmingham | Jewellers |
| R2/11<br>15 February 1906<br>Sent by E A Lilley<br>Two sizes | 76 Stanmore Road<br>Edgbaston<br>Birmingham | P9/L/73,74<br>***#2093,4***<br> | **Edward LILLEY**<br>113 Warstone Lane<br>Birmingham | Manufacturing jewellers |

| REGISTRATION DETAILS | MAKER'S PRIVATE ADDRESS and DETAILS | PLATE and MARK DETAILS | MAKER/COMPANY and BUSINESS ADDRESS | MAKER'S TRADE |
|---|---|---|---|---|
| R1/96<br>21 March 1899<br>Sent by E W Linnett | Private address same as business | P9/L/6<br>***#2095***<br>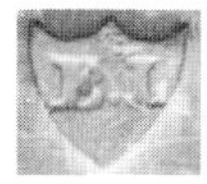 | **Edward William LINNETT** *<br>King Street<br>Coventry | Silver watchcase manufacturer |
| MR1/143<br>MR3/183<br>J3 1672-91<br>J3/416 | Mark seen in conjunction with a bird/duck which probably indicates a Liverpool connection. Spoons, tankard *c*.1700 | Predates P1<br>***#2096***<br>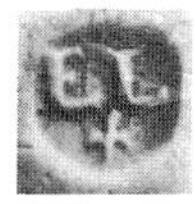 | **Edward LEWIS**<br>Water Street<br>Liverpool | Silversmith |
| LPB/16<br>7 February 1881 | | P3/B/x1<br>***#2097***<br> | **Eli Lewis BARNETT**<br>66 Great Hampton Street<br>Birmingham | Jeweller |
| R1/11<br>4 May 1895<br>Sent by E Langridge & Co | 107 Hollydale Road<br>Peckham<br>London SE | P5/L/658<br>***#2098***<br> | **Edward LANGRIDGE**<br>**Alfred LANGRIDGE**<br>**Frederick John LANGRIDGE**<br>trading as **E LANGRIDGE & CO** *<br>51 New Oxford Street and<br>209 Shaftsbury Avenue<br>London WC | Silversmiths and general engravers |
| R1/237<br>22 July 1905<br>Sent by E Loe & Co | 1 Hemberton Road<br>Clapham, London SW<br>13 Beresford Road<br>Canonbury, London W | P9/L/68,69<br>***#2099,2100***<br> | **Ernest LOE**<br>**Lewis SOLOMON** trading as<br>**E LOE & CO**<br>95 Hatton Garden<br>London | Manufacturing jewellers |
| R2/138<br>21 June 1911<br>Sent by Charles Lucas | Private address same as business | P13/L/59-61<br>***#2101-3***<br> | **Edward LYON** trading as<br>**Edward LYON & CO**<br>22 Charleville Road<br>London W | Jewellers |
| LPB/36 SP32/2<br>26 February 1884<br>Sent by Pope & Phelps | No mark in LPB, only initials ELG | P5/G/x1<br>***#2104***<br> | **Edwin Lewis GYDE** *<br>125 Vyse Street<br>Birmingham | Jeweller |
| Missing register<br>*c*.1892 | | P5/E/443<br>***#2105***<br> | | |
| R1/171<br>22 June 1902<br>Sent by T Nightingale | Elton<br>Four Oaks<br>Warwickshire | P9/G/36<br>***#2106***<br> | **Edwin Lewis GYDE**<br>32 Frederick Street<br>Birmingham | Manufacturing jeweller |
| R3/53<br>27 March 1930<br>Sent by Edith Lilian Williams | Private address same as business | P15/W/94<br>***#2107***<br> | **Edith Lilian WILLIAMS (Mrs)**<br>Rockmount<br>Clifton Road<br>Birkenhead | Art worker |
| R3/143<br>18 April 1953<br>Sent by E L Mansfield<br>Two sizes | 243 Manby Road<br>Chorlton-cum-Hardy<br>Manchester 21 | P21/M/30,31<br>***#2108,9***<br> | **Ethel Lilian MANSFIELD**<br>No business address entered | Student |
| R3/147<br>26 November 1953<br>Sent by E Millington<br>Three sizes | 1 Barlow Moor Road<br>Didsbury, Manchester 20<br>Moved 15 October 1959 to 31 Sandiacre Road<br>Wythenshawe<br>Manchester 23 | P21/M/36-38<br>***#2110-2***<br> | **Ernest MILLINGTON**<br>No business address entered | Student |
| PDB 1815-32<br>GTD1815-1829<br>PP1/187 | Two Edward Maddocks mentioned in trade directories | P1/25/x1<br>***#2113***<br> | **Edward MADDOCK II**<br>Ormond Street (1807-30)<br>Liverpool | Watchcase maker and silverware |

| REGISTRATION DETAILS | MAKER'S PRIVATE ADDRESS and DETAILS | PLATE and MARK DETAILS | MAKER/COMPANY and BUSINESS ADDRESS | MAKER'S TRADE |
|---|---|---|---|---|
| PP1/187<br>PP2/350<br>PDB 1798-1815<br>Goldware<br>J1/373<br>MR3/93<br>GTD1785-1818<br>SOT/127 | Seen on watchcases 1792 and 1803 | P1/24/x2<br>***#2114,5***<br><br><br>P1/28/x3<br>***#2116-8***<br><br> | **Edward MADDOCK I**<br>Cumberland Street (1791)<br>Plumb Street (1793)<br>Edmund Street (1795)<br>Liverpool | Watchcase maker and goldware |
| LPB/56 SP27/7<br>26 November 1884<br>Sent by S Quilliam & Son | Entry in WCI p75, also in Slater's Directory for 1894. No mark in LPB, just EM | P5/M/x1<br>***#2119***<br> | **Edward MORRISON**<br>Cumberland Square<br>Parsonstown (now Birr)<br>Ireland | Watchmaker and jeweller |
| LPB/54<br>31 December 1879 | | P3/M/x3<br>***#2120-2***<br> | **MOJON & MONTANDON** *<br>120/121 Newgate Street<br>London | Watch manufacturer and importer |
| R3/180<br>13 June 1961<br>Sent by E M Boase | 21 Glendyke Road<br>Liverpool 18 | P21/B/66<br>***#2123***<br>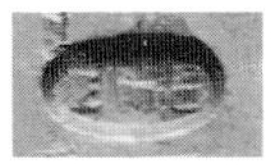 | **Elizabeth M BOASE**<br>No business address entered | Housewife |
| R1/147<br>15 May 1901<br>Sent by R Mackenzie | 7 Mannering Road [1]<br>Sefton Park<br>Victoria Park [2]<br>Wavertree<br>Liverpool | P9/C/51<br>***#2124***<br><br> | **E M CRAWFORD** [1]<br>**Robert MACKENZIE** [2] trading as<br>**E M CRAWFORD**<br>34 Bold Street<br>Liverpool | Umbrella manufacturers |
| R1/185<br>17 February 1903<br>Sent by R Mackenzie | Victoria Park<br>Wavertree<br>Liverpool | P9/C/81<br>***#2125***<br><br> | **Robert MACKENZIE** trading as<br>**E M CRAWFORD**<br>34 Bold Street<br>Liverpool | |
| Missing register<br>*c.*1891<br>Similar mark entered<br>BAO 11 October 1897 | | P5/E/372<br>***#2126***<br> | **Edward Masters EVANS** trading as<br>**E M EVANS & SON**<br>64 Northampton Street<br>Birmingham | Jewellers |
| Missing register<br>*c.*1886<br>Similar mark BAO<br>20 September 1887 | | P5/L/23<br>***#2127***<br><br> | **Edward Moses LEVETUS**<br>47 Vittoria Street<br>Birmingham | Jeweller |
| Missing register<br>*c.*1890<br>Similar mark entered<br>BAO 12 August 1890 | | P5/M/311<br>***#2128***<br><br> | **E MANDER & SON**<br>31 Branston Street<br>Birmingham | Jewel case and photographic frame makers |
| PDB 1826-8<br>MR3/95 | Gold rings | P1/26/x1<br>***#2129***<br><br> | **Edward NIGHTINGALE**<br>Manchester | Goldsmith |
| J1 1859-66 GSJW/139<br>Not in SPB or LPB | May be struck in error on P2 | P2/N/x3<br>***#2130-2***<br><br> | **Elias NATHAN**<br>6 Victoria Street<br>Manchester | Optician and silversmith |
| Not in SPB or LPB so struck 1860-3 | | P3/N/x1<br>***#2133***<br><br> | | |
| SPB/11<br>8 February 1866 | | P3/N/x3<br>***#2134-6***<br><br> | | |

| REGISTRATION DETAILS | MAKER'S PRIVATE ADDRESS and DETAILS | PLATE and MARK DETAILS | MAKER/COMPANY and BUSINESS ADDRESS | MAKER'S TRADE |
|---|---|---|---|---|
| Missing register<br>*c.*1893 | | P5/N/525<br>***#2137***  | **Unidentified** | |
| R2/54<br>25 January 1908<br>Sent by Edward Needham | 62 Oakfield Road<br>Birmingham<br>(Ed: Clerk should have entered 41 and 42) | P9/N/34,35<br>***#2138,9***  | **Edward NEEDHAM** trading as<br>**Edward NEEDHAM & CO**<br>102 Great Hampton Street<br>Birmingham | Wholesale jewellers |
| R2/213<br>6 August 1917<br>Sent by Edward Needham | 5 Hillcrest Road<br>Moseley<br>Birmingham | P15/N/6–8<br>***#2140-2***  | | Manufacturers and wholesale jewellers |
| R1/50<br>17 August 1897<br>Two sizes<br>Sent by E O Marples | 28 Poplar Road<br>Birmingham | P5/Z*sic*/866x2<br>***#2143,4*** 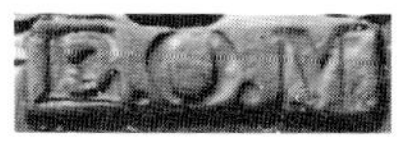 | **Edward Osborne MARPLES**<br>117a Carver Street<br>Birmingham | Silversmith |
| R1/143<br>21 February 1901<br>Sent by Edwin Page | 137 Albert Road<br>Aston<br>Birmingham | P9/P/96<br>***#2145***  | **Edwin PAGE**<br>33 Hylton Street<br>Birmingham | Chain manufacturer |
| R1/127<br>23 May 1900<br>Sent by<br>W H Carrington & Co | 3 St Patrick's Terrace<br>Inchicore | P9/P/67<br>***#2146***  | **Edward POWER**<br>**John POWER** trading as<br>**POWER BROTHERS**<br>36 Parliament Street and<br>31 Sinclair Place<br>Dublin | Tobacconists |
| R1/140<br>30 January 1901 | 137 Albert Road<br>Aston<br>Birmingham | P9/P/80,81,83<br>***#2147-9***  | **Edwin PAGE**<br>33 Hylton Street<br>Birmingham | Chain manufacturer |
| LPB/64<br>25 November 1879 | Not in 1879 directory | P3/P/x3<br>***#2150-2***  | **Edward POWELL**<br>No business address listed | Silversmith or jeweller |
| Missing register<br>*c.*1893<br>Similar mark entered CAO 30 January 1901 | | P5/P/529<br>***#2153*** 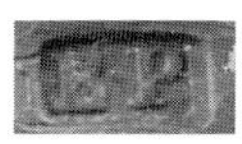 | **Edwin PAGE**<br>33 Hylton Street<br>Birmingham | Chain manufacturer |
| Missing register<br>*c.*1891 | | P5/P/355<br>***#2154***  | | |
| R2/222<br>8 July 1919<br>Sent by Ernest Payne | 9 Richmond Road<br>Bearwood | P15/P/116<br>***#2155***  | **Ernest PAYNE**<br>104 Vyse Street<br>Birmingham | Manufacturer jeweller |
| R3/75<br>31 March 1935<br>Sent by H J Pilcher Clayton | Private address same as business | P15/K*sic*/224<br>***#2156***  | **Miss Elspeth Pilcher CLAYTON**<br>19 Byron Road<br>Sheffield 7 | Horseshoe charms |
| LPB/72<br>12 May 1882<br>Sent by Edward Roek Fritz & Charles | | P3/R/x3<br>***#2157-9***  | **E ROEK** trading as<br>**ROEK & DREYFUS** *<br>3 doors south of Ray Street<br>Farringdon Road<br>London | Gold chain makers |
| | | P3/R/x2<br>***#2160,1***  | | |
| R2/209<br>5 December 1916<br>Sent by E Riheiro | Private address same as business | P15/R/18<br>***#2162*** 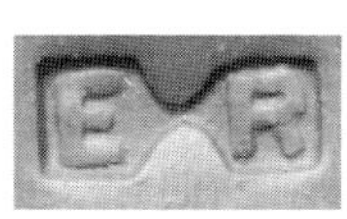 | **Emmanuel RIHEIRO**<br>90 Charlotte Street<br>High Town<br>Manchester | Gold and silver mounter and engraver |

| REGISTRATION DETAILS | MAKER'S PRIVATE ADDRESS and DETAILS | PLATE and MARK DETAILS | MAKER/COMPANY and BUSINESS ADDRESS | MAKER'S TRADE |
|---|---|---|---|---|
| R3/158<br>15 June 1956<br>Sent by E Reddish<br>Two sizes | 45 Crow Hill North<br>Alkrington<br>Middleton<br>Nr Manchester | P21/R/25,26<br>***#2163,4***<br> | **Elizabeth REDDISH**<br>No business address entered | Student |
| LPB/4<br>17 November 1877 | | P3/R/x2<br>***#2165,6***<br> | **Evan ROBERTS**<br>37 Albion Street<br>Gayborn<br>Manchester | Watchmaker |
| R3/101<br>26 September 1941<br>Sent by Edward Daniel Rowland | 37 High Street<br>Abercarn<br>Monmouth | P21/R/2<br>***#2167***<br> | **Edward ROWLAND**<br>Edward Daniel Rowland<br>Greenwich House<br>35 High Street<br>Abercarn, Monmouthshire | Jeweller |
| R3/127<br>3 December 1948<br>Sent by Ernest Green<br>Two sizes | Trevelyn<br>Summerhill<br>Nr Wrexham | P21/G/19,20<br>***#2168,9***<br> | **Ernest GREEN**<br>19 Central Arcade<br>Hope Street<br>Wrexham | Manufacturing jeweller |
| R2/32<br>29 January 1907<br>Sent by Elliott & Sheldon | Hingeston Street<br>120 New John Street West<br>Birmingham | P9/E/21 and 0*sic*<br>***#2170,1***<br> | **Charles ELLIOTT**<br>**Henry SHELDON** trading as<br>**ELLIOTT & SHELDON**<br>Back of 10 Tenby Street<br>Birmingham | Jewellers |
| | | P9/E/22<br>***#2172***<br> | | |
| R3/11<br>22 July 1922<br>Sent by Evelyn Sumner<br>Two sizes | Copenhurst<br>Waterloo<br>Liverpool | P/15/S/56,57<br>***#2173,4***<br> | **Evelyn SUMNER**<br>Liverpool School of Art<br>Hope Street<br>Liverpool | Silversmith |
| R3/143<br>18 April 1953<br>Sent by E Stewart<br>Two sizes | 97 Claude Road<br>Chorlton-cum-Hardy<br>Manchester 21 | P21/S/52,53<br>***#2175,6***<br>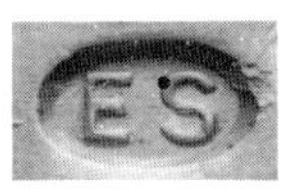 | **Mrs Edna STEWART**<br>No business address entered | Student |
| R2/16<br>21 April 1906<br>Sent by E Simmons | 38 Milner Square<br>London W | P9/S/99<br>***#2177***<br> | **Ernest SIMMONS** trading as<br>**E & R SIMMONS** *<br>359 City Road<br>London EC | Wholesale optician |
| Missing register<br>*c.*1889<br>Two sizes | | P5/S/213x2<br>***#2178,9***<br>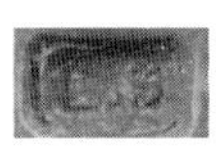 | **Unidentified** | |
| R1/84<br>16 November 1898<br>Sent by E Smith | 33 Soho Hill<br>Handsworth<br>Birmingham | P9/S/10<br>***#2180***<br> | **Edward SMITH**<br>1 Augusta Street<br>Birmingham | Manufacturing jeweller |
| R1/78<br>24 August 1894<br>Sent by Edward Smith | 2 Louser Place<br>Prescot Street<br>Birmingham | P5/S/574<br>***#2181***<br> | **Edward SMITH**<br>9 Hampton Buildings<br>Hey Hill<br>Birmingham | Jeweller |
| PP1/187<br>WTD 1856<br>CWMP 1850-74<br>Similar mark entered<br>BAO 10 March 1856 | | P2/X*sic*/x3<br>***#2182-4***<br> | **Edward SALISBURY**<br>Sovereign Place<br>Chapel Fields (1850)<br>77 The Butts (1874)<br>Coventry | Watchcase maker |
| R3/100<br>15 July 1941<br>Sent by E Simpson | 15 Cranbrook Road<br>Handsworth<br>Birmingham | P21/S/12<br>***#2185***<br> | **Ernest SIMPSON**<br>102 Vyse Street<br>Birmingham | Jeweller |

 ES–ET

| REGISTRATION DETAILS | MAKER'S PRIVATE ADDRESS and DETAILS | PLATE and MARK DETAILS | MAKER/COMPANY and BUSINESS ADDRESS | MAKER'S TRADE |
|---|---|---|---|---|
| R1/16<br>10 October 1895<br>Punch cancelled<br>5 November 1910<br>Sent by Lucas Brothers Ltd | Grove House<br>The Grove<br>Highgate Road<br>London NW | P5/E/691<br>*#2186*<br>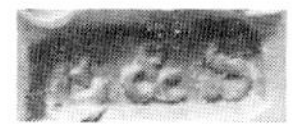 | **Edward Henry EDWARDS**<br>**John Frederick EDWARDS**<br>**Charles Alfred EDWARDS**<br>trading as **EDWARDS & SONS** *<br>161 Regent Street<br>London | Silversmiths |
| R2/123<br>5 November 1910<br>LAO 4660<br>Sent by Grey & Co | Homestead<br>Blenheim Road<br>St Albans<br>12 Church Road<br>Hampstead | P13/E/17<br>*#2187*<br> | **John Frederick EDWARDS**<br>**Charles Alfred EDWARDS** *<br>159 and 161 Regent Street<br>London | Stationers, silversmiths, etc |
| R3/29<br>23 May 1925<br>Sent by Stokes & Ireland<br>Three sizes | | P15/E/28-30<br>*#2188-90*<br> | **EDWARD & SONS** *<br>Charlotte Robertson Edward<br>William Cunningham Rankin<br>92 Buchanan Street<br>Glasgow | Jewellers and silversmiths |
| R3/45<br>12 January 1929<br>Sent by A Wilcox of 15 Nursery Road, B'ham | 15 Nursery Road, B'ham | P15/E/39<br>*#2191*<br> | | |
| 21 December 1929 | | P15/E/40<br>*#2192*<br>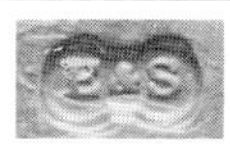 | | |
| 19 December 1931 | | P15/E/42<br>*#2193*<br> | | |
| 9 February 1933 | | P15/E/43<br>*#2194*<br> | | |
| R3/56<br>9 February 1931<br>Sent by A Wilcox | | P15/E/41<br>*#2195*<br> | **EDWARD & SONS** *<br>92 Buchanan Street<br>Glasgow | |
| R2/59<br>19 May 1908<br>Sent by Adie Brothers | 15 Yateley Road<br>Edgbaston<br>25 Rotten Park Road<br>Edgbaston<br>Birmingham | P13/B/21-23<br>*#2196-8*<br> | **Herbert W ADIE**<br>**Percy J ADIE** trading as<br>**E S BARNSLEY & CO** *<br>45 Frederick Street<br>Birmingham | Manufacturing silversmiths |
| | | P13/B/20<br>*#2199*<br> | | |
| R3/52<br>11 February 1930<br>Sent by Ethel S Martin | 20 Avondale Road<br>Hoylake<br>Cheshire | P15/M/65,66<br>*#2200,1*<br> | **Ethel S MARTIN**<br>City School of Art<br>Hope Street<br>Liverpool | Student |
| R3/177<br>14 February 1961<br>Sent by E S Scains | 52 Broadway Avenue<br>Wallasey<br>Cheshire | P21/S/87<br>*#2202*<br> | **Eric Stanley SCAINS**<br>No business address entered | Student |
| R2/234<br>24 September 1920<br>Sent by Edward Stillwell & Son Ltd | | P15/S/44<br>*#2203*<br> | **Edward STILLWELL & SON LTD** *<br>E Digby Stillwell (Director)<br>25/26/27 Barbican and<br>6 Little Britain and<br>29 Saville Row<br>London W | Manufacturing jewellers |
| J1 1861 | | Not on P1, P2 or P3<br>*#2204* **E T?** | **Edward TATLER**<br>Chester | Silversmith |

ET–EW

| REGISTRATION DETAILS | MAKER'S PRIVATE ADDRESS and DETAILS | PLATE and MARK DETAILS | MAKER/COMPANY and BUSINESS ADDRESS | MAKER'S TRADE |
|---|---|---|---|---|
| LPB/80<br>21 February 1881<br>Sent by Coley Brothers | William Swan, electro-plater, at number 3½ in 1881.<br>Number 3 not in 1881 Kelly | P3/T/x2<br>***#2205,6***<br> | **Edward TRUMAN**<br>3 Regent Parade<br>Birmingham | Trade not identified |
| R3/176<br>24 January 1961<br>Sent by E Thornley | 91 Deane Church Lane<br>Bolton<br>Lancashire | P21/T/44<br>***#2207***<br> | **Edith THORNLEY**<br>No business address entered | Student of silversmithing |
| R3/2<br>29 April 1921<br>Sent by A Noel | Private address same as business | P15/D/60<br>***#2208***<br> | **Edgar T DAILLEY**<br>41 Charles Street<br>Hatton Garden<br>London EC | Manufacturing jeweller |
| LPB/86<br>4 April 1879 | Ashley House<br>Claremount Road<br>Soho Park<br>Birmingham | P3/V/x3<br>***#2209-11***<br> | **Edward VAUGHTON**<br>4 Warstone Lane<br>Birmingham | Jeweller |
| R3/81<br>13 November 1935<br>Sent by Viners Ltd | | P15/V/17<br>***#2212***<br> | **VINERS LTD**<br>Common seal of company affixed in the presence of:-<br>A Viner (Director)<br>P Johnson (Secretary)<br>Bath Street (Registered Office)<br>Sheffield | Cutlery manufacturers and silversmiths |
| Missing register<br>*c.*1886 | | P5/V/38<br>***#2213***<br> | **Edward VAUGHTON** ?<br>4 Warstone Lane<br>Birmingham | Jeweller |
| R1/74<br>29 September 1898<br>Sent by L E Neale<br>Marlow & Vaughton<br>R Parker<br>J H Wynn<br>J Hayward<br>G Smallwood<br>T S Osborn | | P9/V/1<br>***#2214***<br> | **Edward VAUGHTON**<br>88 Vyse Street<br>Birmingham | Manufacturing jeweller |
| Missing register<br>*c.*1892 | | P5/V/444<br>***#2215***<br> | | Jeweller |
| Not in R2 as expected - March to October 1909<br>Similar mark CAO 29 September 1898 and December 1900 | | P13/V/3<br>***#2216***<br> | **Edward VAUGHTON**<br>4 Warstone Lane<br>Birmingham | |
| R3/81<br>24 January 1953 | | P21/V/6<br>***#2217***<br> | **VINERS LTD**<br>Common seal of company affixed in the presence of:-<br>A Viner (Director)<br>P Johnson (Secretary)<br>Bath Street (Registered Office)<br>Sheffield | Cutlery manufacturers and silversmiths |
| R3/12<br>17 October 1922<br>Sent by Ernest Woodcock | 157 Lutterworth Road<br>Northampton | P15/W/57<br>***#2218***<br> | **Ernest WOODCOCK**<br>King Street<br>Northampton | Gold and silver worker |

| REGISTRATION DETAILS | MAKER'S PRIVATE ADDRESS and DETAILS | PLATE and MARK DETAILS | MAKER/COMPANY and BUSINESS ADDRESS | MAKER'S TRADE |
|---|---|---|---|---|
| Not in R2 as expected<br>Between February<br>and May 1920 | Not registered at BAO or LAO | P15/W/54<br>***#2219***  | **Unidentified** but see next entry | |
| R2/236<br>29 January 1921<br>Sent by Edith Watson | 27 Princess Avenue<br>Liverpool | P15/W/58<br>***#2220***  | **Edith WATSON**<br>The School of Art<br>Liverpool | Student in silver |
| R3/158<br>29 September 1958<br>Sent by W Whittaker<br>Two sizes | 48 Highfield Road<br>Cheadle Hulme<br>Cheshire | P21/W/80,81<br>***#2221,2*** 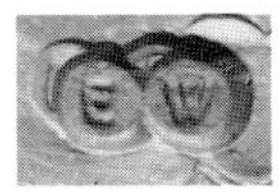 | **Ethel WHITTAKER**<br>No business address entered | Student |
| PP1/187<br>Similar mark LAO<br>4 December 1854 and<br>BAO 26 July 1844 | CWMP 1850 | P2/belowW/x5<br>***#2223-7***  | **Edward WAITHMAN** *<br>Spon Street<br>Coventry | Watchcase maker |
| CWMP 1874 PP3/83<br>Not in SPB or LPB so<br>struck 1860-63<br>Similar mark entered<br>LAO 30 October 1862 | | P3/W/x3<br>***#2228-30***  | **Edward WILDAY** *<br>77 Court, Brown's Building<br>Spon Street<br>100 Spon Street (1874)<br>Coventry | Watchcase maker |
| R1/209<br>8 March 1904<br>Sent by R Smart | 40 Cambridge Road<br>King's Heath | P9/W/108<br>***#2231***  | **Ernest Robert WRIGHT**<br>60 Northampton Street<br>Birmingham | Ring manufacturer |
| LPB/88<br>1 December 1880 | See EW & S on page 38 | P3/W/x1<br>***#2232***  | **Edwin WHITEHOUSE**<br>52 Vyse Street<br>Birmingham | Gold chain maker |
| LPB/86<br>6 March 1883 | | P3/W/x1<br>***#2233***  | | |
| Missing register<br>*c.*1887 | | P5/W/70<br>***#2234***  | | |
| SPB/23<br>11 August 1869 | | P3/W/x3<br>***#2235-7***  | **Ebenezar WHITE** *<br>42 Spon Street<br>Coventry | Watchcase maker |
| R1/180<br>19 November 1902<br>Sent by Eaton &<br>Wrighton | 82 Westfield Road<br>King's Heath<br>Dunbeath<br>Radnor Road<br>Handsworth | P9/E/11<br>***#2238***  | **Frederick Henry EATON**<br>**Ernest WRIGHTON** trading as<br>**EATON & WRIGHTON** *<br>33 Tenby Street<br>Birmingham | Manufacturing jewellers |
| R2/144<br>23 September 1911<br>Sent by Eaton &<br>Wrighton<br>BAO 19.418, 19.419 | Westover<br>Beaconsfield Road<br>Four Oaks<br>Dunbeath<br>Radnor Road<br>Handsworth | P13/E/24,25<br>***#2239,40***  | **Frederick Henry EATON**<br>**Ernest WRIGHTON** trading as<br>**EATON & WRIGHTON** *<br>121 Vyse Street<br>Birmingham | |
| R2/163<br>15 October 1912<br>Sent by F H Eaton | Westover<br>Four Oaks<br>Wycliff Road<br>Handsworth<br>Birmingham | P13/E/26,27<br>***#2241,2***  | | |

| REGISTRATION DETAILS | MAKER'S PRIVATE ADDRESS and DETAILS | PLATE and MARK DETAILS | MAKER/COMPANY and BUSINESS ADDRESS | MAKER'S TRADE |
|---|---|---|---|---|
| R2/177<br>10 October 1913<br>Sent by F H Eaton | Westover<br>Four Oaks<br>Wycliff Road<br>Handsworth<br>Birmingham | P13/E/30-35<br>*#2243-8*<br> | **Frederick Henry EATON**<br>**Ernest WRIGHTON** trading as<br>**EATON & WRIGHTON** *<br>33 Tenby Street<br>Birmingham | Manufacturing jewellers |
| R2/199<br>13 September 1915<br>Sent by Eaton & Wrighton<br>BAO 22.965 to 22.969<br>Two sizes | Westover<br>Beaconsfield Road<br>Four Oaks<br>Wycliff Road<br>Handsworth<br>Birmingham | P15/E/7-11<br>*#2249-53*<br> | | |
| R3/29<br>2 September 1925<br>Sent by Ernest Wrighton | Westover<br>Sutton Coldfield<br>Hill House Hotel<br>Handsworth<br>Birmingham | P15/E/32,33<br>*#2254,5*<br> | | |
| R3/168<br>8 July 1959<br>Sent by Eaton & Wrighton | | P21/E/13<br>*#2256*<br> | **EATON & WRIGHTON LTD** *<br>Sealed in the presence of:-<br>L P Wasty? (Director)<br>E Durley? (Secretary)<br>121 Vyse Street<br>Birmingham 18 | |
| LPB/50<br>1 November 1881<br>CWMP 1874 | | P3/L/x3<br>*#2257-9*<br> | **Edward William LINNETT** *<br>42 Spon Street (1874)<br>King Street (1881)<br>Coventry | Gold and silver dial maker, watchcase maker and springer |
| R2/116<br>13 August 1910<br>Sent by Lawson, Ward & Gammage<br>Two sizes | 191 Beckenham Road<br>Penge | P13/P/141,142<br>*#2260,1*<br> | **Ernest Walter PAYNE**<br>191 Beckenham Road<br>Penge and<br>High Street<br>Bromley<br>Kent | Gold and silversmith, watchmaker and jeweller |
| R3/13<br>14 November 1922<br>Sent by E Whitehouse & Son | Knowle<br>Warwick<br>Coleshill<br>Warwick | P15/W/59,60<br>*#2262,3*<br> | **Albert WHITEHOUSE**<br>**Frank WHITEHOUSE** trading as<br>**E WHITEHOUSE & SON**<br>52 Vyse Street<br>Birmingham | Gold chain manufacturers |
| R2/122<br>3 November 1910<br>Sent by E Whitehouse & Son | Barnt Green<br>Worcestershire<br>Knowle<br>Worcestershire | P13/W/81-86<br>*#2264-9*<br> | | |
| R3/110<br>24 August 1945<br>All previous EW&S valid<br>Sent by E Whitehouse & Son Ltd | | No new marks<br>*#2270* | **E WHITEHOUSE & SON LTD**<br>Sealed by:-<br>R H Whitehouse (Director)<br>A E B Whitehouse (Secretary)<br>52 Vyse Street<br>Birmingham | Jewellers |
| 10 June 1948 | | P21/W/49<br>*#2271*<br> | | |

| REGISTRATION DETAILS | MAKER'S PRIVATE ADDRESS and DETAILS | PLATE and MARK DETAILS | MAKER/COMPANY and BUSINESS ADDRESS | MAKER'S TRADE |
|---|---|---|---|---|
| Missing register<br>*c.*1890<br>Similar mark entered LAO 3 April 1873 and BAO 27 September 1893 | | P5/S/327<br>***#2272***<br> | **Edward William STILLWELL** trading as<br>**Edward STILLWELL & SON** *<br>47 Augusta Street (1867)<br>Birmingham<br>6 Little Britain (1881)<br>London<br>88 Vyse Street (1890)<br>Birmingham | Manufacturing jewellers<br><br>Later masonic jewellers |
| R1/19<br>7 December 1895<br>Sent by E Whitehouse & Son | Water Orton<br>Birmingham | P5/X*sic*/712<br>***#2273***<br> | **Edwin WHITEHOUSE**<br>**Albert WHITEHOUSE** trading as<br>**E WHITEHOUSE & SON**<br>52 Vyse Street<br>Birmingham | Gold chain manufacturers |
| R1/208<br>26 February 1904<br>Sent by A Whitehouse<br>Four sizes | Dorridge<br>Barnt Green | P9/W/104-107<br>***#2274-7***<br> | | Gold and silver chain manufacturers |
| R2/77<br>3 April 1909<br>Sent by E Whitehouse & Son<br>Three sizes | Barnt Green<br>Nr Birmingham<br>Knowle<br>Nr Birmingham | P13/W/49-54<br>***#2278-83***<br> | | Gold and silver chain makers |
| R2/98<br>23 November 1909<br>Sent by E W Sanders & Co<br>BAO 15.204,15.208 | 161 Church Lane<br>Handsworth<br>Birmingham | P13/S/49<br>***#2284***<br><br>P13/S/48<br>***#2285***<br> | **Ernest W SANDERS** trading as<br>**E W SANDERS & CO**<br>15 Vyse Street<br>Birmingham | Manufacturing jewellers |

| REGISTRATION DETAILS | MAKER'S PRIVATE ADDRESS and DETAILS | PLATE and MARK DETAILS | MAKER/COMPANY and BUSINESS ADDRESS | MAKER'S TRADE |
|---|---|---|---|---|
| R2/218<br>11 March 1919<br>Sent by Imperial Tobacco Co | 67 Airedale Avenue<br>Chiswick<br>London W4 | P15/A/13<br>***#2286***<br> | **BARRATT & CO**<br>F Archer (Manager)<br>266 King Street<br>Hammersmith<br>London WC | Fancy goods manufacturers |
| LPB/14<br>23 May 1885<br>No mark in LPB | 8th name in LPB/14<br>9th mark on P5/A | P5/A/x1<br>***#2287***<br> | **Frank ALLEN**<br>146½ Hockley Hill<br>Birmingham | Jeweller |
| R1/51<br>22 September 1897<br>Sent by F Allardice | Aneina House<br>Inderwick Road<br>Hornsey<br>London N | P5/A/871<br>***#2288***<br> | **Frank ALLARDICE** trading as<br>**J ALLARDICE**<br>2 Carthusian Street<br>London EC | Stick mounters |
| R1/27<br>18 April 1896<br>Sent by B H Joseph & Son | 129 High Street<br>Eton | P5/R/758<br>***#2289***<br> | **Frederick Arthur ROWELL** trading as<br>**H MERRICK**<br>Eton College<br>Eton | Watchmaker and silversmith |
| R3/158<br>8 October 1960<br>Sent by F A Welsh | | P21/W/96<br>***#2290***<br> | **F A WELSH (LIVERPOOL)**<br>Sealed in the presence of:-<br>F A Welsh (Director)<br>E R Clotworthy (Secretary) | Manufacturing jewellers |
| 7 April 1962 | | P21/W/101<br>***#2291***<br> | 10 Dale Street (Registered Office)<br>Liverpool 2 and<br>The Works<br>3 Hood Street | |
| 23 August 1956<br>P21/W/78 cancelled<br>16 April 1957 | | P21/W/76-79<br>***#2292-5***<br> | Liverpool 1 | |
| 16 April 1957 | | P21/W/84,85<br>***#2296,7***<br> | | |
| R1/138<br>14 December 1900<br>Sent by S Farren<br>Lancashire Watch Co<br>W Ehrhardt (Ed: Watch manufacturer) | West Villas<br>Stockton-on-Tees | P9/W/45<br>***#2298***<br> | **Frederick Arthur WOODROFFE**<br>58 High Street<br>Stockton-on-Tees | Goldsmith and watchmaker |
| R1/190<br>11 April 1903<br>Sent by R Parkes | | P9/W/94<br>***#2299***<br> | | Wholesale jeweller |
| R2/115<br>15 July 1910<br>BAO 16.634 Sent by Frederick Banks | Mascot<br>Cotton Lane<br>Moseley | P13/B/83<br>***#2300***<br> | **Frederick BANKS**<br>149 Warstone Lane<br>Birmingham | Manufacturing jeweller |
| Not in R2 as expected<br>Between 9 September and 18 October 1910 | | P13/B/88<br>***#2301***<br> | | |
| R2/213<br>14 November 1917<br>Sent by Louis Emanuel Hart<br>Two sizes | 436 Gillott Road<br>Edgbaston<br>283 Wheelers Street<br>Lozells<br>Birmingham | P15/B/75-85<br>***#2302-12***<br> | **Louis Emanuel HART** (acting Partner)<br>**Frank BONEHAM** trading as<br>**F BONEHAM & CO**<br>Hartington Buildings<br>Branston Street<br>Birmingham | Manufacturing jewellers |

| REGISTRATION DETAILS | MAKER'S PRIVATE ADDRESS and DETAILS | PLATE and MARK DETAILS | MAKER/COMPANY and BUSINESS ADDRESS | MAKER'S TRADE |
|---|---|---|---|---|
| LPB/16<br>16 June 1880<br>MR3/118<br>Sent by Francis Butt | | P3/B/x1<br>***#2313***<br> | **Alfred Wathew BUTT** *<br>69 Eastgate Row South<br>Chester | Goldsmith, silversmith, jeweller, watch and clock maker |
| SPB/7<br>5 September 1865 | | P3/B/x3<br>***#2314-6***<br> | **Francis BUTT** *<br>69 Eastgate Row South<br>Chester | |
| SPB/14<br>no day/month 1867 | | P3/B/x3<br>***#2317-9***<br> | **Francis BUTT** *<br>Birdcage Street<br>Chester | |
| R1/26<br>13 April 1896<br>Sent by F Blumenstein | 226 Upland Road<br>London E | P5/B/753<br>***#2320***<br> | **Franz BLUMENSTEIN**<br>37 Great Arthur Street<br>London | Stick mounter |
| Missing register<br>*c.*1886 | | P5/B/35<br>***#2321***<br> | | |
| LPB/16<br>23 August 1881 | | P3/B/x1<br>***#2322***<br> | **Frederick BANKS**<br>149 Warstone Lane<br>Birmingham | Jeweller |
| R1/95<br>18 March 1899<br>Sent by Frederick Banks | Private address same as business | P9/B/14,15<br>***#2323,4***<br> | | 15-carat gold brooch and scarf pin maker |
| R2/35<br>20 March 1907<br>Sent by Fred S Banks<br>Style of punch cancelled 15 July 1910 | Mascot<br>Cotton Lane<br>Moseley | P9/O*sic*/187<br>***#2325***<br> | **Frederick S BANKS** trading as<br>**F BANKS**<br>149 Warstone Lane<br>Birmingham | Jeweller |
| R2/70<br>14 January 1909<br>Sent by Frederick Barnes | 9 Turville Road<br>Handsworth<br>Birmingham | P13/B/44<br>***#2326***<br> | **Frederick BARNES**<br>43 Frederick Street<br>Birmingham | Jeweller |
| Not in R2 as expected<br>Between September and October 1909 | | P13/B/67<br>***#2327***<br> | | |
| R2/215<br>19 March 1918<br>Sent by F Banks | 163 Whitehead Road<br>Aston<br>Birmingham | P15/B/96<br>***#2328***<br> | **Frank BANKS**<br>11 Regent Place<br>Birmingham | General silversmith |
| R2/93<br>25 September 1909<br>Sent by J Eldridge | 32 Allerton Road<br>Lordship Road<br>Stoke Newington<br>London N | P13/B/66<br>***#2329***<br> | **Frederick BOYTON** trading as<br>**F BOYTON & CO** *<br>47 Hatton Garden<br>London EC | Manufacturing silversmiths |
| LPB/84<br>20 November 1882<br>Sent by R Case | Smart & Co, tobacconists, at this address 1875, 1882 and 1884 | P3/F/x2<br>***#2330,1***<br> | **FEILDING BROTHERS**<br>159 Fenchurch Street<br>Birmingham | Stick importers |
| R3/184<br>I June 1962<br>Sent by F Benoy Ltd | | P21/B/69<br>***#2332***<br>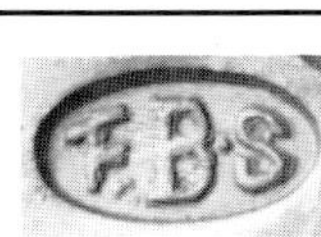 | **F BENOY LTD**<br>11 Pillory Street<br>Nantwich | Watchmakers, jewellers and silversmiths |

| REGISTRATION DETAILS | MAKER'S PRIVATE ADDRESS and DETAILS | PLATE and MARK DETAILS | MAKER/COMPANY and BUSINESS ADDRESS | MAKER'S TRADE |
|---|---|---|---|---|
| R1/2<br>31 October 1894<br>Sent by F Coulthurst | 141 Clifton Street<br>Old Trafford<br>Manchester | P5/C/616<br>*#2333*<br> | **Frederick COULTHURST**<br>3 Todd Street<br>Corporation Street and<br>43 Edge Street<br>Shudehill<br>Manchester | Silver engraver |
| R3/100<br>26 June 1941<br>Sent by F Collinge | 67 Long Street<br>Middleton<br>Manchester | P21/C/17<br>*#2334*<br>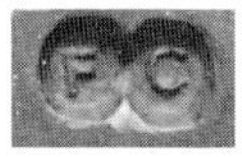 | **Florence COLLINGE** trading as<br>**RUSHBRIDGES**<br>24 King William Street<br>Blackburn | Jewellers |
| 29 October 1941 | | P21/C/19<br>*#2335*<br> | | |
| R2/130<br>11 March 1911<br>Sent by Frank Cobb<br>Two sizes | 145 Burngreave Road<br>Sheffield | P13/C/89, 90<br>*#2336,7*<br> | **Frank COBB** trading as<br>**Frank COBB & CO** *<br>Howard Street<br>Sheffield | Silversmiths and cutlers |
| Missing register<br>*c.*1891 Incuse mark<br>BAO 16 May 1889 | | P5/B/351a<br>*#2338*<br> | **Frederick Charles BERKELEY**<br>77 Carver Street<br>Birmingham | Pencil case maker |
| | | P5/B/351b<br>*#2339*<br> | | |
| | | P5/B/351c<br>*#2340*<br> | | |
| R3/168<br>1 July 1959<br>Sent by F C J Walsh | 193 Orwell Road<br>Kirkdale<br>Liverpool 4 | P21/W/91<br>*#2341*<br> | **Francis Charles John WALSH**<br>College of Art<br>Hope Street<br>Liverpool | Student |
| R2/150<br>20 February 1912<br>Sent by Lowe & Sons<br>Two sizes | 17 Eaton Road<br>Chester<br>Stone Bridge House<br>Chester | P13/L/64-71<br>*#2342-9*<br> | **J Cecil LOWE**<br>**G F LOWE** trading as<br>**LOWE & SONS** *<br>11 Bridge Street Row<br>Chester | Silversmiths |
| R3/41<br>26 May 1928<br>Sent by selves | | P15/P/211,212<br>*#2350,1*<br>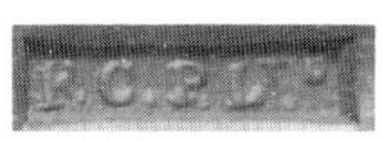 | **F C PARSONS LTD**<br>16 Vyse Street<br>Birmingham | Wholesale and manufacturing jewellers |
| R2/7<br>30 November 1905<br>Sent by F C Rowan | 25 Courcy Road<br>Hornsey<br>London N | P9/R/69<br>*#2352*<br> | **Frederick Charles ROWAN**<br>58a Hatton Garden<br>London EC | Goldsmith and diamond mounter |
| R1/76<br>26 November 1898<br>Sent by F C Smith | 9 Church Street<br>Lozells<br>Aston<br>Birmingham | P9/S/12<br>*#2353*<br> | **Frederick Charles SMITH**<br>32 Tenby Street<br>Birmingham | Jeweller |
| R1/129<br>25 July 1900<br>Sent by F & C Taylor | 48 Anglesea Avenue<br>Harpurhey<br>Manchester | P9/T/16<br>*#2354*<br> | **Fred TAYLOR**<br>**Charles TAYLOR**<br>68 Corporation Street<br>Manchester | Pipe, stick and umbrella mounters |
| R3/116<br>12 December 1950<br>Sent by F A Welch | 28 Barlow Avenue<br>Bebington | P21/W/56,57<br>*#2355,6*<br> | **Frederick Albert WELCH**<br>3 Hood Street<br>Liverpool | Practical jeweller |

| REGISTRATION DETAILS | MAKER'S PRIVATE ADDRESS and DETAILS | PLATE and MARK DETAILS | MAKER/COMPANY and BUSINESS ADDRESS | MAKER'S TRADE |
|---|---|---|---|---|
| R3/116<br>12 December 1950<br>14 April 1953<br>All FCW punches cancelled<br>23 August 1956 | | P21/W/63<br>*#2357*<br> | **Frederick Albert WELCH**<br>3 Hood Street<br>Liverpool | Practical jeweller |
| R3/168<br>14 May 1959<br>Sent by F C Welch | Private address same as business | P21/W/89<br>*#2358*<br> | **Frederick Charles WELCH**<br>3 Brimstage Avenue<br>Higher Bebington<br>Wirral<br>Cheshire | |
| R2/65<br>23 September 1908<br>Sent by Frederick Charles Welch<br>Punch with stops between letters cancelled 29 April 1959 and transferred to Albert Welch | 55 Granville Road<br>Higher Tranmere | P13/W/33<br>*#2359*<br> | **Frederick Charles WELCH**<br>62 The Arcade<br>Lord Street<br>Liverpool | Working jeweller |
| R3/116<br>27 February 1947<br>Sent by F A Welch<br>Taking over punches from Frederick Charles Welch | 28 Barlow Avenue<br>Bebington | No new marks<br>*#2360* | **Frederick Albert WELCH**<br>3 Hood Street<br>Liverpool | Practical jeweller |
| R1/56<br>4 January 1898<br>Sent by Fred Doyle<br>R1 has both P5/D/916 and 917 | 11 Denmark Road<br>Moss Side<br>Manchester | P5/D/917<br>*#2361*<br> | **Fred DOYLE**<br>1 Tarriff Street<br>Dale Street<br>Manchester | Stick and umbrella mounter |
| R1/121<br>14 February 1900 | | P9/D/16<br>*#2362*<br> | **Fred DOYLE**<br>Argyle Buildings<br>Hanging Ditch<br>Manchester | |
| R2/105<br>8 March 1910<br>Sent by Francis Arthur Darton | Clare Lodge<br>Woodford | P13/D/27<br>*#2363*<br> | **Francis Arthur DARTON**<br>Sole proprietor of **F DARTON & CO** *<br>142 St John Street and<br>52 Clerkenwell Road<br>London | Manufacturing opticians |
| R1/231<br>15 April 1905<br>Sent by Otto Fulda | Russell Square Mansions<br>Southampton Row<br>London WC | P9/D/47<br>*#2364*<br> | **Otto FULDA** trading as<br>**FULDA & DAVID** *<br>11 Hatton Garden<br>London EC | Watch manufacturers |
| LPB/96<br>22 April 1882 | | P3/D/x3<br>*#2365-7*<br> | **Frank DAVIS**<br>50 Augusta Street<br>Birmingham | Jeweller and fancy ring maker |
| Missing register<br>*c.*1890 | | P5/D/332<br>*#2368*<br> | **Unidentified** | |
| R1/45<br>1 June 1897<br>Sent by Benson Brothers<br>R Fennell | 7 Crossfield Road [1]<br>Hampstead, London NW<br>8 Steels Road [2]<br>Haverstock Hill<br>London NW | P5/D/846<br>*#2369*<br> | **Otto FULDA** [1]<br>**Jacques DAVID** [2] trading as<br>**FULDA & DAVID** *<br>11 Hatton Garden<br>London | Watch manufacturers |

| REGISTRATION DETAILS | MAKER'S PRIVATE ADDRESS and DETAILS | PLATE and MARK DETAILS | MAKER/COMPANY and BUSINESS ADDRESS | MAKER'S TRADE |
|---|---|---|---|---|
| R1/120<br>8 February 1900<br>Sent by R J Pike | 7 Crossfield Road [1]<br>Hampstead, London NW<br>8 Steels Road [2]<br>Haverstock Hill<br>London NW | P9/D/15<br>***#2370***<br> | **Otto FULDA** [1]<br>**Jacques DAVID** [2] trading as<br>**FULDA & DAVID** *<br>11 Hatton Garden<br>London | Watch manufacturers |
| Missing register<br>*c.*1889 | | P5/B/269<br>***#2371***<br> | **Unidentified** | |
| LPB/32 SP26/5<br>15 January 1884<br>Only initials FF in LPB | | P5/F/x1<br>***#2372***<br> | **Frederick FLINT & CO** *<br>24 Clerkenwell Road<br>London EC | Manufacturing and wholesale jewellers |
| R3/159<br>4 December 1956<br>Sent by E F Flockton<br>Two sizes | 14 Brixton Avenue<br>Withington<br>Manchester 20 | P21/F/31,32<br>***#2373,4***<br> | **Elizabeth Frances FLOCKTON**<br>No business address entered | Student |
| R1/193<br>18 May 1903<br>Sent by F F Clarkson | Private address same as business | P9/C/91&0*sic*<br>***#2375,6***<br> | **Frank Finley CLARKSON** *<br>Market Place<br>Northallerton<br>Yorkshire also London | Silversmith |
| R2/9<br>20 January 1906<br>Sent by F F Clarkson | | P9/D*sic*/233<br>***#2377***<br> | | |
| R2/62<br>15 June 1908<br>Sent by Frank Finlay Clarkson<br>Two sizes | Market Place<br>Northallerton | P13/C/32,33<br>***#2378,9***<br> | | |
| R2/78<br>7 April 1909<br>Sent by A Bailey | Beechfield<br>Barnt Green<br>Beechfield<br>Barnt Green<br>Birmingham | P13/F/7<br>***#2380***<br> | **Walter FETTER**<br>**Walter Hickman FETTER** trading as<br>**FETTER, FORBES & CO**<br>24 & 26 Hylton Street<br>Birmingham | Manufacturing jewellers |
| | | P13/F/6<br>***#2381***<br> | | |
| SPB/23<br>31 January 1876<br>See also AB for A Bedford, General Manager Waltham Co, UK<br>Two sizes | US citizen. Mark only seen on silver cases 1875/6 and 1876/7 with Waltham movements. Cases believed to have been made by Dennison & Wigley of Birmingham. | P3/S/x7<br>***#2382-8***<br> | **Frederick Francis SEELAND** *<br>(Ed: Assistant Manager)<br>**WALTHAM WATCH COMPANY**<br>Waltham Buildings<br>Holborn Circus<br>London | Watchcase maker and USA watch importer (Agent) |
| SPB/4<br>Undated –<br>3 March 1876 or<br>20 October 1876<br>Two sizes | Seeland was in process of becoming General Manager of International Watch Company of Schaffhausen, Switzerland. He started 24 October 1876 and stayed 3 years before returning to USA in disgrace for fraud. | P3/S/x2<br>***#2389,90***<br> | **Frederick Francis SEELAND** *<br>Schaffhausen<br>Switzerland | |
| R1/151<br>13 July 1901 | Private address same as business | P9/G/27<br>***#2391***<br> | **Frank GOUGH**<br>30 Rochdale Road<br>Blackley<br>Manchester | Tobacconist |

| REGISTRATION DETAILS | MAKER'S PRIVATE ADDRESS and DETAILS | PLATE and MARK DETAILS | MAKER/COMPANY and BUSINESS ADDRESS | MAKER'S TRADE |
|---|---|---|---|---|
| R2/191<br>13 January 1915<br>Sent by Friedman & Gottliffe | 26 Dorset Avenue<br>Leeds<br>54 Harehill Avenue<br>Leeds<br>55 Cowper Street<br>Leeds | P15/F/9-11<br>***#2392-4***<br> | **FRIEDMAN & GOTTLIFFE LTD**<br>S Mitchell (Secretary)<br>A Friedman (Director)<br>L Gottliffe (Director)<br>24, 26 Central Road<br>Key Hill Drive<br>Birmingham | Manufacturing jewellers |
| R3/7<br>18 February 1922<br>Sent by F Tennant | 54 Harehill Avenue<br>Chapel Town<br>Leeds<br>55 Cowper Street<br>Chapel Town<br>Leeds | P15/F/22<br>***#2395***<br>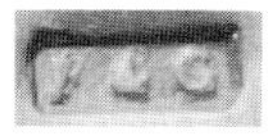 | **FRIEDMAN & GOTTLIFFE LTD**<br>A Friedman (Partner)<br>L Gottliffe (Partner)<br>24, 26 Central Road<br>Leeds and<br>10 New Street<br>Newcastle upon Tyne and<br>Key Hill Drive<br>Birmingham | Wholesale and manufacturing jewellers |
| R3/21<br>26 March 1924<br>Sent by S Mitchell | 54 Harehill Avenue<br>Chapel Town<br>Leeds<br>55 Cowper Street<br>Chapel Town<br>Leeds | P15/F/26,27<br>***#2396,7***<br> | **A FRIEDMAN**<br>**L GOTTLIFFE** trading as<br>**FRIEDMAN & GOTTLIFFE LTD**<br>115 Vicars Lane<br>Leeds and<br>Key Hill Drive<br>Birmingham | |
| R1/148<br>24 May 1901<br>Cancelled and punch defaced<br>20 July 1901<br>Sent by<br>W H Carrington | Private address same as business | P9/G/26<br>***#2398***<br> | **Frank GOUGH**<br>30 Barns Green<br>Blackley<br>Manchester | Tobacconist |
| R1/57<br>25 January 1898<br>Sent by<br>F W Goldsmith | 22 St Peter's Road<br>Birmingham | P5/G/922<br>***#2399***<br> | **Frederick William GOLDSMITH**<br>trading as **F GOLDSMITH**<br>90 Spencer Street<br>18 Vyse Street (later - undated)<br>Birmingham | Manufacturing jeweller |
| R2/20<br>12 June 1906<br>Sent by Friedman & Gottliffe | 38 Hamilton Avenue<br>74 Grange Avenue<br>Leeds | P9/F/28<br>***#2400***<br> | **Aaron FRIEDMAN**<br>**Lazarus GOTTLIFFE** trading as<br>**FRIEDMAN & GOTTLIFFE**<br>5 Upper Mill Hill<br>Leeds | Wholesale jewellers |
| R1/50<br>19 August 1897<br>Sent by W H<br>Carrington & Co | Edge Hill<br>Alexander Road<br>Gloucester | P5/Z*sic*/868<br>***#2401***<br> | **Frederick George HOUGHTON**<br>51 Deansgate<br>Bolton | Tobacconist |
| R1/207<br>5 February 1904<br>Sent by P Ford | 6 Broughton Road<br>Handsworth | P9/F/19<br>***#2402***<br> | **FORD & GALLOWAY LTD**<br>P Ford (Director)<br>47 Frederick Street<br>Birmingham | Wholesale jewellers and manufacturers |
| R3/174<br>17 September 1960<br>Sent by F G Roberts<br>Two sizes | 145 Birchfield Road<br>Widnes<br>Lancashire | P21/R/33,34<br>***#2403,4***<br> | **Frederick Gerrard ROBERTS**<br>No business address entered | Student |
| R2/39<br>14 May 1907<br>Sent by<br>F G Rowbotham<br>Two sizes | 102 Alexandra Road<br>Acocks Green<br>Birmingham | P9/R/88,89<br>***#2405,6***<br> | **Frederick George ROWBOTHAM**<br>(late **G ROWBOTHAM & SON**)<br>30 Spencer Street<br>Birmingham | Ring manufacturers |

| REGISTRATION DETAILS | MAKER'S PRIVATE ADDRESS and DETAILS | PLATE and MARK DETAILS | MAKER/COMPANY and BUSINESS ADDRESS | MAKER'S TRADE |
|---|---|---|---|---|
| R3/22<br>7 May 1924 | | P15/H/78<br>***#2407***<br>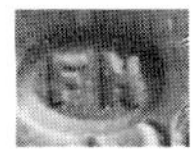 | **THE GOLDSMITH & SILVERSMITH RETAIL**<br>Frank Hallett (Ed: Director?)<br>No business address entered | Retail goldsmiths and silversmiths |
| R3/172<br>19 May 1960<br>Sent by F Hunt<br>Two sizes | 3 Thorns Avenue<br>Sharples<br>Bolton | P21/H/79,80<br>***#2408,9***<br>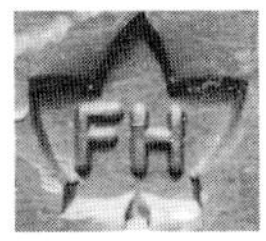 | **Frank HUNT**<br>No business address entered | Student of silversmithing |
| R3/132<br>29 April 1950<br>Sent by C J Hooper | 1 Tynesdale Crescent [1]<br>Great Barr<br>9 Shelford Road [2]<br>Great Barr<br>Birmingham 22 | P21/F/13<br>***#2410***<br> | **Frederick William FLETCHER** [1]<br>**Charles John HOOPER** [2] trading as<br>**FLETCHER & HOOPER**<br>114 Branston Street<br>Hockley<br>Birmingham 18 | Manufacturing jewellers |
| R2/222<br>1 August 1919<br>Sent by F Hiscocks | 17 Marsland Road<br>Sale<br>Manchester | P15/H/51<br>***#2411***<br> | **F HISCOCKS**<br>22 Longston Buildings<br>Cannon Street<br>Manchester | Ring mounter and setter |
| Missing register<br>*c.*1888 | | P5/H/178<br>***#2412***<br> | **Unidentified** | |
| R1/44<br>11 May 1897<br>Sent by F Highland | 27 Northumberland Grove<br>Park Lane<br>Tottenham<br>London | P5/Z*sic*/841<br>***#2413***<br> | **Frederick HIGHLAND** *<br>21 Camomile Street<br>London EC | Fancy leather worker |
| R1/110<br>30 August 1899<br>Sent by F Hollis | Private address same as business | P9/H/19<br>***#2414***<br> | **Frederick HOLLIS**<br>24 George Street<br>Lozells<br>Birmingham | Jeweller |
| R2/109<br>4 May 1910<br>Sent by Fisher & Holmes<br>Clerk entered Francis & Holmes in error | 55 Douglas Road<br>Birmingham<br>102 Handsworth Wood Road<br>Birmingham | P13/F/20<br>***#2415***<br> | **John FISHER**<br>**Donald Francis HOLMES** trading as<br>**FISHER & HOLMES**<br>72 Branston Street<br>Birmingham | Manufacturing jewellers, ring makers and diamond mounters |
| R2/118<br>9 September 1910<br>Sent by Frank Harding | 43 Mainwaring Road<br>Seacombe | P13/H/61<br>***#2416***<br> | **Frank HARDING**<br>31a Tarleton Street<br>Liverpool | Wholesale and working jeweller |
| R2/121<br>20 October 1910<br>Sent by T S Osborn<br>BAO 15.841<br>Cancelled<br>6 June 1912 | | P13/H/65<br>***#2417***<br> | | Manufacturing jeweller |
| R3/43<br>14 September 1928<br>Sent by H Hall & Sons | 56 Somerset Road [1]<br>Handsworth<br>43 Tenbury Road [2]<br>King's Heath<br>Birmingham | P15/A/49<br>***#2418***<br> | **W L MARRAN** [1]<br>**N L MARRAN** [2] trading as<br>**F H ADAMS & CO**<br>262 New John Street West<br>Birmingham | Manufacturing silversmiths |
| R1/190<br>20 April 1903<br>Sent by F H Cose | Private address same as business | P9/C/87<br>***#2419***<br>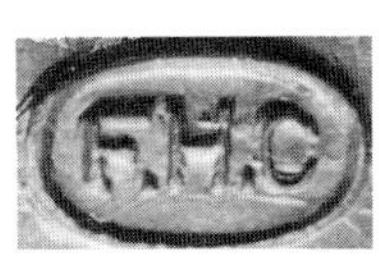 | **Frederick Hugh COSE**<br>126 Heneage Street<br>Birmingham | Pipe manufacturer |

| REGISTRATION DETAILS | MAKER'S PRIVATE ADDRESS and DETAILS | PLATE and MARK DETAILS | MAKER/COMPANY and BUSINESS ADDRESS | MAKER'S TRADE |
|---|---|---|---|---|
| R1/9<br>18 April 1895<br>Sent by Frederick Hutchinson | 60 Albion Street<br>Birmingham | P5/H/652<br>***#2420***<br> | **Frederick HUTCHINSON** trading as<br>**F HUTCHINSON & CO**<br>60 Albion Street<br>Birmingham | Jewellers |
| R2/47<br>12 October 1907<br>Sent by F H Dingley | Private address same as business | P9/D/58<br>***#2421***<br> | **Francis Henry DINGLEY**<br>186 Albert Road<br>Handsworth<br>Birmingham | Signet and fancy rings, hollow and solid |
| R1/174<br>20 August 1902<br>Sent by F H Eaton | 122 Westfield Road<br>King's Heath<br>Birmingham | P9/E/9<br>***#2422***<br> | **Frederick Henry EATON**<br>33 Tenby Street<br>Birmingham | Manufacturing jeweller |
| R1/173<br>29 July 1902<br>Sent by F H Eaton | | P9/E/8<br>***#2423***<br> | | |
| R3/35<br>11 December 1926<br>Sent by A E Jones<br>Two sizes | Somerville<br>Haines Hill<br>Taunton | P15/F/30,31<br>***#2424,5***<br> | **FRANKLIN & HARE LTD**<br>28 The Parade<br>Taunton | Jewellers |
| R2/1<br>18 August 1905<br>Sent by Twine & Gilpin | St Annes<br>Four Oaks | P9/M/93<br>***#2426***<br> | **Frank H MANNOX**<br>45 Warstone Lane<br>Birmingham | Manufacturing jeweller |
| 20 September 1909<br>Sent by Ward Brothers | | P13/M/22<br>***#2427***<br> | | |
| R1/217<br>2 July 1904<br>Sent by Frederick Harding<br>Two sizes | 312 Hagley Road<br>Edgbaston<br>The Laurels<br>St Bernard's Road<br>Orton<br>Birmingham | P9/H/62,63<br>***#2428,9***<br> | **Frederick HARDING**<br>**Arthur W HARDING** trading as<br>**F HARDING & SON**<br>56/58 Spencer Street<br>Birmingham | Silversmiths and electroplate manufacturers |
| R2/135<br>15 May 1911<br>Sent by Frank Howard Wilde | Private address same as business | P13/W/91<br>***#2430***<br> | **Frank Howard WILDE**<br>22 Alcester Road<br>Moseley<br>Birmingham | Ring maker and diamond mounter |
| | | P2/J/x2<br>***#2431,2***<br> | **Unidentified** | |
| R2/95<br>16 October 1909<br>Sent by T Johnson | 6 Rheidol Terrace<br>Islington North<br>London | P13/T/9<br>***#2433***<br> | **H FRANCIS**<br>**T JOHNSON** trading as<br>**FRANCIS & JOHNSON**<br>6 Rheidol Terrace<br>Islington North<br>London | Pipe mounters and repairers |
| R1/190<br>16 April 1903<br>Sent by F J Bennett | Wood Cottage<br>Baccus Road<br>Birmingham | P9/B/105, 01*sic*<br>***#2434,5***<br> | **Frederick John BENNETT**<br>127½ Branston Lane<br>Birmingham | Jeweller |

| REGISTRATION DETAILS | MAKER'S PRIVATE ADDRESS and DETAILS | PLATE and MARK DETAILS | MAKER/COMPANY and BUSINESS ADDRESS | MAKER'S TRADE |
|---|---|---|---|---|
| LPB/18<br>18 January 1884<br>No mark in LPB | | P5/B/x1<br>*#2436*  | **Frederick Joseph BRAHAM**<br>29 Richard Street<br>Spencer Street<br>Birmingham | Manufacturing optician |
| LPB/98<br>11 August 1885<br>No mark in LPB<br>Sent by W Butler | | P5/B/x1<br>*#2437*  | | |
| Missing register<br>*c* 1890 | | P5/B/278<br>*#2438*  | | |
| R3/108<br>9 April 1945<br>Sent by Frederick Joseph Collins | | P21/C/22<br>*#2439*  | **Frederick Joseph COLLINS**<br>7 Great King Street<br>Hockley<br>53 Gt Hampton Street (4 March 1946)<br>Birmingham 18<br>73 Alum Rock Road (15 December 1953)<br>Saltley<br>Birmingham 8 | Silversmith |
| R1/95<br>9 March 1899<br>Sent by F J Cockle | 2 Japan Street<br>Cheetham Hill<br>Manchester | P9/C/10<br>*#2440*  | **Frank Josiah COCKLE** trading as<br>**CLIFT & COCKLE**<br>19a Corporation Street<br>51 Arcade Chambers ( later - undated)<br>St Mary's Gate | General engravers and piercers |
| R1/66<br>8 June 1898<br>Sent by F J Cockle | | P5/aboveC/957<br>*#2441*  | Manchester | General engraving |
| R1/188<br>17 March 1903<br>Sent by J & R Griffin | 137 Heathfield Road<br>Birmingham | P9/Q*sic*/158<br>*#2442*  | **Francis Joseph PARKES**<br>Harford Street<br>Birmingham | Wholesale jeweller |
| R2/9<br>1 February 1906<br>Sent by J & R Griffin | | P9/Q*sic*/230<br>*#2443*  | | |
| R2/86<br>29 June 1909<br>BAO 9.301<br>Sent by J Hayward | | P13/P/87[1] *sic*<br>*#2444*  | **Francis Joseph PARKES**<br>45 Tenby Street North<br>Birmingham | Jeweller |
| R2/155<br>18 April 1912<br>Sent by R Parkes & Co | | P13/Q*sic*/211-216<br>*#2445-50*  | | Wholesale jeweller |
| R2/1<br>28 August 1905<br>MR3/139<br>Sent by Stokes & Ireland | Ronaldsha<br>Winchester | P9/R/68<br>*#2451*  | **Frederick James ROSS**<br>**George Malcolm ROSS**<br>**Herbert Frederick ROSS** trading as<br>**J ROSS & SON** *<br>43/44 High Street<br>Winchester | Silversmiths and jewellers |
| R3/165<br>16 December 1958<br>Sent by F Kitson<br>Two sizes | 13 Alresford Road<br>Salford 6<br>Lancashire | P21/K/18,19<br>*#2452,3*  | **Frank KITSON**<br>No business address entered | Student silversmith |
| R3/23<br>20 September 1924<br>Sent by Benson Brothers | 42 Radnar Road<br>Handsworth<br>Birmingham<br>162 Poland Road<br>Edgbaston | P15/K/16<br>*#2454*  | **Herbert Fritz KUNDERD**<br>**Fritz KUNDERD**<br>26 Frederick Street<br>Birmingham | Watch merchants |

| REGISTRATION DETAILS | MAKER'S PRIVATE ADDRESS and DETAILS | PLATE and MARK DETAILS | MAKER/COMPANY and BUSINESS ADDRESS | MAKER'S TRADE |
|---|---|---|---|---|
| R3/71<br>24 May 1934<br>Sent by Elite Bracelet Man'g Co Ltd<br>Regent Place<br>Birmingham | 162 Poland Road<br>Edgbaston | P15/K/21<br>***#2455***<br> | **Herbert Fritz KUNDERD**<br>**Fritz KUNDERD**<br>26 Frederick Street<br>Birmingham | Watch merchants |
| LPB/46<br>5 May 1881<br>Similar mark entered LAO 1879 | Struck in error on P2 rather than P3 GTD 1865 | P2/K/x3<br>***#2456-8***<br> | **Frederick KAY** *<br>51 Wynyatt Street<br>Goswell Road<br>London | Watchcase maker |
| LPB/52<br>7 March 1884<br>Sent by J Ahronsberg<br>No mark in LPB only FL written | | P5/L/x1<br>***#2459***<br> | **Frederick LYNE**<br>10 Perry Road<br>Bristol | Goldsmith and jeweller |
| R2/49<br>2 November 1907<br>Sent by Frederick Lyne | Private address same as business | P9/L/91<br>***#2460***<br> | **Frederick LYNE**<br>5 Perry Road<br>Bristol | Working goldsmith |
| R3/89<br>2 March 1938<br>Sent by R Jones | 5 Warstone Parade East<br>Birmingham<br>21 Old Shoreham Road<br>Hove | P21/L/3<br>***#2461***<br> | **Frank Fincher LONDON**<br>34 Queens Road<br>Brighton | Masonic outfitter and furnisher |
| R2/68<br>10 November 1908<br>Sent by Frank Lees | 3 Alexandra Terrace<br>Bedford Road<br>Rock Ferry | P13/L/5<br>***#2462***<br> | **Frank LEES**<br>65 St Paul's Road<br>Nelson Road<br>Rock Ferry (ed. near Birkenhead) | Umbrella and walking stick manufacturer |
| R3/71<br>26 April 1934<br>Sent by Samuel Hope<br>126 Vyse Street<br>Birmingham | 88 Clough Road [1]<br>Rotherham<br>7 Broomfield Grove [2]<br>Rotherham | P15/L/43<br>***#2463***<br> | **Francis Sydney LOWE** [1]<br>**Harold Ernest LOWE** [2] trading as<br>**Francis LOWE & SONS**<br>24/26 Effingham Street<br>Rotherham<br>Yorkshire | Jewellers |
| R2/104<br>4 March 1910<br>BAO 17.569 to 17.574<br>Sent by Coley Brothers | 12 Woodstock Road<br>Redland<br>Bristol<br>12 Woodstock Road<br>Redland<br>Bristol | P13/F/11-16<br>***#2464-9***<br> | **FEARS LTD**<br>Amos Daniel Fear (Managing Director)<br>Amos Reginald Portius Fear (Director and Secretary)<br>4 Bristol Bridge<br>Bristol | Watchmakers and jewellers |
| R2/164<br>16 October 1912<br>Sent by Coley Brothers | | P13/F/29<br>***#2470***<br> | **FEARS LTD**<br>A Reginald P Fear (Secretary)<br>Amos D Fear (Managing Director)<br>Bristol Bridge<br>Bristol | Wholesale jewellers |
| R3/15<br>26 April 1923<br>Sent by J Taylor Foot | 34 Bellot Street<br>Manchester<br>41 Dannock Road<br>London W | P15/F/24,25<br>***#2471,2***<br> | **Isaac FOSTER**<br>**James FAY** trading as<br>**FOSTER & CO (MANCHESTER) LTD**<br>10 Watling Street<br>Shudehill<br>Manchester | Wholesale watch and clock warehouse |
| R2/69<br>10 December 1908<br>Sent by Fredericks Ltd | Lynhurst [1]<br>Woodward Road<br>London SE<br>498 Lordship Lane [2]<br>London SE | P13/F/4<br>***#2473***<br>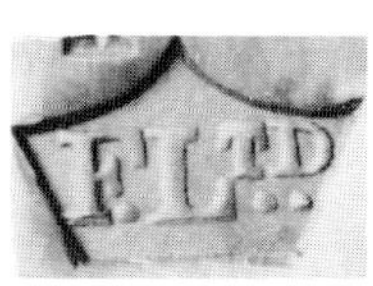 | **FREDERICKS LTD** *<br>F W Bambridge [1] (Director)<br>W G Harris [2] (Director)<br>20 Holborn Viaduct<br>London EC | Goldsmiths and silversmiths |

| REGISTRATION DETAILS | MAKER'S PRIVATE ADDRESS and DETAILS | PLATE and MARK DETAILS | MAKER/COMPANY and BUSINESS ADDRESS | MAKER'S TRADE |
|---|---|---|---|---|
| R2/69<br>1 January 1909<br>impression<br>taken of # 5 | Lynhurst [1]<br>Woodward Road<br>London SE<br>498 Lordship Lane [2]<br>London SE | P13/F/5<br>*#2474*<br> | **FREDERICKS LTD** *<br>F W Bambridge [1] (Director)<br>W G Harris [2] (Director)<br>20 Holborn Viaduct<br>London EC | Goldsmiths and silversmiths |
| Missing register<br>*c.*1891 | See Mills and Marson below | P5/M/371<br>*#2475*<br> | **Unidentified** | |
| Missing register<br>*c.*1892<br>Similar mark entered<br>BAO 12 May 1903 | | P5/F/437<br>*#2476*<br> | **FERGUSON & McBEAN**<br>41 Union Street<br>Inverness | Jewellers |
| R2/37<br>5 November 1910<br>Sent by Smith & Co<br>Punch returned to be altered, wrong style | 216 Soho Hill<br>Handsworth | P13/M/38<br>*#2477*<br> | **Frederick MARSON** *<br>109 Spencer Street<br>Birmingham | Manufacturing jewellers |
| R1/132<br>25 September 1900<br>Sent by Francis Mills | 25 Hayden Road<br>Handsworth<br>Birmingham | P9/M/25<br>*#2478*<br> | **Francis MILLS**<br>32½ Frederick Street<br>Birmingham | Ring manufacturer |
| R3/146<br>4 November 1953<br>Sent by F Metcalfe | 71 School Lane<br>Didsbury<br>Manchester 20 | P21/M/35<br>*#2479*<br> | **Fred METCALFE**<br>No business address entered | Student |
| Not in R1 as expected | Post-1898 as on P9<br>Could be Marson #2482? | P9/M/19<br>*#2480*<br> | **Unidentified** | |
| R2/140<br>27 July 1911<br>Sent by A Moore | 18 Britannia Road<br>Westcliff-on-Sea | P13/M/45<br>*#2481*<br> | **Frederick MOULE** *<br>95 Aldersgate Street<br>London EC | Wholesale jeweller |
| R1/33<br>29 September 1896<br>Sent by Frederick Marson<br>Two sizes | 216 Soho Hill<br>Birmingham | P5/M/790x2<br>*#2482,3*<br> | **Frederick MARSON** *<br>41 and 47 Hylton Street<br>Birmingham | Goldsmith |
| R1/81<br>31 October 1898<br>Sent by F Marson<br>J Morris | | P9/M/3<br>*#2484*<br> | | Manufacturing jeweller |
| R1/126<br>11 May 1900<br>Sent by F Marson | | P9/M/21<br>*#2485*<br> | **Frederick MARSON** *<br>109 Spencer Street<br>Birmingham | |
| R1/131<br>31 August 1900<br>Sent by F Marson<br>C G Heaven | | P9/M/24<br>*#2486*<br> | | |
| R1/171<br>8 July 1902<br>Sent by F Marson | | P9/M/39<br>*#2487*<br> | | |
| R2/37<br>19 April 1907<br>Sent by Smith & Co | | P9/M/113<br>*#2488*<br> | | |

| REGISTRATION DETAILS | MAKER'S PRIVATE ADDRESS and DETAILS | PLATE and MARK DETAILS | MAKER/COMPANY and BUSINESS ADDRESS | MAKER'S TRADE |
|---|---|---|---|---|
| R2/175<br>27 August 1913<br>Sent by self<br>Two sizes | 216 Soho Hill<br>Handsworth | P15/M/1-4<br>***#2489-92***<br> | **Frederick MARSON** *<br>90 Spencer Street<br>Birmingham | Manufacturing jeweller |
| R2/220<br>8 May 1919<br>Sent by F Marson | F Marson<br>140 Hampstead Road<br>Handsworth | P15/M/30–32<br>***#2493-5***<br> | | |
| R2/180<br>14 November 1913<br>Sent by Coley Brothers | 18 Britannia Road<br>Westcliff-on-Sea | P13/M/62<br>***#2496***<br> | **Frederick MOULE** *<br>95 Aldersgate Street<br>London EC | Wholesale jeweller |
| R2/142<br>29 August 1911<br>Sent by Albert Medley | 143 Gell Street [1]<br>Sheffield | P13/F/27<br>***#2497***<br> | **FORD & MEDLEY LTD**<br>Albert Medley [1] (Director)<br>137 Arundel Street<br>Sheffield | Cutlers and silversmiths |
| R1/80<br>13 October 1894<br>Sent by T S Osborn<br>F C Berkeley | Annotated "*sunk* (cameo?) punch on P5 and *cutting* (incuse?) punch"<br>See #2503 below | P5/M/599<br>***#2498***<br> | **F MORDAN & CO** *<br>Albion Works<br>City Road<br>London EC | Jewellers |
| R2/171<br>6 May 1913<br>Sent by F Marson & Co<br>Punch withdrawn<br>19 August 1913 | 216 Soho Hill<br>Handsworth<br>11 Terrace Road<br>Handsworth<br>Birmingham | P13/M/57-60<br>***#2499-2502***<br> | **Frederick MARSON**<br>**Harry JONES** trading as<br>**F MARSON & CO** *<br>90 Spencer Street<br>Birmingham | Manufacturing jewellers and silversmiths |
| Missing register<br>*c.*1892 | Presumably the *sunk* punch mentioned at #2498 | P5/M/419<br>***#2503***<br> | **F MORDAN & CO** * ? | Jewellers |
| M/23 not in R1 as expected | | P9/M/23<br>***#2504***<br> | | |
| R3/178<br>18 March 1961<br>Sent by F M Wallis<br>Two sizes | Lividons<br>343 Upton Lane<br>Widnes<br>Lancashire | P21/W/98,99<br>***#2505,6***<br> | **Frances Mary WALLIS**<br>No business address entered | Student |
| R3/174<br>13 October 1960<br>Sent by F Neville | 6 East Rise<br>Lichfield Park<br>Sutton Coldfield<br>Warwickshire | P21/N/12<br>***#2507***<br> | **Frank NEVILLE**<br>c/o **H SAMUEL LTD** *<br>Hunters Road Works<br>Hockley<br>Birmingham 19 | Silversmith and designer |
| Missing register<br>*c.*1886<br>Similar mark BAO<br>8 December 1898 and incuse mark 1881 | | P5/N/37<br>***#2508***<br> | **Frederick NARBOROUGH**<br>53 Green Street<br>Doriton<br>Birmingham | Whip mounter |
| R2/131<br>24 March 1911<br>Sent by Frank Ogden | Private address same as business | P13/O/11<br>***#2509***<br> | **Frank OGDEN**<br>155 Waterloo Street<br>Oldham | Working jeweller |
| R2/162<br>6 October 1912<br>Sent by Frank Ogden | | P13/O/16<br>***#2510***<br> | | Manufacturing jeweller |
| R2/67<br>23 October 1908<br>Sent by Banyard & Co | 11 Victoria Street<br>Urmston Lane | P13/B/40<br>***#2511***<br> | **F O BANYARD** trading as<br>**BANYARD & CO**<br>32 Back Turner Street<br>Manchester | Umbrella and walking stick mounters |

| REGISTRATION DETAILS | MAKER'S PRIVATE ADDRESS and DETAILS | PLATE and MARK DETAILS | MAKER/COMPANY and BUSINESS ADDRESS | MAKER'S TRADE |
|---|---|---|---|---|
| R2/141<br>10 August 1911<br>Sent by B Wade | Both – private address same as business | P13/O/13<br>***#2512***  | **F A OLD**<br>**T OLD** trading as<br>**F A OLD & SON**<br>19 Above Bar<br>Southampton | Wholesale tobacconists |
| Missing register<br>*c.*1886<br>Two sizes | | P5/P/24x2<br>***#2513,4***   | **Unidentified** | |
| R2/98<br>29 November 1909<br>Sent by T C Smith | 154 Gerrard Street<br>Aston<br>Birmingham<br>46 St Thomas Road<br>Gravelly Hill<br>Birmingham | P13/F/10<br>***#2515***   | **George FISHER**<br>**Alfred Walter POOLE** trading as<br>**FISHER & POOLE**<br>21/23 Spencer Street<br>Birmingham | Manufacturing jewellers |
| R2/197<br>11 June 1915<br>Sent by A W Poole | 84 Francis Road<br>Erdington<br>29 Leyton Road<br>Handsworth<br>Birmingham | P15/F/12,13<br>***#2516,7***   | **Alfred Walter POOLE**<br>**George F FISHER** trading as<br>**FISHER & POOLE**<br>56 Spencer Street<br>Birmingham | Manufacturing jewellers |
| LPB/7<br>18 June 1878 | Culme has Castelberg, Petitpierre Co at this address in 1876 | P3/P/x3<br>***#2518-20***   | **Fritz PETITPIERRE** *<br>58 Holborn Viaduct<br>London | Watchcase maker |
| LPB/30<br>28 October 1880<br>Sent by E Vaughton | | P3/F/x3<br>***#2521-3***   | **William FOLLIS and**<br>**Francis William PAYTON**<br>7 Hylton Street<br>Birmingham | Jewellers |
| R1/97<br>28 March 1899<br>Sent by W Walker | Beech Hirst [1]<br>South Croydon<br>Surrey<br>Mapleton [2]<br>Edenbridge, Kent<br>Balls Park [3]<br>Hertford | P9/P/26<br>***#2524***   | **Henry John DAVIS** [1]<br>**Samuel Henry Faudel PHILLIPS** [2]<br>**Sir George Faudel PHILLIPS** [3] Bart<br>**Benjamin Samuel PHILLIPS** [3]<br>trading as<br>**FAUDEL, PHILLIPS & SONS** *<br>40 Newgate Street<br>London<br><br>All three Phillips shown as JPs (Justice of Peace or Magistrate) | Warehousemen and manufacturers |
| R1/66<br>24 May 1898<br>Sent by Hollins & Jacques<br>T Breadsmore | | P5/Q*sic*/956<br>***#2525***  | | Warehousemen |
| Not in R1 as expected<br>Similar mark entered LAO 26 October 1886 | | P5/R/877<br>***#2526***   | **Frederick RYMELL** *<br>12 Jordan Well<br>Coventry | Watchcase maker |
| R3/128<br>11 March 1949<br>Previous entry R3/106 cancelled<br>Sent by F & R Beach | | P21/B/31<br>***#2527***   | **F & R BEACH LTD**<br>Sealed in the presence of:-<br>N M Beach (Director)<br>R W Beach (Secretary)<br>184 Warstone Lane<br>Birmingham | Manufacturing jewellers |
| R2/13<br>9 March 1906<br>Sent by C H Cheshire | 163 Bounkfield Place<br>Edinburgh | P9/R/74<br>***#2528***   | **FENTON RUSSELL & CO LTD**<br>J L Fenton (Director)<br>12, 16 George IV Bridge<br>Edinburgh | Wholesale jewellers |
| R2/14<br>30 March 1906<br>Two sizes Sent by Haseler Brothers | Birchlea<br>Liberton<br>Midlothian | P9/R/75,76<br>***#2529,30***   | | |

| REGISTRATION DETAILS | MAKER'S PRIVATE ADDRESS and DETAILS | PLATE and MARK DETAILS | MAKER/COMPANY and BUSINESS ADDRESS | MAKER'S TRADE |
|---|---|---|---|---|
| R2/13<br>9 March 1906<br>Sent by C H Cheshire | 163 Bounkfield Place<br>Edinburgh | P9/R/73<br>***#2531***  | **FENTON RUSSELL & CO LTD**<br>J L Fenton (Director)<br>12, 16 George IV Bridge<br>Edinburgh | Wholesale jewellers |
| LPB/4<br>31 October 1877<br>LPB mark shown<br>Sent by J Sharpe<br>J LeComber | | Not on P3<br>***#2532*** 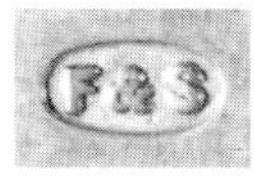 | **FATTORINI & SONS** *<br>Bradford | Watch manufacturers and importers |
| Not in R1 as expected<br>P5/F/777 suggests later than 1894 | | P5/F/777<br>***#2533***  | | |
| R3/4<br>9 April 1923<br>Sent by Clark & Sewill<br>Frank Fattorini | Rockwood<br>Skipton<br>2 Hugley Grove<br>Edgbaston | P15/F/23<br>***#2534*** 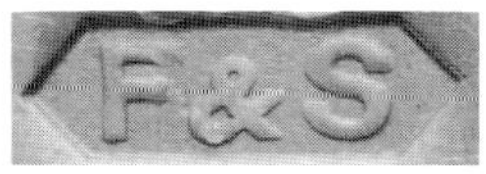 | **Thomas FATTORINI (BIRMINGHAM) LTD** *<br>Thomas Fattorini (Partner)<br>Frank Fattorini (Partner)<br>5 Hockley Street<br>Birmingham | Medal and badge makers |
| LPB/32 SP26/3<br>24 October 1883<br>Sent by Richard Nevill<br>Vyse Street<br>Birmingham | No mark in LPB only F&S penned | P5/F/x1<br>***#2535***  | No name or address entered<br>**FATTORINI & SONS** *<br>21 Kirkgate and 27 Westgate<br>Bradford | Silversmiths, watch importers and medallists |
| Missing register<br>*c.*1886 | | P5/F/1<br>***#2536***  | | |
| Missing register<br>*c.*1886<br>Similar mark entered BAO 14 June 1888 | | P5/F/46<br>***#2537***  | | |
| R1/101<br>17 May 1899<br>Sent by Stephen Farren | 5 Blenheim Mount [1]<br>Bradford<br>2 St Paul's Road [2]<br>Bradford | P9/F/2<br>***#2538***  | **John FATTORINI** [1] *<br>**Edward FATTORINI** [2] *<br>Kirkgate and Westgate<br>Bradford | Watch makers and jewellers |
| R1/131<br>19 September 1900<br>Sent by C H Cheshire | | P9/F/6<br>***#2539***  | **John FATTORINI** [1]<br>**Edward FATTORINI** [2] trading as<br>**John FATTORINI & SONS** *<br>Kirkgate and Westgate<br>Bradford | Silversmiths |
| R1/208<br>25 February 1904<br>Sent by R Nevill | | P9/F/20,21<br>***#2540,1***  | **John FATTORINI**<br>**Edward FATTORINI** trading as<br>**FATTORINI & SONS** *<br>21 Kirkgate and 27 Westgate<br>Bradford | Jewellers |
| R1/168<br>29 May 1902 | | P9/F/16<br>***#2542***  | **John FATTORINI**<br>**Edwin** (*sic*) **FATTORINI** trading as<br>**FATTORINI & SONS** *<br>21 Kirkgate and 27 Westgate<br>Bradford | |
| R2/60<br>20 May 1908<br>Sent by H Moreton | | P13/F/I<br>***#2543***  | **Edward FATTORINI** trading as<br>**FATTORINI & SON** *<br>21 Kirkgate and 27 Westgate<br>Bradford | Jewellers and silversmiths |

| REGISTRATION DETAILS | MAKER'S PRIVATE ADDRESS and DETAILS | PLATE and MARK DETAILS | MAKER/COMPANY and BUSINESS ADDRESS | MAKER'S TRADE |
|---|---|---|---|---|
| R2/87<br>10 July 1909<br>Sent by Joseph Moore | 2 St Paul's Road<br>Bradford | P13/F/8<br>***#2544***<br> | **Edward FATTORINI**<br>**John FATTORINI** trading as<br>**FATTORINI & SON** *<br>21 Kirkgate and 27 Westgate<br>Bradford | Jewellers |
| On wrong plate if Fattorini<br>Similar mark BAO<br>10 December 1885 | May also be Frisch & Schierwater – see below | P1/32/x1<br>***#2545***<br> | | |
| R1/203<br>11 November 1903<br>Sent by J G Newbold | 1 Rockfield Terrace<br>Dundee | P9/F/17<br>***#2546***<br> | **William Wilson FAIRWEATHER**<br>trading as **FAIRWEATHER & SON**<br>sole partner of the firm<br>108 Seagate<br>Dundee | Tobacco manufacturer |
| R1/141<br>7 February 1901<br>Sent by F Simpson | Private address same as business | P9/S/38<br>***#2547***<br> | **Frederick SIMPSON** *<br>10 Royston Crescent<br>Roseberry Avenue<br>London EC | Manufacturing jeweller |
| R1/141<br>6 February 1901<br>Sent by F S Banks | Barnt Green<br>Worcestershire | P9/B/33<br>***#2548***<br> | **Frederick Sidney BANKS**<br>41 Northampton Street<br>Birmingham | Jeweller |
| Missing register<br>*c.*1890<br>Adjacent P5/B/327 | | P5/B/x1<br>***#2549***<br> | | |
| Missing register<br>*c.*1887 | | P5/B/97<br>***#2550***<br> | | |
| Missing register<br>*c.*1886 | | P5/B/0*sic*<br>***#2551***<br> | | |
| R1/86<br>24 November 1898<br>Sent by Fred S Banks<br>Two sizes | 141 Heathfield Road<br>Handsworth<br>Birmingham | P9/B/9,10<br>***#2552,3***<br> | | Silver and gold brooch maker |
| R1/115<br>26 October 1899 | | P9/B/24<br>***#2554***<br> | | |
| R1/220<br>23 September 1904<br>Sent by F S Banks | Rose Lea<br>Barnt Green<br>Birmingham | P9/XYZ*sic*/125,126<br>***#2555,6***<br> | | Manufacturer of brooches and pins |
| GSWJ/184 | | P1/20/x14<br>***#2557-70***<br> | **FRISCH & SCHIERWATER** ?<br>97 Hanover Street<br>Liverpool | Wholesale watch manufacturers and importers |
| | | P1/10/x3<br>***#2571-3***<br>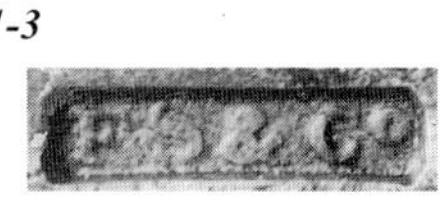 | | |
| | | P1/15/x3<br>***#2574-6***<br>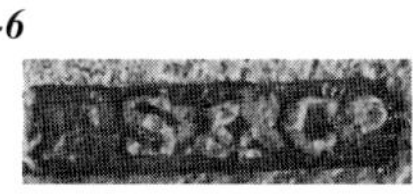 | | |
| Missing register<br>*c.*1890<br>Incuse FSR mark entered BAO<br>25 November 1889 | | P5/R/324<br>***#2577***<br> | **Frank Saul ROTHSCHILD** *<br>17 Little Britain<br>London | Pipe mounter |

| REGISTRATION DETAILS | MAKER'S PRIVATE ADDRESS and DETAILS | PLATE and MARK DETAILS | MAKER/COMPANY and BUSINESS ADDRESS | MAKER'S TRADE |
|---|---|---|---|---|
| R1/221<br>4 October 1904<br>Sent by Bacon & Bill and Hemming & Hazlewood<br>4 February 1909 | Ashleigh<br>Mayfield Road<br>Moseley | P9/S/79<br>***#2578***<br><br>P13/T*sic*/7<br>***#2579***<br> | **Frederick STONE**<br>65 Northampton Street<br>Birmingham | Wholesale jeweller |
| Missing register<br>*c.*1887<br>Similar mark entered LAO 28 January 1889 | See also AWFT | P5/T/116a<br>***#2580***<br><br>P5/T/116b<br>***#2581***<br> | **Frederick TRAHERN** *<br>Clifton Villas<br>Allesley Old Road<br>Chapel Fields<br>Coventry | Gold watchcase maker |
| R3/90<br>10 May 1938<br>Sent by F W Trahern | Private address same as business | P21/T/1<br>***#2582***<br> | **Frederick William TRAHERN**<br>**Alfred Wickes TRAHERN** trading as<br>**F T TRAHERN & SONS** *<br>51 Allesley Old Road<br>28 Baginton Road (from16January1939)<br>Coventry | Watchcase manufacturers |
| R3/166<br>13 March 1959<br>Sent by F Tyldesley<br>Two sizes | 33 Peelwood Avenue<br>Little Hulton<br>Walkden | P21/T/36,37<br>***#2583,4***<br> | **Frank TYLDESLEY**<br>No business address entered | Student silversmith |
| R2/116<br>26 July 1910<br>Sent by Frank Turner | Private address same as business | P13/T/22<br>***#2585***<br> | **Frank TURNER** *<br>51 Stanley Road<br>Earlsdon<br>Coventry | Gold watchcase manufacturer |
| R1/31<br>1 July 1896<br>Sent by F R Tyrer | 13 St John's Square<br>London EC | P5/T/781<br>***#2586***<br> | **Francis Robert TYRER** *<br>30 Linton Street<br>New North Road<br>London | Register and purse mounter |
| R1/62<br>8 March 1898<br>P5/T/940 in R1 but 904 on P5<br>Sent by Fred Taylor | Private address same as business | P5/T/904<br>***#2587***<br> | **Fred TAYLOR** *<br>7 Roberts Place<br>Bowling Green Lane<br>Clerkenwell<br>London | Gold and silver mounter |
| R2/133<br>25 April 1911<br>Sent by Frank Templeton | Private address same as business | P13/T/32<br>***#2588***<br> | **Frank TEMPLETON**<br>14 Kent Street<br>Rochdale | Silver mounter |
| R2/19<br>29 May 1906<br>Sent by F T Krauth | Hazeldene<br>Vicarage Road<br>Olton<br>Birmingham | P9/K/41<br>***#2589***<br> | **F T KRAUTH**<br>124 Great Hampton Street<br>Birmingham | Watchmaker |
| R3/18<br>25 August 1923<br>Sent by F Tennant | 25 Alexander Road<br>Acocks Green<br>Birmingham | P15/T/46<br>***#2590***<br> | **F TENNANT LTD**<br>F Tennant (Manager)<br>46 Hylton Street<br>Birmingham | Jewellers |
| R3153<br>7 December 1954<br>Sent by F T Perkins | 16 Broughville Drive<br>Manchester | P21/P/60<br>***#2591***<br> | **Frank Trevor PERKINS**<br>No business address entered | Student of silversmithing |

| REGISTRATION DETAILS | MAKER'S PRIVATE ADDRESS and DETAILS | PLATE and MARK DETAILS | MAKER/COMPANY and BUSINESS ADDRESS | MAKER'S TRADE |
|---|---|---|---|---|
| LPB/86<br>12 June 1882<br>Sent by J Hallet | | P3/V/x3<br>***#2592-4***<br> | **Frederick VENOUR** junior<br>3 Richard Street<br>Birmingham | Silversmith |
| Missing register<br>*c.*1886 | | P5/V/13<br>***#2595***<br> | | |
| Missing register<br>*c.*1888<br>Similar mark entered<br>BAO April 1890 | | P5/V/195<br>***#2596***<br> | **Frederick VENOUR & SON** ?<br>3 Richard Street<br>Birmingham | |
| J1 1851 | | Not on P1<br>***#2597*** **F W?** | **Frederick Walter WARD**<br>Address unknown | Silversmith |
| LPB/90<br>12 January 1884<br>No mark in LPB only<br>FW | | P5/W/x1<br>***#2598***<br> | **Frank WILDAY**<br>90 The Butts<br>Coventry | Watchcase maker |
| R1/73<br>31 August 1898<br>Sent by F Weiner | Private address same as business | P9/W/1<br>***#2599***<br> | **Ferdinand WEINER**<br>10 Brow Side<br>Everton<br>Liverpool | Silver mounter and pipe maker |
| R1/128<br>7 June 1900<br>Sent by F Weiner | | P9/W/37<br>***#2600***<br> | 26 Pembroke Place<br>Liverpool | Pipe maker and mounter in gold and silver |
| LPB/90<br>15 August 1882<br>No mark in LPB only<br>FW | | P5/W/x1<br>***#2601***<br> | **Frank WILDAY**<br>90 The Butts<br>Coventry | Watchcase maker |
| LPB/86<br>27 May 1880 | | P3/W/x3<br>***#2602-4***<br> | **Frederick WAGSTAFF**<br>36 Horse Fair<br>Birmingham | Jeweller |
| SPB/5<br>8 December 1864 | | P3/W/x5<br>***#2605-9***<br> | **Frederick WILKINS** *<br>42 Spon Street<br>Coventry | Watchcase maker |
| Missing register<br>*c.*1886 | | P5/W/12<br>***#2610***<br> | **Unidentified** | |
| SPB/8<br>1 November 1872 | | P3/W/x3<br>***#2611-3***<br> | **F WRIGHT**<br>46 Cochrane Street<br>Liverpool | Trade not identified |
| R1/161<br>7 February 1902<br>Sent by Frederick Wright | Private address same as business | P9/W/64<br>***#2614***<br> | **Frederick WRIGHT** *<br>127 Spon Street<br>Coventry | Watchcase manufacturer |
| LPB/30<br>29 July 1879 | | P3/F/x2<br>***#2615,6***<br> | **John Joseph FULFORD and William WYNN**<br>40 Northampton Street<br>Birmingham | Jewellers |

| REGISTRATION DETAILS | MAKER'S PRIVATE ADDRESS and DETAILS | PLATE and MARK DETAILS | MAKER/COMPANY and BUSINESS ADDRESS | MAKER'S TRADE |
|---|---|---|---|---|
| SPB/11<br>8 February 1866 | | P3/W/x3<br>***#2617-9***<br> | **Frederick WILKINS** *<br>42 Spon Street<br>Coventry | Watchcase maker |
| Missing register<br>*c.*1886 | See other FW marks | P5/W/x1<br>***#2620***<br> | **Unidentified** | |
| R1/9<br>28 March 1895<br>Sent by W Aitken<br>Four sizes | 2 Turville Road<br>Handsworth<br>Birmingham | P5/X*sic*/648x4<br>***#2621-4***<br> | **Florence WARDEN**<br>2 Turville Road<br>Handsworth<br>Birmingham | Silversmith |
| Not in R1 as expected but post-1898 as on P9 | Possibly Florence Warden see above | P9/W/9<br>***#2625***<br> | **Unidentified** | |
| R1/34<br>19 October 1896<br>Sent by E Langridge & Co | 26 Chester Terrace<br>Regent Road<br>London | P5/X*sic*/797<br>***#2626***<br> | **Frederick WICK**<br>8 and 10 Great Titchfield Street<br>London | Leather goods manufacturer |
| R1/67<br>21 June 1898<br>Sent by Charles John | Private address same as business | P5/aboveA/961<br>***#2627***<br> | **Charles JOHN** trading as<br>**Frederick W ARLEY**<br>253 Burbury Street<br>Birmingham | Silver chain maker |
| LPB/92<br>20 July 1882 | | P3/B/x1<br>***#2628***<br> | **Frederick William BAUER**<br>52 Albion Street<br>Birmingham | Wholesale jeweller |
| LPB/62<br>21 February 1883<br>No name or address listed | | P3/B/x1<br>***#2629***<br> | | |
| LPB/18 undated but next to one for<br>23 September 1884<br>No mark in LPB<br>Sent by J Postons | | P5/B/x1<br>***#2630***<br> | | |
| R2/236<br>18 January 1921<br>Sent by<br>F W Bennett | Private address same as business | P15/B/150<br>***#2631***<br> | **Frederick William BENNETT**<br>85 Gerrard Street<br>Aston<br>Birmingham | Gold ring maker |
| R2/158<br>25 June 1912<br>Sent by E L Merle<br>Two sizes | 120 Iverson Road<br>London NW | P13/D*sic*/150,151<br>***#2632,3***<br> | **Francis Wride COLE** *<br>7 Midland Parade<br>West End Lane<br>London NW | Tobacconist |
| R2/120<br>18 October 1910<br>Sent by R E Cole | 113 Vyse Street<br>Birmingham | P13/C/84,85<br>***#2634,5***<br> | **Ralph Edgar COLE** trading as<br>**F W COLE**<br>113 Vyse Street<br>Birmingham | Gold and silver chain maker |
| R1/64<br>2 April 1898<br>Sent by W Mills<br>Cancelled<br>18 October 1910<br>deceased | | P5/aboveC/948<br>***#2636***<br> | **Frank William COLE**<br>113 Vyse Street<br>Birmingham | Gold and silver watch chain maker |

| REGISTRATION DETAILS | MAKER'S PRIVATE ADDRESS and DETAILS | PLATE and MARK DETAILS | MAKER/COMPANY and BUSINESS ADDRESS | MAKER'S TRADE |
|---|---|---|---|---|
| Missing register<br>*c.*1888 | | P5/W/172<br>***#2637***<br> | **Unidentified** | |
| R1/91<br>15 February 1899<br>Sent by W Aitken<br>Three sizes | 2 Turnville Road<br>Handsworth<br>Birmingham<br><br>See also WA | P9/W/11-13<br>***#2638-40***<br> | **William AITKEN** * trading as<br>**F WALTERS & CO**<br>37 and 38 Vyse Street<br>Birmingham | Silversmiths |
| R2/146<br>28 October 1911<br>BAO 14.339<br>Sent by<br>F W Devereux | 33 Mostyn Road<br>Handsworth<br>Birmingham | P13/D/38<br>***#2641***<br> | **Frederick William DEVEREUX**<br>70 Vyse Street<br>Birmingham and<br>44 Hockley Hill (1939)<br>Birmingham | Manufacturing jeweller |
| R3/4<br>27 July 1921<br>Sent by F W Hoyle | 2 Harold Street<br>Egremont<br>Wallasey | P15/H/67<br>***#2642***<br> | **Frederick William HOYLE**<br>City School of Art<br>Liverpool | Silversmith student |
| SPB/7<br>15 June 1865<br>GSJW/134 1861 | | P3/L*sic*/x1<br>***#2643***<br> | **Frederick William PROMOLI**<br>30 Church Street<br>Liverpool | Silversmith and jeweller |
| LPB/64<br>5 November 1881 | | P3/P/x1<br>***#2644***<br> | **Francis William PAYTON**<br>7 Hylton Street<br>Birmingham | Jeweller |
| R2/187<br>16 May 1914<br>Sent by A E Pearson | 70 Grosvenor Road<br>Harborne | P15/P/61<br>***#2645***<br> | **Albert Edward PEARSON** trading as<br>**F W PEARSON & CO**<br>72 Vyse Street<br>Birmingham | Manufacturing jewellers, sleeve links, etc |
| Missing register<br>*c.*1892<br>Cameo mark entered<br>BAO 23 April 1896 | | P5/S/433<br>***#2646***<br> | **F W SHIPTON**<br>25, 27 Corn Exchange Chambers<br>Hanging Ditch<br>Manchester | Pipe and stick mounter |
| R1/64<br>29 March 1898<br>Sent by James Ossian Lloyd<br>Two sizes | 185 Coventry Road<br>Birmingham | P5/T/947a,b<br>***#2647,8***<br><br>P5/T/947c,d<br>***#2649,50***<br> | **James Ossian LLOYD** (Secretary)<br>**Frederick W TURTON LTD** *<br>Frederick Street Works<br>Birmingham | Manufacturing jewellers and silversmiths |
| Missing register<br>*c.*1888<br>Similar mark entered<br>LAO 4 January 1887 | | P5/W/156<br>***#2651***<br> | **Frederick and Walter WEBB** *<br>33 St John Street Road<br>Clerkenwell<br>London | Gold watchcase makers |
| R1/169<br>2 June 1902<br>Sent by self and<br>H Griffith & Sons | Private address same as business | P9/XYZ/4<br>***#2652***<br>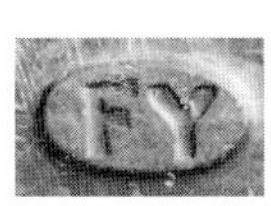 | **Frederick YOUNG**<br>12 Junction Street<br>Coventry | Watchcase maker |

| REGISTRATION DETAILS | MAKER'S PRIVATE ADDRESS and DETAILS | PLATE and MARK DETAILS | MAKER/COMPANY and BUSINESS ADDRESS | MAKER'S TRADE |
|---|---|---|---|---|
| Missing register<br>*c.*1887<br>Similar mark entered LAO 20 March 1902 | | P5/A/83<br>***#2653***<br> | **George Smith ABBOTT** *<br>63 Aldermanbury<br>London EC | Manufacturers agent |
| Not in R1 as expected - possibly in missing register | Mark may be same date as previous one as they are struck together on P5 but could be post 1898 | P5/B/783<br>***#2654***<br>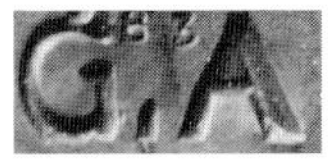 | | |
| R1/223<br>5 December 1904<br>Sent by E J Rudge | 9 Carlton Vale<br>Maida Vale<br>London | P9/A/58<br>***#2655***<br> | **George ARONSON**<br>16 Hatton Garden<br>London EC | Wholesale jeweller |
| R2/116<br>22 July 1910<br>Sent by<br>G H Johnston & Co | Farnborough<br>Kent | P13/F/22<br>***#2656***<br>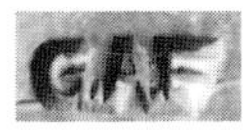 | **G Allen FROST** trading as<br>**G A FROST**<br>95 Hatton Garden<br>London | Wholesale jewellers |
| R2/123<br>10 November 1910<br>Sent by A Wilcox | | P13/F/23<br>***#2657***<br>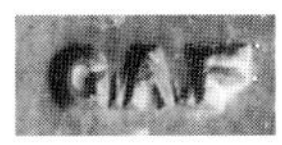 | | |
| R2/150<br>26 January 1912<br>Sent by George Alfred Retchford | Private address same as business | P13/R/45<br>***#2658***<br> | **George Alfred RETCHFORD**<br>77 St Ancocks Street<br>Birmingham | Jeweller |
| R3/40<br>23 April 1928<br>Sent by selves | 37 Portland Road [1]<br>Edgbaston<br>Birmingham | P15/S/81<br>***#2659***<br> | **ELITE BRACELET MANUFACTURING CO LTD**<br>George Arnold Stoll[1] (Managing Director)<br>37 Portland Road<br>Edgbaston (undated, moved to)<br>Regent Street<br>Birmingham | Jewellers |
| 21 November 1930 | | P15/S/94,95<br>***#2660,1***<br> | | |
| 6 May 1934 | | P15/S/102<br>***#2662***<br>§<br> | | |
| 6 May 1934 | | P15/S/103<br>***#2663***<br>§<br> | | |
| 6 December 1947<br>Three sizes | | P21/S/29-31<br>***#2664-6***<br>§<br> | | |
| R3/123<br>22 April 1948<br>Sent by Elite Bracelet Manufacturing Co Ltd | Sealed in the presence of Ryf and Gosling | No new mark<br>***#2667*** | **ELITE BRACELET MANUFACTURING CO LTD**<br>M Ryf (Director)<br>J N Gosling (Secretary)<br>Regent Works<br>Regent Street<br>Birmingham 1 | Manufacturing jewellers |
| R3/171<br>12 February 1960<br>Sent by G A Tate<br>Two sizes | | P21/T/40,41<br>***#2668,9***<br> | **George Arthur TATE**<br>12 Collingwood Road<br>Manchester 19 | Silversmith and goldsmith |
| PP1/187<br>GTD1805-20<br>PMR 1816-41 | | P1/19/x1<br>***#2670***<br>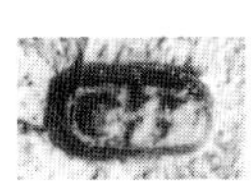 | **George BROWN**<br>48 Sawney Pope Street (1816)<br>Liverpool | Goldsmith and watchcase maker |

| REGISTRATION DETAILS | MAKER'SPRIVATE ADDRESS and DETAILS | PLATE and MARK DETAILS | MAKER/COMPANY and BUSINESS ADDRESS | MAKER'S TRADE |
|---|---|---|---|---|
| R3/85<br>9 December 1936<br>Sent by Ernest Guy Booker | 6 Newland Gardens<br>Chesterfield | P21/B/1<br>***#2671***  | **Ernest Guy BOOKER**<br>St Mary's Modern School<br>Cross Street<br>Chesterfield | Ecclesiastical metal worker and enameller |
| R1/176<br>7 October 1902<br>Sent by self<br>Two sizes | 5 Ash Grove [1]<br>Chester<br>9 Cambriam View [2]<br>Chester | P9/B/94,95<br>***#2672,3***  | **George John Hemsley BROWN** [1]<br>**Frederick George BROWN** [2]<br>2 Eastgate Row<br>Chester | Jewellers and silversmiths |
| R3/76<br>22 June 1935<br>Sent by M P Smith | Carrick House<br>Curzon Park<br>Chester | P15/G*sic*/217<br>***#2674***  | | Jewellers and silversmiths |
| 20 March 1941 | | P21/G*sic*/12<br>***#2675***  | | |
| Missing register<br>*c*.1893 | See G Buckner | P5/B/523<br>***#2676***  | **Unidentified** | |
| R1/41<br>25 March 1897<br>Sent by E Langridge & Co | 19 Leinster Square<br>Bayswater<br>London W | P5/aboveB/826<br>***#2677***  | **Gustav BUCKNER**<br>13 Carter Lane, St Paul's<br>London EC | Fancy goods dealer and silversmith |
| R2/33<br>8 February 1907<br>Sent by E J Rudge | Trentham<br>Howard Road<br>New Malden<br>Surrey | P9/XYZ*sic*/185<br>***#2678***  | **George BAYLIE**<br>21 Key Hill<br>Birmingham | Jeweller |
| R1/232<br>1 May 1905<br>Sent by G Bedingham | 79 St Asaph Road<br>Brockley<br>London SE | P9/XYZ*sic*/132<br>***#2679***  | **George BEDINGHAM** *<br>34 Paternoster Row<br>London EC | Silversmith |
| R1/234<br>19 May 1905 | | P9/XYZ*sic*/133<br>***#2680***  | | |
| Missing register<br>*c*.1892 | | P5/B/429<br>***#2681*** 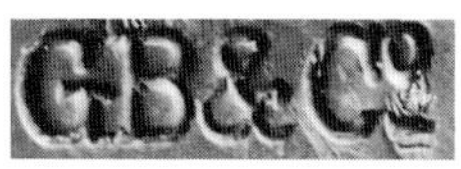 | **Unidentified** | |
| Missing register<br>*c*.1892 | | P5/B/428<br>***#2682***  | **Unidentified** | |
| R2/222<br>29 July 1919<br>Sent by Bacon & Bill | Roselea<br>Queens Drive<br>8 Balmoral Crescent<br>74 Albert Road<br>Glasgow<br>18 Grosvenor Road<br>Newcastle upon Tyne | P15/B*sic*/103<br>***#2683***  | **Barnett GERBER**<br>**Matthew L GERBER**<br>**Hyman GERBER**<br>**J LAZARUS** trading as<br>**GERBER BROTHERS & CO**<br>127 Argyle Street<br>Glasgow and<br>14 Cloth Market<br>Newcastle upon Tyne | Wholesale jewellers |
| R3/12<br>7 September 1922<br>Two sizes Sent by George Bouverat | 39 Brighton Road<br>Moseley, Birmingham<br>17 Yew Tree Road<br>Edgbaston, Birmingham | P15/B/162,163<br>***#2684,5*** 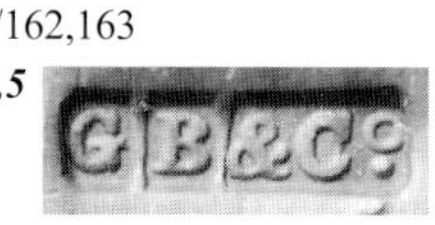 | **George BOUVERAT**<br>**Jean BOUVERAT**<br>30 Frederick Street<br>Birmingham | Watch manufacturers and importers |
| R3/47<br>9 July 1929<br>Sent by self | 423 City Road [1]<br>Edgbaston<br>Birmingham<br>17 Yew Tree Road [2]<br>Edgbaston<br>Birmingham | P15/B/197<br>***#2686***  | **George BOUVERAT & CO** trading as<br>**SWISS AGENCY**<br>George Bouverat[1] (Partner)<br>Jean Bouverat[2] (Partner)<br>30 Frederick Street<br>Birmingham | |

| REGISTRATION DETAILS | MAKER'S PRIVATE ADDRESS and DETAILS | PLATE and MARK DETAILS | MAKER/COMPANY and BUSINESS ADDRESS | MAKER'S TRADE |
|---|---|---|---|---|
| R3/62<br>5 April 1932<br>Sent by G Bryan & Co | 13 Lozells Street<br>Lozells<br>Birmingham | P15/B/207<br>***#2687***  | **G BRYAN & CO**<br>George Thomas Bryan (Proprietor)<br>Standard Works<br>52 Great Hampton Street<br>Birmingham | Silversmiths |
| R3/45<br>12 February 1929<br>Sent by George Birkett Fisher<br>Two sizes<br><br>Punches cancelled 31 October 1930 and P15/F/38 style substituted | Private address same as business | P15/F/35<br>***#2688*** <br>P15/F/36<br>***#2689***  | **George Birkett FISHER**<br>419 Poulton Road<br>Wallasey<br>Cheshire | Silversmith |
| R3/55<br>28 October 1930<br>Sent by G B Fisher | | P15/F/38<br>***#2690***  | **George Birkett FISHER**<br>109 Seaview Road<br>Wallasey | |
| R3/126<br>18 September 1948<br>Sent by The Gem Box Ltd | Sealed in the presence of both | P21/G/18<br>***#2691***  | **THE GEM BOX LTD**<br>R H Watkins (Director)<br>D T Watkins (Secretary)<br>60 Caroline Street<br>Birmingham 3 | Manufacturing jewellers |
| R1/174<br>25 August 1902<br>Sent by T Nightingale | 125 City Road<br>Birmingham | P9/G/37<br>***#2692***  | **Walter J GINDER** trading as<br>**GINDER BROTHERS**<br>47 Frederick Street<br>Birmingham | Jewellers |
| R1/222<br>18 November 1904<br>Sent by J Hayward | | P9/G/56<br>***#2693***  | | Speciality gem rings |
| Missing register<br>*c.*1886 | | P5/G/28<br>***#2694***  | **Unidentified** | |
| LPB/34<br>30 September 1881<br>LPB mark shown | | Not on P3<br>***#2695***  | **GINDER BROTHERS**<br>8 Augusta Street<br>Birmingham | Jewellers |
| R1/66<br>11 June 1898<br>Sent by George Carol | 9 Stafford Road<br>Handsworth<br>Birmingham | P5/aboveC/958<br>***#2696***  | **George CAROL**<br>54 St Paul's Square<br>Birmingham | Manufacturer of studs and links |
| R3/149<br>30 December 1953<br>Sent by G Craven | 5 Greave Road<br>Offerton<br>Southport<br>Cheshire | P21/C/65<br>***#2697***  | **Geoffrey CRAVEN**<br>No business address entered | Student |
| R3/154<br>15 December 1954<br>Sent by G Collis<br>Two sizes | The Cottage<br>Oaklands<br>Horton<br>Cheshire | P21/C/71,72<br>***#2698,9***  | **Geoffrey COLLIS**<br>No business address entered | General silversmithing and jewellery |
| R1/27<br>16 April 1896<br>Sent by Roek & Dreyfus | George Chandler<br>12 Newman Street<br>Oxford Street<br>London | P5/aboveC/755<br>***#2700***  | **George CHANDLER** trading as<br>**George CHANDLER & SON** *<br>12 Newman Street, Oxford Street<br>London | Goldsmiths |
| R1/225<br>5 January 1905<br>Sent by F O Banyard | New House<br>Mill Mellon<br>Derbyshire | P9/D*sic*/216<br>***#2701***  | **George CHELL**<br>Soap Street<br>Thomas Street<br>Manchester | Manufacturing agent |

| REGISTRATION DETAILS | MAKER'S PRIVATE ADDRESS and DETAILS | PLATE and MARK DETAILS | MAKER/COMPANY and BUSINESS ADDRESS | MAKER'S TRADE |
|---|---|---|---|---|
| Missing register<br>*c.*1886 | | P5/C/15<br>***#2702***  | **Unidentified** | |
| Missing register<br>*c.*1889 | | P5/C/219<br>***#2703***  | **Unidentified** | |
| LPB/20<br>28 July 1880<br>No address entered<br>Similar mark entered<br>BAO 16 January 1882 | CWMP 1874-96 | P3/C/x2<br>***#2704,5***  | **George COATES**<br>Manor House (BAO 1882)<br>Holyhead Road<br>Coventry | Watchcase maker |
| R2/53<br>9 January 1908<br>Sent by J Hayward<br>Cancelled<br>7 March 1911<br>Three sizes | YMCA<br>Dale End<br>Birmingham | P9/G/0, 93-95<br>***#2706-9***  | **Joseph Curmin GINDER**<br>**Walter Conroy COUCH** trading as<br>**GINDER & COUCH**<br>11 Hockley Street<br>Birmingham | Wholesale jewellers |
| R2/130<br>7 March 1911<br>Sent by J Ginder | 116 Thornhill Road<br>Handsworth<br>116 Thornhill Road<br>Handsworth | P13/G/34,35<br>***#2710,1***  | **Joseph Curmin GINDER**<br>**Walter Conroy COUCH**<br>Gem Buildings<br>Frederick Street<br>Birmingham | Ring manufacturers |
| R2/181<br>6 December 1913<br>Sent by Ginder & Couch | Ashlow Croft<br>Heath, Warwickshire<br>Fredalma<br>Solihull<br>33 Alcester Road<br>Moseley<br>96 William Road, Common Hill | P15/G/10,11<br>***#2712,3***  | **Joseph Curmin GINDER**<br>**Walter Conroy COUCH**<br>**Walter Joseph GINDER**<br>**William Henry GINDER** trading as<br>**GINDER & COUCH**<br>21 and 44 Frederick Street<br>Birmingham | Ring makers |
| R2/195<br>29 April 1915<br>Sent by William Albert Smith | 33 Alcester Road<br>Moseley<br>Birmingham | P15/G/25–27<br>***#2714-6***  | **Joseph Curmin GINDER**<br>**Walter Conroy COUCH**<br>**Walter Joseph GINDER**<br>**William Henry GINDER**<br>Gem Buildings<br>Hockley Hill<br>Birmingham | Manufacturing jewellers |
| R2/101<br>15 January 1910<br>Sent by Edward Arthur Carpenter | The Gables<br>Northwood<br>6 Hyde Park Mansions<br>London | P13/G/15<br>***#2717*** 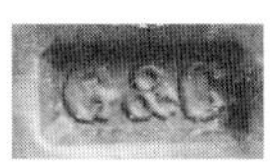 | **George GREEN** *<br>**Edward Arthur CARPENTER** *<br>61, 63 Beak Street<br>London | Goldworkers |
| Not in R2 as expected<br>Between 21 March 1917 and 12 October 1920 | | P15/G/34<br>***#2718***  | **GINDER & COUCH** (see above) | Manufacturing jewellers |
| R1/88<br>11 January 1899<br>Sent by T R Arnott<br>E Wilday<br>E W Linnett | CWMP 1874-96 | P9/C/6<br>***#2719***  | **Samuel George WOOTTON** trading as<br>**G CROFT & CO**<br>7 St Michael's Churchyard<br>Coventry | Watch manufacturers |
| Missing register<br>*c.*1886 | | P5/C/45<br>***#2720***  | | |
| R1/168<br>14 May 1902<br>Cancelled<br>25 January 1904<br>Sent by Green & Cadbury | Sutton Coldfield<br>Birmingham | P9/G/33<br>***#2721***  | **GREEN & CADBURY LTD**<br>Ivel Cadbury (Director)<br>96 Great Hampton Street Works<br>Birmingham | Manufacturing silversmiths |

| REGISTRATION DETAILS | MAKER'S PRIVATE ADDRESS and DETAILS | PLATE and MARK DETAILS | MAKER/COMPANY and BUSINESS ADDRESS | MAKER'S TRADE |
|---|---|---|---|---|
| R1/88<br>24 December 1898<br>Sent by G & C Hodgetts | Waverhill Road<br>Handsworth<br>111 Lewood Road<br>Handsworth | P9/H/5<br>*#2722*  | **Charles Victor HODGETTS**<br>**George Henry HODGETTS** trading as<br>**G & C HODGETTS**<br>28 Spencer Street<br>Birmingham | Manufacturing jewellers |
| R1/100<br>8 May 1899<br>Sent by John Haseler | 5 Radnor Road [1]<br>Handsworth<br>243 Mary Street [2]<br>Birmingham<br>(Ed: G=George, C=Carter) | P9/H/13<br>*#2723*  | **John HASELER** [1]<br>**William Frederick HOLMES** [2] trading as<br>**G C HASELER & CO**<br>59 Vittoria Street<br>Birmingham | Manufacturing jewellers |
| R2/40<br>18 May 1907<br>Sent by John Haseler | Westover<br>Beaconfield Road<br>Birmingham | P9/H/95<br>*#2724*  | **John HASELER** trading as<br>**G C HASELER & CO**<br>59 Vittoria Street<br>Birmingham | |
| R2/28<br>27 October 1906<br>Sent by John Haseler | Westover<br>Four Oaks<br>Sutton Coldfield | P9/H/86<br>*#2725*  | | |
| CWMP 1850, PP1/187<br>Identical mark LAO 30 May 1862 and BAO 6 September 1860 | Not in SPB or LPB so struck 1860-3 | P3/I/x3<br>***#2726-8***  | **George & Christopher JONES** *<br>22 West Orchard (Fleet Street 1850)<br>Coventry | Watchcase makers |
| GSJW/139,140<br>J1 1853<br>PP3/83 | | P2/L/x3<br>***#2729-31***  | **George Cliff LOWE**<br>26 St Anne's Street<br>Manchester | Watchmaker, clockmaker, jeweller and silversmith |
| R2/6<br>11 November 1905<br>Sent by G Culver Ltd | 77 Lordship Park<br>Stoke Newington<br>London N | P9/D*sic*/222<br>*#2732*  | **George CULVER LTD** *<br>Optical Works<br>White Lion Street, Pentonville<br>London N | Manufacturing opticians |
| R1/159<br>13 January 1902<br>Sent by George William Bayliss | 21 Gloucester Road [1]<br>Finsbury Park<br>London | P9/C/74<br>*#2733*  | as above with<br>George William Bayliss [1] (Secretary) | Jewellers |
| R1/206<br>25 January 1904<br>Sent by Green & Cadbury | Tudor Hill<br>Sutton Coldfield | P9/G/54<br>*#2734*  | **GREEN & CADBURY LTD**<br>Joel Cadbury (Director)<br>Great Hampton Street<br>Birmingham | Manufacturers of silver fancy goods |
| Missing register<br>*c.* 1892 | See other G & Co marks | P5/G/443<br>*#2735* 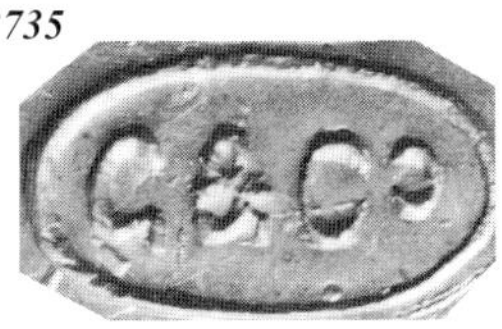 | **Unidentified** | |
| R1/46<br>15 June 1897<br>Sent by S C Grove | 112 Carpenters Road<br>Lozells<br>Birmingham | P5/G/848<br>*#2736*  | **Silas Cornelius GROVE** trading as<br>**GROVE & CO**<br>169 Hockley Hill<br>Birmingham | Jewellers |
| R1/128<br>31 May 1900<br>Sent by Grove & Co | | P9/G/16<br>*#2737*  | as above but at<br>167 Hockley Hill<br>Birmingham | Manufacturing jewellers |
| R2/40<br>29 May 1907<br>Sent by Kiva Goldberg<br>Punches 86 and 87 returned to be altered to 88 and 89 | 20 Elizabeth Street<br>Cheetham<br>Manchester | P9/G/86,87<br>***#2738,9***  | **Kiva GOLDBERG** trading as<br>**GOLDBERG & CO** *<br>38a and 40 Lancaster Avenue<br>Fennel Street | Watches and watchmakers materials |
| | | P9/G/84,85,88,89<br>***#2740-3***  | Manchester | |

| REGISTRATION DETAILS | MAKER'S PRIVATE ADDRESS and DETAILS | PLATE and MARK DETAILS | MAKER/COMPANY and BUSINESS ADDRESS | MAKER'S TRADE |
|---|---|---|---|---|
| R2/71<br>16 January 1909<br>Sent by B H Joseph & Co | Glenart<br>Windsor Park<br>Belfast | P13/G/4<br>*#2744*<br> | **GIBSON & CO** *<br>John A Pryde (Director) *<br>Donegal Place<br>Belfast | Jewellers |
| Missing register<br>*c.*1888<br>Similar mark BAO<br>20 July 1889 | | P5/G/185<br>*#2745*<br> | **GILPIN & CO**<br>9 Augusta Street<br>Birmingham<br>or | Jewellers |
| Missing register<br>*c.*1891<br>Similar mark entered<br>BAO 15 July 1890 | | P5/G/336<br>*#2746*<br> | **GEORGE & CO**<br>42 Vyse Street<br>Birmingham | Gem ring makers |
| Missing register<br>*c.*1887<br>Similar mark entered<br>BAO 5 June 1896 | | P5/G/74<br>*#2747*<br> | **C GRIFFITHS & CO**<br>105 Carver Street<br>Birmingham | Silversmiths |
| R1/180<br>18 November 1902<br>Sent by H Grifffith & Sons | | P9/G/38<br>*#2748*<br> | **GIBSON & CO LTD** *<br>Donegal Place<br>Dublin | Goldsmiths and silversmiths |
| R1/202<br>30 October 1903<br>Sent by Haseler Brothers | Glenart<br>10 Windsor Park<br>Belfast | P9/G/52<br>*#2749*<br> | John A Pryde (Director) * | |
| R2/74<br>11 March 1909<br>Sent by Alfred Marston | | P13/G/7<br>*#2750*<br>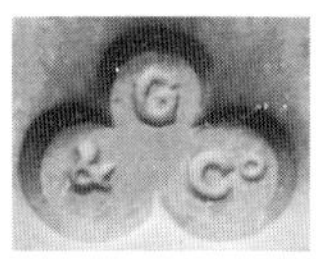 | **GIBSON & CO** *<br>Donegal Place<br>Belfast | |
| R2/169<br>6 March 1913<br>Sent by Stokes & Ireland Ltd | | P15/G/2<br>*#2751*<br> | **GIBSON & CO LTD** *<br>John Pryde (Director)<br>Donegal Place<br>Belfast | |
| R2/114<br>5 July 1910<br>Sent by J W Wynn | Donegal Place<br>Belfast | P13/G/22,23<br>*#2752,3*<br>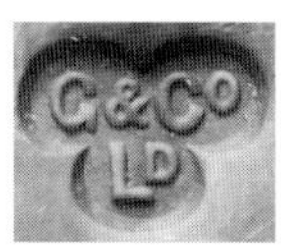 | **GIBSON & CO** *<br>John A Pigot (Director)<br>Donegal Place<br>Belfast | |
| R2/157<br>25 May 1912<br>Sent by W Aitken<br>Two sizes | 10 Windsor Park<br>Belfast | P13/G/41,42<br>*#2754,5*<br> | **GIBSON & CO LTD** *<br>John Pryde (Secretary)<br>Donegal Place and<br>Castle Place<br>Belfast | |
| R3/183<br>31 March 1962<br>Sent by selves | | P21/G/48<br>*#2756*<br> | **GARRARD & CO LTD** *<br>112 Regent Street<br>London W1 | Jewellers |
| 24 July 1962 | | P21/G/50<br>*#2757*<br> | | |
| R1/119<br>3 January 1900<br>Sent by G Dresden | 149 Kingsley Road<br>Liverpool | P9/D/14<br>*#2758*<br> | **George DRESDEN** *<br>42 South John Street<br>Liverpool | Wholesale agent and commercial jeweller |

| REGISTRATION DETAILS | MAKER'S PRIVATE ADDRESS and DETAILS | PLATE and MARK DETAILS | MAKER/COMPANY and BUSINESS ADDRESS | MAKER'S TRADE |
|---|---|---|---|---|
| R1/127<br>31 May 1900<br>Sent by G Dresden | 149 Kingsley Road<br>Liverpool | P9/D/17<br>***#2759***<br> | **George DRESDEN** *<br>42 South John Street<br>Liverpool | Foreign agent |
| R2/86<br>7 July 1909<br>Sent by<br>George Dresden<br>Two sizes | 26 Cavendish Road<br>London | P13/D/19,20<br>***#2760,1***<br> | **George DRESDEN** *<br>10 Hatton Gardens<br>London | Jeweller |
| R2/127<br>30 January 1911<br>Two sizes Sent by<br>George Dresden<br><br>Two sizes | 26 Cavendish Road<br>Brondesbury | P13/D/32,34<br>***#2762,3***<br><br>P13/D/26,33<br>***#2764,5***<br>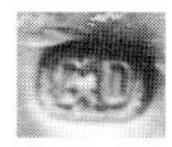 | | Jewellery manufacturers agent |
| R3/83<br>25 March 1936<br>Sent by B H Britton & Sons<br>35 Hockley Hill<br>Birmingham | Common seal of company affixed in the presence of:-<br>Georges H S Dimier ? | P15/D/93<br>***#2766***<br> | **DIMIER BROTHERS & CO LTD** *<br>Atlantic House<br>45/50 Holborn Viaduct<br>London EC1 | Watch importers and manufacturers |
| R3/22<br>20 May 1924<br>Sent by George Thomas Davis | 102 Packington Street<br>Islington | P15/D/71<br>***#2767***<br> | **George Thomas DAVIS**<br>332c Goswell Road<br>London EC | Gold and silver mounter |
| R2/161<br>24 September 1912<br>Sent by Charles Peach & Son | Sheringham [1]<br>Jersey Road<br>Osterley Park<br>Middlesex | P15/G/1<br>***#2768***<br> | **THE GOPHIR DIAMOND COMPANY LTD**<br>E H E Giles [1] (Director)<br>61, 98, 145 and 176 Regent Street<br>London W | Jewellers |
| R2/190<br>9 September 1914<br>Sent by The Gophir Diamond Co Ltd | | P15/G/23,24<br>***#2769,70***<br> | | |
| R1/46<br>15 June 1897<br>Sent by J Gammage | 17 Leucian Place<br>Newcastle upon Tyne | P5/D/849<br>***#2771***<br> | **George Albert DAVISON**<br>**George DAVISON** trading as<br>**George DAVISON & CO**<br>60 to 64 Gray Street<br>Newcastle upon Tyne | Watchmakers, jewellers and manufacturers |
| R2/108<br>16 April 1910<br>BAO 17.458<br>Sent by Frank Edmonds | Walsall Road<br>Four Oaks<br>Oakfield Road<br>Selly Park<br>Birmingham | P13/E/15<br>***#2772***<br>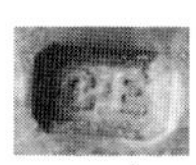 | **Henry EDMONDS**<br>**Frank EDMONDS** trading as<br>**G EDMONDS**<br>Soho Hill Works<br>Birmingham | Manufacturing jewellers |
| MR1/36<br>J1 1585<br>J3/389 | Paten *c.*1590<br>Working *c.*1585 – 1605 | Predates P1<br>***#2773***<br>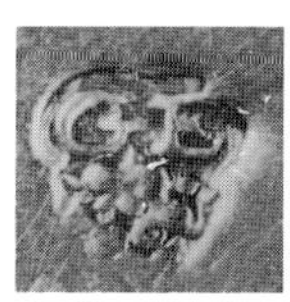 | **Griffith EDWARDES I**<br>Chester | Silversmith |
| MR1/36-38<br>J1 1607-40 died<br>J3/389 | Communion cup *c.*1620<br>Free 1607 | Predates P1<br>***#2774***<br> | **Griffith EDWARDES II**<br>Chester | Silversmith |
| R2/226<br>18 January 1920<br>Sent by A E Jones | 13 Queens Gate<br>Glasgow<br>Alipore<br>Skelmorlie<br>Ayrshire | P15/E/16<br>***#2775***<br> | **George EDWARD**<br>**Arthur EDWARD**<br>92 Buchanan Street<br>Glasgow | Jewellers and silversmiths |

| REGISTRATION DETAILS | MAKER'S PRIVATE ADDRESS and DETAILS | PLATE and MARK DETAILS | MAKER/COMPANY and BUSINESS ADDRESS | MAKER'S TRADE |
|---|---|---|---|---|
| R3/14<br>24 March 1923<br>Sent by Docker & Burn<br>Three sizes | St Germains<br>Bearsden<br>Alipore<br>Skelmorlie<br>Ayrshire | P15/E/18-24<br>***#2776-82***  | **George EDWARD**<br>**Arthur EDWARD**<br>92 Buchanan Street<br>Glasgow | Jewellers and silversmiths |
| R1/180<br>18 November 1902<br>Sent by E J Trevitt | 179 Heathfield Road<br>Birmingham | P9/C/78<br>***#2783***  | **Enoch James TREVITT** trading as<br>**G E CRAMP** *<br>121 Vyse Street<br>Birmingham | Ring makers |
| R1/57<br>21 January 1898<br>Sent by E Durban & Co<br>Edward Brothers | 96 Thornhill Road<br>Handsworth<br>Birmingham | P5/aboveC/921<br>***#2784***  | **George Edward CRAMP** *<br>121 Vyse Stret<br>Birmingham | Manufacturing jeweller |
| R1/119<br>30 January 1900<br>Sent by E J Trevitt | 179 Heathfield Road<br>Handsworth<br>Birmingham | P9/C/32,33<br>***#2785,6***  | **Enoch James TREVITT** trading as<br>**G E CRAMP** *<br>20 Vyse Street<br>Birmingham | Jewellers |
| R2/1<br>25 August 1905<br>Sent by G Edwards | 41 Havelock Road<br>Birchfields<br>Birmingham<br>Authority to use M Spiro punch<br>5 September 1905 | P9/E/17<br>***#2787***  | **George EDWARDS**<br>16 Hockley Street<br>Birmingham | Ring makers |
| R2/71<br>19 January 1909<br>Sent by George Edwards<br>Dissolved partnership<br>23 May 1911 | 41 Havelock Road<br>Handsworth<br>Birmingham | P13/E/7<br>***#2788***  | **William Henry EDWARDS**<br>**George EDWARDS** trading as<br>**G EDWARDS & CO**<br>16 Hockley Street<br>Birmingham | |
| LPB/34<br>12 February 1883 | | P3/G/x3<br>***#2789-91***  | **George Edward GEE**<br>58 Tenby Street<br>Birmingham | Jeweller |
| Missing register<br>*c.*1886 | | P5/G/16<br>***#2792***  | | |
| R3/124<br>9 June 1948<br>Sent by Miss George | Private address same as business | P21/G/15<br>***#2793*** 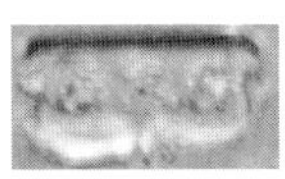 | **Gwyneth Edwina GEORGE (Miss)**<br>84 Mitton Road<br>Gorse Hill, Stretford<br>Lancashire | Art student |
| R3/163<br>20 March 1958<br>Sent by G E Gate | Grisedale<br>High Portinscale<br>Keswick | P21/G/41<br>***#2794***  | **George Elliott GATE**<br>No business address entered | Silversmith and jewellery |
| 1 December 1956 | | P21/G/45<br>***#2795***  | | |
| R1/63<br>19 March 1898<br>Sent by G E Hawkins | 223 Church Hill Road<br>Handsworth<br>Birmingham | P5/*Zsic*/944<br>***#2796***  | **George Ernest HAWKINS**<br>15, 16 Legge Lane<br>Birmingham | Manufacturing silversmith |
| R3/145<br>23 June 1953<br>Sent by G E Parry | 134 Birchfields Róad<br>Manchester 14 | P21/P/53<br>***#2797***  | **Gwen Enid PARRY**<br>No business address entered | Student |
| R1/160<br>29 January 1902<br>Sent by G E Walton Ltd | 7 Stanmore Road<br>Edgbaston<br>Birmingham | P9/W/63<br>***#2798***  | **G E WALTON LTD** *<br>Arthur Joseph Mason (Manager and Secretary)<br>52 Hylton Street<br>Birmingham | Manufacturing jewellers |

| REGISTRATION DETAILS | MAKER'S PRIVATE ADDRESS and DETAILS | PLATE and MARK DETAILS | MAKER/COMPANY and BUSINESS ADDRESS | MAKER'S TRADE |
|---|---|---|---|---|
| R1/168<br>12 May 1902<br>Sent by G E Walton Ltd | Nelleslie<br>Stanmore Road<br>Edgbaston<br>Birmingham | P9/W/68-70<br>***#2799-2801***  | **G E WALTON LTD** *<br>52, 54 Hylton Street<br>Birmingham | Manufacturing jewellers |
| R1/233<br>18 May 1905<br>Sent by selves | | P9/V*sic*/127-132<br>***#2802-7***  | | |
| R2/7<br>8 December 1905 | | P9/V*sic*/138<br>***#2808***  | | |
| R2/68<br>19 November 1908<br>Sent by Andrew Moodie | 88 Alexander Street<br>Acocks Green<br>Birmingham | P13/W/35-37<br>***#2809-11***  | **G E WALTON & CO LTD** *<br>Andrew Moodie (General Manager)<br>52 Hylton Street<br>Birmingham and<br>56, 61 Hatton Garden<br>London | Jewellers silversmiths and metal workers |
| R2/114<br>1 July 1910<br>Sent by Andrew Moodie<br>BAO 17833<br>17.834-17.842 | | P13/W/76-78<br>***#2812-4***  | **G E WALTON LTD** *<br>Andrew Moodie (Secretary)<br>52 Hylton Street<br>Birmingham | Manufacturing jeweller |
| R2/49<br>2 November 1907<br>Sent by<br>G E Walton Ltd | | P13/W/15-17<br>***#2815-7***  | **G E WALTON LTD** *<br>Arthur Joseph Mason (Secretary)<br>52, 54 Hylton Street<br>Birmingham | |
| R2/49<br>2 November 1907<br>Sent by G E Walton Ltd | Nelleslie<br>Stanmore Road<br>Edgbaston<br>Birmingham | P13/W/12-14<br>***#2818-20***  | **G E WALTON LTD** *<br>52, 54 Hylton Street<br>Birmingham | |
| R1/160<br>29 January 1902<br>Sent by G E Walton Ltd | 7 Stanmore Road<br>Edgbaston<br>Birmingham | P9/W/62<br>***#2821***  | **G E WALTON LTD** *<br>Arthur Joseph Mason (Manager and Secretary)<br>52 Hylton Street<br>Birmingham | |
| R1/183<br>29 January 1903<br>Sent by G E Walton Ltd | 15 Stanmore Road<br>Edgbaston<br>Birmingham | P9/W/86-88<br>***#2822-4***  | **G E WALTON LTD** *<br>Arthur Joseph Mason (Secretary)<br>52, 54 Hylton Street<br>Birmingham and<br>59 Hatton Garden<br>London EC | Wholesale jewellers |
| R2/114<br>1 July 1910<br>BAO 17.833,<br>17.834-17.842<br>Sent by Andrew Moodie | 88 Alexander Street<br>Acocks Green<br>Birmingham | P13/W/73-75<br>***#2825-7***  | | Manufacturing jewellers |
| LPB/90<br>31 August 1883<br>No mark in LPB only initials GEW | | P5/W/x1<br>***#2828***  | **WALTON & CO** *<br>15 Hylton Street<br>Birmingham | Gold chain makers |
| LPB/98<br>5 July 1884<br>No address in LPB | | P5/W/x1<br>***#2829***  | **George Edwin WALTON** *<br>Hylton Street<br>Birmingham | |
| R1/229<br>9 March 1905<br>Sent by self | Water Orton | P9/F/25<br>***#2830***  | **George FREEMAN**<br>68 Regent Place<br>Birmingham | Chain maker |

| REGISTRATION DETAILS | MAKER'S PRIVATE ADDRESS and DETAILS | PLATE and MARK DETAILS | MAKER/COMPANY and BUSINESS ADDRESS | MAKER'S TRADE |
|---|---|---|---|---|
| R2/135<br>12 May 1911<br>Sent by<br>George F Bickerton<br>BAO 16.948<br>Two sizes | 48 Crompton Road<br>Handsworth<br>Birmingham | P13/B/122,123<br>***#2831,2***<br> | **George Frank BICKERTON**<br>41 Hylton Street<br>Birmingham | Manufacturing jeweller |
| R2/163<br>15 October 1912<br>Sent by George F Bickerton | | P13/B/133<br>***#2833***<br> | | |
| R2/28<br>17 November 1906<br>Sent by J Gammage<br>Cancelled<br>15 May 1914 | Woburn Lodge<br>Oak Hill<br>Surbiton<br>Surrey | P9/XYZ*sic*/179-181<br>***#2834-6***<br> | **George Herbert BRAVINGTON**<br>**Frank William BRAVINGTON**<br>trading as **G & F BRAVINGTON**<br>298 Pentonville Road<br>London | Jewellers |
| Missing register<br>*c.*1889 | | P5/C/266<br>***#2837***<br> | **Unidentified** | |
| R3/138<br>5 July 1952<br>Sent by G F Cramer<br>Two sizes | 31 Totnes Road<br>Sale, Cheshire (later)<br>Glebe Cottage<br>Hastingfield, Cambs | P21/C/55,56<br>***#2838,9***<br> | **George Frederick CRAMER**<br>No business address entered | Student |
| R2/218<br>6 February 1919<br>Sent by G F Coverdale | 23 Rotherwick Green<br>Golders Green<br>London NW4 | P15/C/70-72<br>***#2840-2***<br>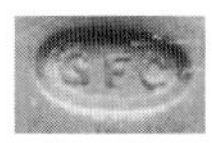 | **George Frederick COVERDALE**<br>1 Hatton Garden<br>London EC | Wholesale jeweller |
| R2/209<br>26 October 1916<br>MR3/131 Two sizes<br>Sent by George Frederick Lowe | 29 Dee Banks<br>Chester | P15/L/15–20<br>***#2843-8***<br> | **George Frederick LOWE** trading as **LOWE & SON** *<br>11 Bridge Street Row<br>Chester | Goldsmith and silversmiths |
| R3/87<br>24 June 1937 Re-entry of marks 15 to 20 on P15<br>Sent by G F Lowe | St Werburgh Row<br>Chester | No new marks<br>***#2849*** | **Mrs G F LOWE** trading as **LOWE & SONS** *<br>11 Bridge Street Row<br>Chester | Gold and silversmiths and antique silver |
| R3/160<br>22 February 1957<br>Sent by G F Turton<br>Two sizes | Private address same as business | P21/T/31,32<br>***#2850,1***<br> | **George Frederick TURTON**<br>91 Kimberley Road<br>Nuthall<br>Nr Nottingham | No trade entered |
| R1/44<br>7 May 1897<br>Sent by E Langridge | 19 Southcote Road<br>London N | P5/W/839<br>***#2852***<br> | **George Frederick WALKER**<br>42 Bassinghall Street<br>London EC | Fancy goods manufacturer |
| LPB/92<br>23 July 1883 | | P3/X*sic*/x2<br>***#2853,4***<br> | **George Frederick WAKEFIELD**<br>57 Northampton Street<br>Birmingham | Jeweller |
| LPB/6<br>8 January 1878 | 12 West Seacombe Terrace<br>Seacombe | P3/W/x1<br>***#2855***<br> | **George Frederick WRIGHT**<br>21 Tarleton Street<br>Liverpool | Watch manufacturer |
| Missing register<br>*c.*1890<br>Roman letters mark<br>BAO 28 January 1885 | | P5/G/272<br>***#2856***<br> | **George GOODMAN**<br>52 Caroline Street<br>Birmingham | Pin maker and factor |
| Missing register<br>*c.*1891 | See also George Goodman and George Green | P5/G/343<br>***#2857***<br> | **Unidentified** | |

| REGISTRATION DETAILS | MAKER'S PRIVATE ADDRESS and DETAILS | PLATE and MARK DETAILS | MAKER/COMPANY and BUSINESS ADDRESS | MAKER'S TRADE |
|---|---|---|---|---|
| Missing register<br>*c.*1894 | See George Goodman or George Green | P5/G/546<br>***#2858***<br> | **Unidentified** | |
| R1/13<br>13 July 1895<br>Sent by Dennison, Wigley & Co | Northwood<br>London | P5/G/674 but not on plates<br>***#2859*** | **George GREEN** *<br>14 Rathbone Place<br>Oxford Street<br>London | Jeweller |
| R1/21<br>12 February 1896<br>Authority to D & L Spiers and J Fenton<br>G Green | The Oaks<br>Northwood<br>Rickmansworth<br>62 Hyde Park Mansions<br>London | P5/G/726<br>***#2860***<br> | **George GREEN** *<br>**Edward Arthur CARPENTER** *<br>14 Rathbone Place<br>London | Goldsmiths and jewellers |
| R1/84<br>16 November 1898<br>Sent by G Green for Green & Carpenter | The Gables [1]<br>Northwood<br>Rickmansworth<br>6 Hyde Park Mansions [2]<br>London W | P9/G/4<br>***#2861***<br> | **George GREEN** [1]<br>**Edward Arthur CARPENTER** [2]<br>trading as **GREEN & CARPENTER** *<br>61, 63 Beak Street<br>Regent Street<br>London | Manufacturing jewellers |
| R2/36<br>3 April 1907<br>Sent by Alexander George | 164 High Street<br>East Ham<br>Eynsham<br>Oxford | P9/G/82<br>***#2862***<br> | **Alexander GEORGE**<br>**Edward James GIBBONS** trading as **GEORGE & GIBBONS**<br>162 High Street<br>East Ham<br>Essex | Pawnbrokers, jewellers and silversmiths |
| R2/211<br>21 March 1917<br>Sent by W J Ginder | 96 Oakfield Road<br>33 Alcester Road<br>Birmingham<br>164 Pett Street<br>Sydney | P15/G/30–33<br>***#2863-6***<br> | **William H GINDER**<br>**W J GINDER J C GINDER**<br>trading as **GINDER & GINDER**<br>20 Hockley Hill<br>Birmingham | Ring manufacturers |
| R2/224<br>11 October 1919<br>Sent by Ginder & Ginder | 43 Heathfield Road<br>Handsworth<br>25 Holly Hill<br>Handsworth<br>Birmingham | P15/G/38<br>***#2867***<br> | **W H GINDER J C GINDER** trading as **GINDER & GINDER**<br>20 Hockley Hill<br>Birmingham | |
| R3/2<br>15 April 1921<br>Sent by Twine & Gilpin | Kismet<br>Middleton Road<br>Golders Green<br>London NW3 | P15/N/9<br>***#2868***<br> | **G & G NATHAN**<br>Gordon Ellis Nathan<br>25a Hatton Garden<br>London EC1 | Ring makers |
| R3/15<br>25 March 1923<br>Sent by Gordon Hillcox | Private address same as business | P15/H/75<br>***#2869***<br> | **Gordon HILLCOX**<br>42 Osborn Road<br>Handsworth<br>Birmingham | Goldsmith and silversmith |
| R3/44<br>19 October 1928<br>Sent by Villiers & Jackson<br>3 Hockley Hill<br>Birmingham | Newlyn<br>Hockley Hill<br>Wylde Green<br>Birmingham | P15/H/104<br>***#2870***<br> | **Ilyla George HOLDEN** trading as **George HOLDEN**<br>29 Hockley Hill<br>Birmingham | Pencil case makers |
| R1/42<br>13 May 1897<br>Sent by R Parker | 280 Pershore Road<br>Birmingham | P5/*Zsic*/842<br>***#2871***<br> | **George William HARVEY**<br>43 Warstone Lane<br>Birmingham | Jeweller |
| PP1/187<br>PP3/83<br>Similar mark entered LAO 13 June 1863 | Not in SPB or LPB so struck 1860-3 | P3/H/x3<br>***#2872-4***<br> | **George John HAMMON** *<br>Providence House<br>Earlsdon<br>Coventry | Watchcase maker |

| REGISTRATION DETAILS | MAKER'S PRIVATE ADDRESS and DETAILS | PLATE and MARK DETAILS | MAKER/COMPANY and BUSINESS ADDRESS | MAKER'S TRADE |
|---|---|---|---|---|
| R3/51<br>15 January 1930<br>Sent by George Edward Hunt | Private address same as business | P15/I*sic*/109<br>***#2875***<br> | **George Edward HUNT**<br>10 Bull Street<br>Harborne<br>Birmingham | Artist and craftsman |
| R1/208<br>25 February 1904<br>cancelled 17 November 06<br>Sent by Lawson, Ward & Gammage | Woburn Lodge Hill<br>Surbiton, Surrey<br>Strathmore<br>Hatch End<br>Middlesex | P9/B/115-117<br>***#2876-8***<br> | **G H BRAVINGTON**<br>298 Pentonville Road<br>London | Jeweller and silversmith |
| R2/133<br>22 April 1911<br>Sent by G J Bendall | Private address same as business | P13/B/119<br>***#2879***<br> | **Gordon James BENDALL**<br>**Harry BENDALL** trading as<br>**G & H BENDALL**<br>8 Wells Street, Lozells<br>Birmingham | Working jewellers |
| LPB/40<br>20 January 1884<br>Sent by Horton & Allday | No mark in LPB | P5/H/x1<br>***#2880***<br> | **George HEATH & CO** *<br>146 Aldersgate<br>London | Manufacturing jewellers |
| LPB/40<br>14 February 1884<br>No mark in LPB | | P5/H/x1<br>***#2881***<br> | **George Henry HIBBERD** *<br>82 New North Road<br>London | Goldsmith |
| R3/42<br>18 July 1928<br>Sent by W J Pellow Ltd | Craiglands<br>Victoria Road<br>Wednesfield<br>Staffordshire | P15/J/34<br>***#2882***<br> | **G H JACKSON**<br>Wolverhampton Street<br>Willenhall, Staffordshire | Wholesale and retail jeweller |
| R3/170<br>25 October 1959<br>Sent by G H Mason | 130 Templeton Road<br>Birmingham 22A | P21/M/50<br>***#2883***<br> | **George Hammond MASON**<br>37 Warstone Lane<br>Birmingham 18 | Manufacturing jeweller |
| LPB/46<br>21 July 1883 | | P5/N/x1<br>***#2884***<br>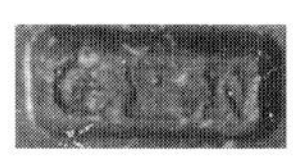 | **George Hewitt NOON**<br>Ruby Buildings, Frederick Street<br>Birmingham | Jeweller and gold ring manufacturer |
| R1/204<br>11 December 1903<br>Sent by H G Plant | Erdington [1]<br>Birmingham<br>111 City Road [2]<br>Birmingham | P9/Q*sic*/188<br>***#2885***<br>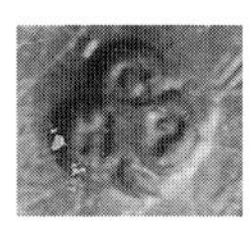 | **Henry Griffin PLANT** [1]<br>**L A WACARON** [2] (name indistinct)<br>61 Albion Street<br>Birmingham | Manufacturing jewellers |
| R1/140<br>MR3/183<br>J3/423<br>Mark entered *c*.1701 | | P1/8/x1<br>***#2886***<br>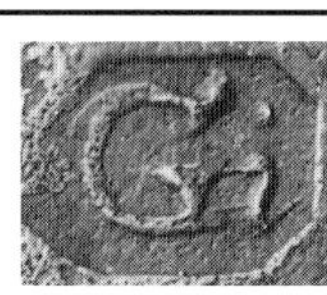 | **Thomas GITTIN(S)**<br>Shrewsbury | Silversmith |
| | | P1/8/x1<br>***#2887***<br> | | |
| R3/185<br>28 June 1962<br>Sent by G Jones | 17 Sandringham Avenue<br>Vicars Cross<br>Chester | P21/IJ/19<br>***#2888***<br>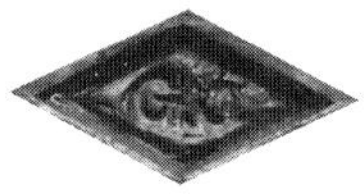 | **Grahame JONES**<br>The Assay Office<br>13/15 Goss Street<br>Chester | Goldsmith |
| Not in R3 as expected Between March and July 1962 | | P21/G*sic*/49<br>***#2889***<br> | | |

| REGISTRATION DETAILS | MAKER'S PRIVATE ADDRESS and DETAILS | PLATE and MARK DETAILS | MAKER/COMPANY and BUSINESS ADDRESS | MAKER'S TRADE |
|---|---|---|---|---|
| R3/161<br>7 May 1957<br>Sent by N Futter | 6 Penrhyn Drive<br>Prestwich<br>Lancashire | P21/IJ/12<br>***#2890***<br> | **Nathan FUTTER** trading as<br>**GEMCRAFT JEWELLERS**<br>68-70 Lancaster Avenue<br>Fennel Street<br>Manchester 4 | Manufacturing and repairing jewellers |
| Missing register<br>*c.*1892<br>Two sizes | See L G Jackson below | P5/J/411x2<br>***#2891,2***<br> | **Unidentified** | |
| R1/108<br>3 August 1899<br>Sent by L G Jackson | 4 Stanley Terrace<br>Coventry | P9/J/19<br>***#2893***<br> | **Leonard George JACKSON**<br>4 Stanley Terrace<br>Coventry | Gold watch pendant maker |
| Missing register<br>*c.*1890 | | P5/J/303<br>***#2894***<br>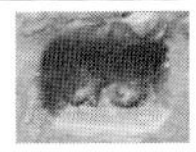 | **Unidentified** | |
| Missing register<br>*c.*1892<br>Two sizes | | P5/J/411x2<br>***#2895,6***<br>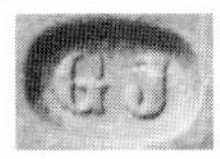 | **Unidentified** | |
| R1/142<br>13 February 1901<br>Sent by L G Jackson<br>Destroyed 18 Nov 03 | Private address same as business | P9/J/32<br>***#2897***<br> | **Leonard George JACKSON**<br>Allesley Old Road<br>4 Stanley terrace<br>Coventry | Gold watch pendant manufacturer |
| R1/203<br>20 November 1903 | | P9/J/38<br>***#2898***<br>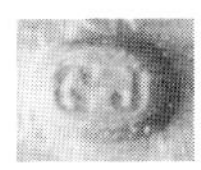 | | |
| Missing register<br>*c.*1886 | | P5/J/11<br>***#2899***<br>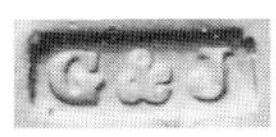 | **Unidentified** | |
| R2/211<br>28 March 1917<br>BAO 22.724<br>Sent by G J Bendall | 8 Wells Street<br>Lozells<br>Birmingham | P15/B/66<br>***#2900***<br> | **Gordon James BENDALL**<br>24 Spencer Street<br>Birmingham | Manufacturing jeweller |
| R2/224<br>Undated between<br>11 October and<br>7 November 1919<br>Sent by G J Bendall<br>Two sizes | | P15/B/106-9<br>***#2901-4***<br> | | Wholesale and manufacturing silversmith |
| R1/208<br>3 March 1904<br>Sent by C J Hunt | 31 Daulby Street<br>Liverpool | P9/H/57<br>***#2905***<br>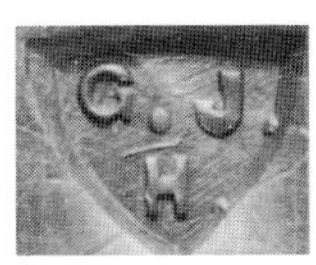 | **George J HUNT**<br>North Crescent Chambers<br>3 Lord Street<br>Liverpool | Jeweller and silversmith |
| PP1/187<br>GTD 1859-68<br>Similar marks entered<br>LAO 23 April 1856 | | P2/H/x3<br>***#2906-8***<br> | **George John HAMMON** *<br>7 Ashby Street, Clerkenwell<br>London | Watchcase maker |
| | | P2/H/x4<br>***#2909-12***<br> | | |
| R3/166<br>3 March 1959<br>Sent by London<br>Assay Office<br>Gutter Lane EC2<br>Two sizes | | P21/IJ/14,16<br>***#2913,4***<br> | **Georg JENSEN**<br>15 New Bond Street<br>London W1 | Silversmith |
| Not in R1 as expected<br>Roman font cameo<br>mark entered LAO in<br>1895, etc | | P5/K/662a<br>***#2915***<br> | **George KENNING** *<br>1-3 Little Britain<br>London and | Goldsmith and masonic medals |
| | | P5/K/662b<br>***#2916***<br> | 1 Monument Place<br>Liverpool and<br>47 Bridge Street<br>Manchester | |

| REGISTRATION DETAILS | MAKER'S PRIVATE ADDRESS and DETAILS | PLATE and MARK DETAILS | MAKER/COMPANY and BUSINESS ADDRESS | MAKER'S TRADE |
|---|---|---|---|---|
| R3/125<br>30 July 1948<br>Sent by G K Kitson<br>Two sizes | Westwood<br>29 Southport Road<br>Chorley<br>Lancs | P21/K/6,7<br>***#2917,8***<br> | **Geoffrey Knowles KITSON**<br>Manchester Municipal School of Art<br>Cavendish Street, All Saints<br>Manchester 15 | Full-time student<br>Gold and Silversmithing Department |
| LPB/52<br>4 March 1885<br>Sent by Ernest Leeson | 5 Havelock Road<br>Handsworth<br>Birmingham | P5/L/x1<br>***#2919***<br> | **Ernest LEESON**<br>**George K LEESON**<br>125½ Vyse Street<br>Birmingham | Manufacturing jewellers |
| Missing register<br>*c.*1890 | | P5/L/283<br>***#2920***<br> | | |
| Missing register<br>*c.*1890 | | P5/L/282<br>***#2921***<br> | **George K LEESON**<br>125½ Vyse Street<br>Birmingham | |
| R1/77<br>20 December 1898<br>Sent by Ernest Leeson | | P9/L/2<br>***#2922***<br> | **Ernest LEESON**<br>**George K LEESON**<br>125½ Vyse Street<br>Birmingham | |
| R2/72<br>5 February 1909<br>Sent by G E Lancelott | 15 Soho Avenue<br>Handsworth<br>Birmingham | P13/L/6<br>***#2923***<br> | **G E LANCELOTT LTD**<br>G E Lancelott (Director)<br>49 Tenby Street North<br>Birmingham | Electroplate and silver goods |
| R1/88<br>4 January 1899<br>Sent by G W Nettleton | Private address same as business | P9/L/3<br>***#2924***<br> | **George LANE**<br>22 Crown Street<br>Halifax | Cigar and pipe importer |
| MR2/97-112<br>MR3/90<br>GMSC/53-63<br>PDB 1791-1840 | Gold rings and large variety of plate 1791-1840 | P1/25/x2<br>***#2925,6***<br>type 1<br> | **George LOWE I** and **II** (G)<br>Chester and Gloucester | Goldsmiths and silversmiths |
| Similar mark entered LAO 21 January1791 | | P1/25/x2<br>***#2927,8***<br> | | |
| PDB 1815<br>MR3/90<br>J1 1847-74 | | P2/L/x2<br>***#2929,30***<br>type 3<br> | **George LOWE II**<br>Gloucester | |
| PDB 1791-1840<br>MR2/97-112<br>MR3/90-3, 193<br>SIL/44<br>SOT/77-83 | Known to have worked 1791-1837<br>Entries in PDB after 1837 refer to sons John and Thomas Lowe<br>SIL/52 | P1/4/x3<br>***#2931-3***<br> | **George LOWE I** (G)<br>The Cross<br>Bridge Street Row East (1804)<br>Chester | |
| | Double lobed mark seen until 1838 may be George I and II or John and Thomas working from Gloucester | P1/25/x1<br>***#2934***<br>type 2<br> | | |
| SPB/17<br>1 May 1868 | Identical to his earlier pre-1841 mark on P2 | P3/L/x3<br>***#2935-7***<br> | **George LOWE**<br>Gloddaith Street<br>Llandudno | |
| GMSC/53-63 | Found on silverware 1791-1821 | P1/25/x2<br>***#2938,9***<br> | **George LOWE I** and **II** (G)<br>Chester and Gloucester | |
| R1/215<br>14 June 1904<br>Sent by<br>George L Allen<br>Two sizes | Private address same as business | P9/A/53-56<br>***#2940-3***<br> | **George Leonard ALLEN** *<br>6 Shirlock Road<br>Gospel Oak<br>London NW | Silversmith |

| REGISTRATION DETAILS | MAKER'S PRIVATE ADDRESS and DETAILS | PLATE and MARK DETAILS | MAKER/COMPANY and BUSINESS ADDRESS | MAKER'S TRADE |
|---|---|---|---|---|
| R2/38<br>30 April 1907<br>Sent by Marston & Bayliss<br>Two sizes | Private address same as business | P9/A/86,87<br>***#2944,5***<br> | **George Leonard ALLEN** *<br>10 Lichfield Road<br>Cricklewood<br>London NW | Silversmith |
| Missing register<br>*c.*1892 | | P5/M/447<br>***#2946***<br> | **Unidentified** | |
| LPB/54<br>12 May 1879 | | P3/M/x3<br>***#2947-9***<br> | **George James MANSELL** *<br>Spon End<br>Coventry | Watch manufacturer |
| LPB/56 SP27/5<br>Undated *c.*1884<br>Only GM in LPB Sent by E Culver | See also WGM #9043-51 | P5/M/x1<br>***#2950***<br>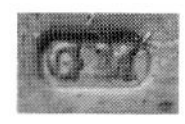 | **Walter & George MYERS** *<br>68 Northampton Street<br>Birmingham | Wholesale jewellers and factors |
| Missing register<br>*c.*1892 | See W G Myers above | P5/M/434<br>***#2951***<br> | **Unidentified** | |
| R2/234<br>12 October 1920<br>Sent by The Gold Mesh Bag Co Ltd | 7 Dawson Place [1]<br>Bayswater<br>London W | P15/D*sic*/57 and P15/G/40<br>***#2952,3***<br> | **THE GOLD MESH BAG CO LTD** *<br>Mr Weston Dresden [1] (Managing Director)<br>11 Kirby Street<br>Hatton Garden<br>London | Gold and silver mesh bag manufacturers |
| R3/118<br>19 June 1947<br>Sent by W H Tandy & Son<br>122 Vyse Street<br>Birmingham 18 | | P21/M/20,21<br>***#2954,5***<br> | **Gordon MAITLAND & CO LTD**<br>Sealed in the presence of:-<br>A H Spencer (Director)<br>A E H Hawley (Secretary)<br>King William Street House<br>Arthur Street, London Bridge<br>London EC4 | Wholesale jewellers |
| R3/159<br>4 January 1957<br>Sent by G M McDonald<br>Two sizes | 2 Kings Crescent East<br>Chester | P21/M/47,48<br>***#2956,7***<br> | **Greta Margaret MACDONALD**<br>No business address entered | Student silversmith |
| R1/152<br>14 August 1901<br>Sent by W H Carrington | Birchroyd [1]<br>St Annes on the Sea (*sic*)<br>Sunnybank [2]<br>Didsbury | P9/M/32<br>***#2958***<br> | **George MAKIN** [1]<br>**Joseph MAKIN** [2] trading as<br>**George MAKIN & SON**<br>58 Shudehill<br>Manchester | Wholesale jewellers |
| R3/135<br>29 May 1951<br>Sent by G M Wilkinson<br>Two sizes | Private address same as business | P21/W/60,61<br>***#2959,60***<br> | **Grace Monica WILKINSON**<br>Penketh Grange<br>Nr Warrington<br>Lancashire | None entered |
| R1/45<br>9 May 1897<br>MR3/136<br>Sent by Nathan & Hayes | Argent House [1]<br>Handsworth<br>7 Clarendon Road [2]<br>Edgbaston | P5/N/561a<br>***#2961***<br> | **George NATHAN** [1]<br>**Ridley HAYES** [2] trading as<br>**NATHAN & HAYES** *<br>285 Icknield Street<br>Birmingham | Silversmiths |
| R1/197<br>4 July 1903<br>Sent by G Nathan | 243 Hagley Road<br>Birmingham<br>Hall Road<br>Birmingham | P9/N/25<br>***#2962***<br> | **George NATHAN**<br>**Ridley HAYES** trading as<br>**NATHAN & HAYES** *<br>Howard Street<br>Birmingham | Manufacturing silversmiths |

| REGISTRATION DETAILS | MAKER'S PRIVATE ADDRESS and DETAILS | PLATE and MARK DETAILS | MAKER/COMPANY and BUSINESS ADDRESS | MAKER'S TRADE |
|---|---|---|---|---|
| R2/152<br>12 March 1912<br>Sent by George Nathan | 243 Hagley Road<br>Birmingham | P13/N/33<br>***#2963***<br> | **George NATHAN** * trading as<br>**NATHAN & HAYES** *<br>Howard Street<br>Birmingham and<br>13 Hatton Garden<br>London | Manufacturing silversmiths |
| R3/176<br>28 January 1961<br>Sent by G H Hart | The Ivy House<br>Chipping Campden<br>Gloucestershire | P21/H/82<br>***#2964***<br> | **George Henry HART** FRSA<br>**The GUILD OF HANDICRAFT** *<br>Sheep Street<br>Chipping Campden<br>Gloucestershire | Goldsmith craftsman |
| R3/109<br>25 June 1945<br>Sent by B H Britton & Sons Ltd<br>35 Hockley Hill<br>Birmingham 18 | | P21/G/7<br>***#2965***<br> | **GOULD & PALMER LTD**<br>Sealed in the presence of:-<br>W P Gould (Director)<br>A F Weedon (Secretary)<br>67, 68 Hatton Garden<br>London EC1 | Wholesale jewellers and watch importers |
| R1/62<br>26 February 1898<br>Sent by W H Carrington Ltd | 27 Upper Brook Street<br>Manchester | P5/P/937a<br>***#2966***<br> | **George POLLARD**<br>Moseley Street<br>Manchester | Tobacconist |
| R1/104<br>20 June 1899<br>Sent by G A Peters | Private address same as business | P9/P/40<br>***#2967***<br>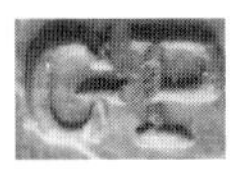 | **George Albert PETERS** *<br>151 Balls Pond Road<br>London N | Pipe and stick mounter |
| R1/62<br>26 February 1898<br>Sent by W H Carrington Ltd | 27 Upper Brook Street<br>Manchester | P5/P/937b<br>***#2968***<br> | **George POLLARD**<br>Moseley Street<br>Manchester | Tobacconist |
| R1/6<br>28 January 1895<br>Sent by W H Carrington & Co<br>Manchester | 18 Oxford Street<br>Chorlton-cum-Medlock<br>Manchester<br>See also AP over GP #475 | P5/P/x1<br>***#2969***<br> | **George POLLARD**<br>12 Princess Street<br>Manchester | |
| | | P5/P/below634<br>***#2970***<br> | | |
| R3/92<br>15 November 1938<br>Sent by S L Platnauer<br>Two sizes | Private address same as business | P21/P/4,5<br>***#2971,2***<br> | **Septimus Louis PLATNAUER**<br>trading as **G PLATNAUER**<br>51 Vyse Street<br>Birmingham | Manufacturing jewellers |
| R2/165<br>10 November 1912<br>Sent by Charles Lucas | 67 Oakfield Hill<br>Birmingham | P13/Q*sic*/212-215<br>***#2973-6***<br> | **Gertrude PLATNAUER**<br>61 Branston Street<br>Birmingham | Manufacturing jewellers and silversmiths |
| R2/200<br>5 October 1915<br>Sent by R C Roden<br>Two sizes | Private address same as business | P15/P/66–71<br>***#2977-82***<br> | **Gertrude PLATNAUER**<br>51 Vyse Street<br>Birmingham | Manufacturing jewellers |
| R2/228<br>5 March 1920<br>Sent by G Platnauer<br>Three sizes | 53 Wheeleys Road<br>Edgbaston | P15/P/118–131<br>***#2983-6***<br>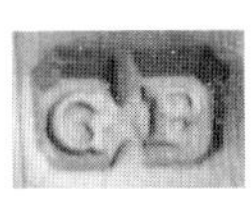 | **Gertrude PLATNAUER**<br>51 Vyse Street<br>Birmingham | Manufacturing jewellers and silversmiths |
| Not in R2 as expected<br>*c.* April 1917 | | P15/B/71<br>***#2987***<br> | **Unidentified** | |

| REGISTRATION DETAILS | MAKER'S PRIVATE ADDRESS and DETAILS | PLATE and MARK DETAILS | MAKER/COMPANY and BUSINESS ADDRESS | MAKER'S TRADE |
|---|---|---|---|---|
| R3/123<br>29 May 1948<br>Sent by G P Nix | Private address same as business | P21/N/6<br>***#2988***<br> | **Gerald Patrick NIX**<br>Woodside, Woodland Road<br>Whitby<br>Wirral | Art metalworker |
| R1/35<br>22 October 1896<br>Sent by G Robinson | 124 Coplone Street<br>Birmingham | P5/R/798 and P5/W*sic*//798<br>***#2989,90***<br> | **George ROBINSON**<br>15a Pitsford Street<br>Hockley<br>Birmingham | Silversmith |
| SPB/17<br>1 May 1868 | | P3/R/x3<br>***#2991-3***<br>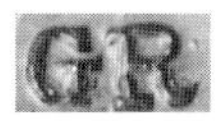 | **George READER**<br>1 Hertford Place<br>Coventry | Watch manufacturer |
| SPB/3 undated<br>no name or address given in SPB | | P3/R/x3<br>***#2994-6***<br> | | |
| LPB/72<br>2 April 1881<br>Sent by<br>E Vaughton | | P3/R/x1<br>***#2997***<br> | **George REED**<br>140 Kingsland High Street<br>London | Jeweller |
| LPB/74<br>20 October 1883<br>No mark in LPB | Third entry on LPB/74 but fifth mark in wrong square-W | P5/W*sic*/x1<br>***#2998***<br> | | |
| R2/180<br>22 November 1913<br>MR3/138<br>Sent by J & R Griffin Ltd | Bank Street<br>Teignmouth | P9/R/108<br>***#2999***<br> | **George ROSSITER**<br>11 Bank Street<br>Teignmouth and<br>15 Victoria Street<br>Paignton and<br>20 Courtenay Street<br>Newton Abbot | Goldsmiths and silversmith |
| R3/22<br>7 May 1924<br>Sent by J & R Griffin Ltd | 21 Fore Street<br>Tiverton | P15/R/32<br>***#3000***<br> | 11 Bank Street<br>Teignmouth and<br>20 Courtenay Street<br>Newton Abbott and<br>21 Fore Street<br>Tiverton | Retail goldsmith and silversmith |
| GTD 1859-68<br>PP1/187<br>GSJW/136<br>J1 1855-75<br>PMR 1851-1871 | Seen on watchcases 1861/2 and 1876/7 | P2/R/x3<br>***#3001-3***<br> | **George ROBERTS**<br>14 Plover Street (1851)<br>50 Stafford Street (1859-62)<br>Hope House, Stanley Street (1868)<br>50 Stafford Street (Shop) (1868)<br>Liverpool | Watchcase maker, watch maker and watch importer |
| | | P2/R/x3<br>***#3004-6***<br> | | |
| | | P2/R/x3<br>***#3007-9***<br> | | |
| R2/5<br>9 November 1905<br>Sent by selves<br>Three sizes | 125 Wills Street<br>Lozells, Birmingham<br>52 Church Street<br>Lozells, Birmingham | P9/XYZ*sic*/142-144<br>***#3010-2***<br>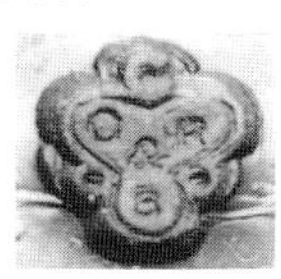 | **George BRYAN**<br>**Ralph BRYAN** trading as<br>**G & R BRYAN**<br>7 Pitsford Street<br>Birmingham | Silversmiths |
| R3/59<br>11 September 1931<br>Sent by Charles Peach & Son Ltd<br>235 Icknield Street<br>Birmingham | 17 South Cliff Avenue<br>Eastbourne<br>Sussex | P15/B/203<br>***#3013***<br> | **George Richard BALDOCK** trading as<br>**G R BALDOCK & CO** *<br>1 Hatton Garden<br>London EC1 | Wholesale jewellers |

| REGISTRATION DETAILS | MAKER'S PRIVATE ADDRESS and DETAILS | PLATE and MARK DETAILS | MAKER/COMPANY and BUSINESS ADDRESS | MAKER'S TRADE |
|---|---|---|---|---|
| PCR-1773<br>MR2/192 | | Not on P1<br>*#3014* **G S?** | **George SMITH**<br>Warrington | Silversmith |
| R3/128<br>15 February 1949<br>Sent by G Scherner<br>Two sizes | 16 Clarendon Crescent<br>Eccles<br>Lancashire | P21/S/42,43<br>*#3015,6*  | **Gladys SCHERNER**<br>No business address entered | Student of metal work |
| Missing register<br>*c.*1889 | Large "&" but plain font!<br>See # 3022 | P5/G/214<br>*#3017*  | **GOODALL & SKELTON**<br>192 Warstone Lane<br>Birmingham | Jewellers |
| R2/15<br>31 March 1906<br>Sent by self | Private address same as business | P9/S/96<br>*#3018*  | **G STACEY**<br>6 Park Street<br>Minehead<br>Somerset | Jeweller, gold and silversmith |
| R1/15<br>5 September 1895<br>Sent by H Griffith & Sons | St Mary's Road [1]<br>Stechford<br>School Road [2]<br>Moseley | P5/S/685<br>*#3019*  | **George SNOOK** [1]<br>**Charles BERKELEY** [2] trading as<br>**George SNOOK & CO**<br>Borough Works<br>Floodgate Street<br>Birmingham | Thimble manufacturers |
| LPB/36 SP32/1<br>30 January 1884<br>No mark in LPB | | SP32/1(Not on P5)<br>*#3020*  | **GARNER & STEVENS**<br>48 Kilverts Building<br>Withy Grove<br>Manchester | Working jewellers |
| Missing register<br>*c.*1886 | Small "&" like mark above | P5/G/51<br>*#3021*  | | |
| R1/52<br>7 October 1897<br>Sent by Goodall & Skelton | 101 Nursery Road [1]<br>Aston<br>95 Brewers Street [2]<br>Aston | P5/G/876<br>*#3022*  | **Edward GOODALL** [1]<br>**William James SKELTON** [2] trading as<br>**GOODALL & SKELTON**<br>192 Warstone Lane<br>Birmingham | Jewellers |
| R3/5<br>6 November 1921<br>Sent by G A Suter | 66 Wilton Road<br>Handsworth<br>Birmingham | P15/S/51<br>*#3023* 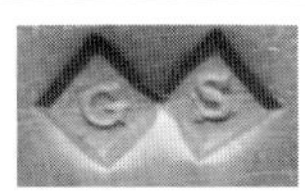 | **George Alfred SUTER**<br>146½ Hockley Hill<br>Birmingham | Jeweller |
| 14 July 1923 | | P15/S/62<br>*#3024* 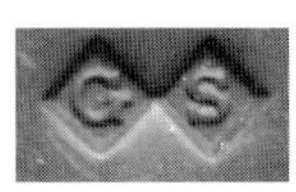 | | |
| R3/96<br>1 February 1940<br>Sent by Walter Hands<br>26 Spencer Street<br>Birmingham | 32 Westminster Road<br>Handsworth | P21/S/8,9<br>*#3025,6*  | **George SUTER**<br>109 Spencer Street<br>Birmingham | |
| R1/143<br>21 February 1901<br>Sent by G Smallwood | Bowyer Road<br>Birmingham | P9/S/39<br>*#3027*  | **George SMALLWOOD**<br>33 St Paul's Square<br>Birmingham | Jeweller and ring maker |
| R2/6<br>18 November 1905<br>Sent by Gopsill & Sanders | Boldmere Road<br>Wyle Road Green (*sic*)<br>(Ed: Wylde Green?)<br>Ravensea<br>Church Lane<br>Handsworth | P9/G/64<br>*#3028*  | **Thomas Frank Lloyd GOPSILL**<br>**Ernest Wilfred SANDERS** trading as<br>**GOPSILL & SANDERS**<br>15 Vyse Street<br>Birmingham | Goldsmiths and jewellers |
| R3/54<br>1 August 1930<br>Sent by T J Skelton | 86 Vyse Street<br>Birmingham | P15/G/55<br>*#3029* 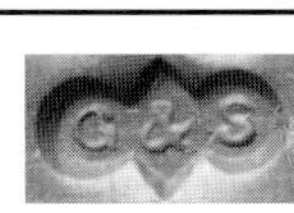 | **GREEN & SON**<br>George Green (Sole Proprietor)<br>75 Meadow Street<br>Preston | Jewellers and watchmakers |

| REGISTRATION DETAILS | MAKER'S PRIVATE ADDRESS and DETAILS | PLATE and MARK DETAILS | MAKER/COMPANY and BUSINESS ADDRESS | MAKER'S TRADE |
|---|---|---|---|---|
| R3/16<br>5 May 1923<br>Sent by G Stockwell | 14 Aldersmead Road<br>New Beckenham<br>Kent | P15/S/61<br>***#3030***<br>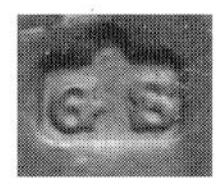 | **George STOCKWELL** trading as<br>**STOCKWELL & CO LTD** *<br>16, 18 Finsbury Street<br>London EC | Continental carriers |
| R2/50<br>15 November 1907<br>Sent by Lancashire Watch Co | Thornham House<br>Manchester Road<br>Southport | P13/B/2<br>***#3031***<br> | **George Stephen BURT**<br>Warrington Road<br>Prescot | Watch manufacturer |
| R2/37<br>13 April 1907<br>Sent by W Neale & Sons | 152 Elsley Road<br>Lavender Hill<br>London SW | P9/G/83<br>***#3032***<br> | **GOLDSMITHS & SILVERSMITHS CO LTD** *<br>James William Rice (Secretary)<br>112 Regent Street<br>London W | Jewellers and silversmiths |
| R3/78<br>26 August 1935<br>Sent by Roberts & Belk Ltd<br>Furnival Works<br>Sheffield | Common seal affixed in the presence of directors and secretary | P15/G/59<br>***#3033***<br>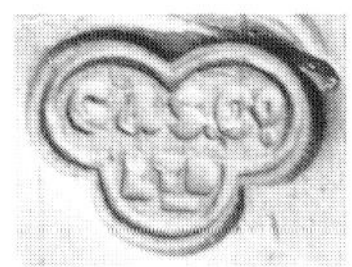 | **GOLDSMITHS & SILVERSMITHS CO LTD** *<br>E G Godwin, John J Hodges (Directors)<br>J W Isaacs (Assistant Secretary)<br>112 Regent Street (Registered Office)<br>London W1 | Goldsmiths, silversmiths and jewellers |
| Missing register<br>*c.*1890<br>Similar mark entered BAO 17 March 1893 | | P5/S/324<br>***#3034***<br> | **George SMITH**<br>24 Merchant's Quay<br>Dublin | Pipe merchant |
| R2/172<br>3 June 1913<br>Sent by G S Elcose | 6 Lucy Street<br>Lower Broughton | P13/E/29<br>***#3035***<br> | **George Stephen ELCOSE**<br>37 Blackfriars Street<br>Manchester | General jeweller |
| Missing register<br>*c.*1892 | | P5/T/415<br>***#3036***<br> | **Unidentified** | |
| R1/51<br>1 October 1897<br>Sent by C H Collins | 16 Mattocks Lane<br>Ealing<br>London W | P5/T/874<br>***#3037***<br> | **George TAYLOR** trading as<br>**George TAYLOR & CO**<br>4 Long Lane<br>London EC | Jewellers |
| R1/12<br>8 June 1895<br>Sent by J Gammage | 47 Sanderson Road [1]<br>Newcastle<br>16 Oxford Street [2]<br>Newcastle | P5/D/666<br>***#3038***<br> | **George DAVISON** [1]<br>**Thomas DAVISON** [2] trading as<br>**George & Thomas DAVISON**<br>80 to 84 Grey Street<br>Newcastle upon Tyne | Watchmakers and jewellers |
| LPB/54<br>31 March 1881 | Trade from 1881 census records | P3/M/x1<br>***#3039***<br> | **George T MYATT**<br>2 Geelong Terrace<br>Birmingham | Gold ring maker |
| SPB/12<br>20 April 1870 | Born Chester *c.*1858 | P3/R/x3<br>***#3040-2***<br> | **George Thomas ROWLANDS**<br>Provident House<br>Watergate Street<br>Chester | Jeweller and silversmith |
| R2/126<br>27 January 1911<br>Sent by E J Rudge | 216 St Paul's Road<br>Birmingham | P13/T/30<br>***#3043***<br>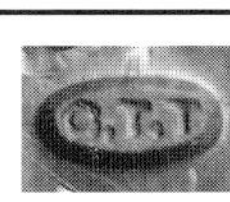 | **George Turner TABBERNER**<br>2 Warstone Parade East<br>Birmingham | Manufacturing jeweller |
| R1/47<br>15 July 1897<br>Sent by G Unite & Sons | 391 Gillott Road<br>Edgbaston<br>Birmingham | P5/V*sic*/855<br>***#3044***<br> | **Harry LYDE** trading as<br>**George UNITE & SONS** *<br>65 Caroline Street<br>Birmingham | Silversmiths and goldsmiths |

| REGISTRATION DETAILS | MAKER'S PRIVATE ADDRESS and DETAILS | PLATE and MARK DETAILS | MAKER/COMPANY and BUSINESS ADDRESS | MAKER'S TRADE |
|---|---|---|---|---|
| R1/70<br>18 October 1898<br>Sent by<br>G Unite & Sons<br>Two sizes | 391 Gillott Road<br>Edgbaston<br>Birmingham | P9/U/1,2<br>***#3045,6***<br> | **Harry LYDE** * trading as<br>**George UNITE** *<br>65 Caroline Street<br>Birmingham | Silversmiths and goldsmiths |
| 18 October 1898 | | P9/U/3<br>***#3047***<br> | | |
| Missing register<br>*c.*1893<br>Similar mark LAO<br>18 September 1903 | | P5/G/518<br>***#3048***<br> | **GOURDEL, VALES & CO** *<br>57 Great Marlborough Street<br>London W | Goldsmiths and silversmiths |
| R1/154<br>5 October 1901<br>Sent by W J Pellow | Eldon Lodge[1]<br>Lee<br>Kent<br>11 Oxford Mansions [2]<br>Oxford Street<br>London<br>33 Algiers Road [3]<br>Ladywall<br>Kent | P9/G/30<br>***#3049***<br> | **Thomas Edward NALTY** [1]<br>**Edward Thomas NALTY** [2]<br>**Herbert NALTY** [3] trading as<br>**GOURDEL, VALES & CO** *<br>57 Great Marlborough Street<br>London and<br>8 Rue Pavillon<br>Paris<br>France | Wholesale jewellers |
| R2/96<br>26 October 1909<br>Sent by W Vale & Sons | 48 St Gabriels Road<br>Cricklewood<br>London NW<br>75 London Lane<br>Bromley, Kent | P13/V/4-9<br>***#3050-5***<br> | **Edward Thomas NALTY** *<br>**Herbert NALTY** *<br>57 Great Marlborough Street<br>London W | |
| R2/146<br>24 October 1911<br>Sent by C Horner Ltd | 48 St Gabriels Road<br>Cricklewood<br>Carlton House<br>London Lane<br>Bromley<br>Kent | P13/V/17<br>***#3056***<br> | **Edward Thomas NALTY**<br>**Herbert NALTY** trading as<br>**GOURDEL, VALES & CO** *<br>57 Great Marlborough Street<br>London | |
| R1/85<br>23 November 1898<br>Sent by Groves Brothers<br>Have authority from A G Griffiths to use their punch | 16 Guthric Street [1]<br>Birmingham<br>123 Carpenters Road [2]<br>Aston<br>Birmingham | P9/G/5,6<br>***#3057,8***<br> | **Thomas E C GROVES** [1]<br>**Arthur Henry GROVES** [2] trading as<br>**GROVES BROTHERS**<br>169 Hockley Hill<br>Birmingham | Jewellers and ring manufacturers |
| Missing register<br>*c.*1889 | | P5/G/264<br>***#3059***<br> | | |
| R2/129<br>1 March 1911<br>Sent by W H Carrington & Co | 5 Eastborough<br>Scarborough | P13/W/87<br>***#3060***<br> | **George WHIRRETT**<br>5,7 Eastborough<br>Scarborough and<br>2 Royal Hotel Shop<br>St Nicholas Street<br>Scarborough | Tobacconist |
| Missing register<br>*c.*1889 | See also G W marks | P5/W/244<br>***#3061***<br> | **Unidentified** | |
| R1/184<br>7 February 1903<br>Sent by G Widmer | 289 Edge Lane<br>Liverpool | P9/W/92<br>***#3062***<br> | **Gabriel WIDMER** *<br>289 Edge Lane and<br>27 Beech Street<br>Liverpool | Watch importer and wholesale jeweller |
| R2/13<br>8 March 1906<br>Sent by J & R Griffin | | P9/V*sic*/140<br>***#3063***<br> | **Gabriel WIDMER** *<br>27 Beech Street<br>Liverpool | Merchant |

| REGISTRATION DETAILS | MAKER'S PRIVATE ADDRESS and DETAILS | PLATE and MARK DETAILS | MAKER/COMPANY and BUSINESS ADDRESS | MAKER'S TRADE |
|---|---|---|---|---|
| R2/162<br>27 September 1912<br>Sent by B Wade | 251 The Rye<br>Peckham SE | P13/W/125<br>***#3064***  | **G WARD**<br>60 Gresham Road<br>London | Tobacconist |
| PDB 1785-1805<br>Variety of plate, rings and buckles<br>MR2/196-203<br>MR3/100-2<br>SIL/39,42,46,50<br>SOT/70-2<br>GMSC/37-43 | George Walker I. Free 1767 admitted to Company 1770, died 1809<br>George Walker II admitted to Company 1794, Free 1799. Practised only as a wine merchant | P1/14/x5<br>***#3065-9*** 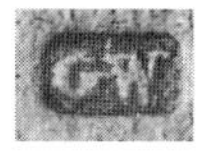<br>P1/26/x1<br>***#3070*** <br>P1/26/x1<br>***#3071***  | **George WALKER I**<br>Eastgate Street<br>Chester | Goldsmith and silversmith |
| MR3/143<br>Similar mark entered SAO 28 May 1846 | J1/379 1840-58 | P2/W/x1<br>***#3072***  | **George WARD**<br>6 Exchange Street<br>Manchester or | Silversmith |
| J1/379 1845-93 | | P2/W/x3<br>***#3073-5***  | **George Lowe WHITEHOUSE**<br>Chester or | Silversmith |
| J1/379 1878 | | P2/W/x2<br>***#3076,7***  | **George Henry WILLIAMS**<br>Chester | Silversmith |
| LPB/12<br>14 July 1883 | | P3/W/x1<br>***#3078***  | **George WING** *<br>66 Winston Road<br>Stoke Newington<br>London | Jeweller |
| Missing register<br>*c.*1888 | See also Walker & White | P5/W/137<br>***#3079***  | **Unidentified** | |
| R1/119<br>20 January 1900<br>Sent by George Watts<br>Three sizes | Private address same as business | P9/W/30, 31, 32<br>***#3080-2***  | **George WATTS** trading as<br>**G WATTS & CO** *<br>10 Meredith Street, Clerkenwell<br>London | Silversmiths and mounters |
| LPB/90<br>12 September 1883<br>Sent by Joseph Jackson | No mark in LPB | P5/W/x1<br>***#3083*** 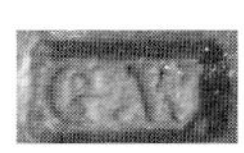 | **George WHITE**<br>Exchange Street<br>Manchester | Umbrella manufacturer |
| Missing register<br>*c.*1889<br>Similar mark entered LAO 20 October 1887 | Absorbed by H Williamson 1902 | P5/B/212<br>***#3084***  | **George William BRADDOCK** *<br>214 Goswell Road<br>London | Silversmith |
| LPB/24<br>1 December 1879<br>No name or address in LPB | GSJW/263 1861 at<br>1 Carver Street<br>Birmingham | P3/D/x3<br>***#3085-7***  | **George William DAWSON**<br>53 Hockley Street<br>Birmingham | Goldsmith and jeweller |
| R1/69<br>13 October 1898<br>Sent by G W Harvey | Private address same as business | P9/H/2<br>***#3088***  | **George William HARVEY**<br>9 Market Street<br>Wellington<br>Salop | Jeweller and watchmaker |
| Missing register<br>*c.*1890 | This and/or the next mark seen on thimbles marked for 1892,97,99,1900,02,05,14,17 | P5/H/324<br>***#3089***  | **G W HARVEY & CO** ?<br>(see next entry) | |

| REGISTRATION DETAILS | MAKER'S PRIVATE ADDRESS and DETAILS | PLATE and MARK DETAILS | MAKER/COMPANY and BUSINESS ADDRESS | MAKER'S TRADE |
|---|---|---|---|---|
| Missing register<br>*c.*1892 | | P5/H/423<br>***#3090***<br>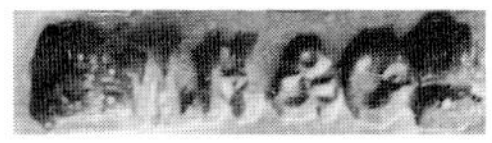 | **G W HARVEY & CO** ?<br>(see next entry) | |
| R1/190<br>3 April 1903<br>Sent by R Parkes | Bracebridge Road<br>Four Oaks | P9/H/50<br>***#3091***<br> | **G W HARVEY & CO**<br>E Tanner (Director?)<br>45 Frederick Street<br>Birmingham | Wholesale jewellers |
| R2/126<br>28 January 1911<br>Sent by R Parkes & Co<br>BAO 17.674 | Elvaston<br>Moseley<br>Elmhurst<br>Solihull | P13/H/69<br>***#3092***<br> | **G W HARVEY & CO**<br>J A Tanner<br>C E Tanner (Senior Partner)<br>48 Frederick Street<br>Birmingham | Manufacturer jeweller |
| R3/13<br>6 December 1922<br>Sent by C Walker-Litherland Ltd | Private address same as business | P15/W/61<br>***#3093***<br> | **George WHITFIELD & CO**<br>Harry Hill (Director)<br>20 Bradshaw Street<br>Manchester | Merchants and agents |
| R1/68<br>14 July 1898<br>Sent by<br>G W Nettleton | Private address same as business | P9/N/964<br>***#3094***<br> | **George William NETTLETON**<br>30 King Cross Street<br>Halifax | Tobacco pipe manufacturer |
| R1/68<br>14 July 1898<br>Sent by<br>W H Carrington | | P5/N/914<br>***#3095***<br> | | Briar pipe manufacturer |
| R2/121<br>27 October 1910<br>Sent by H Tattershall | 26 Hilton Road [1]<br>Leeds | P13/S/60<br>***#3096***<br> | **SINGLETON & COLE LTD**<br>C W Harvey [1] (Manager)<br>11, 16 Camson Street<br>Birmingham and<br>The Square<br>Walsall and<br>Dudley Street<br>Wolverhampton and<br>43 Paradise Street<br>Liverpool and<br>22 Mardel<br>Shrewsbury | Pipe mounters and dealers |
| Not in R3 as expected<br>*c.* November 1921 | | P15/S/52<br>***#3097***<br>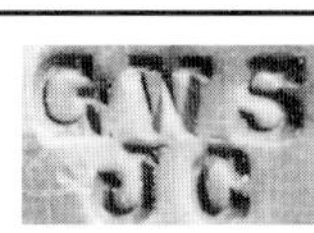 | | |
| R3/17<br>26 July 1923<br>Sent by George Waterson & Son Ltd | | P15/W/69,70<br>***#3098,99***<br>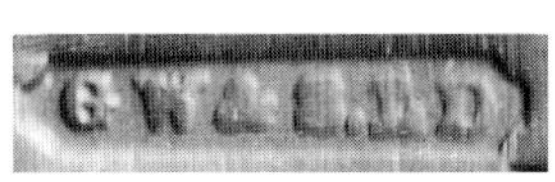 | **George WATERSON & SON LTD**<br>Allan Waterson (Director)<br>Warrington Works<br>Edinburgh and<br>8 St Bride Street<br>London EC | Manufacturing stationers |
| R2/97<br>13 November 1909<br>Sent by Sidney T Oldridge<br>BAO 15.54? | 110 Hallam Street<br>London W | P13/G/14<br>***#3100***<br> | **Sidney Thomas OLDRIDGE** trading as **GREY & CO** *<br>7 Market Place<br>Oxford Street<br>London W | General mounters |
| R2/119<br>4 October 1910<br>BAO 15.540<br>LAO 4172<br>Sent by self | | P13/G/25<br>***#3101***<br> | | Manufacturing silversmiths |

| REGISTRATION DETAILS | MAKER'S PRIVATE ADDRESS and DETAILS | PLATE and MARK DETAILS | MAKER/COMPANY and BUSINESS ADDRESS | MAKER'S TRADE |
|---|---|---|---|---|
| R2/174<br>29 July 1913<br>Sent by Sidney Thomas Oldridge | 110 Hallam Street<br>London W | P15/G/5-7<br>***#3102-4***<br> | **Sidney Thomas OLDRIDGE** trading as<br>**GREY & CO** *<br>7 Market Place<br>Oxford Street<br>London W | Silversmiths |
| R3/6<br>16 January 1922<br>Sent by John W R Middleton | 23 Carburton Street<br>London W1 (both) | P15/G/43<br>***#3105***<br> | **John Richmond MIDDLETON**<br>**John William Richmond MIDDLETON**<br>(Ed: trading as **GREY & CO** * )<br>24½ Upper Charlton Street<br>Great Portland Street<br>London W1 | Manufacturing silversmiths |

| REGISTRATION DETAILS | MAKER'S PRIVATE ADDRESS and DETAILS | PLATE and MARK DETAILS | MAKER/COMPANY and BUSINESS ADDRESS | MAKER'S TRADE |
|---|---|---|---|---|
| R1/14<br>24 July 1895<br>Sent by C Horner | Stony Lane<br>Moseley | P5/A/677<br>***#3106***<br> | **Harry ALLDAY** trading as<br>**HORTON & ALLDAY** *<br>195,196 Warstone Lane<br>Birmingham | Chain manufacturers |
| R3/117<br>29 April 1947<br>Sent by H Ackers | Private address same as business | P21/A/4<br>***#3107***<br> | **Harry ACKERS**<br>192 West Park Drive<br>Blackpool | Student at Manchester School of Art |
| 24 May 1949<br>Two sizes | | P21/A/8,9<br>***#3108,9***<br>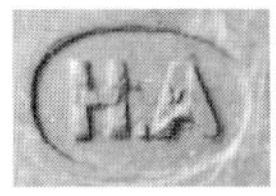 | | |
| R2/100<br>23 December 1909<br>Sent by H Arkinstall | 3 Chester Road<br>Nr Sutton<br>1 Bayswater Road<br>Birmingham | P13/A/21<br>***#3110***<br>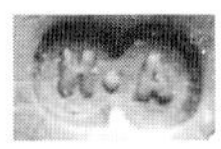 | **Herbert ARKINSTALL**<br>**Walter Discombe WALTON** trading as<br>**H ARKINSTALL**<br>7 St George's Place<br>Birmingham | Jewellers |
| PDB 1805-33<br>MR3/75<br>PP1/187<br>GTD 1800-25 | Gold rings, medals, spoons, snuff box | P1/9/x2<br>***#3111,2***<br> | **Hugh ADAMSON**<br>Ray Street<br>Liverpool | Watchcase maker, gold and silversmith |
| | | P1/29/x2<br>***#3113,4***<br> | | |
| | | P1/30/x2<br>***#3115,6***<br> | | |
| | | P1/32/x1<br>***#3117***<br> | | |
| LPB/12<br>16 February 1880 | | P3/A/x3<br>***#3118-20***<br> | **Henry Hyde ASTON** *<br>12 Regent Place<br>Birmingham | Gold wedding and keeper ring manufacturer |
| | Seen on 1806 watchcase | P1/28/x2<br>***#3121,2***<br> | **Hugh ADAMSON**<br>Ray Street<br>Liverpool | Watchcase maker, gold and silversmith |
| R3/76<br>6 June 1935<br>Sent by Atkin Brothers | Common seal of company affixed in the presence of director and secretary | P15/A/53<br>***#3123***<br> | **ATKIN BROTHERS (SILVERSMITHS) LTD** *<br>Harry Atkin (Director)<br>Harold J Atkin (Secretary)<br>Truro Works (Registered Office)<br>Sheffield | Manufacturers of silver goods |
| Missing register<br>*c.*1891 | | P5/A/393<br>***#3124***<br> | **Unidentified** | |
| R2/81<br>8 May 1909<br>Sent by H Aston Ltd<br>BAO 13.695 | Merelands [1]<br>Trinity Road<br>Handsworth<br>Birmingham | P13/A/11<br>***#3125***<br> | **H ASTON LTD**<br>F Powell [1] (Managing Director)<br>1 Regent Street<br>Birmingham | Gold wedding ring makers |
| LPB/38<br>6 February 1882<br>LPB mark shown | | Not on P3<br>***#3126***<br> | **HORTON & ALLDAY** *<br>195 Warstone Lane<br>Birmingham | Manufacturing silversmiths |
| LPB/40<br>2 August 1883<br>No mark in LPB | | P5/H/x1<br>***#3127***<br> | | |

| REGISTRATION DETAILS | MAKER'S PRIVATE ADDRESS and DETAILS | PLATE and MARK DETAILS | MAKER/COMPANY and BUSINESS ADDRESS | MAKER'S TRADE |
|---|---|---|---|---|
| R1/4<br>16 November 1894<br>Sent by Villiers & Jackson | Birch Lane<br>Moseley | P5/H/622<br>*#3128*  | **Harry ALLDAY** trading as<br>**HORTON & ALLDAY** *<br>195 Warstone Lane<br>Birmingham | Silversmiths |
| R2/24<br>18 September 1906<br>Sent by selves<br>Two sizes | Meadsfoot<br>Four Oaks<br>Warwickshire | P9/H/82,83<br>*#3129,30*  | **Harry ALLDAY** trading as<br>**HORTON & ALLDAY** *<br>195 Warstone Lane<br>Birmingham and<br>47 Poland Street<br>London W | |
| LPB/14<br>20 July 1885 | 9th name on LPB/14 best matches this 10th mark on P5/A | P5/A/x1<br>*#3131*  | **Henry ALLEN** *<br>9 Tenby Street<br>Birmingham | Gold signet, gem and fancy ring maker |
| R2/84<br>26 May 1909<br>Sent by Henry Allen<br>BAO 3.388 | 126 Greenfield Road<br>Harborne | P13/A/13<br>*#3132*  | | Jeweller |
| R2/22<br>31 July 1906<br>Sent by Benson Brothers | Private address same as business | P9/A/79<br>*#3133*  | **Henry Alfred ASTELL**<br>20 Trinity Road<br>Birchfield<br>Birmingham | Watch factor |
| R3/97<br>17 April 1940<br>Sent by H A Daulby<br>Two sizes | 27 Totland Grove<br>Newton Park<br>Chester | P21/D/4,5<br>*#3134,5*  | **Helen Audrey DAULBY**<br>City School of Art<br>Liverpool | Art student |
| R3/137<br>20 March 1952<br>Sent by H A Dodd<br>Two sizes | Private address same as business | P21/D/20,21<br>*#3136,7*  | **Hilda Almond DODD**<br>4 The Crescent<br>Chorley<br>Lancashire | Craftworker |
| R3/26<br>6 February 1925<br>Sent by H A Mason | Private address same as business | P15/M/64<br>*#3138*  | **Howard Arthur MASON**<br>164 High Street<br>Smethwick<br>Staffordshire | Manufacturing jeweller |
| Missing register<br>*c.*1886<br>Mark with pellet<br>BAO 8 June 1883 | | P5/A/55<br>*#3139*  | **Henry ALLDAY & SON** *<br>130 Warstone Lane<br>Birmingham | Chain manufacturers |
| LPB/82 SP24/1<br>10 August 1884<br>No mark in LPB | | P5/T/x1<br>*#3140*  | **Henry Alfred TAYSON**<br>169 Hockley Hill<br>Birmingham | Jeweller |
| R2/147<br>23 November 1911<br>Sent by Harold A Underwood | 128 Pershore Road<br>Edgbaston<br>Birmingham | P13/U/6<br>*#3141*  | **Harold Archer UNDERWOOD**<br>217a Brearley Street, Hockley<br>Birmingham | Manufacturing jeweller |
| R3/162<br>25 June 1957<br>Sent by H A Walsh | 97 Duchy Drive<br>Bradford 9<br>Yorkshire | P21/W/87<br>*#3142*  | **Harold Augustus WALSH**<br>No business address entered | Craft teacher |
| R3/165<br>26 0ctober 1958<br>Sent by W J Pellow Ltd, 31 Vyse Street<br>Birmingham 18 | | P21/H/78<br>*#3143*  | **HILL BROTHERS (WHOLESALE) LTD**<br>37 Renfrew Lane<br>Glasgow C2 | Wholesale jewellers |
| R2/152<br>20 March 1912<br>Sent by E L Merle | Private address same as business | P13/B/129<br>*#3144* 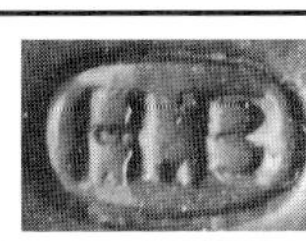 | **Henry BEAL**<br>93 Forest Road<br>Walthamstow | Briar pipe manufacturer |

| REGISTRATION DETAILS | MAKER'S PRIVATE ADDRESS and DETAILS | PLATE and MARK DETAILS | MAKER/COMPANY and BUSINESS ADDRESS | MAKER'S TRADE |
|---|---|---|---|---|
| No entry in R1.<br>Between 12 March 1901 and 9 July 1901.<br>Has similar frame to P9/B/37[7]. | | P9/B/37<br>***#3145***<br> | **Edwin Collier HARWOOD**<br>**Thomas HARWOOD** trading as<br>**HARWOOD BROTHERS**<br>2 Old Post Office Place<br>Liverpool | Tobacconists and fancy goods dealers |
| R2/233<br>21 September 1920<br>Clerk should have struck 64!<br>Sent by T C Nixon | Private address same as business | P15/H/44<br>***#3146***<br> | **HIRST BROTHERS & CO LTD**<br>T C Nixon<br>57 Roscoe Street<br>Oldham | Wholesale manufacturing jewellers |
| R1/10<br>28 April 1895<br>Sent by Stainton Brothers | Thornhill Road<br>Handsworth<br>Linwood Road<br>Handsworth | P5/H/653<br>***#3147***<br>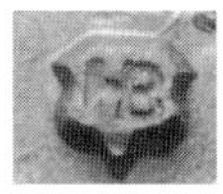 | **William HAYES** and **Harry HAYES**<br>trading as **HAYES BROTHERS** *<br>73 Great Hampton Street<br>Birmingham | Silversmiths |
| Similar mark entered LAO 13 November 1852 | | P2/B/x5<br>***#3148-52***<br> | **Henry BAMFORD** *<br>18 Myddelton Street, Clerkenwell<br>London | Watchcase maker |
| Missing register<br>*c.*1887 | See other H B marks | P5/B/105<br>***#3153***<br> | **Unidentified** | |
| LPB/92<br>10 September 1882 | | P3/H/x2<br>***#3154,5***<br> | **HARDY BROTHERS** *<br>19 Charterhouse Street<br>Holborn Circus<br>London | Exporters of jewellery, watches and electroplate |
| SPB/16<br>18 October 1874 | | P3/B/x3<br>***#3156-8***<br> | **Henry BUTTERWORTH**<br>Town Hall Buildings<br>7 Yorkshire Street<br>Rochdale, Lancashire | Watchmaker and jeweller |
| R1/189<br>25 March 1903<br>Sent by T C Smith | Hawthorns<br>Oakland Road<br>Moseley | P9/B/102<br>***#3159***<br> | **Herbert BUSHELL**<br>32 Northampton Street<br>Birmingham | Manufacturing jeweller |
| R1/197<br>7 July 1903<br>Sent by H J Batson | Lyndale<br>Platts Road<br>Rosslyn<br>Keefes Road<br>Cricklewood<br>London NW | P9/B/108<br>***#3160***<br> | **Henry John BATSON**<br>**Albert Edward BATSON** trading as<br>**J BATSON & SON** *<br>42/43 Brewer Street<br>London W | Silversmiths |
| R2/166<br>22 November 1912<br>Sent by H Bushell | 31 Wycliffe Road<br>Handsworth<br>Birmingham | P13/B/135<br>***#3161***<br> | **Harold Bushell** trading as<br>**H BUSHELL & CO**<br>Laurel Works<br>Farm Street and<br>38, 40 Tenby Street North<br>Birmingham | Silver and electroplate manufacturing |
| R1/236<br>10 July 1905<br>Sent by<br>F Goldsmith & Co | 61 Union Street West<br>Oldham | P9/H/71,72<br>***#3162,3***<br> | **HIRST BROTHERS & CO LTD**<br>Alfred Hirst (Managing Director)<br>Roscoe Street<br>Oldham | Jewellers |
| R1/237<br>19 July 1905<br>Sent by James Harrison | 208 Waterloo Street<br>Oldham | P9/H/73<br>***#3164***<br> | details as above<br>Charles Adams (Secretary)<br>Roscoe Street<br>Oldham and<br>26 Withy Grove<br>Manchester | Wholesale jewellers |

| REGISTRATION DETAILS | MAKER'S PRIVATE ADDRESS and DETAILS | PLATE and MARK DETAILS | MAKER/COMPANY and BUSINESS ADDRESS | MAKER'S TRADE |
|---|---|---|---|---|
| R2/37<br>16 April 1907<br>Sent by Alfred Hirst | 61 Union Street W<br>Oldham | P9/H/92<br>***#3165***<br> | **HIRST BROTHERS & CO LTD**<br>Alfred Hirst (Director)<br>Roscoe Street<br>Oldham | Wholesale and manufacturing jewellers |
| 22 January 1915 one old punch cancelled | | P15/H/22<br>***#3166***<br> | | |
| 4 December 1919 | | P15/H/53-55<br>***#3167-9***<br> | | |
| R1/163<br>8 March 1902<br>Sent by Harwood Brothers | Both private addresses<br>105 Manor Road<br>Liscard | P9/H/38[7]*sic*<br>***#3170***<br> | **Edwin Collier HARWOOD**<br>**Thomas HARWOOD**<br>trading as **HARWOOD BROTHERS**<br>2 Old Post Office Place<br>Liverpool | Tobacconists and fancy goods dealers |
| R1/162<br>28 February 1902<br>Sent by A H Tongue<br>cancelled<br>13 October 1911 | Clifton Villa<br>Manse Road<br>Blackpool | P9/H/37[7]*sic*<br>***#3171***<br> | | Importers of tobacconist goods |
| R1/161<br>11 February 1902<br>Sent by C Horner | 208 Waterloo Road<br>Oldham | P9/H/49<br>***#3172***<br> | **HIRST BROTHERS & CO LTD**<br>Charles Adams (Director and Secretary)<br>8 Curzon Street<br>Oldham | Wholesale jewellers |
| R3/20<br>12 December 1923<br>Sent by C Horner Ltd | Hairstrup<br>Shepherd Hill<br>17 Ilfracombe Avenue<br>Southend-on-Sea<br><br>See also #3175 below | P15/H/76<br>***#3173***<br> | **HARDY BROTHERS** *<br>S H Hardy (Director)<br>J P Petterton (Secretary)<br>32 Old Burlington Street<br>London | Jewellers and silversmiths |
| R1/188<br>24 March 1903<br>Sent by N Haseler | 199 Holly Road<br>Handsworth<br>118 Thornhill Road<br>Birmingham | P9/H/49[7]*sic*<br>***#3174***<br> | **Noble HASELER** *<br>**Edward John HASELER** *<br>53 Branston Street<br>Birmingham | Manufacturing jewellers |
| R2/114<br>1 July 1910<br>Sent by Stokes & Ireland Ltd<br>Two sizes | Cholmoley Lodge<br>Highgate<br>29 Talbot Road<br>Highgate<br>London<br>Also in Sydney and Brisbane Australia | P13/H/55-60<br>***#3175-80***<br> | **HARDY BROTHERS LTD** *<br>Samuel Hardy (Director)<br>Samuel Houston Hardy (Director)<br>left 19 Charterhouse Street and<br>17, 18 West Smithfield<br>London E | Jewellers and silversmiths |
| R3/18<br>30 August 1923<br>Sent by Stokes & Ireland | Devonia<br>Baring Road<br>Cowes | P15/B/168<br>***#3181***<br> | **Herbert S BENZIE** *<br>61 High Street<br>Cowes<br>Isle of Wight | Jeweller and silversmith |
| R2/124<br>18 November 1910<br>BAO 18.441<br>18.442<br>Sent by Roland Bushell | Both at<br>Hambleton<br>Upper Colwall<br>Malvern | P13/B/91,92<br>***#3182,3***<br> | **Herbert BUSHELL & SON LTD**<br>Herbert Bushell (Managing Director)<br>Roland Bushell (Director)<br>32 Northampton Street<br>Birmingham | Manufacturing jewellers |
| Missing register<br>*c.*1887<br>Similar mark BAO<br>27 November 1883 | see also *#3174* | P5/H/72<br>***#3184***<br> | **HASELER BROTHERS** *<br>Harlington Buildings<br>53 Branston Street<br>Birmingham | Silversmiths and electroplate manufacturers |

| REGISTRATION DETAILS | MAKER'S PRIVATE ADDRESS and DETAILS | PLATE and MARK DETAILS | MAKER/COMPANY and BUSINESS ADDRESS | MAKER'S TRADE |
|---|---|---|---|---|
| LPB/38<br>26 March 1881<br>Sent by E Whitacker | | P3/H/x3<br>***#3185-7***  | **HARDING BROTHERS**<br>10 Augusta Street<br>Birmingham | Silversmiths |
| Missing register<br>*c.*1890 | | P5/H/301<br>***#3188***  | | |
| LPB/40<br>26 March 1884<br>No mark in LPB just HB. | 14th mark on P5 and 14th name on LPB page 40 | P5/H/x1<br>***#3189***  | | |
| LPB/40<br>9 November 1883<br>No mark by name | 5th mark on P5 and 5th name in LPB/40. Note this address used by W H Haseler so may be link to Haseler Brothers | P5/H/x1<br>***#3190***  | **John HORTON**<br>**James HORTON** trading as<br>**HORTON BROTHERS**<br>12 Richard Street<br>Birmingham | Jewellers |
| Missing register<br>*c.*1886 | See other HB marks | P5/H/44<br>***#3191*** 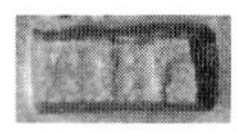 | **Unidentified** | |
| R2/159<br>12 July 1912<br>Sent by<br>Roland Bushell<br>Two sizes<br><br>Roman font one size | Hambleton<br>Upper Colwall<br>Malvern | P15/B/7-25<br>***#3192-3210***  | **Herbert BUSHELL & SON LTD**<br>Roland Bushell (Director)<br>32 Northampton Street<br>Birmingham | Manufacturing gold and silversmiths |
| | | P15/B/1-6<br>***#3211-6***  | | |
| Not in R2 as expected<br>*c.* December 1915 | | P15/H/27<br>***#3217***  | **HIRST BROTHERS & CO LTD**<br>8 Curzon Street<br>Oldham | Wholesale jewellers |
| R3/143<br>23 April 1953<br>Sent by H G Crook | 7 Sandringham Drive<br>Wallasey<br>Cheshire | P21/C/60<br>***#3218***  | **Harold George CROOK**<br>No business address entered | Student |
| R2/207<br>30 August 1916<br>Sent by H Camrass | Private address same as business | P15/C/66<br>***#3219***  | **H CAMRASS**<br>29 South Portland Street<br>Glasgow | Manufacturing jeweller |
| R2/226<br>14 January 1920<br>Sent by Henry Clark | Both at<br>110 Grant Avenue<br>Sefton Park<br>Liverpool | P15/C/76<br>***#3220*** 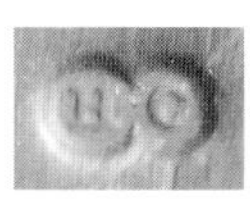 | **Henry CLARK**<br>**William CLARK**<br>112 Allerton Road, Mossley Hill<br>Liverpool | Manufacturing jewellers |
| SPB/4<br>3 March 1876 | | P3/C/x2<br>***#3221,2***  | **HUTCHENSE & COOPER**<br>54 Duke Street<br>Liverpool | Trade not identified |
| PDB 1828-39<br>MR3/79<br>J1 1831-42 | Medals and toiletry wares<br><br>Square marked 1785 | P1/21/x2<br>***#3223,4***  | **Henry CLOSE**<br>Liverpool | Silversmith |
| LPB/22<br>29 September1883<br>No mark in LPB – just HC written | | P5/C/x1<br>***#3225***  | **Henry CHADWICK** *<br>49a Islington<br>Liverpool | Watchcase maker |
| R3/137<br>8 March 1952<br>Sent by H C Abbott<br>Two sizes | Private address same as business | P21/A/14,15<br>***#3226,7***  | **Henry Charles ABBOTT**<br>130 Stuart Road<br>Crosby<br>Liverpool 23 | Artist craftsman and silversmith |

| REGISTRATION DETAILS | MAKER'S PRIVATE ADDRESS and DETAILS | PLATE and MARK DETAILS | MAKER/COMPANY and BUSINESS ADDRESS | MAKER'S TRADE |
|---|---|---|---|---|
| R2/31<br>12 January 1907<br>Sent by H Banks | Ashcroft, Kinston Road<br>Olton<br>Bryman, Westfield Road<br>Acocks Green | P9/*Osic*/183,184<br>***#3228,9***<br> | **Harry BANKS**<br>**Charles BANKS**<br>41 Northampton Street<br>Birmingham | Manufacturing jewellers |
| R3/36<br>29 November 1927<br>Sent by H & C Banks | Ashcroft<br>Kinela Road, Alton<br>Mascot<br>St Bernards Road<br>Alton | P15/B/72,73<br>***#3230,1***<br> | **Harry BANKS**<br>**Charles BANKS** trading as<br>**H & C BANKS**<br>41 Northampton Street<br>Birmingham | |
| LPB/20<br>20 May 1881 | | P3/C/x1<br>***#3232***<br> | **Harry CLARKE & CO**<br>35 Northampton Street<br>Birmingham | Jeweller |
| R2/185<br>26 March 1914<br>BAO 18.757 Sent by H Clifford Davis | Elsinore<br>Barnt Green<br>Birmingham | P15/D/20<br>***#3233***<br> | **Henry Clifford DAVIS**<br>Harford Street<br>Birmingham | Manufacturing silversmiths |
| R3/67<br>9 July 1933<br>Sent by H C Davis | Common seal of company affixed in the presence of Director | P15/D/86<br>***#3234***<br> | **H Clifford DAVIS LTD**<br>H Clifford Davis ( Managing Director)<br>23 Warstone Lane<br>Birmingham 18 | |
| R3/142<br>11 March 1953<br>Sent by H C Davis Ltd | | P21/D/26,27<br>***#3235,6***<br> | **H Clifford DAVIS LTD**<br>23 Warstone Lane<br>Birmingham 18 | |
| R2/109<br>28 April 1910<br>Sent by H Clifford Davis | Elsinore<br>Barnt Green<br>Birmingham | P13/D/30<br>***#3237***<br> | **H Clifford DAVIS**<br>121 Vyse Street<br>Birmingham | |
| R2/180<br>22 November 1913<br>Sent by L Selwyn Davis | | P15/D/9<br>***#3238***<br> | **H Clifford DAVIS**<br>Harford Street<br>Birmingham | |
| R3/136<br>18 October 1960<br>Sent by Smith, Ewen & Stylic Ltd | Sealed in the presence of director and secretary | P21/F/33<br>***#3239***<br> | **H C FREEMAN LTD** *<br>Harry W E Richards (Director)<br>C H Phillips (Secretary)<br>31 Hatton Garden<br>London EC1 | Wholesale jewellers |
| Missing register<br>*c.*1888<br>Similar marks LAO 10 August 1894 | see also next entry | P5/F/152a<br>***#3240***<br> | **Henry Charles FREEMAN** *<br>31 Hatton Garden<br>London EC | Silversmith |
| R1/49<br>31 May 1894<br>Annotated *532 Old Number* Sent by Charles Horner ES Barnsley & Co | 67 Water Lane<br>Brixton<br>London SW | P5/F/532a<br>***#3241***<br> | **Henry Charles FREEMAN** *<br>31 Hatton Garden<br>London | |
| Missing register<br>*c.*1886 | | P5/F/30<br>***#3242***<br> | | |
| Missing register<br>*c.*1888 | | P5/F/152b<br>***#3243***<br> | | |
| Missing register<br>*c.*1894 | | P5/F/532b<br>***#3244***<br> | | |

| REGISTRATION DETAILS | MAKER'S PRIVATE ADDRESS and DETAILS | PLATE and MARK DETAILS | MAKER/COMPANY and BUSINESS ADDRESS | MAKER'S TRADE |
|---|---|---|---|---|
| R1/16<br>20 September 1895<br>Sent by Lucas Brothers Ltd | 67 Water Lane<br>Brixton<br>London SW | P5/F/688<br>*#3245*  | **Henry Charles FREEMAN** *<br>31 Hatton Garden<br>London | Silversmith |
| R3/136<br>8 February 1952<br>Sent by Smith, Ewen & Stylic Ltd | | P21/F/16<br>*#3246*  | **H C FREEMAN LTD** *<br>Harry W E Richards (Director)<br>C H Phillips (Secretary)<br>31 Hatton Garden<br>London EC1 | Wholesale jewellers |
| R3/77<br>5 July 1935<br>Sent by H C Lowe<br>Ground off 5.9.1958 – deceased | Private address same as business | P15/L/44<br>*#3247*  | **Hugh Cawley LOWE**<br>51 Green Lane<br>Vicars Cross<br>Chester | Goldsmith |
| R1/63<br>10 March 1898<br>Sent by H Perkins<br>G Peters<br>A J Cole | 7 Deptford Bridge Street [1]<br>Gordan Villa, Jersey Road [2]<br>23 Albert Mansions [3]<br>South Lambeth Road<br>London | P5/Z*sic*/941<br>*#3248*  | **Arthur John McCONNELL** [1]<br>**Charles Benjamin HALL** [2]<br>**Andrew James GRAY** [3] trading as<br>**HARRINGTON & CO**<br>34 Wilson Street<br>Islington<br>London | Importers of tobacconists fancy goods |
| R1/103<br>3 June 1899<br>Sent by A H Tongue | 140 Courthill Road [1]<br>Lewisham<br>23 Albert Mansions [2]<br>South Lambeth Road<br>London SE<br>7 Deptford Bridge Street [3]<br>London SE | P9/H/15<br>*#3249*  | **Charles Benjamin HALL** [1]<br>**Andrew James GRAY** [2]<br>**Arthur John McCONNELL** [3] trading as<br>**HARRINGTON & CO**<br>34 and 34a Wilson Street<br>Islington<br>London | |
| R1/39<br>10 February 1897<br>Sent by Louis Houel per H Ferguson | 1 Wembury Street<br>Harpurhey | P5/Z*sic*/814<br>*#3250*  | **Louis Houel** trading as<br>**HOUEL & CO**<br>13 Sugar Lane<br>Manchester | Umbrella and walking stick manufacturers |
| R2/73<br>4 March 1909<br>Sent by Walter Davies<br>Three sizes | 32 Hamilton Road<br>Ealing<br>8 Old Court House Street<br>Calcutta | P13/H/11-32<br>*#3251-72* 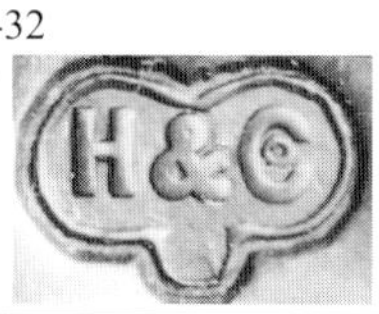 | **Walter DAVIES**<br>**William SMITH** trading as<br>**HAMILTON & CO** *<br>16 Eastcheap<br>London | Jewellers and silversmiths |
| R2/82<br>14 May 1909<br>BAO 16.249,250 251, 252 Sent by Walter Davies | | P13/H/33-36<br>*#3273-6*  | | |
| R2/185<br>17 March 1914<br>Sent by Remfrey Davies & Co<br>Two sizes | Downhurst<br>Ealing<br>London W<br>8 Old Court House Street<br>Calcutta | P15/H/7-18<br>*#3277-88* 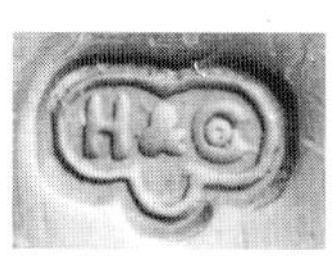 | **Walter DAVIES William SMITH**<br>**John MacLAREN** trading as<br>**HAMILTON & CO** *<br>16 Eastcheap<br>London and<br>Calcutta, Delhi and Simla<br>India | |
| Mark only on SPB/3 – no name, date or address SPB/3 suggests 1864<br>J1/380 1842 but no address listed | Very tentative attribution<br><br>See also Harman & Co, Hargreaves & Co and SH for Samuel Hayne | P3/H/x3<br>*#3289-91*  | **HAYNE & CO** *<br>**Samuel Holditch Thomas HAYNE**<br>**Dudley Frank CATER** trading as<br>**HAYNE & CO** (1836-48) then<br>**Samuel HAYNE & CO** * (from 1864)<br>16 Red Lion Street<br>London | Manufacturing silversmiths |

| REGISTRATION DETAILS | MAKER'S PRIVATE ADDRESS and DETAILS | PLATE and MARK DETAILS | MAKER/COMPANY and BUSINESS ADDRESS | MAKER'S TRADE |
|---|---|---|---|---|
| SPB/23<br>No date, name or address in SPB<br>*c.* January 1869 | See comments above | P3/M*sic*/x3<br>***#3292-4***  | See previous entry | See previous entry |
| R1/29<br>2 June 1896<br>Sent by W Walker<br>H Perkins<br>E J Oakley | Edmond House [1]<br>Hinsbury, Rochester<br>91 Hythe Street [2]<br>Dartford, Kent<br>31 Margarets Bank [3]<br>Rochester | P5/Q*sic*/770<br>***#3295***<br> | **Charles Benjamin HALL** [1]<br>**Arthur John McCONNELL** [2]<br>**Charles George BROGDEN** [3] trading as<br>**HARRINGTON & CO**<br>34 Wilson Street<br>Islington<br>London | Importers of tobacconist fancy goods |
| LPB/84<br>3 October 1882 | | P3/H/x1<br>***#3296***  | **HARMAN & CO**<br>121 Vyse Street<br>Birmingham | Manufacturing jewellers |
| R3/27<br>18 March 1925<br>Sent by J & R Griffin Ltd | 37 Cleveley Road<br>London NW<br>16 Upper Phillmore Gardens<br>London W8 | P15/H/87<br>***#3297***  | **Harry Lewis HAYMAN**<br>**Harold Lachman HAYMAN** trading as<br>**HAYMAN & CO** *<br>3 Coleman Street<br>London E | Export merchants |
| R2/86<br>29 June 1909<br>Sent by T Hale | 391 Oxford Street<br>London<br>Long Market Street<br>Cape Town | P13/H/38<br>***#3298***  | **Henry** and **Charles HIGHMAN** trading as<br>**HIGHMAN & CO**<br>391 Oxford Street<br>London | Wholesale jewellers |
| Not in R1 as expected<br>*c.*1899 | See other H&Co | P9/H/20<br>***#3299***  | **Unidentified** | |
| R2/237<br>27 January 1921<br>Sent by Remfrey Davies & Co<br>Two sizes | 9 Muswell Avenue<br>Muswell Hill<br>London<br>8 Old Court House Street<br>Calcutta | P15/H/46–65<br>***#3300-19***  | **William SMITH**<br>**John Frank SMITH**<br>**Ernest Fenton LAWSON**<br>**Charles Harry PRATT** trading as<br>**HAMILTON & CO LTD** *<br>16 Eastcheap<br>London and<br>Calcutta, Delhi and Simla, India | Jewellers and silversmiths |
| Not in R3 as expected - between October 1926 and September 1927<br>Five sizes | | P15/I*sic*/94–101<br>***#3320-7*** 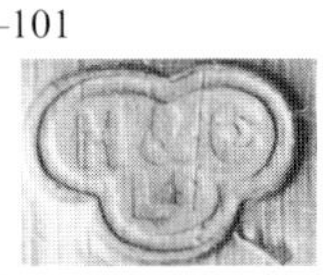 | | |
| LPB/76<br>26 November 1880 | See also JS&Co | P3/S/x2<br>***#3328,9***  | **Henry Charles SPIERS**<br>40 Warstone Lane<br>Birmingham | Gold chain manufacturers |
| R2/118<br>27 September 1910<br>Sent by Nicholas & Foye | Chiddingfold<br>Surrey | P13/C/79<br>***#3330***  | **Henry COOPER James COOPER**<br>**John COOPER** (partners) trading as<br>**Henry COOPER & SONS** *<br>Chiddingfold<br>Surrey | Walking stick manufacturers |
| Missing register<br>*c.*1887<br>Cameo HCW mark<br>LAO 2 March 1859 | In business to 20th century | P5/W/69<br>***#3331***  | **Henry Charles WALES** trading as<br>**WALES & McCULLOCH** *<br>56 Cheapside<br>London | Watch manufacturers, jewellers and silversmiths |
| R1/211<br>30 March 1904<br>Sent by Cristford & Norris Ltd | 42 Sandown Road<br>Birmingham<br>Somerset Road<br>Handsworth | P9/D*sic*/204-207<br>***#3332-5***  | **Harold CRISTFORD**<br>**William NORRIS** trading as<br>**CRISTFORD & NORRIS LTD**<br>118 Vyse Street<br>Birmingham | Manufacturing silversmiths |

| REGISTRATION DETAILS | MAKER'S PRIVATE ADDRESS and DETAILS | PLATE and MARK DETAILS | MAKER/COMPANY and BUSINESS ADDRESS | MAKER'S TRADE |
|---|---|---|---|---|
| R3/171<br>12 February 1960 | | P21/D/29<br>***#3336*** 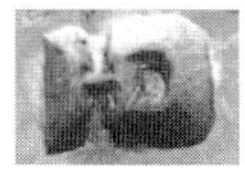 | **THE DAVID MANUFACTURING CO LTD**<br>16/17 Northampton Street<br>Birmingham 18 and | Manufacturing jewellers |
| 22 April 1961 | | P21/D/34<br>***#3337***  | 104 Vyse Street (Registered Office)<br>Birmingham 18 | |
| LPB/26 SP25/2<br>12 September 1883<br>No mark in LPB<br>Ist name in LPB/26 and 2nd mark on P5 | Garner & Stevens, working jewellers, at this address in 1885.<br>Wm H Diggles listed as ale-house owner in 1885. | P5/D/x1<br>***#3338*** 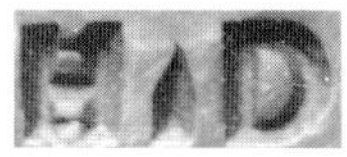 | **William H DIGGLES**<br>48 Kilverts Buildings<br>Manchester | Working jeweller? |
| LPB/26 SP25/1<br>12 September 1883<br>No mark in LPB | 1st name in LPB/26 and 1st mark on P5 | P5/D/x1<br>***#3339***  | | |
| R2/12<br>3 March 1906<br>Sent by J & R Griffin | 6 Crediton Road<br>West Hampstead<br>London NW | P9/D/52<br>***#3340***  | **Henry DOBB LTD**<br>R Rendell Dobb<br>5-17 Westbourne Grove<br>London W | Silversmiths and drapers |
| R3/107<br>12 January 1945<br>Sent by Harold David Stewart | 152 Wolverhampton Road<br>Warley<br>Birmingham | P21/S/16<br>***#3341***  | **Harold David STEWART**<br>22 Vyse Street<br>Hockley<br>Birmingham 18 | Toolmaker and die-sinker |
| R1/193<br>13 May 1903<br>Sent by H Emmanuel | 36 Beaufort Road<br>Edgbaston | P9/E/12b<br>***#3342*** 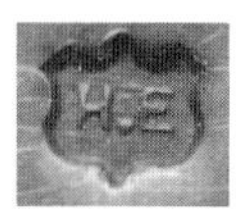 | **Harry EMMANUEL**<br>10a Arthur Place<br>Summer Hill<br>3 Pitsford Street later (undated)<br>Vyse Street<br>Birmingham | Silversmith |
| R3/164<br>9 May 1958<br>Sent by H Eakers | 65 Moscow Drive<br>Liverpool 14 2 May 1962<br>29 Malvern Avenue<br>Bowring Park<br>Liverpool 14 | P21/E/11<br>***#3343*** 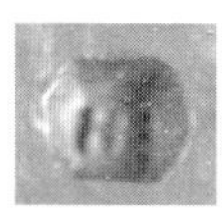 | **Harry EAKERS**<br>c/o A Hill Room 14<br>6 Wood Street<br>Liverpool | Practical jeweller |
| Missing register<br>*c.*1890 | | P5/H/307<br>***#3344***  | **Unidentified** | |
| Missing register<br>*c.*1893 | | P5/H/526<br>***#3345***  | **Unidentified** | |
| R2/22<br>31 July 1906<br>MR3/116<br>Sent by Barker Brothers<br>Three sizes | Tudor Hill<br>Sutton Coldfield<br>Tudor Hill<br>Sutton Coldfield<br>Weybridge<br>Surrey | P9/XYZ*sic*/174-176<br>***#3346-8***  | **Herbert Edward BARKER**<br>**Frank Ernest BARKER**<br>**Frederick WALLIS** trading as<br>**BARKER BROTHERS** *<br>Constitution Hill<br>Birmingham and<br>292 High Holborn<br>London | Silversmiths |
| Not in R2 as expected - between 21 May 1913 and 15 May 1914 | | P15/B/47<br>***#3349***  | | |

| REGISTRATION DETAILS | MAKER'S PRIVATE ADDRESS and DETAILS | PLATE and MARK DETAILS | MAKER/COMPANY and BUSINESS ADDRESS | MAKER'S TRADE |
|---|---|---|---|---|
| Not in R2 as expected<br>*c.* June 1920 | | P15/B/148<br>***#3350***  | **BARKER BROTHERS** *<br>Constitution Hill<br>Birmingham and<br>292 High Holborn<br>London | Silversmiths |
| Not in R2 as expected<br>*c.* January 1921 | | P15/B/149<br>***#3351*** 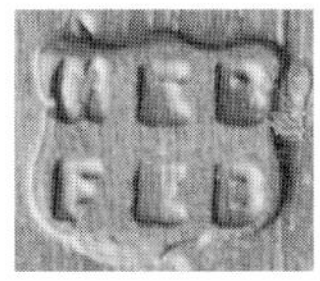 | | |
| R3/30<br>10 November 1925<br>Sent by Barker Brothers<br>Three sizes<br>Punches cancelled and New style entered 1 March 1936 | Tudor Hill, Sutton Coldfield<br>Holm Wood, Four Oaks<br>Sutton Coldfield<br>Beaconsfield Road<br>Camberley<br>Avondale, West Byfield<br>Heathcourt, Four Oaks<br>Sutton Coldfield<br>The Shubbery<br>Sherbourne Road<br>Sutton Coldfield | P15/B/177-179<br>***#3352-4***  | **BARKER BROTHERS LTD** *<br>Herbert Edward Barker (All directors)<br>Frank Ernest Barker<br>Olive Joseph Levi<br>Frederick Wallis<br>Cyril Otley Fletcher<br>David Harper<br>Unity Works, Constitution Hill<br>Birmingham and<br>292 High Holborn<br>London | Silversmiths and electroplate manufacturers |
| R2/32<br>24 January 1907<br>Sent by Imperial Tobacco Co | 124 Princes Road<br>Liverpool | P9/E/20<br>***#3355***  | **Herbert WOEF** trading as<br>**H EBERT & CO**<br>State Insurance Buildings<br>Liverpool | Jewellers and silversmiths |
| Missing register<br>*c.*1894<br>Similar mark LAO<br>20 December 1892 | | P5/H/531<br>***#3356***  | **Thomas Alfred SCOTT** [1] (Joint Managing<br>**Josiah Timmis SMITH** [2] Directors)<br>**HAWKSWORTH, EYRE & CO LTD** *<br>60 Rockingham Street<br>Sheffield | Silversmiths |
| R2/147<br>14 November 1911<br>Sent by Coley Brothers | Private address same as business | P13/J/56<br>***#3357***  | **Hugh Edward JONES**<br>11 Mayfield Road<br>Alexandra Park<br>Manchester | Wholesale jeweller |
| R2/221<br>6 June 1919<br>Sent by Harold Edwin Landon | Hortindale Bottom<br>Grange-over-Sands?<br>Nr Carnforth | P15/L/21,22<br>***#3358,9*** 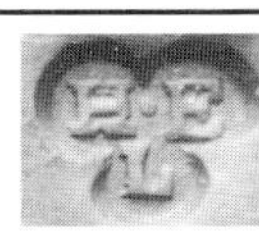 | **Harold Edwin LANDON**<br>82 Church Street<br>Lancaster | Manufacturing silversmith and jeweller |
| Not in R3 as expected - between April 1925 and January 1928<br>Mark not registered at BAO | | P15/L/33<br>***#3360***<br>§  | | |
| R1/25<br>18 March 1896<br>Sent by Hawksworth, Eyre & Co | 60 Rockingham Street [1]<br>Sheffield<br>Rhine Hill [2]<br>Stratford-upon-Avon | P5/Z*sic*/744<br>***#3361***  | **Thomas Alfred SCOTT** [1]<br>**Josiah Timmis SMITH** [2]<br>(Managing Directors) trading as<br>**HAWKSWORTH, EYRE & CO LTD** *<br>60 Rockingham Street<br>Sheffield | Silversmiths |
| R1/76<br>29 November 1898<br>Sent by H E Venour | 81 Albert Road<br>Handsworth<br>Birmingham | P9/V/2<br>***#3362***  | **Henry Edward VENOUR**<br>21 Vyse Street<br>Birmingham | Manufacturing jeweller |
| PDB 1838<br>MR3/81 | Gold rings | Not on P1<br>***#3363*** **H F?** | **Henry FISHWICK**<br>Liverpool | Goldsmith |

| REGISTRATION DETAILS | MAKER'S PRIVATE ADDRESS and DETAILS | PLATE and MARK DETAILS | MAKER/COMPANY and BUSINESS ADDRESS | MAKER'S TRADE |
|---|---|---|---|---|
| R2/24<br>31 August 1906<br>Sent by H Farrer | 37 Elizabeth Street<br>Accrington | P9/F/29<br>*#3364*<br> | **Henry FARRER**<br>37 Elizabeth Street<br>Accrington<br>1 Commercial Street later, undated<br>Church | Mounter and pipe repairer |
| R1/22<br>4 March 1896<br>Sent by Herbert Ferguson | 24 Yerby Terrace<br>Queen's Road<br>Manchester | P5/F/732<br>*#3365*<br> | **Herbert FERGUSON**<br>13 Sugar Lane<br>Manchester | Pipe and stick mounter |
| R3/183<br>24 March 1962<br>Sent by<br>Hayes & Finch Ltd<br>Two sizes | 5 Halshead Avenue<br>Whiston<br>near Prescot, Lancashire | P21/H/89<br>*#3366*<br> | **HAYES & FINCH LTD**<br>30/38 Vernon Street<br>Liverpool 2 | Church furnishers and candle makers |
| PDB 1838 Gold rings<br>MR3/81<br>Two sizes | | P2/F/x4<br>*#3367-70*<br> | **Henry FISHWICK**<br>Liverpool | Goldsmith |
| PP1/187 PP3/83<br>GTD 1830-65<br>GSJW/135 | J1 1843-65<br>GSJW/135 | | or<br>**Hugh FISHWICK**<br>9 Tarleton Street<br>Liverpool | Watchcase maker |
| R1/213<br>8 June 1904<br>Sent by<br>H Friedlander | 16 Mornington Avenue<br>West Kensington<br>London | P9/F/22<br>*#3371*<br> | **Harry FRIEDLANDER** *<br>51 Milton Street<br>London EC | Manufacturing jewellers and importers |
| R2/188<br>23 July 1914<br>Sent by Hall & Fitzgerald<br>Two sizes<br>Cancelled<br>24 March 1962 | 6 Hillside<br>Cotham<br>Bristol<br>23 Fernback Road<br>Bristol | P15/H/19,20<br>*#3372,3*<br> | **William Sydney HALL**<br>**Edward Thurston DAVIES** trading as<br>**HALL & FITZGERALD** *<br>147 Temple Street<br>Bristol | Merchants of tobacconists fancy goods |
| R1/156<br>31 October 1901<br>Sent by C Horner<br>cancelled<br>24 March 1962 | Clifton Down House<br>Bristol | P9/H/47<br>*#3374*<br> | **William Sydney HALL**<br>**Henry Edgar FITZGERALD** trading as<br>**HALL & FITZGERALD** *<br>20 Victoria Street<br>Bristol | Fancy goods merchants |
| Not in SPB or LPB so struck 1860-3 | | P3/F/x3<br>*#3375-7*<br> | **Hugh FISHWICK**<br>9 Tarleton Street<br>Liverpool | Watchcase maker |
| Not in R2 as expected. Between 23 March 1910 and<br>4 May 1910 | | P13/F/19<br>*#3378*<br>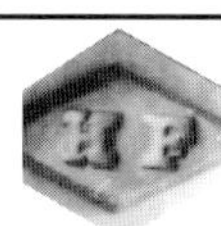 | **Unidentified** | |
| Not in R2 as expected - dated<br>August 1911 to<br>October 1912 | | P13/F/28<br>*#3379*<br> | **Unidentified** | |
| LPB/30<br>13 April 1882 | | P3/F/x3<br>*#3380-2*<br> | **Henry FITTER & SONS** *<br>3, 4 Hylton Street<br>Birmingham | Gold chain manufacturers |
| SPB/5<br>5 June 1865 | | P3/G/x2<br>*#3383,4*<br> | **Hugh GREEN**<br>20 Percival Square<br>Liverpool | Watchcase maker |
| R3/173<br>16 June 1960<br>Sent by<br>H Goldwhite<br>Two sizes | 49 Manley Road<br>Whalley Range<br>Manchester 16 | P21/G/46,47<br>*#3385,6*<br> | **Harold GOLDWHITE**<br>No business address entered | Student |

| REGISTRATION DETAILS | MAKER'S PRIVATE ADDRESS and DETAILS | PLATE and MARK DETAILS | MAKER/COMPANY and BUSINESS ADDRESS | MAKER'S TRADE |
|---|---|---|---|---|
| SPB/5<br>5 June 1865 | | P3/G/x4<br>***#3387-90***<br> | **Hugh GREEN**<br>20 Percival Square<br>Liverpool | Watchcase maker |
| Missing register<br>*c.*1888 | | P5/G/176<br>***#3391***<br> | | |
| PDB 1808-10<br>MR3/85<br>J1 1808-10 | Gold rings | P1/28/x2<br>***#3392,3***<br> | **HEMMINGWAY & GLOVER**<br>Manchester | Goldsmiths |
| Missing register<br>*c.*1886 SP32/6<br>Similar mark entered LAO 4 April 1891 | | P5/G/6<br>***#3394***<br> | **Henry GRIFFITH** *<br>159 Warstone Lane<br>Birmingham | Gold and silver case pencil manufacturers |
| R1/223<br>18 November 1904<br>Sent by Haseler Brothers | 106 Ivor Road<br>Sparkhill<br>Birmingham | P9/G/57<br>***#3395***<br> | **H GREAVES LTD** *<br>Alfred Hill (Managing Director)<br>35/36 New Street<br>Birmingham | Silversmiths |
| Missing register<br>*c.*1886<br>Similar mark BAO 10 November 1883 | | P5/H/65<br>***#3396***<br> | **HALL & GOODE** *<br>23 Bartletts Passage Building<br>Holborn Circus<br>London | Jewellers and silversmiths |
| LPB/34<br>24 June 1880 | | P3/G/x2<br>***#3397,8***<br> | **Henry GREEN**<br>15 President Street East<br>King Square<br>London | Watchcase maker |
| Missing register<br>*c.*1888 | | P5/G/144<br>***#3399***<br> | | |
| Missing register<br>*c.*1886<br>Mark with pellet BAO 28 July 1898 | | P5/G/28<br>***#3400***<br> | **Henry GREAVES** *<br>35/36 New Street<br>Birmingham | Portmanteau manufacturer |
| R1/223<br>18 November 1904<br>Sent by Haseler Brothers | Struck for one lot of work and returned to be altered | P9/G/0*sic*<br>***#3401***<br> | **H GREAVES LTD** *<br>Alfred Hill (Managing Director)<br>35/36 New Street<br>Birmingham | Silversmith |
| Not in R3 as expected but index has H Gilpin with mark P15/G/50 annotated *c.*1926 | | P15/G/50<br>***#3402***<br> | **Henry GILPIN**<br>9 Augusta Street<br>Birmingham | Jeweller |
| R3/47<br>29 June 1929<br>Sent by E Horton | 18 Bank Street<br>Hulme<br>Manchester | P15/B/196<br>***#3403***<br> | **Henry George BARTLETT**<br>11 Seven Stairs Building<br>16 Withy Grove<br>Manchester | Jeweller |
| R2/109<br>28 April 1910<br>Sent by<br>H G Croneen<br>3 December 1932<br>Four sizes | 1 Kingswood Villas<br>New Brompton<br>Gillingham<br>Kent | P13/C/65-68<br>***#3404-7***<br> | **Horace George CRONEEN**<br>5, 7, 9 High Street<br>New Brompton<br>Gillingham<br>Kent | Medal maker and silversmith |
| | | P15/K*sic*/219<br>***#3408***<br> | | |

| REGISTRATION DETAILS | MAKER'S PRIVATE ADDRESS and DETAILS | PLATE and MARK DETAILS | MAKER/COMPANY and BUSINESS ADDRESS | MAKER'S TRADE |
|---|---|---|---|---|
| R3/127<br>13 January 1949<br>Sent by H G Russell | 98 Holliday Road<br>Birmingham 21 | P21/R/6<br>***#3409***<br> | **Herbert George RUSSELL**<br>103 Vyse Street, Hockley<br>Birmingham | Jewellers materials |
| R3/150<br>20 February 1954<br>Sent by Secretary of the Company | | P21/G/31-36<br>***#3410-5***<br> | **Henry GRIFFITH & SONS LTD**<br>Tachbrook Road<br>Leamington Spa | Manufacturing jewellers |
| | | P21/G/25-30<br>***#3416-21***<br> | | |
| R3/86<br>8 February 1937<br>Sent by Henry Griffith & Sons | The Lawn [1]<br>26 Newbold Terrace<br>Leamington Spa<br>Chesford Bridge House [2]<br>Kenilworth<br>53 Kenilworth Road [3]<br>Leamington Spa<br>41 Avenue Road [4]<br>Leamington Spa | P21/G/1<br>***#3422***<br>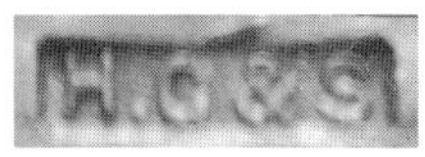 | **Henry GRIFFITH & SONS** *<br>Frederic Griffith[1]<br>Frederic Priestley Griffith[2] (All<br>John Goodwin Lucas [3] Partners)<br>William Goodman Ward [4]<br>Tachbrook Road<br>Leamington Spa | |
| R2/155<br>11 April 1912<br>BAO 20.025 20.026<br>Two sizes Sent by<br>H Griffith & Sons | The Nook<br>Lapworth<br>Warwickshire | P13/G/39-44<br>***#3423-8***<br> | **Frederic GRIFFITH** trading as<br>**H GRIFFITH & SONS** *<br>131 Warstone Lane<br>Birmingham | |
| Missing register<br>*c.*1887 | | P5/G/78<br>***#3429***<br> | **Henry GRIFFITH & SONS** *<br>131 Warstone Lane<br>Birmingham | |
| Missing register<br>*c.*1890 | | P5/G/324<br>***#3430***<br> | | |
| Missing register<br>*c.*1890<br>Next to P5/G/324 | | P5/G/x1<br>***#3431***<br> | | |
| R1/97<br>28 March 1899<br>Sent by H Griffith & Sons Ltd | Ericsholme<br>St Bernard's Road<br>Olton<br>near Birmingham | P9/G/10<br>***#3432***<br> | **Frederic Griffith** (Director) trading as<br>**Henry GRIFFITH & SONS LTD***<br>131 Warstone Lane<br>Birmingham | |
| R2/17<br>26 April 1906<br>Sent by H Griffith & Sons | | P9/G/74<br>***#3433***<br> | | |
| R1/73<br>28 August 1898<br>Sent by H Griffith & Sons Ltd<br>C Drefus<br>I J Evans & Son | | P9/G/1<br>***#3434***<br> | | |
| R1/97<br>28 March 1899<br>Sent by H Griffith & Sons Ltd | | P9/G/9<br>***#3435***<br> | | |
| | | P9/G/11<br>***#3436***<br>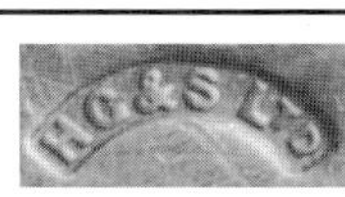 | | |

| REGISTRATION DETAILS | MAKER'S PRIVATE ADDRESS and DETAILS | PLATE and MARK DETAILS | MAKER/COMPANY and BUSINESS ADDRESS | MAKER'S TRADE |
|---|---|---|---|---|
| R3/27<br>27 March 1925<br>Sent by<br>H K Harrrison<br><br>27 February 1928 | Private address same as business | P15/H/89<br>***#3437*** 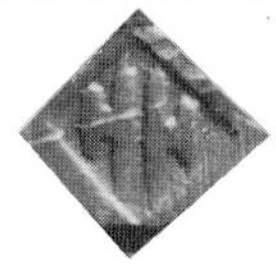<br><br>P15/I*sic*/103<br>***#3438***  | **Helen Kinsey HARRISON**<br>8 Lancaster Avenue<br>Sefton Park<br>Liverpool | Artist |
| R2/231<br>13 May 1920<br>Sent by Hubert Hall<br>Two sizes | 109 Burbury Street<br>Birmingham | P15/H/39,40<br>***#3439,40***  | **Hubert HALL**<br>223a Great King Street<br>107 Unett Street later-undated<br>Birmingham | Silversmith glass mounting and boxes |
| R1/140<br>14 January 1901<br>Sent by John Haseler | 5 Radnor Road [1]<br>Handsworth<br>Loughton [2]<br>Water Orton<br>Birmingham | P9/H/39<br>***#3441*** 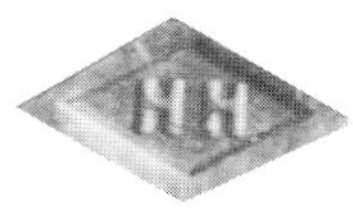 | **John HASELER** [1]<br>**William Frederick HOLMES** [2]<br>trading as **HASELER & HOLMES**<br>59 Vittoria Street<br>Birmingham | Manufacturing jewellers |
| R3/52<br>4 March 1930<br>Sent by The Civic Co Ltd, 81 Fulham Palace Road<br>Hammersmith, W6 | Private address same as business | P15/I*sic*/110<br>***#3442***  | **Harry HARTLEY**<br>20 Gainsborough Gardens<br>Golders Green<br>London NW11 | Gold and silver worker |
| R3/110<br>7 September 1945<br>Sent by Hadley & Hadley | 16 Holliday Road [1]<br>Handsworth<br>Birmingham<br>78 Newton Road [2]<br>Birmingham | P21/H/21<br>***#3443*** 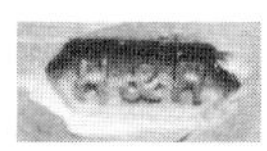 | **Arthur HADLEY**[1] (Partners)<br>**Cornelius HADLEY**[2] trading as<br>**HADLEY & HADLEY**<br>38 Spencer Street, Hockley<br>Birmingham | Manufacturing jewellers |
| R3/126<br>24 September 1948<br>Sent by H Holmes | Kingston<br>8 Grove Lane<br>Timperly<br>Cheshire | P21/H/47<br>***#3444***  | **Harold HOLMES**<br>Lamberts Buildings<br>Tipping Street<br>Altrincham | Art metalworker |
| PDB 1822-30<br>MR3/86<br>J1 1827-31 | Gold rings, skewers, coffin plates, etc. Mary Huntingdon working on her own before 1822.<br>See also MH | P1/30/x1<br>***#3445***  | **H M & S HUNTINGDON**<br>38 Bridge Street Row<br>Chester | Goldsmiths and silversmiths |
| GTD 1865-87 | | P2/H/x3<br>***#3446-8***  | **Henry HULL**<br>Liverpool | Watchcase maker |
| LPB/38<br>24 October 1881 | Entry reads like Harrison but Henry Harris at this address in 1881 | P3/H/x3<br>***#3449-51***  | **Henry HARRIS & CO**<br>30 Warstone Lane<br>Birmingham | Watch manufacturers |
| GTD 1865-87 | This larger mark may be for silverware | P2/H/x1<br>***#3452***  | **Henry HULL**<br>Liverpool | Watchcase maker |
| R2/225<br>7 November 1919<br>Sent by<br>H Henderson | 254 Great King Street<br>Birmingham | P15/H/52<br>***#3453***  | **Herbert HENDERSON**<br>52 Vittoria Street<br>Birmingham | Manufacturing jeweller |
| R3/26<br>31 December 1924<br>Sent by Helen Holmes<br>Two sizes | Private address same as business | P15/H/84,85<br>***#3454,5***  | **Helen HOLMES**<br>16 Maculary<br>Bath | Metalworker |

| REGISTRATION DETAILS | MAKER'S PRIVATE ADDRESS and DETAILS | PLATE and MARK DETAILS | MAKER/COMPANY and BUSINESS ADDRESS | MAKER'S TRADE |
|---|---|---|---|---|
| R1/21<br>5 February 1896<br>Sent by Lucas Brothers Ltd | 36 Marquise Road<br>Finsbury Park<br>London | P5/H/723<br>***#3456***<br> | **Harry HOWITT** *<br>17 Holborn<br>London EC | Wholesale jeweller |
| R1/52<br>12 October 1897<br>Sent by Hemming & Hazlewood<br>Two sizes | 118 Trafalgar Road<br>Moseley<br>Birmingham | P5/*Zsic*/878x2<br>***#3457,8***<br> | **George Henry HAZLEWOOD**<br>trading as<br>**HEMMING & HAZLEWOOD** *<br>60 Spencer Street<br>Birmingham | Jewellers |
| LPB/8<br>25 September 1884<br>No mark in LPB | Kelly 1883 | P5/H/x1<br>***#3459***<br> | **Henry HAYLETT** *<br>39 Spencer Street<br>Clerkenwell<br>London | Gold chain maker |
| PP1/164<br>Entered similar mark BAO 29 May 1816 | Unique font style is similar to the WH of her late husband, William Howard | P1/31/x3<br>***#3460-2***<br> | **Hannah HOWARD**<br>(late William Howard)<br>Lombard Street<br>Liverpool | Watchcase maker |
| R2/205<br>12 May 1916<br>Sent by Imperial Tobacco Co | Private address same as business | P15/H/35<br>***#3463***<br>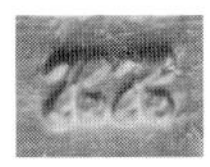 | **Harry Jutsum HARTSHORN**<br>53 Stundale Road<br>West Kensington<br>London | Dealer in fancy goods |
| R2/217<br>3 February 1919<br>Sent by Imperial Tobacco Co | | P15/H/42<br>***#3464***<br> | **Harry Jutsum HARTSHORN**<br>5 Auriol Road<br>West Kensington<br>London | |
| R1/8<br>18 February 1895<br>Sent by T P Hewitt Lancashire Watch Company, Prescot | | P5/aboveB/642<br>***#3465***<br> | **Howard H BERTON**<br>123 Vyse Street<br>Birmingham | Watch manufacturer and importer |
| Missing register<br>*c.*1891 | D = Dublin ? | P5/D/363<br>***#3466***<br> | **Unidentified** | |
| R2/212<br>10 May 1919<br>Sent by H H Friend | 30 Hamstead Road<br>Handsworth<br>Birmingham | P15/F/17<br>***#3467***<br> | **Henry Herbert FRIEND**<br>25, 27 Soho Hill<br>Birmingham | Manufacturing jeweller |
| 18 July 1917 | | P15/F/16<br>***#3468***<br> | | |
| R1/118<br>20 December 1899<br>Sent by Jones & Crompton | Trenant<br>Woodville Road<br>Barnet<br>137 Tulse Hill<br>London SW | P9/H/23<br>***#3469***<br> | **Henry Stanley HOBSON**<br>**George F HOBSON** trading as<br>**Henry HOBSON & SON** *<br>67, 69 Hounsditch<br>London | Cutlers and electroplate dealers |
| R3/77<br>25 July 1935<br>Sent by H Huntley & Sons | 204 Erdington Hall Road [1]<br>Erdington<br>25 Emmanuel Road [2]<br>Wylde Green<br>Sutton Coldfield | P15/*Isic*/125<br>***#3470***<br> | **Harold GARDNER** [1]<br>**Edward Stanley GARDNER-POWELL** [2]<br>trading as **H HUNTLEY & SONS**<br>6 Vyse Street<br>Birmingham | Manufacturing jewellers |
| 17 June 1938 | | P21/H/3,4<br>***#3471,2***<br> | | |

| REGISTRATION DETAILS | MAKER'S PRIVATE ADDRESS and DETAILS | PLATE and MARK DETAILS | MAKER/COMPANY and BUSINESS ADDRESS | MAKER'S TRADE |
|---|---|---|---|---|
| R1/175<br>15 September 1902<br>Sent by H Griffith & Sons | 141 Tulse Hill [1]<br>London<br>Trenant [2]<br>Woodville Road<br>Barnet, London | P9/H/44[7]*sic*<br>***#3473***<br> | **George Frederick HOBSON** [1]<br>**Henry Stanley HOBSON** [2] trading as<br>**H HOBSON & SON** *<br>67, 69 Houndsditch<br>London and<br>23 Carver Street<br>Sheffield | Silversmiths and general merchants |
| R1/40<br>27 February 1897<br>Sent by W Aitken<br>W Davenport<br>Two sizes | 137 Tulse Hill<br>London SW | P5/Z*sic*/819x2<br>***#3474,5***<br> | **George Frederick HOBSON** trading as<br>**Henry HOBSON & SON** *<br>67, 69 Houndsditch<br>London | Cutlers and silversmiths |
| R1/53<br>1 November 1897<br>Sent by<br>W H Carrington<br>J Taylor | 187 High Street<br>Lincoln<br>(Ed: this shop established 1870 still named Higgs Brothers selling tobacco, etc in 2002) | P5/aboveD/903<br>***#3476***<br> | **George HIGGS** and **Fred HIGGS**<br>trading as **HIGGS BROTHERS**<br>187 High Street<br>Lincoln and<br>Boar Lane<br>Newark and<br>35 Southgate<br>Sleaford | Tobacconists |
| Missing register<br>*c.*1888<br>Mark with full stop<br>BAO 25 March 1881 | | P5/J/157<br>***#3477***<br> | **Howard JAMES**<br>63 Great Hampton Street<br>Birmingham | Jeweller |
| R1/138<br>1 December 1900<br>Sent by Hollins & Jacques<br>Two sizes | Llanfair<br>Westminster Road, Handsworth<br>Lime House<br>Rink? Road<br>Handsworth | P9/H/37,38<br>***#3478,9***<br> | **Henry HOLLINS**<br>**Frederick JACQUES** trading as<br>**HOLLINS & JACQUES** *<br>120 Branston Street<br>Birmingham | Manufacturing silversmiths |
| R2/2<br>17 August 1905<br>Sent by J H Horton<br>cancelled until new punch #77 received | 248 Alcester Road<br>Mosely<br>Birmingham | P9/H/74<br>***#3480***<br> | **Frederick Hart HORTON**<br>**Charles JOLLIFFE** trading as<br>**HORTON & JOLLIFFE**<br>37 Warstone Lane<br>Birmingham | Jewellers |
| 14 February 1906 | 163 Milcote Road<br>Bearwood<br>Birmingham | P9/H/77<br>***#3481***<br> | | |
| R3/136<br>3 January 1952<br>Sent by E Isherwood | 58 Keys Road [1]<br>Prestwick<br>16 Burrage Road [2]<br>Bagaley, Manchester<br>14 Chelmsford Street [3]<br>Oldham<br>Lancashire | P21/B/36<br>***#3482***<br> | **Edmund ISHERWOOD** [1]<br>**Stanley CLAYTON** [2]<br>**Wilfred CARTWRIGHT** [3] trading as<br>**Herbert J BARTON**<br>Swan Chambers<br>2 Garden Street<br>Manchester 4 | Working jewellers |
| R3/81<br>12 November 1935<br>Sent by T J Skelton | 86 Vyse Street<br>Birmingham<br>Hilbrew<br>52 Wordhurst Road<br>Edgbaston, Birmingham | P15/G*sic*/221<br>***#3483***<br> | **Harold James BRIGHTLEY**<br>8 Augusta Street<br>Hockley<br>Birmingham | Manufacturing jeweller |
| R2/172<br>10 May 1913<br>Sent by Trevine & Gilpin | 20 Sutton Court<br>Chiswick | P15/C/28<br>***#3484***<br> | **H J COOPER & CO LTD** *<br>Grendon Kent (Secretary)<br>22 Thavies Inn<br>London EC | Wholesale jewellers |
| R2/164<br>24 October 1912<br>BAO 20.617 20.640<br>Sent by F Marson | 22 Powis Gardens<br>Golders Green<br>London N W | P15/C/2,3,13-19<br>***#3485-93***<br> | | |

| REGISTRATION DETAILS | MAKER'S PRIVATE ADDRESS and DETAILS | PLATE and MARK DETAILS | MAKER/COMPANY and BUSINESS ADDRESS | MAKER'S TRADE |
|---|---|---|---|---|
| R2/207<br>8 July 1916<br>Sent by F Marson | 11 Purbeck Mansions<br>Chiswick<br>London W | P15/C/54-65<br>***#3494-3505***<br> | **H J COOPER & CO LTD** *<br>Grendon Kent (Director)<br>22, 23 Thavies Inn<br>London EC | Wholesale jewellers |
| R3/15<br>6 April 1923<br>Sent by F Marson<br>Two sizes | 153 Herne Hill<br>London EC | P15/C/121–144<br>***#3506-29***<br> | **H J COOPER & CO LTD** *<br>H J Cooper (Director)<br>22 Thavies Inn<br>London EC | |
| R3/44<br>23 October 1928<br>Sent by F H Adams & Co<br>262 New John Street West, Birmingham | 11 Pretend Mansions [1]<br>Chiswick N14<br>153 Herne Hill [2]<br>London SE<br>41 Grove Park Gardens [3]<br>Chiswick W4 | P15/C/189-200<br>***#3530-41***<br> | **H J COOPER CO LTD** *<br>Grendon Kent[1] (Director)<br>H Cooper [2] (Director)<br>Mrs C A Cooper[3] (Director)<br>22, 23 Thavies Inn<br>London EC1 | |
| R3/6<br>16 January 1922<br>Sent by F Marson | | P15/C/98,100-106<br>***#3542-9***<br> | **H J COOPER & CO LTD** *<br>22 Thavies Inn<br>London EC1 | |
| | | P15/C/99<br>***#3550***<br> | | |
| R2/133<br>1 May 1911<br>BAO 18.856-18.905<br>Sent by James Rooker<br>Two sizes | 22 Powis Gardens<br>Golders Green<br>London NW | P13/C/92-132<br>***#3551-91***<br> | **H J COOPER & CO LTD** *<br>22, 23 Thavies Inn<br>London EC | |
| | (Ed: Letter "C" from number 133 continues on square D) | P13/D*sic*/133-142<br>***#3592-3601***<br> | | |
| R2/164<br>24 October 1912<br>Sent by F Marson<br>BAO 20.617 20.640 | 22 Powis Gardens<br>Golders Green<br>London NW | P15/C/1,4-12,20<br>***#3602-12***<br> | **H J COOPER & CO LTD** *<br>Grendon Kent (Secretary)<br>22 Thavies Inn<br>London EC | |
| R2/187<br>15 May 1914<br>Sent by H J Cooper & Co Ltd | 20 Sutton Court [1]<br>Chiswick<br>London W | P15/C/32-43<br>***#3613-24***<br> | **H J COOPER & CO LTD** *<br>Grendon Kent [1] (Secretary)<br>22, 23 Thavies Inn<br>London | |
| Missing register<br>*c.*1893 | | P5/C/517<br>***#3625***<br> | **H J COOPER & CO LTD** *<br>22 Thavies Inn<br>Holborn<br>London EC | Manufacturing jewellers |
| R1/148<br>7 June 1901<br>Sent by H J Cooper Ltd | 140 Wellesley Road<br>Chiswick<br>London | P9/C/52-67<br>***#3626-41***<br> | **H J COOPER & CO LTD** *<br>Grendon Kent (Director)<br>22, 23 Thavies Inn<br>Holborn Circus<br>London | Wholesale jewellers |
| Missing register<br>*c.*1889<br>Similar mark entered<br>LAO 30 June 1898 | | P5/C/254<br>***#3642***<br> | | |
| R1/101<br>30 May 1899<br>Sent by C Lyster & Sons<br>H J Cooper | 13 Loughborough Road<br>Brixton | P9/C/12-25<br>***#3643-56***<br> | **Henry James COOPER**<br>Managing Director on behalf of<br>**H J COOPER & CO LTD** *<br>22 Thavies Inn, Holborn<br>London EC | |

| REGISTRATION DETAILS | MAKER'S PRIVATE ADDRESS and DETAILS | PLATE and MARK DETAILS | MAKER/COMPANY and BUSINESS ADDRESS | MAKER'S TRADE |
|---|---|---|---|---|
| R1/149<br>18 June 1901<br>Sent by H J Cooper Ltd | 13 Loughborough Road<br>Brixton | P9/C/69,70<br>***#3657,8***<br> | **Henry James COOPER**<br>Managing Director on behalf of<br>**H J COOPER & CO LTD** *<br>22 Thavies Inn, Holborn<br>London EC | Wholesale jewellers |
| R1/205<br>22 December 1903<br>Sent by Williams & Franks | 140 Wellesley Road<br>Gunnersbury<br>London W<br>NB: P9/C/120-199 unused | P9/C/98-116, P9/Dsic/117-119, 200, 201<br>***#3659-82***<br> | | |
| R2/99<br>3 December 1909<br>Sent by Frederick Marson | 1 Cromwell Mansions<br>Ravenscourt Park<br>London W | P13/C/45-56<br>***#3683-94***<br> | | Manufacturing jewellers |
| R2/112<br>8 June 1910<br>Sent by J & R Griffin Ltd | | P13/C/75<br>***#3695***<br> | | Wholesale jewellers |
| Missing register<br>*c.*1893 | | P5/C/517<br>***#3696***<br> | **H J COOPER & CO LTD** *<br>22 Thavies Inn<br>Holborn<br>London EC | |
| R1/65<br>25 April 1898<br>Sent by H J Cooper<br>Authority to<br>G E Walton & Co Ltd | 13 Loughborough Road<br>Brixton<br>London | P5/aboveC/952a<br>***#3697***<br>§<br> | **Henry James COOPER**<br>Managing Director on behalf of<br>**H J COOPER & CO LTD** *<br>22 Thavies Inn<br>Holborn<br>London EC | |
| R1/65<br>25 April 1898 | | P5/aboveC/952b<br>***#3698***<br>§<br>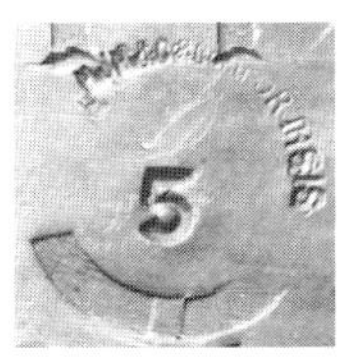 | | |
| R2/99<br>2 December 1909<br>Sent by H Howitt | Douglas<br>Eversleigh Road<br>Finchley<br>London | P13/H/43-45<br>***#3699-3701***<br> | **Harry Joseph HOWITT** *<br>18 Cross Street<br>Hatton Garden<br>London EC | Jeweller |
| SPB/6<br>18 May 1872<br>Sent by H Mansell | | P3/N/x3<br>***#3702-4***<br> | **Henry J NICHOLLS**<br>30 Williamson Street<br>Liverpool | Watch manufacturer |
| Missing register<br>*c.*1886 | | P5/N/26<br>***#3705***<br> | | |
| R1/184<br>10 February 1903<br>Sent by R J Pike | 30 Union Street<br>Coventry | P9/N/16<br>***#3706***<br> | **Henry John NORRIS** *<br>Hertford Works<br>Coventry | Watch manufacturer |
| R3/58<br>11 January 1931<br>Sent by Kinsey Brothers & Patrick Ltd | Private address same as business<br><br>Common seal of company affixed in the presence of the directors and secretary | P15/P/230<br>***#3707***<br> | **KINSEY BROTHERS & PATRICK LTD**<br>W B Patrick (Director)<br>Harold J Patrick (Director)<br>Clarence Patrick (Secretary)<br>15 Vyse Street (Registered Office)<br>Birmingham | Manufacturing jewellers |

| REGISTRATION DETAILS | MAKER'S PRIVATE ADDRESS and DETAILS | PLATE and MARK DETAILS | MAKER/COMPANY and BUSINESS ADDRESS | MAKER'S TRADE |
|---|---|---|---|---|
| R2/105<br>5 March 1910<br>LAO 5039,5940<br>Sent by H Jackson & Sons<br>Two sizes | For all partners<br>4 Meridith Street<br>London EC | P13/J/27,28<br>***#3708,9***<br> | **Henry Philip JACKSON**<br>**Samuel James JACOBS**<br>**Richard Alfred JACOBS** trading as<br>**H JACKSON & SONS** *<br>4 Meredith Street<br>Clerkenwell<br>London EC | Silversmiths |
| SPB/19<br>9 September 1869<br>Similar mark entered<br>LAO 5 October 1869 | See his roman font mark below | P3/K/x3<br>***#3710-2***<br> | **Herbert KERBY** *<br>Spon Street<br>Coventry | Watchcase maker |
| R1/49<br>13 August 1897<br>Sent by W Walker | 93 Manor Road<br>London N | P5/K/864<br>***#3713***<br> | **Henry KAUFMAN** *<br>91, 93 Milton Street<br>London | Tobacconist and fancy goods manufacturer |
| R2/35<br>22 March 1907<br>Sent by J G Newbold | 100 Manor Road<br>London N | P9/K/45<br>***#3714***<br> | **H KAUFMAN** trading as<br>**H KAUFMAN & CO** *<br>91, 93 Milton Street<br>London EC | Tobacco pouch manufacturers |
| LPB/44<br>24 November 1883<br>No mark in LPB | | P5/K/x1<br>***#3715***<br> | **Hugh KYLE**<br>Warstone Building<br>Warstone Lane<br>Birmingham | Jeweller |
| SPB/19<br>9 September 1869 | See his plain font mark above | P3/K/x3<br>***#3716-8***<br> | **Herbert KERBY** *<br>Spon Street<br>Coventry | Watchcase maker |
| R1/75<br>7 October 1898<br>Sent by Harriet Kent | Private address same as business | P9/K/3<br>***#3719***<br> | **Harriet KENT**<br>3 Pembroke Street<br>Birmingham | Jeweller |
| R2/21<br>13 July 1906<br>Sent by H Lawrence | 48 Priory Road<br>South Hampstead<br>London NW | P9/L/76<br>***#3720***<br> | **Henry LAWRENCE**<br>44 Hatton Garden<br>London EC | Manufacturing optician |
| R2/26<br>12 October 1906<br>Sent by H Lawrence | | P9/L/77<br>***#3721***<br> | | |
| R1/18<br>9 May 1894<br>Sent by Henry Lillie | | P5/L/559<br>***#3722***<br> | **Henry LILLIE**<br>65 Margate Street<br>Cavendish Square<br>London | Engraver |
| R2/94<br>30 September 1909<br>Sent by H Lambin | 29 Wyke Gardens<br>Clapham Road<br>London SW | P13/L/29<br>***#3723***<br>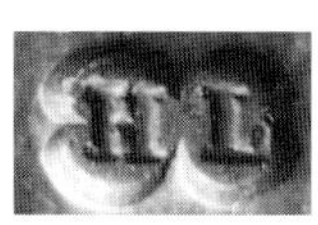 | **Henri LAMBIN** *<br>Audrey House<br>Ely Place<br>Holborn Circus<br>London EC | Silversmith |
| R1/144<br>27 February 1901<br>Sent by H L Brown | Kenyon House<br>Brincliffe Crescent<br>Sheffield | P9/B/35<br>***#3724***<br> | **H L BROWN** trading as<br>**H L BROWN & SON** *<br>65 Market Place<br>Sheffield | Jewellers |

| REGISTRATION DETAILS | MAKER'S PRIVATE ADDRESS and DETAILS | PLATE and MARK DETAILS | MAKER/COMPANY and BUSINESS ADDRESS | MAKER'S TRADE |
|---|---|---|---|---|
| R3/72<br>16 May 1934<br>Sent by<br>Samuel Hope<br>126 Vyse Street<br>Birmingham<br>Clerk entered May but entry made between 20 June and 13 August! | In 2002 still trading as H L Brown & Son Ltd with premises in Sheffield, Derby, York, Doncaster, Scarborough and Lincoln | P15/B/214<br>*#3725*<br> | **H L BROWN & SON LTD** *<br>65 Market Place (Registered Office)<br>Sheffield and<br>92 Regent Street<br>London and<br>17 High Street<br>Doncaster and<br>Corn Market<br>Derby and<br>28 Burlington Street<br>Chesterfield and<br>22 College Street<br>Rotherham | Jewellers |
| Missing register<br>*c.*1889<br>Similar mark LAO<br>15 July 1892 | see also *#3724* | P5/B/256<br>*#3726*<br> | **Harris Leon BROWN** *<br>65 Market Place<br>Sheffield | Watchmaker and jeweller |
| R1/229<br>8 March 1905<br>Sent by Herbert Lees | Parkleigh<br>Pine Road<br>Didsbury | P9/L/64<br>*#3727*<br> | **Herbert LEES** trading as<br>**H LEES & CO** and<br>**TATE, BROADHURST & LEES**<br>60 Swan Street<br>Manchester | Umbrella and walking stick manufacturers |
| R2/59<br>14 May 1908<br>Sent by C Walker | 122 Landsdowne Road<br>Didsbury | P13/L/I<br>*#3728*<br> | **Herbert LEES** trading as<br>**H LEES & CO**<br>60 Swan Street<br>Manchester | |
| R2/219<br>29 April 1919<br>Sent by J G Slide & Co | Private address same as business | P15/H/45-50<br>*#3729-34*<br> | **HINDS LTD**<br>W Hinds (Managing Director)<br>24c King Street<br>Hammersmith<br>London | Wholesale and manufacturing jewellers |
| LPB/58<br>25 October 1882 | | P3/L/x3<br>*#3735-7*<br> | **Henry LAWSON**<br>**John WARD** (Ed: trading as)<br>**LAWSON & WARD** *<br>5 Hatton Garden<br>London | Manufacturing jewellers |
| Missing register<br>*c.*1887 | | P5/W/88<br>*#3738*<br> | | |
| Missing register<br>*c.*1889<br>Similar mark entered CAO 25 October 1882 | | P5/W/215<br>*#3739*<br> | | |
| R3/82<br>16 March 1936<br>Sent by T J Skelton<br>86 Vyse Street<br>Birmingham | Private address same as business | P15/M/78<br>*#3740*<br> | **Harry Laxton MELHUISH** trading as<br>**H L MELHUISH**<br>22 High Street<br>Wimbledon<br>London SW19 | Jeweller |
| R3/64<br>27 August 1932<br>Sent by<br>Albion Chain Co<br>39 Albion Street<br>Birmingham | | P15/H/112<br>*#3741*<br> | **W HINDS LTD**<br>Common seal of company affixed in the presence of:-<br>William Hinds (Director)<br>T N Hinds (Director)<br>James Dawson (Secretary)<br>26 King Street (Registered Office)<br>Hammersmith<br>London W6 | Jewellers |

| REGISTRATION DETAILS | MAKER'S PRIVATE ADDRESS and DETAILS | PLATE and MARK DETAILS | MAKER/COMPANY and BUSINESS ADDRESS | MAKER'S TRADE |
|---|---|---|---|---|
| Missing register<br>*c.*1887 | | P5/Y/115<br>***#3742***  | **Unidentified** | |
| Missing register<br>*c.*1889 | | P5/M/255<br>***#3743***  | **Henry Edward MEYER** trading as<br>**J L MEYER, SONS & CO** *<br>8 Lawrence Lane<br>London EC | Pipe merchants |
| R1/106<br>18 July 1899<br>Sent by Haseler & Milner | Hall Road<br>Handsworth<br>Birmingham | P9/H/17<br>***#3744***  | **Arnold & Herbert HASELER** trading as<br>**HASELER & MILNER**<br>31 Tenby Street<br>Birmingham | Manufacturing jewellers |
| LPB/54<br>5 February 1880 | | P3/N*sic*/x3<br>***#3745-7***  | **Henry MATTOCKS & CO**<br>2 Trafalgar Street<br>Coventry | Watchmakers |
| R2/5<br>8 November 1905<br>Sent by J G Newbold | 12 Elm Park Gardens<br>London SW | P9/M/94<br>***#3748***  | **Henry MEYER** *<br>72 Aldersgate Street<br>London EC | Pipe merchants |
| R2/226<br>26 January 1920<br>Sent by Harry Mindel | Private address same as business | P15/M/35<br>***#3749***  | **Harry MINDEL**<br>16 Morgan Street<br>Bow<br>London E | Wholesale manufacturing jeweller |
| R1/106<br>18 July 1899<br>Sent by Haseler & Milner | Hall Road<br>Handsworth<br>Birmingham | P9/H/16<br>***#3750***  | **Arnold** and **Herbert HASELER**<br>trading as **HASELER & MILNER**<br>31 Tenby Street<br>Birmingham | Manufacturing jewellers |
| LPB/74<br>28 October 1884<br>No mark in LPB | | P5/H/x1<br>***#3751***  | **HASELER & MILNER**<br>31 Tenby Street<br>Birmingham | |
| R2/6<br>11 November 1905<br>Old punch P9/H/16 recut<br>Sent by Herbert Haseler | 135 Holly Road<br>Handsworth<br>Hall Road<br>Handsworth | P9/H/76<br>***#3752***  | **Herbert HASELER**<br>**Arnold HASELER** trading as<br>**HASELER & MILNER**<br>31 Tenby Street<br>Birmingham | |
| R2/229<br>13 April 1920<br>Sent by Harry Morser | 8 Oakhill Road<br>Surbiton<br>Surrey | P15/M/37<br>***#3753*** 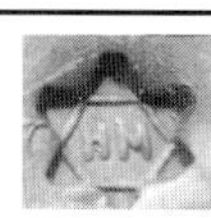 | **Harry MORSER**<br>329 High Holborn<br>London WC | Manufacturer of jewellery |
| SPB/15<br>20 August 1867 | | P3/M/x3<br>***#3754-6***  | **H MANSELL**<br>40 Mount Street<br>Coventry | Watchcase maker |
| SPB/22<br>8 January 1876<br>No name or address in SPB | | P3/M/x3<br>***#3757-9***  | | |
| R1/52<br>20 October 1897<br>Sent by A H Tongue | 4 Henry Road<br>Finsbury Park<br>London | P5/M/879<br>***#3760***  | **Theodore TWIST** trading as<br>**J L MEYER, SONS & CO** *<br>8 Lawrence Lane<br>London EC | Pipe merchants |
| R1/96<br>25 March 1899<br>Sent by R Pattenden | 12 Glen Park Gardens<br>London SW | P9/M/10<br>***#3761***  | **Henry Edward MEYER** *<br>8 Lawrence Lane<br>London EC | Pipe importers |

| REGISTRATION DETAILS | MAKER'S PRIVATE ADDRESS and DETAILS | PLATE and MARK DETAILS | MAKER/COMPANY and BUSINESS ADDRESS | MAKER'S TRADE |
|---|---|---|---|---|
| Missing register<br>*c.*1890<br>Similar mark entered<br>BAO 28 August 1899 | | P5/M/326<br>***#3762***<br> | **Henry Edward MEYER** *<br>8 Lawrence Lane<br>London EC | Pipe importers |
| R1/4<br>23 November 1894<br>Sent by A Brooker<br>for D & L Spiers<br>Three sizes | 13 Augustan Road<br>Edgbaston<br>Birmingham | P5/M/625x4<br>***#3763-6***<br> | **Lionel SPIERS** trading as<br>**D & L SPIERS** also as<br>**Henry MATTHEWS** *<br>45 Vittoria Street<br>Birmingham | Goldsmiths and silversmiths |
| R1/20<br>8 January 1896<br>Sent by<br>E Langridge & Co<br>C Widmer & Sons<br>Stainsby & Coupland | 24 Canonbury Villas<br>Islington<br>London | P5/M/718a<br>***#3767***<br> | **Henry MARSHALL** *<br>Highbury Leather Works<br>22 Corsica Street<br>Highbury<br>London | Purse and cigar case manufacturers |
| R1/153<br>18 September 1901 | | P9/M/33<br>***#3768***<br> | **Walter Henry MARSHALL**<br>**George Robert MARSHALL**<br>trading as **H MARSHALL** *<br>18, 20 & 22 Corsica Street<br>Highbury<br>London | Fancy leather goods importers |
| Missing register<br>*c.*1891<br>Similar mark entered<br>LAO 14 May 1886 | | P5/M/379<br>***#3769***<br> | **Henry E MEYER** *<br>8 Lawrence Lane<br>London EC | Pipe importer |
| R1/155<br>16 October 1901 | | P9/M/34<br>***#3770***<br> | **Harry MANISON**<br>85½ Great Hampton Street<br>Birmingham | Manufacturing jeweller |
| R1/20<br>8 January 1896<br>Sent by E Langridge<br>& Co<br>C Widmer & Sons<br>Stainsby & Coupland | 24 Canonbury Villas<br>Islington<br>London | P5/M/718b<br>***#3771***<br> | **Henry MARSHALL** *<br>Highbury Leather Works<br>22 Corsica Street<br>Highbury<br>London | Purse and cigar case manufacturer |
| R1/113<br>4 October 1899<br>Sent by Henry<br>Moreton | 16 Charles Road<br>Handsworth<br>Birmingham | P9/M/16<br>***#3772***<br> | **Henry MORETON**<br>11 Pitsford Street<br>Birmingham | Manufacturer of silver and electroplate goods |
| Not in R1 as expected | Possibly Haseler & Milner | P5/H/774<br>***#3773***<br> | **Unidentified** | |
| R2/52<br>11 December 1907<br>Sent by Herbert<br>Maryon | Yewbarrow Lodge Studio<br>Grange-over-Sands<br>Lancaster | P9/M/122<br>***#3774***<br> | **Herbert MARYON**<br>Yewbarrow Lodge Studio<br>Grange-over-Sands<br>Lancaster<br>University College<br>Reading | Artist and craftsman |
| R2/182<br>16 January 1914<br>Sent by H Morser | 8 Crescent Road<br>Kingston Hill<br>London SW | P15/M/5<br>***#3775***<br> | **Harry MORSER** *<br>35 Hatton Garden<br>London | Jeweller |
| R3/106<br>14 September 1944<br>Sent by Hilda M<br>Beach | 16 Heath Street<br>Birmingham 18 | P21/B/22<br>***#3776***<br> | **Hilda M BEACH**<br>184 Warstone Lane<br>Birmingham 18 | Manufacturing jeweller |

| REGISTRATION DETAILS | MAKER'S PRIVATE ADDRESS and DETAILS | PLATE and MARK DETAILS | MAKER/COMPANY and BUSINESS ADDRESS | MAKER'S TRADE |
|---|---|---|---|---|
| Missing register<br>*c.*1891<br>Cameo mark LAO<br>6 December 1899 | Very tentative attribution | P5/M*sic*/351<br>***#3777***<br>  | **Henry Moxhay COHEN** *<br>7 Manchester Avenue<br>Aldersgate Street<br>London EC | Stick mounter |
| R1/106<br>10 July 1899<br>Sent by A J Cheshire | Goodwood House<br>Southend | P9/E/4<br>***#3778***<br> | **A Leon EMMANUEL** trading as<br>**H M EMMANUEL & SON**<br>12, 13 Ordinance Road<br>Portsea | Silversmiths and jewellers |
| 10 July 1899 | | P9/E/3<br>***#3779***<br> | | |
| R3/11<br>22 August 1922<br>Sent by Henry Mander | Private address same as business | P15/M/46<br>***#3780***<br>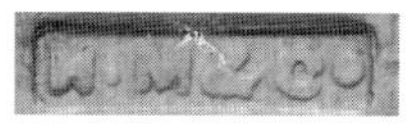 | **Henry MANDER** trading as<br>**H MANDER & CO**<br>Spon Works<br>Coventry | Wholesale jewellers |
| R2/235<br>22 October 1920<br>Sent by Geo F Bickerton | | P15/M/41<br>***#3781***<br> | | |
| R2/74<br>11 March 1909<br>Sent by W Sharman | 90 Maida Vale<br>20 Sheldon Road<br>London NW | P13/M/7<br>***#3782***<br>  | **Harold M MERTON**<br>**Daniel JACOBS** trading as<br>**Daniel JACOBS**<br>12 Moore Lane<br>London EC | Merchants |
| SPB/15 undated between 20 June 1866 and 4 December 1867 | | P3/N/x3<br>***#3783-5***<br>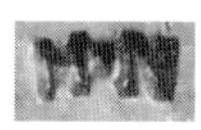 | **Henry NICHOLLS**<br>5 Hunter Street<br>Liverpool | Watch manufacturer |
| R3/142<br>27 March 1953<br>Sent by Elite Bracelet Manufacturing Co<br>Regent Street<br>Birmingham | | P21/N/7<br>***#3786***<br>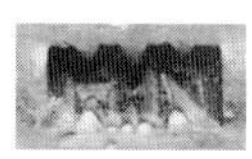 | **Louis NEWMARK LTD**<br>Prefect Works<br>542/548 Purley Way<br>Croydon<br>Surrey | Watch manufacturers |
| LPB/38<br>30 May 1883 | | P3/H/x1<br>***#3787***<br> | **HOLLIS & NEWMAN** *<br>58 Tenby Street North<br>Birmingham | Jewellers |
| R1/184<br>10 February 1903<br>Sent by W E Hollis | Conway House<br>Wood End Road<br>Gravelly Hill<br>The Hawthornes<br>Hyde Green, Birmingham | P9H/46[7]*sic*<br>***#3788***<br> | **William Edward HOLLIS**<br>**Arthur NEWMAN** trading as<br>**HOLLIS & NEWMAN** *<br>62 Tenby Street North<br>Birmingham | Manufacturing jewellers |
| LPB/40<br>3 November 1883<br>No mark in LPB | | P5/H/x1<br>***#3789***<br> | | |
| Missing register<br>*c.*1890 | | P5/H/287<br>***#3790***<br> | | |
| Missing register<br>*c.*1891 | | P5/H/394<br>***#3791***<br>  | | |
| R1/85<br>25 April 1894<br>Sent by Hollis & Newman<br>W H & F Rabone<br>Marlow & Vaughton | | P5/N/553<br>***#3792***<br> | **H NATHAN & CO** *<br>102 Fore Street<br>London | Wholesale jewellers |

| REGISTRATION DETAILS | MAKER'S PRIVATE ADDRESS and DETAILS | PLATE and MARK DETAILS | MAKER/COMPANY and BUSINESS ADDRESS | MAKER'S TRADE |
|---|---|---|---|---|
| R2/43<br>10 July 1907<br>Sent by<br>J & R Griffin | 10 Hereford Mansions<br>London W | P9/H/96<br>***#3793***<br> | **S HOFFNUNG & CO**<br>B Sinauer (Secretary)<br>102 Fore Street<br>London E | Merchants |
| MR2/4,7,87<br>J3/398 | Admonished for sub-standard spoons 1730 | P1/1/x1<br>***#3794***<br> | **Peter HOPWOOD**<br>Preston<br><br>or | Silversmith |
| MR1/142<br>J3/398<br>Free 1680 | This mark struck post-1701 so may be a little late for Howell? See also his TH mark ***#9884*** | P1/6/x2<br>***#3795,6***<br> | **Thomas HOWELL**<br>Chester | Silversmith |
| R2/138<br>29 June 1911<br>Sent by<br>H Pritchard | 47 Ayris Road<br>Brooks Bar<br>Manchester | P13/Q*sic*/204<br>***#3797***<br> | **Henry PRITCHARD**<br>11a Sugar Lane<br>Withy Grove<br>Manchester | Working jeweller and diamond mounter |
| 29 August 1950<br>New punch | | P21/P/39<br>***#3798***<br> | | |
| R3/105<br>30 March 1943<br>Sent by Samuel Henry Phillips | 20 Treton Road<br>Handsworth Wood<br>Birmingham | P21/P/11<br>***#3799***<br> | **Samuel Henry PHILLIPS**<br>16 Hockley Street<br>Birmingham 18 | Jeweller |
| R1/40<br>19 February 1897<br>Sent by H Perkins<br>H Tongue | Private address same as business | P5/P/818<br>***#3800***<br> | **Henry PERKINS** *<br>179 Tottenham Court Road<br>London | Pipe and stick mounter |
| R1/65<br>2 May 1898<br>Sent by W Walker | Private address same as business<br>At 33 Compton Street by September 1908 | P5/Q*sic*/954<br>***#3801***<br> | | |
| LPB/70<br>10 June 1885 | | P5/P/x1<br>***#3802***<br> | **Henry POPE**<br>15 Pitsford Street<br>Birmingham | Jeweller |
| R2/143<br>9 September 1911<br>Sent by H Pope<br>44, 46 Allen Road<br>Birmingham | | P13/Q*sic*/207<br>***#3803***<br> | **Henry POPE**<br>15a Pitsford Street<br>Birmingham | |
| Missing register<br>*c.*1890 | | P5/P/286<br>***#3804***<br> | | |
| R2/54<br>16 January 1908<br>Sent by Cyril Harris | Albert Palmer<br>191 Waterloo Road<br>Smethwick<br>243 Burberry Street<br>Lozells | P9/H/101<br>***#3805***<br> | **Albert E PALMER**<br>**Cyril HARRIS** trading as<br>**HARRIS & PALMER**<br>98 Spencer Street<br>Birmingham | Ring manufacturers |
| R1/127<br>31 May 1900<br>Sent by H P Bowdler | Private address same as business | P9/B/29<br>***#3806***<br> | **Henry Peter BOWDLER**<br>138 Alwyn Street<br>Liverpool | Watchmaker |
| R3/74<br>10 January 1935<br>Sent by T J Skelton<br>86 Vyse Street<br>Birmingham | | P15/F/41<br>***#3807***<br> | **Hannah Phoebe FLIGELSTONE**<br>22 City Road<br>Cardiff | Jeweller |

| REGISTRATION DETAILS | MAKER'S PRIVATE ADDRESS and DETAILS | PLATE and MARK DETAILS | MAKER/COMPANY and BUSINESS ADDRESS | MAKER'S TRADE |
|---|---|---|---|---|
| R1/45<br>22 May 1897<br>Sent by Percy Haseler<br>Two sizes | 60 St Peters Row [1]<br>Handsworth<br>187 Heathfield Road [2]<br>Handsworth | P5/*Zsic*/843x2<br>***#3808,9***<br> | **Henry HASELER** [1]<br>**Percy HASELER** [2] trading as<br>**H & P HASELER**<br>36 Hylton Street<br>Birmingham | Jewellers |
| LPB/62<br>20 January 1883 | | P3/O/x1<br>***#3810***<br> | **Henry Pitman ORCHARD**<br>30 Snape Street<br>Birmingham | Jeweller |
| R3/38<br>12 July 1927<br>Sent by self | Rockwood<br>Skipton | P15/P/200<br>***#3811***<br> | **Frank FATTORINI** trading as<br>**H PEARSON LTD**<br>Seymour Place<br>Old Trafford<br>Manchester | General merchants |
| R3/24<br>22 October 1924<br>Sent by E Whitehouse & Son | Rockwood<br>Skipton | P15/P/193<br>***#3812***<br> | **H PEARSON LTD**<br>Thomas Fattorini<br>Frank Fattorini<br>Seymour Grove<br>Old Trafford<br>Manchester | |
| R3/41<br>11 July 1928<br>Sent by Eaton & Wrighton | 121 Vyse Street<br>Birmingham<br>Rockwood [1]<br>Skipton | P15/P/213<br>***#3813***<br> | **H PEARSON LTD**<br>Wilfred Fattorini [1] (Director)<br>1 Newmarket Street<br>Skipton (Reg Office)<br>Seymour Place<br>Old Trafford<br>Manchester | |
| R3/71<br>28 April 1934<br>Sent by Samuel Hope<br>126 Vyse Street<br>Birmingham | Rockwood [1 2]<br>Skipton<br>Laurel Bank [3]<br>Ilkley<br>Yorkshire | P15/P/238<br>***#3814***<br> | **H PEARSON LTD**<br>Thomas Fattorini [1] (Director)<br>Frank Fattorini [2] (Director)<br>Wilfred Fattorini [3] (Director)<br>Seymour Place<br>Old Trafford<br>Manchester | Jewellers |
| PDB 1785-7<br>SOT/125-6<br>MR3/97<br>PP1/187<br>PP2/349 | Seen on the case of a watch by Henry Rose, Liverpool, 1779 | Not on P1<br>***#3815***<br> | **Henry RIGBY**<br>76 Castle Street (in 1774)<br>23 John Street (1777-80)<br>Liverpool | Watch and watchcase maker |
| PDB 1785-7<br>SOT/125-6<br>MR3/97<br>PP1/187, PP2/349 | Seen on the silver case of a watch by Henry Rigby, Liverpool, 1781 | Not on P1<br>***#3816***<br> | | |
| R1/80<br>13 October 1894<br>Sent by H C Richarde | 33 St John Street Road<br>Clerkenwell<br>London | P5/R/611<br>***#3817***<br> | **Henry Charles RICHARDE** *<br>70 Wynyatt Street<br>Clerkenwell<br>London EC | Silversmith and engraver |
| Missing register<br>*c.*1887 Similar mark<br>LAO 23 Nov 1892 | see also mark above | P5/R/87<br>***#3818***<br> | | |
| Missing register<br>*c.*1887 | | P5/R/111<br>***#3819***<br>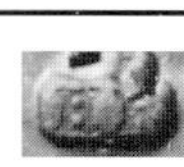 | | |
| R2/92<br>16 September 1909<br>Sent by Heaps, Rosenberg & Co<br>Dissolved part'ship 13 July 1911 | 89 Wretham Road<br>Birmingham<br>69 Conybere Street<br>Birmingham | P13/R/28<br>***#3820***<br> | **Louis HEAPS**<br>**Louis ROSENBERG** trading as<br>**HEAPS, ROSENBERG & CO**<br>78 Vittoria Road<br>Birmingham | Manufacturing jewellers |

| REGISTRATION DETAILS | MAKER'S PRIVATE ADDRESS and DETAILS | PLATE and MARK DETAILS | MAKER/COMPANY and BUSINESS ADDRESS | MAKER'S TRADE |
|---|---|---|---|---|
| R2/140<br>20 July 1911<br>Sent by Louis Rosenberg<br>BAO 16.973<br>Originally 28 | Belmont House<br>Belgrave Road<br>Birmingham | P13/R/33<br>***#3821***<br> | **Louis ROSENBERG** trading as<br>**HEAPS, ROSENBERG & CO**<br>46 Warstone Lane<br>Birmingham | Manufacturer of signet and dress rings, etc |
| R2/156<br>23 May 1912<br>Sent by Handcock & Walker<br>clerk entered HS 44 but this is ES&S | Private address same as business | P15/S/39?<br>***#3822***<br> | **H SHOERATTS**<br>Hengestbury Road<br>Southbourne<br>Hampshire | Fancy leather goods |
| R1/85<br>16 November 1898<br>Sent by Robert Pike ? (indistinct)<br>W J Spencer through T P Hewitt | 2 Southwood Road<br>Liverpool | P9/S/9<br>***#3823***<br> | **Edgar SAMUEL** trading as<br>**Harriet SAMUEL** *<br>97, 99, 101 Market Street<br>Manchester | Jeweller |
| R1/65<br>15 April 1898<br>Sent by Hart & Sons per W Walker | 119 Sutherland Avenue [1]<br>8 St John's Wood Park [2]<br>London | P5/*Zsic*/950<br>***#3824***<br>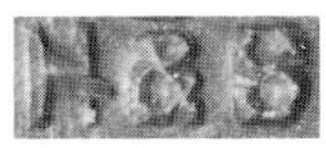 | **David HART** [1]<br>**Montague HART** [2] trading as<br>**HART & SONS** *<br>23 Goswell Road<br>London | Fancy goods warehousemen |
| R1/153<br>18 September 1901<br>Sent by W Walker | Norfolk House[1]<br>Chorleywood<br>Herts<br>119 Sutherland Avenue [2]<br>London W | P9/H/45<br>***#3825***<br> | **Montague HART** [1] **David HART** [2]<br>trading as **HART & SONS** *<br>23 Goswell Road<br>London | |
| R2/233<br>16 September 1920<br>Sent by Imperial Tobacco Co | Private address same as business | P15/S/43<br>***#3826***<br> | **Harry Leonard SHEEN**<br>8 Luxor Street<br>London SE5 | Dealer in fancy goods |
| R2/214<br>2 February 1918<br>Sent by Hyman Subenberg | 31 Tower Essex Street<br>Birmingham | P15/S/31<br>***#3827***<br> | **Hyman SUBENBERG**<br>26 Spencer Street<br>Birmingham | Gold ring maker |
| Not in R2 as expected - between February and November 1918 | | P15/S/34<br>***#3828***<br> | | |
| R1/13<br>2 July 1895<br>Sent by F Doyle<br>J H Rowland also authority to C Walker | Ivy House<br>Parsonage Road<br>Heaton Chapel<br>Manchester | P5/H/671<br>***#3829***<br> | **George HUXLEY** trading as<br>**HUXLEY & SIDEBOTHAM** *<br>60, 68 Newton Street and<br>37, 39 Ancoats Street<br>Manchester | Umbrella stick and cane manufacturers |
| Missing register<br>*c.*1891<br>Similar marks entered LAO 8 January 1909 | see mark above | P5/H/357a<br>***#3830***<br> | | |
| | | P5/H/357b<br>***#3831***<br> | | |
| R3/153<br>5 October 1954<br>Sent by R L Hughes | Glenwood<br>Llangollen | P21/H/71<br>***#3832***<br> | **Robert Llewellyn HUGHES** trading as<br>**HUGHES & SON**<br>37 Castle Street<br>Llangollen | Watchmakers and jewellers, goldsmiths and silversmiths |
| Missing register<br>*c.*1886 | | P5/S/18<br>***#3833***<br>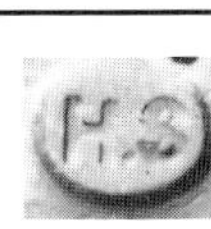 | **Edgar SAMUEL** trading as<br>**Harriet SAMUEL** *<br>97, 99, 101 Market Street<br>Manchester | Jeweller |

| REGISTRATION DETAILS | MAKER'S PRIVATE ADDRESS and DETAILS | PLATE and MARK DETAILS | MAKER/COMPANY and BUSINESS ADDRESS | MAKER'S TRADE |
|---|---|---|---|---|
| R2/201<br>13 November 1915<br>Sent by F W Cole | Private address same as business | P15/S/23-25<br>***#3834-6***<br> | **Harry SAPIRO**<br>8 Hartington Road<br>Liverpool | Wholesale jeweller |
| R3/13<br>24 October 1922<br>Sent by Henry Spiro | 16 Newsham Drive<br>Liverpool | P15/S/58<br>***#3837***<br> | **Henry SPIRO**<br>Bank Chambers<br>2 Moss Street<br>Liverpool | General merchant |
| Not in R2 as expected - between May and September 1920 | | P15/S/42<br>***#3838***<br>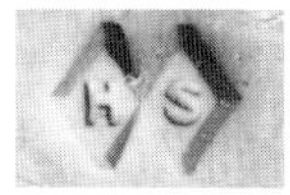 | | |
| R1/10<br>30 April 1895<br>Sent by Edgar Samuel | 17 Northumberland Street<br>Higher Broughton<br>Manchester | P5/S/656<br>***#3839***<br>§<br> | **Edgar SAMUEL** trading as<br>**H SAMUEL** *<br>97, 99, 101 Market Street<br>Manchester | Watch manufacturers |
| R3/58<br>4 July 1931<br>Sent by Smith, Ewen & Stylic Ltd<br>42 Frederick Street<br>Birmingham | 27 Woodfield Avenue [1]<br>Streatham, London SW16<br>43 Parklands Road [2]<br>Streatham<br>London SW16 | P15/I*sic*/111<br>***#3840***<br> | **William Arthur HILDYARD** [1]<br>**Joshua SHINDLER** [2] trading as<br>**HILDYARD & SHINDLER**<br>65 Hatton Garden<br>London EC1 | Watchcase manufacturers |
| PP1/187<br>J1 1849-66<br>Similar mark entered LAO 16 January 1849 | | P2/S/x4<br>***#3841-4***<br> | **Henry J STEWART**<br>170 Park Lane<br>Liverpool | Watchcase maker |
| R3/49<br>4 October 1929<br>Sent by Smith, Ewen & Stylic Ltd<br>42 Frederick Street<br>Birmingham | | P15/S/90<br>***#3845***<br> | **H SAMUEL LTD** *<br>John Ashton (Secretary)<br>Hunters Road Works<br>Hockley<br>Birmingham | Manufacturing jewellers |
| LPB/76<br>29 April 1882 | Precursor of H Samuel High Street Jewellers<br>See also HSAMUEL #3565 Page 209 | P3/S/x1<br>***#3846***<br> | **Harriet SAMUEL** *<br>97 Market Street<br>Manchester | Watch manufacturer and importer |
| Missing register<br>*c.*1894 | | P5/S/556<br>***#3847***<br> | | |
| R2/17<br>5 May 1906<br>Sent by H Samuel | Wyelands<br>St John's Road<br>Buxton | P9/S/100-102<br>***#3848-50***<br> | **H SAMUEL** *<br>Market Street<br>Manchester | Watchmaker and jeweller |
| R2/52<br>3 November 1907<br>Sent by Allen Brothers | 1 Princess Gate<br>London | P13/S/5<br>***#3851***<br> | **Edgar Samuel EDGAR** trading as<br>**H SAMUEL** *<br>91 Market Street<br>Manchester | |
| R1/199<br>11 August 1903<br>Sent by F C Hawkford | 18 Spring Road<br>19 Snow Hill<br>Birmingham | P9/H/52<br>***#3852***<br>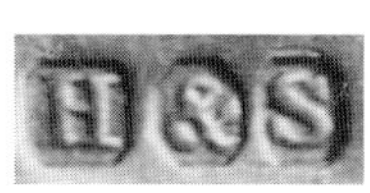 | **Francis Charles HAWKFORD**<br>trading as<br>**Charles Singleby HAWKFORD**<br>136 New Street<br>Birmingham | Tobacconist |
| LPB/34<br>24 May 1880 | | P3/D*sic*/x1<br>***#3853***<br> | **Henry HYDE & SONS**<br>47 Warstone Terrace<br>Warstone Lane<br>Birmingham | Jewellers |

| REGISTRATION DETAILS | MAKER'S PRIVATE ADDRESS and DETAILS | PLATE and MARK DETAILS | MAKER/COMPANY and BUSINESS ADDRESS | MAKER'S TRADE |
|---|---|---|---|---|
| PP1/187<br>J1 1849-66<br>Similar mark entered LAO 13 July 1858 | | P2/S/x2<br>***#3854,5***<br> | **Henry J STEWART**<br>170 Park Lane<br>Liverpool | Watchcase maker |
| | | P2/X*sic*/x3<br>***#3856-8***<br> | | |
| SPB/12 entry SPB/15 mark<br>Undated – 1870-3<br>Sent by J Tayton | Entry and mark on different pages | P3/S/x3 (SPB/15)<br>***#3859-61***<br> | **Henry STUART** *<br>13 Hope Street<br>Liverpool | Watchcase and watch manufacturer |
| SPB/17<br>6 April 1873<br>SPB mark shown.<br>Sent by Yardley & Buckland | See also JS and RY over WB | Not on P3<br>***#3862***<br> | **John STUART**<br>13 Hope Street<br>Liverpool | |
| R2/219<br>29 April 1919<br>Sent by A Hyams | 142 Victoria Park Road and<br>5 Brunswick Street<br>London E | P15/H/51<br>***#3863***<br> | **Arthur HYAMS**<br>**Morris STRUMINGHER**<br>5 Brunswick Street<br>Hackney Road<br>London E | Chain, bracelet and ring makers |
| R2/184<br>27 February 1914<br>Sent by Imperial Tobacco Co | Private address same as business | P15/S/6<br>***#3864***<br> | **Harry SHEEN**<br>8 Luxor Street<br>Camberwell<br>London SE | Fancy goods dealer |
| LPB/78 SP31/3<br>24 May 1884<br>No mark in LPB | See also HS | P5/S/x1<br>***#3865***<br> | **Harriet SAMUEL** *<br>99 Market Street<br>Manchester | Watch manufacturer and importer |
| Missing register<br>*c.*1894 | | P5/S/538a<br>***#3866***<br> | **Henry STOKES**<br>43 Tenby Street<br>Birmingham | Jeweller |
| Missing register<br>*c.*1894<br>Similar mark entered BAO 20 June 1892 | | P5/S/538b<br>***#3867***<br> | | |
| R3/130<br>12 January 1950<br>Sent by H S Hodgson<br>Two sizes | 31 Ulster Road<br>Bowsham<br>Lancaster | P21/H/51,52<br>***#3868,9***<br> | **Henry Stockdale HODGSON**<br>College of Arts & Crafts<br>Storey Institute<br>Lancaster | Teacher |
| R2/236<br>14 December 1920<br>Sent by H S Hack | The Grove<br>Westend<br>Nr Stonehouse<br>Glos | P15/H/45<br>***#3870***<br> | **Henry Stanley HACK**<br>Bourne Mill<br>Brimscombe<br>Nr Stroud<br>Gloucestershire | Umbrella stick and parasol stick manufacturer |
| R1/55<br>1 December 1897<br>Sent by A H Tongue | 409 Beverley Road<br>Hull | P5/aboveD/911<br>***#3871***<br> | **William HART**<br>**Herbert William HART** trading as<br>**William HART & SON**<br>14, 15 Waterworks Street<br>Hull | Importers of tobacconists fancy goods |
| R3/117<br>18 April 1947<br>Sent by H S Hack Ltd<br>- P15/H/45 cancelled 8 June 1948 | Sealed in the presence of the director and secretary | No new mark<br>***#3872*** | **H S HACK LTD**<br>H S Hack (Director)<br>M C Denby (Secretary)<br>Bourne Mill, Brimscombe<br>Nr Stroud, Gloucestershire | Umbrella and walking stick manufacturers |

| REGISTRATION DETAILS | MAKER'S PRIVATE ADDRESS and DETAILS | PLATE and MARK DETAILS | MAKER/COMPANY and BUSINESS ADDRESS | MAKER'S TRADE |
|---|---|---|---|---|
| R2/215<br>28 February 1918<br>Sent by H S Hack | Lewiston Villa<br>Brinscombe<br>Nr Stroud<br>Gloucestershire | P15/H/40<br>*#3873*<br> | **Henry Stanley HACK**<br>Bourne Mill<br>Brimscombe<br>Nr Stroud<br>Gloucestershire | Wholesale umbrella, parasol and walking stick manufacturer |
| R3/124<br>8 June 1948<br>Sent by H S Hack Ltd<br>All previous entries cancelled | | P21/H/43<br>*#3874*<br> | | |
| R2/120<br>15 October 1910<br>Sent by Harrods Stores Ltd<br>Per Stokes & Ireland<br>Cancelled<br>25 September 1911<br>Two sizes | 26 Granard Road [1]<br>Wandsworth Common<br>London | P13/H/63,64<br>*#5875,6*<br> | **HARRODS STORES LTD**<br>George Sheald [1] (Secretary)<br>Brompton Road<br>London SW | General merchants, silversmith and jewellers |
| R2/8<br>23 December 1905<br>Sent by J G Newbold | 22 Fellows Road<br>London NW<br>Manor Mansions<br>Belsize Grove<br>London NW | P9/S/93-95<br>*#3877-9*<br> | **Henry SIMON**<br>**Maurice STRAUSS** style of firm<br>**SIMON, (Emile) VUILLARD & STRAUSS** *<br>4 Edward Place<br>London EC | Tobacco pipe manufacturers |
| R2/28<br>5 November 1906<br>Sent by J G Newbold | 22 Fellows Road<br>London NW<br>4a Belsize Grove<br>London NW | P9/S/108-110<br>*#3880-2*<br> | **Henry SIMON**<br>**Maurice STRAUSS** trading as **SIMON & STRAUSS** *<br>4 Edward Place<br>London EC | |
| R2/184<br>13 March 1914<br>Sent by Handcock & Walker | 4 Belsize Grove<br>London NW<br>2 Lancaster Place<br>London NW | P15/S/7-9<br>*#3883-5*<br> | **Maurice STRAUSS** *<br>**Henry SIMON** *<br>108,110 Golden Lane<br>London EC | |
| R1/206<br>5 February 1903<br>Sent by J & R Griffin | Summer Hill<br>Nuneaton | P9/S/71<br>*#3886*<br> | **Henry SLINGSBY** trading as<br>**H SLINGSBY & SON**<br>Seymour Street<br>Nuneaton | Regalia manufacturers |
| R3/107<br>22 November 1944<br>Sent by Henry Sidney Thomas | 63 Mapleton Road<br>Hall Green<br>Birmingham 28 | P21/T/10<br>*#3887*<br> | **Henry Sidney THOMAS**<br>97a Vittoria Road<br>Hockley<br>Birmingham 18 | Ring mounter and repairer |
| PP1/187<br>GTD 1852-69<br>J1 1852-69<br>PMR 1849-65 | | P2/T/x4<br>*#3888-91*<br> | **Henry TARLETON**<br>13 Highfield Street (1853-64)<br>17 Holford Street (1865)<br>Liverpool | Watch and watchcase manufacturer |
| SPB/2<br>18 July 1871 | | P3/T/x3<br>*#3892-4*<br> | **Henry TARLETON**<br>13 Highfield Street<br>Liverpool | |
| R2/84<br>9 June 1909<br>Sent by Henry Tattersall | 14 Peel Street<br>Hanlet<br>Leeds | P13/T/15<br>*#3895*<br> | **Harry TATTERSALL**<br>5 Dodsworth Courts<br>40 Briggate<br>Leeds | Silver mounters, tobacco pipe and walking stick makers |

| REGISTRATION DETAILS | MAKER'S PRIVATE ADDRESS and DETAILS | PLATE and MARK DETAILS | MAKER/COMPANY and BUSINESS ADDRESS | MAKER'S TRADE |
|---|---|---|---|---|
| Not in R2 as expected<br>Between January and<br>March 1922 | See previous entry<br>Mark not registered at BAO | P15/T/38<br>*#3896*<br> | **Harry TATTERSALL**<br>5 Dodsworth Courts<br>40 Briggate<br>Leeds | Silver mounters tobacco pipe and walking stick makers |
| | Possibly punched in error on plate 1 instead of plate 2 | P1/32/x4<br>*#3897-3900*<br> | **Henry TARLETON**<br>13 Highfield Street<br>Liverpool | Watch and watchcase manufacturer |
| LPB/80<br>15 January 1882 | BAO 1879 has him at<br>28a Richard Street | P3/T/x1<br>*#3901*<br> | **Henry THOMPSON**<br>25 Warstone Lane<br>Birmingham | Jeweller |
| Missing register<br>*c.*1888 | T badly formed and over-struck | P5/H/177<br>*#3902*<br> | **Unidentified** | |
| Missing register<br>*c.*1888 | | P5/T/173<br>*#3903*<br> | **Unidentified** | |
| R1/60<br>9 February 1898<br>Sent by F J H Thomas<br>Durban & Co<br>C Horner | Water Orton<br>Nr Birmingham | P5/T/931<br>*#3904*<br> | **Francis John Horace THOMAS**<br>**Joseph THOMAS**<br>40 St Paul's Square<br>Birmingham | Jewellers |
| R1/88<br>20 December 1898<br>Sent by H Tongue | Private address same as business | P9/T/7<br>*#3905*<br> | **Henry TONGUE** *<br>37 Hunters Vale<br>Birmingham | Pipe mounter |
| | | P9/T/8<br>*#3906*<br> | | |
| R1/57<br>20 January 1898<br>Sent by<br>W E Thomason<br>Five sizes<br>MR3/120 | 227 Churchill Road [1]<br>Handsworth<br>107 Hamstead Road [2]<br>Handsworth<br>Birmingham | P5/T/920x5<br>*#3907-11*<br> | **Joseph John RICHARDSON** [1]<br>**William Edwin THOMASON** [2]<br>trading as<br>**HILLIARD & THOMASON** * and<br>**John THOMASON & NEPHEWS** *<br>1, 3, 5 Spencer Street<br>Birmingham | Silversmiths |
| Missing register<br>*c.*1887 | | P5/H/99<br>*#3912*<br> | **Unidentified** | |
| LPB/18<br>26 August 1884<br>Sent by Horton &<br>Allday | | P5/B/x1<br>*#3913*<br> | **Henry Titterton BROCKWELL** *<br>8 Brooke Street<br>London EC | Cut glass manufacturer |
| R2/139<br>6 July 1911<br>Sent by H Clifford<br>Davis<br>BAO 18.703 | Warwick Hall<br>Bromsgrove<br>Birmingham | P13/T/39<br>*#3914*<br> | **A J PEPPER** trading as<br>**H TERRY & CO**<br>29 Newhall Hill<br>Birmingham | Silversmiths |
| R1/105<br>28 June 1899<br>Sent by H J Dumelow | 90 Lodge Road<br>Hockley<br>Birmingham | P9/D/10<br>*#3915*<br> | **Henry James DUMELOW**<br>39 Northampton Street<br>Birmingham | Stud and link manufacturer |
| No entry in R1<br>Estimated May to<br>November 1900 | | P9/D/18<br>*#3916*<br> | | |

| REGISTRATION DETAILS | MAKER'S PRIVATE ADDRESS and DETAILS | PLATE and MARK DETAILS | MAKER/COMPANY and BUSINESS ADDRESS | MAKER'S TRADE |
|---|---|---|---|---|
| SPB/38<br>24 November 1880 | | P3/Hx1<br>***#3917***<br> | **HARRIS & USHER**<br>123 Vyse Street<br>Birmingham | Jewellers |
| Missing register<br>*c.*1887<br>Similar mark entered LAO 15 December 1887 | | P5/V/83<br>***#3918***<br> | **Henry VOSE** *<br>24 Gloucester Street<br>Clerkenwell<br>London | Manufacturing jeweller |
| R2/137<br>9 June 1911<br>Sent by Alfred Vander<br>Two sizes | 7 Spencer Gardens<br>Eltham<br>11 Gourock Road<br>Eltham | P13/V/15,16<br>***#3919,20***<br> | **Henry VANDER**<br>**Alfred VANDER** trading as<br>**C J VANDER** *<br>12 Betterton Street<br>Drury Lane<br>London | Silversmiths |
| R1/213<br>30 April 1904<br>Sent by W J Wyatt<br>Two sizes | White Lodge<br>Acre Lane<br>Brixton | P9/Q*sic*/189-200<br>***#3921-32***<br>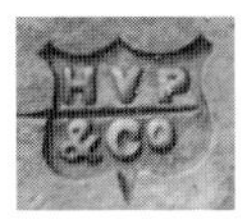 | **Harold Vyvyan PITHEY** trading as<br>**H V PITHEY & CO** *<br>10 Lower John Street<br>Golden Square<br>London | Goldsmiths and silversmiths |
| R2/27<br>30 April 1904<br>Sent by Eels Brothers & Brown<br>Two sizes | 2 Becmead Avenue<br>Streatham<br>London SW | P9/U*sic*/256-267<br>***#3933-44***<br> | **H V PITHEY & CO** *<br>26 Great Pulteney Street<br>London W | |
| R2/139<br>6 July 1911<br>Sent by H Clifford Davis<br>BO17.445 | 13 Northampton Road<br>Addiscombe<br>Surrey<br>Staines<br>Middlesex | P13/Q*sic*/205<br>***#3945***<br> | **Harold Vivian PITHEY**<br>**Charles Arthur HOLDEN** trading as<br>**H V PITHEY & CO** *<br>26 Great Pulteney Street<br>London | |
| R3/108<br>22 February 1945<br>Sent by Harold Victor Woolley | Private address same as business | P21/W/39<br>***#3946***<br> | **Harold Victor WOOLLEY**<br>7, 8, 8A Station Terrace<br>Blackpool | Jeweller, ring maker and silversmith |
| PP1/187<br>Similar mark entered BAO 24 May 1847 | | P2/V*sic*/x3<br>***#3947-9***<br> | **Henry WELLS**<br>Bond Street<br>Coventry | Watchcase maker |
| LPB/88<br>25 November 1879<br>Sent by C Brown & Co | See also HWLtd | P3/X*sic*/x3<br>***#3950-2***<br> | **Henry WILLIAMSON** *<br>Farringdon Road<br>London | Watch and watchcase manufacturer |
| LPB/64<br>17 October 1882<br>Sent by Fulford ?<br>Two sizes | | P3/W/x2<br>***#3953,4***<br> | | |
| R3/186<br>16 August 1962<br>Sent by<br>A H Westwood<br>Two sizes | 35 The Green<br>Castle Bromwich | P21/W/110,111<br>***#3955,6***<br> | **Arthur Hamil WESTWOOD**<br>Birmingham Assay Office<br>Newhall Street<br>Birmingham 3 | Assayer |
| R3/33<br>14 September 1926<br>Sent by W Weston<br><br>1 January 1929<br>Punch recut and registered | 46 Cecil Street<br>Glasgow | P15/H/92<br>***#3957***<br>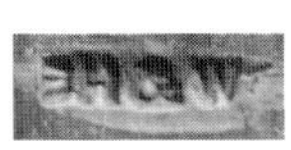<br>P15/I*sic*/106<br>***#3958***<br> | **James Taylor Niven WATSON**<br>**William HECTOR** trading as<br>**HECTOR & WATSON**<br>19 Waterloo Street<br>Glasgow and<br>1a Great King Street<br>Birmingham | Gem ring manufacturers |

| REGISTRATION DETAILS | MAKER'S PRIVATE ADDRESS and DETAILS | PLATE and MARK DETAILS | MAKER/COMPANY and BUSINESS ADDRESS | MAKER'S TRADE |
|---|---|---|---|---|
| R3/77<br>20 August 1935<br>Sent by Weston & Sons<br>28 Hylton Street<br>Birmingham | Parkleven<br>Kilmacolm<br>Renfrewshire | P15/H/126<br>***#3959***<br> | **James Taylor Niven WATSON**<br>trading as **HECTOR & WATSON**<br>19 Waterloo Street<br>Glasgow | Wholesale jewellers |
| R3/148<br>8 December 1953<br>Sent by H Waywell<br>Two sizes | 2 Hawkhurst Avenue<br>Fulwood<br>Preston<br>Lancs | P21/W/70,71<br>***#3960,1***<br> | **Horatio WAYWELL**<br>No business address entered | Silversmith |
| R1/237<br>13 July 1905<br>Sent by Hugh Wallis | Carn Brae<br>Hazel Road<br>Altrincham | P9/V*sic*/135<br>***#3962***<br> | **Hugh WALLIS**<br>7 Market Street<br>2 Station Buildings (undated, moved to)<br>Altrincham | Artist and designer |
| R2/33<br>18 February 1907<br>Sent by Hugh Wallis | | P9/V*sic*/165<br>***#3963***<br> | as above<br>2 Station Road<br>Stamford New Road<br>Altrincham<br>Cheshire | Designer and art metalworker |
| R3/115<br>5 November 1946<br>Sent by B M Wallis<br>Took over P*sic*/W/162 of Hugh Wallis deceased | Private address same as business | No new mark<br>***#3964*** | **Brian Mills WALLIS** trading as<br>**Hugh WALLIS**<br>72 The Downs<br>Altrincham<br>Cheshire | Art metalworker |
| Not in R3 as expected<br>*c.* March 1923 | | P15/H/74<br>***#3965***<br> | **M G HEPBURN** trading as<br>**HEPBURN & WILCOX**<br>36 Tenby Street<br>Birmingham | Manufacturing jewellers |
| Not in R3 as expected<br>*c.* March 1925 | | P15/H/86<br>***#3966***<br> | | |
| R1/47<br>26 June 1897<br>Sent by Harry Wainwright | 36 Wateley Road<br>Handsworth<br>Birmingham | P5/aboveA/853<br>***#3967***<br>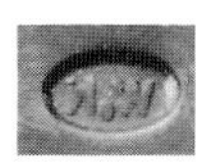 | **Harry WAINWRIGHT**<br>1 Regent Street<br>Birmingham | Jeweller |
| J1 1838-40 | | P2/W/x3<br>***#3968-70***<br> | **Henry WALKER**<br>Chester | Silversmith |
| | | P2/X*sic*/x3<br>***#3971-3***<br> | | |
| LPB/88<br>8 July 1881<br>No name or address in LPB | | P3/W/x1<br>***#3974***<br> | **Henry WILLIAMSON** *<br>Farringdon Road<br>London | Watch and watchcase manufacturer |
| LPB/68<br>7 February 1883<br>LPB mark shown<br>Sent by Jeffries & Smith | | Not on P3<br>***#3975***<br> | | |
| LPB/68<br>1 November 1882<br>Sent by J Whilter | | P3/W/x1<br>***#3976***<br> | | |

| REGISTRATION DETAILS | MAKER'S PRIVATE ADDRESS and DETAILS | PLATE and MARK DETAILS | MAKER/COMPANY and BUSINESS ADDRESS | MAKER'S TRADE |
|---|---|---|---|---|
| LPB/68<br>2 November 1882<br>LPB mark shown | | Not on P3<br>***#3977***  | **Henry WILLIAMSON** *<br>Farringdon Road<br>London | Watch and watchcase manufacturer |
| LPB/90<br>24 March 1884 | | P5/W/x1<br>***#3978*** 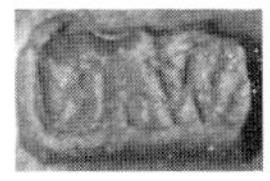 | | |
| LPB/98<br>13 March 1885<br>No mark in LPB<br>Sent by C Roek | | P5/W/x1<br>***#3979***  | | |
| LPB/98<br>30 June 1885<br>No mark in LPB | | P5/W/x1<br>***#3980***  | | |
| Missing register<br>*c.*1886 | | P5/W/18<br>***#3981***  | | |
| Missing register<br>*c.*1886 | | P5/W/33<br>***#3982***  | | |
| Missing register<br>*c.*1888 | | P5/W/178<br>***#3983***  | | |
| LPB/84<br>29 November 1882 | | P3/W/x1<br>***#3984***  | **Henry WOOD**<br>47 Wood Street<br>Liverpool | Jeweller |
| R3/8<br>5 April 1922<br>Sent by M G Hepburn | 760 Western Road<br>Wylde Green<br>Birmingham | P15/H/71,72<br>***#3985,6***  | **M G HEPBURN** trading as<br>**HEPBURN & WILCOX**<br>36 Tenby Street<br>Birmingham | Manufacturing jewellers |
| Not in R3 as expected<br>*c.* June 1924 | | P15/H/79<br>***#3987*** 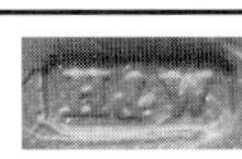 | | |
| R2/183<br>6 February 1914<br>Sent by Handcock & Walker | 6 Colebrook Row<br>London N<br>19 Woodside Gardens<br>London N | P15/H/6<br>***#3988***  | **W A N HANDCOCK**<br>**William P WALKER** (Ed: trading as<br>**HANDCOCK & WALKER** * )<br>58 Pentonville Road<br>London N | Pipe mounters |
| R1/200<br>8 September 1903<br>Sent by G Unite & Son | Private address same as business | P9/W/101<br>***#3989***  | **Henry WELLS** *<br>15 High Street<br>Shrewsbury | Jeweller, silversmith and optician |
| R2/165<br>8 November 1912<br>Sent by Stokes & Ireland Ltd | Bowbrook Bank<br>Shrewsbury | P13/W/1<br>***#3990***  | **Henry WELLS** *<br>15, 17 High Street<br>Shrewsbury | Jeweller and silversmith |
| R3/2<br>21 April 1921<br>Sent by Stokes & Ireland Ltd | Private address same as business | P15/W/39<br>***#3991***  | **Henry WELLS** *<br>18, 19 High Street<br>Shrewsbury | |

| REGISTRATION DETAILS | MAKER'S PRIVATE ADDRESS and DETAILS | PLATE and MARK DETAILS | MAKER/COMPANY and BUSINESS ADDRESS | MAKER'S TRADE |
|---|---|---|---|---|
| Missing register<br>*c*.1886 | Similar mark entered BAO 27 September 1866 and with full stops<br>28 March 1890 | P5/A/63<br>***#3992***<br> | **H W ASHFORD**<br>38, 40 Hylton Street<br>Birmingham | Jeweller |
| LPB/18<br>25 January 1884<br>No mark in LPB | Similar mark entered<br>LAO 12 April 1876 | P5/B/x1<br>***#3993***<br>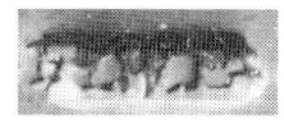 | **Henry White BAMFORD** *<br>25 Northampton Square<br>London EC | Watchcase maker |
| R2/172<br>27 May 1913<br>Sent by Adie Brothers<br>Two sizes | 16 St Helen's Place<br>London EC | P15/W/4,5<br>***#3994,5***<br> | **Harold WALTER** trading as<br>**Harold WALTER & CO**<br>Buenos Aires<br>Brazil | Jewellers and silversmiths |
| R2/89<br>24 July 1909<br>Sent by C Horner | Coleyford<br>Devon | P13/G/11<br>***#3996***<br> | **E W Thadaway HORNER** trading as<br>**Henry W GLESSON**<br>50 Clerkenwell Road<br>London | Manufacturing jewellers |
| SPB/22<br>14 January 1876 | | P3/G/x2<br>***#3997,8***<br> | **Henry William GRIFFIN** *<br>2 King Square<br>London | Watchcase maker |
| R1/25<br>20 March 1896<br>Sent by Henry W King<br><br>Two sizes | Stanford<br>Muswell Avenue<br>Muswell Hill<br>London | P5/K/748a<br>***#3999***<br>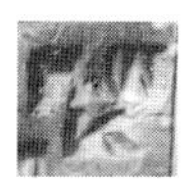 | **Henry William KING** trading as<br>**Henry W KING & SON** *<br>Silverdale Works<br>15 Charterhouse Street<br>London | Silversmiths and jewellers |
| | | P5/K/748b,c<br>***#4000,1***<br> | | |
| R2/130<br>11 March 1911<br>BAO 17.241, 18.717, 15.719<br>Sent by Phillips & Mayell Ltd | Winchester House<br>Upper Tulse Hill<br>London SW<br>Winchester House<br>Upper Tulse Hill SW<br>Hughenden, Cator Road<br>Sydenham<br>26 Kensington Park Gardens W<br>22 Palace Road<br>Streatham Hill<br>5 Fourth Avenue<br>Hove (Brighton, Sussex)<br>Park View, Alton Road<br>Rockhampton<br>Cator Road<br>Sydenham<br>26 Kensington Park Gardens, London<br>Ixworth Court<br>Stanhope Road<br>Highgate<br>London | P13/W/89,90<br>***#4002,3***<br> | **Henry WILLIAMSON**<br>**Charles Herbert WILLIAMSON**<br>**William Edward TUCKER**<br>**Francis George NEWBOLT**<br>**Thomas Abercrombie WELTON**<br>trading as<br>**Henry WILLIAMSON LTD** *<br>81 Farringdon Road<br>London EC | Wholesale jewellers |
| R2/153<br>20 March 1912<br>Sent by Phillip & Mayell | | P13/W/112-115<br>***#4004-7***<br> | **Henry WILLIAMSON**<br>**Charles Herbert WILLIAMSON**<br>**William Edward TUCKER**<br>**Francis George NEWBOLT**<br>**Thomas Abercrombie WELTON**<br>(all Directors) trading as<br>**H WILLIAMSON LTD** *<br>81 Farrendon Road<br>London | |
| Missing register<br>*c*.1894<br>Similar mark entered CAO 26 March 1901 | | P5/W/547<br>***#4008***<br> | **Henry WILLIAMSON** *<br>81 Farringdon Road<br>London<br>7/9/11 Spencer Street<br>Birmingham<br>Holyhead Road<br>Coventry | |

| REGISTRATION DETAILS | MAKER'S PRIVATE ADDRESS and DETAILS | PLATE and MARK DETAILS | MAKER/COMPANY and BUSINESS ADDRESS | MAKER'S TRADE |
|---|---|---|---|---|
| R1/2<br>31 October 1894<br>Sent by W F Twine<br>R Parke<br>Stainsby & Coupland<br>W J Pellow<br>Marlow & Vaughton<br>Two sizes | 32 Wilmington Square<br>London | P5/W/618x2<br>***#4009,10***<br> | **Henry WILLIAMSON** * (Governing Director)<br>**Alfred WILLIAMSON** (Director)<br>**Charles Herbert WILLIAMSON** * (Director)<br>**James Samuel Blackett** * (Secretary)<br>81 Farringdon Road<br>London EC | Wholesale jewellers |
| Not in R1 as expected | | P5/X*sic*/944<br>***#4011***<br> | | |
| R1/70<br>17 October 1898<br>Sent by Marlow & Vaughton | Winchester House [1, 2]<br>Upper Tulse Hill<br>London SW<br>1 Palace Houses [3]<br>Bayswater Road<br>London W<br>5 Forgate Street [4]<br>London EC<br>Glenthouse [5]<br>New Southgate<br>London N | P9/W/2-4<br>***#4012-4***<br> | **Henry WILLIAMSON** [1]<br>**Charles Herbert WILLIAMSON** [2]<br>**Francis Walter GILPIN** [3]<br>**Thomas Abercrombie WELTON** [4]<br>**William Edward TUCKER** [5]<br>trading as **H WILLIAMSON LTD** *<br>81 Farringdon Road<br>London EC | Jewellers |
| R1/98<br>26 April 1899<br>Sent by Benson Brothers to use<br>F Goldsmith & Co<br>W H Rosson<br>C M Wrighton | | P9/W/17<br>***#4015***<br> | | Wholesale jewellers and manufacturers |
| | | P9/W/26<br>***#4016***<br> | | |
| R1/108<br>17 August 1899<br>Sent by J Ashwin | Wheeleys Road<br>Edgbaston<br>Birmingham | P9/W/23<br>***#4017***<br> | **Henry WILLIAMSON LTD** *<br>John Ashwin (Director)<br>7, 9, 11 Spencer Street<br>Birmingham | Watch manufacturers and silversmiths |
| R1/144<br>26 March 1901<br>Sent by H Williamson Ltd<br>HWLtd mark used from 29 October 1904 through Haseler & Holmes<br>Two sizes | Winchester House [1]<br>Upper Tulse Hill<br>London SW<br>5 Moorgate Street [2]<br>London<br>Hughenden [3]<br>Cator Road<br>Sydenham<br>Oakley Lodge [4]<br>Weybridge | P9/W/46-55<br>***#4018-27***<br> | **Henry WILLIAMSON** [1]<br>**Thomas Abercrombie WELTON** [2]<br>**William Edward TUCKER** [3]<br>**Francis George NEWBOLT** [4]<br>trading as **H WILLIAMSON LTD** *<br>81 Farringdon Road<br>London and<br>7/9/11 Spencer Street<br>Birmingham and<br>Holyhead Road<br>Coventry | Wholesale jewellers |
| R2/56<br>11 March 1908<br>Sent by J Smith<br>Per Mr S. Phelps | Winchester House<br>Upper Tulse Hill, Lon SW<br>Hughenden, Cator Road<br>Sydenham<br>26 Kensington Park Gardens, London<br>20 Cophall Avenue, London EC | P13/W/26<br>***#4028***<br> | **Henry WILLIAMSON**<br>**Charles Herbert WILLIAMSON**<br>**William Edward TUCKER**<br>**Francis George NEWBOLT**<br>**Thomas Abercombie WELTON**<br>trading as **H WILLIAMSON LTD** *<br>81 Farrendon Road<br>London | |

| REGISTRATION DETAILS | MAKER'S PRIVATE ADDRESS and DETAILS | PLATE and MARK DETAILS | MAKER/COMPANY and BUSINESS ADDRESS | MAKER'S TRADE |
|---|---|---|---|---|
| 20 February 1909<br>Annotated No.18 but clerk should have struck 48! | Winchester House<br>Upper Tulse Hill, Lon SW<br>Hughenden, Cator Road<br>Sydenham<br>26 Kensington Park Gardens, London<br>20 Copthall Avenue<br>London EC | P13/W/48?<br>***#4029***<br> | **Henry WILLIAMSON**<br>**Charles Herbert WILLIAMSON**<br>**William Edward TUCKER**<br>**Francis George NEWBOLT**<br>**Thomas Abercombie WELTON**<br>trading as **H WILLIAMSON LTD** *<br>81 Farrendon Road<br>London | Wholesale jewellers |
| R2/57<br>1 April 1908<br>Sent by C Horner | Winchester House<br>Upper Tulse Hill, Lon SW<br>Hughenden<br>Cator Road<br>Sydenham<br>2 Copthall Avenue<br>London EC<br>2 Kings Bench Walk<br>Temple, London EC | P13/W/27-32<br>***#4030-5***<br> | **Henry WILLIAMSON**<br>**Charles Herbert WILLIAMSON**<br>**William Edward TUCKER**<br>**Thomas Abercrombie WILTON**<br>**Francis George NEWBOLT**<br>trading as **H WILLIAMSON LTD** *<br>81 Farringdon Road<br>London | |
| R2/98<br>19 November 1909<br>Sent by H Williamson Ltd | Winchester House [1]<br>Upper Tulse Hill<br>London SW | P13/W/61-66<br>***#4036-41***<br> | **H WILLIAMSON LTD** *<br>C H Williamson [1] (Director)<br>81 Farringdon Road,<br>London EC<br>Holyhead Road<br>Coventry<br>7, 9, 11 Spencer Street<br>Birmingham<br>Bureau Chaux de Fonds<br>Switzerland | |
| R2/107<br>5 April 1910<br>Sent by H Williamson Ltd<br>Four sizes<br>BAO 11.778<br>16.486 15.378<br>16.494 | Winchester House<br>Upper Tulse Hill<br>London SW<br>Hughendon, Cator Road<br>Sydenham<br>26 Kensington Park Gdns<br>London W<br>22 Palace Road<br>Streatham Hill, London SW | P13/W/69-72<br>***#4042-5***<br> | **Henry WILLIAMSON**<br>**Charles Herbert WILLIAMSON**<br>**William Edward TUCKER**<br>**Francis George NEWBOLT**<br>**Thomas Abercombie WELTON**<br>(all directors) trading as<br>**H WILLIAMSON LTD** *<br>81 Farringdon Road<br>London EC | |
| R2/130<br>11 March 1911<br>Sent by Phillips & Mayell Ltd<br>BAO 17.241,18.717<br>15.719 | Winchester House<br>Upper Tulse Hill, SW<br>Winchester House<br>Upper Duke Hill SW<br>Hughenden, Cator Road<br>Sydenham<br>26 Kensington Park Gdns W<br>22 Palace Road<br>Streatham Hill, London SW | P13/W/88<br>***#4046***<br> | **Henry WILLIAMSON**<br>**Charles Herbert WILLIAMSON**<br>**William Edward TUCKER**<br>**Francis George NEWBOLT**<br>**Thomas Abercombie WELTON**<br>trading as **Henry WILLIAMSON LTD** *<br>81 Farringdon Road<br>London EC | |
| R2/199<br>19 August 1915<br>Sent by E Page | Winchester House [1]<br>Upper Tulse Hill<br>London SW | P15/W/15<br>***#4047***<br> | **H WILLIAMSON LTD** *<br>C H Williamson [1] (Director)<br>81 Farringdon Road<br>London and<br>7, 9, 11 Spencer Street<br>Birmingham | |
| Not in R3 as expected - between October & May 1916. | | P15/W/30<br>***#4048***<br> | | |
| R3/23<br>31 June 1924<br>Sent by J & R Griffin Ltd | | P15/H/81-83<br>***#4049-51***<br> | **HOWARD & WALSH LTD**<br>Thomas Walsh (Secretary)<br>84 Yorkshire Street<br>Oldham and<br>336 Middleton Road<br>Oldham | Watchmakers and jewellers |

| REGISTRATION DETAILS | MAKER'S PRIVATE ADDRESS and DETAILS | PLATE and MARK DETAILS | MAKER/COMPANY and BUSINESS ADDRESS | MAKER'S TRADE |
|---|---|---|---|---|
| R1/71<br>27 October 1898<br>Sent by J Gammage<br>T Hale<br>W H Rosson | Winchester House<br>Upper Tulse Hill<br>London SW | P9/W/5<br>***#4052***<br> | **HOWARD & WALSH LTD**<br>Thomas Walsh (Secretary)<br>84 Yorkshire Street<br>Oldham and<br>336 Middleton Road<br>Oldham | Wholesale jewellers and manufacturers |
| R1/32<br>14 August 1896<br>Sent by H Hughes<br><br>New punch<br>28 January 1897 | Larkfield [1]<br>Wilmslow, Cheshire<br>Cheshire View [2]<br>Pendleton<br>Now out of the firm | P5/Z*sic*/786a<br>***#4053***<br><br>P5/Z*sic*/786b<br>***#4054***<br> | **Herbert HUGHES** [1]<br>**G H YOUNG** [2]<br>sole partners trading as<br>**HUGHES & YOUNG**<br>75 Thomas Street<br>Manchester | Umbrella manufacturers |
| PP3/83<br>Similar mark entered<br>LAO 24 October 1862 | Not in SPB or LPB so struck 1860-3 | P3/V*sic*/x3<br>***#4055-7***<br> | **Henry YARDLEY** *<br>28 Moat Street<br>Coventry | Watchcase maker |
| LMS 1834<br>PP1/187<br>PMR 1832-62<br><br>On plate 2 but not plate 3 so 1841-60 | Square marked 1787 | P1/23/x6<br>***#4058-63***<br><br>P2/A/x4<br>***#4064-7***<br>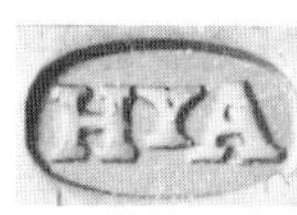 | **Henry ADAMSON**<br>49 Milton Street (1832)<br>7 Scarlett Street (1843)<br>26 Downe Street (1851-5)<br>9 Tomlinson Place (1862)<br>Liverpool | Watchcase maker |

| REGISTRATION DETAILS | MAKER'S PRIVATE ADDRESS and DETAILS | PLATE and MARK DETAILS | MAKER/COMPANY and BUSINESS ADDRESS | MAKER'S TRADE |
|---|---|---|---|---|
| R3/182<br>18 November 1961<br>Sent by I Abbott | 53 Sharples Avenue<br>Bolton<br>Lancashire | P21/A/31<br>***#4068***  | **Miss Inez ABBOTT**<br>No business address entered | Student |
| LPB/12<br>6 November 1882 | | P3/A/x2<br>***#4069,70***  | **J AHRONSBERG** *<br>28 Upper Hockley Street<br>Birmingham | Ring manufacturer |
| | | P3/A/x2<br>***#4071,2***  | | |
| LPB/14<br>27 October 1883<br>No mark in LPB | 4th name in LPB/14 and 4th mark on P5 | P5/A/x1<br>***#4073***  | **J AHRONSBERG** *<br>37 Albion Street<br>Birmingham | |
| LPB/14<br>22 March 1884<br>No mark in LPB | 6th name in LPB/14 and 6th mark on P5 | P5/A/x1<br>***#4074***  | | |
| PDB 1785-98<br>MR3/75<br>PP1/187<br>PP2/346,7<br>Similar mark entered<br>BAO *c*.1785 | Watchcases and snuff boxes | P1/19/x1<br>***#4075***  | **John ADAMSON**<br>25 North Street<br>18 Johnson Street from 1790<br>Liverpool | Watchcase maker and silversmith |
| | | P1/31/x1<br>***#4076*** 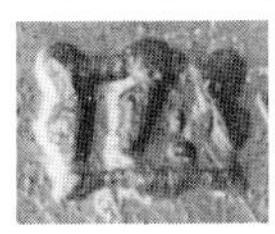 | | |
| Similar mark entered<br>BAO *c*.1785 | | P1/24/x1<br>***#4077***  | | |
| PDB 1796-8<br><br>PP1/187 | Watchcases<br>See also IA | P1/27/x5<br>***#4078-82***  | **John ADAMSON & SON**<br>63 Pitt Street<br>Liverpool | Watchcase makers |
| R1/68<br>27 July 1898<br>Sent by W Walker | 113 Wilberforce Road<br>Finsbury Park<br>London | P9/B/1<br>***#4083***  | **Isaac BRAZER**<br>67 Golden Lane<br>London | Fancy goods dealer |
| R3/161<br>21 March 1957<br>Sent by I E Burgl | The Small House<br>Cuddington<br>Northwich<br>Cheshire | P21/B/52<br>***#4084***  | **Isabel Edith BURGL**<br>No business address entered | Amateur silversmith |
| 21 October 1960 | | P21/B/61<br>***#4085***  | | |
| PDB 1785-98<br>Similar mark entered<br>at BAO *c*.1785<br>MR3/76,7<br>LTB 1790-1814<br>GTD 1785-98 | Square marked 1786<br><br>PP1/187<br>PP2/347 | P1/22/x10<br>***#4086-95***  | **James BARTON & CO**<br>Cumberland Street (1787)<br>55 Key Street (from 1811)<br>Liverpool | Watchcase makers |
| | | P1/28/x2<br>***#4096,7***  | | |

| REGISTRATION DETAILS | MAKER'S PRIVATE ADDRESS and DETAILS | PLATE and MARK DETAILS | MAKER/COMPANY and BUSINESS ADDRESS | MAKER'S TRADE |
|---|---|---|---|---|
| PDB 1831-2 MR3/78 | Medals | P1/18/x5<br>***#4098-4102***<br>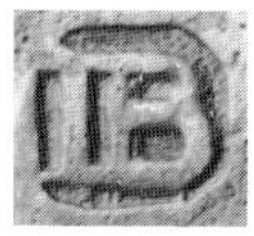 | **John BROOKS**<br>Liverpool | Silversmith |
| | Square marked 1787 | P1/23/x2<br>***#4103,4***<br> | | |
| R3/101<br>1 September 1941<br>Sent by Irwin Brothers | 81 Orchard Avenue [1]<br>Blackpool<br>8 Kinder Row [2]<br>Hayfield<br>Derbys | P21/IJ/1<br>***#4105***<br> | **Leonard IRWIN**[1]<br>**Albert IRWIN**[2] trading as<br>**IRWIN BROTHERS**<br>78, 78a, 80 Lancaster Avenue<br>Fennel Street<br>Manchester | Manufacturing jewellers |
| PDB 1785<br>MR3/79<br>PP1/187<br>PP2/349<br>LGSJ/109 | Watchcases<br>Loomes has longcase clockmaker b.1742, working 1775 to 1794 (died)<br>See also JC for John Clarke or John Coakley | P1/32/x3<br>***#4106-8***<br>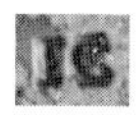 | **John CLIFTON**<br>16 Fazakerley Street<br>Liverpool | Watchcase maker |
| R3/10<br>20 July 1922<br>MR3/118<br>Sent by Iverna Cubbin | Hillcote (4 December 1956)<br>Bidston Village<br>Birkenhead | P15/C/108<br>***#4109***<br> | **Iverna CUBBIN**<br>City School of Art<br>Liverpool | Student in silver work |
| LPB/20<br>24 February 1880 | | P3/C/x3<br>***#4110-2***<br> | **Israel COHEN**<br>Soho Hill<br>Birmingham | Jeweller |
| LPB/58<br>6 February 1883 | | P3/C/x2<br>***#4113,4***<br> | **Israel COHEN**<br>Summer Hill<br>Birmingham | |
| Missing register<br>*c.*1887<br>Similar mark without pellet entered BAO 30 November 1876 | | P5/C/111<br>***#4115***<br> | **Israel COHEN**<br>Wellesley Villas<br>Soho Hill<br>Birmingham | |
| Missing register<br>*c.*1891 | | P5/C/373<br>***#4116***<br>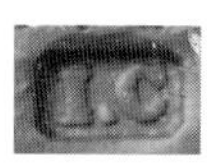 | | |
| | ? I & C M or I & G M | P2/M/x2<br>***#4117,8***<br> | **Unidentified** | |
| R2/69<br>13 November 1908<br>Sent by L Isaac | 223 Romford Road<br>Forest Gate<br>Sussex | P13/I/1<br>***#4119***<br> | **Louis ISAAC** * trading as<br>**ISAAC & CO**<br>103 Hatton Garden<br>London EC | Importers of foreign merchandise |
| Missing register<br>*c.*1890<br>Similar mark entered BAO 29 April 1889 | | P5/C/332<br>***#4120***<br> | **Israel COHEN & SON** *<br>66 Great Hampton Street<br>Birmingham | Jewellers |
| R1/6<br>26 January 1894<br>Sent by<br>J Windridge Manager to the said I Cohen & Son | | P5/C/633<br>***#4121***<br> | **Israel COHEN** trading as<br>**I COHEN & SON** *<br>66 Great Hampton Street and<br>66/67 Vyse Street<br>Birmingham | Manufacturing jewellers |

| REGISTRATION DETAILS | MAKER'S PRIVATE ADDRESS and DETAILS | PLATE and MARK DETAILS | MAKER/COMPANY and BUSINESS ADDRESS | MAKER'S TRADE |
|---|---|---|---|---|
| PDB 1816<br>MR3/80 | Gold rings<br>Seven strikings may indicate high-volume maker such as James Duke | P1/12/x7<br>***#4122-8***<br>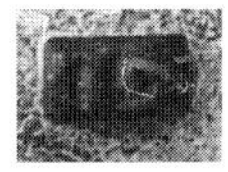 | **James DUKE**<br>Manchester or | Goldsmith |
| PDB 1838-40<br>MR3/80 | Gold rings and spoons<br>See also JD marks for James Dixon and Joseph Duke | P1/16/x5<br>***#4129-33***<br> | **Joseph DUKE II**<br>Pepper Street<br>Chester or | Goldsmith and silversmith |
| PDB 1836-38<br>MR3/80 | Gold rings<br>Note that one JD and three ID marks match the four duty book names | P1/31/x2<br>***#4134,5***<br> | **Joseph DUTTON**<br>Eastgate Street<br>Chester | Goldsmith |
| MR2/75-7<br>MR3/80,192<br>PCR-1773<br>J1/378<br>J3 1769-72<br>GMSC/44-6 | Mugs 1769, chamber stick 1771 and spoon 1772<br><br>Free 1767 | Not on P1<br>***#4136***<br> | **James DIXON**<br>Eastgate Street<br>Northgate Street (moved here–undated)<br>Chester | Silversmith |
| MR2/75<br>MR3/80,192 SIL/37,44<br>J1 1752-76<br>J3/400 1771-80<br>GMSC/35,36 | Sauceboats 1772,1774, marrow scoop 1776, caster *c.*1778 and ladle 1780<br>Caster has assay marks but date letter is missing | Not on P1<br>***#4137***<br> | **Joseph DUKE I**<br>Pepper Street<br>Chester | Silversmith |
| MR1/142<br>MR2/115<br>MR3/183<br>J3/423 | Working late seventeenth century - buried 2 August 1706.<br><br>Apprenticed 25 December 1703 to John Bingley.<br>Previously assigned to Henry Jewell of Knutsford. | P1/10/x1<br>***#4138***<br> | **Henry JENCKES**<br>Shrewsbury | Silversmith |
| | | P1/10/x1<br>***#4139***<br> | | |
| J1/379 1839-46 | | Not on P1<br>***#4140*** **I E?** | **James EVANS**<br>Chester | Silversmith |
| PDB 1794-1807<br>MR3/81<br>PP1/187<br>PP2/351,352<br>PMR 1796-1824 | Watchcases gold rings and snuff box<br><br>Seen on a case of a watch by M I Tobias 1818 | P1/27/x2<br>***#4141,2***<br> | **John ELLISON**<br>5 Crosshall Street (1796)<br>148 New Scotland Road (1821)<br>Liverpool | Watchcase maker, gold and silversmith |
| PDB 1824-37<br>MR3/8 | After John Ellison senior's death in 1823 the firm became Ellison & Company | No separate mark seen<br>***#4143*** | **ELLISON & COMPANY**<br>Liverpool | |
| PDB 1784-90 Gold rings, buttons, buckles, mugs, skewers, etc<br>MR2/81-3<br>MR3/81 | John Fisher and the next four names are candidates for this mark. Curiously there are no early JF marks that might fit. Seen on skewer 1782. | Not on P1<br>***#4144***<br> | **John FISHER**<br>Harrington Street<br>Liverpool | Gold and silversmith |

| REGISTRATION DETAILS | MAKER'S PRIVATE ADDRESS and DETAILS | PLATE and MARK DETAILS | MAKER/COMPANY and BUSINESS ADDRESS | MAKER'S TRADE |
|---|---|---|---|---|
| PDB 1785-1819<br>MR2/83<br>MR3/82 | Gold rings, coat buttons, caddy spoons, teaspoons and skewers<br><br>James France is a second good candidate for this mark | See mark above<br>***#4144a*** | **James FRANCE**<br>Manchester<br>or | Goldsmith and silversmith |
| PDB 1790<br>MR3/81 | Spoons, soup ladle and wine funnel - Falconer perhaps unlikely as only seen on skewer | See mark above<br>***#4144b*** | **Joseph FALCONER**<br>Chester<br>or | Silversmith |
| PDB 1813-6<br>MR3/81 | Gold rings<br>Entry is rather late and mark a little large for rings | See mark above<br>***#4144c*** | **John FOWLER**<br>Manchester<br>or | Goldsmith |
| Liverpool Directory of 1766 | | See mark above<br>***#4144d*** | **John FAZAKERLEY**<br>Liverpool | Silversmith |
| Missing register<br>*c.*1889 | | P5/F/257<br>***#4145***  | **Unidentified** | |
| Missing register<br>*c.*1894 | | P5/F/533<br>***#4146***  | **Unidentified** | |
| R3/55<br>18 November 1930<br>Sent by selves | 12 Rondu Road [1]<br>London NW2 | P15/F/37<br>***#4147***  | **I FREEMAN & SON LTD** *<br>Adelaide Freeman [1] (Secretary)<br>37/38 Hatton Garden<br>23 Hatton Garden (23 May 1928)<br>London EC1 | Antique and modern silver, silver-plated goods dealers |
| R1/41<br>15 March 1897<br>Sent by Isiah Friend<br>Authority to<br>W H Leather<br>R J Wakefield | Private address same as business | P5/F/824<br>***#4148*** 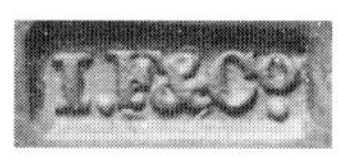 | **Isiah FRIEND** trading as<br>**Isiah FRIEND & CO**<br>39 Balshall Heath Road<br>Edinburgh | Jewellers |
| R3/87<br>11 June 1937<br>Sent by I F Hooper | 24 Allerton Drive<br>Liverpool 18 | P21/H/1<br>***#4149***  | **Isabel Florence HOOPER**<br>No business address entered | Artist craftsman |
| GTD 1851 GSJW/134<br>J1 1852-68<br>Similar mark BAO<br>5 November 1857 | | P2/Q/x1<br>***#4150***  | **John Fryer QUICK**<br>7 Parker Street<br>Liverpool | Jeweller |
| R3/39<br>18 November 1927<br>Sent by selves | 12 Rondu Road [1]<br>London NW2 | P15/F/32<br>***#4151***  | **I FREEMAN & SON LTD** *<br>Adelaide Freeman [1] (Secretary)<br>37/38 Hatton Garden<br>23 Hatton Garden (23 May 1928)<br>London EC1 | Antique and modern silver, silver-plated goods dealers |
| LMS 1848<br>MR3/144<br>J1 1843-52<br>CMC/134 | Name seen engraved on watch *c.*1860 - successor to Richard Richardson IV who died in 1822<br>Wathew's son-in-law Francis Butt continued the business | P2/W/x2<br>***#4152,3*** <br>P2/W/x2<br>***#4154,5*** <br>P2/W/x4<br>***#4156-9***  | **John F WATHEW**<br>Bridge Street<br>69 Eastgate Row (1846-50)<br>Chester | Watch maker and jeweller |
| R1/44<br>11 May 1897<br>Sent by Isaac Green | Private address same as business | P5/G/840<br>***#4160*** 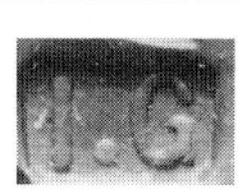 | **Isaac GREEN**<br>46 Waterloo Road<br>Strangeways<br>Manchester | Jeweller and silversmith |

| REGISTRATION DETAILS | MAKER'S PRIVATE ADDRESS and DETAILS | PLATE and MARK DETAILS | MAKER/COMPANY and BUSINESS ADDRESS | MAKER'S TRADE |
|---|---|---|---|---|
| PDB 1786-97<br>PCR-1773<br>MR3/83 | Gold rings<br>Square marked 1786<br>See also JG | P1/22/x1<br>***#4161***  | **John GILBERT**<br>Liverpool or | Goldsmith |
| PDB 1810-13 Gold rings<br>MR3/83 | | P1/24/x2<br>***#4162,3*** 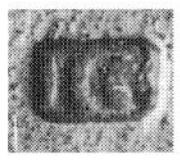 | **James GLOVER**<br>Manchester | Goldsmith |
| R2/4<br>17 October 1905<br>Sent by Isaac Goldberg | Private address same as business | P9/G/63<br>***#4164***  | **Isaac GOLDBERG** *<br>42 Settles Street<br>Commercial Road<br>London E | Jeweller |
| R3/140<br>6 December 1952<br>Sent by E Whitehouse & Son<br>52 Vyse St<br>Birmingham | Flat 2, 81-85 Tufton Street<br>London SW1 | P21/G/23<br>***#4165***  | **Ivor GORDON LTD**<br>55 Hatton Garden<br>London EC1 | Manufacturing jewellers and goldsmiths |
| Not in SPB or LPB so struck 1860-3<br>Similar mark entered BAO 31 January 1862 | | P3/H/x3<br>***#4166-8***  | **John HAYES**<br>50 Hampton Street<br>Birmingham | Silversmith |
| SPB/19<br>28 January 1869 | Old punch defaced<br>CWMP 1874-83 | P3/H/x3<br>***#4169-71***  | **John HAMMON**<br>25 York Street<br>Coventry | Watchcase maker |
| PDB 1792<br>MR3/84<br>PP1/187<br>GTD 1777-84 | Gold rings<br>Square marked 1785<br>See also JH | P1/21/x1<br>***#4172***  | **Isaac HADWINE III (HADWEN)**<br>34 Pool Lane (1766 to 1799)<br>Liverpool<br>or | Goldsmith and watchmaker |
| PDB 1790-2<br>MR3/86<br>GMSC/77 | Gold rings, skewers, wine labels, buttons, chalice<br>Square marked 1786<br>See also JH | P1/22/x1<br>***#4173*** 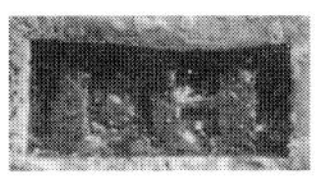 | **Joseph HEWITT**<br>Liverpool | Goldsmith and silversmith |
| SPB/13<br>20 June 1866 | Charles Harris at this address in 1874<br>CWMP 1886-1901 | P3/H/x1<br>***#4174***  | **John HARRIS** *<br>6 York Street (1866)<br>3 Hertford Place (1886)<br>Coventry | Watchcase maker |
| PP1/187<br>Similar mark entered LAO 27 February 1852 and BAO 18 June 1857 | | P2/E/x3<br>***#4175-7***  | **Joseph Harris ELLIOTT** *<br>7 Skinner Street (1852)<br>London<br>Butts (15 September 1854)<br>Coventry | Watchcase maker |
| R2/38<br>26 April 1907<br>Sent by selves | 10 Canning Street<br>17 Longdale Road<br>94 Huskinson Street<br>Liverpool | P9/H/93<br>***#4178***  | **Lewis HARRIS Isaac HARRIS**<br>**Alfred SOLOMON** trading as<br>**I HARRIS & SON** *<br>5 Bold Street<br>Liverpool | Manufacturing jewellers |
| Not in R2 as expected - between 23 July 1914 and 13 September 1915 | | P15/H/21<br>***#4179***  | | |
| R3/36<br>20 September 1927<br>Sent by Henry Griffith & Sons<br>Leamington Spa | 10 Canning Street [1]<br>Liverpool | P15/I*sic*/102<br>***#4180***  | **I HARRIS & SONS LTD** *<br>Lewis Harris[1] (Director)<br>12 Rotunda Buildings<br>5 Bold Street<br>Liverpool | Wholesale diamond merchants |

| REGISTRATION DETAILS | MAKER'S PRIVATE ADDRESS and DETAILS | PLATE and MARK DETAILS | MAKER/COMPANY and BUSINESS ADDRESS | MAKER'S TRADE |
|---|---|---|---|---|
| Not in R3 as expected<br>*c.* January 1924 | | P15/H/73<br>***#4181***<br> | **I HARRIS & SONS LTD** *<br>Liverpool | Wholesale diamond merchants |
| MR2/91,92<br>Not in PDB | Definitely II pellet between.<br>Late square so may be just before 1841 | P1/32/x1<br>***#4182***<br> | **John JONES**<br>Chester or | Silversmith |
| GTD 1798-9<br>Not in PDB | | | **James JOHNSON**<br>Key Street<br>Liverpool | Watchcase maker |
| SPB/14<br>8 January 1877<br>Sent by SR<br>(Ed: Samuel & Rogers?)<br>GSJW/157 1861 | See JJH and J&JH | P3/H/x3<br>***#4183-5***<br>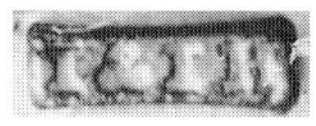 | **Joseph & John HARGREAVES**<br>18 School Lane<br>Liverpool | Watch manufacturers |
| LPB/98 SP28/5<br>16 July 1884<br>Sent by C Harris | CWMP 1896-1936 | P5/N/x1<br>***#4186***<br> | **J NEWSOME** *<br>14/15 The Butts<br>Coventry | Watch manufacturer |
| Missing register<br>*c.*1888 | | P5/N/182<br>***#4187***<br> | | |
| LPB/60 SP28/1,2<br>7 November 1884<br>Sent by J Sharpe | | P5/N/x1<br>***#4188***<br> | **Isaac Jabez Theo NEWSOME** *<br>14/15 The Butts<br>Coventry | |
| R3/98<br>13 January 1941<br>Sent by W I Kirby | 24 Kenilworth Road<br>Childwall<br>Liverpool 16 | P21/K/2<br>***#4189***<br>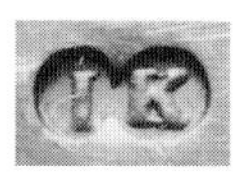 | **William Isaac KIRBY**<br>6a Richmond Street<br>Liverpool 1 | Working jeweller |
| PDB 1821-2<br>MR3/89<br>LGSJ 1825 | Gold rings<br>See also JH | P1/30/x3<br>***#4190-2***<br> | **John KIND**<br>1 Church Street<br>Liverpool | Goldsmith |
| MG/140<br>Similar mark entered NAO 1740s | Tablespoon 1747<br>Possibly journeyman in Chester | Not on P1<br>***#4193***<br> | **John LANGLANDS** (G)<br>Newcastle | Silversmith |
| R1/92<br>17 February 1899<br>Sent by W Aitken | 165 Kensington Park Road<br>London SE | P9/L/4<br>***#4194***<br>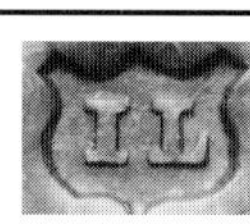 | **Isadore LEAPMAN**<br>179, 181 Victoria Street<br>London SW | Jeweller and silversmith |
| MR1/42-51<br>MR2/51, 220<br>MR3/179<br>SIL/22<br>J1 1585-1612<br>J3/389 | Free 1565<br>Church plate, spoon *c.*1574<br><br>J1 has John Lynglay | Predates P1<br>***#4195***<br> | **John LINGLEY I**<br>Bridge Street<br>Chester | Silversmith |
| | Mace inscribed 1606 | Predates P1<br>***#4196***<br> | **John LINGLEY I**<br>Bridge Street, Chester | |
| | Free 1592 | | **John LINGLEY II**<br>Chester | |
| | Church plate inscribed 1625<br>Free 1585 | | **Joseph LINGLEY I**<br>Chester | |
| | Free 1616<br>Seal top spoon *c.*1620 | Predates P1<br>***#4197***<br> | **Joseph LINGLEY II**<br>Chester | |

| REGISTRATION DETAILS | MAKER'S PRIVATE ADDRESS and DETAILS | PLATE and MARK DETAILS | MAKER/COMPANY and BUSINESS ADDRESS | MAKER'S TRADE |
|---|---|---|---|---|
| PDB 1834-39<br>MR3/97<br>PP1/187 | Gold rings<br>See also JLS and IS | P1/19/x5<br>***#4198-4202***  | **Joseph Lewis SAMUEL**<br>Liverpool | Goldsmith and watchcase maker |
| | | P2/S/x2<br>***#4203,4***  | | |
| | Square marked 1787 | P1/23/x2<br>***#4205,6***  | | |
| MR2/112-113<br>MR3/90,127<br>SOT/86<br>J1 1840-41; 1826-66 | This mark thought to have been used from 1839<br><br>See also I&TL | P1/11/x3<br>***#4207-9***<br>type 2  | **John & Thomas LOWE**<br>Bridge Street Row<br>Chester | Silversmiths |
| | | P1/13/x4<br>***#4210-3***<br>type 2  | | |
| | | P2/L/x2<br>***#4214,5***<br>type 2  | | |
| R3/147<br>8 December 1953<br>Sent by I Meek | 6 Carlton Road<br>Manchester 16 | P21/M/39<br>***#4216*** 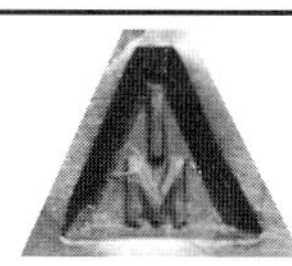 | **Irene MEEK**<br>No business address entered | Student |
| Not in R3 as expected - between April 1947 and April 1948.<br>Two sizes | Not registered at BAO | P21/M/23,24<br>***#4217,8***  | **Unidentified** | |
| PDB 1811<br>MR3/94<br>J1 1811 | Gold rings<br>See also JM | P1/32/x2<br>***#4219,20***  | **Joseph MORTON**<br>Manchester | Goldsmith |
| | | P2/M/x3<br>***#4221-3***  | or | |
| J1 1825-6 | | P1/21/x2<br>***#4224,5*** 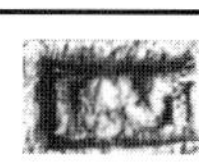 | **J MILLER**<br>Liverpool | Silversmith |
| R2/228<br>5 March 1920<br>Sent by<br>I M Hutchfield<br>Two sizes | Alexandra Road<br>Acocks Green<br>Birmingham | P15/H/57,58<br>***#4226,7***  | **I M HUTCHFIELD**<br>Harford Works<br>Harford Street<br>Birmingham | Manufacturing silversmith |
| R1/18<br>26 November 1895<br>Sent by Stokes & Ireland | Redhill<br>Sevenoaks<br><br>Chislehurst | P5/*Osic*/698<br>***#4228***  | **John Marshall SPINK**<br>**Charles Frederick SPINK**<br>**Samuel Martin SPINK** trading as<br>**SPINK & SON** *<br>17, 18 Piccadilly<br>London W and<br>1, 2 Gracechurch Street<br>London EC | Silversmiths and goldsmiths |

| REGISTRATION DETAILS | MAKER'S PRIVATE ADDRESS and DETAILS | PLATE and MARK DETAILS | MAKER/COMPANY and BUSINESS ADDRESS | MAKER'S TRADE |
|---|---|---|---|---|
| R1/118<br>12 December 1899<br>Sent by John M Spink<br>Three sizes | Southborough<br>Sevenoaks<br>Chislehurst<br>Kent | P9/S/29-31<br>*#4229-31*<br> | **John Marshall SPINK**<br>**Samuel Martin SPINK**<br>**Charles Frederick SPINK** trading as<br>**SPINK & SON** *<br>17, 18 Piccadilly and<br>1, 2 Gracechurch Street and<br>7 Golden Square<br>London | Diamond merchants, silversmiths and medallists |
| MR2/118-20<br>SIL/51<br>J3/418<br>J3 1746-95 (died) | Skewers and spoons 1783 | Not on P1<br>*#4232*<br>type 1<br> | **John OLLIVANT**<br>Manchester | Silversmith |
| | Spoon *c*1760 with mark struck four times without assay office marks | Not on P1<br>*#4233*<br>type 2<br> | | |
| PP1/187<br>Similar mark entered LAO 25 March 1854 | See also JOK&Co | P2/K/x2<br>*#4234,5*<br> | **John O'KEEFFE** *<br>16 Queen's Row, Pentonville Hill<br>London | Watchcase maker |
| R2/26<br>7 October 1906<br>Sent by I Pothecary | 95 Trinity Road<br>Wimbledon<br>Surrey | P9/U*sic*/255<br>*#4236*<br> | **Isaac POTHECARY** *<br>19 Woodstock Street<br>New Bond Street<br>London W | Manufacturing goldsmith and silversmith |
| J1 1863-6<br>PP1/187<br>GTD 1863-77<br>PMR 1851-68 | Not in SPB or LPB so struck 1860-3 | P3/R/x3<br>*#4237-9*<br> | **John RICHARDS**<br>66 Brownhill Hill (1851)<br>166 Mount Pleasant (1855)<br>4 Chestnut Street (1859)<br>13 Hunter Street (1860)<br>96 Seel Street (1862)<br>53 Hunter Street West (1864-8)<br>Liverpool<br>or | Watchmaker |
| | | P2/Q*sic*/x3<br>*#4240-2*<br> | | |
| | | P2/R/x3<br>*#4243-5*<br> | | |
| PDB 1795<br>MR3/96<br>GTD 1796<br>PP1/187<br>PP2/352 | Watchcases<br>Not in SPB or LPB so struck 1860-3 | P3/R/x3<br>*#4246-8*<br> | **James RICHARDS**<br>Marybone<br>Bevington Bush Road<br>Liverpool | Watchcase maker |
| | | P1/26/x2<br>*#4249,50*<br> | | |
| | | P1/27/x1<br>*#4251*<br> | | |
| R1/64<br>23 March 1898<br>Sent by L E Neale | 33 Carrington Street<br>Glasgow | P5/R/946<br>*#4252*<br> | **Israel ROSENTHAL**<br>60 St Enoch Square<br>Glasgow | Jeweller |
| R3/156<br>24 September 1955<br>Sent by I Roth<br>Two sizes | St Michaels<br>Spath Road<br>Didsbury<br>Manchester 20 | P21/R/23,24<br>*#4253,4*<br> | **Isobel ROTH**<br>No business address entered | Student of silversmithing |
| PDB 1820-22<br>MR3/87 PP1/187 | Medals and snuff boxes | P1/30/x3<br>*#4255-7*<br> | **JONES & REEVES**<br>Liverpool | Silversmith |

| REGISTRATION DETAILS | MAKER'S PRIVATE ADDRESS and DETAILS | PLATE and MARK DETAILS | MAKER/COMPANY and BUSINESS ADDRESS | MAKER'S TRADE |
|---|---|---|---|---|
| Missing register<br>*c.*1892 | | P5/R/441<br>***#4258***  | **Unidentified** | |
| Missing register<br>*c.*1890 | | P5/C/291<br>***#4259***  | **Unidentified** | |
| Missing register<br>*c.*1890 | | P5/C/277<br>***#4260***  | **Unidentified** | |
| R1/130<br>1 August 1900<br>Sent by W H Leather | 39 Carlyle Road<br>Edgbaston<br>Birmingham | P9/R/17<br>***#4261***  | **Israel ROSENTHAL** trading as<br>**ROSENTHAL & CO**<br>1 Regent Place<br>Birmingham | Jewellers |
| J1 1842-7 | | P2/G/x2<br>***#4252,3***  | **J R GOEPELL**<br>Liverpool | Silversmith |
| MR3/140<br>Not in PDB<br>Similar mark SAO<br>21 February 1839 | Jacob L Samuel of Liverpool entered similar mark BAO 15 May 1839 | P2/S/x2<br>***#4264,5***  | **Isaac SIMMONS** *<br>9 St Anne's Square<br>Manchester | Silversmith and medallist |
| MR2/191<br>MR3/50,51 | Free Brother of the Goldsmiths' Company 1763<br><br>Mark seen only on brass coin weights 1772 | Not on P1<br>***#4266***  | **John SCASEBRICK**<br>Chester | Assay Master<br><br>Not seen on silverwares |
| R1/61<br>21 February 1898<br>Sent by J Houlston | 22 Frederick Street<br>Birmingham | P5/O*sic*/935<br>***#4267***  | **Isaac SUMMERS**<br>22 Frederick Street<br>Birmingham | Wholesale jeweller |
| Not in SPB or LPB so struck 1860-3 | Jacob L Samuel is another possibility – see IS above | P3/S/x3<br>***#4268-70***  | **Isaac SIMMONS** *<br>9 St Anne's Square<br>Manchester | Silversmith and medallist |
| LPB/76<br>26 June 1880<br>Sent by Mayell Brothers | | P3/S/x2<br>***#4271,2***  | **SILVERSTON & CO**<br>25 Summerhill Terrace<br>Birmingham | Factors |
| Missing register<br>*c.*1886 | | P5/S/5<br>***#4273***  | **SILVERSTON & CO**<br>25 Summerhill Terrace<br>Birmingham | Factors |
| Missing register<br>*c.*1886 | | P5/S/36<br>***#4274***  | **SILVERSTON & CO**<br>25 Summerhill Terrace<br>Birmingham | Factors |
| R1/83<br>9 November 1898<br>Sent by Kinsey Brothers & Patrick | 33 Portland Road<br>Edgbaston<br>Birmingham | P9/S/8<br>***#4275***  | **Isaac SILVERSTON** trading as<br>**Isaac SILVERSTON & CO**<br>19, 20 Summerhill Terrace<br>Birmingham | Wholesale jewellers |
| R2/21<br>13 July 1906<br>Sent by I Silverston | 24 Clarendon Road<br>Edgbaston<br>Birmingham | P9/S/01*sic*,103,104<br>***#4276-8***  | **Isaac SILVERSTON** trading as<br>**Isaac SILVERSTON & CO**<br>19, 20 Summerhill Terrace<br>Birmingham | Wholesale jewellers |
| LPB/34<br>19 October 1882<br>Similar mark entered LAO 9 August 1884 | | P3/G/x1<br>***#4279***  | **I S GREENBERG & CO** *<br>44 Frederick Street<br>Birmingham | Plateworkers, manufacturers and jewellers |

| REGISTRATION DETAILS | MAKER'S PRIVATE ADDRESS and DETAILS | PLATE and MARK DETAILS | MAKER/COMPANY and BUSINESS ADDRESS | MAKER'S TRADE |
|---|---|---|---|---|
| Missing register<br>*c.*1888 | | P5/G/163<br>***#4280***  | **I S GREENBERG & CO** *<br>44 Frederick Street<br>Birmingham | Plateworkers, manufacturers and jewellers |
| Missing register<br>*c.*1890 | | P5/G/325<br>***#4281***  | | |
| Missing register<br>*c.*1889 | | P5/G/213<br>***#4282***  | | |
| R1/210<br>12 March 1904<br>Sent by D Sherrett & Co | 48 Calthorpe Road<br>Edgbaston | P9/G/55<br>***#4283*** 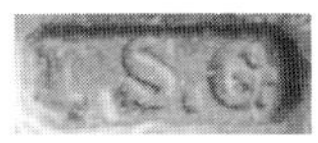 | **Israel Sigmund GREENBERG** trading as **I S GREENBERG & CO** *<br>125/126 Great Hampton Street<br>Birmingham | Wholesale jewellers |
| R2/60<br>28 May 1908<br>Sent by J & R Griffin Ltd | | P13/G/2<br>***#4284***  | **I S GREENBERG** trading as<br>**I S GREENBERG & CO** *<br>126 Great Hampton Street<br>Birmingham | Factors |
| R2/78<br>7 April 1909<br>Sent by E Whitehouse & Son<br>BAO 11.419 | | P13/G/8<br>***#4285***  | | Jewellers |
| R2/174<br>14 July 1913<br>Sent by selves | 15 Portland Road<br>Edgbaston<br>Birmingham | P15/G/4<br>***#4286***  | **I S GREENBERG**<br>(Managing Director) trading as<br>**I S GREENBERG & CO** *<br>125, 126 Great Hampton Street and<br>1, 2 Hall Street<br>Birmingham | Jewellers and silversmiths |
| R2/151<br>24 February 1912<br>Sent by<br>H S Greenberg & Co<br>BAO 15.545 | 9 Rotten Park Road<br>Edgbaston<br>Birmingham | P13/G/38<br>***#4287***  | **Herbert S GREENBERG** *<br>126 Great Hampton Street<br>Birmingham | Jewellers and factors |
| R3/97<br>19 April 1940<br>Sent by<br>B H Britton & Sons | | P21/G/4<br>***#4288***  | **I S GREENBERG & CO LTD** *<br>126 Great Hampton Street<br>Birmingham 18 | Merchants |
| R1/20<br>27 January 1896<br>Sent by W Aitken<br>Kinsey Brothers & Patrick<br>Three sizes | | P5/G/719x3<br>***#4289-91***  | **Israel Sigmond GREENBERG** *<br>126 Great Hampton Street<br>Birmingham | Wholesale jewellers and silversmiths |
| PDB 1814-33<br>MR2/194<br>MR3/99 | Gold rings and silver wares | P1/26/x1<br>***#4292***  | **John TWEMLOW**<br>Chester or | Goldsmith and silversmith |
| PDB 1825<br>MR3/98 | Gold rings | P1/32/x3<br>***#4293-5***  | **J TAYLOR**<br>Liverpool or | Goldsmith |
| GSJW/136<br>PP3/83 | Not in SPB or LPB so struck 1860-3 | P3/T/x3<br>***#4296-8***  | **John TAYLOR**<br>18 Tarleton Street<br>Liverpool or | Watchcase maker |
| J1 1861 | | P1/25/x3<br>***#4299-4301***  | **Joseph TETTER**<br>Liverpool | Silversmith |

| REGISTRATION DETAILS | MAKER'S PRIVATE ADDRESS and DETAILS | PLATE and MARK DETAILS | MAKER/COMPANY and BUSINESS ADDRESS | MAKER'S TRADE |
|---|---|---|---|---|
| PP1/188<br>GTD 1805-11 | See also I*E and TE/HF | P1/30/x3<br>***#4302-4***  | **John & Timothy ELLISON**<br>Liverpool | Watchcase makers |
| MR2/112<br>MR3/90, 127<br>SOT/86<br>J1 1840-1 | See also IL over TL | P1/4/x3<br>***#4305-7***<br>type 1  | **John & Thomas LOWE**<br>Chester | Silversmiths |
| | | P1/11/x3<br>***#4308-10*** 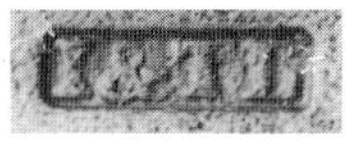 | | |
| | | P2/L/x2<br>***#4311,12***  | | |
| R2/204<br>2 April 1916<br>Sent by I Tropp & Son | 102 Hartington Road<br>Liverpool<br>102 Hartington Road<br>Liverpool | P15/T/26<br>***#4313***  | **Isaac TROPP**<br>**Harry TROPP** trading as<br>**I TROPP & SON**<br>Cooper Buildings<br>Church Street<br>Liverpool | Wholesale jewellers |
| | Incuse mark typically used by watchcase maker | P1/32/x1<br>***#4314*** 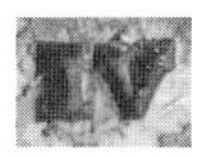 | **John VICARS**<br>Liverpool or | Watch maker |
| J1 1869-78 | | | **Isaac VICARS**<br>Manchester | Silversmith |
| SPB/17<br>4 December 1867 | | P3/V/x3<br>***#4315-7***  | **Isaac VICKERS**<br>108 Market Street<br>Lancaster | Watch and clockmaker and jeweller |
| R3/5<br>26 November 1921<br>Sent by Israel Victor Weinberg | 20 Hankin Street<br>Stepney<br>London E1 | P15/W/50,51<br>***#4318,9*** 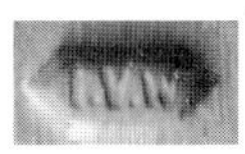 | **Israel Victor WEINBERG**<br>17 Jamaica Street<br>Stepney<br>London E1 | Chain and ring maker |
| R1/33<br>10 October 1896<br>Sent by I Wasserberg | 35 Devonshire Road<br>Higher Broughton<br>Manchester | P5/X*sic*/792<br>***#4320***  | **Isidor WASSERBERG**<br>35 Kilverts Building<br>High Grove<br>Manchester | Jeweller |
| PP1/188<br>GTD 1825-9<br>Similar mark BAO<br>18 February 1835 | See also JW | P1/29/x2<br>***#4321,2***  | **James WIDOWSON**<br>4 Shakespeare Gardens<br>Spon Street<br>Coventry or | Watchcase maker |
| PMR 1823-34 | | P1/30/x2<br>***#4323,4***  | **John WIDDOWSON**<br>17 Edmund Street (1825)<br>Liverpool | Watchcase maker |
| Missing register<br>*c.*1891<br>Similar mark entered<br>LAO 30 June 1888 | | P5/W/354<br>***#4325***  | **Ignatz WEISS** *<br>Auckland House<br>36 Basinghall Street<br>London EC | Silversmith |
| MR2/205,208<br>SOT/114-7<br>SIL/42,50<br>PCR-1773<br>J3/416 1777-1801 | Beaker 1778<br>See also J W | Not on P1<br>***#4326***<br>type 2 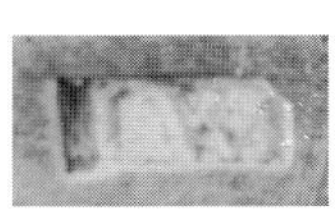 | **Joseph WALLEY**<br>1, 2 Water Street<br>Liverpool | Silversmith |

| REGISTRATION DETAILS | MAKER'S PRIVATE ADDRESS and DETAILS | PLATE and MARK DETAILS | MAKER/COMPANY and BUSINESS ADDRESS | MAKER'S TRADE |
|---|---|---|---|---|
| PDB 1805-36<br>MR2/205 | Gold rings and silverware<br>Seen on watchcase 1810 | P1/17/x2<br>***#4327,8***<br> | **John WALKER I**<br>Chester | Goldsmith and silversmith |
| MR3/102<br>J1 1834-40 | See also JW | P1/31/x2<br>***#4329,30***<br> | | |
| MR2/205,208<br>SOT/114-7<br>SIL/42,50<br>PCR-1773 | See also JW type 2 | P1/reverse/x1<br>***#4331***<br> | **Joseph WALLEY**<br>1, 2 Water Street<br>Liverpool | Silversmith |
| J3/416 1777-1801 | Square marked 1785 | P1/21/x1<br>***#4332***<br>type 1<br> | | |
| | These marks on back of plate 1 appear to be similar to previous one | P1/reverse/x6<br>***#4333-8***<br>type 1<br> | | |
| PDB 1805-36<br>MR2/205<br>MR3/102-<br>J1 1834-40 | Gold rings and silverware | P1/30/x3<br>***#4339-41***<br> | **John WALKER I**<br>Chester | Gold rings and silverware |
| R2/193<br>31 March 1915 | 9 Woodcroft Avenue<br>Mill Hill<br>London NW | P15/I/1<br>***#4342***<br> | **THE ILLINOIS WATCH CASE CO LTD** *<br>Joseph Wright (Managing Director)<br>64, 65 Holborn Viaduct<br>London EC | Watchcase manufacturers |
| | (Ed: this company located in Elgin, Illinois, USA) | P15/I/2<br>***#4343***<br> | | |
| Not in J1<br>Similar mark entered LAO 13 July 1825 | | P1/29/x3<br>***#4344-6***<br> | **J Wil$^{on}$** (*sic*) **PIPE** (G p370)<br>Market Street<br>Manchester or | Goldsmith |
| LLCC 1834 | Possibly the same person as above? | | **Isaac PIPE**<br>29 Market Street<br>Manchester or | Clockmaker |
| GTD 1857-90 | Possibly struck in error on P1 instead of P2 or P3<br><br>See also mark ***#2423*** | | **James W PETERS**<br>3 London Road<br>Liverpool | Watchmaker |
| SOT/128<br>PCR-1773 | Seen on the case of a watch by S Barrow of Billinge, Lancs, 1775<br><br>See also TG | Not on P1<br>***#4347***<br> | **John WYKE and Thomas GREEN**<br>Wykes Court<br>Dale Street<br>Liverpool | Watch and watchcase manufacturers |

| REGISTRATION DETAILS | MAKER'S PRIVATE ADDRESS and DETAILS | PLATE and MARK DETAILS | MAKER/COMPANY and BUSINESS ADDRESS | MAKER'S TRADE |
|---|---|---|---|---|
| R2/38<br>23 April 1907<br>Sent by J Adelman | 25 Fenney Street<br>Higher Broughton | P9/A/85<br>***#4348***  | **Joseph ADELMAN** *<br>27 Corporation Street<br>Manchester | Ring mounter |
| R2/81<br>12 May 1909<br>Sent by J Aldcroft | 79 Bent Street<br>Cheetham Hill<br>Manchester | P13/A/12<br>***#4349***  | **James ALDCROFT**<br>27 Kilverts Buildings<br>Shudehill<br>Manchester (undated - moved to)<br>1 Cathedral Gates<br>Cateaton Street<br>Manchester | Diamond mounter and working jeweller |
| R1/157<br>28 November 1901<br>Sent by J Adelman<br>cancelled<br>16 January 1904 | 31 Elizabeth Street<br>Cheetham<br>Manchester | P9/A/31<br>***#4350*** 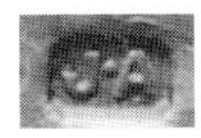 | **Joseph ADELMAN** *<br>76, 78 Lancaster Avenue<br>Fennel Street<br>Manchester | Ring manufacturer |
| Not in R1 as expected | See other J A marks | P5/A/606<br>***#4351***  | **Unidentified** | |
| R1/31<br>25 June 1896<br>Sent by J Adelman | 50 Cheetham Street<br>Cheetham Hill Road<br>Manchester | P5/A/779<br>***#4352*** 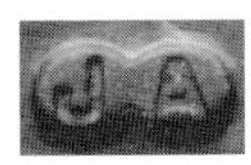 | **Joseph ADELMAN** *<br>72a Lancaster Avenue<br>Fennel Street<br>Manchester | Jeweller |
| R1/159<br>17 January 1902<br>Sent by J Appleby | Private address same as business | P9/A/32<br>***#4353*** 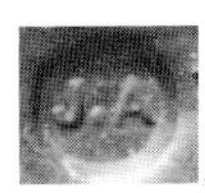 | **Joseph APPLEBY**<br>64 Bridge Street West<br>Birmingham | Seal maker |
| PDB 1819<br>MR3/76 | Gold rings | P1/17/x3<br>***#4354-6***  | **J ATKER/ATKINS**<br>address unknown<br>or | Goldsmith |
| PDB 1833-9<br>MR3/76 | Medals<br><br>See also IA | P1/31/x2<br>***#4357,8***  | **John & Joseph ARMSTRONG**<br>Deansgate<br>Manchester | Silversmiths |
| LPB/14<br>14 September 1883<br>No mark in LPB<br>Sent by Jackson Brothers | 2nd name in LPB/14 and 2nd mark on P5 | P5/A/x1<br>***#4359*** 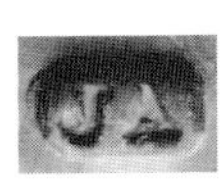 | **John ABRAHALL & CO**<br>1 Pitsford Street and<br>Vyse Street<br>Birmingham | Jewellers |
| LPB/14<br>6 February 1885<br>No mark in LPB | This 8th mark on P5 follows the A A mark (7th) for Allday & Allday, but could be Abrahall – see above | P5/A/x1<br>***#4360*** 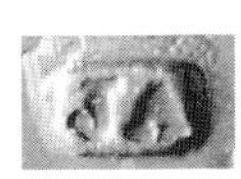 | **John ALLDAY & SON** *<br>8 Warstone Lane<br>Birmingham | Jewellers |
| Missing register<br>*c.*1891 | See other J A marks | P5/A/339b<br>***#4361***  | **Unidentified** | |
| R1/117<br>30 November 1899<br>Sent by J Adelman | 31 Elizabeth Street<br>(Manchester ?) | P9/A/15<br>***#4362***  | **Joseph ADELMAN** *<br>76, 78 Lancaster Avenue<br>Fennel Street<br>Manchester | Fancy ring maker |
| R1/235<br>10 June 1905<br>Sent by J Adelman | 379 Cheetham Street<br>Manchester | P9/A/61<br>***#4363***  | **Joseph ADELMAN** *<br>31 Withy Grove<br>Manchester | Manufacturing jeweller |

| REGISTRATION DETAILS | MAKER'S PRIVATE ADDRESS and DETAILS | PLATE and MARK DETAILS | MAKER/COMPANY and BUSINESS ADDRESS | MAKER'S TRADE |
|---|---|---|---|---|
| MR2/57<br>MR3/75<br>SOT/129 | Wine label *c.*1786-96 and watchcase 1794/5 | Not on P1<br>***#4364***<br> | **John ADAMSON**<br>8 Hales Street (1781-8)<br>Johnson Street (1787-95)<br>25 North Street (1795)<br>Liverpool | Silversmith |
| Missing register<br>*c.*1887 | See other J A marks | P5/A/95<br>***#4365***<br> | **Unidentified** | |
| Missing register<br>*c.*1891 | See other J A marks | P5/A/339a<br>***#4366***<br>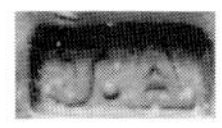 | **Unidentified** | |
| LPB/12<br>5 November 1880<br>No name by mark just JA<br>LPB mark shown<br>Sent by B H Joseph & Co | See Abrahall entry above | Not on P3<br>***#4367***<br>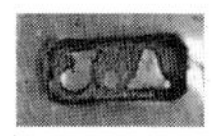 | **John ABRAHALL & CO**<br>1 Pitsford Street and<br>Vyse Street<br>Birmingham | Jewellers |
| Not in R1 as expected<br>*c.* March 1896 | See other J A marks | P5/A/733<br>***#4368***<br> | **Unidentified** | |
| R1/205<br>16 January 1904<br>Sent by J Adelman | 31 Elizabeth Street<br>Cheetham<br>Manchester | P9/A/52<br>***#4369***<br> | **Joseph ADELMAN** *<br>78 Lancaster Avenue<br>Fennel Street<br>Manchester and<br>31 Withy Grove<br>Manchester | Ring manufacturer |
| LPB/12<br>26 August 1881 | | P3/A/x2<br>***#4370,1***<br> | **James ADAMS** *<br>40 Barr Street West<br>Birmingham | Goldsmith |
| Missing register<br>*c.*1886 | See other J A marks | P5/A/68<br>***#4372***<br>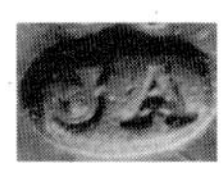 | **Unidentified** | |
| R1/57<br>19 January 1898<br>Sent by William Henry Adams | 31 Whitton Road [1]<br>Aston Parvy<br>56 Aston Lane [2]<br>Perry Barr<br>Birmingham | P5/aboveA/919<br>***#4373***<br> | **Charles Edward ADAMS** [1]<br>**William Henry ADAMS** [2] trading as<br>**James ADAMS**<br>211 Barr Street<br>Birmingham | Jewellers |
| PDB1817-26<br>MR3/75<br>PP1/188<br>LGSJ 1825 | Gold rings, medals, jewellery and watchcases<br><br>Mark seen on 1816 watchcase<br><br>See also IA | P1/27/x2<br>***#4374,5***<br>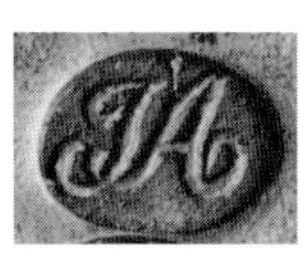 | **John ABBOTT**<br>21 Copperas Hill<br>6 Richmond Street (1825)<br>Liverpool | Goldsmith and silversmith |
| R2/14<br>16 March 1906<br>Sent by J A Britton & Son<br>BAO 12.245 | 179 Maiden Vale<br>51 Finsbury Park Road<br>36 Houndsditch<br>London | P9/XYZ*sic*/171<br>***#4376***<br> | **Joseph A BRITTON**<br>**Solomon J BRITTON**<br>**Samson J BRITTON** trading as<br>**J A BRITTON & SON**<br>18/19 Houndsditch<br>London | Jewellers and silversmiths |

| REGISTRATION DETAILS | MAKER'S PRIVATE ADDRESS and DETAILS | PLATE and MARK DETAILS | MAKER/COMPANY and BUSINESS ADDRESS | MAKER'S TRADE |
|---|---|---|---|---|
| R1/116<br>7 November 1899<br>R1 has P9/C/28<br>Sent by<br>W H Carrington & Co | Private address same as business | P9/C/30<br>*#4377*<br>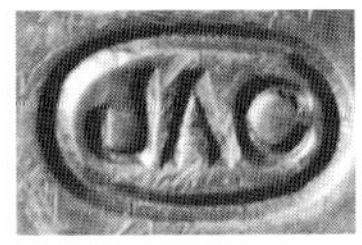 | **John Alexander CARRINGTON**<br>Bridge Street<br>Bakewell | Tobacconist |
| R2/199<br>6 September 1915<br>Sent by J Alex Culver Ltd | Private address same as business | P15/C/47<br>*#4378*<br> | **J Alex CULVER LTD** *<br>26 Spencer Street<br>London EC | Manufacturing jewellers |
| LPB/20<br>1 January 1881 | | P3/C/x1<br>*#4379*<br> | **James Adam CHALK** *<br>6 Queen Street, Percival Street<br>Clerkenwell<br>London | Watchcase maker |
| Missing register<br>*c.*1892 | | P5/A/449<br>*#4380*<br> | **Unidentified** | |
| R3/114<br>3 June 1946<br>Sent by<br>J A C Waplington | 27 Leopold Avenue<br>Handsworth Wood<br>Birmingham 20 | P21/W/42<br>*#4381*<br>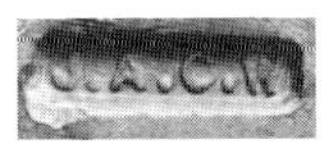 | **John Alfred Charles WAPLINGTON**<br>30 Frederick Street<br>Birmingham (moved 9 September 1952 to)<br>58 Hockley Hill<br>Birmingham 1 | Manufacturing jeweller |
| SPB/9 undated<br>November 1865 to February 1866<br>Sent by John Richards | 53 Hunter Street<br>Liverpool | P3/H/x1<br>*#4382*<br> | **Joseph & Abraham HARRIS**<br>26 Berry Street<br>Liverpool | Watch manufacturers |
| Not in SPB<br>Probably punched on P2 in error | | P2/H/x4<br>*#4383-6*<br> | | |
| LPB/40<br>3 September 1883<br>No mark in LPB | | P5/H/x1<br>*#4387*<br> | | |
| R3/57<br>13 May 1931<br>Sent by J A Jackson | Paxcroft<br>Erith Lane<br>Padgate<br>Warrington | P15/J/37<br>*#4388*<br>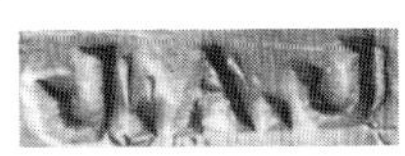 | **James Arthur JACKSON**<br>No business address entered | None entered |
| R3/87<br>21 April 1937<br>Sent by J A Leece<br>Two sizes | 48 Percy Street<br>Liverpool | P21/L/1,2<br>*#4389,90*<br> | **John Arthur LEECE**<br>17 Blair Street<br>Liverpool | Engineer |
| R3/87<br>November 1944<br>Sent by J A Leece | | P21/L/7<br>*#4391*<br> | | |
| 25 October 1946<br>Recut | Died 9 May 1947 | P21/L/21<br>*#4392*<br> | | |
| R3/109<br>16 July 1945<br>Sent by John Andrew Leece<br>Five sizes | Private address same as business | P21/L/8-12<br>*#4393-7*<br> | **John Andrew LEECE** junior<br>48 Percy Street<br>Liverpool 8<br>Lancashire | Welder and motor engineer |

| REGISTRATION DETAILS | MAKER'S PRIVATE ADDRESS and DETAILS | PLATE and MARK DETAILS | MAKER/COMPANY and BUSINESS ADDRESS | MAKER'S TRADE |
|---|---|---|---|---|
| LPB/96<br>18 April 1882 | Also at BAO | P3/M/x3<br>***#4398-4400***  | **John Alfred MACKENZIE**<br>250 Icknield Street<br>Birmingham | Ring maker |
| R1/174<br>1 September 1902<br>Sent by E J Rudge | Private address same as business | P9/M/41<br>***#4401***  | **John Alfred MACKENZIE**<br>35 Soho Hill<br>Birmingham | Jeweller |
| Missing register<br>*c.*1890<br>Similar mark entered<br>LAO 12 April 1882 | | P5/J/328<br>***#4402***  | **John Abraham NORTON**<br>70 Newman Street<br>London W | Gold chain maker |
| R2/63<br>30 July 1908<br>Sent by Charles A Cheshire | Waterloo Place | P13/J/1<br>***#4403*** 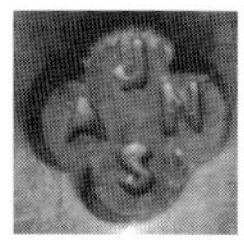 | **JUNIOR ARMY & NAVY STORES**<br>Charles G Selfe (Secretary)<br>John Bathurst (General Manager)<br>York House<br>15 Regent Street<br>London | Silversmiths and jewellers |
| R3/151<br>2 April 1954<br>Sent by A J Rhodes<br>Two sizes | 106 Loxford Street<br>Hulme<br>Manchester 15 | P21/R/21,22<br>***#4404,5***  | **Anthony Joseph RHODES**<br>No business address entered | Student |
| R1/172<br>15 July 1902<br>Sent by Joseph Aitkin | 40 Sandon Road<br>Edgbaston<br>Two Ashes<br>Sutton Coldfield | P9/A/39<br>***#4406***  | **Joseph AITKIN**<br>**John ASHFORD** trading as<br>**J AITKIN & SON**<br>79/81 Spencer Street<br>Birmingham | Makers of studs and links |
| R1/59<br>31 January 1898<br>Sent by W Hammon | | P5/aboveA/925<br>***#4407***  | **Edward Joseph ADKINS** trading as<br>**J ADKINS & SONS**<br>29 Fleet Street<br>Coventry | Watch manufacturers |
| R1/21<br>30 January 1896<br>Sent by R J Pike<br>CWMP 1883-1901 | 29 Fleet Street<br>Coventry | P5/S/722<br>***#4408***  | | |
| Missing register<br>*c.*1886 | | P5/A/20<br>***#4409***  | | |
| R2/95<br>21 October 1909<br>Sent by John Allday | 11 Vernon Road<br>Edgbaston<br>Birmingham | P13/A/19, 20 and<br>P13/J*sic*/21,22<br>***#4410-3***  | **John ALLDAY & SON LTD** *<br>John Allday (Director)<br>8, 9 Warstone Lane<br>Birmingham | Manufacturing jewellers |
| Missing register<br>*c.*1886 | | P5/W/36<br>***#4414***  | **Unidentified** | |
| R2/112<br>8 June 1910<br>Sent by B Wade | Brookside<br>Marlborough Road<br>Long Eaton<br>Derbyshire | P13/B/77<br>***#4415***  | **Ernest Vincent BROWN** trading as<br>**Josiah BROWN**<br>24 Market Street<br>Nottingham<br>39, 41 High Street<br>Long Eaton<br>Derbyshire<br>Church Street<br>Ripley<br>Derbyshire | Tobacconists and importers |

| REGISTRATION DETAILS | MAKER'S PRIVATE ADDRESS and DETAILS | PLATE and MARK DETAILS | MAKER/COMPANY and BUSINESS ADDRESS | MAKER'S TRADE |
|---|---|---|---|---|
| R2/134<br>6 May 1911<br>Sent by E Vincent Brown | Brookside<br>Marlborough Road<br>Long Eaton | P13/B/120<br>***#4416***<br> | **Ernest Vincent BROWN** trading as<br>**Josiah BROWN**<br>Church Street<br>Ripley<br>Derbyshire and<br>24 Market Street<br>Nottingham and<br>Oxford Buildings<br>High Street<br>Long Eaton<br>Nottinghamshire | Tobacconists |
| R2/175<br>27 August 1913<br>Sent by H Comoy & Co | | P15/B/48<br>***#4417***<br> | **E Vincent BROWN** trading as<br>**Josiah BROWN**<br>39, 41 High Street<br>Long Eaton<br>Church Street | Wholesale tobacconists |
| 7 November 1927 | | P15/B/189<br>***#4418***<br>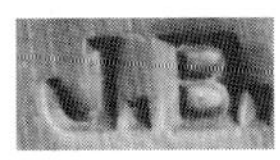 | Ripley<br>24 Market Street<br>Nottingham | |
| R2/121<br>20 October 1910<br>Sent by George Bradbury | 78 Sycamore Road<br>Smethwick<br>Birmingham | P13/B/90<br>***#4419***<br> | **George BRADBURY** trading as<br>**J BRADBURY**<br>20 Caroline Street<br>Birmingham | Manufacturing jeweller |
| R2/189<br>5 August 1914<br>Sent by Jack Brower | 22 Greenfield Street<br>Commercial Road<br>London E | P15/B/36<br>***#4420***<br> | **Jack BROWER**<br>85 Commercial Road<br>London E | Gold chains and bracelets |
| R2/205<br>7 June 1916<br>Sent by Joseph Bolloten | Private address same as business | P15/B/64<br>***#4421***<br> | **Joseph BOLLOTEN**<br>17 Arundel Avenue<br>Liverpool | Diamond merchant |
| R3/101<br>19 August 1941<br>Sent by Stanley Harris Bennett | 30 Carnaervon Road<br>Bristol 6 | P21/B/16<br>***#4422***<br> | **Stanley Harris BENNETT** trading as<br>**John BENNETT**<br>82 Park Street<br>Bristol 1 | Jeweller |
| R1/49<br>12 August 1897<br>Sent by W Walker | Primrose Buildings<br>Frayer Street<br>London | P5/aboveB/862<br>***#4423***<br>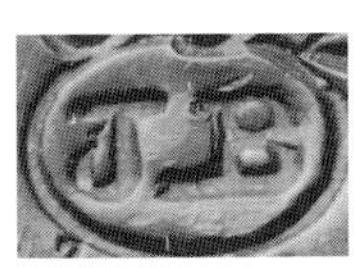 | **Arthur Wolf JAY**<br>**David Fack JAY** trading as<br>**JAY BROTHERS**<br>Johannesburg SA and<br>120 London Wall<br>London EC | Tobacco merchants |
| MR2/58-9 | No date letter on snuff box *c.*1791 | Not on P1<br>***#4424***<br> | **James BARTON**<br>Liverpool | Watch and watchcase manufacturer |
| CWMP 1850<br>Similar mark entered BAO 31 October 1850 | | P2/B/x3<br>***#4425-7***<br> | **Joseph BATES**<br>7 Cox Street<br>Gosford Street (1850)<br>Coventry or | Watchcase maker |
| J1 1846-9 | | P2/B/x2<br>***#4428,9***<br> | **J BURBIDGE**<br>Liverpool | Silversmith |
| LPB/18<br>9 November 1883<br>No mark in LPB | | P5/B/x1<br>***#4430***<br> | **John BUNCE**<br>12 North Street<br>Bristol | Watchmaker |

| REGISTRATION DETAILS | MAKER'S PRIVATE ADDRESS and DETAILS | PLATE and MARK DETAILS | MAKER/COMPANY and BUSINESS ADDRESS | MAKER'S TRADE |
|---|---|---|---|---|
| Missing register<br>*c.*1886 | See other J B marks | P5/B/14<br>***#4431***  | **Unidentified** | |
| Missing register<br>*c.*1887 | See other J B marks | P5/B/106<br>***#4432***  | **Unidentified** | |
| Missing register<br>*c.*1890 | See other J B marks | P5/B/267<br>***#4433***  | **Unidentified** | |
| Missing register<br>*c.*1891 | See other J B marks | P5/B/363<br>***#4434***  | **Unidentified** | |
| R1/37<br>14 December 1896<br>Sent by A H Tongue | 64 Brewery Street<br>Warrington | P5/aboveB/809<br>***#4435***  | **Joseph BESWICK**<br>58 Horse Market Street<br>Warrington | Tobacconist |
| R3/5<br>10 November 1921<br>Sent by E & N Speak | Private address same as business | P15/A*sic*/19<br>***#4436***  | **J BRAHAM LTD** *<br>Cecil F Hawley (Managing Director)<br>Gerrard Street<br>London W1 | Manufacturing goldsmiths and silversmiths |
| R2/232<br>23 June 1920<br>Sent by W Clark & Sons | Viewfield<br>Currie<br>Midlothian | P15/B/147<br>***#4437***  | **John BETHUNE**<br>19, 21, 23 Clerk Street<br>Edinburgh | Regalia manufacturer |
| LPB/18<br>25 March 1884<br>Similar mark entered LAO 23 October 1878 by Albert Beer | No mark in LPB<br>at this address | P5/B/x1<br>***#4438*** 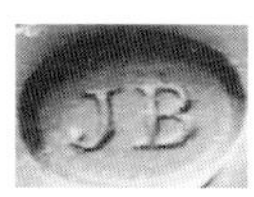 | **John BEER**<br>19 Trenchard Street<br>Bristol | Silversmith |
| R1/4<br>21 November 1894<br>Sent by J Blocksidge | 27 Crabtree Road<br>Birmingham | P5/aboveB/623<br>***#4439*** 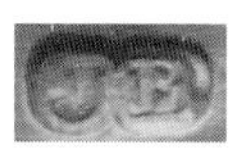 | **John BLOCKSIDGE**<br>Back of 33 Vyse Street<br>Birmingham | Jeweller |
| LPB/4<br>17 December 1877<br>Sent by Myer Brothers | | P3/B/x2<br>***#4440,1***  | **JOSEPH BROTHERS**<br>94 Vyse Street<br>Birmingham | Wholesale jewellers and factors |
| R3/14<br>8 March 1923<br>Sent by R Nevill | Waverley Hotel<br>Whitley Bay | P15/B/165,166<br>***#4442,3***  | **Joseph BERNSTONE**<br>57 Northumberland Street<br>Newcastle | Jeweller and silversmith |
| R1/206<br>5 February 1904<br>Sent by J Baker | Private address same as business | P9/B/114<br>***#4444***  | **John BAKER**<br>45 Northfield Road<br>Harborne | Manufacturing jeweller |
| R2/25<br>25 September 1906<br>Sent by John Broughton | Private address same as business | P9/XYZ*sic*/177<br>***#4445*** 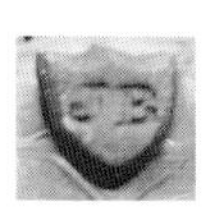 | **John BROUGHTON**<br>297 Wilmslow Road<br>Fallowfield<br>Manchester | Agent |
| R3/76<br>26 June 1935<br>Sent by S Blanckensee & Sons Ltd | 28 Vicarage Park<br>Belfast | P15/B/218<br>***#4446***  | **Joseph BERRINGER**<br>36 North Street<br>Belfast | Jeweller |
| R3/101<br>5 December 1941<br>Sent by Stanley Harris Bennett<br>Two sizes | 30 Caernarvon Road<br>Bristol 6 | P21/B/17,18<br>***#4447,8***  | **Stanley Harris BENNETT** trading as **John BENNETT**<br>131 Gloucester Road<br>Bristol 6 | Jeweller |

| REGISTRATION DETAILS | MAKER'S PRIVATE ADDRESS and DETAILS | PLATE and MARK DETAILS | MAKER/COMPANY and BUSINESS ADDRESS | MAKER'S TRADE |
|---|---|---|---|---|
| MR2/68-9<br>SOT/190<br>J3/416<br>J3 *c*.1734-52 | Tumbler cup *c*.1735 | Not on P1<br>***#4449***<br>type 1<br> | **John BRANCKER**<br>2 Castle Street<br>Liverpool | Silversmith |
| MR2/68<br>SIL/42 | Brandy saucepan 1741 | Not on P1<br>***#4450***<br>type 2<br> | | |
| Missing register<br>*c*.1889 | See next entry | P5/B/259<br>***#4451***<br> | **Joseph B BROWN** | See below |
| R1/156<br>29 October 1901<br>Sent by A H Tongue | Briarville<br>Southcliffe<br>Withensea<br>Yorks | P9/B/81<br>***#4452***<br> | **Joseph BROWN**<br>41 Brook Street<br>Hull | Fancy goods dealer |
| R1/24<br>17 March 1896<br>Sent by A H Tongue | 54 Fountain Street<br>Hull | P5/aboveB/742<br>***#4453***<br> | **Joseph B BROWN**<br>41 Brook Street<br>Hull | Importer of tobacconists goods |
| R2/40<br>16 May 1907<br>Cancelled<br>18 July 1908<br>Two sizes<br>Sent by C Stanley Bennett | 87 Bethune Road<br>Stamford Hill<br>London<br>5 Barnstaple Mansions<br>Roseberry Avenue<br>London | P9/O*sic*/198-202<br>***#4454-8***<br> | **John Baker BENNETT**<br>**Leonard John BENNETT**<br>**Charles Stanley BENNETT**<br>**Henry James HUBBERT** trading as<br>**J B BENNETT & CO** *<br>7 Charterhouse Street<br>London EC temporarily at<br>58a Hatton Garden<br>London EC | Wholesale jewellers |
| R2/41<br>1 June 1907<br>Sent by C Stanley Bennett per C E Evans<br>Cancelled 18 July 1908 | 5 Barnstaple Mansions<br>Roseberry Avenue<br>London<br>See also *#833* Impression taken 30 May 1909 P13/B/47 | P9/O*sic*/205-207<br>***#4459-61***<br> | **J B BENNETT & CO LTD** *<br>C Stanley Bennett (Director)<br>58a Hatton Garden<br>London EC | |
| R2/40<br>16 May 1907<br>Sent by C Stanley Bennett<br>Cancelled<br>18 July 1908<br>Three sizes | 87 Bethune Road<br>Stamford Hill<br>London<br>5 Barnstaple Mansions<br>Roseberry Avenue<br>London | P9/O*sic*/188-197, 203,204<br>***#4462-73***<br> | **John Baker BENNETT**<br>**Leonard John BENNETT**<br>**Charles Stanley BENNETT**<br>**Henry James HUBBERT** trading as<br>**J B BENNETT & CO** *<br>7 Charterhouse Street<br>London EC temporarily at<br>58a Hatton Garden<br>London EC | |
| R2/192<br>23 January 1915<br>Sent by Jacques Brown<br>Two sizes | Mayville<br>Tarvin Road<br>Chester | P15/B/58,61<br>***#4474,5***<br> | **Jacques BROWN & CO**<br>Bells Building<br>34 St John Street<br>38 Chapel Walks (from 12 August 1915)<br>South Castle Street<br>Liverpool | General exporters and importers |
| LPB/84<br>11 December 1882 | | P3/B/x1<br>***#4476***<br> | **John BOYD & CO**<br>5 Mason Street<br>Manchester | London, Birmingham and Sheffield warehousemen |
| R1/128<br>31 May 1900<br>Sent by F Goldsmith & Co | Sanders Road [1]<br>Edgbaston<br>60 Gough Road [2]<br>Edgbaston<br>Birmingham | P9/B/30<br>***#4477***<br> | **Leon BLANCKENSEE** [1]<br>**Frank MOSS** [2] trading as<br>**J BLANCKENSEE & CO** *<br>48 Frederick Street<br>Birmingham | Watch manufacturers |

| REGISTRATION DETAILS | MAKER'S PRIVATE ADDRESS and DETAILS | PLATE and MARK DETAILS | MAKER/COMPANY and BUSINESS ADDRESS | MAKER'S TRADE |
|---|---|---|---|---|
| R3/29<br>22 May 1925<br>Sent by Alfred Wilcox | Private address same as business | P15/B/176<br>*#4478*<br> | **John BULL & CO (BEDFORD) LTD**<br>47-49 High Street<br>Bedford | Gold and silversmiths |
| R3/41<br>11 July 1928<br>Sent by selves<br>Two sizes | | P15/C/187,188<br>*#4479,80*<br> | **John B CHATTERLEY & SONS LTD** *<br>Albert E Chatterley (Director)<br>F M Chatterley (Director)<br>111-119 Newtown Road<br>Birmingham | Silversmiths and electroplate manufacturers |
| R2/220<br>6 June 1919<br>Sent by James Booker Ltd | | P15/B/99<br>*#4481*<br> | **James BOOKER LTD**<br>Minis G Pelsin (Manager)<br>29 Hylton Street and 100 Spencer Street<br>Birmingham | Manufacturing jewellers |
| R3/116<br>4 February 1947<br>Sent by J B Morris<br>Two sizes | Private address same as business | P21/M/18,19<br>*#4482,3*<br> | **John Barrymore MORRIS**<br>12 Chester Avenue<br>Southport | Silversmith |
| R3/177<br>3 March 1961<br>Sent by T P C Mulholland | 70 Gurney Court Road<br>St Albans<br>Hertfordshire | P21/M/53<br>*#4484*<br> | **Jean Barbara MULHOLLAND**<br>No business address entered | Housewife |
| R3/144<br>23 May 1953<br>Sent by J B Moss | Sandilands<br>12 Sandringham Road<br>Birkdale<br>Southport, Lancashire | P21/M/32<br>*#4485*<br> | **Joan Barrington MOSS**<br>No business address entered | Art student |
| LPB/72<br>19 July 1882 | | P3/R/x1<br>*#4486*<br> | **John Bayton ROBINSON**<br>167½ Hockley Hill<br>Birmingham | Trade not identified |
| | | P3/R/x1<br>*#4486a*<br> | | |
| R1/85<br>22 November 1898<br>Sent by I Jonas | 8 Ampton Road<br>Edgbaston<br>Birmingham | P9/J/2<br>*#4487*<br> | **Isaac JONAS** trading as<br>**JONAS BROTHERS**<br>1 Vyse Street, Birmingham and<br>34 Ely Place, Holborn, London | Jewellers, factors and manufacturers |
| R2/227<br>9 February 1920<br>Sent by P Jackson<br>P15/J/18 impression taken 7 December 1920 | Private address same as business | P15/J/14,18<br>*#4488,9*<br> | **JACKSON BROTHERS**<br>P Jackson (Sole Proprietor)<br>4 Carlingford Road<br>Liverpool | Wholesale dealers in watches and jewellery |
| R1/30<br>12 June 1896<br>Sent by J B Salmon | 10 Dunham Street<br>Hulme<br>Manchester | P5/Y*sic*/775<br>*#4490*<br> | **John Buxton SALMON**<br>20b Hanging Ditch<br>Manchester | Pipe and stick mounter |
| LPB/42<br>26 August 1880 | | P3/I*sic*/x1<br>*#4491*<br> | **JACKSON BROTHERS**<br>60½ Great Hampton Street<br>Birmingham | Manufacturing jewellers |
| Missing register<br>*c.*1890 | | P5/J/315<br>*#4492*<br>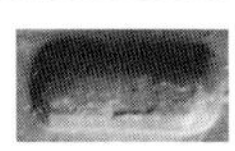 | | |
| Missing register<br>*c.*1890 | | P5/J/347<br>*#4493*<br>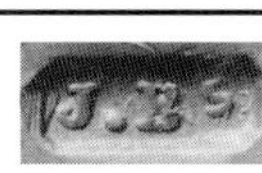 | | |
| R2/64<br>8 September 1908<br>Sent by Wright & Perry | 72 Portland Road<br>Edgbaston<br>Birmingham | P13/J/2<br>*#4494*<br> | **George JAMES** trading as<br>**JAMES BROTHERS**<br>37 Tenby Street and<br>16 Frederick Street<br>Birmingham | Jewellers |

| REGISTRATION DETAILS | MAKER'S PRIVATE ADDRESS and DETAILS | PLATE and MARK DETAILS | MAKER/COMPANY and BUSINESS ADDRESS | MAKER'S TRADE |
|---|---|---|---|---|
| R2/52<br>11 December 1907<br>Sent by R Chandler<br>Two sizes | 35 Alva Street<br>10 Forbes Road and<br>4 Church Hill Place<br>Edinburgh | P13/B/4-7<br>***#4495-8***<br> | **John BARTLEMAN** senior<br>**Thomas BARTLEMAN** trading as<br>**J BARTLEMAN & SON**<br>44 Hanover Street<br>Edinburgh | Gold and silversmiths |
| R3/38<br>8 September 1927<br>Sent by selves | | P15/J/29<br>***#4499***<br><br>§ | **JUNGHANS BROTHERS LTD** *<br>N Colton (Managing Director)<br>55 Hatton Garden<br>London EC1 | Clock and watch importers |
| PP1/188<br>GTD 1870<br>PMR 1834-68 | See also IC | P2/C/x4<br>***#4500-3***<br> | **James CAVE**<br>42 Eldon Place (1851-71)<br>Liverpool | Watchcase maker |
| R2/115<br>5 July 1910<br>Sent by B Wade | 11 Duke Street [1]<br>Edinburgh | P13/C/77,78<br>***#4504,5***<br>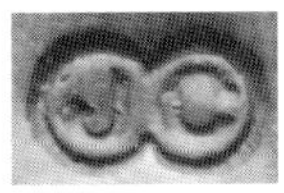 | **Joseph COTTON LTD**<br>James Arkman Smith [1] (Secretary)<br>172 Eastern Road and<br>7 Frederick Street<br>Edinburgh | Tobacco and snuff manufacturers |
| Missing register<br>*c.*1894 | | P5/C/539<br>***#4506***<br>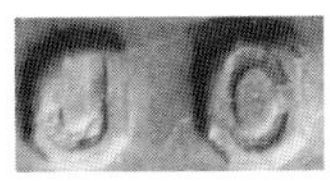 | **Unidentified** | |
| Missing register<br>*c.*1889 | | P5/C/234<br>***#4507***<br> | **Unidentified** | |
| R2/70<br>22 December 1908<br>Sent by B Wade | 40 Blacket Place [1]<br>Edinburgh | P13/C/35<br>***#4508***<br>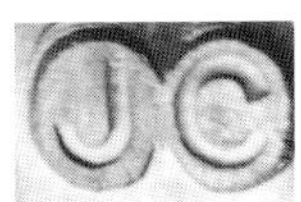 | **John COTTON LTD**<br>James Arkman Smith [1] (Secretary)<br>172 Eastern Road<br>Edinburgh and<br>7 Frederick Street<br>Edinburgh | Tobacco manufacturers |
| R3/51<br>14 December 1929<br>Sent by T J Skelton<br>119 Vyse Street<br>Birmingham | 68 Abbotsford Place [1]<br>Glasgow C5 | P15/C/202-206<br>***#4509-13***<br> | **Joseph CUTLER** [1]<br>118 Howard Street<br>Glasgow C1 | Wholesale jeweller |
| R3/52<br>20 February 1930<br>Sent by R Jones | 5 Warstone Parade East<br>Birmingham | P15/C/207<br>***#4514***<br> | | |
| R3/60<br>18 November 1931<br>Sent by T J Skelton<br>86 Vyse Street<br>Birmingham | 1 Springhill Terrace [1]<br>Glasgow S1 | P15/K*sic*/210<br>***#4515***<br>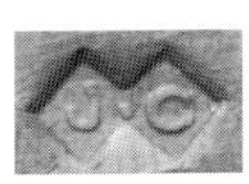 | | |
| R3/60<br>18 November 1931<br>Sent by T J Skelton<br>86 Vyse Street<br>Birmingham | | P15/K*sic*/211<br>***#4516***<br>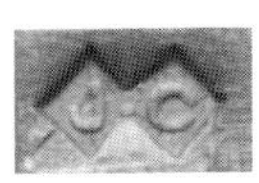 | | |
| PDB 1813-30 Gold rings and silverware<br>MR2/73<br>MR3/78<br>LGSJ 1825 | Very small cameo perhaps indicates use for rings?<br>This mark and the next one may also be for John Clifton IC or James Critchley of Liverpool, watchcase maker J1 1821-8 | P1/19/x1<br>***#4517***<br> | **John CLARKE**<br>45 Hanover Street<br>Liverpool or<br><br>**John COAKLEY**<br>see next entry | Goldsmith and silversmith |

| REGISTRATION DETAILS | MAKER'S PRIVATE ADDRESS and DETAILS | PLATE and MARK DETAILS | MAKER/COMPANY and BUSINESS ADDRESS | MAKER'S TRADE |
|---|---|---|---|---|
| PDB 1828-33<br>MR2/73<br>MR3/79<br>GTD 1829<br>J1 1828-34<br>GMSC/79,80<br>Similar mark LAO<br>3 September 1832 | Spoons and flatware<br>Square marked 1785<br>See also IC | P1/21/x1<br>***#4918***<br> | **John COAKLEY** (G)<br>18 Arley Street<br>Liverpool or<br>**John CLARKE**<br>see entry above | Goldsmith and silversmith |
| R3/166<br>14 February 1959<br>Sent by J Creed<br>Two sizes | Lightfoot Lane<br>Heswall<br>Wirral<br>Cheshire | P21/C/78,79<br>***#4519,20***<br> | **John CREED**<br>City College of Art<br>Hope Street<br>Liverpool 1 | Student artist craftsman |
| LPB/92<br>23 September 1882 | Entry reads like Cohen but could be John Culver who was at this address 1882 to 1886 | P3/C/x3<br>***#4521-3***<br> | **John CULVER** *<br>28 Spencer Street<br>London | Gold chain maker |
| R1/151<br>12 July 1901<br>Sent by self | Augustine House<br>Queens Road N<br>London | P9/C/71<br>***#4524***<br> | **John CULVER** *<br>26 Spencer Street<br>Clerkenwell<br>London | Manufacturing jeweller |
| Not in R2 as expected<br>*c.* March 1917 to August 1919 | | P15/G*sic*/between 33 and 34<br>***#4525***<br> | **James CAMERON**<br>(see next entry) | |
| R2/212 no date or mark number - between April and June 1917<br>Sent by Jessie Cameron | 15 North Place<br>Cheltenham | P15/C/69 ?<br>***#4526***<br> | **James CAMERON**<br>7 Bennington Street<br>Cheltenham | Walking stick mounter and manufacturer |
| Missing register<br>*c.*1893 | | P5/C/477<br>***#4527***<br>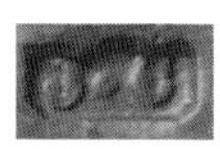 | **Unidentified** | |
| SPB/7<br>21 June 1865 | | P3/C/x3<br>***#4528-30***<br> | **John CHADWICK**<br>52 Kensington Terrace<br>Kirkdale<br>Liverpool | Watchmaker |
| R1/100<br>12 May 1899<br>Sent by Herbert Crompton Three sizes | Wilton House<br>St James Road<br>Edgbaston, Birmingham<br>E S Jones<br>33 Olive Road<br>Edgbaston, Birmingham | P9/J/13-15<br>***#4531-3***<br> | **Herbert** (Hubert BAO/LAO) **CROMPTON**<br>trading as **JONES & CROMPTON** *<br>(late **E S JONES**)<br>36 Spencer Street<br>Birmingham | Silversmiths |
| Missing register<br>*c.*1889<br>Similar mark entered LAO 27 October 1886 | | P5/B/263<br>***#4534***<br> | **John Clegg BUTTERWORTH** *<br>83 Clifton Street<br>Lytham<br>Lancashire | Silversmith |
| R1/82<br>4 November 1898<br>Sent by James Morris | 225 Great Kings Street<br>Hockley<br>Birmingham | P9/J/1<br>***#4535***<br> | **James MORRIS**<br>**John BRAY** trading as<br>**JAMES & CO**<br>83½ Hampton Street<br>Birmingham | Jewellers |
| R1/219<br>30 August 1904<br>Sent by W J Holmes | Trelyn<br>Sutton Coldfield | P9/D*sic*/212<br>***#4536***<br> | **J COLLYER & CO LTD**<br>C B Barnett (Secretary and Director)<br>50 Hockley Hill<br>Birmingham | Electroplaters and silversmiths |

| REGISTRATION DETAILS | MAKER'S PRIVATE ADDRESS and DETAILS | PLATE and MARK DETAILS | MAKER/COMPANY and BUSINESS ADDRESS | MAKER'S TRADE |
|---|---|---|---|---|
| R2/51<br>26 November 1907<br>Sent by John Culver Ltd<br>Two sizes | 4 Dukes Avenue<br>Muswell Hill<br>London | P13/C/6,7<br>*#4537,8*<br> | **John CULVER LTD** *<br>John Culver (Director)<br>26 Spencer Street<br>Clerkenwell<br>London | Manufacturing jewellers |
| R3/99<br>29 May 1941<br>Sent by J C Murray<br>Two sizes | 42 Melrose Avenue<br>Sutton Coldfield | P21/M/10,11<br>*#4539,40*<br> | **John Charles MURRAY**<br>12 Northampton Street<br>Birmingham 18 | Manufacturing jeweller |
| R1/170<br>11 June 1902<br>Sent by J C Plimpton & Co<br>Two sizes | Penkett Road<br>Liscard<br>Cheshire<br>50 Grove Street<br>Liverpool | P9/Q*sic*/151-156<br>*#4541-6*<br> | **John Cohen PLIMPTON**<br>**S Raleigh KIRKNESS** trading as<br>**J C PLIMPTON & CO**<br>112/114/116 Old Hall Street<br>Liverpool and<br>34 Curtain Road<br>London | American import/export merchants |
| R1/201<br>1 October 1903<br>Sent by J C Plimpton | Penkett Road<br>Liscard<br>The Hollies<br>Wavertree | P9/Q*sic*/187<br>*#4547*<br> | details as above<br>Liverpool address only | Merchants |
| Missing register<br>*c*.1888<br>Similar mark entered BAO 4 June 1888 | | P5/C/198<br>*#4548*<br> | **Joseph COOK & SON**<br>6, 7 Carver Street<br>Birmingham | Silversmiths |
| R2/73<br>24 February 1909<br>Sent by Charles Horner | Hibernia<br>Gravelly Hill North<br>nr Birmingham | P13/C/37<br>*#4549*<br> | **J COOK & SONS LTD**<br>William Henry Hall (Director)<br>Hibernian Works,<br>Livery Street<br>Birmingham | Manufacturing jewellers |
| R2/79<br>16 April 1909<br>Sent by W H Hall<br>BAO 13.557, 13.558 | | P13/C/41,42<br>*#4550,1*<br> | **Joseph COOK & SON LTD**<br>W H Hall (Director)<br>Hiberian Works<br>Livery Street<br>Birmingham | |
| Missing register<br>*c*.1892 | On square C so surname likely to begin with "C" | P5/C/448<br>*#4552*<br> | **Joseph COHEN & SON** | Tobacconists furnishers |
| R1/63<br>23 March 1898<br>Sent by A H Tongue | 2 Alfred Terrace<br>Glasgow | P5/aboveC/945<br>*#4553*<br> | **Morris Tobias COHEN** trading as<br>**Joseph COHEN & SON**<br>80 Buchannan Street<br>Glasgow | |
| Missing register<br>*c*.1890 | | P5/C/300<br>*#4554*<br> | **Joseph COOK & SON**<br>6, 7 Carver Street<br>Birmingham | Silversmiths |
| Missing register<br>*c*.1888<br>Similar mark entered BAO 22 January 1889 | | P5/C/196<br>*#4555*<br> | | |
| R2/147<br>22 November 1911<br>Sent by R Parkes & Co<br>BAO 6.154 | Elleslie<br>Kilmarnock | P13/D*sic*/147<br>*#4556*<br> | **J Wilson WALLACE** trading as<br>**J CAMERON & SON**<br>13 King Street<br>Kilmarnock | Manufacturing jewellers |
| R1/221<br>7 October 1904<br>Sent by S Mordan & Co | Leigh Holme<br>Streatham<br>London SW | P9/V/6<br>*#4557*<br>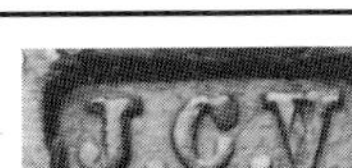 | **John Collard VICKERY** *<br>179/181/183 Regent Street and<br>1 New Burlington Place<br>London | Goldsmith, silversmith and jeweller |

| REGISTRATION DETAILS | MAKER'S PRIVATE ADDRESS and DETAILS | PLATE and MARK DETAILS | MAKER/COMPANY and BUSINESS ADDRESS | MAKER'S TRADE |
|---|---|---|---|---|
| R2/4<br>16 October 1905<br>Sent by Cohen & Charles | Acquired by James Walker Ltd in 1903 and thence to H Samuel Ltd in 1985 | P9/V/9<br>***#4558***  | **John Collard VICKERY** *<br>179/181/183 Regent Street<br>London | Goldsmith, silversmith and jeweller |
| R2/24<br>14 September 1906<br>Sent by Saunders & Shepherd | Leigh Holme<br>Streatham<br>London SW | P9/V/16<br>***#4559***  | **John Collard VICKERY** *<br>179/181/183 Regent Street<br>London | |
| R2/45<br>6 September 1907<br>Sent by John Millward Banks | | P9/V/17<br>***#4560***  | **John Collard VICKERY** *<br>183 Regent Street<br>London | Jeweller and silversmith |
| R2/198<br>17 July 1915<br>Sent by Horace Woodward Co<br>BAO 22.841 | | P15/V/1<br>***#4561***  | **John Collard VICKERY** *<br>177 to 183 Regent Street<br>London | Goldsmith, silversmith and jeweller |
| R3/9<br>20 May 1922<br>Sent by Docker & Burn | | P15/V/10<br>***#4562***  | **John Collard VICKERY** *<br>John Collard Vickery<br>177 to 183 Regent Street<br>London W1 | Silversmith |
| R3/181<br>7 November 1961<br>Sent by J C Webb | Orchard House Cottage<br>Holywell Hill<br>St Albans<br>Hertfordshire | P21/W/107<br>***#4563***  | **John Christopher WEBB**<br>Orchard House Studios<br>Holywell Hill<br>St Albans<br>Hertfordshire | Silversmith |
| J1 1841<br>CMC/100 | | P2/D/x3<br>***#4564-6***  | **John DAVIES**<br>Eastgate (1846)<br>Foregate (1860)<br>Chester | Clockmaker, watchmaker and silversmith |
| Not in SPB or LPB so struck 1860-3 | | P3/D/x3<br>***#4567-9***  | | |
| R3/105<br>28 May 1943<br>Sent by Joseph Dixon | 42 Lea Hill Road<br>Birmingham 20 | P21/D/7<br>***#4570***  | **Joseph DIXON**<br>50 Vyse Street<br>Birmingham 18 | Jeweller |
| LPB/24<br>11 October 1879 | | P3/D/x3<br>***#4571-3***  | **James DODSWORTH** *<br>2 Chesterfield Street<br>Liverpool | Watch and watchcase manufacturer |
| R2/81<br>11 May 1909<br>Sent by Isaac Birkett | 21 Geriant Street<br>Liverpool<br>9 Vanguard Street<br>Liverpool | P13/D/18<br>***#4574***  | **Henry TURNER**<br>**Isaac BIRKETT** trading as<br>**DODSWORTH BROTHERS**<br>16 Richmond Street<br>Liverpool | |
| PDB 1816<br>MR3/80 | Gold rings<br>Also see ID | P1/16/x3<br>***#4575-7*** | **James DUKE**<br>Manchester or | Goldsmith |
| PDB 1838-40<br>MR3/80 | Gold rings and silver spoons |  | **Joseph DUKE II**<br>Chester or | Goldsmith and silversmith |
| PDB 1836-8<br>MR3/80<br>CMC/102 | Gold rings | | **Joseph DUTTON**<br>Eastgate Row (1834-50)<br>Chester | Goldsmith, clockmaker and watchmaker |

| REGISTRATION DETAILS | MAKER'S PRIVATE ADDRESS and DETAILS | PLATE and MARK DETAILS | MAKER/COMPANY and BUSINESS ADDRESS | MAKER'S TRADE |
|---|---|---|---|---|
| R1/150<br>10 July 1901<br>Sent by self | 13 Tynwald Hill<br>Stoneycroft<br>Liverpool | P9/D/23<br>***#4578***<br> | **John DWERRYHOUSE**<br>52 Castle Street<br>Liverpool | Jeweller |
| LPB/18<br>6 September 1884<br>No mark in LPB | | P5/B/x1<br>***#4579***<br> | **John Daniels BENSON**<br>64 Vyse Street<br>Birmingham | Jeweller |
| R3/116<br>15 April 1947<br>Sent by J D Cherry<br>Two sizes | Private address same as business | P21/C/34,35<br>***#4580,1***<br> | **Joan Dorothy CHERRY**<br>Rylcroft<br>Langham Road<br>Bowdon<br>Cheshire | Student in gold and silversmithing |
| R2/81<br>7 May 1909<br>Sent by J Daffern | 13 Bromshill Road<br>Harlesden<br>London NW | P13/D/17<br>***#4582***<br> | **Joseph DAFFERN** trading as<br>**J DAFFERN & CO**<br>23 Hatton Garden<br>London EC | Medallists and club badge makers |
| R3/148<br>8 December 1953<br>Sent by J D Kelly<br>Mark not struck on P21 as expected! | 65 Stewards Avenue<br>Widnes<br>Lancashire | P21/K/14<br>**#4583**<br>**J D K?** | **John Derek KELLY**<br>No business address entered | Silversmith |
| LPB/46<br>11 April 1883<br>LPB mark shown | Not at BAO or LAO<br>See entry for Reid & Son for possible relative.<br>Name not in 1881 census, but seen in *Birmingham Life in* 1868 as a writer. | Not on P3<br>***#4584***<br>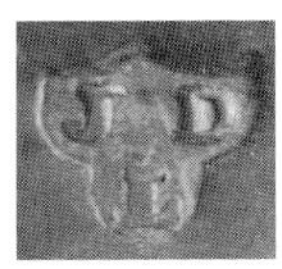 | **J Deverill LANGFORD**<br>Business address not entered | Trade not identified |
| R1/42<br>26 March 1897<br>Sent by E Langridge & Co | William Henry Appleby<br>Managing Director<br>26 Clarke Street<br>Sheffield | P5/D/827<br>***#4585***<br> | **James DEWSNAP LTD** *<br>10 St Thomas Street<br>Sheffield and<br>35 Ely Place<br>Holborn<br>London EC | Fancy leather goods manufacturers |
| R1/17<br>15 October 1895<br>Sent by Levi & Salaman<br>T Able<br>Westwood & Sons<br>F W Turton Ltd<br>F Hewson<br>W Turner<br>C E Turner<br>E S Jones<br>Lines, Bunn & Mason<br>Synyer & Beddoes<br>Myatt & Pulligne<br>Lucas & Co<br>C Wilkes | 71 Crescent Road<br>Sheffield | P5/D/692<br>***#4586***<br> | **William Petchford DEAKIN**<br>**John DEAKIN**<br>**Albert DEAKIN** trading as<br>**James DEAKIN & SON** *<br>Sidney Walk<br>Matilda Street<br>Sheffield and<br>14 Charterhouse Street<br>London | Silversmiths |
| R1/154<br>1 October 1901<br>Sent by Charles Frederick Dyson | The Limes [1]<br>Weston<br>The Limes [2]<br>Weston<br>Haly Park [3]<br>Leeds | P9/D/24<br>***#4587***<br>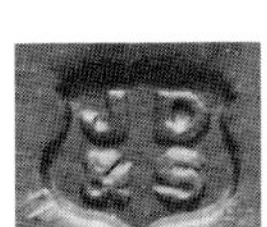 | **John DYSON** [1]<br>**John P DYSON** [2]<br>**Charles F DYSON** [3] trading as<br>**John DYSON & SON** *<br>Briggate<br>Leeds and<br>Westgate<br>Wakefield | Watchmakers, jewellers and silversmiths |

| REGISTRATION DETAILS | MAKER'S PRIVATE ADDRESS and DETAILS | PLATE and MARK DETAILS | MAKER/COMPANY and BUSINESS ADDRESS | MAKER'S TRADE |
|---|---|---|---|---|
| R2/210<br>5 December 1916<br>Sent by Charles Frederick Dyson | Croft House<br>Weeton<br>Leeds<br>Weston Hall<br>Weeton<br>Leeds | P15/D/30<br>***#4588***<br> | **Charles Frederick DYSON**<br>**John P DYSON** trading as<br>**John DYSON & SON** *<br>24, 25, 26 Briggate<br>Leeds and<br>13 Cross Square<br>Wakefield | Watchmakers and jewellers |
| R3/65<br>30 November 1932<br>Sent by J Deakin & Sons Ltd | | P15/D/79-84<br>***#4589-94***<br> | **James DEAKIN & SONS LTD** *<br>Sidney Works<br>Matilda Street<br>Sheffield | Silversmiths |
| R3/80<br>I November 1935<br>Sent by J Dixon & Sons Ltd<br>Two sizes | | P15/D/92 and P21/D/1<br>***#4595,6***<br>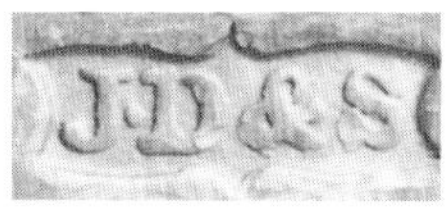 | **James DIXON & SONS LTD** *<br>Sealed by:-<br>S Constantine (Director)<br>A Dearden (Secretary)<br>Cornish Place (Registered Office)<br>Sheffield | Silversmiths |
| Missing register<br>*c* 1888 | | P5/D/156a<br>***#4597***<br> | **John DEAKIN**<br>**William DEAKIN** | Silversmiths |
| Missing register<br>*c.*1888<br>Three sizes<br>Similar mark entered BAO 26 May 1888 | | P5/D/156b-d<br>***#4598-4600***<br> | | |
| Missing register<br>*c.*1888 | | P5/D/156e<br>***#4601***<br> | | |
| R1/83<br>15 November 1898<br>Sent by F W Turton & Co<br>Levi & Salaman<br>Reynolds & Westwood<br>F Hewson of London<br>C E Turner<br>W Vale & Sons | 18 Moncrief Road<br>Sharlon<br>Sheffield | P9/D/4-7<br>***#4602-5***<br>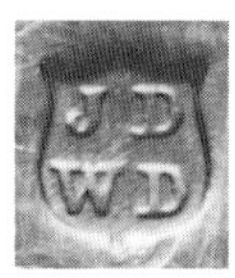 | **William P DEAKIN** (Chairman and Managing Director)<br>trading as<br>**James DEAKIN & SONS LTD** *<br>Sydney Works<br>Matilda Street<br>Sheffield and<br>14 Charterhouse Street<br>Sheffield (*sic*) (in error for London ?) | |
| R1/176<br>25 September 1902<br>Sent by E Mander & Son | | P9/D/35,36<br>***#4606,7***<br> | **James DEAKIN & SON** *<br>Albert Deakin (Director)<br>Sidney Works<br>Sheffield | Silversmiths and cutlers |
| R2/54<br>21 January 1908<br>Sent by WJ Myatt & Co<br>Three sizes | Osborne Road<br>Brincliffe<br>Sheffield | P9/D/64-71 and P13/D/1,2<br>***#4608-17***<br> | | Silversmiths |
| R2/107<br>4 April 1910<br>Sent by Clark & Sewell<br>Two sizes | Osborne Road<br>Sheffield<br>33 Kenwood Park Road<br>Sheffield<br>44 Kingsfield Road<br>Sheffield | P13/D/28,29<br>***#4618,9***<br> | **John DEAKIN** (Director)<br>**William Petchford DEAKIN**<br>**Albert DEAKIN** trading as<br>**James DEAKIN & SONS LTD** *<br>Sidney Works<br>Sheffield | Manufacturing silversmiths |

| REGISTRATION DETAILS | MAKER'S PRIVATE ADDRESS and DETAILS | PLATE and MARK DETAILS | MAKER/COMPANY and BUSINESS ADDRESS | MAKER'S TRADE |
|---|---|---|---|---|
| R2/130<br>9 March 1911<br>Sent by D & L Spiers<br>Two sizes | 33 Kenwood Park Road<br>Sheffield<br>Osborne Road<br>Sheffield<br>44 Kingsfield Road<br>Sheffield | P13/D/35,36<br>*#4620,1*<br>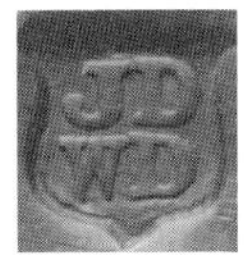 | **William P DEAKIN**<br>**John DEAKIN**<br>**Albert DEAKIN** trading as<br>**James DEAKIN & SONS** *<br>Sidney Works<br>Matilda Street<br>Sheffield and<br>14 Charterhouse Street<br>London EC | Manufacturing silversmiths |
| R2/168<br>24 February 1913<br>Sent by Baldwin & Marriott<br>Two sizes | 33 Kenwood Park Road<br>Sharrow, Sheffield<br>Osborne Road<br>Nether Edge, Sheffield<br>44 Kingsfield Road, Sharrow<br>Sheffield<br>Kenwood Road, Sharrow<br>Sheffield | P15/D/1,2<br>*#4622,3*<br> | | |
| R2/173<br>7 June 1913<br>Sent by Napper & Davenport<br>Two sizes | | P15/D/3,4<br>*#4624,5*<br> | | |
| R2/173<br>13 June 1913<br>Sent by Napper & Davenport<br>Two sizes | | P15/D/5,6<br>*#4626,7*<br> | | |
| R2/175<br>29 July 1913<br>Sent by L Smith & Co<br>Two sizes | | P15/D/7,8<br>*#4628,9*<br> | | |
| R2/183<br>10 February 1914<br>Sent by Clark & Sewell<br>Three sizes | | P15/D/10-14<br>*#4630-34*<br>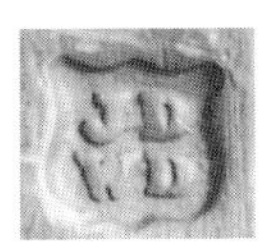 | | |
| R2/199<br>17 August 1915<br>Sent by A & J Zimmerman | 33 Kenwood Park Road<br>Sharrow, Sheffield<br>85 Osborne Road<br>Nether Edge, Sheffield<br>44 Kingsfield Road, Sharrow<br>Sheffield<br>Kenwood Bank, Sharrow<br>Sheffield | P15/D/25, 26<br>*#4635,6*<br> | **William P DEAKIN**<br>**John DEAKIN**<br>**Albert DEAKIN**<br>**James Henry DEAKIN** trading as<br>**James DEAKIN & SONS LTD** *<br>Sidney Works<br>Matilda Street<br>Sheffield | |
| Not in R3 as expected<br>*c.*1925 | | P15/D/67-70,77<br>*#4647-41*<br>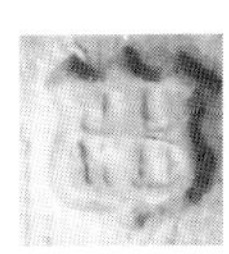 | **James & William DEAKIN** *<br>Sidney Works<br>Matilda Street<br>Sheffield | |
| J1/379 1839-46 | Mark not seen | Not on P1<br>*#4642* **J E?** | **James EVANS**<br>Chester | Silversmith |
| SPB/10<br>14 June 1873<br>defaced 2 August 1877 | Purchased Benson Brothers, watchcase makers 1 September 1902 and cancelled all BB punches | P3/E/x3<br>*#4643-5*<br> | **James Buckley EASTHAM**<br>10 Springfield<br>St Anne Street<br>Liverpool | Watchcase maker |

| REGISTRATION DETAILS | MAKER'S PRIVATE ADDRESS and DETAILS | PLATE and MARK DETAILS | MAKER/COMPANY and BUSINESS ADDRESS | MAKER'S TRADE |
|---|---|---|---|---|
| SPB/10<br>14 June 1873<br>defaced 2 August 1877 | Purchased Benson Brothers, watchcase makers 1 September 1902 and cancelled all BB punches | P3/E/x3<br>***#4646-8***<br> | **James Buckley EASTHAM**<br>10 Springfield<br>St Anne Street<br>Liverpool | Watchcase maker |
| SPB/10<br>2 August 1877 | | P3/E/x2<br>***#4649,50***<br> | | |
| R2/58<br>2 April 1908<br>Sent by Benson Brothers | 9 Rock Point Avenue<br>New Brighton<br>18 Rock Point Avenue<br>New Brighton<br>2 Vale Drive<br>New Brighton | P13/E/I<br>***#4651***<br> | **William Hilton BENSON**<br>**John BENSON**<br>**George Walter BENSON** trading as<br>**J EASTHAM**<br>72 Wood Street<br>Liverpool | Watchcase manufacturers |
| Not in R2 as expected<br>*c.* February to September 1915 | | P15/E/6<br>***#4652***<br>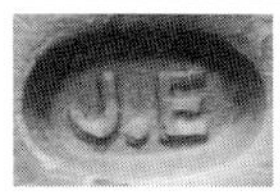 | | |
| R3/173<br>8 June 1960<br>Sent by J Edmonton | Private address same as business | P21/E/17,18<br>***#4653,4***<br>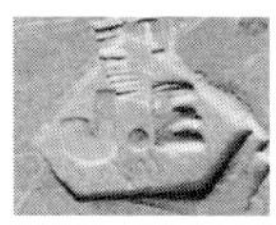 | **John EDMONTON**<br>Moss Bank<br>20 Throstle Grove<br>Slyne-with-Hest<br>Lancaster | Metalworker |
| R1/174<br>1 September 1902<br>Sent by Benson Brothers<br>Cancelled<br>2 April 1908 | 10 Vaughton Road [1]<br>New Brighton<br>41 Halkyn Avenue [2]<br>Liverpool<br>2 Vale Drive [3]<br>New Brighton | P9/E/10<br>***#4655***<br> | **John BENSON** [1]<br>**William Hilton BENSON** [2]<br>**George Walter BENSON** [3]<br>**BENSON BROTHERS** trading as<br>**J EASTHAM**<br>72 Wood Street<br>Liverpool | Watchcase manufacturers |
| R2/133<br>28 April 1911<br>Sent by Joseph Ettlinger<br>Two sizes | 19 Park Square<br>Regents Park<br>London NW | P13/E/20,21<br>***#4656,7***<br> | **Joseph ETTLINGER** *<br>176 Regent Street<br>London W | Fancy goods dealer (wholesale) |
| R1/200<br>22 August 1903<br>Sent by G K Leeson | Cork Hotel<br>Brighton | P9/E/14<br>***#4658***<br> | **John ELKAN** *<br>35/23/14 (*sic*) Liverpool Street<br>London EC | Jeweller |
| R1/231<br>12 April 1905<br>Sent by John Eldridge | 45 Wandsworth Bridge Road<br>Fulham<br>London SW | P9/E/16<br>***#4659***<br> | **John ELDRIDGE** *<br>9 Kenton Street<br>Brunswick Square<br>London WC | Manufacturing goldsmith and silversmith |
| R3/5<br>19 October 1921<br>Sent by J E Ashworth | 39 Heathfield Road<br>Acton<br>London W | P15/A/17,18<br>***#4660,1***<br> | **John E ASHFORTH**<br>28 Ely Place<br>Holborn Circus<br>London EC1 | Silversmith |
| R3/54<br>22 June 1930<br>Sent by J E Bradley | Private address same as business | P15/B/200<br>***#4662***<br> | **J E BRADLEY**<br>182 Brighton Street<br>Wallasey<br>Cheshire | Watchmaker and jeweller |
| New punch<br>undated | | P21/B/28<br>***#4663***<br>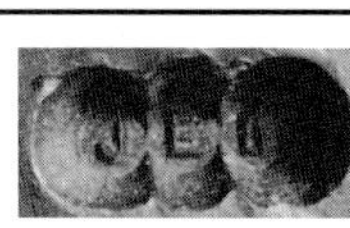 | | |
| R2/131<br>20 March 1911<br>Sent by J E Barnett<br>BAO 18.150 | Private address same as business | P13/B/117<br>***#4664***<br> | **James Edward BARNETT**<br>17 Larpent Avenue<br>Putney<br>London SW | Silver novelties, inventor and manufacturer |

| REGISTRATION DETAILS | MAKER'S PRIVATE ADDRESS and DETAILS | PLATE and MARK DETAILS | MAKER/COMPANY and BUSINESS ADDRESS | MAKER'S TRADE |
|---|---|---|---|---|
| LPB/68<br>4 August 1883 | | P3/C/x1<br>***#4665***  | **Joshua Edward CARTWRIGHT** *<br>17 Warstone Parade<br>Warstone Lane<br>Birmingham | Goldsmith and silversmith |
| R3/150<br>19 January 1954<br>Sent by J E Lamb | 12 River Parade<br>Preston<br>Lancashire | P21/L/34<br>***#4666***  | **John Edward LAMB**<br>No business address entered | Teacher of metalwork |
| R1/74<br>12 September 1898<br>Sent by J E Pool | Private address same as business | P9/P/3<br>***#4667***  | **John Edward** (*sic*) **POOL**<br>328 Lodge Road<br>Hockley<br>Birmingham | Jeweller |
| R2/98<br>19 November 1909<br>Sent by John Edwin Pool | 33 Park Road<br>Hockley<br>Birmingham | P13/P/107<br>***#4668***  | **John Edwin POOL**<br>33 Park Road<br>Hockley<br>Birmingham | Manufacturing jeweller |
| Not in R2 as expected<br>*c.* March to May 1909<br>Similar mark BAO<br>11 September 1912 | The Priory<br>Goldhurst Terrace<br>West Hampstead | P13/S/32<br>***#4669***  | **Joseph Edward SUTTON** *<br>25 President Street<br>London EC | Chain maker |
| Not in R2 as expected<br>*c.* November to December 1911 | | P13/S/81<br>***#4670*** 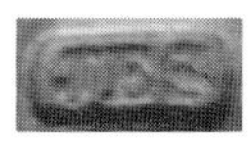 | | |
| R2/223<br>4 September 1919<br>Sent by Joseph Elliot & Son | 1 Tapton House Road<br>Sheffield | P15/E/13<br>***#4671*** 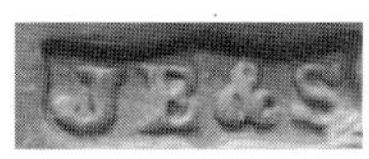 | **Joseph G ELLIOT** trading as<br>**NIXON & SON**<br>4 Hollis Croft<br>Sheffield | Silversmiths |
| Not in R3 as expected<br>*c.*1923 Two sizes<br>Similar mark BAO<br>11 September 1923 | | P15/W/62,63<br>***#4672,3***  | **John Eli WEETMAN**<br>15A Harford Street<br>Birmingham | Jeweller |
| R2/218<br>20 February 1919<br>Sent by John E Weetman | Private address same as business | P15/W/42<br>***#4674***  | **John Eli WEETMAN**<br>204 Burbury Street<br>Aston<br>Birmingham | Gold chain and ring manufacturer |
| R2/221<br>28 June 1919<br>Sent by John Fitton | Private address same as business | P15/F/18<br>***#4675***  | **John FITTON**<br>76 Lees Road<br>Oldham | Pawnbroker and jeweller |
| R2/169<br>6 March 1913<br>Sent by James Fenton | Westfield Road<br>Edgbaston<br>41 Algernon Road<br>Edgbaston<br>Birmingham | P15/F/1<br>***#4676*** 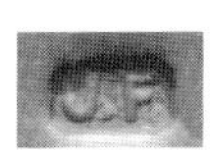 | **Allan H ELKINGTON**<br>**Ernest BOWKER** trading as<br>**James FENTON**<br>74 Great Hampton Street<br>Birmingham | Manufacturing jewellers |
| R2/48<br>19 October 1907<br>Sent by Joseph Flynn | 109 Leonard Road<br>Handsworth<br>Birmingham | P9/F/32<br>***#4677***  | **Joseph FLYNN**<br>45 Branston Street<br>Birmingham | Manufacturing jewellers |
| LPB/84<br>22 November 1882<br>Sent by C Bradford | | P3/F/x3<br>***#4678-80***  | **James FENTON**<br>74 Great Hampton Street<br>Birmingham | Silversmith, jeweller and thimble specialist |
| R2/27<br>20 October 1906<br>Sent by James Fawson | 32 Florence Road<br>Handsworth<br>Birmingham | P9/F/30<br>***#4681***  | **James FAWSON**<br>27 Northampton Street<br>Birmingham | Jeweller |

| REGISTRATION DETAILS | MAKER'S PRIVATE ADDRESS and DETAILS | PLATE and MARK DETAILS | MAKER/COMPANY and BUSINESS ADDRESS | MAKER'S TRADE |
|---|---|---|---|---|
| LPB/30<br>13 May 1881 | | P3/F/x1<br>***#4682***<br> | **Joseph FRAY**<br>Northampton Street<br>Birmingham | Jeweller |
| Missing register<br>*c.*1886 | | P5/F/27<br>***#4683***<br> | **J FRAY** or **James FENTON** | |
| Missing register<br>*c.*1886 | | P5/F/51<br>***#4684***<br> | **J FRAY** or **James FENTON** | |
| SPB/11<br>2 February 1870 | CWMP 1874 has him as Dial Maker and Springer<br><br>38 Mount Street (1874) | P3/F/x3<br>***#4685-7***<br> | **John FLECKNER** *<br>Warwick Street<br>Earlsdon<br>Coventry | Watchcase maker |
| SPB/16<br>18 March 1875<br>CWMP 1886-1901 | | P3/F/x2<br>***#4588,9***<br> | **Joseph FELTHAM** *<br>62 Spon Street<br>Coventry | Watchcase maker |
| LPB/30<br>18 October 1881<br>LPB mark shown | | Not on P3<br>***#4690***<br> | **James FENTON**<br>74 Great Hampton Street<br>Birmingham | Silversmith, jeweller and thimble specialist |
| R1/134<br>20 October 1900<br>Sent by Lancashire Watch Co | 24 Heywood Street<br>Cheetham<br>Manchester | P9/F/9<br>***#4691***<br> | **Joseph FIRESTONE**<br>7 Kilverts Buildings<br>Withy Grove<br>Manchester | Jeweller |
| R2/111<br>24 May 1910<br>Sent by J Freeman | 104 Richmond Road<br>Barnsbury<br>London N | P13/F/21<br>***#4692***<br> | **Joseph FREEMAN** *<br>104 Richmond Road, Barnsbury<br>London N | Hollow and solid keeper ring maker |
| R2/189<br>29 July 1914 and<br>14 August 1914<br>Sent by E J Rudge | Parkfoot<br>Walton<br>Warrington | P15/F/7<br>***#4693***<br> | **John FINLAYSON**<br>42 Horsemarket Street<br>Warrington | Retail jeweller |
| R3/96<br>19 November 1939<br>Sent by J Fawson | 12 Kensington Road<br>Birmingham 29 | P21/F/6<br>***#4694***<br> | **James FAWSON**<br>13 Northampton Street<br>Birmingham 18 | Jeweller |
| R1/224<br>23 December 1904<br>Sent by J Feinknope<br>Two sizes | Private address same as business | P9/F/23,24<br>***#4695,6***<br> | **J FEINKNOPE**<br>28 Great Garden Street<br>Whitechapel<br>London E | Jewellers |
| R2/145<br>2 October 1911<br>Sent by B Wade | 17 Roe Lane [1]<br>Southport | P13/A/32<br>***#4697***<br>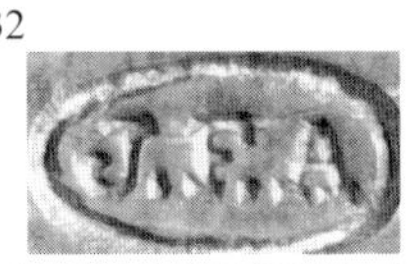 | **J F ASHTON LTD**<br>J F Ashton [1] (Managing Director)<br>20 Wallgate<br>Wigan | Tobacconists |
| SPB/22<br>22 November 1875 | | P3/B/x2<br>***#4698,9***<br> | **J & F BROWN**<br>5 Mount Pleasant<br>Liverpool | Watch manufacturers |
| Missing register<br>*c.*1889<br>Similar mark entered BAO 6 April 1882 | | P5/B/225<br>***#4700***<br> | **Joseph & F BROMAGE**<br>113 Vyse Street<br>Birmingham | Jewellers |
| R2/192<br>2 February 1915<br>Sent by A Hewlett<br>BAO 20.411 | 11 Manley Road<br>Whalley Range<br>Manchester<br>3 Manor Avenue<br>Whalley Range<br>Manchester | P15/S/14<br>***#4701***<br> | **James Frederick STUBBS**<br>**Frank STUBBS** trading as<br>**J F & F STUBBS**<br>17 Thomas Street<br>Manchester | Wholesale jewellers |

| REGISTRATION DETAILS | MAKER'S PRIVATE ADDRESS and DETAILS | PLATE and MARK DETAILS | MAKER/COMPANY and BUSINESS ADDRESS | MAKER'S TRADE |
|---|---|---|---|---|
| R2/179<br>11 November 1913<br>Sent by J H Wynn | 11 Manley Road<br>Whalley Range<br>Manchester<br>3 Manor Avenue<br>Whalley Range<br>Manchester | P13/S/115<br>***#4702***<br> | **James Frederick STUBBS**<br>**Frank STUBBS** trading as<br>**J F & F STUBBS**<br>17 Thomas Street<br>Manchester | Wholesale jewellers |
| PP3/83<br>Not in SPB or LPB so struck 1860-3 | Struck above incuse JFH&Co mark on P3 so probably John Francis Harbinson of Belfast. | P3/H/x3<br>***#4703-5***<br>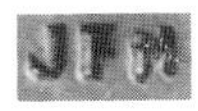 | **John Francis HARBINSON**<br>79 High Street<br>Belfast | Watch and clock maker |
| SPB/3<br>21 March 1864<br>Sent by Samuel Quilliam | 32 Elizabeth Street<br>Liverpool | P3/H/x3<br>***#4706-8***<br>§<br>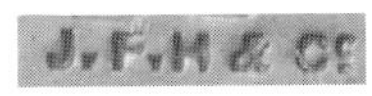 | | |
| SPB/19<br>28 January 1869<br>Sent by H Williamson<br>SPB mark shown | | Not on P3<br>***#4709***<br>§<br>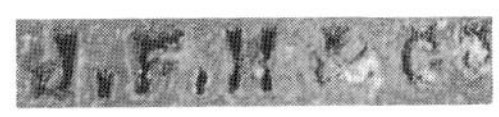 | | |
| Missing register<br>*c.*1886<br>Entered incuse mark LAO 5 November 1883 | | P5/L/66a<br>***#4710***<br> | **John Frederick LOWDEN** *<br>21 Walbrook and<br>1 Ludgate Circus<br>London or | Tobacconist |
| Missing register<br>*c.*1886<br>Cameo mark LAO<br>27 November 1883 | | P5/L/66b<br>***#4711***<br> | **John Francis LATHAM**<br>27 Pall Mall<br>London | Wilkinson Sword silversmiths |
| Missing register<br>*c.*1886 | | P5/L/66c<br>***#4712***<br> | **Unidentified**<br>See previous two entries | |
| Missing register<br>*c.*1888 | | P5/R/158<br>***#4713***<br> | **Unidentified** | |
| R2/50<br>11 November 1907<br>Sent by Joseph Fergus Todd | 77 Highfield Road<br>Rock Ferry | P9/T/71<br>***#4714***<br> | **Joseph Fergus TODD**<br>59 The Arcade<br>Lord Street<br>Liverpool | General engraver and piercer |
| R2/171<br>10 May 1913<br>Sent by John Gatecliff | Private address same as business | P13/G/58<br>***#4715***<br> | **John GATECLIFF**<br>28 Greenhead Lane<br>Utley<br>Keighley | Artist and craftsman |
| J1 1842-61 | | P2/G/x2<br>***#4716,7***<br> | **John GARNER**<br>Chester | Silversmith |
| Missing register<br>*c.*1891 | See below | P5/G/347<br>***#4718***<br> | **J GAMMAGE**<br>26 Clerkenwell Road<br>London EC | Ring manufacturers |
| R2/11<br>6 February 1906<br>Sent by Rink & Dalby | 5 St Paul's Square<br>Preston<br>Lancashire | P9/G/66<br>***#4719***<br> | **James Richard GOODWIN**<br>Orchard Street<br>Preston<br>Lancashire | Umbrella and walking stick maker |
| R3/94<br>31 March 1939<br>Sent by J Green | Private address same as business | P21/G/3<br>***#4720***<br> | **Joseph GREEN**<br>127 Pinehurst Avenue<br>Anfield<br>Liverpool 4 | Teacher |

| REGISTRATION DETAILS | MAKER'S PRIVATE ADDRESS and DETAILS | PLATE and MARK DETAILS | MAKER/COMPANY and BUSINESS ADDRESS | MAKER'S TRADE |
|---|---|---|---|---|
| PDB 1810-13<br>MR3/83<br>J1 1812 | Gold rings | P1/32/x1<br>***#4721***<br> | **James GLOVER**<br>Manchester or | Goldsmith |
| PDB 1786-97<br>MR3/83 | Gold rings<br>See also IG | | **John GILBERT**<br>Liverpool | Goldsmith |
| Missing register<br>*c.*1886 | | P5/G/53x3<br>***#4722-4***<br> | **J GAMMAGE**<br>See below | Ring manufacturers |
| R1/3<br>18 April 1899<br>Sent by J E Gammage<br>G H Gammage | | No mark for this entry<br>***#4725*** | Transfer of business to<br>**John Ellis GAMMAGE &**<br>**George Henry GAMMAGE**<br>trading as **J GAMMAGE** *<br>26 Clerkenwell Road<br>London EC | Wedding, keeper and signet ring manufacturers |
| R1/137<br>17 November 1900<br>Sent by J Gammage | Seven Sisters Road<br>Finsbury Park<br>London | P9/G/18,20,21<br>***#4726-8***<br> | **John Ellis GAMMAGE**<br>**George Henry GAMMAGE**<br>trading as **J GAMMAGE** *<br>26 Clerkenwell Road<br>London EC | Ring manufacturers |
| R1/164<br>12 March 1902<br>Sent by J E Gammage | 25 Collingswood Avenue<br>Fortes Green<br>Braisiler<br>Regents Park Road<br>Church End, Finchley | P9/G/31,32<br>***#4729,30***<br> | | |
| R1/199<br>21 August 1903<br>Sent by J E Gammage<br>Two sizes | 25 Collingswood Avenue<br>Fortes Green | P9/G/43-51<br>***#4731-9***<br> | **John Ellis GAMMAGE** trading as<br>**LAWSON, WARD & GAMMAGE LTD** *<br>26 Clerkenwell Road<br>London and<br>5 Hatton Garden<br>London EC | Manufacturing jewellers |
| R2/19<br>29 May 1906<br>Sent by J E Gammage | | P9/G/75-80<br>***#4740-5***<br> | | |
| R2/107<br>5 April 1910<br>Sent by Lawson Ward & Gamage | Down View<br>Arterberry Road<br>Wimbledon<br>London<br>Newlands<br>Great North Road<br>Highgate<br>London | P13/G/16-21<br>***#4746-51***<br> | **Henry LAWSON**<br>**John Ellis GAMMAGE** trading as<br>**LAWSON, WARD & GAMMAGE LTD** *<br>26 Clerkenwell Road<br>London and<br>Ely Place<br>Tenby Street<br>Birmingham | |
| R1/137<br>17 November 1900<br>Sent by J Gammage | Seven Sisters Road<br>Finsbury Park<br>London | P9/G/19<br>***#4752***<br> | **John Ellis GAMMAGE**<br>**George Henry GAMMAGE** trading as<br>**J GAMMAGE** *<br>26 Clerkenwell Road<br>London EC | Ring manufacturers |
| R2/123<br>9 November 1910<br>Sent by Lawson, Ward & Gammage Ltd | Downview<br>Arterberry Road<br>Wimbledon<br>Newlands<br>Great North Road<br>Highgate | P13/G/26-31<br>***#4753-8***<br> | **Henry LAWSON**<br>**John Ellis GAMMAGE**<br>in the style of firm<br>**LAWSON, WARD & GAMMAGE LTD** *<br>26 Clerkenwell Road<br>London | Manufacturing jewellers |

| REGISTRATION DETAILS | MAKER'S PRIVATE ADDRESS and DETAILS | PLATE and MARK DETAILS | MAKER/COMPANY and BUSINESS ADDRESS | MAKER'S TRADE |
|---|---|---|---|---|
| R2/183<br>27 January 1914<br>Sent by Lawson, Ward & Gammage | 2 Perham Crescent<br>West Kensington<br>Newlands<br>Great North Road<br>Highgate<br>London | P15/G/12-17<br>***#4759-64***<br> | **LAWSON, WARD & GAMMAGE LTD** *<br>Henry Lawson (Director)<br>John Ellis Gammage (Director)<br>26 Clerkenwell Road<br>London and<br>Ely Place<br>Tenby Street<br>Birmingham | Manufacturing jewellers |
| R2/89<br>23 July 1909<br>Sent by James Griffiths | 11 Hall Road<br>Handsworth<br>Birmingham | P13/G/10<br>***#4765***<br> | **James GRIFFITHS**<br>97 Spencer Street<br>Birmingham | Jeweller |
| R1/169<br>30 May 1902<br>Sent by Green & Cadbury C o | Raseleigh<br>Malvern Road<br>Acocks Green<br>Birmingham | P9/G/34<br>***#4766***<br> | **Joseph GLOSTER**<br>35 Vyse Street<br>Birmingham | Silversmith |
| GSJW/134, 183<br>PP3/83 | | P1/3/x3<br>***#4767-9***<br> | **J G BRADLEY**<br>Orrell Place<br>32 Lord Street<br>Liverpool | Wholesale watchmaker and importer |
| R1/7<br>12 February 1895<br>Sent by J & R Griffin | Glenholme [1]<br>Wycliffe Road<br>Rose Villa [2]<br>Salisbury Road<br>Birchfields | P5/G/637<br>***#4770***<br> | **Joseph James GRIFFIN** [1]<br>**Richard Charles GRIFFIN** [2] trading as<br>**J & R GRIFFIN**<br>28 Hylton Street<br>Birmingham | Manufacturing jewellers |
| Missing register<br>*c.*1887<br>Similar mark entered BAO 29 August 1883 | J G Graves entered a similar mark at BAO 21 February 1898 which may be relevant | P5/G/131<br>***#4771***<br> | **J G GLOVER**<br>7½ Warstone Lane<br>Birmingham | Jeweller |
| R1/146<br>30 April 1901<br>Sent by G K Leeson | Hillside<br>Crookes Road<br>Sheffield | P9/G/23<br>***#4772***<br> | **John George GRAVES**<br>Division Street<br>Sheffield | Jeweller, watch maker and general factor |
| R1/146<br>2 May 1901<br>Sent by J Hayward | | P9/G/24<br>***#4773***<br> | | |
| R1/196<br>24 June 1903<br>Sent by J Hayward<br>This punch recut | | P9/G/40<br>***#4774***<br> | Details as above<br>West Street<br>Sheffield | General factor |
| R1/197<br>23 July 1903<br>Sent by Lancashire Watch Co<br>S Farren | Riverdale<br>Sheffield | P9/G/41<br>***#4775***<br> | Details as above<br>Division Street<br>Sheffield | Jeweller and merchant |
| R1/104<br>19 June 1899<br>Sent by T P Hewitt | Hillside<br>Crookes Road<br>Sheffield<br>Philanthropist and early provider of credit facilities for mail order. Sold Ehrhardt watches. Started with 8 staff in 1884 which grew to 2000 by 1902. | P9/G/12<br>***#4776***<br> | | Watchmaker and jeweller |
| R3/140<br>10 February 1953<br>Sent by J G Jardalla<br>Two sizes | Private address same as business | P21/IJ/6,7<br>***#4777,8***<br>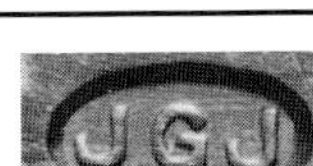 | **Josephine Georgina JARDALLA**<br>1 Ilford Avenue<br>Great Crosby<br>Liverpool 23 | Student |

| REGISTRATION DETAILS | MAKER'S PRIVATE ADDRESS and DETAILS | PLATE and MARK DETAILS | MAKER/COMPANY and BUSINESS ADDRESS | MAKER'S TRADE |
|---|---|---|---|---|
| SPB/23<br>11 January 1869 | | P3/I*sic*/x3<br>***#4779-81***<br> | **John Gibborn JACOB**<br>56 Church Street<br>Liverpool | Watch manufacturer |
| R3/92<br>2 November 1938<br>Sent by J Gloster Ltd | | P21/G/2<br>***#4782***<br>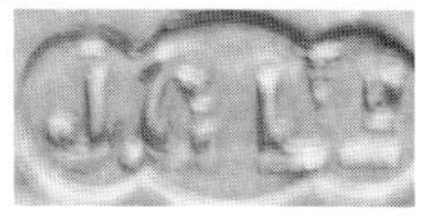 | **Joseph GLOSTER LTD**<br>Lion Silver Works<br>Hockley Hill<br>Birmingham | Manufacturing silversmiths |
| R3/142<br>11 March 1953<br>Sent by J Gloster Ltd | 4 Sharmans Cross [1]<br>425 Streetsbrook Road [2]<br>Solihull<br>Lane House, Levens[3], Kendal<br>Garth, Broad Oaks Road [4]<br>17 Dovehouse Lane [5]<br>66 School Lane [6]<br>Solihull | P21/H*sic*/24<br>***#4783***<br> | **Joseph GLOSTER LTD**<br>Directors: G Gloster [1]<br>E Gloster [2]<br>L J Gloster [3]<br>C F Gloster [4]<br>O E Gloster [5]<br>R W Grinesley [6]<br>33 Hockley Hill<br>Birmingham 18 | |
| R1/152<br>3 August 1901<br>Sent by J G Newbold<br>Punch withdrawn<br>8 May 1903 | 57 Ravenscroft Street<br>Hackney Road<br>London N | P9/N/11,12<br>***#4784,5***<br> | **James George NEWBOLD** *<br>226 St John Street<br>Clerkenwell<br>London | Pipe mount manufacturer |
| R2/59<br>19 May 1908<br>Sent by J G Newbold<br>Three sizes | 226 St John Street<br>Clerkenwell<br>London EC | P13/N/1-3<br>***#4786-8***<br> | **James George NEWBOLD** *<br>226 St John Street<br>Clerkenwell and<br>58 Pentonville Road<br>London EC | Gold and silver pipe mount manufacturer |
| R1/192<br>8 May 1903<br>Sent by J G Newbold | | P9/N/22<br>***#4789***<br>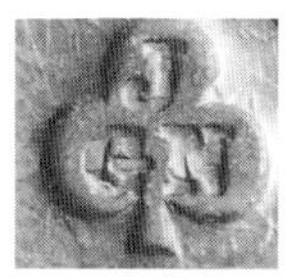 | | Gold and silver mounter |
| R1/236<br>1 July 1905<br>Sent by J G Newbold | | P9/N/34<br>***#4790***<br>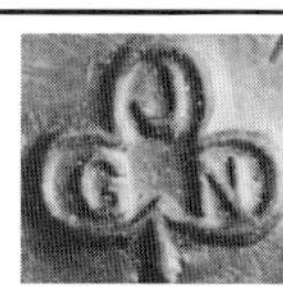 | | Pipe mount manufacturer |
| R2/14<br>21 March 1906<br>Sent by J G Newbold<br>Two sizes | | P9/N/36,37<br>***#4791,2***<br> | | Gold and silver pipe mount manufacturer |
| R1/114<br>17 October 1899<br>Sent by J G Styles<br>BAO 2.594 | 64 Union Street<br>Smethwick<br>Birmingham | P9/S/27<br>***#4793***<br> | **Joseph Gray STYLES**<br>62 Branston Street<br>Birmingham | Jeweller |
| R1/160<br>27 January 1902<br>Sent by J G Styles | Hawthorne House<br>Smethwick<br>Birmingham | P9/S/41-43<br>***#4794-6***<br> | **Joseph Gray STYLES**<br>55 Albion Street<br>Birmingham | Wholesale jeweller |
| LPB/36 SP32/3<br>17 May 1884 | | P5/G/x1<br>***#4797***<br> | **John GOODE & SONS** *<br>3 Regent Place<br>Birmingham | Gold chain manufacturers |
| R2/96<br>22 October 1909<br>Sent by John Goode & Son<br>BAO 6.941, 13.626<br>Two sizes | The Glebe<br>Moseley<br>Ashleigh Road<br>Solihull<br>Birmingham | P13/G/12,13<br>***#4798,9***<br> | **Albert Conrad GOODE**<br>**Ernest William GOODE** trading as<br>**John GOODE & SONS** *<br>60 Regent Place<br>Birmingham and<br>60 Hatton Garden<br>London | |

| REGISTRATION DETAILS | MAKER'S PRIVATE ADDRESS and DETAILS | PLATE and MARK DETAILS | MAKER/COMPANY and BUSINESS ADDRESS | MAKER'S TRADE |
|---|---|---|---|---|
| R2/96<br>24 August 1911<br>BAO 14.659<br>Replacement mark | Details as for previous entry | P13/G/37<br>***#4800***  | **John GOODE & SON**<br>Details as for previous entry | |
| R1/15<br>8 July 1895<br>Sent by<br>W W Cashmore<br>Annotated JH 681 | Dora Road<br>Small Heath<br>Birmingham | P5/H/681 not found<br>***#4801***<br>**J H?** | **Joseph HAWKINS**<br>28 Spencer Street<br>Birmingham | Jeweller |
| Not in R1 as expected | | P5/H/569<br>***#4802***  | | |
| LPB/38<br>13 May 1880<br>LPB mark shown<br>CWMP 1891 | | Not on P3<br>***#4803***  | **John HAWLEY** *<br>35 Cow Lane<br>Coventry | Watch manufacturer |
| Missing register<br>*c.*1889 | | P5/H/255<br>***#4804***  | **Unidentified** | |
| R3/170<br>6 January 1960<br>Sent by selves | 47 Wiltshire Street [1]<br>Salford 7<br>42 Aldwyn Crescent [2]<br>Hazel Grove<br>Stockport | P21/IJ/17<br>***#4805***  | **Henry Joseph JONES** [1]<br>**Thomas Augustine HAZLEY** [2]<br>trading as **JONES & HAZLEY**<br>Douglas Chambers<br>63 Corporation Street<br>Manchester 4 | Jewellers to the trade |
| R3/120<br>11 December 1947<br>Sent by J Hollings<br>Two sizes | 27 Bolton Avenue<br>East Didsbury<br>Manchester 19 | P21/H/39,40<br>***#4806,7***  | **John HOLLINGS**<br>Manchester School of Domestic Economy<br>Westborne<br>231 Wilmslow Road<br>Rusholme | Handicraft teacher |
| R1/174<br>19 August 1902<br>Two sizes Sent by<br>James Harrison | Chanty Road<br>Moseley | P9/H/42[7], 43[7] *sic*<br>***#4808,9***  | **James HARRISON**<br>16 Tenby Street<br>Birmingham | Ring maker |
| R2/55<br>21 February 1908<br>Sent by James Harrison | Saterbury Road<br>Moseley<br>Birmingham | P9/H/102,103<br>***#4810,11***  | **Francis F HARRISON**<br>**Wilfred J HARRISON**<br>**James HARRISON**<br>16 Tenby Street<br>Birmingham | Manufacturing jewellers |
| Not in R2 as expected<br>*c.* July 1914 to<br>September 1915 | | P15/H/24<br>***#4812*** 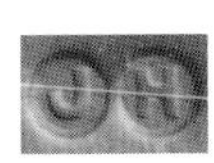 | | |
| R3/83<br>24 March 1936<br>Sent by W J Pellow Ltd<br>31 Hylton Road<br>Birmingham | Manor Croft [1]<br>68 Fennal Road<br>Harborne<br>Birmingham | P15/H/121<br>***#4813*** 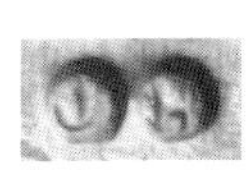 | **James HARRISON & SONS**<br>Francis F Harrison [1] (Sole Proprietor)<br>16 Tenby Street<br>Birmingham | |
| R3/99<br>18 March 1941<br>Sent by J Harrison & Sons Ltd | 183 Ravenhurst Road [1]<br>Harborne<br>Birmingham | P21/H/16<br>***#4814*** 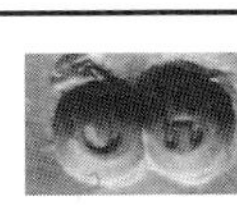 | **James HARRISON & SONS LTD**<br>Common seal of company affixed in the presence of:-<br>Trevor Harrison [1] (Managing Director)<br>Sidney Williams (Secretary)<br>16 Tenby Street<br>Birmingham | |
| 12 November 1949 | | P21/H/50<br>***#4815*** 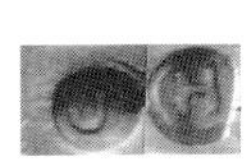 | | |
| 16 May 1961 | | P21/H/84<br>***#4816***  | | |

| REGISTRATION DETAILS | MAKER'S PRIVATE ADDRESS and DETAILS | PLATE and MARK DETAILS | MAKER/COMPANY and BUSINESS ADDRESS | MAKER'S TRADE |
|---|---|---|---|---|
| R3/115<br>26 November 1946<br>Sent by R & K M Beach<br>184 Warstone Lane<br>Birmingham | K M Beach also listed | P21/H/35<br>***#4817***<br> | **J HARRISON & SONS LTD**<br>63 Warstone Lane<br>Birmingham | Manufacturing jewellers |
| R2/216<br>22 October 1918<br>Sent by Jos A Hodel | 139 Upper Canning Street<br>Liverpool | P15/H/41<br>***#4818***<br> | **Jos A HODEL**<br>School of Art<br>Liverpool | Instructor of silverworkers and jewellers |
| PDB 1830-5 MR3/85<br>PP1/188<br>GTD 1820-62<br>J1 1830-57<br>GSJW/135 GMSC/83 | Note that James Helsby, a WCM of 26 Trueman Street (same address as Thomas Helsby) may have used this incuse mark. John Helsby born 1796 (1841 Census), probably son of Thomas Helsby by his first wife Margaret. Successor to Thomas Helsby with own entries in PDB from 1830. | P1/25/x1<br>***#4819***<br> | **John HELSBY**<br>45 Bevington Hill (1823)<br>5 then 4 Trueman Street (1829-37)<br>6 Hunter Street (1839-49)<br>42 Springfield (1851-7)<br>20 Moss Street (1861)<br>8 Moss Street (1862) | Silversmith, watchcase maker<br><br>Gold and silver assayer |
| | | P2/H/x3<br>***#4820-2***<br> | Pembroke Gardens (1864)<br>6 Belgrave Terrace (1871)<br>Liverpool | |
| Missing register<br>*c* 1887 | | P5/H/84<br>***#4823***<br> | **Unidentified** | |
| Missing register<br>*c.*1891 | | P5/H/349<br>***#4824***<br>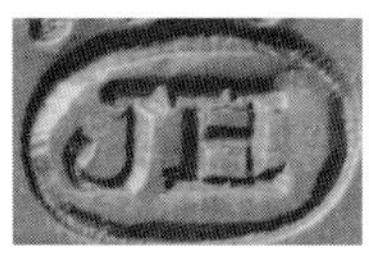 | **Unidentified** | |
| PDB 1833<br>MR3/84 | Silver boxes<br>Very small mark so may be for rings | P1/15/x4<br>***#4825-8***<br> | **John HACK**<br>Town unspecified or | Silversmith |
| PDB 1813-14<br>MR3/85 | Gold rings<br>Small mark might indicate use for rings<br>See also IH | P1/22/x1<br>***#4829***<br> | **John HEMMINGWAY**<br>13 Tarleton Street<br>Manchester or | Goldsmith |
| PDB 1837-9<br>MR3/85 | Gold rings<br>Square marked 1786 | | **James HEMMING**<br>Liverpool | Goldsmith |
| | See also TH, TH&Co, TH&Son | P2/H/x2<br>***#4830,1***<br> | **John HELSBY**<br>Liverpool See above | Watchcase maker |
| Not in R1<br>P5/H/566 also used for JMT mark | | P5/H/566<br>***#4832***<br> | **Unidentified** | |
| Missing register<br>*c.*1894 | | P5/H/549<br>***#4833***<br> | **Unidentified** | |
| Missing register<br>*c.*1888 | | P5/H/187<br>***#4834***<br> | **Unidentified** | |
| PDB 1833<br>MR3/84 | Silver boxes<br>Small mark might indicate use for rings | P1/13/x3<br>***#4835-7***<br> | **John HACK**<br>Town unspecified or | Silversmith |
| PDB 1813-14<br>MR3/85 | Gold rings<br>See also IH | P1/13/x3<br>***#4838-40***<br> | **John HEMMINGWAY**<br>13 Tarleton Street<br>Manchester or | Goldsmith |
| PDB 1837-9<br>MR3/85 | Gold rings | | **James HEMMING**<br>Liverpool | Goldsmith |

| REGISTRATION DETAILS | MAKER'S PRIVATE ADDRESS and DETAILS | PLATE and MARK DETAILS | MAKER/COMPANY and BUSINESS ADDRESS | MAKER'S TRADE |
|---|---|---|---|---|
| Not in R1 as expected | | P5/H/568<br>***#4841***  | **Unidentified** | |
| SPB/23<br>9 May 1876 | | P3/M*sic*/x2<br>***#4842,3***  | **Jesse HALLAM** *<br>24 Hertford Place<br>Coventry | Watchcase maker |
| LPB/40<br>9 November 1883<br>No mark in LPB just J H | This mark in 3rd position on P5 but LPB entry is indecipherable<br>Address of W H Haseler | P5/H/x1<br>***#4844***  | **John HORTON** *<br>12 Richard Street<br>Birmingham | Jeweller |
| LPB/38<br>27 January 1881 | | P3/H/x1<br>***#4845***  | **James HARRISON**<br>16 Tenby Street<br>Birmingham | Jeweller |
| LPB/8<br>17 July 1885<br>No mark in LPB just JH | | P5/H/x1<br>***#4846***  | **Joseph HAWKINS**<br>59 Albion Street<br>Birmingham | Chain and locket maker |
| | See John Helsby above | P2/H/x3<br>***#4847-9***  | **John HELSBY**<br>Liverpool see above | Watchcase maker |
| MDGC 1866<br>CWMP 1874-09<br>PP3/83<br>Similar mark LAO<br>9 September 1869 | Not in SPB or LPB<br>so struck 1860-3 | P3/H/x3<br>***#4850-2***  | **John HEWITT** *<br>9 Russell Terrace<br>Chapel Fields<br>Coventry | Watch manufacturer |
| R1/91<br>14 February 1899<br>Sent by R J Pike | Private address same as business | P9/H/8<br>***#4853*** 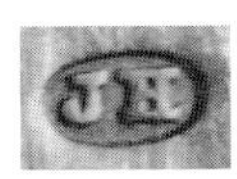 | **John HEWITT** *<br>Holyhead Road<br>Coventry | |
| Missing register<br>*c.*1890 | | P5/H/319<br>***#4854***  | **Unidentified** | |
| LPB/40<br>9 November 1883 | | P5/H/x1<br>***#4855***  | **John HORTON** *<br>12 Richard Street<br>Birmingham | Jeweller |
| LPB/36<br>19 September 1884<br>No mark just initials JH | See HBs | P5/H/x1<br>***#4856***  | | |
| LPB/8<br>24 August 1885<br>Similar mark entered LAO 27 October 1858 | | P5/H/x1<br>***#4857*** 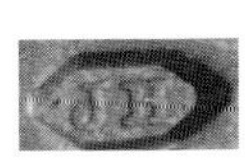 | **Jonathan HAZELL** *<br>25 Gloucester Street, Clerkenwell<br>London | Manufacturing jeweller |
| Missing register<br>*c.*1886 | | P5/H/3<br>***#4858***  | **Unidentified** | |
| Missing register<br>*c.*1889<br>Similar mark entered BAO 19 May 1887 | | P5/H/218<br>***#4859***  | **Jonathan HOWELL** trading as<br>**Henry HOWELL & CO** *<br>180 Old Street<br>London EC | Cane and stick mounters |
| R1/31<br>22 July 1896<br>Sent by Edwards Brothers | 86 Thornhill Road<br>Handsworth<br>Birmingham | P5/H/783<br>***#4860***  | **Joseph HAYWARD**<br>41 Frederick Street<br>Birmingham | Jeweller |
| R1/145<br>6 April 1901<br>Sent by Joseph Haywood | Punch recut<br>23 December 1903 | P9/H/43,56<br>***#4861,2***  | | Ring manufacturer |

| REGISTRATION DETAILS | MAKER'S PRIVATE ADDRESS and DETAILS | PLATE and MARK DETAILS | MAKER/COMPANY and BUSINESS ADDRESS | MAKER'S TRADE |
|---|---|---|---|---|
| R1/218<br>21 July 1904<br>Sent by Joseph Hayward | 86 Thornhill Road<br>Handsworth<br>Birmingham | P9/H/65<br>***#4863***<br> | **Joseph HAYWARD**<br>41 Frederick Street<br>Birmingham | Ring manufacturer |
| R1/232<br>29 April 1905<br>Sent by Joseph Hayward<br>Punch P9/H/65 recut | | P9/H/70<br>***#4864***<br> | | |
| R2/12<br>3 March 1906<br>Sent by J Hayward<br>P13/H/72 taken<br>10 May 1911 | | P9/H/78<br>***#4865***<br> | | Jeweller |
| CWMP 1835<br>Similar mark entered BAO 7 July 1824 | Successor to William Howard | P1/29/x2<br>***#4866,7***<br> | **James HEALES**<br>Spon Street (1835)<br>Coventry | Watchcase maker |
| R2/157<br>18 June 1912<br>Sent by B Wade | 174 Fitzwilliam Road<br>Rotherham | P13/H/85<br>***#4868***<br>§<br>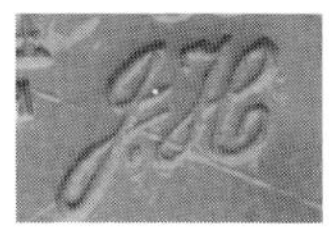 | **Joseph HILEY**<br>31a College Street<br>Rotherham | Tobacconist |
| SPB/12<br>6 August 1873<br>Sent by Samuel & Rogers | | P3/G*sic*/x3<br>***#4869-71***<br> | **Joseph & Abraham HARRIS**<br>28 Berry Street<br>Liverpool | Watch manufacturers |
| R1/36<br>23 November 1896<br>Sent by J L Duncan & Co | 48 Preston Road<br>Blackburn | P5/Z*sic*/805<br>***#4872***<br> | **James HARGREAVES**<br>36 King William Street<br>Blackburn<br>Lancashire | Tobacconist |
| R3/134<br>19 December 1950<br>Sent by Smith, Ewen & Stylic Ltd<br>42 Frederick Street<br>Birmingham | | P21/C/51<br>***#4873***<br>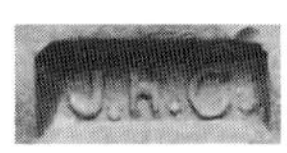 | **J H CRAWCOUR LTD**<br>Nassau House<br>122 Shaftsbury Avenue<br>London W1 | Manufacturing jewellers, goldsmiths and silversmiths |
| R1/165<br>26 March 1902<br>Sent by Benson Brothers | Warren Drive<br>New Brighton<br>2 Buckingham Avenue<br>Liverpool | P9/H/39[7] *sic*<br>***#4874***<br> | **Thomas Townsend RUSSELL** *<br>**Bernard Alfred RUSSELL** * trading as<br>**J HARGREAVES & CO**<br>12 Church Street<br>Liverpool | Watch manufacturers |
| SPB/16<br>12 March 1875<br>Sent by Samuel & Rogers<br>James Eastham | See also J & JH | P3/H/x1 and P3/M*sic*/x3<br>***#4875-8***<br> | **J HARGREAVES & CO**<br>11 Slater Street<br>Liverpool | |
| LPB/28<br>5 July 1883<br>Sent by Hugh Green | | P3/H/x1<br>***#4879***<br> | **J HARGREAVES & CO**<br>17 Norton Street<br>Derby Road<br>Liverpool | |
| LPB/40<br>29 November 1883<br>Sent by Hugh Green<br>No mark in LPB | | P5/H/x1<br>***#4880***<br> | | |
| R1/2<br>26 October 1894<br>Sent by J Eastham<br>Benson Brothers | | P5/H/615<br>***#4881***<br> | | |

| REGISTRATION DETAILS | MAKER'S PRIVATE ADDRESS and DETAILS | PLATE and MARK DETAILS | MAKER/COMPANY and BUSINESS ADDRESS | MAKER'S TRADE |
|---|---|---|---|---|
| R1/71<br>25 October 1898<br>Sent by James Eastham | 24 Carlton Road<br>New Brighton<br>Cheshire | P9/H/3<br>***#4882***<br> | **Martin SHORT**<br>Sole proprietor trading as<br>**J HARGREAVES & CO**<br>17 Norton Street<br>Liverpool | Watch manufacturers |
| R2/213<br>20 July 1917<br>Sent by Harold Deakin<br>No square or mark # entered in R2<br>These marks best fit the dates | 192 Compton Road<br>Handsworth<br>Birmingham<br>7 Compton Road<br>Handsworth<br>Birmingham | P15/D/33<br>***#4883***<br>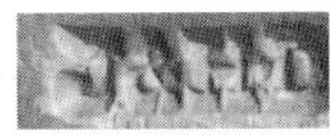<br>P15/D/31<br>***#4884***<br> | **John DEAKIN**<br>**Harold DEAKIN** trading as<br>**J & H DEAKIN**<br>354 New John Street<br>Hockley<br>Birmingham | Manufacturing jewellers |
| PP3/83<br>Not in SPB or LPB so struck 1860-3<br>Similar mark entered LAO 3 July 1860 | See also IHE | P3/E/x3<br>***#4885-7***<br> | **Joseph Harris ELLIOTT** *<br>7 Skinner Street (1852)<br>London<br>The Butts (15 September 1854)<br>Coventry | Watchcase maker |
| R3/153<br>23 November 1954<br>Sent by<br>J H Hopkinson | 10 Moorcroft Road<br>Liverpool 18 | P21/H/72<br>***#4888***<br> | **John Hubert HOPKINSON**<br>No business address entered | Schoolmaster |
| R1/200<br>18 September 1903<br>Sent by J A Hutchings | Arosfa<br>Deganwy<br>North Wales | P9/H/53<br>***#4889***<br> | **John Hanmer HUTCHINGS**<br>14 St Werberg Street<br>Chester | Artist |
| R2/202<br>4 January 1916<br>Sent by Jose Hermano de Netto Lourenco | Private address same as business | P15/L/12<br>***#4890***<br>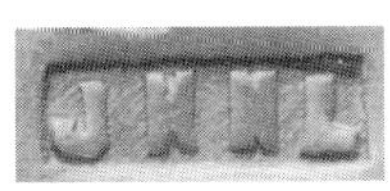 | **Jose Hermano de NETTO LOURENCO**<br>Cartref<br>Aigburth Road<br>Liverpool | Importer of silver mesh bags |
| CWMP 1886-1901<br>PP3/83<br>Similar mark entered LAO 18 May 1861 | Not in SPB or LPB so struck 1860-3 | P3/S/x3<br>***#4891-3***<br> | **John HARRIS & John SCOTT** trading as<br>**HARRIS & SCOTT** *<br>Old Allesley Road<br>3 Hertford Place (1886-1901)<br>Coventry | Watchcase makers |
| R2/34<br>12 March 1907<br>Sent by C Horner | 11 Marlborough Road<br>Sheffield | P9/*Usic*/279<br>***#4894***<br> | **John Henry POTTER**<br>Brockingham Works<br>Division Street<br>Sheffield | Manufacturing silversmith and cutler |
| R3/60<br>18 November 1931<br>Sent by T J Skelton<br>86 Vyse Street<br>Birmingham | Private address same as business | P15/P/233<br>***#4895***<br> | **James Henry PROFFITT**<br>145, 147 Great Moor Street<br>Bolton<br>Lancashire | Jeweller |
| Missing register<br>*c.*1890 | | P5/R/319<br>***#4896***<br> | **John Henry ROWLAND** | Pipe and stick mounter |
| R1/48<br>26 July 1897<br>Sent by<br>J H Rowland | 15 Elm Grove<br>Sale<br>Cheshire | P5/R/860<br>***#4897***<br> | **John Henry ROWLAND**<br>34 Great Ancoats Street<br>Manchester | |
| R1/79<br>26 September 1894<br>Sent by John H Rowland | Crossford Bridge<br>Sale<br>Cheshire | P5/R/593<br>***#4898***<br>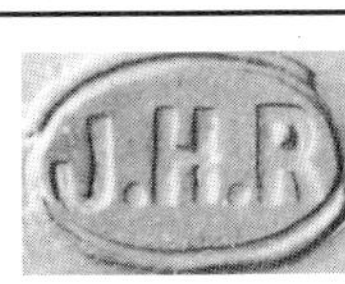 | details as above<br>11 Todd Street<br>Manchester | |

| REGISTRATION DETAILS | MAKER'S PRIVATE ADDRESS and DETAILS | PLATE and MARK DETAILS | MAKER/COMPANY and BUSINESS ADDRESS | MAKER'S TRADE |
|---|---|---|---|---|
| R2/42<br>26 June 1907<br>Sent by John Henry Rowland | 10 Well Lane<br>Rock Ferry | P9/R/91<br>***#4899***<br> | **John Henry ROWLAND**<br>64 Hanover Street<br>Liverpool | Stick mounter and pipe mounter |
| R3/150<br>23 February 1954<br>Sent by<br>W J Pellow Ltd<br>34 Hylton Street<br>Birmingham 18 | | P21/H/68<br>***#4900***<br> | **B T GREENING LTD** also trading as<br>**J HORTON & SON** *<br>30 Hatton Garden<br>London EC1 | Wholesale jewellers |
| R3/107<br>8 January 1945<br>Sent by Joseph Hawkings & Son | Private address same as business | P21/H/18<br>***#4901***<br>§<br> | **Joseph HAWKINGS & SON**<br>131 Welton Road<br>Near Crumpsall<br>Manchester 8 | Briar pipe manufacturers, repairers and metal spinners |
| R2/202<br>30 December 1915<br>Sent by Joseph Hayward & Son Ltd | 86 Thornhill Road<br>Handsworth<br>65 Leyton Road<br>Handsworth | P15/H/28<br>***#4902***<br> | **Joseph HAYWOOD**<br>**Percy C HAYWARD**<br>**H A HAYWARD** trading as<br>**Joseph HAYWARD & SON**<br>41 Frederick Street<br>Birmingham | Manufacturing jewellers |
| R2/103<br>Undated<br>*c.* September 1916 to March 1918<br>Sent by Charles Horner Ltd | Gladsmuir<br>Harpenden<br>Hertfordshire | P15/H/38<br>***#4903***<br> | **J HORTON & SON** *<br>B T Greening (Governing Director)<br>30 Hatton Garden<br>London and<br>21 Hylton Street<br>Birmingham | Wholesale jewellers |
| R1/73<br>8 September 1898<br>Sent by J H Silvers | 18 Douglas Road<br>Handsworth<br>Birmingham | P9/S/3<br>***#4904***<br> | **James Henry SILVERS**<br>43 Warstone Lane<br>Birmingham | Wholesale jeweller |
| R3/163<br>31 October 1957<br>Sent by W J Pellow Ltd<br>31 Vyse Street<br>Birmingham 18 | | P21/H/75<br>***#4905***<br> | **J HORTON & SON** *<br>30 Hatton Garden<br>London EC1 | Jewellers |
| R2/103<br>5 February 1910<br>Sent by Charles Horner Ltd | Gladsmuir<br>Harpenden<br>Hertfordshire | P13/H/47,48<br>***#4906,7***<br> | **J HORTON & SON** *<br>B T Greening (Governing Director)<br>30 Hatton Garden<br>London and<br>21 Hylton Street<br>Birmingham | Wholesale jewellers |
| Missing register<br>*c.*1886<br>Similar mark entered LAO 30 July 1901 | | P5/H/67<br>***#4908***<br> | **Joshua HORTON & SON** *<br>57 High Street<br>Whitechapel | Goldsmiths and silversmiths |
| R1/202<br>6 November 1903<br>Sent by J & R Griffin adjacent 53 | Gladsmuir<br>Spenser Road<br>Harpenden<br>Herts | P9/G*sic*/01*sic*<br>***#4909***<br> | **Benjamin Thomas GREENING**<br>trading as **J HORTON & SON** *<br>30 Hatton Garden<br>London | Wholesale jewellers |
| R3/95<br>25 May 1939<br>Sent by B T Greening<br>30 Hatton Garden (Head Office)<br>London<br>Three sizes | | P21/H/9-12<br>***#4910-13***<br> | **B T GREENING LTD** trading as<br>**J HORTON & SON** *<br>9 Tenby Street<br>Birmingham | Wholesale jewellers |

| REGISTRATION DETAILS | MAKER'S PRIVATE ADDRESS and DETAILS | PLATE and MARK DETAILS | MAKER/COMPANY and BUSINESS ADDRESS | MAKER'S TRADE |
|---|---|---|---|---|
| R3/95<br>6 April 1954<br>Sent by B T Greening<br>30 Hatton Garden<br>London | | P21/H/69<br>***#4914***<br><br> | **B T GREENING LTD** trading as<br>**J HORTON & SON** *<br>9 Tenby Street<br>Birmingham | Wholesale jewellers |
| 30 January 1958 | | P21/H/76<br>***#4915***<br> | | |
| R1/213<br>29 April 1904<br>Sent by J & R Griffin | Gladsmuir<br>Milton Road<br>Harpenden<br>Herts | P9/H/58<br>***#4916***<br> | | Manufacturing jewellers and silversmiths |
| R2/46<br>27 September 1907<br>Sent by H Reeves | | P9/H/97-99<br>***#4917-9***<br><br> | Details as above<br>30 Hatton Garden<br>London and<br>21 Hylton Street<br>Birmingham | Wholesale jewellers |
| 6 April 1954 | | P21/H/65<br>***#4920***<br> | **B T GREENING LTD** trading as<br>**J HORTON & SON** *<br>9 Tenby Street<br>Birmingham | |
| R2/122<br>28 October 1910<br>Sent by Arthur Wells | 43 Hall Road<br>Handsworth<br>43 Hall Road<br>Handsworth | P13/S/61<br>***#4921***<br> | **John Henry STELL**<br>**Arthur WELLS** trading as<br>**J H STELL & CO**<br>16 Frederick Street<br>Birmingham | Gold chain manufacturers |
| R2/91<br>21 August 1909<br>Sent by John Oliver Taylor | Bishops Road<br>Sutton Coldfield | P13/T/16<br>***#4922***<br> | **John Oliver TAYLOR**<br>**Harry Langley TAYLOR** trading as<br>**J & H TAYLOR**<br>54 Tenby Street North<br>Birmingham | Gold spectacles and eyeglasses |
| R2/106<br>15 March 1910<br>Sent by C B Ustonson<br>2 impressions | Lynton<br>Bishops Road<br>Sutton Coldfield<br>25 Stanley Road<br>New Southgate<br>London | P13/T/20<br>***#4923***<br> | **J & H TAYLOR LTD**<br>J O Taylor (Director)<br>H L Taylor (Director)<br>C B Ustonson (Director)<br>33 Kirby Street<br>Hatton Garden<br>London | Wholesale opticians |
| LPB/86<br>27 October 1882<br>Sent by Pope & Phelps<br>LPB mark shown | | Not on P3<br>***#4924***<br> | **Joseph Hayes TAYLOR** *<br>70 Spencer Street<br>Birmingham | Manufacturer of coloured gold charms, seals, keys, compasses and chain appendages |
| R1/203<br>20 November 1903<br>Sent by<br>J A MacKenzie | 30 Hadden Road<br>Rock Ferry | P9/W/102<br>***#4925***<br><br> | **John Horace WARD**<br>35 Market Street<br>Birkenhead | Jeweller |
| Missing register<br>*c.*1892 | | P5/W/431<br>***#4926***<br> | **John Henry WYNN** | Ring maker |
| R1/97<br>14 April 1899<br>Sent by J H Wynn | 16 St John Street<br>Lozells<br>Birmingham | P9/W/16<br>***#4927***<br> | **John Henry WYNN**<br>44 Hylton Street<br>Birmingham | |
| R1/121<br>22 February 1900<br>Sent by J H Wynn | | P9/W/33,34<br>***#4928,9***<br><br> | | |

| REGISTRATION DETAILS | MAKER'S PRIVATE ADDRESS and DETAILS | PLATE and MARK DETAILS | MAKER/COMPANY and BUSINESS ADDRESS | MAKER'S TRADE |
|---|---|---|---|---|
| R1/176<br>25 September 1902<br>Sent by J H Wynn | 43 South Road<br>Handsworth<br>Birmingham | P9/W/73,74<br>*#4930,1*  | **John Henry WYNN**<br>42/44 Hylton Street<br>Birmingham | Ring maker |
| R1/184<br>6 February 1903<br>Sent by J H Wynn | 17 Claremont Road<br>Handsworth | P9/W/89-91<br>*#4932-4*  | | |
| R1/212<br>15 April 1904<br>Sent by J H Wynn | | P9/W/110,111<br>*#4935,6*  | | Jeweller |
| Not in R2 as expected<br>*c.* February to June 1919 | | P15/W/46<br>*#4937*  | | |
| R3/103<br>25 August 1942<br>Sent by James H Windle | 21 Westdale Gardens<br>Manchester 19 | P21/W/33<br>*#4938*  | **James H WINDLE**<br>3 Cateaton Street<br>Manchester | Manufacturing jeweller |
| R3/110<br>14 September 1945<br>Sent by<br>James H Windle<br>Two sizes | | P21/W/40,43-5<br>*#4939-42*  | | |
| LPB/44<br>9 August 1883 | 2nd name on LPB/44 and 2nd mark on P5/J | P5/J/x1<br>*#4943*  | **John IZON**<br>39 Spencer Street<br>Birmingham | Jeweller |
| Missing register<br>*c.*1891<br>Similar mark LAO<br>12 December 1898 | See also James Jackson below | P5/J/389<br>*#4944*  | **Joshua JACOBS** trading as<br>**JACOBS BROTHERS** *<br>40 Broad Street<br>London EC | Foreign agents |
| R2/70<br>29 December 1908<br>Sent by J Joel | 38 Waterloo Road<br>Salford | P13/J/4<br>*#4945*  | **Joe JOEL**<br>19 Corporation Street<br>Manchester | Jeweller |
| R2/230<br>19 April 1920<br>Sent by T J Skelton<br>Two sizes | Private address same as business | P15/J/15,16<br>*#4946,7*  | **Joseph JACOBSON**<br>264 Buchanan Street<br>Glasgow | Wholesale jeweller |
| PP1/188<br>SPR 1798/9 | See also II | P1/29/x2<br>*#4948,9*  | **James JOHNSON**<br>Key Street<br>Liverpool or | Watchcase maker |
| MR2/91,92 | | | **John JONES**<br>Chester | Silversmith |
| R1/109<br>26 August 1899<br>Sent by Vale Brothers & Sermon<br>Two sizes<br>MR3/121 | 107 Bedford Court Mansion<br>Bedford Square<br>London | P9/J/20,21<br>*#4950,1*  | **James Charles JAY** (Chairman)<br>**JAY, Richard ATTENBOROUGH & CO** *<br>142, 144 Oxford Street<br>London W | Silversmiths and jewellers |
| SPB/17<br>6 April 1873 | See below | P3/I*sic*/x2<br>*#4952,3*  | **James JACKSON** *<br>36 Helmet Row, St Lukes<br>London | Watchcase maker |
| R1/78<br>24 September 1894<br>Sent by W H Pierce & Co | 42 Yarbury Street<br>Moss Side<br>Manchester | P5/J/591<br>*#4954*  | **Samuel Hindle EVANS**<br>**Thomas Humphrey EVANS**<br>trading as **John JAMES**<br>24 Old Mill Gate<br>Manchester | Tobacconists |

 JJ–JJ

| REGISTRATION DETAILS | MAKER'S PRIVATE ADDRESS and DETAILS | PLATE and MARK DETAILS | MAKER/COMPANY and BUSINESS ADDRESS | MAKER'S TRADE |
|---|---|---|---|---|
| R1/42<br>3 April 1897<br>Sent by J M Banks<br>CH Cheshire<br>Minshall & Latimer | Private address same as business | P5/J/829<br>***#4955***<br> | **James Charles JAY** *<br>142, 144 Oxford Street<br>London | Silversmith |
| LPB/42<br>8 June 1881<br>LPB mark shown | | Not on P3<br>***#4956***<br>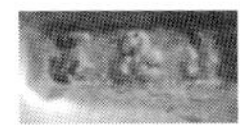 | **JONES & JACKSON**<br>43 Hockley Street<br>Birmingham | Gem ring makers |
| | See also James and Joseph Jackson | P2/I*sic*/5<br>***#4957-61***<br> | **Joseph JONES**<br>Chester or | Silversmith |
| SPB/20<br>30 March 1875<br>No mark in SPB | | P2*sic*/I/x1<br>***#4962***<br>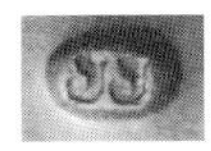 | **Joseph JACKSON**<br>Victoria Buildings<br>Corporation Street<br>Manchester | Working jeweller |
| Similar mark entered LAO 21 July 1851 | | P2/I/x5<br>***#4963-7***<br> | **James JACKSON & SON** *<br>6 Norman Street<br>St Luke's<br>London | Watchcase makers |
| SPB/4<br>22 March 1877 | | P3/D/x2<br>***#4968,9***<br>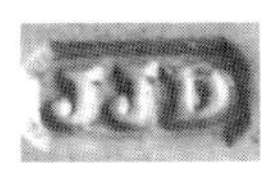 | **James J DAGG**<br>242 Scotland Road<br>Liverpool | Watch manufacturer |
| LPB/24<br>6 August 1880 | | P3/D/x2<br>***#4970,1***<br> | | |
| R1/62<br>1 March 1898<br>Sent by<br>G W Nettleton | 18 Glen View<br>Halifax | P5/Z*sic*/939<br>***#4972***<br> | **Jean Jacques FORRER**<br>18 Glen View<br>Halifax | Cigar and pipe importer |
| SPB/14<br>8 January 1877<br>Sent by SR (possibly Samuel & Rogers) | see also JJH and I&IH | P3/G*sic*/x3<br>***#4973-5***<br> | **Joseph & John HARGREAVES**<br>11 Slater Street<br>Liverpool | Watch manufacturers |
| SPB/1<br>5 February 1864<br>Sent by James Walker, Earlsdon Coventry | | P3/H/x3<br>***#4976-8***<br> | **Joseph & John HARGREAVES**<br>40 Slater Street<br>Liverpool | |
| SPB/7<br>29 November 1865 | | P3/H/x3<br>***#4979-81***<br>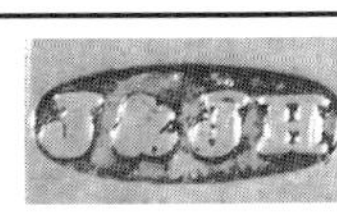 | | |
| SPB/11<br>6 February 1866 | | P3/H/x1<br>***#4982***<br> | | |
| R1/130<br>4 August 1900<br>Sent by<br>W H Carrington & Co | 25 Upper Camden Street<br>Dublin | P9/K/12<br>***#4983***<br> | **James J KIRK**<br>37 Upper Camden Street and<br>Harcourt Road<br>Dublin | Tobacconist and cigar bonder |
| R1/100<br>9 May 1899<br>Sent by Hermann Stanger | 40 Clissold Road<br>London N | P9/S/18<br>***#4984***<br> | **Hermann STANGER** trading as<br>**J J STANGER**<br>34 Gracechurch Street<br>London | Ring manufacturer |

| REGISTRATION DETAILS | MAKER'S PRIVATE ADDRESS and DETAILS | PLATE and MARK DETAILS | MAKER/COMPANY and BUSINESS ADDRESS | MAKER'S TRADE |
|---|---|---|---|---|
| R1/13<br>5 July 1895<br>Sent by W Aitken | 14 Beaufort Road<br>Edgbaston<br>Birmingham | P5/J/673<br>***#4985***<br>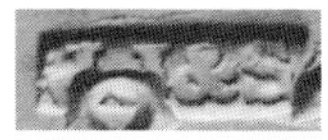 | **Joseph JOSEPH** trading as<br>**Joseph JOSEPH & SONS**<br>59 Caroline Street<br>Birmingham | Jewellers |
| Missing register<br>*c.*1891<br>Roman incuse LAO<br>18 November 1886 | | P5/W/377<br>***#4986***<br> | **John James WOOD**<br>212 Strand<br>London W2 | Tobacconist |
| R3/148<br>8 December 1953<br>Sent by J D Kelly<br>Mark not on P21 as expected | 65 Stewards Avenue<br>Widnes<br>Lancashire | P21/K/14<br>***#4987*** **J K?** | **John Derek KELLY**<br>No business address entered | Silversmith |
| Missing register<br>*c.*1889 | | P5/K/242a<br>***#4988***<br> | **Jacob KOPPENHAGEN** trading as<br>**KOPPENHAGEN BROTHERS**<br>4 Queen Street<br>Cheapside<br>London EC | Cigar importers |
| Missing register<br>*c.*1889 | | P5/K/242b<br>***#4989***<br> | | |
| Missing register<br>*c.*1889 | | P5/K/242c<br>***#4990***<br> | | |
| Missing register<br>*c.*1886<br>Similar mark LAO<br>5 November 1889 | | P5/K/63<br>***#4991***<br> | | |
| R3/148 undated<br>Between March and November 1902 | | P9/K/27<br>***#4992***<br> | | |
| Missing register<br>*c.*1893 | | P5/K/525<br>***#4993***<br> | | |
| R1/68<br>26 July 1898<br>Sent by J Kirk | Orchard Street<br>Erdington | P9/K/2<br>***#4994***<br> | **Joseph KIRK**<br>68 Vyse Street<br>Birmingham | Jeweller |
| R1/93<br>27 February 1899<br>Sent by J Kirk | | P9/K/5<br>***#4995***<br> | | |
| SPB/1<br>16 October 1863<br>CWMP 187 | | P3/K/x2<br>***#4996,7***<br> | **Jeremiah KIRK**<br>Summerland Place (1850)<br>57 The Butts (1863)<br>Coventry | Watchcase maker |
| LPB/46<br>30 July 1878 | | P3/K/x2<br>***#4998,9***<br> | **Joseph KNIGHT**<br>29 Upper Hockley Street<br>Birmingham | Gold chain maker |
| R1/10<br>9 May 1895<br>Sent by Henry W King | Stamford<br>Muswell Hill<br>London N | P5/K/657<br>***#5000***<br> | **John Percy KING**<br>**Henry William KING** trading as<br>**KING & SON**<br>3, 5 Charterhouse Street<br>London | Jewellers and silversmiths |

| REGISTRATION DETAILS | MAKER'S PRIVATE ADDRESS and DETAILS | PLATE and MARK DETAILS | MAKER/COMPANY and BUSINESS ADDRESS | MAKER'S TRADE |
|---|---|---|---|---|
| SPB/23<br>16 September 1876<br>Sent by J L Tolman<br>Old punch destroyed | | P3/L/x3<br>***#5001-3***  | **John LECOMBER**<br>121 Derby Road<br>Bootle<br>Lancashire | Watch manufacturer |
| R2/162<br>4 October 1912<br>Sent by J Lawrence | 55 Hall Road<br>Handsworth<br>Birmingham | P13/L/74<br>***#5004*** 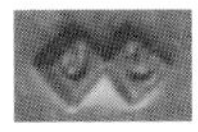 | **James LAWRENCE**<br>91a Vittoria Street<br>Birmingham | Jeweller |
| SPB/14<br>8 January 1877 | | P3/L/x3<br>***#5005-7***  | **John LECOMBER**<br>43 Slater Street<br>Liverpool | Watch manufacturer |
| SPB/22<br>5 August 1872<br>Sent by G Roberts | | P3/L/x4<br>***#5008-11***  | **John LECOMBER** (crossed out)<br>121 Derby Road<br>Liverpool | Watch manufacturer |
| LPB/62 between July 1882 and January 1883 | | Not on P3<br>***#5012***  | **J & E LECOMBER**<br>12 Mount Street<br>Liverpool | Watch manufacturers |
| Missing register<br>*c.*1887 | | P5/L/106<br>***#5013*** 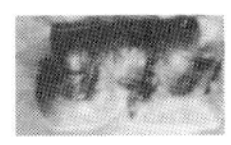 | | |
| MR3/90<br>SIL/54<br>SOT/86<br>J1 1842-64<br>GMSC/67-70 | Free 1842 | P2/L/x3<br>***#5014-6***  | **John LOWE** *<br>6 Bridge Street Row (1846-60)<br>Chester | Silversmith, clockmaker and watchmaker |
| | | P2/L/x3<br>***#5017-9***  | | |
| | | P2/L/x4<br>***#5020-3***  | | |
| SIL/52 | | P2/L/x3<br>***#5024-6*** 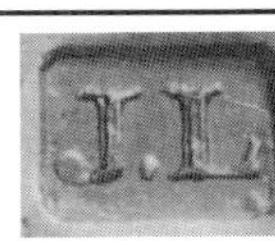 | | |
| | | P2/L/x4<br>***#5027-30***  | | |
| SPB/3<br>16 July 1864 | See also JL over GL | P3/L/x3<br>***#5031-3***  | **LOWE & SONS** *<br>Bridge Street<br>Chester | Silversmiths and jewellers |
| R2/17<br>28 April 1906<br>Sent by A Moore | 80 Evering Road<br>Stoke Newington | P9/L/75<br>***#5034***  | **John LAZAMS**<br>28 Houndsditch<br>London EC | Watchmaker and jeweller |
| R2/3<br>6 October 1905<br>Sent by Joseph Letowsky | 17 Osborne Street<br>Whitechapel<br>London | P9/L/70<br>***#5035***  | **Joseph LETOWSKY** *<br>12 Osborne Street<br>Whitechapel<br>London E | Chain and bracelet maker |
| R1/182<br>22 December 1902<br>Sent by J Letowsky | Private address same as business | P9/L/40<br>***#5036***  | **Joseph LETOWSKY** *<br>3 Great Garden Street<br>Whitechapel<br>London E | Chain maker |
| R2/28<br>1 November 1906<br>Sent by self | 44 Paignton Road<br>Birmingham | P9/L/82<br>***#5037*** 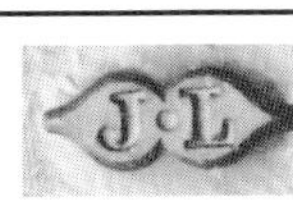 | **Joseph LYDDIATT**<br>39 Monument Road<br>Birmingham | Jeweller |

| REGISTRATION DETAILS | MAKER'S PRIVATE ADDRESS and DETAILS | PLATE and MARK DETAILS | MAKER/COMPANY and BUSINESS ADDRESS | MAKER'S TRADE |
|---|---|---|---|---|
| R2/228<br>6 March 1920<br>Sent by J Lyddiatt | 6 Handsworth Road<br>Birmingham | No new mark<br>***#5038*** | **Joseph LYDDIATT**<br>52 Hockley Hill<br>Birmingham | Gold and silver jewellery |
| R3/48<br>26 September 1929<br>Sent by J Lyddiatt | 12 Havistock Road<br>Handsworth Wood<br>Birmingham | P15/L/38<br>***#5039*** 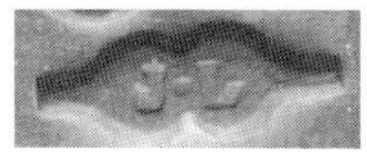 | | Gold and silversmith |
| R2/181<br>9 December 1913<br>Sent by J Leton | Private address same as business | P13/L/75<br>***#5040***  | **Joseph LETON**<br>17 Osborn Street<br>London | Chain and bracelet maker |
| R1/109<br>30 August 1899<br>Sent by James Lloyd | 209 Bar Street West<br>Birmingham | P9/L/12<br>***#5041***  | **James LLOYD**<br>209 Bar Street West<br>Birmingham | Jeweller and pipe maker |
| R2/120<br>12 October 1910<br>Sent by Joseph Latten | Private address same as business | P13/L/45<br>***#5042***  | **Joseph LATTEN**<br>3 Little Halifax Street<br>Chicksand Street<br>Spitalfields<br>London E | Jeweller |
| R3/104<br>16 February 1943<br>Sent by John Lawrence Barber | Private address same as business | P21/B/19<br>***#5043***  | **John Lawrence BARBER**<br>27 Upper Northgate Street<br>Chester | Dentist |
| R1/112<br>18 September 1899<br>Sent by W Ehrhardt | Holmdale<br>Bradninch<br>Devonshire | P9/L/14<br>***#5044***  | **John LONG** trading as<br>**John LONG & CO**<br>Bradninch<br>Devonshire | Watchmakers |
| R1/233<br>6 May 1905<br>Sent by R Archer & Son<br>next to P9/L/70 | Rosslyn<br>Oxford Road<br>Moseley<br>Birmingham | P9/L/65 and P9/H*sic*/0*sic*<br>***#5045,6***  | **James LUCKING** trading as<br>**James LUCKING & CO**<br>5 Corporation Street<br>Birmingham | Opticians and spectacle makers |
| R3/9<br>11 April 1922<br>Sent by J L Duncan | 12 Curzon Road<br>Southport | P15/D/63<br>***#5047***  | **John Louis DUNCAN** trading as<br>**DUNCANS**<br>64 Shudehill and<br>17 Thomas Street<br>Manchester | Pipe makers, mounters and repairers |
| R2/162<br>1 October 1912<br>Sent by R E Duncan | Rock Cliff<br>Monton<br>Eccles | P13/D/55<br>***#5048***  | **John Louis DUNCAN**<br>17 Thomas Street<br>64 Shudehill (undated new address)<br>Manchester | Tobacconist and sundries man |
| R2/216<br>30 November 1918<br>Sent by W Sharman | Rockcliff<br>Monton<br>Near Manchester | P15/D/32<br>***#5049***  | **John Lewis DUNCAN**<br>trading as **DUNCANS**<br>64 Shudehill (late 17 Thomas Street)<br>Manchester | Wholesale tobacconist and fancy goods dealer |
| R1/79<br>25 September 1894<br>Sent by W A Stevens<br>40 Kilverts Buildings<br>Manchester | Stonycroft<br>Whitefield<br>Lancashire | P5/D/592<br>***#5050***  | **John L DUNCAN** trading as<br>**J L DUNCAN & CO**<br>6 Thomas Street and<br>1 Soap Street<br>Manchester | Tobacconists and fancy goods importers |
| Not in R1 as expected - mark P5/D/698 already used for IMS 26 November 1895 | | P5/D/698a<br>***#5051*** 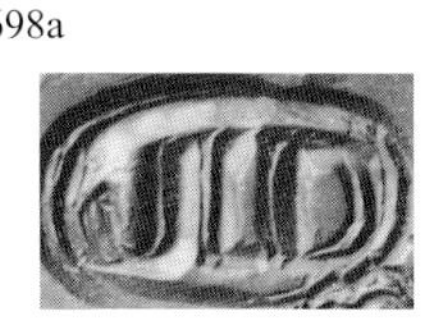 | | |

| REGISTRATION DETAILS | MAKER'S PRIVATE ADDRESS and DETAILS | PLATE and MARK DETAILS | MAKER/COMPANY and BUSINESS ADDRESS | MAKER'S TRADE |
|---|---|---|---|---|
| Mark struck twice next to mark above | | P5/D/698b<br>***#5052***<br>§  | **John L DUNCAN** trading as<br>**J L DUNCAN & CO**<br>6 Thomas Street and<br>1 Soap Street<br>Manchester | Tobacconists and fancy goods importers |
| LPB/52<br>4 January 1886<br>No mark in LPB<br>MR3/129 | 7th name in LPB/52 and 7th mark on P5/L<br><br>See also JL | P5/L/5<br>***#5053***  | **LOWE & SONS** *<br>6 Bridge Street Row<br>Chester | Silversmiths and jewellers |
| R1/35<br>27 October 1896<br>Sent by Lowe & Sons - Authority to Platnauer & Co | Stone Bridge [1]<br>Chester<br>25 Hough Green [2]<br>Chester | P5/L/801<br>***#5054***  | **John Foulkes LOWE** [1]<br>**George Bennett LOWE** [2] trading as<br>**LOWE & SONS** *<br>6 Bridge Street Row<br>Chester | Silversmiths |
| R2/27<br>25 October 1906<br>Sent by W Aitken<br>Two sizes | 48 Liverpool Road<br>Chester | P9/L/78,79<br>***#5055,6***  | **George Bennett LOWE** trading as<br>**LOWE & SONS** *<br>11 Bridge Street Row<br>Chester | |
| R2/73<br>26 February 1909<br>Sent by W Aitken<br>Cancelled<br>20 February 1912<br>Partner deceased | Stone Bridge<br>Chester<br>Onnley House<br>Liverpool Road<br>Chester | P13/L/7<br>***#5057***  | **John Foulkes LOWE**<br>**George Bennett LOWE** trading as<br>**LOWE & SONS** *<br>11 Bridge Street Row<br>Chester | |
| R3/185<br>30 June 1962<br>Sent by Lowe & Sons<br>Three sizes | Aikman Gardens [1]<br>The Groves<br>Chester<br>Arglow College [2]<br>Chesières Villars<br>Switzerland | P21/L/59-61<br>***#5058-60***  | **John ffoulkes LOWE** [1]<br>**Miss Margaret Joyce LOWE** [2] (Equal Partners) trading as<br>**LOWE & SONS** *<br>11 Bridge Street Row<br>Chester | Goldsmiths and silversmiths |
| Missing register<br>*c.*1890 | | P5/L/327<br>***#5061***  | **Unidentified** | |
| PP1/188<br>GTD 1835-58 | See also ILS and IS | P1/24/x6<br>***#5062-7***  | **Joseph Lewis SAMUEL**<br>Liverpool | Watchcase maker |
| | | P1/24/x3<br>***#5068-70***  | | |
| R2/96<br>4 November 1909<br>Sent by J L Shure | 287 Amhurst Road<br>Stoke Newington<br>London | P13/S/47<br>***#5071***  | **Julius Louis SHURE**<br>287 Amhurst Road<br>Stoke Newington<br>London | Chain and bracelet maker |
| R2/209<br>22 November 1916<br>Sent by J L Shure<br>(entered)<br>sent at first but not accepted | Private address same as business | P15/S/28<br>***#5072***  | **Louis SHURE**<br>(**Julius Louis SHURE** full name accepted)<br>287 Amhurst Road<br>Stoke Newington<br>London N | Gold chain, bracelet and ring makers |
| MR3/135<br>J1 1846-73<br>GTD 1844-73<br>SOT/122-3 | See also MAYER #5870 | P2/M/x2<br>***#5073,4***  | **Joseph MAYER** *<br>68/70 Lord Street<br>Liverpool | Watchmaker and clockmaker |

| REGISTRATION DETAILS | MAKER'S PRIVATE ADDRESS and DETAILS | PLATE and MARK DETAILS | MAKER/COMPANY and BUSINESS ADDRESS | MAKER'S TRADE |
|---|---|---|---|---|
| R1/60<br>9 February 1898<br>Sent by John Martin | Private address same as business | P5/*Zsic*/930<br>***#5075***   | **John MARTIN** *<br>32a Colebrooke Row<br>Islington<br>London N | Watchcase maker |
| SPB/7<br>21 June 1865<br>Sent by F Wright<br>Two sizes | | P3/M/x2<br>***#5076,7***   | **John McCORMACK**<br>no address given<br>(Ed: Waterford Buildings<br>Richmond Street, Liverpool) | |
| R3/95<br>3 July 1939<br>Sent by P J Moss | Private address same as business | P21/M/9<br>***#5078***  | **Phyllis Joan MOSS**<br>6 Beaufort Road<br>Brooklands<br>Cheshire | Silversmith |
| MR3/135<br>J1 1846-73<br>GTD 1844-73<br>SOT/122-3 | | P2/M/x2<br>***#5079,80***   | **Joseph MAYER** *<br>68/70 Lord Street<br>Liverpool | Watchmaker and clockmaker |
| | | P2/M/x2<br>***#5081,2***   | | |
| Missing register<br>*c.*1888 | | P5/M/177<br>***#5083***  | **Unidentified** | |
| R2/97<br>4 November 1909<br>Sent by Joseph Moore<br>No. 29 rejected | 14 Holly Road<br>Handsworth<br>Birmingham | P13/M/29<br>***#5084***   | **J E MOORE**<br>**Frank MOORE** trading as<br>**Joseph MOORE**<br>13 Petsford Street<br>Birmingham | Die sinkers and medallists |
| No. 30 cut in place and accepted | Trenarter<br>Chester Road<br>Edgbaston<br>Birmingham | P13/M/30<br>***#5085***   | | |
| R2/44<br>7 August 1907<br>Sent by Joseph Myers | 40 Burlington Road<br>South Shore<br>Blackpool | P9/M/115,116<br>***#5086,7***   | **Joseph MYERS**<br>3 Kilverts Building<br>Withy Grove<br>Manchester | Watch manufacturers and jewellers agent |
| R3/154<br>12 March 1955<br>Sent by J Mathews<br>Two sizes | Private Patients Home<br>Lorne Street<br>Manchester 13 | P21/M/42,43<br>***#5088,9***   | **Jessie MATHEWS**<br>No business address entered | Student of silversmithing |
| Missing register<br>*c.*1891 | | P5/M/336<br>***#5090***  | **Unidentified** | |
| Missing register<br>*c.*1892<br>Similar mark BAO<br>22 December 1892 | | P5/M/439<br>***#5091***   | **John MARSHALL**<br>82 Oxford Street<br>Ripley | Jeweller |
| PDB 1825-6<br>MR3/94 | Variety of plate<br>See also IM | P1/25/x2<br>***#5092,3***   | **John MILLER**<br>Newcastle | Silversmith |
| LPB/54<br>5 March 1880 | | P3/M/x2<br>***#5094,5***  | **John MOORE**<br>12 Caroline Street<br>Birmingham | Gold chain maker |
| R1/107<br>3 August 1899<br>Sent by J Mantle | 87 Church Hill Road<br>Handsworth<br>Birmingham | P9/M/14<br>***#5096***  | **Frederick MANTLE**<br>160 Warstone Lane<br>Birmingham | Manufacturing jeweller |

| REGISTRATION DETAILS | MAKER'S PRIVATE ADDRESS and DETAILS | PLATE and MARK DETAILS | MAKER/COMPANY and BUSINESS ADDRESS | MAKER'S TRADE |
|---|---|---|---|---|
| R1/107<br>3 August 1899 | 87 Church Hill Road<br>Handsworth<br>Birmingham | P9/M/15<br>***#5097***  | **Frederick MANTLE**<br>160 Warstone Lane<br>Birmingham | Manufacturing jeweller |
| LPB/54<br>2 September 1880 | | P3/M/x1<br>***#5098***  | **James MASON**<br>49 Hockley Street<br>Birmingham | Jeweller |
| LPB/92<br>28 May 1883<br>Sent by A Griffiths<br>LPB mark shown | | Not on P3<br>***#5099***  | **John MANTLE**<br>160 Warstone Lane<br>Birmingham | Chain maker |
| R2/100<br>15 December 1909<br>Sent by J Mantle & Sons<br>Three sizes | 123 Wentworth Road<br>Harborne<br>Birmingham | P13/M/32-34<br>***#5100-2***  | **J MANTLE & SONS**<br>J Stafford Mantle (Secretary)<br>160 Warstone Lane<br>Birmingham | Chain and jewellery manufacturers |
| R3/86<br>10 February 1937<br>Sent by<br>S Blanckensee & Son Ltd | | P21/M/4<br>***#5103***  | **John MORTIMER**<br>18 Kirkgate<br>Ripon<br>Yorkshire | Watchmaker and silversmith |
| LPB/54<br>24 February 1879<br>Two sizes | | P3/M/x6<br>***#5104-9***  | **John MANGER** *<br>9 Bartletts Passage Buildings<br>Holborn Circus<br>London | Watchcase maker |
| Missing register<br>*c.*1892<br>Similar mark entered BAO 7 July 1893 | | P5/M/444<br>***#5110*** 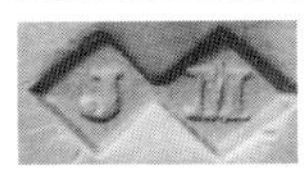 | **Joseph MOORE** *<br>4 Spon End<br>Coventry | Watchcase manufacturer |
| R1/86<br>30 November 1898<br>Sent by J M Banks<br>MR3/116 | 47 Heathfield Road<br>Handsworth<br>Birmingham | P9/B/11<br>***#5111***  | **John Millward BANKS** *<br>6, 7 Northampton Street<br>Birmingham | Goldsmith and jeweller |
| R1/131<br>30 August 1900<br>Sent by Coley Brothers | 50 Carpenter Road<br>Birmingham | P9/B/32<br>***#5112*** 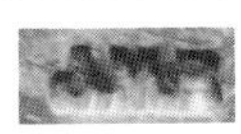 | | |
| LPB/18<br>5 July 1884<br>Sent by Pope & Phelps | | P5/B/x1<br>***#5113*** 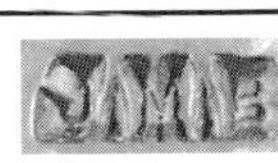 | | |
| Missing register<br>*c.*1886 | | P5/B/15<br>***#5114***  | | |
| R2/35<br>15 March 1907<br>Sent by J M Bassett | 17 Ospringe Road<br>London NW | P9/*Osic*/186<br>***#5115***  | **James Mapleton BASSETT** *<br>39 Kings Square, Clerkenwell<br>London EC7 | Manufacturing goldsmith and jeweller |
| R3/164<br>24 June 1958<br>Sent by Mrs J M Brown | 2 Bidstone Road<br>Oxton<br>Birkenhead | P21/B/54<br>***#5116***  | **Mrs Jane McCracken BROWN**<br>No business address entered | Student |
| Not in R2 as expected<br>*c.* August 1914 to January 1915 | | P15/B/57<br>***#5117***  | **John Millward BANKS** * | Jeweller and silversmith |
| R1/150<br>9 July 1901<br>Sent by self<br>Four sizes | 50 Carpenter Road<br>Edgbaston<br>Birmingham | P9/B/74-79<br>***#5118-23***  | **John Millward BANKS** *<br>6, 7 Northampton Street<br>Birmingham and<br>12, 14 Beake Street (Showroom)<br>Regent Street, London W | |

| REGISTRATION DETAILS | MAKER'S PRIVATE ADDRESS and DETAILS | PLATE and MARK DETAILS | MAKER/COMPANY and BUSINESS ADDRESS | MAKER'S TRADE |
|---|---|---|---|---|
| Missing register<br>*c.*1888<br>Similar mark BAO<br>2 December 1897 | | P5/B/143<br>***#5124***  | **John M BANKS**<br>6 Northampton Street<br>Birmingham | Goldsmith and jeweller |
| R2/35<br>15 March 1907<br>Sent by J M Bassett | 17 Ospringe Road<br>London NW | P9/O*sic*/0*sic*<br>***#5125***  | **James Mapleton BASSETT** *<br>39 Kings Square<br>Clerkenwell<br>London EC7 | Manufacturing goldsmith and jeweller |
| LPB/86<br>8 November 1882 | | P3/B/2<br>***#5126***  | **John Millward BANKS** *<br>6 Northampton Street<br>Birmingham | Goldsmith and jeweller |
| Missing register<br>*c.*1893 | | P5/B/524<br>***#5127***  | | |
| Not in R1 as expected<br>Sent by J M Banks | Heathfield Road<br>Handsworth | P5/B/624<br>***#5128***  | **John Millward BANKS** *<br>6, 7 Northampton Street<br>Birmingham | Silversmith and jeweller |
| R1/72<br>28 July 1898<br>Sent by J M Banks<br>Four sizes | Heathfield Road<br>Handsworth<br>Birmingham<br>Seen on mustard pot 1898 | P9/B/2a-d<br>***#5129-32***  | | |
| R1/72<br>28 July 1898<br>Two sizes | | P9/B/2e,f<br>***#5133,4***  | | |
| R1/150<br>9 July 1901<br>Sent by self | 50 Carpenter Road<br>Edgbaston<br>Birmingham | P9/B/38-73<br>***#5135-40***  | **John Millward BANKS** *<br>6, 7 Northampton Street<br>Birmingham and<br>12, 14 Beake Street (Showroom)<br>Regent Street, London W | |
| R1/144<br>12 March 1901<br>Sent by J M Banks | | P9/B/36<br>***#5141***  | | Goldsmith, silversmith and diamond merchant |
| | | P2/M/x3<br>***#5142-4***  | **Unidentified** | |
| | | P2/M/x3<br>***#5145-7***  | **Unidentified** | |
| R3/17<br>28 June 1923<br>Sent by Jack M Cutler | 3 Rolston Drive<br>Ivor<br>Glasgow | P15/C/145-147<br>***#5148-50***  | **Jack M CUTLER**<br>72 Great Clyde Street<br>Glasgow | Wholesale jewellers |
| R1/105<br>1 July 1899<br>Sent by S Usher | 62 Thorpe Road [1]<br>Kingston upon Thames<br>Surrey | P9/M/13<br>***#5151***  | **John MYERS & CO LTD**<br>William Edward JONES[1] (Secretary)<br>131, 135 Westminster Bridge Road<br>London | Watchmakers and jewellers |
| R2/57<br>18 March 1908<br>Sent by James Marlow | 80 Putney Road<br>Handsworth<br>Staffordshire | P13/M/1-4<br>***#5152-5***  | **James MARLOW**<br>4 Warstone Lane<br>Birmingham | Goldsmith and jeweller |

| REGISTRATION DETAILS | MAKER'S PRIVATE ADDRESS and DETAILS | PLATE and MARK DETAILS | MAKER/COMPANY and BUSINESS ADDRESS | MAKER'S TRADE |
|---|---|---|---|---|
| R3/51<br>7 January 1930<br>Sent by Janet Mathieson Gill | 141 Dullis Terrace<br>Aberdeen and<br>Flat 10, 152 Princes Road<br>Liverpool | P15/G/54<br>***#5156***<br> | **Janet Mathieson GILL, DA**<br>City School of Art<br>Liverpool | Professional teacher |
| | | P2/H/x3<br>***#5157-9***<br> | **Unidentified** | |
| R1/48<br>20 July 1897<br>Sent by W Walker | 68 Gunterstone Road<br>West Kensington<br>London | P5/J/857<br>***#5160***<br> | **Joshua Michael JACOBS** *<br>6 Castle Street<br>Falcon Square<br>London EC | Merchant |
| R2/190<br>9 September 1914<br>Sent by Handcock & Walker | 16 Ebbofleet Road<br>Cricklewood | P15/J/5<br>***#5161***<br> | **Joshua Michael JACOBS** trading as<br>**J M JACOBS & CO** *<br>Finsbury Court<br>Finsbury Pavement<br>London E C | Exporters and dealers in pipes, etc |
| R2/127<br>8 February 1911<br>Sent by J M Jackson | 8 Warbour Lane<br>Milnrow | P13/J/46<br>***#5162***<br> | **Joseph Marshall JACKSON**<br>88 Yorkshire Street<br>Rochdale and<br>76 Market Street<br>Shaw | Umbrella manufacturer |
| R2/167<br>27 January 1913<br>Sent by Emma McKnight | Private address same as business<br>Widow of James? | No new mark<br>***#5163*** | **Emma McKNIGHT**<br>21 Barras Lane<br>Coventry | Silver watchcase maker |
| R1/78<br>30 August 1894<br>Sent by James McKnight<br>CWMP 1901 | 25 Norfolk Street<br>Coventry | P5/M*sic*/586a<br>***#5164***<br> | **James McKNIGHT** *<br>25 Norfolk Street (1894)<br>21 Barras Lane (1901)<br>Coventry | |
| | Seen on watchcase 1895 | P5/M*sic*/586b<br>***#5165***<br> | | |
| R3/186<br>24 August 1962<br>Sent by Lt Col M J Perreau | Dalwood<br>Gold Hill<br>Lower Bourne<br>Fareham<br>Surrey | P21/P/63<br>***#5166***<br> | **Lt Col Montague John PERREAU**<br>No business address entered<br><br>**LAST ENTRY AT CHESTER**<br>**Signed A GODWIN Warden** | Student silversmith |
| R2/140<br>28 July 1911<br>Sent by J M Plower | 13 Greenbank Road<br>Sefton Park<br>Liverpool | P13/Q*sic*/206<br>***#5167***<br> | **Johan Milton PLOWER**<br>15 Old Post Office Place<br>off Church Street<br>Liverpool | Dealer in Indian goods |
| R3/10<br>26 May 1922<br>Sent by Joseph Myers | 82 Osborn Road<br>Blackpool<br>26 Lapwing Lane<br>Withington<br>Manchester | P15/M/45<br>***#5168***<br> | **Joseph MYERS**<br>**Reginald MYERS** trading as<br>**Joseph MYERS & SON**<br>8 Green Street<br>Tib Street<br>Manchester | Manufacturing agents |
| R2/235<br>22 October 1920<br>Sent by Joseph Myers | 82 Osborn Road<br>Blackpool<br>38 Wicklow Road<br>Chorlton-cum-Hardy | P15/M/42<br>***#5169***<br>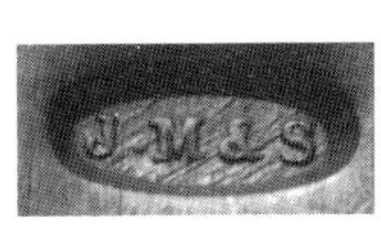 | | Manufacturing jewellers, agents and importers |

| REGISTRATION DETAILS | MAKER'S PRIVATE ADDRESS and DETAILS | PLATE and MARK DETAILS | MAKER/COMPANY and BUSINESS ADDRESS | MAKER'S TRADE |
|---|---|---|---|---|
| R1/107<br>31 July 1899<br>Sent by W H<br>Carrington & Co | 4 Cavendish Street<br>Grimsby | P9/T/11<br>***#5170***<br> | **James Michael TIERNEY** trading as<br>**J M TIERNEY LTD**<br>110 Cleethorpes Road<br>Grimsby | Tobacconists |
| R1/64<br>6 June 1894<br>Sent by W H<br>Carrington & Co | 21 Cavendish Street<br>Grimsby | P5/T/566<br>***#5171***<br> | **James Michael TIERNEY**<br>20 Cleethorpes Road<br>Grimsby | Cigar and tobacconist |
| CWMP 1874-91<br>Similar mark LAO<br>28 April 1861, BAO<br>3 November 1853 | PP3/83<br>Not in SPB or LPB so struck<br>1860-3<br>See also N&F | P3/N/x5<br>***#5172-6***<br> | **James NEALE** *<br>Ryley Street and Hill Street<br>Coventry | Watchcase maker |
| Missing register<br>*c.*1886 | | P5/N/11<br>***#5177***<br> | **J NEWSOME** *<br>14/15 The Butts<br>Coventry | Watch and watchcase manufacturer |
| LPB/6<br>7 February 1878 | See also IJTN | P3/N/x2<br>***#5178,9***<br> | | |
| LPB/58<br>23 March 1880<br>Sent by J Sharpe | | P3/N/x2<br>***#5180,1***<br> | | |
| LPB/98<br>16 July 1884<br>Sent by C Harris<br>No mark or initial | | Not on P5<br>***#5182***<br> | **J NEWSOME** *<br>No business address entered | |
| R2/46<br>12 September 1907<br>Sent by S Mordan &<br>Co | Private address same as business | P9/K/47<br>***#5183***<br> | **J N KUHN** trading as<br>**J N KHUN & CO** *<br>61, 63 Shaftesbury Avenue<br>London | Manufacturers and importers of fancy goods |
| R2/182<br>22 January 1914<br>Sent by Coley<br>Brothers | Hope House<br>Rye, Sussex<br>Watchwell Chambers [1]<br>Rye, Sussex | P15/M/6<br>***#5184***<br> | **J N MASTERS**<br>Lewis Amon [1] (Secretary)<br>Hope House, Rye<br>Sussex | Watchmakers and jewellers |
| SPB/8<br>18 November 1872 | | P3/O/x3<br>***#5185-7***<br> | **James OLIVER** *<br>4 King's Square, Goswell Road<br>London | Watchcase maker |
| PP1/124<br>Similar mark entered<br>LAO 28 January 1858 | Possibly struck on plate 1 in error for plate 2 or 3 | P1/6/x3<br>***#5188-90***<br> | **James OVERAN** *<br>30 Smith Street<br>Clerkenwell<br>London<br>or | Watch pendant maker |
| PP1/188<br>Similar mark LAO<br>16 April 1883 | Possibly struck on plate 1 in error for plate 2 or 3 | | **James OLIVER**<br>8 Wellington Street<br>London | Watchcase maker |
| LPB/76<br>13 April 1882<br>Sent by Nathan<br>Brothers<br>No mark in LPB | | P3/S/x3<br>***#5191-3***<br> | **Jacob Otto SCHULER**<br>190 Warstone Lane<br>Birmingham | Manufacturing jeweller, wholesale and export and diamond merchants |
| LPB/78 SP31,32<br>6 May 1884<br>Sent by Roek &<br>Dreyfus | | P5/S/x1<br>***#5194***<br> | | |

| REGISTRATION DETAILS | MAKER'S PRIVATE ADDRESS and DETAILS | PLATE and MARK DETAILS | MAKER/COMPANY and BUSINESS ADDRESS | MAKER'S TRADE |
|---|---|---|---|---|
| Missing register<br>*c* 1886 | | P5/S/5<br>***#5195***<br> | **Jacob Otto SCHULER** ?<br>190 Warstone Lane<br>Birmingham | Diamond merchants |
| R3/144<br>16 May 1953<br>Sent by J O'H Tobin | Flat 3<br>116 Edge Lane<br>Stretford | P21/T/19<br>***#5196***<br> | **John O'Hara TOBIN**<br>Department of Bacteriology<br>York Place<br>Manchester 3 | Student |
| GTD 1824-29<br>PP3/83<br>IoK cameo mark<br>LAO 25 March 1854 | Attribution based on IoK cameo mark | P2/K/x2<br>***#5197,8***<br> | **John O'KEEFFE** *<br>16 Queen's Row<br>Pentonville Road<br>London | Watchcase maker |
| R1/109<br>24 August 1899<br>Sent by W H Carrington | Littlecot<br>Stoneygate<br>Leicester | P9/P/41<br>***#5199***<br> | **William SEDGWICK** trading as<br>**John PROCTOR**<br>51 Gallow Tree Gate and<br>89 Grafton Street<br>Leicester | Tobacconist |
| SPB/12<br>2 October 1873 | | P3/P/x2<br>***#5200,1***<br> | **Joseph PENNLINGTON**<br>14 Oxton Road<br>Birkenhead | Watch manufacturer |
| R3/130<br>18 February 1950<br>Sent by J Prince<br>Two sizes | 55 Daisybank Road<br>Victoria Park<br>Manchester 14 | P21/P/31,32<br>***#5202,3***<br> | **John PRINCE**<br>No business address entered | Student |
| R1/200<br>15 September 1903<br>Sent by Joseph Peskin | 27 Dunk Street<br>Spitalfields<br>London | P9/Q*sic*/186<br>***#5204***<br> | **Jacob PESKIN** *<br>27 Dunk Street<br>Spitalfields<br>London E | Goldworker |
| R3/108<br>8 March 1945<br>Sent by John Pass<br>Two sizes | Private address same as business | P21/P/14, 15<br>***#5205,6***<br> | **John PASS**<br>9 Wellesley Avenue<br>Haslington<br>Crewe | Freelance silversmith, watchmaker and jeweller |
| PP1/187,188<br>GTD 1807<br>PMR 1807-24 | A John Pinnington 1806 to 1847 also recorded as a watchcase maker at Moffat Place, Liverpool | P1/6/x8<br>***#5207-14***<br> | **John PENNINGTON**<br>32 Leeds Street (1807)<br>Liverpool or | Watch and watchcase manufacturer |
| PMR 1841-71 | See also P&R for Plumb & Rigby | | **James PLUMB**<br>20 Downe Street (1841)<br>1 Barrow Street (1871)<br>Liverpool or | Watch and watchcase manufacturer |
| PDB 1831<br>MR2/120, MR3/95<br>J1/1831<br>PMR 1830-9 | Box lids | P1/17/x3<br>***#5215-7***<br> | **John PARSONAGE**<br>Richmond Row (1841)<br>Liverpool or | Watch and watchcase maker |
| GTD 1880<br>PMR 1861-71<br>Not in SPB or LPB so struck1860-3 | See also P&R for Plumb & Rigby | P3/P/x3<br>***#5218-20***<br>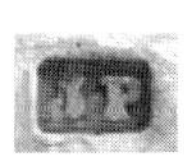 | **John PLUMB**<br>48 Prospect Street (1861)<br>27 Plan Street (1871)<br>Liverpool or | Watch and watchcase maker |
| GTD 1825-*c.*1890 | | | **Joseph PENLINGTON**<br>39 Church Street (1828-34)<br>3 St George's Crescent (1848-79)<br>Liverpool | Watch manufacturer |
| LPB/68<br>20 December 1882 | | P3/P/x3<br>***#5221-3***<br> | **John POSTONS**<br>58 Northampton Street<br>Birmingham | Chain maker |

| REGISTRATION DETAILS | MAKER'S PRIVATE ADDRESS and DETAILS | PLATE and MARK DETAILS | MAKER/COMPANY and BUSINESS ADDRESS | MAKER'S TRADE |
|---|---|---|---|---|
| R1/65<br>22 April 1898<br>Sent by Adelman & Broadhead | Higher House<br>Lastock Park<br>Bradford | P5/Q*sic*/951<br>***#5224***<br> | **James PRESTON**<br>36 Bradshaw Gate<br>Bolton | Jeweller |
| R2/18<br>16 May 1906<br>Sent by J Adelman | Hazlehurst<br>Green Lane<br>Bolton<br>Fairfield<br>Heston<br>Bolton | P9/Q*sic*/251<br>***#5225***<br> | **Robert J TYSON** (Executor)<br>**Edward HOPE** (Executor)<br>trading as **James PRESTON**<br>2 Deansgate<br>Bolton | Jewellers, etc |
| R3/154<br>10 December 1954<br>Sent by selves<br>Two sizes | 135 Queen Street<br>Crewe | P21/P/61,62<br>***#5226,7***<br> | **Josef PRONCZUK**<br>**Selina Ann GOSLING** trading as<br>**CHARMS**<br>9 High Street (and from 24 February 1958)<br>265 Edleston Road<br>Crewe, Cheshire | Manufacturing jewellers |
| | Square marked 1786<br>See other J P marks above | P1/22/x1<br>***#5228***<br> | **Unidentified** | |
| R1/137<br>21 November 1900<br>Sent by A W Wilson | 59 Boulton Road<br>Handsworth<br>Birmingham | P9/P/76<br>***#5229***<br> | **John PREEDY**<br>33 Tenby Street<br>Birmingham | Ring maker |
| LGSJ 1825 | | P2/P/x2<br>***#5230,1***<br> | **JONES & PAINTER**<br>44 Church Street<br>Liverpool | Working jewellers |
| R1/172<br>18 July 1902<br>Sent by J Preedy | Anselms Road<br>Handsworth<br>36 Waverley Road<br>Handsworth | P9/Q*sic*/157<br>***#5232***<br> | **John PREEDY**<br>**H WILCOX** trading as<br>**J PREEDY & CO**<br>14 Vyse Street<br>Birmingham | Goldsmiths and silversmiths |
| R2/4<br>11 October 1905<br>Sent by J Preedy | 3 Broughton Road<br>Handsworth<br>Birmingham | P9/Q*sic*/229<br>***#5233***<br> | | Ring makers and diamond mounters |
| R1/111<br>5 September 1899<br>Sent by C Lyster & Son | 211 Regent Street<br>Tottenham Court Road<br>London | P9/P/43<br>***#5234***<br> | **John POUND**<br>**John Lulham POUND**<br>**Percy Herbert POUND** trading as<br>**John POUND & CO** *<br>81 Leadenhall Street<br>6 Piccadilly<br>378 Strand<br>London | Silversmiths and cutlers |
| LPB/42<br>2 March 1883 | | P3/H/x1<br>***#5235***<br> | **John Price HUNT**<br>25 Warstone Lane<br>Birmingham | Manufacturing jeweller |
| R3/115<br>16 July 1946<br>Sent by J P McGeoch<br>Two sizes | Private address same as business | P21/M/16,17<br>***#5236,7***<br> | **James Paul MACGEOCH**<br>The Cottage<br>Stockham<br>Near Runcorn<br>Cheshire (moved 1 February 1952 to)<br>Mona Lodge<br>Ramsey<br>Isle of Man | Private silver worker |
| R2/184<br>18 February 1914<br>Sent by Ginder & Couch | 23 Polworth Gardens<br>Edinburgh | P15/P/60<br>***#5238***<br> | **James PATERSON**<br>John Paterson (Sole Partner)<br>17 St Giles Street<br>Edinburgh | Wholesale jewellers |

| REGISTRATION DETAILS | MAKER'S PRIVATE ADDRESS and DETAILS | PLATE and MARK DETAILS | MAKER/COMPANY and BUSINESS ADDRESS | MAKER'S TRADE |
|---|---|---|---|---|
| R2/185<br>18 March 1914<br>Sent by Richard Nevill | 16 Nettlecombe Avenue<br>Southsea | P13/Q*sic*/216<br>***#5239***<br> | **Cyril Robarts PURSER** trading as<br>**John PURSER & SONS** *<br>181 Commercial Road<br>Portsmouth<br>18 Wine Street<br>Bristol<br>25 High Street<br>Newport<br>2 Queen Street<br>Cardiff<br>263 Oxford Street<br>Swansea | Jewellers |
| R3/31<br>22 December 1925<br>Sent by T J Skelton<br>84 Vyse Street<br>Birmingham | 1 Greenwich Road<br>Cardiff | P15/P/196-198<br>***#5240-2***<br> | **William Watson PAIRMAN** trading as<br>**John PAIRMAN & SONS**<br>1 St John's Square<br>Cardiff<br>263 Oxford Road<br>Swansea<br>35 Castle Street<br>Bristol | Jewellers |
| R3/63<br>2 July 1932<br>Sent by S Blanckensee<br>& Sons Ltd<br>63 Albion Street<br>Birmingham | | P15/P/235<br>***#5243***<br>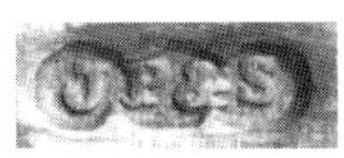 | | |
| LPB/64<br>4 May 1882 | | P3/P/x3<br>***#5244-6***<br>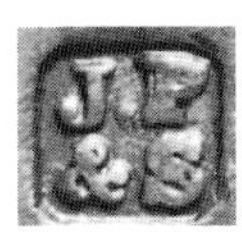 | **Joel PHILLIPS & SON**<br>3 Bury Street<br>St Mary's Axe<br>London | Watchmakers |
| R3/58<br>24 August 1931<br>Sent by<br>P F Jackson Ltd<br>35 Frederick Street<br>Birmingham | | P15/P/232<br>***#5247***<br> | **John PURSER & SONS LTD** *<br>Common seal of company affixed in the presence of<br>R E Pickett (Managing Director)<br>L A Vernon (Secretary)<br>181 Commercial Road (Registered Office)<br>Portsmouth | Goldsmiths and silversmiths |
| R3/65<br>27 February 1933<br>Sent by T J Skelton<br>86 Vyse Street<br>Birmingham | Brantwood [1]<br>St Helen's Parade<br>Southsea | P15/P/236<br>***#5248***<br> | **John PURSER & SONS LTD** *<br>R E Pickett (Director)<br>Mrs D Pickett wife of above (Director)<br>Miss G Pickett [1] (Director)<br>181 Commercial Road<br>Portsmouth | |
| R3/82<br>6 March 1936<br>Sent by S Blanckensee<br>& Sons Ltd<br>19-35 Regent Place<br>Birmingham<br>Two sizes | | P15/P/241-244<br>***#5249-52***<br> | **John PURSER & SONS LTD** *<br>R E Pickett (Managing Director)<br>181 Commercial Road<br>Portsmouth | |
| R3/135<br>17 May 1951<br>Sent by J P Wheldon | 58 Leigh Logie Camp<br>Crimond<br>Lonmay<br>Aberdeenshire | P21/W/59<br>***#5253***<br> | **John Potter WHELDON**<br>Crimond School<br>Lonmay<br>Aberdeenshire and | Educational |
| 20 May 1952 | (moved 6 July 1954 to) Darnall<br>Skendleby<br>nr Spilsby, Lincolnshire | P21/W/62<br>***#5254***<br>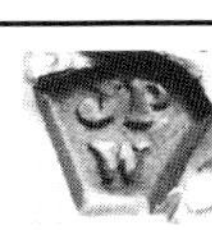 | Invercaldy School<br>by Fraserburgh<br>Aberdeenshire | |

| REGISTRATION DETAILS | MAKER'S PRIVATE ADDRESS and DETAILS | PLATE and MARK DETAILS | MAKER/COMPANY and BUSINESS ADDRESS | MAKER'S TRADE |
|---|---|---|---|---|
| Missing register<br>*c.*1890 | See other JR marks | P5/R/326<br>***#5255***<br> | **Unidentified** | |
| SPB/15<br>20 August 1867<br>Sent by J Fleckner | | P3/R/x3<br>***#5256-8***<br> | **Joseph ROBINSON**<br>7 House Court<br>The Butts<br>Coventry | Watchmaker |
| Missing register<br>*c.*1891<br>Similar mark LAO<br>10 November 1880 | | P5/R/373<br>***#5259***<br> | **John ROTHERHAM & SONS** *<br>27 Spon Street<br>Coventry | Watch and watchcase manufacturers |
| R3/130<br>6 January 1950<br>Sent by J Randle | Private address same as business | P21/R/8<br>***#5260***<br> | **James RANDLE**<br>182 Berkeley Road<br>East Hay Mills<br>Birmingham 25 | Manufacturing jeweller |
| Missing register<br>*c.*1887<br>Similar mark BAO<br>20 September 1890 | Similar mark entered LAO<br>7 March 1881 | P5/R/94<br>***#5261***<br>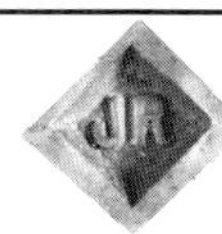 | **ROTHERHAM & SONS** *<br>Spon Street<br>Coventry | Watch and watchcase manufacturers |
| R1/184<br>5 February 1903<br>Sent by Joshua Richards | 16 Sycamore Road<br>Handsworth<br>Birmingham | P9/R/54<br>***#5262***<br> | **Joshua RICHARDS**<br>Export Work<br>New Spring Street<br>Birmingham | Manufacturing jeweller |
| LPB/72<br>24 April 1882 | Kelly 1880 has address at 2A Charing Cross, Birkenhead – General Agent for Waltham Watch Company of USA | P3/R/x3<br>***#5263-5***<br> | **James ROBERTS** *<br>2A Oxton Road and<br>3 Regent Place<br>Liverpool | Watch manufacturer |
| R2/35<br>21 March 1907<br>Sent by Joseph Ridge | 30 Oakholm Road<br>Sheffield | P9/R/82<br>***#5266***<br> | **Joseph RIDGE** trading as<br>**John ROUND & SON LTD** *<br>Tudor Works<br>Sheffield | Silversmiths |
| R2/36<br>26 March 1907 | | P9/R/86,87<br>***#5267,8***<br> | | |
| R2/35<br>21 March 1907<br>Sent by Joseph Ridge | | P9/R/83<br>***#5269***<br>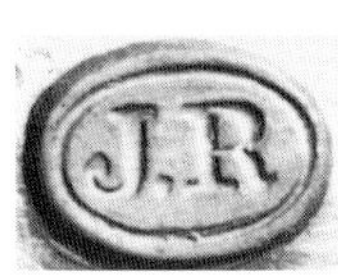 | | |
| R2/36<br>26 March 1907 | | P9/R/84,85<br>***#5270,1***<br> | | |
| R2/42<br>4 July 1907 | | P9/R/93<br>***#5272***<br> | | |

| REGISTRATION DETAILS | MAKER'S PRIVATE ADDRESS and DETAILS | PLATE and MARK DETAILS | MAKER/COMPANY and BUSINESS ADDRESS | MAKER'S TRADE |
|---|---|---|---|---|
| R2/63<br>29 July 1908<br>Sent by Joseph Ridge<br>Two sizes | 35 Thornsitt Road<br>Sheffield | P13/R/2-6<br>***#5273-7***  | **Joseph RIDGE** *<br>Tudor Works<br>Sheffield | Silversmith |
| SPB/9 undated - November 1865 to February 1866<br>GSJW/138<br>Sent by<br>Samuel & Rogers<br>72 Wood Street<br>Liverpool | | P3/R/x1<br>***#5278***  | **Joseph ROSENTHAL**<br>58 Swan Street<br>Manchester | Silversmith and jeweller |
| LPB/7<br>4 March 1879 | | P3/V*sic*/x2<br>***#5279,80***  | **James ROOKER**<br>148 Warstone Lane<br>Birmingham | Gold and silver chain maker and jeweller |
| Missing register<br>*c.*1891 | See other JR marks | P5/R/351<br>***#5281***  | **Unidentified** | |
| R1/29<br>19 May 1896<br>Sent by Stainsby & Coupland | Private address same as business | P5/R/768<br>***#5282***  | **John ROSS**<br>47 Colebrook Row<br>Islington<br>London | Purse and pocket book maker |
| R1/86<br>30 November 1898<br>Sent by James Rooker | Private address same as business | P9/R/3,4<br>***#5283,4***  | **James ROOKER**<br>148 Warstone Lane<br>Birmingham | Gold and silver chain maker and jeweller |
| SPB/17<br>8 July 1875<br>Sent by J Sharpe | | P3/R/x1<br>***#5285***  | **James RICHARDSON** *<br>Percy House<br>Holyhead Road<br>Coventry | Watch and watchcase manufacturer |
| SPB/6<br>2 October 1876 | | P3/R/x1<br>***#5286***  | | |
| Missing register<br>*c.*1886 | See other JR marks | P5/R/49<br>***#5287***  | **Unidentified** | |
| Missing register<br>*c.*1886 | See other JR marks | P5/R/64<br>***#5288***  | **Unidentified** | |
| Missing register<br>*c.*1889 | See other JR marks | P5/R/256<br>***#5289*** 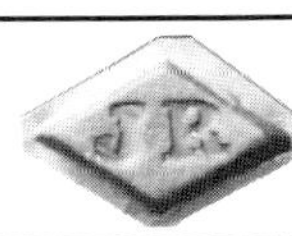 | **Unidentified** | |
| SPB/9 undated November 1865 to February 1866<br>Sent by Samuel & Rogers | CWMP 1874 | P3/R/x2<br>***#5290,1***  | **Joseph RADGES**<br>14 The Butts<br>Coventry | Watch manufacturer |
| R2/45<br>28 August 1907<br>Sent by James Francis Richardson | 536 Stoney Stanton Road<br>Coventry | P9/R/100<br>***#5292***  | **James Francis RICHARDSON** *<br>127 Spon Street<br>Coventry | Gold watchcase manufacturer |
| R2/63<br>30 July 1908<br>Sent by E Vaughton | 208 Analley Road<br>Hull | P13/R/7–12<br>***#5293-8***  | **Joseph ROSENTHAL**<br>1, 2 Anne Street<br>Hull and<br>128 Market Street<br>Johannesburg | Jeweller and silversmith |

| REGISTRATION DETAILS | MAKER'S PRIVATE ADDRESS and DETAILS | PLATE and MARK DETAILS | MAKER/COMPANY and BUSINESS ADDRESS | MAKER'S TRADE |
|---|---|---|---|---|
| R2/64<br>5 September 1908<br>Sent by E Vaughton | 208 Analley Road<br>Hull | P13/R/13–18<br>***#5299-5304***<br> | **Joseph ROSENTHAL**<br>1, 2 Anne Street<br>Hull | Jeweller and silversmith |
| R2/149<br>19 December 1911<br>Punch was entered especially for ladies' silver bags | James Charles Jay<br>Oak House<br>Ganwick<br>Barnet N | P13/A/37<br>***#5305***<br> | **JAY RICHARD ATTENBOROUGH & CO LTD** *<br>142, 144 Oxford Street<br>London W | Silversmiths |
| Missing register<br>*c.*1891 | See other JR&Bs marks | P5/R/388<br>***#5306***<br> | **Unidentified** | |
| R2/2<br>16 September 1905<br>Sent by R Chandler<br>Two sizes | Oak House<br>Ganwick<br>Barnet N | P9/A/62-73<br>***#5307-18***<br> | **JAY RICHARD ATTENBOROUGH & CO LTD** *<br>James Charles Jay (Director?)<br>142/144 Oxford Street<br>London W | Silversmiths |
| R2/26<br>16 October 1906<br>Sent by Barker Brothers<br>Four sizes | | P9/A/80-83<br>***#5319-22***<br> | **James Charles JAY** trading as<br>**JAY, RICHARD ATTENBOROUGH & CO LTD** *<br>details as above | |
| R3/73<br>21 December 1934<br>Sent by W J Dingley<br>77 Warstone Lane<br>Birmingham | | P15/J/40<br>***#5323***<br> | **JAY RICHARD ATTENBOROUGH & CO LTD** *<br>Common seal of company affixed in the presence of:-<br>Walter W Scott (Director)<br>D W Scott (Director)<br>Arthur C C Sinclair (Director)<br>142/144 Oxford Street (Registered Office)<br>London W1 | Goldsmiths and silversmiths |
| R3/4<br>11 August 1921<br>Sent by Jay Richard Attenborough & Co Ltd | 37 Imperial Avenue<br>Westcliff-on-Sea | P15/J/25<br>***#5324***<br> | **JAY RICHARD ATTENBOROUGH & CO LTD** *<br>142, 144 Oxford Street<br>London W1 | Jewellers and silversmiths |
| R3/23<br>20 September 1924<br>Sent by Vale & Simmons | Oak House<br>Ganwick<br>Barnett N<br>Powis Court, Potters Bar<br>Highlands, Imperial Ave<br>Westcliff<br>Arlington, Cannon Hill<br>Old Southgate | P15/A/44<br>***#5325***<br> | **JAY RICHARD ATTENBOROUGH & CO LTD** *<br>James Charles Jay (Director)<br>Walter William Scott (Director)<br>Horace Alexander Miles (Secretary)<br>Stephen Grounds<br>142–144 Oxford Street<br>London W1 | Jewellers, silversmiths and watchmakers |
| R3/44<br>2 October 1928<br>Sent by H Clifford Davis | Oak House [1]<br>Ganwick, Barnett N<br>Powis Court, [2] Potters Bar<br>Highlands, Imperial Ave,<br>Westcliff<br>Arlington, [3] Cannon Hill<br>Old Southgate | P15/A/50<br>***#5326***<br>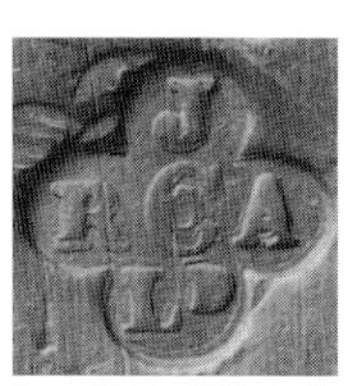 | **JAY RICHARD ATTENBOROUGH & CO LTD** *<br>James Charles Jay [1] (Director)<br>Walter William Scott [2] (Director)<br>Stephen Grounds [3] (Director)<br>142–144 Oxford Street<br>London W1 | Goldsmiths and silversmiths |

| REGISTRATION DETAILS | MAKER'S PRIVATE ADDRESS and DETAILS | PLATE and MARK DETAILS | MAKER/COMPANY and BUSINESS ADDRESS | MAKER'S TRADE |
|---|---|---|---|---|
| R2/164<br>26 October 1912<br>Sent by self | Private address same as business | P13/D/56<br>***#5327***<br> | **John Richard DAVIES**<br>3 Waverley Terrace<br>Newton<br>Chester | No trade entered<br><br>Jeweller? |
| R2/19<br>29 May 1906<br>Sent by Robert J Fleming | 57 Loveday Road<br>Ealing<br>Middlesex | P9/F/27<br>***#5328***<br> | **John FLEMING**<br>**Robert James FLEMING** trading as<br>**J & R FLEMING**<br>52 Grays Inn Road<br>London WC | Wholesale opticians |
| R1/154<br>1 October 1901<br>Sent by J & R Griffin | Nordene [1]<br>Radnor Road, Handsworth<br>Glenholme [2]<br>Wyecliff Road, Handsworth<br>Birmingham | P9/G/29<br>***#5329***<br>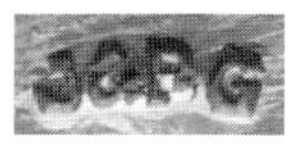 | **Joseph James GRIFFIN** [1]<br>**Richard Charles GRIFFIN** [2]<br>28 Hylton Street<br>Birmingham | Manufacturing jewellers |
| R2/170<br>11 April 1913<br>Sent by J & R Griffin Ltd | Nordene<br>Radnor Road<br>Handsworth | P13/G/51-54<br>***#5330-3***<br> | **J & R GRIFFIN LTD**<br>Joseph J Griffin (Director)<br>Link Works<br>Soho Hill<br>Birmingham | Silversmiths |
| R1/14<br>30 July 1895<br>Sent by J J Griffin | 94 Albert Road [1]<br>Aston<br>21 Salisbury Road [2]<br>Birchfields<br>Birmingham | P5/G/679<br>***#5334***<br> | **Joseph James GRIFFIN** [1]<br>**Richard Charles GRIFFIN** [2] trading as<br>**J & R GRIFFIN**<br>28 Hylton Street<br>Birmingham | Manufacturing jewellers |
| R2/170<br>23 June 1914 | | P15/G/19<br>***#5335***<br> | **J & R GRIFFIN LTD**<br>Joseph J Griffin (Director)<br>Link Works<br>Soho Hill<br>Birmingham | Silversmiths |
| 7 July 1914 | Ceased business 1926 – voluntary liquidation | P15/G/20-22<br>***#5336-8***<br> | **J & R GRIFFIN LTD**<br>Joseph J Griffin (Director)<br>Link Works<br>Soho Hill<br>Birmingham | |
| R1/228<br>1 March 1905<br>Sent by J J Griffin | | P9/G/58<br>***#5339***<br> | **J & R GRIFFIN**<br>Joseph James Griffin (Director)<br>105 Hockley Street<br>Birmingham | Manufacturing jewellers |
| R1/231<br>13 April 1905<br>Sent by J & R Griffin | Nordene<br>Radnor Road<br>Handsworth | P9/G/59-61<br>***#5340-2***<br> | | |
| R2/3<br>5 October 1905<br>Sent by Joseph J Griffin | | P9/G/62<br>***#5343***<br> | **J & R GRIFFIN**<br>Joseph J Griffin<br>105, 109 Hockley Street<br>Birmingham | Jewellers |
| Not in R2 as expected<br>*c.*1913 | | P13/G/55-57<br>***#5344-6***<br><br>§ | | |
| R3/80<br>24 October 1935<br>Sent by J R Talbot | | P15/T/79<br>***#5347***<br> | **J R TALBOT LTD**<br>J R Talbot (Director)<br>M Linday (Secretary)<br>36 Northampton Street (Reg'd Office)<br>Birmingham | Manufacturing jewellers |

| REGISTRATION DETAILS | MAKER'S PRIVATE ADDRESS and DETAILS | PLATE and MARK DETAILS | MAKER/COMPANY and BUSINESS ADDRESS | MAKER'S TRADE |
|---|---|---|---|---|
| R3/168<br>10 June 1959<br>Sent by J R Yorke-Radleigh | Private address same as business | P21/R/32<br>***#5348***  | **James Richard YORKE-RADLEIGH**<br>H M Inspector of Education<br>99 Belgrave Road<br>London SW1 | Amateur silversmith |
| R1/39<br>11 February 1897<br>Sent by<br>W H Carrington | Private address same as business | P5/O/*sic*/815<br>***#5349***  | **John STONE**<br>60 Cheetham Hill Road<br>Manchester | Tobacconist |
| R3/117<br>16 April 1947<br>Sent by J Simpson | 68 Streetley Road<br>Erdington<br>Birmingham 23 | P21/S/25,26<br>***#5350,1***  | **John SIMPSON**<br>5 Warstone Parade East<br>Birmingham | Silversmith |
| Not in R1 as expected - mark P5/S/763 entered 30 April 1896 | See James Swann & Joseph Sewill | P5/S/764<br>***#5352***  | **Unidentified** | |
| SPB/19<br>28 January 1869<br>Similar mark entered LAO 30 April 1872 | Sent by H Mansell | P3/S/x3<br>***#5353-5***  | **Joseph SEWILL**<br>35 South Castle Street<br>Liverpool | Watch manufacturer |
| CWMP 1874-83<br>Similar mark entered LAO 21 June 1869 | Could also be J Stuart, see below | P3/S/x3<br>***#5356-8***  | **Joseph SHARPE ***<br>39 Mount Street (1869)<br>Sovereign Place (1859)<br>The Butts<br>Coventry | Watchcase maker |
| R3/88<br>29 August 1956<br>Sent by Joseph Smith & Sons (Birmingham) Ltd | | P21/S/66<br>***#5359***  | **Joseph SMITH & SONS (BIRMINGHAM) LTD**<br>Common seal of company affixed in the presence of:-<br>S P Smith (Director)<br>B Payton-Smith (Secretary)<br>39-41 Vittoria Street<br>Birmingham | Manufacturing jewellers |
| LPB/62<br>1 March 1883 | | P3/S/x2<br>***#5360,1***  | **John SKINNER**<br>4 Northampton Street<br>Birmingham | Jeweller |
| Missing register<br>*c.*1890<br>Similar mark entered LAO 31 October 1879 | | P5/S/274<br>***#5362*** 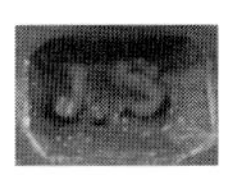 | **Joseph SEWILL**<br>35 South Castle Street<br>Liverpool | Watch and watchcase manufacturer |
| Missing register<br>*c.*1886 | Star motif might indicate cog-wheels and a watch manufacturer such as Sewill | P5/S/54<br>***#5363***  | | |
| R1/163<br>12 March 1902<br>Sent by J Swan | 39 John Street<br>Lozells<br>Birmingham | P9/S/43<br>***#5364***  | **James SWAN**<br>32 Northampton Street<br>Birmingham | Silversmith |
| R3/49<br>21 October 1929<br>Sent by J Smithies | Private address same as business | P15/S/91<br>***#5365***  | **James SMITHIES**<br>Manchester Road<br>Wilmslow<br>Cheshire | Metal craftsman |
| LPB/42<br>2 November 1882 | | P3/S/x1<br>***#5366***  | **JEFFRIES & SMITH**<br>43 Hockley Street<br>Birmingham | Jewellers |

| REGISTRATION DETAILS | MAKER'S PRIVATE ADDRESS and DETAILS | PLATE and MARK DETAILS | MAKER/COMPANY and BUSINESS ADDRESS | MAKER'S TRADE |
|---|---|---|---|---|
| R1/200<br>8 September 1903<br>Sent by J Adelman | Hambro House<br>Mayfield Road<br>Whalley Range<br>48 Bishop Street<br>Moss Side<br>Manchester | P9/J/37<br>***#5367***<br> | **Hugh Edward JONES**<br>**James Frederick STUBBS**<br>trading as **JONES & STUBBS**<br>28 Shudehill<br>Manchester | Wholesale jewellers |
| PP1/182<br>GTD 1834-80<br>Not in SPB or LPB so struck 1860-3<br>Similar mark LAO<br>29 December 1859 | | P2/V*sic*/x3<br>***#5368-70***<br> | **Joseph SHARPE**<br>39 Mount Street (1869)<br>Sovereign Place (1859)<br>11 Mount Street (1874)<br>Holyhead Road (1883)<br>The Butts<br>Coventry | Watchcase maker |
| | May also be J Stuart trading as H Stuart & Co of 13 Hope Street, Liverpool | P2/S/x2<br>***#5371,2***<br> | | |
| Not in SPB or LPB so struck 1860-3<br>Similar mark LAO<br>26 August 1862 | | P3/S/x3<br>***#5373-5***<br>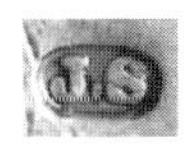 | **Joseph SEWILL** *<br>61 South Castle Street<br>Liverpool | Watchcase maker |
| SPB/5<br>27 January 1865 | See also H S | P3/Sx3<br>***#5376-8***<br> | **John STUART** trading as<br>**H STUART & CO** *<br>13 Hope Street<br>Liverpool | Watchcase makers |
| SPB/2<br>29 December 1870<br>Similar mark entered LAO 21 March 1863 | Mark struck on paper not the lead sheet | P3/Sx3<br>***#5379-81***<br> | **Joseph SHARPE** *<br>39 Mount Street<br>Coventry | Watchcase maker |
| R1/45<br>28 May 1897<br>Sent by W H Ashford | 22 Carpenter Road<br>Edgbaston<br>Birmingham | P5/S/845<br>***#5382***<br> | **John SILVERSTON**<br>18 Summer Hill Terrace<br>Birmingham | Wholesale jeweller |
| R1/234<br>6 June 1905<br>Sent by A J Cheshire | 10 Rotten Park Road<br>Edgbaston | P9/S/88<br>***#5383***<br> | **John SILVERSTON**<br>43 Frederick Street<br>Birmingham | Wholesale jeweller |
| R3/88<br>16 August 1937<br>Sent by Joseph Smith & Sons (Birmingham) Ltd | | P21/S/4<br>***#5384***<br>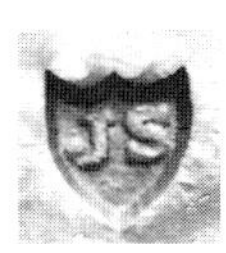 | **Joseph SMITH & SONS (BIRMINGHAM) LTD**<br>Common seal of company affixed in the presence of:-<br>S P Smith (Director)<br>B Payton-Smith (Secretary)<br>39-41 Vittoria Street<br>Birmingham | Manufacturing jewellers |
| 28 March 1941 | | P21/S/11<br>***#5385***<br>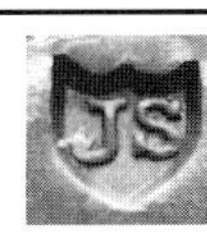 | | |
| 12 May 1943 | | P21/S/15<br>***#5386***<br>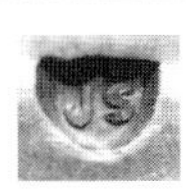 | | |
| 12 October 1946 | | P21/S/24<br>***#5387***<br> | | |
| 25 October 1947 | | P21/S/28<br>***#5388***<br>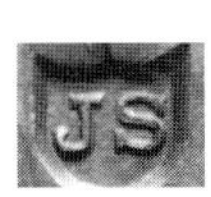 | | |

| REGISTRATION DETAILS | MAKER'S PRIVATE ADDRESS and DETAILS | PLATE and MARK DETAILS | MAKER/COMPANY and BUSINESS ADDRESS | MAKER'S TRADE |
|---|---|---|---|---|
| R2/68<br>12 November 1908<br>Sent by Joseph Smith & Sons | 27 Churchill Road<br>Handsworth<br>Birmingham | P13/S/12<br>***#5389***<br>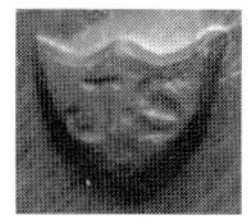 | **Joseph SMITH & SONS LTD**<br>C P Smith (Director)<br>S P Smith (Director)<br>63 Vittoria Street<br>Birmingham | Manufacturing jewellers |
| PDB 1835-40<br>MR2/193 —<br>MR3/97<br>SOT/120-1<br>SIL/52,53,54<br>GMSC/81,82 | Flatware<br>First registered at Newcastle in 1832 | P1/7/x5<br>***#5390-4***<br>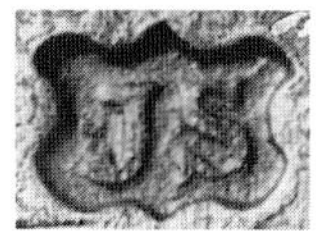 | **John SUTTER**<br>29 Standish Street (1839)<br>8 Fleet Street (1843)<br>12 Williamson Street (1857-60)<br>College Lane (1868-74)<br>Liverpool | Silversmith |
| R1/111<br>5 September 1899<br>Sent by John G Slide | 5 Poplar Avenue<br>Edgbaston<br>Birmingham | P9/S/25<br>***#5395***<br> | **John George SLIDE**<br>16 Frederick Street<br>Birmingham | Manufacturing jeweller |
| R2/121<br>27 October 1910<br>Sent by J G Slide | 49 Poplar Avenue<br>Edgbaston<br>Birmingham | P13/S/59<br>***#5396***<br> | **John George SLIDE**<br>18 Albion Street<br>Birmingham | Ring maker |
| R3/138<br>17 May 1952<br>Sent by J Sudlow | 2 Edmund Street<br>Failsworth<br>Lancashire | P21/S/49,50<br>***#5397,8***<br> | **John SUDLOW**<br>No business address entered | Student silversmith |
| R2/50<br>19 November 1907<br>Sent by John Smith | 52 City Road<br>Edgbaston | P13/S/4<br>***#5399***<br> | **John SMITH**<br>8 Tenby Street<br>Birmingham | Medal, lockets and pendant makers |
| R3/31<br>1 December 1925<br>Sent by Jessie Sidebotham<br>Two sizes | Private address same as business | P15/S/69-72<br>***#5400-3***<br>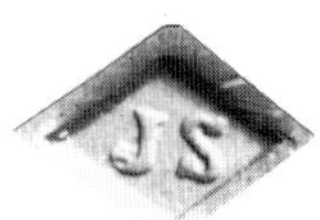 | **Jessie SIDEBOTHAM**<br>41 Devonshire Road<br>Heaton Moor<br>Stockport | Craftworker in gold and silver |
| LPB/28<br>30 June 1883<br>Sent by S Usher | Allen & Martin, jewellers, at this address in 1882 PO directory | P3/S/x1<br>***#5404***<br> | **J SEYWORTH**<br>70 Great Hampton Street<br>Birmingham | Jeweller ? |
| LPB/28<br>19 June 1883 | | P3/I*sic*/x2<br>***#5405,6***<br> | | |
| LPB/76<br>9 December 1879 | See HGS | P3/W*sic*/x2<br>***#5407,8***<br> | **John SPIERS & CO** *<br>Warstone Lane<br>Birmingham | Manufacturing jewellers |
| R1/59<br>27 January 1898<br>Sent by J Haywood | 24 Westfield Road<br>Edgbaston<br>Birmingham | P5/Y*sic*/924<br>***#5409***<br> | **John SPIERS Isaac SPIERS** trading as **John SPIERS & CO** *<br>117 Vyse Street<br>Birmingham | Manufacturing jewellers and mounters |
| R2/177<br>22 October 1913<br>Sent by John G Slide | 17 Melville Road<br>Edgbaston<br>Oakleigh<br>West Bromwich | P13/S/114<br>***#5410***<br> | **John George SLIDE**<br>**Gordon W FIELD** trading as<br>**John G SLIDE & CO**<br>18 Albion Street<br>Birmingham | Manufacturing jewellers |
| R1/172<br>16 July 1902<br>Sent by J H Wynn | Gravelly Hill<br>Erdington<br>Birmingham | P9/S/48<br>***#5411***<br> | **John SATCHWELL & CO LTD**<br>1 Station Street<br>Birmingham | Jewellers and fancy goods dealers |
| R1/150<br>9 July 1901<br>Sent by W J Myatt & Co<br>Four sizes | 16 Weatheroak Road<br>Spark Hill | P9/P/100-103<br>***#5412-5***<br> | **John S PULLINGER**<br>28 Horse Fair<br>Birmingham | Factor |

| REGISTRATION DETAILS | MAKER'S PRIVATE ADDRESS and DETAILS | PLATE and MARK DETAILS | MAKER/COMPANY and BUSINESS ADDRESS | MAKER'S TRADE |
|---|---|---|---|---|
| R1/97<br>20 April 1899<br>Sent by J Sherwood & Sons<br><br>Two sizes | 1 Eastbourne House<br>Lichfield Road<br>Sutton Coldfield<br><br>27 Handsworth Wood Road<br>Handsworth<br>3 Ivanhoe Rectory Road<br>Sutton Coldfield<br>Birmingham | P9/S/15<br>***#5416*** <br>P9/S/13,14<br>***#5417,8***  | **William SHERWOOD**<br>**George SHERWOOD**<br>**Wilfred SHERWOOD** trading as<br>**John SHERWOOD & SONS** *<br>Regent Works<br>Regent Street<br>Birmingham | Silversmiths |
| Missing register<br>*c.*1890<br>Similar mark LAO<br>19 September 1892 | Worked for Rotherham & Son for 12½ years | P5/W/317a<br>***#5419***  | **Joseph Samuel WILDAY** *<br>2 St Thomas' Villas<br>Butts<br>Coventry | Watchcase maker |
| Missing register<br>*c.*1890 | | P5/W/316<br>***#5420***  | | |
| Missing register<br>*c.*1887<br>Similar mark entered LAO 10 May 1889 | | P5/W/131<br>***#5421***  | | |
| Missing register<br>*c.*1890<br>Similar mark entered LAO 1 October 1894 | | P5/W/317b<br>***#5422***  | | |
| SPB/8<br>5 May 1875<br>Sent by H Green | 59 Percival Street<br>Liverpool | P3/T/x1<br>***#5423***  | **James TAYLOR**<br>4 Gill Street<br>Liverpool | Watchmaker |
| SPB/6<br>21 July 1876<br>Sent by J LeComber | 121 Derby Road<br>Bootle<br>Lancs | P3/T/x1<br>***#5424***  | | |
| R3/169<br>22 September 1959<br>Sent by J Twiss<br>Two sizes | 1 Heyes Terrace<br>Old Heyes Road<br>Timperley<br>Altrincham, Cheshire | P21/T/38,39<br>***#5425,6*** 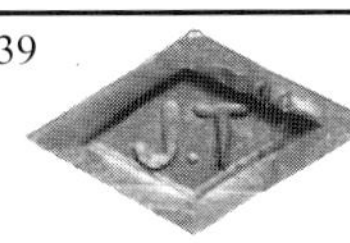 | **Joan TWISS**<br>No business address entered | Student silversmith |
| SPB/11<br>8 February 1866<br>Two sizes | | P3/T/x2<br>***#5427,8***  | **John Gaskins TAYTON & SONS** *<br>17 Trafalgar Street<br>Coventry | Watchcase makers |
| LPB/80<br>31 July 1880 | | P3/T/x1<br>***#5429*** 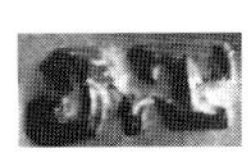 | **Joseph TOWNS**<br>169 Gosford Street<br>Coventry | Agent |
| R2/140<br>22 July 1911<br>Sent by Joseph Taylor | 57 Albert Road<br>Handsworth<br>Birmingham | P13/T/40<br>***#5430***  | **Joseph TAYLOR**<br>York Terrace<br>13½ Hockley Hill<br>Birmingham | Pipe mounter |
| PDB 1825<br>MR3/98 | Gold rings<br>This small mark may indicate use for rings<br>See also IT | P1/25/x2<br>***#5431,2***  | **John TAYLOR**<br>Chester or | Goldsmith |
| PDB 1814-33<br>MR2/194<br>MR3/99<br>SIL/52<br>GMSC/66 | Gold rings and silverware | P1/29/x2<br>***#5433,4***  | **John TWEMLOW**<br>Boughton<br>Chester | Goldsmith and silversmith |

| REGISTRATION DETAILS | MAKER'S PRIVATE ADDRESS and DETAILS | PLATE and MARK DETAILS | MAKER/COMPANY and BUSINESS ADDRESS | MAKER'S TRADE |
|---|---|---|---|---|
| LPB/80<br>24 September 1878 | See his other mark in Monograms section<br><br>Late of 30 Augusta Street Birmingham | P3/T/x1<br>*#5435*<br> | **James THORNTON**<br>54 Guest Street<br>Hockley Hill<br>Birmingham | Jeweller |
| LPB/80<br>13 February 1880 | See JTS | P3/T/x3<br>*#5436-8*<br> | **John TROUP & SONS** *<br>36 Hatton Garden<br>London | Watch and clock makers and jewellers |
| LPB/82 SP24/2<br>12 August 1885<br>Sent by F W Cole<br>H Pope<br>No mark in LPB | See JTS | P5/T/x1<br>*#5439*<br> | | |
| R1/113<br>7 October 1899<br>Sent by Villiers & Jackson<br>Hemming & Hazlewood | Wigmore House<br>3 South Tottenham Road<br>London | P9/T/10<br>*#5440*<br> | **Frederick William TROUP** trading as<br>**John TROUP & SONS** *<br>36 Hatton Garden<br>London | Wholesale jewellers and watchmakers |
| R3/22<br>31 May 1924<br>Sent by James T Birchall | 53 Heywood Street<br>Moss Side<br>Manchester | Mark not on P15/B<br>*#5441*<br>**J T B?** | **James Thomas BIRCHALL**<br>83 Heywood Street<br>Moss Side<br>Manchester | Worker in all metals |
| R3/66<br>17 May 1933<br>Sent by J Birchall | Private address same as business | P15/B/212<br>*#5442*<br> | **James Thomas BIRCHALL**<br>13 Waltham Road<br>Alexandra Road S<br>Manchester 16 | Designer and craftsman in metals |
| 18 June 1941<br>Transferred 21 November 1955 to Mary Birchall | | P21/B/13<br>*#5443*<br> | | |
| R3/134<br>21 November 1950<br>Sent by M Birchall<br>Widow's entry? | | No new mark<br>*#5444* | **Mary BIRCHALL** trading as<br>**James Thomas BIRCHALL**<br>20 Central Drive, Long Lane<br>Cheadle<br>Cheshire | Silversmith |
| R2/197<br>9 July 1915<br>Sent by James Thomas Cottrill Punch transferred to J T Cottrill & Sons Ltd<br>11 October 1941 | 23 Rushden Road<br>Levenshulme<br>Manchester | P15/C/46<br>*#5445*<br> | **James Thomas COTTRILL**<br>50, 51 Kilverts Buildings<br>Withy Grove<br>Manchester | Working jeweller and ring maker |
| R3/102<br>11 October 1941<br>Sent by J T Cottrill & Sons Ltd | | P21/C/18<br>*#5446*<br> | **J T COTTRILL & SONS LTD**<br>Sealed in the presence of:-<br>J T Cottrill (Director)<br>E Cottrill (Secretary)<br>Bank Buildings<br>2 Nicholas Croft<br>High Street<br>Manchester 4 | Manufacturing and wholesale jewellers |
| LPB/30<br>27 July 1881 | | P3/F/x1<br>*#5447*<br> | **FREEMAN & CO**<br>59 Northampton Street<br>Birmingham | Jewellers |

| REGISTRATION DETAILS | MAKER'S PRIVATE ADDRESS and DETAILS | PLATE and MARK DETAILS | MAKER/COMPANY and BUSINESS ADDRESS | MAKER'S TRADE |
|---|---|---|---|---|
| Missing register<br>*c*.1886 | | P5/F/52<br>***#5448***  | **FREEMAN & CO**<br>59 Northampton Street<br>Birmingham | Jewellers |
| LPB/58<br>8 March 1883 | | P3/N/x1<br>***#5449***  | **James Thomas NEWMAN** *<br>42 Spencer Street<br>London | Watchcase maker |
| R2/175<br>5 September 1913<br>Sent by J T Pendlebury Ltd | 8 Burford Avenue<br>Manchester<br>19 Oak Road<br>Higher Crumpsall<br>35 Oak Road<br>Higher Crumpsall | P15/P/57<br>***#5450*** 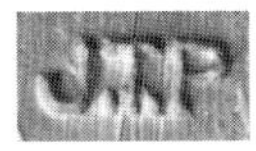 | **James Thomas PENDLEBURY**<br>**Arthur Percy PENDLEBURY**<br>**Jonathan PENDLEBURY** trading as<br>**J T PENDLEBURY LTD**<br>12a Thorniley Brow<br>Dantzic Street<br>Manchester | Manufacturing jewellers and watchcase makers |
| Missing register<br>*c*.1894 Similar mark<br>CAO 11 October 1905 | | P5/P/549<br>***#5451***  | **James Thomas PENDLEBURY**<br>12a Thorniley Brow<br>Manchester | Manufacturing jewellers and gold case makers |
| R2/3<br>11 October 1905<br>Sent by James T Pendlebury | 28 Delauneys Road<br>Crumpsall<br>Manchester | P9/Q*sic*/228<br>***#5452***  | | |
| R2/28<br>5 November 1906<br>Sent by J T Pendlebury | 17 Woodlands Road<br>Cheetham Hill<br>Manchester | P9/U*sic*/268<br>***#5453***  | | Manufacturing and wholesale jeweller |
| Missing register<br>*c*.1889 | | P5/P/232<br>***#5454***  | | |
| R2/178<br>25 October 1913<br>Sent by J T Pendlebury Ltd | 8 Burford Avenue<br>Manchester<br>19 Oak Road<br>Higher Crumpsall<br>35 Oak Road<br>Higher Crumpsall | P15/P/58<br>***#5455***  | **James Thomas PENDLEBURY**<br>**Arthur Percy PENDLEBURY**<br>**Jonathan PENDLEBURY** trading as<br>**J T PENDLEBURY LTD**<br>12a Thorniby Brow<br>Dantzic Street<br>Manchester | Manufacturing jewellers and watchcase makers |
| R1/46<br>12 June 1897<br>Sent by R Parker | Wigmore House<br>South Tottenham Road<br>London | P5/T/847<br>***#5456***  | **John TROUP & SONS** *<br>36 Hatton Garden<br>London | Watch and clockmakers and jewellers |
| Missing register<br>*c*.1887 | | P5/T/72<br>***#5457***  | | |
| Missing register<br>*c*.1886 | | P5/T/9<br>***#5458***  | | |
| Missing register<br>*c*.1891 | | P5/T/346<br>***#5459***  | | |
| LPB/68<br>4 December 1882<br>No name or address listed | | P3/T/x3<br>***#5460-2***  | | |
| LPB/80<br>16 February 1880 | | P3/T/x1<br>***#5463***  | | |

| REGISTRATION DETAILS | MAKER'S PRIVATE ADDRESS and DETAILS | PLATE and MARK DETAILS | MAKER/COMPANY and BUSINESS ADDRESS | MAKER'S TRADE |
|---|---|---|---|---|
| LPB/80<br>6 May 1881<br>Sent by E Whitehouse | | P3/X*sic*/x1<br>***#5464***  | **John TROUP & SONS** *<br>36 Hatton Garden<br>London | Watch and clockmakers and jewellers |
| Missing register<br>*c.*1891 | | P5/T/333<br>***#5465***  | | |
| R1/212<br>19 April 1904<br>returned via Twine & Gilpin 17 May 1907 to be altered to original | | P9/T/0*sic*<br>between 29 and 30<br>***#5466***  | | |
| R1/209<br>11 March 1904<br>Sent by W E Houlston<br>Two sizes | 3 High Road<br>Tottenham | P9/T/47,48<br>***#5467,8***  | **Frederick William TROUP** trading as **J TROUP & SONS** *<br>36 Hatton Garden<br>London | Manufacturing jewellers |
| R1/212<br>19 April 1904<br>Sent by A E Jenkins | 53 Park Avenue<br>Wood Green<br>98 Claremont Road<br>Forest Gate<br>21 Grange Terrace<br>Wood Green | P9/T/51,52<br>***#5469,70***  | **Henry Graham THOMPSON**<br>**John THOMPSON** (senior ?)<br>**John THOMPSON** (junior ?) trading as **J THOMPSON & SONS** *<br>31 Clerkenwell Road<br>London EC | Jewellers |
| R2/40<br>18 May 1907<br>Sent by Twine & Gilpin<br>Punch returned to be altered – adjacent 62 | 98 Claremont Road<br>Forest Gate<br>Atworth<br>Wood Green | P9/T/0*sic*<br>***#5471***  | **John THOMPSON**<br>**Henry Graham THOMPSON** trading as **J THOMPSON & SON** *<br>31 Clerkenwell Road<br>London EC | |
| R2/40<br>29 May 1907 | | P9/T/62<br>***#5472***  | | |
| R2/80<br>27 April 1909<br>Sent by E Whitehouse & Son | 1 The Avenue<br>Muswell Hill<br>Middlesex | P13/T/10-12<br>***#5473-5***  | | |
| R2/141<br>26 August 1911<br>Sent by C Horner Ltd | | P13/T/47<br>***#5476***  | | |
| R2/143<br>12 September 1911<br>Sent by C Horner | | P13/T/48-50<br>***#5477-9***  | | |
| Missing register<br>*c.*1889<br>Incuse mark in oval cameo entered BAO 9 June 1896 | | P5/T/259<br>***#5480***  | **John TELFER & SONS**<br>33 Clayton Street<br>Newcastle upon Tyne | Tobacco manufacturers, etc |
| SPB/1<br>15 February 1864 | | P3/W/x3<br>***#5481-3***  | **James Thomas WHITE** *<br>1 Northampton Square<br>Clerkenwell<br>London | Watchcase maker |
| R2/173<br>6 June 1913<br>Sent by Barker Brothers | Private address same as business | P15/U/1<br>***#5484***  | **James Ward USHER** trading as **James USHER & SONS**<br>192 High Street<br>Lincoln | Jewellers and silversmiths |

| REGISTRATION DETAILS | MAKER'S PRIVATE ADDRESS and DETAILS | PLATE and MARK DETAILS | MAKER/COMPANY and BUSINESS ADDRESS | MAKER'S TRADE |
|---|---|---|---|---|
| R2/207<br>2 September 1916<br>Sent by Stokes & Ireland | Private address same as business | P15/V/4-6<br>***#5485-7***<br> | **John VINCENT**<br>86 St Mary's Street<br>Weymouth | Silversmith and goldsmith |
| R3/169<br>8 August 1959<br>Sent by J V Robinson<br>Two sizes | Robin Cottage<br>Mill Lane<br>Cuddington<br>Nr Northwich | P21/S*sic*/85,86<br>***#5488,9***<br> | **James Valentine ROBINSON**<br>No business address entered | Amateur silversmith |
| R1/217<br>19 July 1904<br>Sent by J V Horton & Son | 2 Lime Grove<br>Manchester | P9/H/64<br>***#5490***<br> | **J V HORTON** *<br>20 Caroline Street<br>Birmingham | Manufacturing jewellers and ring makers |
| Missing register<br>*c.*1892<br>J1 1862-1900 | Tentative attribution | P5/W/443<br>***#5491***<br> | **John WOOLEY**<br>Chester | Silversmith |
| R3/127<br>3 February 1949<br>Sent by John Walker<br>Three sizes | Private address same as business | P21/W/50-52<br>***#5492-4***<br> | **John WALKER**<br>28 Hurstville Road<br>Chorlton<br>Manchester 21 | Student |
| R3/183<br>10 April 1962<br>Sent by Mrs J Wright | 8 New Springs<br>Smith Hills Dean<br>Bolton<br>Lancashire | P21/W/108<br>***#5495***<br> | **Mrs Joan WRIGHT**<br>No business address entered | Student silversmith |
| R1/40<br>6 March 1897<br>Sent by J White | Private address same as business | P5/W/821<br>***#5496***<br> | **Joseph WHITE**<br>44 Oughton Place<br>Highgate<br>Birmingham | Armourer |
| LGSJ 1825 | See also IW | P1/28/x3<br>***#5497-9***<br> | **James WORDLEY** *<br>69 Lord Street<br>Liverpool or | Goldsmith |
| CMC/45, 137 | Free 1732 | | **John WRENCH**<br>Chester or | Watchmaker |
| CMC/45, 46 | Free 1742 | | **John WARRINGTON**<br>Chester | Clockmaker and watchmaker |
| CWMP 1850<br>PP3/83<br>Similar mark entered LAO 14 September 1854 | | P2/belowW/x3<br>***#5500-2***<br> | **James WALKER** *<br>Onion Place (1850)<br>Spon Street<br>Albert Street (1854)<br>Coventry | Watchcase maker |
| LPB/92<br>2 June 1882 | | P3/W/x1<br>***#5503***<br> | **James WIDMER** *<br>55 Holborn Viaduct<br>London | Watchcase maker |
| LPB/68<br>1 November 1882 | | P3/W/x3<br>***#5505-6***<br> | **Joseph WHITTEN**<br>12 Spencer Street<br>Birmingham | Jeweller |
| Missing register<br>*c.*1891<br>Similar mark BAO 5 September 1881<br>Similar mark entered BAO 27 April 1882 | | P5/W/344<br>***#5507***<br> | **James WHEELER**<br>147 Hugleston Street<br>Birmingham or | Jeweller |
| | | | **Joseph WHITTEN**<br>12 Spencer Street<br>Birmingham | Jeweller |

| REGISTRATION DETAILS | MAKER'S PRIVATE ADDRESS and DETAILS | PLATE and MARK DETAILS | MAKER/COMPANY and BUSINESS ADDRESS | MAKER'S TRADE |
|---|---|---|---|---|
| MR2/205-6, 208<br>SIL/42<br>J3/416 1777-1801<br>GMSC/75,76 | Skewer, forks 1777, 1778 and ladle 1800/1<br><br>See also IW | Not on P1<br>***#5508***<br>type 1 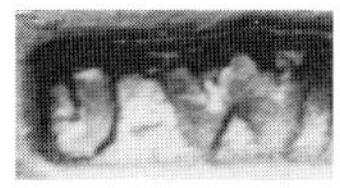 | **Joseph WALLEY**<br>1, 2 Water Street<br>Liverpool | Silversmith |
| SPB/6<br>23 July 1875<br>Sent by J Tayton | | P3/X*sic*/x2<br>***#5509,10***  | **James WINDRIDGE**<br>1/2 Swanswell Terrace<br>Coventry | Watch manufacturer |
| LPB/90<br>18 August 1883 | | P5/W/x1<br>***#5511***  | **James WOODHOUSE** *<br>31 Wynyatt Street<br>Clerkenwell<br>London | Watchcase maker |
| Missing register<br>*c.*1889 | | P5/W/262<br>***#5512***  | | |
| PDB 1785-8<br>MR3/88 | Silverware | P1/29/x2<br>***#5513,4***  | **JONES & WALLEY**<br>**(Ed: Also WALLEY & JONES)**<br>Liverpool | Silversmiths |
| SPB/2<br>13 May 1871 | | P3/W/x3<br>***#5515-7***  | **Joseph WALTON** *<br>7 Upper Charles Street<br>Northampton Square<br>Clerkenwell<br>London | Watchcase maker |
| R1/45<br>24 May 1897<br>Sent by A G Griffiths | Northfield Road<br>King's Norton<br>Worcestershire | P5/X*sic*/844<br>***#5518***  | **Joseph WOODWARD**<br>73 Constitution Hill<br>Birmingham | Wholesale jeweller |
| LPB/92<br>23 November 1881<br>LPB mark shown | | Not on P3<br>***#5519*** 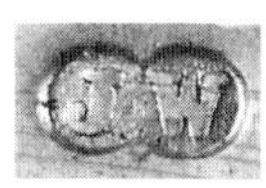 | **John WOODMAN** *<br>33 Smith Street<br>Clerkenwell<br>London | Watchcase maker |
| R1/235<br>10 June 1905<br>Sent by J Woodroffe | Private address same as business | P9/V*sic*/134<br>***#5520***  | **Joseph WOODROFFE**<br>129 Park Road<br>Hockley<br>Birmingham | Jeweller |
| R2/155<br>30 March 1912<br>Sent by W J Myatt & Co | Yale House<br>Streatham<br>458 Brixton Road<br>London SW | P13/W/117,118<br>***#5521,2***  | **Sidney SANDERS**<br>**William METHERELL** trading as<br>**SANDERS & CO & James WALKER**<br>248 Oxford Street<br>London | Jewellers and silversmiths |
| Missing register<br>*c.*1888<br>Similar marks entered LAO 5 February 1880, 26 July 1882, etc | | P5/B/139<br>***#5523***  | **James William BENSON** *<br>62, 64 Ludgate Hill<br>London EC | Jewellers and watch manufacturers |
| No corresponding entry in R1 | | P5/B/665<br>***#5524***  | | |
| Missing register<br>*c.*1886 | | P5/B/22a<br>***#5525***  | | |

| REGISTRATION DETAILS | MAKER'S PRIVATE ADDRESS and DETAILS | PLATE and MARK DETAILS | MAKER/COMPANY and BUSINESS ADDRESS | MAKER'S TRADE |
|---|---|---|---|---|
| Missing register<br>*c.*1886 | | P5/B/55<br>***#5526***<br> | **James William BENSON** *<br>62, 64 Ludgate Hill<br>London EC | Jewellers and watch manufacturers |
| Missing register<br>*c.*1886 | | P5/B/22b<br>***#5527***<br> | | |
| Missing register<br>*c.*1890 | | P5/B/316<br>***#5528***<br> | | |
| R2/120<br>18 October 1910<br>Sent by J W Barrett<br>BAO 13.108<br>LAO 2112 | 318 Birchfield Road<br>Handsworth<br>Birmingham | P13/B/89<br>***#5529***<br> | **John William BARRETT**<br>7 Warstone Lane<br>Birmingham | Jeweller |
| R1/104<br>15 June 1899<br>Sent by H Griffith & Sons Ltd | Glenbrook [1]<br>Carnarvon Road<br>Forest Gate<br>London E | P9/B/20<br>***#5530***<br> | **James William BENSON** *<br>**Edward John Sanders MILLS** [1]<br>Secretary to the Company<br>62, 64 Ludgate Hill<br>London EC | Jewellers |
| Not in R2 as expected<br>*c.* May 1911 | | P13/B/124<br>***#5531***<br> | **J W BENSON LTD** *<br>58, 60 Ludgate Hill<br>London EC | Watchmakers, goldsmiths and silversmiths |
| R1/56<br>4 January 1898<br>Sent by E J Rudge<br>W Mills<br>Allen Brothers<br>W H Collins<br>Edwards Brothers<br>917 in R1 but 916 on P5 | Southbourne<br>Acocks Green<br>Birmingham | P5/C/916<br>***#5532***<br> | **John William CALDICOTT** *<br>1 Great Hampton Street<br>Birmingham | Manufacturing jeweller and bullion dealer |
| LPB/20<br>4 March 1882<br>No mark or initial in LPB | This mark may be J W C but has not been found on a plate – J C is another possibility | Not on P3<br>***#5533*** **J W C?** | **James Walter CROWTHER**<br>60 Shudehill<br>Manchester | Watchmaker and jeweller |
| R2/119<br>8 October 1910<br>Sent by J W Caldicott<br>Three sizes | 28 Stanmore Road<br>Birmingham | P13/C/80-82<br>***#5534-6***<br>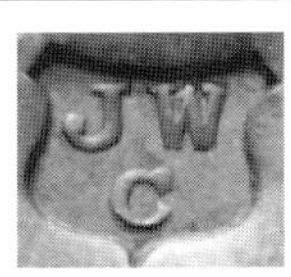 | **John William CALDICOTT**<br>(Successor to W G Knight & Co)<br>32 Spencer Street<br>Birmingham | Manufacturing silversmith |
| R3/170<br>26 September 1959<br>Sent by J W Earl<br>Three sizes | 85 Leigh Road<br>Boothstown<br>Walkden<br>near Manchester | P21/E/15-17<br>***#5537-9***<br> | **John Wesley EARL**<br>No business address entered | Student silversmith |
| R1/173<br>24 July 1902<br>Sent by Wakely & Wheeler<br>Two sizes<br>Cancelled 2 January 1954 R2/149 | Ardbeg Road<br>Dulwich<br>1 Lisgar Terrace<br>West Kensington<br>London | P9/W/71,72<br>***#5540,1***<br> | **James WAKELY**<br>**Frank Clarke WHEELER** trading as<br>**WAKELY & WHEELER** *<br>66 Hatton Garden<br>London and<br>14 Forde Street<br>Dublin | Silver plate manufacturers |
| R3/112<br>22 February 1946<br>Sent by John William Guyton<br>Two sizes | Private address same as business | P21/G/9,10<br>***#5542,3***<br> | **John William GUYTON**<br>Rosslyn<br>Hawarden Road<br>Caergwle<br>Wales | Gold and silversmith |

| REGISTRATION DETAILS | MAKER'S PRIVATE ADDRESS and DETAILS | PLATE and MARK DETAILS | MAKER/COMPANY and BUSINESS ADDRESS | MAKER'S TRADE |
|---|---|---|---|---|
| R3/112<br>17 April 1947 | Private address same as business | P21/G/14<br>***#5544***<br> | **John William GUYTON**<br>Rosslyn<br>Hawarden Road<br>Caergwle<br>Wales | Gold and silversmith |
| R3/161<br>20 April 1957<br>Sent by J W Hollis | 9 Alvanley Road<br>Liverpool 12 | P21/H/74<br>***#5545***<br> | **John William HOLLIS**<br>No business address entered | Student |
| R2/152<br>16 March 1912<br>Sent by Kirwan & Co | 145 Highbury New Road<br>Walthamstow<br>Moved 22 June 1916 to<br>Lower Grosvenor Place<br>London SW | P13/K/5<br>***#5546***<br>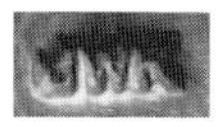 | **John William KIRWAN** trading as<br>**J W KIRWAN & CO** *<br>84 Hatton Garden<br>London and<br>6 Vyse Street<br>Birmingham | Goldsmiths |
| Missing register<br>*c.*1890 | | P5/K/271<br>***#5547***<br> | **John William KIRWAN** trading as<br>**KIRWAN & CO** *<br>48 Frederick Street<br>Birmingham and<br>84 Hatton Garden<br>London | Jewellers |
| Missing register<br>*c.*1892 | | P5/K/424b<br>***#5548***<br> | **John William KIRWAN** trading as<br>**KIRWAN & CO** *<br>48 Frederick Street<br>Birmingham and<br>84 Hatton Garden<br>London | Jewellers |
| Missing register<br>*c.*1892 | | P5/L*sic*/422<br>***#5549***<br> | | |
| Missing register<br>*c.*1886 | | P5/K/23<br>***#5550***<br> | | |
| Missing register<br>*c.*1892 | | P5/K/424a<br>***#5551***<br> | | |
| R1/80<br>24 April 1894<br>Sent by James Fenton<br>W G Matthews<br>C Robinson<br>Wright & Perry<br>R Parker<br>G C Haseler & Co | | P5/K/554<br>***#5552***<br> | | |
| P1/154<br>1 October 1901<br>Sent by Harry Josiah Wilkins<br>Manager to J W Kirwan | 68 Highbury Hill<br>London N | P9/K/16-21<br>***#5553-8***<br> | **John William KIRWAN** trading as<br>**J W KIRWAN & CO** *<br>84 Hatton Garden<br>London and<br>6 Vyse Street<br>Birmingham | Goldsmiths |
| R2/26<br>12 October 1906<br>Sent by Twine & Gilpin | 68 Highbury Hill<br>145 Highbury New Park<br>London N from 12 June 1911 | P9/K/44<br>***#5559***<br> | | |

| REGISTRATION DETAILS | MAKER'S PRIVATE ADDRESS and DETAILS | PLATE and MARK DETAILS | MAKER/COMPANY and BUSINESS ADDRESS | MAKER'S TRADE |
|---|---|---|---|---|
| R3/11<br>22 August 1922<br>Sent by Sidney Sanders | Thurston Towers [1]<br>Streatham<br>147 Hurlingham Road [2]<br>London SW | P15/W/55, 56<br>***#5560,1***<br> | **James WALKER LTD** *<br>Sidney Sanders [1]<br>Stanley Brimsmead Squire [2]<br>85 High Street<br>Streatham<br>London SW16 | Jewellers and silversmiths |
| R3/9<br>17 May 1922<br>Sent by S R Ward & Son | Newton Towers [1]<br>Streatham<br>London SW<br>109 Harlington Road [2]<br>London SW | P15/W/53<br>***#5562***<br> | | |
| R3/38<br>9 November 1927<br>Sent by Henry Griffith & Sons | 99 Gracefield Gardens [1]<br>Streatham<br>London SW16 | P15/W/90<br>***#5563***<br> | **James WALKER LTD** *<br>D'Arcy Eville Lewis [1] (Secretary)<br>85 High Road<br>Streatham<br>London SW16 (and numerous branches) | |
| R3/48<br>24 August 1929<br>Sent by Albion Chain Co | Newton Towers [1]<br>Streatham<br>London SW<br>109 Harlington Road [2]<br>London SW | P15/W/93<br>***#5564***<br> | **James WALKER LTD** *<br>Sidney Sanders [1]<br>Stanley Brimsmead [2] Squire<br>85 High Street<br>Streatham<br>London SW16 | |
| LPB/34<br>2 June 1883<br>Sent by J Eastham | See also mark ***#4344-6*** | P3/P/x3<br>***#5565-7***<br> | **James W PETERS**<br>3 London Road<br>Liverpool | Watch manufacturer |
| LPB/34<br>6 July 1883<br>LPB mark shown | | Not on P3<br>***#5568***<br> | | |
| R2/139<br>17 July 1911<br>Sent by J & R Griffin & Son | 38 Haycott Road<br>West Kensington<br>London | P13/S/65<br>***#5569***<br> | **John Walter SPURRIER** *<br>15 Wool Exchange<br>London EC | Silversmith |
| R1/155<br>8 October 1901<br>Sent by F Coulthurst | Brook Lane<br>Alderley Edge | P9/S/40<br>***#5570***<br> | **John STOVELL** [1]<br>**William STOVELL** [2] trading as<br>**J & W STOVELL**<br>98 Shudehill<br>Manchester | Umbrella and walking stick manufacturers |
| R1/22<br>17 February 1896<br>Sent by J W Smith | Laburnum Villa<br>Albert Road<br>Stechford | P5/O*sic*/728<br>***#5571***<br> | **John William SMITH**<br>29 and later 14 Tenby Street<br>Birmingham | Jeweller |
| R1/156<br>5 November 1901<br>Sent by Stokes & Ireland | Glanmore<br>Rathdown Road<br>Dublin | P9/W/61<br>***#5572***<br> | **James Arthur WEIR**<br>**John Hunt WEIR** trading as<br>**J WEIR & SONS**<br>3 Wicklow Place<br>Dublin | Silversmiths |
| R3/26<br>7 January 1925<br>Sent by J W Templer | 34 Copeland Road<br>Leyton<br>London | P15/T/47<br>***#5573***<br> | **James Walter TEMPLER**<br>34 Copeland Road<br>Leyton<br>London and<br>164 High Street<br>Smethwick and<br>105 Vyse Street<br>Birmingham | Manufacturing jeweller |

| REGISTRATION DETAILS | MAKER'S PRIVATE ADDRESS and DETAILS | PLATE and MARK DETAILS | MAKER/COMPANY and BUSINESS ADDRESS | MAKER'S TRADE |
|---|---|---|---|---|
| R3/67<br>27 May 1933<br>Sent by J W Templer | 34 Copeland Road<br>Leyton<br>London E17 | P15/T/69<br>***#5574***<br> | **James Walter TEMPLER**<br>34 Copeland Road<br>Leyton<br>London E17 and<br>105 Vyse Street<br>Birmingham | Wholesale and manufacturing jeweller |
| R3/68<br>1 August 1933<br>Sent by J W Templer | | P15/T/70<br>***#5575***<br> | | |
| R1/213<br>30 April 1904<br>Sent by J W Tiptaft | 22 Whately Road<br>Handsworth<br>Staffs | P9/T/53<br>***#5576***<br> | **James Walter TIPTAFT**<br>25 Northampton Street<br>Birmingham | Jeweller |
| R2/151<br>7 March 1912<br>Sent by Johnson Walker & Tolhurst<br>Two sizes | The Grange<br>West Drayton<br>Percy Lodge<br>Winchmore Hill<br>Rosslyn<br>Copers Cope Road<br>Beckenham | P13/J/57-59<br>***#5577-9***<br> | **Ernest Alfred WALKER**<br>**Guy WALKER**<br>**George TOLHURST** trading as<br>**JOHNSON WALKER & TOLHURST LTD** *<br>Ernest E Greenwood (Secretary)<br>80 Aldersgate Street<br>London EC | Manufacturing jewellers and silversmiths |
| R3/42<br>2 August 1928<br>Sent by Hadley & Hadley | 34 Copeland Road<br>Leyton<br>London E17 | P15/T/49<br>***#5580***<br> | **James Walter TEMPLER**<br>trading as **J W TEMPLER & CO**<br>105 Vyse Street<br>Birmingham<br>68 Spencer Street<br>Birmingham<br>34 Copeland Road<br>Leyton<br>London E17 | Wholesale and manufacturing jewellers |
| R2/46<br>2 October 1907<br>Sent by C Dreyfus | Hurst Cottage<br>Reigate<br>Surrey<br>Percy Lodge<br>Winchmore Hill<br>London N<br>Rosslyn<br>Copers Cope Road<br>Beckenham | P9/J*sic*/57<br>***#5581***<br> | **Brownfield TOLHURST**<br>**Guy WALKER**<br>**George TOLHURST** trading as<br>**JOHNSON, WALKER & TOLHURST LTD** *<br>80 Aldersgate Street<br>London EC and<br>172 New Bond Street<br>London W | Wholesale jewellers and silversmiths |
| R1/78<br>10 September 1894<br>Sent by J W Watson<br>Authority to W Sexton<br>A H Ratcliff<br>mark shown as 589 in register | 4 John Street<br>Bradford | P5/W/587<br>***#5582***<br> | **J W WATSON**<br>51 North Parade and<br>6 Charles Street<br>Bradford | Jeweller |
| R1/113<br>11 October 1899<br>Sent by Johnson & Yates<br>Two sizes | 86 Haliston Street [1]<br>Hulme<br>Manchester<br>169 St Mary's Road [2]<br>Moston<br>Manchester | P9/J/22,23<br>***#5583,4***<br> | **Charles JOHNSON** [1]<br>**Thomas YATES** [2] trading as<br>**JOHNSON & YATES**<br>Collegiate Chambers<br>24 Old Millgate<br>Manchester | Jewellers and diamond mounters |

| REGISTRATION DETAILS | MAKER'S PRIVATE ADDRESS and DETAILS | PLATE and MARK DETAILS | MAKER/COMPANY and BUSINESS ADDRESS | MAKER'S TRADE |
|---|---|---|---|---|
| PP1/188, CWMP 1850<br>Similar mark entered LAO 4 May 1858 and BAO 24 April 1844 | | P2/Y/x4<br>*#5585-8*<br>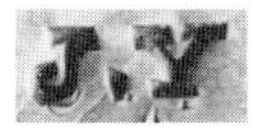 | **John YARDLEY** *<br>Craven Street (1850)<br>41 Mount Street (1858)<br>Coventry | Watchcase maker |
| Missing register *c.*1887<br>Similar mark entered LAO 9 February 1884 | | P5/Y/76<br>*#5589*<br> | **John YARDLEY** *<br>Craven Street (1850)<br>4 Poddycroft Terrace (1885)<br>Coventry | Watchcase maker |
| SPB/2<br>12 June 1871<br>CWMP 1874-83 | | P3/Y/x3<br>*#5590-2*<br> | **Joseph YARDLEY** *<br>55 Spon Street<br>Coventry | Watchcase maker |
| R1/32<br>23 September 1896<br>Sent by A H Tongue | 40 Stanley Street<br>Aberdeen | P5/Y/788<br>*#5593*<br>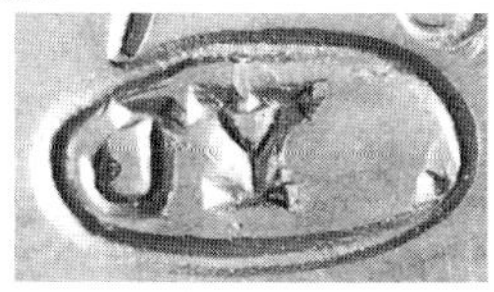 | **James YALE**<br>17 Union Buildings<br>Aberdeen | Tobacconist |
| LPB/98<br>18 November 1885<br>No mark, initial or address listed | | P5/Y/x1<br>*#5594*<br> | **John YARDLEY** *<br>Craven Street (1850)<br>4 Poddycroft Terrace (1885)<br>Coventry | Watchcase maker |
| R2/13<br>14 March 1906<br>Sent by J G Crowther<br>BAO 10.103<br>SAO 410 | 21 Wharncliffe Rood<br>Broomhall<br>Sheffield<br><br>First reference to registrations at other assay offices | P9/Dsic/224<br>*#5595*<br>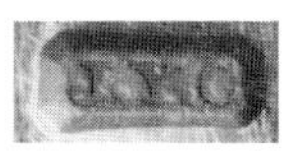 | **James Guest CROWTHER** trading as **John Yeoman COWLISHAW & Edmund BELL** Incorporated<br>25 Paradise Street and<br>Room 40, Soho Works<br>Summerfield Street<br>Sheffield | Fruit knife manufacturers |
| R1/186<br>3 March 1903<br>Sent by E D Yates | 169 St Mary's Road<br>Moston<br>Manchester | P9/XYZ/6<br>*#5596*<br> | **Edward Dootson YATES** trading as **James YATES & SON**<br>Collegiate Chambers<br>24 Old Millgate<br>Manchester | Ring mounters and jewellers |
| R1/206<br>29 January 1904<br>Sent by E D Yates | | P9XYZ/7<br>*#5597*<br> | Details as above<br>86 Lancaster Avenue<br>Fennel Street<br>Manchester | |
| R2/83<br>22 May 1909<br>Sent by Edward Dootson Yates | 15 Herschel Street<br>Lighthouse<br>Manchester | P13/XYZ/1<br>*#5598*<br> | **Edward Dootson YATES**<br>84, 86 Lancaster Avenue<br>Fennel Street<br>Manchester | Ring mounter and manufacturing jeweller |
| R1/123<br>24 March 1900<br>Sent by Edward Yates | 169 St Mary's Road<br>Moston<br>Manchester | P9/XYZ/1<br>*#5599*<br> | **James YATES & Edward YATES** trading as **James YATES & SON**<br>84, 86 Lancaster Avenue<br>Fennel Street, Manchester | Ring manufacturers and jewellers |
| R2/174<br>10 July 1913<br>Sent by S Zeving | Private address same as business | P15/XYZ/1<br>*#5600*<br> | **Samuel ZEVING** trading as **J ZEVING**<br>32 Great Garden Street<br>London | Silversmith |

| REGISTRATION DETAILS | MAKER'S PRIVATE ADDRESS and DETAILS | PLATE and MARK DETAILS | MAKER/COMPANY and BUSINESS ADDRESS | MAKER'S TRADE |
|---|---|---|---|---|
| Not in SPB, LPB or R1<br><br>Date unknown as mark is not numbered | Punched at bottom of square K so not an early 1883 mark – also near P5/K/812 for Kinsey Brothers & Patrick (*#5618*). Square K suggests surname beginning with K: B suggests brothers. See other KB marks. | P5/K/x1<br>***#5601***<br> | **Unidentified** | |
| R1/93<br>23 February 1899<br>Sent by W Walker | Registered Office same as business address | P9/K/4<br>***#5602***<br> | **Luke KIPPAX** (Managing Director)<br>trading as<br>**KIPPAX BROTHERS LTD**<br>St James Street<br>Accrington | Briar pipe manufacturers, fancy goods importers and dealers in tobacconists goods |
| R1/94<br>1 March 1899<br>Sent by Kippax Brothers | 37 Colne Road<br>Burnley | P9/K/6<br>***#5603***<br> | Registered Office same as business address | |
| R1/116<br>24 November 1899<br>Sent by Kippax Brothers Ltd | Padiham Road [1]<br>Burnley<br>12 Colne Road [2]<br>Burnley | P9/K/10<br>***#5604***<br> | **Luke KIPPAX** [1] (Director)<br>**Thomas SHEPLEY** [2] (Secretary)<br>trading as **KIPPAX BROTHERS**<br>St James Street<br>Accrington | |
| R1/229<br>10 March 1905<br>Sent by Kippax Brothers | 183 Manchester Road<br>Burnley<br>15 Marlborough Street<br>Accrington | P9/K/35<br>***#5605***<br> | **Luke KIPPAX**<br>**James MITCHELL** trading as<br>**KIPPAX BROTHERS**<br>St James Street<br>Accrington | |
| R2/156<br>24 April 1912<br>Sent by E Edmonds<br>BAO 17.819 | Poynton Villas<br>Grove Park<br>Redland<br>Bristol | P13/K/6<br>***#5606***<br> | **Charles Wilson KEMP** trading as<br>**KEMP BROTHERS** *<br>Union Street and Fairfax Street<br>Bristol | Silversmiths |
| R2/158<br>25 June 1912<br>Sent by E Edmonds | | P13/K/7<br>***#5607***<br> | | |
| R3/19<br>31 October 1923<br>Sent by Dingley Brothers<br>Three sizes | 1 Grove Park<br>Woodstock Avenue<br>26 Carnarvon Road<br>1 Grove Park<br>26 Carnavon Road<br>Hammersmith Road<br>Bristol | P15/B*sic*/169-171<br>***#5608-10***<br> | **Charles Wilson KEMP**<br>**Charles Milford KEMP**<br>**Arthur Sidney KEMP**<br>**Herbert Cunliffe KEMP**<br>**Ella Gladys GIBBS**<br>**Henry Edgar TYRRELL**<br>Union Street and Fairfax Street<br>Bristol | |
| Missing register<br>*c.*1890 | | P5/K/302<br>***#5611***<br> | **KIRWAN & BOLDING** *<br>47 Warstone Lane<br>Birmingham | Jewellers |
| SPB/11<br>5 June 1877<br>Sent by Samuel & Rogers | | P3/B/x2<br>***#5612,13***<br> | | |
| LPB/16<br>9 July 1880<br>Sent by E Vaughton | | P3/B/x1<br>***#5614***<br> | | |
| LPB/46<br>31 January 1881<br>Sent by Coley Brothers | | P3/K/x1<br>***#5615***<br> | **KIRWAN & BOLDING** *<br>48 Frederick Street<br>Birmingham | |
| Missing register<br>*c.*1886 | | P5/K/64<br>***#5616***<br> | | |

| REGISTRATION DETAILS | MAKER'S PRIVATE ADDRESS and DETAILS | PLATE and MARK DETAILS | MAKER/COMPANY and BUSINESS ADDRESS | MAKER'S TRADE |
|---|---|---|---|---|
| R2/6<br>17 November 1905<br>Sent by Kay Brothers | 21 Angle Street<br>Burnley<br>5 Cromwell Street<br>Burnley | P9/K/40<br>*#5617*<br> | **Ernest KAY**<br>**Benjamin LAYCOCK** trading as<br>**KAY BROTHERS**<br>31 Standish Street<br>Burnley | Walking stick and umbrella manufacturers and mounters |
| R1/37<br>26 January 1897<br>Sent by J B Patrick | Cavendish House [1]<br>42 Holly Road [2]<br>51 Whaterly Road [3]<br>Handsworth<br>(Ed: Clerk wrote Joseph Benjamin Kinsey instead of correct Patrick) | P5/K/812a<br>*#5618*<br> | **John Albert KINSEY** [1]<br>**William Allen KINSEY** [2]<br>**Joseph Benjamin PATRICK** [3] trading as<br>**KINSEY BROTHERS & PATRICK**<br>56 Albion Street<br>Birmingham | Keeper ring manufacturers |
| R2/106<br>19 March 1910<br>Sent by Taylor & Hancock | 7 Queen Street<br>Oxford<br>27 Bartlemas Road<br>Oxford | P13/K/4<br>*#5619*<br> | **Anthony Leonard KIRNER**<br>**Anthony KIRNER** trading as<br>**KIRNER BROTHERS**<br>7 Queen Street<br>Oxford | Jewellers and watchmakers |
| R1/37<br>26 January 1897 | Read as KBSP | P5/K/812b<br>*#5620*<br> | **KINSEY BROTHERS & PATRICK**<br>56 Albion Street<br>Birmingham | Keeper ring manufacturers |
| R1/181<br>5 December 1903<br>Sent by Kinnear & Co | The Shanty<br>Mossley Hill<br>Liverpool | P9/K/29<br>*#5621*<br> | **Charles Maxwell KINNEAR** trading as<br>**KINNEAR & CO**<br>8 Bradshaw Street<br>Shude Hill<br>Manchester | Tobacconists and fancy goods importers |
| R1/178<br>3 November 1902<br>Sent by Kinnear & Co | | P9/K/28<br>*#5622*<br> | | |
| R1/198<br>10 August 1903<br>Sent by Kinnear & Co | | P9/K/32<br>*#5623*<br> | | |
| R1/80<br>9 October 1894<br>Sent by Stainton Brothers | Saint Dennis House<br>Worcester | P5/K598<br>*#5624*<br> | **William Kilbourne KAY** trading as<br>**KAY & CO** *<br>4 Foregate Street and<br>Shrub Hill<br>Worcester | Watchmakers, watch importers and wholesale jewellers |
| Missing register<br>*c.*1892 | | P5/K/423<br>*#5625*<br> | | |
| R1/188<br>23 March 1903<br>Sent by H Bushell | Infirmary Walk<br>Worcester | P9/K/30<br>*#5626*<br> | **KAY & CO LTD** *<br>T Russell Dyke (Secretary)<br>Shrub Hill<br>Worcester | |
| Missing register<br>*c.*1892 | | P5/K/411<br>*#5627*<br> | | |

| REGISTRATION DETAILS | MAKER'S PRIVATE ADDRESS and DETAILS | PLATE and MARK DETAILS | MAKER/COMPANY and BUSINESS ADDRESS | MAKER'S TRADE |
|---|---|---|---|---|
| R2/22<br>3 August 1906<br>Sent by Kay & Co | Infirmary Walk<br>Worcester | P9/K/43<br>***#5628,9***<br> | **KAY & CO LTD** *<br>**William Kilbourne KAY**<br>Managing Director<br>4 Foregate Street<br>Worcester | Wholesale jewellers and watch importers |
| R1/145<br>22 April 1901<br>Sent by T P Hewitt | | P9/K/14<br>***#5630***<br> | | General merchants |
| R1/146<br>27 April 1901<br>Sent by H Stoker | | P9/K/13<br>***#5631***<br> | | |
| R1/42<br>7 April 1897<br>Sent by R F Carsberg<br>H Williamson & Co<br>J & R Griffin<br>W J Pellow | Heron Lodge<br>Worcester | P5/K/830<br>***#5632***<br> | **KAY & CO LTD** *<br>William Kilbourne Kay (Managing Director)<br>4 Foregate Street<br>Worcester | Wholesale jewellers and watch importers |
| Missing register<br>*c.*1886 | | P5/K/44<br>***#5633***<br>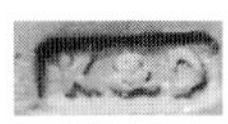 | **KENDAL & DENT** * | Jewellers and watch importers |
| Missing register<br>*c.*1894 | | P5/K/547<br>***#5634***<br> | | |
| R1/66<br>8 June 1894<br>Sent by S Usher<br>J Gammage | | P5/K/567<br>***#5635***<br> | **KENDAL & DENT** *<br>106 Cheapside<br>London | |
| R1/122<br>24 February 1900<br>Sent by Benson Brothers<br>Two sizes | Oxford Lodge<br>Kensington<br>Surrey | P9/K/11a,b<br>***#5636,7***<br> | **James Francis KENDAL** trading as<br>**KENDAL & DENT** *<br>106 Cheapside<br>London | |
| R1/34<br>16 October 1896<br>Sent by<br>W H Carrington & Co<br>Manchester | Private address same as business | P5/K/794<br>***#5638***<br> | **James Joseph KELLY**<br>34 Upper Camden Street<br>Dublin | Tobacconist |
| R1/24<br>16 March 1896<br>Sent by John Percy King | The Cedars<br>Upper Park Road<br>New Southgate<br>London | P5/K/739<br>***#5639***<br> | **John Percy KING** trading as<br>**KING & SONS** *<br>3/5 Charterhouse Street and<br>222/224 Goswell Road<br>London | Goldsmiths and silversmiths |
| R1/26<br>11 April 1896 | | P5/K/753<br>***#5640***<br> | | |

| REGISTRATION DETAILS | MAKER'S PRIVATE ADDRESS and DETAILS | PLATE and MARK DETAILS | MAKER/COMPANY and BUSINESS ADDRESS | MAKER'S TRADE |
|---|---|---|---|---|
| R3/184<br>27 April 1962<br>Sent by K I Makinson | The Millstone<br>Trenddyn<br>Mold<br>Flintshire | P21/M/55<br>***#5641***  | **Mrs Kathleen Irene MAKINSON**<br>No business address entered | Amateur silversmith |
| R3/21<br>2 May 1924<br>Sent by Ward Brothers (Birmingham) Ltd<br>Two sizes | Inishmore<br>Robin Hood Lane<br>Hall Green<br>4 Crocketts Road<br>Handsworth<br>Birmingham | P15/K/14,15<br>***#5642,3***  | **Kenneth KNIGHT LTD**<br>Norman F Wilson (Director)<br>Edna Florence Cartwright (Secretary)<br>33 Barker Street, Villa Cross<br>Birmingham | Manufacturing jewellers and silversmiths |
| R3/106<br>21 January 1944<br>Sent by Kenneth Kirkpatrick Drury | Private address same as business | P21/D/8,9<br>***#5644,5***  | **Kenneth Kirkpatrick DRURY**<br>Upperlands<br>Harborough<br>Near Leicester | Silversmith (doctor of medicine) |
| R1/154<br>20 September 1901<br>Sent by Kinnear Ltd | The Shanty<br>Mossley Hill<br>Liverpool | P9/K/15<br>***#5646***  | **Charles Maxwell KINNEAR** trading as **KINNEAR LTD**<br>57 Park Lane, Liverpool and<br>8 Bradshaw Street<br>Manchester | Pipe and stick mounters |
| R1/158<br>10 December 1901<br>Sent by Kinnear Ltd | | P9/K/22<br>***#5647***  | | |
| R2/228<br>5 March 1920<br>Sent by J W More | 14 Chaucer Mansions [1]<br>Queens Club Gardens<br>London<br>2 St George's Terrace<br>Regent's Park<br>London<br>74 Westwaugh Road<br>Dudley Hill<br>Birmingham | P15/K/37<br>***#5648***  | **KIRWAN CO LTD** *<br>J W More [1] (Director)<br>S Tompkins (Secretary)<br>Mr Seal<br>84 Hatton Garden<br>London and<br>6 Vyse Street<br>Birmingham | Wholesale jewellers |
| R3/171<br>17 February 1960<br>Sent by J K Mold | 7 Wyvern Road<br>Moreton<br>Wirral, Cheshire | P21/M/51<br>***#5649***  | **John Kirby MOLD**<br>No business address entered | Teacher of metalwork |
| R3/4<br>11 July 1921<br>Sent by Stokes & Ireland | 44 Belsize Park<br>Hampstead<br>London | P15/M/44<br>***#5650***  | **Kokichi MIKIMOTO**<br>37, 38 Hatton Garden<br>London EC1 | Jeweller and pearl merchant |
| R3/145<br>28 July 1953<br>Sent by K M John | 66 Town Road<br>Neath | P21/IJ/11<br>***#5651***  | **Kathleen May JOHN**<br>No business address entered | Student of silverwork |
| R3/179<br>4 May 1961<br>Sent by K N Widdup | The Sheeling<br>34 Hall Park<br>Lancaster | P21/W/103<br>***#5652***  | **Kenneth Noel WIDDUP**<br>34 Church Street<br>Lancaster | Dental surgeon |
| 13 June 1961 | | P21/W/105<br>***#5653***  | | |

| REGISTRATION DETAILS | MAKER'S PRIVATE ADDRESS and DETAILS | PLATE and MARK DETAILS | MAKER/COMPANY and BUSINESS ADDRESS | MAKER'S TRADE |
|---|---|---|---|---|
| R3/70<br>20 April 1934<br>Sent by T J Skelton<br>86 Vyse Street<br>Birmingham<br>Two sizes | 180 Balgrayhill Road<br>Glasgow N | P15/K/18-20<br>***#5654-6***<br>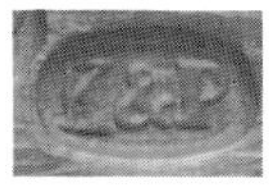 | **John Oliver EARLY** trading as<br>**KERR & PHILLIPS**<br>25 Gordon Street<br>Glasgow | Wholesale jewellers and silversmiths |
| R2/80<br>27 April 1909<br>Sent by<br>J & R Griffin<br>Cancelled<br>23 April 1912 new punch entered<br>BAO 11.145<br>LAO 2425 | Poynton Villa<br>Grove Park<br>Redland | P13/K/2<br>***#5657***<br> | **Charles Wilson KEMP** trading as<br>**KEMP BROTHERS** *<br>4 Union Street<br>Bristol | Silversmiths |
| R3/25<br>12 November 1924<br>Sent by K Stewart<br>Two sizes | Private address same as business | P15/S/64,65<br>***#5658,9***<br> | **Kenneth STEWART**<br>3 Widecombe Terrace<br>Bath | Artist craftsman |
| R1/231<br>12 April 1905<br>Sent by Rob Hilton | The Northgate<br>Chester and<br>Keswick | P9/K/36<br>***#5660***<br> | **KESWICK SCHOOL OF INDUSTRIAL ARTS**<br>Robert Hilton (Director)<br>Keswick | School of industries |
| R1/231<br>22 April 1905<br>Sent by Rob Hilton | | P9/K/37<br>***#5661***<br> | | |

| REGISTRATION DETAILS | MAKER'S PRIVATE ADDRESS and DETAILS | PLATE and MARK DETAILS | MAKER/COMPANY and BUSINESS ADDRESS | MAKER'S TRADE |
|---|---|---|---|---|
| R1/160<br>23 January 1902<br>Sent by W Walker | 31 Great Alie Street<br>London E | P9/L/22<br>***#5662***  | **Haggman LYNN**<br>**Isidore AARONS** trading as<br>**LYNN & AARONS**<br>37 Commercial Road<br>London E | Tobacconists and fancy goods dealers |
| R2/133<br>20 April 1911<br>Sent by J G Newbold | 67 Canfield Gardens<br>London NW<br>99b Marylebone Road<br>London NW | P13/O/12<br>***#5663***  | **Louis ORLIK**<br>**Alfred ORLIK** trading as<br>**L & A ORLIK** *<br>62 Barbican<br>London EC | Tobacconists and fancy goods importers |
| R2/150<br>26 January 1912<br>Sent by J G Newbold | | P13/O/14,15<br>***#5664,5***  | | Pipe importers |
| R2/89<br>23 July 1909<br>Sent by C H Dumenil Ltd | | P13/O/2,3<br>***#5666,7***  | | Smokers requirements |
| R2/109<br>4 May 1910<br>Sent by L & A Orlik | | P13/O/5,6<br>***#5668,9*** 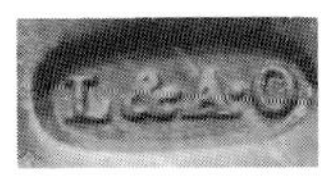 | | Smokers requisites |
| R2/115<br>14 July 1910<br>Sent by C H Dumenil Ltd | | P13/O/7-9<br>***#5670-2***  | | Tobacconists and fancy goods importers |
| R3/125<br>10 July 1948<br>Sent by L Bock<br>Two sizes | Private address same as business | P21/B/29,30<br>***#5673,4***  | **Ladislav BOCK**<br>24a High Street<br>Whitchurch<br>Salop | Silversmith, goldsmith and jeweller |
| Missing register<br>*c.*1887 | | P5/B/77<br>***#5675***  | **Unidentified** | |
| LPB/16<br>25 March 1880<br>Sent by A Russell & Co | | P3/B/x2<br>***#5676,7***  | **L BEAVER** *<br>37 Cross Street<br>Manchester | Jeweller |
| R1/165<br>26 March 1902<br>Sent by Joseph Jackson | 335 Moss Lane East<br>Manchester | P9/B/90<br>***#5678***  | **Marcus BEAVER** trading as<br>**L BEAVER** *<br>7 and 9 St Ann's Street<br>Manchester | |
| LPB/50<br>11 March 1880<br>Sent by Mayell Brothers<br>Nathan Brothers | | P3/L/x2<br>***#5679,80***  | **LEWIS BROTHERS**<br>26 Hylton Street<br>Birmingham | Wholesale jewellers |
| Missing register<br>*c.*1888 | | P5/L/191<br>***#5681***  | | |
| Missing register<br>*c.*1890 | | P5/L/326<br>***#5682***  | | |
| R1/208<br>1 March 1904<br>Sent by W H Ashford | Westbourne<br>Birchfield | P9/L/45,46<br>***#5683,4***  | **Frederick Eric LEWIS**<br>**Edward LEWIS**<br>**Frank LEWIS** trading as<br>**LEWIS BROTHERS**<br>Mark Waters (Manager)<br>35 Hale Street<br>Birmingham | |

| REGISTRATION DETAILS | MAKER'S PRIVATE ADDRESS and DETAILS | PLATE and MARK DETAILS | MAKER/COMPANY and BUSINESS ADDRESS | MAKER'S TRADE |
|---|---|---|---|---|
| Not in R3 as expected<br>*c.* April 1925 to<br>January 1928 | | P15/L/34<br>***#5685***  | **LEWIS BROTHERS** | Wholesale jewellers |
| R3/57<br>9 April 1931<br>Sent by Kinsey Brothers & Patrick Ltd, Vyse Street<br>Birmingham | Westbourne<br>Birchfield<br>Birmingham | P15/L/41<br>***#5686***  | **LEWIS BROTHERS**<br>35 Hall Street<br>Birmingham | |
| LPB/50<br>6 June 1882<br>Sent by Nathan Brothers<br>John Ward | PO directory 1882 | P3/L/x1<br>***#5687***  | **LEWIS BROTHERS**<br>187 Warstone Lane<br>Birmingham | Jewellers |
| LPB/50<br>7 December 1881<br>LPB mark shown | | Not on P3<br>***#5688***  | **LOACH BROTHERS**<br>59 Albion Street<br>Birmingham | Jewellers |
| Missing register<br>*c.*1886 | | P5/L/60<br>***#5689***  | | |
| R1/55<br>4 May 1894<br>Sent by Lucas Brothers | | P5/L/557<br>***#5690***  | **LUCAS BROTHERS LTD**<br>22 Hylton Street<br>Birmingham | Jewellers |
| R2/154<br>26 March 1912<br>Sent by Loach Brothers<br>BAO 19.642 | 364 Gillot Road<br>Birmingham | P13/L/72<br>***#5691***  | **Joseph LOACH** trading as<br>**LOACH BROTHERS**<br>59 Albion Street<br>Birmingham | Gem and fancy ring manufacturers |
| Missing register<br>*c.*1889<br>Similar mark entered BAO 24 January 1887 | | P5/L/225<br>***#5692***  | **LOACH BROTHERS**<br>59 Albion Street<br>Birmingham | Jewellers |
| LPB/52<br>3 July 1884<br>No name or address given | | P5/B/x1<br>***#5693***  | **Unidentified** | |
| No entry in LPB to match | | P5/L/x1<br>***#5694***  | **Unidentified** | |
| R3/88<br>5 July 1937<br>Sent by L Colquitt | Private address same as business | P21/C/2<br>***#5695***  | **Leonard COLQUITT**<br>23 Chepstow Avenue<br>Wallasey<br>Cheshire | Artist craftsman |
| 24 June 1938 | | P21/C/7<br>***#5696*** 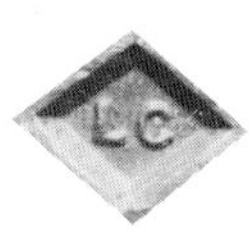 | | |
| R1/136<br>1 November 1900<br>Sent by Louis Cohen | Private address same as business | P9/C/42<br>***#5697***  | **Louis COHEN**<br>32 Bristol Street<br>Edinburgh | Working jeweller and manufacturer |
| R1/60<br>7 February 1898<br>Sent by Lionel Carper | 16 Battersea Road<br>London EC | P5/aboveC/929<br>***#5698***  | **Lionel CORPER** trading as<br>**L CORPER & CO**<br>43 Old Street<br>London | Gold and silver mounters |

| REGISTRATION DETAILS | MAKER'S PRIVATE ADDRESS and DETAILS | PLATE and MARK DETAILS | MAKER/COMPANY and BUSINESS ADDRESS | MAKER'S TRADE |
|---|---|---|---|---|
| R2/126<br>27 January 1911<br>Sent by Leonard Crossley | Private address same as business | P13/C/87<br>***#5699***<br>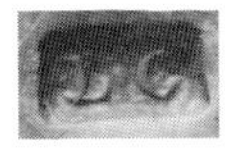 | **Leonard CROSSLEY**<br>13 Hockley Hill<br>Birmingham | Diamond mounter |
| R2/138<br>5 July 1911<br>Sent by Lydia Cooper | 5a Parade Mansions<br>Golders Green<br>London NW | P13/D*sic*/143<br>***#5700***<br> | **Lydia COOPER**<br>5a Parade Mansions<br>Golders Green and<br>3 The Mall Studio<br>Parkhill Road, Hampstead<br>London NW | Trade not entered. Worker in silver? |
| R2/55<br>12 February 1908<br>Sent by C M Wrighton | 14 Crediton Road<br>West Hampstead<br>London NW | P9/L/92<br>***#5701***<br> | **Samuel JACOB** trading as<br>**LAMES & CO**<br>4, 5 Holborn Circus<br>London | Wholesale jewellers |
| R2/116<br>26 July 1910<br>Sent by F W Cole<br>Two sizes | Private address same as business | P13/L/42,43<br>***#5702,3***<br> | **William LANGLEY** trading as<br>**LANGLEY & CO**<br>271 Pershore Road<br>Birmingham | Wholesale jewellers |
| R2/188<br>22 May 1914<br>Sent by F W Cole | | P15/L/2<br>***#5704***<br> | **William LANGLEY**<br>123 Pershore Road<br>Birmingham | Manufacturing jeweller |
| R2/200<br>12 October 1915<br>Sent by Leonard Ward | 129 Villa Street<br>Birmingham<br>54 Thornhill Road<br>Handsworth<br>39 Guest Street<br>Birmingham | P15/L/11<br>***#5705***<br>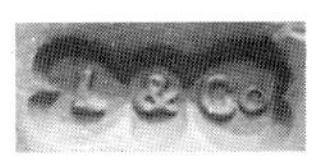 | **Archibald Leslie WAIN**<br>**Leonard WARD**<br>**Allan Ewart COOK** trading as<br>**LESLIE & CO**<br>129 Villa Street, Hockley<br>Birmingham | Manufacturing jewellers |
| R3/146<br>14 October 1953<br>Sent by Lillman & Co | 7 Wyndham Street [1]<br>Marylebone<br>London W1<br>39 Field Road [2]<br>Bloxwich, Staffordshire | P21/L/33<br>***#5706***<br> | **LILLMAN & CO**<br>Benjamin Newman [1]<br>Edmund Lilley [2]<br>59 Caroline Street<br>Birmingham 3 | Manufacturing jewellers |
| R2/197<br>9 July 1915<br>Sent by Ginder & Couch<br>BAO 5.550 | 18 Woodburn Avenue<br>Glasgow<br>48 Albert Drive<br>Glasgow | P15/L/7<br>***#5707***<br> | **LAWSON & CO LTD**<br>Alice Mackinnon<br>Thomas B Lawson (Director)<br>85 Buchanan Street<br>Glasgow | Jewellers |
| Missing register<br>*c.*1887 | | P5/L/107<br>***#5708***<br> | **LAMB & CO** | Wholesale jewellers |
| R1/43<br>27 April 1897<br>Sent by W J Pellow<br>Hollis & Newman<br>Payton, Pepper & Son Ltd<br>Mayell Brothers | Hotel Cecil<br>Strand<br>London WC<br>Culme has Ferdinand Livingstone and Wood Exchange – also see next entry | P5/L/834<br>***#5709***<br> | **Frederick** (*sic*) **LIVINGSTONE** trading as<br>**LAMB & CO**<br>149 Wood Exchange *<br>London EC | |
| R1/166<br>3 April 1902<br>Sent by Payton, Pepper & Co | | P9/L/28-33<br>***#5710-15***<br> | **Ferdinand LIVINGSTONE** trading as<br>**LAMB & CO** *<br>147(*sic*) Wool(*sic*) Exchange<br>London EC | |
| R1/37<br>19 December 1896<br>Sent by George A Richards | 67 Water Street [1]<br>Brixton, London<br>28 Lancaster Road [2]<br>Strand Green, London<br>See also LBrsLtd | P5/L/810<br>***#5716***<br> | **Henry Charles FREEMAN** [1] *<br>**George Augustus FREEMAN** [2] (Partners)<br>trading as<br>**LUCAS & CO**<br>22 Hylton Street<br>Birmingham | Silversmiths |

| REGISTRATION DETAILS | MAKER'S PRIVATE ADDRESS and DETAILS | PLATE and MARK DETAILS | MAKER/COMPANY and BUSINESS ADDRESS | MAKER'S TRADE |
|---|---|---|---|---|
| R3/93<br>22 February 1939<br>Sent by L C W Holt | Stoneycroft<br>Marine Park<br>West Kirby<br>Cheshire | P21/H/8<br>*#5717*  | **Lawrence C Whalley HOLT**<br>Art School<br>Town unlisted (Liverpool ?) | Art student |
| R2/98<br>23 November 1909<br>Sent by Britton & Son<br>Two sizes | 73 Vyse Street<br>Birmingham | P13/L/30,31<br>*#5718,9*  | **O LEONARDT** trading as<br>**O LEONARDT & CO**<br>73 Vyse Street<br>Birmingham | Wholesale jewellers |
| R1/215<br>21 June 1904<br>Sent by L Duff | 100 Alexandra Road<br>London NW | P9/D/43<br>*#5720*  | **Lionel DUFF**<br>44 Hatton Garden<br>London EC | Manufacturing jeweller |
| R3/7<br>23 March 1922<br>Sent by Henry James Lester | Marle Hill<br>Chalford<br>Woodview<br>Chalford | P15/L/24<br>*#5721*  | **Henry James LESTER**<br>**Arthur DAMSELL** trading as<br>**LESTER & DAMSELL**<br>High Street<br>Chalford<br>Nr Stroud<br>Gloucestershire | Manufacturers of umbrella mounts |
| R1/23<br>7 March 1896<br>Sent by Louis C Dettmer | 35 Breakspear Road<br>London EC | P5/D/736<br>*#5722*  | **Louis Charles DETTMER** trading as<br>**CALIPE, DETTMER & CO** *<br>21 Poland Street<br>Oxford Street<br>London | Jewellers |
| PP1/188<br>GTD 1816 | | P1/12/x7<br>*#5723-9*  | **LITHERLAND, DAVIS & CO**<br>63 Church Street<br>Liverpool | Watch and watchcase manufacturers |
| R2/203<br>3 February 1916<br>Sent by W J Skelton | Private address same as business | P15/E/12<br>*#5730*  | **Lyon EPRILE**<br>15 Hope Park Terrace<br>Edinburgh<br>Scotland | Wholesale jeweller |
| R3/158<br>23 November 1956<br>Sent by E Leadbeater<br>Two sizes | 25 Meadowbank<br>Chorltonville<br>Manchester | P21/L/35,36<br>*#5731,2*  | **Edith LEADBEATER**<br>No business address entered | Housewife |
| Missing register<br>*c.*1886 | | P5/E/52<br>*#5733*  | **Unidentified** | |
| R1/86<br>2 December 1898<br>Sent by Lewis Neale | Grange Road<br>Olton<br>Birmingham | P9/N/2<br>*#5734*  | **Lewis Edwin NEALE**<br>55 Northampton Street<br>Birmingham | Jeweller |
| R1/212<br>19 April 1904<br>Sent by L E Neale | | P9/N/32<br>*#5735*  | | Ring manufacturer |
| LPB/58<br>23 June 1880 | | P3/I*sic*/x1<br>*#5736*  | | Jeweller |
| R1/230<br>8 April 1905 | | P9/N/33<br>*#5737*  | | |
| R1/231<br>11 April 1905 | | No new mark<br>*#5738* | | |

| REGISTRATION DETAILS | MAKER'S PRIVATE ADDRESS and DETAILS | PLATE and MARK DETAILS | MAKER/COMPANY and BUSINESS ADDRESS | MAKER'S TRADE |
|---|---|---|---|---|
| R3/135<br>28 February 1951<br>Sent by L Furness<br>Two sizes | Private address same as business<br><br>NB: First entry in new ***Biro*** pen | P21/F/14,15<br>***#5739,40***<br> | **Leslie FURNESS**<br>6 Roseleigh Avenue<br>Burnage<br>Manchester 19 | Student |
| Missing register<br>*c.*1892<br>Similar mark entered<br>BAO 24 October 1890 | | P5/F/427<br>***#5741***<br>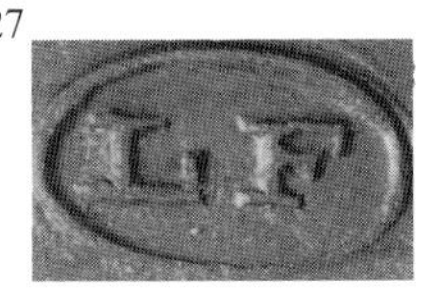 | **Lesser FRIEDLANDER** *<br>3 Houndsditch<br>London | Importer |
| R3/153<br>16 July 1954<br>Sent by Nathan Futter<br>(Dir) and Ann Futter | Both of 6 Penrhyn Drive<br>Bristwick<br>Lancashire | P21/G/38,39<br>***#5742,3***<br>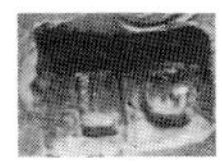 | **L GRINGAS LTD**<br>68, 68a and 69 Fennel Street<br>Manchester 4 | Manufacturing and repairing jewellers |
| R1/131<br>16 August 1900<br>Sent by W Walker | 1 Herbert House [1]<br>Stockwell Street<br>London SW<br>35 Warmesley Road [2]<br>Hornsey<br>London | P9/R/18,19<br>***#5744,5***<br> | **Ludwig GUNZEL** [1]<br>**Edward ROSENBERGER** [2] trading as<br>**GUNZEL & ROSENBERGER**<br>7 Victoria Avenue<br>Bishopsgate Street<br>London EC | Wholesale dealers in tobacconists goods |
| R1/152<br>13 September 1901<br>Sent by James George<br>Newbold | | P9/G/28<br>***#5746***<br> | | Tobacconists and fancy goods importers |
| Missing register<br>*c.*1891 | | P5/G/384<br>***#5747***<br> | | |
| R2/206<br>29 June 1916<br>Sent by Last &<br>Gregory Ltd | 21 Livingstone Road<br>Handsworth<br>47 Woodstock Road<br>Handsworth<br>Birmingham | P15/L/13,14<br>***#5748,9***<br> | **A R GREGORY** (Director)<br>**M LAST** trading as<br>**LAST & GREGORY LTD**<br>59 Key Hill<br>Birmingham | Manufacturing jewellers |
| R1/149<br>14 June 1901<br>Sent by Carrington<br>Brothers | Samplers Villas [1]<br>Crossgates, Leeds<br>11 Eldon Terrace [2]<br>Leeds | P9/L/21<br>***#5750***<br> | **William George LEATHERBARROW** [1]<br>**James Cookson HUME** [2] trading as<br>**LEATHER (*sic*) & HUME**<br>49 Aire Street<br>Leeds | Umbrella manufacturers |
| R1/121<br>16 February 1900<br>Sent by W H Leather<br>J Gammage | Private address same as business | P9/H/25<br>***#5751***<br> | **Leopold HEINZELMANN** *<br>60 Atlantic Road<br>Brixton<br>London SW | Manufacturing jeweller |
| R2/131<br>16 March 1911<br>Sent by<br>L Heinzelmann | | P13/H/70,71<br>***#5752,3***<br> | | Wholesale jeweller |
| R1/214<br>27 May 1904<br>Sent by Nathan &<br>Hayes Two sizes | Private address same as business | P9/H/60,61<br>***#5754,5754a***<br> | **Lewis HART** *<br>160 Victoria Street<br>London SW | Silversmith |
| R1/39<br>10 February 1897<br>Sent by Louis Houel<br>per H Ferguson | 1 Wembury Street<br>Harpurhey<br>This mark probably H & Co double struck – see *#3250* | P5/Z*sic*/814<br>***#5755***<br> | **Louis HOUEL** trading as<br>**HOUEL & CO**<br>13 Sugar Lane<br>Manchester | Umbrella and walking stick manufacturers |
| LPB/44<br>No mark in LPB just<br>the year 1885 | $8^{th}$ name on LPB/44 and $8^{th}$ mark on P5/J | P5/J/x1<br>***#5756***<br> | **Louis JACOB**<br>Hayden Road, Soho Hill<br>Birmingham | Silversmith |

| REGISTRATION DETAILS | MAKER'S PRIVATE ADDRESS and DETAILS | PLATE and MARK DETAILS | MAKER/COMPANY and BUSINESS ADDRESS | MAKER'S TRADE |
|---|---|---|---|---|
| R3/157<br>23 March 1956<br>Sent by L J Becker | Private address same as business | P21/B/47<br>*#5757*<br> | **Lucas John BECKER**<br>Holmeside, St Margaret's Road<br>Bowden<br>Cheshire | Antique dealer |
| LPB/44<br>30 November 1883<br>Sent by Pope & Phelps<br>No mark in LPB | 3rd name on LPB/44 and 3rd mark on P5/J<br>Not in 1882 or 1883 directories so trade unknown | P5/J/x1<br>*#5758*<br> | **L JACKSON & CO**<br>Naden Road<br>Soho Hill<br>Birmingham | Jewellers? |
| LPB/42<br>15 October 1879 | | P3/I*sic*/x1<br>*#5759*<br> | **Lyon Joseph JOSEPH**<br>88 Vyse Street<br>Birmingham | Factor |
| LPB/42<br>18 November 1880 | | P3/I*sic*/x1<br>*#5760*<br> | | |
| R3/18<br>16 September 1923<br>Sent by Candelent & Adams | Braenor<br>Eastwood Avenue | P15/L/27<br>*#5761*<br> | **Louis Jules LEVY** trading as<br>**Louis J LEVY & CO**<br>16 St Enoch Square<br>Glasgow and<br>27 Donegall Place<br>Belfast | Wholesale jewellers and diamond merchants |
| R2/214<br>1 February 1918<br>Sent by L J Wright | Private address same as business | P15/W/38-40<br>*#5766-8*<br> | **Lott John WRIGHT**<br>37 Woodland Road<br>Northfield<br>Birmingham | Manufacturing jeweller |
| R2/43<br>22 July 1907<br>Sent by Lott John Wright | | P13/W/1-4<br>*#5762-5*<br> | **Lott John WRIGHT**<br>11 Priory Road<br>Sheffield | Manufacturers agent |
| R1/136<br>7 November 1900<br>Sent by L J Wright | 2 Chatham Grove<br>Withington<br>Manchester | P9/W/42,43<br>*#5769,70*<br> | **Lott John WRIGHT**<br>17 Thomas Street<br>Manchester | Wholesale jeweller |
| R1/95<br>10 March 1899<br>Sent by J Hayward | 206 Hamstead Road [1]<br>Handsworth<br>213 Heathfield Road [2]<br>Handsworth, Birmingham<br>Telegraphic address "Ruby"<br>Birmingham | P9/L/5<br>*#5771*<br> | **Edward LINGARD** [1]<br>**Joseph William LINGARD**[2] trading as<br>**LAWRENCE & LINGARD**<br>Tenby Street North<br>Birmingham | Manufacturing jewellers |
| LPB/50<br>4 September 1882 | | P3/L/x3<br>*#5772-4*<br> | **LAWRENCE & LINGARD**<br>4 Gladstone Buildings<br>Richmond Street<br>Birmingham | |
| R1/189<br>1 April 1903<br>Sent by Mills & Gilpin | 107 Blondesbury Villas<br>London NW | P9/C/83<br>*#5775*<br> | **Lionel Louis COHEN** *<br>60 Hatton Garden<br>London | Ring manufacturer |
| R2/61<br>6 June 1908<br>Sent by Harry Emmanuel | 87 Burton Road<br>Brixton<br>London SW | P13/L/4<br>*#5776*<br> | **Leopold BOEKBINDER** (Managing Dir)<br>**James de Lara COHEN**<br>**B MOCATTA**<br>**Walker S HAIR**<br>**Montague WOOD**<br>**Herbert VIGERS** (Secretary) trading as<br>**LEOPOLD LTD** *<br>40 Hatton Garden, London EC<br>65 and 67 Regent Street, London<br>36 and 37 King Street, Cheapside, EC<br>67 Rue de la Victorie<br>Paris | Goldsmiths, silversmiths and jewellers |

| REGISTRATION DETAILS | MAKER'S PRIVATE ADDRESS and DETAILS | PLATE and MARK DETAILS | MAKER/COMPANY and BUSINESS ADDRESS | MAKER'S TRADE |
|---|---|---|---|---|
| R1/224<br>14 December 1904<br>Sent by L Mander | 71 Elizabeth Street<br>Cheetham<br>Manchester | P9/M/86<br>***#5777*** 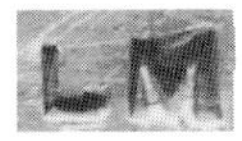  | **Louis MANDER**<br>24 Market Place<br>Manchester | Manufacturing jeweller and diamond mounter |
| Not in R1 as expected<br>*c.* Jan to April 1907<br>Similar mark BAO<br>4 November 1898 | | P9/M/0*sic*<br>***#5778***   | **Lucy MANDER**<br>13-14 Hollier Street<br>Birmingham | Pipe mount maker |
| R2/138<br>16 June 1911<br>Sent by Louis Mander | 60 Brunswick Street<br>Cheetham<br>Manchester | P13/M/44<br>***#5779***   | **Louis MANDER**<br>20 Cannon Street<br>Manchester | Manufacturing jeweller |
| R3/13<br>25 October 1922<br>Sent by Elizabeth Murphy<br>Two sizes<br><br>11 November 1929 | Private address same as business<br><br>P15/M/67 undated<br>*c.* July 1927 | P15/M/48,67<br>***#5780,1***  <br>P15/M/73<br>***#5782*** 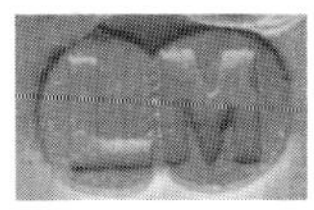  | **Elizabeth MURPHY**<br>28 Princes Avenue<br>Liverpool | No trade entered<br>Student? |
| R3/142<br>24 March 1953<br>Sent by L M Coventry<br>Two sizes<br><br>17 November 1959 | 22 Shrewsbury Road<br>Oxton<br>Birkenhead | P21/C/58,59<br>***#5783,4*** 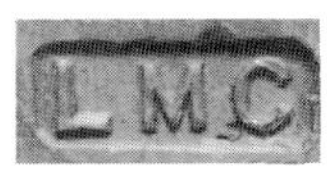 <br>P21/C/83<br>***#5785*** 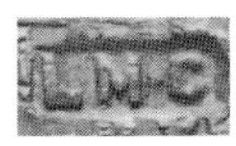  | **Laura Mary COVENTRY**<br>No business address entered | Designer craftworker |
| R3/121<br>31 January 1948<br>Sent by Lillian Mary Pinson Two sizes | Auldgirth<br>Victoria Park<br>Manchester 14 | P21/P/19,20<br>***#5786,7***   | **Lillian Mary PINSON**<br>No business address entered | Student |
| R3/139<br>4 October 1952<br>Sent by L M Stubbs<br><br>Undated<br>*c.* December 1953<br><br>29 May 1958 | 78 Fieldton Road<br>West Derby<br>Liverpool 11 | P21/S/51<br>***#5788***  <br>P21/S/54<br>***#5789*** <br>P21/S/74<br>***#5790***  | **Lillian Molyneux STUBBS**<br>174 Hoylake Street<br>Moreton, Wirral<br>Liverpool 46 | Student metal worker |
| R3/79<br>2 October 1935<br>Sent by B H Britton & Sons<br>35 Hockley Hill<br>Birmingham | 58 Portland Street<br>London W1 | P15/N/25<br>***#5791***   | **Louis NEWMARK**<br>**Elizabeth NEWMARK** trading as<br>**Louis NEWMARK LTD**<br>44 Hatton Garden<br>London EC1 | Watch and clock importers |
| R2/237<br>31 January 1921<br>Sent by Handcock & Walker<br>Two sizes | 23 Lindfield Gardens<br>London NW3 | P15/O/4,5<br>***#5792,3***   | **Louis ORLIK** *<br>62 Barbican<br>London EC3 | Briar pipe maker |
| R1/166<br>7 April 1902<br>Sent by B Wade | 17 Orchard Street<br>Neath | P9/Q*sic*/125<br>***#5794***   | **Oliver Llewellyn PARKER**<br>Opposite Gwyn Hall<br>Neath | Tobacconist |
| R2/65<br>18 September 1908<br>Sent by Leo Rathausky | 43 Half Moon Crescent<br>Barnsbury<br>London N | P13/R/23<br>***#5795***   | **Leo RATHAUSKY** *<br>43 Half Moon Crescent<br>Barnsbury<br>London N | Gold and silver mounter |

| REGISTRATION DETAILS | MAKER'S PRIVATE ADDRESS and DETAILS | PLATE and MARK DETAILS | | MAKER/COMPANY and BUSINESS ADDRESS | MAKER'S TRADE |
|---|---|---|---|---|---|
| R3/134<br>13 July 1950<br>Sent by S Watson<br>Two sizes | Private address same as business | P21/L/31,32<br>***#5796,7*** |  | **LAKELAND RURAL INDUSTRIES**<br>(Directed by Stanley Watson, ARPS,FRSA)<br>Grange, Borrowdale<br>Cumberland | Wood and metal workers |
| R2/206<br>22 June 1916<br>Sent by H G Raynor | 44 Godwin Road<br>Forest Gate<br>London | P15/R/7<br>***#5798*** |  | **Louis RAYNOR LTD**<br>H G Rayner (Secretary)<br>25a Hatton Garden<br>London | Manufacturers agents and merchants |
| R2/210<br>6 December 1916<br>Sent by Louis Raynor Ltd | | P15/R/8<br>***#5799*** |  | **H G RAYNOR** for<br>**Louis RAYNOR LTD**<br>25a Hatton Garden<br>London | Commission agents and general merchants |
| LPB/50<br>29 April 1880<br>Sent by John Ward | | P3/L/x2<br>***#5800,1*** | 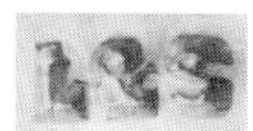 | **Phineas Harris LEVI &**<br>**Joseph Wolff SALAMAN** trading as<br>**LEVI & SALAMAN** *<br>18/19/20 Upper Hockley Street<br>Birmingham | Silversmiths |
| Missing register<br>*c.*1886<br>Similar mark entered LAO 28 July 1896 | See also Leon Steiner | P5/S/30<br>***#5802*** |  | **Louis SYMELMAN** *<br>56 York Road, Kings Cross<br>London N | Watchmaker |
| R2/129<br>28 February 1911<br>Sent by Levi & Salaman | 4 Greenfield Crescent<br>Birmingham<br>Sutton Coldfield<br>4 Greenfield Crescent<br>Birmingham | P13/L/47<br>***#5803*** |  | **LEVI & SALAMAN LTD** *<br>Joseph Wolff Salaman (Director)<br>Clive Joseph Levi (Director)<br>Lewis Henry Salaman (Director)<br>143 Newhall Street<br>Birmingham and<br>2 Hansell Street<br>London EC | Manufacturing silversmiths |
| R3/24<br>27 September 1924<br>Sent by Last & Smith | 47 Woodstock Road<br>Handsworth<br>13 Broughton Street<br>Hockley<br>Birmingham | P15/L/30,31<br>***#5804,5*** |  | **William Nelson LAST**<br>**Alfred John SMITH** trading as<br>**LAST & SMITH**<br>162 Hockley Hill<br>Birmingham | Manufacturing jewellers |
| B 1813-29<br>PP3/83<br>PMR 1813-48 | Succeeded by his son Sylvester Lewis Samuel<br><br>See also JLS | P1/10/x3<br>***#5806-8*** |  | **Lewis SAMUEL & CO** (G)<br>4 Lord Street (1824)<br>48 Lord Street (1848)<br>Liverpool | Watch manufacturers, silversmiths and watchcase makers |
| Missing register<br>*c.*1887 Similar mark without full-stop BAO 24 March 1882 | See also Louis Symelman | P5/S/118<br>***#5809*** |  | **Leon STEINER** *<br>16 Percival Street, Clerkenwell<br>London | Watchmaker |
| LPB/50<br>18 March 1880<br>Sent by John Ward | | P3/L/x3<br>***#5810-12*** |  | **LEVI & SALAMAN** *<br>18/19/20 Upper Hockley Street<br>Birmingham | Silversmiths and jewellers |
| LPB/46<br>7 April 1883<br>Sent by J Ward | | P3/L/x2<br>***#5813,14*** |  | **LEVI & SALAMAN** *<br>10 York Street<br>Hockley<br>Birmingham | |
| R1/107<br>2 August 1899<br>Sent by Levi & Salaman | 4 Greenfield Crescent<br>Edgbaston<br>Birmingham<br>Driffield<br>Sutton Coldfield | P9/L/10,11<br>***#5815,16*** |  | **Levi SALAMAN**<br>**Joseph Wolff SALAMAN**<br>**Phineas Harris LEVI**<br>**Clive Joseph LEVI** trading as<br>**LEVI & SALAMAN** *<br>143 Newhall Street<br>Birmingham | Manufacturing silversmiths |

| REGISTRATION DETAILS | MAKER'S PRIVATE ADDRESS and DETAILS | PLATE and MARK DETAILS | MAKER/COMPANY and BUSINESS ADDRESS | MAKER'S TRADE |
|---|---|---|---|---|
| R1/177<br>21 October 1902<br>Sent by self | Private address same as business | P9/S/52<br>***#5817***<br> | **Lewis SIGALOV**<br>60 Settle Street<br>Commercial Road<br>London EC | Jeweller |
| R2/106<br>11 March 1910<br>Sent by Hirst Brothers & Co Ltd<br>BAO 14.024 | 38 Fern Street<br>Coppice<br>Oldham | P13/S/51<br>***#5818***<br>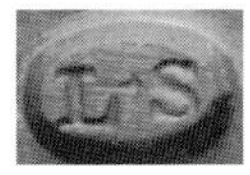 | **Law SWALLOW**<br>8 Curzon Street<br>Oldham | Jeweller |
| R2/128<br>11 February 1911<br>Sent by L Schlund | 2 Ballbeck Road<br>Highbury<br>London N | P13/S/63<br>***#5819***<br> | **Leon SCHLUND & CO** * trading as<br>**THE LONDON REFINING & METALLURGICAL WORKS**<br>32 Clerkenwell Road<br>London EC | Assayers and refiners |
| R1/179<br>15 November 1902<br>Sent by selves<br>Two sizes | 32 Hamstead Road<br>Handsworth<br>Birmingham | P9/S/57,58<br>***#5820,1***<br>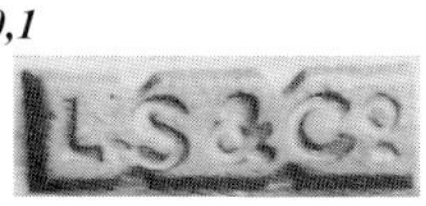 | **Lionel SMITH** trading as<br>**Lionel SMITH & CO**<br>56 Spencer Street<br>Birmingham | Manufacturing goldsmiths and silversmiths |
| R2/179<br>14 November 1913<br>Sent by selves | | P13/S/116<br>***#5822***<br> | | |
| R2/203<br>16 February 1916<br>Sent by Lionel Smith | 1 Endsleigh Street<br>London NW | P15/S/26,27<br>***#5823,4***<br> | **Lionel SMITH & CO LTD**<br>Lionel Smith (Director)<br>56 Spencer Street<br>Birmingham | Silversmiths |
| R2/134<br>6 May 1911<br>Sent by J & R Griffin Ltd<br>BAO 18.512 | Bellwood<br>13 Forbes Road<br>Edinburgh | P13/L/48<br>***#5825***<br> | **George Brown LATIMER** trading as<br>**LATIMER & SONS**<br>143–147 Lothian Road<br>Edinburgh | Goldsmiths |
| R2/80<br>1 May 1909<br>Sent by J & R Griffin | | P13/L/12<br>***#5826***<br> | **George Brown LATIMER** (sole partner) trading as<br>**LATIMER & SONS**<br>143–147 Lothian Road<br>Edinburgh | Jewellers |
| Missing register<br>*c.*1887<br>Similar mark BAO<br>26 February 1884 | | P5/W/77<br>***#5827***<br> | **LAWSON, SON & WARD**<br>5 Hatton Garden<br>London | Manufacturing jewellers |
| Not in SPB or LPB so struck 1860-3 | Lewis Thomas, clockmaker in Chester 1750 is too early, but may be related | P3/T/x1<br>***#5828***<br> | **Unidentified** | |
| | | P3/T/x3<br>***#5829-31***<br> | **Unidentified** | |
| CMC/137 | Very tentative attribution | P1/16/x4<br>***#5832-5***<br> | **Lewis WYATT**<br>Mill Street (1828-9)<br>Macclesfield<br>192 Higher Hillgate (1834)<br>Stockport | Clockmaker and watchmaker |
| Missing register<br>*c.*1890<br>Similar mark CAO<br>19 February 1902 | | P5/L/295a<br>***#5836***<br>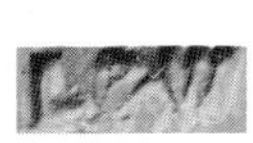 | **Henry LAWSON &**<br>**John Barron WARD** trading as<br>**LAWSON & WARD** *<br>5 Hatton Garden<br>London EC | Wholesale jewellers |

| REGISTRATION DETAILS | MAKER'S PRIVATE ADDRESS and DETAILS | PLATE and MARK DETAILS | MAKER/COMPANY and BUSINESS ADDRESS | MAKER'S TRADE |
|---|---|---|---|---|
| Missing register<br>*c.*1890 | | P5/L/295b<br>***#5837***<br> | **LAWSON & WARD** *<br>5 Hatton Garden<br>London EC | Wholesale jewellers |
| Missing register<br>*c.*1892<br>Two sizes | | P5/L/399a,b<br>***#5838,5838a***<br> | | |
| R1/162<br>19 February 1902<br>Sent by J Gammage | Wimbledon [1]<br>London SW<br>Dimera [2]<br>Streatham<br>London SW | P9/L/24-26<br>***#5839-41***<br> | **Henry LAWSON** [1]<br>**John Barron WARD** [2] trading as<br>**LAWSON & WARD** *<br>5 Hatton Garden<br>London EC | |
| LPB/88<br>30 November 1881<br>No name or address<br>LPB mark shown<br>Similar mark LAO<br>24 November 1879 | | Not on P3<br>***#5842***<br> | **Louis WEILL** *<br>3 Holborn Circus<br>London | Watch manufacturer |
| R1/62<br>4 June 1894<br>Sent by W Walker | 69 Gibson Square<br>London N<br>Michael Weiss, tobacconist, of 65/66 Basinghall Street in 1894 (renumbering ?) may be related | P5/W/565<br>***#5843***<br> | **Leopold WEISS**<br>62, 63 Basinghall Street<br>London EC | Tobacconist ? |
| R1/210<br>12 March 1904<br>Sent by Lawson, Ward & Gammage | Down View<br>Arterberry Road<br>Wimbledon<br>106 Leigham Court Road<br>Streatham<br>25 Collingwood Avenue<br>Fortis Green, London N<br>Braceside<br>Regents Park Road<br>Church End<br>Finchley | P9/L/53-58<br>***#5844-9***<br> | **Henry LAWSON**<br>**B WARD**<br>**J E GAMMAGE**<br>**G H GAMMAGE** trading as<br>**LAWSON, WARD & GAMMAGE** *<br>5 Hatton Garden and<br>26 Clerkenwell Road<br>London | Manufacturing jewellers |
| R1/209<br>4 March 1904<br>Sent by J E Gammage<br>cancelled and recut<br>22 March 1904 | | P9/L/47-52<br>***#5850-5***<br> | | |
| R3/19<br>27 October 1923<br>Sent by Benson Brothers | Beechwood Road<br>Sanderstead?, Surrey<br>Melrose<br>Royston Park Road<br>Hatch End, Middlesex<br>20 Church Crescent<br>Church End<br>Finchley<br>Heath Drive<br>Potters Bar<br>Coverdale<br>Chorleywood, Herts | P15/L/28<br>***#5856***<br> | **LAWSON, WARD & GAMMAGE** *<br>Henry Lawson (Director)<br>John Ellis Gammage (Director)<br>George Henry Gammage (Director)<br>Sydney Herbert Gammage (Director)<br>Ernest William Wedge (Director)<br>26 Clerkenwell Road<br>London and<br>24 Berry Street<br>London and<br>Ely Place<br>Tenby Street<br>Birmingham | |
| LPB/96<br>25 September 1880 | | P3/Y*sic*/x2<br>***#5857,8***<br> | **Laurence W ZIMMERMAN**<br>98 Seal Street<br>Liverpool | Watch manufacturer |

| REGISTRATION DETAILS | MAKER'S PRIVATE ADDRESS and DETAILS | PLATE and MARK DETAILS | MAKER/COMPANY and BUSINESS ADDRESS | MAKER'S TRADE |
|---|---|---|---|---|
| R3/154<br>30 March 1955<br>Sent by M J Allen | 142 Darnley Road<br>Gravesend<br>Kent | P21/A/22<br>***#5859***<br> | **Madeline Jane ALLEN**<br>No business address entered | Student silversmith |
| R3/102<br>17 December 1941<br>Sent by J W Mason & Co | 14 Glenavon Road [1]<br>Birmingham 14<br>92 Hugh Road [2]<br>Smethwick | P21/M/13<br>***#5860***<br> | **Jeremiah William MASON** [1]<br>**Frank ADDERLEY** [2] trading as<br>**J W MASON & CO**<br>61 Northampton Street<br>Birmingham | Manufacturing jewellers |
| MR1/143<br>MR2/115<br>J3/398 | Free 1721<br><br>See also TM | P1/15/x1<br>***#5861***<br>type 1a<br> | **Thomas MADDOCK**<br>Chester | Silversmith |
| | Spoons 1716-20 | P1/15/x1<br>***#5862***<br>type 1b<br> | | |
| | Tumbler cup and seal 1730 | P1/15/x1<br>***#5863***<br>type 2a<br>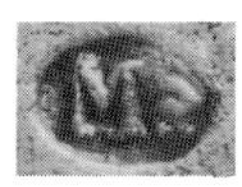 | | |
| | | P1/15/x1<br>***#5864***<br>type 2b<br> | | |
| R3/151<br>13 April 1954<br>Sent by W J Pellow Ltd<br>31 Hylton Street<br>Birmingham | 8 Gainsborough Road [1]<br>Southport | P21/B*sic*/41<br>***#5865***<br> | **Maurice ABELSON & CO**<br>Sole Proprietor Maurice Abelson [1]<br>23 Lord Street<br>Southport | Wholesale manufacturing jewellers and diamond merchants |
| Not in R3 as expected<br>Mar 1925 to Oct 1926<br>Cut corners oblong cameo mark LAO<br>6 September 1907 | | P15/H/90,91<br>***#5866,7***<br> | **Marc Alfred HOLLAND** *<br>45 Holborn Viaduct<br>London EC | Importer of foreign gold and silver watchcases |
| R2/92<br>8 September 1909<br>Sent by Marc Alfred Holland | 38 Tavistock Square<br>London | P13/H/41,42<br>***#5868,9***<br> | **Marc Alfred HOLLAND** *<br>46a Holborn Viaduct<br>London | Watch manufacturer |
| GTD 1844-73<br>MR3/135<br>SOT/122-3 | See also JM #5073,4 | P2/M/x1<br>***#5870***<br> | **Joseph MAYER** *<br>68/70 Lord Street<br>Liverpool | Goldsmith and silversmith |
| R1/169<br>3 June 1902<br>Sent by Marples & Beasley | 1 St Mary Road<br>Smethwick<br>24 South Road<br>Handsworth | P9/M/37<br>***#5871***<br> | **Edward Osborne MARPLES**<br>**Joseph Henry BEASLEY** trading as<br>**MARPLES & BEASLEY**<br>15 Albion Street<br>Birmingham | Jewellers |
| R3/169<br>18 August 1959<br>Sent by M Barnett | 105 Grove Hall Court<br>St John's Wood<br>London NW8 | P21/B/57<br>***#5872***<br> | **Maurice BARNETT**<br>40 Hatton Garden<br>London EC1 | Manufacturing jeweller |

| REGISTRATION DETAILS | MAKER'S PRIVATE ADDRESS and DETAILS | PLATE and MARK DETAILS | MAKER/COMPANY and BUSINESS ADDRESS | MAKER'S TRADE |
|---|---|---|---|---|
| R1/132<br>2 October 1900<br>Sent by Alfred Marston<br>Two sizes | 49 Havelock Road [1]<br>Handsworth<br>141 Park Road [2]<br>Hockley<br>Birmingham | P9/M/025,026<br>*#5873,4*<br> | **Alfred MARSTON** [1]<br>**Walter BAYLISS** [2] trading as<br>**MARSTON & BAYLISS** *<br>20a Branston Street<br>Birmingham | Silversmiths |
| R2/23<br>17 August 1906<br>Sent by W Bayliss<br><br>Punches cancelled 22 October 1906 and partnership dissolved | 263 Icknield Street<br>Birmingham<br>49 Havelock Road<br>Birmingham | P9/M/106<br>*#5875*<br><br>P9/M/105<br>*#5876*<br> | **Walter BAYLISS**<br>**Alfred MARSTON** trading as<br>**MARSTON & BAYLISS** *<br>263 Icknield Street<br>Birmingham | Manufacturing jewellers |
| R3/156<br>21 October 1955<br>Sent by M Buck<br>Two sizes | Vonga House<br>4 Frenchwood Knoll<br>Preston<br>Lancs | P21/B/43,44<br>*#5877,8*<br> | **Mary BUCK**<br>No business address entered | Amateur silversmith |
| R3/67<br>29 May 1933<br>Sent by M Barnes | Wasdale<br>St Anthony's Road<br>Blundellsands<br>Liverpool | P15/B/213<br>*#5879*<br> | **Marjory BARNES**<br>City School of Art<br>Liverpool | Jewellery and metalwork student |
| R1/169<br>3 June 1902<br>Sent by Marples & Beasley<br>Two sizes | 1 St Mary Road<br>Smethwick<br>24 South Road<br>Handsworth | P9/M/35,36<br>*#5880,1*<br> | **Edward Osborne MARPLES**<br>**Joseph Henry BEASLEY** trading as<br>**MARPLES & BEASLEY**<br>15 Albion Street<br>Birmingham | Jewellers |
| LPB/84<br>22 November 1882 | | P3/M/x2<br>*#5882,3*<br> | **Edward MOORE BROTHERS**<br>38 London Street<br>Derby | Jewellers |
| R1/194<br>5 June 1903<br>Sent by M Bachmer | Private address same as business | P9/B/106<br>*#5884*<br> | **Morris BACHMER**<br>14 Bold Place<br>Liverpool | Diamond mounter and ring maker |
| R2/97<br>13 November 1909<br>Sent by Marcus Beaver | Oakley<br>Fallowfield<br>Manchester | P13/B/70<br>*#5885*<br> | **Marcus BEAVER** *<br>7, 9 St Ann Street<br>Manchester | Jeweller and silversmith |
| R2/216<br>3 May 1918<br>Sent by Benson Brothers | 21 St Peters Road<br>Handsworth<br>56 Orchard Road<br>Erdington<br>Birmingham | P15/B/93<br>*#5886*<br> | **Henry BOSLEY** (Director)<br>**Theodore BOSLEY** (Director)<br>trading as<br>**MITCHELL BOSLEY & CO LTD**<br>74, 75 Bath Street<br>Birmingham | Electroplate manufacturers |
| R1/232<br>2 May 1905<br>Sent by Marples & Beasley<br>Three sizes | Holly Road<br>Edgbaston<br>South Road<br>Handsworth | P9/M/90-92<br>*#5887-9*<br> | **Edward Osborne MARPLES**<br>**Joseph Henry BEASLEY** trading as<br>**MARPLES & BEASLEY**<br>15 Albion Street<br>Birmingham | Jewellers and silversmiths |
| R1/149<br>2 July 1901<br>Sent by Haseler & Holmes<br>Two sizes | 22 Dunsmore Road [1]<br>Stamford Hill<br>19 Rosendale Road [2]<br>Dulwich, London | P9/M/28,29<br>*#5890,1*<br> | **John Baker BENNETT** [1]<br>**Ernest MURRELL** (*sic*) [2] trading as<br>**MURRLE, BENNETT & CO** *<br>13 Charterhouse Street<br>London EC | Jewellers |

| REGISTRATION DETAILS | MAKER'S PRIVATE ADDRESS and DETAILS | PLATE and MARK DETAILS | MAKER/COMPANY and BUSINESS ADDRESS | MAKER'S TRADE |
|---|---|---|---|---|
| R1/188<br>18 March 1903<br>Sent by C Horner | 62 Thrale Road<br>Streatham Park<br>87 Bethune Road<br>Stamford Hill<br>London | P9/B*sic*/85,101<br>***#5892,3***<br> | **Ernest MURRLE**<br>**John Baker BENNETT** trading as<br>**MURRLE, BENNETT & CO** *<br>13 Charterhouse Street<br>London EC | Wholesale jewellers |
| R1/195<br>16 June 1903<br>Sent by C Horner<br>Three sizes | | P9/M/49-67 and P9/B/82-89<br>***#5894-5920***<br> | | |
| R2/206<br>5 July 1916<br>Sent by Philip H Manison<br>BAO 23.507 23.508<br>Two sizes | 524 Chester Road<br>Erdington<br>Birmingham | P15/M/23,24<br>***#5921,2***<br> | **MANISON BAYLISS & CO LTD**<br>Philip Henry Manison (Principal)<br>63 Tenby Street North<br>Birmingham | Goldsmiths and silversmiths |
| R2/200<br>15 October 1915<br>Sent by Magen Brothers | 5 Greenfield Street<br>Stepney<br>59 New Road<br>Stepney<br>London | P15/M/19<br>***#5923***<br> | **Pinkus MAGEN**<br>**Abraham Emanuel MAGEN** trading as<br>**MAGEN BROTHERS**<br>5 Greenfield Street<br>Stepney<br>London | Gold ring, chain and bracelet manufacturers |
| | | P15/M/18<br>***#5924***<br> | | |
| R1/79<br>3 October 1894<br>Sent by Minshall & Latimer | Private address same as business | P5/M/595<br>***#5925***<br> | **Charles Dew MILLER**<br>**Richard William Bentley MILLER**<br>trading as **MILLER BROTHERS** *<br>78 Newgate Street<br>London | Jewellers |
| R2/207<br>26 July 1916<br>Sent by J & R Griffin Ltd<br>BAO 28 374 | 16 Vineyard Hill<br>Wimbledon<br>Surrey | P15/M/25<br>***#5926***<br> | **MILLER BROTHERS LONDON LTD** *<br>WC Miller (Director)<br>16–18 Beak Street<br>Regent Street<br>London W | Factors and merchants |
| R1/40<br>8 March 1897<br>Sent by Stokes & Ireland<br>Chas Vale | 49 Albion Street [1]<br>London<br>6 Stanhope Terrace [2]<br>London | P5/M/822<br>***#5927***<br> | **William GIBSON** [1]<br>**John Lawrence LANGMAN** [2] trading as<br>**MAPPIN BROTHERS** *<br>220 Regent Street<br>66 Cheapside, London and<br>The Queens Works, Bakers Hill<br>Sheffield | Silversmiths |
| R1/19<br>3 January 1896<br>Sent by James Moore | 46 Stafford Street<br>Derby | P5/M/716<br>***#5928***<br> | **James MOORE** trading as<br>**MOORE BROTHERS & CO**<br>14 Curzon Street<br>Derby | Goldsmiths and jewellers |
| R1/36<br>21 November 1896<br>Sent by Villiers & Jackson<br>R1 has P5/M/804 in error for P5/M/805. | Clapham Park<br>Sutton<br>London | P5/M/805<br>***#5929***<br> | **Charles Dew MILLER**<br>**Richard William Bentley MILLER**<br>trading as **MILLER BROTHERS** *<br>78 Newgate Street<br>London | Wholesale jewellers |
| R3/103<br>11 January 1943<br>Sent by Moore Brothers & Co Ltd | | P21/M/14<br>***#5930***<br> | **MOORE BROTHERS & CO (JEWELLERS ) LTD**<br>Sealed in the presence of:-<br>Arthur Charles Moore (Director)<br>GL Hufton (Director Secretary)<br>14 Curzon Street (Registered Office)<br>Derby | Manufacturing jewellers |

| REGISTRATION DETAILS | MAKER'S PRIVATE ADDRESS and DETAILS | PLATE and MARK DETAILS | MAKER/COMPANY and BUSINESS ADDRESS | MAKER'S TRADE |
|---|---|---|---|---|
| R2/99<br>15 December 1909<br>Sent by<br>W R Macdonall | 35 Hillary Street<br>Leeds | P13/M/31<br>*#5931*<br> | **William Robertson MACDONALL**<br>trading as **MAX BROTHERS**<br>Boar Lane Chambers<br>Basinghall Street<br>Leeds | Manufacturing goldsmiths and jewellers |
| R2/213<br>11 December 1917<br>Sent by Benson Brothers | 5 The Drive<br>Kersal | P15/S/30<br>*#5932*<br> | **Marks Barnett SHIBKO**<br>11 Kilverts Building<br>Withy Grove<br>Manchester | Watch importer |
| R2/230<br>13 May 1920<br>Sent by B Shibko | | P15/S/40, 41<br>*#5933,4*<br> | **Marks Barnett SHIBKO**<br>12a Withy Grove<br>Manchester | |
| SPB/13<br>6 October 1877 | | P3/M/x2<br>*#5935,6*<br> | **MEYERS** or **MAYERS BROTHERS**<br>Caroline Street<br>Birmingham | |
| Missing register<br>*c.*1892 | | P5/C/417<br>*#5937*<br> | **Unidentified** | |
| R3/42<br>31 July 1928<br>Sent by F Massingham | 3 Highbury Avenue<br>Thornhill Road<br>Handsworth<br>Birmingham | P15/M/63<br>*#5938*<br> | **F MASSINGHAM** trading as<br>**W A MASSINGHAM**<br>55 Northampton Street<br>Birmingham | Medallist and badge maker |
| LPB/54<br>5 July 1880<br>Sent by B H Joseph & Co | | P3/M/x1<br>*#5939*<br> | **MACKAY & CHISHOLME** *<br>57 Princess Street<br>Edinburgh | Jewellers, gold and silversmiths, dealers in antique silver and curiosities |
| R1/224<br>20 December 1904<br>Sent by C Horner | Hill Crest, Lyttelton Road<br>Edgbaston<br>74 Portland Road<br>Edgbaston | P9/M/87<br>*#5940*<br> | **Walter Henry MARKS** *<br>**Samuel Tobias COHEN**<br>92/94/96 Camden Street<br>Birmingham | Wholesale jewellers |
| R1/214<br>28 May 1904<br>Sent by J & R Griffin | 4 Lyttelton Road<br>Edgbaston<br>74 Portland Road<br>Edgbaston | P9/M/79<br>*#5941*<br> | **Walter Henry MARKS** *<br>**Samuel Tobias COHEN**<br>94/96 Camden Street<br>Birmingham | Jewellers and silversmiths |
| Missing register<br>*c.*1887 | | P5/M/73<br>*#5942*<br> | **Unidentified** | |
| LPB/92<br>26 September 1882 | | P3/M/x1<br>*#5943*<br> | **McCLELLAND BROTHERS & CO (Hugh & John)** *<br>The Crescent<br>59 Cambridge Street<br>Birmingham | Jewellers and factors |
| LPB/56 SP27/1<br>19 January 1884<br>Sent by E Whitehouse<br>No mark in LPB | | P5/M/x1<br>*#5944*<br> | **McCLELLAND & DUFFUS**<br>63 Warstone Lane<br>Birmingham | Manufacturing jewellers |
| LPB/34<br>14 Sep1882<br>Sent by Pope & Phelps | | P3/G/x2<br>*#5945,6*<br> | **McGREGOR & GARDNER**<br>7 Princess Square<br>Glasgow | Wholesale jewellers and watchmakers |
| R3/11<br>28 July 1922<br>Sent by Ernest Woodcock | 157 Lutterworth Road<br>Northampton<br>Pinner<br>North London | P15/M/47<br>*#5947*<br> | **MIDLAND CHAIN & MESH CO**<br>Ernest Woodcock (Director)<br>Sigfreid Simon (Director)<br>King Street<br>Northampton | Manufacturers of chain and mesh |

| REGISTRATION DETAILS | MAKER'S PRIVATE ADDRESS and DETAILS | PLATE and MARK DETAILS | MAKER/COMPANY and BUSINESS ADDRESS | MAKER'S TRADE |
|---|---|---|---|---|
| R2/45<br>31 August 1907<br>Sent by Martin Hall & Co<br>Two sizes | 99 Rustling Road<br>Sheffield | P9/M/119,120<br>*#5948,9*<br> | **MARPLES & CO** *<br>Harry Wilkins (Director)<br>18 Ludgate Hill<br>Birmingham | Manufacturing silversmiths |
| R1/105<br>24 June 1899<br>Sent by Thomas Nightingale | | P9/M/12<br>*#5950*<br> | **Richard Charles MARSH** trading as **MARSH & CO**<br>17 New Street and<br>18 Union Passage<br>Birmingham | Jewellers and watchmakers |
| R1/205<br>23 December 1903<br>Sent by Durban & Co | 6-26 Cathcart Hill<br>London N | P9/M/70-75<br>*#5951-6*<br> | **MARION & CO** *<br>George Frederick Bishop (Secretary)<br>22/23 Soho Square<br>London | Wholesale fancy goods dealers |
| LPB/50<br>21 November 1878 | | P3/M/x2<br>*#5957,8*<br>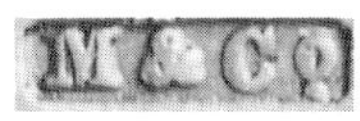 | **MARLOW & CO**<br>6/7/8 Spencer Street<br>Coventry | Watch manufacturers |
| R1/22<br>18 February 1896<br>Sent by John Horton | Farquhar House<br>Richmond Hill<br>Edgbaston | P5/M/729<br>*#5959*<br> | **Richard Charles MARSH** trading as **MARSH & CO**<br>76 High Street and<br>17 New Street<br>Birmingham | Jewellers |
| R2/167<br>11 January 1913<br>Sent by E H Durban | 10 Annesbury Road<br>Moseley<br>Birmingham | P13/M/56<br>*#5960*<br> | **Edward Henry DURBAN** trading as **E MEYERS & CO**<br>95 Spencer Street<br>Birmingham | Jewellers and precious stone dealers |
| R1/171<br>6 July 1902<br>Sent by W Manton | 6-26 Cathcart Hill<br>London N | P9/M/38<br>*#5961*<br> | **MARION & CO LTD** *<br>George Frederick Bishop (Director)<br>William Piper (Secretary)<br>22/23 Soho Square<br>London W | Manufacturers and fancy goods warehousemen |
| R3/43<br>9 October 1928<br>Sent by S Blanckensee & Sons Ltd | The Beeches [1]<br>Trumpington<br>Cambs<br>17 Glossop Road [2]<br>Cambridge 2 | P15/M/70<br>*#5962*<br>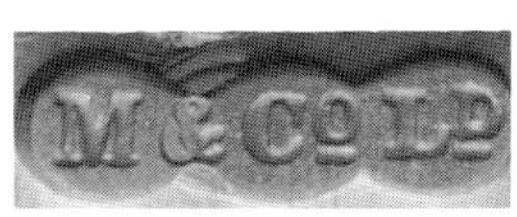 | **MUNSEY & CO LTD** *<br>Edwin Jackson[1] (Director and Chairman)<br>Leslie Edwin Jackson[2] (Director)<br>Frank Clarabut Jackson[1] (Director)<br>19, 20 Market Hill<br>Cambridge | Silversmiths and jewellers |
| R2/192<br>23 January 1915<br>Sent by Chas Peach & Son<br>Two sizes | 83 Water Lane<br>Brixton<br>London SW | P15/M/14,15<br>*#5963,4*<br> | **MOZON & CO LTD**<br>E W Wright (Managing Director)<br>12 Bartletts Passage Buildings<br>London EC | Watch and clock manufacturers |
| R2/211<br>20 April 1917<br>Sent by S Blanckensee<br>Two sizes | Bushmead<br>Tennison Road<br>Cambridge | P15/M/26,27<br>*#5965,6*<br> | **MUNSEY & CO** *<br>Edwin Jackson (Director)<br>19, 20 Market Street<br>Cambridge | Silversmiths and jewellers |
| R3/123<br>8 May 1948<br>Sent by M C Spence<br>Two sizes | Mildmay<br>Blackburn Place<br>Liverpool 8 | P21/S/40,41<br>*#5967,8*<br> | **Margaret Clara SPENCE**<br>City School of Art<br>Liverpool | Art metalworker |
| R3/8<br>25 March 1922<br>Sent by<br>W A Massingham | 109 Church Lane<br>Handsworth<br>Birmingham | P15/D/64<br>*#5969*<br> | **Matthew DAVIES**<br>102 Vyse Street<br>Birmingham | Jewellers factor |

| REGISTRATION DETAILS | MAKER'S PRIVATE ADDRESS and DETAILS | PLATE and MARK DETAILS | MAKER/COMPANY and BUSINESS ADDRESS | MAKER'S TRADE |
|---|---|---|---|---|
| R3/183<br>11 April 1962<br>Sent by M A Duggan | 92 Gorsey Lane<br>Wallasey<br>Cheshire | P21/D/36<br>***#5970***  | **Mrs Mary Agnes DUGGAN**<br>No business address entered | Amateur |
| R2/202<br>21 December 1915<br>Sent by Maurice Dewhurst | Private address same as business | P9*sic*/B*sic*/62<br>***#5971***  | **Maurice DEWHURST** trading as<br>**J WINTERBOTTOM**<br>30 Manchester Street<br>Oldham | Jeweller |
| 16 December 1921 | | P15/D/61<br>***#5972***  | | |
| R1/194<br>26 May 1903<br>Sent by M Davies | 317 Hagley Road<br>Birmingham | P9/D/41<br>***#5973***  | **Montague DAVIES** (*sic*)<br>21 Frederick Street<br>Birmingham | Gold chain manufacturer |
| LPB/24<br>5 February 1880 | | P3/D/x3<br>***#5974-6***  | **Montague DAVIS**<br>Regent Street<br>Birmingham | |
| R3/9<br>20 May 1922<br>Sent by M Dewhurst | Wincliff<br>West Drive<br>Cleveleys | P15/D/62<br>***#5977***  | **Maurice DEWHURST**<br>(Managing Director)<br>**DEWHURST & CO**<br>San Sea Works<br>Cleveleys, Liverpool and<br>82 Lancaster Avenue<br>Manchester | Manufacturing and wholesale jewellers |
| Missing register<br>*c.*1886<br>Similar mark LAO<br>10 December 1886 | | P5/L/55<br>***#5978***  | **Marcus David LOEWENSTARK** *<br>210 Strand<br>London WC | Masonic jewellers |
| R3/23<br>10 July 1924<br>Sent by M Evans | Private address same as business | P15/E/26<br>***#5979***  | **M EVANS**<br>Gwalin<br>Sandfield Road<br>West Derby<br>Liverpool | Art student |
| R1/183<br>28 January 1903<br>Sent by J H Wynn | 139 Amhurst Road<br>Hackney Down | P9/E/12a<br>***#5980***  | **Maurice EMANUEL** *<br>12 Cullum Street<br>Fenchurch Street<br>London EC | Wholesale jeweller |
| R2/186<br>5 May 1914<br>Sent by Thomas E Osborn | | P15/E/4<br>***#5981***  | **Maurice EMANUEL** *<br>27 Billiter Street<br>London | Jeweller |
| R3/35<br>no day December 1926<br>Sent by S Blanckensee & Son Ltd | 6 The Firs<br>Hulse Road<br>Northampton | P15/E/36<br>***#5982*** 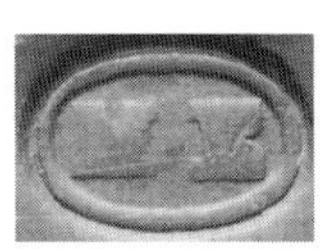 | **M EMANUEL**<br>11 High Street<br>Northampton | Silversmith |
| R2/18<br>25 May 1906<br>Sent by E Harper | 36 Cheltenham Road<br>Chorlton-cum-Hardy<br>Manchester | P9/H/81<br>***#5983***  | **Mary Ellen HARPER** trading as<br>**M E HARPER**<br>Pigots Court<br>68a Corporation Street<br>Manchester | Jeweller, etc |
| R3/151<br>3 April 1954<br>Sent by<br>M E MacDowell | 67 Beech Road<br>Stockport | P21/M/41<br>***#5984***  | **Mary Eveline MacDOWELL**<br>No business address entered | Student |

| REGISTRATION DETAILS | MAKER'S PRIVATE ADDRESS and DETAILS | PLATE and MARK DETAILS | MAKER/COMPANY and BUSINESS ADDRESS | MAKER'S TRADE |
|---|---|---|---|---|
| R2/105<br>8 March 1910<br>Sent by W Reeves | 22 Belsize Park<br>London W | P13/F/17<br>***#5985***<br>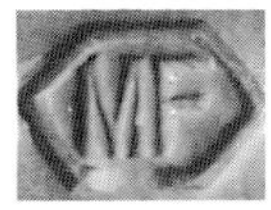 | **Maurice FLIXHER**<br>22 Ropemakers Street<br>London SE | Fancy goods importer |
| R3/125<br>15 September 1948<br>Sent by M L Fremaux | 8 Monument Grove<br>Waterloo<br>Liverpool 22 | P21/F/12<br>***#5986***<br> | **Maurice Leon FREMAUX**<br>None entered – Liverpool School of Art? | Art student |
| 16 August 1955 | | P21/F/30<br>***#5987***<br>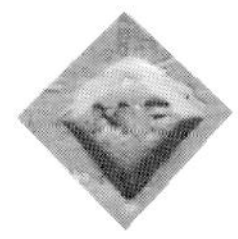 | | |
| R2/201<br>21 October 1915<br>Sent by Handcock & Walker | 18 Evelyn Mansions<br>Carlisle Place<br>London SW<br>20 Charing Cross Mansions<br>Glasgow | P15/F/15<br>***#5988***<br> | **M A FRIEDLANDER**<br>**Julia FRIEDLANDER** trading as<br>**A FRIEDLANDER & CO**<br>23 Royal Exchange Square and<br>74 Buchanan Street<br>Glasgow | Wholesale tobacconists and silver mounters |
| Missing register<br>*c.*1889 | | P5/F/237<br>***#5989***<br> | **Unidentified** | |
| R1/25<br>18 March 1896<br>Sent by Stokes & Ireland | Grafton Street<br>Dublin<br>Ireland | P5/F/745a<br>***#5990***<br> | **Michael FACK**<br>32 Grafton Street<br>Dublin | Jeweller and silverplate beater |
| | | P5/F/745b<br>***#5991***<br> | | |
| R1/24<br>14 March 1896<br>Sent by A H Tongue | 6 Huntley Gardens<br>Glasgow | P5/F/738<br>***#5992***<br> | **Montague Alexander FRIEDLANDER**<br>trading as<br>**FRIEDLANDER & CO**<br>23 Royal Exchange Square<br>Glasgow | Wholesale tobacconists |
| MR3/82 | | P1/32/x4<br>***#5993-6***<br> | **M FRANCE**<br>Manchester | Silversmith |
| R1/109<br>26 August 1899<br>Sent by M Freeman<br>cancelled 23 Mar 1910 | 25 Compton Road<br>Highbury<br>London N | P9/F/3<br>***#5997***<br> | **Maurice FREEMAN** *<br>26 Clerkenwell Road<br>London EC | Manufacturing silversmith |
| R1/235<br>29 June 1905<br>Sent by M Freeman | 147 Fordwych Road<br>Cricklewood<br>London | P9/F/26<br>***#5998***<br> | **Maurice FREEMAN** *<br>22 Clerkenwell Road<br>London | Silversmith |
| R2/107<br>23 March 1910<br>Sent by S Lyons<br>MF punch used twice<br>cancelled 23 Mar 1910 | 11 Manston Road<br>Brondesbury<br>London | P13/F/18<br>***#5999***<br> | **Harry FREEMAN** trading as<br>**Maurice FREEMAN** *<br>22 Clerkenwell Road<br>London | Silversmith |
| R2/190<br>14 August 1914<br>Sent by C J Plunkett & Co | Private address same as business | P15/F/8<br>***#6000***<br> | **Margaret FENN**<br>Parsoncot<br>Great Missenden<br>Buckinghamshire | Private person |

| REGISTRATION DETAILS | MAKER'S PRIVATE ADDRESS and DETAILS | PLATE and MARK DETAILS | MAKER/COMPANY and BUSINESS ADDRESS | MAKER'S TRADE |
|---|---|---|---|---|
| R2/118<br>15 September 1910<br>Sent by Charles Peach & Son | 2 Westfield Road<br>Edgbaston<br>Birmingham | P13/G/24<br>***#6001***<br> | **Marcus GUMPELSON**<br>187 Warstone Lane<br>Birmingham | Jeweller |
| R2/76<br>27 March 1909<br>Sent by W H George<br>BAO 15.053 | 310 Monument Road<br>Birmingham<br>42 Havelock Road<br>Handsworth<br>Birmingham | P13/M/11<br>***#6002***<br> | **Walter Hudson GEORGE**<br>**Henry MATTHEWS** trading as<br>**MATTHEWS & GEORGE**<br>38 Vyse Street<br>Birmingham | Jewellers |
| R1/47<br>24 June 1897<br>Sent by J Hayward<br>C G Heaven | Private address same as business | P5/G/852<br>***#6003***<br> | **Mark GOLDMAN** *<br>241 Cheetham Hill Road<br>Manchester | Jeweller |
| Missing register<br>*c*.1887 | | P5/M/129<br>***#6004***<br> | **Unidentified** | |
| R2/164<br>29 October 1912<br>Sent by Coley Brothers | Private address same as business | P13/G/44<br>***#6005***<br> | **Maurice GOLDING**<br>216 Walworth Road<br>London | Watchmaker and jeweller |
| R1/214<br>12 May 1904<br>Sent by W George | Ivanhoe<br>Havelock Road<br>310 Monument Road<br>Birmingham | P9/M/78<br>***#6006***<br> | **Henry MATTHEWS**<br>**Walter Hudson GEORGE** trading as<br>**MATTHEWS & GEORGE**<br>38 Vyse Street<br>Birmingham | Manufacturing jewellers |
| LPB/62<br>27 October 1881<br>Similar mark entered BAO 19 July 1882 | 22 Portland Street (BAO)<br>Edgbaston<br>No name in LPB<br>LPB mark shown | Not on P3<br>***#6007***<br> | **Maurice GRATZ & CO**<br>7 Vyse Street<br>Birmingham | Jewellers |
| R1/93<br>25 February 1899<br>Sent by<br>H W Collingwood | Park Road<br>Middlesbrough | P9/C/9<br>***#6008***<br> | **H William COLLINGWOOD** sole partner trading as **COLLINGWOOD & SON***<br>66 Linthorpe Road<br>Middlesbrough and<br>5 Johnson Street (no town listed) and<br>21 New Bridge Street<br>Newcastle-under-Lyme and<br>25 Church Street<br>West Hartlepool | Jewellers |
| R1/160<br>21 January 1902<br>Sent by F T Trahern | | P9/C/75<br>***#6009***<br> | **Horatio Nelson COLLINGWOOD**<br>trading as<br>**M G COLLINGWOOD & SON** *<br>66 Linthorpe Road<br>Middlesbrough | Watch manufacturers and jewellers |
| R3/129<br>21 June 1949<br>Sent by Mayers & Harrison Ltd | | P21/M/26<br>***#6011***<br> | **MAYERS & HARRISON LTD**<br>Sealed in the presence of:-<br>A Mayers (Director)<br>L Mayers (Secretary)<br>215 Great Jackson Street<br>Manchester 15 | Musical instrument makers |
| R3/156<br>15 September 1955<br>Sent by Mayers & Harrison Ltd | | P21/M/46<br>***#6010***<br> | | |
| R3/121<br>7 January 1948<br>Sent by M Hellwig | Hope Lodge<br>5 Poplar Road<br>Oxton<br>Birkenhead | P21/H/41<br>***#6012***<br> | **Marianne HELLWIG**<br>None entered – Liverpool School of Art? | Student |

| REGISTRATION DETAILS | MAKER'S PRIVATE ADDRESS and DETAILS | PLATE and MARK DETAILS | MAKER/COMPANY and BUSINESS ADDRESS | MAKER'S TRADE |
|---|---|---|---|---|
| R3/173<br>1 June 1960<br>Sent by M Heal | Winchfield<br>66 Hillfoot Avenue<br>Hunts Cross<br>Liverpool | P21/H/81<br>***#6012a***<br> | **Miss Monica HEAL**<br>No business address entered | Student silversmith |
| R1/112<br>4 October 1899<br>Sent by W Mills | Private address same as business | P9/H/21<br>***#6013***<br> | **Myer HARRINSON** *<br>27 Norton Street<br>Liverpool | Watch manufacturer and jeweller |
| Sent by L E Neale | | P9/H/22<br>***#6014***<br> | | |
| PDB 1815-22<br>MR2/89,90<br>MR3/86<br>SOT/85<br>GMSC/65 | Coffin plates, jugs, labels and skewers | P1/30/x2<br>***#6015,6***<br> | **Mary HUNTINGDON**<br>Bridge Street Row<br>Chester or | Silversmith |
| PDB 1822-30 | Goldware and silver tableware | | **Hannah Maria HUNTINGDON** and **S HUNTINGDON**<br>Bridge Street Row<br>Chester | Goldsmiths and silversmiths |
| R1/49<br>12 August 1897<br>Sent by Benson Brothers | Private address same as business | P5/*Zsic*/863<br>***#6017***<br> | **Myer HARRINSON**<br>27 Norton Street<br>Liverpool | Watch manufacturer and importer |
| R3/88<br>4 November 1937<br>Sent by Joseph Smith & Sons (B'ham) Ltd<br>63 Vittoria Street<br>Birmingham | | P21/M/6<br>***#6018***<br>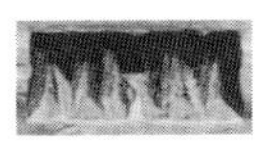 | **M H MEYER LTD**<br>Sealed in the presence of:-<br>Philip Green (Director)<br>Harold E Woolston (Secretary)<br>60, 62 Clerkenwell Road<br>London EC1 | Wholesale jewellers |
| R2/86<br>29 June 1909<br>Sent by J & R Griffin Ltd | 99 Broadhurst Gardens<br>London NW | P13/M/17<br>***#6019***<br> | **Theodore MEYER** trading as **M H MEYER**<br>156 Houndsditch<br>London | Wholesale fancy jeweller |
| R2/118<br>23 September 1910<br>Sent by Charles Horner Ltd | | P13/M/37<br>***#6020***<br> | **Theodore MEYER**<br>**Bertha MEYER**<br>60, 62 Clerkenwell Road<br>London | Wholesale jewellers |
| R3/16<br>15 June 1923<br>Sent by H Griffith & Son | | P15/M/61<br>***#6021***<br> | **Theodore MEYER** (Managing Director) trading as **M H MEYER LTD**<br>60, 62 Clerkenwell Road<br>London EC | |
| R3/14<br>7 February 1923<br>Sent by W H Tandy & Sons | | P15/M/49<br>***#6022***<br> | **M H MEYER LTD**<br>Theodore Meyer<br>60, 62 Clerkenwell Road<br>London EC | |
| PP1/188<br>GTD 1794-1840 | | P1/16/x2<br>***#6023,4***<br> | **Myer I TOBIAS**<br>2 Dorans Lane<br>Lord Street<br>Liverpool | Watch manufacturer |
| R1/53<br>2 November 1897<br>Sent by M Jacobinsky | Private address same as business | P5/J/904<br>***#6025***<br> | **Marks JACOBINSKY** *<br>2 Green Street, New Road<br>Whitechapel<br>London | Jeweller |
| | | P9/J/12<br>***#6026***<br> | | |

| REGISTRATION DETAILS | MAKER'S PRIVATE ADDRESS and DETAILS | PLATE and MARK DETAILS | MAKER/COMPANY and BUSINESS ADDRESS | MAKER'S TRADE |
|---|---|---|---|---|
| Missing register<br>*c.*1889<br>Similar mark entered<br>LAO 31 August 1903 | | P5/M/243<br>***#6027***<br> | **Morton BRITTON**<br>**James PHELPS** trading as<br>**MORTON & JAMES** *<br>68 Britannia Street<br>London | Stick mounters |
| R1/179<br>14 November 1902<br>Sent by Male & Jones | 14 Richmond Road<br>Olton<br>Birmingham | P9/M/42,43<br>***#6028,9***<br> | **Frederick MALE** trading as<br>**MALE & JONES**<br>21 Hylton Street<br>Birmingham | Jewellers |
| R3/156<br>20 September 1955<br>Sent by M J Atyer | 16 The Circuit<br>Withington<br>Manchester 20 | P21/A/24<br>***#6030***<br> | **Mary Joyce ATYER**<br>College of Housecraft<br>High Street<br>Manchester 13 | Lecturer |
| R3/141<br>17 February 1953<br>Sent by M J Brickell<br>Two sizes | Glenhurst<br>53 Selborne Street<br>Preston | P21/B/37,38<br>***#6031,2***<br> | **Miss Marie Josephine BRICKELL**<br>No business address entered | Student |
| LPB/34<br>1 December 1880 | | P3/G/x3<br>***#6033-5***<br> | **Michael Joseph GOLDSMITH**<br>21/22 Vittoria Street<br>Birmingham | Jeweller |
| Missing register<br>*c.*1887<br>Similar mark entered<br>LAO 6 February 1886 | | P5/J/123<br>***#6036***<br> | **Matthew John JESSOP** *<br>11 Hatton Garden<br>London EC | Wholesale jewellers |
| R1/130<br>3 August 1900<br>Sent by<br>J J Evans & Co | 57 Christchurch Road<br>Streatham<br>London | P9/J/29<br>***#6037***<br> | **Matthew John JESSOP** *<br>10 Hatton Garden<br>London | Jewellers and silversmiths manufacturers agency |
| R3/133<br>2 May 1950<br>Sent by M Keegan<br>Two sizes | 278 Brooklands Road<br>Wythenshawe<br>Manchester | P21/K/12,13<br>***#6038,9***<br> | **Mary KEEGAN**<br>No business address entered | Student |
| LPB/46<br>1 January 1881 | | P3/K/x3<br>***#6040-2***<br> | **Michael KLEAN & CO** *<br>70 Myddelton Street<br>Clerkenwell | Watch manufacturers |
| R1/61<br>17 February 1898<br>Sent by Maurice Krumm | 26 Finsbury Square<br>London EC | P5/K/932<br>***#6043***<br> | **Maurice KRUMM**<br>1, 2 and 3 Falcon Square<br>Aldersgate Street<br>London | Silver mounter and leather goods manufacturer |
| R1/191<br>27 April 1903<br>Sent by Wright & Perry<br>annotated *(0) struck on punch* | 20 Buckland Crescent<br>London NW<br>7 Buckland Crescent<br>London NW | P9/K/31<br>***#6044***<br> | **Simeon KLEAN**<br>**Moss FRIDLANDER** trading as<br>**M KLEAN & CO** *<br>70 Myddleton Street, Clerkenwell<br>London | Diamond mounters |
| LPB/50<br>20 July 1882<br>Sent by E F Booth | 1881 census has this man from Birmingham staying at hotel in Bishopswearmouth, Durham | P3/L/x3<br>***#6045-7***<br> | **Moses LEVENBERG**<br>16, 17 Vyse Street<br>Birmingham | Commercial traveller and export merchant |

| REGISTRATION DETAILS | MAKER'S PRIVATE ADDRESS and DETAILS | PLATE and MARK DETAILS | MAKER/COMPANY and BUSINESS ADDRESS | MAKER'S TRADE |
|---|---|---|---|---|
| R2/189<br>30 July 1914<br>Sent by M Lee | Private address same as business | P15/L/6<br>***#6048***  | **Matthew LEE**<br>72 Gloucester Street, London Road<br>Liverpool | Manufacturer and repairer |
| R3/166<br>13 March 1959<br>Sent by M Longworth | 79 Wolfenden Street<br>Bolton | P21/L/38<br>***#6049***  | **Margaret LONGWORTH**<br>No business address entered | Student silversmith |
| R3/111<br>6 January 1946<br>Sent by Marian Littlewood<br>Two sizes | 12 White Street<br>Warrington<br>Lancashire | P21/L/19,20<br>***#6050,1***  | **Marian LITTLEWOOD**<br>Manchester Municipal School of Art<br>Manchester | Student of silversmithing |
| LPB/56 SP27/11<br>14 November 1885 | | P5/M/x1<br>***#6052***  | **MINSHULL & LATIMER** *<br>102 Vyse Street<br>Birmingham | Silversmiths |
| Missing register<br>*c.*1886 | | P5/M/58<br>***#6053***  | | |
| Missing register<br>*c.*1887 | | P5/M/95<br>***#6054***  | | |
| R2/37<br>13 April 1907<br>Sent by J Gammage | 11 Highbury Hill<br>London | P9/L/88-90<br>***#6055-7***  | **Mason LEETE** trading as<br>**Mason LEETE & CO** *<br>91 Aldersgate Street<br>London EC | Manufacturing jewellers |
| R3/173<br>21 May 1960<br>Sent by M L D Noblett<br>Two sizes | 8 Royston Avenue<br>Whalley Range<br>Manchester 16 | P21/N/9,10<br>***#6058,9***  | **Mary Lilian Dorning NOBLETT**<br>No business address entered | Silversmith |
| R1/106<br>28 July 1899<br>Sent by Grove Brothers<br>J & R Griffin | 31 Francis Road<br>Edgbaston<br>Birmingham | P9/J/18<br>***#6060***  | **Montague Leonard JACKSON**<br>11 Northampton Street<br>Birmingham | Wholesale jeweller |
| R1/124<br>10 April 1900<br>Sent by<br>W J Spencer | Private address same as business | P9/L/16<br>***#6061***  | **Morris Lawrence LEVY**<br>70 Cranford Street<br>Smethwick | Watchcase maker |
| Not in R3 as expected<br>*c.* July 1921<br>Similar mark entered<br>LAO 22 June 1914 | | P15/M/40<br>***#6062***  | **MARTIN'S LTD** *<br>H C Sydnercombe (Secretary)<br>210 Piccadilly<br>London W | Cigar shippers, gold and silver dealers |
| R3/54<br>7 June 1930<br>Sent by Munos Ltd | Private address same as business | P15/M/75<br>***#6063***  | **MUNOS LTD**<br>J W Field (Director)<br>Valley Works<br>Chalford<br>Glos | Stick manufacturers |
| LPB/54<br>13 July 1880 | | P3/M/x1<br>***#6064***  | **Henry MANTON**<br>**James Henry MOLE** *<br>33/34 Edmund Street<br>Birmingham | Gold chain makers |
| Missing register<br>*c.*1889 | | P5/M/246<br>***#6065***  | | |
| R1/70<br>22 October 1898<br>Sent by Coley Brothers | Park Avenue[1]<br>Soho Hill, Birmingham<br>York Road [2]<br>Edgbaston, Birmingham | P9/M/2<br>***#6066***  | **James WOODWARD** [1]<br>**Wilfred Bernard MOLE** [2] trading as<br>**MANTON & MOLE** *<br>Warstone Lane<br>Birmingham | Goldsmiths |

| REGISTRATION DETAILS | MAKER'S PRIVATE ADDRESS and DETAILS | PLATE and MARK DETAILS | MAKER/COMPANY and BUSINESS ADDRESS | MAKER'S TRADE |
|---|---|---|---|---|
| LPB/56 SP27/6<br>26 November 1884<br>No mark in LPB just MM | | P5/M/x1<br>***#6067***<br> | **MARSON & MOSELEY**<br>2½ Augusta Street<br>Birmingham | Jewellers |
| R3/140<br>23 January 1953<br>Sent by M M Foster<br>Three sizes | Private address same as business | P21/F/22-24<br>***#6068-70***<br> | **Mrs Margaret MacQueen FOSTER**<br>Cottesmore<br>Grantham Avenue, Lower Walton<br>Warrington | Art student |
| R3/73<br>26 November 1934<br>Sent by S Blanckensee & Sons Ltd<br>19-35 Regent Place<br>Birmingham | | P15/H/123,124<br>***#6073,4***<br><br>P15/H/121,122<br>***#6071,2***<br> | **M M HENDERSON LTD**<br>Common seal of company affixed in the presence of:-<br>W Gordon Henderson (Director)<br>Dora F S Henderson (Secretary)<br>84 Argyle Street (Registered Office)<br>Glasgow | Jewellers and silversmiths |
| R1/29<br>30 May 1896<br>Sent by Stainsby & Coupland<br>E Langridge | Private address same as business | P5/M/679<br>***#6075***<br> | **Leon MARION**<br>**Henry GULSON** (Guibout in Culme)<br>**George BISHOP**<br>**John Pattison KIRK**<br>**Frank BISHOP** trading as<br>**MARION & CO** *<br>51 New Oxford Street<br>London | Silversmiths, etc |
| R1/129<br>14 July 1900<br>Sent by H Griffith & Sons | | P9/M/22<br>***#6076***<br> | **MARION & CO** *<br>22, 23 Soho Square<br>London | Fancy goods, etc. |
| R1/144<br>1 March 1901<br>Sent by J E Sutters | 54 Parliament Hill<br>Hampstead<br>London | P9/M/27<br>***#6077***<br> | **MAPPIN & WEBB LTD** *<br>James Leary (Managing Director)<br>2 Queen Victoria Street and<br>158 to 162 Oxford Street, London EC and<br>The Royal Works<br>Sheffield | Jewellers and silversmiths |
| R2/157<br>14 June 1912<br>cancelled<br>15 June 1912<br>Two sizes | Frederick Waite[1]<br>Dularant<br>24 Third Avenue<br>Manor Park<br>London N | P13/M/48,49<br>***#6078,9***<br> | **MAPPIN & WEBB** *<br>Walter Joseph Mappin (Chairman)<br>John Newton Mappin (Director)<br>Herbert Joseph Mappin (Director)<br>Stanley Arthur Mappin (Director)<br>Walter Thorpe Maddock (Director)<br>A Gordon Maginnis (Director)<br>Henry Portlock (Director)<br>Frederick Waite [1] (Secretary)<br>158, 162 Oxford Street (Reg Office)<br>London W | Goldsmiths and silversmiths |
| R3/17<br>21 July 1923<br>Sent by Synyer & Beddoes | | P15/M/62<br>***#6080***<br>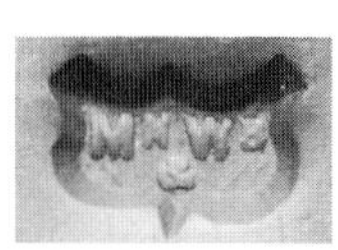 | **MAPPIN & WEBB LTD** *<br>158 Oxford Street<br>London | |
| R2/158<br>28 June 1912<br>Sent by Frederick Waite<br>Two sizes | 24 Third Avenue<br>Manor Park<br>London N | P13/M/50,51<br>***#6081,2***<br> | **MAPPIN & WEBB (1908) LTD** *<br>Frederick Waite (Secretary)<br>Registered Office<br>158 and 162 Oxford Street<br>London | |

| REGISTRATION DETAILS | MAKER'S PRIVATE ADDRESS and DETAILS | PLATE and MARK DETAILS | MAKER/COMPANY and BUSINESS ADDRESS | MAKER'S TRADE |
|---|---|---|---|---|
| R3/176<br>10 January 1961<br>Sent by selves | 4 Kinnard Street<br>Belfast 15 | P21/B/65<br>***#6083***<br> | **Michael O'BOYLE**<br>**Rose O'BOYLE**<br>5-7 Chapel Lane, Belfast South 1<br>Northern Ireland | Devotional goods depot |
| LPB/50<br>17 March 1883 | | P3/P/x3<br>***#6084-6***<br> | **Marks PERKS**<br>43 Vyse Street<br>Birmingham | Jeweller |
| R3/184<br>6 June 1962<br>Sent by M Poole | 57 Warwick Road<br>Heaton Moor<br>Stockport<br>Cheshire | P21/P/61,62<br>***#6087,8***<br> | **Maurice POOLE**<br>Manchester Grammar School<br>Rusholme<br>Manchester 13 | Schoolmaster<br>Head of handicraft department |
| R3/36<br>25 March 1927<br>Sent by Margaret Prescott | Private address same as business | P15/P/199<br>***#6089***<br> | **Margaret PRESCOTT**<br>**(Mrs J Mulleneux PRESCOTT)**<br>3 Bentley Road<br>Princes Park<br>Liverpool | Art student |
| R3/137<br>20 March 1952<br>Sent by H A Dodd<br>Two sizes | Private address same as business | P21/R/10,11<br>***#6090,1***<br> | **Madge REEDER**<br>Newstead<br>Blackburn Road<br>Heapey, near Chorley<br>Lancashire | Craftworker |
| R3/159<br>6 December 1956<br>Sent by M Reynolds<br>Two sizes | Pinehurst<br>Sefton Road<br>Archer Park<br>Middleton<br>Manchester | P21/R/27,28<br>***#6092,3***<br>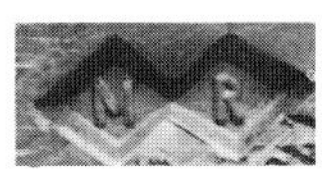 | **Margaret REYNOLDS**<br>No business address entered | Student of silversmithing |
| LPB/72<br>10 July 1880 | Kelly 1880 | P3/R/x1<br>***#6094***<br> | **MILLS & REYNOLDS**<br>17 Caroline Street<br>Birmingham | Jewellers |
| LPB/72<br>13 July 1880<br>Sent by F W Cole<br>LPB mark shown | | Not on P3<br>***#6095***<br> | | |
| R2/5<br>2 November 1905<br>Sent by Max Stollsteimer | 45 Milford Road<br>East Dulwich SE | P9/S/92<br>***#6096***<br> | **Max STOLLSTEIMER** *<br>81 Hatton Garden<br>London EC | Agent and merchant |
| R1/163<br>11 March 1902<br>Sent by J H Wynn | 41 Milford Road<br>Lordship Lane<br>East Dulwich SE | P9/S/44<br>***#6097***<br> | | Jewellers agent |
| R1/235<br>30 June 1905<br>Sent by Max Schoder | 16 Gubyon Avenue<br>Herne Hill<br>London | P9/S/89<br>***#6098***<br>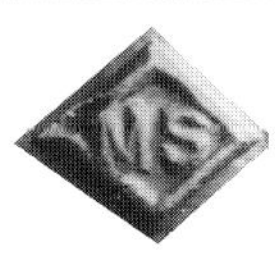 | **Max SCHODER** *<br>**RICHTER & GLUCK**<br>23 Thavies Inn, Holborn Circus<br>London EC | Manufacturing jewellers |
| PDB 1814-15<br>MR3/97 | Gold rings | P1/31/x1<br>***#6099***<br> | **M SOLOMON**<br>Liverpool<br>or | Goldsmith |
| PMR 1861 | In 1861 census employed 40 men and 20 boys | P1/32/x2<br>***#6100,1***<br> | **Mary Smith SAMUEL**<br>16 Faulkner Street (1861)<br>Liverpool | Gold watchcase maker |
| Missing register<br>*c.*1887<br>Similar mark entered<br>LAO 25 March 1886 | | P5/S/76<br>***#6102***<br> | **Max STEYERMAN** *<br>33 Holborn Viaduct<br>London EC | Watchcase maker |

| REGISTRATION DETAILS | MAKER'S PRIVATE ADDRESS and DETAILS | PLATE and MARK DETAILS | MAKER/COMPANY and BUSINESS ADDRESS | MAKER'S TRADE |
|---|---|---|---|---|
| R1/191<br>21 April 1903<br>Sent by L E Neale | 30 South Road<br>Handsworth | P9/S/61<br>***#6103***<br> | **Maurice SPIRO**<br>73 Great Hampton Street<br>Birmingham | Jeweller |
| Not in R2 as expected<br>*c.* April to October 1913 | See other MS marks | P13/S/112<br>***#6104***<br> | **Unidentified** | |
| R2/196<br>29 May 1915<br>Sent by Ginder & Couch | Cathcart<br>Glasgow | P15/M/17<br>***#6105***<br> | **Henry MUIR**<br>**James B MUIR**<br>**John Macgregor MUIR** trading as<br>**MUIR & SON**<br>182 Argyle Street and 1 Union Street<br>Glasgow | Jewellers |
| R2/156<br>23 May 1912<br>Sent by L E Neale<br>BAO18.771,18.773<br>18.777,18.779 | 20 Duchess Road<br>Edgbaston | P13/S/85-88<br>***#6106-9***<br> | **Morris** (*sic*) **SPIRO**<br>21 Hockley Hill<br>Birmingham | Manufacturing jeweller |
| J1 1861-81<br>PP3/83<br>Not in SPB or LPB so struck 1860-3 | | P3/R/x2<br>***#6110,1***<br> | **Mary SAMUEL**<br>**Arthur ROGERS** *<br>**(SAMUEL & ROGERS *)**<br>72 Wood Street<br>Liverpool | Watchcase makers |
| Similar mark entered LAO 30 October 1860 | See also S&R | P3/S/x2<br>***#6112,3***<br> | | |
| R1/2<br>31 October 1894<br>Sent by S Lotheim | 152 Bristol Road and<br>85 Sterling Road<br>Birmingham | P5/L/617<br>***#6114***<br> | **Moritz Lotheim**<br>**Simon Lotheim** trading as<br>**M & S LOTHEIM**<br>35 Vittoria Street<br>Birmingham | Manufacturing silversmiths |
| R2/77<br>2 April 1909<br>Sent by Maxfield & Son Ltd<br>Sheffield<br>1914 | Plane Hurst Hill<br>Hill Park<br>70 Devonshire Street and<br>Thame Hurst<br>West Hampstead<br>London | P13/M/12<br>***#6115***<br> | **MAXFIELD & SONS LTD** *<br>J E Ashford (Director)<br>C Friswell (Director)<br>S W Oliver (Director)<br>10 Upper John Street, London and<br>Enterprise Works<br>Sheffield | Manufacturing silversmiths |
| R1/16<br>11 September 1895<br>Sent by<br>W H Carrington | 10 Burlington Street<br>Manchester | P5/T/687<br>***#6116***<br> | **Marcus THEMANS**<br>26 Piccadilly<br>Manchester | Tobacconist |
| R1/61<br>23 February 1898<br>Sent by Allen & Co<br>T Phillips | 10 Burlington Street<br>Manchester | P5/T/936<br>***#6117***<br> | **Marcus THEMANS**<br>26 Piccadilly<br>Manchester | Tobacconist |
| R2/74<br>11 March 1909<br>Sent by Themans & Co | 346 Moss Lane East<br>Manchester | P13/T/8<br>***#6118***<br> | **Marcus THEMANS**<br>**Henry THEMANS** trading as<br>**THEMANS & CO**<br>26 Piccadilly<br>Manchester | Tobacconists and licensed silver dealers |

| REGISTRATION DETAILS | MAKER'S PRIVATE ADDRESS and DETAILS | PLATE and MARK DETAILS | MAKER/COMPANY and BUSINESS ADDRESS | MAKER'S TRADE |
|---|---|---|---|---|
| R2/123<br>12 November 1910<br>Sent by Themans & Co | 346 Moss Lane East<br>Manchester | P13/T/28<br>***#6119***<br>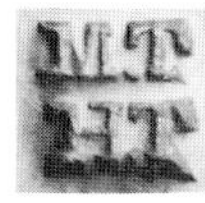 | **Marcus THEMANS**<br>**Henry THEMANS**<br>26 Piccadilly<br>Manchester | Tobacconists and licensed silver dealers |
| R3/152<br>7 May 1954<br>Sent by<br>M Kosciukiewicz<br>Two sizes | Private address same as business | P21/K/16,17<br>***#6120,1***<br><br>P21/K/15<br>***#6122***<br> | **M KOSCIUKIEWICZ**<br>**Teresa KOSCIUKIEWICZ**<br>Name changed by deed poll 1 April 1954 to **KAYE**. Husband and Wife joint ownership trading as<br>**THE CLOCK SHOP**<br>30 Queen Street, Rhyll<br>North Wales | Watch makers and jewellers |
| R2/205<br>7 June 1916<br>Sent by Chas Horner Ltd | 15 Wavertree Road<br>Streatham<br>25 Meteor Road<br>Westcliff-on-Sea | P15/M/22<br>***#6124***<br> | **Charles MULLAND**<br>**William George UPCOTT** *<br>112–118 Fore Street<br>London E C | Manufacturers agents |
| Missing register<br>*c.*1887<br>Similar mark entered BAO 28 March 1889 | | P5/M/134<br>***#6123***<br> | **James MARLOW**<br>**Ernest Vernon VAUGHTON**<br>41 Frederick Street<br>Birmingham | Manufacturing jewellers |
| R1/137<br>8 November 1900<br>Sent by<br>M E Wittenberg | 10 Avenue Parade<br>Accrington<br>Cheshire (*sic*) | P9/W/44<br>***#6125***<br> | **Max Ehrigott WITTENBERG**<br>Back Owen Street<br>Accrington<br>Cheshire (*sic*) | Pipe manufacturer and mounter |
| LPB/54<br>21 March 1879 | James Mattocks at this address in 1881 census as a Newsagent! | P3/M/x3<br>***#6126-8***<br> | **MATTOCKS & WHITEHEAD**<br>11 Well Street<br>Coventry | Watchmakers |
| R3/179<br>6 May 1961<br>Sent by M Wright | Oakenclough<br>North End Lane<br>Halewood<br>near Liverpool | P21/W/104<br>***#6129***<br>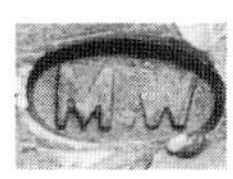 | **Maurice WRIGHT**<br>No business address entered | Student |
| R3/140<br>29 January 1953<br>Sent by selves<br>Registered Office<br>156-162 Oxford Street<br>London | | P21/W/83<br>***#6130***<br> | **MAPPIN & WEBB LTD** *<br>Royal Works<br>Queens Road<br>Sheffield | Manufacturing silversmiths |
| R1/220<br>21 September 1904<br>Sent by J E Sutters | 54 Parliament Hill<br>Hampstead<br>London | P9/M/81<br>***#6131***<br> | **MAPPIN & WEBB LTD** *<br>Henry Portlock (Secretary)<br>2 Queen Victoria Street and<br>158 to 162 Oxford Street and<br>22 Regent Street<br>London W and<br>The Royal Works<br>Sheffield and<br>Library Building<br>Johannesburg and<br>Jardine Public<br>Nice | Jewellers and silversmiths |
| R2/234<br>5 October 1920<br>Sent by M Woolf | 44 Vallance Road<br>London E | P15/W/57<br>***#6132***<br> | **Morris WOOLF**<br>67 Whitechapel Road<br>London E | Manufacturing jeweller |
| Missing register<br>*c.*1890<br>Similar mark entered BAO 14 July 1891 | | P5/W/296<br>***#6133***<br> | **Myra WILDE**<br>Back of 50 Tenby Street<br>Birmingham | Goldsmith |

| REGISTRATION DETAILS | MAKER'S PRIVATE ADDRESS and DETAILS | PLATE and MARK DETAILS | MAKER/COMPANY and BUSINESS ADDRESS | MAKER'S TRADE |
|---|---|---|---|---|
| R1/220<br>21 September 1904<br>Sent by J E Sutters | 54 Parliament Hill<br>Hampstead<br>London | P9/M/82<br>***#6134***<br> | **MAPPIN & WEBB LTD** *<br>Henry Portlock (Secretary)<br>2 Queen Victoria Street and<br>158 to 162 Oxford Street and<br>22 Regent Street<br>London W and<br>The Royal Works<br>Sheffield and<br>Library Building<br>Johannesburg and<br>Jardine Public<br>Nice | Jewellers and silversmiths |
| R3/106<br>7 January 1944<br>Sent by T E Hughes<br>22 Vyse Street<br>Birmingham 18 | | P21/W/37<br>***#6135***<br> | **M WACHENHEIMER & CO LTD**<br>Sealed in the presence of:-<br>M Wachenheimer (Director)<br>E G Wachenheimer (Director)<br>43 Great Marlborough Road (Registered Office)<br>London W1 | Manufacturing and wholesale jewellers |
| R3/107<br>20 November 1944<br>Sent by Montal Watch Fittings Ltd | | P21/F/8<br>***#6136***<br> | **MONTAL WATCH FITTINGS LTD**<br>Sealed in the presence of:-<br>John Gantner (Director)<br>E Geary (Secretary)<br>Icknield Street (Registered Office)<br>Birmingham 18 | Manufacturers of watch fittings |
| R3/81<br>7 November 1935<br>Sent by R Jones | The Mount<br>29 Craiglockhart<br>Edinburgh | P15/M/77<br>***#6137***<br>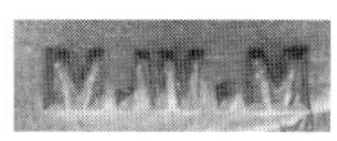 | **Margaret White MACDOUGALL**<br>102 George Street<br>Edinburgh | Jeweller |
| Missing register<br>*c.*1886 | | P5/W/54<br>***#6138***<br> | **Unidentified** | |
| R2/94<br>28 September 1909<br>Sent by Harold Wright Wilcox<br><br>9 October 1909 No59<br>same punch recut | Northwood<br>St Bernard's Road<br>Olton | P13/W/57<br>***#6139***<br><br>P13/W/59<br>***#6140***<br> | **Harold Wright WILCOX** trading as<br>**Matthew WILCOX & SON**<br>111 Spencer Street<br>Birmingham | Silversmiths |
| Missing register<br>*c.*1887<br>Similar mark entered LAO 13 December 1887 | | P5/W/87<br>***#6141***<br> | **Matthew William WHITE** trading as<br>**JOHNSON & WHITE** *<br>20 Red Lion Road<br>Clerkenwell<br>London | Manufacturing gold and silversmiths |
| R1/226<br>31 January 1905<br>Sent by E Durban & Co<br>Two sizes | 24 Westfield Road<br>Birmingham | P9/M/88,89<br>***#6142,3***<br> | **Isaac MYERS** trading as<br>**MYERS BROTHERS**<br>117 Vyse Street<br>Birmingham | Merchants and manufacturing jewellers |

| REGISTRATION DETAILS | MAKER'S PRIVATE ADDRESS and DETAILS | PLATE and MARK DETAILS | MAKER/COMPANY and BUSINESS ADDRESS | MAKER'S TRADE |
|---|---|---|---|---|
| LPB/7<br>29 May 1878 | | P3/N/x2<br>***#6144,5***<br> | **NEWMARK & ABRAHAMS** *<br>128 Houndsditch<br>London E | Jewellers |
| R3/145<br>23 May 1853<br>Sent by N Brown | Fairfield<br>465 Chester Road<br>Old Hartford<br>Cheshire | P21/B/39<br>***#6146***<br> | **Norman BROWN**<br>No business address entered | Amateur silversmith |
| MR1/124-30<br>MR3/181<br>SIL/44<br>J1 1668-1712<br>J3/389 | Communion cup and cover 1678, paten 1683, communion cups dated *c.*1677-85 and tankard 1690<br>Free 1669<br>See also Bu #982 | Pre-dates P1<br>***#6147***<br>type 1<br> | **Nathaniel BULLEN**<br>Chester | Silversmith |
| | Trefid spoons, late 17th century | Pre-dates P1<br>***#6148***<br>type 3<br> | | |
| R3/185<br>24 July 1962<br>Sent by Nayler Brothers | 32 Thorncliff Court<br>Kings Avenue<br>London SW4 | P21/N/17<br>***#6149***<br> | **Cyril Thomas SMITH**<br>**Phyllis SMITH** trading as<br>**NAYLER BROTHERS** *<br>45 Broadwick Street<br>London W1 | Manufacturing silversmiths |
| LPB/58<br>22 October 1879 | | P3/N/x2<br>***#6150,1***<br> | **NATHAN BROTHERS** *<br>103 Vyse Street<br>Birmingham | Jewellers |
| R1/50<br>9 September 1897<br>Sent by Nathan Brothers | Campden Square [1]<br>London<br>Hampton-in-Arden [2]<br>Warwickshire | P5/B/870<br>***#6152***<br> | **Maurice NATHAN** [1]<br>**Frederick NATHAN** [2] trading as<br>**NATHAN BROTHERS** *<br>120 Vyse Street<br>Birmingham | Manufacturing jewellers |
| R3/108<br>20 March 1945<br>Sent by Nathan Brothers | 87 Fountain Road [1]<br>Birmingham 17<br>73 Fountain Road [2]<br>Birmingham 17 | P21/N/4<br>***#6153***<br>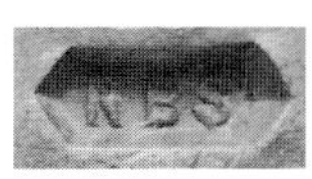 | **NATHAN BROTHERS** *<br>Reuben Nathan[1]<br>Leonard Nathan[2]<br>120 Vyse Street<br>Birmingham 18 | |
| R2/149<br>19 January 1912<br>Sent by W O Davies<br>BAO 19.653 | 1 South Villas<br>Camden Square<br>London<br>23 Portland Road<br>Edgbaston<br>Birmingham | P13/N/32<br>***#6154***<br> | **Maurice NATHAN**<br>**Frederick NATHAN** trading as<br>**NATHAN BROTHERS** *<br>120 Vyse Street, Birmingham and<br>92 Hatton Garden<br>London | |
| PDB 1798-1815<br>MR2/74<br>MR3/80,192<br>PP1/188<br>SOT/67,80<br>SIL/40, GMSC/78 | Gold rings, medals, conche shell, jug and labels | P1/28/x2<br>***#6155,6***<br> | **Nicholas CUNLIFFE**<br>4 Castle Street (1790)<br>16 Sir Thomas' Buildings (1794)<br>Daulby Street (1825)<br>Liverpool | Goldsmith and silversmith |
| R2/167<br>5 December 1912<br>Sent by N Reading | Inglewood<br>Moseley<br>Briskley Done<br>Moseley | P13/R/47<br>***#6157***<br> | **Nathaniel C READING**<br>**Althans BLACKBURN** (*sic*)<br>(Ed: Should be Blackwell as per next entry?)<br>trading as **N READING & CO**<br>33 and 35 Hall Street<br>Birmingham | Gold and silver chain manufacturers |

| REGISTRATION DETAILS | MAKER'S PRIVATE ADDRESS and DETAILS | PLATE and MARK DETAILS | MAKER/COMPANY and BUSINESS ADDRESS | MAKER'S TRADE |
|---|---|---|---|---|
| R3/15<br>31 March 1923<br>Sent by F C Parsons<br>BAO has Althans Blackwell with signature | Inglewood<br>Wake Green Road<br>Moseley<br>30 Chortney Road<br>Moseley | P15/R/30<br>*#6158*<br> | **N C READING**<br>**Arthur** (*sic*) **BLACKWELL**<br>trading as **N C READING & CO**<br>30–35 Hall Street<br>Birmingham | Manufacturing jewellers |
| LPB/60 SP28/3<br>7 November 1884 | | P5/N/x1<br>*#6159*<br> | **NATHAN & DAVIS**<br>2 Gladstone Buildings, Richmond Street<br>Birmingham | Jewellers |
| R3/155<br>16 July 1955<br>Sent by N E Fisher | Private address same as business | P21/F/29<br>*#6160*<br> | **Norah Eileen FISHER**<br>30 York Road<br>Birkdale<br>Southport | Student |
| R1/139<br>12 January 1901<br>Sent by<br>F Coulthurst<br>Partnership dissolved<br>21 September 1913 | 13 Elm Street<br>3 Elm Street<br>Waterloo Road<br>Manchester | P9/N/10<br>*#6161*<br> | **Nicholas RUSHFORTH**<br>**Edward FOYE** trading as<br>**NICHOLAS & FOYE**<br>38 Hanover Street, Shudehill<br>Manchester | Umbrella and walking stick manufacturers |
| PP1/188<br>Similar mark BAO<br>14 December 1854 | | P2/N/x2<br>*#6162,3*<br> | **James NEALE** *<br>**Samuel FREEMAN** *<br>Victoria Buildings, Hill Street<br>Coventry | Watchcase makers |
| R3/137<br>8 March 1952<br>Sent by N H Fryer<br>Two sizes | Private address same as business | P21/F/17,18<br>*#6164,5*<br> | **Norman Hilary FRYER**<br>45 Cinnamon Lane<br>Fearnhead<br>Warrington | Artist craftsman and silversmith |
| R3/57<br>20 May 1931<br>Sent by T J Skelton<br>86 Vyse Street<br>Birmingham | | P15/N/17,18<br>*#6166,7*<br><br>P15/N/19,20<br>*#6168,9*<br> | **NORTHERN GOLDSMITHS CO** *<br>Crossley Cooke<br>Albert Thomas Pettinger<br>1-7 Blackett Street<br>85, 87 Westgate Road<br>Newcastle upon Tyne<br>9, 10 Blackwell Gate<br>Darlington<br>10 Fawcett Street<br>Sunderland<br>92 Deansgate<br>Manchester<br>11 Church Street<br>Oswestry | Jewellers watchmakers and silversmiths |
| R2/203<br>29 January 1916<br>Sent by The Northern Goldsmith Co | Croft House Grange [1]<br>Park Road<br>Newcastle upon Tyne | P15/N/3<br>*#6170*<br> | **NORTHERN GOLDSMITHS & SILVERSMITH CO** *<br>A T Pettinger [1] acting under power of attorney for Crossley Cooke<br>1, 3 Blackett Street<br>Newcastle upon Tyne | Jewellers and silversmiths |
| R3/76<br>27 May 1935<br>Sent by Charles Packer & Co Ltd<br>P15/N/3,17,18,20 confirmed | Re-entry owing to exchange of proprietors.<br>Common seal affixed in the presence of:-<br>Crossley Cooke (Director)<br>John Usher (Secretary) | No new marks<br>*#6171* | **NORTHERN GOLDSMITHS CO**<br>1 Blackett Street<br>Newcastle upon Tyne<br>**Charles PACKER & CO LTD** *<br>76 Regent Street (Registered Office)<br>London W1 | Goldsmiths and silversmiths |

| REGISTRATION DETAILS | MAKER'S PRIVATE ADDRESS and DETAILS | PLATE and MARK DETAILS | MAKER/COMPANY and BUSINESS ADDRESS | MAKER'S TRADE |
|---|---|---|---|---|
| R3/80<br>15 October 1935<br>Sent by Roberts & Belk Ltd<br>Furnival Works<br>Sheffield | | P15/N/26<br>***#6172***<br> | **NORTHERN GOLDSMITHS CO**<br>**Charles PACKER & CO LTD** *<br>(Proprietors)<br>Common seal of company affixed in the presence of:-<br>A T Pettinger (Director)<br>J Lees (Secretary)<br>76 Regent Street (Registered Office)<br>London W1 | Goldsmiths and silversmiths |
| R3/51<br>11 February 1930<br>Sent by N G Lainas | 19 Stoneby Drive<br>Wallasey | P15/L/40<br>***#6173***<br> | **Niobe George LAINAS**<br>City School of Art<br>Hope Street<br>Liverpool | Student |
| R2/105<br>9 March 1910<br>Sent by Nathaniel Greenside Prince | 68 Victoria Road<br>Aldershot<br>Hants | P13/P/137,138<br>***#6174,5***<br> | **Nathaniel Greenside PRINCE** *<br>Audrey House<br>Ely Place<br>London EC | Jewellery manufacturers agent |
| R2/157<br>6 June 1912<br>Sent by J Harding | 43 Mainwaring Road<br>Seacombe | P13/H/84<br>***#6176***<br> | **Nelly HARDING**<br>28 Tarleton Street<br>Liverpool | Manufacturing jeweller |
| R1/67<br>30 June 1898<br>Sent by F Coulthurst<br>Cancelled<br>17 January 1901 | 36 Sudell Street<br>Manchester<br>84 Elizabeth Street<br>Cheetham<br>Manchester | P5/N/962<br>***#6177***<br> | **Nicholas RUSHWORTH**<br>**Thomas Edward HARDY** trading as<br>**NICHOLAS & HARDY**<br>38 Hanover Street<br>Manchester | Umbrella and walking stick manufacturers |
| PDB 1822-6<br>MR3/94<br>J1 1822-29 | Gold rings | P1/19/x7<br>***#6178-84***<br> | **NEWTON & HYDE**<br>Manchester or | Goldsmith |
| PDB 1834<br>MR3/86 | Toy spoons | | **N HORT**<br>Town unspecified | Silversmith |
| R1/197<br>4 July 1903<br>Sent by G Nathan between P9/N/25 and 26 | 243 Hagley Road<br>Birmingham<br>Hall Road<br>Birmingham | P9/N/0*sic*<br>***#6185***<br> | **George NATHAN**<br>**Ridley HAYES** trading as<br>**NATHAN & HAYES** *<br>Howard Street<br>Birmingham | Manufacturing silversmiths |
| R1/45<br>9 May 1897<br>Sent by Nathan & Hayes | Argent House [1]<br>Handsworth<br>7 Clarendon Road [2]<br>Edgbaston<br>See also GNRH and #2963, R.H #6796 | P5/N/561b<br>***#6186***<br> | **George NATHAN** [1]<br>**Ridley HAYES** [2] trading as<br>**NATHAN & HAYES** *<br>285 Icknield Street<br>Birmingham | Silversmiths |
| R2/110<br>13 May 1910<br>Sent by Newcastle Handicrafts Co<br>Two sizes | College Road<br>Barras Bridge<br>Newcastle on Tyne | P13/N/25,26<br>***#6187,8***<br> | **NEWCASTLE HANDICRAFTS CO**<br>Charles Irwin (Secretary)<br>College Road<br>Barras Bridge<br>Newcastle upon Tyne | Jewellers, silver and metal work |
| Three sizes<br>same date | 65 Quayside<br>Newcastle on Tyne | P13/N/22-24<br>***#6189-91***<br> | | |
| R3/148<br>8 December 1953<br>Sent by N J Price | 521 Mather Avenue<br>Liverpool 19 | P21/P/54<br>***#6192***<br> | **Nancy Jones PRICE**<br>No business address entered | Metal worker and jeweller |

| REGISTRATION DETAILS | MAKER'S PRIVATE ADDRESS and DETAILS | PLATE and MARK DETAILS | MAKER/COMPANY and BUSINESS ADDRESS | MAKER'S TRADE |
|---|---|---|---|---|
| R3/172<br>14 May 1960<br>Sent by Gerrard Kayman | | P21/K/20<br>***#6193*** 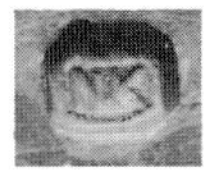 | **N KAYMAN LTD**<br>11 Hatton Garden<br>London EC1 | No trade entered |
| GTD 1818-29<br>PP1/188<br>PMR 1816-41 | Son of Nicholson Lee | P2/L/x2<br>***#6194,5***  | **Nathaniel LEE**<br>32 Leeds Street (1818)<br>36 Ray Street (1821)<br>2 Ray Street (1823-30)<br>Liverpool | Watchcase maker |
| | | P2/L/x2<br>***#6196,7***  | | |
| | Possibly the plate 1 incuse marks used by Nicholson Lee | P1/28/x2<br>***#6198,9***  | | |
| | Possibly the plate 1 incuse marks used by Nicholson Lee | P1/29/x2<br>***#6200,1***  | | |
| PDB 1796-1817<br>GTD1796-1817<br>MR2/95<br>MR3/89,193<br>PP1/188<br>PP2/352,353 | Gold rings, snuff boxes and tipstaffs<br><br>It is possible he used the plate 1 incuse marks for watchcases. | P1/27/x3<br>***#62002-4***  | **Nicholson LEE**<br>34 Ray Street (1796)<br>143 Scotland Road (1823-34)<br>Liverpool | Watchcase maker and goldsmith |
| R1/5<br>19 December 1894<br>Sent by J Johnston | 13 Nicholson Square<br>Edinburgh | P5/M/629<br>***#6205***  | **Nicholas MARTINET**<br>11 to 17 Nicolson Square<br>Edinburgh | Wholesale merchants |
| Missing register<br>*c.*1891 | | P5/M/393<br>***#6206***  | | |
| R2/79<br>22 April 1909<br>Sent by Nathan Rosenweig | 22 Elton Square<br>Broughton<br>Salford<br>Manchester | P13/R/24<br>***#6207***  | **Nathan ROSENWEIG**<br>10 to 12 Elton Street<br>Lower Broughton, Salford, Manchester<br>Left this address 16 July 1909<br>217 Bury New Road, Higher Broughton<br>Manchester | Stick manufacturer and cane importer |
| R2/168<br>28 February 1913<br>Sent by Mary Rushworth | 13 Birch Lane<br>Longsight<br>Manchester | P15/N/1<br>***#6208*** 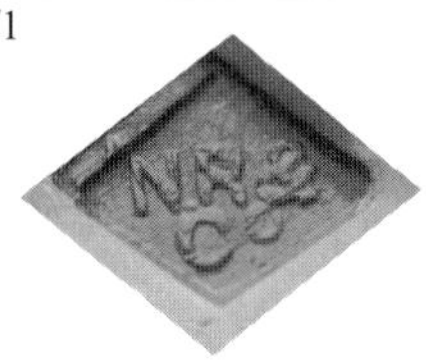 | **Nicholas RUSHWORTH** trading as<br>**Nicholas RUSHWORTH & CO**<br>38 Dantzig Street<br>Shudehill<br>58 Miller Street (new address undated)<br>Manchester | Umbrella and walking stick mounters and manufacturers |
| R3/160<br>20 February 1957<br>Sent by N Smith<br>Three sizes | Private address same as business | P21/S/67-69<br>***#6209-11***  | **Norman SMITH**<br>12a Sharpes Avenue<br>Scotforth<br>Lancaster<br>Lancashire | Jeweller and silversmith |

| REGISTRATION DETAILS | MAKER'S PRIVATE ADDRESS and DETAILS | PLATE and MARK DETAILS | MAKER/COMPANY and BUSINESS ADDRESS | MAKER'S TRADE |
|---|---|---|---|---|
| R2/182<br>6 January 1914<br>Sent by N Steingold | Private address same as business | P15/S/4<br>***#6212***<br> | **Nathan STEINGOLD** *<br>30 Commercial Road<br>London | Gold chain maker |
| R1/101<br>13 May 1899<br>Sent by Nock & Sanders | Heathfield Road<br>Handsworth<br>Chester Road<br>Sutton Coldfield | P9/N/6<br>***#6213***<br> | **Henry B NOCK**<br>**Alfred H SANDERS** trading as<br>**NOCK & SANDERS**<br>57 Tenby Street North<br>Birmingham | Jewellers |
| Missing register<br>*c.*1887 | | P5/N/81<br>***#6214***<br> | | |
| R3/182<br>2 March 1962<br>Sent by N J Tudor-Thomas | 20 Brooklands Avenue<br>Fulwood<br>Preston<br>Lancashire | P21/T/46,47<br>***#6215,6***<br> | **Neville James TUDOR-THOMAS**<br>No business address entered | Student silversmith |
| R3/85<br>7 October 1936<br>Sent by T J Skelton<br>86 Vyse Street<br>Birmingham<br>Two sizes | 186 Hampstead Road [1]<br>Handsworth<br>Birmingham<br>2 Edgbaston Road [2]<br>Smethwick<br>Birmingham | P21/T/1,2<br>***#6217,8***<br> | **Norman TIPTAFT LTD**<br>Norman Tiptaft [1]<br>Hilda Tiptaft [1]<br>Ethel Morgan [2]<br>Lombard House<br>Great Charles Street<br>Birmingham | Marketing specialists to the jewellery trade |
| R3/122<br>10 March 1948<br>Sent by N V Hall & Son | 26 Colebourne Road [1]<br>Kings Heath<br>Birmingham 14<br>62 Keswick Road [2]<br>Sheldon<br>Birmingham 26 | P21/H/42<br>***#6219***<br>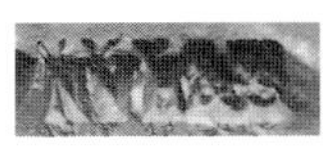 | **Noel Victor HALL** [1]<br>**Eric Noel HALL** [2] trading as<br>**N V HALL & SON**<br>33 Frederick Street<br>Birmingham 1 | Manufacturing jewellers |
| PP3/83<br>Not in SPB or LPB so struck 1860-3<br>Similar mark LAO 25 June 1862 and BAO26 February 1864 | | P3/W/x3<br>***#6220-2***<br> | **Noah WRIGHT** *<br>86 The Butts (1862)<br>13 Trafalgar Street (1867)<br>24 Southport Street (1867)<br>Coventry | Watchcase maker |
| SPB/12<br>23 August 1873 | CWMP 1883 has Wright & Son, gold and silver watchcase makers | P3/W/x3<br>***#6223-5***<br> | **Noah WRIGHT** *<br>136 Spon Street (1873)<br>127 Spon Street (1880)<br>Coventry | Watch pendant maker |
| Missing register<br>*c.*1890 | | P5/W/326<br>***#6226***<br> | | |

| REGISTRATION DETAILS | MAKER'S PRIVATE ADDRESS and DETAILS | PLATE and MARK DETAILS | MAKER/COMPANY and BUSINESS ADDRESS | MAKER'S TRADE |
|---|---|---|---|---|
| R1/124<br>23 April 1900<br>Sent by H T Olney | Chichester Road [1]<br>Croydon<br>Hallwood? [2]<br>Smithdown?, Sydenham<br>Redcott [3]<br>Forest Hill<br>Holmburydean [4]<br>Sydenham<br>Aldrincham Road [5]<br>Sydenham | P9/O/4<br>*#6227*<br> | **Frederick William AMSDEN** [1]<br>**Ernest AMSDEN** [2]<br>**Stanley AMSDEN** [3]<br>**Frank AMSDEN** [4]<br>**Henry Thomas OLNEY** [5] trading as<br>**OLNEY, AMSDEN & SONS**<br>9, 10, 11 Falcon Street<br>London | Haberdashers, trimming and fancy warehousemen |
| R3/99<br>12 May 1941<br>Sent by J M Perkins | | P21/O/1<br>*#6228*<br> | **OLLIVANT & BOTSFORD LTD** *<br>Sealed by:-<br>Nancy W Bake (Cashier)<br>John Marsden Perkins (Director and Secretary)<br>12/14 St Ann Street<br>Manchester | Jewellers and silversmiths |
| 24 June 1960 | | P21/O/5,6<br>*#6229,30*<br> | | |
| Missing register<br>*c.*1889<br>Similar mark BAO<br>23 September 1878 | | P5/O/222<br>*#6231*<br> | **OSBORNE & BAILEY**<br>52 Northampton Street<br>Birmingham | Goldsmiths |
| LPB/62<br>15 March 1882 | | P3/O/x3<br>*#6232-4*<br> | **OSBORNE & CO**<br>6, 7, 8 Spencer Street<br>Birmingham | Jewellers |
| R3/153<br>12 October 1954<br>Sent by O Edwards | 2E Huskisson Street<br>Liverpool 8 | P21/E/10<br>*#6235*<br> | **Miss Olive EDWARDS**<br>No business address entered | Student |
| R2/49<br>31 October 1907<br>Sent by O E Summers<br>Two sizes | 49 Beresford Road<br>Hornsey<br>London | P13/S/2,3<br>*#6236,7*<br> | **Oliver Ellington SUMMERS**<br>(Successor to G E Pickering)<br>3 Percival Street<br>Clerkenwell<br>London | Manufacturing jeweller |
| | Possibilities include a member of the France family of Manchester (see Elizabeth and James) – may also be two names such as Ollivant & France, both of Manchester | P1/24/x4<br>*#6238-41*<br> | **Unidentified** | |
| R2/65<br>9 September 1908<br>Sent by J & R Griffin | 149 Ferne Park Road<br>Hornsey<br>London N | P13/F/2<br>*#6242*<br> | **Oreste FRANZI & CO** *<br>Herbert Frederick Thorne (Manager)<br>5 Castle Street<br>London | Merchants |
| R3/127<br>15 February 1949<br>Sent by Oliver Heywood<br>Two sizes | 3 Windsor Drive<br>Park Road<br>Timperley<br>Cheshire | P21/H/48,49<br>*#6243,4*<br>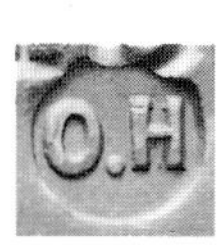 | **Oliver HEYWOOD**<br>No business address entered<br>Liverpool School of Art? | Art student |

| REGISTRATION DETAILS | MAKER'S PRIVATE ADDRESS and DETAILS | PLATE and MARK DETAILS | MAKER/COMPANY and BUSINESS ADDRESS | MAKER'S TRADE |
|---|---|---|---|---|
| R2/201<br>13 November 1915<br>Sent by O H Hancocks | 19 Chinley Avenue<br>Moston | P15/H/26<br>***#6245***<br> | **O H HANCOCKS**<br>82 Lancaster Avenue<br>Fennel Street<br>Manchester | Diamond mounter and jeweller |
| R2/233<br>24 September 1920<br>Sent by Owen Jones | 22 Hereford Street<br>Oldham | P15/J/17<br>***#6246***<br> | **Owen JONES**<br>2 Waterloo Street<br>Oldham | Engraver, badge and medal maker |
| R3/119<br>11 October 1947<br>Sent by Outhwaite & Litherland | Ardlen [1]<br>The Ridgeway<br>Gayton, The Wirral<br>75 Moor Lane [2]<br>Crosby<br>Crantock [3]<br>Harbour Road<br>Preston<br>1 Ashford Road [4]<br>Meols<br>Lancashire | P21/O/4<br>***#6247***<br> | **Thomas Oscar OUTHWAITE** [1]<br>**Henry Raymond LITHERLAND** [2]<br>**George Henry COTTRAM** [3]<br>**Thomas Reynolds OUTHWAITE** [4]<br>trading as<br>**OUTHWAITE & LITHERLAND**<br>3 Eberle Street<br>Liverpool and<br>11-13 Pembroke Place<br>Liverpool 3 and<br>23-25 Bridge Street<br>Litherland<br>Liverpool 21 | Auctioneers and valuers |
| R1/114<br>18 October 1899<br>Sent by Okell & Owen | Barrow<br>Chester<br>Kingswood Road<br>South Oxton<br>Bidston Road<br>Oxton | P9/O/3<br>***#6248***<br>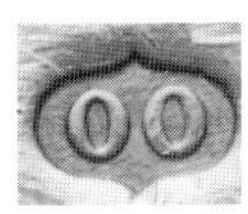 | **George OKELL**<br>**George McLAREN**<br>**Richard Robert OWEN** trading as<br>**OKELL & OWEN**<br>17 St James' Street<br>Liverpool and<br>Bombay<br>India | East India merchants |
| R2/82<br>14 May 1909<br>Sent by G H Johnstone & Co | Formans Road<br>Sparkhill<br>Birmingham | P13/P/86<br>***#6249***<br> | **Owen POWELL**<br>39 Northampton Street<br>Birmingham | Manufacturing jeweller |
| R3/6<br>6 February 1922<br>Sent by<br>W A Massingham | Private address same as business | P15/O/6<br>***#6250***<br> | **OWEN & ROBINSON LTD** *<br>31 Upper Head Row (Registered Office)<br>Leeds | Jewellers |
| R2/93<br>22 September 1909<br>Sent by William Neale & Son | Bamfield<br>Ashton upon Mersey | P13/O/4<br>***#6251***<br> | **James W BOTSFORD** trading as<br>**OLLIVANT & BOTSFORD** *<br>12, 14 St Ann Street<br>Manchester | Silversmiths |
| R2/51<br>21 November 1907<br>Sent by Akerman Co | 75 Hurstbourne Road<br>Forest Hill<br>London SE | P13/W/19<br>***#6252***<br> | **Richard Owen WILLIAMS** *<br>18 Bartletts Passage Buildings<br>Holborn Circus<br>London and<br>56 Frederick Street<br>Birmingham | Silversmiths |
| R2/117<br>26 August 1910<br>Sent by J G Newbold | 75 Hurstbourne Road<br>Forest Hill<br>London SE<br><br>See also RW #7487, etc | P13/W/80<br>***#6253***<br>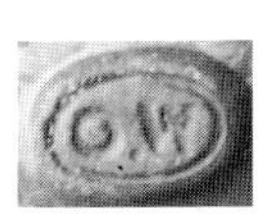 | **Richard Owen WILLIAMS** trading as<br>**R Owen WILLIAMS** *<br>18 Bartletts Passage Buildings<br>Holborn Circus<br>London EC and<br>94 Vyse Street<br>Birmingham | Wholesale silversmiths and mounters |

| REGISTRATION DETAILS | MAKER'S PRIVATE ADDRESS and DETAILS | PLATE and MARK DETAILS | MAKER/COMPANY and BUSINESS ADDRESS | MAKER'S TRADE |
|---|---|---|---|---|
| R2/227<br>27 February 1920<br>Sent by R Owen Williams Ltd | 153 Perry Vale<br>Forest Hill<br>London SE | P15/W/53<br>***#6254***<br> | **Richards Owen WILLIAMS** trading as<br>**R Owen WILLIAMS LTD** *<br>76–78 Grays Inn Road<br>Holborn<br>London<br>Caldercot Works<br>24 St Marys Street<br>St Pauls<br>Birmingham | Silversmiths and electroplate manufacturers |
| R2/231<br>18 May 1920<br>Sent by R Owen Williams | 153 Perry Vale<br>Forest Hill<br>London SE | P15/W/56<br>***#6255***<br> | **R Owen WILLIAMS** *<br>76–78 Grays Inn Road<br>Holborn<br>London WC | Silversmith |
| R2/51<br>21 November 1907<br>Sent by Akerman Co | 75 Hurstbourne Road<br>Forest Hill<br>London SE | P13/W/18<br>***#6256***<br> | **Richard Owen WILLIAMS** *<br>18 Bartletts Passage Buildings<br>Holborn Circus<br>London and<br>56 Frederick Street<br>Birmingham | |
| R2/41<br>15 June 1907<br>Sent by J & R Griffin | Caldicot<br>75 Hurstbourne Road<br>Forest Hill<br>London | P9/V*sic*/171<br>***#6257***<br> | **R Owen WILLIAMS** *<br>18 Bartletts Passage Buildings<br>London EC and<br>56 Frederick Street<br>Birmingham | |
| LPB/96<br>16 April 1880 | | P3/Y/x2<br>***#5258***<br>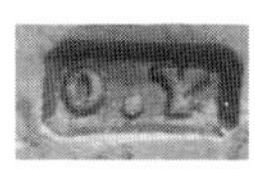 | **Oliver YOUNG**<br>27 Sandhill<br>Newcastle upon Tyne | Watchmaker |

| REGISTRATION DETAILS | MAKER'S PRIVATE ADDRESS and DETAILS | PLATE and MARK DETAILS | MAKER/COMPANY and BUSINESS ADDRESS | MAKER'S TRADE |
|---|---|---|---|---|
| R3/166<br>12 March 1959<br>Sent by E P R Baker | 3 Bilston Road<br>Oxton<br>Birkenhead | P21/B/56<br>***#6260***  | **Mrs Esther Phoebe Rosa BAKER**<br>No business address entered | Trade not entered |
| LPB/64<br>3 April 1880 | | P3/P/x2<br>***#6261,2***  | **PLATNAUER BROTHERS** *<br>1 St Paul's Square, Ludgate Hill<br>Birmingham | Watch manufacturers and importers |
| PMR 1824-55 | | P1/26/x1<br>***#6263***  | **Patrick BELL**<br>Ray Street (1829)<br>13 Blenheim Street (1845)<br>9 Baptist Street (1849-51)<br>15 Thornton Place (1853-5)<br>Wellington Road<br>Liverpool | Watchcase maker |
| LPB/66<br>23 August 1883<br>Sent by Mr Briault<br>No mark in LPB just P&B initials | | P5/P/x1<br>***#6264***  | **George William PICKERING** *<br>**& BRIAULT**<br>3 Percival Street<br>Clerkenwell<br>London | Jewellers |
| Not in LPB | | P3/B*sic*/x1<br>***#6265***  | **PLATNAUER BROTHERS** *<br>1 St Paul's Square<br>Ludgate Hill<br>Birmingham | Watch manufacturers and importers |
| Missing register<br>*c.*1887 | | P5/P/114<br>***#6266***  | | |
| Missing register<br>*c.*1886 | | P5/P/73<br>***#6267***  | | |
| Missing register<br>*c.*1888 | | P5/P/168<br>***#6268***  | | |
| LPB/64<br>3 April 1880<br>Two sizes | | P3/P/x2<br>***#6269,70***  | | |
| LPB/72<br>10 March 1880<br>Sent by Mayell Brothers | | P3/B*sic*/x3<br>***#6271-3***  | | |
| LPB/28<br>28 June 1883<br>Sent by J Harris | | P3/P/x3<br>***#6274-6***  | | |
| LPB/92<br>28 August 1882 | | P3/Q*sic*/x1<br>***#6277*** 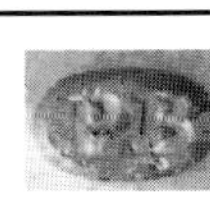 | | |
| PMR 1824-55 | See entry above for other business addresses | P1/26/x1<br>***#6278***  | **Patrick BELL**<br>Ray Street (1829)<br>Liverpool | Watchcase maker |
| R2/153<br>26 March 1912<br>Sent by Thos Perks & Son<br>BAO 19.152 | 78 Stanmore Road<br>Edgbaston<br>Birmingham | P13/B/130<br>***#6279*** 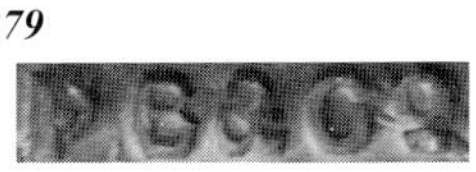 | **Philip BASH** trading as<br>**Philip BASH & CO**<br>27 Hylton Street<br>Birmingham | Wholesale jewellers |
| R1/124<br>10 April 1900<br>Sent by J & R Griffin<br>73 Vyse Street<br>Birmingham | | P9/B/26<br>***#6280***  | **Philip BASH** trading as<br>**P BASH & CO**<br>27 Hylton Street<br>Birmingham | Jewellers |

| REGISTRATION DETAILS | MAKER'S PRIVATE ADDRESS and DETAILS | PLATE and MARK DETAILS | MAKER/COMPANY and BUSINESS ADDRESS | MAKER'S TRADE |
|---|---|---|---|---|
| R2/111<br>26 May 1910<br>Sent by T Perks & Son | 78 Stanmore Road<br>Edgbaston<br>Birmingham | P13/B/76<br>***#6281***  | **Philip BASH** trading as<br>**Philip BASH & CO**<br>27 Hylton Street<br>Birmingham | Jewellers factors |
| R2/170<br>17 April 1913<br>Sent by W Clark & Son | | P15/B/44<br>***#6282***  | | Jewellers |
| R2/1<br>31 July 1905<br>Sent by J & R Griffin | | P9/XYZ*sic*/135<br>***#6283***  | | Jewellers factors |
| R3/7<br>11 March 1922<br>Sent by T J Skelton | | P15/B/160,161<br>***#6284,5*** 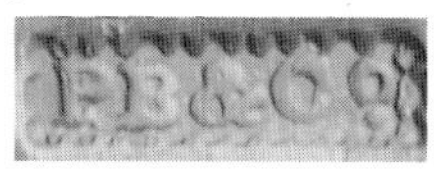 | **Philip BASH** trading as<br>**P BASH & CO**<br>83 Vyse Street<br>Birmingham | |
| R3/12<br>11 October 1922<br>Sent by T J Skelton | | P15/B/164<br>***#6286***  | | |
| R1/151<br>11 July 1901<br>Sent by selves<br>Two sizes | Lismore [1]<br>Erdington<br>Birmingham<br>Lismore [2]<br>Erdington<br>Birmingham | P9/P/104-117<br>***#6287-90***  | **Frederick William PEACH** [1]<br>**Ernest William PEACH** [2] trading as<br>**PEACH BROTHERS**<br>34 Northampton Street<br>Birmingham | Manufacturing jewellers |
| R2/197<br>11 June 1915<br>Sent by T S Osborn<br>BAO 20.653 | Private address same as business | P15/P/65<br>***#6291***  | **Ernest Arthur PEACH**<br>**Frederick William PEACH** trading as<br>**PEACH BROTHERS**<br>235 Icknield Street<br>Birmingham | |
| MR1/34-5<br>J3/389 | Incuse mark might indicate a location or building rather than Peter Conway who probably used a cameo mark | Pre-dates P1<br>***#6292***  | **Pott Chapel**<br>Pott Shrigley Parish<br>Chester or | Place name |
| | Working from 1533, died 1606<br>Paten *c*.1576 | | **Peter CONWAY**<br>Chester | Silversmith |
| PP1/188<br>WTD 1850 | CWMP 1874-96 | P2/C/x3<br>***#6293-5***  | **Philip COHEN**<br>1 Oxford Terrace<br>Coventry | Watch manufacturer and watchcase maker |
| | | P2/C/x3<br>***#6296-8***  | | |
| | | P2/C/x3<br>***#6299-6301*** 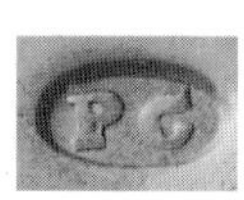 | | |
| SPB/19<br>3 June 1868<br>Sent by James Walker<br>Earlsdon, Coventry | | P3/C/x3<br>***#6302-4***  | | |
| Missing register<br>*c*.1887<br>Similar mark entered<br>BAO 3 October 1894 | | P5/P/81<br>***#6305***  | **PEERS & CLARKE**<br>2 Warstone Parade<br>Birmingham | Jewellers |

| REGISTRATION DETAILS | MAKER'S PRIVATE ADDRESS and DETAILS | PLATE and MARK DETAILS | MAKER/COMPANY and BUSINESS ADDRESS | MAKER'S TRADE |
|---|---|---|---|---|
| R2/50<br>19 November 1907<br>Sent by Dobson & Son | Toorak<br>Hollycroft Avenue<br>Hampstead<br>4 Parsipal Road<br>Hampstead | P9/D/62<br>***#6306***<br> | **Percy H DOBSON**<br>**Charles W DOBSON** trading as<br>**DOBSON & SONS** *<br>200 Piccadilly<br>London | Goldsmiths and silversmiths |
| Missing register<br>*c.*1886 | See Perry & Co below | P5/P/23<br>***#6307***<br><br> | **Unidentified** | |
| R2/26<br>6 October 1906<br>Sent by Perry & Co Ltd | 14 Arden Road<br>Handsworth<br>Staffordshire | P9/U*sic*/254<br>***#6308***<br> | **PERRY & CO**<br>J Martyn Smith (Director)<br>William Willey (Director)<br>Herbert Smith (Director)<br>36 Lancaster Street<br>Birmingham | Manufacturing jewellers and silversmiths |
| R2/119<br>30 September 1910<br>Sent by Perry & Co Ltd | Elslie, Church Lane<br>Handsworth Wood<br>Disposed of stud business 14 November 1916 to Moore Abbott & Co | P13/P/143<br>***#6309***<br> | **PERRY & CO LTD**<br>C J Hampton (Secretary)<br>36 Lancaster Street<br>Birmingham | Manufacturers of articles in gold and silver |
| R1/64<br>2 April 1898<br>Sent by<br>W G Dickins | Church Road<br>Moseley | P5/Q*sic*/949<br>***#6310***<br>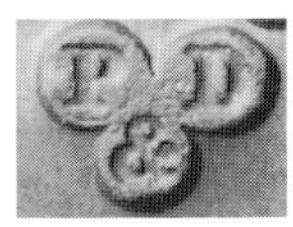 | **W G DICKINS** trading as<br>**PEMBROOK & DICKINS**<br>43 Hall Street<br>Birmingham | Silversmiths and electroplate manufacturers |
| Missing register<br>*c.*1890 | | P5/B/276<br>***#6311***<br><br> | **Unidentified** | |
| R3/157<br>15 March 1956<br>Sent by P D Sloane<br>5 December 1957 | 11 Thornton Road<br>Rock Ferry<br>Birkenhead | P21/S/65<br>***#6312***<br>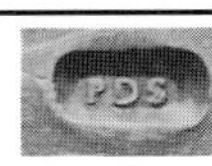<br><br>P21/S/77<br>***#6313***<br><br> | **Patricia Dorothy SLOANE**<br>No business address entered | Student silversmith |
| MR1/148-57<br>SOT/31-5<br>SIL/48 | Large variety of plate 1701 to 1727<br>Free 1676/7<br>See also PP | P1/5/x1<br>***#6314***<br>type 4a<br><br> | **Peter PEMBERTON I**<br>Eastgate Street<br>Chester<br><br>and | Silversmith |
| | Free 1690 | P1/5/x1<br>***#6315***<br>type 4b<br><br> | **Thomas PEMBERTON**<br>Eastgate Street<br>Chester | Silversmith |
| R3/125<br>16 July 1948<br>Sent by E C Preston | Private address same as business | P21/P/28<br>***#6316***<br>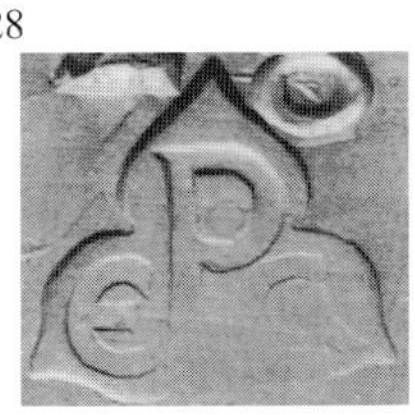 | **Edward Carter PRESTON**<br>88 Bulford Street South<br>Liverpool 7 | Sculptor |
| R3/38<br>29 August 1927<br>Sent by selves<br>Two sizes | Keston [1]<br>Hathaway Lane<br>Stratford-upon-Avon<br>The Cottage [2]<br>Loxley Lane<br>Stratford-upon-Avon | P15/P/201,202<br>***#6317,8***<br><br> | **F A BALL** [1]<br>**F BALL** [2] trading as<br>**PERMANENT ENAMEL CO**<br>Arden Street, Stratford-upon-Avon and<br>24 Branston Street<br>Birmingham | Manufacturing jewellers and enamellers |

| REGISTRATION DETAILS | MAKER'S PRIVATE ADDRESS and DETAILS | PLATE and MARK DETAILS | MAKER/COMPANY and BUSINESS ADDRESS | MAKER'S TRADE |
|---|---|---|---|---|
| R2/171<br>10 May 1913<br>Sent by Stokes & Ireland<br>Three sizes | | P15/P/40-54<br>***#6319-33***<br> | **John PEARCE**<br>**Charles BROOK**<br>**John PEARCE jnr**<br>**Arthur PEARCE** (Secretary) trading as<br>**PEARCE & SONS LTD** *<br>Bond Street<br>Leeds and<br>Lendal<br>York and<br>34 Gallowtree Gate<br>Leicester | Gold and silversmiths |
| R1/67<br>21 June 1898<br>Sent by R Parkes<br>J & R Griffin<br>Kinsey Brothers & Patrick<br>Grove Brothers<br>Two sizes | R1 has #960, P5 has #906 | P5/J/906x2<br>***#6334,5***<br> | **Percy Frederick JACKSON**<br>34 Warstone Lane<br>Birmingham | Wholesale jeweller |
| R3/3<br>18 May 1928<br>Sent by P F Jackson | 184 Hamstead Road<br>Handsworth<br>Birmingham | P15/J/31-33<br>***#6336-8***<br> | **Percy Frederick JACKSON**<br>35 Frederick Street<br>Birmingham | |
| R3/62<br>21 March 1932<br>Sent by R Jones | 5 Warstone Parade East<br>Birmingham | P15/J/38<br>***#6339***<br> | | |
| R3/3<br>27 May 1921<br>Sent by P F Jackson | 184 Hamstead Road<br>Handsworth<br>Birmingham | P15/J/28<br>***#6340***<br> | | |
| R3/62<br>August 1944<br>Sent by P F Jackson Ltd<br>July 1946 | | P21/J/2<br>***#6341***<br> | **P F JACKSON LTD**<br>35 Frederick Street<br>Birmingham | Jewellers and silversmiths |
| | | P21/J/3<br>***#6342***<br> | | |
| R1/227<br>13 February 1905<br>Sent by P F Jackson | 184 Hamstead Road<br>Handsworth<br>Birmingham | P9/J/52-54<br>***#6343-5***<br> | | Jewellers |
| R1/4<br>6 November 1894<br>Sent by E Vaughton<br>F Martin | 31 Francis Road<br>Edgbaston<br>Birmingham | P5/J/621<br>***#6346***<br> | **Percy Frederick JACKSON**<br>64 Spencer Street<br>34 Warstone Lane (from 3 September 1896)<br>Birmingham | Wholesale jewellers |
| R2/94<br>12 October 1909<br>Sent by P F Jackson<br>BAO 16.908, 16.919 | 184 Hamstead Road<br>Handsworth<br>Birmingham | P13/J/7-18<br>***#6347-58***<br> | | |
| R2/51<br>26 November 1907<br>Sent by J Hayward<br>BAO 13.918 | | P13/J/38<br>***#6359***<br> | | |
| R2/121<br>19 October 1910<br>Sent by P F Jackson<br>BAO 18.215 to 18.226 | | P13/J/29-40<br>***#6360-71***<br> | | |

| REGISTRATION DETAILS | MAKER'S PRIVATE ADDRESS and DETAILS | PLATE and MARK DETAILS | MAKER/COMPANY and BUSINESS ADDRESS | MAKER'S TRADE |
|---|---|---|---|---|
| R3/3<br>1 November 1927<br>Sent by P F Jackson Ltd | 184 Hamstead Road<br>Handsworth<br>Birmingham | P15/J/30<br>***#6372***  | **Percy Frederick JACKSON**<br>35 Frederick Street<br>Birmingham | Wholesale jewellers |
| R3/49<br>19 October 1929<br>Sent by P F Jackson Ltd | | P15/J/1<br>***#6373***  | | Jewellers and silversmiths |
| R3/57<br>2 April 1931<br>Sent by Kinsey Brothers & Patrick Ltd, Vyse Street, Birmingham | | P15/J/36<br>***#6374***  | | Wholesale jewellers |
| R1/170<br>13 June 1902<br>Sent by E J Rudge | 282 Hamstead Road<br>Birmingham | P9/J/34<br>***#6375***  | **Percy Frederick JACKSON**<br>69 Great Hampton Street<br>Birmingham | |
| R3/112<br>4 February 1946<br>Sent by<br>Paul P Gutfreund | Private address same as business | P21/G/8<br>***#6376***  | **Paul P GUTFREUND**<br>87 Serpentine Road<br>Kendal | Artistic goods |
| 13 August 1946 | | P21/G/13<br>***#6377***  | | |
| 13 July 1948 | | P21/G/17<br>***#6378*** 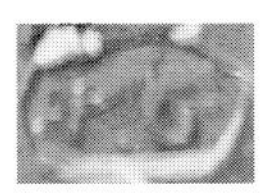 | | |
| R3/126<br>22 October 1948<br>Sent by Paul P Goodfriend<br>re-entry | Private address same as business<br>Formerly Paul P Gutfreund name changed by deed poll dated 25 September 1948 advertised in Westmorland Gazette | P21/G/8,13,16, 17<br>***#6379-82*** 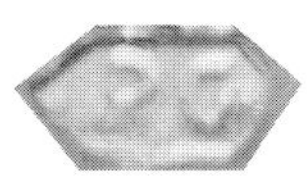 | **Paul P GOODFRIEND**<br>87 Serpentine Road<br>Kendal | Artistic silverworker |
| R3/124<br>9 June 1948<br>Sent by Philip Hilton | Private address same as business | P21/H/44<br>***#6383***  | **Philip HILTON**<br>302 Evington Road<br>Leicester | Jeweller and optician |
| 23 July 1953 | | P21/H/66<br>***#6384***  | | |
| PP1/169, 188 | | P2/P/x2<br>***#6385,6***  | **PACKWOOD & HARRIS**<br>**David PACKWOOD**<br>Summerland, The Butts<br>Coventry | Watch manufacturers and watchcase makers |
| SPB/24<br>30 March 1871<br>CWMP 1874 | Mark on P3 looks like BH, PH or RH, but is actually EH (*#1991-3*) | P3/H/x3<br>***#6387-9*** 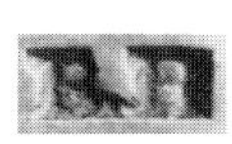 | **Edward HICKMAN** *<br>Old Allesley Road<br>Coventry | Watchcase maker |
| PP1/188<br>Similar mark CAO<br>14 October 1863 | Possibly mispunched for plate 3 | P2/P/x2<br>***#6390,1***  | **PENLINGTON & HUTTON**<br>3 St George's Crescent (*c.*1868)<br>Liverpool | Watch, chronometer and watchcase makers |
| PP1/188<br>CWMP 1850<br>Similar mark entered BAO 25 July 1810 | | P1/14/x3<br>***#6392-4*** 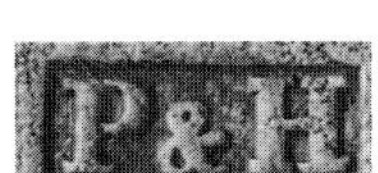 | **PACKWOOD & HARRIS**<br>**David PACKWOOD**<br>Summerland, The Butts<br>Coventry | Watch manufacturers and watchcase makers |

| REGISTRATION DETAILS | MAKER'S PRIVATE ADDRESS and DETAILS | PLATE and MARK DETAILS | MAKER/COMPANY and BUSINESS ADDRESS | MAKER'S TRADE |
|---|---|---|---|---|
| SPB/1<br>16 October 1863<br>GSJW/136 1861 | | P3/P/x2<br>***#6395,6***<br>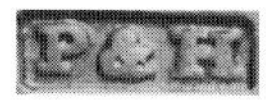 | **PENLINGTON & HUTTON**<br>3 St George's Crescent<br>Liverpool | Chronometer watch manufacturers |
| R1/96<br>24 March 1899<br>Sent by R Nevill | 20 Sydenham Road<br>Bristol | P9/P/25<br>***#6397***<br> | **John George HARPER** trading as<br>**PLEASANCE & HARPER**<br>4 Wine Street<br>Bristol | Watchmakers and jewellers |
| R2/8<br>9 January 1906<br>Sent by S Usher Ltd | 86 Redland Road<br>Bristol | P9/Q*sic*/229[7] *sic*<br>***#6398***<br> | | Jewellers |
| R2/20<br>4 July 1906<br>Sent by S Usher Ltd | | P9/U*sic*/253<br>***#6399***<br> | | |
| R1/205<br>24 December 1903<br>Sent by P H Faulkner | 4 Witton Road<br>Six Ways<br>Aston<br>Birmingham | P9/F/18<br>***#6400***<br> | **Philip Henry FAULKNER**<br>15 Branston Street<br>Birmingham | Jeweller |
| R3/71<br>24 May 1934<br>Sent by Samuel Hope<br>126 Vyse St, Birm | | P15/P/239<br>***#6401***<br> | **PLEASANCE & HARPER LTD**<br>4 Wine Street<br>Bristol | Jewellers |
| R2/171<br>1 May 1913<br>Sent by P J Jones | 59 Gosford Street<br>Coventry | P13/J/61<br>***#6402***<br>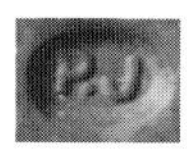 | **Percy John JONES** *<br>Back of 31 Norfolk Street<br>Coventry | Gold watchcase maker |
| R3/91<br>27 September 1938<br>Sent by P J Finch<br>Two sizes | 80 Lansdowne Road<br>Handsworth<br>Birmingham | P21/F/3-5<br>***#6403-5***<br> | **Percy James FINCH**<br>14b Tenby Street<br>Birmingham | Manufacturing silversmith |
| R3/132<br>18 April 1950<br>Sent by P J Vickers<br>Two sizes | 8 Woodbine Crescent<br>Stockport | P21/V/4,5<br>***#6406,7***<br> | **Peter Julian VICKERS**<br>No business address entered<br>Liverpool School of Art? | Student |
| R3/112<br>13 February 1946<br>Sent by<br>Phyllis Kerrison Smith<br>Two sizes | Private address same as business | P21/S/20,21<br>***#6408,9***<br> | **Phyllis Kerrison SMITH**<br>4 Barlow Fold<br>Romiley<br>Cheshire | Craftsman |
| R3/100<br>30 June 1941<br>Sent by selves | Sealed by the Directors and Secretary | P21/P/8<br>***#6410***<br> | **PARSONS THE JEWELLERS LTD**<br>Cyril G Parsons (Director)<br>L D Parsons (Director)<br>W H Goodenough (Secretary)<br>10 and 12 Clare Street<br>Bristol and<br>Sun Buildings (Registered Office)<br>1 Clare Street<br>Bristol | Jewellers |
| PDB 1835<br>MR3/89,123<br>SIL/53,54<br>SOT/134-5<br>J1 1842-7 | Spoons, toddy ladle and badge | P1/7/x3<br>***#6411-3***<br> | **Patrick LEONARD**<br>Jackson's Square<br>Green Gate<br>Salford<br>Manchester | Silversmith |
| Similar mark entered<br>SAO 15 October 1835 | | P2/L/x2<br>***#6414,5***<br> | | |

| REGISTRATION DETAILS | MAKER'S PRIVATE ADDRESS and DETAILS | PLATE and MARK DETAILS | MAKER/COMPANY and BUSINESS ADDRESS | MAKER'S TRADE |
|---|---|---|---|---|
| LPB/50<br>8 December 1881 | | P3/L/x1<br>***#6416***<br>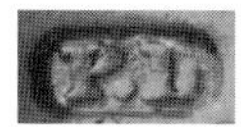 | **Philip LEWIS**<br>96 Digbeth Street<br>Birmingham | Jeweller |
| R1/99<br>3 May 1899<br>Sent by<br>J Gammage | Private address same as business | P9/L/8<br>***#6417***<br> | **Percy LAWRENCE**<br>35 Brompton Road<br>London SW | Jeweller |
| R2/194<br>13 April 1915<br>Sent by Gertrude Duckworth | 38 Bronwich Street[1]<br>Bolton | P15/P/62<br>***#6418***<br> | **PRESTON LTD**<br>Gertrude Duckworth[1] (Managing Director)<br>2 Deansgate<br>Bond Street<br>Bolton | Jewellers and silversmiths |
| R3/94<br>10 March 1939<br>Sent by P Marsh<br>Two sizes | Balholm<br>Bertram Drive<br>Meols<br>Wirral<br>Cheshire | P21/M/7,8<br>***#6419,20***<br> | **Phyllis MARSH**<br>No business address entered | Private jewellery and metalworker |
| R2/205<br>3 June 1916<br>Sent by Pinkus Magen | Private address same as business | P15/M/21<br>***#6421***<br>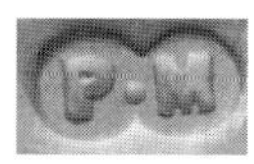 | **Pinkus MAGEN**<br>46 Princess Square, Cable Street<br>London E | Jeweller, ring and chain maker |
| R2/68<br>3 November 1908<br>Sent by William James Mayell<br>Cancelled<br>24 April 1912<br>Ltd Co Two sizes | The Laurels<br>Warwick Road<br>Olton<br>Warwickshire | P13/P/5,6<br>***#6422,3***<br> | **PHILLIPS & MAYELL LTD**<br>William John Mayell (Managing Director)<br>27 Tenby Street<br>Birmingham | Jewellers |
| R2/231<br>18 May 1920<br>Sent by J Taylor Foot<br>Two sizes | 28 Earlstom Road<br>Wallasey<br>Grosvenor Galleries<br>Harrogate | P15/P/156,157<br>***#6424,5***<br> | **Archibald PHILLIPS**<br>**Robert Raynor MACCONNELL**<br>25 Castle Street<br>Liverpool and<br>Grosvenor Galleries<br>Harrogate | Fine art and oriental dealers |
| R2/233<br>18 September 1920<br>Sent by W J Mayell<br>Two sizes | Private address same as business | P15/P/160-168<br>***#6426-34***<br> | **PHILLIPS & MAYELL LTD**<br>W J Mayell (Director)<br>27 Tenby Street<br>Birmingham | Gold chain makers and goldsmiths |
| PDB 1793-6<br>MR3/94 | Gold rings | P1/19/x1<br>***#6435***<br>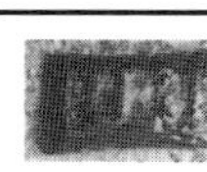<br>P1/27/x1<br>***#6436***<br> | **Peter MOLYNEUX**<br>Liverpool | Goldsmith |
| R2/235<br>2 December 1920<br>Sent by P Magen | Private address same as business | P15/M/43<br>***#6437***<br> | **Pinkus MAGEN**<br>61 Chapel Road<br>London E1 | Ring and chain maker |
| Missing register<br>*c.*1891<br>Similar incuse mark without frame entered BAO 30 July 1890 | | P5/D/334<br>***#6438***<br> | **Peter Martin DOYLE**<br>79 Quay<br>Waterford City<br>Ireland | Tobacconist |
| R1/32<br>15 September 1896<br>Sent by W J Mayell (Secretary) | | P5/P/787<br>***#6439***<br> | **PHILLIPS & MAYELL LTD**<br>51 Albion Street<br>Birmingham | Gold chain makers |

| REGISTRATION DETAILS | MAKER'S PRIVATE ADDRESS and DETAILS | PLATE and MARK DETAILS | MAKER/COMPANY and BUSINESS ADDRESS | MAKER'S TRADE |
|---|---|---|---|---|
| R2/156<br>24 April 1912<br>Sent by Phillips & Mayell<br>BAO 20.048,20.049<br>20.050, 20.051<br>Two sizes | Warwick Road<br>Olton | P13/Q*sic*/217-220<br>***#6440-3***<br> | **PHILLIPS & MAYELL LTD**<br>W J Mayell (Director)<br>27 Tenby Street<br>Birmingham | Jewellers |
| GTD 1835-70<br>Three sizes | | P1/3/x3<br>***#6444-6***<br> | **Peter NORRIS**<br>56 Great Crosshall Street<br>Liverpool | Watch and watchcase manufacturer |
| R3/26<br>7 January 1925<br>Sent by Stylic Watch Case Co<br>153 Farringdon Road<br>London | | P15/W/77<br>***#6447***<br> | **BRADLEY BRITISH OVERSEAS LTD** *<br>No business address entered<br>(Ed: Culme has Percy Nind-Ward at<br>12 St Andrew Street, Holborn Circus) | Export and import shipping agents |
| LPB/96<br>27 April 1882<br>No name or address entered<br>GSJW/102 1861 | | P3/C/x3<br>***#6448-50***<br> | **P N CASPER**<br>16 Bury Street<br>St Mary Axe<br>London EC | Watch manufacturer to the trade |
| Missing register<br>*c.*1890 | Ist edition Jackson. See also E Power, Dublin, 1901 | P5/P/275<br>***#6451***<br> | **T POWER & SON**<br>Liverpool or<br><br>**POWER BROTHERS**<br>Dublin | Silversmiths |
| LPB/66<br>31 May 1884<br>No mark just PP initials | | P5/P/x1<br>***#6452***<br> | **POPE & PHELPS**<br>15 Tenby Street<br>Birmingham | Jewellers |
| R3/31<br>17 November 1925<br>Sent by Peach M Page | Private address same as business | P15/P/195<br>***#6453***<br> | **Peach M PAGE**<br>2 Kings Mount<br>Oxton<br>Birkenhead | Artist and craftsman |
| 22 December 1927<br>Sent by Peach M Page | | P15/P/203<br>***#6454***<br> | | |
| ? ? 1936 only year entered | | P21/P/41<br>***#6455***<br> | | |
| LPB/64<br>25 November 1879 | | P3/P/x3<br>***#6456-8***<br> | **Henry POPE & Stephen PHELPS**<br>52 Frederick Street<br>Birmingham | Jewellers |
| R1/22<br>24 February 1896<br>Sent by Poyser & Privett | 27 St James Walk [1]<br>Clerkenwell<br>6 Clarence Road [2]<br>Leytonstone | P5/P/731<br>***#6459***<br> | **Arthur Wellesley POYSER** [1] *<br>**Benjamin Alfred PRIVETT** [2] *<br>trading as **POYSER & PRIVETT**<br>27 St James Walk, Clerkenwell<br>London | Stick and pipe mounter |
| MR1/148-57 MR3/184<br>SIL/30/1,45/6,48<br>J1 1677-1706<br>J3/389 | Two communion cups *c.*1685<br>Free 1677<br>Mark seen with single wheatsheaf mark | Pre-dates P1<br>***#6460***<br>type 1<br> | **Peter PEMBERTON I**<br>Chester | Silversmith |
| J1 | This mark noted only in Jackson<br>Porringer 1690-92 | Pre-dates P1<br>***#6461***<br> | | |

| REGISTRATION DETAILS | MAKER'S PRIVATE ADDRESS and DETAILS | PLATE and MARK DETAILS | MAKER/COMPANY and BUSINESS ADDRESS | MAKER'S TRADE |
|---|---|---|---|---|
| J1 | This mark noted only in Jackson Free 1676/7 Trefid spoon 1692 | Pre-dates P1<br>***#6462***  | **Peter PEMBERTON I**<br>Chester | Silversmith |
| MR1/148-57<br>MR3/184<br>SIL/30/1,45/6,48<br>J1 1677-1706 J3/389 | Communion cups and cover, spoons *c*.1694-97 | Pre-dates P1<br>***#6463***<br>type 2  | | |
| | Miniature porringer, marrow spoon *c*.1695-1701 | Pre-dates P1<br>***#6464***<br>type 3  | | |
| LPB/62<br>17 February 1883 | | P3/P/x2<br>***#6465,6***  | **PEPPER, PAYTON & CO** *<br>23 Richard Street<br>Birmingham | Jewellers and silversmiths |
| LPB/70<br>17 July 1885<br>Sent by S Phelps<br>Only PP&Co entered in LPB | | P5/P/x1<br>***#6467***  | | |
| R1/94<br>1 March 1899<br>Sent by H Payton junior | 50 Wellington Road<br>Edgbaston<br>Birmingham | P9/P/22<br>***#6468***  | **Henry PAYTON** junior (Director)<br>trading as<br>**PAYTON, PEPPER & SONS LTD** *<br>3, 4, 5 Vyse Street<br>Birmingham | Jewellers |
| R1/111<br>15 September 1899<br>Sent by H Payton junior | 50 Wellington Road<br>Edgbaston<br>Birmingham | P9/P/53-58<br>***#6469-74***  | | |
| R1/161<br>11 February 1902<br>Sent by John Smith<br>8 Tenby Street<br>Birmingham | 23 Frederick Street<br>Birmingham | P9/P/119<br>***#6475***  | **PAYTON, PEPPER & SONS LTD** *<br>Robert Edward Dowsett (Secretary)<br>3, 4 and 5 Vyse Street and<br>23 Frederick Street<br>Birmingham | Manufacturing jewellers |
| R2/78<br>5 April 1909<br>Sent by H Payton | Hedingham<br>Edgbaston<br>Birmingham | P13/P/79-83<br>***#6476-80***  | **PAYTON, PEPPER LTD** *<br>Henry Payton (Managing Director)<br>3, 4 and 5 Vyse Street<br>Birmingham | Jewellers |
| R2/78<br>7 April 1909<br>Sent by H Payton | | P13/P/84<br>***#6481***  | **PAYTON, PEPPER LTD** *<br>3, 4 and 5 Vyse Street<br>Birmingham | |
| R2/112<br>21 June 1910<br>Sent by C Horner<br>23 Frederick Street | Aston Manor<br>Birmingham | P13/P/139<br>***#6482*** 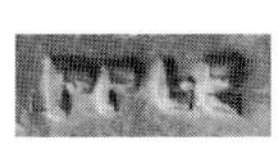 | **PAYTON, PEPPER & SONS LTD** *<br>R E Dowsett (Secretary)<br>3, 4 and 5 Vyse Street<br>Birmingham | Manufacturing jewellers |
| R2/114<br>Undated, between October 1913 and February 1914 | | P15/P/59<br>***#6483***  | | |
| R2/194<br>14 April 1928<br>Sent by Payton Pepper & Sons Ltd | | P15/P/204-208<br>***#6484-8***  | **PAYTON, PEPPER & SONS LTD** *<br>R E Dowsett (Secretary)<br>3, 4, 5 Vyse Street<br>Birmingham and<br>34 Ely Place, Holborn<br>London | |

| REGISTRATION DETAILS | MAKER'S PRIVATE ADDRESS and DETAILS | PLATE and MARK DETAILS | MAKER/COMPANY and BUSINESS ADDRESS | MAKER'S TRADE |
|---|---|---|---|---|
| R3/56<br>4 March 1948<br>Sent by Geo L Joseph<br>3 Vyse Street, Birm | | P21/P/21<br>***#6489***  | **PAYTON PEPPER & SONS LTD** *<br>Geo L Joseph (Managing Director)<br>3-5 Vyse Street<br>Birmingham | Manufacturing jewellers |
| 6 January 1931 | | P15/P/225<br>***#6490***  | | |
| 19 March 1948 | | P21/P/22<br>***#6491*** 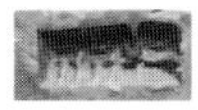 | | |
| 19 March 1948 | | P21/P/23<br>***#6492*** 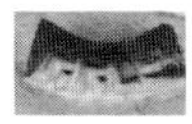 | | |
| R1/94<br>1 March 1899<br>Sent by H Payton junior | 50 Wellington Road<br>Edgbaston<br>Birmingham | P9/P/21<br>***#6493***  | **Henry PAYTON junior** (Director)<br>trading as<br>**PAYTON, PEPPER & SONS LTD** *<br>3-5 Vyse Street<br>Birmingham | Jewellers |
| R2/114<br>1 July 1910<br>Sent by C Horner Ltd | 23 Frederick Road [1]<br>Aston Manor | P13/P/140<br>***#6494***  | **PAYTON, PEPPER & SONS LTD** *<br>R C Dowsett [1] (Secretary)<br>3-5 Vyse Street<br>Birmingham | Manufacturing jewellers |
| 12 November 1919 | | P15/P/114<br>***#6495***  | | |
| R3/56<br>6 January 1931<br>Sent by Geo L Joseph<br>3 Vyse Street<br>Birmingham<br>Three sizes | | P15/P/226-229<br>***#6496-9***  | | |
| 13 July 1935 | | P15/P/240<br>***#6500***  | | |
| R3/68<br>28 October 1933<br>Sent by Payton, Pepper & Sons Ltd | | P15/P/237<br>***#6501***  | | |
| Not in R3 as expected<br>*c.*1920 to 1927 | | P15/P/100-105,171-182, 187-192<br>***#6502-25***  | | |
| R2/194<br>24 April 1915<br>Sent by Payton Pepper & Sons<br>BAO 22.525, 22.527 | | P15/P/63, 64<br>***#6526,7***  | | |
| R1/111<br>15 September 1899<br>Sent by H Payton junior | 50 Wellington Road<br>Edgbaston<br>Birmingham | P9/P/47-51<br>***#6528-32***  | **Henry PAYTON** junior (Director)<br>trading as<br>**PAYTON, PEPPER & SONS LTD** *<br>3-5 Vyse Street<br>Birmingham | Jewellers |
| R1/94<br>1 March 1899 | | P9/P/20<br>***#6533***  | | |
| R1/111<br>15 September 1899 | | P9/P/44-46<br>***#6534-6***  | | |

| REGISTRATION DETAILS | MAKER'S PRIVATE ADDRESS and DETAILS | PLATE and MARK DETAILS | MAKER/COMPANY and BUSINESS ADDRESS | MAKER'S TRADE |
|---|---|---|---|---|
| R1/118<br>20 December 1899<br>Sent by W Walker | Private address same as business | P9/R/12<br>***#6537***<br> | **William Thomas Price TAYLOR**<br>**Ralph RIMMEL** trading as<br>**PRICE, RIMMEL & CO**<br>205 Seven Sisters Road<br>Finsbury Park<br>London N | Wholesale fancy goods importers |
| R1/141<br>5 February 1901<br>Sent by J H Rowland | 46 Alma Street [1]<br>Halifax<br>10 Westbury Terrace [2]<br>Halifax | P9/P/82<br>***#6538***<br> | **Arthur POYSER** [1]<br>**John Henry ROWLAND** [2] trading as<br>**POYSER & ROWLAND**<br>Argyle Chambers<br>45 Hanging Ditch<br>Manchester | Pipe and stick mounters |
| PP1/188<br>GTD 1845<br>PMR 1845 | | P2/P/x2<br>***#6539,40***<br> | **James PLUMB**<br>**William RIGBY**<br>1 Holly Street (1845)<br>Liverpool | Watchcase makers |
| R3/135<br>6 March 1951<br>Sent by P Sumner<br>Two sizes | Private address same as business | P21/S/46,47<br>***#6541,2***<br> | **Peggy SUMNER**<br>49 Albert Road<br>Hale<br>Altrincham | Hobby |
| Missing register<br>*c.*1888 | Punched slightly overlapping *#6579* (P5/P/86a) so assumed to be the same company | P5/P/86b<br>***#6543***<br> | **PHELPS BROTHERS**<br>50 Spencer Street<br>Birmingham | Jewellers |
| R3/113<br>15 March 1946<br>Sent by P A Sampson<br>Two sizes | Private address same as business | P21/S/22,23<br>***#6544,5***<br> | **Miss Pauline Alwyne SAMPSON**<br>The Red House<br>Crumpsall Hospital<br>Manchester 8 | Student craftsman |
| R1/72<br>11 August 1898<br>Sent by Edgar Perks | Sunny Side<br>Holland Road<br>Sutton Coldfield | P9/P/1<br>***#6546***<br> | **Edgar PERKS** trading as<br>**Thomas PERKS & SONS**<br>84 Vyse Street<br>Birmingham | Goldsmiths and silversmiths |
| R1/190<br>16 April 1903<br>Sent by T Perks & Son | 89 Holly Road<br>Handsworth<br>91 Princess Road<br>Edgbaston<br>BAO has T Perks & Son at 84 Vyse Street | P9/Q*sic*/183<br>***#6547***<br> | **George Harold CARTER**<br>**Louis HADDEN** trading as<br>**T PERKS & SON** (*sic*)<br>48(*sic*) Vyse Street<br>Birmingham | Manufacturering jewellers |
| LPB/6<br>21 May 1878 | | P3/P/x6<br>***#6548-53***<br> | **PENDLETON & SONS**<br>19 Northampton Street<br>Birmingham | Jewellers |
| LPB/66<br>26 March 1885<br>No mark just P&S | | P5/P/x1<br>***#6554***<br> | | |
| LPB/28<br>11 June 1883 | | P3/P/x1<br>***#6555***<br> | | |
| LPB/66<br>25 October 1883<br>No mark just P&S initials | | P5/P/x1<br>***#6556***<br> | | |
| Missing register<br>*c.*1887<br>Four sizes | | P5/P/112x4<br>***#6557-60***<br> | | |

| REGISTRATION DETAILS | MAKER'S PRIVATE ADDRESS and DETAILS | PLATE and MARK DETAILS | MAKER/COMPANY and BUSINESS ADDRESS | MAKER'S TRADE |
|---|---|---|---|---|
| R1/109<br>26 August 1899<br>Sent by<br>E T Pendleton | 24 Mayfield Road<br>Handsworth<br>43 St Peter's Road<br>Handsworth<br>Birmingham | P9/P/42<br>***#6561***<br> | **Ernest Thomas PENDLETON**<br>**Lewis William PENDLETON** trading as<br>**W PENDLETON & SONS**<br>19 Northampton Street<br>Birmingham | Manufacturing jewellers |
| R1/124<br>7 April 1900<br>Sent by W Pendleton & Sons<br>Two sizes | 14 (*sic*) Mayfield Road<br>43 St Peter's Road<br>Handsworth<br>Staffordshire | P9/P/63-65<br>***#6562-4***<br> | | |
| R1/150<br>3 July 1901<br>Sent by W Pendleton & Sons | 24 Mayfield Road [1]<br>Handsworth<br>43 St Peter's Road [2]<br>Handsworth, Birmingham<br>Dissolved partnership 10 Dec. 1910. Business carried on as usual by Ernest Thomas Pendleton | P9/P/98,99<br>***#6565,6***<br> | **Ernest Thomas PENDLETON** [1]<br>**Lewis William PENDLETON** [2] trading as<br>**W PENDLETON & SONS**<br>19 Northampton Street<br>Birmingham | Jewellers |
| R2/130<br>8 March 1911<br>Sent by W Pendleton & Sons | 24 Mayfield Road<br>Handsworth<br>Birmingham | P13/Q*sic*/194<br>***#6567***<br> | **Ernest Thomas PENDLETON** trading as<br>**W PENDLETON & SONS**<br>19 Northampton Street<br>Birmingham | |
| R2/136<br>26 May 1911<br>Sent by W Pendleton & Sons | | P13/Q*sic*/202,203<br>***#6568,9***<br>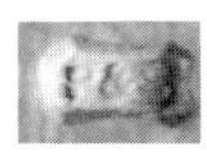 | | |
| R1/235<br>29 June 1905<br>Sent by Stokes & Ireland | Roundhay<br>Leeds<br>Ilkley<br>Leeds | P9/Q*sic*/227<br>***#6570***<br> | **John PEARCE**<br>**William PEARCE** trading as<br>**PEARCE & CO** *<br>Bond Street<br>Leeds and<br>Lendal<br>York | Gold and silversmiths |
| R2/39<br>30 April 1907<br>Sent by W Aitken<br>Two sizes | Exton<br>Ilkley<br>Yorkshire | P9/U*sic*/299,300<br>***#6571,2***<br> | **PEARCE & SON** *<br>T Archer Pearce (Secretary)<br>Bond Street<br>Gallowtree Gate<br>Leeds and<br>Lendal<br>Yorkshire | Silversmiths |
| R2/195<br>27 April 1915<br>Sent by Paul Sharp | 14 Harold Place<br>Birmingham | P15/S/16<br>***#6573***<br> | **Paul SHARP** trading as<br>**Paul SHARP & CO**<br>58 Albion Street<br>Birmingham | Ring makers |
| R3/84<br>7 May 1936<br>Sent by T J Skelton<br>86 Vyse Street<br>Birmingham<br>Two sizes | | P15/XYZ/245,246<br>***#6574,5***<br> | **P S PHILLIPS & CO LTD**<br>Isidor Rosenthal (Managing Director)<br>Mrs Bianca Rosenthal (Director)<br>Harold Rosenthal (Director)<br>1, 2, 3, 4 and 11 Ann Street<br>Hull<br>Yorkshire | Jewellers and silversmiths |
| R3/101<br>9 September 1941<br>Sent by C Peach & Sons Ltd<br>235 Icknield Street<br>Birmingham 18 | | P21/P/9<br>***#6576***<br> | **E J PEARSON & SONS LTD** *<br>Sealed in the presence of:-<br>Alfred E Pearson (Managing Director)<br>H G Blake (Secretary)<br>39 West Heath Drive<br>London NW11 | Leather goods, watch strap and watch guard manufacturers |

| REGISTRATION DETAILS | MAKER'S PRIVATE ADDRESS and DETAILS | PLATE and MARK DETAILS | MAKER/COMPANY and BUSINESS ADDRESS | MAKER'S TRADE |
|---|---|---|---|---|
| R2/170<br>29 April 1913<br>Sent by P Spicer & Son | Selbourne, Leamington<br>Clarendon Avenue<br>Leamington<br>Radway House<br>Leamington | P13/S/111<br>***#6577***<br> | **Peter SPICER**<br>**William Sydney SPICER**<br>**Gilbert Harry SPICER**<br>Victoria Terrace<br>Leamington and<br>60 Academy Street<br>Inverness | Silversmiths |
| Undated *c.* 1936 | | P15/S/5<br>***#6578***<br> | | |
| Missing register<br>*c.*1888<br>Similar mark entered BAO 9 August 1888 | | P5/P/86a<br>***#6579***<br> | **PHELPS BROTHERS**<br>50 Spencer Street<br>Birmingham | Jewellers |
| LPB/64<br>27 July 1880 | | P3/P/x2<br>***#6580,1***<br> | **PEARCE & THOMPSON**<br>40 Vyse Street<br>Birmingham | Jewellers |
| | | P3/R*sic*/x1<br>***#6582***<br> | | |
| Not in LPB as expected<br>*c.*1883 | Purdon & Boyd Ltd, silversmiths of 126 Great Tindall Street, Birmingham, noted in 1915. Robert Purdon director of Willmots Ltd in 1906, optical case makers of Conduit Hill, Evesham, Worcestershire | P5/P/x1<br>***#6583***<br> | **PURDON** | |
| R3/77<br>16 July 1935<br>Sent by P V Carroll<br>Two sizes | Private address same as business | P15/K*sic*/225,226<br>***#6584,5***<br> | **Phyllis Vale CARROLL**<br>Verdala Tower<br>Allerton<br>Liverpool 18 | Silversmith |
| R1/116<br>7 November 1899<br>Sent by<br>W H Carrington & Co<br>Clerk entered 30 in R1 | Sweaborg<br>Dialstone Lane<br>Stockport | P9/W/28<br>***#6586***<br>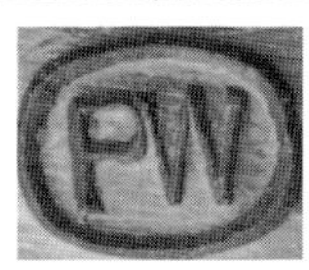 | **Peter WALTERS**<br>Heaton Lane<br>Stockport | Tobacconist |
| R2/150<br>6 February 1912<br>Sent by T J Skelton<br>BAO 15.212 | 3 Abbotsford Place<br>Glasgow | P13/W/105<br>***#6587***<br>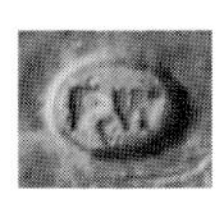 | **Philip WOOLFSON**<br>165 Trongate<br>Glasgow | Wholesale jeweller |
| R2/159<br>25 July 1912<br>Sent by S R William & Co | | P13/W/123<br>***#6588***<br> | | |
| R2/191<br>16 January 1915<br>Sent by J H Wynn | | P15/W/12<br>***#6589***<br> | | |
| R2/230<br>19 April 1920<br>Sent by Benson Brothers | 38 Morrison House Road<br>Glasgow | P15/W/48<br>***#6590***<br> | | |
| R3/54<br>30 August 1930<br>Sent by Elite Bracelet Co Ltd<br>Regent Street<br>Birmingham | | P15/P/224<br>***#6591***<br> | **PERRIN WATCH CO LTD**<br>Common Seal of the Company affixed in the presence of :-<br>M Ryf (Director)<br>S W Thomas (Secretary)<br>1 Hatton Garden (Registered Office)<br>London EC1 | Watch importers |

| REGISTRATION DETAILS | MAKER'S PRIVATE ADDRESS and DETAILS | PLATE and MARK DETAILS | MAKER/COMPANY and BUSINESS ADDRESS | MAKER'S TRADE |
|---|---|---|---|---|
| Missing register<br>*c.*1890 | See *#6586* | P5/W/316<br>***#6592***<br>  | **Peter WALTERS**<br>Heaton Lane<br>Stockport | Tobacconist |
| R1/131<br>16 August 1900<br>Sent by Price & Williams | 66 Wiggin Street<br>Birmingham<br>173 Montague Road<br>Smethwick | P9/P/68<br>***#6593***<br>  | **James PRICE**<br>**Samuel WILLIAMS** trading as<br>**PRICE & WILLIAMS**<br>Back 105 Vyse Street<br>Birmingham | Manufacturing jewellers |
| R3/25<br>2 December 1924<br>Sent by Percy William Benton | Private address same as business | P15/B/175<br>***#6594***<br>  | **Percy William BENTON**<br>83 Church Street<br>Lozells<br>Birmingham | Jeweller |
| R3/131<br>2 March 1951<br>Sent by selves | | P21/P/33-38<br>***#6595-6600***<br>  | **PLATINUM WATCH CASE CO LTD**<br>Sealed in the presence of:-<br>N G Glikston (Director)<br>A G Du Plat (Secretary)<br>Treasure House<br>19/21 Hatton Garden<br>London EC1 | Watchmakers and jewellers |
| R3/99<br>15 May 1941<br>Sent by P & W Phillips | 8 Fields Park Terrace [1]<br>Cross Keys<br>11 Tredegar Road [2]<br>Risca<br>Monmouthshire | P21/P/7<br>***#6601***<br>  | **Percy PHILLIPS** [1]<br>**Wilfred PHILLIPS** [2]<br>The Bridge<br>Pontywain<br>Cross Keys<br>Monmouthshire and<br>11 Tredegar Road<br>Risca<br>Monmouthshire | Retail watchmakers, jewellers and opticians |
| 15 August 1942 | | P21/P/10<br>***#6602***<br>  | | |
| LPB/74<br>9 March 1885<br>Sent by J Eastham | | P5/R/x1<br>***#6603***<br>  | **Philip William ROBERTS**<br>249 Park Road<br>Liverpool | Watch manufacturer |

| REGISTRATION DETAILS | MAKER'S PRIVATE ADDRESS and DETAILS | PLATE and MARK DETAILS | MAKER/COMPANY and BUSINESS ADDRESS | MAKER'S TRADE |
|---|---|---|---|---|
| SPB/8<br>21 June 1877<br>Sent by H Mansell | | P3/C/x3<br>***#6604-6***<br> | **QUILLIAM (Samuel) * & COOPER**<br>1 Rathbone Street<br>Liverpool | Watch and watchcase manufacturers |
| LPB/4<br>14 November 1877<br>Sent by H Green<br>Samuel & Rogers<br>LPB mark shown | | Not on P3<br>***#6607***<br> | | |
| LPB/4<br>15 November 1877<br>LPB mark shown | | Not on P3<br>***#6608***<br> | | |
| R2/220<br>6 June 1919<br>Sent by D Quilley | Holly Lodge [1]<br>Stewart Crescent<br>Wood Green [2]<br>18 Highfield Avenue<br>Hornsey<br>44 Thorold Road [3]<br>Wood Green | P15/Q/1,2<br>***#6609,10***<br> | **David QUILLEY** [1]<br>**Joseph Samuel CURTOIS** [2]<br>**David Henry QUILLEY** [1]<br>**Albert Stanley QUILLEY** [3]<br>**Charles William QUILLEY** [1]<br>**Charles William COUCHLEY** [1]<br>trading as<br>**QUILLEY SONS & CURTOIS**<br>380 St John Street<br>London | Manufacturing jewellers |

| REGISTRATION DETAILS | MAKER'S PRIVATE ADDRESS and DETAILS | PLATE and MARK DETAILS | MAKER/COMPANY and BUSINESS ADDRESS | MAKER'S TRADE |
|---|---|---|---|---|
| MR2/129 | Skewer 1788 | Not on P1<br>***#6611***  | **Unidentified** | |
| Missing register<br>*c.* 1892 | | P5/A/438<br>***#6612***  | **Unidentified** | |
| R1/143<br>18 February 1901<br>Sent by T P Hewitt<br>R J Pike<br>(Watchcase makers associated with Lancashire Watch Company, Prescot) | 4 Oxford Street [1]<br>Edinburgh<br>10 Parkside Terrace [2]<br>Edinburgh | P9/A*sic*/25<br>***#6613***  | **Simon ROSEN** [1] and<br>**Charles ALEXANDER** [2] trading as<br>**ROSEN & ALEXANDER**<br>10 Drummond Street<br>Edinburgh | Wholesale jewellers |
| PDB 1833<br>MR3/75 | Spoons<br>Square marked 1787<br>Struck inverted at top of square<br>Possibly later than 1787 | P1/23/x5<br>***#6614-8***  | **Robert ADAMSON**<br>Liverpool or | Silversmith |
| PP1/188<br>GTD 1834-53<br>J1 1840<br>PMR 1837-55 | | P2/A/x1<br>***#6619*** <br>P2/A/x1<br>***#6620*** 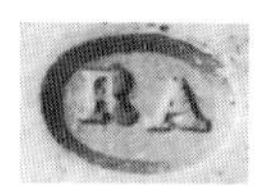 | **Richard ADAMSON**<br>40 Peter Street (1837)<br>81 Peter Street (1839-47)<br>31 St Vincent Street (1851-5)<br>27 Great Richmond Street (1861)<br>Liverpool | Watchcase maker |
| R1/226<br>31 January 1905<br>Sent by R Archer & Son | 153 Adelaide Road<br>London NW<br>28 Chandos Road<br>London NW | P9/A/59<br>***#6621*** 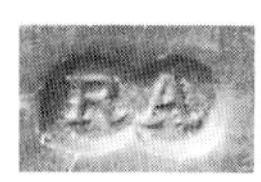 | **Reuben ARCHER**<br>**Ernest Albert ARCHER** trading as<br>**R ARCHER & SON** *<br>17 Myddleton Street<br>Clerkenwell<br>London | Manufacturing opticians |
| R1/125<br>27 April 1900 and<br>R1/126<br>4 May 1900<br>Sent by E Vaughton | 9 DeVere Gardens [1]<br>Kensington<br>London | P9/R/13<br>***#6622***  | **Saul Philip ARONSON** [1]<br>**George Alfred ARONSON**<br>**Samuel ARONSON** trading as<br>**ROSENTHAL, ARONSON & CO** *<br>26 Fore Street<br>London EC and<br>Melbourne<br>Australia | Australian merchants |
| R1/127<br>11 May 1900<br>Sent by Wright & Hadgkiss | DeVere Gardens<br>South Kensington<br>London<br>Melbourne<br>Australia | P9/R/15<br>***#6623***  | **Saul Philip ARONSON**<br>**George Alfred ARONSON**<br>trading as<br>**ROSENTHAL, ARONSON & CO** *<br>26 Fore Street<br>London EC and<br>Melbourne<br>Australia | |
| R1/128<br>14 June 1900<br>Sent by Hollis & Newman | DeVere Gardens<br>Kensington | P9/R/16<br>***#6624***  | **Samuel** (*sic*) **Philip ARONSON**<br>**George Alfred ARONSON** trading as<br>**ROSENTHAL, ARONSON & CO** *<br>Address as above | |
| R3/43<br>28 Sept 1928<br>Sent by F Marson<br>Birmingham | 5 Casiobury Terrace<br>Southend–on–Sea | P15/J/35<br>***#6625***  | **R A JONES & SONS LTD** *<br>Edward Cecil Jones (Managing Director)<br>76, 78 High Street<br>Southend-on-Sea<br>193 Hampton Court Road<br>Westcliff-on-Sea | Jewellers watch and clockmakers |

| REGISTRATION DETAILS | MAKER'S PRIVATE ADDRESS and DETAILS | PLATE and MARK DETAILS | MAKER/COMPANY and BUSINESS ADDRESS | MAKER'S TRADE |
|---|---|---|---|---|
| R2/134<br>4 May 1911<br>Sent by Ginder & Couch<br>BAO 16.981 | All partners<br>Redholm<br>Royal Terrace<br>Southend-on-Sea<br>Essex | P13/J/48<br>***#6626***<br> | **Robert Arthur JONES**<br>**Arthur Percy JONES**<br>**Edward Cecil JONES** trading as<br>**R A JONES & SONS** *<br>76, 78 High Street<br>Southend-on-Sea<br>Essex | Jewellers and watchmakers |
| R2/224<br>11 October 1919<br>Sent by Ginder & Ginder | Southend-on-Sea<br>The Cliff<br>Thamesmouth | P15/J/12<br>***#6627***<br> | **Robert Arthur JONES** *<br>(Sole Proprietor)<br>76, 78 High Street<br>Southend-on-Sea | Watchmakers and jewellers |
| R3/22<br>28 May 1924<br>Sent by W H Leather & Son | | P15/J/26<br>***#6628***<br> | **R A JONES & SONS LTD** *<br>E Cecil Jones (Director and Secretary)<br>76, 78 High Street<br>Southend-on-Sea | Diamond merchants, jewellers and watchmakers |
| R3/28<br>17 April 1925<br>Sent by J & R Griffin Ltd | | P15/J/27<br>***#6629***<br>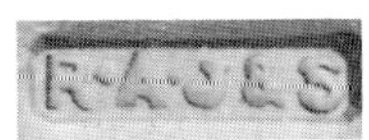 | **R A JONES & SONS LTD** *<br>E Cecil Jones<br>76, 78 High Street<br>Southend-on-Sea | Jewellers |
| R2/144<br>22 September 1911<br>Sent by H G Rayner | 14 Grosvenor Road<br>Forest Gate<br>Essex | P13/A*sic*/31<br>***#6630***<br> | **Horace RAYNER AGENCIES LTD**<br>H G Rayner (Director)<br>25 Hatton Garden<br>London E C | Manufacturing agents and importers |
| R3/50<br>8 November 1929<br>Sent by R Jones<br>Birmingham | 11 Berwick Drive [1]<br>Gt Crosby, Liverpool<br>Tern Hill [2]<br>Milner Road<br>Keswall Hills<br>Cheshire | P15/P/222<br>***#6631***<br> | **R A PARKIN & SON**<br>George Parkin [1] (Director)<br>Arthur Parkin [2] (Director)<br>18 Paradise Street<br>Liverpool | Jewellers |
| R3/76<br>1 July 1935<br>Sent by Roberts & Belk Ltd<br>Four sizes | Common seal of company affixed in the presence of Belk and Clayton | P15/R/52-55<br>***#6632-5***<br> | **ROBERTS & BELK LTD** *<br>W H Belk (Chairman of Directors)<br>C H Clayton (Secretary)<br>Furnival Works (Registered Office)<br>Furnival Street<br>Sheffield 1 | Electroplaters, silversmiths and cutlers |
| PDB 1787<br>MR2/64<br>MR3/77<br>PP1/188<br>PP2/350<br>GTD 1787-93 | Watchcases | P1/26/x1<br>***#6636***<br>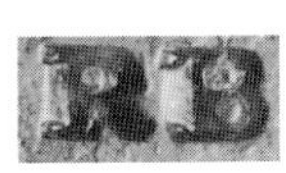 | **Richard BOULGER**<br>Saint Nicholas Parish (1784)<br>Liverpool | Watchcase maker |
| PDB 1787-1814<br>MR2/64-8<br>MR3/77-8<br>SIL/46<br>CMC/92<br>GMSC/64 | Gold rings, silver buttons, labels, beakers, coffin plates, dog collars and flatware<br>Square marked 1787<br><br>R Burgess of Liverpool mentioned in Jl 1843 to 1851 is another possibility | P1/23/x2<br>***#6637,8***<br> | **Robert BOWERS I & II**<br>3 Bridge Street (1782)<br>19 Bridge Street Row (1783)<br>Higher Bridge Street (1792)<br>Eastgate Row (1801-5)<br>Chester | Goldsmith and silversmith |
| | | P1/32/x2<br>***#6639,40***<br> | | Silversmith |
| LPB/18<br>20 November 1884<br>No mark in LPB<br>Similar marks LAO<br>9 March 1876 and<br>27 November 1886 | RB mark on P5 best match | P5/B/x1<br>***#6641***<br> | **Richard Macaire BALL** *<br>31 Sudeley Street<br>Nelson Terrace<br>City Road<br>London | Watchcase maker |

| REGISTRATION DETAILS | MAKER'S PRIVATE ADDRESS and DETAILS | PLATE and MARK DETAILS | MAKER/COMPANY and BUSINESS ADDRESS | MAKER'S TRADE |
|---|---|---|---|---|
| R2/144<br>25 September 1911<br>Sent by Sibray Hall & Co<br>Five sizes | Harris Mansions [1]<br>London SW | P13/U*sic*/127-194<br>***#6642-6709***<br> | **HARRODS STORES LTD** *<br>Sir Alfred J Morton, Bart (Chairman)<br>R Burbridge [1] (Managing Director)<br>Herbert Bennett (Director)<br>Edgar Cohen (Director)<br>T H Harvey Samuel (Director)<br>Wm Mendel (Director)<br>R H Griffiths (Secretary)<br>87 to 135 Brompton Road<br>London | Merchants, shippers and bankers |
| R3/78<br>10 September 1935<br>Sent by S Blanckensee & Sons<br>Two sizes | High Bank<br>Stapleton<br>Darlington | P15/G*sic*/219,220<br>***#6710,11***<br> | **Alfred James LASCELLES**<br>(Sole proprietor) trading as<br>**R BOND & CO**<br>Kings Head Buildings<br>Darlington | Jewellers and silversmiths |
| R2/23<br>22 August 1906<br>Sent by Roden Brothers & Co | Silver Birch Road<br>Erdington<br>Leward Road<br>Handsworth | P9/R/78<br>***#6712***<br> | **Alfred George RODEN**<br>**Walter Henry BRINDLEY** trading as<br>**RODEN BROTHERS & CO**<br>11 Hockley Street<br>Birmingham | Wholesale jewellers |
| R2/8<br>16 December 1905<br>Sent by<br>L J Blankensie<br>Two sizes | Sandow Road<br>Birmingham<br>60 Gough Road<br>Birmingham<br>NB: Different spelling from similar name Blanckensee | P9/R/70,71<br>***#6713,4***<br> | **Leon Julius BLANKENSIE**<br>**Elizabeth BLANKENSIE**<br>**Frank MOSS** trading as<br>**RIDLEY BROTHERS & MERTON**<br>67 Vittoria Street and<br>48 Frederick Street<br>Birmingham | Manufacturing jewellers |
| R3/69<br>25 October 1933<br>Sent by L W Rudell | 20 Lark Road<br>Edgbaston<br>Birmingham | P15/R/51<br>***#6715***<br> | **Leon Wilfred RUDELL** trading as<br>**RUDELL BROTHERS**<br>34 Frederick Street<br>Birmingham | Manufacturing jewellers |
| LPB/4<br>27 November 1877 | Mark seen on watchcase of UK manufacturer.<br>WCI p85 working 1880 to 1894 | P3/R/x1<br>***#6716***<br> | **RANKIN BROTHERS**<br>5 Castle Lane<br>Belfast | Jewellers and watch and watchcase importers ? |
| LPB/72<br>5 March 1881 | | P3/R/x1 & P3/V*sic*/x2<br>***#6717-9***<br> | | |
| Missing register<br>*c.* 1886<br>Similar mark LAO<br>6 December 1907 | See Culme #11908 | P5/R/33<br>***#6720***<br> | **ROBINSON BROTHERS** *<br>5 Hampstead Road<br>London NW | Jewellers |
| R1/142<br>12 February 1901<br>Sent by J W Rolason<br>C W Holmes | 25 Hamstead Road [1]<br>Birmingham<br>2 Radnor Road [2]<br>Handsworth | P9/R/30<br>***#6721***<br> | **John William ROLASON** [1]<br>**Joseph Gilbert ROLASON** [2] trading as<br>**ROLASON BROTHERS**<br>81 Vyse Street<br>Birmingham | Manufacturing jewellers and silversmiths |
| R1/159<br>8 January 1902<br>Sent by John W Rolason | | P9/R/42,43<br>***#6722,3***<br> | | |
| R1/192<br>1 May 1903<br>Sent by Rolason Brothers<br>Two sizes | | P9/R/55-59<br>***#6724-8***<br> | | |

| REGISTRATION DETAILS | MAKER'S PRIVATE ADDRESS and DETAILS | PLATE and MARK DETAILS | MAKER/COMPANY and BUSINESS ADDRESS | MAKER'S TRADE |
|---|---|---|---|---|
| R2/32<br>2 February 1907<br>Sent by Rolason Brothers | 25 Hamstead Road [1]<br>Birmingham<br>2 Radnor Road [2]<br>Handsworth | P9/R/79-81<br>***#6729-31***<br> | **John William ROLASON** [1] and<br>**Joseph Gilbert ROLASON** [2]<br>trading as **ROLASON BROTHERS**<br>81 Vyse Street<br>Birmingham | Manufacturing jewellers and silversmiths |
| R3/145<br>30 June 1953<br>Sent by R H M Creighton | Grantchester<br>164 Wilton Road, Shirley<br>Southampton, Hampshire<br>54 Kenilworth Avenue<br>from 22 March 1954<br>Reading, Berkshire | P21/C/62<br>***#6732***<br> | **Robert Henry Mason CREIGHTON**<br>No business address entered | Student |
| R3/167<br>28 April 1959<br>Sent by R Comer | 18 Harcourt Road<br>Altrincham | P21/C/81<br>***#6733***<br> | **Ramon COMER**<br>Regional College of Art<br>All Saints<br>Manchester | Student |
| R2/82<br>15 May 1909<br>Sent by Robert Crompton | 14 Clarendon Road<br>Edgbaston<br>Birmingham | P13/C/43<br>***#6734***<br>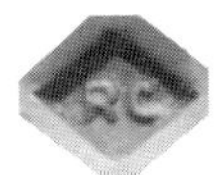 | **Robert CROMPTON**<br>36 Northampton Street<br>Birmingham | Jeweller |
| R2/39<br>10 May 1907<br>Sent by self | 10 Hamilton Street<br>Hoole | P9/*Esic*/241,242<br>***#6735,6***<br> | **Robert CAWLEY**<br>The High Cross<br>Chester | Watchmaker |
| PP3/18, 43 | Working 1704-29 - mark seen on empty silver watchcase *c*.1700 in Prescot Museum, Lancashire | Not on P1<br>***#6737***<br>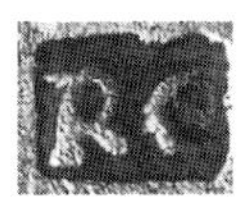 | **Robert CHANTRELL**<br>West Derby<br>Liverpool | Watchcase maker |
| LPB/22<br>3 March 1884<br>No mark alongside name | Entry may also be read as Cushey but Carsberg worked at this address from 1879 to 1906. RC mark between AC and RMC on P5. | P5/C/x1<br>***#6738***<br> | **Robert Frederick CARSBERG** *<br>16 Lever Street<br>Goswell Road<br>London | Gold chain maker |
| PP1/169,188<br>CWMP 1874<br>Similar mark entered BAO 5 October 1854 | | P2/C/x3<br>***#6739-41***<br>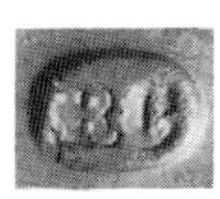 | **Robert CAUSER** *<br>Jordan Well<br>Coventry | Watchcase maker |
| R2/45<br>16 August 1907<br>Sent by self | 10 Hamilton Street<br>Hoole | P13/C/2<br>***#6742***<br>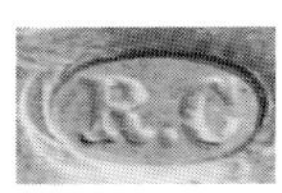 | **Robert CAWLEY**<br>The High Cross<br>Chester | Watchmaker and jeweller |
| R2/48<br>23 October 1907<br>Sent by self | Private address same as business | P13/C/5<br>***#6743***<br> | **Raul CIRNE**<br>11 Nicholas Road<br>Chorlton-cum-Hardy<br>Manchester | Agent |
| R2/51<br>30 November 1907<br>Sent by R Chandler<br>Four sizes | Alderbrook Road<br>Solihull | P13/C/8-11<br>***#6744-7***<br> | **James MARRISON** trading as<br>**R CHANDLER**<br>101 and 108 Spencer Street<br>Birmingham | Silversmiths |
| R3/175<br>13 December 1960<br>Sent by R C Layfield | 135 Bowring Park Road<br>Liverpool 14 | P21/L/48<br>***#6748***<br> | **Richard Charles LAYFIELD**<br>99 Grange Road<br>Birkenhead<br>Cheshire | Opthalmic optician |
| 4 January 1961 | | P21/L/53<br>***#6749***<br> | | |

| REGISTRATION DETAILS | MAKER'S PRIVATE ADDRESS and DETAILS | PLATE and MARK DETAILS | MAKER/COMPANY and BUSINESS ADDRESS | MAKER'S TRADE |
|---|---|---|---|---|
| R2/12<br>27 February 1906<br>Sent by Nicholas & Foye | 22 Cable Street<br>Manchester<br>22 Cable Street<br>Manchester | P9/R/72<br>***#6750***<br> | **James RUSHWORTH**<br>**Nicholas RUSHWORTH** trading as<br>**RUSHWORTH & CO**<br>3 Elm Street, Hightown<br>Manchester | Stick manufacturers |
| R3/79<br>23 September 1935<br>Sent by Payton, Pepper & Sons Ltd<br>3-5 Vyse Street<br>Birmingham | Wynhurst [1]<br>Arbroath Road<br>West Ferry, Dundee<br>5 Seafield Terrace [2]<br>Broughty Ferry<br>Dundee | P15/R/56<br>***#6751***<br>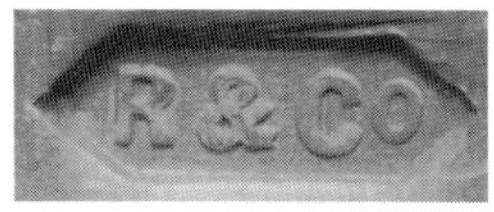 | **Joan KIRKCALDY** [1]<br>**John SHELLAND** [2] (Partners)<br>trading as **RATTRAY & CO**<br>32-36 Nethergate<br>Dundee | Jewellers and silversmiths |
| R2/177<br>1 October 1913<br>Sent by Lawson Ward & Gamage | 29 Broadway<br>Wimbledon<br>London | P13/R/48<br>***#6752***<br>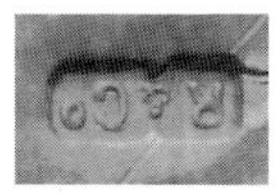 | **Walter Richard RELF** trading as<br>**RELF & CO**<br>29 Broadway and 13 Market Broadway<br>Wimbledon and<br>140 High Street<br>Wandsworth | Jewellers and silversmiths |
| R1/216<br>28 June 1904<br>Sent by E E Plimmer<br>S Mordan & Co<br>Two sizes | Greyfriars<br>Chester<br>Almere<br>Clifford Street<br>Shrewsbury | P9/R/64,65,0*sic*<br>***#6753-5***<br> | **ROBINSON & CO** *<br>Alfred Wathew Butt (Chairman)<br>Ernest Edward Plimmer (Man'g Director)<br>9 and 10 The Square and<br>8 Market Street<br>Shrewsbury | Goldsmiths and silversmiths |
| R3/46<br>23 May 1929<br>Sent by selves through Deakin & Francis | | P15/R/43<br>***#6756***<br><br>§ | **ROBINSON & CO LTD** *<br>G E Plimmer (Director)<br>9 and 10 The Square<br>Shrewsbury | |
| Missing register<br>*c.*1887<br>Similar mark entered BAO 3 April 1889 | | P5/R/77<br>***#6757***<br> | **Albert Charles REVELL**<br>**(late REVELL & CO)**<br>33 Vyse Street<br>Birmingham | Jewellers |
| Missing register<br>*c.*1890 | | P5/R/302<br>***#6758***<br> | | |
| R1/139<br>12 December 1900<br>Sent by Adie & Lovekin<br>D & L Spiers<br>The Douglas Clock Co.<br>7 King Street<br>St James, London | | P9/R/26<br>***#6759***<br> | **James REICHENBERG** trading as<br>**REICHENBERG & CO** *<br>106 Hatton Garden<br>London EC | Importers of watches |
| R2/192<br>29 January 1915<br>Sent by A C Revell<br>BAO 22.540 | 114 Leonard Road<br>Birchfield<br>Birmingham | P15/R/5<br>***#6760***<br>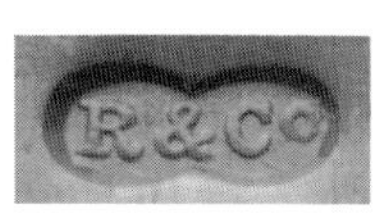 | **Albert Charles REVELL**<br>**Maurice SPIRO** trading as<br>**REVELL & CO**<br>59 Key Hill<br>Birmingham | Manufacturing jewellers |
| R3/172<br>16 April 1960<br>Sent by R Dunlop<br>Two sizes | 45 Sharples Avenue<br>Bolton<br>Lancashire | P21/D/30,31<br>***#6761,2***<br> | **Robert DUNLOP**<br>No business address entered | Student |
| R1/225<br>5 January 1905<br>Sent by F O Banyard<br>Banyard & Co<br>Cancelled<br>3 November 1906 | 86 Crowther Street<br>Bradford<br>125 College Road<br>Bradford | P9/R/66<br>***#6763***<br> | **Arthur B RINK**<br>**Arthur DALBY** trading as<br>**RINK & DALBY**<br>1 Leeds Road<br>Bradford<br>Yorkshire | Umbrella and walking stick makers |

| REGISTRATION DETAILS | MAKER'S PRIVATE ADDRESS and DETAILS | PLATE and MARK DETAILS | MAKER/COMPANY and BUSINESS ADDRESS | MAKER'S TRADE |
|---|---|---|---|---|
| Missing register<br>*c.*1890 | | P5/R/328<br>***#6764*** 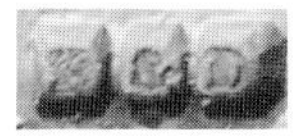 | **ROEK & DREYFUS** * | Gold chain makers and manufacturing jewellers |
| LPB/74<br>26 January 1885<br>No mark in LPB | | P5/R/x1<br>***#6765***  | **Edward ROEK &<br>Charles DREYFUS** *<br>111 Farringdon Road<br>3 doors south of Ray Street<br>London | |
| LPB/74<br>12 February 1885 | | P5/R/x1<br>***#6766***  | | |
| Missing register<br>*c.*1886 | | P5/R/14<br>***#6767***  | | |
| Missing register<br>*c.*1886 | | P5/R/12<br>***#6768***  | | |
| Missing register<br>*c.*1891 | | P5/R/335<br>***#6769***  | | |
| R3/169<br>21 August 1959<br>Sent by R J K Ellis | Grasmere<br>Tram Road<br>Buckley<br>Flintshire | P21/E/14<br>***#6770***  | **Randolph John Keith ELLIS**<br>No business address entered | |
| Missing register<br>*c.*1893 | | P5/A/510<br>***#6771***  | **Unidentified** | |
| R2/223<br>15 August 1919<br>Sent by Regal Watch Case Co Ltd | 70 Wake Green Road<br>Moseley<br>Birmingham | P15/R/21<br>***#6772*** 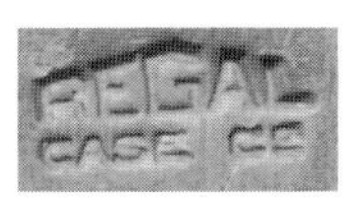 | **THE REGAL WATCH (*sic*) CO**<br>(ed: The Regal Watch Case? Co)<br>W F Smith (Managing Director)<br>32-44 Branston Street<br>Birmingham | Watchcase manufacturers |
| R3/167<br>11 April 1959<br>Sent by R E Stone<br>Two sizes | 95 Eaton Avenue<br>Wembley<br>Middlesex | P21/S/75-77<br>***#6773-5***  | **Robert Edgar STONE**<br>20 Garrick Street<br>London WC2 | Goldsmith and silversmith |
| LPB/80<br>20 September 1879<br>No name or address listed | | P3/T/x2<br>***#6776,7***  | **Richard Edwin THOMPSON**<br>Albion Street<br>Birmingham | Factor |
| PDB 1795-1804<br>Gold rings and buttons<br>MR3/81 | Mark seen on buckle without date letter, 1797 to *c.*1810. Richard Ferris of Exeter is another possibility. | Not on P1<br>***#6778***  | **Richard FISHER**<br>Manchester and Liverpool | Goldsmith and silversmith |
| R1/113<br>4 October 1899<br>Sent by R J Pike<br>CWMP 1896-1901 | Private address same as business | P9/F/4<br>***#6779***  | **Richard FENNELL**<br>Mount Street, Chapel Fields<br>Coventry | Watch manufacturer |
| R1/151<br>27 July 1901<br>Sent by Edward Brothers | Private address same as business | P9/F/12<br>***#6780***  | **Randolf FISCHER**<br>167 Hockley Hill<br>Birmingham | Watchmaker and jeweller |
| MR1/38-41<br>J1/369<br>J3/389 | Free 1594-5<br>Part of the Chester Mace started *c.*1620 and refashioned in 1668<br>Jackson read this as George Oulton – mentioned 1658 | Pre-dates P1<br>***#6781***  | **Richard GREGORY**<br>Chester | Silversmith |

| REGISTRATION DETAILS | MAKER'S PRIVATE ADDRESS and DETAILS | PLATE and MARK DETAILS | | MAKER/COMPANY and BUSINESS ADDRESS | MAKER'S TRADE |
|---|---|---|---|---|---|
| PDB 1791-1803<br>MR2/83<br>MR3/83<br>PP1/188<br>SIL/42 | Variety of plate and gold rings 1791 to 1803 | P1/26/x2<br>***#6782,3*** |  | **Robert GREEN**<br>Liverpool | Goldsmith and silversmith |
| Missing register<br>*c.*1886 SP32/7<br>Similar mark entered LAO 9 December 1885 | CWMP 1886-1901 | P5/G/11<br>***#6784*** |  | **Robert GRAVENOR** *<br>141 Spon Street (1886)<br>35 Craven Street (1891)<br>7 The Butts (1901)<br>Coventry | Watchcase maker |
| R1/182<br>24 January 1903<br>Sent by R G Merrick | Private address same as business | P9/M/44<br>***#6785*** |  | **Richard George MERRICK**<br>53 Lever Street, Goswell Road<br>London EC<br>New address (undated)<br>124 St John Street<br>London | Watchmaker |
| R1/28<br>11 May 1896<br>Sent by Robert Hilton<br>MR3/120 | Melidin<br>Near Rhyl<br>North Wales | P5/D*sic*/767<br>***#6786*** |  | **Robert HILTON**<br>Luscombe<br>Allerford<br>Taunton | Artist |
| R2/68<br>13 November 1908<br>Sent by W H Leather | 22 Carlton Avenue<br>Sefton Park<br>Liverpool | P13/H/4<br>***#6787*** |  | **Robert HARRIS** also trading as<br>**Robert HARRIS & CO** *<br>22 Carlton Avenue<br>Sefton Park<br>Liverpool<br>34 Hatton Garden<br>London | Wholesale Jewellers |
| Missing register<br>*c.*1890 | See RH below | P5/H/294<br>***#6788*** |  | **Ridley HAYES** * | Silversmiths |
| Missing register<br>*c.*1886 | | P5/H/17a<br>***#6789*** |  | | |
| Missing register<br>*c.*1886 | | P5/H/48<br>***#6790*** |  | | |
| R1/45<br>9 May 1897<br>Sent by Nathan & Hayes | Argent House [1]<br>Handsworth<br>7 Clarendon Road [2]<br>Edgbaston<br>See N&H #6185 and GNRN #2963 | P5/N/561<br>***#6791*** |  | **George NATHAN** [1]<br>**Ridley HAYES** [2] trading as<br>**NATHAN & HAYES** *<br>285 Icknield Street<br>Birmingham | |
| PDB 1799-1800<br>MR3/84 | Gold rings | P1/3/x3<br>***#6792-4*** |  | **Richard HARPER**<br>Liverpool<br>or | Goldsmith |
| J1 1841-3 | | | | **Richard HALL**<br>Chester | Silversmith |
| Missing register<br>*c.*1886 | See RH above | P5/H/17b<br>***#6795*** |  | **Ridley HAYES** *<br>285 Icknield Street<br>Birmingham | Silversmith |

| REGISTRATION DETAILS | MAKER'S PRIVATE ADDRESS and DETAILS | PLATE and MARK DETAILS | MAKER/COMPANY and BUSINESS ADDRESS | MAKER'S TRADE |
|---|---|---|---|---|
| Missing register<br>*c.*1886 | | P5/H/43<br>***#6796***  | **Ridley HAYES** *<br>285 Icknield Street<br>Birmingham | Silversmith |
| Missing register<br>*c.*1891 | | P5/H/337<br>***#6797***  | | |
| PDB 1799-1800<br>MR3/84 | Gold rings | P1/5/x3<br>***#6798-6800*** 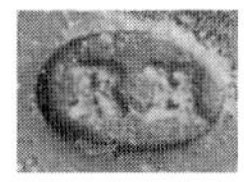 | **Richard HARPER**<br>Liverpool<br>or | Goldsmith |
| J1 1841-3 | | | **Richard HALL**<br>Chester | Silversmith |
| Missing register<br>*c.*1888 | CWMP 1874-76 | P5/H/197<br>***#6801***  | **Rowland HILL** * | Watch manufacturers |
| R1/19<br>17 December 1895<br>Sent by R J Pike | | P5/H/715<br>***#6802***  | **Rowland HILL** trading as<br>**Thomas HILL & CO** *<br>Hearsall House (1883)<br>50 Spon End (1895)<br>Coventry | |
| Missing register<br>*c.*1889<br>Similar mark entered<br>LAO 1 January 1874 | | P5/H/251<br>***#6803***  | **Robert HARPER** *<br>16 Red Lion Street<br>Clerkenwell<br>London | Silversmith |
| Missing register<br>*c.* March 1890<br>Similar mark with pellets entered BAO<br>23 September 1890 | | P5/C/281<br>***#6804***  | **Robert Howard CONSTANTINE**<br>34½ Great Hampton Street<br>Birmingham | Jeweller |
| PP3/83<br>Not in SPB or LPB so struck 1860-63<br>Similar mark entered<br>LAO 13 March 1860 | | P3/I/x3<br>***#6805-7***  | **Robert Henry JONES** *<br>51 Wynyatt Street<br>Clerkenwell<br>London | Watchcase maker |
| R3/139<br>26 November 1952<br>Sent by R H Forbes<br>Two sizes | 14 Gill Bent Road<br>Cheadle Hulme, Cheshire<br>10 Laurel Grove (undated)<br>Bingley, Yorkshire | P21/F/19,20<br>***#6808,9***  | **Richard Hutchinson FORBES**<br>Regional College of Art<br>Manchester | Student |
| R1/60<br>4 June 1894<br>Sent by W Walker<br>A H Tongue | 34 Leighton Court Road<br>West Streatham | P5/H/564<br>***#6810***  | **Robert HOVENDEN**<br>**Albert HOVENDEN**<br>**Charles William HOVENDEN** trading as<br>**R HOVENDEN & SONS** *<br>91, 95 City Road, Finsbury<br>London EC | Merchants |
| R1/230<br>10 April 1905<br>Sent by R Williams | 186 Stapleton Hall Road<br>Strand Green<br>London | P9/H/69<br>***#6811*** 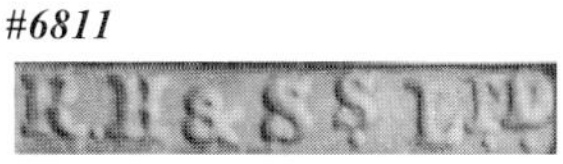 | **R HOVENDEN & SON LTD** *<br>T C Rowe (Secretary)<br>29/33 Berners Road and 89/95 City Road<br>London | General merchants and warehousemen |
| R1/115<br>24 October 1899<br>Sent by R H Whittaker | 245 Vauxhall Bridge Road<br>London SW | P9/W/27<br>***#6812***  | **Richard Healey WHITTAKER** *<br>46 Wilton Road<br>London SW | Watchmaker, jeweller and silversmith |
| MR1/175<br>Free 1715<br>Tumbler cup 1715 | Ri with dotted in cut corners cameo surround is assumed to be that of Ridge who made it uniquely different from the style used by Richardson during the same period | Not on P1<br>***#6813*** 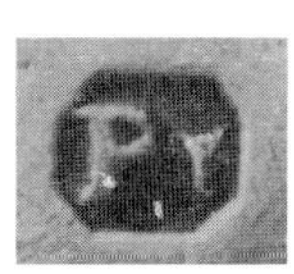 | **Jonathan RIDGE**<br>Chester | Silversmith |

| REGISTRATION DETAILS | MAKER'S PRIVATE ADDRESS and DETAILS | PLATE and MARK DETAILS | MAKER/COMPANY and BUSINESS ADDRESS | MAKER'S TRADE |
|---|---|---|---|---|
| MR1/160-72<br>MR2/134-8<br>MR3/187-8<br>SIL/12,16,18,20,37,48<br>J1 1701-14 at least<br>J3/400 | Stand patens 1710<br>Free 1703 but worked earlier<br>He came from Worcester<br>See also Ri | Pre-dates P1<br>***#6814***<br>type 2  | **Richard RICHARDSON I**<br>Eastgate Street<br>Chester (from Worcester) | Silversmith |
| MR1/160-172<br>MR3/185-6<br>GMSC/10<br>SIL/12,16,18,34,39,48, 49 | Free 1703, but worked earlier - mark seen 1704-25 Corporate and church plate, cups, spoons, taper stick and tobacco box | P1/2/x1<br>***#6815***<br>type 3  | | |
| MR1/160-72<br>MR3/185-6<br>GMSC/10<br>SIL/12,16,18,34,39,48 49 | Free 1703, but worked earlier<br>Mark seen 1709-24 on corporate and church plate, cups, spoons, taper stick and tobacco box | P1/2/x1<br>***#6816***<br>type 4  | | |
| MR1/160-72<br>MR2/134-8<br>MR3/187-8<br>SIL/12,16,18,20,37,48<br>J1 1701-14 at least<br>J3/400 | Spoons *c.*1713, 1718 | Not on P1<br>***#6817***<br>type 4a  | | |
| SIL/32,39 | Mugs 1721 | Not on P1<br>***#6818***<br>type 5  | | |
| MR1/172-5<br>MR2/221<br>MR3/189-90 | Free 1720-21<br>Mark seen 1720-25 on church plate, flatware, coffee pot stand and coconut cup | P1/14/x1<br>***#6819***<br>type 1a  | **William RICHARDSON**<br>Chester | Silversmith |
| SIL/20 | | P1/14/x1<br>***#6820***<br>type 1b 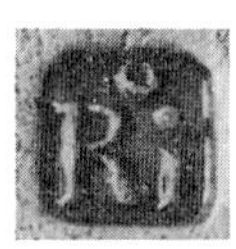 | | |
| PDB 1788-1822<br>MR3/87<br>PP1/188<br>SOT/118<br>J3/416 | Gold rings<br>Son-in-law of Joseph Walley, went into partnership as Jones & Walley in 1785, dissolved March 1788<br>Square marked 1787 | P1/23/x1<br>***#6821***<br>type 1  | **Robert JONES**<br>17 Strand Street (1786)<br>Castle Street (1788-96)<br>Liverpool | Watchmaker, watchcase maker, goldsmith and silversmith |
| | Square marked 1787 | P1/23/x1<br>***#6822***<br>type 2  | | |
| PDB 1811-31<br>MR3/88 | Gold rings and tableware | | **R JONES & CO**<br>Liverpool | |
| PDB 1813-32<br>MR3/88<br>LGSR 1825 | Gold rings and labels | | **R JONES & SON**<br>71 Castle Street and<br>2 Water Street<br>Liverpool | |

| REGISTRATION DETAILS | MAKER'S PRIVATE ADDRESS and DETAILS | PLATE and MARK DETAILS | MAKER/COMPANY and BUSINESS ADDRESS | MAKER'S TRADE |
|---|---|---|---|---|
| PDB 1788-1822<br>MR2/91-3<br>MR3/87<br>J1 *c*.1788-1826<br>J3/400 | Large variety of plate<br>1788-1800 | Not on P1<br>***#6823***<br>type 3  | **Robert JONES**<br>Liverpool | Silversmith |
| R2/103<br>8 February 1910<br>Sent by R Jones | 4 Grove Hill Road<br>Handsworth<br>Birmingham | P13/J/26<br>***#6824***  | **Reuben JONES**<br>5 Warstone Parade East<br>Birmingham | Manufacturing jeweller, chains seals, etc |
| R3/167<br>14 April 1959<br>Sent by A J Barton | Velshreda House<br>8 Wellesbourne Grove<br>Stratford-upon-Avon | P21/IJ/15<br>***#6825***  | **Alfred John BARTON** trading as<br>**Reuben JONES**<br>5 Warstone Parade East<br>Birmingham | Masonic jewellers |
| Missing register<br>*c*.1887 | See Reuben Jones | P5/J/127a<br>***#6826***  | **Unidentified** | |
| R2/102<br>4 February 1910<br>Sent by Imperial Tobacco Co<br>LAO 3004, 3005 | 64 Hatfield Road<br>Bedford Park<br>London W | P13/J/24,25<br>***#6827,8***  | **Reuben JORDAN** *<br>64 Hatfield Road<br>Bedford Park<br>London W | Silversmith |
| R2/184<br>27 February 1914<br>Sent by Imperial Tobacco Co | | P15/J/2,3<br>***#6829,30***  | **Reuben JORDAN** *<br>14 Brackley Road<br>Chiswick<br>London W4 | |
| R3/1<br>12 April 1921<br>Sent by The Civic Company Ltd | | P15/J/19,20<br>***#6831,2***  | | |
| R1/134<br>20 October 1900<br>Sent by R Jones | 78 Gower Street<br>Lozells<br>Aston<br>Birmingham | P9/J/30<br>***#6833***  | **Reuben JONES**<br>5 Warstone Parade East<br>Birmingham | Jeweller |
| 15 October 1935 | | P15/J/41,42<br>***#6834,5***  | | |
| R2/189<br>28 July 1914<br>Sent by self<br>Two sizes | 6 Thornhill Road<br>Handsworth<br>Birmingham | P15/J/4,6-8,11<br>***#6836-40***  | **Richard JONES**<br>9 Claremont Road, Hockley<br>Birmingham | Manufacturer of rings, brooches and pendants |
| Missing register<br>*c.* 1887<br>Richard similar mark BAO 18 October 1882<br>Reuben similar mark BAO 27 September 1888 | | P5/J/127b<br>***#6841***  | **Richard JONES** or **Reuben JONES**<br>4 Key Hill Drive<br>Birmingham | Jeweller |
| R1/134<br>2 April 1932<br>Sent by R Jones | 4 Grove Hill Road<br>Handsworth<br>Birmingham | P15/J/39<br>***#6842***  | **Reuben JONES**<br>5 Warstone Parade East<br>Birmingham | Manufacturing jeweller, chains seals, etc |
| R1/35<br>23 October 1896<br>Sent by F T Trahern<br>Authority to EW Linnett | Private address same as business | P5/J/799<br>***#6843***  | **Robert JONES** trading as<br>**Robert JONES & CO**<br>28 Market Street<br>Rhosllanerchrugog, near Ruabon | Watch manufacturers |
| LPB/26 SP25/6<br>30 April 1885<br>No mark in LPB | | P5/D/x1<br>***#6844***  | **Robert James DICK**<br>46 Hylton Street<br>Birmingham | Jeweller |

| REGISTRATION DETAILS | MAKER'S PRIVATE ADDRESS and DETAILS | PLATE and MARK DETAILS | MAKER/COMPANY and BUSINESS ADDRESS | MAKER'S TRADE |
|---|---|---|---|---|
| R1/180<br>28 November 1902<br>Sent by Kinnear Brothers | Redcroft<br>Bramhall<br>Cheshire | P9/L/39<br>***#6845***<br> | **William Robert ALLEN** trading as<br>**R J LEA**<br>45 Market Street and<br>12 Market Place and<br>19 Oxford Street and<br>55a Piccadilly<br>Manchester and<br>12 Talbot Street<br>Blackpool | Tobacconist |
| R1/228<br>3 March 1905<br>Sent by M E Wittenberg & Co | | P9/L/63<br>***#6846***<br> | **William Robert ALLEN** trading as<br>**R J LEA**<br>45 Market Street<br>Manchester | |
| R1/233<br>16 May 1905<br>Sent by R Wade<br>Leeds | | P9/L/66<br>***#6847***<br> | **William Robert ALLEN** trading as<br>**R J LEA**<br>45 Market Street and<br>12 Market Place and<br>19 Oxford Street and<br>55a Piccadilly<br>Manchester and<br>12 Talbot Street<br>Blackpool | |
| Missing register<br>*c.*1889 | | P5/L/236<br>***#6848***<br> | | |
| R1/54<br>1 November 1897<br>Sent by<br>W H Carrington | 43 Heaton Moor Road<br>Heaton Moor<br>Manchester | P5/L/905 Mark not found<br>***#6849*** | **William Robert ALLEN** trading as<br>**R J LEA**<br>Market Street and<br>Market Place and<br>Piccadilly<br>Manchester | |
| R3/89<br>11 February 1938<br>Sent by R J Noscoe | Private address same as business | P21/N/3<br>***#6850***<br> | **Robin John NOSCOE**<br>26 Highton Road<br>Woolton<br>Liverpool | Assistant advertising manager |
| LPB/62<br>19 July 1882 | | P3/O/x3<br>***#6851-3***<br> | **Richard James OLIVER** *<br>1 Northampton Square<br>Clerkenwell<br>London | Watchcase maker |
| R1/201<br>7 October 1904<br>Sent by A T Oliver | 76 Durham Road<br>Manor Park<br>London E | P9/O/6<br>***#6854***<br> | **Richard James OLIVER** *<br>31 Wynyatt Street, Clerkenwell<br>London EC | Gold and silver watchcase maker |
| SPB/8<br>11 January 1873 | CWMP 1874-1900 | P3/P/x3<br>***#6855-7***<br> | **Robert John PIKE** *<br>Cromwell Street<br>Earlsdon<br>Coventry | Watchcase maker |
| Missing register<br>*c.*1890<br>Similar mark LAO<br>14 September 1891 | | P5/P/x1<br>***#6858***<br> | | |

| REGISTRATION DETAILS | MAKER'S PRIVATE ADDRESS and DETAILS | PLATE and MARK DETAILS | MAKER/COMPANY and BUSINESS ADDRESS | MAKER'S TRADE |
|---|---|---|---|---|
| LPB/86<br>25 June 1880<br>Sent by Pope & Phelps | | P3/P/x2<br>***#6859,60***  | **Robert John PIKE** *<br>3 Cromwell Street<br>Coventry | Watchcase maker |
| Missing register<br>*c.*1890<br>Similar mark entered LAO 9 January 1893 | | P5/P/x1<br>***#6861***  | | |
| Missing register<br>*c.*1890<br>Similar mark LAO 14 September 1891 | | P5/P/324<br>***#6862***  | | |
| R3/59<br>7 September 1931<br>Sent by W R Manton | 322 Hamstead Road<br>Handsworth<br>Birmingham | P15/T/59,60<br>***#6863,4***  | **Roland James TAYLOR**<br>31 Northampton Street<br>Birmingham | Jeweller |
| R3/4<br>23 August 1921<br>Sent by C J Ward | 11 Fairfield Crescent<br>Liverpool<br>Dinus Lane<br>Huyton<br>6 Clarendon Road<br>Egremont, Cheshire | P15/W/48<br>***#6865***  | **Richard Joseph WARD**<br>**Charles John WARD**<br>**Thomas Walton WARD**<br>10 and 12 St Anne Street<br>Liverpool | Band instrument manufacturers, silverplaters and silversmiths |
| R1/44<br>3 May 1897<br>Sent by R J Wakefield<br>MR3/141 | Private address same as business | P5/X*sic*/838<br>***#6866***  | **Richard John WAKEFIELD**<br>48 Tenby Street North<br>Birmingham | Manufacturer of silver jewellery |
| LPB/46<br>14 September 1880<br>Sent by H Mansell | 9 Clarence Street<br>Liverpool | P3/K/x3<br>***#6867-9***  | **Richard KIRKMAN**<br>Liverpool | Watchcase maker |
| R1/17<br>21 October 1895<br>Sent by selves | 35 Oxford Street [1]<br>Old Trafford<br>Manchester<br>Lime View [2]<br>High Lane<br>Stockport | P5/R/694<br>***#6870***  | **John Henry ROWLAND** [1]<br>**Charles William KIBBLE** [2] trading as<br>**ROWLAND & KIBBLE**<br>19/20 Argyle Chambers<br>Manchester | Silversmiths |
| R1/234<br>9 June 1905<br>Sent by B Wade | Both at<br>Golf Avenue<br>Monfieth | P9/K/38<br>***#6871***  | **Richard KENNEDY**<br>**James KENNEDY**<br>7 Reform Street and<br>110 Seagate<br>Dundee | Tobacconists |
| PDB 1802<br>MR3/89<br>PP1/188<br>GTD 1805-7<br>PMR 1803-27 | Silver seals | P1/28/x2<br>***#6872,3*** 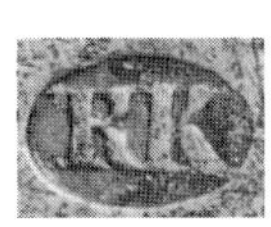 | **Richard KILSHAW**<br>Crosshall Street (1803)<br>15 Sir Thomas Buildings (1804)<br>9 Cook Street (1805)<br>Liverpool | Watchmaker, watchcase maker and silversmith |
| PP1/66-8, 169, 188<br>CWMP 1850-1901<br>Similar marks entered BAO 9 Nov 1854 and LAO 24 Feb 1855 | | P2/R/x4<br>***#6874-7*** 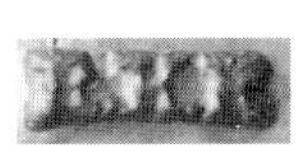 | **Richard Kevitt ROTHERHAM** *<br>Spon Street<br>Coventry | Watch and watchcase manufacturer |
| R1/216<br>29 June 1904<br>Sent by A J Cole & Co | 47b Welbeck Street<br>London W | P9/L/61<br>***#6878***  | **Rudolf LICHTBLAN**<br>2 Hanover Court<br>Milton Street<br>London EC | Pipe manufacturer |
| R1/110<br>5 September 1899<br>Sent by R Liebisch | 27 Church Street<br>Southport | P9/L/13<br>***#6879***  | **Richard LIEBISCH**<br>10 Lever Street<br>Manchester | Importer and manufacturer |

| REGISTRATION DETAILS | MAKER'S PRIVATE ADDRESS and DETAILS | PLATE and MARK DETAILS | MAKER/COMPANY and BUSINESS ADDRESS | MAKER'S TRADE |
|---|---|---|---|---|
| B 1734<br>PMR 1712-45 | | P2/L/x2<br>***#6880,1***<br> | **Robert LAITHWAIT**<br>Dale Street (1728)<br>Liverpool or | Watchcase maker |
| PP1/188<br>GTD 1832-53<br>PMR 1827-53 | | P2/L/x2<br>***#6882,3***<br>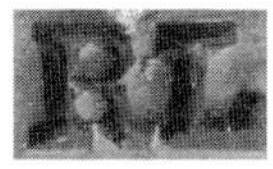 | **Richard LUCAS**<br>Cheapside (1827)<br>47 Cheapside (1847)<br>35 Cheapside (1849-53)<br>Liverpool | Watchcase maker |
| | | P1/12/x3<br>***#6884-6***<br> | | |
| PDB 1830-9<br>MR3/93<br>J1 1830-42 | Silverware | P1/7/x4<br>***#6887-90***<br> | **Robert LOWE**<br>Preston<br>or | Silversmith |
| PDB 1832-9<br>MR3/93 | Silver medals<br>Square marked 1787 | P1/23/x1<br>***#6891***<br> | **Richard LUCAS**<br>Liverpool | Silversmith |
| | Square marked 1785 | P1/26/x1<br>***#6892***<br> | | |
| | | P2/L/x2<br>***#6893,4***<br> | | |
| | | P2/L/x2<br>***#6895,6***<br> | | |
| | | P1/21/x6<br>***#6897-6902***<br> | | |
| Missing register<br>*c.*1890<br>Similar mark entered<br>BAO 29 May 1891 | | P5/R/329<br>***#6903***<br>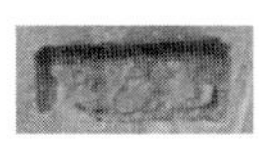 | **READING & LEA**<br>45a Frederick Street<br>Birmingham | Manufacturing jewellers |
| R3/118<br>17 July 1947<br>Sent by R L Dearman<br>Two sizes | 2 Eileengrove West<br>Rusholme<br>Manchester 14 | P21/D/15,16<br>***#6904,5***<br> | **Richard Lionel DEARMAN**<br>c/o Manchester Education Committee<br>Education Offices<br>Deansgate<br>Manchester 3 | Teacher |
| R1/193<br>23 May 1903<br>Sent by J Sloan | Leek Road<br>Buxton<br>74 Upper Parliament Street<br>Liverpool<br>28 Albert Road<br>Birkenhead | P9/R/60-63<br>***#6906-9***<br> | **Stanley RUSSELL**<br>**Walter RUSSELL** trading as<br>**RUSSELL'S LTD** *<br>Jas Sloan (Director)<br>18 Church Street<br>Liverpool and<br>10 Exchange Street<br>Manchester and<br>Lloyd Street<br>Llandudno | Watch manufacturers and jewellers |
| LPB/38<br>No name, address or date listed – *c.*1882<br>Similar mark entered<br>LAO 11 October 1870 | R L Hector of 10 Miller Street, Glasgow, is another possibility | Not on P3 LPB mark shown<br>***#6910***<br> | **Richard Leowe HENRY** *<br>12 Thavies Inn<br>London | Jeweller |
| R1/90<br>3 February 1899<br>Sent by<br>R Ll B Rathbone | Private address same as business | P9/R/7<br>***#6911***<br> | **Richard Llewelyn B RATHBONE**<br>37 Northumberland Terrace<br>Everton, Liverpool and<br>174 Buckingham Palace Road<br>London | Designer and maker of artistic metalwork |

| REGISTRATION DETAILS | MAKER'S PRIVATE ADDRESS and DETAILS | PLATE and MARK DETAILS | MAKER/COMPANY and BUSINESS ADDRESS | MAKER'S TRADE |
|---|---|---|---|---|
| R1/138<br>1 December 1900<br>Sent by<br>R Ll B Rathbone<br>Three sizes | Private address same as business | P9/R/23-25<br>***#6912-4***<br> | **Richard Llewelyn B RATHBONE**<br>37 Northumberland Terrace<br>Everton<br>Liverpool annotated *Left*<br>3 Ravenscourt Square (new address?)<br>Hammersmith<br>London | Designer and worker in metals |
| Not in R3 as expected<br>*c.*1922<br>Similar mark LAO<br>25 November 1905 | | P15/R/22<br>***#6915***<br> | **RUSSELL'S LTD** *<br>18 Church Street<br>Liverpool | Watch and chronometer makers |
| PDB 1786-92<br>MR3/94 | Gold rings, silver medals, buttons and buckles | Not on P1<br>***#6916*** **R M?** | **Richard MORROW**<br>Liverpool | Goldsmith and silversmith |
| Missing register<br>*c.*1886 | | P5/M/35<br>***#6917***<br> | **Unidentified** | |
| R1/56<br>5 January 1898<br>Sent by R Marsh | Avon Villa<br>Cambridge Road<br>King's Heath<br>Birmingham | P5/*Zsic*/918<br>***#6918***<br> | **Robert MARSH**<br>16 Hockley Street<br>Birmingham | Gold chain manufacturer |
| Missing register<br>*c.*1886<br>Similar mark entered<br>LAO 23 October 1885 | | P5/M/60<br>***#6919***<br> | **Robert Moffat MARPLES** *<br>7 Cripplegate Buildings, Wood Street<br>London EC | Watchcase maker and watch importer |
| R1/51<br>1 October 1897<br>Sent by E Langridge<br>& Co | 62 Wortham Road<br>London | P5/M/875<br>***#6920***<br> | **Robert MARSHALL** *<br>226 High Holborn<br>London | Pocket book maker and silversmith |
| LPB/72<br>13 May 1881 | | P3/R/x3<br>***#6921-3***<br> | **William ROBINSON**<br>**Arthur George McKEWAN**<br>36 Hockley Street<br>Birmingham | Jewellers |
| LPB/22<br>30 June 1884 | | P5/C/x1<br>***#6924***<br> | **Robert Miller CRAIG**<br>37 Dean Street<br>Newcastle upon Tyne | Manufacturing gold and silversmith , watchmaker and jeweller |
| R3/47<br>6 June 1929<br>Sent by T J Skelton | Gladeside Cottage<br>Rosehill<br>Rednal<br>Worcestershire | P15/R/46<br>***#6925***<br> | **RODIME MANUFACTURING CO**<br>George Ruden (Managing Director)<br>Dorothy Ruden<br>184 Warstone Lane<br>Birmingham | Jewellers and silversmiths |
| R2/45<br>31 August 1907<br>Sent by Martin Hall &<br>Co<br>Two sizes | 99 Rustlings Road<br>Sheffield | P9/M/117,118<br>***#6926,7***<br> | **MARTIN HALL & CO LTD** *<br>Mr Harry Wilkins (Director)<br>18 Ludgate Hill<br>Birmingham and<br>Audrey House<br>Ely Place<br>London and<br>Shrewsbury Works<br>Sheffield | Manufacturing jewellers and silversmiths |
| R2/43<br>24 July 1907<br>Sent by Martin Hall &<br>Co | Cairns Chambers<br>Sheffield<br>Bank Street, Sheffield<br>Shrewsbury Works<br>Shrewsbury Works<br>Veronah<br>Walm Lane<br>Willesden, London | P9/M/114<br>***#6928***<br> | **Alfred Ernest MAXFIELD**<br>**Philip Kenyon WAKE**<br>**Richard MARTIN**<br>**Harry WILKINS** (Managing Director)<br>**John Mackay ENSELL** trading as<br>**MARTIN, HALL & CO LTD** *<br>Shrewsbury Works<br>Sheffield | Silver, electroplate and cutlery manufacturers |

| REGISTRATION DETAILS | MAKER'S PRIVATE ADDRESS and DETAILS | PLATE and MARK DETAILS | MAKER/COMPANY and BUSINESS ADDRESS | MAKER'S TRADE |
|---|---|---|---|---|
| R2/88<br>21 July 1909<br>Sent by Frank E Butler<br>Two sizes | Moltrasis<br>Balsall Heath Road<br>Edgbaston<br>Birmingham | P13/M/18-21<br>***#6929-32***<br> | **MARTIN HALL & CO** *<br>Frank E Butler (Works Manager)<br>Henry Wilkins (Managing Director)<br>18 Ludgate Hill<br>Birmingham<br>Audrey House, Ely Place<br>London<br>Shrewsbury Works<br>Sheffield | Manufacturing silversmiths |
| R3/179<br>2 May 1961<br>Sent by R M Wallis | Livildons<br>343 Upton Lane<br>Widnes<br>Lancashire | P21/W/102<br>***#6933***<br> | **Raymond Marriage WALLIS**<br>No business address entered | Amateur |
| R2/208<br>19 September 1916<br>Sent by Richard Nevill | 164 Hamstead Road<br>Handsworth<br>Birmingham | P15/N/4<br>***#6934***<br> | **Walter A NEVILL** trading as<br>**Richard NEVILL** *<br>48 Vyse Street<br>Birmingham | Ring makers |
| Missing register<br>*c.*1888 | | P5/N/183<br>***#6935***<br> | | |
| R1/187<br>5 March 1903<br>Sent by R Nevill | 55 Soho Hill<br>Handsworth<br>Birmingham | P9/N/19-21<br>***#6936-8***<br> | **Richard Arthur NEVILL**<br>**Walter Austin NEVILL** trading as<br>**R NEVILL** *<br>48 Vyse Street<br>Birmingham | Gem ring makers |
| R1/207<br>23 February 1904<br>Sent by W A Nevill<br>Two sizes | | P9/N/26-30<br>***#6939-43***<br> | | Manufacturing jewellers |
| R2/178<br>24 October 1913<br>Sent by Richard Nevill | | P13/N/36,37<br>***#6944,5***<br> | **Richard NEVILL** *<br>48 Vyse Street<br>Birmingham | Ring manufacturer |
| LPB/58<br>10 September 1880<br>LPB marks shown<br>Two sizes | | Not on P3<br>***#6946,7***<br> | **Richard NEVILL** *<br>34 Vyse Street<br>Birmingham | Manufacturing jeweller |
| R2/211<br>29 March 1917<br>Sent by Richard Nevill | 164 Hamstead Road<br>Handsworth<br>Birmingham | P15/N/5<br>***#6948***<br>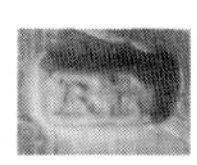 | **Richard NEVILL** *<br>Walter Nevill (Proprietor)<br>48 Vyse Street<br>Birmingham | |
| Not in R3 as expected<br>*c.*1917 | | P15/N/10-12<br>***#6949-51***<br> | | |
| PP1/189<br>Similar mark entered<br>BAO 2 May 1827 | Square marked 1786 | P1/22/x1<br>***#6952***<br>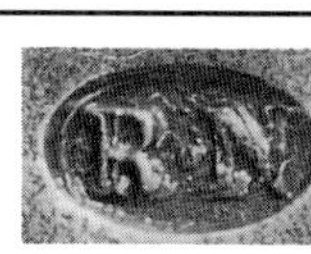 | **Richard NEALE**<br>Coventry | Watchcase maker |
| R3/65<br>30 December 1932<br>Sent by R L Nicholson<br>Two sizes | Fron Hall<br>Aipht<br>Bodfari<br>Denbigh | P15/N/21,22<br>***#6953,4***<br> | **Richard Lavoisier NICHOLSON**<br>24 Fenwick Street and<br>2 Maryland Street<br>Liverpool | Trade not entered |
| R3/121<br>6 January 1948<br>Sent by R N Naylor | 10 George Mount<br>Birkenhead | P21/N/5<br>***#6955***<br> | **Robert Norman NAYLOR**<br>City School of Art<br>Liverpool | Jewellery student |

| REGISTRATION DETAILS | MAKER'S PRIVATE ADDRESS and DETAILS | PLATE and MARK DETAILS | MAKER/COMPANY and BUSINESS ADDRESS | MAKER'S TRADE |
|---|---|---|---|---|
| MR1/175,180<br>MR3/190<br>GMSC/6 | Free 1681-2.<br>Mark seen 1703-19 on church plate, flatware and tumbler cups | P1/1/x1<br>***#6956***<br>type 2  | **Thomas ROBINSON**<br>Goss Lane<br>Chester | Silversmith |
| PP1/183<br>Similar mark entered LAO 5 Sep 1845 and CAO 4 Dec 1867 | | P2/O/x3<br>***#6957-9***  | **Richard OLIVER** *<br>19 Galway Street<br>London or | Watchcase maker |
| GSJW/136<br>PP1/189<br>J1 1858-79 | | P2/O/x3<br>***#6960-2***  | **Robert OVER**<br>15 Highfield Street<br>Liverpool | Watchcase maker |
| SPB/17<br>4 December 1867 | | P3/O/x3<br>***#6963-5***  | **Richard OLIVER** *<br>10 Galway Street<br>St Luke's<br>London | Watchcase maker |
| LPB/62<br>27 July 1882<br>No name or address listed | | P3/O/x3<br>***#6966-8***  | | |
| LPB/22<br>29 September 1883<br>No name or address<br>Sent by Henry Chadwick<br>49A Islington<br>Liverpool | | P5/O/x1<br>***#6969***  | | |
| R3/18<br>13 September 1923<br>Sent by J L Duncan | East Bank<br>99 Castle Street<br>Bolton | P15/P/187<br>***#6970***  | **Robert PARKINSON**<br>39 Newport Street<br>Bolton | Tobacco manufacturer and dealer |
| R3/124<br>6 July 1948<br>Sent by Richard Partington<br>Two sizes | Private address same as business | P21/P/26,27<br>***#6971,2***  | **Richard PARTINGTON**<br>26 Gatley Road<br>Cheadle<br>Cheshire | Student |
| R1/93<br>24 February 1899<br>Sent by R Parker | 19 Stafford Road<br>Handsworth<br>Birmingham | P9/P/14-19<br>***#6973-8***  | **Richmond PARKER**<br>51 Vyse Street<br>Birmingham | Jeweller |
| R1/21<br>11 February 1896<br>Sent by R Parker | 51 Vyse Street<br>Birmingham | P5/P/725<br>***#6979***  | | Ring maker |
| R1/96<br>21 March 1899<br>Sent by R Pattenden | 78 Forest Road<br>Dalston<br>London NE | P9/P/24<br>***#6980*** 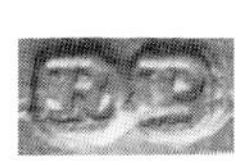 | **Richard PATTENDEN**<br>13 Meredith Street, Clerkenwell<br>London | Pipe mounter |
| R3/48<br>24 September 1929<br>Sent by selves | | P15/P/221<br>***#6981***  | **R PARKE & CO**<br>76 Vyse Street<br>Birmingham | Manufacturing jewellers |
| MR2/129 | Free 1730, died 1739<br>Jackson records a spoon *c.*1730 | P1/17/x2<br>***#6982,3***  | **Robert PYKE**<br>Chester and Wrexham | Silversmith |
| PDB 1787-92<br>MR3/95<br>CMC/124 | Silver buttons 1779<br><br>This mark may also be for Robert Pyke | P1/26/x2<br>***#6984,5***  | **Robert PRESTON**<br>Eastgate (1783)<br>Chester | Silversmith |

| REGISTRATION DETAILS | MAKER'S PRIVATE ADDRESS and DETAILS | PLATE and MARK DETAILS | MAKER/COMPANY and BUSINESS ADDRESS | MAKER'S TRADE |
|---|---|---|---|---|
| Missing register<br>*c.*1891 | | P5/P/382<br>***#6986***<br> | **Robert PRINGLE & SONS** * | |
| LPB/64<br>29 April 1882 | | P3/P/x3<br>***#6987-9***<br> | **Robert PRINGLE & CO** *<br>42 Clerkenwell Road<br>London | Wholesale manufacturing jewellers, electroplate and jewellers materials |
| Missing register<br>*c.*1887 | | P5/P/103<br>***#6990***<br> | | |
| Missing register<br>*c.*1891 | | P5/P/385<br>***#6991***<br>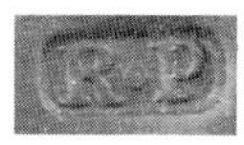 | **Robert PRINGLE & CO** *<br>42 Clerkenwell Road<br>London | Jewellers |
| R1/72<br>26 August 1898<br>Sent by Ward Brothers<br>J H Workall<br>J Hayward<br>R Pringle & Sons<br>G K Leeson<br>J Houlston | 28 Arundel Square<br>London N | P9/P/2a<br>***#6992***<br> | **Robert PRINGLE** trading as<br>**Robert PRINGLE & SONS**<br>40, 42 Clerkenwell Road<br>London EC | |
| R1/72<br>21 December 1898 | | P9/P/7-12<br>***#6993-8***<br> | | |
| R1/103<br>31 May 1899<br>Sent by R Pringle & Sons<br>H Moreton<br>Two sizes | 28 Arundel Square [1]<br>London N<br>49 Duckett Road [2]<br>Harringay<br>London N | P9/P/33-39<br>***#6999-7005***<br> | | Wholesale jewellers and silversmiths |
| R1/115<br>26 October 1899<br>Sent by R Pringle<br>C Lyster & Son<br>Three sizes | | P9/P/59-62<br>***#7006-9***<br> | | Jewellers and silversmiths |
| R1/142<br>14 February 1901<br>Sent by R Pringle<br>H Moreton | | P9/P/84-95<br>***#7010-21***<br> | | |
| R1/170<br>5 June 1902<br>Sent by R Pringle & Sons | 19 Highbury Crescent<br>London N<br>Hillside<br>Crouch Hill | P9/Q*sic*/128-132,136,137,141, 143,147,149,150<br>***#7022-33***<br> | **Robert PRINGLE**<br>**Robert PRINGLE junior**<br>**William PRINGLE** trading as<br>**Robert PRINGLE & SONS** *<br>40/42 Clerkenwell Road<br>London | Jewellers and silversmiths |
| R2/17<br>21 April 1906<br>Sent by R Pringle & Sons<br>BAO 12.471-12.489 | | P9/Q*sic*/249,250<br>***#7034,5***<br> | | Jewellers |
| R3/56<br>1 January 1931<br>Sent by Robert Pringle & Sons Ltd<br>All previously entered punches are valid | Company seal was affixed in the presence of both directors:- | No new punches entered<br>***#7036*** | **Robert PRINGLE & SONS (LONDON) LTD** *<br>Robert Pringle (Director)<br>R Pringle junior (Secretary)<br>40, 42 Clerkenwell Road (Registered<br>London EC1 Office) | Wholesale and manufacturing jewellers, silversmiths etc |

| REGISTRATION DETAILS | MAKER'S PRIVATE ADDRESS and DETAILS | PLATE and MARK DETAILS | MAKER/COMPANY and BUSINESS ADDRESS | MAKER'S TRADE |
|---|---|---|---|---|
| R3/115<br>25 October 1946<br>Sent by Steele & Dolphin<br>119 Vyse Street<br>Birmingham | | P21/P/16<br>***#7037***<br> | **Robert PRINGLE & SONS (LONDON) LTD** *<br>Robert Pringle (Director)<br>R Pringle Junior (Secretary)<br>40, 42 Clerkenwell Road (Registered Office)<br>London EC1 | Wholesale and manufacturing jewellers, silversmiths, etc |
| Missing register<br>*c.*1894 | | P5/P/545<br>***#7038***<br>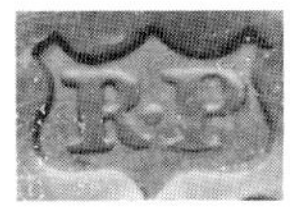 | | |
| R1/103<br>31 May 1899 | Common Seal of the Company was affixed in the presence of the directors | P9/P/27-32<br>***#7039-44***<br> | **Robert PRINGLE & SONS (LONDON) LTD** *<br>Robert Pringle (Director)<br>R Pringle Junior (Secretary)<br>40, 42 Clerkenwell Road (Registered Office)<br>London EC1 | Jewellers and silversmiths |
| R1/132<br>21 September 1900<br>Sent by Robert Pringle & Sons<br>Ward Brothers | | P9/P/69-74<br>***#7045-50***<br> | | |
| R1/72<br>26 August 1898<br>Two sizes | | P9/P/2b,c<br>***#7051,2***<br>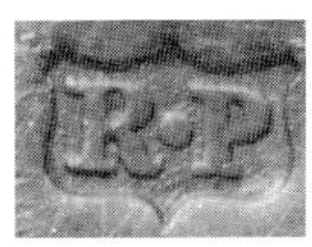 | | |
| R1/170<br>5 June 1902 | London N<br>92 Hillfield Drive<br>Hornsey Drive<br>London | P9/Q*sic*/126,127,133-135,138-140, 142,144-146,148<br>***#7053-65***<br> | | |
| R1/188<br>24 March 1903<br>Sent by R Pringle & Sons<br>Two sizes | 19 Highbury Crescent, N<br>Hillside<br>Crouch Hill, N<br>92 Hillfield Avenue<br>Hornsey, N<br>19 Highbury Crescent<br>London N | P9/Q*sic*/159-182<br>***#7066-89***<br> | **Robert PRINGLE**<br>**Robert PRINGLE** junior<br>**William PRINGLE**<br>**James PRINGLE** trading as<br>**Robert PRINGLE & SONS** *<br>40/42 Clerkenwell Road<br>London | |
| R1/221<br>6 October 1904<br>Sent by Robert Pringle & Sons<br>Three sizes | 19 Highbury Crescent, N<br>Hillside<br>Crouch Hill, London N<br>Melsome<br>Hillfield Avenue<br>Hornsey, London N<br>19 Highbury Crescent, N | P9/Q*sic*/202-226<br>***#7090-4***<br> | **Robert PRINGLE**<br>**Robert PRINGLE** junior<br>**William PRINGLE**<br>**James PRINGLE** trading as<br>**Robert PRINGLE & SONS** *<br>40/42 Clerkenwell Road and<br>20 Great Sutton Street<br>London | |
| R2/17<br>21 April 1906<br>BAO 12.471- 12.489<br>SAO #774 to 778<br>Robert Pringle snr died 23 June 1907<br>Two sizes | Crouch End, N<br>Melrose, Hillfield Avenue<br>Hornsey, N<br>19 Highbury Crescent, N<br>Rozel<br>Hendon Avenue, Finchley<br>London N | P9/Q*sic*/232-240, 243,245-248<br>***#7095-7108***<br> | **Edwin PRINGLE** trading as<br>**Robert PRINGLE & SONS** *<br>40/42 Clerkenwell Road<br>London | |
| R2/36<br>30 March 1907<br>LAO (61) 3254, 3252, 3251, 3250<br>Four sizes | | P9/U*sic*/281-299<br>***#7109-27***<br> | and 20 Great Sutton Street<br>London EC | |

| REGISTRATION DETAILS | MAKER'S PRIVATE ADDRESS and DETAILS | PLATE and MARK DETAILS | MAKER/COMPANY and BUSINESS ADDRESS | MAKER'S TRADE |
|---|---|---|---|---|
| R2/74<br>11 March 1909<br>Sent by R Pringle & Sons<br>Three sizes | 107 Crouch Hill, London N<br>Melrose, Hillfield Avenue<br>Hornsey<br>19 Highbury Crescent<br>London N<br>Rozel, Hendon Avenue<br>Finchley | P13/P/7-78<br>***#7128-99***<br> | **Robert PRINGLE**<br>**William PRINGLE**<br>**James PRINGLE**<br>**Edwin PRINGLE** trading as<br>**Robert PRINGLE & SONS** *<br>40, 42 Clerkenwell Road and<br>19, 20 Great Sutton Street<br>London EC | Jewellers and silversmiths |
| 22 April 1909<br>Per Mr C Horner | | P13/P/85<br>***#7200***<br> | | |
| R2/89<br>24 July 1909<br>Sent by Robert Pringle & Sons<br>Two sizes | 107 Crouch Hill<br>London<br>Melrose, Hillfield Avenue<br>Hornsey<br>19 Highbury Crescent<br>London N<br>Rozel, Hendon Avenue<br>Finchley | P13/P/87-98<br>***#7201-12***<br> | | |
| R2/101<br>7 January 1910<br>Sent by Robert Pringle & Sons<br>Two sizes | | P13/P/110-133<br>***#7213-36***<br> | | |
| R2/123<br>4 November 1910<br>Sent by R Pringle & Sons<br>Three sizes | | P13/P/145-149<br>***#7237-41***<br> | | |
| R2/129<br>1 March 1911<br>Sent by R Pringle & Sons<br>Six sizes | | P13/Q*sic*/167-193<br>***#7242-68***<br>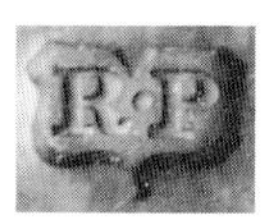 | | |
| R2/170<br>17 April 1913<br>Sent by R Pringle & Sons<br>Five sizes | | P15/P/1-39<br>***#7269-7307***<br> | | Manufacturing silversmiths |
| R2/210<br>6 December 1916<br>Sent by R Pringle & Sons<br>Six sizes | | P15/P/75–99<br>***#7308-32***<br> | | Jewellers and silversmiths |
| R2/219<br>29 April 1919<br>Sent by R Pringle & Sons<br>Six sizes | | P15/P/106–115<br>***#7333-42***<br> | **Robert PRINGLE**<br>**William PRINGLE**<br>**James PRINGLE**<br>**Edwin PRINGLE** trading as<br>**Robert PRINGLE & SONS** *<br>40 and 42 Clerkenwell Road, and<br>19 and 20 Great Sutton Street<br>London EC | |
| R2/230<br>15 April 1920<br>Sent by R Pringle & Sons<br>Six sizes | 25 Coolhurst Road, London N8<br>Melrose<br>Highfield Crescent<br>Hornsey<br>19 Highbury Crescent<br>London N<br>Rozel, Hendon Avenue<br>Finchley, London N | P26/P/132–155<br>***#7343-66***<br> | | |

| REGISTRATION DETAILS | MAKER'S PRIVATE ADDRESS and DETAILS | PLATE and MARK DETAILS | MAKER/COMPANY and BUSINESS ADDRESS | MAKER'S TRADE |
|---|---|---|---|---|
| R3/14<br>3 March 1923<br>Sent by R Pringle & Son | 25 Coolhurst Road<br>Crouch End, London<br>19 Highbury Crescent<br>London N5<br>Melrose<br>Hillfield Avenue<br>Hornsey Royal<br>Hendon Avenue<br>Church End, Finchley | P15/P/184<br>***#7367***<br> | **Robert PRINGLE**<br>**James PRINGLE**<br>**William PRINGLE**<br>**Edwin PRINGLE** trading as<br>**Robert PRINGLE & SONS** *<br>40, 42 Clerkenwell Road and<br>17 to 20 Great Sutton Street<br>London EC | Manufacturing jewellers and silversmiths |
| R3/163<br>22 February 1958<br>Sent by W J Pellow Ltd<br>31 Vyse Street<br>Birmingham 18 | | P21/P/71<br>***#7368***<br> | **Robert PRINGLE & SONS (LONDON) LTD** *<br>Sealed in the presence of both directors:-<br>W E Pringle (Director)<br>R Pringle (Secretary)<br>36-42 Clerkenwell Road<br>London EC1 | Wholesale merchants |
| R3/65<br>29 November 1932<br>Sent by selves | | P15/R/50<br>***#7369***<br> | **THE FORGE LTD**<br>Common seal of company affixed in presence of Roberts and Hodson:-<br>Richard Pryce Roberts (Director)<br>Philip Hodson (Secretary)<br>Beechlawn (Registered Office)<br>Beechwood Road<br>Aigburth<br>Liverpool | Art metal workers |
| 1 October 1937 | | P21/R/1<br>***#7370***<br> | | |
| R3/178<br>19 April 1961<br>Sent by R P Semple<br>Two sizes | 13 Cadogan Street<br>Princes Park<br>Liverpool 8 moved 17 May 1962 to 104 Bishops Road<br>Fulham, London SW6 | P21/S/88,89<br>***#7371,2***<br> | **Raymond Peter SEMPLE**<br>No business address entered | Silversmith |
| R2/19<br>31 May 1906<br>Sent by Richard & Quilley | 71 Devonshire Road<br>Palmers Green EC<br>84 Lymington Avenue<br>Wood Green<br>London EC | P9/R/77<br>***#7373***<br> | **Arthur William RICHARD**<br>**David QUILLEY** trading as<br>**RICHARD & QUILLEY** *<br>9 Albermarle Street, Clerkenwell<br>London EC | Goldsmiths |
| R2/58<br>13 April 1908<br>Sent by AW Richard | | P13/R/1<br>***#7374***<br> | as above<br>24 Red Lion Street, Clerkenwell<br>London EC | Manufacturing jewellers |
| MR1/160-72<br>MR2/134-8<br>MR3/185-9<br>SIL/12,22,40, 49<br>J1 1701-14 at least<br>J3/400<br>GMSC/11-13 | Communion cups *c.*1699<br><br>He came from Worcester - Free 1703, but worked earlier - died Jan 1729/30<br>This mark seen 1727-30 on a large variety of plate | Pre-dates P1<br>***#7375***<br>type 1<br> | **Richard RICHARDSON I**<br>Eastgate Street<br>Chester | Silversmith |
| | | P1/2/x1<br>***#7376***<br>type 6<br> | | |
| | This mark seen 1724-9 | P1/2/x1<br>***#7377***<br>type 7<br>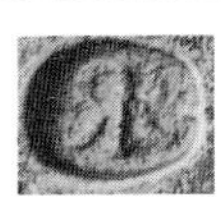 | | |
| MR2/145<br>SIL/29,39,40<br>GMSC/21-32 | Free 1736, died 1769 | P1/2/x1<br>***#7378***<br>type 2<br>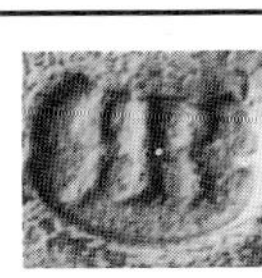 | **Richard RICHARDSON II**<br>Eastgate Street<br>Chester | Silversmith |

| REGISTRATION DETAILS | MAKER'S PRIVATE ADDRESS and DETAILS | PLATE and MARK DETAILS | MAKER/COMPANY and BUSINESS ADDRESS | MAKER'S TRADE |
|---|---|---|---|---|
| LPB/72<br>14 July 1880<br>Sent by Woodman & Son LPB marks | Redmond not in 1880 directories but Richard Redman (*sic*) at this address | Not on P3 LPB mark shown<br>***#7379***<br> | **Richard REDMOND (REDMAN ?)**<br>170 Edmund Street<br>Birmingham | Trade not identified |
| R3/123<br>30 October 1948<br>Sent by Elite Bracelet Man Co Ltd | | P21/R/5<br>***#7380***<br> | **ELITE BRACELET MANUFACTURING CO LTD**<br>Sealed in the presence of Ryf and Gosling:-<br>R Ryf (Director)<br>J N Gosling (Secretary)<br>Regent Works, Regent Street<br>Birmingham 1 | Manufacturing jewellers |
| R3/123<br>17 June 1953<br>Ed: P21/R/16 already used for WR. Clerk probably forgot to enter the punch mark on plate 21 | | P21/R/16 Mark not found<br>***#7381*** | | |
| R3/55<br>16 September 1930<br>Sent by Ryf & Marchands Ltd | Private address same as business | P15/R/49<br>***#7382***<br> | **RYF & MARCHANDS LTD**<br>Common Seal of Company affixed in the presence of:-<br>M Ryf (Director)<br>S W Thomas (Secretary)<br>1 Hatton Garden (Registered Office)<br>London EC1 | Watch importers |
| R3/115<br>19 July 1946<br>Sent by Haydn Marples | Tottey<br>33 Welch Road<br>Birkdale<br>35 Duke Street [1]<br>Southport<br>86 Old Park Lane [2]<br>Southport | P21/R/3<br>***#7383***<br> | **Charles Thomas REVELL** [1]<br>**Albert Edward ROBINSON** [2] trading as<br>**C T REVELL & CO**<br>79 Shakespear Street<br>Southport<br>Lancashire | Manufacturing jewellers |
| R1/182<br>17 December 1902<br>Sent by R Rohleder | Doenberg Wood Road<br>Whalley Range<br>Manchester | P9/R/53<br>***#7384***<br> | **Robert ROHLEDER**<br>29 Dale Street<br>Manchester | Merchant in umbrella cloth and materials |
| MR2/149-73<br>MR3/194-6<br>SIL/12,39,40,42,49<br>GMSC/21-32 | This mark seen 1739 to 1766 | Not on P1<br>***#7385***<br>type 5a<br> | **Richard RICHARDSON II**<br>Eastgate Street<br>Chester | Silversmith |
| | Pan, cake basket and chamber stick all 1765 | Not on P1<br>***#7386***<br>type 5b<br> | | |
| | Tumbler cup<br>1766 | Not on P1<br>***#7387***<br>type 5c<br> | | |
| | Balaster jug and beer jug 1750, communion cup 1760 | Not on P1<br>***#7388***<br>type 5d<br> | | |
| PDB 1784-90<br>MR2/179-85<br>MR3/96,197<br>SIL/12,40,42,49<br>J1 1734-87<br>J3/400<br>GMSC49,50 | Large variety of plate including skewer 1778<br>Free of the Goldsmiths' Company<br>23 October 1779 and died 1822 | Not on P1<br>***#7389***<br>type 1a<br> | **Richard RICHARDSON IV**<br>Eastgate Street<br>Chester | Goldsmith and silversmith |
| | Soup ladle 1777 | Not on P1<br>***#7390***<br>type 1b<br> | | |

| REGISTRATION DETAILS | MAKER'S PRIVATE ADDRESS and DETAILS | PLATE and MARK DETAILS | MAKER/COMPANY and BUSINESS ADDRESS | MAKER'S TRADE |
|---|---|---|---|---|
| PDB 1784-90<br>MR2/179-85<br>MR3/96, 197<br>SIL/12,40,42,49 | Tumbler cup 1780 | Not on P1<br>***#7391***<br>type 4  | **Richard RICHARDSON IV**<br>Eastgate Street<br>Chester | Goldsmith and silversmith |
| J1 1734-87<br>J3/400<br>GMSC49,50 | Square marked 1785<br>This mark at top of square so may have been entered 1785 - large variety of plate | P1/21/x1<br>***#7392***<br>type 2a  | | |
| Not in SPB or LPB so struck 1860-3<br>Similar mark entered BAO 5 August 1873 | See also *#7379* | P3/R/x1<br>***#7393***  | **Richard REDMAN**<br>170 New Edmund Street<br>Birmingham | Factor, wholesale jeweller and gunsmith |
| R1/234<br>8 June 1905<br>Sent by R Richardson | Springvale House<br>Park Lane<br>Sheffield | P9/R/67<br>***#7394***  | **Richard RICHARDSON**<br>Cornwall Works<br>Scotland Street<br>Sheffield | Silversmith |
| MR2/149-73<br>MR3/194-6<br>SIL/12,39,40,42,49<br>GMSC/21-32 | Beaker 1764 | Not on P1<br>***#7395***<br>type 5e  | **Richard RICHARDSON II**<br>Eastgate Street<br>Chester | Silversmith |
| PDB 1784-90 | Very large variety of plate 1783-88 | Not on P1<br>***#7396***<br>type 2b  | **Richard RICHARDSON IV**<br>Eastgate Street<br>Chester | Goldsmith and silversmith |
| MR2/188-191<br>MR3/197-8<br>SIL/12,19,20,32,40,44<br>J1 died 1768<br>J3/400<br>GMSC/34,35 | Beaker, pap boat, porringer 1739-48 | Not on P1<br>***#7397***<br>type 3a  | **Richard RICHARDSON II**<br>Eastgate Street<br>Chester and<br><br>**William RICHARDSON II**<br>Eastgate Street<br>Chester | Silversmiths |
| | Flagon, communion cup, tea caddy and tray | Not on P1<br>***#7398***<br>type 3b  | | |
| | Paten, communion cup 1741-7 | Not on P1<br>***#7399***<br>type 3c  | | |
| | Beer jug 1751, tray 1751 | Not on P1<br>***#7400***<br>type 4  | | |
| | Cruet stand 1753 | Not on P1<br>***#7401***<br>type 5f  | | |
| | Spoons 1763 | Not on P1<br>***#7402***<br>type 8  | | |
| | Beaker 1768 and communion cup 1769<br>Mark seen 1764 to 1769 replaced the earlier type 5 | Not on P1<br>***#7403***<br>type 6  | | |
| | This mark only found with date letter R for 1767 on an asparagus tray | Not on P1<br>***#7404***<br>type 7  | | |

| REGISTRATION DETAILS | MAKER'S PRIVATE ADDRESS and DETAILS | PLATE and MARK DETAILS | MAKER/COMPANY and BUSINESS ADDRESS | MAKER'S TRADE |
|---|---|---|---|---|
| MR1/109<br>MR2/171<br>MR3/196 GMSC/47,48 | Type 1 mark is more commonly seen - same as Richard Richardson II type 6<br>Seen 1769-70 | Not on P1<br>***#7405***<br>type 1<br> | **Richard RICHARDSON III**<br>Eastgate Street<br>Chester | Silversmith |
| SIL/12 | Wares seen 1771-79 | Not on P1<br>***#7406***<br>type 1a<br> | | |
| PDB 1784-90<br>MR2/179<br>MR3/96, 197<br>SIL/12<br>J1 1734-87<br>J3/400<br>GMSC49,50 | Free 1779 of the Goldsmiths' Company<br>23 October 1779 and died 1822 | Not on P1<br>***#7407***<br>type 3<br> | **Richard RICHARDSON IV**<br>Eastgate Street<br>Chester | Silversmith |
| R2/124<br>29 November 1910<br>Sent by M Freeman | Earlston Road<br>Liscard, Cheshire<br>Brooklands<br>Beresford Road<br>Wallesey<br>Malpas Grove<br>Wallesey | P13/C/86<br>***#7408***<br> | **Archibald PHILLIPS**<br>**Reginald Stanley CROSS**<br>**Robert Raynor MACCONNALL**<br>trading as **Reginald R CROSS and CROSS & PHILLIPS**<br>25 Castle Street<br>52 Church Street<br>1 Exchange Street E<br>Liverpool | Fine art dealers |
| R2/91<br>19 August 1909<br>Sent by Robert Reid & Co | 28 St Albans Road<br>Westbury Park<br>Bristol | P13/R/27<br>***#7409***<br> | **Robert James REID** trading as<br>**Robert REID & CO** *<br>2 Dean Street<br>Portland Square<br>Bristol | Jewellers |
| SPB/4<br>28 April 1876<br>Sent by Henry Green | | P3/S/x2<br>***#7410,11***<br> | **Robert SUTTON**<br>32 Lowther Street<br>Whitehaven, Cumberland | Chronometer and watchmaker, jeweller and optician |
| R2/104<br>5 March 1910<br>Sent by Ralph Scholes | 23 Hyde Road<br>Woodley<br>Cheshire | P13/S/50<br>***#7412***<br> | **Ralph SCHOLES**<br>23 Hyde Road<br>Woodley<br>Cheshire | Manufacturer of jewellery in silver and gold |
| R2/90<br>14 August 1909<br>Sent by Ruben Segal | 42 Carnarvon Street<br>Cheetham<br>Manchester | P13/S/43<br>***#7413***<br> | **Ruben SEGAL**<br>42 Carnarvon Street<br>Cheetham<br>Manchester | Jeweller, diamond mounter, setter and electroplate gilder |
| R3/94<br>17 March 1939<br>Sent by<br>R W R Spelman<br>Three sizes | Solsboro<br>Granville Road<br>Timperley<br>Cheshire | P21/S/5-7<br>***#7414-6***<br> | **Richard Whately Raynold SPELMAN**<br>28 Railway Street<br>Altrincham | Jeweller |
| R2/152<br>12 March 1912<br>Sent by Charles Peach & Son | Keresley Grange<br>Coventry<br>Gate House<br>Kenilworth<br>Allesley<br>Coventry | P13/R/46<br>***#7417***<br> | **Hugh ROTHERHAM**<br>**Kevitt ROTHERHAM**<br>**Ewan ROTHERHAM**<br>(Ed: trading as **ROTHERHAM & SON**) *<br>Spon Street, Coventry and<br>1 Holborn Circus<br>London | Watch manufacturers |

| REGISTRATION DETAILS | MAKER'S PRIVATE ADDRESS and DETAILS | PLATE and MARK DETAILS | MAKER/COMPANY and BUSINESS ADDRESS | MAKER'S TRADE |
|---|---|---|---|---|
| R3/83<br>16 April 1936<br>Sent by Smith, Ewen & Stylic Ltd<br>Frederick Street<br>Birmingham | | P15/R/57<br>***#7418***<br> | **ROTHERHAM & SONS LTD** *<br>Common seal of company affixed in the presence of:-<br>K Rotherham (Director)<br>Ernst Milne (Secretary)<br>Spon Street,<br>Coventry | Watch manufacturers |
| R3/84<br>16 May 1936<br>Sent by Rotherham & Sons Ltd | Common seal of company affixed in the presence of Rotherham and Nelson | P15/R/58<br>***#7419***<br> | **ROTHERHAM & SONS (COVENTRY) LTD** *<br>Hugh Rotherham (Director)<br>Ernest Nelson (Secretary)<br>Spon Street (Registered Office)<br>Coventry | Watch manufacturers and engineers |
| R3/28<br>16 May 1925<br>Sent by Rotherham & Sons Ltd<br>Two sizes | Keresley Grange<br>Coventry<br>The Gate House, Kenilworth<br>Aston Hill<br>Near Leamington | P15/R/36-41<br>***#7420-5***<br> | **Hugh ROTHERHAM**<br>**Kevitt ROTHERHAM**<br>**Ewan ROTHERHAM**<br>(Ed: trading as **ROTHERHAM & SON**) *<br>Spon Street<br>Coventry and<br>1 Holborn Circus<br>London | Watch manufacturers |
| LPB/74<br>10 October 1884<br>Similar mark BAO<br>24 September 1885 | 8th mark on P5 and 8th on LPB/74 | P5/R/x1<br>***#7426***<br> | **A T ROWLANDS & SON** *<br>46 Sir Thomas' Building<br>Liverpool | Pipe mounters |
| Missing register<br>*c.*1886 | | P5/R/44<br>***#7427***<br> | | |
| PP1/189<br>J1 1838-58 | | P2/S/x2<br>***#7428,9***<br> | **Ralph SAMUEL** *<br>72 Wood Street<br>Liverpool | Watch and watchcase maker |
| | | P2/S/x2<br>***#7430,1***<br> | | |
| | | P2/S/x2<br>***#7432,3***<br> | | |
| R1/132<br>26 September 1900<br>Sent by R Smart | 101 Mardock Road<br>Handsworth<br>Birmingham | P9/S/36<br>***#7434***<br> | **Richard SMART**<br>105 Vyse Street<br>Birmingham | Manufacturing jeweller |
| R3/36<br>15 August 1927<br>Sent by W J Dingley | 77 Warstone Lane [1]<br>Birmingham<br>Ridings<br>Addington<br>2 Shooters Hill Road [2]<br>Blackheath, Surrey<br>9 St Germans Place [3]<br>Blackheath, Surrey | P15/S/80<br>***#7435***<br> | **George E HUTCHINSON** [1]<br>**W L HUTCHINSON** [2]<br>**H DAILEY** [3]<br>**E J HUTCHINSON** [3] trading as<br>**SPENCER & CO** *<br>19, 21 Great Queen Street<br>London WC2 | Masonic jewellers |
| PP1/66-68, 189<br>CWMP 1850-1939<br>Similar mark entered BAO 7 April 1841 | | P1/3/x3<br>***#7436-8***<br> | **ROTHERHAM & SONS**<br>4 Spon Street<br>Coventry | Watch and watchcase manufacturers |
| R1/76<br>15 August 1894<br>Sent by T P Hewitt | 3 Wardle Terrace [1]<br>Newcastle<br>20 Perry Park Road [2]<br>Tynemouth<br>98 Mary's Terrace [3]<br>Whitely | P5/R/573<br>***#7439***<br> | **Thomas Arthur REID**[1]<br>**Walter Cecil REID** [2]<br>**Francis James LANGFORD** [3]<br>trading as **REID & SONS** *<br>41 Grey Street and 48 Grainger Street<br>Newcastle upon Tyne | Watch and clock manufacturers and jewellers |

| REGISTRATION DETAILS | MAKER'S PRIVATE ADDRESS and DETAILS | PLATE and MARK DETAILS | MAKER/COMPANY and BUSINESS ADDRESS | MAKER'S TRADE |
|---|---|---|---|---|
| R3/21<br>6 March 1924<br>Sent by Benson Brothers | Yeale, Gosforth<br>Newcastle upon Tyne<br>Norismore, Long Centre<br>Northumberland<br>1 Victoria Avenue<br>Whitley Bay<br>Hardwick, Gosforth<br>Newcastle upon Tyne | P15/R/31<br>***#7440***<br> | **Christain Leopold REID** *<br>**William Septimus LECTE** *<br>**Percival Vincent Stanley LANGFORD**<br>**William Herbert LECTE**<br>(Ed: trading as **REID & SON LTD**?) *<br>23–27 Blackett Street and<br>48 Granger Street<br>Newcastle upon Tyne | Goldsmiths and silversmiths |
| R3/52<br>14 February 1930<br>Sent by Benson Brothers | | P15/R/47<br>***#7441***<br>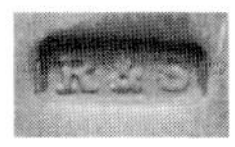 | **ROTHERHAM & SONS** *<br>Spon Street<br>Coventry | Watch manufacturers |
| | | P2/S/x2<br>***#7442,3***<br> | **Ralph SAMUEL** *<br>72 Wood Street<br>Liverpool | Watch and watchcase maker |
| Similar mark entered LAO 7 April 1843 and BAO 20 June 1850 | 1855 watchcase | P2/X*sic*/x3<br>***#7444-6***<br> | | |
| | | P2/S/x2<br>***#7447,8***<br> | | |
| | | P2/S/x2<br>***#7449,50***<br> | | |
| R2/148<br>29 November 1911<br>Sent by Robert Stebbings<br>LO 3874 | Granville Road<br>Clacton-on-Sea | P13/S/80<br>***#7451***<br> | **Robert STEBBINGS**<br>18 Myddleton Street<br>London EC | Manufacturing silversmiths |
| R2/183<br>6 February 1914<br>Sent by W Neale & Son<br>26 Highbury<br>London | Overton<br>Longbenton | P15/R/3,4<br>***#7452,3***<br> | **Christian Leopold REID**<br>**William Septimus LECTE** trading as<br>**REID & SON** *<br>Gem Buildings<br>Blackett Street and<br>48 Granger Street<br>Newcastle upon Tyne | Goldsmiths and silversmiths |
| R2/87<br>14 July 1909<br>Sent by Clarence Flint | 73 Clarnston Road<br>Crumpsall<br>Manchester | P13/S/41<br>***#7454***<br> | **Alfred Ernest ROBINSON** trading as<br>**ROBINSON SMITH & CO**<br>68 Spencer Street<br>Birmingham<br>27 Bradshaw Street, Shudehill<br>Manchester | Jewellers |
| R1/17<br>31 October 1895<br>Sent by E Vaughton | 31 Portland Road<br>Birmingham | P5/S/695<br>***#7455***<br> | **Henry SPIERS** trading as<br>**R SPIERS & CO**<br>2 Vyse Street<br>Birmingham | Jewellers |
| R3/98<br>6 February 1941<br>Sent by R S Horne<br>11 Abbey Gardens<br>Southport<br>All previous punches for R S Horne valid.<br>27 February 1941 new mark P21/H/15 | 168 Stamford Road [1]<br>Waterhead<br>Oldham<br>59 Church Street [2]<br>Lozells<br>Birmingham | P21/H/15<br>***#7456***<br> | **John Stott HALLEY** [1]<br>**Frank Unite HARRIS** [2] trading as<br>**R S HORNE**<br>9 Corporation Street<br>Manchester | Manufacturing jewellers |

| REGISTRATION DETAILS | MAKER'S PRIVATE ADDRESS and DETAILS | PLATE and MARK DETAILS | MAKER/COMPANY and BUSINESS ADDRESS | MAKER'S TRADE |
|---|---|---|---|---|
| R3/98<br>26 March 1946 | | P21/H/34<br>***#7457***<br> | **John Stott HALLEY** [1]<br>**Frank Unite HARRIS** [2] trading as<br>**R S HORNE**<br>9 Corporation Street<br>Manchester | Manufacturing jewellers |
| R2/5<br>25 October 1905<br>Sent by R S Horne | 4 Grenville Street<br>Moss Side<br>Manchester | P9/H/75<br>***#7458***<br> | **R S HORNE**<br>Parsonage Buildings<br>29 Blackfriars Street<br>Manchester | Working jewellers |
| R3/134<br>30 November 1950<br>Sent by R S Partington | Private address same as business | P21/P/40<br>***#7459***<br> | **Richard Scott PARTINGTON**<br>22a Sapling Road<br>Bolton<br>Lancashire (moved 16 June 1962)<br>1 Woodlands Road<br>Worsley<br>Nr Manchester | Student |
| R2/66<br>14 October 1908<br>Sent by C E Smart | 61 Mostyn Road<br>Handsworth<br>61 Mostyn Road<br>Handsworth<br>125 Newdock Road<br>Handsworth<br>Birmingham | P13/S/9<br>***#7460***<br> | **Richard SMART**<br>**Charles Edward SMART**<br>**Bertram Thomas SMART** trading as<br>**R SMART & SON**<br>105 Vyse Street<br>Birmingham | Ring makers |
| LPB/72<br>14 June 1881 | | P3/R*sic*/x1<br>***#7461***<br> | **Richard Samuel WILKINS**<br>55 Warwick Street<br>Leamington Spa<br>Warwickshire | Watchmaker and jeweller |
| R1/79<br>26 September 1894<br>Sent by Richard Stainsby<br>William Coupland | 54 Arundell Square<br>Barnsbury<br>Packington Street<br>Islington | P5/S/594<br>***#7462***<br> | **Richard STAINSBY**<br>**William COUPLAND** *<br>32 Willmington Square, Clerkenwell<br>London EC | Jewellers, silver purse lock and general mounters |
| R2/32<br>2 February 1907<br>Sent by Thomason and Haseler Brothers | Viewfield<br>Partick<br>Glasgow | P9/I*sic*/126<br>***#7463***<br> | **William SORLEY** trading as<br>**R & W SORLEY** *<br>93 St Vincent Street and<br>24b Benfield Street<br>Glasgow | Jewellers, watchmakers and silversmiths |
| R3/147<br>21 November 1953<br>Sent by R Taylor | 159 Withington Road<br>Whalley Range<br>Manchester 16 | P21/T/22,23<br>***#7464,5***<br> | **Ruth TAYLOR**<br>No business address entered | Student |
| SPB/3<br>13 May 1864 | | P3/T/x1<br>***#7466***<br> | **Richard TARLETON**<br>8 Ray Street<br>Liverpool | Watchcase maker |
| R1/32<br>30 July 1896<br>Sent by R Turner<br>Authority to<br>Wittenburg & Bateson | Ash Villa<br>Langton<br>Near Preston | P5/T/784<br>***#7467***<br> | **Richard TURNER**<br>29 Fishergate and<br>45 Church Street<br>Preston | Tobacconist, cigar merchant and fancy goods dealer |
| Missing register<br>*c.*1887 | | P5/T/108<br>***#7468***<br> | | |
| LPB/16<br>30 November 1880 | | P3/B/x1<br>***#7469***<br> | **Richard Thomas BOWMAN** *<br>78 Goswell Road<br>London | Jewellers |

| REGISTRATION DETAILS | MAKER'S PRIVATE ADDRESS and DETAILS | PLATE and MARK DETAILS | MAKER/COMPANY and BUSINESS ADDRESS | MAKER'S TRADE |
|---|---|---|---|---|
| LPB/68<br>21 October 1882 | | P3/B/x1<br>*#7470*  | **Richard Thomas BOWMAN** *<br>78 Goswell Road<br>London | Jeweller |
| R3/151<br>1 April 1954<br>Sent by R T Noonan | 25 Heyburn Road later<br>35 Canning Road<br>Liverpool | P21/N/8<br>*#7471*  | **Raymond Thornton NOONAN**<br>No business address entered | Student silversmith |
| R1/152<br>19 August 1901<br>Sent by George Frederick Westwood | Wyecliff Road [1]<br>Handsworth<br>Highfield [2]<br>Stafford | P9/R/34-37<br>*#7472-5*  | **Samuel John REYNOLDS** [1]<br>**George Frederick WESTWOOD** [2]<br>trading as **REYNOLDS & WESTWOOD**<br>10 Vyse Street<br>Birmingham | Silversmiths |
| PP1/189<br>PCR-1773 | | P1/30/x1<br>*#7476*  | **Ralph WAKEFIELD**<br>Dale Street<br>Liverpool | Watchcase maker |
| MR2/222<br>MR3/191<br>J3/390 | Spoon *c.*1687-90 | Pre-dates P1<br>*#7477*  | **Richard WYTHE**<br>Chester | Silversmith |
| GTD 1742-76 | | P1/17/x2<br>*#7478,9*  | **Ralph WALKER**<br>Liverpool | Silversmith |
| SPB/2<br>25 August 1870 | | P3/W/x7<br>*#7480-6*  | **R & R WRIGHT**<br>24 Tarleton Street<br>Liverpool | Watch manufacturers |
| R2/117<br>13 August 1910<br>Sent by Benson Brothers<br>Punch entered for Mr Williams own use | 50 Laurel Road<br>Liverpool<br>West Wood<br>Warren Drive<br>New Brighton<br>Millside<br>Higher Bebington | P13/W/79<br>*#7487*  | **Robert Owen WILLIAMS** (Partner)<br>**Thomas Townsend RUSSELL**<br>**Bernard Alfred RUSSELL**<br>trading as **Thos RUSSELL & SON** *<br>12 Church Street<br>Liverpool | Watch manufacturers |
| Missing register<br>*c.*1890<br>Similar mark entered BAO 10 October 1888<br>Similar mark entered BAO 28 May 1890 | | P5/R/268<br>*#7488*  | **RIGBY & WILSON**<br>17, 19 Geach Street<br>Birmingham or<br>**REYNOLDS & WESTWOOD**<br>44 Vyse Street<br>Birmingham | Spur makers<br>Jewellers |
| R1/52<br>19 August 1901<br>Two sizes | | P9/R/31-33,38,39<br>*#7489-93*  | **REYNOLDS & WESTWOOD**<br>44 Vyse Street<br>Birmingham | Jewellers |
| R1/169<br>2 June 1902<br>Sent by Henry Griffith & Sons | 57 North Main Street [1]<br>Wexford<br>36 Wicklow Street [2]<br>Dublin | P9/R/48<br>*#7494*  | **RICHARDS** [1] **&**<br>**WALSH** [2]<br>36 Wicklow Street<br>Dublin | Watchmakers and jewellers |
| SPB/6<br>7 June 1872 | | P3/W/x1<br>*#7495*  | **Richard WASHINGTON**<br>44 William Henry Street<br>Liverpool | Watch manufacturer |
| Not in SPB but see entry above | | P2/V*sic*/x3<br>*#7496-8*  | **R & R WRIGHT**<br>24 Tarleton Street<br>Liverpool | Watch manufacturers |

| REGISTRATION DETAILS | MAKER'S PRIVATE ADDRESS and DETAILS | PLATE and MARK DETAILS | MAKER/COMPANY and BUSINESS ADDRESS | MAKER'S TRADE |
|---|---|---|---|---|
| GTD 1742-76 | | P1/29/x2<br>***#7499,7500***<br> | **Ralph WALKER**<br>Liverpool | Silversmith |
| Missing register<br>*c.*1887<br>Mark without full stop entered BAO 23 June 1897 | | P5/W/80<br>***#7501***<br> | **Robert WADDINGTON**<br>The Terrace<br>Earlsdon<br>Coventry | Watch manufacturer |
| MR1/67<br>J3 1596-8 died<br>J3/418<br>MR1/378 also has Richard Warmingshaw 1577 to 1609 | Communion cup *c.*1620 at Cheadle | Pre-dates P1<br>***#7502***<br> | **Robert WELSHMAN**<br>Manchester | Silversmith |
| MR1/180-4<br>MR2/221<br>MR3/191<br>SIL/32/3,40/1,47<br>J1 1682-92<br>J3/389<br>GMSC/7,8 | Paten, tankard, spoons and jug *c.*1683<br>Free 1682/3 - died 1703 | Pre-dates P1<br>***#7503***<br> | **Ralph WALLEY**<br>Eastgate Street<br>Chester | Silversmith |
| Did not register with the new assay office in 1701 | Spoons *c.*1687-92 | Pre-dates P1<br>***#7504***<br> | | |
| LPB/62<br>20 January 1883 | | P3/H/x1<br>***#7505***<br> | **Reginald Walter HEWETT & CO**<br>103 Vyse Street<br>Birmingham | Jewellers |
| R2/225<br>12 December 1919<br>Sent by Regal Watch Case Co Ltd | 70 Wake Green Road [1]<br>Moseley<br>Birmingham | P15/R/23<br>***#7506***<br> | **THE REGAL WATCH CASE CO**<br>Walter F Smith [1] (Director)<br>44 Branston Street<br>Birmingham | Watchcase manufacturers |
| R3/28<br>22 April 1925<br>Sent by Benson Brothers | Connaught House<br>Ballards Lane<br>London N3 | P15/R/34,35<br>***#7507,8***<br> | **THE ROME WATCH CO**<br>Harold Auguste Neale<br>Raymond Keith Neale<br>87 Hatton Garden<br>London | Watch importers |
| R3/130<br>7 February 1950<br>Sent by Rolex Watch Co | | P21/R/9<br>***#7509***<br> | **ROLEX WATCH CO LTD** *<br>Sealed in the presence of:-<br>A M Wickhorn (Director)<br>E Reynolds (Secretary)<br>1 Green Street | Watch importers |
| 25 July 1952<br>Punch replaced by B H Britton Ltd<br>Punch returned to B H Britton Ltd | | P21/R/12<br>***#7510***<br> | Mayfair<br>London W1 | |
| R3/183<br>31 March 1962<br>Sent by R W Ellwood<br>Two sizes | Buena Vista Farm<br>Frisby-on-the-Wreake<br>Leicestershire | P21/E/24,25<br>***#7511,12***<br>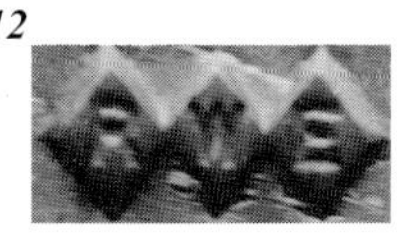 | **Robert William ELLWOOD**<br>No business address entered | Metalwork teacher |

| REGISTRATION DETAILS | MAKER'S PRIVATE ADDRESS and DETAILS | PLATE and MARK DETAILS | MAKER/COMPANY and BUSINESS ADDRESS | MAKER'S TRADE |
|---|---|---|---|---|
| R2/97<br>13 November 1909<br>Sent by W Neale & Sons | Monkfield<br>Old Southgate | P13/J/23<br>***#7513***<br> | **Robert William JAY** trading as<br>**JAYS** *<br>55 King Street<br>Brighton | Silversmiths |
| R2/67<br>20 October 1908<br>Sent by W Neale & Sons | | P13/J/3<br>***#7514***<br>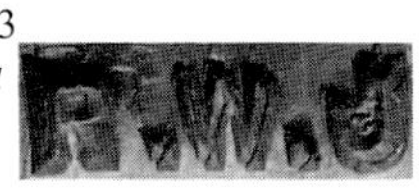 | as above | |
| R2/122<br>3 November 1910<br>Sent by Nathan & Hayes | | P13/J/41<br>***#7515***<br> | **Robert William JAY** trading as<br>**JAYS** *<br>55 Kings Road<br>Brighton and<br>366 Essex Road<br>London and<br>73 Charlotte Street<br>London | Jewellers and silversmiths |
| R3/51<br>7 February 1930<br>Sent by Roy William Patrick | Private address same as business | P15/P/223<br>***#7516***<br> | **Roy William PATRICK**<br>Melville<br>Greenbank Drive<br>Sefton Park<br>Liverpool | Civil engineer |
| R2/66<br>13 October 1908<br>Sent by William Neale & Sons | Viewfield House<br>Partick<br>89 Hyndland Road<br>Glasgow | P13/S/10<br>***#7517***<br> | **William SORLEY**<br>**William STEELE** trading as<br>**R & W SORLEY** *<br>93 St Vincent Street and<br>24 Renfield Street<br>Glasgow | Jewellers, silversmiths and watchmakers |
| R3/28<br>16 May 1925<br>Sent by Stokes & Ireland | Rockcliff<br>Bridge of Weir<br>Renfrewshire | P15/S/66<br>***#7518***<br> | **R & W SORLEY** *<br>107-109 West George Street<br>Glasgow | Jewellers and silversmiths |
| R3/46<br>14 May 1929<br>Sent by C Perry<br>Two sizes | | P15/S/86,87<br>***#7519,20***<br> | | |
| SPB/15 undated between June 1866 and December 1867<br>LPB mark shown | CWMP 1873-86 | Not on P3<br>***#7521***<br> | **Richard YARDLEY** *<br>132 Spon Street<br>Coventry | Gold and silver watchcase makers |
| SPB/4<br>25 September 1871 | | P3/Y/x3<br>***#7522-4***<br>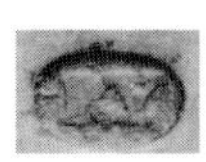 | | |
| SPB/19 undated<br>No name or address in SPB – just this incuse mark - *c.*1874 | | P3/Y/x3<br>***#7525-7***<br> | **YARDLEY & BUCKLAND** *<br>132 Spon Street<br>Coventry | |
| SPB/17 1868 only<br>Similar mark entered LAO 1 January 1868<br>Sent by Yardley & Buckland | H Stuart entered his own HS oval cameo mark just below this mark as Manager of Yardley & Buckland | P3/Y/x3<br>***#7528-30***<br> | **YARDLEY & BUCKLAND** *<br>H Stuart (Manager)<br>132 Spon Street<br>Coventry | |

| REGISTRATION DETAILS | MAKER'S PRIVATE ADDRESS and DETAILS | PLATE and MARK DETAILS | MAKER/COMPANY and BUSINESS ADDRESS | MAKER'S TRADE |
|---|---|---|---|---|
| R1/48<br>23 July 1897<br>Sent by J Hayward<br>A Revell & Co | 51 Mildmay Park [1]<br>London N<br>51 Pyrland Road [2]<br>London N | P5/A/859<br>*#7531*<br> | **Joseph ABRAHAMS** [1]<br>**Edward LYON** [2] trading as<br>**Samuel ABRAHAMS & SONS** *<br>36 Clerkenwell Road<br>London | Jewellers |
| R2/177<br>9 October 1913<br>Sent by self | Private address same as business | P13/A/39<br>*#7532*<br>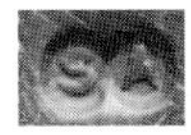 | **Solomon ABELMAN** *<br>58 Buxton Street<br>Vallance Road and<br>233 Kingsland Road (28 January 1915)<br>London | Gold chain and bracelet maker |
| MR1/180<br>LGM *c.*1699<br>J3/423 | Free 1701 | P1/11/x1<br>*#7533*<br>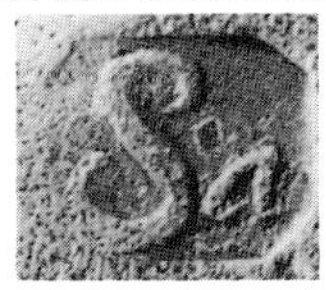<br>P1/11/x1<br>*#7534*<br> | **Robert SANFORD**<br>Shrewsbury | Silversmith |
| R3/34<br>undated - between October 1926 and November 1926<br>Sent by Stylic Watch Case Co | 423 City Road<br>Edgbaston<br>Birmingham | P15/S/76<br>*#7535*<br> | **George BOUVERAT** trading as<br>**SWISS AGENTS**<br>30 Frederick Street<br>Birmingham | Watchcase manufacturers and importers |
| R3/45<br>13 February 1929<br>Sent by James Mathey & Fils<br>Tramelan<br>Switzerland | 423 City Road [1]<br>Edgbaston<br>Birmingham<br>17 Yew Tree Road [2]<br>Edgbaston<br>Birmingham | P15/S/82, 83<br>*#7536,7*<br> | **George BOUVERAT & CO** trading as<br>**SWISS AGENCY**<br>George Bouverat[1]<br>Jean Bouverat[2]<br>30 Frederick Street<br>Birmingham | |
| LPB/14<br>21 November 1883<br>No mark in LPB<br>Sent by Coley Bros | 5th name on LPB/14 and 5th mark on P5/A | P5/A/x1<br>*#7538*<br> | **Samuel ABRAHAMS & SONS** *<br>136 Houndsditch<br>London | Jewellers |
| Missing register<br>*c.*1886 | | P5/A/5<br>*#7539*<br>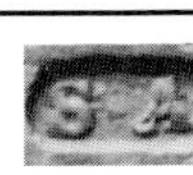 | | |
| Missing register<br>*c.*1887 | | P5/A/73<br>*#7540*<br> | | |
| R1/34<br>14 October 1896<br>Sent by T Cleaver<br>J Harris<br>E W Linnett | Private address same as business<br>R1 has #793½ (*sic*)<br>CWMP 1874-1901 | P5/A/792<br>*#7541*<br>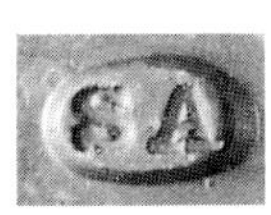 | **Samuel ALEXANDER** *<br>11 Percy Street<br>Coventry | Watch manufacturer |
| R2/21<br>21 July 1906<br>Sent by S Alexander | 11 Percy Street and<br>51 Waverley Road<br>Coventry | P9/A/78<br>*#7542*<br>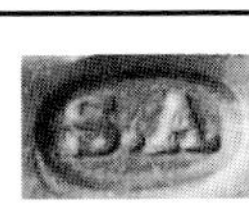 | | |
| R1/172<br>18 July 1902<br>Sent by W F Twine<br>Cancelled 18 Sept 03<br>*old punch lost* | 120 Victoria Road<br>Maida Vale<br>London W<br>9 Carlton Vale<br>London | P9/S/49<br>*#7543*<br> | **Borris SEGAL**<br>**George ARONSON** trading as<br>**SEGAL & ARONSON** *<br>16 Hatton Garden<br>London EC | Watch importers and wholesale jewellers |

| REGISTRATION DETAILS | MAKER'S PRIVATE ADDRESS and DETAILS | PLATE and MARK DETAILS | MAKER/COMPANY and BUSINESS ADDRESS | MAKER'S TRADE |
|---|---|---|---|---|
| R1/201<br>18 September 1903<br>Sent by J H Wynn | 7 Inglewood Road<br>West Hampstead | P9/S/66<br>*#7544*  | **Borris SEGAL**<br>**George ARONSON** trading as<br>**SEGAL & ARONSON** *<br>16 Hatton Garden<br>London EC | Watch importers and wholesale jewellers |
| R3/178<br>22 March 1961<br>Sent by S A Abrahams | 17 Greenhill Road<br>Allerton<br>Liverpool 18 | P21/A/30<br>*#7545*  | **Selwyn Arthur ABRAHAMS**<br>No business address entered | Student |
| SPB/13<br>17 November 1866 | | P3/S/x3<br>*#7546-8*  | **SCALES BROTHERS**<br>26 Finkle Street<br>Kendal, Cumberland | Watch and clock manufacturers and jewellers |
| R1/233<br>17 May 1905<br>Sent by Synyer & Beddoes Ltd | Hampton–in–Arden<br>151 Bristol Road<br>Bristol | P9/S/87<br>*#7549*  | **Harry SYNYER**<br>**Charles Joseph BEDDOES** trading as<br>**SYNYER & BEDDOES** *<br>32 Vyse Street<br>Birmingham | Manufacturing silversmiths |
| R3/67<br>10 July 1933<br>Sent by Synyer & Beddoes Ltd | Common seal of company affixed in presence of H Clifford Davis | P15/S/101<br>*#7550*  | **H Clifford DAVIS** trading as<br>**SYNYER & BEDDOES LTD** *<br>H Clifford Davis (Managing Director)<br>23 Warstone Lane<br>Birmingham 18 | Silversmiths |
| R2/169<br>12 March 1913<br>Sent by Stokes & Ireland | 61 High Street [1]<br>Cowes<br>Caring [2 & 3]<br>Northwood Park<br>Cowes | P13/S/42<br>*#7551* 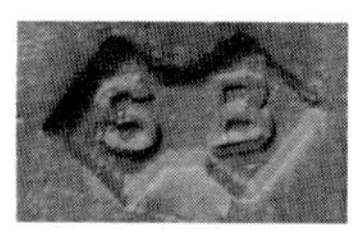 | **Herbert Simpson BENZIE** [1]<br>**Norman BENZIE** [2]<br>**Karl Theodore BENZIE** [3] trading as<br>**Simpson BENZIE** *<br>61 High Street<br>Cowes | Jewellers and silversmiths |
| PDB 1831 Medals<br>MR2/59<br>MR3/78<br>CMC/75 | *Chester Courant* of 22 April 1831 lists Bryars as a "Seller of fashionable London Jewellery and Foreign Fancy Goods, Musical Clocks and Watchmaker" | Not on P1<br>*#7552*  | **Samuel BRYARS**<br>Watch Manufactory<br>Eastgate Street Row (1831-4)<br>Chester | Silversmith and medallist |
| LPB/58<br>8 February 1883 | See associated pellet (·) mark below | P3/S/x1a<br>*#7553*  | **SMITH BROTHERS**<br>233 Icknield Street<br>Birmingham | Jewellers |
| Missing register<br>*c.*1887 | On square-S so may be S- Brothers | P5/S/100<br>*#7554*  | | |
| Missing register<br>*c.*1890 | On square-S so may be S- Brothers | P5/S/324<br>*#7555*  | | |
| LPB/58<br>8 February 1883 | See associated dot (.) mark above | P3/S/x1b<br>*#7556*  | | |
| Missing register<br>*c.*1886<br>Similar mark LAO<br>21 May 1891 | Square B suggests surname beginning with "B", but see similar mark above registered for Smith Brothers | P5/B/46<br>*#7557*  | **Samuel BEAUMONT** *<br>39 Croft Road<br>Coventry | Silver watchcase maker |
| Missing register<br>*c.*1889<br>Similar mark LAO<br>21 May 1891 | | P5/B/242<br>*#7558*  | | |
| Not in R1 as expected | | P5/aboveB/x1<br>*#7559*  | **Unidentified** | |

| REGISTRATION DETAILS | MAKER'S PRIVATE ADDRESS and DETAILS | PLATE and MARK DETAILS | MAKER/COMPANY and BUSINESS ADDRESS | MAKER'S TRADE |
|---|---|---|---|---|
| R2/124<br>29 November 1910<br>Sent by S Bateman<br>BAO 18.402 | 429 City Road<br>Birmingham | P13/B/93<br>***#7560***<br> | **Samuel BATEMAN**<br>38 Vyse Street<br>Birmingham | Diamond mounter and jeweller |
| R3/175<br>11 November 1960<br>Sent by S Barder & Co Ltd Two sizes | | P21/B/62<br>***#7561***<br> | **S BARDER & CO LTD**<br>101/102 Hatton Garden<br>London EC1 | Wholesale jewellers |
| R2/160<br>7 September 1912<br>Sent by Sutherland Brown & Co | The Lydiate<br>Heswall, Cheshire<br>5 Alresford Road<br>Aigburth<br>Dumsbin<br>Heswall, Cheshire | P13/B/132<br>***#7562***<br>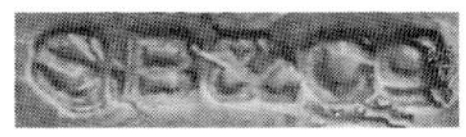 | **James SUTHERLAND**<br>**David Preston SUTHERLAND**<br>**Montague John BROWN** trading as<br>**SUTHERLAND BROWN & CO**<br>51 South John Street<br>Liverpool | Commission merchants |
| R1/9<br>28 March 1895<br>Sent by Saunders Brothers & Co | 203 Albert Road [1]<br>Aston<br>Blossomfield [2]<br>Clarence Road<br>King's Heath | P5/S/647<br>***#7563***<br> | **Walter James SAUNDERS** [1]<br>**John SAUNDERS** [2] trading as<br>**SAUNDERS BROTHERS & CO**<br>3, 4 Augusta Street<br>Birmingham | Jewellers |
| R2/210<br>24 January 1917<br>Sent by J W Cole | 1 Lansdown Road<br>Harrow<br>101 Forburgh Road<br>Stamford Hill<br>London N | P15/B/65<br>***#7564***<br>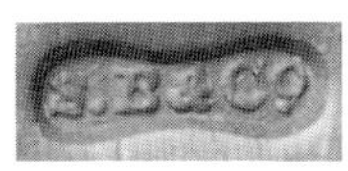 | **Samuel BARDER**<br>**Laurence MOSS**<br>101 and 102 Hatton Garden<br>London | Wholesale jewellers |
| R1/161<br>7 February 1902<br>Sent by Samuel B Landeck<br>cancelled<br>26 March 1907<br>Deceased | Private address same as business | P9/L/23<br>***#7565***<br> | **Samuel Boyce (Boaz) LANDECK** *<br>4 South Villas<br>Campden Square<br>London NW | Importer of foreign silver plate |
| R1/106<br>6 July 1899<br>Sent by W H Leatlick | 35 Duncam Street<br>Glasgow | P9/S/24<br>***#7566***<br> | **J H SPENCELAND** (Managing Director)<br>**SPENCELAND BROTHERS LTD**<br>23, 25 Main Street<br>Gorbels<br>Glasgow | Wholesale jewellers |
| R3/167<br>28 April 1959<br>Sent by A Stone (Director) | Avalon<br>251 Blackley New Road<br>Manchester 9 | P21/S/78-80<br>***#7567-9***<br> | **STONE BROTHERS (JEWELLERS) LTD**<br>107 Market Street<br>Manchester 1 | Manufacturing and wholesale jewellers |
| 6/7 May 1959 | | P21/S/81,82<br>***#7570,1***<br> | | |
| 16 May 1959 | | P21/S/83,84<br>***#7572,3***<br> | | |
| R1/227<br>21 February 1905<br>Sent by Smith & Bartlam | 34 Woodstock Road<br>Handsworth<br>133 Limewood Road<br>Birmingham | P9/S/84<br>***#7574***<br> | **Edward Ernest SMITH**<br>**William BARTLAM** trading as<br>**SMITH & BARTLAM** *<br>3½ Regent Parade, Caroline Street<br>Birmingham | Jewellers and silversmiths |
| R1/229<br>14 March 1905<br>Sent by Smith & Bartlam | Woodcock (*sic*) Road<br>Handsworth<br>(Ed: No Woodcock Road in Handsworth)<br>133 Limewood Road<br>Handsworth | P9/S/85<br>***#7575***<br>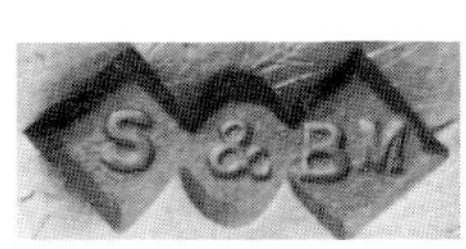 | | |

| REGISTRATION DETAILS | MAKER'S PRIVATE ADDRESS and DETAILS | PLATE and MARK DETAILS | MAKER/COMPANY and BUSINESS ADDRESS | MAKER'S TRADE |
|---|---|---|---|---|
| R1/179<br>28 October 1902<br>Sent by W H Ashford | Parkenham Road<br>Edgbaston<br>Bristol Road<br>Edgbaston<br>Bolehall<br>Tamworth | P9/S/53-55<br>***#7576-8***<br> | **George SYDENHAM**<br>**Robert SYDENHAM**<br>**William SYDENHAM** trading as<br>**SYDENHAM BROTHERS** *<br>Tenby Street<br>Birmingham | Wholesale jewellers |
| R1/191<br>30 April 1903<br>Sent by W Bradbury | | P9/S/62<br>***#7579***<br> | | |
| R2/117<br>19 August 1910<br>Sent by G H Johnstone & Co | 83 Stamore Road<br>Edgbaston<br>Birmingham | P13/S/56<br>***#7580***<br> | **SYDENHAM BROTHERS LTD** *<br>Tenby Street<br>Birmingham | Manufacturing jewellers merchants |
| R2/165<br>6 November 1912<br>Sent by Sydenham Brothers<br>W E Old | | P13/S/108,109<br>***#7581,2***<br> | **SYDENHAM BROTHERS** *<br>Ernest Old (Director)<br>Tenby Street North<br>Birmingham | Jewellers |
| R2/176<br>11 September 1913<br>Sent by George Freeman | | P15/S/1<br>***#7583***<br> | **SYDENHAM BROTHERS LTD** *<br>Tenby Street<br>Birmingham | Wholesale and manufacturing jewellers |
| Missing register<br>*c.*1892 | Both Sydenham Brothers of New Edmund Street (late Tenby Street), Birmingham, and Sheldon Brothers Jewellers of 9 Tenby Street, later Vyse Street, used several SBROS punches at BAO | P5/S/425a<br>***#7584***<br> | | |
| Missing register<br>*c.*1889 | | P5/S/252<br>***#7585***<br> | | |
| R1/111<br>14 September 1899<br>Sent by H H Smith | 206 Albert Road<br>Handsworth<br>206 Albert Road<br>Handsworth<br>23 Whately Road<br>Handsworth<br>Birmingham | P9/S/26<br>***#7586***<br> | **William George SMITH**<br>**Harry Hinde SMITH**<br>**Fred Hinde SMITH** trading as<br>**SMITH BROTHERS**<br>41 Frederick Street<br>Birmingham | Manufacturing jewellers |
| LPB/7<br>15 June 1878<br>Sent by J Rooker | | P3/T*sic*/x1<br>***#7587***<br> | **SYDENHAM BROTHERS** *<br>54 New Edmund Street<br>Birmingham | Manufacturing jewellers and factors |
| LPB/76<br>8 March 1880<br>Sent by Mayell Brothers | | P3/S/x1<br>***#7588***<br> | | |
| Missing register<br>*c.*1892 | | P5/S/425b<br>***#7589***<br> | See Sydenham Brothers above<br>Saunders Brothers & Co #7598 | |
| R1/168<br>6 May 1902<br>Sent by J Smith | 36 Sandon Road<br>Birmingham<br>38 Sandon Road<br>Birmingham | P9/S/47<br>***#7590***<br> | **Charles Thomas SHELDON**<br>**William Samuel SHELDON** trading as<br>**SHELDON BROTHERS** *<br>6 Vyse Street<br>Birmingham | Manufacturing jewellers |
| R2/198<br>31 July 1915<br>Sent by Geo A Smawley | 20 Osborne Road<br>Handsworth<br>41 Upper Grosvenor Road<br>Handsworth Wood<br>Birmingham | P15/S/22<br>***#7591***<br> | **George Alfred SMAWLEY**<br>**Gordon Ernest SMAWLEY** trading as<br>**SMAWLEY BROTHERS**<br>58 Tenby Street North<br>Birmingham | Jewellers |

| REGISTRATION DETAILS | MAKER'S PRIVATE ADDRESS and DETAILS | PLATE and MARK DETAILS | MAKER/COMPANY and BUSINESS ADDRESS | MAKER'S TRADE |
|---|---|---|---|---|
| R2/185<br>18 March 1914<br>Sent by Shoep (*sic*) Brothers<br>Per Benson Brothers<br>BAO 15.500 | 7 Wynnstay Grove<br>Fallowfield<br>Manchester | P15/S/10<br>***#7592***<br> | **Jacob SHOEPS**<br>**Henry SHOEPS** trading as<br>**SHOEP** (*sic*) **BROTHERS**<br>76 Shudehill<br>Manchester | Wholesale jewellers |
| Missing register<br>*c.*1886 | Mark not annotated but adjacent P5/S/36<br>See Saunders Brothers below | P5/S/x1<br>***#7593***<br>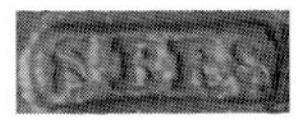 | **Unidentified** | |
| Missing register<br>*c.*1891 | | P5/S/386<br>***#7594***<br> | | |
| Missing register<br>*c.*1887 | | P5/S/112<br>***#7595***<br> | | |
| Missing register<br>*c.*1886 | | P5/S/37<br>***#7596***<br> | | |
| Missing register<br>*c.*1888 | | P5/S/136<br>***#7597***<br> | | |
| LPB/78 SP31/5<br>13 January 1885 | | P5/S/x1<br>***#7598***<br> | **SAUNDERS BROTHERS**<br>3 Augusta Street<br>Birmingham | Jewellers |
| LPB/16<br>6 August 1879<br>MR3/117 | | P3/F*sic*/x3<br>***#7599-7601***<br> | **S BLANCKENSEE & SON** *<br>8 Great Charles Street<br>Birmingham | Jewellers, watch manufacturers and importers |
| R3/103<br>25 September 1942<br>Sent by S R Williams & Co<br>105 Vyse Street<br>Birmingham | 43 Uphill Road<br>Mill Hill<br>London NW7 | P21/S/13<br>***#7602***<br> | **SWAN BROTHERS** *<br>Sydney Bartlett Swan (Proprietor)<br>70 Hatton Garden<br>London EC1 | Manufacturing jewellers |
| LPB/98<br>2 March 1885<br>No name, address or punch entered just SB&S<br>Sent by T E Sutton | | P5/B/x1<br>***#7603***<br> | **S BLANCKENSEE & SON** *<br>8 Great Charles Street<br>Birmingham | Jewellers, watch manufacturers and importers |
| Missing register<br>*c.*1886<br>Similar marks without full stop entered BAO 21 April 1879, etc | | P5/B/17<br>***#7604***<br> | | |
| Missing register<br>*c.*1886<br>Similar marks without full stop entered BAO 21 April 1879, etc | | P5/B/40<br>***#7605***<br> | | |
| R2/118<br>9 September 1910<br>Sent by S Blanckensee & Son | 26 Duchess Road [1]<br>Edgbaston | P13/B/86,87<br>***#7606,7***<br> | **S BLANCKENSEE & SON LTD** *<br>W Davies [1] (Secretary)<br>14, 15 Frederick Street and<br>72, 73 Great Hampton Street<br>Birmingham | Manufacturing jewellers and silversmiths |
| R2/168<br>25 February 1913<br>Sent by Blanckensee & Son<br>BAO 20.952 to 20.961 | | P15/S/37-41<br>***#7608-12***<br> | **S BLANCKENSEE & SON LTD** *<br>W Davies [1] (Secretary)<br>14 and 15 Frederick Street and<br>72 and 73 Great Hampton Street<br>Birmingham | |

| REGISTRATION DETAILS | MAKER'S PRIVATE ADDRESS and DETAILS | PLATE and MARK DETAILS | MAKER/COMPANY and BUSINESS ADDRESS | MAKER'S TRADE |
|---|---|---|---|---|
| R1/155<br>16 October 1901<br>Sent by S Blanckensee Ltd | Private address same as business | P9/B/80<br>***#7613***<br> | **S BLANCKENSEE LTD** *<br>14 and 15 Frederick Street<br>Birmingham | Manufacturing jewellers and silversmiths |
| R2/16<br>19 April 1906<br>Sent by S Blanckensee<br>A Hewlett | 22 Duchess Road<br>Edgbaston<br>Birmingham | P9/XYZ*sic*/172<br>***#7614***<br>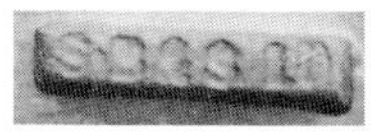 | **S BLANCKENSEE & SON LTD** *<br>14 and 15 Frederick Street<br>Birmingham and<br>35 Ely Place<br>London EC | Wholesale manufacturing jewellers and silversmiths |
| R3/109<br>10 May 1945<br>Sent by H Gilpin<br>89 Vyse Street<br>Birmingham 18 | | P21/S/18<br>***#7615***<br> | **S B SCHLESINGER & CO LTD**<br>Sealed in the presence of:-<br>B Schlesinger (Director)<br>A F Newton (Secretary)<br>Colonial Buildings<br>59-61 Hatton Garden<br>London EC1 | Manufacturing jewellers |
| R2/118<br>9 September 1910<br>Sent by S Blanckensee & Sons<br>P13/B/87 entered in R2 BAO 17.543 | 26 Duchess Road [1]<br>Edgbaston | P13/B/85<br>***#7616***<br> | **S BLANCKENSEE & SON LTD** *<br>W Davies (Secretary) [1]<br>14 and 15 Frederick Street and<br>72 and 73 Great Hampton Street<br>Birmingham | Manufacturing jewellers and silversmiths |
| R2/124<br>29 November 1910<br>Sent by Smith & Ewen for them<br>BAO 18.297,18.298 18.299, 18.301 | | P13/B/104<br>***#7617***<br> | | |
| Missing register<br>*c.*1890<br>Similar marks without raised D in LD entered BAO<br>31 January 1890 | | P5/B/327<br>***#7618***<br>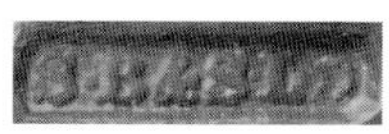 | **S BLANCKENSEE LTD** *<br>8 Great Charles Street<br>Birmingham | |
| R1/198<br>23 July 1903<br>Sent by S Blanckensee Ltd | 10 Queen's Gardens<br>Hyde Park<br>London W | P9/B/109<br>***#7619***<br> | **S BLANCKENSEE & SON LTD** *<br>Julius Blanckensee (Managing Director)<br>14 Frederick Street<br>Birmingham | Manufacturing jewellers |
| R1/203<br>10 October 1903<br>Sent by S Blanckensee Ltd | Secretary's address<br>26 Duchess Road<br>Birmingham | P9/B/112<br>***#7620***<br> | **S BLANCKENSEE & SON LTD** *<br>W Davies (Secretary)<br>14/15 Frederick Street<br>Birmingham | Wholesale manufacturing jewellers |
| R1/217<br>1 July 1904<br>Sent by S Blanckensee Ltd | Queens Hotel<br>Birmingham | P9/XYZ*sic*/123<br>***#7621***<br> | **S BLANCKENSEE & SON LTD** *<br>15 Frederick Street<br>Birmingham and<br>35 Ely Place<br>London | Manufacturing jewellers |
| R2/56<br>14 March 1908<br>Sent by S Blanckensee & Son<br>Two sizes | 26 Duchess Road<br>Edgbaston<br>Birmingham | P13/B/12-17<br>***#7622-7***<br> | **S BLANCKENSEE & SON LTD** *<br>W Davies (Secretary)<br>73 Great Hampton Street<br>Birmingham<br>14 and 15 Frederick Street<br>Birmingham<br>35 Ely Place<br>Holborn<br>London | Goldsmiths and silversmiths |

| REGISTRATION DETAILS | MAKER'S PRIVATE ADDRESS and DETAILS | PLATE and MARK DETAILS | MAKER/COMPANY and BUSINESS ADDRESS | MAKER'S TRADE |
|---|---|---|---|---|
| R2/124<br>29 November 1910<br>Sent by Thomas Mitchell for<br>S Blanckensee & Son<br>BAO18.297-18.299<br>18.301<br>Three sizes | 26 Duchess Road [1]<br>Edgbaston | P13/B/94-102<br>***#7628-36***<br> | **S BLANCKENSEE & SON LTD** *<br>Walter Davies [1] (Secretary)<br>14/15 Frederick Street and<br>72/73 Great Hampton Street<br>Birmingham | Manufacturing jewellers and silversmiths |
| R2/168<br>25 February 1913<br>Sent by<br>S Blanckensee & Son<br>BAO 20.952- 20.961 | | P15/S/32-36<br>***#7637-41***<br>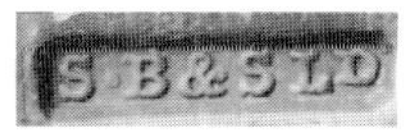 | | |
| R3/109<br>10 May 1945<br>Sent by H Griffin<br>89 Vyse Street<br>Birmingham 18 | | P21/S/17<br>***#7642***<br> | **S B SCHLESINGER & CO LTD** *<br>Sealed in the presence of:-<br>B Schlesinger (Director)<br>A F Newton (Secretary)<br>Colonial Buildings<br>59-61 Hatton Garden<br>London EC1 | Manufacturing jewellers |
| R2/57<br>24 March 1908<br>Sent by S Blanckensee & Son<br>No plate or mark number in R2 as expected. Next entry in R2 is P13/B/19 | 26 Duchess Road<br>Edgbaston<br>Birmingham | P13/B/18?<br>***#7643***<br> | **S BLANCKENSEE & SON LTD** *<br>14/15 Frederick Street<br>Birmingham and<br>73 Great Hampton Street<br>Birmingham and<br>35 Ely Place<br>Holborn<br>London | Goldsmiths and silversmiths |
| R2/212<br>24 April 1917<br>Sent by S Blanckensee & Son | 26 Duchess Road [1]<br>Edgbaston<br>Birmingham | P15/S/68–70<br>***#7644-6***<br>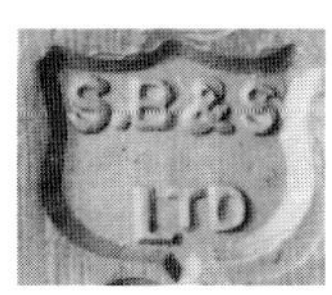 | **S BLANCKENSEE & SON LTD** *<br>Walter Davies [1] (Secretary)<br>14/15 Frederick Street and<br>72/73 Great Hampton Street<br>Birmingham and<br>Institute Works<br>Howard Street<br>Sheffield and<br>22 Hatton Garden<br>London | Manufacturing silversmiths |
| R3/37<br>22 June 1927<br>Sent by selves | | P15/B/187,188<br>***#7647,8***<br> | **S BLANCKENSEE & SON LTD** *<br>W Davies (Secretary)<br>14-16 Frederick Street and<br>72-73 Great Hampton Street<br>Birmingham | Jewellers and silversmiths |
| R3/41<br>9 July 1928<br>Sent by selves | 26 Duchess Road [1]<br>Edgbaston<br>Birmingham | P15/B/190-195<br>***#7649-54***<br>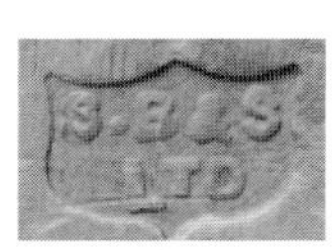 | **S BLANCKENSEE & SON LTD** *<br>Walter Davies [1] (Secretary)<br>72/73 Great Hampton Street and<br>14/15 Frederick Street and<br>19-35 Regent Street<br>Birmingham | Silversmiths and manufacturers |
| PDB 1838<br>MR3/79 | Medals 1838 | Not on P1<br>*# 7655* **S C?** | **Samuel CLOSE**<br>Liverpool | Silversmith |

| REGISTRATION DETAILS | MAKER'S PRIVATE ADDRESS and DETAILS | PLATE and MARK DETAILS | MAKER/COMPANY and BUSINESS ADDRESS | MAKER'S TRADE |
|---|---|---|---|---|
| R2/25<br>25 September 1906<br>Sent by S Cheshelsky | Private address same as business | P9/D*sic*/236<br>***#7656***<br> | **Samuel CHESHELSKY**<br>39 Brownlow Hill<br>Liverpool | Jeweller |
| R3/93<br>7 March 1939<br>Sent by S Crooke | Private address same as business | P21/C/12<br>***#7657***<br><br> | **Stanley CROOKE**<br>155 Grove Street<br>Liverpool | Silverwork and jewellery |
| R2/173<br>11 June 1913<br>Sent by<br>W H Carrington & Co | Lapwing Lodge<br>Didsbury | P15/C/30<br>***#7658***<br><br> | **Squire Sydney CARRINGTON**<br>**William Arthur CARRINGTON**<br>Style of firm<br>**William Henry CARRINGTON & CO**<br>34 Thomas Street<br>Manchester | Tobacconists and fancy goods dealers |
| Not in R3 as expected<br>*c.* April 1929 to April 1921 | | P15/C/94<br>***#7659***<br> | | |
| R3/79<br>7 October 1935<br>Sent by Shipton & Co Ltd | | P15/S/104<br>***#7660***<br>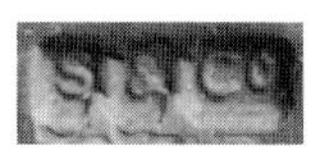 | **SHIPTON & CO LTD**<br>Common seal of company affixed in the presence of:-<br>A G Shipton (Director)<br>G Chaplin (Secretary)<br>29-31 Spencer Street (Registered Office)<br>Birmingham 18 | Jewellers |
| 15 July 1937 | | P21/S/3<br>***#7661***<br> | | |
| Between May 1945 and February 1946 | | P21/S/19<br>***#7662***<br><br> | | |
| 3 December 1953 | | P21/S/55,56<br>***#7663,4***<br> | | |
| R2/191<br>9 January 1915<br>Sent by Lawson, Ward & Gamage<br>Head Office<br>53 Berners Street<br>London | | P15/S/12,13<br>***#7665,6***<br> | **SANDERS & CO LTD**<br>William Wetherell (Director)<br>53 Berners Street<br>London W | Goldsmiths |
| R2/168<br>20 February 1913<br>Sent by Ahronsberg Brothers | Portland Road and<br>Clarendon Road<br>Edgbaston<br>Birmingham | P13/S/110<br>***#7667***<br> | **Albert AHRONSBERG**<br>**Judas** (*sic*) **AHRONSBERG**<br>**Lionel AHRONSBERG** trading as<br>**SYDNEY & CO** *<br>Alfred Chambers (Manager)<br>Powell Street<br>Birmingham<br>Century Buildings<br>Summer Hill Road<br>Birmingham | Manufacturing silversmiths |
| R2/23<br>21 August 1906<br>Sent by Ahronsberg Brothers | 46 Portland Road<br>Edgbaston<br>Birmingham | P9/S/106<br>***#7668***<br><br> | **Judah AHRONSBERG**<br>**Albert AHRONSBERG**<br>**Lionel AHRONSBERG** trading as<br>**AHRONSBERG & CO** *<br>Century Buildings<br>Summerhill Road<br>Birmingham | Wholesale jewellers |

| REGISTRATION DETAILS | MAKER'S PRIVATE ADDRESS and DETAILS | PLATE and MARK DETAILS | MAKER/COMPANY and BUSINESS ADDRESS | MAKER'S TRADE |
|---|---|---|---|---|
| R1/179<br>12 November 1902<br>Sent by Albert Ahronsberg for Sydney Brothers | 46 Portland Road<br>Birmingham | P9/S/56<br>***#7669***<br> | **Judah AHRONSBERG**<br>**Albert AHRONSBERG**<br>**Lionel AHRONSBERG** trading as<br>**SYDNEY & CO** *<br>24/25 Powell Street<br>Birmingham | Merchants and manufacturers |
| R1/196<br>27 June 1903<br>Sent by selves<br>L & A Ahronsberg | 46 Portland Road<br>Edgbaston<br>23 Clarendon Road<br>Edgbaston<br>Birmingham | P9/S/65<br>***#7670***<br> | | Manufacturers and importers |
| R2/29<br>27 November 1906<br>Sent by J & R Griffin<br>Three sizes | 23 Clarendon Road<br>Edgbaston, Birmingham<br>46 Portland Road<br>Edgbaston<br>46 Portland Road<br>Edgbaston | P9/S/111-113<br>***#7671-3***<br> | **Judah AHRONSBERG**<br>**Albert AHRONSBERG**<br>**Lionel AHRONSBERG** trading as<br>**SYDNEY & CO** *<br>Summerhill Road<br>Birmingham | Wholesale jewellers |
| R2/149<br>13 December 1911<br>Sent by Ahronsberg Brothers<br>Three sizes | Portland Road<br>Edgbaston<br>Birmingham | P13/S/82-84<br>***#7674-6***<br> | **Judah AHRONSBERG**<br>**Albert AHRONSBERG**<br>**Sydney AHRONSBERG** trading as<br>**AHRONSBERG BROTHERS** * and<br>**SYDNEY & CO** *<br>Century Buildings<br>Summerhill Road<br>Birmingham | Manufacturing silversmiths |
| Missing register<br>*c.*1891<br>Similar mark entered CAO 12 November 1902 | | P5/S/322<br>***#7677***<br> | **SYDNEY & CO** *<br>(Partners Judah, Albert and Lionel Ahronsberg)<br>24, 25 Powell Street<br>Birmingham | Merchants and manufacturers |
| R1/227<br>18 February 1905<br>Sent by C Horner | 291 Hagley Road<br>Birmingham | P9/S/83<br>***#7678***<br> | **Siegfried Emil STEINHART**<br>trading as **STEINHART & CO** *<br>14 Newhall Street<br>Birmingham | Export merchants |
| R1/103<br>9 June 1899<br>Sent by Steinhart & Co | | P9/S/21-23<br>***#7679-81***<br> | | |
| R1/129<br>30 June 1900<br>Sent by S E Steinhart<br>Two sizes | | P9/S/34,35<br>***#7682,3***<br> | | |
| R2/176<br>1 October 1913<br>Sent by S Ward & Son | 53 Bermos? Street [1]<br>London | P13/S/113<br>***#7684***<br> | **SANDERS & CO LTD**<br>H Hussey [1] (Secretary)<br>458, 460 Brixton Road<br>London SW | Jewellers |
| R2/71<br>23 January 1909<br>Sent by Selfridge & Co Ltd<br>(H Gordon Selfridge)<br><br>Four sizes | 17 Arlington Street<br>London SW<br><br>Registered Offices<br>4 London Wall Bridge<br>Blomfield Street<br>London EC | P13/S/13-26<br>***#7685-98***<br> | **SELFRIDGE & CO** *<br>H Gordon Selfridge (Director)<br>B F Popham (Director)<br>G W Steines (Director)<br>H Musker (Director)<br>G F Assinder (Director)<br>398–422 Oxford Street<br>33–45 Somerset Street<br>40–52 Duke Street<br>London W | Wholesale and retail merchants |

| REGISTRATION DETAILS | MAKER'S PRIVATE ADDRESS and DETAILS | PLATE and MARK DETAILS | MAKER/COMPANY and BUSINESS ADDRESS | MAKER'S TRADE |
|---|---|---|---|---|
| R2/160<br>3 September 1912<br>Sent by W Neale & Son Ltd | 17 Arlington Street<br>London W | P13/S/89<br>*#7699*  | **SELFRIDGE & CO LTD** *<br>Harry Gordon Selfridge (Director)<br>Oxford Street<br>London W | Merchants |
| LPB/24 undated between 11 and 17 October 1879<br>Entry lacks name or address - before SD&S | See SD&S #7725-30 | P3/D/x3<br>***#7700-2***  | **Samuel DICKINSON & SON**<br>1 Rathbone Street<br>Liverpool | Watch manufacturers |
| Missing register<br>*c.*1889 | | P5/D/251a-d<br>***#7703-6***  | | |
| R3/35<br>24 February 1927<br>Sent by Smith, Ewen & Stylic Ltd | 8 Ferncroft Avenue<br>Hampstead<br>London | P15/D/76<br>***#7707***  | **Sylvain DREYFUS**<br>**J DREYFUS** trading as<br>**M DREYFUS**<br>Moorgate Station Chambers<br>Moorfield Street<br>London EC2 | Watch manufacturers |
| R3/66<br>6 April 1933<br>Sent by B H Britton & Sons<br>35 Hockley Hill<br>Birmingham | 8 Ferncroft Avenue [1 2]<br>Hampstead<br>London NW3 | P15/D/85<br>***#7708***  | **Moise DREYFUS** proprietors<br>George Dreyfus [1]<br>Sylvain Dreyfus [2]<br>Moorgate Station Chambers<br>Moorfield<br>London EC2 | |
| R3/107<br>9 November 1944<br>Sent by Steele & Dolphin | 7a St Augustines Road [1]<br>Birmingham<br>305 Tiverton Road [2]<br>Selly Oak<br>Birmingham | P21/D/10-12<br>***#7709-11***  | **STEELE & DOLPHIN**<br>Elliot Steele [1]<br>Benjamin Dolphin [2]<br>119 Vyse Street<br>Birmingham 18 | Manufacturing jewellers |
| R3/110<br>18 October 1945<br>Sent by Steele & Dolphin<br>Re-entry of marks P21/D/10-12 for Limited Co | | No new marks<br>***#7712*** | **STEELE & DOLPHIN**<br>Sealed in the presence of:-<br>C Hames (Director)<br>E Steele (Director and Secretary)<br>119 Vyse Street<br>Birmingham 18 | |
| LPB/84<br>30 November 1882<br>Sent by J Fleckner | | P3/D/x3<br>***#7713-5***  | **Stewart DAWSON & CO** *<br>2 Randolph Place<br>Liverpool | Watch manufacturers |
| Missing register<br>*c.*1891<br>Similar mark entered BAO 17 October 1881 | | P5/D/338<br>***#7716***  | | |
| R1/35<br>23 October 1896<br>Sent by T P Hewitt Dennison & Wigley | 91 Ashley Gardens<br>Victoria Street<br>London | P5/*Osic*/800<br>***#7717***  | **David Stewart DAWSON**<br>James MacWilliam (Acting Manager)<br>trading as **Stewart DAWSON & CO** *<br>96 Newgate Street<br>London EC | |
| R1/157<br>6 December 1901<br>Sent by T P Hewitt | 19 Torrington Square<br>London WC | P9/D/27<br>***#7718***  | **Stewart DAWSON & CO** *<br>William Makins<br>20 Hatton Garden<br>London EC | Watch manufacturers and jewellers |

| REGISTRATION DETAILS | MAKER'S PRIVATE ADDRESS and DETAILS | PLATE and MARK DETAILS | MAKER/COMPANY and BUSINESS ADDRESS | MAKER'S TRADE |
|---|---|---|---|---|
| R3/27<br>9 April 1925<br>Sent by S D Levy | 322 Cheetham Hill Road<br>Manchester | P15/L/32<br>***#7719***<br> | **Samuel David LEVY**<br>**Sidney LEVY**<br>31 and 33 Withy Grove<br>Manchester | Manufacturing jewellers |
| R2/92<br>14 September 1909<br>Sent by W Neale & Sons<br>Three sizes | 12 Hyde Park Place [1]<br>London W | P13/D/21-25<br>***#7720-4***<br>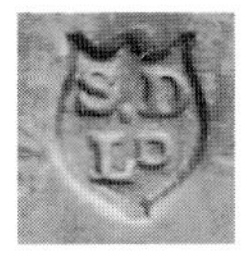 | **Stewart DAWSON & CO LTD** *<br>Percy Stewart Dawson [1]<br>19 and 21 Hatton Garden and<br>73 and 79 Regent Street<br>London | Goldsmiths, silversmiths and diamond merchants |
| LPB/68<br>15 December 1882<br>Sent by E Barrett | 54 Hockley Hill<br>Birmingham | P3/D/x1<br>***#7725***<br> | **Samuel DICKINSON & SON**<br>125 Duke Street<br>Liverpool | Watch manufacturers |
| Missing register<br>*c.*1886 | | P5/D/64<br>***#7726***<br>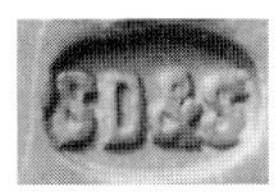 | | |
| LPB/24<br>17 October 1879<br>Sent by Samuel & Rogers, Liverpool<br>LPB mark shown | | Not on P3<br>***#7727***<br> | **Samuel DICKINSON & SON**<br>1 Rathbone Street<br>Liverpool | |
| LPB/24<br>10 November 1879<br>Sent by W Sexton<br>Coventry | | P3/D/x3<br>***#7728-30***<br> | **Samuel DICKINSON & SON**<br>125 Duke Street<br>Liverpool | |
| R1/217<br>12 July 1904<br>Sent by H V Pithey & Co per<br>W J Myatt & Co<br>Two sizes | 39 Regent Street<br>London | P9/S/75,76<br>***#7731,2***<br> | **SWAN & EDGAR LTD**<br>Charles John Vollhardt (Secretary)<br>39 Regent Street near Piccadilly<br>London | General drapery and fancy goods |
| R1/230<br>28 March 1905<br>Sent by J & R Griffin | 19 St Nicholas Road<br>W Tooting<br>London SW | P9/S/86<br>***#7733***<br> | | Linen drapers |
| R2/217<br>10 January 1919<br>Sent by Smith & Ewen (Aeroparts) Ltd<br>Two sizes | 70 Wake Green Road<br>Moseley<br>Birmingham | P15/S/37,38<br>***#7734,5***<br>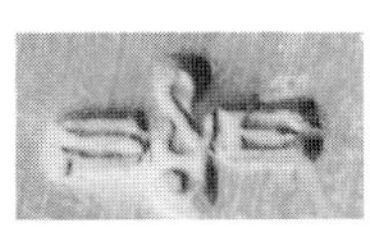 | **SMITH & EWEN (AEROPARTS) LTD**<br>Walter F Smith (Director)<br>32–44 Branston Street and<br>53 Tennant Street<br>Birmingham | Watchcase manufacturers |
| R2/84<br>9 June 1909<br>Sent by Smith & Ewen | The Birches<br>Hall Green<br>Birmingham | P13/S/35,36<br>***#7736,7***<br> | **Thomas SMITH** trading as<br>**SMITH & EWEN**<br>42 Frederick Street<br>Birmingham | Gold and silver bracelets, brooches and pendants |
| R3/35<br>16 November 1926<br>Sent by Smith, Ewen & Stylic Ltd<br>Two sizes | | P15/E/77-79<br>***#7738-40***<br> | **SMITH, EWEN & STYLIC LTD**<br>42 Frederick Street<br>Birmingham | Watch manufacturers |
| R3/95<br>15 November 1939<br>Sent by S E Cooke | 50 Marlborough Road<br>Castle Bromwich | P21/C/13<br>***#7741***<br> | **Stanley Ernest COOKE**<br>4 Northampton Street<br>Birmingham | Jeweller |

| REGISTRATION DETAILS | MAKER'S PRIVATE ADDRESS and DETAILS | PLATE and MARK DETAILS | MAKER/COMPANY and BUSINESS ADDRESS | MAKER'S TRADE |
|---|---|---|---|---|
| R3/95<br>12 June 1941 | 50 Marlborough Road<br>Castle Bromwich | P21/C/16<br>***#7742***<br> | **S E COOKE (BIRMINGHAM) LTD**<br>from 1 October 1960<br>191 Warstone Lane<br>Birmingham | Jewellers |
| R3/157<br>25 April 1956<br>Sent by W P Heaven | 28 Fosseway<br>Lichfield<br>Staffordshire | No new marks<br>***#7743*** | **William Peter HEAVEN** trading as<br>**S E COOKE**<br>191 Warstone Lane<br>Birmingham | Manufacturing jewellers |
| R1/87<br>23 December 1898<br>Sent by W Walker | 26 Adamson Road<br>South Hampstead<br>London<br>NB: Culme has Jellinek | P9/J/10<br>***#7744***<br> | **Sigmund Edmund JELLINECK** *<br>5 Lauderdale Buildings<br>Aldersgate Street<br>London EC | Importer and manufacturer |
| R1/222<br>15 November 1904<br>Sent by E Wettenberg | Rookwood<br>Brooklands<br>Ashelstone<br>Didsbury | P9/E/15<br>***#7745***<br> | **Samuel H EVANS**<br>**Thomas H EVANS**<br>24 Old Millgate<br>Manchester | Tobacco merchants |
| R3/146<br>9 October 1953<br>Sent by S Fildes<br>Two sizes | 6 Kingsmere Avenue<br>Manchester 19 | P21/F/25,26<br>***#7746,7***<br> | **Stella FILDES**<br>No business address entered | Student |
| CWMP 1874-83<br>PP3/83<br>Not in SPB or LPB so struck 1860-63<br>Similar mark entered LAO 25 April 1862 | See also related JN #5172 and N&F marks #6162,3 | P3/F/x3<br>***#7748-50***<br>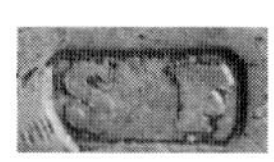 | **Samuel FREEMAN** *<br>5 Trafalgar Street (1862)<br>16 Hertford Terrace (1874-83)<br>Coventry | Watchcase maker |
| R3/35 undated – between October and November 1926<br>Sent by W Griffiths & Sons Ltd | The Crescent<br>Galway | P15/F/29<br>***#7751***<br> | **Stephan FALLER**<br>Williamsgate Street<br>Galway | Jeweller |
| Missing register<br>*c.*1886<br>Similar mark entered LAO 9 September 1886 and 23 July 1889 | Seen on thimbles 1889 and 1890 | P5/F/20<br>***#7752***<br> | **Samuel FOSKETT** *<br>32 Great Sutton Street<br>Clerkenwell<br>London EC | Thimble maker |
| Not in R1 as expected<br>*c.*1898 | | P9/F/1<br>***#7753***<br> | | |
| R1/134<br>20 October 1900<br>Sent by S Farren<br>Lancashire Watch Company | 19 Station Row<br>Prescot | P9/F/10<br>***#7754***<br> | **Stephen FARREN**<br>19 Station Row<br>Prescot | Watchmaker |
| R1/158<br>20 December 1901<br>Sent by S Farren - provisional Two sizes | | P9/F/13-15<br>***#7755-7***<br> | **Stephen FARREN**<br>Lancashire Watch Company<br>(Prescot, Lancs) | |
| R2/222<br>15 August 1919<br>Sent by A Pickering Co | 48 Sandford Road<br>Bradford | P15/G/37<br>***#7758***<br> | **Samuel GERSHAM**<br>7 Woodbine Street<br>Birkenhead Road<br>Bradford, Yorkshire | Umbrella and walking stick mounter |
| SPB/14<br>2 June 1874<br>Sent by H Green | | P3/G/x2<br>***#7759,60***<br> | **Samuel GREENHOUGH**<br>45 Newport Street<br>Bolton<br>Lancashire | Goldsmith and silversmith |

| REGISTRATION DETAILS | MAKER'S PRIVATE ADDRESS and DETAILS | PLATE and MARK DETAILS | MAKER/COMPANY and BUSINESS ADDRESS | MAKER'S TRADE |
|---|---|---|---|---|
| PP1/189<br>GTD1746<br>Similar mark entered LAO 15 August 1718 | Buried 1746 PMR | P1/16/x1<br>***#7761***<br> | **Solomon GIBBS** (G)<br>"at ye Bakers in Phillip Lane near Addle Street"<br>London (later in Liverpool) or | Watchcase maker |
| | Probate in 1756 PMR | | **Samuel GERRARD**<br>Liverpool | Watchcase maker |
| R1/171<br>18 June 1902<br>Sent by Benson Brothers | Private address same as business | P9/G/35<br>***#7762***<br> | **S GLASS**<br>3 Elizabeth Street<br>Cheetham<br>Manchester | Jeweller |
| R1/209<br>3 March 1904<br>Sent by J H T Green | 215 Newhall Street<br>Birmingham | P9/S/74<br>***#7763***<br> | **John Hugh Thomas GREEN** trading as<br>**SHARPE & GREEN**<br>215 Newhall Street and<br>5 Vittoria Street<br>Birmingham | Manufacturing jewellers |
| LPB/36<br>13 December 1884<br>No mark in LPB<br>SP32/4 | | P5/G/x1<br>***#7764***<br> | **Samuel GARSIDE**<br>12½ St Paul's Square<br>Birmingham | Silver chain maker |
| SPB/15 undated between 20 June 1866 and 4 December 1867<br>Sent by Samuel & Rogers | | P3/G/x3<br>***#7765-7***<br> | **Sampson GOLDSTONE**<br>2 Orton? Place<br>Stock Street, Cheetham (undated)<br>Manchester | Watch manufacturer |
| R2/190<br>6 October 1914<br>Sent by H Griffith & Sons | 68 Panmire Road [1]<br>Sheffield | P15/G/11<br>***#7768***<br> | **THE SHEFFIELD GOLDSMITHS CO**<br>W Griffiths [1] (Director)<br>11 Fargate<br>Sheffield | Jewellers and goldsmiths |
| R3/85<br>? January 1937<br>Sent by Roberts & Belk Ltd<br>Furnival Works<br>Sheffield | | P21/S/2<br>***#7769***<br> | **THE SUSSEX GOLDSMITHS & SILVERSMITHS CO LTD** *<br>Sealed by<br>W D Popley (Director and Secretary)<br>C P Flowers (Director)<br>4 Palace Place (Registered Office)<br>Brighton and<br>13 Pavilion Buildings<br>Castle Square<br>Brighton | Goldsmiths and silversmiths |
| R1/72<br>17 August 1898<br>Sent by S & G Glass | 3 Elizabeth Street<br>6 Elizabeth Street<br>Manchester | P9/G/2a<br>***#7770***<br> | **S G GLASS** trading as<br>**S & G GLASS**<br>Cathedral Street<br>Manchester | Jewellers |
| | | P9/G/2b<br>***#7771***<br> | | |
| R1/72<br>17 August 1898<br>Curiously, no name was entered, but the clerk entered a BB shield mark as used by Benson Brothers. | | P9/G/2c<br>***#7772***<br>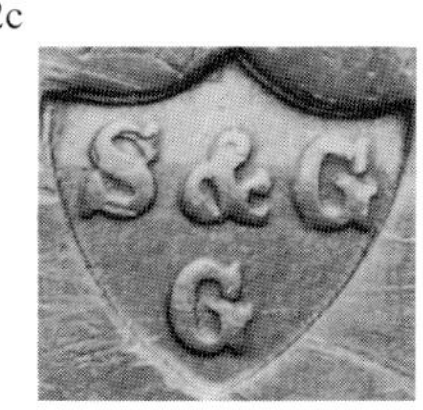 | **S & G GLASS**<br>Cathedral Street<br>Manchester | |

| REGISTRATION DETAILS | MAKER'S PRIVATE ADDRESS and DETAILS | PLATE and MARK DETAILS | MAKER/COMPANY and BUSINESS ADDRESS | MAKER'S TRADE |
|---|---|---|---|---|
| R1/23<br>7 March 1896<br>Sent by A H Tongue | 41 Clerkenwell Road<br>London EC<br>Fancy goods department turned over to Imperial Tobacco Co of 58 Holborn Viaduct, 1 July 1904 | P5/O*sic*/735<br>***#7773***<br> | **SALMON (Barnett) & GLUCKSTEIN** *<br>41 Clerkenwell Road<br>London EC | Tobacconists |
| R1/9<br>9 April 1895<br>Sent by George & Samuel Greenough | 45 Newport Street<br>82 Bradford Street<br>Haulgh<br>Bolton | P5/G/649<br>***#7774***<br> | **George GREENOUGH**<br>**Samuel GREENOUGH** trading as<br>**Samuel GREENOUGH & SONS**<br>45 Newport Street<br>Bolton | Watch manufacturers, jewellers and silversmiths |
| R2/87<br>7 July 1909<br>Sent by Sam Johnson Howes | Livingstone Road<br>King's Heath<br>Birmingham | P13/H/39<br>***#7775***<br> | **Sam Johnson HOWES**<br>41 Frederick Street<br>Birmingham | Manufacturing jeweller |
| R3/70<br>18 April 1934<br>Sent by selves | Westdean [1]<br>Blackroot Road<br>Sutton Coldfield<br>Cleveland [2]<br>Cremorne Road<br>Four Oaks, Warwickshire | P15/I*sic*/113-120<br>***#7776-83***<br> | **Rose HOPE** [1]<br>**Samuel Henry HOPE** [2] trading as<br>**Samuel HOPE** *<br>126 Vyse Street<br>Birmingham | Manufacturing jewellers |
| LPB/7<br>21 June 1878<br>Mark not in LPB | | P3/H/x1<br>***#7784***<br> | **Samuel HOPE**<br>126 Vyse Street<br>Birmingham | Wedding ring manufacturer |
| LPB/38<br>25 November 1880 | | P3/H/x1<br>***#7785***<br> | **Samuel HOLDER**<br>70 Great Colmore Street<br>Birmingham | Jeweller |
| MR1/141 | Communion cup inscribed 1710 in St Matthews, Douglas, Isle of Man. Goldsmith recorded in diary written in Crosby, Liverpool, 30 April 1725 | Not on P1<br>***#7786***<br> | **S HIGGENS**<br>Liverpool | Silversmith |
| MR1/141<br>MR3/183<br>SOT 108-9<br>J3/416 | Punch ladle and mugs 1692-1719<br>NB: Shield cameo perhaps matches name in which case this is a Britannia mark not used before 1697 which does not match the 1692 item | Not on P1<br>***#7787***<br> | **Robert SHIELDS**<br>Water Street<br>Liverpool | Silversmith |
| J1/380 1842 | Address from Culme | P2/H/x2<br>***#7788,9***<br>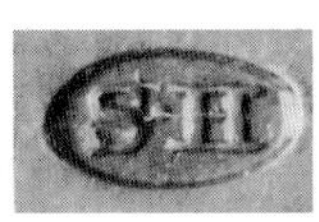 | **Samuel Holditch Thomas HAYNE**<br>**Dudley Frank CATER** trading as<br>**HAYNE & CO** (until 1848) then<br>**Samuel HAYNE & CO** * (from 1864)<br>16 Red Lion Street<br>London or<br><br>**Samuel HILL**<br>3 Mary Anne Street, Liverpool or<br><br>**S HUNTINGDON**<br>Chester | Manufacturing silversmiths<br><br>Watch manufacturer<br><br>Silversmith |
| R2/217<br>5 February 1919<br>Sent by Sydney James Hall | Private address same as business | P15/H/43<br>***#7790***<br> | **Sydney James HALL** trading as<br>**Sydney HALL CO**<br>57 Hockley Hill<br>Birmingham | Ring makers and manufacturing jewellers |
| R3/152<br>5 June 1954<br>Sent by S H Gadsby | 30 White Moss Avenue<br>Manchester 21 | P21/G/37<br>***#7791***<br> | **Stanley Herbert GADSBY**<br>No business address entered | Student |

| REGISTRATION DETAILS | MAKER'S PRIVATE ADDRESS and DETAILS | PLATE and MARK DETAILS | MAKER/COMPANY and BUSINESS ADDRESS | MAKER'S TRADE |
|---|---|---|---|---|
| R3/177<br>23 February 1961<br>Sent by S H Jowett | 20 Westminster Avenue<br>Morecambe<br>Lancashire | P21/IJ/18<br>***#7792***<br> | **Sidney Hill JOWETT**<br>No business address entered | Dental surgery student, silversmith |
| R1/7<br>15 February 1895<br>Sent by Allen Brothers Baker & Hinks | | P5/S/638<br>***#7793***<br> | **Solomon Henry SCHWERSEE**<br>18 Bevis Marks<br>London EC and<br>Birmingham | Jeweller |
| R2/93<br>25 September 1909<br>Sent by C E Adams | 154 Highbury New Park<br>London | P13/S/45<br>***#7794***<br> | | |
| R1/71<br>27 October 1898<br>Sent by W Mills<br>J J Johnson | 50 Petherton Road<br>London N | P9/S/7<br>***#7795***<br> | | |
| R1/186<br>25 February 1903<br>Sent by J H Wynn | 154 Highbury New Park<br>London N | P9/S/60<br>***#7796***<br> | | |
| Missing register<br>*c.*1890 | | P5/S/321<br>***#7797***<br> | | |
| LPB/88<br>13 January 1880 | | P3/W/x1<br>***#7798***<br> | **Samuel Hillyard WHITE**<br>28 Augusta Street<br>Birmingham | Jeweller |
| LPB/88<br>13 May 1880 | | P3/W/x1<br>***#7799***<br> | | |
| Not in R1 as expected | | P5/S/724<br>***#7800***<br> | **William Henry STOKES**<br>**Arthur George IRELAND** trading as<br>**STOKES & IRELAND** *<br>83, 84 Great Hampton Street<br>Birmingham | Silversmiths |
| R3/31<br>21 January 1931<br>Sent by S Blanckensee & Son<br>Three sizes | 26 Duchess Road<br>Edgbaston<br>Birmingham | P15/S/73-75<br>***#7801-3***<br>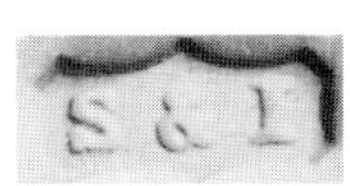 | **S BLANCKENSEE & SON** trading as<br>**STOKES & IRELAND** *<br>W Davis (Secretary)<br>14-16 Frederick Street and<br>72-73 Great Hampton Street<br>Birmingham | Manufacturing jewellers and silversmiths |
| Missing register<br>*c.*1891 | | P5/S/333a<br>***#7804***<br> | | |
| Missing register<br>*c.*1891 | | P5/S/333b<br>***#7805***<br> | | Silversmiths |
| R1/26<br>2 April 1896<br>Sent by Stokes & Ireland<br>Not on P5 as expected but on P9<br>Three sizes | Shirley House<br>Acocks Green<br>Birmingham | P9/S/752a-c<br>***#7805-8***<br> | **STOKES & IRELAND LTD** *<br>Theodore Schwarz (Schwarck) (Director)<br>83, 84 Great Hampton Street<br>Birmingham | |

| REGISTRATION DETAILS | MAKER'S PRIVATE ADDRESS and DETAILS | PLATE and MARK DETAILS | MAKER/COMPANY and BUSINESS ADDRESS | MAKER'S TRADE |
|---|---|---|---|---|
| R1/220<br>29 September 1904<br>Sent by Stokes & Ireland<br>Two sizes | Woodcroft<br>Acocks Green<br>Birmingham | P9/S/77,78<br>***#7809,10***<br> | **STOKES & IRELAND LTD** *<br>T Schwarck (Director)<br>83/84 Great Hampton Street<br>Birmingham | Silversmiths |
| R2/232<br>5 June 1920<br>Sent by S R Ward & Son | Private address same as business | P21/P/158<br>***#7811***<br> | **Saul PINCES**<br>**Isaac PINCES**<br>135 Edmond Street<br>Birmingham | Wholesale jewellers |
| R2/110<br>6 May 1910<br>Sent by Bacon & Bill | Westward House<br>Westcliff–on–Sea | P13/S/54<br>***#7812***<br> | **Samuel Isidore SIMPSON** trading as<br>**S I SIMPSON & SON** *<br>60, 62 Clerkenwell Road<br>London EC | Wholesale jewellers |
| SPB/6<br>22 November 1871 | CWMP 1886-91 | P3/I/x2<br>***#7813,4***<br> | **Samuel JACKSON** *<br>6 Albert Street (1874)<br>6 Meadow Street (1886-91)<br>Coventry | Watchcase maker |
| Missing register<br>*c.*1889 | | P5/D/247<br>***#7815***<br>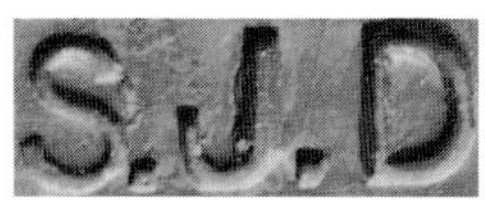 | **S J O'DONNELL** | |
| R1/15<br>20 July 1895<br>Sent by J H Rowland | 367 Oxford Road<br>Manchester | P5/D/682<br>***#7816***<br> | **Silvester Joseph O'DONNELL**<br>7 Palace Street<br>Manchester | Umbrella manufacturer |
| R1/24<br>18 March 1896<br>Sent by Smith, Salamon & Co | | P5/D/743<br>***#7817***<br> | | |
| Not in R1 as expected<br>*c.*1896 | | P5/E/765<br>***#7818***<br> | **Unidentified** | |
| SPB/5<br>29 November 1865 | CWMP | P3/I/x3<br>***#7819-21***<br> | **Samuel JACKSON** *<br>**Edward HICKMAN** *<br>76 Spon End<br>Coventry | Watchcase makers |
| R3/7<br>28 February 1922<br>Sent by S J Hall | 2 Stoneleigh Road<br>Birchfield<br>Birmingham | P15/H/70<br>***#7822***<br> | **Sydney James HALL**<br>80½ Branston Street<br>77 Spencer Street (from 21 September 1940)<br>Birmingham | Manufacturing jeweller |
| R3/112<br>28 January 1946<br>Sent by R S Walker | 755 Walsall Road<br>Great Barr<br>Birmingham | P21/H/23<br>***#7823***<br>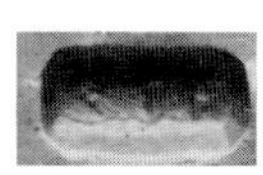 | **Ralph Stanley WALKER** trading as<br>**Sydney J HALL**<br>31 Northampton Street<br>Birmingham 18 | Manufacturing jeweller and silversmith |
| 5 February 1946<br>cancelled and recut | | P21/H/24<br>***#7824***<br> | | |
| R3/1<br>12 March 1921<br>Sent by E Whitehouse & Son | Altyer<br>Benhill Road<br>Sutton<br>Surrey | P15/R/29<br>***#7825***<br> | **Stephen J ROSE**<br>2 Ridgmount Street,<br>Tottenham Court Road<br>London WC1 | Jeweller and medallist |
| 8 June 1948 | | P21/R/4<br>***#7826***<br>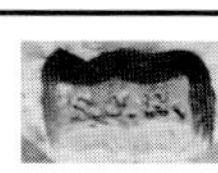 | | |

| REGISTRATION DETAILS | MAKER'S PRIVATE ADDRESS and DETAILS | PLATE and MARK DETAILS | MAKER/COMPANY and BUSINESS ADDRESS | MAKER'S TRADE |
|---|---|---|---|---|
| R3/139<br>22 November 1952<br>Sent by S J Rose & Son<br>Two sizes | Deepdale [1]<br>Surrey Road<br>Bournemouth<br>The Old Rectory [2]<br>Ranmore<br>91 Queens Road [3]<br>Richmond, Surrey | P21/R/13,14<br>***#7827,8***<br> | **Gertrude Necada (Nicola?) ROSE** [1]<br>**Julian Stephen ROSE** [2]<br>**Arthur Brian ROSE** [3] trading as<br>**S J ROSE & SON**<br>19 Ridgemount Street<br>London WC1 | Manufacturing goldsmiths and silversmiths |
| R2/214<br>18 January 1918<br>Sent by S J Shipton | 16 Grosvenor Road<br>Handsworth<br>Birmingham | P15/S/32<br>***#7829***<br> | **Sydney John SHIPTON**<br>91 Vyse Street<br>Birmingham | Manufacturing jeweller |
| R2/37<br>18 April 1907<br>Sent by W H Carrington & Co Ltd | 114 High Street<br>Chorlton-cum-Medlock<br>Manchester | P9/K/46<br>***#7830***<br> | **Solomon KUIT**<br>**Morris KUIT** trading as<br>**A KUIT**<br>27 Oxford Street<br>Manchester<br>1 Lord Street<br>9 Lime Street<br>2 Victoria Street<br>Liverpool<br>377 Lord Street<br>7 Leyland Arcade<br>Southport<br>Lancashire | Retail tobacconists |
| R3/46<br>27 May 1929<br>Sent by W J Pellow Ltd<br>31 Hylton Street<br>Birmingham | 2 Hermitage Gardens<br>Edinburgh | P15/L/37<br>***#7831***<br>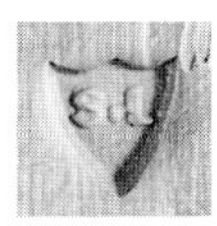 | **Sydney LATIMER**<br>70 George Street and<br>143, 145 and 147 Lothian Road<br>Edinburgh | Goldsmith |
| R2/27<br>26 October 1906<br>Sent by Imperial Tobacco Ltd | Private address same as business | P9/L/80,81<br>***#7832,3***<br> | **Samuel LYONS**<br>10 Doddington Grove<br>Kennington<br>London SE | Dealer in fancy goods |
| R2/113<br>28 June 1910<br>Sent by Imperial Tobacco Co | 169 The Grove<br>Hammersmith<br>London W | P13/L/38-41<br>***#7834-7***<br> | **Samuel LYONS**<br>169 The Grove<br>Hammersmith<br>London W<br>Late of 10 Doddington Grove<br>Kennington<br>London SE | |
| R2/61<br>28 May 1908<br>Sent by Imperial Tobacco Co<br>Two sizes | 10 Doddington Grove<br>London SE | P13/L/2,3<br>***#7838,9***<br>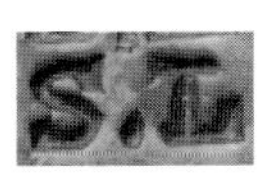 | **Samuel LYONS**<br>10 Doddington Grove<br>Kennington<br>London SE | |
| R2/80<br>27 April 1909<br>Sent by Imperial Tobacco Co<br>Three sizes | | P13/L/9-11<br>***#7840-2***<br> | | |
| R2/99<br>10 December 1909<br>Sent by Imperial Tobacco Co | | P13/L/32<br>***#7843***<br>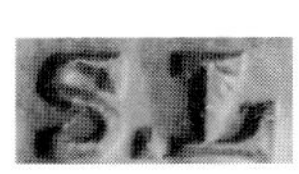 | | |
| R2/104<br>26 February 1910<br>Sent by Imperial Tobacco Co<br>Two sizes | | P13/L/34,35<br>***#7844,5***<br> | | |

| REGISTRATION DETAILS | MAKER'S PRIVATE ADDRESS and DETAILS | PLATE and MARK DETAILS | MAKER/COMPANY and BUSINESS ADDRESS | MAKER'S TRADE |
|---|---|---|---|---|
| R2/135<br>9 May 1911<br>Sent by Imperial Tobacco Co<br>Two sizes | Private address same as business | P13/L/49-57<br>***#7846-54***<br>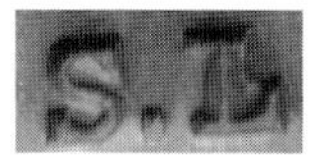 | **Samuel LYONS**<br>169 The Grove<br>Hammersmith<br>London | Dealer in fancy goods |
| R2/226<br>4 February 1920<br>Sent by The Imperial Tobacco Co Ltd | | P13/L/76<br>***#7855***<br>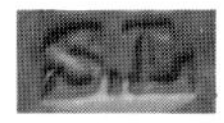 | | Silversmith |
| LPB/52<br>31 October 1883<br>No mark in LPB | Hulley's 1881 directory | P5/L/x1<br>***#7856***<br> | **Solomon LYON**<br>38 Frederick Street<br>Birmingham | Watch manufacturer and jeweller |
| Missing register<br>*c.*1891 | | P5/L/345<br>***#7857***<br> | | |
| R2/186<br>11 May 1914<br>Sent by Stuart Lehrer | Private address same as business | P15/L/1<br>***#7858***<br>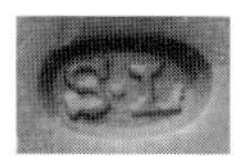 | **Stuart LEHRER**<br>3 Commercial Street<br>London E | Goldsmith |
| R2/116<br>13 August 1910<br>Sent by Samuel Le Bass | 105 Sth Circular Road<br>Dublin | P13/B/84<br>***#7859***<br> | **Samuel Le BASS**<br>5 Fleet Street<br>Dublin | Silversmith |
| R3/131<br>15 March 1950<br>Sent by S L Evans | Private address same as business | P21/E/9<br>***#7860***<br> | **Sydney Lloyd EVANS**<br>106 Brockin Avenue<br>Liverpool 18 | Silversmith and goldsmith |
| R3/53<br>29 May 1930<br>Sent by W Manton | 60 Tenby Street North<br>Birmingham | P15/S/93<br>***#7861***<br> | **SUCKLING LTD**<br>Joseph Suckling (Director)<br>William Suckling (Director)<br>Kingsway House<br>Albion Street and<br>Phoenix House<br>Vyse Street<br>Birmingham | Silversmiths and electroplate manufacturers |
| 4 February 1931<br>Three sizes | | P15/S/96-98<br>***#7862-4***<br>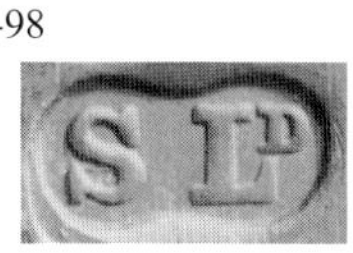 | | |
| PP1/189<br>GTD 1841-5<br>GSJW/136 | 16 Percy Street<br>Liverpool in 1848 | P2/S/x3<br>***#7865-7***<br> | **Sylvester Lewis SAMUEL** *<br>50 Lord Street (1848)<br>2 York Street (1849)<br>Liverpool | Watch manufacturer |
| Not in SPB or LPB so struck 1860-3 | In 1865 listed as American Merchant and Commission Agent | P3/S/x3<br>***#7868-70***<br> | | |
| | | P2/S/x6<br>***#7871-6***<br> | | |
| Similar mark entered LAO 20 November 1849 | | P2/S/x2<br>***#7877,8***<br> | | |
| Not in SPB or LPB so struck 1860-3 | | P3/S/x3<br>***#7879-81***<br> | | |
| Similar mark entered LAO 20 August 1858 | | P2/T *sic*/x3<br>***#7882-4***<br>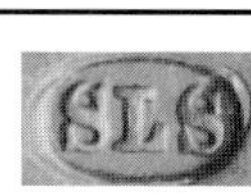 | | |

| REGISTRATION DETAILS | MAKER'S PRIVATE ADDRESS and DETAILS | PLATE and MARK DETAILS | MAKER/COMPANY and BUSINESS ADDRESS | MAKER'S TRADE |
|---|---|---|---|---|
| PP1/189<br>GTD 1841-5<br>GSJW/136<br>Similar mark entered<br>LAO 20 August 1858 | | P2/T *sic*/x3<br>***#7885-7*** 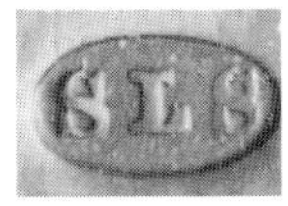 | **Sylvester Lewis SAMUEL** *<br>50 Lord Street (1848)<br>2 York Street (1849)<br>Liverpool | Watch manufacturer |
| | | P2/S/x2<br>***#7888,9***  | | |
| | | P2/S/x2<br>***#7890,1*** 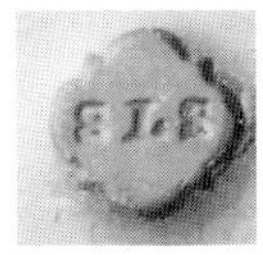 | | |
| | | P2/X*sic*/x3<br>***#7892-4*** 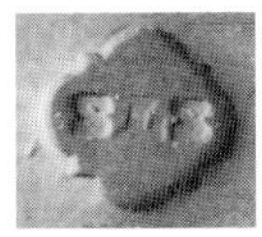 | | |
| R3/117<br>16 May 1947<br>Sent by S E Cooke<br>191 Warstone Lane<br>Birmingham 18 | | P21/S/27<br>***#7895***  | **STANLEY (FANCY GOODS) LTD**<br>Scaled in the presence of:-<br>S Aarons? (Director)<br>H Slyomovier? (Secretary)<br>Greville Buildings<br>12 Cherry Street<br>Birmingham 2 | Manufacturers and distributors of art jewellery and fancy goods |
| R3/85<br>3 October 1936<br>Sent by H Huntley & Sons<br>6 Vyse Street<br>Birmingham | 16 Clarence Gardens<br>Hampstead<br>London | P21/UV/1<br>***#7896***  | **S & L ULLMANN** *<br>Louis Ullmann<br>102 Hatton Garden<br>London EC1 | Jewellers |
| R2/14<br>23 March 1906<br>Sent by S McLardy | Basford Mount<br>Higher Crumpsall | P9/M/101<br>***#7897***  | **Samuel McLARDY** *<br>67 Shude Hill<br>Manchester | Tobacco pipe manufacturer |
| R1/199<br>19 August 1903<br>Sent by W H Newman | 2 Vincent Square<br>London SW | P9/M/68<br>***#7898***  | **Stanley D MACKINDER** trading as<br>**FRENCH TOBACCO CO**<br>40 Gerrard Street<br>London W | Tobacco and fancy goods dealers |
| R2/191<br>2 December 1914<br>Sent by Samuel McLardy<br>P15/M/7 cancelled | Basford Mount<br>Higher Crumpsall | P15/M/13<br>***#7899*** 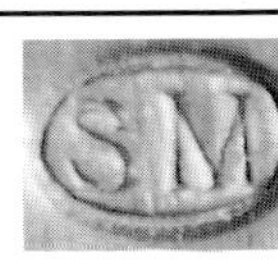 | **Samuel McLARDY** *<br>20 Swan Street<br>Manchester | Pipe manufacturer and mounter |
| R3/184<br>13 April 1962<br>Sent by<br>S W R Mottram | 30 Hartington Road<br>Chorlton-cum-Hardy<br>Manchester 21 | P21/M/54<br>***#7900***  | **Sydney William Royle MOTTRAM**<br>No business address entered | Student of silversmithing |
| R1/120<br>13 February 1900<br>Sent by J Adelman | Private address same as business | P9/M/18<br>***#7901***  | **Solomon MENDELSON**<br>39 Pimblett Street<br>Cheetham<br>Manchester | Jeweller |
| R1/201<br>17 October 1903<br>Sent by G K Leeson | 34 Myddleton Square<br>London EC | P9/S/70<br>***#7902***  | **William SMOLLENS** trading as<br>**SMOLLENS & MITCHELL**<br>52 Hatton Garden<br>London EC | Wholesalers jewellers |

| REGISTRATION DETAILS | MAKER'S PRIVATE ADDRESS and DETAILS | PLATE and MARK DETAILS | MAKER/COMPANY and BUSINESS ADDRESS | MAKER'S TRADE |
|---|---|---|---|---|
| R2/163<br>15 October 1912<br>Sent by Sanders & Mackenzie<br>Three sizes | 161 Church Lane<br>Handsworth<br>Alexandra Road<br>Acocks Green<br>Birmingham | P13/S/105-107<br>***#7903-5***<br> | **Ernest Wilfred SANDERS**<br>**Henry Arthur MACKENZIE** trading as<br>**SANDERS & MACKENZIE**<br>101, 103 Spencer Street<br>Birmingham | Manufacturing silversmiths |
| R2/165<br>20 November 1912<br>Sent by J G Newbold | 84 Friar Park<br>North Finchley<br>London | P13/B/134<br>***#7906***<br>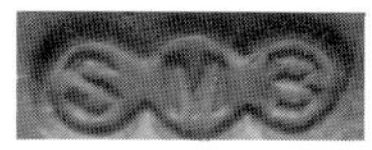 | **Samuel M BULL**<br>6 Nisbet Place<br>Homerton<br>London NE | Importer and maker of tobacconists goods |
| Missing register<br>*c.*1890 | | P5/L/303<br>***#7907***<br> | **Samuel McLARDY & CO** *<br>16 Miller Street<br>Manchester | Tobacco pipe manufacturer |
| Not in R2 as expected<br>*c.* 9 May 1911 to 21 June 1911<br>Similar mark CAO 17 February 1914 and BAO 12 October 1898 | | P13/L/58<br>***#7908***<br> | **Samuel McLARDY** *<br>16 Miller Street<br>Birmingham | |
| R2/183<br>17 February 1914<br>Sent by Handcock & Walker | | P15/M/7<br>***#7909***<br> | **Samuel McLARDY** *<br>20 Swan Street<br>Manchester | |
| R3/46<br>25 April 1919<br>Sent by Souvenir Manufacturing Co Ltd | 125 Brandswood Road [1]<br>King's Heath<br>Birmingham<br>30 Heathcroft [2]<br>Hampstead Way<br>London NW | P15/S/85<br>***#7910***<br> | **SOUVENIR MANUFACTURING CO LTD**<br>Geoffrey Lawson Barnes[1] (Managing Director)<br>Gladys Kathleen Lawson Barnes[1] (Director)<br>William Roscoe Evison [2] (Director)<br>15 Vyse Street<br>Birmingham | Manufacturing jewellers |
| R1/151<br>27 July 1901<br>Sent by J Gammage | 1 Albert Court<br>Prince Consort Road<br>South Kensington<br>London | P9/M/30,31<br>***#7911,12***<br> | **Simon MAYER**<br>111 Hatton Garden<br>London | Shipper |
| Not in R1 as expected - between P9/M69 and P9/M/70 | | P9/M/0*sic*<br>***#7913***<br> | See other SM&Co | |
| Not in R2 as expected<br>*c.* December 1914 | | P15/M/12<br>***#7914***<br>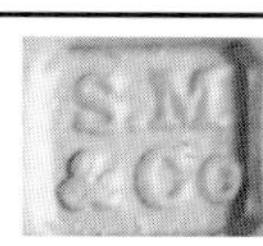 | **Unidentified** | |
| R1/206<br>23 January 1904<br>Sent by S Mordan & Co | Mantrom<br>Headenham<br>Finchley N | P9/M/76<br>***#7915***<br> | **S MORDAN & CO** *<br>Alfred Bridges (Secretary)<br>41 City Road<br>London EC and<br>11 Warwick Street<br>Regent Street<br>London W | Manufacturing silversmiths |
| R2/6<br>14 November 1905<br>Sent by S Mordan | Secretary's address<br>Elsmere, Dynoke Road<br>Hornchurch<br>Romford | P9/M/95-100<br>***#7916-21***<br> | **S MORDAN & CO** *<br>H Symonds (Managing Director)<br>41 City Road<br>London EC | |

| REGISTRATION DETAILS | MAKER'S PRIVATE ADDRESS and DETAILS | PLATE and MARK DETAILS | MAKER/COMPANY and BUSINESS ADDRESS | MAKER'S TRADE |
|---|---|---|---|---|
| R2/30<br>13 December 1906<br>Sent by E G Chapman | 52 Ripley Road<br>Seven Kings<br>Essex | P9/M/108-112<br>***#7922-26***<br> | **S MORDAN & CO LTD** *<br>Edward George Chapman (Secretary)<br>41 City Road and<br>11 Warwick Street<br>Regent Street<br>London | Manufacturing goldsmiths and silversmiths |
| R2/83<br>15 May 1909<br>Sent by E G Chapman | 12 Gartmore Road<br>Goodways<br>Essex | P13/M/13<br>***#7927***<br> | | Goldsmiths and silversmiths |
| R2/84<br>11 June 1909<br>Sent by S Mordan & Co | | P13/M/14-16<br>***#7928-30***<br>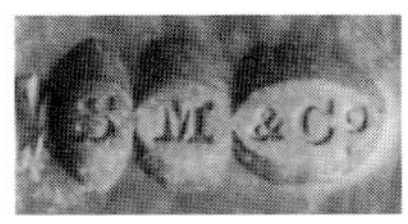 | **S MORDAN & CO** *<br>E G Chapman (Secretary)<br>41 City Road<br>2 Belfast Chambers<br>Beak Street<br>London W | Manufacturing goldsmiths and silversmiths |
| R2/96<br>21 October 1909<br>Sent by E G Chapman | 48 Upper Grosvenor Road<br>Tunbridge Wells<br>Sunnyside<br>Woodland Avenue<br>Hornchurch<br>12 Gartmore Road<br>Goodways, Essex | P13/M/23-28<br>***#7931-6***<br> | **S MORDAN & CO LTD** *<br>James Pulley (all three Managing Directors)<br>Harry Lambert Symond<br>Edward George Chapman<br>41 City Road<br>London<br>2 Belfast Chambers<br>Beak Street<br>London | Goldsmiths and silversmiths |
| R2/235<br>24 November 1920<br>Sent by Stylic Manufacturing Co Ltd | 70 Wake Green Road<br>Moseley<br>105 Hatton Garden<br>London | P15/M/45,46<br>***#7937,8***<br> | **STYLIC MANUFACTURING CO LTD**<br>W F Smith<br>A M Lederman<br>32–44 Branston Street<br>Birmingham | Watchcase manufacturers |
| R2/237<br>17 February 1921<br>Sent by Stylic Manufacturing Co | | P15/M/47,48<br>***#7939,40***<br> | **STYLIC MANUFACTURING CO LTD**<br>W F Smith (Director)<br>Branston Street<br>Birmingham | Watchcase manufacturers |
| R1/92<br>18 February 1899<br>Sent by Alfred Bridges, Secretary<br>Dennison & Wigley<br>MR3/135 | 7 Grove Hill<br>South Woodford<br>Essex | P9/M/9<br>***#7941***<br> | **Sampson MORDAN & CO LTD** *<br>Alfred Bridges (Secretary)<br>41, 43 City Road<br>London EC | Manufacturing silversmiths and pencil case makers |
| R1/222<br>8 November 1904<br>Sent by S Mordan & Co | Montrose<br>Hendon Lane<br>Finchley<br>London N | P9/M/83-85<br>***#7942-4***<br> | **S MORDAN & CO LTD** *<br>41 City Road<br>9 Warwick Street<br>Regent Street<br>London | Silversmiths |
| R1/129<br>21 June 1900<br>Sent by S M Levi | 51 York Road<br>Edgbaston<br>24 Frederick Road<br>Edgbaston | P9/L/19<br>***#7945***<br> | **Samuel M LEVI**<br>**Charles M LEVI**<br>16 Frederick Street<br>Birmingham | Manufacturing silversmiths |
| R2/88<br>23 July 1909<br>Sent by Samuel M Levi<br>Two sizes | 13 Portland Road<br>Edgbaston<br>24 Frederick Street | P13/L/15,16<br>***#7946,7***<br> | **Samuel M LEVI**<br>**Charles M LEVI**<br>67, 68, 69 Vyse Street<br>Birmingham | |

| REGISTRATION DETAILS | MAKER'S PRIVATE ADDRESS and DETAILS | PLATE and MARK DETAILS | MAKER/COMPANY and BUSINESS ADDRESS | MAKER'S TRADE |
|---|---|---|---|---|
| R3/175<br>29 December 1960<br>Sent by S Nieviaski | Private address same as business | P21/N/13,14<br>***#7948,9***<br> | **Samuel NIEVIASKI**<br>14 Princess Court<br>Bryanston Place<br>London W1 | Manufacturer and importer |
| Missing register<br>*c.*1893 | | P5/N/513<br>***#7950***<br> | **Sebastian NOTTON** * | |
| R1/33<br>14 October 1896<br>Sent by A H Tongue | 510 Caledonian Road<br>Holloway<br>London N | P5/N/793a<br>***#7951***<br> | **Sebastian NOTTON** *<br>32-38 Whitecross Street<br>London EC | Pipe importer |
| | | P5/N/793b<br>***#7952***<br> | | |
| R1/236<br>30 June 1905<br>Sent by Sothers & Orchard | 96 Thornhill Road<br>Handsworth<br>38 Broughton Road<br>Handsworth | P9/S/90<br>***#7953***<br> | **William George SOTHERS**<br>**Edward Steadman ORCHARD** trading as<br>**SOTHERS & ORCHARD**<br>113 Spencer Street<br>Birmingham | Jewellers |
| R1/57<br>26 January 1898<br>Sent by W Walker | Private address same as business | P5/O/923<br>***#7954***<br> | **Louis SECKEL**<br>84 Warwick Road, Maida Vale<br>**Sina OPPENHEIMER** *<br>282 Elgin Terrace, Maida Vale<br>London W | Pipe merchants and manufacturers |
| R1/72<br>23 August 1898<br>Sent by Louis Seckel<br>G Peters<br>J Cole | 282 Elgin Avenue<br>Maida Vale<br>London W | P9/O/1<br>***#7955***<br> | **Louis SECKEL**<br>**Sina OPPENHEIMER** trading as<br>**OPPENHEIMER, SECKEL & CO** *<br>6 New Zealand Avenue<br>London EC | |
| R1/153<br>19 September 1901<br>Sent by J G Newbold<br>W G Stiffin | | P9/O/5<br>***#7956***<br>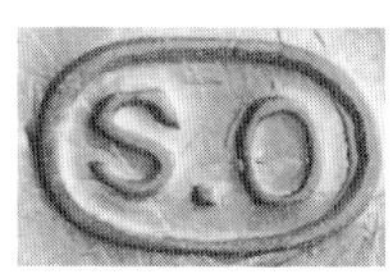 | **Sina OPPENHEIMER** *<br>6 New Zealand Terrace<br>London | |
| R2/31<br>24 January 1907<br>Sent by Sothers & Orchard<br>Three sizes | Neville, Kingsbury Road<br>Gravelly Hill<br>38 Broughton Road<br>Handsworth | P9/S/117-121, P9/I*sic*/117-125<br>***#7957-70***<br> | **William George SOTHERS**<br>**Edward Steadman ORCHARD** trading as<br>**SOTHERS & ORCHARD**<br>113 Spencer Street<br>Birmingham | Silversmiths |
| R3/122<br>1 April 1948<br>Sent by Samuel Pitt | 3 Bishop Road [1]<br>Sutton Coldfield<br>196 Eachelhurst Road [2]<br>Sutton Coldfield | P21/P/24,25<br>***#7971,2***<br>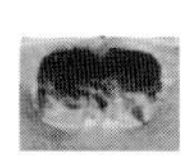 | **William PITT** [1]<br>**Oliver William PITT** [2] trading as<br>**Samuel PITT**<br>61 Albion Street<br>Birmingham 1 | Manufacturing jewellers |
| R3/150<br>23 April 1954<br>Sent by Smith & Pepper Ltd | | P21/S/61,62<br>***#7973,4***<br>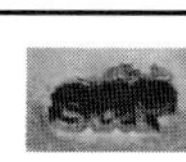 | **SMITH & PEPPER LTD**<br>77 and 78 Vyse Street<br>Birmingham 18 | Manufacturing jewellers |
| R3/136<br>9 June 1951<br>Sent by S Pryatt<br>Two sizes | Private address same as business | P21/P/42,43<br>***#7975,6***<br>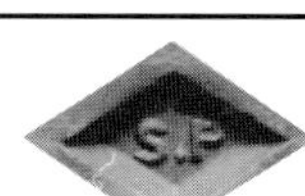 | **Sidney PRYATT**<br>52 Lansdowne Road<br>West Didsbury<br>Manchester 20 | Student |

| REGISTRATION DETAILS | MAKER'S PRIVATE ADDRESS and DETAILS | PLATE and MARK DETAILS | MAKER/COMPANY and BUSINESS ADDRESS | MAKER'S TRADE |
|---|---|---|---|---|
| R3/150<br>20 January 1954<br>Two sizes | | P21/S/57-60<br>***#7977-80***<br> | **SMITH & PEPPER LTD**<br>77, 78 Vyse Street<br>Birmingham 18 | Manufacturing jewellers |
| 29 April 1954 | | P21/S/63,64<br>***#7981,2***<br> | | |
| R3/14<br>20 February 1923<br>Sent by B Pedlingham | 29 Francis Road<br>Stechford<br>148 Station Road<br>Stechford | P15/S/59<br>***#7983***<br> | **Sampson SANDERS**<br>**Bernard Albert PEDLINGHAM**<br>53 Great Hampton Street<br>Birmingham | Silversmiths |
| R2/103<br>18 February 1910<br>Sent by Stephen Phelps | 211 Barclay Road<br>Warley<br>Birmingham | P13/P/136<br>***#7984***<br> | **Stephen PHELPS**<br>97 Camden Street<br>Birmingham | Manufacturing jeweller |
| LPB/70<br>6 June 1885<br>No mark in LPB | | P5/P/x1<br>***#7985***<br> | **Stephen PHELPS**<br>50 Albion Street<br>Birmingham | Jeweller |
| Missing register<br>*c.*1887 | | P5/P/117<br>***#7986***<br>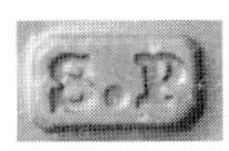 | | |
| R1/139<br>17 December 1900<br>Sent by S Pitt | Woodbine Lodge<br>Vesey Road<br>Wylde Green<br>Nr Sutton Coldfield | P9/P/77,78<br>***#7987,8***<br> | **Samuel PITT**<br>61 Albion Street<br>Birmingham | Jeweller |
| R1/165<br>25 March 1902<br>Sent by A Jackson | 12 Courtfield Gardens<br>South Kensington<br>London SW | P9/A/33,34,35<br>***#7989-91***<br> | **Saul P ARONSON** trading as<br>**ROSENTHAL, ARONSON & CO** *<br>26 Fore Street<br>London | Australian merchants |
| R2/131<br>27 March 1911<br>Sent by S P Aronson<br>Punch P9/A/35 recut | | P13/A/27<br>***#7992***<br> | **Samuel** (*sic*) **P ARONSON** trading as<br>**ROSENTHAL, ARONSON & CO** *<br>26 Fore Street<br>London | |
| R2/149<br>16 December 1911<br>Sent by J Griffiths | | P13/A/36<br>***#7993***<br>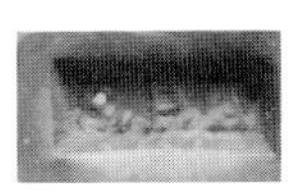 | **Saul Philip ARONSON** *<br>26 Fore Street<br>London EC | |
| Missing register<br>*c.*1890 | | P5/Q/325b<br>***#7994***<br>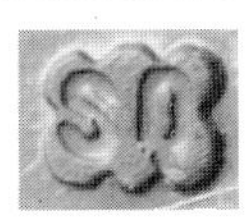 | **Samuel QUILLIAM** * | Watchcase maker and watch manufacturer |
| Missing register<br>*c.*1890 | | P5/Q/325a<br>***#7995***<br>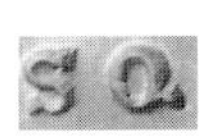 | **Samuel QUILLIAM** *<br>32 Elizabeth Street<br>Liverpool | |
| J1 1861-82<br>Similar mark entered LAO 5 July 1859 | | P2/Q/x4<br>***#7996-9***<br> | **Samuel QUILLIAM** *<br>28 Elizabeth Road and<br>32 Elizabeth Road (factory)<br>Liverpool | |
| Missing register<br>*c.*1891 | | P5/Q/378<br>***#8000***<br> | | |
| SPB/8<br>2 July 1872<br>Old punch destroyed | | P3/Q/x3<br>***#8001-3***<br>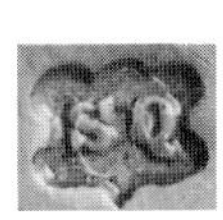 | **Samuel QUILLIAM** *<br>32 Elizabeth Street<br>Liverpool | |

| REGISTRATION DETAILS | MAKER'S PRIVATE ADDRESS and DETAILS | PLATE and MARK DETAILS | MAKER/COMPANY and BUSINESS ADDRESS | MAKER'S TRADE |
|---|---|---|---|---|
| Missing register<br>*c.*1889 | | P5/R/217<br>***#8004***<br> | **Unidentified** | |
| SPB/3<br>18 February 1864<br>GSJW/136 1861 | | P3/S/x3<br>***#8005-7***<br> | **SAMUEL * (Mary) &**<br>**ROGERS * (Arthur)**<br>72 Wood Street<br>Liverpool | Watchcase manufacturers |
| SPB/3<br>16 July 1864 | | P3/S/x3<br>***#8008-10***<br> | | |
| Missing register<br>*c.*1887 SP33/1<br>Similar mark entered<br>LAO 5 March 1870 | | P5/E/77<br>***#8011***<br> | **Samuel Robert EDWARDS** *<br>15 Alfred Street<br>City Road<br>London | Goldsmith |
| R2/7<br>21 November 1905<br>Sent by S R Edwards | Private address same as business | P9/E/18<br>***#8012***<br> | **Samuel Robert EDWARDS** *<br>54 Northampton Square<br>Clerkenwell<br>London | Gold chain maker and general jeweller |
| R1/167<br>29 April 1902<br>Sent by S R Williams | 15 Wilton Road<br>Smethwick<br>Birmingham | P9/W/66<br>***#8013***<br>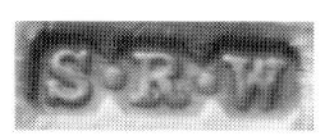 | **Samuel Roger WILLIAMS**<br>Back of 105 Vyse Street<br>Birmingham | Jeweller |
| R2/48<br>23 October 1947 | Manor Lane<br>Quinton<br>27 Anglesey Street<br>Lozells<br>Birmingham | P21/W/45<br>***#8014***<br> | **Samuel Roger WILLIAMS**<br>**Francis Robert JONES** trading as<br>**S R WILLIAMS & CO**<br>105 Vyse Street<br>Birmingham | Manufacturing jewellers |
| R2/48<br>22 October 1907<br>Sent by S R Williams &Co | | P13/W/11<br>***#8015***<br> | | |
| R2/212<br>23 June 1917<br>Sent by S Schonberg | 142 Coronation Avenue<br>Stoke Newington | P15/S/29<br>***#8016***<br> | **Solomon SCHONBERG** *<br>30b Great Sutton Street<br>Clerkenwell<br>London EC | Manufacturing jeweller |
| R2/227<br>17 February 1920<br>Sent by S Schonberg Co | 142 Coronation Avenue<br>Stoke Newington<br>46 Fircroft Road<br>Upper Tooting<br>188 High Holborn<br>London WC1 | No new mark<br>***#8017*** | **Solomon SCHONBERG** (Secretary)<br>**Arthur John GLAYSHER**<br>**Barnett NIMERZOWSKY** trading as<br>**S SCHONBERG LTD** *<br>30 Great Sutton Street<br>Clerkenwell<br>London | Manufacturing jewellers |
| R3/15<br>26 April 1923<br>Sent by S Simon | Private address same as business | P15/S/60<br>***#8018***<br> | **Seigfried SIMON**<br>97 Hatton Garden<br>London EC | Gold and silver worker |
| Not in SPB or LPB so struck 1860-3 | | P3/S/x3<br>***#8019-21***<br> | **Selim SAMUEL** * | Watchcase maker |
| LPB/86<br>13 October 1882<br>KOC/186 | In partnership with Philip Cohen as Cohen and Samuel at this address 1878-81<br>Ed: Culme has Samuel Selim | P3/S/x2<br>***#8022,3***<br> | **Selim SAMUEL** *<br>1 Oxford Street (*sic*)<br>(Ed: Should be Terrace)<br>Chapel Fields<br>Coventry | |

| REGISTRATION DETAILS | MAKER'S PRIVATE ADDRESS and DETAILS | PLATE and MARK DETAILS | MAKER/COMPANY and BUSINESS ADDRESS | MAKER'S TRADE |
|---|---|---|---|---|
| R1/66<br>21 May 1898<br>Sent by C H Cheshire<br>Two sizes | Lavington<br>Putney Heath<br>London SW | P5/Y*sic*/955a,b<br>***#8024,5***<br> | **Samuel SMITH** trading as<br>**S SMITH & SON** *<br>9 Strand<br>London | Jewellers |
| Missing register<br>*c.*1890 | | P5/S/278<br>***#8026***<br>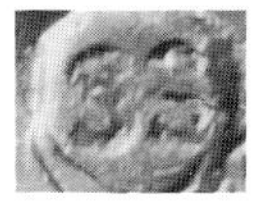 | **Unidentified** | |
| Missing register<br>*c.*1891<br>Similar mark entered<br>BAO 10 March 1893 | | P5/S/395<br>***#8027***<br> | **Sidney SMITH**<br>98 Vyse Street<br>Birmingham | Jeweller |
| Missing register<br>*c.*1892<br>adjacent P5/S/33 | 10 Dundee Street<br>Hulme<br>Manchester | P5/S/x1<br>***#8028***<br> | **SMITH, SALMON & Co**<br>20b Hanging Ditch<br>Manchester | Pipe and stick mounters and engravers |
| R2/119<br>30 September 1910<br>Sent by<br>G Stephenson | High Toft [1]<br>Hornsey Lane<br>London and<br>Elm Glen, Bognor<br>14 Woodburn Place [2]<br>Russell Square, London WC | P13/S/58<br>***#8029***<br> | **Gordon STEPHENSON** [1]<br>**Louis SMITH** [2] trading as<br>**SMITH & STEPHENSON** *<br>34 Hatton Garden<br>London | Wholesale jewellers |
| R2/161<br>19 September 1912<br>Sent by W Aitken<br>BAO 20.416-20.420<br>20.378 | Brightshowe<br>St Annes on Sea<br>4 Rutlan Drive<br>Kesal<br>9 Fairhaven Road<br>St Annes on Sea | P13/S/88-103<br>***#8030-45***<br> | **H G STEPHENSON**<br>**H M STEPHENSON**<br>**V G STEPHENSON** trading as<br>**STEPHENSON & SON**<br>24, 26 St Ann's Square<br>Manchester | Silversmiths |
| R1/226<br>27 January 1905<br>Sent by S Carrington | 171 High Street<br>Chorlton-on-Medlock<br>Manchester | P9/D*sic*/217<br>***#8046***<br> | **Squire Sydney CARRINGTON**<br>trading as<br>**William Henry CARRINGTON & CO**<br>34 Thomas Street<br>Manchester | Tobacconists and fancy goods dealers |
| R1/228<br>2 March 1905<br>Sent by S Carrington | | P9/D*sic*/219<br>***#8047***<br> | | |
| R1/157<br>30 November 1901<br>Sent by<br>W H Carrington | | P9/C/73<br>***#8048***<br> | | Tobacconists |
| R2/208<br>26 September 1916<br>Sent by W H<br>Carrington & Co | 89 Newport Road<br>Chorlton-cum-Hardy | P15/C*sic*/67<br>***#8049***<br> | **Frank GOUGH**<br>c/o **W H CARRINGTON & CO**<br>34 and 36 Thomas Street<br>Manchester | Pipe and stick mounters |
| R1/133<br>17 October 1900<br>Sent by W Walker | 67 High Street<br>Aldershot | P9/S/37<br>***#8050***<br> | **Francis PHILLIPS** trading as<br>**S SNELL & CO**<br>17 George Street and 13 Bradford Street<br>Plymouth<br>32 Fore Street<br>Devonport | Tobacconists |
| R1/20<br>6 January 1896<br>Sent by Smith, Salmon<br>& Co | 10 Dundee Street<br>Hulme<br>Manchester | P5/O*sic*/717<br>***#805***<br>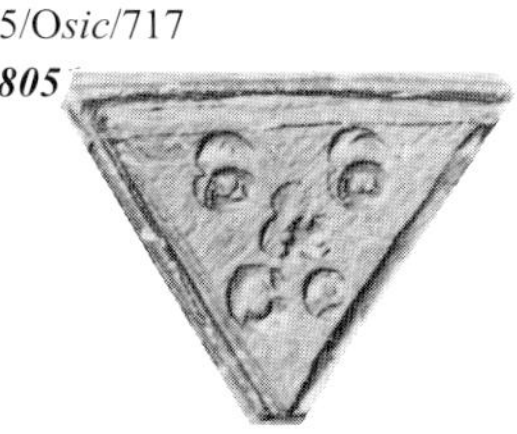 | **George Alfred SMITH**<br>**John Buxton SALMON**<br>**Richard William WILSON**<br>trading as **SMITH, SALMON & CO**<br>20b Hanging Ditch<br>Manchester | Pipe and stick mounters and engravers |

| REGISTRATION DETAILS | MAKER'S PRIVATE ADDRESS and DETAILS | PLATE and MARK DETAILS | MAKER/COMPANY and BUSINESS ADDRESS | MAKER'S TRADE |
|---|---|---|---|---|
| R1/165<br>26 March 1902<br>Sent by W Mills | 84 Westmorland Road<br>Newcastle upon Tyne | P9/S/46<br>***#8052***  | **Solomon SEGAL & CO**<br>16 Scotswood Road<br>Newcastle upon Tyne | Wholesale jewellers |
| R2/179 and 180<br>14 November 1913<br>Sent by A Moore | 4 Mowbray Road<br>Brondesbury<br>London NW | P15/S/3<br>***#8053***  | **Solomon SEGAL** trading as<br>**S SEGAL & CO**<br>114 Fore Street<br>London | Jewellers merchants |
| R2/24<br>19 September 1906<br>Sent by Lawson, Ward & Gammage Ltd | 187 High Road<br>Streatham<br>71 Rye Lane<br>Peckham | P9/S/107<br>***#8054***  | **Sidney SAUNDERS**<br>**William WETHERELL** trading as<br>**S SAUNDERS & CO**<br>458/460 Brixton Road<br>London | Jewellers |
| R2/179<br>28 October 1913<br>Sent by H Griffith & Sons | 12 Kensington Hall Gardens<br>London | P15/S/2<br>***#8055***  | **Montague GRANT** trading as<br>**SOVEREIGN SUPPLY STORES**<br>435 Strand<br>London WC | Jewellers |
| R1/22<br>15 February 1896<br>Sent by<br>James Scotland<br>A H Tongue | 538 Manchester Road [1]<br>Bury<br>48 Poplar Green [2]<br>Manchester<br>3 Granville Street [3]<br>Murne? Green | P5/O*sic*/727<br>***#8056*** 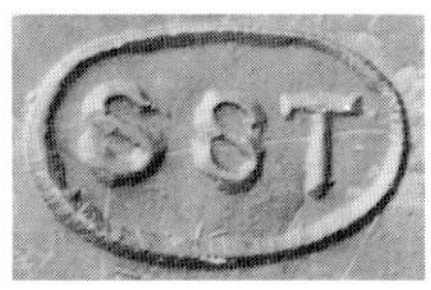 | **John William SAYNOR** [1]<br>**James SCOTLAND** [2]<br>**William TOFT** [3] trading as<br>**SAYNOR, SCOTLAND & TOFT**<br>4 Bradshaw Street<br>Manchester | Pipe mounters and importers |
| R3/179<br>22 April 1961<br>Sent by S Tennant | 7 Palmerston Road<br>Wallasey<br>Cheshire | P21/T/45<br>***#8057***  | **Sheila TENNANT**<br>No business address entered | Student |
| MR2/193<br>GMSC/52<br>LLCC/148<br>Liv Dir 1767, 1773 | Two skewers 1788 with duty mark, but not in PDB. Working 1735 to 1793<br>Tentative attribution | Not on P1<br>***#8058***  | **Stephen TILLINGHAST**<br>Castle Street<br>Liverpool | Silversmith, watchmaker, watchcase maker and tax gatherer |
| R1/135<br>26 October 1900<br>Sent by S Usher | 93 Jerningham Road<br>New Cross<br>London SE | P9/T/19<br>***#8059***  | **Stephen TREE** *<br>120, 122 Great Dover Street<br>Borough<br>London EC | Manufacturing jeweller |
| LPB/84<br>22 March 1881 | | P3/U/x2<br>***#8060,1***  | **Samuel USHER**<br>123 Vyse Street<br>Birmingham | Ring maker |
| LPB/84<br>21 September 1882<br>LPB mark shown | | Not on P3<br>***#8062***  | | |
| LPB/84<br>21 September 1882<br>LPB mark shown | | Not on P3<br>***#8063***  | | |
| Not in R1 as expected | | P5/V*sic*/831<br>***#8064***  | | |
| LPB/84<br>22 March 1881 | | P3/U/x3<br>***#8065-7*** 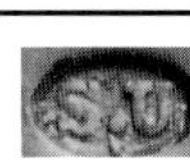 | | |
| R1/82<br>8 November 1898<br>Sent by S Usher<br>T Hale, W H Collins | Vicarage Road<br>Handsworth<br>Birmingham | P9/U/4<br>***#8068***  | | Jeweller |
| R1/142<br>13 February 1901<br>Sent by S Usher<br>J Raymond<br>B Lucas, B Lucas jnr | | P9/U/5,6<br>***#8069,70*** 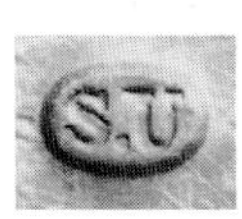 | | Ring maker |

| REGISTRATION DETAILS | MAKER'S PRIVATE ADDRESS and DETAILS | PLATE and MARK DETAILS | MAKER/COMPANY and BUSINESS ADDRESS | MAKER'S TRADE |
|---|---|---|---|---|
| R1/232<br>5 May 1905<br>Sent by selves<br>Three sizes | 18 Radnor Road<br>Handsworth<br>Birmingham | P9/U/8-10<br>***#8071-3***  | **Samuel USHER LTD**<br>G W Usher (Secretary)<br>123 Vyse Street<br>Birmingham | Manufacturing jewellers and goldsmiths |
| R2/59<br>8 May 1908<br>Sent by S Usher Ltd<br>cancelled<br>25 Nov1911 new shape entered.<br>G W Usher, secretary | | P13/U/1-4<br>***#8074-7***  | **Samuel USHER LTD**<br>123 Vyse Street<br>Birmingham | Manufacturing jewellers |
| R2/147<br>24 November 1911<br>Sent by G W Usher | Thorpe Cottage<br>Ashleigh Road<br>Solihull<br>Birmingham | P13/U/7-11<br>***#8078-82***  | **Samuel USHER**<br>**Frank Edward USHER**<br>**John Mark USHER**<br>**Gustavus William USHER**<br>123 Vyse Street<br>Birmingham | |
| R2/191<br>26 October 1914<br>Sent by Samuel Usher Ltd<br>Two sizes | Thorpe Cottage [1]<br>Ashleigh Road<br>Solihull<br>Birmingham | P15/S/2-7<br>***#8083-8***  | **Samuel USHER LTD**<br>G W Usher [1] (Director)<br>123 Vyse Street<br>Birmingham | Gold ring, brooch and bracelet makers |
| R2/207<br>18 July 1916<br>Sent by Gustavus William Usher | | P15/U/8–12<br>***#8089-93***  | | Manufacturing jewellers |
| R2/160<br>3 September 1912<br>Sent by G W Usher | Thorpe Cottage<br>Ashleigh Road<br>Solihull<br>Warwickshire | P13/U/13-18<br>***#8094-99***  | | Manufacturing goldsmiths |
| R1/59<br>3 February 1898<br>Sent by Simmons & Venour | 6 Harborne Road [1]<br>Edgbaston<br>86 Albert Road [2]<br>Handsworth<br>Birmingham | P5/Y*sic*/927<br>***#8100*** 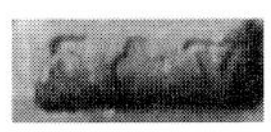 | **Bernard Rintel SIMMONS** [1]<br>**Henry Edward VENOUR** [2] trading as<br>trading as Vyse Street<br>Birmingham | Manufacturing jewellers |
| R1/204<br>12 December 1903<br>Sent by selves | 23 Deane Road<br>Fairfield<br>Liverpool | P9/W/103 and 01*sic*<br>***#8101,2***  | **THE LANG CO LTD**<br>Samuel Wade (Manager)<br>48 Copperas Hill<br>Liverpool | Fountain pen makers |
| R3/58<br>13 July 1931<br>Sent by Smith, Ewen & Stylic Ltd<br>42 Frederick Street<br>Birmingham | 93 Bethune Road<br>Stamford Hill | P15/W/98<br>***#8103***  | **Simon WINEGARTEN** trading as<br>**WINEGARTEN**<br>145 Bishopsgate<br>London EC2 | Manufacturing jewellers |
| J1 1858-70<br>Similar mark entered<br>SAO 18 August 1858 | | P2/W in margin below/x3<br>***#8104-6***  | **S & S (Samuel) WARD**<br>20 St Mary's Gate<br>Manchester | Silversmiths |
| R3/49<br>26 October 1929<br>Sent by S W Goode<br>Two sizes | 69 Westminster Road<br>Handsworth<br>Birmingham | P15/G/52,53<br>***#8107,8***  | **S W GOODE & CO**<br>11-13 Prescot Street<br>Birmingham | Goldsmiths and jewellers |
| R2/86<br>29 June 1909<br>Sent by Samuel William Goode | | P13/S/9<br>***#8109***  | **Samuel William GOODE** trading as<br>**S W GOODE & CO**<br>11 Prescot Street<br>Birmingham | Manufacturing jewellers |

| REGISTRATION DETAILS | MAKER'S PRIVATE ADDRESS and DETAILS | PLATE and MARK DETAILS | MAKER/COMPANY and BUSINESS ADDRESS | MAKER'S TRADE |
|---|---|---|---|---|
| R2/166<br>27 November 1912<br>Sent by S W Goode & Co | 69 Westminster Road<br>Handsworth<br>Birmingham | P13/G/50<br>***#8110***<br> | **Samuel William GOODE** trading as<br>**S W GOODE & CO**<br>11 Prescot Street<br>Birmingham | Manufacturing jewellers |
| 17 July 1929 | | P15/G/52<br>***#8111***<br> | | |
| R1/42<br>9 April 1897<br>Sent by J Fleckner | Private address same as business<br>CWMP 1896-1900 | P5/R/831<br>***#8112***<br> | **Samuel William READ** *<br>37 Craven Street<br>Coventry | Watch manufacturer |
| R1/74<br>21 September 1898<br>Sent by C Harris | | P9/R/1<br>***#8113***<br> | | |
| Missing register<br>*c.*1889<br>Similar mark entered<br>BAO 20 January 1887 | | P5/S/253<br>***#8114***<br> | **Samuel Walton SMITH**<br>57 Cambridge Street<br>Birmingham | Silversmith |
| LPB/96<br>16 April 1880 | CWMP 1883-1924 as a watch manufacturer | P3/Y/x2<br>***#8115,6***<br> | **Samuel YEOMANS** *<br>48 Spon Street<br>Coventry | Watchcase maker |
| LPB/94<br>30 May 1884<br>Sent by S Jackson | | P5/Y/x1<br>***#8117***<br>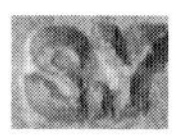 | | |
| SPB/14<br>29 August 1874<br>Sent by S R<br>(Samuel & Rogers?) | | P3/Y/x3<br>***#8118-20***<br> | | |
| Missing register<br>*c.*1886<br>Similar mark entered<br>BAO 19 June 1890 | | P5/Y/48<br>***#8121***<br>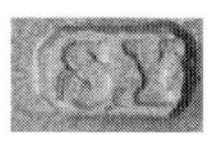 | | |
| Missing register<br>*c.*1888<br>Similar mark entered<br>BAO 14 April 1897 | | P5/Y/166<br>***#8122***<br> | | |
| Missing register<br>*c.*1886 | | P5/Y/45<br>***#8123***<br> | | |
| R2/138<br>17 June 1911<br>Sent by Benson Brothers | 40 Coundon Road<br>13 Northumberland Road<br>40 Coundon Road<br>Coventry | P13/XYZ/2<br>***#8124***<br> | **Frederick Samuel YEOMANS** *<br>**George W YEOMANS** *<br>**Charles H YEOMANS** *<br>48 Spon Street<br>Coventry | Watchmakers |
| R1/180<br>29 November 1902<br>Sent by S Zyto | Private address same as business | P9/XYZ/5<br>***#8125***<br> | **Sigmund ZYTO** *<br>15 St Mark's Street<br>Goodman's Fields<br>London E | Chain maker |

| REGISTRATION DETAILS | MAKER'S PRIVATE ADDRESS and DETAILS | PLATE and MARK DETAILS | MAKER/COMPANY and BUSINESS ADDRESS | MAKER'S TRADE |
|---|---|---|---|---|
| MR1/180<br>*c.*1699<br>LGM | | P1/12/x1<br>***#8126***<br> | **-- TAYLOR**<br>Nantwich | Silversmith |
| LPB/14<br>13 October 1883<br>No mark in LPB | 3rd name in LPB/14 and 3rd mark on P5/A | P5/A/x1<br>***#8127***<br> | **Thomas ACOTT & CO** *<br>4 Vyse Street<br>Birmingham | Goldsmiths |
| R1/78<br>30 August 1894<br>Sent by Thomas Able | | P5/A/585<br>***#8128***<br> | **Thomas ABLE**<br>56 Tenby Street North<br>Birmingham | Jeweller |
| PP1/189<br>GTD 1825-9 | Star between letters might indicate allusion to wheels and watch mechanisms - see Thomas Russell's TR mark | P1/31/x1<br>***#8129***<br> | **Thomas ADAMSON**<br>83 Gerrard Street (1816)<br>Liverpool | Watchcase maker |
| PDB 1791<br>MR2/57<br>MR3/75,76<br>J1 1791<br>PP1/189<br>SIL/26<br>SOT/136 | Gold rings, buttons and badge | P1/32/x2<br>***#8130,1***<br> | **Thomas APPLEBY**<br>Manchester | Goldsmith and silversmith |
| | May be Adamson, Armit or Appleby | P1/29/x2<br>***#8132,3***<br> | **Unidentified** | |
| PDB 1832-5<br>MR3/76<br>PTD 1824-43<br>J1 1793<br>GMSC/85 | Masonic medals<br>Square marked 1786<br>J1 has watchcase 1793 but no corresponding entry in the PDB and suggests Thomas Appleby. Perhaps a mis-reading of date for 1814 in which case duty not due | P1/22/x4<br>***#8134-7***<br> | **Thomas ARMITT**<br>65 Chapel Street<br>Manchester | Medallist |
| SOT/26 reports this mark on a badge as 1810 but probably is 1832 | Square marked 1787 | P1/23/x1<br>***#8138***<br> | | |
| Missing register<br>*c.*1890<br>Similar mark BAO<br>2 November 1911 and incuse mark 1897 | | P5/A/292<br>***#8139***<br> | **Thomas ARMSTRONG & BROTHER**<br>88-90 Deansgate<br>Manchester | Optician, watchmaker and clockmaker |
| Missing register<br>*c.*1894 | See Thomas Able #72<br>**PROBABLY LAST MARK IN MISSING REGISTER** | P5/A/552b<br>***#8140***<br> | **Thomas ABLE**<br>56 Tenby Street North<br>Birmingham | Jeweller |
| R1/153<br>19 September 1901<br>Sent by Frederick Thomas Trahern<br>Two sizes | 69 Hunkers Road [1]<br>Newcastle upon Tyne<br>35 Edwards Road [2]<br>Whitley Bay<br>1 Wardle Terrace [3]<br>Newcastle upon Tyne | P9/R/40,41<br>***#8141,2***<br> | **Thomas Arthur REID** [1]<br>**Francis James LANGFORD** [2]<br>**Christian Leopold REID** [3] trading as<br>**REID & SON** *<br>41 Grey Street<br>Newcastle upon Tyne | Goldsmiths, silversmiths and watchmakers |
| R1/1<br>28 April 1894<br>Sent by T E Aston | | P5/A/555<br>***#8143***<br> | **Thomas ASTON & SON**<br>95 Spencer Street<br>Birmingham | Eye glass manufacturers |

| REGISTRATION DETAILS | MAKER'S PRIVATE ADDRESS and DETAILS | PLATE and MARK DETAILS | MAKER/COMPANY and BUSINESS ADDRESS | MAKER'S TRADE |
|---|---|---|---|---|
| Missing register<br>*c.*1888 | Mark badly struck -<br>T Able or T Aston & Son or Co | P5/A/174<br>***#8144***<br> | **Unidentified** | |
| PDB 1831<br>MR3/77 | Spectacle frames | Not on P1<br>***#8145*** **T B?** | **T M BOWEN**<br>Liverpool | Goldsmith and silversmith |
| R3/105<br>24 April 1943<br>Sent by Thomas Arthur Brown | Private address same as business | P21/B/20<br>***#8146***<br> | **Thomas Arthur BROWN**<br>29 St Michael's Hill<br>Handsworth<br>Birmingham 19 | Manufacturing jeweller |
| R3/56<br>28 January 1931<br>Sent by Kinsey Brothers & Patrick Ltd<br>17 Vyse Street<br>Birmingham | 1 Bedford Road [1]<br>Crouch End<br>London N<br>13 Nursery Close [2]<br>Shirley<br>Croydon<br>Surrey | P15/T/57<br>***#8147***<br> | **TIDY & BLANCHARD**<br>George Tidy [1] (Partner)<br>John Stephen Owen Blanchard [2] (Partner)<br>37 Hatton Garden<br>London EC1 | Wholesale jewellers |
| R3/175<br>11 November 1960<br>Sent by Tidy & Blanchard | | P21/T/63<br>***#8148***<br> | **TIDY & BLANCHARD**<br>37/38 Hatton Garden<br>London EC1 | Manufacturers and wholesale jewellers |
| R3/56<br>17 April 1957<br>Sent by Kinsey Brothers & Patrick Ltd<br>17 Vyse Street<br>Birmingham | | P21/T/35<br>***#8149***<br> | **TIDY & BLANCHARD**<br>George Tidy [1] (Partner)<br>John Stephen Owen Blanchard [2] (Partner)<br>37 Hatton Garden<br>London EC1 | Wholesale jewellers |
| SPB/16<br>13 April 1870 | | P3/B/x3<br>***#8150-2***<br> | **Thomas BULL**<br>50 Gas Street<br>Coventry | Watch pendant maker |
| LPB/80<br>22 July 1881<br>LPB mark shown | Henry Thompson, jeweller, 25 Warstone Lane, Birmingham, and George Henry Brookes, Jeweller, Kelly 1882 | Not on P3<br>***#8153***<br> | **THOMPSON & BROOK**<br>address illegible – possibly Birmingham | Jewellers ? |
| R3/56<br>29 November 1956<br>Punch recut | | P21/T/28<br>***#8154***<br> | **TIDY & BLANCHARD**<br>George Tidy [1] (Partner)<br>John Stephen Owen Blanchard [2] (Partner)<br>37 Hatton Garden<br>London EC1 | Wholesale jewellers |
| 17 April 1957 | | P21/T/34<br>***#8155***<br> | | |
| R1/185<br>23 February 1903<br>Sent by T Bishton<br>Two sizes | 106 Leonard Street<br>Handsworth<br>Birmingham | P9/B/98,99<br>***#8156,7***<br> | **Thomas BISHTON** *<br>146½ Hockley Hill<br>Birmingham | Jeweller and silversmith |
| R1/75<br>1 October 1898<br>Sent by<br>W H Carrington & Co | 66 Hinkley Road<br>Lester (*sic*) | P9/B/4<br>***#8158***<br> | **T BLACKMAN**<br>10 Cheapside<br>Lester (*sic*)<br>Leicester probably | Tobacconist |

| REGISTRATION DETAILS | MAKER'S PRIVATE ADDRESS and DETAILS | PLATE and MARK DETAILS | MAKER/COMPANY and BUSINESS ADDRESS | MAKER'S TRADE |
|---|---|---|---|---|
| R1/145<br>2 April 1901<br>Sent by A J Cheshire | 116 Heathfield Road<br>Handsworth<br>Birmingham | P9/T/21<br>***#8159***<br> | **W F TURNBULL** and<br>**J E TURNBULL** trading as<br>**TURNBULL BROTHERS**<br>179 Warstone Lane<br>Birmingham | Jewellers and silversmiths |
| Missing register<br>*c.*1888<br>Similar mark BAO<br>23 September 1898 | | P5/T/174<br>***#8160***<br> | **TURNBULL BROTHERS**<br>63 Northampton Street<br>Birmingham | Jewellers and jet workers |
| R2/92<br>10 September 1909<br>Sent by W Fisher<br>BAO 9.465 | 2 Albert Road<br>Handsworth<br>Sussex Cottage<br>Lichfield Road<br>Four Oaks, Warwickshire | P13/T/17<br>***#8161***<br> | **William Foster TURNBULL**<br>**Joseph Edwin TURNBULL** trading as<br>**TURNBULL BROTHERS**<br>179 Warstone Lane<br>Birmingham | Wholesale jewellers |
| R3/155<br>26 April 1955<br>Sent by Taylor Brothers | 50 Sherwood Road [1]<br>Hall Green<br>66 Clarence Road [2]<br>King's Norton | P21/T/26<br>***#8162***<br> | **Thomas Arthur TAYLOR** [1]<br>**Montgomery TAYLOR** [2] trading as<br>**TAYLOR BROTHERS**<br>11 Hockley Street<br>Birmingham 18 | Manufacturing jewellers |
| Missing register<br>*c.*1892<br>Similar mark BAO<br>23 September 1891 | | P5/T/424<br>***#8163***<br> | **TURNER BROTHERS**<br>2 Alfred Street<br>Warstone Lane<br>Birmingham | Silversmiths |
| R1/27<br>16 April 1896<br>Sent by C E Turner | Private address same as business | P5/T/756<br>***#8164***<br> | **Charles Edward TURNER** trading as<br>**TURNER BROTHERS**<br>2 Alfred Street<br>Warstone Lane then<br>Pemberton Street<br>Birmingham | |
| R3/81<br>27 November 1935<br>Sent by T Bradbury & Sons | | P15/G*sic*/222<br>***#8165***<br>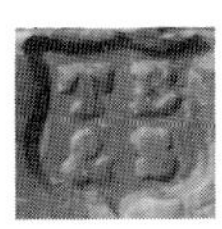 | **Thomas BRADBURY & SONS LTD** *<br>Common seal of company affixed in the presence of:-<br>T Bradbury (Director)<br>S W Turner (Director)<br>G H Cottram (Secretary)<br>22 and 24 Arundel Street<br>Sheffield 1 | Silversmiths |
| Not in R1 as expected<br>*c.*1895 | *Jewellery making In Birmingham*, p187 | P5/T/622<br>***#8166***<br>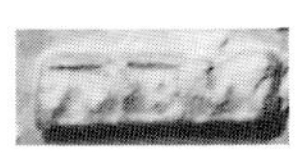 | **T B TRAWFORD?**<br>41 Frederick Street<br>Birmingham | Jeweller |
| R1/6 undated but next to entry for<br>28 January 1895<br>Sent by A H Landless | Hope Cottage<br>Flixton<br>Manchester | P5/aboveC/635<br>***#8167***<br> | **James Henry CONRY**<br>**Josephine Teresa CONRY**<br>**Mary CONRY**<br>**Rose CONRY** trading as<br>**T CONRY**<br>2 Oak Street<br>Thomas Street<br>Manchester | Umbrella manufacturers |
| R2/202<br>14 January 1916<br>Sent by A A Thorne<br>Edwin Clark | 146 Wheeler Street<br>Birmingham<br>20 Station Road<br>Handsworth<br>Birmingham | P15/T/25<br>***#8168***<br>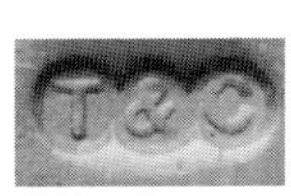 | **Alfred Albert THORNE**<br>**Edwin CLARK** trading as<br>**THORNE & CLARK**<br>91 Vyse Street<br>Birmingham | Ring makers |
| SPB/6 date indistinct<br>?1877 | | P3/C/x3<br>***#8169-71***<br> | **Thomas CARRAN**<br>50 Stafford Street<br>Liverpool | Watchcase maker |

| REGISTRATION DETAILS | MAKER'S PRIVATE ADDRESS and DETAILS | PLATE and MARK DETAILS | MAKER/COMPANY and BUSINESS ADDRESS | MAKER'S TRADE |
|---|---|---|---|---|
| PDB 1837-9<br>MR3/80<br>GTD 1846-60<br>GSJW/135<br>J1 1837-55 | Gold rings and medals<br>Square marked 1787<br>Town not mentioned in PDB | P1/23/x2<br>***#8172,3***<br> | **Thomas CUBBIN**<br>251 Crown Street<br>Liverpool | Goldsmith and medallist |
| PP1/170 | | P2/C/x3<br>***#8174-6***<br><br>P2/J*sic*/x1<br>***#8177***<br>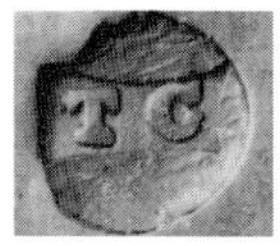 | **Thomas CUBBIN**<br>Great King Street<br>Hockley<br>Birmingham | Watchcase maker |
| LPB/34<br>3 May 1883 | | P3/C/x3<br>***#8178-80***<br> | **Thomas CURRYER** *<br>32 Southampton Square<br>London | Goldsmith and jeweller |
| Missing register<br>*c.*1886<br>Similar mark entered<br>LAO 25 January 1887<br><br>Similar mark entered<br>LAO 15 August 1887 | Seen on Waltham watchcase<br>1887 | P5/C/21<br>***#8181***<br> | **Thomas COBB** *<br>77 Farringdon Road<br>London EC<br>or<br>**Thomas CLEAVER** *<br>8 York Street, The Butts<br>Coventry | Watchcase maker<br><br>Watchcase maker |
| Missing register<br>*c.*1888<br>Similar mark entered<br>LAO 14 June 1890 | | P5/C/188<br>***#8182***<br> | **Thomas CAUSER** *<br>Hope Cottage<br>Hill Street<br>Coventry | Watchcase maker |
| R1/198<br>10 August 1903<br>Sent by J G Newbold | 23 Muswell Road<br>Muswell Hill<br>Strand Green | P9/G/42<br>***#8183***<br> | **Thomas Claud GOODING**<br>**Edward Ryan[1] GOODING**<br>(Ed: Rhymer[1] in #8185)<br>37 Farringdon Road<br>London | Tobacconists, etc |
| R1/134<br>17 October 1900<br>Sent by W Walker | 35 Argyle Terrace<br>Workington | P9/G/17<br>***#8184***<br> | **Thomas Critchly GARSTANG**<br>4 Finkle Street<br>Workington and<br>1 Main Street<br>Keswick | Tobacconist and cigar merchant |
| R1/91<br>16 February 1899<br>Sent by W Walker | 2 Ravenscroft Park [1]<br>High Barnett<br>29 Mount View [2]<br>Stroud Green<br>London | P9/G/8<br>***#8185***<br> | **Thomas Claud GOODING** [1]<br>**Edward Rhymer GOODING** [2]<br>trading as<br>**Thomas C GOODING & CO**<br>37 Farringdon Street (*sic*)<br>London | Pipe dealers |
| | TC&CB or TC&GB or TG&GB | P1/9/x3<br>***#8186-8***<br> | **Unidentified** | |
| R3/94<br>13 March 1939<br>Sent by<br>W T Toghill & Co<br>26 February 1949 | The Old House<br>Station Road<br>Knowle<br>Warwickshire | P21/T/2<br>***#8189***<br><br>P21/T/18<br>***#8190***<br>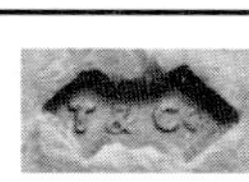 | **William Thomas TOGHILL** trading as<br>**W T TOGHILL & CO**<br>38 Vyse Street<br>Birmingham | Manufacturing goldsmiths and silversmiths |

| REGISTRATION DETAILS | MAKER'S PRIVATE ADDRESS and DETAILS | PLATE and MARK DETAILS | MAKER/COMPANY and BUSINESS ADDRESS | MAKER'S TRADE |
|---|---|---|---|---|
| Missing register<br>*c.*1890 | | P5/T/285<br>***#8191***  | **Unidentified** | |
| LPB/22<br>22 January 1884 | | P5/C/x1<br>***#8192***  | **Thomas CARTWRIGHT & SONS**<br>173 Hockley Street<br>Birmingham | Jewellers |
| SPB/23<br>16 September 1876<br>GSJW/137 1861 | Late John Richards | P3/T/x3<br>***#8193-5***  | **Thomas C TOLMAN**<br>53 Hunter Street<br>Liverpool | Watchcase maker and case springer |
| R1/20<br>28 January 1896<br>Sent by Tom Ducrow | 27 Upper Gough Street<br>Birmingham | P5/D/721<br>***#8196***  | **Tom DUCROW**<br>40 St Paul's Square<br>Birmingham | Silversmith |
| R2/153<br>22 March 1912<br>BAO 14.775, 14.776<br>Sent by T Ducrow<br>Two sizes | Yardley Village<br>Birmingham | P13/D/40,41<br>***#8197,8*** 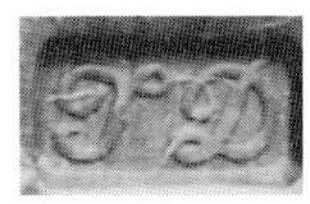 | **Tom DUCROW (or DUCROU)**<br>22 Vittoria Street<br>Birmingham | Manufacturing silversmith |
| Missing register<br>*c.*1886 | | P5/D/36<br>***#8199*** 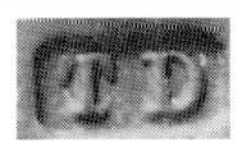 | **Unidentified** | |
| R1/73<br>3 August 1894<br>Sent by T Dodwell<br>CWMP 1896-1900 | Private address same as business | P5/D/571<br>***#8200***  | **Thomas DODWELL**<br>45 Bond Street<br>Coventry | Watchcase maker |
| R1/123<br>23 March 1900<br>Sent by W Walker | 64 Bensham Manor Road<br>Thornton Heath<br>Surrey | P9/L/15<br>***#8201***  | **Thomas D LOECKER**<br>42 Tabernacle Street, Finsbury<br>London EC | Importer of tobacconists fancy goods |
| R2/10<br>5 February 1906<br>Sent by J G Newbold | 32 Dugnall Park<br>Sellhurst<br>London | P9/L/72<br>***#8202***  | **Thomas M de LOEKER** trading as<br>**VAN ANDELEST FIOLET**<br>42 Tabernacle Street<br>Finsbury<br>London EC | Clay pipe manufacturers and fancy goods importers |
| R1/156<br>13 January 1901<br>Sent by L Smith & Co | Highgate Lodge<br>Campden Hill<br>Kensington<br>London W | P9/D/26<br>***#8203***  | **Thomas De La RUE & CO LTD** *<br>William Thomas Shaw (Director)<br>Bunhill Row<br>London | Manufacturing stationers |
| R1/177<br>3 October 1902<br>Sent by Lionel Smith & Co Cancelled 31 January 1905 | 30 Dracot Place<br>London SW | P9/D/38-40<br>***#8204-6***  | **Thomas De La RUE & CO LTD** *<br>W Auld (Director)<br>110 Bunhill Row<br>London EC | Wholesale jewellers |
| Missing register<br>*c.*1891 | "D" square suggests surname beginning with "D" and "M" might indicate Manchester | P5/D/376<br>***#8207***  | **Unidentified** | |
| R2/54<br>29 January 1908<br>Sent by Thomas E Aitkin<br>Four sizes | Coversham<br>Botteville Road<br>Acocks Green<br>Birmingham | P9/A/96-99<br>***#8208-11***  | **Thomas Edward AITKIN**<br>40 St Paul's Square<br>Birmingham | Manufacturing silversmith |

| REGISTRATION DETAILS | MAKER'S PRIVATE ADDRESS and DETAILS | PLATE and MARK DETAILS | MAKER/COMPANY and BUSINESS ADDRESS | MAKER'S TRADE |
|---|---|---|---|---|
| R3/96<br>5 December 1939<br>Sent by T E Hughes | 49 Tennal Road<br>Harborne<br>Birmingham 32 | P21/H/13<br>***#8212***<br> | **Thomas Edgar HUGHES**<br>45 Vyse Street<br>22 Vyse Street (from 1944)<br>Birmingham | Manufacturing metal mounter |
| 25 February 1940 | | P21/H/17<br>***#8213***<br> | | |
| R3/118<br>12 June 1947<br>Sent by T E Hughes | Private address same as business | P21/H/37<br>***#8214***<br> | **Thomas Edward HUGHES**<br>7 Warstone Lane<br>Birmingham 18 | Manufacturing jeweller |
| R1/153<br>18 September 1901<br>Sent by T E Hughes | 54 New Spring Street<br>Birmingham | P9/H/46<br>***#8215***<br> | **Thomas Edward HUGHES**<br>98 Spencer Street<br>Birmingham | |
| PP1/189<br>GTD 1825-9<br>PMR 1822-37 | See also related I*E and ITE marks | P1/30/x2<br>***#8216,7***<br> | **Timothy ELLISON and Henry FISHWICK**<br>5 Tarleton Street<br>Liverpool | Watchcase makers |
| R3/56<br>3 February 1931<br>Sent by T E Ketterer | Bonaventure<br>London Road<br>Brentwood<br>Essex | P15/K/17<br>***#8218***<br> | **T E KETTERER & CO LTD**<br>Common Seal of the Company was affixed in the presence of:-<br>Thomas Edward Ketterer (Director)<br>Bernadine Ketterer (Secretary)<br>1 Hatton Garden<br>London EC1 | Watch importers |
| R1/35<br>6 November 1896<br>Sent by W H Cotton<br>A G Griffiths<br>Two sizes | 300 Hagley Road<br>Birmingham | P5/M/802a,b<br>***#8219,8220***<br> | **Thomas Edward MANNOX**<br>84 Worcester Street<br>Birmingham | Jeweller |
| R3/4<br>27 July 1921<br>Sent by Clark & Sewill<br>Frank Fattorini | Rockwood<br>Skipton<br>2 Hayley Grove<br>Edgbaston | P15/F/21<br>***#8221***<br> | **Thomas FATTORINI (BIRMINGHAM) LTD** *<br>Thomas Fattorini (Partner)<br>Frank Fattorini (Partner)<br>5 Hockley Street<br>Birmingham | Medal and badge makers |
| LPB/30<br>21 June 1879 | | P3/F/x1<br>***#8222***<br>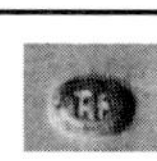 | **Thomas FRAZER** *<br>10 Thavies Inn<br>London | Watchcase maker |
| | | P3/F/x1<br>***#8223***<br> | | |
| R3/140<br>26 November 1952<br>Sent by T Fleming | 35 Brompton Road<br>Stretford<br>Manchester | P21/F/21<br>***#8224***<br> | **Thomas FLEMING**<br>Domestic and Trades College<br>West Bourne<br>Manchester | Student |
| PDB 1820-2<br>MR3/82 | Gold rings<br><br>See also IF | P1/30/x2<br>***#8225,6***<br>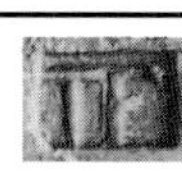 | **Thomas FOXALL**<br>Address unknown | Goldsmith |
| R1/32<br>13 August 1896<br>Sent by T P Hewitt<br>Benson Brothers<br>Dennison & Wigley | TF impression taken of punch received by R J Pike, Coventry, 8 December 1905 | P5/F/785<br>***#8227***<br> | **Thomas FATTORINI** *<br>Caroline Square<br>Skipton<br>Yorkshire | Jewellers |
| Not in LPB or R1 as expected | | P5/F/01*sic*<br>***#8228***<br>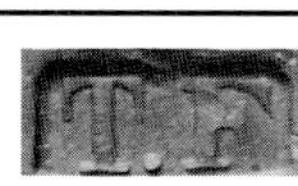 | | |

| REGISTRATION DETAILS | MAKER'S PRIVATE ADDRESS and DETAILS | PLATE and MARK DETAILS | MAKER/COMPANY and BUSINESS ADDRESS | MAKER'S TRADE |
|---|---|---|---|---|
| LPB/30<br>20 November 1880 | | P3/F/x3<br>***#8229-31***<br>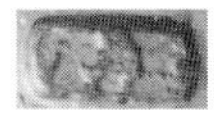 | **Thomas FOLLIS**<br>Warstone Buildings<br>Warstone Lane<br>Birmingham | Jeweller |
| R1/149<br>25 June 1901<br>Sent by T Fattorini | Greenmount<br>Skipton | P9/F/11<br>***#8232***<br> | **Thomas FATTORINI** *<br>Caroline Square<br>Skipton | Watch and jewellery manufacturer |
| R2/129<br>7 March 1911<br>Sent by<br>W W Cashmore | | P13/F/24<br>***#8233***<br> | | Jewellers |
| R2/181<br>1 January 1914<br>Sent by Ginder & Couch<br>Three sizes | Rockwood<br>Skipton | P15/F/5,6,19<br>***#8234-6***<br>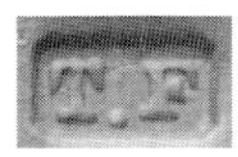 | **Thomas FATTORINI** *<br>Caroline Square<br>Skipton and<br>Knowsley Street<br>Bolton | |
| R3/70<br>20 April 1934<br>Sent by Samuel Hope<br>126 Vyse Street<br>Birmingham | Rockwood [1 2]<br>Skipton<br>Laurel Bank [3]<br>Ilkley, Yorkshire | P15/F/39<br>***#8237***<br>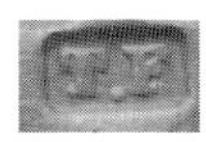 | **Thomas FATTORINI (SKIPTON) LTD** *<br>Thomas Fattorini [1] (Director)<br>Frank Fattorini [2] (Director)<br>Wilfred Fattorini [3] (Director)<br>1-7 Newmarket Street<br>Skipton<br>Yorkshire | |
| R2/181<br>1 January 1914<br>Sent by Ginder & Couch<br>Two sizes | Rockwood<br>Skipton | P15/F/2-4<br>***#8238-40***<br> | **Thomas FATTORINI** *<br>Caroline Square<br>Skipton and<br>Knowsley Street<br>Bolton | |
| LPB/80<br>3 May 1881 | Kelly 1881 | P3/F/x2<br>***#8241,2***<br> | **TROUP & FORD**<br>91 Vyse Street<br>Birmingham | Jewellers |
| R2/3<br>23 September 1905<br>Sent by Twine & Gilpin | Rosslyn<br>Alexander Road<br>Acocks Green<br>53 Mostyn Road<br>Handsworth<br>Birmingham | P9/T/56<br>***#8243***<br> | **W F TWINE**<br>**H GILPIN** trading as<br>**TWINE & GILPIN**<br>89 Vyse Street<br>Birmingham | Manufacturing jewellers |
| R1/204<br>1 December 1903<br>Sent by selves | | P9/T/41<br>***#8244***<br> | | |
| PP1/191<br>GTD 1865-82 | | P2/G/x6<br>***#8245-50***<br> | **Thomas GREEN II**<br>44 Gerrard Street<br>Liverpool or<br><br>**Thomas GROVE** *<br>55 Wellington Street<br>Goswell Road<br>London | Watchcase maker<br><br>Watchcase maker |
| PP3/83<br>Not in SPB or LPB so struck 1860-3<br>Similar mark LAO<br>30 September 1859 | | P3/G/x3<br>***#8251-3***<br> | **Thomas GROVE** *<br>55 Wellington Street<br>Goswell Road<br>London | Watchcase maker |

| REGISTRATION DETAILS | MAKER'S PRIVATE ADDRESS and DETAILS | PLATE and MARK DETAILS | MAKER/COMPANY and BUSINESS ADDRESS | MAKER'S TRADE |
|---|---|---|---|---|
| PDB 1785-90<br>MR3/83<br>PP1/189<br>PP2/346<br>PCR-1773<br>Similar mark entered<br>BAO *c*.1782 | See also related IW over TG mark | P1/19/x1<br>***#8254***<br><br>P2/G/x2<br>***#8255,6***<br> | **Thomas GREEN I**<br>Temple Street (1781)<br>Wyke's Court, Dale Street (1782)<br>Sir Thomas Building (1790)<br>1 and 2 Wykes Court, Dale Street (1794-1811)<br>Wire Works (1796-1804)<br>Liverpool | Watchcase maker |
| Not in SPB<br>Similar mark entered<br>LAO 7 November 1856 | | P2/G/x2<br>***#8257,8***<br> | **Thomas GROVE** *<br>22 Norman's Buildings<br>St Lukes<br>London EC | Watchcase maker |
| R3/159<br>12 January 1957<br>Sent by T G Galilee | 2 Cornwall Road<br>Widnes<br>Lancashire | P21/G/40<br>***#8259***<br> | **Thomas George GALILEE**<br>No business address entered | Student silversmith |
| | See Thomas Green and Thomas Grove | P2/G/x2<br>***#8260,1***<br> | **Unidentified** | |
| MR1/139-40<br>J1 1687-96<br>J3/416 | Church plate *c*.1697-1701<br>Free 1686 | Pre-dates P1<br>***#8262***<br> | **Timothy GARDNER**<br>Chester | Silversmith |
| R1/34<br>16 October 1896<br>Sent by Stokes & Ireland Ltd | 3 Melville Terrace<br>Stirling | P5/D/795<br>***#8263***<br>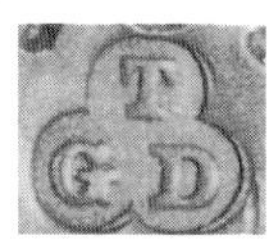 | **George Turnbell DRUMMOND**<br>5 Murray Place<br>Stirling | Goldsmith and silversmith |
| R1/137<br>13 November 1900<br>Sent by T P Hewitt<br>J Harris | The Avenue<br>Linthorpe Road<br>Middlesbrough | P9/P/75<br>***#8264***<br> | **Thomas Gibson POOLE**<br>52 Linthorpe Road<br>Middlesbrough | Jeweller |
| R1/214<br>18 May 1904<br>Sent by T Hancox | 124 Heathfield Road<br>Handsworth | P9/H/59<br>***#8265***<br> | **Thomas HANCOX**<br>15 Tenby Street<br>Birmingham | Manufacturing jeweller and silversmith |
| Missing register<br>*c*.1889 | | P5/H/212<br>***#8266***<br> | **Unidentified** | |
| R1/140<br>30 January 1901<br>Sent by Thomas Hale | 207 Lozells Road<br>Handsworth<br>Birmingham | P9/H/41<br>***#8267***<br> | **Thomas HALE**<br>56 Branston Street<br>Birmingham | Gold brooch and locket maker |
| R2/66<br>8 October 1908<br>Sent by Thomas Hale | 158 Hamstead Road<br>Handsworth<br>Birmingham<br>Staffs | P13/H/3<br>***#8268***<br> | | Manufacturing jewellers |
| R3/133<br>13 July 1950<br>Sent by T W Harding<br>Two sizes | St Hellier, Buxton Road<br>Chinley, Stockport<br>Lodge Wood Cottage<br>Taxal (27 September 1960)<br>Whaley Bridge | P21/H/59,60<br>***#8269,70***<br> | **Trevor Wilson HARDING**<br>No business address entered | Student silversmith |
| PDB 1793-1811<br>MR2/87<br>MR3/84<br>PP1/51,189<br>PP2/351<br>SIL/28 | Watchcases and snuff boxes<br>Working on own 1793 to 1816.<br>Seen on the case of a watch by Morris Tobias 1815<br>See TH&Co, TH&Son and TH/ JH | P1/28/x2<br>***#8271,2***<br> | **Thomas HELSBY**<br>26 Trueman Street (1793-6)<br>15, 16, 17 Vauxhall Road (1800-5)<br>26, 28 Vauxhall Road (1806-25)<br>Liverpool | Watchcase and snuff box maker |

| REGISTRATION DETAILS | MAKER'S PRIVATE ADDRESS and DETAILS | PLATE and MARK DETAILS | MAKER/COMPANY and BUSINESS ADDRESS | MAKER'S TRADE |
|---|---|---|---|---|
| See above entry | Seen on Liverpool watchcases 1800 and 1806 | P1/28/x1<br>***#8273***<br> | **Thomas HELSBY**<br>26 Trueman Street (1793-6)<br>15, 16, 17 Vauxhall Road (1800-5)<br>26, 28 Vauxhall Road (1806-25)<br>Liverpool | Watchcase and snuff box maker |
| Missing register<br>*c.*1891<br>Similar mark entered LAO 20 March 1882 | | P5/H/381<br>***#8274***<br> | **Thomas HALL** *<br>22 Bouverie Street<br>London EC | Silversmith |
| R2/89<br>30 July 1909<br>Sent by E Whitehouse & Son<br>BAO 7.689 | 27 Rotten Park Road<br>Edgbaston<br>Birmingham | P13/H/40<br>***#8275***<br> | **Tobias HIRSCHFIELD** *<br>99 Vyse Street<br>Birmingham | Jeweller |
| R2/122<br>31 October 1910<br>Sent by L E Neale<br>BAO 16.653<br>16.654, 16.655 | | P13/H/66-68<br>***#8276-8***<br> | | |
| PDB 1785<br>MR3/84<br>PP1/189<br>PP2/350<br>GTD 1784-99 | | P1/17/x3<br>***#8279-81***<br>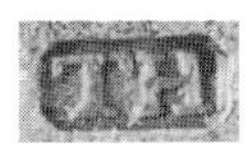 | **Thomas HARRISON**<br>1 Finney Lane (1774-1803)<br>Liverpool | Watchcase maker |
| On plate 2 so post 1841 | See other TH marks | P2/H/x2<br>***#8282,3***<br> | **Unidentified** | |
| PDB 1788-9<br>MR2/87<br>MR3/86 | Spoon, skewer, buckles, seals, labels, gorget, tongs 1787-9 | P1/24/x1<br>***#8284***<br> | **Thomas HILL**<br>Chester | Silversmith |
| SPB/5<br>2 October 1876<br>Sent by J McCormack | 32 Rydal Street<br>Everton | P3/H/x2<br>***#8285,6***<br> | **Charles** (*sic*) **HUGHES**<br>4 Waterford Buildings<br>14 Richmond Street<br>Liverpool | Watchmaker |
| LPB/40<br>4 December 1883<br>Sent by J Fleckner | | P5/H/x2<br>***#8287,7a***<br> | **Thomas HILL & CO**<br>Hearsall House<br>Chapel Fields<br>Coventry | Watch manufacturer |
| LPB/40<br>3 March 1884 | | P5/H/x2<br>***#8288,8a***<br> | | |
| LPB/8<br>8 October 1884<br>No mark in LPB | | P5/H/x1<br>***#8289***<br> | | |
| Missing register<br>*c.*1887 | | P5/H/82<br>***#8290***<br> | | |
| Missing register<br>*c.*1887 | | P5/H/92<br>***#8291***<br> | | |
| R1/9<br>18 April 1895<br>Sent by Tom Hayes | 98 Thornhill Road<br>Handsworth<br>Birmingham | P5/H/651<br>***#8292***<br> | **Tom HAYES** *<br>21 Spencer Street<br>Birmingham | Silversmith |

| REGISTRATION DETAILS | MAKER'S PRIVATE ADDRESS and DETAILS | PLATE and MARK DETAILS | MAKER/COMPANY and BUSINESS ADDRESS | MAKER'S TRADE |
|---|---|---|---|---|
| R1/178<br>13 October 1902<br>Sent by selves | Thornhill Road<br>Handsworth<br>Coppice Road<br>Moseley | P9/T/29<br>***#8293***<br> | **Roland James TAYLOR**<br>**Mortimer William HANCOCK** trading as<br>**TAYLOR & HANCOCK**<br>31 Northampton Street<br>Birmingham | Jewellers |
| R2/2<br>1 September 1905<br>Sent by Wright & Hadgkiss<br>Old punch P9/T/29 recut | 332 Church Hill<br>Handsworth<br>Coppice Road<br>Moseley, Birmingham | P9/T/55<br>***#8294***<br> | | |
| R2/58<br>9 April 1908<br>Sent by J Hayward | Ashdene<br>Handsworth Road<br>Birmingham<br>Coppice Road<br>Moseley, Birmingham | P13/T/1,2<br>***#8295,6***<br> | **Robert** (*sic*) **James TAYLOR**<br>**Mortimer William HANCOCK** trading as<br>**TAYLOR & HANCOCK**<br>31 Northampton Street<br>Birmingham | |
| R2/141<br>1 August 1911<br>Sent by M W Hancock | Hamstead Road<br>Handsworth<br>Coppice Road<br>Moseley, Birmingham | P13/T/41-46<br>***#8297-8302***<br> | **Roland James TAYLOR**<br>**Mortimer William HANCOCK** trading as<br>**TAYLOR & HANCOCK**<br>31 Northampton Street<br>Birmingham | |
| PDB 1793-1811 | Mark seen on watchcase 1792<br>His first entry in PDB dated 29 April 1793 matches perfectly.<br>See other marks and addresses | P1/26/x1<br>***#8303***<br> | **Thomas HELSBY**<br>26 Trueman Street<br>Liverpool | Watchcase maker |
| PP1/189<br>GTD 1816-34 | See other TH marks | P1/26/x1<br>***#8304***<br>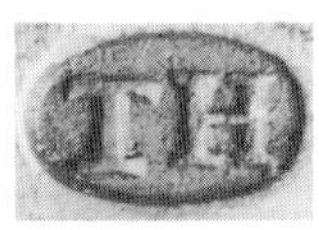 | **Thomas HULL**<br>36 Cottenham Street<br>Liverpool or | Watchcase maker |
| | See other marks and addresses | P1/28/x2<br>***#8305,6***<br>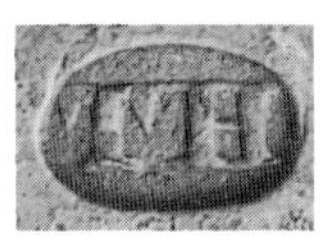 | **Thomas HELSBY**<br>26 Trueman Street<br>Liverpool | Watchcase maker |
| R2/176<br>30 September 1913<br>Sent by T Harvey | Squirrells Heath<br>Essex<br>Treyerlyn<br>Harold Wood<br>Essex | P13/H/86<br>***#8307***<br> | **Thomas E HARVEY**<br>**John J HARVEY** trading as<br>**T HARVEY** *<br>10 Cullum Street<br>London | Manufacturers agents and jewellers |
| R2/15<br>30 March 1906<br>Sent by T Hartmann | 42 Forest Drive<br>East Leytonstone | P9/H/80<br>***#8308***<br>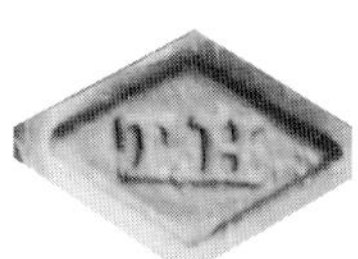 | **Theodor HARTMANN** *<br>14 Paternoster Row<br>London EC | Importer of silverware |
| R1/75<br>7 October 1898<br>Sent by Thomas Hale | 207 Lozells Road<br>Handsworth<br>Birmingham | P9/H/1<br>***#8309***<br>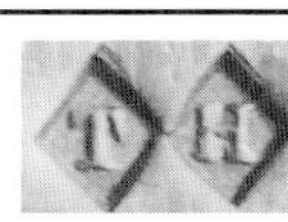 | **Thomas HALE**<br>5 Hortins Buildings<br>Branston Street<br>Birmingham | Manufacturing jeweller |
| R1/91<br>10 February 1899<br>Sent by T Hale<br>Cancelled<br>January 1901 | | P9/H/6,7<br>***#8310,11***<br>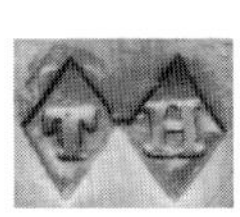 | | |
| R3/49<br>26 September 1929<br>Sent by R Jones | 5 Warstone Parade East<br>Birmingham | P15/B/198<br>***#8312***<br> | **Thomas Herbert BLISS** trading as<br>**Thomas BLISS & CO**<br>Kingsway House<br>103 Kingsway<br>London WC2 | Masonic jewellers |

| REGISTRATION DETAILS | MAKER'S PRIVATE ADDRESS and DETAILS | PLATE and MARK DETAILS | MAKER/COMPANY and BUSINESS ADDRESS | MAKER'S TRADE |
|---|---|---|---|---|
| R2/125<br>17 December 1910<br>Sent by Edward John Haseler<br>BAO 18.526 | 199 Holly Road<br>Handsworth<br>119 Thornhill Road<br>Handsworth<br>Birmingham | P13/T/29<br>*#8313*<br> | **Noble HASELER**<br>**Edward John HASELER** trading as<br>**THOMASON & HASELER BROTHERS**<br>24 Northwood Street *<br>Birmingham | Silversmiths |
| R3/102<br>6 July 1942<br>Sent by T & H Crathorne Ltd | | P21/C/21<br>*#8314*<br>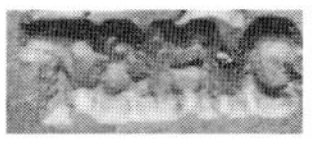 | **T & H CRATHORNE LTD**<br>T Crathorne (Director)<br>51 Newhall Hill<br>Birmingham | Manufacturing jewellers |
| GTD 1816-38<br>PP1/51,189 | Seen on the case of a watch by Morris Tobias 1825 and on a snuff box 1825 | P1/29/x2<br>*#8315,6*<br> | **Thomas HELSBY & CO**<br>22 Northampton Street (1827)<br>Liverpool | Watchcase makers |
| R1/114<br>12 October 1899<br>Sent by W Walker | 52 Devonshire Road<br>Aberdeen | P9/D/12<br>*#8317*<br>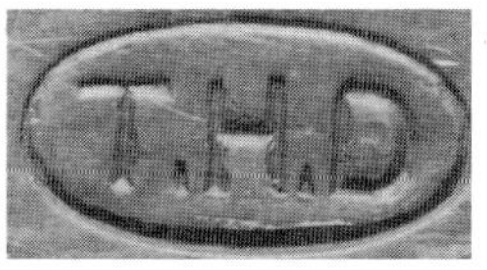 | **Thomas Henry DAVIS**<br>140 Union Street<br>Aberdeen | Fancy goods merchant |
| R2/145<br>13 October 1911<br>Sent by E C Harwood | Both of<br>Hillside Street<br>Georges Road<br>Wallasey<br>Cheshire | P13/H/81<br>*#8318*<br> | **Edwin Collier HARWOOD**<br>**Thomas HARWOOD** trading as<br>**HARWOOD BROTHERS**<br>18 and 20 Richmond Street<br>Liverpool | Importers of tobacconists fancy goods |
| GTD 1820-30<br>PP1/51,189 | Seen on watchcases 1815, 1819, 1821 and 1822<br><br>See also related TH and TH&Co marks | P1/31/x2<br>*#8319,20*<br> | **Thomas HELSBY**<br>**John HELSBY**<br>26 Vauxhall Road (1807-25)<br>Liverpool | Watchcase makers |
| R3/18<br>23 October 1923<br>Sent by Nicholas Rushworth & Co | Bryn Eden<br>Llanwnda<br>Caernarvonshire | P15/L/29<br>*#8321*<br>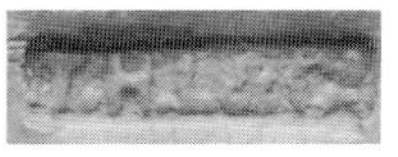 | **Charles Handley LAWSON** trading as<br>**T H LAWSON & CO**<br>6 Watling Street, Manchester and<br>62-63 Basinghall Street<br>London EC | Umbrella manufacturers |
| R1/48<br>5 August 1897<br>Sent by E J Rudge<br>J R Griffin | 28 Wickham Road<br>Beckenham<br>Kent | P5/M/861<br>*#8322*<br> | **Thomas Harold MARCH** trading as<br>**T H MARCH & CO** *<br>101 Hatton Garden<br>London EC | Wholesale jewellers |
| Undated | | P9/M/20<br>*#8323*<br> | | |
| R1/187<br>12 March 1903<br>Sent by W R & F Rabone | 126 Marlborough Road<br>London N | P9/M/46-48<br>*#8324-6*<br> | **T H MARCH & CO** *<br>G T C Welsford (Secretary)<br>17 Hatton Garden<br>London EC | |
| R3/25<br>15 November 1924<br>Sent by Florence Annie Moss | | P15/B/174<br>*#8327*<br> | **Florence Annie MOSS** trading as<br>**Thomas BROWN**<br>12 London Road<br>Liverpool | Jeweller |
| R2/51<br>3 November 1907<br>Sent by T H Rothwell | Ash Grove<br>Llanfairfechan | P9/R/105<br>*#8328*<br> | **Thomas Henry ROTHWELL**<br>Ash Grove<br>Llanfairfechan | Repousee worker |

| REGISTRATION DETAILS | MAKER'S PRIVATE ADDRESS and DETAILS | PLATE and MARK DETAILS | MAKER/COMPANY and BUSINESS ADDRESS | MAKER'S TRADE |
|---|---|---|---|---|
| R2/142<br>1 September 1911<br>Sent by A J Hirschfeld<br>BAO 19.194 | Rotten Park Road<br>Edgbaston<br>Birmingham | P13/H/80<br>*#8329*<br> | **Tobias HIRSCHFELD**<br>**Alex HIRSCHFELD** trading as<br>**T HIRSCHFELD & SON** *<br>99 Vyse Street<br>Birmingham | Manufacturing jewellers |
| PDB 1816-26<br>PDB 1827 Gold rings, snuff boxes and spoons | Eldest son John involved in 1816 at the age of 20 (see John Helsby).<br>Second son William joined in 1827 aged 20 years | P1/31/x3<br>*#8330-2*<br>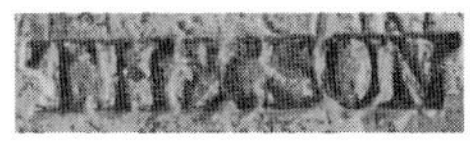 | **Thomas HELSBY & SON(S)**<br>26 Vauxhall Road (1807-21)<br>28 Vauxhall Road (1821-5)<br>Liverpool | Goldsmiths, silversmiths and watchcase makers |
| R1/135<br>29 October 1900<br>Sent by<br>T H Woodward | Private address same as business | P9/W/41<br>*#8333*<br> | **Thomas Hall WOODWARD**<br>1 Farringdon Road and North Finchley<br>London | Manufacturing jeweller |
| LGSJ 1825 | | P1/23/x1<br>*#8334*<br> | **Thomas JONES**<br>50 Lord Street<br>Liverpool | Goldsmith |
| R3/143<br>14 April 1953<br>Sent by T Jolly<br>Two sizes | 35 Woodcote Road<br>West Timperley<br>Altrincham<br>Cheshire | P21/IJ/9,10<br>*#8335,6*<br> | **Thomas JOLLY**<br>No business address entered | Silversmith |
| R2/61<br>6 June 1908<br>Sent by T Tomkins | 39 Victoria Road<br>Urmston<br>124 Davyhulme Road<br>Davyhulme | P13/T/3<br>*#8337*<br> | **Tom TOMKINS**<br>**Henry JACKSON** trading as<br>**TOMKINS & JACKSON**<br>46 Back Turner<br>Manchester | Umbrella and walking stick mounters |
| LPB/44<br>8 September 1884<br>Sent by T E Sutton<br>No mark in LPB | 5th name on LPB/44 and 5th mark on P5/J | P5/J/x1<br>*#8338*<br>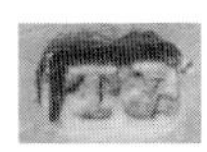 | **Thomas JONES** *<br>395 City Road<br>London | Wholesale jeweller and watch manufacturer |
| Missing register<br>*c.*1891 | | P5/J/398<br>*#8339*<br>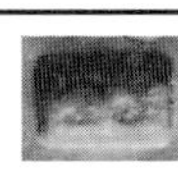 | **Unidentified** | |
| Missing register<br>*c.*1890<br>Similar mark BAO June 1917 | Plain font T&JB struck lightly | P5/B/232<br>*#8340*<br> | **Thomas & John BRAGG** *<br>18 Vittoria Street<br>Birmingham | General and masonic goldsmiths and jewellers |
| R3/186<br>14 August 1962<br>Sent by<br>T J Boucher | 30 Finchdean House<br>Tangley Grove<br>London SW15 | P21/B/74<br>*#8341*<br> | **Thomas James BOUCHER**<br>School of Silversmithing<br>Royal College of Art<br>Kensington Gore<br>London SW7 | Silversmithing |
| LPB/56 SP27/4<br>22 August 1884<br>Sent by J Sharpe<br>No mark in LPB just TJM | CWMP 1886-1901 | P5/M/x1<br>*#8342*<br>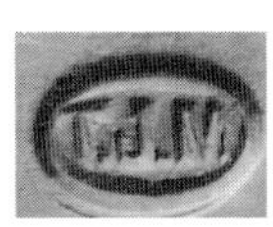 | **Thomas MERCER & SONS**<br>Hertford Place<br>Coventry | Watch manufacturers and jewellers |
| Missing register<br>*c.*1886<br>Similar mark entered BAO 4 June 1886 | | P5/M/59<br>*#8343*<br>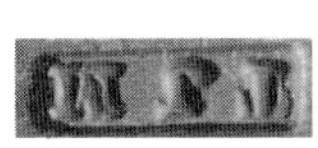 | | |
| R2/75<br>17 March 1909<br>Sent by T J Skelton | Ivanmere<br>Station Road<br>Wylde Green<br>Birmingham | P13/S/28-31<br>*#8344-7*<br> | **Thomas James SKELTON**<br>86 Vyse Street<br>Birmingham | Jeweller |
| R2/145<br>4 October 1911<br>Sent by Thomas James Shelton<br>Four sizes | Elton House<br>Western Road<br>Wylde Green<br>Birmingham | P13/S/66-79<br>*#8348-61*<br> | | |

| REGISTRATION DETAILS | MAKER'S PRIVATE ADDRESS and DETAILS | PLATE and MARK DETAILS | MAKER/COMPANY and BUSINESS ADDRESS | MAKER'S TRADE |
|---|---|---|---|---|
| R3/42<br>30 August 1928<br>Sent by T J Skelton | | P15/T*sic*/50-55<br>***#8362-7***<br> | **Thomas James SKELTON**<br>86 Vyse Street<br>Birmingham | Jeweller |
| R3/122<br>1 April 1948<br>Sent by<br>T J Skelton<br>Two sizes | 71 Leonard Road [1]<br>Handsworth, Birmingham<br>7 Hudson Road [2]<br>Handsworth Wood<br>Birmingham 20 | P21/S/34-39<br>***#8368-73***<br> | **Percy John SKELTON** [1]<br>**Elivia Millicent DODGE** [2] trading as<br>**T J SKELTON**<br>86 Vyse Street<br>Birmingham 18 | Manufacturing jewellers |
| Not in R1 as expected<br>Similar mark without full stops entered<br>LAO 25 May 1886 | | P5/W/747<br>***#8374***<br> | **Thomas Jones WATSON** *<br>12 Leverington Street<br>King Square, Goswell Road<br>London EC | Dress case fittings |
| Missing register<br>*c.*1886 | | P5/K/34<br>***#8375***<br> | **Unidentified** | |
| R2/82<br>12 May 1909<br>Sent by Travers Kessell & Co | 36 Crouch End Road<br>Crouch End<br>London N | P13/T/14<br>***#8376***<br> | **Arthur A TRAVERS** trading as<br>**TRAVERS KESSELL & CO** *<br>65 Hatton Garden<br>London EC | Fancy jewellers |
| R2/166<br>22 November 1912<br>Sent by C Horner | Ivy Lodge<br>Woodford Green<br>The Cottage, Betchworth<br>Fairmead, Theydon Bois<br>Orchard House, Pushhill Road<br>Wallington<br>Bindrose, Farm House<br>Amersham Common<br>Ivy Lodge, Woodford Green | P13/T/53<br>***#8377***<br> | **Walter KERNSLEY**<br>**Edward TOZER**<br>**A H TOZER**<br>**R MILLBOURNE**<br>**H TOZER**<br>**D KERNSLEY** trading as<br>**TOZER, KERNSLEY & FISHER LTD**<br>84 Fenchurch Street<br>London EC | Shipping merchants |
| R2/18<br>19 May 1906<br>Sent by J & R Griffin | Mole Cottage<br>Bore Hill, Surrey<br>Ivy Lodge, Woodford Green<br>Fair Mead, Epping<br>The Chase, Hadley Common<br>Parkfield, Parkhill Road<br>Wallington | P9/T/61<br>***#8378***<br> | **Edward TOZER**<br>**Walter KERNSLEY**<br>**Augustus H TOZER**<br>**Henry Edward FISHER**<br>**Robert MILLBOURNE** trading as<br>**TOZER, KERNSLEY & FISHER**<br>84 Fenchurch Street<br>London | |
| R2/79<br>22 April 1909<br>Sent by E Whitehouse & Son<br>BAO 11.554 | Ivy Lodge, Woodford Green<br>Essex<br>The Cottage, Betchworth<br>Surrey<br>Fairmead, Theydon Bois<br>Essex<br>The Chase, Hadley Common<br>Parkfield, Parkhill Road<br>Wallington, Surrey | P13/T/9<br>***#8379***<br> | **Walter KERNSLEY**<br>**Edward TOZER**<br>**Augustus H TOZER**<br>**Henry FISHER**<br>**Robert MILLBOURNE** trading as<br>**TOZER, KERNSLEY & FISHER LTD**<br>84 Fenchurch Street<br>London EC | |
| R1/223<br>15 November 1904<br>Sent by Thomas Lennie | Private address same as business | P9/L/62<br>***#8380***<br> | **Thomas LENNIE**<br>45 Brighton Street<br>Seacombe<br>Cheshire | Jeweller and watchmaker |
| R3/175<br>2 December 1960<br>Sent by T H Lennon | 41 Rockville Street<br>Falls Road<br>Belfast | P21/L/47<br>***#8381***<br> | **Thomas Henry LENNON**<br>College Jewellery Repair Centre<br>41 Fountain Street<br>Belfast | Practical jeweller |
| LPB/52<br>4 August 1883 | | P5/L/x1<br>***#8382***<br> | **T LORTON**<br>61 Lower Tower Street<br>Birmingham | Gem and fancy ring maker |

| REGISTRATION DETAILS | MAKER'S PRIVATE ADDRESS and DETAILS | PLATE and MARK DETAILS | MAKER/COMPANY and BUSINESS ADDRESS | MAKER'S TRADE |
|---|---|---|---|---|
| Missing register<br>*c.*1887<br>Similar mark without full stops entered BAO June 1890 | | P5/B/75<br>***#8383***<br> | **Thomas Lumsden BROWN**<br>St Catherine Street<br>Cupar | Jeweller |
| R1/173<br>7 August 1902<br>Sent by Latham & Morton | Acocks Green [1]<br>Nr Birmingham<br>Birchfield [2]<br>Birmingham | P9/L/38,44<br>***#8384,5***<br> | **Thomas LATHAM** [1]<br>**Ernest MORTON** [2] trading as<br>**LATHAM & MORTON** *<br>115/116 Vyse Street<br>Birmingham | Silversmiths |
| Recut to similar marks P9/L/43,44<br>6 February 1904<br>Two sizes | | P9/L/36,37,43<br>***#8386-8***<br> | | |
| R3/16<br>9 June 1923<br>Sent by T J Skelton | 58 Somerset Road<br>Handsworth<br>16 Robert Road<br>Handsworth | P15/M/60<br>***#8389***<br> | **Thomas Lynton MOTT**<br>**Charles Arthur MOTT**<br>79 Vyse Street<br>Birmingham | Jewellers |
| R3/85<br>3 September 1936<br>Sent by Thomas L Mott Ltd | | P21/M/2,3<br>***#8390,1***<br> | **Thomas L MOTT LTD**<br>Sealed by<br>C F Gaunt, JP<br>C C Mott (Director, Secretary)<br>79 Vyse Street (Registered Office)<br>Birmingham 18 | Manufacturing jewellers |
| LPB/54 undated 19th to 21st November 1878 No name or address | | P3/M/x2<br>***#8392,3***<br> | **Thomas Lynton MOTT**<br>50 Hockley Hill<br>Birmingham | Jewellers |
| R3/16<br>9 June 1923<br>Three sizes | 58 Somerset Road<br>Handsworth<br>16 Robert Road<br>Handsworth | P15/M/50-59<br>***#8394-8403***<br> | **Thomas Lynton MOTT**<br>**Charles Arthur MOTT**<br>79 Vyse Street<br>Birmingham | |
| R3/85<br>3 September 1936<br>Sent by Thomas L Mott Ltd | | P21/M/1<br>***#8404***<br> | | |
| R1/218<br>9 August 1904<br>Sent by T Perks & Sons | 45 Heathfield Road<br>Handsworth<br>Birmingham | P9/M/80<br>***#8405***<br> | **Thomas Lynton MOTT**<br>40 Heathfield Road<br>Handsworth<br>Birmingham | Wholesale jeweller and factor |
| R2/24<br>19 September 1906<br>Sent by F Goldsmith & Co | | P9/M/107<br>***#8406***<br> | | Wholesale jeweller |
| R2/111<br>24 May 1910<br>Sent by Thomas Perks & Sons | | P13/M/36<br>***#8407***<br> | **Thomas Lynton MOTT**<br>79 Vyse Street<br>Birmingham | Wholesale and manufacturing jeweller |
| R2/134<br>3 May 1911<br>Sent by R Parkes & Co BAO 18.254 | | P13/M/41<br>***#8408***<br> | | Manufacturing jeweller |
| R2/81<br>6 May 1909<br>Sent by Saunders & Shepherd | 131 Kings Road<br>Brighton | P13/L/13<br>***#8409***<br> | **Fenton Bowman LAWSON** trading as<br>**T LAWSON & SON** *<br>16 Old Steine and 131 Kings Road<br>Brighton | Watchmakers, jewellers and silversmiths |
| R3/155<br>23 August 1955<br>Sent by T MacInerny<br>Two sizes | Private address same as business | P21/M/44,45<br>***#8410,11***<br>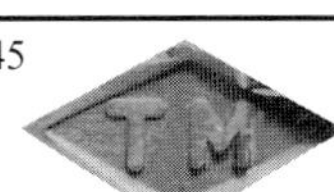 | **Thomas MACINERNY**<br>8 Kingston Road<br>Didsbury<br>Manchester 20 | Student |

| REGISTRATION DETAILS | MAKER'S PRIVATE ADDRESS and DETAILS | PLATE and MARK DETAILS | MAKER/COMPANY and BUSINESS ADDRESS | MAKER'S TRADE |
|---|---|---|---|---|
| SPB/13<br>20 June 1866<br>SPB mark shown | CWMP 1874 | Not on P3<br>***#8412*** 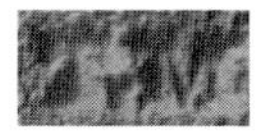 | **Thomas MILLS** *<br>83 Cromwell Street<br>Chapel Fields<br>Coventry | Watchcase maker |
| Missing register<br>*c.*1886 | | P5/M/52<br>***#8413***  | | |
| PDB 1786-92<br>MR3/94<br>PP1/189 | Gold buttons | P1/17/x3<br>***#8414-6***  | **Thomas MORROW**<br>Liverpool<br>or | Goldsmith |
| PMR/1861 | Thomas Moreland CMC/119 watch and clockmaker Northgate Street, Chester (1843-68) may be too late | P1/27/x1<br>***#8417***  | **Thomas MEAK**<br>65 Rodney Street<br>Liverpool | Watchcase maker |
| LPB/96<br>25 February 1882 | | P3/M/x1<br>***#8418*** 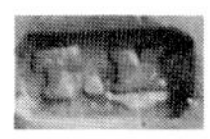 | **Thomas MORRALL**<br>259 New John Street West<br>Birmingham | Jeweller |
| R1/173<br>11 August 1902<br>Sent by C Horner | Water Orton [1]<br>Warwickshire<br>50 Summerfield Crescent [2]<br>Birmingham | P9/T/26<br>***#8419***  | **Horace THOMAS** [1]<br>**Walter MARSHALL** [2]<br>40 St Paul's Square<br>Birmingham | Wholesale jewellers |
| R1/205<br>9 January 1904<br>Sent by Loach Brothers | | P9/T/42<br>***#8420***  | | |
| R2/196<br>29 May 1915<br>Sent by T S Osborn | Water Orton<br>Near Birmingham<br>Harborne<br>Near Birmingham | P15/T/20-24<br>***#8421-5***  | **Horace THOMAS**<br>**Walter MARSHALL** trading as<br>**THOMAS & MARSHALL**<br>30 Frederick Street<br>Birmingham | Jewellers |
| MR1/143-5<br>MR2/183<br>SIL/46 | Tumbler cups, pap boat, bowl and marrow scoop1726-42 | P1/15/x1<br>***#8426***<br>type 3a  | **Thomas MADDOCK**<br>Chester | Silversmith |
| | See also his Ma mark<br>Free 1721 | P1/15/x1<br>***#8427***<br>type 3b  | | |
| MR1/145<br>J3/390 | Spoon *c.*1699 | Predates P1<br>***#8428***  | **Thomas MARSH**<br>Chester | Silversmith |
| Missing register<br>*c.*1892 | T M de L | P5/L/441<br>***#8429***  | **Unidentified** | |
| R2/94<br>30 September 1909<br>Sent by T M Taylor<br>LAO 14.082 | 109 High Street<br>Cowes<br>Isle of Wight | P13/T/18,19<br>***#8430,1***  | **T M TAYLOR** trading as<br>**T M TAYLOR & SON** *<br>109 High Street, Cowes<br>Isle of Wight | Watchmakers, jewellers and opticians |
| R2/122<br>1 November 1910<br>Sent by T M Taylor<br>*Entered at Chester, Birmingham, LAO and Sheffield (see form)* | | P13/T/27<br>***#8432***  | | |
| | | P13/T/26<br>***#8433***  | | |
| One block punch rejected | | P13/T/23-25<br>***#8434-6***  | | |

| REGISTRATION DETAILS | MAKER'S PRIVATE ADDRESS and DETAILS | PLATE and MARK DETAILS | MAKER/COMPANY and BUSINESS ADDRESS | MAKER'S TRADE |
|---|---|---|---|---|
| R2/114<br>28 June 1910<br>Sent by Thomas Newton | 64 Percival Street<br>Chorlton-on-Medlock<br>Manchester | P13/N/27<br>***#8437***  | **Thomas NEWTON**<br>13 Sugar Lane<br>Manchester | Stick mounting |
| PDB 1827-40<br>MR2/118<br>J1 1828-45 | Gold rings | P1/19/x1<br>***#8438*** <br>P2/N/x3<br>***#8439-41***  | **Thomas NEWTON**<br>9 Chapel Walks (1883)<br>Manchester<br>68 Bradshaw Street (1851)<br>Hulme<br>Manchester | Jeweller, goldsmith and silversmith |
| R1/112<br>26 September 1899<br>Sent by Thos Nightingale | 76 Aberdeen Street<br>Birmingham | P9/N/7<br>***#8442***  | **Thomas NIGHTINGALE**<br>33 Tenby Street<br>Birmingham | Jeweller and diamond mounter |
| LPB/92<br>23 December 1881 | CWMP 1883-91 | P3/B/x1<br>***#8443***  | **Thomas Newnham BELL** *<br>3 Spon Street<br>Coventry | Gold watchcase maker |
| R2/148<br>13 December 1911<br>Sent by T Nightingale & Son | 370 Bearwood Road<br>Smethwick | P13/N/28<br>***#8444***  | **Thomas NIGHTINGALE**<br>**Frank NIGHTINGALE** trading as<br>**T NIGHTINGALE & SON**<br>33 Tenby Street<br>Birmingham | Jewellers and ring makers |
| Registered different style mark at LAO<br>3 November 1830 | | P1/28/x2<br>***#8445,6***  | **Thomas OLLIVANT II** (G)<br>16 Exchange Street<br>Manchester or | Smallworker |
| GTD 1851-75<br>J1 1850 | | | **Thomas OVER**<br>Liverpool | Watchmaker |
| GTD 1807<br>PMR 1805-32 | | P1/30/x2<br>***#8447,8*** <br>P1/30/x2<br>***#8449,50***  | **Thomas PENNINGTON**<br>20 Leeds Street (1805)<br>51 Leeds Street (1810)<br>15 Downe Street (1816-18)<br>12 Baptist Street (1825)<br>3 Collingwood Street (1827-32)<br>Liverpool | Watch and watchcase manufacturer |
| PCR-1773<br>J1/373<br>MR2/128 | Seen on beaker 1786 with duty mark but name not in PDB<br><br>Seen on skewer 1787 | P1/19/x1<br>***#8451*** <br>Not on P1<br>***#8452***  | **Thomas PRITCHARD**<br>Shrewsbury | Silversmith |
| R1/216<br>23 June 1904<br>Sent by D Jones per Pannett & Son | 28 Pandora Road [1]<br>West Hampstead<br>London NW | P9/Q*sic*/201<br>***#8453***  | **T D PANNETT & SON LTD** *<br>David Jones [1] (Representative)<br>6 Carlisle Street<br>Soho Square<br>London W | Manufacturing jewellers |
| PDB 1785-6<br>MR2/128<br>MR3/95<br>SOT/127<br>PP2/349 | Silver watchcase 1784 and watch by William Spalding of Liverpool<br><br>His widow married a watchcase maker David Beyendorfe | Not on P1<br>***#8454*** 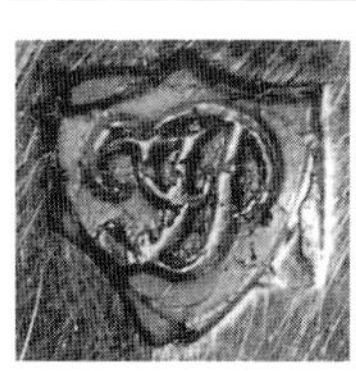 | **Thomas PIERPOINT**<br>12 Southside<br>St Paul's Square<br>Liverpool | Watchcase maker |

| REGISTRATION DETAILS | MAKER'S PRIVATE ADDRESS and DETAILS | PLATE and MARK DETAILS | MAKER/COMPANY and BUSINESS ADDRESS | MAKER'S TRADE |
|---|---|---|---|---|
| SPB/19<br>10 December 1868<br>Sent by Hugh Green<br>Liverpool | | P3/B/x6<br>***#8455-60***  | **Thomas Powell BATES**<br>62 Duke Street<br>Liverpool | Watch manufacturer |
| SPB/3<br>13 May 1864<br>no address with this entry | Thos Powell Bates in Directory | P3/B/x3<br>***#8461-3***  | **Thomas Pearson** (*sic*) **BATES** | |
| SPB/13<br>8 February 1867<br>Sent by John Richards | 53 St Martin's Street<br>Liverpool | P3/B/x3<br>***#8464-6***  | **Thomas P BATES**<br>62 Duke Street<br>Liverpool | |
| SPB/16<br>21 January 1875<br>Sent by Samuel & Rogers | | P3/B/x1<br>***#8467***  | **Thomas P BATES**<br>62 Duke Street<br>Liverpool | |
| R3/177<br>3 March 1961<br>Sent by<br>T P C Mulholland | 70 Gurney Court Road<br>St Albans<br>Hertfordshire | P21/M/52<br>***#8468***  | **Thomas Patrick Cunningham MULHOLLAND**<br>No business address entered | Research chemist |
| LPB/64<br>20 August 1880 | | P3/P/x1<br>***#8469***<br>§  | **Thomas POWERS & CO**<br>7 Police Street<br>Manchester | Artistic workers in metal |
| Missing register<br>*c.*1892 | | P5/H/414<br>***#8470***  | | Watch and watchcase manufacturer |
| R1/136<br>7 November 1900<br>Sent by T P Hewitt | Whitehouse<br>Eccleston Park<br>Nr Prescot | P9/H/34<br>***#8471*** 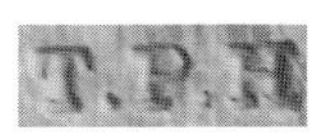 | **Thomas Peter HEWITT** (Mng. Director)<br>Lancashire Watch Company<br>Prescot | Machine watch manufacturers |
| R1/101<br>17 May 1899<br>Sent by<br>Stephen Farren<br>T R Arnott | | P9/H/14<br>***#8472***  | **Thomas Peter HEWITT**<br>**THE LANCASHIRE WATCH CO LTD***<br>Prescot (Registered Office & Works)<br>Lancashire | Watch and watchcase manufacturers |
| LPB/64<br>28 July 1882 | PO directory 1882 | P3/P/x3<br>***#8473-5***  | **Thomas PRIME & SON** *<br>19 Northwood Street<br>Birmingham | Silversmiths |
| Missing register<br>*c.*1889 | | P5/R/249<br>***#8476***  | **Thomas RUSSELL** * | Watch and watchcase manufacturer and clock retailer |
| PP1/189<br>J1 1850-1901 | | P2/R/x2<br>***#8477,8***  | **Thomas RUSSELL** *<br>20 Slater Street (1848)<br>30 Slater Street (1859)<br>Liverpool | |
| | | P2/R/x3<br>***#8479-81***  | | |
| Not in SPB or LPB so struck 1860-3 | | P3/R/x3<br>***#8482-4*** 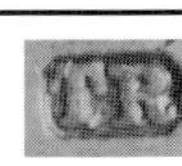 | | |
| Not in R2 as expected - between 26 June and 4 July 1907<br>Similar mark entered LAO 17 July 1907 | | P9/R/92<br>***#8485***  | **Thomas Townsend RUSSELL**<br>1 Minster Buildings<br>12 Church Street<br>Liverpool | Importer of watchcases |
| SPB/22<br>19 January 1876<br>Sent by Harris of Coventry | | P3/R/x2<br>***#8486,7***  | **Thomas RUSSELL & SON** *<br>30 Slater Street<br>Liverpool | |

| REGISTRATION DETAILS | MAKER'S PRIVATE ADDRESS and DETAILS | PLATE and MARK DETAILS | MAKER/COMPANY and BUSINESS ADDRESS | MAKER'S TRADE |
|---|---|---|---|---|
| LPB/80<br>20 September 1879<br>LPB mark shown | | Not on P3<br>***#8488***  | **Alfred RUSSELL**<br>late Theo Russell & Son<br>24 Tarleton Buildings<br>Liverpool | Watch and watchcase manufacturer |
| No entry in LPB<br>*c.*1883 | Seen on Thomas Russell gold watchcase 1892 | P5/R/x1<br>***#8489***  | **Thomas RUSSELL** *<br>30 Slater Street<br>Liverpool | Watch and watchcase manufacturer |
| Missing register<br>*c.*1890 | | P5/R/312<br>***#8490***  | | |
| Missing register<br>*c.*1890 | | P5/R/313<br>***#8491***  | | |
| Not in R1 as expected<br>*c.*1895 | | P5/R/698a<br>***#8492***  | | |
| R1/95<br>15 March 1899<br>Sent by Benson Brothers | | P9/R/138<br>***#8493***  | **Thomas RUSSELL & SON** *<br>12 Church Street<br>Liverpool | Watch manufacturers |
| R2/221<br>26 June 1919<br>Sent by Thomas Restall<br>No mark no. in R2 | 95 Whitehall Road<br>Birmingham<br>R2 Index has T Restall | P15/R/19?<br>***#8494***  | **Norman** (*sic*) **RESTALL**<br>56 Albion Street<br>Birmingham | Jeweller and silversmith |
| SPB/22<br>11 October 1875<br>Sent by James Eastham | | P3/R/x2<br>***#8495,6***  | **Thomas RUSSELL** *<br>30 Slater Street<br>Liverpool | Watch and watchcase manufacturer |
| LPB/80<br>20 August 1881<br>LPB mark shown | | Not on P3<br>***#8497***  | **TANDY & RUDGE**<br>205½ Vyse Street<br>Birmingham | Jewellers |
| R2/221<br>26 June 1919<br>Sent by Thomas Restall | No mark numbers entered – number 20 matches<br>R2 Index has T Restall | P15/R/20?<br>***#8498*** 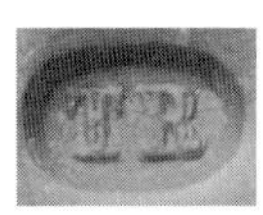 | **Norman** (*sic*) **RESTALL**<br>56 Albion Street<br>Birmingham | Jeweller and silversmith |
| Similar mark entered LAO 16 July 1850 | | P2/R/x2<br>***#8499,8500***  | **Thomas RUSSELL & SON** *<br>30/32 Slater Street (1860)<br>Liverpool | Watch manufacturers |
| Not in R1 as expected<br>*c.*1895 | | P5/R/698b<br>***#8501***  | | |
| Similar mark entered LAO 3 August 1848 | | P2/R/x2<br>***#8502, 3*** 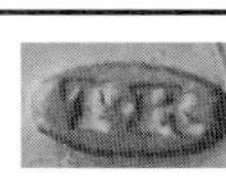 | | |
| LPB/72<br>14 August 1880 | | P3/R/x1<br>***#8504***  | **Thomas RUSSELL** *<br>10 Church Street<br>Liverpool | |
| LPB/74<br>18 June 1884<br>Sent by J H Dodsworth | No mark in LPB/74 just TR* | P5/R/x1<br>***#8505***  | | |
| R2/53<br>19 December 1907<br>Sent by Thos Reeves | 15 Albert Road<br>Aston Manor<br>Birmingham | P9/R/106<br>***#8506*** 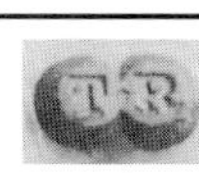 | **Thomas REEVES**<br>105 Vyse Street<br>Birmingham | Enameller and jeweller |

| REGISTRATION DETAILS | MAKER'S PRIVATE ADDRESS and DETAILS | PLATE and MARK DETAILS | MAKER/COMPANY and BUSINESS ADDRESS | MAKER'S TRADE |
|---|---|---|---|---|
| R1/1<br>7 May 1894<br>Sent by T R Arnott<br>Cutting punch | CWMP 1896-1901 | P5/A/558<br>***#8507***  | **Thomas Richard ARNOTT** *<br>Wilderau House<br>33 Chester Street<br>Coventry | Watchcase maker |
| Missing register<br>*c.*1889 | | P5/A/263<br>***#8508***  | | |
| Missing register<br>*c.*1893 | | P5/R/474<br>***#8509***  | **RUSSELL'S LTD** * | |
| R1/82<br>9 November 1898<br>Sent by Benson Brothers | 28 Alford Road<br>Birkenhead<br><br>(Ed: This company separated from next entry *c.*1894) | P9/R/2<br>***#8510***  | **James SLOAN** (Director)<br>**RUSSELL'S LTD** *<br>18 Church Street<br>Liverpool | Watch manufacturers |
| R2/233<br>29 June 1920<br>Sent by Benson Brothers<br>Two sizes | Warren Drive<br>New Brighton<br>Brompton<br>Egerton Park Road<br>Rock Ferry<br>12 Laurel Road<br>Fairfields, Liverpool<br>Mill Hill, London | P15/R/25,26<br>***#8511,2***  | **Thomas Townsend RUSSELL**<br>**Bernard Alfred RUSSELL**<br>**Robert Owen WILLIAMS**<br>**Joseph WRIGHT** trading as<br>**Thomas RUSSELL & SON** *<br>12 Church Street<br>Liverpool | Watch manufacturers |
| Missing register<br>*c.*1888<br>Adjacent P5/W/156<br>Similar mark entered BAO 10 October 1895 | | P5/W/x1<br>***#8513***  | **T R WITHECOMB** | Pipe manufacturer |
| Missing register<br>*c.*1890<br>Similar mark with pellets entered BAO 8 October 1894 | | P5/X*sic*/321<br>***#8514***  | **T R WITHECOMB** | |
| R1/11<br>24 May 1895<br>Sent by B Wade<br>Leeds<br>W H Carrington Co<br>H Perkins | 77 Dulcie Grove<br>Manchester | P5/X*sic*/661<br>***#8515***  | **Thomas Robert WITHECOMB**<br>16,18 Victoria Street<br>66 Market Street and<br>Hanging Ditch<br>Manchester | Tobacconist |
| Undated | | P9/W/36<br>***#8516***  | | |
| Missing register<br>*c.*1886 | See mark #8505 which includes a star wheel | P5/W/57<br>***#8517***  | **Thomas Robert WITHECOMB** or<br>**T R RUSSELL** | |
| Not in R1 as expected | | P5/T/999<br>***#8518***  | **E J TREVITT & SONS** | |
| R1/69<br>13 October 1898<br>Sent by E J Trevitt | 179 Heathfield Road [1]<br>Handsworth<br>194 Church Hill Road [2]<br>Handsworth<br>Birmingham | P9/A/1-3<br>***#8519-21*** 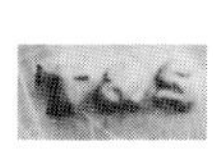 | **Enoch James TREVITT** [1]<br>**Charles James TREVITT** [2]<br>trading as **E J TREVITT & SONS**<br>29 Augusta Street<br>Birmingham | Jewellers |

| REGISTRATION DETAILS | MAKER'S PRIVATE ADDRESS and DETAILS | PLATE and MARK DETAILS | MAKER/COMPANY and BUSINESS ADDRESS | MAKER'S TRADE |
|---|---|---|---|---|
| R2/66<br>8 October 1908<br>Sent by E J Trevitt | The Limes<br>Stechford<br>Glentrees<br>Ashleigh Road, Solihull | P13/T/4-6<br>***#8522-4***  | **E J TREVITT**<br>**A W TREVITT** trading as<br>**E J TREVITT & SONS**<br>29 and 30 Augusta Street<br>Birmingham | Jewellers and silversmiths |
| R2/146<br>19 October 1911<br>Sent by E J Trevitt | The Limes<br>Stechford<br>Ashleigh Road | P13/T/51<br>***#8525***  | | |
| R3/94<br>21 January 1954 | Details same as for marks *#8617-22* | P21/T/24,25<br>***#8526,7***  | **W H TANDY & SONS**<br>122 Vyse Street<br>Birmingham | Gold ring manufacturers |
| R1/130<br>30 July 1900<br>Sent by A W Trevitt | 85 Whitehall Road<br>Handsworth<br>Birmingham | P9/T/17,18<br>***#8528,9*** 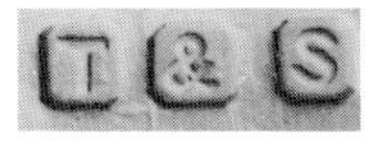 | **Charles James TREVITT &**<br>**Alfred Walter TREVITT** (Partners)<br>trading as **E J TREVITT & SONS**<br>29 Augusta Street<br>Birmingham | Jewellers and silversmiths |
| R1/177<br>10 October 1902<br>Sent by C J Trevitt | 194 Church Hill Road [1]<br>Handsworth<br>85 Whitehall Road [2]<br>Handsworth | P9/T/27,28<br>***#8530,1***  | **Charles James TREVITT** [1]<br>**Alfred Wallace** (*sic*) **TREVITT**[2]<br>trading as **E J TREVITT & SONS**<br>29 Augusta Street<br>Birmingham | |
| R1/203<br>14 November 1903 | | P9/T/31-40<br>***#8532-41***  | | |
| R2/47<br>3 October 1907<br>Sent by selves | The Limes<br>Stechford<br>Glentrees<br>Ashleigh Road<br>Solihull | P9/T/63,64<br>***#8542,3***  | | |
| R2/146<br>20 August 1919 | | P15/T/27, 28<br>***#8544,5*** 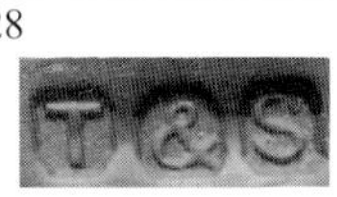 | | |
| 10 January 1922 | Seen on cigarette case 1927 | P15/T/36,37<br>***#8546,7***  | | |
| R3/88<br>1 October 1937<br>Sent by E J Trevitt & Sons Ltd<br>All punches previously entered for E Trevitt and Sons | | No new punches<br>***#8548*** | **E J TREVITT & SONS LTD**<br>Sealed in the presence of:-<br>Herbert O Worrall (Director)<br>K L Trevitt (Secretary)<br>29 Augusta Street (Registered Office)<br>Birmingham | |
| R2/198<br>13 July 1915<br>Sent by T Stewart | Private address same as business | P15/S/20<br>***#8549***  | **Tom STEWART**<br>28 The Crescent<br>Northwich | Artist |
| | | P15/S/21<br>***#8550***  | | |
| R1/37<br>17 February 1897<br>Sent by Houel & Co<br>F Coulthurst | 392 Regent Road [1]<br>Salford<br>126 Duke Street [2]<br>Old Trafford<br>Manchester | P5/T/817<br>***#8551***  | **James TELFORD** [1]<br>**Arthur Polycarp SPEAKMAN** [2]<br>6 Pool Street<br>Manchester | Umbrella and walking stick mounters |

| REGISTRATION DETAILS | MAKER'S PRIVATE ADDRESS and DETAILS | PLATE and MARK DETAILS | MAKER/COMPANY and BUSINESS ADDRESS | MAKER'S TRADE |
|---|---|---|---|---|
| R1/113<br>10 October 1899<br>Sent by Telford & Speakman | 392 Regent Road [1]<br>Salford<br>160 Duke Street [2]<br>Old Trafford<br>Manchester | P9/T/12<br>***#8552***<br> | **James TELFORD** [1]<br>**Arthur Polycarp SPEAKMAN** [2]<br>6 Pool Street<br>Manchester | Manufacturers of umbrellas and walking sticks |
| R3/60<br>15 October 1931<br>Sent by Kinsey Brothers & Patrick Ltd<br>17 Vyse Street<br>Birmingham | Oak Cottage<br>Belwell Lane<br>Four Oaks<br>Warwickshire | P15/T/67<br>***#8553***<br> | **Harold Stewart TURNER** trading as<br>**TURNER & SOMERS**<br>22 Frederick Street<br>Birmingham | Gold and silversmiths |
| PP3/27 | Seen on watch case *c*.1725 | P1/18/x1<br>***#8554***<br> | **Thomas SMALLEY**<br>Chester | Watchcase maker and silversmith |
| Missing register<br>*c*.1891 | | P5/T/346<br>***#8555***<br> | **W H TANDY & SONS**<br>122 Vyse Street<br>Birmingham | Ring manufacturers |
| R1/47<br>10 July 1897<br>Sent by C Wade | Private address same as business | P5/Y*sic*/854<br>***#8556***<br> | **Thomas SALISBURY**<br>5 Abington Street<br>Northampton | Tobacconist |
| LPB/78 SP31/6<br>13 February 1885<br>Sent by Tandy & Rudge | No mark in LPB | P5/S/x1<br>***#8557***<br> | **Thomas SMITH**<br>42 Frederick Street<br>Birmingham | Jewellers |
| R2/198<br>13 July 1915<br>Sent by T Stewart | Private address same as business | P15/S/19<br>***#8558***<br> | **Tom STEWART**<br>28 The Crescent<br>Northwich | Artist |
| R1/29<br>5 June 1896<br>Sent by W H Tandy<br>Edwards Brothers | 119 Crompton Road<br>Birmingham | P5/T/772<br>***#8559***<br> | **William Harry TANDY**<br>**William TANDY**<br>**George TANDY** trading as<br>**W H TANDY & SONS**<br>122 Vyse Street<br>Birmingham | Ring manufacturers |
| R1/76<br>26 November 1898<br>Sent by W H Tandy & Sons | 12 Stamford Road [1]<br>Handsworth<br>17 Crompton Road [2]<br>Handsworth<br>Birmingham | P9/T/4-6<br>***#8560-2***<br> | **William Steward TANDY** [1]<br>**Harry George TANDY** [2] trading as<br>**W H TANDY & SONS**<br>122 Vyse Street<br>Birmingham | |
| R1/159<br>21 January 1902<br>Sent by William Steward Tandy | 64 Broughton Road [1]<br>34 Broughton Road [2]<br>12 Stamford Road [3]<br>all in Handsworth<br>Birmingham | P9/T/22,23<br>***#8563,4***<br> | **William H TANDY** [1]<br>**Henry George TANDY** [2]<br>**William Steward TANDY** [3] trading as<br>**WH TANDY & SON**<br>112 Vyse Street<br>Birmingham | |
| R1/207<br>16 February 1903 | | P9/T/43-46<br>***#8565-8***<br> | **W H TANDY & SONS** see previous entry for Directors<br>112 Vyse Street<br>Birmingham | |
| R2/47<br>4 October 1907<br>Sent by William Steward Tandy | 35 Wall Road<br>34 Thornhill Road<br>Handsworth<br>See WHT&S #9266<br>P13/T/21 used for one lot 15 June 1909 | P9/T/65-70<br>***#8569-74***<br> | **William Steward TANDY**<br>**Harry George TANDY** trading as<br>**TANDY & SON**<br>122 Vyse Street<br>Birmingham | |

| REGISTRATION DETAILS | MAKER'S PRIVATE ADDRESS and DETAILS | PLATE and MARK DETAILS | MAKER/COMPANY and BUSINESS ADDRESS | MAKER'S TRADE |
|---|---|---|---|---|
| R2/136<br>17 May 1911<br>Sent by William S Tandy | 51 Heathfield Road<br>Handsworth<br>Coniston<br>Merton Road<br>Moseley, Birmingham | P13/T/33-38<br>*#8576-81*<br> | **William S TANDY**<br>**Harry G TANDY** trading as<br>**W H TANDY & SONS**<br>122 Vyse Street<br>Birmingham | Ring manufacturers |
| R2/189<br>18 November 1913<br>Sent by W S Tandy | | P15/T/2-13<br>*#8582-93*<br> | | |
| R2/195<br>12 May 1915<br>Sent by W S Tandy | 51 Heathfield Road<br>Handsworth<br>Coniston<br>Merton Road, Moseley | P15/T/14-19<br>*#8594-9*<br> | | |
| R2/237<br>3 March 1921<br>Sent by W S Tandy | 112 Church Lane<br>Handsworth Wood<br>12 Forest Road<br>Moseley, Birmingham | P15/T/30–35<br>*#8600-5*<br> | | |
| R3/20<br>2 January 1924<br>Sent by William Stewart Tandy | | P15/T/41-45<br>*#8606-10*<br> | | Manufacturing jewellers |
| R3/59<br>24 September 1931<br>Sent by W H Tandy & Sons | 112 Church Road [1]<br>Handsworth Wood<br>Birmingham<br>12 Forest Road [2]<br>Moseley, Birmingham | P15/T/61- 66<br>*#8611-16*<br> | **W H TANDY & SONS**<br>William Stewart Tandy [1] (Acting<br>Harry George Tandy [2] Partners)<br>122 Vyse Street<br>Birmingham | |
| R3/75<br>16 April 1935<br>Sent by W H Tandy & Sons | 112 Church Lane<br>112 Church Lane<br>Handsworth<br>12 Forest Row<br>Moseley, Birmingham<br>109 Sherwood Road<br>Hall Green, Birmingham | P15/T/72-77<br>*#8617-22*<br> | **William Stewart TANDY**<br>**Ronald Hickman TANDY**<br>**Harry George TANDY**<br>**Harold George TANDY** trading as<br>**W H TANDY**<br>122 Vyse Street<br>Birmingham | Jewellers and ring makers |
| R3/94<br>17 March 1939 | | P21/T/3-9<br>*#8623-9*<br> | **W H TANDY & SONS**<br>122 Vyse Street<br>Birmingham | Gold ring manufacturers |
| 12 March 1948 | | P21/T/14-16<br>*#8630-2*<br> | | |
| 15 January 1948 | | P21/T/17<br>*#8633*<br> | | |
| R3/160<br>22 February 1957<br>Sent by W H Tandy & Sons | 109 Sherwood Road [1]<br>Hall Green<br>Birmingham 28<br>Green Gables [1]<br>Little Aston Park<br>Staffs | P21/T/29,30<br>*#8634,5*<br> | **Harold George TANDY** [1]<br>**Ronald Hickman TANDY** [2] trading as<br>**W H TANDY & SONS**<br>122 Vyse Street<br>Birmingham 18 | Manufacturing jewellers |
| R1/50<br>19 August 1897<br>Sent by W H Carrington & Co | Private address same as business | P5/aboveB/867<br>*#8636*<br> | **Thomas Southwark BROWN**<br>12 Bradshaw Gate<br>Bolton | Tobacconist |

| REGISTRATION DETAILS | MAKER'S PRIVATE ADDRESS and DETAILS | PLATE and MARK DETAILS | MAKER/COMPANY and BUSINESS ADDRESS | MAKER'S TRADE |
|---|---|---|---|---|
| R3/104<br>24 February 1943<br>Sent by T S Osborn | 97 Whitehall Road<br>Handsworth<br>Birmingham 21 | P21/O/2,3<br>***#8637,8***<br> | **Thomas Edward OSBORN** trading as<br>**Thomas S OSBORN**<br>9 Key Hill Drive<br>Hockley<br>Birmingham 18 | Manufacturing jewellers |
| R3/54<br>5 June 1930<br>Sent by T S Osborn | | P15/O/8<br>***#8640***<br> | **T S OSBORN**<br>9 Key Hill Drive<br>Hockley<br>Birmingham 18 | |
| R1/101<br>31 May 1899<br>Sent by T S Osborn | 129 Holly Road<br>Handsworth<br>Birmingham | P9/O/2<br>***#8639***<br> | **Thomas Samuel OSBORN**<br>9 Key Hill Drive<br>Hockley<br>Birmingham | Jeweller and fancy ring maker |
| Not in R2 as expected<br>*c.* January 1921<br>Similar mark entered BAO 9 October 1907 by T S Osborn | | P15/O/1-3<br>***#8641-3***<br> | | |
| R3/122<br>7 February 1948<br>Sent by Thomas Tushingham | Private address same as business | P21/T/13<br>***#8644***<br> | **Thomas TUSHINGHAM**<br>The Ronce<br>Torbank Road<br>Huyton<br>Liverpool | Haulage contractor |
| R2/148<br>9 December 1911<br>Sent by Thomas Tweedale | Private address same as business | P13/T/52<br>***#8645***<br>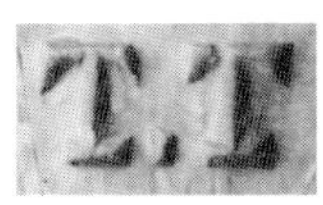 | **Thomas TWEEDALE**<br>64 Hanover Street<br>Liverpool | Briar and meerschaum pipe manufacturer |
| LPB/80<br>27 January 1879 | | P3/T/x3<br>***#8646-8***<br> | **Thomas TRAHERN** *<br>11 Ravensdon Street<br>Kennington Park Road<br>London | Watchcase maker |
| Missing register<br>*c.*1886 | | P5/T/55<br>***#8649***<br> | | |
| Missing register<br>*c.*1886 | | P5/W/19a<br>***#8650***<br> | **Unidentified** | |
| R1/82<br>5 November 1898<br>Sent by T W Wright | 20 Douglas Street<br>Manchester | P9/W/8<br>***#8651***<br>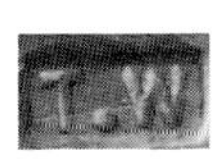 | **Thomas Weston WRIGHT**<br>18 Corporation Street<br>Manchester | Jeweller |
| R1/167<br>29 April 1902<br>Sent by R J Wakefield | 6 Brookside Terrace<br>Sunderland | P9/W/67<br>***#8652***<br>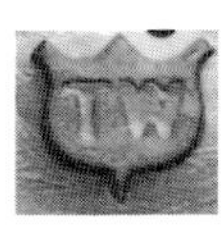 | **Thomas WILLIAMSON**<br>8/12/15/17 New Arcade<br>Sunderland | Jeweller and fancy goods dealer |
| | Square marked 1786 | P1/22/x2<br>***#8653,4***<br> | **Unidentified** | |
| PDB 1832-7<br>MR2/214<br>MR3/103 | Box covers and spoons | P1/14/x1<br>***#8655***<br> | **Thomas WOOLFIELD**<br>Liverpool<br>or | Silversmith |
| PDB 1830-6<br>MR3/103<br>J1 1832-40 | Gold rings, spoons and coffin plates | P1/15/x2<br>***#8656,7***<br> | **Thomas WALKER**<br>Chester | Goldsmith and silversmith |

| REGISTRATION DETAILS | MAKER'S PRIVATE ADDRESS and DETAILS | PLATE and MARK DETAILS | MAKER/COMPANY and BUSINESS ADDRESS | MAKER'S TRADE |
|---|---|---|---|---|
| PDB 1830-6<br>MR3/103<br>J1 1832-40 | Gold rings, spoons and coffin plates | P1/16/x4<br>***#8658-61***  | **Thomas WOOLFIELD**<br>Liverpool<br>or | Silversmith |
| | Square marked 1786 | P1/22/x4<br>***#8662-5***  | **Thomas WALKER**<br>Chester | Goldsmith and silversmith |
| | Square marked 1787 | P1/23/x3<br>***#8666-8***  | | |
| | | P1/Reverse/x3<br>***#8669-71***  | | |
| LMS 1878<br>J1 1852-1903 | | P2/W/x2<br>***#8672,3***  | **Thomas WOOLLEY**<br>36 Bridge Street Row<br>Chester | Clockmaker and jeweller |
| | | P2/W/x2<br>***#8674,5***  | | |
| SPB/23<br>11 January 1869<br>SPB mark shown<br>MR3/145 | | Not on P3<br>***#8676***  | | |
| SPB/23<br>16 September 1876<br>SPB mark shown | | Not on P3<br>***#8677*** 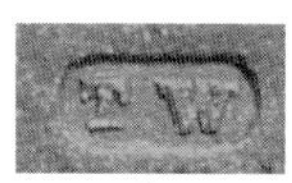 | **Thomas WHEELER**<br>160 Lancaster Road<br>Preston<br>Lancashire | Watchmaker and jeweller |
| SPB/4<br>20 October 1871<br>Sent by Samuel & Rogers<br>Liverpool | CWMP 1874-83 | P3/W/x3<br>***#8678-80***  | **Thomas WALLEN** *<br>King Street<br>Coventry | Watchcase and watch manufacturer |
| LPB/90<br>19 January 1884 | | P5/W/x1<br>***#8681***  | **Thomas WEBB** *<br>4 Craven Street<br>Chapel Fields<br>Coventry | Watchcase maker |
| Missing register<br>*c.*1886 | | P5/W/19b<br>***#8682***  | **Unidentified** | |
| Missing register<br>*c.*1891 | | P5/W/337<br>***#8683***  | **Unidentified** | |
| R1/13<br>25 June 1895<br>Sent by T Woolnough | 17 Freegrove Road<br>Holloway<br>London | P5/X*sic*/669<br>***#8684*** 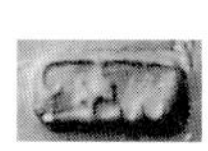 | **Thomas WOOLNOUGH** *<br>128 Farringdon Road<br>London EC | Gold chain maker |
| R1/195<br>6 June 1903<br>Sent by T A Roberts | | P9/W/99<br>***#8685***  | | |

| REGISTRATION DETAILS | MAKER'S PRIVATE ADDRESS and DETAILS | PLATE and MARK DETAILS | MAKER/COMPANY and BUSINESS ADDRESS | MAKER'S TRADE |
|---|---|---|---|---|
| GTD 1859<br>PP1/189<br>J1 1849-51<br>PMR 1847-65 | | P2/W/x2<br>***#8686,7***<br><br>P2/W/x2<br>***#8688,9***<br> | **Thomas WILSON**<br>9 Clare Street (1847-51)<br>15 Radcliffe Street (1853)<br>11 Martin Street (1855)<br>30 Chapel Place (1857-62)<br>41 Dee Street (1864-5)<br>Liverpool | Watchcase maker and watchmaker |
| R1/230<br>16 March 1905<br>Sent by A C Tongue | Percy Villas<br>Weston Road<br>Wylde Green<br>Hollyhurst<br>Highbridge Road, Wylde Green | P9/T/54<br>***#8690***<br> | **Arthur Charles TONGUE**<br>**George Arthur WALKER** trading as<br>**TONGUE & WALKER**<br>46 Warstone Lane<br>Birmingham | Jewellers |
| R3/72<br>20 June 1934<br>Sent by Samuel Hope<br>126 Vyse Street<br>Birmingham | 24 Weston Road<br>Wylde Green<br>Birmingham | P15/T/71<br>***#8691***<br> | **Frank TONGUE** trading as<br>**TONGUE & WALKER**<br>46 Warstone Lane<br>Birmingham | Manufacturing jewellers |
| SPB/4<br>17 March 1877<br>Two sizes | | P3/X*sic*/a,b<br>***#8692,3***<br> | **Thomas WHEELER**<br>160 Lancaster Road<br>Preston | Watchmaker and jeweller |
| Missing register<br>*c.*1888 | | P5/W/151<br>***#8694***<br> | | |
| LPB/88<br>9 February 1881 | | P3/W/x1<br>***#8695***<br> | **T WILLIS & CO**<br>65 Northampton Street<br>Birmingham | Jewellers |
| LPB/68<br>17 October 1882 | | P3/V*sic*/x2<br>***#8696,7***<br> | | |
| Missing register<br>*c.*1889 | Large mark might indicate tobacconist<br><br>S might denote Son(s) or Sheffield | P5/S/254<br>***#8698***<br> | **Unidentified** | |
| R3/145<br>30 June 1953<br>Sent by G W Travis<br>(Director)<br>Three sizes | 62 Kingfield Road<br>Sheffield 2 | P21/W/65-67<br>***#8699-8701***<br> | **TRAVIS WILSON & CO LTD**<br>Clarence Works<br>Bath Street<br>Sheffield 1 | Silversmiths |
| R1/70<br>22 October 1898<br>Sent by B H Joseph & Co<br>Two sizes | Chislett Road<br>West Hampstead<br>London NW | P9/D/2a,b<br>***#8702,3***<br> | **Thomas William DOBSON** trading as<br>**DOBSON & SONS** *<br>32 Piccadilly<br>London | Goldsmiths and silversmiths |

| REGISTRATION DETAILS | MAKER'S PRIVATE ADDRESS and DETAILS | PLATE and MARK DETAILS | MAKER/COMPANY and BUSINESS ADDRESS | MAKER'S TRADE |
|---|---|---|---|---|
| R2/75<br>18 March 1909<br>Sent by T W Dickson<br>BAO 15.061,15.062 | 5 The Grove<br>Villa Road<br>Handsworth<br>Birmingham | P13/D/9<br>***#8704***<br> | **Thomas W DICKSON**<br>64 Hockley Hill<br>Birmingham | Manufacturing jeweller and silversmith |
| | | P13/D/8<br>***#8705***<br> | | |
| R3/40<br>12 April 1928<br>Sent by J H Wynn Ltd | 8 Hewitt Road<br>London N8 | P15/L/36<br>***#8706***<br> | **Tom William LACK**<br>59 Hatton Garden<br>London EC1 | Silversmith |
| R3/43<br>4 September 1928<br>Sent by C Lucas | Fairlawn<br>Woodford Bridge<br>Essex | P15/M/69<br>***#8707***<br> | **Thomas William MARTIN** *<br>72 Queens Road<br>Dalston<br>London E8 | Wholesale jeweller |
| R3/45<br>22 January 1929<br>Sent by T Martin | | P15/M/71<br>***#8708***<br> | | |
| R3/69<br>15 November 1933<br>Sent by Coley Brothers<br>119 Vyse Street<br>Birmingham | | P15/M/76<br>***#8709***<br> | | |
| PP1/189<br>J1 1849-51<br>Similar mark entered<br>LAO 5 June 1847 | | P2/W/x2<br>***#8710,11***<br> | **Thomas Willis WILLIN** *<br>6 Percival Street<br>London | Watchcase maker |
| Not in R3 as expected<br>*c.* May 1921 | | P15/W/41<br>***#8712***<br> | **THE WOOD WORKERS CO** | |
| R2/159<br>19 July 1912<br>Sent by Daniel Rowles | Rodborough Court<br>Stroud | P13/W/122<br>***#8713***<br> | **Sir Alfred APPERLY J P**<br>**Charles A APPERLY** trading as<br>**THE WOOD WORKERS CO**<br>Daniel Rowles (Acting Secretary)<br>Bliss Mills<br>Chalford<br>Gloucestershire | Umbrella, parasol and walking stick manufacturers |

| REGISTRATION DETAILS | MAKER'S PRIVATE ADDRESS and DETAILS | PLATE and MARK DETAILS | MAKER/COMPANY and BUSINESS ADDRESS | MAKER'S TRADE |
|---|---|---|---|---|
| R3/34<br>18 October 1926<br>Sent by U E Harper | Private address same as business | P15/I*sic*/93<br>***#8714***<br> | **U E HARPER**<br>35 Moses Street<br>Dimple<br>Liverpool | Art student |
| R1/136<br>1 November 1900<br>Sent by<br>W H Carrington & Co | 88 West Derby Street<br>Liverpool<br>13 Jubilee Drive<br>Liverpool | P9/L/20<br>***#8715***<br>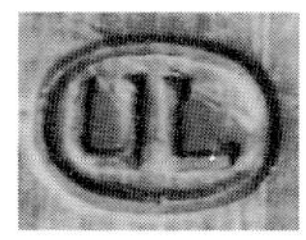 | **George Henry LAKE**<br>**Charles WHITE** trading as<br>**U LAKE**<br>2 James Street and<br>26 Fenwick Street<br>Liverpool | Tobacconists |

| REGISTRATION DETAILS | MAKER'S PRIVATE ADDRESS and DETAILS | PLATE and MARK DETAILS | MAKER/COMPANY and BUSINESS ADDRESS | MAKER'S TRADE |
|---|---|---|---|---|
| R1/43<br>27 April 1897<br>Sent by Chas Vale<br>Two sizes | Maney<br>Sutton Coldfield | P5/M*sic*/835a,b<br>***#8716,7***<br>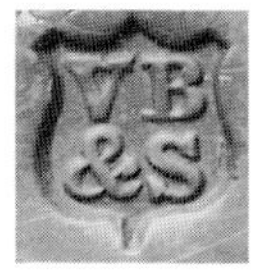 | **Charles VALE** trading as<br>**VALE BROTHERS & SERMON** *<br>27 Spencer Street<br>Birmingham | Silversmiths |
| R2/218<br>25 March 1919<br>Sent by Vera Hillary | Private address same as business | P15/H/44<br>***#8718***<br> | **Vera HILLARY**<br>84 Cavendish Street<br>Keighley | Art craftsman |
| PDB 1819 Gold rings<br>MR3/100<br>PP1/66-8, 189<br>CWMP 1822-35 | Started by Samuel Vale in 1747, later traded from 1754 as Vale, Howlette and Carr. Baillie lists this as the earliest watch manufacturing company in Coventry. Closed 1973.<br>See also associated V&R and RKR marks | P1/10/x3<br>***#8719-21***<br> | **VALE & HOWLETTE** *<br>**(VALE & COMPANY)**<br>Spon Street<br>Coventry | Goldsmiths and watch and watchcase manufacturers |
| SP30/1 Not in LPB<br>*c.*1883<br>Similar mark entered BAO February 1890 | On plate 5 so post August 1883 | P5/V/x1<br>***#8722***<br> | **VILLIERS & JACKSON**<br>3 Hockley Hill<br>Birmingham | Pencil case makers |
| R1/212<br>15 April 1904<br>Sent by Villiers & Jackson | Mayfield<br>Station Road<br>Solihull | P9/V/5<br>***#8723***<br> | **Walter JACKSON** trading as<br>**VILLIERS & JACKSON**<br>3 Hockley Hill<br>Birmingham | Gold and silver pencil case manufacturers |
| R1/232<br>28 April 1905<br>Sent by Villiers & Jackson | | P9/V/7<br>***#8724***<br> | | |
| R2/61<br>6 June 1908<br>Sent by Walter Jackson | | P13/V/1<br>***#8725***<br>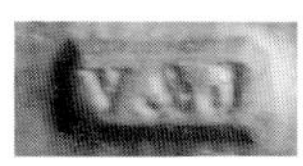 | | |
| R2/76<br>24 March 1909<br>Sent by Walter Jackson | | P13/V/2<br>***#8726***<br>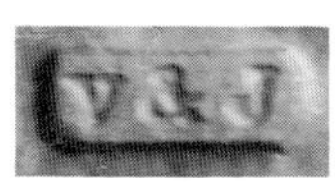 | | |
| R2/134<br>9 May 1911<br>Sent by Walter Jackson | | P13/V/13,14<br>***#8727,8***<br> | | |
| R2/206<br>29 June 1916<br>Sent by Walter Jackson | | P15/V/2,3<br>***#8729,30***<br> | | |
| R2/214<br>4 January 1918<br>Sent by Villiers & Jackson Two sizes | | P15/V/7-10<br>***#8731-4***<br> | | |
| Recut<br>22 September 1922<br>Two sizes | | P15/V/11-13<br>***#8735-7***<br> | | |
| R2/85<br>19 June 1909<br>Sent by S Blanckensee & Son | 71 Aberdare Gardens<br>London NW | P13/L/14<br>***#8738***<br> | **Victor LUXENBURG** trading as<br>**THE GOLDSMITHS EMPORIUM** *<br>90 Fleet Street and<br>97 Regent Street and<br>63 Fleet Street and<br>38 Cheapside and<br>148 Oxford Street (Head Department)<br>London | Goldsmiths and jewellers |

| REGISTRATION DETAILS | MAKER'S PRIVATE ADDRESS and DETAILS | PLATE and MARK DETAILS | MAKER/COMPANY and BUSINESS ADDRESS | MAKER'S TRADE |
|---|---|---|---|---|
| R2/90<br>30 July 1909<br>Sent by J R Griffin Ltd | 71 Aberdare Gardens<br>London NW | P13/L/17-28<br>***#8739-50***<br> | **Victor LUXENBURG** trading as<br>**THE GOLDSMITHS EMPORIUM** *<br>90 Fleet Street and<br>97 Regent Street and<br>63 Fleet Street and<br>38 Cheapside and<br>148 Oxford Street (Head Department)<br>London | Goldsmiths and jewellers |
| R1/128<br>14 June 1900<br>Sent by John Harris | 46 Cecil Street<br>Glasgow | P9/L/18<br>***#8751***<br> | **Victor LEVY** trading as<br>**Victor LEVY & CO**<br>40 Union Street<br>Glasgow and<br>43 Frederick Street<br>Birmingham | Watch manufacturers and jewellers |
| R2/31<br>22 January 1907<br>Sent by Ralph Levy | 76 Sardens Terrace<br>Glasgow<br>47 Leby Bank Garden<br>Glasgow | P9/L/83<br>***#8752***<br> | **Victor LEVY**<br>**Ralph LEVY** trading as<br>**Victor LEVY & CO**<br>40 Union Street<br>Glasgow and<br>43 Frederick Street<br>Birmingham | Wholesale jewellers |
| R3/178<br>16 March 1961<br>Sent by V M Evans | 205 Finney Lane<br>Heald Green<br>Cheadle<br>Cheshire | P21/E/19<br>***#8753***<br> | **Violet Moorly EVANS**<br>No business address entered | Student silversmith |
| 20 October 1961 | | P21/E/20<br>***#8754***<br>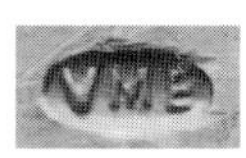 | | |
| PDB 1819<br>MR3/100<br>PP1/66-8,189<br>CWMP 1822-35<br>Similar mark entered<br>BAO 6 February 1822 | Gold rings | P1/30/x2<br>***#8755,6***<br> | **VALE & ROTHERHAM** *<br>Spon Street<br>Coventry | Goldsmiths and watch and watchcase manufacturers |
| | | P1/30/x2<br>***#8757,8***<br> | | |
| | | P1/30/x2<br>***#8759,60***<br> | | |
| Similar mark entered<br>BAO 6 February 1822<br>and 18 August 1824 | | P1/29/x1<br>***#8761***<br>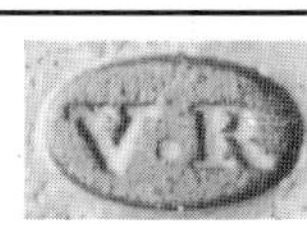 | | |
| R2/108<br>18 April 1910<br>Sent by E Durban & Co | The Grove<br>Old Southgate<br>London<br>3 Wilmington House<br>Highbourn Crescent, London | P13/V/10-12<br>***#8762-4***<br> | **Alfred THOMPSON** *<br>**George Henry Weston VINE** *<br>85 Aldersgate Street and<br>38 Basinghall Street<br>London | Wholesale jewellers |
| R3/28<br>2 May 1925<br>Sent by Benson Brothers | 12 Dunstan Road<br>Golders Green<br>London NW | P15/V/14,15<br>***#8765,6***<br> | **George Henry Weston VINE**<br>trading as **VINE & THOMPSON** *<br>and as **S RICHARDS**<br>86 Aldersgate Street and<br>38 Basinghall Street<br>London | |

| REGISTRATION DETAILS | MAKER'S PRIVATE ADDRESS and DETAILS | PLATE and MARK DETAILS | MAKER/COMPANY and BUSINESS ADDRESS | MAKER'S TRADE |
|---|---|---|---|---|
| R3/174<br>5 July 1960<br>Sent by V Webb<br>Two sizes | 6 Longshaw Street<br>Bewsey<br>Warrington<br>Lancashire | P21/W/93,94<br>***#8767,8***<br><br> | **Mrs Vera WEBB**<br>No business address entered | Student of jewellery |
| R3/66<br>7 April 1933<br>Sent by B H Britton & Sons<br>35 Hockley Hill<br>Birmingham | 5 Aberdeen Gardens<br>London NW6 | P15/V/16<br>***#8769***<br><br> | **VERTEX WATCH CO**<br>Claude Octavius Asher Lyons (Proprietor)<br>Diamond House?<br>37 and 38 Hatton Garden<br>London EC | Watch importers |

| REGISTRATION DETAILS | MAKER'S PRIVATE ADDRESS and DETAILS | PLATE and MARK DETAILS | MAKER/COMPANY and BUSINESS ADDRESS | MAKER'S TRADE |
|---|---|---|---|---|
| R2/128<br>24 February 1911<br>Sent by A H Tongue | The Oaks<br>Alderley Edge<br>Cheshire | P13/A/26<br>***#8770***<br>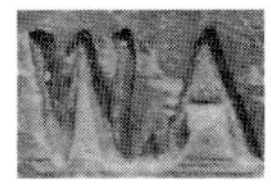 | **Walter ALLEN**<br>Thomas Street and<br>Shudehill<br>Manchester | Tobacconist wholesaler |
| Missing register<br>*c.*1893 | | P5/A/521<br>***#8771***<br> | **Unidentified** | |
| Not in R2 as expected<br>*c.* October 1916 to March 1919<br>Similar mark entered BAO 1 June 1917 | | P15/A/11<br>***#8772***<br> | **W ADAMS LTD**<br>Herbert Edward Hooper Adams (Managing Director)<br>Walker George Adams (Director)<br>211 Barr Street<br>Birmingham | Silversmiths |
| R2/90<br>13 August 1909<br>Sent by William Adams<br>Cancelled<br>5 March 1910 | 77 Hall Street<br>Handsworth<br>Birmingham | P13/A/17,18<br>Two sizes<br>***#8773,4***<br>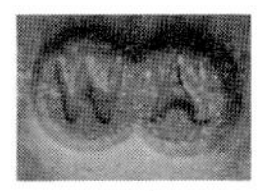 | **William ADAMS**<br>211 Barr Street<br>Birmingham | Goldsmith and silversmith |
| R2/105<br>5 March 1910<br>Sent by William Adams Ltd<br>P13/A/17,18 re-entered | 77 Hall Road<br>Handsworth<br>49 Stafford Road<br>Handsworth<br>Birmingham | P13/A/23,24<br>Two sizes<br>***#8775,6***<br>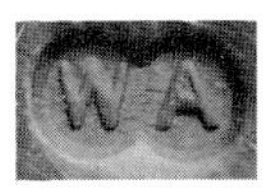 | **William ADAMS LTD**<br>W E Adams (Secretary)<br>Herbert Adams (Director)<br>211 Barr Street<br>Hockley<br>Birmingham | Manufacturing jewellers and silversmiths |
| R2/229<br>11 March 1920<br>Sent by F Winwood | 90 Clifford Road<br>Birmingham<br>25 Paddington Road<br>Handsworth<br>Birmingham | P15/W/54<br>***#8777***<br>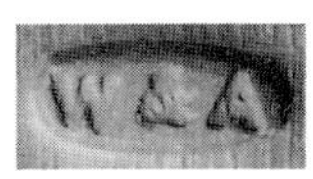 | **Frederick WINWOOD**<br>**William Leonard ASPREY** trading as<br>**WINWOOD & ASPREY**<br>184a Wheeler Street<br>Birmingham | Jewellers and silversmiths |
| R1/18<br>8 November 1895<br>Sent by Rowland & Kibble | Woodside<br>Wilmslow<br>Cheshire | P5/W/697<br>***#8778***<br> | **Walter ALLEN**<br>9 Cannon Street<br>Manchester | Pipe manufacturer |
| R2/43<br>30 July 1907<br>Sent by self | 77 Huddleton Road<br>Furnell Park<br>London W | P9/A/90<br>***#8779***<br> | **William ADAMS** *<br>5 Edward Street<br>Wardour Street<br>London moved (undated) to<br>Baronsmere Road<br>East Finchley<br>London | Goldsmith and silversmith |
| LPB/90<br>15 January 1884<br>No mark just W&A entered | | P5/W/x1<br>***#8780***<br> | **WARDEN & AITKEN**<br>26 Upper Hockley Street<br>Birmingham | Jewellers |
| R1/91<br>15 February 1899<br>Sent by W Aitken<br>Two sizes MR3/116 | 2 Turnville Road<br>Handsworth<br>Birmingham<br>See also FW&Co | P9/A/6,7<br>***#8781,2***<br> | **William AITKEN** *<br>37, 38 Vyse Street<br>Birmingham | Silversmith |
| R1/115<br>7 November 1899<br>Sent by W Aitken<br>Two sizes | | P9/A/13,14<br>***#8783,4***<br> | | |
| Missing register<br>*c.*1893<br>Similar mark entered BAO 18 May 1892 | | P5/A/519<br>***#8785***<br> | | Jeweller |

| REGISTRATION DETAILS | MAKER'S PRIVATE ADDRESS and DETAILS | PLATE and MARK DETAILS | MAKER/COMPANY and BUSINESS ADDRESS | MAKER'S TRADE |
|---|---|---|---|---|
| R1/157<br>20 November 1901<br>Sent by W Aitken<br>Two sizes | 141 Heathfield Road<br>Handsworth<br>Birmingham | P9/A/27-30<br>***#8786-9***<br> | **William AITKEN** *<br>37, 38 Vyse Street<br>Birmingham | Silversmith |
| R1/175<br>18 September 1902<br>Sent by W Aitken<br>Two sizes | | P9/A/40,41<br>***#8790,1***<br> | **William AITKEN** *<br>Eagle Works<br>78 Summer Row<br>Birmingham | |
| R2/83<br>19 May 1909<br>Sent by Alfred Morton | (Business address and private)<br>15 Perrymead Street<br>Parsons Green<br>London SW | P13/E/8-10<br>***#8792-4***<br>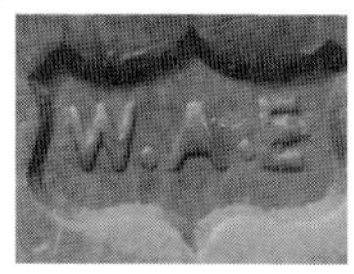 | **William Ambrose EMERSON**<br>Chancery Lane Safe Deposit Company<br>Chancery Lane<br>London WC<br>This address not accepted | Silversmith |
| R3/144<br>22 May 1953<br>Sent by W A Geddes | Private address same as business | P21/G/24<br>***#8795***<br> | **William Andrew GEDDES**<br>29 Bamber Avenue, Sale<br>Manchester | Watchmaker and jeweller |
| R2/228<br>6 March 1920<br>Sent by<br>W A Massingham | 123 Thornhill Road<br>Handsworth<br>Birmingham | P15/M/36<br>***#8796***<br> | **William Alfred MASSINGHAM**<br>55 Northampton Street<br>Birmingham | Manufacturing jewellers |
| R3/150<br>15 January 1954<br>Sent by W M Muir Ltd | Grasmere [1]<br>Styal Road<br>60 Broad Walk [2]<br>Seatoller [3]<br>Weston Road<br>Wilmslow<br>Cheshire | P21/M/40<br>***#8797***<br>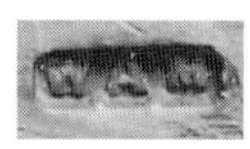 | **William M MUIR LTD**<br>Mrs T Muir [1] (Director)<br>W A Muir [2] (Director)<br>R E Muir [3] (Director)<br>45-47 Stockport Road<br>Manchester 12 | Jewellers and pawnbrokers |
| R3/137<br>4 March 1952<br>Sent by N A Harper<br>W A Perry & Co<br>Two sizes | | P21/P/44,45<br>***#8798,9***<br> | **W A PERRY LTD**<br>9 and 11 Corporation Street<br>Birmingham and<br>47 Temple Row (Registered Office)<br>Birmingham 2 | Retail goldsmiths and jewellers |
| Missing register<br>*c.*1891 | | P5/S/391<br>***#8800***<br> | **Unidentified** | |
| Missing register<br>*c.*1888 | | P5/S/192<br>***#8801***<br> | **Unidentified** | |
| R3/98<br>13 March 1941<br>Sent by W A Smith | 14 Leyton Road<br>Handsworth<br>Birmingham 21 | P21/S/10<br>***#8802***<br>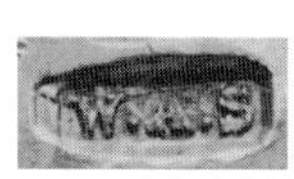 | **William Albert SMITH**<br>61 Northampton Street<br>Birmingham 18 | Manufacturing jeweller |
| R1/46<br>17 June 1897<br>Sent by Arthur Watts | West Bridgeford<br>Nottinghamshire | P5/aboveA/850<br>***#8803***<br> | **Arthur WATTS**<br>Station Street<br>Nottingham | Tobacconist |
| R2/96<br>12 November 1909<br>Sent by W A Wooley<br>BAO 16.449 | 30 Sycamore Road<br>Smethwick<br>Birmingham | P13/W/60<br>***#8804***<br> | **Walter Albert WOOLEY**<br>30 Sycamore Road, Smethwick<br>Birmingham | Jewellers |
| R2/213 and 214<br>28 July 1917<br>Sent by W A Wooley | 108 Wigons Road<br>Bearwood<br>Birmingham | P15/W/36<br>***#8805***<br> | **Harold WOOLEY** trading as<br>**W A WOOLEY**<br>44 Warstone Lane<br>Birmingham | Ring makers and jeweller |

| REGISTRATION DETAILS | MAKER'S PRIVATE ADDRESS and DETAILS | PLATE and MARK DETAILS | MAKER/COMPANY and BUSINESS ADDRESS | MAKER'S TRADE |
|---|---|---|---|---|
| R3/53<br>21 May 1930<br>Sent by W A Wooley<br>Two sizes | 130 Milcote Road<br>Bearwood<br>Birmingham | P15/W/95,96<br>***#8806,7***<br>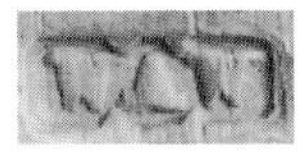 | **Walter Albert WOOLEY**<br>44 Warstone Lane<br>Birmingham | Manufacturing goldsmith |
| R2/100<br>18 December 1909<br>Sent by W Neale<br>& Sons | Buck Lodge<br>Norwich | P13/B/71<br>***#8808***<br> | **R Windsor BISHOP** trading as<br>**W BISHOP**<br>41 and 43 London Street<br>Norwich | Silversmiths and jewellers |
| R2/195<br>28 April 1915<br>Sent by Hirst Brothers Ltd | 161 Chamber Road<br>Oldham | P15/B/59<br>***#8809***<br> | **William BERRY**<br>130 Yorkshire Street<br>Oldham | Jewellers and diamond merchants |
| R3/128<br>3 May 1949<br>Sent by Wilfred Brown | | P21/B/32<br>***#8810***<br> | **Wilfred BROWN**<br>25 Seymour Avenue<br>Morecambe | Master grocer |
| R2/91<br>25 August 1909<br>Sent by W Bayliss<br>Two sizes<br>BAO 16.513,16.685 | Elesmere Avenue<br>Acocks Green<br>Birmingham | P13/B/64,65<br>***#8811,2***<br> | **Walter BAYLISS** *<br>60 Branston Street<br>Birmingham | Silversmith |
| R1/34<br>17 October 1896<br>Sent by Wittenberg & Bateson<br>Dissolved partnership<br>5 January 1900 | 3 Holly Bank [1]<br>Hawthorn Cottage [2]<br>Accrington | P5/X*sic*/796<br>***#8813***<br> | **Max Ehrigott Aaron WITTENBERG** [1]<br>**Frederick William BATESON** [2]<br>trading as **M E Aaron WITTENBERG & BATESON**<br>142a Back Wellington Street<br>Accrington | Pipe manufacturers |
| LPB/82<br>23 February 1881 | | P3/B/x1<br>***#8814***<br> | **William BUTLER**<br>28 Richard Street<br>Birmingham | Jeweller |
| R1/175<br>13 September 1902<br>Sent by W Bradbury | 58 Barker Street<br>Lozells | P9/B/93<br>***#8815***<br> | **William BRADBURY**<br>69 Hockley Hill<br>Birmingham | Silversmith |
| PDB 1823-6<br>MR3/76<br>J1 1823-6 | Gold rings and pencil cases | P1/29/x2<br>***#8815,7***<br> | **William BALL**<br>Liverpool | Goldsmith and silversmith |
| Missing register<br>*c.*1888<br>Similar mark LAO<br>29 September 1890 | | P5/B/155<br>***#8818***<br> | **William Thomas BULLOCK** *<br>10 Cherry Street<br>Coventry | Watchcase maker |
| LPB/88<br>3 March 1880<br>Sent by Mayell Brothers | | P3/W/x1<br>***#8819***<br> | **WELCH & BANKS**<br>62 Summer Hill Terrace<br>Birmingham | Jewellers |
| LPB/94 undated but during 1884<br>Sent by Mr Floyd | Brothers are Bernard, David & Samuel - see also WOLFFE BROTHERS #8843 | P5/W/x1<br>***#8820***<br> | **WOLFFE BROTHERS** *<br>94 Vyse Street<br>Birmingham | Watch manufacturers |
| R3/60<br>20 October 1931<br>Sent by H S Smets ?<br>107 Vyse Street<br>Birmingham | Private address same as business | P15/B/206<br>***#8821***<br> | **Walter BREAKELL**<br>Ellowes Hall<br>Sedgley<br>Staffs<br>(Mr Dudley) | Teacher |

| REGISTRATION DETAILS | MAKER'S PRIVATE ADDRESS and DETAILS | PLATE and MARK DETAILS | MAKER/COMPANY and BUSINESS ADDRESS | MAKER'S TRADE |
|---|---|---|---|---|
| R2/50<br>19 November 1907<br>Sent by W Boucher & Co | 77 Church Street<br>Aston Manor<br>Disposed of business to Alfred Charles Goss | P13/B/3<br>***#8822***<br> | **Mrs L CLARK** trading as<br>**W BOUCHER & CO**<br>5 Warstone Parade East<br>Birmingham | Gold chain manufacturers and jewellers |
| R2/56<br>14 March 1908<br>Sent by Alfred Charles Goss | 86 South Road<br>Handsworth<br>Birmingham | P13/B/11<br>***#8823***<br> | **Alfred Charles GOSS** trading as<br>**W BOUCHER & CO**<br>5 Warstone Parade<br>Birmingham | Jewellers |
| R2/83<br>19 May 1909<br>Sent by Alfred C Goss | 13 Norton Street<br>Birmingham | P13/B/49<br>***#8824***<br> | **Alfred Charles GOSS** trading as<br>**W BOUCHER & CO**<br>5 Warstone Parade East<br>Birmingham | |
| R1/189<br>26 March 1903<br>Sent by W M Briggs<br>Two sizes | The Hollies<br>11 Victoria Road<br>Broomhall Park | P9/B/103,104<br>***#8825,6***<br> | **William BRIGGS & CO**<br>William Marriott Briggs (Director)<br>33 Andrew Street<br>Wicker<br>Sheffield | Silversmiths and electroplate manufacturers |
| R2/143<br>15 September 1911<br>Sent by Williams Ltd<br>Four sizes | 221 Beaumont Road [1]<br>Bourneville<br>Birmingham | P13/W/99-102<br>***#8827-30***<br>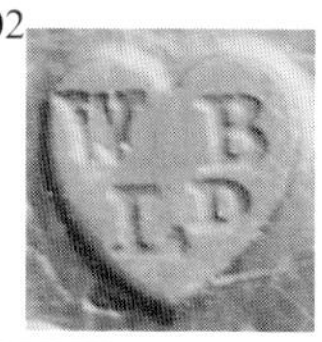 | **WILLIAMS (BIRMINGHAM) LTD** *<br>James Green [1] (Secretary)<br>Silver Works<br>Goodman Street<br>Birmingham | Manufacturing silversmiths |
| R3/59<br>3 October 1931<br>Sent by W P Bonaston | Private address same as business | P15/B/204<br>***#8831***<br> | **William Pearson BONASTON**<br>115 Royston Street<br>Liverpool | Machine insurance clerk |
| R2/103<br>11 February 1910<br>Sent by<br>W B Perkins<br>Two sizes | 61 Church Street<br>Lozells<br>Aston Manor<br>Birmingham | P13/P/134,135<br>***#8832,3***<br> | **William Burnett PERKINS**<br>11 Vyse Street<br>Birmingham | Manufacturing jeweller and silversmith |
| R2/106<br>15 March 1910<br>Sent by W H<br>Carrington & Co | Whitworth House<br>High Street<br>Manchester | P13/R/30<br>***#8834***<br> | **William Barnes RUSSELL**<br>Piccadilly and<br>St Mary's Gate<br>Manchester | Tobacconist |
| R1/117<br>27 November 1899<br>Sent by W H<br>Carrington<br>C Hitchin<br>Cancelled<br>15 March 1900 | Whitworth House<br>C-on-M<br>(Ed: Chorlton-on-Medlock)<br>Manchester | P9/R/11<br>***#8835***<br> | **William Barnes RUSSELL**<br>Piccadilly<br>Manchester | |
| Missing register<br>*c.*1888<br>Two sizes | Another possibility may be William Bainbridge Reynolds Ltd, Art metal workers<br>7b Old Town<br>Clapham<br>London SW | P5/R/184a,b<br>***#8836,7***<br> | | |
| Missing register<br>*c.*1888 | | P5/R/184c<br>***#8838***<br> | | |

| REGISTRATION DETAILS | MAKER'S PRIVATE ADDRESS and DETAILS | PLATE and MARK DETAILS | MAKER/COMPANY and BUSINESS ADDRESS | MAKER'S TRADE |
|---|---|---|---|---|
| Missing register<br>*c.*1888 | | P5/R/184d<br>***#8839***<br>  | **William Barnes RUSSELL**<br>Piccadilly<br>Manchester | Tobacconist |
| R1/29<br>9 June 1896<br>Sent by Henry Wood | 44 Difford Road<br>Burbury Street<br>Birmingham | P5/X*sic*/773<br>***#8840***<br>  | **Henry WOOD** trading as<br>**WOOD BROTHERS**<br>63 Great Hampton Street<br>Birmingham | Silver chain manufacturers |
| R1/162<br>22 February 1902<br>Sent by C Horner | 25 Belloff Street [1]<br>Cheetham<br>Woodleigh [2]<br>Egerton Road<br>Fallowfield | P9/W/65<br>***#8841***<br> | **B M WENGOLD** [1]<br>**S H WENGOLD** [2] trading as<br>**WENGOLD BROTHERS**<br>84 Corporation Street<br>Manchester | Wholesale jewellers |
| R1/176<br>25 September 1902<br>Sent by T Wilson | 93 Leconfield Road<br>Highbury New Park<br>London N | P9/W/75<br>***#8842***<br> | **Thomas William WILSON** trading as<br>**WILSON BROTHERS** *<br>8 Skinner Street, Clerkenwell<br>London | Gold chain maker |
| LPB/88<br>13 January 1880 | | P3/W/x1<br>***#8843***<br> | **WOLFE BROTHERS**<br>75 Buchanan Street<br>Glasgow | Watch manufacturers and importers and wholesale jewellers |
| R1/46<br>18 June 1897<br>Sent by Ward Brothers<br>W Bradbury | Antrobus Road<br>Handsworth<br>Birmingham | P5/aboveA/851<br>***#8844***<br> | **Samuel Robert WARD**<br>**Charles Augustus WARD** trading as<br>**WARD BROTHERS**<br>124 Branston Street<br>Birmingham | Manufacturing jewellers |
| R2/34<br>12 March 1907<br>Sent by C A Ward | 54 Thornhill Road<br>Handsworth<br>Birmingham | P9/V*sic*/168<br>***#8845***<br>  | **Charles Augustus WARD**<br>124 Branston Street<br>Birmingham | Brooch manufacturer |
| R3/74<br>6 February 1935<br>Sent by Ward Brothers | | P15/W/110<br>***#8846***<br>  | **WARD BROTHERS (BIRMINGHAM) LTD**<br>Common seal of company affixed in the presence of:-<br>L Ward (Director)<br>G G Ward (Secretary)<br>124 Branston Lane (Registered Office)<br>Hockley<br>Birmingham | Manufacturing jewellers |
| R3/106<br>18 March 1944<br>Sent by Ward Brothers (Birmingham) Ltd | | P21/W/38<br>***#8847***<br>  | | |
| R2/90<br>14 August 1909<br>Sent by W B Small | 30 Clapton Mount<br>Halifax | P13/S/42<br>***#8848***<br>  | **William Bromley SMALL**<br>39 Crown Street<br>Halifax | Jeweller |
| R1/215<br>14 June 1904<br>Sent by A Batt for W Batt & Son | 77 Watson Road<br>23 Beech Hill Road<br>Sheffield | P9/XYZ*sic*/122<br>***#8849***<br>  | **Albert S BATT**<br>**Thomas BATT**<br>**Arthur BATT** trading as<br>**W BATT & SON** *<br>17 Sycamore Road<br>Sheffield | Silversmiths and cutlers |

| REGISTRATION DETAILS | MAKER'S PRIVATE ADDRESS and DETAILS | PLATE and MARK DETAILS | MAKER/COMPANY and BUSINESS ADDRESS | MAKER'S TRADE |
|---|---|---|---|---|
| R3/33<br>16 July 1926<br>Sent by A V Base<br>Three sizes | 10 Great Wall Street<br>Hall Green, Birmingham<br>D R Base<br>48 Belgrave Road<br>Edgbaston<br>Birmingham | P15/B/180-182<br>***#8850-2***  | **William BASE & SONS**<br>D R Base<br>A V Base<br>18 Kenyon Street<br>Birmingham | Gold and silversmiths |
| R3/104<br>10 February 1943<br>Sent by William Bernard Wallis | Private address same as business | P21/W/36<br>***#8853***  | **William Bernard WALLIS**<br>39 Laxey Road<br>Birmingham 16 | Jewellers |
| R3/102<br>11 March 1942<br>Sent by William John Cole | 93 Longdon Road<br>Knowle<br>Warwickshire | P21/C/20<br>***#8854***  | **William John COLE**<br>Back 119 Branston Street<br>Birmingham | Silversmith |
| LPB/20<br>19 August 1880 | | P3/C/x2<br>***#8855,6***  | **William CROWSON**<br>10 Augusta Street<br>Birmingham | Gold chain maker |
| LPB/20<br>9 October 1884 | | P5/C/x1<br>***#8857***  | **W COOK**<br>80 William Street, Broad Street<br>Birmingham | Jeweller |
| R2/132<br>28 March 1911<br>Sent by F O Banyard | Rosamond Street<br>Salford | P13/C/91<br>***#8858***  | **William CHADWICK**<br>3 Hanson Court<br>Manchester | Stick mounter |
| R3/167<br>26 March 1959<br>Sent by W Cartwright | c/o 29 Chelmsford Street<br>Oldham 7 | P21/C/80<br>***#8859***  | **William CARTWRIGHT**<br>Gordon Chambers<br>15 King Street<br>Huddersfield | Jeweller and diamond mounter |
| 5 March 1960 | | P21/C/85<br>***#8860***  | Room 3 (from 5 March 1960)<br>Market Hall<br>Huddersfield | |
| R2/107<br>4 April 1910<br>Sent by Hirst Brothers & Co Ltd<br>BAO 12.470 | 371 Park Road<br>Oldham | P13/C/63<br>***#8861*** 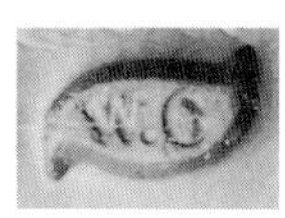 | **MESSRS COOKSON**<br>11 Manchester Street and<br>32 High Street and<br>217 Manchester Street<br>Oldham | Watchmakers and jewellers |
| R1/198<br>24 July 1903<br>Sent by Waldron & Cheshire | Middlemore Road<br>Northfield<br>116 Gillot Road<br>Birmingham | P9/W/100<br>***#8862***  | **George WALDRON**<br>**Walter William CHESHIRE** trading as<br>**WALDRON & CHESHIRE**<br>47 Vyse Street<br>Birmingham | Manufacturing jewellers |
| Missing register<br>*c.*1886<br>Similar mark entered<br>LAO 5 May 1886 | | P5/C/22<br>***#8863***  | **William CHINN** *<br>37 Hill Street<br>Coventry | Watchcase maker |
| CMC 1846<br>J1 1845 | | P2/C/x3<br>***#8864-6***  | **William CROFTON**<br>Bridge Street Row<br>Chester | Watchmaker and clockmaker |
| PDB 1822-3<br>MR3/79<br>J1 1822-4 | Gold rings | P1/29/x3<br>***#8867-9***  | **William CRUMPSTY**<br>Liverpool<br>or | Goldsmith |
| PDB 1815 | Gold rings | P1/29/x2<br>***#8870,1***  | **William CLARKE**<br>Liverpool | Goldsmith |

| REGISTRATION DETAILS | MAKER'S PRIVATE ADDRESS and DETAILS | PLATE and MARK DETAILS | MAKER/COMPANY and BUSINESS ADDRESS | MAKER'S TRADE |
|---|---|---|---|---|
| GSJW/105<br>PP3/83<br>Similar mark LAO<br>7 November 1855 | Not in SPB or LPB so struck<br>1860-3 | P3/C/x3<br>***#8872-4***<br> | **William CARTER** *<br>7 President Street East, Goswell Road<br>London EC | Watchcase maker |
| Missing register<br>*c.*1888 | | P5/C/141<br>***#8875***<br> | **Unidentified** | |
| Missing register<br>*c.*1888 | | P5/C/142<br>***#8876***<br> | **Unidentified** | |
| Similar mark entered<br>LAO 10 January 1843 | | P1/5/x3<br>***#8877-9***<br> | **William Charles BACON** *<br>9 President Street West, Goswell Road<br>London | Watchcase maker |
| Missing register<br>*c.*1888<br>Similar mark entered<br>LAO 1 August 1891 | Silversmith William Charles Brewer also entered similar mark LAO 24 November 1886 | P5/B/181<br>***#8880***<br> | **William Cotton BIRD** *<br>10 Norfolk Street<br>Coventry | Watchcase maker |
| R1/130<br>31 July 1900<br>Sent by Walter Coulthard | 48 Hampton Road [1]<br>Birchfield<br>Birmingham<br>68 Trinity Road [2] | P9/C/37<br>***#8881***<br> | **Walter COULTHARD** [1]<br>**Henry PORTER** [2]<br>**Nathaniel PORTER** [3] trading as<br>**W COULTHARD & CO**<br>59 Northampton Street<br>Birmingham | Silversmiths |
| MR3/113<br>Two sizes | Birchfield<br>Birmingham<br>17 Wellington Road [3]<br>Handsworth<br>Birmingham | P9/C/35,36<br>***#8882,3***<br>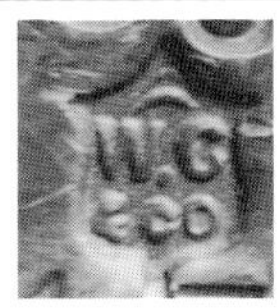 | | |
| R2/53<br>16 January 1908<br>Sent by G Waldron | Bathurst Villa<br>Bristol Road<br>Northfields and<br>16 Goldsmith Road<br>King's Heath, Birmingham | P13/W/20<br>***#8884***<br> | **George WALDRON**<br>**Charles DAWSON**<br>47 Vyse Street<br>Birmingham | Manufacturing jewellers |
| R2/219<br>9 January 1918<br>Sent by Whitehouse & Cox | 15 Borneo Street<br>Walsall | P15/W/37<br>***#8885***<br> | **E Irwin MILLER** (Chairman)<br>**Harry C COX** (Managing Director)<br>**George W COX** (Secretary) trading as<br>**WHITEHOUSE, COX & CO LTD**<br>Marsh Street<br>Walsall | Leather and metalware manufacturers |
| R1/14<br>17 July 1895<br>Sent by Wittenberg & Co | 3 Hollybank<br>(Accrington? - town not entered)<br><br>see also *#8892* | P5/X*sic*/675a<br>***#8886***<br> | **Max WITTENBERG** (Managing Director)<br>**WITTENBERG & CO**<br>3 Manchester Road<br>(Accrington? – town not entered) | Briar manufacturers and silver mounters |
| R1/ 81 undated<br>Sent by Wittenberg & Co<br>Entry cancelled | | No new mark<br>***#8886a*** | **Max WITTENBERG** (Managing Director)<br>**WITTENBERG & CO**<br>3 Manchester Road<br>Accrington | |
| R1/41<br>9 March 1897<br>Sent by J W Russell | 84 Whitechapel<br>Liverpool | P5/X*sic*/823<br>***#8887***<br> | **James Williamson RUSSELL** trading as<br>**WILLIAMSON & CO**<br>84 Whitechapel<br>Liverpool | Pipe mounters |
| LPB/84<br>3 October 1882 | | P3/W/x1<br>***#8888***<br> | **WALLBRIDGE & CO**<br>121 Vyse Street<br>Birmingham | Silversmiths |
| LPB/42<br>5 March 1883 | | P3/W/x1<br>***#8889***<br> | **WHITE & CO**<br>7 Vyse Street<br>Birmingham | Jewellers |

| REGISTRATION DETAILS | MAKER'S PRIVATE ADDRESS and DETAILS | PLATE and MARK DETAILS | MAKER/COMPANY and BUSINESS ADDRESS | MAKER'S TRADE |
|---|---|---|---|---|
| R2/139<br>17 July 1911<br>Sent by The Witten Patent Pipe Co Ltd | 235 Upper Brook Street<br>Manchester | P13/W/97<br>***#8890***<br>§ <br>P13/W/98<br>***#8891***  | **THE WITTEN PATENT PIPE CO LTD**<br>Sydney Walker (Director and Secretary)<br>56 Sidney Street<br>Manchester | Pipe manufacturers |
| R1/14<br>17 July 1895<br>Sent by Wittenberg & Co | 3 Hollybank<br>(Accrington? – town not entered)<br>see also *#8886* | P5/X*sic*/675b<br>***#8892***  | **Max WITTENBERG** (Managing Director)<br>**WITTENBERG & CO**<br>3 Manchester Road<br>Accrington ? (Town not entered) | Briar pipe manufacturers and silver mounters |
| R3/24<br>10 October 1924<br>Sent by David Anderson<br>16 June 1931 | 36 Second Avenue<br>Kings Park<br>Cathcart | P15/G/49<br>***#8893*** <br>P15/G/56<br>***#8894***  | **W C GOLDIE & CO LTD**<br>William Cowan Goldie<br>50 Wellington Street<br>Glasgow | Wholesale agent and merchants |
| R1/183<br>4 February 1903<br>Sent by E Booth & Sons<br>R1/195<br>9 June 1903<br>Sent by J Gammage | The Ferns<br>Thames Ditton | P9/S/59<br>***#8895*** <br>P9/S/64<br>***#8896***  | **William Charles SPIKINS**<br>128 High Street, Guildford and<br>69 High Street, Wandsworth and<br>84 High Street, Deptford and<br>80/82 Thames Street<br>Kingston upon Thames | Watchmaker and jeweller |
| R2/104<br>1 March 1910<br>Sent by William Clark (*sic*) & Son William Clark (*sic*) Junior BAO 9049<br>14 January 1928 | Ed: BAO has Clarke see mark *#8900* below with Clarke<br>20 Springfield Road<br>King's Heath and<br>34 Springfield Road<br>King's Heath<br>Birmingham | P13/C/59<br>***#8897*** <br>P15/C/183<br>***#8898***  | **William CLARK** (*sic*) senior<br>**William CLARK** (*sic*) junior<br>40 Vyse Street<br>Birmingham | Manufacturing jewellers |
| Missing register<br>*c.*1886<br>Similar mark entered LAO 21 March 1888 | Very tiny and indistinct WCS mark | P5/S/22<br>***#8899***  | **William Christian SCHULLER** *<br>36 Poland Street<br>London | Diamond merchant and setter |
| R1/112<br>22 September 1899<br>Sent by W Clarke & Son | Endcliffe<br>Institute Road<br>King's Heath<br>Birmingham | P9/C/29<br>***#8900*** 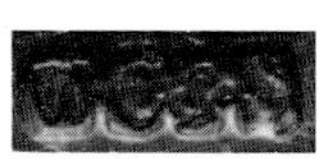 | **William CLARKE & SON**<br>40 Vyse Street<br>Birmingham | Manufacturing jewellers |
| R1/87<br>6 December 1898<br>Sent by Coupland & Monk | 125 St James Road [1]<br>Holloway<br>6 Myddleton Street [2]<br>Clerkenwell | P9/C/2<br>***#8901***  | **William Breeton COUPLAND** [1] *<br>**William MONK** [2] trading as<br>**COUPLAND & MONK**<br>30 St James Walk, Clerkenwell<br>London EC | Silver mounter |
| Mising register<br>c.1886 | | P5/Y/47<br>#8902  | **Unidentified** | |
| R2/20<br>2 July 1906<br>Sent by W Davies | 146 Linwood Road<br>Handsworth<br>Birmingham | P9/D/55<br>#8903  | **William DAVIES**<br>146½ Hockley Hill<br>Birmingham | General ring maker |

| REGISTRATION DETAILS | MAKER'S PRIVATE ADDRESS and DETAILS | PLATE and MARK DETAILS | MAKER/COMPANY and BUSINESS ADDRESS | MAKER'S TRADE |
|---|---|---|---|---|
| R3/90<br>22 August 1938<br>Sent by W Doodson | 22 Halstead Road<br>Gatley<br>Cheshire | P21/D/3<br>***#8904***<br> | **Walter DOODSON**<br>2 Bull's Head Yard, Market Place<br>Manchester | Working jeweller |
| R2/157<br>18 June 1912<br>Sent by P F Jackson<br>Two sizes | 184 Hamstead Road<br>Birmingham | P13/D/43-54<br>***#8905-16***<br> | **Percy Frederick JACKSON** trading as<br>**Walter DUMOLO**<br>35 Frederick Street<br>Birmingham | Wholesale jewellers |
| LPB/26 SP25/4<br>17 May 1884 | | P5/D/x1<br>***#8917***<br> | **William DAVIES**<br>2 Warstone Parade, Warstone Lane<br>Birmingham | Locket maker |
| J1 1854-68<br>Similar mark entered<br>SAO 26 March 1866 | | P2/D/x3<br>***#8918-20***<br> | **William DODGE**<br>25 Market Place<br>Manchester | Silversmith |
| Missing register<br>*c.*1886 | | P5/D/3<br>***#8921***<br>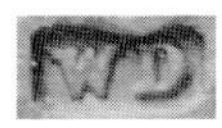 | **Unidentified** | |
| Missing register<br>*c.*1886 | | P5/D/69<br>***#8922***<br> | **Unidentified** | |
| R2/154<br>6 April 1912<br>Sent by Wilsdorf & Davis | Auckland, Auckland Row<br>Norwood, London SE<br>Kingsthorpe<br>Parkstone Avenue<br>Hornchurch<br>Essex | P13/W/119<br>***#8923***<br>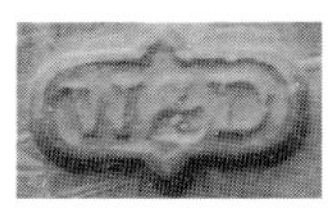 | **Hans WILSDORF**<br>**Alfred James DAVIS** trading as<br>**WILSDORF & DAVIS** *<br>(Ed: Founders and proprietors of Rolex Watch Co)<br>85 Hatton Garden<br>London | Watch manufacturers |
| R2/72<br>27 April 1909<br>Sent by A Wilcox<br>All block letter punches cancelled | 6 St Deverick Terrace<br>Cults<br>by Aberdeen | P13/D/6<br>***#8924***<br> | **William DUNNINGHAM** trading as<br>**W DUNNINGHAM & CO**<br>1 Diamond Street<br>Aberdeen | Manufacturing jewellers and silversmiths |
| 18 February 1909 | | P13/D/3<br>***#8925***<br> | | |
| R2/77<br>3 April 1909<br>Sent by<br>W Dunningham & Co | | P13/D/11<br>***#8926***<br> | **William DUNNINGHAM & CO**<br>1 Diamond Street<br>Aberdeen | |
| 1 May 1909<br>P13/D/14,15 accepted<br>Two sizes | | P13/D/14,15<br>***#8927,8***<br> | | |
| 1 May 1909<br>P13/D/11 recut and re-entered as<br>P13/D/16 | | P13/D/16<br>***#8929***<br> | | |
| PDB 1815<br>MR3/81 | Box mounts | Not on P1<br>***#8930*** **W E?** | **William ELLISON**<br>Liverpool | Silversmith |
| SPB/3<br>No date, name or address listed. *c.*1861<br>Entered mark BAO<br>14 November 1867 | High volume manufacturer using mass-production methods | P3/E/x7<br>***#8931-7***<br>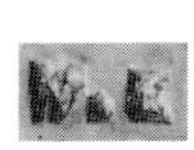 | **William EHRHARDT** *<br>Time Works<br>Barr Street<br>Birmingham | Watchcase and watch manufacturers |
| SPB/23<br>11 January 1869 | John Eagles, watchcase maker, at this address in 1869 | P3/E/x3<br>***#8939-40***<br> | **William EAGLES**<br>10 Park Road<br>Liverpool | Watchcase maker? |

| REGISTRATION DETAILS | MAKER'S PRIVATE ADDRESS and DETAILS | PLATE and MARK DETAILS | MAKER/COMPANY and BUSINESS ADDRESS | MAKER'S TRADE |
|---|---|---|---|---|
| R2/125<br>6 December 1910<br>Sent by Wm Ehrhardt Ltd | Idonea<br>Woodbourne Road<br>Edgbaston<br>Birmingham | P13/E/18<br>***#8941***<br> | **William EHRHARDT LTD** *<br>G V Ehrhardt (Secretary)<br>Time Works, Barr Street<br>Birmingham and<br>17 Hatton Garden<br>London | Watch manufacturers |
| R3/19<br>27 November 1923<br>Sent by William Eels | 28 Church End<br>Hendon<br>London | P15/E/25<br>***#8942***<br> | **William EELS** *<br>12-14 Beak Street<br>London | Silversmith |
| R2/11<br>24 February 1906<br>Sent by W Ehrhardt | 190 Hamstead Road<br>Handsworth<br>Birmingham | P9/E/19<br>***#8943***<br> | **William EHRHARDT** *<br>Wm Ehrhardt (Managing Director)<br>Time Works, Barr Street, Hockley<br>Birmingham | Watch manufacturers |
| LPB/20<br>25 February 1881 | Kelly 1880 | P3/C/x1<br>***#8944***<br> | **William Edward COOPER**<br>30 and 46 Edgbaston Street<br>Birmingham | Manufacturing jeweller |
| R1/228<br>3 March 1905<br>Sent by C Walker | 5 Wellington Grove<br>Stockport | P9/D*sic*/220<br>***#8945***<br> | **Arthur CROKER** trading as<br>**W E CROKER & CO**<br>35 Turner Street<br>Manchester | Umbrella manufacturers |
| Missing register<br>*c.*1894<br>Similar mark entered<br>LAO 22 January 1894 | | P5/D/545<br>***#8946***<br> | **William Edward DIBLEY** *<br>33 Gerrard Street<br>Soho<br>London W | Silversmith |
| R3/75<br>15 March 1935<br>Sent by Kinsey Brothers & Patrick Ltd, 17 Vyse Street Birmingham | 136 Bushmore Road<br>Hall Green<br>Birmingham | P15/G/58<br>***#8947***<br> | **William Edward GINDER**<br>39 Vyse Street<br>Birmingham | Manufacturing jeweller |
| R3/20<br>19 February 1924<br>Sent by J & R Griffin Ltd | The Briars<br>Bolderne Road<br>Sutton Coldfield | P15/H/77<br>***#8948***<br> | **William Ernest HOULSTON** trading as<br>**J & H HOULSTON**<br>105 Spencer Street<br>Birmingham | Jewellers and silversmiths |
| R1/75<br>9 August 1894<br>Sent by W E Lea<br>B Wade | 12 Wilson Street<br>Ardwick<br>Manchester | P5/L/572<br>***#8949***<br> | **Walter Ernest LEA**<br>18 Dale Street<br>Manchester | Stick mounter |
| R2/29<br>16 November 1906<br>Sent by selves | The Hawthorns<br>Acocks Green<br>Birmingham | P9/U*sic*/269<br>***#8950***<br> | **W E PATTERSON** trading as<br>**W E PATTERSON & CO**<br>189 Warstone Lane<br>Birmingham | Manufacturing jewellers |
| R1/77<br>14 February 1900<br>Authority to A Moore<br>*Punch entered in old book 1892* | | P5*sic*/S/337<br>***#8951***<br> | **W E STALLARD**<br>20 Trinity Road<br>Birchfields<br>Birmingham | Jeweller |
| R1/14<br>31 July 1895<br>Sent by A Griffiths<br>No name or address listed | See #8953 | P5/S/678<br>***#8952***<br> | **W E STALLARD or**<br>**William Edward STEVENS** | |

| REGISTRATION DETAILS | MAKER'S PRIVATE ADDRESS and DETAILS | PLATE and MARK DETAILS | MAKER/COMPANY and BUSINESS ADDRESS | MAKER'S TRADE |
|---|---|---|---|---|
| R1/68<br>16 July 1898<br>Sent by R J Pike<br>W Hammon<br>T P Hewitt | | P9*sic*/S/965<br>***#8953***  | **William Edward STEVENS**<br>Brighton Villa<br>Earlsdon<br>Coventry | Watch manufacturer |
| R1/99<br>27 April 1899<br>Sent by John Harris | Private address same as business | P9/S/16<br>***#8954***  | | Watch and cycle manufacturer |
| R1/123<br>17 March 1900<br>Sent by J Fleckner<br>Old punch cancelled | | P9/S/33<br>***#8955***  | | Watch manufacturer |
| R1/99<br>27 April 1899<br>Sent by John Harris | | P9/S/17<br>***#8956***  | | Watch and cycle manufacturer |
| Not in R1 as expected.<br>Perhaps an omission on R1/123 above | | P9/S/32<br>***#8957*** 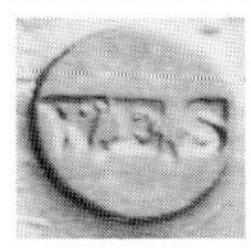 | | |
| PCR-1773<br>PP1/189<br>GTD 1829<br>PMR 1829-61 | Struck inverted | P1/5/x2<br>***#8958,9***  | **William FISHER**<br>3 Burroughs Garden (1829)<br>Liverpool | Watchcase maker |
| R2/69<br>24 November 1908<br>Sent by William Ford | 3 Victoria Street<br>Urmston<br>Manchester | P13/F/3<br>***#8960***  | **William FORD**<br>32 Edge Street<br>off Oak Street<br>Manchester | Umbrella and walking stick mounter |
| LPB/30 SP26/4<br>6 May 1883 | | P3/F/x2<br>***#8961,2***  | **William FOLLIS**<br>42 Vyse Street<br>Birmingham | Jeweller |
| LPB/32<br>26 November 1883<br>Sent by W H Christie | | P5/F/x1<br>***#8963***  | **William FLOWER**<br>4 Weston Street<br>Coventry | Watchcase maker |
| R1/63<br>15 March 1898<br>Sent by Ward & Francis | 2 Miles Buildings [1]<br>130 Far Gosford Road [2]<br>Coventry - authority to use IJT Newsome punch 6 June 1905 | P5/X*sic*/943<br>***#8964***  | **Alfred WARD** [1]<br>**William FRANCIS** [2] trading as<br>**WARD & FRANCIS** *<br>39 Croft Road<br>Coventry | Watchcase makers |
| LPB/16<br>4 June 1880<br>Sent by E Vaughton | | P3/B/x1<br>***#8965***  | **William Fulford BROWN**<br>Northampton Street<br>Birmingham | Jeweller |
| R2/136<br>20 May 1911<br>Sent by W F Gilbert | Private address same as business | P13/G/36<br>***#8966***  | **Walter Fraser GILBERT**<br>87 Foregate Street<br>Leeds | Watchmaker and jeweller |
| Missing register<br>*c.*1887<br>Similar mark LAO<br>6 December 1887 | | P5/G/134<br>***#8967***  | **William Francis GARRUD** *<br>12 Bartletts Passage Building<br>Holborn Circus<br>London EC | Manufacturing jeweller and silversmith |
| Not in R2 as expected<br>*c.* July 1914 to September 1915 | | P15/H/23<br>***#8968***  | **Walter Frederick HOLMES**<br>7 Warstone Parade (East)<br>Birmingham | Manufacturer jewellers |

| REGISTRATION DETAILS | MAKER'S PRIVATE ADDRESS and DETAILS | PLATE and MARK DETAILS | MAKER/COMPANY and BUSINESS ADDRESS | MAKER'S TRADE |
|---|---|---|---|---|
| R2/30<br>29 November and<br>22 December 1906<br>Sent by W F Holmes | Overton<br>Water Orton<br>Warwickshire | P9/H/87,88<br>***#8969,70***<br> | **William Frederick HOLMES** trading as<br>**W F HOLMES**<br>7 Warstone Parade (East)<br>Birmingham | Manufacturing jewellers |
| LPB/46<br>9 April 1883 | | P3/R/x2<br>***#8971,2***<br> | **Walter Hayes RABONE** *<br>**Frank RABONE** *<br>39 Lord Street<br>Birmingham | Jewellers |
| R2/146<br>30 October 1911<br>Sent by Frank Rabone<br>Four sizes | White Lodge<br>Four Oaks<br>Dalecross Grange<br>Barnt Green<br>Birmingham | P13/R/34-43<br>***#8973-82***<br> | **Walter Hayes RABONE** *<br>**Frank RABONE** *<br>49 Frederick Street and<br>39 Albion Street<br>Birmingham | Jewellers, silversmiths and chain makers |
| R3/37<br>22 June 1927<br>Sent by selves | | P15/R/42<br>***#8983***<br> | **S BLANCKENSEE & SON LTD** *<br>trading as **W H & F RABONE** *<br>W Davis (Secretary)<br>14-16 Frederick Street and<br>72-73 Great Hampton Street<br>Birmingham | Jewellers and silversmiths |
| Missing register<br>*c.*1890<br>Similar mark LAO<br>19 September 1892 | | P5/F*sic*/328<br>***#8984***<br> | **Walter Francis READING** *<br>26 St John Street Road<br>Clerkenwell<br>London EC | Pipe mounter |
| R3/29<br>29 July 1925<br>Sent by Stylic Watch Case Co | 70 Wake Green Road<br>Moseley<br>Birmingham | P15/S/67<br>***#8985***<br>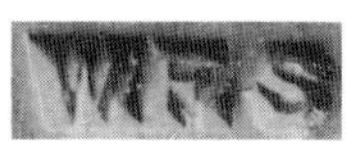 | **STYLIC WATCH CASE CO**<br>W F Smith (Director)<br>42 Frederick Street (Manufactory)<br>Birmingham | Manufacturing jewellers |
| R1/28<br>9 May 1896<br>Sent by W F Twine<br>W Mills<br>Ginder Brothers | 139 Lenox Street<br>Lozells<br>Birmingham | P5/T/766<br>***#8986***<br> | **W F TWINE**<br>44½ Hylton Street<br>Birmingham<br>**TWINE & GILPIN**<br>89 Vyse Street from 27 October1903<br>Birmingham | Manufacturing jewellers |
| R1/67<br>14 June 1898<br>Sent by W & F Terry<br>Russell & Co<br>J Eastham | 13 Moorfield Road<br>Didsbury<br>Manchester | P5/T/959<br>***#8987***<br> | **William TERRY**<br>**Frank Urquart TERRY** trading as<br>**W & F TERRY**<br>70 Stratford Road, Hulme and<br>8 Victoria Street<br>Manchester | Jewellers and watchmakers |
| R1/122<br>2 March 1900<br>Sent by Frank Stone | | P9/T/13<br>***#8988***<br> | | Jewellers |
| R1/147<br>10 May 1901<br>Sent by Walter Glover | Piggots<br>Aleridge<br>Essex | P9/G/25<br>***#8989***<br> | **Walter GLOVER** *<br>17 St John's Square<br>Clerkenwell Road<br>London | Agent |
| R3/34<br>20 September 1926<br>Sent by W Grinstead | Redbourne<br>Harrogate Road<br>Leeds | P15/G/51<br>***#8990***<br> | **W GRINSTEAD** trading as<br>**ENSIGN UMBRELLAS LTD**<br>42 Lowerhead Row<br>Leeds | Stick makers |

| REGISTRATION DETAILS | MAKER'S PRIVATE ADDRESS and DETAILS | PLATE and MARK DETAILS | MAKER/COMPANY and BUSINESS ADDRESS | MAKER'S TRADE |
|---|---|---|---|---|
| R3/98<br>28 February 1941<br>Sent by F H Wright | 262 High Street [1]<br>Bangor<br>28 Brynmore Park [2]<br>Higher Compton<br>Plymouth | P21/W/32<br>***#8991***<br> | **Francis Harry WRIGHT** [1]<br>**Norman Weaver GRIFFITHS** [2]<br>trading as **WRIGHT & GRIFFITHS**<br>262 High Street, Bangor<br>North Wales | Jewellers |
| PP1/189<br>GTD 1829<br>PMR 1825-53 | | P1/3/x3<br>***#8992-4***<br> | **William GRIFFITHS**<br>Richmond Street (1825)<br>6 Highfield Street (1829)<br>64 Vine Street (1834)<br>Sir Thomas' Buildings (1836)<br>Burlington Street (1839)<br>46 Christian Street (1851)<br>Liverpool | Watchcase maker |
| | Looks like WC but struck in square G, but clerk could have entered in wrong square - see also WC for William Crofton | P2/G/x2<br>***#8995,6***<br> | | |
| | | P2/G/x3<br>***#8997-9***<br> | | |
| LPB/6<br>25 April 1878 | | P3/G/x2<br>***#9000,1***<br> | **Walter GREEN**<br>47 Northampton Street<br>Birmingham | Jeweller |
| Missing register<br>*c.*1893 | | P5/G/505<br>***#9002***<br> | **Unidentified** | |
| No corresponding entry in R1 | | P5/G/746<br>***#9003***<br> | **Unidentified** | |
| LPB/34<br>31 January 1881<br>Sent by Coley Brothers | | P3/G/x1<br>***#9004***<br> | **William GRIFFITH**<br>3 Pitsford Street, Vyse Street<br>Birmingham | Jeweller |
| Missing register<br>*c.*1893<br>adjacent P5/G/525 | | P5/G/x1<br>***#9005***<br> | **Unidentified** | |
| No corresponding entry in R1 | | P5/G/577<br>***#9006***<br> | **Unidentified** | |
| SPB/18<br>16 July 1875 | | P3/G/x3<br>***#9007-9***<br> | **William GARDNER** *<br>Yew Bank, Griffin Street<br>Lower Broughton<br>Manchester | Watchmaker |
| R3/113<br>5 March 1946<br>Sent by<br>W G Bradshaw<br>Two sizes | Private address same as business | P21/B/24,25<br>***#9010,11***<br> | **William Griffith BRADSHAW**<br>18 Spring Bridge Road<br>Manchester 16 | Silversmith |
| R2/58<br>13 April 1908<br>Sent by W H Leather | 11 Roseberry Road<br>London N<br>35 Norshead Mansions<br>London W | P13/G/1<br>***#9012***<br> | **Paul Arthur SCHROEPFER**<br>**William GEIGER** trading as<br>**W GEIGER & CO** *<br>91 Hatton Garden<br>London | Manufacturing jewellers |
| R2/9<br>12 January 1906<br>Sent by William Geiger & Co | 14 Howard Street<br>West Hampstead<br>London | P9/G/65<br>***#9013***<br> | **Paul Arthur SCHROEPFER**<br>**William GEIGER** trading as<br>**William GEIGER & CO** *<br>91a Hatton Garden<br>London | |
| R2/23<br>29 August 1906<br>Sent by W Manton | 14 Howard Court<br>Western Lane<br>34 Southerend Mansions<br>Elgin Avenue, London | P9/G/81<br>***#9014***<br> | | |

| REGISTRATION DETAILS | MAKER'S PRIVATE ADDRESS and DETAILS | PLATE and MARK DETAILS | MAKER/COMPANY and BUSINESS ADDRESS | MAKER'S TRADE |
|---|---|---|---|---|
| R3/78<br>23 August 1935<br>Sent by S Blanckensee & Sons Ltd<br>19-35 Regent Place<br>Birmingham | Camden<br>24 New Bridge Hill [1]<br>Broomswood House [2]<br>55 Upper Oldfield Park<br>Bath | P15/D/89-91<br>***#9015-7***<br> | **George Heneage DICKINSON** [1]<br>**William Finch DICKINSON** [2] trading as<br>**W G DICKINSON & SONS**<br>19 New Bond Street<br>Bath | Goldsmiths and silversmiths |
| R3/84<br>9 June 1936<br>Sent by S Blanckensee & Son Ltd<br>19 Regent Street<br>Birmingham | Camden [1]<br>24 New Bridge Hill, Bath<br>Broomswood House [2]<br>55 Upper Oldfield Park<br>Bath | P15/D/94-99<br>***#9018-23***<br> | **W G DICKINSON & SONS**<br>George Heneage Dickinson [1] (Partner)<br>William Finch Dickinson [2] (Partner)<br>19 New Bond Street<br>Bath<br>Somerset | Goldsmiths and silversmiths |
| LPB/28<br>1 December 1880<br>Sent by S Usher | | P3/W*sic*/x1<br>***#9024***<br> | **EDWARDS BROTHERS**<br>32½ Kenyon Street<br>Birmingham | Jewellers |
| SPB/20<br>9 April 1875 | CWMP 1874-1901 | P3/M*sic*/x2<br>***#9025,6***<br> | **William George HAMMON** *<br>8 Russell Terrace<br>Coventry | Watchcase maker |
| SPB/11<br>6 February 1866 | | P3/H/x3<br>***#9027-9***<br> | **William George HAMMON** *<br>86 Sovereign Place<br>Coventry | |
| Missing register<br>*c.*1891 | | P5/H/436<br>***#9030***<br> | | |
| SPB/22<br>7 January 1876 | | P3/M*sic*/x2<br>***#9031,2***<br> | **William George HAMMON** *<br>Portland Terrace<br>Coventry | |
| R2/36<br>27 March 1907<br>Sent by M Freeman | 97 Wood Vale<br>Honour Oak Park | P9/H/91<br>***#9033***<br>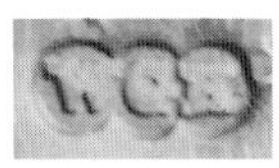 | **W G HARRIS**<br>late A Brahams<br>7 President Street, Goswell Road<br>London EC | Ring manufacturer |
| Not in R2 as expected<br>*c.* May to June 1909 | | P13/H/37<br>***#9034***<br> | | |
| Not in R2 as expected<br>*c.* December 1909 to February 1910 | | P13/H/46<br>***#9035***<br>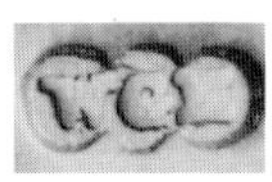 | | |
| R2/161<br>10 September 1912<br>Sent by W G Knight | 14 Heath Road<br>Handsworth<br>Birmingham | P13/K/8<br>***#9036***<br> | **William George KNIGHT**<br>(Agent for Gilbert & Son, Calcutta)<br>43 Hockley Hill<br>Birmingham | Manufacturing silversmith |
| R1/110<br>3 August 1899<br>Sent W G Knight | 21 Albert Road<br>Handsworth<br>Birmingham | P9/K/9<br>***#9037***<br> | **William George KNIGHT** trading as<br>**W G KNIGHT & CO**<br>7½ Warstone Lane<br>Birmingham | |
| R1/110<br>3 August 1899 | | P9/K/8<br>***#9038***<br> | | |
| R2/188<br>3 July 1914<br>Sent by<br>W G Matthews | 183 Antrobus Road<br>Handsworth<br>51 Wellington Road<br>Handsworth | P15/M/9-11<br>***#9039-41***<br> | **Walter George MATTHEWS**<br>**Walter Ernest MATTHEWS** trading as<br>**W G MATTHEWS**<br>26 Hockley Street<br>Birmingham | Manufacturing jewellers |

| REGISTRATION DETAILS | MAKER'S PRIVATE ADDRESS and DETAILS | PLATE and MARK DETAILS | MAKER/COMPANY and BUSINESS ADDRESS | MAKER'S TRADE |
|---|---|---|---|---|
| LPB/54<br>7 July 1881 | | P3/M/x1<br>***#9042*** 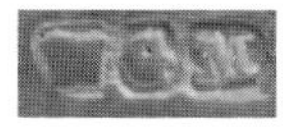 | **Walter George MATTHEWS**<br>16 Upper Hockley Street<br>Birmingham | Jeweller |
| LPB/56 SP27/10<br>16 July 1884<br>Sent by D & L Spiers | | P5/M/x1<br>***#9043***  | **Walter & George MYERS** *<br>68 Northampton Street<br>Birmingham | Wholesale jewellers and factors |
| LPB/6<br>25 March 1878<br>Sent by<br>Benjamin Phelps<br>Myer Brothers | See also GM | P3/M/x2<br>***#9044,5***  | **Walter & George MYERS** *<br>2 Richard Street<br>Spencer Street<br>Birmingham | |
| SP27/2<br>Unclear which entry relates to this mark | | P5/M/x1<br>***#9046***  | | |
| LPB/56 SP27/2<br>14 June 1884<br>Sent by Acott & Co<br>Mark not in LPB | | P5/M/x1<br>***#9047***  | | |
| Missing register<br>*c.*1888 | | P5/M/38<br>***#9048***  | | |
| Missing register<br>*c.*1892 | | P5/M/145<br>***#9049***  | | |
| Missing register<br>*c.*1886 | | P5/M/421<br>***#9050***  | **Walter & George MYERS**<br>68 Northampton Street<br>Birmingham | |
| Missing register<br>*c.*1886 | | P5/M/39<br>***#9051***  | | |
| R2/72<br>6 February 1909<br>Sent by Bacon & Bill<br>BAO 15.597 | The Friary<br>Handsworth Wood<br>61 Hale Road<br>Handsworth | P13/G/6<br>***#9052***  | **Walter G GRIFFITHS**<br>**Arthur GRIFFITHS** trading as<br>**W G GRIFFITHS & SONS**<br>17 Northampton Street<br>Birmingham | Jewellers and ring manufacturers |
| R2/160<br>30 August 1912<br>Sent by J Hayward<br>BAO 19.727 | 22 Holyhead Road<br>Handsworth<br>Birmingham | P13/G/43<br>***#9053***  | | Manufacturing jewellers |
| R2/172<br>21 May 1913<br>Sent by selves | Friary Road<br>Handsworth<br>22 Holyhead Road<br>Handsworth | P13/G/59,60<br>***#9054,5***  | | Jewellers |
| R2/174<br>17 June 1913<br>Sent by Charles Griffiths | | P13/G/61-63<br>***#9056-8***  | **Walter G GRIFFITHS**<br>**Charles GRIFFITHS**<br>17 Northampton Street<br>Birmingham | |
| R1/14<br>22 July 1895<br>Sent by W Aitken<br>E J Rudge<br>R J Wakefield | 61 Hall Road<br>Birmingham | P5/G/676<br>***#9059***  | **Walter GRIFFITHS** trading as<br>**William GRIFFITHS & SON**<br>17 Northampton Street<br>Birmingham | Jewellers |
| R1/186<br>26 February 1903<br>Sent by Eaton & Wrighton | Hall Road<br>Handsworth<br>Holyhead Road<br>Birmingham | P9/G/39<br>***#9060***  | **Arthur GRIFFITHS**<br>**Walter GRIFFITHS** trading as<br>**W GRIFFITHS & SONS**<br>17 Northampton Street<br>Birmingham | Manufacturing jewellers |

| REGISTRATION DETAILS | MAKER'S PRIVATE ADDRESS and DETAILS | PLATE and MARK DETAILS | | MAKER/COMPANY and BUSINESS ADDRESS | MAKER'S TRADE |
|---|---|---|---|---|---|
| R1/145<br>24 April 1901<br>Sent by H Pope | (Arthur Griffiths ?)<br>61 Hall Road<br>Handsworth, Birmingham | P9/G/22<br>***#9061*** |  | **W GRIFFITHS & SONS**<br>17 Northampton Street<br>Birmingham | Wholesale jewellers |
| R2/177<br>17 October 1913<br>Sent by Charles Gilbert<br>26 March 1921 | The Friary<br>Handsworth Wood<br>Birmingham | P15/G/8,9<br>***#9062,3*** |  | **W GRIFFITHS & SONS**<br>17 Northampton Street<br>Birmingham | Manufacturing jewellers |
| | | P15/G/42<br>***#9064*** |  | | |
| Not in R3 as expected *c.* October 1925 to November 1927 | Mark not registered at BAO | P15/W/89<br>***#90655*** | 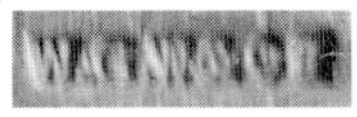 | **Unidentified** | |
| LPB/38<br>19 November 1881 | CWMP 1886 | P3/H/x1<br>***#9066*** |  | **William HICKMAN** *<br>46 Mount Street<br>Coventry | Watchcase maker |
| R1/59<br>5 February 1898<br>Sent by William Hughes | Private address same as business | P5/*Zsic*/928<br>***#9067*** |  | **William HUGHES**<br>39 Hunters Vale, Hockley<br>Birmingham | Jeweller |
| Not in LPB as expected<br>*c.*1886 | | P5/W/x1<br>***#9068*** |  | **Unidentified** | |
| R2/161<br>14 September 1912<br>Sent by Charles Wigley | 45 Douglas Road<br>Handsworth<br>Birmingham<br>Tynkersley House<br>Rowsley, Derbyshire | P13/W/124<br>***#9069*** |  | **Charles John WIGLEY**<br>**Arthur Devereux HALL** trading as<br>**WIGLEY & HALL**<br>87 Vyse Street<br>Birmingham | Jewellers and silversmiths |
| R2/25<br>4 October 1906<br>Sent by W Hands | Private address same as business | P9/H/84<br>***#9070*** |  | **William HANDS**<br>15 St George's Square<br>Forest Gate<br>London | Medallist, silversmith and jeweller |
| R3/117<br>19 April 1947<br>Sent by W Hutt | 41 Quarry Avenue<br>Westby? Castle<br>Birmingham | P21/H/36<br>***#9071*** |  | **William HUTT**<br>184 Warstone Lane<br>Birmingham 18 | Manufacturing jeweller |
| R3/111<br>3 December 1945<br>Sent by Leslie James Anthony Hartley | Hartley<br>Top Flat<br>2 Trafalgar Road<br>Birmingham 13 | P21/H/22<br>***#9072*** |  | **Leslie James Anthony HARTLEY**<br>**THE WAYNE HART CO**<br>184 Warstone Lane<br>Birmingham 18 | Manufacturing and wholesale jewellers |
| R2/204<br>5 May 1916<br>Sent by Walker & Hall<br>Five sizes | Ranby House<br>Nr Retford | P15/W/19-24,27-29<br>***#9073-81*** | 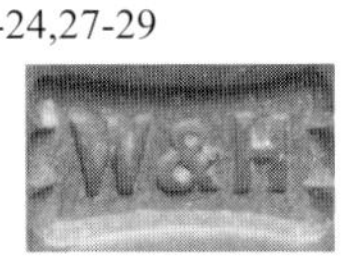 | **WALKER & HALL** *<br>Albert E Bingham (Proprietor)<br>Electro Works<br>Sheffield | Silversmiths |
| R3/68<br>23 October 1933<br>Sent by Walker & Hall Ltd | | P15/W/104<br>***#9082*** |  | **WALKER & HALL LTD** *<br>Common seal of company affixed in the presence of:-<br>J C Riddle (Director)<br>G R Slater (Director)<br>E P Gilbert (Secretary)<br>Electro Works<br>Howard Street<br>Sheffield 1 | Manufacturers of gold and silverplate cutlery and electroplate |

| REGISTRATION DETAILS | MAKER'S PRIVATE ADDRESS and DETAILS | PLATE and MARK DETAILS | MAKER/COMPANY and BUSINESS ADDRESS | MAKER'S TRADE |
|---|---|---|---|---|
| R3/74<br>11 February 1935<br>Sent by Walker & Hall | | P15/W/109<br>***#9083***<br> | **WALKER & HALL LTD** *<br>Common seal of company affixed in presence of:-<br>G R Slater (Director)<br>E P Gilbert (Secretary)<br>Electro Works (Registered Office)<br>Howard Street<br>Sheffield | Manufacturing silversmiths and cutlers |
| 1 September 1938 | | P21/W/2<br>***#9084***<br> | | |
| R3/91<br>24 September 1938<br>Sent by Walker & Hall<br>Electro Plate Works<br>Sheffield 1<br>Three sizes | | P21/W/3-9<br>***#9085-91***<br> | | |
| R3/91<br>26 September 1938<br>Sent by Walker & Hall<br>Electro Plate Works<br>Sheffield 1<br>Two sizes | | P21/W/10,11<br>***#9092,3***<br> | **WALKER & HALL LTD** *<br>Common seal of company affixed in presence of:-<br>G R Slater (Director)<br>E P Gilbert (Secretary)<br>Electro Works (Registered Office)<br>Howard Street<br>Sheffield | Silversmiths and cutlers |
| 3 October 1938<br>Two sizes | | P21/W/13-15<br>***#9094-6***<br> | | |
| 21 October 1938 | | P21/W/16<br>***#9097***<br> | | |
| R3/91<br>27 September 1938<br>Sent by P J Finch<br>14b Tenby Street<br>Birmingham 1 | | P21/W/12<br>***#9098***<br> | | |
| R3/92<br>1 November 1938<br>Sent by Walker & Hall<br>Four sizes<br>P21/W/20,29 cancelled<br>2 September 1941 | Punches lost by Adie Brothers of Birmingham - P21/W/23-26 cancelled 23 July 1947<br>Punches lost by S Blanckensee of Birmingham – P21/W/26,36 cancelled 26 January 1951 -<br>Punches worn out<br>Held by Marples & Beasley | P21/W/17-30<br>***#9099-9112***<br> | **WALKER & HALL LTD** *<br>Common seal of company affixed in the presence of:-<br>G R Slater (Director)<br>E P Gilbert (Secretary)<br>Electro Works (Registered Office)<br>Howard Street<br>Sheffield | |
| R1/156<br>29 October 1901<br>Sent by W Neale & Son | West Lea [1]<br>Ranmoor<br>Ranmoor Grange [2]<br>Ranmoor | P9/W/60<br>***#9113***<br> | **John Edward BINGHAM** [1]<br>**Albert Edward BINGHAM** [2] trading as<br>**WALKER & HALL** *<br>Howard Street<br>Sheffield | Silver and electroplate manufacturers |

| REGISTRATION DETAILS | MAKER'S PRIVATE ADDRESS and DETAILS | PLATE and MARK DETAILS | MAKER/COMPANY and BUSINESS ADDRESS | MAKER'S TRADE |
|---|---|---|---|---|
| R2/25<br>29 September 1906<br>Sent by A E Bingham<br>Four sizes<br>MR3/142 | West Lea<br>Sheffield<br>Ranmoor Grange<br>Sheffield | P9/V*sic*/146-149<br>***#9114-7***<br>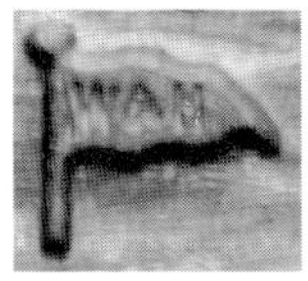 | **John Edward BINGHAM**<br>**Albert Edward BINGHAM** trading as<br>**WALKER & HALL** *<br>Electro Works<br>Sheffield | Silversmiths and cutlers |
| R2/34<br>7 March 1907<br>Sent by Walker & Hall per D & L Spiers<br>Two sizes | | P9/V*sic*/166,7<br>***#9118,9***<br> | **John Edward BINGHAM** Baronet<br>**Albert Edward BINGHAM** trading as<br>**WALKER & HALL** *<br>Howard Street<br>Sheffield | Sterling silver electroplate and cutlery manufacturers |
| 8 October 1908 | Ranby House<br>Retford | P13/W/34<br>***#9120***<br> | | |
| R2/31<br>4 January 1907<br>Sent by selves<br>Five sizes<br>P9/V*sic*/164 added<br>24 January 1907 | Ranby House<br>Retford<br>West Lea<br>Sheffield | P9/V*sic*/150-164<br>***#9121-35***<br> | **Albert Edward BINGHAM**<br>**John Edward BINGHAM** trading as<br>**WALKER & HALL** *<br>Electro Works<br>Sheffield | Silversmiths |
| 28 November 1908<br>P9/W/154,157,160 cancelled and replaced by P13/W/38-40 | | P13/W/38-40<br>***#9136-8***<br> | | |
| SPB/16<br>11 March 1878<br>SPB mark shown | | Not on P3<br>***#9139***<br> | **William HARRIS**<br>11 All Saints<br>Manchester | Working jeweller |
| LPB/6<br>26 March 1878 | | P3/M*sic*/x2<br>***#9140,1***<br> | **William HARRIS**<br>77 Oxford Street<br>Manchester | |
| R2/38<br>29 April 1907<br>Sent by Imperial Tobacco Co | Private address same as business | P9/H/94<br>***#9142***<br> | **William HARRISON**<br>22 Canonbury Street<br>Canonbury<br>London N | Silversmith |
| R2/60<br>28 May 1908<br>Sent by Imperial Tobacco Co | 79 Tollington Road<br>London N | P13/H/I<br>***#9143***<br> | **William HARRISON**<br>79 Tollington Road<br>London N | |
| R2/113<br>24 June 1910<br>Sent by Imperial Tobacco Co | 571 Caledonian Road<br>London N | P13/H/51,52<br>***#9144,5***<br> | **William HARRISON**<br>571 Caledonian Road<br>London N | |
| R2/204<br>27 April 1916<br>Sent by Imperial Tobacco Co<br>Three sizes | Private address same as business | P15/H/31–33<br>***#9146-8***<br> | **William HARRISON**<br>23 Florence Road<br>Finsbury Park<br>London N | |
| R2/225<br>7 January 1920<br>Sent by William Heywood | 14 Serpentine Road<br>Harborne | P15/H/56<br>***#9149***<br> | **William HEYWOOD**<br>100 Vyse Street<br>Birmingham | Brooches, studs and links |

| REGISTRATION DETAILS | MAKER'S PRIVATE ADDRESS and DETAILS | PLATE and MARK DETAILS | MAKER/COMPANY and BUSINESS ADDRESS | MAKER'S TRADE |
|---|---|---|---|---|
| J1 1831-44 | | P1/11/x1<br>***#9150*** | **William HYATT**<br>Worcester<br>or | Silversmith |
| PDB 1830<br>MR3/85<br>J1 1830 | Silver box<br>Born 1807, son of Thomas Helsby by his second wife Ann (née Smith) | 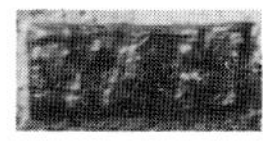 | **William HELSBY**<br>28 Vauxhall Road<br>Liverpool or | Silversmith |
| PDB 1827-36<br>MR3/85 | Gold rings and silver boxes | | **William HEMMING**<br>13 Tarleton Street<br>Liverpool | Goldsmith and silversmith |
| PDB 1785-1801<br>MR3/86<br>PP1/189<br>PP2/347,348<br>Similar mark entered BAO *c.*1789 | Watchcases and medals<br>Seen on 1798 watchcase<br><br>Square marked 1785 | P1/21/x1<br>***#9151***<br> | **William HULL**<br>26 Highfield Street<br>22 Cheapside (1789)<br>Liverpool | Watchcase maker and medals |
| Not in SPB or LPB so struck 1860-3<br>Similar mark entered BAO 28 January 1863 | | P3/H/x3<br>***#9152-4***<br> | **William HAMMON** *<br>86 Sovereign Place, The Butts<br>Coventry<br>or | Watchcase maker |
| Similar mark entered BAO 30 December 1863 | | | **William HEATH**<br>68 Mott Street<br>Birmingham | Jeweller |
| Missing register<br>*c.*1888 | | P5/W/166<br>***#9155***<br> | **Unidentified** | |
| Missing register<br>*c.*1891 | | P5/H/349<br>***#9156***<br> | **Unidentified** | |
| LPB/96<br>22 May 1882<br>Sent by A Griffiths | CWMP 1883 | P3/H/x1<br>***#9157***<br> | **William HAMMON** *<br>Portland Terrace<br>Chapel Fields<br>Coventry | Watchcase maker |
| R2/47<br>9 October 1907<br>Sent by William Hammon | Private address same as business | P9/II/100<br>***#9158***<br> | **William HAMMON** *<br>2 Gloucester Street<br>Coventry | Watchcase manufacturer |
| LPB/8<br>1 May 1885<br>No mark in LPB just entry | | P5/H/x1<br>***#9159***<br> | **William HUTCHINSON**<br>Belgrave Terrace, Lodge Road<br>Birmingham | Jeweller |
| Missing register<br>*c.*1893 | | P5/H/527<br>***#9160***<br> | **Unidentified** | |
| SPB/14<br>10 June 1874 | | P3/W/x2<br>***#9161,2***<br> | **WHITE & HAWKINS**<br>15, 16 Legge Lane<br>Birmingham | Silversmiths, goldsmiths and electroplaters |
| LPB/88<br>11 December 1878 | | P3/W/x1<br>***#9163***<br> | **Louis WEILL & Henry HARBURG** *<br>14 Hatton Garden<br>London EC | Watch manufacturers |
| R1/12<br>20 June 1895<br>Sent by Wigley & Hall | Lonsdale<br>45 Douglas Road<br>Handsworth<br>Birmingham | P5/X*sic*/667<br>***#9164***<br> | **Charles John WIGLEY**<br>**Arthur Devereux HALL** trading as<br>**WIGLEY & HALL**<br>56 Tenby Street North<br>Birmingham | Jewellers and designers |

| REGISTRATION DETAILS | MAKER'S PRIVATE ADDRESS and DETAILS | PLATE and MARK DETAILS | MAKER/COMPANY and BUSINESS ADDRESS | MAKER'S TRADE |
|---|---|---|---|---|
| R1/39<br>15 February 1897<br>Sent by Wright & Hadgkiss | 326 Hamstead Road [1]<br>Stapleton House [2]<br>Harborne | P5/X*sic*/816a<br>***#9165***<br> | **Henry Robert WRIGHT**[1]<br>**William HADGKISS** [2] trading as<br>**WRIGHT & HADGKISS**<br>9 Vyse Street<br>Birmingham | Jewellers |
| J1 1831-44 | | P1/27/x3<br>***#9166-8***<br> | **William HYATT**<br>Worcester<br>or | Silversmith |
| PDB 1830<br>MR3/85<br>J1 1830 | Silver box<br>Born 1807, son of Thomas Helsby by his second wife Ann (nee Smith) | P1/27/x1<br>***#9169***<br> | **William HELSBY**<br>28 Vauxhall Road<br>Liverpool or | Silversmith |
| PDB 1827-36<br>MR3/85 | Gold rings and silver boxes | | **William HEMMING**<br>13 Tarleton Street<br>Liverpool | Goldsmith and silversmith |
| R1/39<br>1 October 1897 | 326 Hamstead Road [1]<br>Stapleton House [2]<br>Harborne | P5/X*sic*/816b<br>***#9170***<br> | **Henry Robert WRIGHT** [1]<br>**William HADGKISS** [2] trading as<br>**WRIGHT & HADGKISS**<br>9 Vyse Street<br>Birmingham | Jewellers |
| R1/134<br>23 October 1900<br>Sent by Wright & Hadgkiss | 326 Hamstead Road<br>St Peters Road<br>Harborne<br>Birmingham | P9/W/38-40<br>***#9171-3***<br> | | Manufacturing jewellers |
| R1/81<br>19 October 1898 | | P9/W/6<br>***#9174***<br> | **WRIGHT & HADGKISS**<br>No address entered | |
| R2/63<br>25 July 1908<br>Sent by William Hewitt | 5 Thorpe Street<br>York | P13/H/2<br>***#9175***<br> | **William HEWITT**<br>City Chambers, Clifford Street<br>York | Engraver |
| R2/204<br>27 April 1916<br>Sent by W Hands | Private address same as business | P15/H/34<br>***#9176***<br> | **Walter HANDS**<br>43 Roland Road, Handsworth<br>Birmingham | Gold ring maker |
| R1/159<br>17 January 1902<br>Sent by W Hughes | Private address same as business | P9/H/48<br>***#9177***<br> | **William HUGHES**<br>Grosvenor House<br>46 Hunter Road, Hockley<br>Birmingham | Jeweller and silversmith |
| R1/218<br>17 August 1904<br>Sent by Howard & Baker | Grasmere<br>Park Avenue<br>Handsworth<br>2 Eaton Villas<br>Bury Old Road<br>Manchester | P9/V*sic*/120<br>***#9178***<br> | **Howard G BARBER**<br>**Hayam George WISE** trading as<br>**WISE & HOWARD**<br>44 Warstone Lane<br>Birmingham | Manufacturing jewellers |
| R1/223<br>23 November 1904<br>Sent by Wise & Howard | | P9/V*sic*/123<br>***#9179***<br> | **Howard G BARBER**<br>**Hayam George WISE** trading as<br>**WISE & HOWARD**<br>44 Warstone Lane<br>Birmingham | |
| R2/56<br>29 February 1908<br>Sent by Howard G Barber | | P13/W/21<br>***#9180***<br> | **Howard G BARBER**<br>**H G WISE** trading as<br>**WISE & HOWARD**<br>44 Warstone Lane<br>Birmingham and<br>Ro. Bose 4290<br>Johannesburg | |

| REGISTRATION DETAILS | MAKER'S PRIVATE ADDRESS and DETAILS | PLATE and MARK DETAILS | MAKER/COMPANY and BUSINESS ADDRESS | MAKER'S TRADE |
|---|---|---|---|---|
| R1/13<br>4 July 1895<br>Sent by W Haddleton | 32 Barford Road<br>Birmingham | P5/H/672<br>***#9181***<br> | **William HADDLETON**<br>15 Pitsford Street<br>Birmingham | Jeweller and silversmith |
| R1/98<br>24 April 1899<br>Sent by W Hughes<br>Second use of 17 – 11th mark in row | Private address same as business | P9/H/1711*sic*<br>***#9182***<br> | **William HUGHES**<br>46 Hunters Road<br>Birmingham | Jeweller |
| PP1/190<br>SNR 1795-7<br>CWMP 1822<br>Similar mark entered BAO February 1813 | See also HH mark of his widow Hannah Howard who continued the business | P1/32/x4<br>***#9183-6***<br> | **William HOWARD**<br>Lombard Street (1797)<br>Liverpool<br>Spon Street (1801)<br>Coventry | Watchcase maker |
| PCR-1773<br>MR2/85<br>GMSC/84<br>J3/400 | Skewers 1772, 1774 and 1779 | Not on P1<br>***#9187***<br> | **William HARDWICK**<br>St Mary Gate<br>Manchester | Silversmith |
| Missing register<br>*c.*1886 | Similar mark with full stops BAO 1 April 1886 for William Henry Ash<br>32 Tenby Street<br>Birmingham | P5/A/67<br>***#9188***<br> | **William Henry ADAMS** | Watch manufacturer |
| Missing register<br>*c.*1888 | | P5/A/135<br>***#9189***<br> | | |
| Missing register<br>*c.*1892 | | P5/A/416<br>***#9190***<br> | | |
| R1/1<br>15 October 1894<br>Sent by Albert Curtis | Cambrian House<br>Coventry<br>CWMP 1886-1909 | P5/A/612a,b<br>***#9191,2***<br> | **William Henry ADAMS**<br>Cambrian House<br>Allesley Old Road<br>Coventry | |
| R1/135<br>1 November 1900<br>Sent by W H Ashford | 306 Hagley Road<br>Edgbaston<br>Birmingham | P9/A/19-24<br>***#9193-8***<br> | **William Henry ASHFORD**<br>40 Frederick Street<br>Birmingham | Gold chain manufacturer |
| Missing register<br>*c.*1888 | Also note cameo mark entered BAO 9 June 1881 for William Henry Clutterbuck, chainmaker, 28 Snape Street, Birmingham<br>See also other WHC marks | P5/C/138<br>***#9199***<br> | **W H CARRINGTON & CO**<br>53 Thomas Street<br>Manchester | Tobacconists and fancy goods dealers |
| Missing register<br>*c.*1886 | | P5/C/66<br>***#9200***<br> | | |
| R3/121<br>15 January 1948<br>Sent by W H Collins & Co Ltd<br>15 March 1952<br>Small punch entered | | P21/C/43<br>***#9201***<br><br>P21/C/54<br>***#9202***<br> | **W H COLLINS & CO LTD**<br>Sealed in the presence of:-<br>W H Collins (Director)<br>C J Usherwood (Secretary)<br>Excelda Works, Rookery Road<br>Handsworth<br>Birmingham 21 | Manufacturing jewellers |
| Missing register<br>*c.*1888<br>Similar mark entered BAO 31 August 1898 | | P5/C/148b<br>***#9203***<br> | **W H CARRINGTON & CO**<br>53 Thomas Street<br>Manchester | Tobacconists and fancy goods dealers |

| REGISTRATION DETAILS | MAKER'S PRIVATE ADDRESS and DETAILS | PLATE and MARK DETAILS | MAKER/COMPANY and BUSINESS ADDRESS | MAKER'S TRADE |
|---|---|---|---|---|
| LPB/20<br>1 October 1881 | CWMP 1896-1909 | P3/C/x2<br>***#9204,5***<br> | **William Henry CHRISTIE** *<br>5 Bull Ring<br>Coventry | Watchcase maker |
| LPB/98<br>14 June 1885 | | P5/C/x2<br>***#9206,7***<br> | **W H CARRINGTON & CO**<br>28 Oak Street<br>Manchester? Town not entered | Tobacconists and fancy goods dealers |
| R3/109<br>23 June 1945<br>Sent by William Henry Creswick<br>Four sizes | Studio Deems<br>Branscombe<br>Devon | P21/C/23-26<br>***#9208-11***<br> | **William Henry CRESWICK**<br>Studio Deems, Branscombe, Beer<br>Devon<br>The White Cottage, Colliton (undated)<br>Devon | Artist in gold and silver |
| Missing register<br>*c.*1891 | | P5/C/399<br>***#9212***<br> | **W H CARRINGTON & CO**<br>53 Thomas Street<br>Manchester | Tobacconists and fancy goods dealers |
| Missing register<br>*c.*1888 | | P5/C/148a<br>***#9213***<br> | | |
| Missing register<br>*c.*1888<br>Similar mark entered BAO 24 April 1891 | | P5/C/148c<br>***#9214***<br>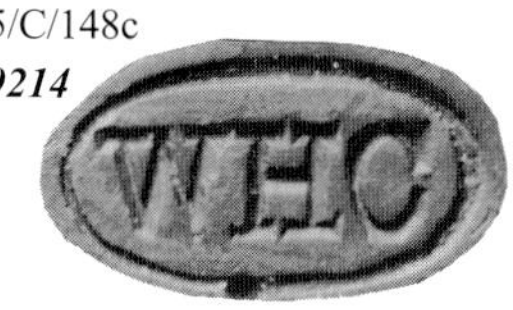 | | |
| R1/218<br>23 July 1904<br>Sent by W H Clark | Private address same as business | P9/D*sic*/211<br>***#9215***<br> | **William Henry CLARK**<br>55 Church Street, Lozells<br>Birmingham | Maker of gold chain guards, etc |
| R2/193<br>Undated-between 26 Feb-31March 1912<br>Sent by John Henry Hollick | | P15/C/45<br>***#9216***<br>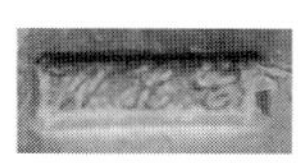 | **W H CLARK LTD**<br>John Henry Hollick (Secretary)<br>Crown Works<br>Hockley Street<br>Birmingham | Manufacturing jewellers |
| LPB/86<br>8 November 1882 | | P3/C/x2<br>***#9217,8***<br> | **W H CARRINGTON & CO**<br>4 Castle Street<br>Oldham Street<br>Manchester | Tobacconists and fancy goods dealers |
| R3/96<br>5 January 1940<br>Sent by<br>W H & D Clark | 130 Thornhill Road<br>Handsworth<br>Birmingham | P21/C/14<br>***#9219***<br> | **W H & D CLARK**<br>109 Spencer Street<br>Birmingham | Manufacturing jewellers |
| R2/193<br>26 August 1940 | Punch struck badly – initial W barely legible | P21/C/49<br>***#9220***<br> | | |
| R2/193<br>(no day) March 1912<br>Sent by John Henry Hollick | Private address same as business | P15/C/79<br>***#9221***<br> | **W H CLARK LTD**<br>John Henry Hollick (Secretary)<br>Crown Works, Hockley Street<br>Birmingham | |
| R3/34<br>19 October 1926<br>Sent by E Whitehouse & Son | 35 Wrexham Road<br>Handsworth<br>Birmingham | P15/C/170<br>***#9222***<br> | **Drayton CLARK**<br>Crown Works<br>Hockley Hill<br>Birmingham | General jewellers |

| REGISTRATION DETAILS | MAKER'S PRIVATE ADDRESS and DETAILS | PLATE and MARK DETAILS | MAKER/COMPANY and BUSINESS ADDRESS | MAKER'S TRADE |
|---|---|---|---|---|
| R3/79<br>7 October 1935<br>Sent by Drayton Clark | 130 Thornhill Road<br>Handsworth<br>Birmingham | P15/N*sic*/214<br>***#9223***<br> | **Drayton CLARK** trading as<br>**W H & D CLARK**<br>109 Spencer Street<br>Birmingham | Manufacturing jewellers |
| R3/61<br>20 January 1932<br>Sent by W A Massingham<br>(F Massingham)<br>53 Northampton Street<br>Birmingham | 61 High Street<br>West Bromwich | P15/K*sic*/212<br>***#9224***<br> | **Drayton CLARK**<br>Crown Works<br>Hockley Hill<br>Birmingham | Jewellers |
| R2/136<br>26 May 1911<br>Sent by W H Edwards | 39 Havelock Road<br>Handsworth<br>Birmingham | P13/E/22<br>***#9225***<br> | **William Henry EDWARDS**<br>16 Hockley Street<br>Birmingham | Jeweller and signet ring maker |
| R3/111<br>3 January 1946<br>Sent by W H Findley | 155 Church Lane<br>Handsworth Wood<br>Birmingham 20 | P21/F/9<br>***#9226***<br> | **W H FINDLEY**<br>169 Hockley Hill<br>Birmingham 18 | Manufacturing jeweller and silversmith |
| R2/224<br>11 October 1919<br>Sent by Ginder & Ginder | Rathgrie<br>Woodcote Green<br>Wallington | P15/T/29<br>***#9227***<br> | **Walter Howard Gamlies TURNER**<br>4-5 Buchanan Buildings<br>Holborn<br>London | Wholesale jeweller |
| Missing register<br>*c.*1891 | | P5/H/369<br>***#9228***<br> | **William Hair HASELER** * | |
| LPB/40<br>10 March 1884<br>No mark entered | | P5/H/x1<br>***#9229***<br> | **William Hair HASELER** *<br>Gladstone Buildings<br>Richmond Street<br>Birmingham | Manufacturing jeweller |
| Missing register<br>*c.*1890 | | P5/H/331<br>***#9230***<br> | | |
| R1/79<br>5 October 1894<br>Sent by C Robinson<br>H & P Haseler<br>WHH entered | | P5/H/596 not found<br>***#9231*** | **William Hair HASELER** *<br>8 Hylton Street<br>Vyse Street<br>Birmingham | Jeweller |
| Missing register<br>*c.*1894 | | P5/H/544<br>***#9232***<br> | **William Hair HASELER** *<br>Gladstone Buildings<br>Richmond Street<br>Birmingham | Manufacturing jeweller |
| R2/109<br>30 April 1910<br>Sent by W H Haseler Ltd | 88 Church Lane<br>Handsworth | P13/H/50<br>***#9233***<br> | **W H HASELER LTD** *<br>Frank Haseler (Director)<br>5 Hylton Street<br>Birmingham | Manufacturing jewellers and silversmiths |
| Missing register<br>*c.*1888 | | P5/H/161<br>***#9234***<br> | | Manufacturer jewellers |
| R2/154<br>26 March 1912<br>Sent by Charles Horner Ltd | Olton<br>Maculove Avenue<br>Colderstone<br>Liverpool | P13/H/83<br>***#9235***<br>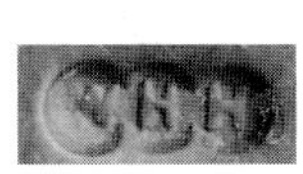 | **Percy George HUNT** trading as<br>**W H HUNT**<br>52 Mount Pleasant<br>Liverpool | Fancy goods importer |

| REGISTRATION DETAILS | MAKER'S PRIVATE ADDRESS and DETAILS | PLATE and MARK DETAILS | MAKER/COMPANY and BUSINESS ADDRESS | MAKER'S TRADE |
|---|---|---|---|---|
| R1/218<br>19 July 1904<br>Sent by B Wade | 7 Avenham Terrace<br>Preston | P9/V*sic*/119<br>***#9236***<br> | **W H & J WOODS LTD**<br>James Nightingale (Director)<br>Derby Street<br>Preston | Tobacco manufacturer |
| R1/53<br>31 May 1894<br>Sent by W H Leather | Private address same as business | P5/L/562a<br>***#9237***<br><br>P5/L/562b<br>***#9238***<br> | **William Henry LEATHER**<br>11 Pitsford Street<br>Birmingham | Jeweller |
| R1/217<br>5 July 1904<br>Sent by H R Wright | 326 Hamstead Road<br>Handsworth<br>Birmingham<br>Stapleton<br>Harborne | P9/V*sic*/116-118<br>***#9239-41***<br> | **Henry Robert WRIGHT**<br>**W HADGKISS** trading as<br>**WRIGHT & HADGKISS**<br>9 Vyse Street<br>Birmingham | Jewellers |
| R1/147<br>9 May 1901<br>Sent by Wright & Hadgkins Ltd | 326 Hamstead Road<br>Birmingham | P9/W/56-58<br>***#9242-4***<br> | **WRIGHT & HADGKISS LTD**<br>Henry Robert Wright (Managing Director)<br>9 Vyse Street<br>Birmingham | |
| R2/137<br>3 June 1911<br>Sent by Wright & Hadgkiss | Springfields [1]<br>Belbroughton<br>Stourbridge | P13/W/93<br>***#9245***<br> | **WRIGHT & HADGKISS**<br>S H Hadgkiss [1] (Director)<br>9 Vyse Street<br>Birmingham | Manufacturing jewellers |
| Not in R2 as expected<br>Between May 1913 and January 1914 | | P15/W/5<br>***#9246***<br> | **Unidentified** | |
| Not in R2 as expected<br>Between October 1915 and May 1916 | | P15/W/18<br>***#9247***<br> | **Unidentified** | |
| Not in R2 as expected<br>Between October 1916 and July 1917 | | P15/W/33<br>***#9248***<br> | **Unidentified** | |
| R3/47<br>4 July 1929<br>Sent by S Blanckensee & Son<br>Birmingham | Private address same as business | P15/M/72<br>***#9249***<br>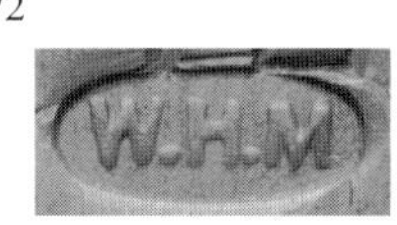 | **William Henry MAY**<br>13-17 Clumber Street<br>Nottingham | Silversmith and jeweller |
| R3/87<br>4 June 1937<br>Sent by W Weston & Sons<br>28 Hylton Street<br>Birmingham | Private address same as business | P21/M/5<br>***#9250***<br> | **Alfred William MILLER** (Proprietor)<br>trading as **William Henry MILLER**<br>Diamond House<br>Snowhill<br>Wolverhampton | Jewellers |
| R3/128<br>27 April 1949<br>Sent by Millers (Jewellers) Ltd | | P21/M/25<br>***#9251***<br> | **MILLERS (JEWELLERS) LTD**<br>Sealed in the presence of:-<br>A W Miller (Director)<br>L R Miller (Secretary)<br>Diamond House, Snow Hill<br>Wolverhampton | |

| REGISTRATION DETAILS | MAKER'S PRIVATE ADDRESS and DETAILS | PLATE and MARK DETAILS | MAKER/COMPANY and BUSINESS ADDRESS | MAKER'S TRADE |
|---|---|---|---|---|
| R1/187<br>13 March 1903<br>Sent by W H Newman | 330 Hagley Road<br>Birmingham | P9/N/22<br>***#9252***<br>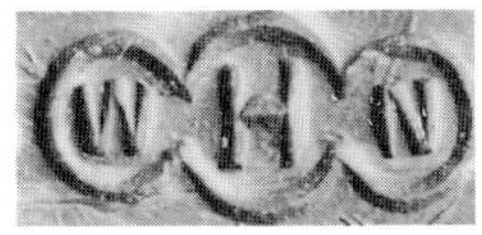 | **W H NEWMAN LTD**<br>Sandpits<br>Birmingham | Pipe mount manufacturers |
| R1/183<br>3 February 1903<br>Sent by W H Newman | | P9/N/15<br>***#9253***<br>§<br> | **William Henry NEWMAN**<br>Sandpits<br>Birmingham | |
| LPB/66<br>27 March 1885<br>No mark in LPB just WHP | Clerk entered Pearce, possibly in error, since similar mark entered LAO 5 March 1890 in the name of William Henry Pierce at this address trading as W H Pierce & Co | P5/P/x1<br>***#9254***<br> | **William Henry PIERCE** *<br>3 Watling Street<br>Shude Hill<br>Manchester | Tobacco pipe manufacturer |
| Missing register<br>*c.*1893 | | P5/P/528<br>***#9255***<br> | | |
| R1/138<br>1 December 1900<br>Sent by W H Reddrop<br>Annotated "Cancelled" | Avendale<br>Holmwood Road<br>Bromley<br>Kent | P9/R21<br>***#9256***<br> | **William Harris REDDROP** trading as **J CAPLIN & CO** *<br>26 Ivy Lane, Newgate Street<br>London | Umbrella and walking stick manufacturers |
| Not in R1 as expected March to May 1902<br>Similar mark LAO 21 April 1902 | | P9/R/45<br>***#9257***<br> | | |
| R1/33<br>28 September 1896<br>Sent by W H Reddrop | 7 Lauriston Place<br>Wimbledon Road<br>London | P5/R/789<br>***#9258***<br> | **William Harris REDDROP** trading as **J CAPLIN & CO** *<br>26 Ivy Lane<br>Newgate Street<br>London | Stick mounters |
| R1/138<br>1 December 1900<br>Sent by W H Reddrop | Avendale<br>Holmwood Road<br>Bromley<br>Kent | P9/R/2<br>***#9259***<br> | | Umbrella and walking stick manufacturers |
| R1/167<br>2 May 1902<br>Sent by W H Reddrop | 19 Holmwood Road<br>Bromley | P9/R/22<br>***#9260***<br> | **William Harris REDDROP**<br>**John CAPLIN** *<br>22 Bartholomew Close<br>London EC | Gold and silver mounters |
| R1/110<br>31 August 1899<br>Sent by W H Rosson | 84 Church Street<br>Lozells<br>Birmingham | P9/R/9<br>***#9261***<br> | **William Henry ROSSON**<br>62 Hockley Street<br>Birmingham | Ring manufacturer |
| R1/207<br>13 February 1904<br>Sent by J & R Griffin<br>Two sizes | 20 Mayfield Road<br>Handsworth | P9/S/72,73<br>***#9262,3***<br> | **William Henry SPARROW**<br>**H WILLIAMSON LTD** *<br>7, 9, 11 Spencer Street<br>Birmingham | Jewellers and silversmiths |
| LPB/80<br>30 August 1881 | | P3/T/x1<br>***#9264***<br> | **William Henry TAYLOR**<br>2 Terrace Street<br>Birmingham | Jeweller |
| R3/7<br>11 March 1922<br>Sent by Stylic Manufacturing Co | Saxonholme<br>41 Pelham Road<br>Gravesend<br>Kent | P15/T/39<br>***#9265***<br> | **Walter Horace THOMPSON** *<br>66 Hatton Garden<br>London EC | Watch importer and agent |

| REGISTRATION DETAILS | MAKER'S PRIVATE ADDRESS and DETAILS | PLATE and MARK DETAILS | MAKER/COMPANY and BUSINESS ADDRESS | MAKER'S TRADE |
|---|---|---|---|---|
| R2/47<br>4 October 1907<br>Sent by William Steward Tandy<br>See also T&S<br>P13/T/21 used 15 June 1909 for one lot of work | 35 Wall Road<br>Handsworth<br>34 Thornhill Road<br>Handsworth | P13/T/21<br>***#9266***<br> | **William Steward TANDY**<br>**Harry George TANDY** trading as<br>**TANDY & SON**<br>112 Vyse Street<br>Birmingham | Ring manufacturers |
| Missing register<br>*c.*1892<br>Incuse WHV mark entered LAO<br>28 October 1886 | | P5/V/445<br>***#9267***<br> | **William Henry VINCE** *<br>25 Spring Grove Terrace<br>Burley Fields<br>Leeds<br>Yorkshire | Silversmith |
| R2/2<br>2 September 1905<br>Sent by W H Vince | 10 Rochester Terrace<br>Leeds | P9/V/8<br>***#9268***<br> | | Tobacconist and fancy goods dealer |
| R3/66<br>19 May 1933<br>Sent by R Parke & Co<br>76 Vyse Street<br>Birmingham | Windyridge [1]<br>Walsall Road<br>Four Oaks<br>Sutton Coldfield | P15/W/103<br>***#9269***<br> | **Richard HINES** [1] trading as<br>**W H WESTON**<br>115 Barr Street (moved May 1937 to)<br>38 Frederick Street<br>Birmingham | Jeweller |
| R1/15<br>29 August 1895<br>Sent by C Horner<br>J Wall | Alban Villa<br>Stourbridge<br>Worcestershire | P5/X*sic*/683<br>***#9270***<br> | **William Harrison WALTER** *<br>31 Newgate Street<br>London | Wholesale jeweller and silversmith |
| Missing register<br>*c.*1888 | | P5/W/25<br>***#9271***<br> | | |
| Missing register<br>*c.*1888 | | P5/W/167<br>***#9272***<br> | | |
| Missing register<br>*c.*1892 | | P5/W/412<br>***#9273***<br> | | |
| R2/94<br>6 October 1909<br>Sent by W H Wilmot Ltd<br>BAO 15.565 | The Warren<br>Four Oaks<br>Cranben<br>Solihull | P13/W/58<br>***#9274***<br> | **W H WILMOT LTD** *<br>W A Crozier (Director)<br>H E Wilmot (Managing Director)<br>Albion Street Works<br>Birmingham | Gold chain makers |
| 16 January 1945 | | P21/W/46<br>***#9275***<br> | | |
| R2/54<br>21 January 1908<br>Sent by W H Young<br>Two sizes | 22 Wilton Road<br>Handsworth<br>Birmingham | P9/XYZ/8-11<br>***#9276-9***<br> | **William Henry YOUNG**<br>7 St George Place, Great Hampton Row<br>Birmingham | Brooches, bracelets and pendant makers |
| Missing register<br>*c.*1886<br>Similar mark entered BAO 29 August 1887 | CWMP 1896-1901 | P5/Y/32<br>***#9280***<br> | **William Henry YARDLEY**<br>18 Duke Street, Chapel Fields<br>Coventry | Watchcase maker |
| PDB 1812-14<br>MR3/89 | Gold rings | P1/28/x6<br>***#9281-6***<br> | **William JONES**<br>**(JONES & ABBOTT)**<br>Liverpool | Goldsmith |
| | Smaller version inverted at top of square | P1/28/x1<br>***#9287***<br> | | |

| REGISTRATION DETAILS | MAKER'S PRIVATE ADDRESS and DETAILS | PLATE and MARK DETAILS | MAKER/COMPANY and BUSINESS ADDRESS | MAKER'S TRADE |
|---|---|---|---|---|
| PDB 1823-6<br>MR3/76 | Gold rings and a pencil case | P1/32/x2<br>***#9288,9***  | **William BALL**<br>Liverpool | Goldsmith and silversmith |
| PDB 1806-13<br>MR3/89<br>PP1/190 | Gold rings | P1/20/x2<br>***#9290,1***  | **William JONES**<br>Liverpool | Goldsmith and watchcase maker |
| SPB/4<br>28 May 1872 | CWMP 1883 located at<br>9 Norfolk Street, Coventry | P3/I/x1<br>***#9292***  | **William JEE** *<br>The Butts<br>Coventry | Watchcase maker |
| SPB/17<br>6 April 1873 | Kelly 1874 | P3/I/x3<br>***#9293-5***  | **William JACKSON**<br>38 Bishop Street<br>Coventry | Watch finisher |
| SPB/17<br>4 December 1867<br>Sent by George Reader | 1 Hertford Place<br>Coventry | P3/I/x3<br>***#9296-8***  | **William JEE** *<br>7 Hertford Place, Butts<br>Coventry | Watchcase maker |
| R2/4<br>19 October 1905<br>Sent by W H Johnson | 219 Albert Road<br>Aston<br>Birmingham | P9/J/55<br>***#9299***  | **William Henry JOHNSON**<br>79 Clifford Street, Aston<br>Birmingham | Silversmiths |
| PDB 1785-6<br>MR3/88,103 | Variety of gold/silverware<br>See also associated J*W mark | P2/W/x2<br>***#9300,1***  | **WALLEY & JONES**<br>later **JONES & WALLEY**<br>Liverpool | Goldsmiths and silversmiths |
| | | P1/32/x2<br>***#9302,3***  | | |
| | | P1/26/x1<br>***#9304*** 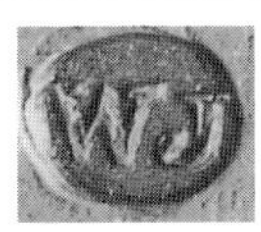 | | |
| Not in SPB or LPB so struck 1860-3 | | P3/I/x3<br>***#9305-7*** 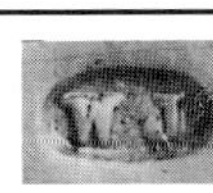 | | |
| R2/65<br>24 September 1908<br>Sent by A Wilcox | 4 Park Crescent<br>Westcliff-on-Sea<br>47 Cheltenham Road<br>Southend-on-sea<br>43 Allendale Terrace<br>Southend-on-sea | P13/C/34<br>***#9308***  | **Walter James CARROLL**<br>**William SADDLETON**<br>**Thomas Charles DICKENSON** trading as<br>**W J CARROLL** *<br>20, 21 London Road<br>Fenchurch Street and<br>33 Walbrook Bank and<br>17,19 Beer Lane<br>London EC | Watchmakers and jewellers |
| LPB/22<br>29 December 1883<br>No mark in LPB | | P5/C/x1<br>***#9309*** 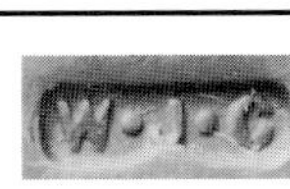 | **William John CARRINGTON**<br>109 Vyse Street<br>Birmingham | Jeweller |
| R1/108<br>22 August 1899<br>Sent by B H Joseph & Co | 17, 19 Beer Lane<br>London | P9/C/26<br>***#9310***  | **Walter James CARROLL**<br>17 and 19 Beer Lane<br>London | Working jeweller and watchmaker |
| Missing register<br>*c.*1887<br>Similar mark entered BAO 22 May 1890 | | P5/D/109<br>***#9311***  | **William James DINGLEY**<br>23 Warstone Lane<br>Birmingham | Jeweller |

| REGISTRATION DETAILS | MAKER'S PRIVATE ADDRESS and DETAILS | PLATE and MARK DETAILS | MAKER/COMPANY and BUSINESS ADDRESS | MAKER'S TRADE |
|---|---|---|---|---|
| LPB/30<br>5 February 1880 | | P3/F/x1<br>***#9312***<br> | **William James FULFORD**<br>11 Key Hill Drive<br>Birmingham | Jeweller |
| R2/223<br>11 October 1919<br>Sent by W J Egginton | 78 Carpenter Road<br>Lozells<br>Birmingham | P15/E/14<br>***#9313***<br>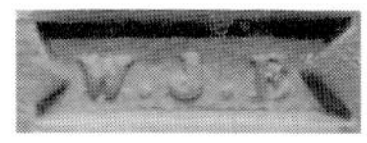 | **William James EGGINGTON**<br>41 Frederick Street<br>Birmingham (moved 25 February 1939 to)<br>42 Warstone Lane<br>Birmingham | Jeweller and setter |
| R2/234<br>25 September 1920<br>Sent by W J Fisher | 87 Albert Road<br>Handsworth<br>Birmingham | P15/F/20<br>***#9314***<br> | **Walter John FISHER**<br>94 Spencer Street<br>Birmingham | Manufacturing jeweller |
| R2/175<br>5 September 1913<br>Sent by Ginger & Couch | 21 Foster Road<br>Chiswick<br>London | P15/T/1<br>***#9315***<br> | **W H G TURNER**<br>1 Gammages Buildings<br>Holborn<br>London EC | Wholesale jeweller |
| R3/90<br>22 June 1938<br>Sent by W J Holmes Ltd | | P21/H/5<br>***#9316***<br> | **William J HOLMES LTD**<br>Sealed in the presence of:-<br>Howard Holmes (Director)<br>E M Hunt (Secretary)<br>173 Hockley Hill (Registered Office)<br>Birmingham | Wholesale jewellers |
| R3/91<br>1 September 1938<br>Sent by Elite Bracelet Manufacturing Co Ltd<br>Regent Street<br>Birmingham | The Spinney<br>Thames Ditton | P21/H/6<br>***#9317***<br> | **William James HUBER**<br>34 Ely Place<br>London EC1 | Watch importer |
| R3/79<br>26 September 1935<br>Sent by B H Britton & Sons<br>35 Hockley Hill<br>Birmingham | | P15/I*sic*/127<br>***#9318***<br> | | |
| Cameo WIH marks entered LAO 1813-35 | | P1/26/x1<br>***#9319***<br> | **William John HAMMON** *<br>35 Clerkenwell Green<br>London | Watchcase maker |
| Incuse WIH mark entered LAO 4 April 1860 | | P2/H/x1<br>***#9320***<br> | | |
| Several cameo WIH marks entered LAO 1813-35 | | P1/26/x1<br>***#9321***<br> | | |
| Several cameo WIH marks entered LAO 1813-35 | | P1/25/x1<br>***#9322***<br> | | |
| R1/99<br>6 May 1899<br>Sent by Wright & Hadgkiss<br>(written in error P9/H/8) | Glendene [1]<br>Ditton Hill<br>Surbiton.<br>4 Vanbrugh Park [2]<br>Blackheath | P9/H/12<br>***#9323***<br> | **William John HUTCHINSON** [1]<br>**Francis William HUTCHINSON** [2]<br>trading as **F HUTCHINSON & CO** *<br>40, 41 Furnival Street<br>London EC | Manufacturing jewellers |

| REGISTRATION DETAILS | MAKER'S PRIVATE ADDRESS and DETAILS | PLATE and MARK DETAILS | MAKER/COMPANY and BUSINESS ADDRESS | MAKER'S TRADE |
|---|---|---|---|---|
| Missing register<br>*c.*1891 | | P5/H/367<br>***#9324***<br> | See other WJH marks | |
| Missing register<br>*c.*1891 | | P5/H/362<br>***#9325***<br>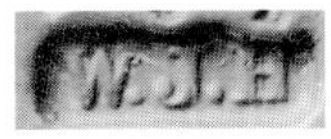 | See other WJH marks | |
| R1/143<br>15 February 1901<br>Sent by W J Holmes<br>Grove Brothers<br>Stainton Brothers | | No mark on P9/H<br>***#9326*** | **William J HOLMES**<br>173 Hockley Hill<br>Birmingham | Jeweller |
| R1/171<br>20 June 1902<br>Sent by W A Ashford | Malvern House<br>Acocks Green<br>Birmingham | P9/H/41[7] *sic*<br>***#9327***<br> | **William J HOLMES**<br>173 Hockley Hill<br>Birmingham | Manufacturing jeweller |
| R2/27<br>18 October 1906<br>Sent by William Holmes | | P9/H/85<br>***#9328***<br> | | Wholesale and manufacturing jeweller |
| R1/12<br>31 May 1895<br>Sent by William J Johnston | Olive Mount<br>Etterby Scaur<br>Carlisle | P5/J/664<br>***#9329***<br>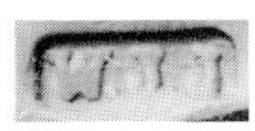 | **William Jackson JOHNSTON**<br>Brown's Lane<br>Carlisle | Goldsmiths |
| R2/216<br>18 November 1918<br>Sent by William J Johnston | 18 Petteril Street<br>Carlisle<br>77 Castle Street<br>Carlisle | P15/J/10<br>***#9330***<br> | **William Jackson JOHNSTON**<br>**William Harold JOHNSTON** trading as<br>**William Harold JOHNSTON & SONS**<br>Goldsmiths Chambers<br>Fisher Street<br>Carlisle | |
| R1/186<br>28 February 1903<br>Sent by W J Johnston | 18 Petteril Street<br>Carlisle | P9/J/36<br>***#9331***<br> | **William Jackson JOHNSTON**<br>Browns Lane (deleted – undated)<br>Goldsmiths Chambers, Fisher Street<br>Carlisle | Goldsmith and silversmith |
| R1/186<br>30 December 1904<br>Sent by W J Johnston | | P9/J/51<br>***#9332***<br> | **William Jackson JOHNSTON**<br>Browns Lane (deleted – undated)<br>Goldsmiths Chambers, Fisher Street<br>Carlisle | |
| R2/216<br>18 November 1918<br>Sent by William J Johnston | 18 Petteril Street<br>Carlisle<br>77 Castle Street<br>Carlisle | P15/J/9<br>***#9333***<br> | **William Jackson JOHNSTON**<br>**William Harold JOHNSTON** trading as<br>**William Harold JOHNSTON & SONS**<br>Goldsmiths Chambers<br>Fisher Street<br>Carlisle | Goldsmiths |
| R2/131<br>18 March 1911<br>Sent by William Jackson Johnston<br>William Harold Johnston | | P13/J/47<br>***#9334***<br> | as above | Goldsmiths and silversmiths |
| Plain font WJM oblong cameo entered LAO 30 September 1879 so only a tentative attribution | | P2/M/x3<br>***#9335-7***<br>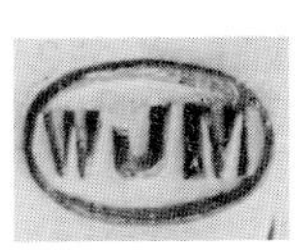 | **William John MASON** *<br>15 and 48 Dagmar Road<br>South Hackney<br>London | Silversmith |

| REGISTRATION DETAILS | MAKER'S PRIVATE ADDRESS and DETAILS | PLATE and MARK DETAILS | MAKER/COMPANY and BUSINESS ADDRESS | MAKER'S TRADE |
|---|---|---|---|---|
| R1/76<br>29 November 1898<br>Sent by W J Myatt & Co | Barnt Green<br>Worcestershire | P9/M/4<br>***#9338*** 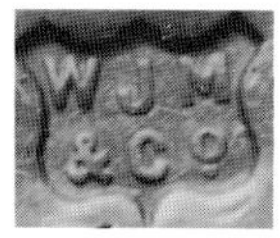 | **William James MYATT** trading as<br>**William James MYATT & CO** *<br>60 Caroline Street<br>Birmingham | Silversmiths and jewellers |
| R1/183<br>4 February 1903<br>Sent by W J Myatt & Co | | P9/M/45<br>***#9339*** 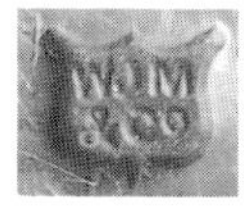 | **W J MYATT & CO** *<br>J L Bloye (Secretary)<br>Graham Street and<br>Frederick Street<br>Birmingham | Manufacturing jewellers |
| R3/138<br>29 March 1952<br>Sent by W J Pellow | | P21/P/46<br>***#9340*** 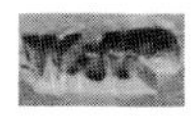 | **W J PELLOW LTD**<br>31 Hylton Street<br>Birmingham | Seal and locket makers |
| 21 August 1952 | | P21/P/47<br>***#9341*** 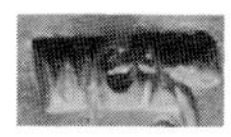 | | |
| 1 April 1953 | | P21/P/51<br>***#9342*** 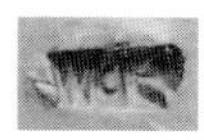 | | |
| 16 June 1953 | | P21/P/52<br>***#9343***  | | |
| 14 September 1954 | | P21/P/59<br>***#9344*** 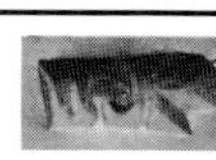 | | |
| 8 October 1955 | | P21/P/67,68<br>***#9345,6***  | | |
| 7 April 1956 | | P21/P/70<br>***#9347***  | | |
| No day October 1956 | | P21/P/72,73<br>***#9348,9***  | | |
| 20 June 1958<br>Two sizes | | P21/P/74,75<br>***#9350,1*** 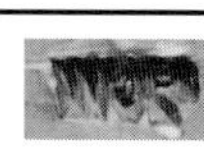 | | |
| R2/32<br>21 November 1947<br>Sent by W J Pellow | 3 Hallewell Road<br>Rotton Park<br>Birmingham | P21/P/18<br>***#9352***  | **William John PELLOW**<br>A B Edge (Secretary)<br>31 Hylton Street<br>Birmingham | Manufacturing jewellers |
| R3/32<br>25 August 1948<br>Sent by W J Pellow | | P21/P/29<br>***#9353*** 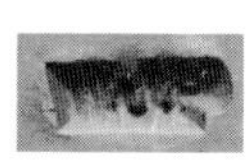 | | |
| 23 October 1948 | | P21/P/30<br>***#9354*** 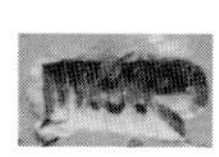 | | |
| R3/138<br>20 January 1954<br>Sent by W J Pellow | | P21/P/55,56<br>***#9355,6***  | **W J PELLOW LTD**<br>31 Hylton Street<br>Birmingham | Seal and locket makers |
| 27 January 1954<br>Two sizes | | P21/P/57,58<br>***#9357,8*** 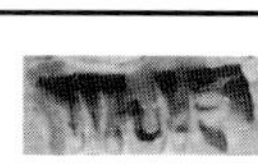 | | |
| 19 September 1955 | | P21/P/63-66<br>***#9359-62***  | | |

| REGISTRATION DETAILS | MAKER'S PRIVATE ADDRESS and DETAILS | PLATE and MARK DETAILS | MAKER/COMPANY and BUSINESS ADDRESS | MAKER'S TRADE |
|---|---|---|---|---|
| R1/162<br>13 February 1902<br>Sent by W J Pellow | Penmere<br>Sutton Coldfield | P9/Q*sic*/121-123<br>***#9363-5***  | **William John PELLOW**<br>31 Hylton Street<br>Birmingham | Seal and locket maker |
| R2/32<br>30 January 1907<br>Sent by A B Edge | 3 Hallewell Road<br>Rotton Park<br>Birmingham | P9/U*sic*/270-277<br>***#9366-73***  | **William John PELLOW**<br>A B Edge (Secretary)<br>31 Hylton Street<br>Birmingham | Manufacturing jewellers |
| 6 May 1938 | | P21/P/1-3<br>***#9374-6***  | | |
| R1/82<br>4 November 1898<br>Sent by W J Pellow | Blackrock Road<br>Sutton Coldfield | P9/P/4-6<br>***#9377-9***  | **William John PELLOW**<br>31 Hylton Street<br>Birmingham | Jeweller |
| Missing register<br>*c.*1886<br>Similar roman mark<br>BAO 26 January 1888 | | P5/P/44<br>***#9380***  | | |
| R1/43<br>26 April 1897<br>Sent by W J Spencer | 160 Anglesey Street<br>Lozells<br>Birmingham | P5/O*sic*/833<br>***#9381***  | **William Joseph SPENCER**<br>146½ Hockley Hill<br>Birmingham | Watchcase manufacturer |
| R2/217<br>22 November 1918<br>Sent by W J Skelton | 59 Soho Road<br>Handsworth<br>Birmingham | P15/S/35<br>***#9382*** 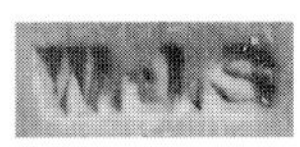 | **William James SKELTON**<br>88 Vittoria Street<br>Birmingham | Manufacturing jeweller |
| R2/91<br>4 September 1909<br>Sent by C Peach<br>& Sons<br>BAO 15.678 | The Dargle<br>Warwick Road<br>Solihull | P13/S/44<br>***#9383***  | **William Josiah SUTTON**<br>73, 75 Spencer Street<br>Birmingham | Gold and silver chains and jewellery |
| R3/162<br>13 July 1957<br>Sent by W J Sutton Ltd | | P21/S/70<br>***#9384***  | **W J SUTTON LTD**<br>Sealed in the presence of:-<br>G W Sutton (Director)<br>G H Sproston (Secretary)<br>73/75 Vyse Street<br>Birmingham 18 | Manufacturing jewellers |
| R2/156<br>17 May 1912<br>Sent by the firm<br>Clerk entered<br>P13/J/47 in error – see<br>WJJ&S #9334 | 74 Trinity Road<br>Handsworth<br>160 Graveley Lane<br>Erdington | P13/J/60<br>***#9385***  | **W JOHNSON & SON LTD**<br>William Henry Johnson (Director)<br>W C Johnson (Secretary)<br>79 Clifford Street<br>Birmingham | Silversmiths |
| R2/156<br>17 May 1912<br>Sent by the firm | | P15/J/1<br>***#9386***  | **W JOHNSON & SON LTD**<br>William Henry Johnson (Director)<br>W C Johnson (Secretary)<br>79 Clifford Street<br>Birmingham | |
| R1/101<br>16 May 1899<br>Sent by<br>W & J Saunders | 205 Albert Road<br>Aston, Birmingham<br>Clarence Road<br>King's Heath<br>Birmingham | P9/S/19,20<br>***#9387,8***  | **Walter James SAUNDERS**<br>**John SAUNDERS** trading as<br>**W & J SAUNDERS** *<br>44 Warstone Lane<br>Birmingham | Jewellers |
| R1/102<br>25 May 1899<br>Sent by W Walker | Beechwood<br>Marblin Park<br>Belfast | P9/K/7<br>***#9389***  | **William KELLY**<br>Foyle Street<br>Londonderry<br>Ireland | Tobacconist |

| REGISTRATION DETAILS | MAKER'S PRIVATE ADDRESS and DETAILS | PLATE and MARK DETAILS | MAKER/COMPANY and BUSINESS ADDRESS | MAKER'S TRADE |
|---|---|---|---|---|
| R1/164<br>12 March 1902<br>Sent by S Farren for Lancashire Watch Company | Heron Lodge<br>Worcester | P9/K/25,26<br>***#9390,1***<br> | **KAY & CO LTD** *<br>Russell Dyke (Secretary)<br>Shrub Hill<br>Worcester | Jewellers |
| R1/224<br>31 December 1904<br>Sent by Lancashire Watch Co Prescot | | P9/K/33<br>***#9392***<br> | **William Kilbourne KAY** *<br>Shrub Hill<br>Worcester | |
| R3/82<br>12 December 1935<br>Sent by Lancasters | Both residing at<br>26 Lime Street<br>Southport | P15/L/45<br>***#9393***<br> | **William LANCASTER**<br>**Ruth LANCASTER** trading as<br>**LANCASTERS**<br>1b Castle Street<br>Southport | Metal crafts |
| Missing register<br>*c.*1889 | | P5/L/245<br>***#9394***<br> | **Unidentified** | |
| R1/15<br>31 August 1895<br>Sent by A J Cheshire | 190 Green Lane<br>London N | P5/L/684<br>***#9395***<br> | **William LEWIS** *<br>14 Myddelton Street, Clerkenwell<br>London | Wholesale jeweller |
| R1/125<br>24 April 1900<br>Sent by C Walker<br>H Litherland Manager<br>Annotated *Old punch defaced* | 22 Prison Road<br>Levenshulme<br>Manchester | P9/L/17<br>***#9396***<br> | **William LINDOP**<br>38 Shude Hill<br>Manchester | Walking stick manufacturer |
| R3/8<br>3 April 1922<br>Sent by C Walker<br>Litherland Ltd | 32 Salisbury Road<br>Chorlton-cum-Hardy<br>Manchester | P15/L/25<br>***#9397***<br> | **William LINDOP**<br>30, 31 and 32 Shudehill and<br>20a Connel Street (Works)<br>Manchester | Walking stick and umbrella manufacturer |
| Missing register<br>*c.*1889 | | P5/L/265<br>***#9398***<br> | **Unidentified** | |
| Missing register<br>*c.*1890 | | P5/L/290<br>***#9399***<br> | **Unidentified** | |
| Missing register<br>*c.*1891 | | P5/L/359<br>***#9400***<br> | **Unidentified** | |
| Similar mark entered BAO 26 March 1817 may be rather early but could be a relative | | P2/L/x2<br>***#9401,2***<br> | **William LINSLEY**<br>33 Great Charlotte Street<br>Birmingham<br>or | Watchcase maker |
| J1 1843-6<br>GSJW/136 | | P2/L/x2<br>***#9403,4***<br> | **William LUCAS**<br>20 Basnett Street<br>Liverpool | Silversmith |
| SOT/124<br>LGM 1698-9<br>PP3/23,45 | Seen on the silver case of a watch by Richard Hough, Liverpool, *c.*1700-10<br>Watchcase maker working *c.*1696-1725 | Pre-dates P1<br>***#9405***<br> | **William LAITHWAIT**<br>Edmund Street<br>Liverpool | Watchcase maker |

| REGISTRATION DETAILS | MAKER'S PRIVATE ADDRESS and DETAILS | PLATE and MARK DETAILS | MAKER/COMPANY and BUSINESS ADDRESS | MAKER'S TRADE |
|---|---|---|---|---|
| A version with cameo surround described in sales records but shape unknown | Seen on the silver case of a watch by George Taylor, Liverpool, *c.*1700 | Pre-dates P1 ***#9406***  | **William LAITHWAIT** Edmund Street Liverpool | Watchcase maker |
| LPB/50 22 October 1880 LPB mark shown | 1881 census has him lodging at 70 Lozells Street, Birmingham W H & F Rabone and Wm Lucket, jewellers, here in 1880 | Not on P3 ***#9407*** 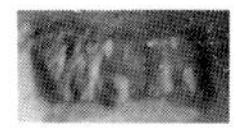 | **Walter W LAKIN** 37 Tenby Street Birmingham | Gold chain maker |
| Missing register *c.*1891 | | P5/L/351 ***#9408***  | **Unidentified** | |
| Not in R1 as expected Between November 1904 and March 1905 Similar mark entered LAO 6 March 1899 | | P9/L/0*sic* ***#9409***  | **William LEWIS** * 14 Myddleton Street, Clerkenwell London EC and 10 Tenby Street Birmingham | Goldsmith |
| | See other WL marks | P2/L/x2 ***#9410,11***  | **Unidentified** | |
| Not in R2 as expected Between October 1910 and February 1911 Similar mark entered BAO 2 March 1915 | | P13/L/46 ***#9412*** 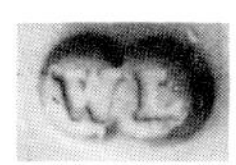 | **William LEWIS** * 14 Myddleton Street, Clerkenwell London EC and 10 Tenby Street Birmingham | Manufacturing jewellers |
| R2/34 14 March 1907 Sent by selves Two sizes | 313 Green Lane Finsbury Park London N1 | P9/L/85a,b ***#9413,4*** 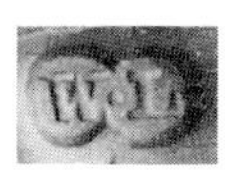 | **William LEWIS** * 45 Rosebury Avenue London and 46 Northampton Street Birmingham | |
| R1/74 24 September 1898 Sent by Kinsey Brothers & Patrick | 192 Hamstead Road [1] Handsworth Church Lane [2] Handsworth | P9/L/1 ***#9415***  | **James Gouldberg PARKES** [1] **Henry LOVERIDGE** [2] trading as **William LOCKE & CO** 141 Hockley Hill Birmingham | Wholesale jewellers |
| R1/185 23 February 1903 Sent by W Locke & Co | | P9/L/42 ***#9416***  | **James G PARKES** **Henry LOVERIDGE** trading as **W LOCKE & CO** 176 Hockley Hill Birmingham | Manufacturing jewellers |
| R2/108 14 April 1910 Sent by Walter Coulthard | 169 Church Street Handsworth Wood Birmingham | P13/C/64 ***#9417***  | **W COULTHARD LTD** Walter Coulthard (Managing Director) 59 and 60 Northampton Street Birmingham | Electroplate manufacturers and silversmiths |
| R2/127 4 February 1911 Sent by Walter L Ginder BAO 18.031 | 37 Soho Avenue Handsworth Birmingham | P13/G/33 ***#9418***  | **Walter Lister GINDER** 26 Hylton Street Birmingham | Manufacturer of rings and jewellery |
| LPB/50 27 April 1882 | | P3/L/x6 ***#9419-24***  | **W L LAWSON** 7 Parker Street and 39 Lord Street Liverpool | Watch manufacturer and jeweller |

| REGISTRATION DETAILS | MAKER'S PRIVATE ADDRESS and DETAILS | PLATE and MARK DETAILS | MAKER/COMPANY and BUSINESS ADDRESS | MAKER'S TRADE |
|---|---|---|---|---|
| R2/223<br>24 August 1919<br>Sent by W L Manton | Private address same as business | P15/M/33,34<br>***#9425,6***<br> | **Walter Louis MANTON**<br>32 Benton Road Sparkhill<br>Birmingham moved 28 March 1952 to<br>29 Tetley Road<br>Birmingham | Jewellery (lockets and seals, etc) |
| R2/232<br>12 June 1920<br>Sent by W L Manton | | P15/M/39 and P15/L*sic*/no num<br>***#9427,8***<br>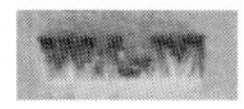 | **W L MANTON**<br>32 Benton Road<br>Sparkhill<br>Birmingham | Jewellery |
| R3/50<br>26 October 1929<br>Sent by S Blanckensee Ltd<br>19-35 Regent Place<br>Birmingham | Whitburn Hall<br>County Durham | P15/L/39<br>***#9429***<br> | **William LISTER & SONS LTD** *<br>William Corrie Grant (Director)<br>James Wadham Grant (Director)<br>32/34 Northumberland Street<br>Newcastle upon Tyne | Goldsmiths, silversmiths and jewellers |
| R3/55<br>15 October 1930<br>Sent by Smith, Ewen & Stylic Ltd<br>42 Frederick Street<br>Birmingham | | P15/W/97<br>***#9430***<br> | **WATCHES LTD**<br>Common Seal of Company affixed in the presence of:-<br>W P Sackville (Director)<br>R N F Lloyd (Secretary)<br>234 Soho Hill (Registered Office)<br>Birmingham | Jewellers |
| Missing register<br>*c.*1891<br>Similar mark entered BAO 15 August 1892 | | P5/M/368<br>***#9431***<br> | **William MILLS**<br>89 Vyse Street<br>Birmingham | Jeweller |
| Not in R1 - between July - September 1902<br>Similar mark entered LAO 22 May 1907 from Acocks Green Birmingham | | P9/M/40<br>***#9432***<br> | **William MAYELL** *<br>2 Spencer Street<br>London and<br>116 Unett Road<br>Birmingham | Gold ring maker |
| R1/68<br>26 June 1894<br>Sent by W Myerstone | Private address same as business | P5/M/568<br>***#9433***<br> | **Woolf MYERSTONE**<br>41 Carnavon Street<br>Cheetham<br>Manchester | Working jeweller |
| PDB 1831-2<br>MR3/94<br>PP1/190<br>Similar mark entered BAO 13 January 1836 | Gold rings | P1/8/x6<br>***#9434-9***<br> | **William MADDOCK**<br>22 Sawney Noke Street<br>Liverpool or | Goldsmith and watchcase maker |
| PP1/190<br>SPR 1725-54 | | P1/18/x1<br>***#9440***<br> | **William MERCER**<br>Moorfields<br>Liverpool | Watch and watchcase manufacturer |
| Not in SPB or LPB so struck 1860-3 | | P3/M/x1<br>***#9441***<br> | | |
| R2/216<br>29 April 1918<br>Sent by Benson Brothers | Private address same as business<br><br>See also Monograms section | P15/M/28<br>***#9442***<br>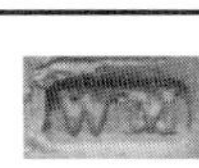 | **William MATTHEWS** *<br>52 Holyhead Road<br>Coventry | Watch manufacturer |
| LPB/54<br>12 February 1880 | | P3/M/x3<br>***#9443-5***<br>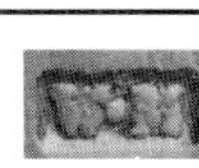 | **MAYELL BROTHERS** *<br>116 Unett Street<br>Birmingham | Ring makers and jewellers |

| REGISTRATION DETAILS | MAKER'S PRIVATE ADDRESS and DETAILS | PLATE and MARK DETAILS | MAKER/COMPANY and BUSINESS ADDRESS | MAKER'S TRADE |
|---|---|---|---|---|
| R1/18<br>27 November 1895<br>Sent by W Manton<br>Hollins & Jaques | 170 Bunns? Street<br>Birmingham | P5/M/699<br>***#9446***<br> | **William MANTON**<br>103 Vyse Street<br>Birmingham | Manufacturing jeweller |
| | | P1/13/x2<br>***#9447,8***<br>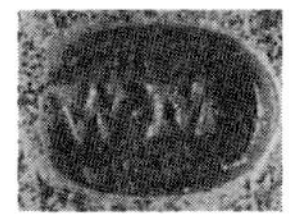 | **William MADDOCK** or<br>**William MERCER**<br>see above | |
| | | P1/14/x1<br>***#9449***<br>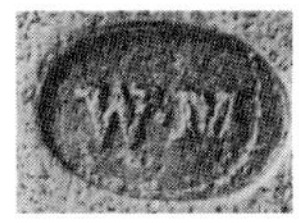 | | |
| | | P1/18/x1<br>***#9450***<br>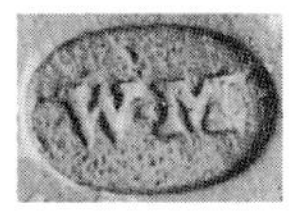 | | |
| | Square marked 1785 | P1/21/x2<br>***#9451,2***<br> | | |
| R2/46<br>20 September 1907<br>Sent by J & R Griffin<br>Two sizes | 43 Torrington Square<br>London | P13/W/5-10<br>***#9453-8***<br> | **Nathaniel RAPHAEL** trading as **THE WARSTONE MANUFACTURING CO** *<br>19 Chapel Street<br>London | Silversmiths |
| R2/158<br>28 June 1912<br>Sent by J & R Griffin Ltd<br>BAO 20.256 | 16 Farquar Road<br>Edgbaston<br>255 Hagley Road<br>Edgbaston<br>Belle Vue<br>Halesowen<br>16 Staplehall Road, Northfield | P13/W/121<br>***#9459***<br> | **Walter Henry MARKS**<br>**Samuel Tobias COHEN**<br>**John Paul WILMOT** trading as **THE WILMOT MANUFACTURING CO** *<br>92-100 Camden Street<br>Birmingham | Silver and electroplate manufacturers |
| SPB/8<br>1 August 1872<br>Sent by S Quilliam | | P3/D/x3<br>***#9460-2***<br> | **William & M DODGE**<br>21 Market Place<br>Manchester | Silversmiths, jewellers and clockmakers |
| SPB/17<br>4 December 1867 | | P3/D/x2<br>***#9463,4***<br> | | |
| R2/230<br>12 May 1920<br>Sent by W H Tandy & Son | 298 Kings Road<br>Chelsea<br>London SW | P15/K/2–7<br>***#9465-70***<br> | **William KNIGHT**<br>63 Hatton Garden<br>London EC | Wholesale jeweller |
| R2/234<br>9 October 1920<br>Sent by J G Slide & Co Two sizes | | P15/K/8–13<br>***#9471-6***<br> | | |
| Missing register<br>*c.*1890 | | P5/W/276<br>***#9477***<br> | **Unidentified** | |
| R1/37<br>19 January 1897<br>Sent by W Mills<br>E Vaughton<br>Two sizes | Gladstone Villa<br>Caroline Road<br>Moseley | P5/N/811a,b<br>***#9478,9***<br> | **Walter NEEDHAM**<br>40 Hill Street<br>Birmingham | Jeweller and watch importer |
| R2/102<br>29 January 1910<br>Sent by W Needham<br>BAO 9091 Two sizes | 19 Edgbaston Road<br>Moseley<br>Birmingham | P13/N/18-21<br>***#9480-3***<br> | **Walter NEEDHAM**<br>34 Vyse Street and<br>37 Hockley Hill (new address)<br>Birmingham | Ring manufacturer and jewellers factor |

| REGISTRATION DETAILS | MAKER'S PRIVATE ADDRESS and DETAILS | PLATE and MARK DETAILS | MAKER/COMPANY and BUSINESS ADDRESS | MAKER'S TRADE |
|---|---|---|---|---|
| R2/102<br>29 January 1910<br>Sent by W Needham<br>Two sizes<br>BAO 9091 | 19 Edgbaston Road<br>Moseley<br>Birmingham | P13/N/17<br>***#9484***<br> | **Walter NEEDHAM**<br>34 Vyse Street<br>Birmingham<br>37 Hockley Hill (new address)<br>Birmingham | Ring manufacturer and jewellers factor |
| R2/235<br>22 October 1920<br>Sent by Robert Needham | Sherburn<br>School Road<br>Hall Green<br>Birmingham | P15/N/9<br>***#9485***<br> | **Walter NEEDHAM**<br>**Robert NEEDHAM**<br>37 Hockley Hill<br>Birmingham | Manufacturing jewellers |
| R1/98<br>26 April 1899<br>Sent by W Neal<br>Cancelled 16 July 08 | Private address same as business<br>CWMP 1896-1909 | P9/N/5<br>***#9486***<br> | **William NEAL** *<br>1 Oxford Terrace, Allesley Old Road<br>Coventry | Gold watchcase maker |
| PP1/186<br>Similar mark entered LAO 17 May 1865 and BAO 3 May 1843 | Not in SPB so struck between 1841 and 1863 | P2/N/x4<br>***#9487-90***<br> | **William NAUL** *<br>48 Albion Street<br>Coventry | Watchcase maker |
| SPB/9<br>16 December 1876 | | P3/N/x3<br>***#9491-3***<br> | | |
| LPB/60 SP28/4<br>19 January 1885 | | P5/N/x1<br>***#9494***<br> | **William NAUL**<br>458 Rochdale Road<br>Manchester | Watch manufacturer |
| LPB/58<br>12 October 1880 | | P3/N/x2<br>***#9495,5a***<br> | **William NORTON**<br>3 Key Hill Drive<br>Birmingham | Jeweller |
| LPB/58<br>23 September 1882 | | P3/N/x3<br>***#9496-8***<br> | **William NEALE** *<br>29 Warstone Lane<br>Birmingham | Bracelet, sovereign purse, match box, cigar and cigarette case manufacturer |
| R2/93<br>25 September 1909<br>Sent by William Neale & Sons | Oakwood<br>Sherbourne Road<br>Acocks Green<br>Birmingham | P13/N/9,10<br>***#9499,9500***<br> | **William NEALE & SON LTD** *<br>Arthur Neale (Director)<br>29 Warstone Lane<br>Birmingham | Goldsmiths and silversmiths |
| R2/100<br>21 December 1909<br>Sent by William Neal & Son Ltd | Langdale<br>Grove Avenue<br>Moseley<br>Birmingham | P13/N/11-16<br>***#9501-6***<br> | **William NEALE & SON LTD** *<br>29 Warstone Lane<br>Birmingham | |
| Missing register<br>*c.*1888<br>Similar mark entered LAO 26 August 1893 | | P5/N/146<br>***#9507***<br> | **William NEAL** *<br>4 Craven Street<br>Coventry | Watchcase maker |
| R2/62<br>16 July 1908<br>Sent by William Neal | 13 Allesley Old Road<br>Coventry | P13/N/4<br>***#9508***<br>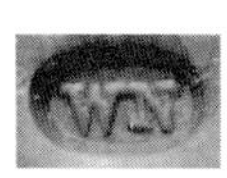 | **William NEAL** *<br>13 Allesley Old Road<br>Coventry | Gold watchcases and locket manufacturer |
| Missing register<br>*c.*1894<br>adjacent P5/N/553 | William Neale possibly | P5/N/x2<br>***#9509,10***<br>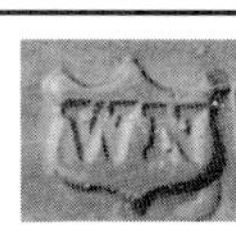 | **Unidentified** | |
| R1/89<br>14 January 1899<br>Sent by E J Rudge | 18 Kilburn Priory<br>London NW | P9/N/3<br>***#9511***<br> | **Walter NATHAN** trading as<br>**Walter NATHAN & BROTHERS**<br>11 Bradford Avenue<br>Redcross Street<br>London EC | Jewellers |

| REGISTRATION DETAILS | MAKER'S PRIVATE ADDRESS and DETAILS | PLATE and MARK DETAILS | MAKER/COMPANY and BUSINESS ADDRESS | MAKER'S TRADE |
|---|---|---|---|---|
| R1/30<br>11 June 1896<br>Sent by W Aitken | 1 Upper Chadwell Street<br>Clerkenwell, London<br><br>NB: Clerk entered Neale *(sic)* | P5/J*sic*/776<br>***#9512***  | **George NEAL**<br>**George Arthur NEAL** trading as<br>**W & G NEAL** *<br>35 Skinner Street, Clerkenwell<br>London | Silversmiths |
| R2/198<br>16 July 1915<br>Sent by W N Last | 12 Regent Road<br>Handsworth<br>47 Woodstock Road<br>Handsworth | P15/L/9<br>***#9513*** 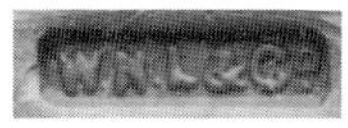<br>P15/L/8,10<br>***#9514,5***  | **William Nelson LAST** trading as<br>**W N LAST & CO**<br>59 Key Hill<br>Birmingham | Manufacturing jewellers |
| R2/149<br>11 January 1912<br>Sent by William Neale & Son Ltd<br>Three sizes<br>BAO 19.633, 34, 41 | 129 Anderton Park Road<br>Moseley<br>Birmingham | P13/N/29-31<br>***#9516-8***  | **William NEALE & SON LTD** *<br>William Neale junior (Secretary)<br>Cox Street<br>St Paul's<br>Birmingham | Goldsmiths and silversmiths |
| R2/179<br>29 October 1913<br>Sent by William Neale & Son Ltd | 129 Anderton Park Road<br>Moseley<br>Acocks Green<br>Birmingham<br>Solihull<br>Birmingham | P15/N/1,2<br>***#9519,20***  | **William NEALE & SON LTD** *<br>William Neale (Director)<br>Arthur Neale (Director)<br>William Neale jnr (Director)<br>William Neale junior (Secretary)<br>34 Cox Street, St Paul's Square<br>Birmingham | |
| R3/24<br>27 September 1924<br>Sent by William Neale & Son | The Croft, Solihull<br>129 Anderton Park Road<br>Moseley<br>Needwood<br>Knowle | P15/N/13-15<br>***#9521-3***  | **William NEALE & SON LTD** *<br>Arthur Neale (Director)<br>William Neale Junior (Director)<br>Harold Neale (Director)<br>34 Cox Street, St Paul's Square<br>Birmingham | |
| R1/122<br>2 March 1900<br>Sent by W Neale & Sons | King's Heath<br>Acocks Green<br>Birmingham | P9/N/8<br>***#9524***  | **William NEALE** (Managing Director)<br>**Arthur NEALE**<br>(ed: trading as William Neale & Son) *<br>29 Warstone Lane<br>Birmingham | |
| Missing register<br>*c.*1889<br>Similar mark entered BAO 15 August 1888 | | P5/O/241a<br>***#9525***  | **William OSBORN** *<br>52 Northampton Street<br>Birmingham | Goldsmith |
| R3/63<br>19 August 1932<br>Sent by T J H Wigley for W Osborn Ltd | Private address same as business | P15/O/11<br>***#9526***  | **W OSBORN LTD** *<br>Thomas John Howell Wigley (Man Dir)<br>Herbert Burton Pickering (Director)<br>51, 52 Northampton Street<br>Birmingham | Manufacturing jewellers |
| R1/8<br>6 March 1895<br>Sent by W Oliver<br>Two sizes | Fern Bank<br>Hall Road<br>Handsworth<br>Birmingham | P5/O/646a,b<br>***#9527,8***  | **William OLIVER**<br>Ely Place, Tenby Street<br>Birmingham | Manufacturing jeweller |
| R1/31<br>30 June 1896<br>Sent by W O Davies | Ivy Cottage<br>Hampton-in-Arden | P5/D/708<br>***#9529***  | **William Oakley DAVIES**<br>2 Warstone Parade<br>Birmingham | Jeweller |
| Not in R3 as expected<br>Similar mark entered BAO 6 January 1919 | | P15/B*sic*/27-29<br>***#9530-2***  | | |

| REGISTRATION DETAILS | MAKER'S PRIVATE ADDRESS and DETAILS | PLATE and MARK DETAILS | MAKER/COMPANY and BUSINESS ADDRESS | MAKER'S TRADE |
|---|---|---|---|---|
| Not in R3 as expected | | P15/B*sic*/18,19<br>***#9533,4***  | **William Oakley DAVIES**<br>2 Warstone Parade<br>Birmingham | Jeweller |
| R2/79<br>22 April 1909<br>Sent by W Oakley Davies | 73 Allesley Road<br>Moseley<br>Birmingham | P13/D/12,13<br>***#9535,6***  | | Manufacturing silversmith |
| Missing register<br>*c.*1889 | Attribution based upon trade directory initials match | P5/O/241b<br>***#9537*** <br>P5/O/241c<br>***#9538***  | **William OWEN**<br>4 Briggate and<br>3 Boar Lane<br>Leeds | Watchmaker, jeweller, clock importer, pawnbroker, cutler and fine art dealer |
| LPB/94 during 1884<br>No mark in LPB<br>Sent by Mr Floyd | See also their WB mark | P5/W/x1<br>***#9539***  | **WOLFFE BROTHERS** *<br>94 Vyse Street<br>Birmingham | Watch manufacturers and jewellers |
| R1/4<br>22 November 1894<br>Sent by W Parry | 20 Churton Road<br>Boughton<br>Chester | P5/W/624<br>***#9540***  | **Ferdinand WRENERBERGER**<br>**William PARRY** trading as<br>**WRENERBERGER & PARRY**<br>20 Churton Road, Boughton<br>Chester | Silver pipe mounters |
| R3/141<br>17 February 1953<br>Sent by W Parker<br>Two sizes | 32 Balderstone Road<br>37 Westcliff (12 December 1953)<br>Preston<br>Lancashire | P21/P/49,50<br>***#9541,2***  | **William PARKER**<br>No business address entered | Student |
| R1/30<br>9 June 1896<br>Sent by H C Wright<br>H T Perry | 17 Putney Road [1]<br>Handsworth, Staffordshire<br>55 Rowland Road [2]<br>Handsworth<br>Staffordshire | P5/X*sic*/774<br>***#9543*** 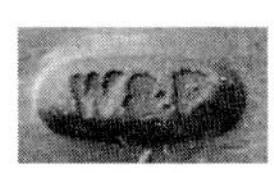 | **Harold Coleman WRIGHT** [1]<br>**Harry Thomas PERRY** [2] trading as<br>**WRIGHT & PERRY** *<br>28 Spencer Street<br>Birmingham | Diamond mounters and jewellers |
| R1/187<br>5 March 1903<br>Sent by Vincent C Smith | Brixton House<br>Walsall<br>Hazledean<br>Nichfield Road<br>Walsall | P9/W/93<br>***#9544***  | **Walter Thomas WINCER** *<br>**Arthur Thomas PLANT** *<br>Brixton Works, Glebe Street<br>Walsall | Fancy goods manufacturers |
| R2/154<br>6 April 1912<br>Sent by B Wade | Private address same as business | P13/Q*sic*/210<br>***#9545***  | **William Henry PETERS**<br>67 Old Christchurch Road<br>Bournemouth | Tobacconist |
| R2/132<br>13 April 1911<br>Sent by William Poorten | 46 DeBurgh Street<br>Cardiff | P13/Q*sic*/201<br>***#9546***  | **William POORTEN**<br>40 Castle Arcade<br>Cardiff | Pipe maker and working jeweller |
| PCR-1773<br>MR2/127<br>J1 has Pennington - in error probably | Made free 1770 – died 1789<br>Seen on serving spoon 1772 | P1/31/x2<br>***#9547,8***  | **William PEMBERTON**<br>Eastgate<br>Chester | Silversmith |

| REGISTRATION DETAILS | MAKER'S PRIVATE ADDRESS and DETAILS | PLATE and MARK DETAILS | MAKER/COMPANY and BUSINESS ADDRESS | MAKER'S TRADE |
|---|---|---|---|---|
| PDB 1810-14<br>MR2/128<br>Registered at BAO<br>1773 to 1801 | Three gold boxes; one in each of 1810, 1813 and 1814 | Not on P1<br>***#9549***<br> | **William PUGH**<br>Suffolk Street<br>Birmingham | Goldsmith and silversmith |
| LPB/68<br>2 December 1882 | | P3/P/x1<br>***#9550***<br> | **William PEARCE**<br>32 Northampton Street<br>Birmingham | Jeweller |
| Not in R1 as expected<br>R1/50 has this mark allocated to EOM | | P5/P/866<br>***#9551***<br> | **Unidentified** | |
| LPB/66<br>23 August 1883 | | P5/P/x1<br>***#9552***<br> | **Walter PARFITT** *<br>61 Myddelton Street<br>Clerkenwell<br>London | Jeweller |
| R1/8<br>1 March 1895<br>Sent by W Priestland | | P5/P/645<br>***#9553***<br> | **William PRIESTLAND**<br>18 Lord Street West<br>Blackburn | Jeweller and electroplater |
| R1/164<br>15 March 1902<br>Sent by W Priestland | 23 Mayfield Terrace<br>Cherry Tree<br>Lancashire | P9/Q*sic*/124<br>***#9554***<br>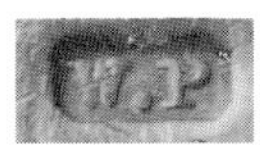 | | Jeweller |
| R2/139<br>6 July 1912<br>Sent by C Lucas<br>BAO 19.021 19.027 19.020 | 115 Church Lane<br>Handsworth Wood<br>Birmingham | P13/W/94-96<br>***#9555-7***<br> | **William Philip WHITEMAN**<br>101 Vyse Street<br>Birmingham | Manufacturing jeweller and silversmith |
| R2/148<br>13 December 1911<br>Sent by W Pendleton & Son | | P13/W/103<br>***#9558***<br> | | |
| R1/167<br>3 May 1902<br>Sent by W I Myatt & Co Ltd<br>Two sizes | 38 Everton Road<br>Sheffield | P9/R/46,47<br>***#9559,60***<br> | **William REDFERN**<br>38 Everton Road<br>Sheffield | Factor |
| R3/141<br>20 February 1953<br>Sent by W Rasburn<br>Two sizes | 13 Woodside Road<br>Manchester 16 | P21/R/15,16<br>***#9561,2***<br> | **Wallace RASBURN**<br>No business address entered | Student |
| R2/53<br>31 December 1907<br>Sent by Walter Reeves | 26 Station Road<br>Tottenham<br>London | P9/R/107<br>***#9563***<br> | **Walter REEVES**<br>45 Mitchell Street, Old Street<br>St Lukes<br>London | Pipe stick and bottle mounter |
| PP1/190<br>GSJW/136<br>J1 1850-75 | | P1/32/x3<br>***#9564-6***<br> | **William ROSKELL** *<br>21 Church Street<br>Liverpool or | Watch and watchcase manufacturer |
| GSJW/148<br>CWMP 1850 | | P1/31/x2<br>***#9567,8***<br> | **William READ**<br>55 Spon End<br>Coventry or | Watchmaker |
| PMR 1835-53<br>Not in SPB or LPB so struck 1860-3 | | P1/31/x2<br>***#9569,70***<br> | **William RIGBY**<br>1 Circus Street (1835)<br>9 Baptist Street (1841-3 and 47)<br>1 Holly Street (1845)<br>6 Upper Sheriff Street (1849)<br>26 Sheriff Street (1853)<br>Liverpool | Watchmaker and watchcase maker |

| REGISTRATION DETAILS | MAKER'S PRIVATE ADDRESS and DETAILS | PLATE and MARK DETAILS | MAKER/COMPANY and BUSINESS ADDRESS | MAKER'S TRADE |
|---|---|---|---|---|
| MR1/172-5<br>MR2/185-7, 221<br>MR3/189,90<br>SIL/12, 19,49<br>GMSC/14<br>J1 1721-51<br>J3/399 | Church plate, flatware and pap-boat<br>This mark smaller version of type 2b<br>Born Worcester 1690 –<br>Free 1720/1 - working *c.*1730<br>See also his Britannia mark Ri | P1/14/x1<br>***#9571***<br>type 2a<br> | **William RICHARDSON I**<br>Chester | Silversmith |
| | | P1/14/x1<br>***#9572***<br>type 2b<br> | | |
| | This example on marrow scoop 1727 struck over another mark | Not on P1<br>***#9573***<br>type 3<br> | | |
| R1/163<br>4 March 1902<br>Sent by W Walker | 41 Corporation Row<br>Clerkenwell<br>London | P9/R/44<br>***#9574***<br> | **William REED** trading as<br>**W REED & CO**<br>36 Crylisbury Street, Clerkenwell<br>London | Tobacco pipe importers |
| LPB/72<br>22 December 1881 | | P3/W*sic*/x1<br>***#9575***<br> | **W RICHMOND**<br>10 Clarendon Buildings<br>Liverpool | Trade not identified |
| SPB/12<br>12 April 1877<br>Sent by J Sharpe | CWMP 1874-96 | P3/R/x2<br>***#9576,7***<br> | **William RANDLES**<br>26 Hill Street<br>Coventry | Watch manufacturer |
| LPB/88<br>8 December 1880 | | P3/R/x1<br>***#9578***<br> | **William RUSSELL**<br>8 Northampton Street<br>Birmingham | Jeweller |
| Similar mark entered BAO *c.*1800 | Could also be Roskell, Russell or Read | P1/31/x2<br>***#9579,80***<br>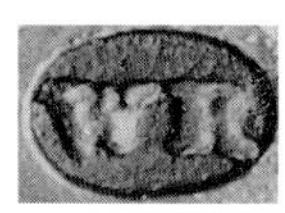 | **William RYLEY**<br>St John's Street<br>Coventry | Watchcase maker |
| SPB/14<br>12 June 1874<br>Sent by James Eastham<br>punched in error on P2 | 10 Springfield<br>St Annes Street<br>Liverpool | P2*sic*/R/x3<br>***#9581-3***<br> | **William ROSKELL** *<br>21 Church Street<br>Liverpool | Watch manufacturer |
| R1/107<br>2 August 1899<br>Sent by White & Reynolds | 10 Hunters Road<br>Birmingham<br>141 Burbury Street<br>Birmingham | P9/W/22<br>***#9584***<br> | **Frank REYNOLDS**<br>**William Alfred WHITE** trading as<br>**WHITE & REYNOLDS**<br>70 Vyse Street<br>Birmingham | Jewellers and silversmiths |
| R2/56<br>10 March 1908<br>Sent by W A White | 222 Burbury Street<br>Lozells and<br>6 Wye Cliff Road<br>Birmingham | P13/W/22-25<br>***#9585-8***<br> | **William A WHITE**<br>**Frank REYNOLDS**<br>58 Northampton Street<br>Birmingham | Manufacturing jewellers and silversmiths |
| R2/229<br>22 March 1920<br>Sent by William W Reeves | 2 Arthur Place<br>Summer Hill Terrace<br>Birmingham | P15/R/24<br>***#9589***<br> | **William REEVES**<br>61 Graham Street<br>St Pauls<br>Birmingham | Locket and ring maker |
| LPB/4<br>21 November 1877<br>LPB mark shown | | Not on P3<br>***#9590***<br> | **William RANDLES**<br>26 Hill Street<br>Coventry | Watch manufacturer |

| REGISTRATION DETAILS | MAKER'S PRIVATE ADDRESS and DETAILS | PLATE and MARK DETAILS | MAKER/COMPANY and BUSINESS ADDRESS | MAKER'S TRADE |
|---|---|---|---|---|
| LPB/74<br>Undated - during 1883<br>Sent by James Neale | | P5/R/x1<br>***#9591***<br> | **William RANDLES**<br>48 Hill Street<br>Coventry | Watch manufacturer |
| LPB/74<br>9 February 1885 | | P5/R/x1<br>***#9592***<br> | **William RANDLES**<br>The Laurels, Hill Street<br>Coventry | Watch manufacturer |
| R2/152<br>30 April 1912<br>Sent by Frank Reynolds | Both at<br>6 Wye Cliff Road<br>Handsworth<br>Birmingham | P13/W/120<br>***#9593***<br> | **Frank REYNOLDS** (Director)<br>**Samuel John REYNOLDS** (Director)<br>trading as<br>**WHITE & REYNOLDS LTD**<br>53 Northampton Street<br>Birmingham | Jewellers and silversmiths |
| 16 March 1912 | | P13/W/106-111<br>***#9594-9***<br> | | |
| R3/162<br>8 May 1957<br>Sent by W R Wilson | 307 Nottingham Road<br>Hill Top<br>Eastwood<br>Notts | P21/W/86<br>***#9600***<br>§<br> | **William Rex WILSON**<br>No business address entered | Silversmithing |
| R2/204<br>5 May 1916<br>Sent by James H White<br>NB: Clerk mis-entered White for Whyte | High Laver<br>(133) Fox Lane<br>Palmers Green<br>26 Copley Park<br>Streatham<br>1 Marmont Street<br>Edinburgh | P15/W/25,26<br>***#9601,2***<br> | **WHITE, REDGROVE & WHYTE** *<br>James Henry White<br>William Raynsford Redgrove<br>Cuthbert George Whyte<br>13 Charterhouse Street<br>London EC | Wholesale jewellers |
| R2/154<br>27 March 1912<br>Sent by Bacon & Bill | 49 Westside<br>Wandsworth Common<br>18 Adamson Road<br>London | P13/W/116<br>***#9603***<br> | **W REED WILLIAMS LTD** *<br>Henry E Merry (Managing Director)<br>W Reed Williams<br>62 Hatton Garden<br>London | Wholesale jewellers |
| R2/182<br>20 January 1914<br>Sent by T S Osborn<br>Mark number not entered in register | 49 Westside [1]<br>Wandsworth Common<br>London | P15/W/7probably<br>***#9604***<br> | **W REED WILLIAMS (1908) LTD** *<br>H E Merrey [1] (Director)<br>66 Hatton Garden<br>London EC | |
| R1/61<br>19 February 1898<br>Sent by T P Hewitt<br>(Ed: – Lancashire Watch Co) | 6 Gardenside Terrace<br>Uddington<br>8 Windsor Quadrant<br>Glasgow | P5/N*sic*/934<br>***#9605***<br> | **Margaret Fulton RUSSELL**<br>**Alexander Whyte DYKES** trading as<br>**William RUSSELL**<br>195 Argyle Street<br>Glasgow | Wholesale jewellers and watch manufacturers |
| SPB/4<br>7 November 1871 | | P3/S/x3<br>***#9606-8***<br> | **William SMITH**<br>40 Mount Pleasant<br>Liverpool | Watchcase maker |
| R2/96<br>26 October 1909<br>Sent by Walter Swann<br>BAO 10.605 | 205 Frederick Street<br>Aston<br>Birmingham | P13/S/46<br>***#9609***<br> | **Walter SWANN**<br>45 Northampton Street<br>Birmingham<br>181 Hockley Street (new address)<br>Birmingham | Jewellers, materials manufacturer |

| REGISTRATION DETAILS | MAKER'S PRIVATE ADDRESS and DETAILS | PLATE and MARK DETAILS | MAKER/COMPANY and BUSINESS ADDRESS | MAKER'S TRADE |
|---|---|---|---|---|
| R2/135<br>16 May 1911<br>Sent by F O Banyard<br>BAO 11.255 | 1 Victoria Street<br>Manchester<br>161 Moorside Road<br>Flixton | P13/W/92<br>***#9610***<br> | **M L WARMSLEY**<br>**G MARSDEN** trading as<br>**WARMSLEY & SON**<br>1 Victoria Street<br>Manchester | Umbrella manufacturers |
| R2/19<br>12 June 1906<br>Sent by W Aitken | 34 FitzWilliam Square<br>Dublin<br>Craigen<br>Sutton Road<br>Howth, Dublin<br>70 Brighton Square<br>Rabgar, Dublin | P9/V*sic*/142-144<br>***#9611-3***<br> | **Langley Archer WEST**<br>**George William THORNLEY** trading as<br>**WEST & SON** *<br>18 and 19 College Green and<br>9 Fleet Street<br>Dublin | Goldsmiths and silversmiths |
| R2/200<br>1 October 1915<br>Sent by Barker Brothers<br><br>Two sizes | Mount Offaley [1]<br>Greystones<br>Co Wicklow | P15/W/16,17<br>***#9614,5***<br>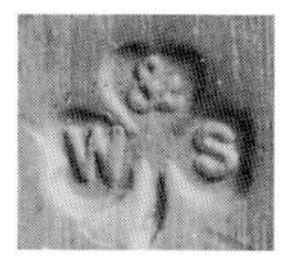 | **WEST & SON** *<br>Langley Archer West [1]<br>Grafton House<br>102, 103 Grafton Street and<br>14 Fade Street<br>Dublin | |
| R2/208<br>5 October 1916<br>Sent by L A West<br>Two sizes | | P15/W/31,32<br>***#9616,7***<br> | **WEST & SON** *<br>(Applicant L A West)<br>Grafton House<br>102 and 103 Grafton Street and<br>14 Fade Street<br>Dublin | Jewellers and silversmiths |
| R3/16<br>13 June 1923<br>Sent by W Neale & Son<br>Three sizes | Mount Offaley<br>Greystones<br>Co Wicklow<br>Graigen<br>Sutton<br>Co Dublin | P15/W/64-66<br>***#9618-20***<br> | **Langley Archer WEST**<br>**George William THORNLEY** trading as<br>**WEST & SON** *<br>Grafton House<br>102 and 103 Grafton Street<br>Dublin | |
| R3/17<br>20 July 1923<br>Sent by Stokes & Ireland | | P15/W/68<br>***#9621***<br> | | |
| R3/30<br>11 October 1925<br>Sent by Deakin & Francis<br>Two sizes | | P15/W/86,87<br>***#9622,3***<br>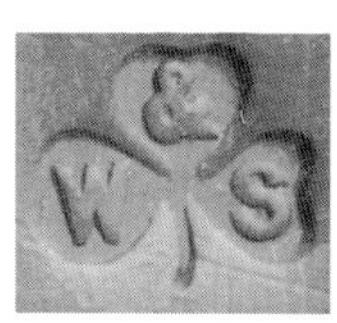 | **Langley Archer WEST** *<br>**George William THORNLEY** *<br>**Lincoln WEST**<br>**Cecil L'Estrange WEST**<br>102-103 Grafton Street<br>Dublin | |
| LPB/76<br>17 February 1880 | | P3/S/x3<br>***#9624-6***<br> | **William SWANSBROOK**<br>60 Church Street<br>Birmingham | Wedding ring manufacturer |
| SPB/19<br>28 January 1869 | | P3/S/x3<br>***#9627-9***<br> | **William SMITH**<br>40 Mount Pleasant<br>Liverpool | Watchcase maker |
| SPB/2<br>27 February 1877 | | P3/S/x2<br>***#9630,1***<br> | **William SKIDMORE** *<br>292 Goswell Road<br>London | Watch pendant maker |

| REGISTRATION DETAILS | MAKER'S PRIVATE ADDRESS and DETAILS | PLATE and MARK DETAILS | MAKER/COMPANY and BUSINESS ADDRESS | MAKER'S TRADE |
|---|---|---|---|---|
| LPB/76<br>8 May 1879 | CWMP 1883-1900 | P3/S/x3<br>***#9632-4***<br> | **William SEXTON** *<br>Norfolk Street<br>Coventry | Watchcase maker |
| Entry in R1 not found | | P5/S/x1<br>***#9635***<br> | **Unidentified** | |
| R2/23<br>13 August 1906<br>Sent by W Sexton | Private address same as business | P9/S/105<br>***#9636***<br> | **William SEXTON** *<br>232 Allesley Road<br>Coventry | Watchcase and pendant manufacturer |
| PP1/190<br>GTD 1845<br>J1 1843<br>PMR 1839-60 | | P2/S/x2<br>***#9637,8***<br> | **William SMITH**<br>55 Prescot Street (1839)<br>Liverpool | Watchmaker or watchcase maker |
| R2/186<br>3 April 1914<br>Sent by James Harrison & Son | 137 Stamford Street<br>Ashton-under-Lyne<br>253 Windsor Road<br>Oldham | P15/W/8-10, P15/P*sic*/0*sic*<br>***#9639-42***<br> | **John Thomas WHITTAKER**<br>**Thomas WHITTAKER** trading as<br>**WHITTAKER & SON**<br>14 Manchester Street<br>Oldham | Jewellers and silversmiths |
| R3/172<br>12 March 1960<br>Sent by W S Barnes | 30 Barnsley Road<br>Goldthorpe<br>Rotherham | P21/B/60<br>***#9643***<br> | **W S BARNES**<br>44 Ling Road, Loughborough<br>Leicestershire | Schoolmaster |
| SPB/17<br>1 May 1868<br>Sent by Hugh Green | SPB mark shown | Not on P3<br>***#9644***<br> | **William Stewart JONES**<br>91 Weston Street, Bolton<br>Lancashire | Watchmaker |
| LPB/54<br>19 November 1878 | CWMP 1874 at 2 Dover Street, Coventry, in 1874 | P3/M/x2<br>***#9645,6***<br> | **Walter Starkey MARSTON**<br>Holyhead Road and<br>9 Spon Street<br>Coventry | Watch manufacturer |
| LPB/4<br>5 November 1877<br>Sent by J Sharpe | | P3/M/x2<br>***#9647,8***<br> | | |
| LPB/86<br>27 October 1882<br>Sent by Pope & Phelps | At 46 in 1882 PO directory - Thomas Smith, jeweller, at 42 Frederick Street, Birmingham | P3/S/x1<br>***#9649***<br>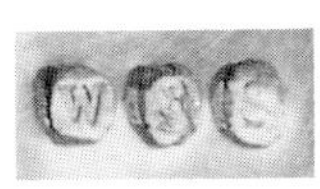 | **A SMITH**<br>46 Frederick Street<br>Birmingham | Jeweller ? |
| R1/119<br>5 January 1900<br>Sent by S H Ward | 29 Antrobus Road [1]<br>Handsworth<br>161 Grove Lane [2]<br>Handsworth<br>Birmingham | P9/W/29<br>***#9650***<br> | **Samuel Herbert WARD** [1]<br>**Samuel Robert WARD** [2] trading as<br>**S WARD & SONS**<br>124 Branston Street (struck out)<br>50 Hockley Street<br>Birmingham | Jewellers |
| R2/104<br>22 February 1910<br>Sent by H Ward | 138 Thornhill Road<br>Handsworth<br>Birmingham | P13/W/68<br>***#9651***<br> | **Samuel Herbert WARD**<br>**Frederick Walter WARD** trading as<br>**S WARD & SONS**<br>50, 52 Hockley Street<br>Birmingham | Manufacturing jewellers |
| R3/83<br>1 May 1936<br>Sent by S Ward & Sons<br>Re-entry of all W&S punches | 296 Jockey Road<br>Sutton Coldfield | No new marks<br>***#9652*** | **William George COSTIN** trading as<br>**S WARD & SONS**<br>10 Branston Lane<br>Birmingham | |

| REGISTRATION DETAILS | MAKER'S PRIVATE ADDRESS and DETAILS | PLATE and MARK DETAILS | MAKER/COMPANY and BUSINESS ADDRESS | MAKER'S TRADE |
|---|---|---|---|---|
| R2/137<br>2 June 1911<br>Sent by selves<br>BAO 17.597, 17.599 | Elstree, Hertfordshire<br>81 Clarkhouse, Sheffield<br>81 Clarkhouse, Sheffield<br>153 Chevening Road<br>Brondesbury, London<br>Tandridge<br>Surrey<br>Leary Greave<br>Sheffield | P13/H/73,74<br>***#9653,4***<br> | **Elford PEARSE**<br>**Herbert HUTTON**<br>**Robert HUTTON**<br>**S C GIBBS**<br>**Wilfred STEEL**<br>**Edward BUTLER** trading as<br>**William HUTTON & SON LTD** *<br>Hanley Street, Birmingham and<br>7 Farringdon Road<br>London | Manufacturing silversmiths |
| R2/142<br>26 August 1911<br>Sent by selves<br>Four sizes | Elstree, Hertfordshire<br>81 Clarkhouse, Sheffield<br>81 Clarkhouse, Sheffield<br>2 Leary Greave<br>Sheffield<br>153 Chevening Road<br>Brondesbury, London<br>New House<br>Oxted<br>Surrey | P13/H/75-78<br>***#9655-8***<br> | **Elford PEARSE**<br>**Herbert HUTTON**<br>**Robert HUTTON**<br>**Edward BUTLER**<br>**Sydney Coral GIBBS**<br>**Wilfred STEEL** trading as<br>**William HUTTON & SON LTD** *<br>West Street, Sheffield and<br>Hanley Street, Birmingham and<br>7 Farringdon Road<br>London | |
| R2/176<br>5 September 1913<br>Sent by Edward Butler<br>Two sizes<br>BAO 21.335-21.337 | Elm Lodge<br>Elstree, Hertfordshire<br>Willow Bank<br>Grindlewood<br>Tapton Villa<br>Sheffield<br>Millhouse Lane<br>Sheffield<br>153 Chevening Road<br>London N10<br>9 Hanley Street<br>Birmingham | P15/H/1-4<br>***#9659-62***<br>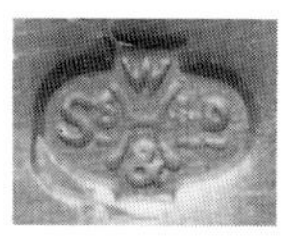 | **Colonel Elford PEARSE**<br>**Herbert HUTTON**<br>**Robert Salmon HUTTON**<br>**Sydney Coral GIBBS**<br>**Wilfred STEEL**<br>**Edward BUTLER** trading as<br>**William HUTTON & SON LTD** *<br>Hanley Street, Birmingham and<br>7 Farringdon Road, London and<br>West Street<br>Sheffield | Silver electroplate and cutlery manufacturers |
| PP1/190<br>WTD 1870<br>CWMP 1883-1900 | Perhaps should have been struck on plate 3 | P2/S/x3<br>***#9663-5***<br> | **William SEXTON** *<br>**Thomas WICKES** *<br>8 Norfolk Street (1883)<br>18 Norfolk Street (1886)<br>Allesley Old Road (1891)<br>2 Hearsall Terrace (1896)<br>Coventry | Gold watchcase makers |
| PDB 1785-7<br>MR3/98<br>PP2/349 | Watchcases<br>Seen on silver watchcase 1780 | Not on P1<br>***#9666***<br> | **William TARLETON**<br>Bixteth Street and Lime Street<br>Liverpool | Watchmaker and goldsmith |
| SPB/9<br>11 January 1877<br>Sent by W Hughes | | P3/X*sic*/x1 & P3/T/x3<br>***#9667-70***<br>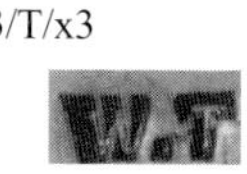 | **William Alfred TATE**<br>11 Church Lane<br>Liverpool | Watch manufacturer |
| R1/36<br>23 November 1896<br>Sent by<br>W Thorneywork | 138 Thornhill Road<br>Handsworth<br>Birmingham | P5/T/806<br>***#9671***<br> | **William THORNEYWORK**<br>40 Northampton Street<br>Birmingham | Goldsmith and silversmith |
| R1/98<br>24 April 1899<br>Sent by<br>W Thorneywork | | P9/T/9<br>***#9672***<br> | **William THORNEYWORK**<br>Tenby Street North<br>Birmingham | |
| R1/170<br>3 June 1902<br>Sent by<br>W Thorneywork | | P9/T/25<br>***#9673***<br> | | Jeweller |

| REGISTRATION DETAILS | MAKER'S PRIVATE ADDRESS and DETAILS | PLATE and MARK DETAILS | MAKER/COMPANY and BUSINESS ADDRESS | MAKER'S TRADE |
|---|---|---|---|---|
| R2/99<br>30 November 1909<br>Sent by S Blanckensee & Son | Laurel Road<br>The Drive<br>Roundhay<br>Leeds | P13/W/67<br>***#9674***<br> | **Frederick Russell TURNER** trading as<br>**WOFFENDEN & TURNER**<br>Land Lane<br>Leeds | Silversmiths and jewellers |
| R1/135<br>29 October 1900<br>Sent by William Turner & Co | 91 Norfolk Road<br>54 Wake Road<br>177 Rushings Road<br>92 Stafford Road<br>Sheffield | P9/T/20<br>***#9675***<br> | **William TURNER**<br>**William Glacier TURNER**<br>**Robert John BROWN**<br>**Harold TURNER** trading as<br>**William TURNER & CO**<br>75 Eyre Street<br>Sheffield | Gold and silver refiners |
| R2/16<br>5 April 1906<br>Sent by William Turton<br>Two sizes | 24 Ventor Road<br>Hockley<br>Birmingham | P9/T/59,60<br>***#9676,7***<br> | **William TURTON**<br>Back 90 Great King Street<br>Hockley<br>Birmingham | Jeweller |
| LPB/6<br>17 April 1878 | | P3/T/x2<br>***#9678,9***<br> | **William Alfred TATE**<br>11 Church Lane<br>Liverpool | Watch manufacturer |
| R2/80<br>27 April 1909<br>Sent by B Wade | 80 Bradford Street<br>Bolton | P13/T/13<br>***#9680***<br> | **Walter TOOLE**<br>77 Bradshawgate and<br>237 St George's Road<br>Bolton | Tobacco and cigar dealer |
| Missing register<br>*c.*1894<br>Similar mark entered LAO 22 August 1894 | | P5/T/535<br>***#9681***<br> | **Walter TICKELL** *<br>62 Paulet Road<br>Camberwell<br>London SE | Silverworker |
| R1/193<br>12 May 1903<br>Sent by Wilson Brothers | The Grange<br>Sidcup<br>Kent | P9/W/95<br>***#9682***<br> | **Walter Crellin TOLHURST** (Manager)<br>**Ernest Alfred WALKER** trading as<br>**JOHNSON, WALKER & TOLHURST** *<br>Brownfield Tolhurst (Secretary)<br>80 Aldersgate Street and<br>172 New Bond Street<br>London | Wholesale jewellers |
| PDB 1787-1823<br>MR2/194<br>MR3/99<br>SIL/52<br>GMSC/51<br>CMC/133 | Gold rings, coffin plates and spoons | P1/27/x2<br>***#9683,4***<br><br>P1/25/x3<br>***#9685-7***<br> | **William TWEMLOW**<br>Nantwich<br>then Chester | Goldsmith, silversmith and watchmaker |
| R2/236<br>11 December 1920<br>Sent by William Thomas Entwistle | 8 Clifford Road<br>Seacombe<br>Cheshire | P15/E/17<br>***#9688***<br> | **William Thomas ENTWISTLE**<br>23 William Street<br>Liverpool | Tobacco pipe manufacturer and mounter |
| R1/212<br>27 April 1904<br>Sent by J & R Griffin<br>Two sizes | 135 Bethune Road<br>London EC | P9/I/6,7<br>***#9689,90***<br> | **William Thomas IMBREY** *<br>16 Holborn Viaduct<br>London EC | Silversmith |
| R2/73<br>26 February 1909<br>Sent by J G Newbold | 93 Gleneldon Road<br>Streatham | P13/O/1<br>***#9691***<br> | **William T OSBORNE** *<br>47 Blackfriars Road<br>London | Fancy goods importers |

| REGISTRATION DETAILS | MAKER'S PRIVATE ADDRESS and DETAILS | PLATE and MARK DETAILS | MAKER/COMPANY and BUSINESS ADDRESS | MAKER'S TRADE |
|---|---|---|---|---|
| SPB/4<br>3 November 1871 | CWMP 1874-86 at 55 Spon Street, Coventry in 1886 | P3/R/x3<br>***#9692-4***<br> | **William Taylor RYLEY**<br>115 Little Park Street<br>Coventry | Watch manufacturer |
| R1/148<br>17 May 1901<br>Sent by W Unite | Private address same as business | P9/U/7<br>***#9695***<br> | **William UNITE**<br>169 New John Street West<br>Birmingham | Jeweller |
| R1/17<br>16 October 1895<br>Sent by W Vale & Son | 217 Heathfield Road<br>107 Albert Road<br>107 Unett Street<br>Birmingham | P5/V/693<br>***#9696***<br> | **Thomas Henry VALE**<br>**William UNITE**<br>**William John CROSS** trading as<br>**William VALE & SON**<br>82, 83 Unett Street<br>Birmingham | Gold and silver pencil case makers |
| R1/197<br>23 July 1903<br>Sent by selves | 177 Albert Road<br>Aston<br>11 Radnor Road<br>Handsworth<br>Birmingham | P9/V/3,4<br>***#9697,8***<br> | **William UNITE**<br>**William John CROSS** trading as<br>**W VALE & SON**<br>82/83 Unett Street<br>Birmingham | General goldsmiths and silversmiths |
| SPB/23<br>31 January 1876 | CWMP 1883 at this address | P3/W/x3<br>***#9699-9701***<br> | **William WICKES** *<br>Portland Terrace<br>Chapel Fields<br>Coventry | Watchcase maker |
| R1/62<br>20 February 1898<br>Sent by W Walker | 43 Mayola Road<br>Lower Clapham<br>London NE | P5/X*sic*/938a<br>***#9702***<br>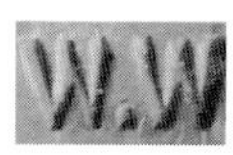 | **William WALKER** *<br>29a, 30 Percival Street<br>Clerkenwell<br>London EC | Pipe mounter |
| | | P5/X*sic*/938b<br>***#9703***<br> | | |
| | | P5/X*sic*/912b<br>***#9704***<br> | | |
| R1/193<br>12 May 1903<br>Sent by W Wilkinson | Cholmeley Park<br>Highgate | P9/W/96<br>***#9705***<br> | **William WILKINSON** *<br>1, 2 Skinner Street<br>38 Clerkenwell Road<br>London EC | Gold ring maker |
| R2/167<br>27 January 1913<br>Sent by W Wilkinson Ltd | Newtownards<br>Cholmeley Park<br>Highgate<br>London N | P13/W/126<br>***#9706***<br> | **W WILKINSON LTD** *<br>S F Wilkinson<br>1, 2 Skinner Street and<br>38 Clerkenwell Road<br>London | Manufacturing goldsmiths |
| SPB/10 no date, name or address entered<br>Similar mark entered LAO 1877 | | P3/W/x3<br>***#9707-9***<br> | **William WILKINSON** *<br>1, 2 Skinner Street<br>London EC | Manufacturing jewellers |
| R1/104<br>15 June 1899<br>Sent by W Watts | 32 Burlington Road<br>Willington | P9/W/20,21<br>***#9710,11***<br> | **William WATTS**<br>41 South King street<br>Manchester | Manufacturing jeweller |
| R1/55<br>7 December 1897<br>Sent by W Walker | | P5/X*sic*/912a<br>***#9712***<br> | **William WALKER** *<br>29a and 30 Percival Street<br>Clerkenwell<br>London EC | Pipe mounter |

| REGISTRATION DETAILS | MAKER'S PRIVATE ADDRESS and DETAILS | PLATE and MARK DETAILS | MAKER/COMPANY and BUSINESS ADDRESS | MAKER'S TRADE |
|---|---|---|---|---|
| R2/8<br>22 December 1905<br>Sent by William Weston | Private address same as business | P9/V*sic*/139<br>***#9713***<br>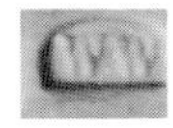 | **William WESTON**<br>43 Hunters Road<br>Hockley<br>Birmingham | Brooches |
| Missing register<br>*c.*1887<br>Similar mark entered LAO 26 January 1887 | | P5/W/102<br>***#9714***<br> | **William WALKER** *<br>29a, 30 Percival Street<br>Clerkenwell<br>London EC | Pipe mounter |
| Missing register<br>*c.*1891 | | P5/W/341<br>***#9715***<br> | | |
| R1/1<br>20 October 1894<br>Sent by W Walker<br>(new punch) | 43 Mayola Road<br>Lower Clapton<br>London EC | P5/X*sic*/613<br>***#9716***<br> | **William WALKER** *<br>29a, 30 Percival Street<br>Clerkenwell<br>London EC | Jeweller |
| R1/110<br>2 September 1899<br>Sent by William Wynn | 75 Whitehall Road<br>Handsworth<br>Birmingham | P9/W/24<br>***#9717***<br> | **William WYNN**<br>27 Northampton Street<br>Birmingham | Ring maker |
| Missing register<br>*c.*1887 | | P5/W/96<br>***#9718***<br> | **Unidentified** | |
| Missing register<br>*c.*1888 | | P5/W/186<br>***#9719***<br> | **Unidentified** | |
| LPB/62<br>1 March 1883<br>Sent by R J Pike | Invented fast beat 2-second centre sweep watch for whippet dog racing | P3/W/x1<br>***#9720***<br> | **William WILLIAMS** *<br>27 Bolton Street, Bury<br>Lancashire | Watch manufacturer and jeweller |
| MR2/50<br>PP1/190<br>CMC/137 | Free 1746 | P1/31/x2<br>***#9721,2***<br> | **William WRENCH**<br>Chester | Clockmaker and watchcase maker |
| GTD 1862<br>PP3/83<br>PMR 1851-64<br>Not in SPB or LPB so struck 1860-3 | | P3/W/x3<br>***#9723-5***<br> | **William WICKES**<br>25 St Brides Street (1851-3)<br>Liverpool | Watchcase maker |
| R1/92<br>22 February 1899<br>Sent by W Walker | 43 Mayola Road<br>Lower Clapham<br>London EC | P9/W/14<br>***#9726***<br>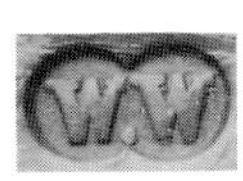 | **William WALKER**<br>29a, 30 Percival Street<br>Clerkenwell<br>London EC | General mounter |
| R1/211<br>25 March 1904<br>Sent by<br>W Wallbridge | Private address same as business | P9/W/109<br>***#9727***<br>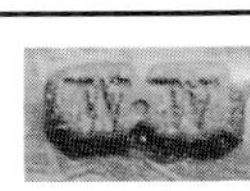 | **Walter WALLBRIDGE**<br>16 Radnor Street<br>Birmingham | Jeweller |
| R1/194<br>26 May 1903<br>Sent by W Williams | 128 Stamford Road<br>New Hall Street<br>263 Hagley Road<br>Birmingham | P9/W/97<br>***#9728***<br>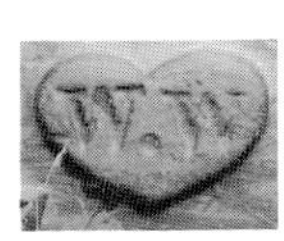 | **William WILLIAMS**<br>**Leigh A ELKINGTON** trading as<br>**WILLIAMS LTD**<br>S J Davies (Director)<br>168-172 Hockley Street<br>Birmingham | Manufacturing jeweller |
| R3/149<br>2 January 1954<br>Sent by Wakley & Wheeler Two sizes<br>Annotated *see Book 1894* | | P21/W/73,74<br>***#9729,30***<br> | **WAKLEY & WHEELER LTD** *<br>Ganton House<br>14-22 Ganton Street<br>London W1 | Manufacturing silversmiths |

| REGISTRATION DETAILS | MAKER'S PRIVATE ADDRESS and DETAILS | PLATE and MARK DETAILS | MAKER/COMPANY and BUSINESS ADDRESS | MAKER'S TRADE |
|---|---|---|---|---|
| R1/181<br>4 December 1902<br>Sent by William Aitken | | P9/W/84<br>***#9731***<br> | **JOHNSON, WALKER & TOLHURST LTD** *<br>Walter Crellin Walker (Director)<br>80 Aldersgate Street<br>London E | Gold and silversmiths |
| Missing register<br>*c.*1891<br>Similar mark entered BAO 27 June 1882 | | P5/C/343<br>***#9732***<br>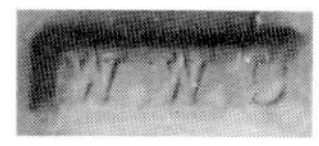 | **William Walter CASHMORE**<br>Warstone Buildings<br>Warstone Lane<br>Birmingham | Chain maker |
| R3/174<br>16 September 1960<br>Sent by European & General Express Co Ltd<br>Building No 1<br>London Airport North<br>Hounslow, Middlesex | | P21/W/95<br>***#9733***<br> | **WORLD WATCH CO LTD**<br>55/59 Saffron Hill<br>London EC1 | Watch importers |
| R2/88<br>21 July 1909<br>Sent by Sydney Fothill<br>Two sizes<br>LAO 4348 and 4353 | 37 Seymour Road<br>Harringey<br>London | P13/W/55,56<br>***#9734,5***<br> | **W WINGROVE & CO LTD** *<br>Sydney Fothill (Secretary)<br>6 Newcastle Place<br>Clerkenwell Green<br>London | Manufacturing jewellers |
| R3/102<br>30 September 1941<br>Sent by Walter Walsh Fraser | 139 Bridge Street West<br>Birmingham 19 | P21/F/7<br>***#9736***<br> | **Walter Walsh FRASER**<br>34 Northampton Street<br>Hockley<br>Birmingham 18 | Jobbing and odd mounting jeweller |
| R3/171<br>15 January 1960<br>Sent by The Assay Office<br>Birmingham | | P21/W/92<br>***#9737***<br>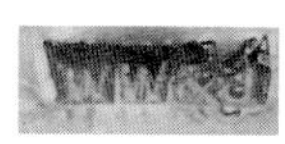 | **W WINGATE & JOHNSON LTD**<br>91-93 Charterhouse Street<br>London EC1 | Forwarding agents |
| R3/99<br>3 June 1941<br>Sent by W W Kemp | | P21/K/5<br>***#9738***<br> | **W W KEMP & SON LTD**<br>R W Kemp (Director and Secretary)<br>58 Corn Street (Registered Office)<br>Bristol 1 | Goldsmiths and silversmiths |
| R2/187<br>16 May 1914<br>Sent by Stanley Frank Wilkinson | Strathdene<br>Shepherds Hill<br>Highgate<br>London N | P15/W/11<br>***#9739***<br> | **W WILKINSON** *<br>Stanley Frank Wilkinson (Director)<br>1, 2 Skinner Street and<br>38 Clerkenwell Road<br>London | Manufacturing goldsmiths |
| R2/194<br>no day April 1915<br>Sent by<br>W G Matthews | Private address same as business | P15/W/13<br>***#9740***<br> | **W WRIGHT LTD**<br>Edward E Grundy (Governing Director)<br>3-6 East Street<br>Brighton<br>Sussex | Jewellers |
| R3/19<br>31 November 1923<br>Sent by W H Tandy & Sons | | P15/W/71<br>***#9741***<br> | **W WRIGHT LTD**<br>7 Stone Street<br>Brighton<br>Sussex | |

| REGISTRATION DETAILS | MAKER'S PRIVATE ADDRESS and DETAILS | PLATE and MARK DETAILS | MAKER/COMPANY and BUSINESS ADDRESS | MAKER'S TRADE |
|---|---|---|---|---|
| SPB/10<br>24 April 1873<br>Sent by William Eaton | 57 King Street<br>Manchester | P3/N/x3<br>***#9742-4***<br> | **Walter W NICHOLSON**<br>86 Exchange Street<br>Manchester | Umbrella manufacturer |
| Missing register<br>*c.*1888<br>Oblong cameo mark<br>BAO 27 June 1882 | | P5/Y/179<br>***#9745***<br> | **William YATEMAN**<br>60 Albion Street<br>Birmingham or | Jeweller |
| Oblong cameo mark<br>entered LAO<br>3 March 1884 | | | **William YANDELL** *<br>8 Hale Street<br>City Road<br>London N | Gold watchcase maker |
| R3/103<br>30 December 1942<br>Sent by W Weston<br>& Sons | 181 Woodland Lane [1]<br>Handsworth<br>Birmingham 20<br>11 Underwood Road [2]<br>Handsworth<br>Birmingham | P21/W/34<br>***#9746***<br>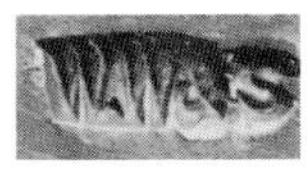 | **William WESTON** [1]<br>**Robert WESTON** [2] trading as<br>**W WESTON & SONS**<br>28 Hylton Street<br>Birmingham 18 | Diamond and signet ring manufacturers |
| R3/152<br>Re-entry of all previous punches | | No new marks<br>***#9747*** | **W WESTON & SON LTD**<br>registered as a new company<br>Sealed in the presence of:-<br>R Weston (Director)<br>E Brown (Secretary)<br>28 Hylton Street<br>Birmingham 18 | Manufacturing jewellers |
| R3/72<br>10 September 1934<br>Sent by W Weston<br>& Son | Both partners at<br>31 St Peter's Road<br>Handsworth<br>Birmingham | P15/W/107<br>***#9748***<br> | **William WESTON**<br>**Robert WESTON** trading as<br>**W WESTON & SON**<br>28 Hylton Street<br>Birmingham | |
| 14 August 1937 | | P21/W/1<br>***#9749***<br> | | |
| 30 December 1942 | | P21/W/35<br>***#9750***<br> | | |
| R2/164<br>18 October 1912<br>Sent by B Wade | 38 De Vere Gardens<br>Ilford<br>Essex<br>35 De Vere Gardens<br>Ilford<br>Essex | P13/XYZ/3<br>***#9751***<br> | **Walter Henry YERBURG**<br>**Sydney Percy YERBURG** trading as<br>**W H YERBURG & SON**<br>109 Bishopsgate<br>London EC<br>79 King William Street<br>London | Tobacconists |

| REGISTRATION DETAILS | MAKER'S PRIVATE ADDRESS and DETAILS | PLATE and MARK DETAILS | MAKER/COMPANY and BUSINESS ADDRESS | MAKER'S TRADE |
|---|---|---|---|---|
| R1/41<br>23 March 1897<br>Sent by<br>W H Carrington & Co | Newland Road<br>Derby | P5/Y/825<br>***#9752***<br> | **Thomas Edward YEOMANS**<br>Market Place and<br>St Peter's Street<br>Derby | Tobacconist |
| R2/87<br>10 July 1909<br>Sent by Samuel<br>Gershon | 12 Browning Street<br>Bradford | P13/S*sic*/40<br>***#9753***<br> | **Samuel GERSHON**<br>**George LESLIE** trading as<br>**THE YORKSHIRE STICK CO**<br>7 Woodbine Street<br>Birkenhead Road<br>Bradford | Umbrella and walking stick manufacturers and mounters |

| REGISTRATION DETAILS | MAKER'S PRIVATE ADDRESS and DETAILS | PLATE and MARK DETAILS | MAKER/COMPANY and BUSINESS ADDRESS | MAKER'S TRADE |
|---|---|---|---|---|
| R1/24<br>17 March 1896<br>Sent by W Sexton<br>Stokes & Ireland | 54 Briggate Street and<br>Commercial Street<br>Leeds | P5/aboveB/741<br>***#9754***<br> | **James Henry BARRACLOUGH**<br>**Herbert BARRACLOUGH** trading as<br>**Z BARRACLOUGH & SON** *<br>54 Briggate and<br>Commercial Street<br>Leeds | Silversmiths and jewellers |
| R1/43<br>1 May 1897<br>Sent by Stokes & Ireland Ltd | Private address same as business<br><br>Seen on a mustard pot 1907 | P5/aboveB/836<br>***#9755***<br> | | |
| R2/135<br>11 May 1911<br>Sent by Adie Brothers Ltd | Both residing at<br>2 St Mary's Road<br>Newton Park<br>Leeds | P13/B/121<br>***#9756***<br> | **James Henry BARRACLOUGH**<br>**Herbert BARRACLOUGH** trading as<br>**Z BARRACLOUGH & SON** *<br>54 Briggate<br>Leeds | |
| R2/172<br>21 May 1913<br>Two sizes<br>Sent by Stokes & Ireland | 16 St Helen's Place<br>London E C | P15/B/45,46<br>***#9757,8***<br> | **James H BARRACLOUGH**<br>**Albert BARRACLOUGH** trading as<br>**Z BARRACLOUGH & SONS** *<br>54 Briggate<br>Leeds | |
| R1/147<br>14 May 1901<br>Sent by A Zinkin | 28 Stafford Buildings [1]<br>13 Stafford Buildings [2]<br>Wentworth Street<br>London E | P9/R/3<br>***#9759***<br> | **Abraham ZINKIN** [1] *<br>**Lewis SILVER** [2] *<br>28 Stafford Buildings<br>Wentworth Street<br>London E | Watchmakers and jewellers |
| R2/195<br>29 April 1915<br>Sent by H Rixon | Le Locle<br>Switzerland<br>La Chaux de Fonds<br>Switzerland<br>1 Woodland Rise [1]<br>Muswell Hill<br>London | P15/XYZ/2<br>***#9760***<br>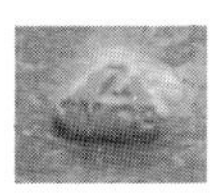 | **THE ZENITH WATCH CO (GREAT BRITAIN)** *<br>James Favie (General Manager)<br>Hehre Lihman (Secretary)<br>H F Roost[1] (Managing Director)<br>119 High Holborn<br>London WC1 | Watch manufacturers |
| R3/83<br>Undated, between 1May and 7May1936<br>Sent by Smith, Ewen & Stylic Ltd<br>42 Frederick Street<br>Birmingham | | P15/XYZ/4<br>***#9761***<br> | **THE ZENITH WATCH CO (GREAT BRITAIN)** *<br>119 High Holborn<br>London WC1 | |
| R2/194<br>13 April 1915<br>Sent by Z Zoltsberg | Private address same as business | P15/XYZ/3<br>***#9762***<br> | **Zisman ZOLTSBERG** *<br>164 Old Montague Street<br>Whitechapel<br>London E | Bracelet and chain maker |

| REGISTRATION DETAILS | MAKER'S PRIVATE ADDRESS and DETAILS | PLATE and MARK DETAILS | MAKER/COMPANY and BUSINESS ADDRESS | MAKER'S TRADE |
|---|---|---|---|---|
| R2/60<br>19 May 1908<br>Sent by Adie Brothers<br>Three sizes | 15 Yateley Road<br>Edgbaston<br>25 Rotten Park Road<br>Edgbaston<br>Birmingham | P13/A/1-3<br>***#9763-5***<br>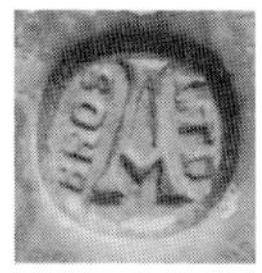 | **Herbert W ADIE**<br>**Percy J ADIE** trading as<br>**ADIE BROTHERS** *<br>45 Frederick Street<br>Birmingham | Manufacturing silversmiths |
| R3/8<br>1 April 1922<br>Sent by Adie Brothers Ltd<br>Four sizes | | P15/A/20-40<br>***#9766-86***<br> | **ADIE BROTHERS LTD** *<br>Percy James Adie (Director)<br>Herbert William Adie (Director)<br>James Percy Adie (Director)<br>45 Frederick Street<br>Birmingham | Goldsmiths and silversmiths |
| R3/109<br>22 August 1945<br>Sent by<br>Arthur Duckworth | 6 Dales Avenue<br>Whitefield<br>Lancashire | P21/D/13<br>***#9787***<br>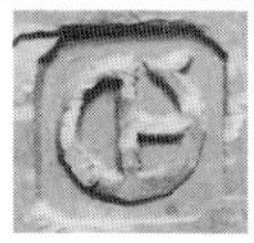 | **Arthur DUCKWORTH**<br>Cross Lane Works<br>Radcliffe<br>Lancashire | Silversmith |
| 28 September 1945 | | P21/D/14<br>***#9788***<br>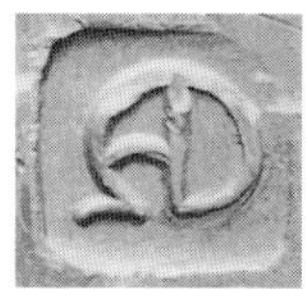 | | |
| 8 December 1948<br>Three sizes | | P21/D/17-19<br>***#9789-91***<br>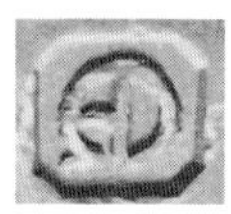 | | |
| R3/61<br>14 December 1931<br>Sent by A H Oritch<br>Two sizes | 23 Sandon Street<br>Liverpool | P15/O/9,10<br>***#9792,3***<br> | **Alexander Hippolyte ORITCH**<br>City School of Art<br>Liverpool | Precious metal worker |
| MR1/158-9<br>SIL/43,44<br>J1 1687-1704<br>J3/390<br>LGM 1699 | Seen on cupping bowl *c.*1690 and taper stick *c.*1697-1701<br><br>Free 1690 | Pre-dates P1<br>***#9794***<br>type 1<br> | **Alexander PULFORD**<br>Chester | Silversmith |
| MR3/184<br>J1 1687-1704<br>J3/390 | Trefid spoon *c.*1686-90 only shown in Jackson and may be the fancy shield cameo type 3b mark | Pre-dates P1<br>***#9795***<br>type 2<br> | | |
| MR2/220<br>J1 1687-1704<br>J3/390<br>GMSC/9 | Mug with reeded handle *c.*1697-1701 struck with both type 3a and type 3b marks | Pre-dates P1<br>***#9796***<br>type 3a<br> | | |
| MR2/220<br>J1 1687-1704<br>J3/390<br>GMSC/9 | Mug with reeded handle *c.*1697-1701 struck with both type 3a and type 3b marks | Pre-dates P1<br>***#9797***<br>type 3b<br>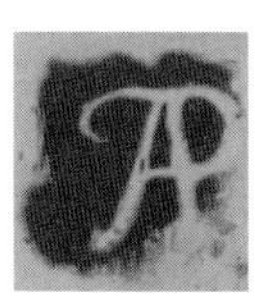 | | |
| R3/39<br>14 March 1928<br>Sent by self | Private address same as business | P15/T/48<br>***#9798***<br>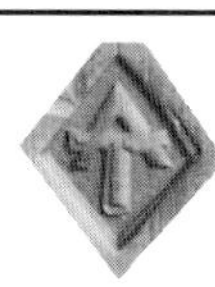 | **Agnes TOMLIN**<br>25 Jermyn Street<br>Princes Park<br>Liverpool | Art student |

| REGISTRATION DETAILS | MAKER'S PRIVATE ADDRESS and DETAILS | PLATE and MARK DETAILS | MAKER/COMPANY and BUSINESS ADDRESS | MAKER'S TRADE |
|---|---|---|---|---|
| R3/129<br>30 November 1949<br>Sent by<br>A Wilkinson | 9 Stanley Park, Litherland<br>Liverpool 21<br>20 Broadway (8 Dec. 1953)<br>Fulwood, Preston | P21/W/55<br>***#9799*** 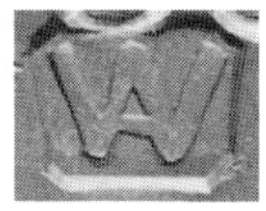 | **Arthur WILKINSON**<br>No business address entered | School teacher |
| Missing register<br>*c*.1893<br>CWCE/129,331 | Attribution based upon trade mark | P5/B/522<br>***#9800***  | **Henry BAND & SON**<br>10 Russell Terrace<br>Chapel Fields<br>Coventry | Watch manufacturers |
| R3/130<br>26 January 1950<br>Sent by C Allen | 28 Grosvenor Terrace<br>Bootham<br>York | P21/A/11<br>***#9801***  | **Charles ALLEN**<br>Archbishop Holgate's Grosvenor School<br>York | Assistant master |
| 31 July 1950 | | P21/A/13<br>***#9802***  | | |
| R1/94<br>6 March 1899<br>Sent by F F Trahern<br>and W Sexton | Elmfield<br>Coventry | P9/H/10<br>***#9803*** 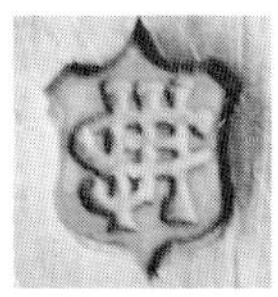 | **Charles J HILL** *<br>Russell House<br>Allesley Old Road<br>Coventry | Watch manufacturer |
| R3/134<br>28 October 1950<br>Sent by A C Miller | Peartree House<br>Holmeswood<br>Rufford | P21/M/27<br>***#9804***  | **Alan Cecil MILLER**<br>Studio and Workshop<br>Holmeswood<br>Rufford | Furniture designer and silversmith |
| 18 April 1958<br>Old punch mislaid,<br>new one entered | NB: Pear-shaped cameo and name of house | P21/M/49<br>***#9805***  | 2 Wright Street (from 18 April 1958)<br>Southport<br>Lancashire<br>Chapel Lane (moved undated)<br>Holmeswood<br>Rufford, nr Ormskirk | |
| R3/131<br>11 March 1950<br>Sent by C N Bertram | Private address same as business | P21/B/34<br>***#9806***  | **Charles Neville BERTRAM**<br>46 Dursbury Boulevard<br>Eastham<br>Cheshire | Sculptor |
| R1/21<br>7 February 1896<br>Sent by C W Shapland<br>Authority to<br>Nathan & Hayes | 207 High Holborn<br>London WC | P5/O*sic*/724<br>***#9807*** 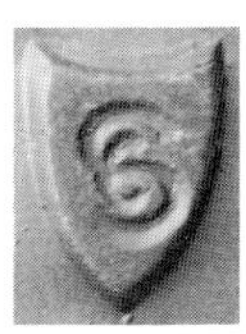 | **Charles William SHAPLAND** *<br>207 High Holborn<br>London WC | Silversmith |
| R3/120<br>6 January 1948<br>Sent by D Avison<br>Two sizes | Beech Lawn<br>Dunham Road<br>Altrincham (3 July 1956)<br>38 Poplar Grove<br>Sale<br>Chester | P21/A/6,7<br>***#9808,9*** 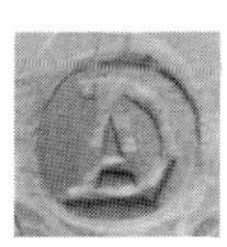 | **Donald AVISON**<br>Municipal School of Art, Manchester<br>19 Everard Street, Crosshand Moor<br>Huddersfield<br>22 Norma Road<br>Liverpool 22 | Silversmith |
| R3/64<br>23 September 1932<br>Sent by D Booth | Summer Hill<br>Gatley Road<br>Gatley | P15/B/210,<br>***#9810***  | **Miss Doris BOOTH**<br>No business address entered | Art silverworker |
| 22 February 1933 | | P15/B/211<br>***#9811***  | | |

| REGISTRATION DETAILS | MAKER'S PRIVATE ADDRESS and DETAILS | PLATE and MARK DETAILS | MAKER/COMPANY and BUSINESS ADDRESS | MAKER'S TRADE |
|---|---|---|---|---|
| R3/182<br>8 February 1962<br>Sent by E Lee | Smithy Cottage<br>Arrowe Park Road<br>Birkenhead | P21/L/56<br>*#9812*<br> | **Edward LEE**<br>No business address entered | Student |
| R3/114<br>3 July 1946<br>Sent by Smith Ewen & Stylic Ltd<br>42 Frederick Street<br>Birmingham 1 | | P21/E/3<br>*#9813*<br><br>P21/E/4<br>*#9814*<br>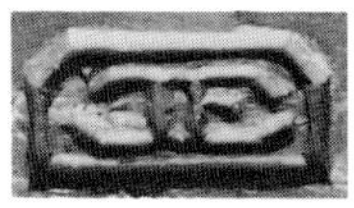 | **EMRICK LTD**<br>Mr Mitcher (Director)<br>Richard Emrick (Director)<br>Audrey House (Registered Office)<br>Ely Place<br>London EC1 | Manufacturing jewellers, importers and exporters |
| R2/181<br>5 December 1913 | | P15/C/31<br>*#9815*<br> | **Gladys COORE**<br>Ladies Residential Club, Cadogan Lodge<br>11 Carlyle Square, Chelsea<br>London | Metalworker |
| R1/120<br>14 February 1900<br>Sent by G Harry Johnstone<br>Two sizes | Headingley<br>Hamstead Hill<br>Birmingham | P9/J/26,27<br>*#9816,7*<br> | **George Hope JOHNSTONE**<br>**George Harry JOHNSTONE** trading as<br>**G H JOHNSTONE & CO** *<br>38 Northampton Street and<br>65 Hatton Garden<br>London EC | Manufacturing jewellers |
| R1/52<br>7 October 1897<br>Sent by J L Duncan Cunnington Bros | 23 Elford Place<br>Roundhay Road<br>Leeds | P5/overA/877<br>*#9818*<br> | **Henry Conyers WEBSTER**<br>46 Briggate<br>Leeds | Pipe mounter |
| R3/180<br>25 July 1961<br>Sent by H Holland | Annadale<br>Salter Beck Road<br>Workington<br>Cumberland | P21/H/85<br>*#9819*<br> | **Hugh HOLLAND**<br>No business address entered | Teacher |
| R3/40<br>4 May 1928<br>Sent by self | 40 South Castle Street<br>Liverpool | P15/E/38<br>*#9820*<br> | **Hilda Margaret ELLIS**<br>City School of Art<br>Liverpool | Art student |
| R2/124<br>22 November 1910<br>Sent by Wigley & Hall | 13 Northampton Road<br>Addiscombe | P13/P/155<br>*#9821*<br> | **Harold Vyvyan PITHEY** (Partner)<br>trading as **H V PITHEY & CO** *<br>26 Great Pulteney Street<br>London | Silversmiths and jewellers |
| R2/127<br>2 February 1911<br>Sent by H V Pithey | 13 Northampton Road<br>Addiscombe<br>Surrey<br>Greenbank<br>Rosefield Road<br>Staines | P13/P/156-158, P13/Q*sic*/159-166<br>*#9822-32*<br> | **Harold Vyvyan PITHEY**<br>**Charles Arthur HOLDEN** trading as<br>**H V PITHEY & CO** *<br>26 Great Pulteney Street<br>London | |

| REGISTRATION DETAILS | MAKER'S PRIVATE ADDRESS and DETAILS | PLATE and MARK DETAILS | MAKER/COMPANY and BUSINESS ADDRESS | MAKER'S TRADE |
|---|---|---|---|---|
| R2/132<br>27 March 1911<br>Sent by H V Pithey | 13 Northampton Road<br>Addiscombe<br>Surrey<br>Greenbank<br>Rosefield Road<br>Staines | P13/Q*sic*/195-200<br>***#9833-8***<br> | **Harold Vyvyan PITHEY**<br>**Charles Arthur HOLDEN** trading as<br>**H V PITHEY & CO** *<br>26 Great Pulteney Street<br>London | Silversmiths |
| R2/21<br>21 July 1906<br>Sent by H N Veitch | Private address same as business | P9/V/10<br>***#9839***<br> | **Henry Newton VEITCH** *<br>10 Barnsley Road<br>Birmingham | Silversmith |
| R2/22<br>8 August 1906<br>Three sizes | | P9/V/11-15<br>***#9840-4***<br> | | |
| R1/42<br>17 April 1897<br>Sent by J Davis | Arening Cottage<br>Near Barnett | P5/D/832<br>***#9845***<br> | **Joseph DAVIS**<br>34 Woodbridge Street<br>Clerkenwell<br>London | Medallist |
| R2/52<br>11 December 1907<br>Sent by John Gatecliff | 28 Greenhead Lane<br>Otley<br>Keighley | P9/G/92, 98<br>***#9846,7***<br> | **John GATECLIFF**<br>28 Greenhead Lane<br>Otley<br>Keighley | Artist |
| R3/132<br>21 March 1950<br>Sent by J Kearton<br>Two sizes | 9 Holly Road<br>Fairfield<br>Liverpool 7 | P21/K/10,11<br>***#9848,9***<br> | **Janet KEARTON**<br>No business address entered | Student |
| R3/106<br>27 January 1944<br>Sent by Joseph Paul | Transvaale<br>Bruce Road<br>Kidderminster | P21/P/12<br>***#9850***<br> | **Joseph PAUL**<br>102 Spencer Street<br>Birmingham | Jewellery manufacturers |
| 22 April 1944 | | P21/P/13<br>***#9851***<br>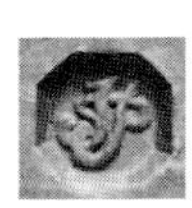 | | |
| MR2/94<br>SOT/52<br>GMSC/19 | Marrow scoop 1742<br>b.1687 Worcester<br>Previously read as D K for Daniel Kirkes | Not on P1<br>***#9852***<br> | **John RICHARDSON** junior<br>Worcester/Chester | Silversmith |
| SPB/2<br>4 May 1871 | | P3/R/x3<br>***#9853-5***<br>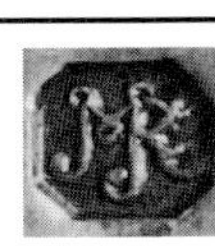 | **J ROTHSCHILD**<br>Caroline Street<br>Birmingham | Jeweller |

| REGISTRATION DETAILS | MAKER'S PRIVATE ADDRESS and DETAILS | PLATE and MARK DETAILS | MAKER/COMPANY and BUSINESS ADDRESS | MAKER'S TRADE |
|---|---|---|---|---|
| LPB/80<br>24 September 1878<br>Similar mark entered<br>BAO 25 March 1875 | | P3/T/x3<br>*#9856-8*<br>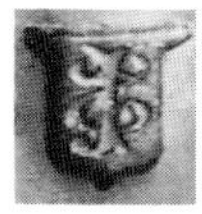 | **James THORNTON** *<br>54 Guest Street, Hockley Hill<br>Birmingham late of<br>30 Augusta Street<br>Birmingham | Jeweller |
| R3/64<br>21 November 1932<br>Sent by Mrs J Wilde<br>Two sizes | Kings View<br>913 Middleton Road West<br>Oldham<br>Lancashire | P15/W/101,102<br>*#9859,60*<br> | **Mrs Jane WILDE**<br>No business address given | Art silverworker |
| Missing register<br>*c.*1887 | REE or KEE<br>Isle of Man? | P5/K/110<br>*#9861*<br>§<br>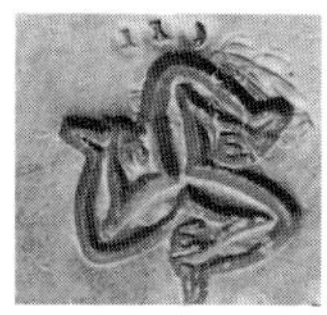 | **Unidentified** | |
| R3/95<br>4 April 1939<br>Sent by L C Barrister | Private address same as business | P21/B/10<br>*#9862*<br> | **Leonard Charles BARRISTER**<br>Howards Lane Farm<br>Eccleston<br>St Helens<br>Lancashire | Silversmith |
| R2/220<br>7 June 1919<br>Sent by G H Mitchell | 46 Sycamore Road<br>Handsworth<br>81 New Spring Street<br>Birmingham | P15/M/29<br>*#9863*<br> | **George Henry MITCHELL**<br>**F A DYKE**<br>300$^{a}$ Camden Street, Brookfield<br>Birmingham | Jewellers |
| R3/46<br>28 May 1929<br>Sent by self<br>Cancelled 4 June 1929 | Private address same as business | P15/R/44<br>*#9864*<br> | **Mary Howarth ROWLINSON**<br>The Homestead<br>Brown Edge<br>Lymm<br>Cheshire | Artist, gold and silversmith |
| 4 June 1929 | | P15/R/45<br>*#9865*<br>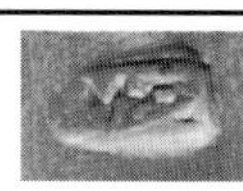 | | |
| R1/133<br>12 October 1900<br>Sent by A H Tongue | 4 Oxford Street<br>Whitely | P9/C/40<br>*#9866*<br> | **Peter Bruce CREASE** trading as<br>**CREASE & CO**<br>St Andrew's Building<br>Galloway Gate<br>Newcastle-upon-Tyne | Wholesale importers of fancy goods |
| MR1/133-5<br>MR2/220<br>MR3/182<br>J1 1651-96<br>J3/390 | Communion cup and cover<br>*c.*1685<br><br>Free 1654 | Pre-dates P1<br>*#9867*<br> | **Peter EDWARDES I**<br>Chester | Silversmith |
| MR1/133-5<br>MR2/220<br>MR3/182<br>LGM 1698<br>J1 1697-1700<br>J3/390<br>GMSC/4 | Communion cups and covers, punch bowl and tobacco box *c.*1687-96, tankard 1687-90 | Pre-dates P1<br>*#9868*<br> | **Peter EDWARDES II**<br>Bridge Street<br>Chester | Silversmith |

| REGISTRATION DETAILS | MAKER'S PRIVATE ADDRESS and DETAILS | PLATE and MARK DETAILS | MAKER/COMPANY and BUSINESS ADDRESS | MAKER'S TRADE |
|---|---|---|---|---|
| MR2/7,89<br>MR3/194 | Communion cup *c*.1732<br>Two sub-standard large spoons mentioned 27 October 1730 | Not on P1<br>***#9869***  | **Peter HOPWOOD**<br>Preston | Silversmith |
| Cripps/133 | Struck four times on a beaker 1728, Lancs. Both types on pair of chalices *c*.1732, Lancs.<br>May be the same mark struck. | Not on P1<br>***#9870***  | | |
| R1/117<br>7 December 1899<br>Sent by R Mander | Lyndhurst<br>Marwem Road<br>Acocks Green<br>Nr Birmingham | P9/M/17<br>***#9871*** 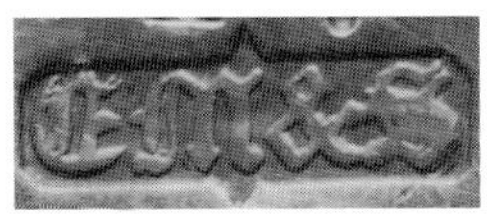 | **Richard MANDER** trading as<br>**Richard MANDER & SON**<br>Branston Street<br>Birmingham | Photo frame makers |
| R2/125<br>2 December 1910<br>Sent by Ruby Orchard | Private address same as business | P13/O/10<br>***#9872***  | **Ruby ORCHARD**<br>The Studio<br>5 Parade Mansions<br>Golders Green<br>London NW | Trade not entered |
| R2/30<br>6 December 1906<br>Sent by self | Private address same as business | P9/F/31<br>***#9873*** 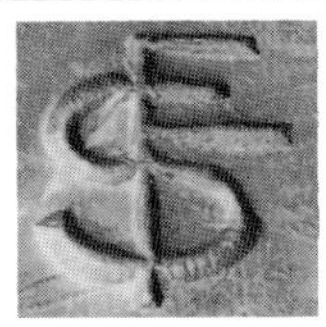 | **Susie FIRTH**<br>42 Hattersley Street<br>Princess Park<br>Liverpool | Trade not entered<br>Student? |
| R3/80<br>3 October 1935<br>Sent by S G Hill<br>Two sizes | 61 Deane Road<br>Liverpool 7 | P15/H/128,129<br>***#9874,5***  | **Stanley George HILL**<br>City School of Art<br>Hope Street<br>Liverpool | Silversmith |
| Undated<br>*c*.1944 | | P21/H/14<br>***#9876***  | | |
| 1 August 1945<br>Two sizes | | P21/H/19,20<br>***#9877,8***  | | |
| R3/50<br>3 December 1929<br>Sent by S Schulze | Private address same as business | P15/S/92<br>***#9879*** 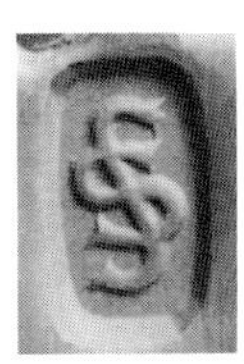 | **Susie Mathilde Charlotte SCHULZE**<br>60 Keppel Road<br>Chorlton-cum-Hardy<br>Manchester | Craftworker, gold and silversmith and handmade jewellery |
| R3/64<br>15 September 1932<br>Sent by<br>Mrs T Campbell<br>Two sizes | 131 Park Road<br>Manchester<br>354 Gorgie Road (13 Oct 1937)<br>Edinburgh | P15/K*sic*/216, 217<br>***#9880,1***  | **Mrs Trudie Gertrude Kate CAMPBELL**<br>No business address given | Art silverworker |
| R2/201<br>25 October 1915<br>Sent by Stokes & Ireland | Croft House<br>Grange Park Road<br>Newcastle upon Tyne | P15/G/28,29<br>***#9882,3***  | **THE GOLDSMITH CO**<br>1,3 Blackett Street<br>Newcastle upon Tyne | Jewellers and silversmiths |

| REGISTRATION DETAILS | MAKER'S PRIVATE ADDRESS and DETAILS | PLATE and MARK DETAILS | MAKER/COMPANY and BUSINESS ADDRESS | MAKER'S TRADE |
|---|---|---|---|---|
| MR1/141, 142 | Spoon *c.*1680 | Pre-dates P1<br>***#9884***  | **Thomas HOWELL**<br>Chester | Silversmith |
| MR1/175-180<br>MR2/221<br>SIL/32,42<br>J1 1682-1712<br>J3/389<br>GMSC/5 | Church plate, tobacco box, jug, porringer, mug, candlesticks *c.*1682-1701and *c.*1719-23<br>Free 1681-2 | Pre-dates P1<br>***#9885***<br>mark<br>type 1  | **Thomas ROBINSON**<br>Goss Lane<br>Chester | Silversmith |
| Missing register<br>*c.*1887<br>Similar mark entered LAO 18 January 1889 | | P5/M/113<br>***#9886***  | **William MATTHEWS** *<br>7 Norfolk Street<br>Coventry | Watchcase maker |
| R3/132<br>26 April 1950<br>Sent by W L Stevenson | 157 Dunburton Road<br>Childwall<br>Liverpool | P21/S/45<br>***#9887*** 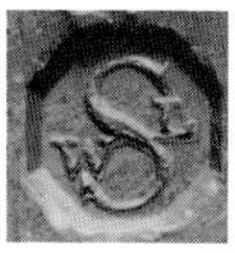 | **William Lennie STEVENSON**<br>College of Art<br>Liverpool | Artist craftsman and designer |

# APPENDICES


Date Profile of Makers' Registrations and Assay Office Dates noted on wares

Volume of Gold and Silver Wares Assayed at Chester

Assay Office Expenses and Staff Salaries

Assay Office Charges for Assays

Liverpool Watchcase Makers

Thimble Makers

Addenda to previous Ridgway Publications

Addenda to Priestley Publication

## DATE PROFILE OF MAKERS' REGISTRATIONS and ASSAY OFFICE DATES NOTED ON WARES

The following histogram has been compiled from two sources of data. For the period before 1863, the table uses the earliest hallmark dates seen on actual wares that can be reasonably attributed to known makers. After 1863, actual Chester registration dates for makers have been used. For the *missing register* period of 1886 to 1894, a linear rate of registration has been assumed in order to calculate a nominal registration year. The graph shows that activity was low before the time of the 1784 Plate Duty Act which introduced stiff penalties for non-compliance. There was another rise in registrations during the 1870s. This did not immediately follow, as might be expected, the Act of 1854 which allowed Midlands workers to use any British assay offices. It is possible there was a time lag before the Birmingham and Coventry watch trade woke up to the fact that there were markets in the Americas and a Chester hallmark would be beneficial. The estimated/actual data by decade beginning with the dates shown is provided in the following table:

| DECADE | NUMBER | DECADE | NUMBER | DECADE | NUMBER |
|---|---|---|---|---|---|
| 1701 | 17 | 1791 | 29 | 1881 | 678 |
| 1711 | 2 | 1801 | 24 | 1891 | 910 |
| 1721 | 15 | 1811 | 27 | 1901 | 1124 |
| 1731 | 7 | 1821 | 49 | 1911 | 558 |
| 1741 | 3 | 1831 | 65 | 1921 | 256 |
| 1751 | 2 | 1841 | 79 | 1931 | 229 |
| 1761 | 1 | 1851 | 70 | 1941 | 170 |
| 1771 | 5 | 1861 | 66 | 1951 | 200 |
| 1781 | 30 | 1871 | 219 | 1961 | 80 |

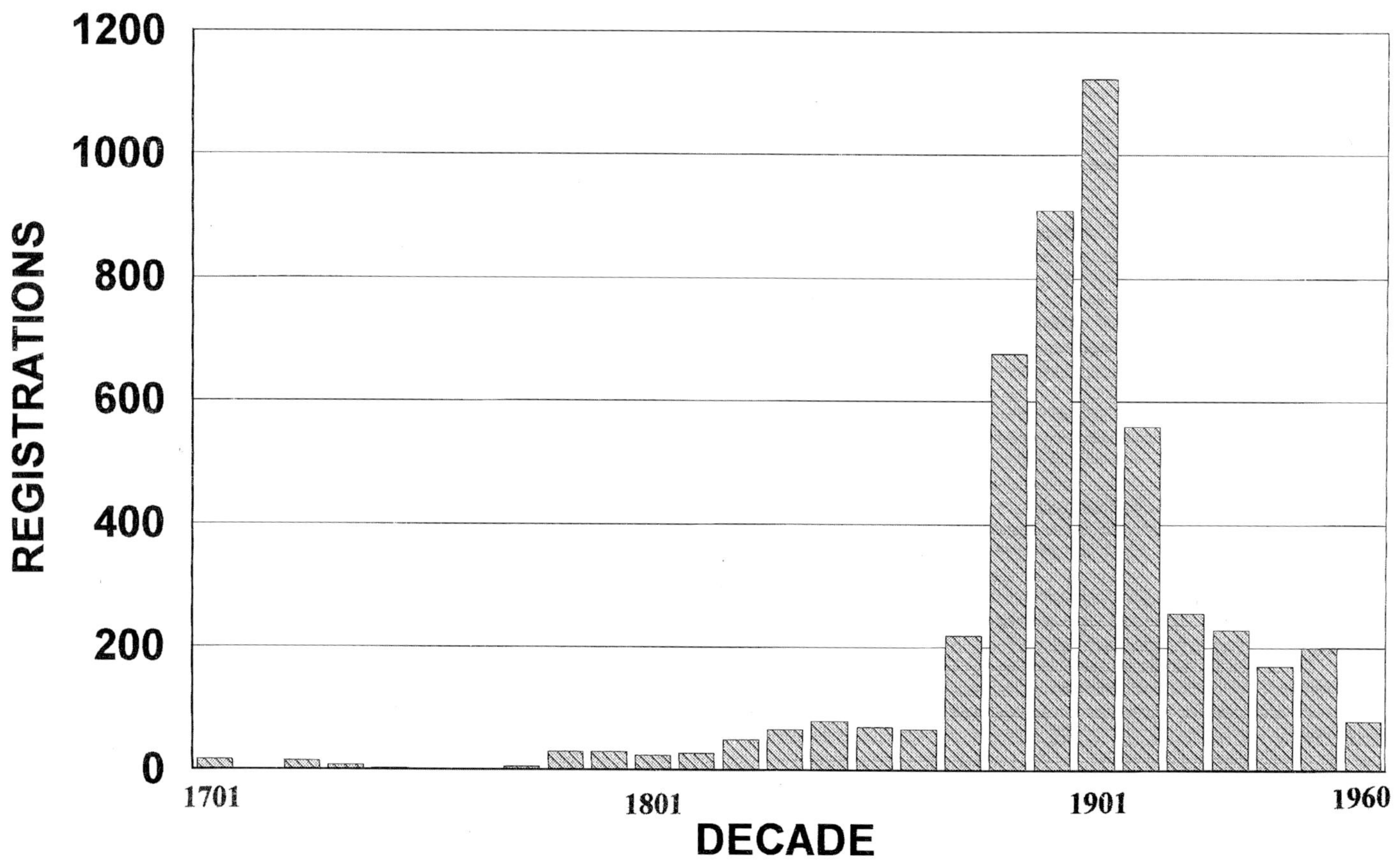

APPENDIX 2

## VOLUME OF GOLD and SILVER WARES ASSAYED AT CHESTER

The following incomplete data (in troy ounces = 31.1 gram) is all that is available on actual volumes assayed at Chester. The data for 1784 to 1839 is taken from the Plate Duty Books, but after 1798 is not representative because from that date watchcases, a major item for assay at Chester, were exempt from assay and therefore not entered in the books. After 1840, five years of data between 1850 and 1854 are preserved but the low weight for silver appears anomalous when viewed against previous years. The data from 1885 onwards does not include the weights of "broken" (sub-standard) wares. For a more detailed account of volumes, see *Chester Silver 1837 to 1962*. Before 1885 the data is for calendar years, afterwards the data is aligned with assay office cycles, i.e. 1st July to 30th June.

| DATE | SILVER & GOLD |
|---|---|
| 1766 | 824 |
| 1767 | 331 |
| 1768 | 314 |
| 1769 | 161 |
| 1770 | 2176 |
| 1771 | 2429 |
| 1772 | 2348 |

| DATE | SILVER | GOLD |
|---|---|---|
| 1785 | 1995 | 66 |
| 1786 | 2645 | 57 |
| 1787 | 3464 | 63 |
| 1788 | 3058 | 68 |
| 1789 | 2571 | 42 |
| 1790 | 1244 | 79 |
| 1791 | 856 | 111 |
| 1792 | 495 | 124 |
| 1793 | 766 | 102 |
| 1794 | 1526 | 89 |
| 1795 | 3749 | 116 |
| 1796 | 4689 | 158 |
| 1797 | 4849 | 164 |
| 1798 | 877 | 83 |
| 1799 | 168 | 102 |
| 1800 | 193 | 85 |
| 1801 | 221 | 112 |
| 1802 | 31 | 72 |
| 1803 | 347 | 175 |
| 1804 | 466 | 157 |
| 1805 | 506 | 152 |
| 1806 | 189 | 152 |
| 1807 | 129 | 164 |
| 1808 | 206 | 121 |
| 1809 | 157 | 156 |
| 1810 | 28 | 219 |
| 1811 | 230 | 156 |
| 1812 | 92 | 149 |
| 1813 | 202 | 265 |
| 1814 | 68 | 216 |
| 1815 | 229 | 142 |
| 1816 | 249 | 191 |
| 1817 | 206 | 179 |
| 1818 | 90 | 185 |
| 1819 | 68 | 197 |
| 1820 | 119 | 193 |
| 1821 | 132 | 176 |
| 1822 | 127 | 162 |
| 1823 | 95 | 154 |
| 1824 | 157 | 166 |

| DATE | SILVER | GOLD |
|---|---|---|
| 1825 | 259 | 168 |
| 1826 | 268 | 122 |
| 1827 | 288 | 128 |
| 1828 | 1352 | 153 |
| 1829 | 2471 | 117 |
| 1830 | 2168 | 72 |
| 1831 | 1940 | 70 |
| 1832 | 1148 | 66 |
| 1833 | 534 | 31 |
| 1834 | 275 | 35 |
| 1835 | 1172 | 35 |
| 1836 | 1287 | 63 |
| 1837 | Incomplete | |
| 1838 | 2970 | 43 |
| 1839 | 2956 | 38 |
| 1840 | Incomplete | |
| 1850 | 106 | 207 |
| 1851 | 186 | 204 |
| 1852 | 115 | 190 |
| 1853 | 106 | 221 |
| 1854 | 124 | 188 |
| 1885 | 84639 | 46937 |
| 1886 | 123380 | 49426 |
| 1887 | 145315 | 42773 |
| 1888 | 195190 | 40310 |
| 1889 | 233121 | 41883 |
| 1890 | 248212 | 51166 |
| 1891 | 246909 | 53715 |
| 1892 | 233491 | 55789 |
| 1893 | 208388 | 61318 |
| 1894 | 227250 | 62442 |
| 1895 | 311624 | 73283 |
| 1896 | 473887 | 97281 |
| 1897 | 556801 | 109187 |
| 1898 | 592783 | 130480 |
| 1899 | 741044 | 148895 |
| 1900 | 889953 | 164958 |
| 1901 | 966885 | 157089 |
| 1902 | 1017631 | 162560 |
| 1903 | 900745 | 169765 |
| 1904 | 864702 | 150221 |
| 1905 | 788807 | 132905 |
| 1906 | 832035 | 135290 |
| 1907 | 1020894 | 133180 |
| 1908 | 889354 | 139010 |
| 1909 | 925714 | 132500 |
| 1910 | 1100956 | 175989 |

| DATE | SILVER | GOLD |
|---|---|---|
| 1911 | 948569 | 165903 |
| 1912 | 971820 | 177651 |
| 1913 | 980498 | 186613 |
| 1914 | 975367 | 188566 |
| 1915 | 549154 | 126671 |
| 1916 | 632215 | 192204 |
| 1917 | 420925 | 134543 |
| 1918 | 292472 | 121762 |
| 1919 | 472247 | 152426 |
| 1920 | 585980 | 180541 |
| 1921 | 374676 | 105061 |
| 1922 | 377232 | 91433 |
| 1923 | 374473 | 71245 |
| 1924 | 380743 | 69038 |
| 1925 | 421368 | 78786 |
| 1926 | 360183 | 71635 |
| 1927 | 323384 | 54238 |
| 1928 | 226320 | 49346 |
| 1929 | 212835 | 51443 |
| 1930 | 188423 | 45275 |
| 1931 | 160317 | 39757 |
| 1932 | 126788 | 25664 |
| 1933 | 118524 | 20716 |
| 1934 | 148629 | 30309 |
| 1935 | 122764 | 31193 |
| 1936 | 132128 | 30100 |
| 1937 | 140153 | 34568 |
| 1938 | 136537 | 36368 |
| 1939 | 146610 | 32904 |
| 1940 | 124207 | 33271 |
| 1941 | 46229 | 20308 |
| 1942 | 30687 | 13490 |
| 1943 | 9162 | 12775 |
| 1944 | 15832 | 11661 |
| 1945 | 48586 | 11661 |
| 1946 | 66808 | 14017 |
| 1947 | 68279 | 19158 |
| 1948 | 53201 | 16632 |
| 1949 | 34129 | 13143 |
| 1950 | 22808 | 9254 |
| 1951 | 24446 | 9126 |
| 1952 | 29147 | 8583 |
| 1953 | 34730 | 9569 |
| 1954 | 45092 | 19313 |
| 1955 | 48980 | 25497 |
| 1956 | 54995 | 20269 |
| 1957 | 64390 | 24473 |
| 1958 | Unknown | Unknown |
| 1959 | 63313 | Unknown |

**APPENDIX 3**

## ASSAY OFFICE EXPENSES and STAFF SALARIES

A report made by the Inspector General of Stamps and Taxes in 1851 referred to Chester. It states that there were only four Chester based goldsmiths, two of whom were appointed as Prime Warden (John Lowe) and assistant Warden (John Garner). The Assay Master was Thomas Lowe, brother of John Lowe, but "not of the trade" and an assistant, a Mr Green. The Prime Warden and the assistant each received £5 a year and the assistant received 3s-6d per day for attendance. The Assay Master received £300 a year less 20% to cover expenses incurred over the recent prosecution of the former Assay Master. He also received the produce of the diet box and the scrapings of gold. The assistant assay master received £2 a week and the clerk, Edward Jones, £20 a year. These salaries were paid out of the charges made for marking silver. The assay days were Thursday and Fridays, though more days were available should the demand increase. The diet box had produced in the last half year of 1851, 2oz 6dwt 18grn of gold and 8 oz of silver. There was also revenue from assaying (see next appendix).

One of the satisfactory results of the Select Committee Report was that it gave a new independence to the Chester Assay Office. The increased income of the Company brought about by the revenue from assays prompted them to review the salaries of their officials. Duty which had been paid on watchcases had ceased in 1794 but the cost of assaying had continued. In August 1856 at the time of the elections the salary of John Lowe, who had done so much in the recent discussions, was raised substantially to £50 a year, that of Mr Green to £80 "for scraping and as a warden". Daniel Davies (auditor and assistant) and Thomas Woolley, weigher, had their salaries raised to £20 each year on condition that they audited the weighing and account books every half year. Members of the Council were to have 30/- a year for an excursion and the apprentices 7s-6d for a similar treat. Another revision of salaries took place 16th August 1862 which again reflected an increase in work. John Lowe had his salary increased from £50 to £100 a year. Thomas Woolley from £50 to £80, James Lowe from 30/- to 40/- a week, E Tatler 21/- to 26/- a week, G Lowe, weigher, £20 to £25 a year, J F Lowe, auditor £20 to £25 a year. John Lowe did not survive long to enjoy the increased salary for he died 11th September 1864. As a mark of the high esteem in which members held him, the Company defrayed his funeral expenses and made an allowance of £5 to each member, and £2-10-0 to each apprentice to provide a suit for mourning on the occasion. He managed to combine civic and church duties with those of an active goldsmith, becoming City Sheriff in 1841, Prime Warden 1854/55 and again in 1864/65. The spiritual needs of the Company and the apprentices were looked after when he appointed the Reverend G L Whitehead as Chaplain to the Company with a yearly stipend of £25.

John's son, John Foulkes Lowe II was elected Warden on the death of his father and George Bennett Lowe became auditor in his place. Thomas, the partner of John Lowe I who had shared the same mark with his late brother was now a very old man and going blind. He could only sign his name with a cross on 22nd September 1864, and on 27th September 1864, at a special meeting convened at the Hall in Goss Street, after twenty years as Assay Master he resigned. The Company considered his retirement and he was granted an allowance of £200 a year or 2/3rds of his former salary. His place as Assay Master was taken by James Foulkes Lowe *an able and skilful man and experienced in assaying gold and silver*. Thomas Lowe died in February 1866, the Company defrayed his funeral expenses as they did for Edward Jones the Clerk in 1867.

Shortly before John Lowe's death in 1864 the Company had planned to acquire land and property which could be used for housing members should the need arise. For this a licence was necessary and the Company sought Counsel's opinion on the matter because there was conflicting legislation regarding the legality of assay offices owning land. Their Counsel, Henry Rowcliffe of Lincoln's Inn, gave advice on the 5th March 1862 and recommended they apply to the Crown to purchase land to the value of £3,345 which they duly submitted on 18th March 1862. The Company had already purchased property in Goss Street where they conducted the assay office, and by the time the Attorney General granted the licence on a payment of £110 on 22nd May 1862 in the 25th year of the reign of Queen Victoria, their assets included land at Pentre, Flintshire and three properties in Back Brook Street, Chester to the value of £2,295; they also owned two houses in Princess Street, property in Whitefriars and a stable to the value of £1,050. By December 1862 their premises in Princess Street had been sold to the Town Council for £500, and the following May the Company added two more acres to the field at Pentre for a sum not exceeding £140. In 1866 the property in Whitefriars was sold for about £1,200 and the following year the Company drew up a number of resolutions connected with the insurance of individual members.

On 3rd August 1889, at the annual meeting which involved the change of date letter, the appointment of the Wardens and other matters were confirmed, and the date of annual meetings changed to 1st July. New punches for the City and Sterling marks with a slight change in style were introduced on 7th October 1889.

There was a regular revision of the amounts paid to the officers and workmen at the assay office: when trade was good, as in 1884, they increased the salary of the Assay Master to £140; but it was reduced in 1886 along with other salaries by a third. In 1895, owing to a new prosperity, the salaries were again listed.

| | | | | | |
|---|---|---|---|---|---|
| James Foulkes Lowe | £50 | W N Godwin | £13 | A N Godwin | £26 |
| Thomas Woolley | £26 | G L Whitehouse | £10 | W F Lowe | £26 |
| John Woolley | £26 | John F Lowe | £26 | G B Lowe | £10 |
| G W Williams | £26 | R E Tatler | £26 | Mrs John Woolley | £ 4 |

They all signed the Company Book except Mrs John Woolley who was not a member of the Company. No woman had ever been elected to the Company during its long history – a custom still observed in 2002.

In the early years of the twentieth century the Company was forced to reduce the salaries to 2/3rds of normal which must have caused considerable hardship to those concerned. One of the results of the Great War was the action taken by the General Workers Union on 8th January 1920 when everyone in the assay office joined in a strong protest and demanded an increase in wages and improved conditions. Regrettably they made their demands at a time when there was a shortage of work. Someone had leaked the amounts received in past years for assaying and had based their demands upon these figures which were in any case strictly confidential. The outcome of this protest hardly benefited the staff. Four boys and two girls were given fourteen days' notice, and in April 1921 four of the younger men were sacked. Those kept on were given a rise of ten shillings per week. Sefton Williams who had joined the Company in 1913 after serving his apprenticeship under his father for seven years, had joined the assay office staff but had been called up. When he returned he was advised by the Company that it would be to his advantage if he remained in the army rather than claim his place at the office again, even though they had made up his pay to the amount that he would have received had he remained. The lean period continued for some time and in 1924 the Company was forced to sell £500 War Stock towards clearing an overdraft at the Bank of £676. They had been financially secure during the war and had invested £4,000 in war stock and Australian investments at 4%, but the lean years that had followed had depleted this considerably.

Birmingham sought to take advantage of the financial problems of the CAO and tried to persuade Chester to drop their Agency in Birmingham. In 1923 Chester made it quite clear that they would not agree to this, even though their agent was far from satisfactory. Instead, in 1930, Harold S Smets of 107 Vyse Street, Birmingham, a dealer in gem stones, was officially appointed as parcels agent to the CAO at Birmingham. After this large quantities of silver came from Birmingham to be assayed at Chester. The advent of this trade from Birmingham, though frowned upon by that city, was a most welcome reward to Chester for their patience during the earlier years of the depression.

Apart from being requested to contribute to a gift for David Lloyd George, the introduction of a 14 carat gold standard and the special Jubilee mark for King George and Queen Mary in 1935, and associated expenditures, very little changed at the assay office until the Second World War. On 5th September 1939, the Company reduced its membership by 20% and ordered a cut of 10% in staff numbers. The War years had a devastating impact on trade unconnected with the war effort, and gold, when permitted, was only used at 9 carat. The Company managed to survive, but in 1946 James Foulkes Lowe died. The new management saw a steady increase in the amount of work passing to Chester, but there was a slow-down in the number of new registrations. In the final decades, the new silversmiths were mainly students enrolling at the Arts and Crafts Colleges in Liverpool and Manchester.

In 1957, the Company allowed the Government's Hallmarking Committee under the chairmanship of Sir Leonard Stone to inspect the assay office records and in due course the Stone Report was issued calling for the closure of Chester but no other assay offices. Plans were laid in Parliament to remove the right of assay and the office closed on 24th August 1962. There were also unsuccessful moves to dissolve the Company but the Company continues to this day in a modified form. The penultimate Chester registration was for Arthur Hamil Westwood, Assay Master at Birmingham, and the final entry was for a student silversmith, one Lt Col Montague John Perreau of Fareham, Surrey.

APPENDIX 4

## ASSAY OFFICE CHARGES FOR ASSAYS

According to the Government Hallmarking Report of 1959, the first reference to paying for assays is contained in the 1700 Act where a sum *not exceeding 6 pence for every pound troy and so proportionately for greater or lesser quantity of plate so assayed and marked* be paid to the assayer. This applied to all assay offices in the land. Section 15 of the 1738 Act details a scale of charges that includes *five farthings (1¼d) for every pair of tea tongs, 3 pence and 3 farthings (3¾d) for a dozen tea-spoons or tea strainers,* etc. Further examples of charges at a later time are shown below.

**1847 Chester Goldsmiths' Company Minutes (MR2/56)**

| | |
|---|---|
| gold watchcase | 9d |
| gold double-bottomed or hunter watchcase | 1s 6d |
| gold or silver watch pendant | 3d |

**1851 Inspector of Stamps Report (MR3/23)**

| | | |
|---|---|---|
| gold watchcase | 1s 6d | |
| gold pendants | 3d | |
| silver watchcase | 4d | |
| silver pendant | 1d | |
| Other articles | 1d | an ounce for silver and 3d for gold. |

**1856 Select Committee Report on Hallmarking**

| | | |
|---|---|---|
| gold watchcases | 1s 6d | |
| gold pendants | 3d | |
| other items | 3d | a piece |

**1957 Parliamentary Report on Hallmarking**

| | | s | d |
|---|---|---|---|
| Gold bracelets and necklets under ¼ ounce | each | 1 | 5 |
| Gold bracelets and necklets under ½ ounce | each | 1 | 9 |
| Gold bracelets and necklets under 1 ounce | each | 2 | 4 |
| Gold bracelets and necklets under 2 ounces | each | 3 | 2 |
| and 6d for every further ounce | | | |
| Gold brooches, buckles, clasps, fancy pins | each | | 9 |
| Gold cases/boxes; cigarette, card, vanity, lighters, etc | each | 1 | 9 |
| Gold chains, Alberts (for watches), dress | each | 3 | 6 |
| Gold pencil cases | each | 1 | 2 |
| Gold pendants, lockets, badges, medals | each | 1 | 0 |
| Gold watchcases under ¼ ounce | each | 1 | 6 |
| Gold watchcases under 1 ounce | each | 2 | 0 |
| Gold watchcases 1 ounce and over | each | 3 | 2 |
| Gold rings | each | | 7 |
| Gold other wares under 1/20 ounce | each | | 5 |
| Gold other wares under ¼ ounce | each | | 7 |
| Gold other wares under ½ ounce | each | 1 | 2 |
| Gold other wares under 1 ounce | each | 1 | 6 |
| Gold other wares under 1½ ounces | each | 1 | 9 |
| Gold other wares under 2 ounces | each | 2 | 0 |
| Gold other wares under 3 ounces | each | 2 | 6 |
| Gold other wares under 5 ounces | each | 3 | 6 |
| and 6d for every further 1 ounce | | | |

*Least parcel of Gold 4s 0d White Gold 3s 0d per parcel extra*

| | | | |
|---|---|---|---|
| Silver wares under ¼ ounce | dozen | 1 | 6 |
| Silver wares under ½ ounce, each of less than three separate pieces | dozen | 1 | 9 |
| Silver wares under ½ ounce, each of three and up to six separate pieces | dozen | 2 | 0 |
| Silver wares under ½ ounce, each of six pieces and over | dozen | 2 | 6 |
| Silver wares ½ ounce and over | ounce | | 5 |
| Silver chain work under ½ ounce | each | | 9 |
| Silver chain work under 1 ounce | each | 1 | 0 |
| Silver chain work over 1 ounce | each | 1 | 6 |

*Least parcel of Silver 3s 6d*

**APPENDIX 5**

## LIVERPOOL WATCHCASE MAKERS

The authors are indebted to Dennis Moore, researcher at the Prescot Clock Museum, Merseyside, for the following information gleaned from records in the Museum and the Bibliography. Some 24 early Liverpool, Merseyside and Chester watchcase makers have been noted working in the 100-year period from 1674, the date of the earliest reference in Liverpool Town records, to 1773, the year in which a Parliamentary Report on Provincial Assay Offices reviewed the status of British goldsmiths and silversmiths and produced a list of craftsmen. The 1773 Report noted that seven Liverpool silversmiths were sending wares to Chester and at least two of these, John Wyke and Thomas Green, were described as watchcase makers. Gabriel Smith, a watchmaker of Chester, was also mentioned in the 1773 report. Not all of the watchcase makers have identifiable maker's marks. The following list shows the watch and case makers with their dates of working:

| | | |
|---|---|---|
| Thomas Barron (Barrow?)<br>Liverpool 1710-42 | Solomon Gibbs, London then<br>Liverpool 1746-? | Roger Prescot<br>Liverpool pre1692-1702 |
| David Beyendorfe, Dublin, London<br>then Liverpool *c.*1760-92 | Thomas Green<br>Liverpool 1773 | Thomas Smalley, Dublin then<br>Liverpool 1725-70 |
| Thomas Boyer<br>Liverpool 1720-27 | John Grimbaldstone<br>Liverpool *c.*1698 | Gabriel Smith<br>Chester 1773 |
| Jonathan Carter<br>Liverpool 1730 | John Hall<br>Liverpool 1745 | William Tarleton<br>Liverpool 1766-1807 |
| Robert Chantrell, West Derby<br>Liverpool 1704-29 | Robert Laithwait<br>Liverpool 1717-45 | Henry Tyrer<br>Liverpool pre1700-4 |
| Joshua Cobham, Dublin then<br>Liverpool 1674-84 | William Laithwait<br>Liverpool 1692-1714 | John Wakefield<br>Liverpool 1769-92 |
| John Eccles<br>Liverpool 1733-96 | Robert Mercer<br>Liverpool 1755 | John Williamson<br>Liverpool 1710-16 |
| Samuel Gerrard<br>Liverpool 1719-51 | John Page<br>Liverpool 1707-? | John Wyke<br>Liverpool pre1773 |

Only a few examples of watchcases have been seen from this early era, and all show just a maker's mark indicating that none of the cases was sent to Chester for assay. However, it is just possible that the raw material silver sheet might have been obtained from reputable sources that guaranteed quality and the assay office may have been involved in checking the bullion raw material. Curiously, no assay office marks have been noted on watchcases before the late eighteenth century even though the Chester/Liverpool area was not exempt from the sporadic searches by the London Goldsmiths' Company who combed the provinces looking for examples of sub-standard wares. Indeed, as early as 1699, watchcase maker William Laithwait was fined by the London Goldsmiths' Company for making sub-standard wares.

The 1773 Parliamentary Report led to the introduction of new assay offices in Birmingham and Sheffield, and all workers within a 20-mile radius of these two towns (later extended to 30 miles) had to use their "local" office. There was no bar against "outsiders" using the new offices as well. The 1773 Report did not force Liverpool watchcase makers to use Chester and there is little evidence for early marked cases. However, the Plate Duty Act of 1st December1784, introduced to raise taxes for the war against France, stipulated that plate should be stamped with the new duty mark and the appropriate duty paid, with severe penalties for non-compliance. The first Plate Duty Book confirms that watchcase makers quickly conformed with the new arrangements. Within the first twelve months of the introduction of the new Tax, nine case makers were submitting wares and a total of 836 cases were assayed, but all did not go well.

Almost immediately the watchcase makers were in trouble with the Chester Goldsmiths' Company. Their Minute Book shows that on 30th July 1785 a letter was sent to twelve Liverpool watchmakers and watchcase makers complaining as follows – *we think it fitting to acquaint you that in future all watchcases sent to this office to be marked must have all the joints and mouldings soldered on. We also recommend that there be no greater quantity of solder about the case than necessary, for provided they appear to be unreasonably loaded, we shall not allow them to be marked.*

The plate duty book shows that almost immediately following the Duty Act, 22-carat gold cases started to be assayed at Chester and by 1798, when duty on cases was repealed, some 84 gold watchcases had been submitted in total. Curiously, none have been seen in museum or private collections. During the same period, 18,321 silver watchcases were assayed. By way of example, William Tarleton, who did so much to foster the art of watch making in Liverpool, and who had advised the 1798 Parliamentary Committee that led to the abolition of the *Timepiece Tax*, submitted 23 gold and 102 silver watchcases during 1785. The following graph shows the extent of watchcase assaying. Note that 1798 shows data for only 4 months. The reduction in volume after the 1792 peak year is probably due to unrest on the Continent with the impending wars with France and later Spain.

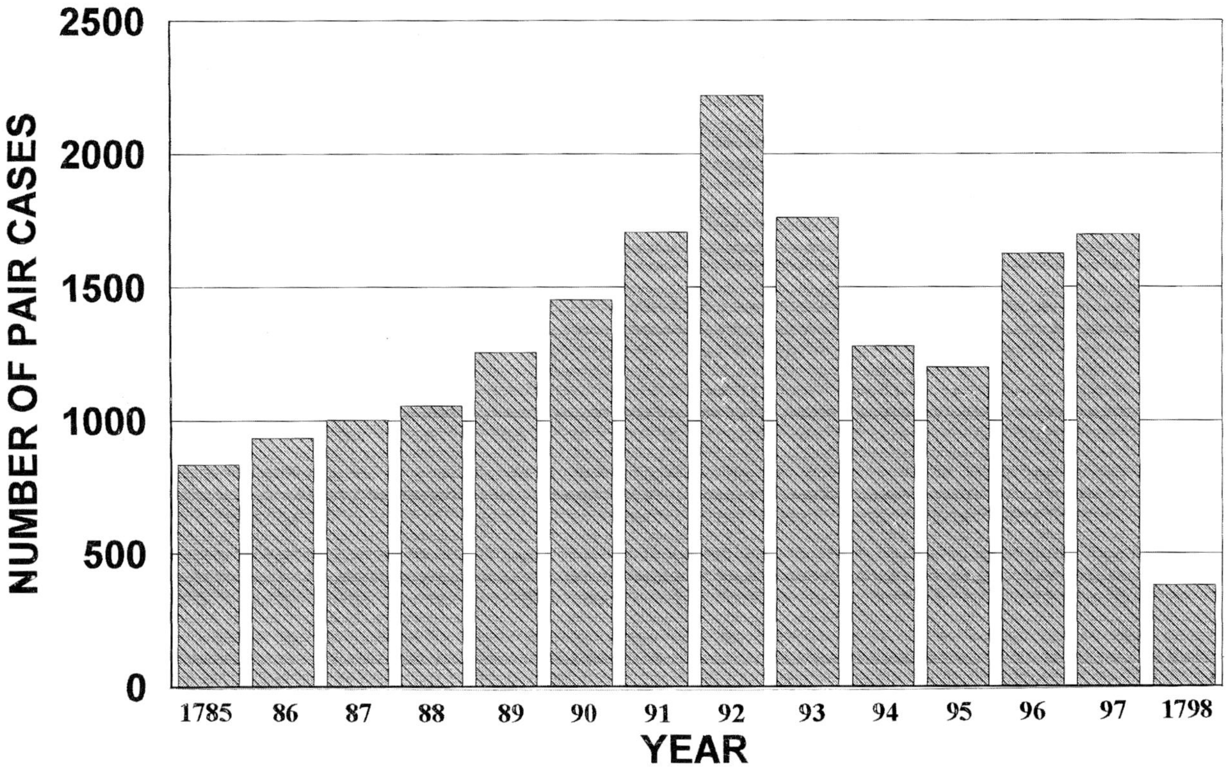


Of particular interest is the fact that three Liverpool case makers in 1789 and a fourth in 1792, transferred their business to Birmingham, but there are no records to explain the incident. Perhaps Chester was becoming too restrictive or it was thought that Birmingham might be more relaxed in their standards. For whatever reason, by 1794/5 these Liverpool makers had returned their business to Chester.

There is an almost sixty year gap in the records before the authorities once again had to castigate the Liverpool watchcase makers as they felt they were attempting to defraud the public. On 11th January 1843 the Company gave further notice – *Some workmen having repeatedly sent to Hall gold and silver watchcases the component parts whereof have been found to differ in goodness and having in some instances resorted to fraudulent schemes of sending parts of a better quality to convey others which are inferior in standard, and the wardens having perceived that some gold case makers after receiving work from the Assay Office, have turned out parts that are good and substituted rims and other parts of a base quality, they think it necessary to give notice that the rims, wires, edges, bottoms and every part must be of the goodness of 22 or 18 carats fine in gold cases and 11 oz 2 pennyweights fine in silver cases that if one part only in gold or silver cases be found deficient in goodness not only that article but every one in the parcel will be defaced and the wardens in discharge of the duty they owe to the public and the fair trader are determined to prosecute all such persons as may be detected in their nefarious practice of changing any parts of their works they have delivered from the Hall...*

A further letter of 9th April 1845 to Ralph Samuel of Liverpool in a similar vein states – *I do hereby give notice that silver work by you on or about the 4th day of this instant sent to the Chester Hall for the purpose of being assayed has after three several assays duly made thereon been found to be of coarser alloy than the standard allowed by law, and is in consequence there of liable to be and will accordingly be cut broken and defaced and in addition thereto you are liable to certain pecuniary and other penalties.*

In 1854 new grades of 9-, 12- and 15- carat gold were introduced and the Act also removed the 30 mile geographical restrictions around Birmingham and Sheffield. As a consequence the Coventry watchcase makers and indeed some of the Birmingham watchcase makers gradually started to transfer business to Chester which led to a marked increase in activity there. A House of Commons Select Committee was established in 1856 to review the future of provincial offices. They were also anxious to discover the truth behind accusations that some wares were being incorrectly assayed, and that false punches were in use on gold wares at Liverpool. It was thought the Act of 1854 was partly responsible for dishonesty in the trade, and Mr Ralph Samuel and Mr John Lowe gave valuable evidence to the Committee.

Ralph Samuel informed the Committee that he was a manufacturer of both gold and silver watchcases, and had been so occupied for the past 25 years. He had in fact virtually monopolised the Liverpool trade for many years. Almost all his work was sent to Chester for assay and the Chester mark was looked upon as the "hallmark" of Liverpool quality. The Chester mark signified to the trade that the watch was of "Liverpool character", and thus had a world-wide reputation, especially in North and South America and in certain manufacturing districts in England. This world reputation for such "Liverpool" cases, having watch movements of equal reputation, made Mr Samuel claim that even if the latter were housed in London assayed cases, they would not have the same market value except in Scotland, where for some reason London watches were deemed preferable. Indeed, Mr Samuel also mentioned he had had orders from some distance, quoting a Mr Kelvey of Gainsborough, Lincolnshire, who felt compelled to have his watches assayed with the so called Liverpool mark.

Ralph Samuel reported that a great many uncased watches or movements were being sent to America where they were encased in gold cases, many of which bore fraudulently forged London and Chester marks and were punched with an 18-carat mark upon 9-carat gold. The bulk of the English trade with the United States was in uncased movements, but a considerable trade was also done in silver watches. Because of the high price of labour in the States it was more profitable for them to concentrate on gold case making. Contrary to the expectations of those who had brought about the 1854 Act, which had lowered the standard of gold, it had not helped the Liverpool gold case makers to compete favourably with those in America. The Americans who had visited Liverpool were willing to place large orders for lower standard gold cases providing that an 18-carat mark could be placed upon them. This Mr Samuel refused to do. His statement is a curious one, for it was the legal requirement for the Chester Assay Office alone to put on the 18-carat and 9-carat marks upon a gold watchcase. It is to his credit that he refused to become party to the fraud. That the Americans were capable of perpetrating the fraud themselves seems clear for they sent fraudulent watches to Australia, where successful gold diggers welcomed them as luxury items. Havana, Buenos Aires, Montevideo, Rio de Janeiro and Pernambucco were additional important markets for such watches. The Committee was told that previous to the "panic in Melbourne", Mr Samuel had enormous trade with Australia sending parcels of 300, 400 and 500 watches at a time.

At the time he himself had shipped £8,000 worth of watches and jewellery and he claimed to be the largest manufacturer in the world, making 200 gold and 400 silver watchcases a week. Had the Liverpool watchcase makers been prepared to do as the Americans had asked, the 1,000 or 2,000 watch movements which were going to America weekly, would go out with watchcases, but Mr Samuel refused to supply unmarked cases for the American market.

The following table shows the extent of watchcase business from 1865 to 1887; unfortunately the import data is incomplete. The units are in troy ounces.

| DATE | GOLD CASES | | SILVER CASES | |
|---|---|---|---|---|
| | HOME | IMPORT | HOME | IMPORT |
| 1865 | 15699 | | 22303 | |
| 1866 | 13504 | | 16216 | |
| 1867 | 10499 | | 17023 | |
| 1868 | 11446 | | 17345 | |
| 1869 | 10858 | | 15583 | |
| 1870 | 12050 | | 14763 | |
| 1871 | 12549 | | 18395 | |
| 1872 | 12919 | | 28993 | |
| 1873 | 12503 | | 36423 | |
| 1874 | 11987 | | 34584 | |
| 1875 | 11595 | | 25776 | |
| 1876 | 10728 | 395 | 24618 | 10224 |
| 1877 | 10189 | 1065 | 24651 | 20704 |
| 1878 | 9429 | 571 | 43345 | 12651 |
| 1879 | 8760 | 1586 | 39262 | 10738 |
| 1880 | 3870 | 1624 | 39653 | 8347 |
| 1881 | 4541 | 1642 | 20158 | 16691 |
| 1882 | 5368 | 347 | 24755 | 8890 |
| 1883 | 4341 | 386 | 29046 | 16322 |
| 1884 | 3369 | 136 | 27680 | 10801 |
| 1885 | 3153 | 39 | 22381 | 7870 |
| 1886 | 2520 | 62 | 19746 | 4470 |
| 1887 | 3334 | 760 | 26257 | 7418 |

# THIMBLE MAKERS

The following data is extracted from *Thimble – Notes and Queries, Number 14,* Spring 1992, published by Edwin F Holmes, and is printed with permission. An enquiry regarding thimbles yielded particulars regarding nearly 700 thimbles with Chester assay marks, a sample considered to be representative of what was happening at Chester. By far the largest number proved to have the mark of Charles Horner, who set up as a thimble manufacturer in Halifax about 1885. The earliest reference to Charles Horner is in the Large Punch Book of Chester Assay Office covering the period 1877 to 1886 where there is an entry dated 2nd December 1884 with the address listed as 21/23 Mortley Street, Halifax. Curiously, there is no mark punched alongside the entry, the book having sheets of tin metal covered with cartridge paper, but there is an unnumbered **C.H** mark in oblong cameo surround on the first line of square H of the 1883 Plate 5 which matches quite well regarding time-frame. There is a framed **CH** incuse mark (number 299) on Plate 5 *c.*1890 which matches a similar mark entered at Birmingham in 1903. The details for this entry are assumed to be in the missing register of 1886 to 1894. The third entry dated 1903, in Register 1, and further listings continue to 1946. His mark was seen on 427 thimbles representing 60% of the sample.

Henry Griffith & Sons of Birmingham was another large manufacturer who made thimbles both for themselves and for their associated company James Walker Ltd. There are three **HG&S** cameo marks dating from about 1887 to 1890 on the 1883 plate but all their corresponding entries are in the missing register. The fourth Chester entry for this company is an HG&SLTD cameo mark entered 1898, with further entries up to 1954. Henry Griffith normally sent their wares to Birmingham but when the latter had too much work, they sometimes resorted to Chester which was open on more days of the week and regularly took Birmingham's excess work. James Walker Ltd entered their first mark at Chester in 1922 and continued until 1929. There were 98 thimbles bearing a Henry Griffith or James Walker mark, representing 14% of the total. The remaining 130 thimbles (26%) involved 41 different makers' marks, only two of which surprisingly have been identified as thimble makers, namely James Swann and Samuel Foskett. In addition, the Chester records show George Snook & Co and James Fenton both of Birmingham as thimble manufacturers.

It had long been suspected that the larger thimble manufacturers must have supplied other firms, but the extent was larger than expected. The figures imply that about 20% of Charles Horner's production of silver thimbles was sold on to wholesale jewellers and manufacturing silversmiths wanting to supply their customers under their own name. We do not know who struck the marks. It is unlikely that Horners held punches belonging to other silversmiths, but it is possible that the retailers had their punches held at Chester to await shipment of thimbles either directly from Horner's or via Horner's agents. Priestley has analysed the Chester Assay Office registers and has noted that Charles Horner entered punches and company details for some 30 other companies, implying quite a strong and widespread relationship between Horner's and the silversmiths they supplied. These included A J Davenport, Henry Charles Freeman, William Harrison Walter, Charles Boyton & Son, Cropp & Farr, Gourdel, Vales & Co, Henry W Gleeson, H Williamson Ltd, Hardy Brothers, Murrle, Bennett & Co, Meyer & Meyer, Mulland & Upcott and Tozer Kemsley Fisher Ltd of London; Abrahall & Bint, Horton & Allday, Thomas & Thomas, Alfred Constantine, Messrs Constantine & Floyd, J Cooke & Sons Ltd, J Horton & Son, Payton, Pepper & Son Ltd, Steinhart & Co, Marks & Cohen and Thomas & Marshall of Birmingham; Eustace George Parker of Altrincham; Hirst Brothers & Co Ltd of Oldham; Hall & Fitzgerald of Bristol; John Henry Potter of Sheffield; Wengold Brothers of Manchester and W H Hunt of Liverpool.

It is unfortunate that many of the thimbles have dates falling within the *missing register* period of 1886 to 1894. However, quite a large proportion have been identified by comparison with records in London, Birmingham and Sheffield assay offices. The following table, derived by Priestley and based upon the article, shows marks, recorded dates and possible attributions for the 130 thimbles which comprised 26 % of the total in the survey.

| | | |
|---|---|---|
| **A.B&Co**<br>oblong | 1898-<br>1909 | **A Bromet & Co**<br>London |
| **AS** joined<br>diamonds | 1907 | **Albert Sydenham**<br>Birmingham |
| **C&SLtd**<br>oblong | 1909 | Unidentified |
| **CS.FS**<br>oblong | 1902,<br>1903 | **Saunders & Shepherd**<br>Birmingham |
| **DF**<br>? | 1898 | **Deeley&Fisher** or<br>**Deakin&Francis**,B'ham |
| **E.G.P**<br>oblong | 1900,<br>1903 | **Eustace Parker**<br>Altrincham |
| **G.G**<br>oblong | 1893 | **George Goodman**<br>Birmingham |
| **G&S**<br>? | 1892 | **Garner & Stevens**<br>Manchester |
| **GWH&Co**<br>incuse | 1892-<br>1917 | Unidentified |
| **HJC**<br>oblong | 1910 | **H J Cooper**<br>London |
| **H&T**<br>oblong | 1895,<br>1900 | **Hilliard &**<br>**Thomason**, Birmingham |
| **H.W.D**<br>oblong | 1895 | **H Williamson** ?<br>HWLTD possibly? |
| **H.W.LTD**<br>oblong | 1889-<br>1913 | **Henry Williamson**<br>**Ltd**, London |
| **I.S&Co**<br>oblong | 1897 | **Isaac Silverston**<br>Birmingham |

| | | |
|---|---|---|
| **J.C**<br>oblong | 1886 | Unidentified |
| **J.C&S**<br>incuse | 1909 | **J Cooke & Son Ltd**<br>Birmingham |
| **J. S**<br>oblong | 1892-<br>1901 | **James Swann**<br>Birmingham |
| **JT**<br>oblong | 1895 | **James Thornton**<br>Birmingham |
| **JT&S**<br>curved | 1890-<br>1906 | **John Thompson &**<br>**Son**, London |
| **M&C**<br>oblong | 1905 | **Marks & Cohen**<br>Birmingham |
| **MN&Co**<br>oblong | 1900-<br>1906 | **Marion & Co**<br>London |
| **O.A.&S**<br>oblong | 1900,<br>1903 | **Olney Amsden & Sons**<br>London |
| **O&E**<br>hour-glass | 1894,<br>1895 | Unidentified |
| **RP**<br>shield | 1898-<br>1915 | **Robert Pringle &**<br>**Sons**, London |
| **RP**<br>oblong | 1906,<br>1907 | **Robert Pringle &**<br>**Sons**, London |
| **S.Bros**<br>oblong | 1896,<br>1900 | **Smith Brothers**<br>Birmingham |
| **S&C** | 1909 | No SC at Chester<br>S&G? or S&Co? |
| **S&Co**<br>? | 1905 | **Steinhart & Co**<br>Birmingham |

| | | |
|---|---|---|
| **SF**<br>oblong | 1889,<br>1890 | **Samuel Foskett**<br>London |
| **S&G**<br>? | 1904 | **Salmon & Gluckstein**<br>London |
| **SG&S**<br>oblong | 1921 | Unidentified |
| **S.J&Co**<br>ellipse | 1897,<br>1893 | Not a Chester mark |
| **ST**<br>? | 1893 | **Stephen Tree**<br>London |
| **TBs**<br>oblong | 1894-<br>1911 | **Turner Brothers**<br>Birmingham |
| **T.M**<br>oblong | 1886 | **Thomas Morrell**<br>Birmingham |
| **T&S**<br>oblong | 1903 | **Tandy & Son**<br>Birmingham |
| **W.G.M**<br>? | nil | **Walter & George**<br>**Myers**, Birmingham |
| **WH**<br>oblong | 1894-<br>1900 | Unidentified |
| **WHC**<br>incuse | 1908 | **W H Collins & Co Ltd**<br>Birmingham |
| **WHW**<br>oblong | 1893-<br>1906 | **William H Walter**<br>London |
| **W.J.H**<br>oblong | 1901,<br>1903 | **William J Holmes**<br>Birmingham |
| | | |

## ADDENDA TO PREVIOUS RIDGWAY PUBLICATIONS

**A P** in shaped cameos ***#9795*** (*Chester Goldsmiths* pages 158-9, and *Chester Silver 1727-1837* page 220)

It appears that the type 2 ornamental shield cameo mark seen on a spoon in the Breadalbane Collection is only listed by Jackson and has not been identified by modern researchers. It is possible it is identical to that listed here as type 3b on a mug of 1697-1701. It should also be noted that type 3a mark in a plain shield mark (recently noted) on the mug is not identical to the type 1 mark seen on a cupping bowl and taper stick.

**D K** in oblong cameo ***# 9852*** (*Chester Silver 1727-1837* pages 133, 188 and 228)

This mark seen on a marrow scoop marked for 1742 and previously identified as possibly D K for Daniel Kirkes of Chester is now considered to be J R and probably ascribed to a John Richardson, possibly the one who entered a mark at London in 1752. The John Richardson listed in the Chester Goldsmiths' Company records as a Brother in 1770 may be too late.

**P C** incuse ***#6292*** (*Chester Goldsmiths* page 34)

These incuse letters on a paten cover in Pott Shrigley Church are now thought to be for Pott Chapel being the precursor church at Pott Shrigley, Cheshire. The attribution to Peter Conway in the last quarter of the sixteenth century seems less likely, particularly since the majority of early makers' punch marks are of the cameo type.

**R i** in diamond-shaped cameo ***#6815*** (*Chester Goldsmiths* pages 160 and 168)

A 1999 revisiting of the type 1a mark on the communion cup at Llanerchymedd Parish Church, Anglesey, reveals that the mark is actually a worn type 3 ornamental shield cameo mark and so type 1a is now considered erroneous.

**S B** incuse # *7552* (*Chester Silver 1727-1837* page 59 and *Chester Silver 1837-1962* page 78)

A recent book on Cheshire Clockmakers shows that Samuel Bryans is actually Samuel Bryars, a Chester watchmaker and jeweller, and that Bryans is a misreading of the entry in the Chester Plate Duty Book.

**TA** pellet after T and A in an escutcheon cameo ***#8134-8*** (*Chester Silver 1837-1962* page 76)

Previously ascribed by Jackson and Ridgway to Thomas Appleby, is now considered to be Thomas Armitt of Manchester, based upon the masonic medal entries in the Plate Duty Book.

**T H** pellet between in oblong cameo ***#8284*** (*Chester Silver 1727-1837* page 87 and *Chester Silver 1837-1962* page 86)

This mark noted on a skewer and spoon of 1787 does not have a pellet between as shown in the above reference and Pickford's Jackson. Rather, the pellet is a remnant of an elongated serif from the right-hand top of the letter "T". The correct mark as shown in the *Compendium* is without pellet and perfectly matches the similar mark punched in square 24 of Plate 1.

## ADDENDA TO PRIESTLEY PUBLICATION *Watchcase Makers of England 1720-1920*

**Gabriel Smith** ***#3014*** (PP1/187)

Jackson has him working 1752 to 1796 and he is mentioned as a watchmaker in the 1773 Parliamentary Report on Assay Offices. No corresponding **G S** maker's mark on plate 1 or entry in Plate Duty Book has yet been found. Possibly also made watchcases.

**I H** pellet between in oblong cameo ***#4173*** (PP1/187)

Probably the mark of Isaac Hadwine working 1766 to 1818 and mentioned in the Plate Duty Book in 1792 when he submitted 45 gold rings. Probably a jeweller who sold goldware and silverware plus watches and clocks, but he cannot be considered a watchcase maker.

**J H over A H** in oblong cameo ***#4869-71*** (New mark for PP1)

New mark for Joseph and Abraham Harris, watchmakers of 28 Berry Street, Liverpool.

**R B** in oblong cameo ***#6637-40*** (PP1/ 188)

Jackson reports seeing this mark on a 1787 watchcase and suggested Robert Boulger but this mark may actually be for Robert Bowers of Chester who is mentioned several times in the Plate Duty Book as a general silversmith. The **RB** incuse mark in square 26 of Plate 1 is likely to be that of Richard Boulger, recorded as a watchcase maker of Liverpool when he married in 1784.

**R G** in oblong cameo ***#6782,3*** (PP1/188)

Recorded by Jackson on a 1799 watch and ascribed to Robert Green of Liverpool. According to the Plate Duty Book he submitted gold rings, skewers, cups and other household items between 1791 and 1803, but no watchcases before 1789 when duty on cases was repealed. He may not have been a mainstream watchcase maker.

**R I** pellet between in oblong cameo ***#6822*** (PP1/188)

Noted by Jackson on 1788 and 1798 watchcases and is probably for Robert Jones. Jackson shows a sovereign's head duty mark against this item but the expected entry does not appear in the Plate Duty Book. There are watchcase entries for another maker on a line adjacent to Jones's entry for flatware in the Plate Duty Book. Jones normally submitted knife blades, forks, skewers, etc, and so this watchcase may have been made by someone else or Jackson recorded the wrong information. It is unlikely that Jones was a watchcase maker.

**T A** pellet after T and A in escutcheon cameo ***#8134-8*** (PP1/189)

Jackson records this mark for Thomas Appleby of Manchester on a watchcase of 1793 with a duty mark, but there is no corresponding entry in the plate duty book. His only entry in the PDB is for gold rings and buttons in 1791. He cannot be considered a watchcase maker. It is now thought this mark best fits Thomas Armitt of Manchester who submitted Masonic medals. See also entry in Appendix 7.

**T H** in oblong cameo ***#8279-81*** (PP1/189)

This mark in square 17 of Plate 1 is probably not attributable to Thomas Helsby in view of his confirmed incuse and oval cameo marks. It may be earlier than 1800 and may be more safely attributed to watchcase maker Thomas Harrison, working in Liverpool 1774-1803.

**T H** in oval cameo ***#8304-6*** (PP1/189)

There are two variants of this mark in square 26 of Plate 1. The one with the tops of the letters in line with one another has been seen on a watchcase marked for 1792 which matches with Thomas Helsby's first entry in the PDB for 29th April 1793. The other version with the top of the "H" slightly above that of the "T" may be the mark of Thomas Hill who submitted gold rings and silver cutlery 1788 to 1789.

**T M** in oblong cameo ***#8414-6*** (PP1/189)

Jackson records this mark for Thomas Morrow on a 1795 watchcase. There is no corresponding entry in the Plate Duty Book but Morrow did submit gold buttons in 1795. He cannot now be considered a watchcase maker.

**V & H** in oblong cameo ***#8719-21*** (PP1/189)

This newly (1999) observed mark only recently deciphered on Plate 1 is conjectured to be V&H for Vale and Howlette, partners in Vale, Howlette and Carr and Vale & Co (1754 to 1790), and precursors of Vale & Rotherham and Rotherham & Son, watch and watchcase makers of Spon Street, Coventry.

**W T** copper plate script incuse ***#9666*** (New mark for PP1)

Newly identified mark for William Tarleton, watchmaker and watchcase maker of Bixteth Street and Lime Street, Liverpool.

# BIBLIOGRAPHY


Appleby, K — *Clockmakers of Cheshire*, Farmhouse Antiques, Boughton, Cheshire, 1999.

Baillie, G H — *Watch & Clockmakers of the World Volume1*, 3rd edition, National Association of Goldsmiths (NAG) Press Ltd, London, 1976.

Boughton, P — *Catalogue of Chester Silver in the Grosvenor Museum, Chester*, Phillimore & Co Ltd, 2000.

Bradbury, F — *History of Old Sheffield Plate*, reprint by J W Northend Ltd, Sheffield, 1968.

Chester Festival Silver Exhibition — *Catalogue of Silver from Chester and other areas including London on Exhibition at the Grosvenor Museum, Chester*, 1973.

Chester Silver Exhibition — *Catalogue of the Chester Silver Exhibition*, held at Sotheby's, Booth Mansion, Watergate Street, Chester, in conjunction with the Grosvenor Museum, 1984.

Cripps, W J — *Old English Plate*, 11th edition, John Murray, London, 1926.

Crisp Jones, K — *The Silversmiths of Birmingham and their marks 1750-1980*, NAG Press, London, 1981.

Culme, John — *Directory of Gold & Silversmiths, Jewellers & Allied Trades 1838-1914, volumes 1 & 2*, Antique Collectors' Club, Woodbridge, Suffolk, 1987.

De Castro, J Paul — *The Law & Practice of Hallmarking Gold & Silver Wares*, 2nd edition, The Technical Press Ltd, London, 1935.

Elmers, C — *The Impact of the 1797 (Timepiece) Tax on Clocks & Watches on the London Trade*, Collectanea Londinensia, Studies in London Archaeology, Special paper No 2, LAMAS, 1978.

Forbes, J S — *Hallmarks – A history of the London Assay Office*, Unicorn Press, London, 1998.

Gill, Dr Margaret — *A Dictionary of Newcastle Goldsmiths*, self-published 1976.

Grimwade, A — *London Goldsmiths 1697-1837*, 2nd edition, Faber & Faber, London, 1982.

Hare, Susan — *Touching Gold & Silver - 500 Years of Hallmarks*, catalogue of a silver exhibition at the Goldsmiths' Hall, London, 1978.

Jackson, Sir C J — *Silver & Gold marks*, 3rd edition edited by Ian Pickford, Antique Collectors' Club, Suffolk, 1989.

Kemp, Dr R — *The Fusee Lever Watch*, John Sherratt & Son Ltd, Altrincham, 1981.

Kochmann, Karl — *Clock & Watch Trademark Index – European Origin*, 2nd edition Antique Clocks Publishing, Concord, California, USA, 1988.

Loomes, Brian — *Watchmakers & Clockmakers of the World Volume 2*, 2nd edition, NAG Press Limited, Colchester, 1989.

Loomes, Brian — *Clockmakers of Northern England*, Mayfield Books, Ashbourne, Derbyshire, 1997.

Lutschaunig, Alfred — *The Book of Hallmarks by the Manager of the Liverpool Assay Office*, J C Hotten, London, 1872.

Mason, Sheena — *Jewellery Making in Birmingham 1750-1995*, Phillimore & Co Ltd, 1998.

McKenna, Joseph — *Clockmakers and Watchmakers of Central England*, Mayfield Books, Ashbourne, Derbyshire, 2002.

Moore, D S and Priestley, P T — *Some Account of Liverpool Watchcase Makers 1785 to 1798*, Antiquarian Horology Journal, Summer 1997.

Prideaux, Sir W S — *Memorials of the Goldsmiths' Company, Extracts of Records 1335-1815*, Eyre & Spottiswoode, London, 1815.

Priestley, P T — *Watchcase Makers of England 1720 to 1920, Bulletin Supplement #20*, National Association of Watch and Clock Collectors (NAWCC), Columbia, Pennsylvania, USA, 1994.

Priestley, P T — *Early Watchcase Makers of England 1631 to 1720, Special Order Supplement #3*, NAWCC, USA, 2000.

Richardson, Jacqueline — *The Sheffield Assay Office Register*, 2nd edition, J W Northend Limited, Sheffield, 1989.

Ridgway, M H — *Chester Goldsmiths from early times to 1726*, John Sherratt & Son Ltd, Altrincham, 1968.

Ridgway, M H — *Chester Silver 1727 to 1837*, Phillimore & Co Ltd, Chichester, West Sussex, 1985.

Ridgway, M H — *Chester Silver 1837 to 1962*, Gee & Son (Denbigh) Ltd, Denbigh, Wales, 1996.

Ridgway, M H — *Church Plate of the St. Asaph Diocese*, Gee & Son (Denbigh) Ltd, Denbigh, Wales, 1997.

Stuart, W G — *Watch & Clockmakers of Ireland*, June Stuart & David A Boles, Celbridge and Dublin, Ireland, 2000.

Tann, Jennifer — *The Birmingham Assay Office 1773-1993*, Assay Office, 1993.

Wadsworth, F — *1996 Facsimile of the London Goldsmiths, Silversmiths, Jewellers, Watchmakers, Opticians & Cutlers Directory, including details of companies in Birmingham, Coventry, Liverpool, Sheffield and Manchester.* Originally published by Collinson & Co, London, 1861.

Wilson R E — *A History of the Sheffield Smelting Company Limited 1760-1960*, Ernest Benn Ltd, London, 1960.

Withers, P and B — *British Coin Weights*, Galata Print Limited, Llanfyllin, Wales, 1993.

# SUBJECT INDEX


Abbreviations key to vi
Acknowledgements vii
Addenda to Maurice Ridgway volumes 501
Addenda to Philip Priestley volumes 502
America, trade with 499
Assay marks, fraudulent 499
Assay Office – Chester 1
Assay Office agencies xii, 495
Assay Office charges 496
Assay Office expenses 494
Assay Office Master(s) xi, xiii
Assay Office premises xi, 494
Assay Office punches xxi
Assay Office registrations – final xxii, 495
Assay Office registrations – overview 492
Assay Office salaries 494, 495
Bibliography 503
Birmingham Assay Office vii, xi
Birmingham Agency 495
Britannia silver marks x, 8
Charles II ix
Charters, Ordinances, Statutes
 1200 Guild Charter ix
 1300 Leopard's head statute 9
 1363 Maker's mark Ordinance 9
 1477 18-carat gold 9
 1576 22-carat gold 9
 1687 Statement – Goldsmiths' ix, x, 1, 7
 1697 Britannia silver x, 1, 8
 1701 Chester Assay Office x, 1
 1720 Sterling silver and Duty 7, 8, 10
 1784 Plate Duty Act 10
 1798 18-carat gold mark 11
 1798 watchcase duty repealed 11
 1820 Memorandum x
 1844 22-carat gold mark 11
 1854 15-, 12- and 9-carat gold mark xi
 1867 Import "F" mark 13
 1887 Foreign Duty mark 13
 1890 Plate Duty repealed 10
 1904 Import City mark 13, 14
 1932 14-carat gold mark 12
Chester Goldsmiths' Company – Arms Title Page
Chester Goldsmiths' & Watchmakers' Company ix
Civil War ix
Coat of Arms – Chester 7
Coinage – Chester ix
Contents v
Copper (metal) plates x, xi, xv
Copper plates – list of xiv
Copper plate – first xvii
Copper plate – second xviii
Copper plate – third xix
Copper plate – last xx, xxi
Crest – Chester 7
Date Letters x, 1–6
Diocese of Chester ix
Duty Allowances 10
Duty marks 7, 10
Duty Drawback mark 10
Earl of Chester ix
Fake marks 14
Foreword viii
Gold marks – general 11
 22 carat 11
 18 carat 11
 15 carat 11
 14 carat 12
 12 carat 11
 9 carat 11
Grosvenor Museum – Chester vii, xiv
Guilds ix
Historical Background ix
Horner, Charles 500
Imported wares marks 13, 14
Inspector General of Stamps xi, 10, 494
Large Punch Book xiv, xv
Lead ingots ix
Legeceastre – Roman Chester ix
Leopard's head mark 1, 9
Lion Passant mark x, 1, 8
Lion's head erased mark 8
Liverpool Assay Office xii
Liverpool trade 498, 499
Liverpool watchcase makers 497, 498, 499
Liverpool watchcases, volumes 498
Liverpool "hallmark" 499
London Goldsmiths' Company ix, xii
Makers' marks tables 20 onwards
Makers' marks tables – how to use 17, 18
Makers' marks tables – pictograms 19
Mint – Chester ix, x
Minute Books – Chester xv
Miscellaneous records xvi
Missing Register xvi
Moneyers – Chester ix
Ordinances (see Charters)
Photographs/plates xvii – xxii
Photography vii
Plate Duty Books xi, xiv, xv
Platinum 12
Registers – Chester Assay Office ix, xiv, xvi
Registers – Chester Goldsmiths' Company xiv
River Dee ix
Samuel, Ralph 498, 499
Sheriff of Chester ix
Small Punch Book xiv, xv
Spurious marks 14
Statutes (see Charters)
Sterling silver marks – unofficial 1
Stone Parliamentary Report xii
Sub-standard wares x, 14
Thimble makers and marks 500
Touch of Paris 9
Town/City mark 1, 7
Trade descriptions 18
Volumes of Gold & Silver Wares assayed 493
Wardens x
Watchcase marks 12, 13
Watchcase makers, admonishment 498
Watchcases, sub-standard 498

Aarons, Isidore **297**
Aarons, S **393**
Abbott & Jones **37**
Abbott, George Smith **159**
Abbott, Henry Charles **186**
Abbott, Ines Miss **219**
Abbott, John **232**
Abel & Katz **40**
Abelman, Solomon **375**
Abelson Brothers **24**
Abelson, George **24**
Abelson, Maurice & Co **307**
Abelson, Myer **24**
Able & Charnell **25, 26, 27**
Able, T *243*
Able, Thomas **23, 25, 26, 403**
Abrahall & Bint **21, 22, 23**
Abrahall, Arthur John **21, 22, 23**
Abrahall, John & Co **231, 232**
Abrahams Brothers **24**
Abrahams, Abraham Levi **29**
Abrahams, Barnett H **62**
Abrahams, Barnett Henry **62**
Abrahams, D **45**
Abrahams, Henry Clarence **62**
Abrahams, J **45**
Abrahams, Joseph **41, 375**
Abrahams, Joseph Henry **62**
Abrahams, Percy Abel **24**
Abrahams, Samuel & Sons **41, 375**
Abrahams, Selwyn Arthur **376**
Ackers, Harry **182**
Acott, Thomas & Co **403**, *447*
Accurist Watches Ltd **54**
Adams, Charles **184, 185**
Adams, Charles Edward **80, 232**, *389*
Adams, F H & Co **146**, *198*
Adams, George **73**
Adams, Herbert Edw Hooper **433**
Adams, James **232**
Adams, W E **433**
Adams, W Ltd **433**
Adams, Walker George **433**
Adams, William **433**
Adams, William Henry **232, 453**
Adams, William Ltd **433**
Adamson, Henry **218**
Adamson, Hugh **182**
Adamson, John **219, 232**
Adamson, John & Son **219**
Adamson, Richard **346**
Adamson, Robert **346**
Adamson, Thomas **403**
Adderley, Frank **307**
Adelman & Broadhead **22**, *43*, **119**, *272*
Adelman, Joseph **22, 119, 231, 232,** *272, 279, 393*
Adie & Lovekin *350*
Adie & Lovekin Ltd **42**
Adie Brothers *116, 135, 215*, **484**
Adie Brothers Ltd *483*
Adie, Herbert William **135, 484**
Adie, Percy James (James Percy) **484**
Adkins, Edward Joseph **234**
Adkins, J & Co **234**
Ahronsberg & Co **382**
Ahronsberg Brothers **24, 383**
Ahronsberg, Albert **24, 382, 383**
Ahronsberg, J *149*, **219**
Ahronsberg, Judah **24, 383**
Ahronsberg, Judas **382**
Ahronsberg, Lionel **24, 382, 383**
Ahronsberg, Sydney **383**
Ainsworth, Anne Helen **35**
Ainsworth, B **56**
Aitchison, James **29**
Aitken, William *62, 109, 110, 112, 124, 157*, **158**, *197, 224, 228, 262, 265, 342, 399*, **433, 434**, *447, 469, 474, 480*
Aitkin, J & Son **234**
Aitkin, Joseph **234**
Aitkin, Thomas Edward **407**
Aitchison & Co **29**
Akerman & Son **29**
Akermann & Co **29**, *77, 329, 330*
Alabaster & Wilson **51**
Albion Chain Co **27, 28, 36, 37**, *201, 289*
Albury Brothers **24**
Albury, Albert **24**
Albury, Judah **24**
Aldcroft, James **231**
Alexander & Lawson **41**
Alexander Clark Co Ltd **29**
Alexander, Charles **346**
Alexander, Samuel **375**
Alexander, William **41**
Allardice, Frank **140**
Allardice, J **140**
Allday & Allday *20, 231*
Allday, Harry **182, 183**
Allday, John **234**
Allday, John & Son **20, 231**
Allday, John & Son Ltd **234**
Allen & Co *30, 320*
Allen & Martin **44**
Allen Brothers **24**, *208, 287, 389*
Allen, Charles **73, 485**
Allen, Frank **140**
Allen, Frederick *44*
Allen, George Leonard **172, 173**
Allen, George Robert **24**
Allen, Henry **183**
Allen, Madeline Jane **307**
Allen, Richard Hooper **24**
Allen, Walter **433**
Allen, William Robert **356**
Allman Pipe Co, The **117**
Allman, David William **117**
Almond, Edward **118**
Alterman & Watson **54**
Alterman, Izek **54**
Ames, Albert Arthur **20**
Amon, Lewis **270**
Amsden, Ernest **328**
Amsden, Frank **328**
Amsden, Frederick William **328**
Amsden, Stanley **328**
Anderson & Son **47, 48**
Anderson, Andrew A **47, 48**
Anderson, Arthur Angus **20**
Anderson, David *440*
Anderson, Eric Gordon **118**
Andrews Corporated Watch Co Ld **55**
Andrews, Alfred Mathew **50**
Andrews, Alfred Nathan **51**
Andrews, Alice **50**
Andrews, Harry Stanley **51**
Andrews, Stanley **50**
Andrews, William **55**
Anglo-Orient Trading Co **45**
Apperley, Alfred Sir **428**
Apperley, Charles A **428**
Appleby, Alfred & Co Ltd **20**
Appleby, Joseph **231**
Appleby, Thomas **403**
Appleby, William Henry **243**
Archer, Ernest Albert **346**
Archer, F **140**
Archer, R & Son **182**, *264*, **346**
Archer, Reuben **346**
Arkinstall, H **182**
Arkinstall, Herbert **157**
Arley, Frederick W **157**
Armitt, Thomas **403**
Armstrong, John & Joseph **231**
Armstrong, Thomas & Brother **403**
Arnott, Thomas R *89, 419*, **421**
Aron Brothers **20**
Aron, Adolphe **20**
Aron, Albert **20**
Aron, Ernest **20**
Aronson, George **375, 376**
Aronson, George Alfred **346**
Aronson, Samuel **346**
Aronson, Saul Philip **346, 397**
Arrowsmith, Alfred Robert **47**
Arrowsmith, Edwin Clement **120**
Ash, William Henry **453**
Ashford, Albert **20**
Ashford, J E **320**
Ashford, John **234**
Ashford, H W **215**, *279*
Ashford, William Henry *49, 84, 120, 122, 124, 129, 297, 378*, **453**
Ashforth, John E **246**
Ashling, George Gilbert **48**
Ashton, Cyril F **66**
Ashton, J F **248**
Ashton, J F Ltd **248**
Ashton, John **208**
Ashwin, John **216**
Asprey & Co **29, 42**
Asprey & Co Ltd **29, 42**
Asprey, Charles George **29**
Asprey, Geo Edward **29**
Asprey, Geo Kenneth **29**
Asprey, Lionel Chas **29**
Asprey, Philip Rolls **29**
Asprey, William Leonard **433**
Assay Office Birm'ham **16, 212**, *480*
Assinder, G F **383**
Astell, Henry Alfred **183**
Aston, H Ltd **182**
Aston, Henry Hyde **182**
Aston, T E *403*
Aston, Thomas & Son **403**
Atker, J **231**
Atkin Brothers (Silversmiths) Ltd **182**
Atkin, Harold J **182**
Atkin, Harry **182**
Atkins & Wigley **52**
Atkins, Chas Herbert **52**
Atkins, J **231**
Atkins, J & Son **234**
Atkins, Joseph **234**
Auld, W **407**
Aunsberg, Merton **62**
Aunsberg, Rebecca **62**
Attrow Jewellery **37**
Atyer, Mary Joyce **316**
Austin, Ambrose Platt **49**
Avery, Charles Robert **97**
Avison, Donald **485**

Bachmer, Morris **308**
Bacon & Bill **57**, *155*, **390**, *447, 473*
Bacon, Charles Walter **57**
Bacon, William Charles **439**
Bacchus & Whitehouse **72**
Bacchus, Bernard Chas **59, 72**
Bailey, A *144*
Bailey, A & Son **37**
Bailey, A J & Son **37, 38**
Bailey, Brian Oswald **37, 38**
Bailey, E **104**
Bake, Nancy W **328**
Baker & Hinks **61**, *389*
Baker & Parker **67**
Baker, Albert & Co **23**
Baker, Edward & Son **118, 119**
Baker, Eli **67**
Baker, Esther Phoebe Rosa **331**
Baker, John **236**
Baker, William **61**
Baldock, George Richard **175**
Baldock, G R & Co **175**
Baldwin & Marriott *245*
Ball & Co **56**
Ball Brothers **56**
Ball, F **333**
Ball, F A **333**
Ball, Richard Macaire **347**
Ball, William **435, 459**
Bamber & Gibson **61**
Bamber, Wilfred **61**
Bambridge, F W **149**
Bamford, Henry **184**
Bamford, Henry White **215**
Band, Charles **74**
Band, Henry & Son **485**
Banks, Charles **187**
Banks, F *49, 81*, **141**
Banks, Frank **141**
Banks, Frederick **140, 141**
Banks, Frederick Sidney **141, 154**
Banks, F S *55*
Banks, H & C **187**
Banks, Harry **187**
Banks, Jn Millward *243, 261*, **267, 268**
Bannister Brothers **57**
Banyard & Co **60, 151**, *350*
Banyard, F O **60, 151**, *350, 438, 474*
Barber Brothers *474*
Barber, Howard G **452**
Barber, John Lawrence **264**
Barber, John Vaughan **57**
Barder, S & Co Ltd **377**
Barder, Samuel **377**
Barker Bros **57**, *110*, **190,191**, *276,284*
Barker Brothers Ltd **191**
Barker Bros Silversmiths Ltd **59**
Barker, Frank Ernest **190, 191**
Barker, Herbert Edward **190, 191**
Barling, Alfred **21**
Barling, B & Sons **21**
Barnard, Edward & Sons Ltd **120**
Barnes, Frederick **141**
Barnes, Geoffrey Lawson **394**
Barnes, Gladys Kathleen Lawson **394**
Barnes, Marjory **308**
Barnes, William **377**
Barnes, W S **475**
Barnett & Scott **70**
Barnett Brothers **57**
Barnett, Barnie **56, 58**
Barnett, C B **240**
Barnett, Eli Lewis **131**
Barnett, James Edward **246**
Barnett, Maurice **307**
Barnett, Samuel **60**
Barnsley, E S & Co **135**, *187*
Barraclough, Albert **483**
Barraclough, Geo Henry **30**
Barraclough, Herbert **483**
Barraclough, Jas Henry **483**
Barraclough, Z & Son **483**
Barratt & Co **140**
Barrett, Andrew & Sons **25**
Barrett, E *385*
Barrett, H A **25**
Barrett, H H **25**
Barrett, John William **287**
Barrett, R J **25**
Barrett, Walter **25**
Barrister, Leonard Charles *488*
Barrow, S **230**
Bartleman, J & Son **239**
Bartleman, John senior **239**
Bartleman, Thomas **239**
Bartlett, Henry George **193**
Barton, Alfred John **354**
Barton, James & Co **219**
Barton, Herbert J **197**
Barton, James **235**
Barwick & Haggas **62**
Base, A V **438**
Base, D R **438**
Base, William & Sons **438**
Bash, Philip **331, 332**
Bash, Philip & Co **331, 332**
Bassett, James Mapleton **268**
Bateman, Samuel **377**
Bates, Albert Alan **22**
Bates, Joseph **235**
Bates, Thomas Powell **419**
Bateson, Fred William **435**
Bateson, Thomas Pearson **419**
Bathurst, John **234**
Batson, Albert Edward **184**
Batson, Henry John **184**
Batson, J & Son **184**
Batt, Albert S **437**
Batt, Arthur **437**
Batt, Thomas **437**
Batt, W & Son **437**
Bauer, E & F **124**
Bauer, Emil & Frank **124**
Bauer, Emil Frederick **124**
Bauer, Frederick William **157**
Baume & Co Ltd **121**
Baxendale, Robert **71**
Baylie, George **160**
Bayliss, Walter **59, 308, 435**
Bayman, Arthur **109**
Beach, F & R Ltd *80*, **152**
Beach, Henry Herbert **90**
Beach, Hilda M **203**
Beach, N M **152**
Beach, R & K M *254*
Beach, R W **152**
Beal, Abraham **21**
Beal, Henry **183**
Beasley, David **108**
Beasley, Douglas Edward **108**
Beasley, Joseph Henry **307**
Beasley, Thomas Chas **60**
Beaver, L **297**
Beaver, Marcus **297, 308**
Becker, Dorothy **99**
Becker, Harry Thomas Alfred **99**
Becker, Lucas John **302**

Beddoes & Co **60, 376**
Bedford, Alfred **22**
Bedingham, George **160**
Beer, John **236**
Beeson, Edith **118**
Belk, W H **347**
Bell, Alexander **23**
Bell, Edmund **291**
Bell, Ernest **119**
Bell, Patrick **331**
Bell, Thos Newnham **418**
Bendall Brothers *99*
Bendall Brothers (Jewellers) Ltd **57**
Bendall, David **65**
Bendall, G & H *28*, **170**
Bendall, Gordon James **65, 170, 171**
Bendall, Harry **170**
Bendall, Henry **65**
Bennett & Thompson **71**
Bennett (1907) Ltd **65**
Bennett, Charles Stanley **237**
Bennett, Clarence Courtney **77**
Bennett, E *23*
Bennett, Eric Arthur Coley **118**
Bennett, Frederick John **147**
Bennett, Frederick William **157**
Bennett, Herbert **348**
Bennett, J B & Co **65, 237**
Bennett, J B & Co Ltd **237**
Bennett, John **235, 236**
Bennett, John Baker **65, 237, 308, 309**
Bennett, Leonard John **237**
Bennett, Philip Henry **71**
Bennett, Stanley Harris **235, 236**
Benny, Alfred **21**
Benoy, F Ltd **141**
Benson Brothers *35, 49,* **56, 57,** *89, 108, 115, 118, 148, 183, 216,* **246,** *256, 294, 306, 310, 315, 343, 370, 372, 373, 379, 387, 402, 408, 421, 431, 466*
Benson, George Walter **246**
Benson, James William **286, 287**
Benson, John **56, 57, 246**
Benson, John Daniels **243**
Benson, J W Ltd **287**
Benson, William Hilton **56, 57, 246**
Benton, Percy William **344**
Benzie, Herbert Simpson **185, 376**
Benzie, Karl Theodore **376**
Benzie, Norman **376**
Benzie, Simpson **376**
Berkeley, Charles **176**
Berkeley, Fred Charles **42,** *151, 304*
Bernstein Brothers **58**
Bernstein Brothers Ltd **58**
Bernstein, Philip **58**
Bernstone, Joseph **236**
Berringer, Joseph **236**
Berry, William **435**
Berton, Howard H **196**
Bertram, Charles Neville **485**
Beswick, Joseph **236**
Bethune, John **236**
Beyendorfe, David **108**
Bickerton, George Frank *204*
Biddulph, Constance **73**
Biddulph, K **125**
Bill, Charles Alfred **127**
Bill, Frank **57**
Bingham, Albert Edw **448, 449, 450**
Bingham, John Edward **449, 450**
Bingley, John **64**
Bint, John William **21, 23**
Birchall, James Thomas **282**
Birchall, Mary **282**
Bird, Charles **64**
Bird, William Cotton **439**
Birkett, Isaac **242**
Birmingham Assay Off **16, 212,** *480*
Birmingham Gold & Silver Chain Co, The **61**
Bishop, Frank **318**
Bishop, George **318**
Bishop, George Frederick **311**
Bishop, R Windsor **435**
Bishop, W **435**
Bishton & Cohen **59**
Bishton & Fletcher **61**
Bishton, Alfred Henry **107**
Bishton, Thomas **404**
Bishtons Ltd **65**
Blackett, James Samuel **216**
Blackburn, Althans **323**
Blackman, Abraham **22**
Blackman, T **404**
Blacksidge, John **236**
Blackwell, Althans **323**
Blackwell, Arthur **324**
Blake, Alfred James **38**
Blake, H G **342**
Blanchard, John Stephen Owen **404**
Blanckensee & Levetus **65**
Blanckensee, Abraham Meyer **44**
Blanckensee, J & Co **237**
Blanckensee, Joel **65**
Blanckensee, Leon **237**
Blanckensee, S **36**
Blanckensee, S Ltd **380,** *466*
Blanckensee, S & Son *99, 116, 348,* **379, 389,** *430, 477*
Blanckensee, S & Son (Lon) Ltd **27**
Blanckensee, S & Son Ltd **27, 36,** *116, 117, 267, 312,* **379, 380, 381**
Blanckensee, S & Sons Ltd *80, 236, 273, 311, 318,* **379,** *446*
Blankensie, Elizabeth **348**
Blankensie, Julius **380**
Blankensie, Leon Julius **348**
Bliss, Thomas & Co **412**
Bliss, Thomas Herbert **412**
Block, Victor **112, 113**
Bloye, J L **462**
Blow & Co **60**
Bloxham, A C Ltd **23**
Blumstein, Franz **141**
Boase, Elizabeth M **132**
Bock, Ladislav **297**
Bolloten, Joseph **235**
Bolton & Redfern Ltd **68**
Bolton, B H & Sons *115*
Bolton, Edwin **68**
Bolton, Kathleen Edith **68**
Bonaston, William Pearson **436**
Bond, R & Co **140, 348**
Boneham, F & Co **140**
Boneham, Frank **140**
Bookbinder, Leopold **302**
Booker, Ernest Guy **160**
Booker, James Ltd **238**
Booth Brothers **58**
Booth, E & Sons *440*
Booth, Edward Foster **124,** *316*
Boots Pure Drug Co Ltd **67, 68**
Borland, Andrew **21**
Bosley, Henry **308**
Bosley, Theodore **308**
Bostock & Rayner (London) Ltd **68**
Botsford, James W **329**
Botshall, Edward **119**
Bott, Edward **119**
Boucher, Thomas James **414**
Boucher, W & Co **436**
Boulger, Richard **347**
Boulton & Fothergill **61**
Bouverat, George **375**
Bouverat, George & Co **375**
Bouverat, Jean **160**
Bowdler, Henry Peter **205**
Bowen, T M **404**
Bowers, Robert I & II **347**
Bowker, Ernest **247**
Bowman Ltd **65**
Bowman, Richard Thos **371, 372**
Bowman, Samuel **65**
Boyd, John & Co **237**
Boyton, Charles **75**
Boyton, Charles & Son Ltd **75**
Boyton, F & Co **141**
Boyton, Frederick **141**
Bradbury, George **235**
Bradbury, J **235**
Bradbury, T **405**
Bradbury, Thomas & Sons Ltd **405**
Bradbury, W *378*
Bradbury, William **435,** *437*
Braddock, George William **179**
Bradford, C **74,** *111, 247*
Bradley British Overseas Ltd **338**
Bradley & Cohn **59**
Bradley James **59**
Bradley, J E **246**
Bradley, J G **251**
Bradshaw, William Griffith **445**
Bragg, Thomas & John **414**
Braham, Edward F Ltd **123, 124**
Braham, Edward Foligne **123, 124**
Braham, Fred James **148**
Braham, J Ltd **236**
Brahams, A **446**
Brancker, Benjamin **56**
Brancker, John **237**
Bravington, Frank William **69**
Bravington, G & F **68**
Bravington, George Herbert **170**
Bravingtons **69**
Bray, J *48*
Bray, John **240**
Brazer, Isaac **219**
Breadsmore, T *152*
Breakell, Walter **435**
Breen Brothers **58**
Breen, Lawrence Joseph **58**
Breen, Philip James **58**
Brewer, William Chas **439**
Brickell, Marie Josephine **316**
Bridges, Alfred **394, 395**
Briggs, William & Co **436**
Briggs, William Marriott **436**
Brightley, Harold James **197**
Brindley, Walter Henry **348**
British Automatic Mesh Co **56**
British Machine Chain Ltd **66**
Britton & Gould **61**
Britton & Hewitt **62**
Britton & Son *300*
Britton & Sons **70**
Britton, Albert **69, 70**
Britton, B H *373*
Britton, B H & Sons *51,* **69,** *228, 303, 384, 432, 460*
Britton, B H & Sons Ltd **69,** *174*
Britton, Chas Ernest **62**
Britton, Charles Henry **69, 70**
Britton, Gould & Co **61**
Britton, Herbert **69, 70**
Britton, J A & Son **232**
Britton, James **44**
Britton, Joseph A **232**
Britton, J W **69**
Britton, Morton **316**
Britton, Richard A **69**
Britton, Samson J **232**
Britton, Solomon J **232**
Britton, Walter **69, 70**
Britton, Walter Haseler **61**
Brix, Chas Aloysius **73**
Broadhead & Adelman *22,* **119**
Broadhead, Edgar **22, 119**
Broadhurst & Lee **65**
Broadhurst, Frank **65**
Broadway & Co Ltd **60**
Broadway, W B **60**
Brockington Brothers **58, 59,** *87*
Brockington, Alfred **21**
Brockington, Geo Samuel **59**
Brockwell, Henry Titterton **211**
Brodrick, Thomas **105**
Brogden, Charles George **189**
Bromage & Hawkins **61**
Bromage, Arthur **21, 61**
Bromage, Joseph & F **248**
Bromet, A & Co **23**
Bromhall, Charles **73**
Brook, Charles **334**
Brooke, Brooke & Co **57, 58**
Brooker, A *203*
Brookes & Crookes **59**
Brooks, Chas Henry Stuart **74**
Brooks, C Ltd **74**
Brooks, John **220**
Broughton, C D **79**
Broughton, John **236**
Brower, Jack **235**
Brown, Alfred Ernest **31**
Brown Brothers **57**
Brown, C & Co *212*
Brown, E **481**
Brown, Ernest Vincent **234, 235**
Brown, Frederick Geo **160**
Brown, George **159**
Brown, George John Hemsley **160**
Brown, Harris Leon **200, 201**
Brown, H L & Son **200**
Brown, H L & Son Ltd **201**
Brown, Jacques & Co **237**
Brown, Jane McCracken **267**
Brown, J & F **248**
Brown, Joseph **237**
Brown, Joseph B **237**
Brown, Josiah **234, 235**
Brown, Montague John **377**
Brown, Norman **323**
Brown, Robert John **477**
Brown, Roy Joseph **37**
Brown, Thomas **413**
Brown, Thomas Arthur **404**
Brown, Thos Lumsden **416**
Brown, Thos Southwark **424**
Brown, Wilfred **435**
Brown, William Fulford **443**
Browns of Chester Ltd **67**
Bruford, Frank **78**
Bryan, G & Co *161*
Bryan, George **175**
Bryan, G & R **175**
Bryan, Ralph **175**
Bryars, Samuel **175, 376**
Buck, Mary **308**
Buckley, Alfred **23**
Buckner, Gustav **160**
Buckton, Christopher **74**
Bull, John & Co (Bedford) Ltd **238**
Bull, Samuel M **394**
Bull, Thomas **404**
Bullen, Nathaniel **19, 71, 323**
Buller & Co **60**
Bullock & Weston **71**
Bullock, W *55*
Bullock, William **71**
Bullock, Will'm Thomas **435**
Bunce Brothers **58**
Bunce, Henry **58**
Bunce, John **58, 235**
Bunce, Thomas **58**
Bunney Ltd **66**
Burbidge, J **235**
Burbridge, R **348**
Burford, Charles E & Co **80**
Burford, Charles Edwin **80**
Burgess Brothers **58**
Burgess, Adam **21**
Burgess, Alfred *22*
Burgess, Bezeliel **56**
Burgess, R **347**
Burgl, Isabel Edith **219**
Burland, B **57**
Burn, F J **108**
Burnett, E **119**
Burrell & Co **56**
Burrows & Mills **66**
Burrows, Chas Turman **101**
Burrows, Chas William **101**
Burrows, C T & Sons **101**
Burrows, F J **101**
Burt, George Stephen **177**
Bushell & Co **59**
Bushell, H *293*
Bushell, H & Co **184**
Bushell, Harold **184**
Bushell, Henry **59**
Bushell, Herbert **184, 185**
Bushell, Herbert & Son Ltd **185, 186**
Bushell, Roland **185**
Butler, Cuthbert **73, 74**
Butler, Edward **476**
Butler, Frank E **360**
Butler, N *58, 66*
Butler, W *49, 150*
Butler, William **435**
Butt & Co Ltd **60**
Butt, Alfred Wathew **53, 141, 350**
Butt, Francis **141**
Butterworth, Henry **184**
Butterworth, John Clegg *240*

Cadbury, Ivel **162**
Cadbury, Joel **163**
Cadle, Percy Edward **73**
Cahoon Brothers Ltd **74**
Cahoon, James M **74**
Cahoon, John **74**
Caldicott, John William **118, 119, 287**

Caldwell, T **116**
Calipe, Dettner & Co **300**
Callaways Ltd **92**
Calom, Charles **75**
Cameron, Alexander **26**
Cameron, J & Son **241**
Cameron, James **240**
Cameron, Jessie *240*
Cameron, J N **60**
Campbell, Trudie Gertrude Kate **489**
Camrass, H **186**
Candelent & Adams **73**, *302*
Candelent, Joseph **73**
Candelesch & Adams **44**
Candland, W H **28**
Caplin, John **75**, **457**
Careless, C **75**
Carol, George **169**
Carpenter, Edward Arthur *162*
Carran, Thomas **405**
Carrington & Co Ltd **78**
Carrington Brothers *301*
Carrington, John Alexander **233**
Carrington, Squire Sydney **382**, **399**
Carrington, W H & Co *47*, *51*, *73*, *109*, *145*, *173*, *174*, *178*, *180*, *197*, *233*, *261*, *270*, *271*, *278*, *294*, *320*, *343*, *356*, *391*, **399**, *404*, *421*, *424*, *429*, *436*, **453**, **454**, **482**
Carrington, W H Ltd *174*
Carrington, W H & Son *25*
Carrington, William Arthur **382**
Carrington, Will Hen & Co **382**, **399**
Carrington, William John **459**
Carroll, Phyllis Vale **343**
Carroll, Walter James **459**
Carruthers, William **80**
Carsberg, Robert Fred'k *294*, **349**
Carter, A **25**
Carter, Albert **26**
Carter, George Harold **341**
Carter, Richard **25**
Carter, William **439**
Cartwright, Edna Florence **295**
Cartwright, Joshua Edward **51**, **247**
Cartwright, Thos & Sons **407**
Cartwright, Wilfred **197**
Cartwright, William **438**
Case, R *141*
Cash, Arthur **26**
Cashmore, Will Walter *253*, *409*, **480**
Cask, W H *40*
Casper, P N **338**
Castelberg, Antoine **25**
Castelberg, Edward **120**
Castelberg, Petitpierre Co **152**
Cater, Dudley Frank **188**, **388**
Causer, Robert **349**
Causer, Thomas **406**
Cave, James **239**
Cawley, Robert **349**
Chadwick, Henry **186**, *361*
Chadwick, John **240**
Chadwick, William **438**
Chalford Stick Co Ltd **99**
Chalk, J A **233**
Chambers, Alfred **382**
Chancellor & Sons **98**, **99**
Chancellor, John **98**, **99**
Chancellor, Jonathan **98**, **99**
Chandler & Son **99**
Chandler, Dorothy **109**
Chandler, F **99**
Chandler, George **161**
Chandler, George & Son **162**
Chandler, George Eugene **99**
Chandler, R *77*, *239*, *276*, **349**
Chantrell, Robert **349**
Chaplin, G **382**
Chapman, Edward George **395**
Charlick, Fred Robert **97**
Charms **272**
Charnell & Line **90**
Charnell, Walter James **25**, **26**, **27**, **90**
Chatelain, Chas Gaston **85**
Chatelain, C G & Fils **85**
Chatelain, Cyril **85**
Chatterley, Albert E **238**
Chatterley, F M **238**
Chatterley, John B & Sons Ltd **238**
Chell, George **161**
Chell, George B **99**
Cherry, Joan Dorothy **243**
Cheshelsky, Samuel **382**
Cheshire Silver Co, The **79**
Cheshire, A J *204*, *279*, *405*, *464*
Cheshire, Alfred James **38**
Cheshire, Charles A *234*
Cheshire, Colen Hewer **76**, *100*, *152*, *153*, *261*, *399*
Cheshire, Walter William **438**
Chester Electro-plate Co **82**
Chibnall, Chas Arthur **73**
Chinn, Benjamin Stuart **71**
Chinn, William **438**
Christian, Edward **120**
Christie, William Henry *443*, **454**
Cirne, Raul **349**
Civic Co Ltd *119*, *122*, *355*
Clark & Sewell *41*, *77*, **98**, *100*, *115*, *244*, *245*
Clark & Sewell Ltd **98**, *408*
Clark Brothers **75**
Clark, Albert Edward **75**
Clark, Alexander **29**
Clark, Alexander Co Ltd **28**
Clark, Alexander Manuf'ing Co **29**
Clark, Drayton **454**, **455**
Clark, Edwin *405*
Clark, Frederick **75**
Clark, George G **81**, **82**
Clark, Henry **186**
Clark, James P **98**
Clark, L Mrs **436**
Clark, Thomas Samuel **103**
Clark, W & Sons *236*, *332*
Clark, W H & D **454**, **455**
Clark, W H Ltd **454**
Clark, William **186**
Clark, William Henry **454**
Clarke & Ward **103**
Clarke Brothers (Liverpool) Ltd **75**
Clarke, Charles *75*
Clarke, H & Co **187**
Clarke, John **239**, **240**
Clarke, William **438**
Clarke, William & Son **440**
Clarke, William junior **440**
Clarke, William senior **440**
Clarkson, Frank Finley **144**
Claydon, Alfred George **97**
Claydon, Robin & Co **97**
Clayton, Angela **25**
Clayton, C H **347**
Clayton, Doris Claire **109**
Clayton, Elspeth Pilcher **133**
Clayton, Stanley **197**
Cleaver, Thomas *375*, **406**
Clewley & Davis **107**
Clewley, Edward John **107**
Clewley, E J & Co **107**
Clift & Cockle **150**
Clifton, John **220**
Clock Shop, The **321**
Close, Henry **186**
Close, Samuel **381**
Clotworthy, E R **140**
Clutterbuck, William Henry **453**
Coakley, John **239**, **240**
Coates, George **162**
Cobb, Frank **142**
Cobb, Frank & Co **142**
Cobb, Thomas **406**
Cockle, Frank Josiah **150**
Cohen & Charles **28**, **76**, **77**, *242*
Cohen & Charles Soloman *76*
Cohen & Co **23**
Cohen & Samuel **398**
Cohen Brothers **94**
Cohen, Abraham **44**
Cohen, Albert **28**, **76**, **77**
Cohen, A & M **44**
Cohen, Arthur Edward **31**, **94**
Cohen, Asher **26**
Cohen, Edgar **348**
Cohen, Henry Moxhay **204**
Cohen, Herman **59**
Cohen, I & Son **220**
Cohen, Isadore **76**, **77**
Cohen, Israel **220**
Cohen, Israel & Son **220**
Cohen, James de Lara **302**
Cohen, Joseph & Son **241**
Cohen, Lionel **94**
Cohen, Lionel Louis **302**
Cohen, Louis **298**
Cohen, M M **97**
Cohen, Morris Tobias **241**
Cohen, Myer **44**
Cohen, Philip **332**
Cohen, Samuel Tobias **310**, **467**
Colbourne Ltd **91**
Colbourne, F **91**
Colbourne, Thomas **92**
Colbourne, Thos Frank **91**, **92**
Cole, A J *46*, *188*
Cole, A J & Co *357*
Cole, Francis Wride **157**
Cole, Frank William *157*
Cole, F W *126*, **157**, *208*, *282*, *299*, *319*
Cole, J *396*
Cole, J W *377*
Cole, Ralph Edgar **157**
Cole, William John **438**
Coley Brothers *21*, *23*, *58*, *61*, *69*, *99*, **105**, **106**, *114*, *136*, *149*, *151*, *267*, *270*, *292*, *314*, *317*, *375*, *428*, *445*
Coley Bros & Leonardt Ltd *33*, **106**
Coley, Alfred George **105**, **106**
Coley, William Arthur **105**, **106**
Coley, William Henry **105**, **106**
Collinge, Florence **142**
Collingwood & Son **98**, **314**
Collingwood, Horatio Nelson **98**, **314**
Collingwood, H William **314**
Collingwood, M G & Son **314**
Collings & Wallace **103**
Collins & Leeson Ltd **90**
Collins Brothers **74**
Collins, Charles Howard **87**
Collins, C H & Sons **87**
Collins, Claude Ernest **81**, **87**, **90**
Collins, Daniel George **112**
Collins, Daniel George Ltd **112**
Collins, Donald **109**
Collins, Donald Reginald **109**
Collins, Ernest Albert Edward **74**
Collins, Fred Joseph **109**, **150**
Collins, George Dawson **87**
Collins, H **74**
Collins, Louis Bonaparte **74**
Collins, Sidney Napolean Cromwell **74**
Collins, Walter H **59**, *287*, *400*, **453**
Collins, W H & Co Ltd *83*, **453**
Collis, Geoffrey **161**
Collyer, J & Co Ltd **240**
Colquitt, Leonard **298**
Colton, N *239*
Colvin, Dorothy Annette Michie **108**
Comberbach, E L & Sons **98**
Comer, Ramon **349**
Comoy, H & Co *235*
Compton & Parry **95**
Comyns, William & Sons Ltd *78*
Connard & Son Ltd **99**
Connard, W **99**
Conry, James Henry **405**
Conry, Josephine Teresa **405**
Conry, Mary **405**
Conry, Rose **405**
Conry, T **405**
Constantine & Floyd **81**, **82**
Constantine & Floyd Ltd **81**
Constantine, Alfred **28**, **81**, **82**
Constantine, Allan **28**
Constantine, Robert Howard **353**
Constantine, S **244**
Conway, Andrew & Co **26**, **27**
Conway, Peter **332**
Cook, Allan Ewart **299**
Cook, Arthur **25**
Cook, W **438**
Cooke & Kelvey **90**
Cooke, Charles **75**, **76**
Cooke, Crossley **324**
Cooke, J & Sons Ltd **241**
Cooke, Joseph & Son **241**
Cooke, S E **386**, *393*
Cooke, S E (B'ham) Ltd **386**
Cooke, Stanley Ernest **385**
Cookson Messrs **438**
Coombs & Co **78**
Coombs, Edgar **78**
Cooper Brothers & Son Ltd **25**
Cooper, Alfred **75**
Cooper, Arthur **75**
Cooper, C A Mrs **198**
Cooper, Charles **75**
Cooper, H **198**
Cooper, Henry **189**
Cooper, Henry & Sons **189**
Cooper, Henry James **198**, **199**
Cooper, H J **198**
Cooper, H J & Co Ltd **197**, **198**, **199**
Cooper, James **189**
Cooper, John **189**
Cooper, Joseph **75**
Cooper, Lydia **299**
Cooper, P E **23**
Cooper, R **94**
Cooper, Thomas **75**
Cooper, Thomas junior **75**
Cooper, William Edward **442**
Cooperative Wholesale Society **105**
Cooperative Wholesale Soc Ltd **104**
Coor, A G Ltd **33**
Cordery, Elizabeth **120**
Coore, Gladys **486**
Corper, L & Co **298**
Corper, Lionel **298**
Corr, Dorothy Ethel **33**
Corton, Geo Hen **329**
Cose, Brook **75**
Cose, Frederick Hugh **146**
Costin, William George **475**
Cotton, Benjamin Marcus **79**
Cotton, B M & Co **79**
Cotton, Ephraim Harris **79**
Cotton, John Ltd **239**
Cotton, Joseph Ltd **239**
Cotton, W H *408*
Cottram, G H **408**
Cottrill & Cattlow Ltd **77**
Cottrill, E **77**, **282**
Cottrill, James Thomas **77**, **282**
Cottrill, J T & Sons Ltd **282**
Couch, Walter Conroy **162**
Couchley, Chas William **345**
Coulshaw, Jones & Kershaw **89**
Coulthard, Albert **25**
Coulthard, Chas Thos **59**
Coulthard, Walter **439**, **465**
Coulthard, W & Co **439**
Coulthard, W Ltd **465**
Coulthurst, Frederick *65*, **142**, *289*, *324*, *325*, *422*
Coupland & Monk **440**
Coupland, William **371**
Coupland, Willm Breeton **440**
Coventry, Laura Mary **303**
Coventry Watch Manuf'g Socy **104**
Coverdale, George Frederick **168**
Cowdrill Brothers **75**
Cowlishaw, John Yeoman **291**
Cox Brothers **75**
Cox, George W **439**
Cox, Harry C **439**
CPS Jewellery Co **96**
Crafts, Alfred John **38**
Craig, Robert Miller **359**
Cramer, George Frederick **168**
Cramp, George Edward **129**
Crathorne, T **413**
Crathorne, T & H Ltd **413**
Craven, Geoffrey **161**
Crawcour, J H Ltd **256**
Crawford, E M **132**
Crawshay, Isa **92**
Crease & Co **488**
Crease, Peter Bruce **488**
Creed, John **240**
Creighton, Arthur **26**
Creighton, Robert Henry Mason **349**
Creswick, William Henry **454**
Criech, Doris Evelyn **110**
Cris(t)ford & Norris **189**
Cris(t)ford & Norris Ltd **189**
Cris(t)ford, Harold **189**
Critchley, James **239**
Croft, G & Son **162**
Crofton, William **438**, **445**
Croker, Arthur **442**
Croker, W E & Co **442**

Crompton, Herbert **240**
Crompton, Robert **349**
Croneen, Horace George **193**
Crook, Harold George **186**
Crooke, Stanley **382**
Cropp & Farr **84**
Cropp & Farr Ltd **83**, **84**
Cropp, Francis **83**
Cropp, H J **83**
Cropp, Horace John Adams **84**
Cropp, John Francis **84**
Crosbee, Arthur Walter **53**
Crosbee, A W & Co **53**
Crosbee, A W & Sons Ltd **53**
Cross & Phillips **368**
Cross, Leslie **78**, **79**
Cross, Leslie Coleman **78**
Cross, Reginald R **368**
Cross, Reginald Stanley **368**
Cross, William James **28**
Cross, William John **478**
Crossley, Leonard **299**
Crown Mounting Repairing Co **93**
Crowson, William **438**
Crowther, J W **287**
Crowther, James Guest **291**
Croydon, Charles & Son **97**
Crozier & Martin **93**
Crozier, W A **458**
Cruickshanks, A & Co **26**
Cruickshanks, Alexander **26**
Crumpsty, William **438**
Cubbin, Ivena **220**
Cubbin, Thomas **406**
Culver, Alfred Ernest **120**
Culver, E *173*
Culver, E & Son **120**
Culver, Edward **120**
Culver, J *38*
Culver, J Alex Ltd **233**
Culver, John **240**, **241**
Culver, John Ltd **241**
Cumming MacDonald Ltd **93**
Cunliffe, Nicholas **323**
Cunnington & Eastwood **80**
Cunnington Brothers *486*
Cunnington, John William **80**
Curryer, Thomas **406**
Curtis, Albert **26**, *453*
Curtis, Cecil Albert Dr **73**
Curtois, Joseph Samuel **345**
Cushey, R F **349**
Cutler, Jack M **268**
Cutler, Joseph **239**

Daffern, J & Co **243**
Daffern, Joseph **243**
Dagg, James J **261**
Dailey, H **369**
Dailley, Edgar T **136**
Dalby, A & Co **30**
Dalby, Arthur **30**, **60**, **350**
Damsell, Arthur **300**
Dance & Duerden **110**
Dance, Albert **110**
Daniel, Emily Doris **110**
Danziger & Isaacs **112**, **113**
Darby, Alfred Horatio **36**
Darnsley, E F & Co *28*, *76*
Darry, Dorothy H **112**
Darton, F & Co **143**
Darton, Francis Arthur **143**
Daulby, Helen Audrey **183**
Daun, H C **99**
Davenport, A J & Co **38**
Davenport, Catherine Jennings **38**
Davenport, W *77*, *197*
Davey, Samuel **84**
David, Jacques **143**, **144**
David Manufacturing Co Ltd **190**
Davies & Co **109**
Davies & Powers **114**, **115**
Davies Brothers **109**
Davies, Daniel **109**
Davies, Edgar **122**
Davies, Edward **107**
Davies, Edward Thurston **192**
Davies, F **126**
Davies, Frederick Joseph **114**
Davies, Henry **107**
Davies, Herbert **107**
Davies, John **242**
Davies, John Richard **277**
Davies, Matthew **311**
Davies, Montague **312**
Davies, Moss & Co **114**
Davies, W **379**, **380**, **381**
Davies, Walter **118**, **381**
Davies, William **114**, **115**, **440**, **441**
Davies, W Oakley *89*, *323*, **469**, **470**
Davis & Co **122**
Davis & Matthews **113**
Davis, Alfred James **441**
Davis, David **114**
Davis, David & Maurice **114**
Davis, Edward **121**, **122**
Davis, Frank **143**
Davis, George Thomas **165**
Davis, Hy Cliff **187**, *211*, *212*, *276*, **376**
Davis, Henry Clifford Ltd **187**
Davis, Henry John **152**
Davis, Isaac **122**
Davis, James **113**
Davis, Joseph **487**
Davis, L Selwyn *187*
Davis, Montague **312**
Davis, Thomas **122**
Davis, Thomas Henry **413**
Davis, W **36**, **389**, **444**
Davis, Walter **27**, **36**, **381**
Davison, George **177**
Davison, George & Co **165**
Davison, George Albert **165**
Davison, George & Thomas **177**
Davison, Thomas **177**
Dawells Patent Pipe Co Ltd **115**
Dawson, Charles **439**
Dawson, David Stewart **384**
Dawson, George Will'am **179**
Dawson, James **201**
Dawson, Percy Stewart **385**
Dawson, Stewart & Co **384**
Dawson, Stewart & Co Ltd **385**
Day, Charles Edward **81**
De Boer, Charles **80**
De Meza, Nathaniel **23**
Deakin & Francis **111**, *350*, *474*
Deakin & Francis Ltd **111**, **112**
Deakin & Nephew **114**
Deakin, Albert **243**, **244**, **245**
Deakin, Harold **257**
Deakin, J & H **257**
Deakin, J & Son *34*
Deakin, James & Sons **243**, **245**
Deakin, James & Sons Ltd **244**, **245**
Deakin, James & William **245**
Deakin, James Henry **245**
Deakin, John **243**, **244**, **245**, **257**
Deakin, Stephen Henry **111**
Deakin,Will Petchford **243**, **244**, **245**
Dearden, A **244**
Dearman, Richard Lionel **357**
Deeby, George **42**
Deely & Fisher **111**
Deguingand, E **122**
Deguingand, F J **122**
Deguingand, P C **122**
De L?, T M **417**
De La Rue, Stewart **113**
De La Rue, Thos & Co Ltd **113**, **407**
De Meza, Nathaniel **23**
Dempsey --- *124*
Denby, M C **209**
De Netto Lourenco, Jose Hermano **257**
Denham, Alfred **30**
Dennison & Wigley **42**, *384*, *408*
Dennison & Wigley Watch Case Co *42*
Dennison Watch Case Co **42**
Dennison Wigley & Co *169*
Dennison, Franklin **42**
Detheridge, Arthur **30**
Dettmer, Louis Charles **300**
Devereux, Frederick William **158**
Dewhurst & Co **312**
Dewhurst, Maurice **312**
Dewsnap & Co **109**
Dewsnap, James Ltd **243**
Dewsnap, John William **109**
Deykin, Chas Pemberton **95**
Dibley, William Edward **442**
Dick, Robert James **355**
Dicken, E *32*
Dickenson, Thomas Charles **459**
Dickins, W G **333**
Dickinson, George Heneage **446**
Dickinson, S & Son **384**, **385**
Dickinson, W G & Sons **446**
Dickinson, William Finch **446**
Dickson, Thomas W **428**
Diem, Charlotte N **125**
Diggles, William Henry **190**
Dimier Brothers **108**, **122**
Dimier Brothers & Co **79**, **108**, **112**
Dimier Brothers & Co Ltd **165**
Dimier Freres & Co **108**
Dimier, Edward **112**, **122**
Dimier, Georges **108**, **112**
Dimmer, George **115**
Dimmer, George junior **115**
Dimmer & Son **115**
Dingley Brothers **108**, *292*
Dingley, Alfred **30**
Dingley, Alfred Harry **108**
Dingley, Francis Henry **147**
Dingley, George Fred **108**
Dingley, Will James *276*, *369*, **459**
Dixon, Christine Tate **79**
Dixon, James **221**
Dixon, James & Sons Ltd **244**
Dixon, Joseph **242**
Dobb, Henry Ltd **190**
Dobb, R Rendall **190**
Dobson, Charles W **333**
Dobson, Percy H **333**
Dobson & Son **333**
Dobson & Sons **427**
Dobson, Thos William **427**
Docker & Burn Ltd **108**, *242*
Docker, F **108**
Dodd, Hilda Almond **183**, *319*
Dodge, Elivia Millicent **415**
Dodge, William **441**
Dodge, William & M **467**
Dodson, Charles Robert **97**
Dodsworth Brothers **242**
Dodsworth, James **242**
Dodsworth, J H *420*
Dodwell, Thomas **407**
Dolphin, Benjamin **384**
Doodson, Walter **441**
Douglas Clock Co *350*
Dow, David **114**
Dowsett, Rob Ed **339**, **340**
Doyle, Frederick **143**, *207*
Doyle, Peter Martin **337**
Dresden, George **56**, *108*
Dresden, Weston **173**
Dreyfus, A & Co **30**
Dreyfus, Auguste **30**
Dreyfus, C *61*, *99*, *194*, *290*
Dreyfus, Charles **79**
Dreyfus, George **384**
Dreyfus, J **384**
Dreyfus, Moise **384**
Dreyfus, Sylvain **384**
Drummond, George Turnbell **410**
Drury, Kenneth Kirkpatrick **295**
Duckworth, Arthur **484**
Duckworth, Gertrude **337**
Ducrou, Tom **407**
Ducrow, Tom **407**
Dudley, A E *31*
Dudley, Mr **435**
Duerden, H **110**
Duff, Lionel **300**
Duggan, Mary Agnes Mrs **312**
Duguid, Christine Catherine **77**
Duke, Bartholomew **117**
Duke, James **221**, **242**
Duke, Joseph I **221**
Duke, Joseph II **221**, **242**
Duley, Albert E **31**
Dumelow, C H Ltd **79**
Dumelow, Henry James **211**
Dumelow, H J *211*
Dumelow, Walter **441**
Dumenil, Charles Henry **79**, **297**
Duncan & Scobbie **115**
Duncan, George Gabriel **115**
Duncan, J L & Co *256*, **254**, **265**
Duncan, Jn Louis **264**, **265**, *361*, *486*
Duncan, R E *264*
Duncans **264**
Dunlop, Robert **350**
Dunningham, W & Co **441**
Dunningham, William **441**
Du Plat, A G *64*, **344**
Durban & Co **109**, *211*, *311*
Durban, E & Co *21*, *54*, **109**, *322*, *431*
Durban, Edward **58**
Durban, Edward Henry **109**, **311**
Durley, E **138**
Dutton, Joseph **221**, **242**
Dwerryhouse, John **243**
Dyke, F A **488**
Dyke, T Russell **293**, **464**
Dykes, Alexander Whyte **54**, **473**
Dyson, Charles Frederick *243*, **244**
Dyson, John **243**
Dyson, John & Son **243**, **244**
Dyson, John P **243**, **244**

Eagles, John **441**
Eagles, William **441**
Eakers, Harry **190**
Eakin, Frank **35**
Earl, John Wesley **287**
Early, John Oliver **296**
Eastham, J *256*, *289*, *344*, *419*, *444*, *472*
Eastham, James Buckley **245**, **246**, *256*, *257*
Eastwood, Annie **30**
Eastwood, George Smith **80**
Eaton & Wrighton *24*, **137**, **138**, *206*, *447*
Eaton & Wrighton Ltd *38*, **138**
Eaton, Bertram **60**
Eaton, Fred Henry **137**, **138**, **147**
Eaton, William *481*
Ebert, H & Co **191**
Eden, Albert Edmund **31**
Edgar, Edgar Samuel **208**
Edge, A B **462**
Edge, W J *462*
Edmonds, E *292*
Edmonds, Frank **165**
Edmonds, G **165**
Edmonds Henry **165**
Edmonton, John **246**
Edward & Sons **110**, **135**
Edward Brothers *106*, *128*, *129*, *351*
Edward, Arthur **110**
Edward, Charles Alfred **135**
Edward, Charlotte Robertson **135**
Edward, David **110**
Edward, David Herbert **110**
Edward, George **110**
Edwards & Sons **135**
Edwards Bros *118*, *255*, *287*, *423*, **446**
Edwards, Arthur **31**, **122**
Edwards, Charles Edward **135**
Edwards, David **80**
Edwards, Edward Henry **135**
Edwards, G **166**
Edwards, G & Co **166**
Edwards, George **166**
Edwards, Griffith I **165**
Edwards, Griffith II **165**
Edwards, John Frederick **135**
Edwards, Olive **328**
Edwards, Peter I & II **488**
Edwards, Samuel Robert **398**
Edwards, William Henry **455**
Eedee Manufacturing Co **122**
Eels Brothers & Brown *212*
Eels, William **442**
Eggington, William James **460**
Ehrhardt, G V **442**
Ehrhardt, William *140*, *264*, **441**, **442**
Elco Clocks & Watches Ltd **121**
Elcose, George Stephen **177**
Eldridge, J *141*
Eldridge, John *246*
Elite Bracelet Manufacturing Co Ltd *149*, *204*, *343*, **366**, **460**
Elkan, John **246**
Elkington & Co Ltd **121**
Elkington, Allan H **247**
Elkington, Chas William **103**
Elkington, Hula G **121**
Elkington, Leigh A **479**
Elkington, Thomas **103**

Elliott & Sheldon **134**
Elliott, Charles **80**, **134**
Elliott, Joseph & Son *247*
Elliott, Joseph G **247**
Elliott, Joseph Harris **223**, **257**
Ellis & Co **121**
Ellis & Co (Birmingham) Ltd **121**
Ellis, Hilda Margaret **486**
Ellis, Randolph John Keith **351**
Ellison & Co **221**
Ellison & Fishwick **408**
Ellison, Charles **80**
Ellison, John **221**
Ellison, John & Timothy **229**
Ellison, Timothy **408**
Ellison, W **441**
Ellwood, Robert Wm **373**
Elston, Charles **80**
Emanuel, Joseph **122**
Emanuel, M **312**
Emary, Cyril **80**
Emerson, Willm Ambrose **434**
Emmanuel, A Leon **204**
Emmanuel, H *190*
Emmanuel, Harry **190**, *302*
Emmanuel, H M & Son **204**
Emmanuel, Maurice **312**
Emrick Ltd **486**
Emrick, Richard **486**
Engley, Charles Richard **97**
Ensell, John MacKay **359**
Ensign Umbrellas Ltd **444**
Entwhistle, William Thos **115**, **477**
Eprile, Lyon **300**
Errington, Chas Hutton **87**
Errington Watch Co *87*
Ettlinger, A T **325**
Ettlinger, Joseph **246**
European & General Express Co Ltd **125**, *480*
Evans Concinnum Metal Works Ltd **53**
Evans & Browns **119**
Evans, Albert Edward **31**
Evans, Annabel **31**
Evans, C E *237*
Evans, Edward & Son *125*
Evans, Edward E **31**
Evans, Edward Masters **132**
Evans, E J **127**
Evans, E M & Son **132**
Evans, I J & Co *194*
Evans, I J & Son *194*
Evans, James **221**, **245**
Evans, J J & Co *316*
Evans, M **312**
Evans, Samuel Hindle **260**, **386**
Evans, Sydney Lloyd **392**
Evans, Thos Humphrey **260**, **386**
Evans, Violet Moorly **431**
Evenson, A **77**
Everett, Edgar **122**
Everington, Alfred **31**
Evetts & Lamb **130**
Evetts, Bert William **130**
Evison, William Roscoe **394**
Fack, Michael **313**
Fairweather & Son **154**
Fairweather, Will Wilson **154**
Falconer, Joseph **222**
Faller, Stephan **386**
Faraday & Davey **73**
Faraday, Charles **84**
Faraday, Chas Adkins **73**
Faraday, Chas Arthur **73**
Faraday, Warren **73**
Farquharson, Chas H **89**
Farrer, Henry **192**
Farren, Steph *140*, *153*, *251*, **386**, *464*
Farror, Jean Jacques **261**
Fattorini & Son **153**, **154**
Fattorini & Sons **153**
Fattorini, Edward **153**, **154**
Fattorini, Edwin **153**
Fattorini, Frank **153**, **206**, **408**, **409**
Fattorini, John **153**, **154**
Fattorini, John & Sons **153**
Fattorini, Thomas **153**, **206**, **408**, **409**
Fattorini, Thos (Bham) Ltd **153**, **408**
Fattorini, Thomas (Skipton) Ltd **409**
Fattorini, Wilfred **206**, **409**
Faudel, Phillips & Sons **152**
Faulkner, Philip Henry **336**
Favie, James **483**
Fawson, James **247**, **248**
Fay, James **149**
Fazakerley, John **222**
Fear, Amos Daniel **149**
Fear, Amos Reginald Portius **149**
Fear, Edwin **123**
Fears Ltd **149**
Feilding Brothers **141**
Feinknope, J **248**
Fekelmeyer, Ferdinand **60**
Feltham, Joseph **248**
Fenn, Margaret **313**
Fennell, Arthur **32**
Fennell, Richard *143*, **351**
Fenton Russell & Co Ltd **152**, **153**
Fenton, James *169*, **247**, **248**, *288*
Fenton, J L **152**
Fenwick, Arthur **32**
Fenwick, Arthur Ltd **32**
Ferguson & McBean **150**
Ferguson, Charles H **87**
Ferguson, H *188*
Ferguson, Herbert **192**
Fetter, Forbes & Co **144**
Fetter, Walter **144**
Fetter, Walter Hickman **144**
Field, F *77*
Field, Gordon W **280**
Field, J W **317**
Fildes, Stella **386**
Finch, Eliza **123**
Finch, Percy James **336**
Finch, P J *449*
Findley, W H **455**
Finlayson, John **248**
Firestone, Joseph **248**
Firth, Susie **489**
Fischer, Randolf **351**
Fisher & Holmes **146**
Fisher & Poole **152**
Fisher, Augustus **415**
Fisher, Charles **83**
Fisher, George **152**
Fisher, George Birkett **11**
Fisher, Henry Edward **415**
Fisher, John **146**, **221**
Fisher, Norah Eileen **324**
Fisher, Richard **351**
Fisher, W *405*
Fisher, Walter John **460**
Fisher, William **443**
Fishwick, Henry **191**, **192**, **408**
Fishwick, Hugh **192**
Fitter, Henry & Sons **192**
Fitton, John **247**
Fleckner, John **248**, *274*, *384*, *402*, *411*, *443*
Fleming, John **277**
Fleming, J & R **277**
Fleming, Robert James **277**
Fleming, Thomas **408**
Fletcher & Hooper **146**
Fletcher, C W **103**, **104**
Fletcher, C W & Son Ltd **103**
Fletcher, C W & Sons Ltd **103**, **104**
Fletcher, Cyril Otley **191**
Fletcher, Frederick Willm **146**
Fletcher, Harold **104**
Fligelstone, Hannah Phoebe **205**
Flint, Clarence *370*
Flint, Frederick & Co **144**
Flixher, Maurice **313**
Flockton, Elizabeth Frances **144**
Flower, William **443**
Flowers, C P **387**
Floyd, Charles Frederick **84**
Floyd, Mr *435*, *470*
Floyd, William Henry **81**, **84**
Flynn, Edwin **123**
Flynn, Joseph **247**
Foliott, John *61*
Follis & Payton **152**
Follis, Thomas **409**
Follis, William **152**, **443**
Foot, J Taylor *149*, *337*
Forbes, Richard Hutchinson **353**
Ford & Galloway Ltd **145**
Ford & Medley Ltd **151**
Ford, P **145**
Ford, William **443**
Forge Ltd, The **365**
Forth, Alfred **32**
Foskett, Samuel **386**
Foster, Barbara Miss **60**
Foster, Betty Mrs **60**
Foster, Isaac **149**
Foster (Manchester) & Co Ltd **149**
Foster, Margaret MacQueen **318**
Fothergill, John **61**
Fothill, Sydney **480**
Fowler, John **222**
Fox, Charles & Co Ltd **89**
Fox, Charles James **89**
Fox, C J & Co **89**
Foxall, Thomas **408**
Foxhall, E **123**
Foye, Edward **324**
Foye, Nicholas *189*
France, Elizabeth **123**, **328**
France, James **222**, **328**
France, M **313**
Francis & Johnson **147**
Francis, Edward **123**
Francis, H **147**
Francis, John Horace **111**
Francis, William **443**
Franklin & Hare Ltd **147**
Franzi, Orester & Co **328**
Fraser, A J & Co **38**
Fraser, Angus Jeffrey **38**
Fraser, Donald **111**
Fraser, Walter Walsh **480**
Fray, Joseph *76*, **248**
Frazer, Thomas **408**
Fredericks Ltd **149**, **150**
Freeman & Co **282**, **283**
Freeman, Adelaide **222**
Freeman, George *378*
Freeman, George Augustus **299**
Freeman, Harry **313**
Freeman, H C Ltd **187**
Freeman, Henry Charles **187**, **188**, **299**
Freeman, I & Son Ltd **222**
Freeman, Joseph **248**
Freeman, M *368*, *446*
Freeman, Maurice **313**
Freeman, Samuel **386**
Fremaux, Maurice Leon **313**
French Tobacco Co **393**
Fridlander, Alfred **32**
Fridlander, Moss **316**
Friedlander & Co **313**
Friedlander, A & Co **313**
Friedlander, Harry **192**
Friedlander, Julia **313**
Freidlander, Lesser **301**
Friedlander, Montague Alexander **313**
Friedman & Gottliffe Ltd **145**
Friedmann, Aaron **145**
Friend, Henry Herbert **196**
Friend, Isiah **222**
Friend, Isiah & Co **222**
Frisch & Schierwater **154**
Friswell, C *320*
Fritz & Charles *133*
Frost, G A **159**
Frost, G A & Co **159**
Frost, G Allen **159**
Fry, C F & Sons **84**
Fry, Charles Edwin **84**
Fryer, Norman Hilary **324**
Fulda & David **143**, **144**
Fulda, Otta **143**, **144**
Fulford -- *212*
Fulford, John Joseph **156**
Fulford, William James **460**
Furness, Leslie **301**
Futter, Ann *301*
Futter, Nathan **171**, *301*
Gadsby, Stanley Herbert **388**
Gaffin, Charles **85**
Galilee, Thomas George **410**
Gammage, George Henry **250**, **306**
Gammage, J *54*, *65*, *89*, *218*, **249**, **250**, *294*, *301*, *317*, *337*, *394*
Gammage, John Ellis **250**, **251**, **306**
Gammage, Sydney Herbert **306**
Ganter, John **322**
Gardner, Harold **196**
Gardner, Timothy **410**
Gardner, William **445**
Gardner-Powell, Edward Stanley **196**
Garner & Stevens **176**
Garner, John **249**
Garrard & Co Ltd **164**
Garrud, William Francis **443**
Garside, Samuel **387**
Garstang, Thos Critchly **164**
Garstin, A & Co **33**
Garstin, Arthur **33**
Garstin, Arthur George **33**
Gate, George Elliott **166**
Gatecliff, John **249**, **487**
Gaunt, C F **416**
Geary, E **322**
Geddes, William Andrew **434**
Gee, George Edward **166**
Geiger, W & Co **445**
Geiger, William **445**
Gem Box Ltd, The **161**
Gemcraft Jewellers **171**
George & Co **164**
George & Gibbons **169**
George, Alexander **169**
George, Gwyneth Edwina **166**
George, Walter Hudson **314**
Gerber Brothers & Co **160**
Gerber, Barnett **61**
Gerber, Hyman **160**
Gerber, Matthew **160**
Gerrard, Samuel **387**
Gershon(am), Samuel **386**, **482**
Gibbons, Edward James **169**
Gibbs, Ella Gladys **292**
Gibbs, S C **476**
Gibbs, Solomon **387**
Gibbs, Sydney Coral **476**
Gibson & Co **116**, **164**
Gibson & Co Ltd **164**
Gibson, Arthur Cecil *21*
Gibson, Robert **61**
Gibson, William **309**
Gieve, J F **116**
Gilbert & Son **446**
Gilbert, Charles *448*
Gilbert, E P **448**, **449**
Gilbert, John **223**, **250**
Gilbert, Walter Fraser **443**
Gill, Janet Mathieson **269**
Gilpin & Co **193**
Gilpin, Francis Walter **216**
Gilpin, H **409**
Gilpin (Twine & Gilpin) **409**
Ginder & Couch *61*, *272*, *299*, *320*, *347*, *409*, *460*
Ginder & Ginder **169**, *455*
Ginder Brothers *444*
Ginder, Joseph Curmin **169**
Ginder, Walter Joseph **169**
Ginder, Walter Lister **465**
Ginder, William Edward **442**
Ginder, William Henry **169**, **442**
Gittens, Thomas **170**
Glass, S **387**
Glass, S G **387**
Glass, S & G **387**
Glaysher, Arthur John **398**
Glazer, Carl **84**
Gleadall, Albert **32**
Glesson, Henry W **215**
Glikston, N G **344**
Gloster, C F **252**
Gloster, E **252**
Gloster, G **252**
Gloster, Joseph **251**
Gloster, Joseph Ltd **252**
Gloster, L J **252**
Gloster, O E **252**
Glover, James **223**, **250**
Glover, J G **251**
Glover, Walter **444**
Goad, Alfred & Son **34**
Goad, Alfred Charles **34**
Goad, Percy & Co **34**
Godfrey, Lewis H **128**
Godwin, A **269**
Godwin, E G **177**
Goepell, J R **226**

Gophir Diamond Co Ltd **165**
Goldberg & Co **163**
Goldberg, Isaac **223**
Goldberg, Kiva **163**
Goldie, W C & Co Ltd **440**
Goldie, William Cowan **440**
Golding, Maurice **314**
Goldman, Mark **314**
Goldmesh Bag Co Ltd **173**
Goldsmith, F **145**, *184*
Goldsmith, F & Co *216, 237, 416*
Goldsmith, Fred Willm **145**
Goldsmith, Michael Joseph **316**
Goldsmith & Silversmith Retail, The **146**
Goldsmiths Company, The **489**
Goldsmiths Emporium **430, 431**
Goldsmiths & Silversmiths Co Ltd **177**
Goldstone, Adolph Lionel **42**
Goldstone, Sampson **387**
Goldwhite, Harold **192**
Gollner, Charles **84**
Gooch, Ephraim **125**
Goodall & Skelton **176**
Goodall, Edward **176**
Goode, Albert Conrad **252**
Goode, Ernest William **252**
Goode, John & Son **252**
Goode, Samuel William **401, 402**
Goode, S W & Co **401, 402**
Goodenough, W H **336**
Goodfriend, Paul P **335**
Gooding, Edwd Rhymer **406**
Gooding, Edward Ryan **406**
Gooding, Thos C & Co **406**
Gooding, Thos Claude **406**
Goodman, George **168**
Goodwin, James Richard **249**
Gopsill & Sanders **176**
Gopsill, Thomas Frank Lloyd **176**
Gordon, Bert **61, 71**
Gordon, Ivor Ltd **223**
Gorham Manufacturing Co *110*
Gosling, J N **366**
Gosling, Selina Ann **272**
Goss, Alfred Charles **436**
Gottliffe, Lazarus **145**
Gough, Edward **124**
Gough, Frank **144, 145, 399**
Gould & Palmer Ltd **174**
Gould, Edward Havelock **61**
Gould, W P **174**
Gourdel, Vale & Co **178**
Graf, Arthur **33**
Grant, James Wadham **466**
Grant, Montague **400**
Grant, William Corrie **466**
Gratz, Maurice **314**
Gravenor, Robert **55**, *123*, **352**
Graves, John George **251**
Gray, Andrew James **188**
Gray, E & Son Ltd **126**
Gray, Joseph **126**
Greaves, Henry **193**
Greaves, H Ltd **193**
Green & Cadbury Co *251*
Green & Cadbury Ltd **163**
Green & Carpenter **169**
Green & Son **176**
Green & Wyke **230**
Green, Charles **84**
Green, Charles S **101**
Green, Charles Stevenson **84**
Green, Chas S & Co Ltd **101**
Green, Charles & Son **84, 85**
Green, Edith Emily **125**
Green, Ernest **134**
Green, George **169, 176**
Green, H *281, 345*
Green, Henry **193**, *368*
Green, Hugh **192, 193**, *256, 386, 419, 475*
Green, Isaac **222**
Green, James **436**
Green, John Hugh Thomas **387**
Green, Joseph **249**
Green, Lionel A **85**
Green, Philip **315**
Green, Robert **352**
Green, Roland **85**
Green, Thomas & Wyke, John **230**
Green, Thomas I **410**
Green, Thomas II **409**
Green, Walter **445**
Greenberg, Herbert S **228**
Greenberg, H S & Co *228*
Greenberg, I S & Co **121, 227, 228**
Greenberg, I S & Co Ltd **228**
Greenberg, Israel Sigmund **121, 228**
Greenhough, George **388**
Greenhough, Samuel **386, 388**
Greenhough, Samuel & Sons **388**
Greening, Benjamin Thomas **71**
Greening, B T Ltd **258, 259**
Greenwood, Ernest E **290**
Gregory, A R **301**
Gregory, Richard **351**
Grey & Co *135*, **180, 181**
Griffin, H **380, 381**
Griffin, Henry William **215**
Griffin, J & R *23, 61, 71, 77, 82, 93, 125, 127, 128, 148, 175, 178, 180, 205, 210, 217, 228*, **251**, *258, 259*, **277**, *294, 296, 305, 309, 310, 317, 328, 330, 331, 332, 334, 347, 383, 385, 413, 415, 431, 457, 467, 477*
Griffin, J & R Ltd *112, 115, 189, 199, 315, 442, 467*
Griffin, Joseph James **251, 277**
Griffin, Richard Charles **251, 277**
Griffith, E & Sons **126**
Griffith, Ernest **126**
Griffith, Frederic **194**
Griffith, Frederic Priestley **194**
Griffith, Henry **193**
Griffith, Henry & Sons **194**, *223, 289, 372*
Griffith, H & Son *97, 315*
Griffith, H & Sons *158, 176*, **194**, *197, 318, 387, 400*
Griffith, H & Sons Ltd *23, 34, 73*, **194**, *287*
Griffith, William **445**
Griffiths & Jones **90**
Griffiths, A **442, 451**
Griffiths, Alfred George **33**, *45, 111, 125, 178, 286, 408*
Griffiths, Arthur *267*, **447**
Griffiths, C & Co **164**
Griffiths, Charles **447**
Griffiths, Ernest **125**
Griffiths, J *113, 397*
Griffiths, James **251**
Griffiths, Norman Weaver **445**
Griffiths, R H **348**
Griffiths, W **387**
Griffiths, Walter **447**
Griffiths, Walter George **447**
Griffiths, W G & Sons **447, 448**
Griffiths, William **445**
Griffiths, William & Co **164**
Griffiths, William & Jones, Christopher **90**
Grimes, Samuel **71**
Grimsdale, Alfred **33**
Grinesley, R W **252**
Gringas, L Ltd **301**
Grinstead, W **444**
Grounds, Stephen **276**
Grove & Co **163**
Grove Brothers *317, 461*
Grove, Silas Cornelius **163**
Grove, Thomas **409, 410**
Groves Brothers **178**, *334*
Groves, Arthur Henry **178**
Groves, Thomas E C **178**
Grundy, Edward E **480**
Grundy, Eric **125**
Guibout, Henry **318**
Guild of Handicraft **174**
Gulson, Henry **318**
Gumpleson, Marcus **314**
Gunn, Arthur Mainwaring **44**
Gunzel & Rosenberger **301**
Gunzel, Ludwig **301**
Gurney, Alfred **32**
Gutfreund, Paul P **335**
Guyton, John William **287, 288**
Gyde, Edwin Lewis **131**
Hack, Henry Stanley **209, 210**
Hack, H S Ltd **209**
Hack, John **254**
Hadden, Louis **341**
Haddleton, William **453**
Hadgkiss & Wright **456**
Hadgkiss, Ada Miss *63*
Hadgkiss, S H **456**
Hadgkiss, William **452, 456**
Hadley & Hadley **195**, *290*
Hadley, Arthur **195**
Hadley, Cornelius **195**
Hadwen(wine), Isaac III **223**
Hair, Walker S **302**
Hale, Thomas *189, 218, 400*, **410, 412**
Hall & Fitzgerald **192**
Hall & Goode **193**
Hall & Wigley *22, 49, 79*, **90, 448, 451**, *486*
Hall, Arthur Devereux **448, 451**
Hall, Charles Benjamin **188, 189**
Hall, Eric Noel **327**
Hall, H & Sons *146*
Hall, Hubert **195**
Hall, Noel Victor **327**
Hall, N V & Son **327**
Hall, Richard **352, 353**
Hall, Sydney Co **388**
Hall, Sydney James **388, 390**
Hall, Thomas **411**
Hall, William Henry **241**
Hall, William Sydney **192**
Hallam, Jesse **255**
Hallet, J *156*
Hallett, Frank **146**
Halley, John Stott **370, 371**
Halliday, Arthur **86**
Hamersley, Donald Edw **110**
Hames, C **384**
Hamilton & Co **188**
Hamilton & Co Ltd **169, 171, 189**
Hamilton, H **116**
Hammon, John **223**
Hammon, William *234, 443*, **451**
Hammon, William George **446**
Hammon, William John **460**
Hampton, C J **335**
Hancock, Mortimer William **412**
Hancock, Roland James **412**
Hand, Arthur **34**
Handcock & Walker *53, 72, 207, 210*, **214**, *303, 313, 394*
Handcock, W A N **214**
Handcocks, O H **329**
Hancox, Thomas **410**
Hands, Arthur **34, 35**, *127*
Hands, Walter *176*, **452**
Hands, William **448**
Harbinson, John Francis **249**
Harburg, Henry **451**
Harding Brothers **186**
Harding, Arthur W **147**
Harding, Frank **146**
Harding, Frederick **147**
Harding, F & Son **147**
Harding, J *325*
Harding, Nelly **325**
Harding, Trevor Wilson **410**
Hardman, Edward John **127**
Hardwick, William **453**
Hardy Brothers **184, 185**
Hardy Brothers Ltd **185**
Hardy, Samuel **185**
Hardy, Samuel Houston **185**
Hardy, Thomas Edward **256, 257**
Hargreaves, J & Co **256**
Hargreaves, James **256**
Hargreaves, Joseph & John **224, 261**
Harling, Henry **451**
Harller, Frank E **59**
Harman & Co **189**
Harmer, Chas James **89**
Harper, David **191**
Harper, George John **336**
Harper, John George **336**
Harper, Mary Ellen **312**
Harper, N A *434*
Harper, Richard **352, 353**
Harper, Robert **353**
Harper, U E **429**
Harrington & Co **188, 189**
Harrinson, Myer **315**
Harris of Coventry *419*
Harris & Palmer **205**
Harris & Scott **212, 257**
Harris & Usher **212**
Harris, Abraham **35**
Harris, C *224, 270, 402*
Harris, Charles **86**
Harris, Cyril **205**
Harris, Frank Unite **370, 371**
Harris, Henry & Co **195**
Harris, I & Sons Ltd **223**
Harris, Isaac **223**
Harris, J *43, 89, 331, 375, 410*
Harris, John **223, 257**, *431, 443*
Harris, Joseph & Abraham **233, 256**
Harris, Leonard **64, 67**
Harris, Lewis **223**
Harris (Packwood &) **335**
Harris, Robert **352**
Harris, Robert & Co **352**
Harris, W G *43, 68*, **446**
Harris, William **450**
Harrison, Francis F **253**
Harrison, Helen Kinsey **195**
Harrison, James *184*, **253, 255**
Harrison, James & Sons **253**, *475*
Harrison, Jas & Sons Ltd *68*, **253, 254**
Harrison, John *122*
Harrison, Thomas **411**
Harrison, Trevor **253**
Harrison, Wilfred J **253**
Harrison, William **450**
Harrods Stores Ltd **210, 348**
Harrold, Charles **86**
Harrold, Charles & Co **86**
Harrop, Edwin George **126**
Hart & Sons **207**
Hart, David **207**
Hart, Dorothy Mary **114**
Hart, E **126**
Hart, E & Co **126**
Hart, Ernest Albert **118**
Hart, George Henry **174**
Hart, Herbert William **209**
Hart, Lewis **301**
Hart, Louis Emanuel **140**
Hart, Montague **207**
Hart, William **209**
Hart, William & Son **209**
Hartley, Harry **195**
Hartley, Leslie James Anthony **448**
Hartmann, Theodor **412**
Hartsholm, Harry Jutsum **196**
Harvey, G W & Co **179, 180**
Harvey, George William **169, 179**
Harvey, John J **412**
Harvey, T **412**
Harvey, Thomas E **412**
Harwood Brothers **184, 185, 413**
Harwood, Edwin Collier **184, 185, 413**
Harwood, Thomas **184, 185, 413**
Haseler & Bill **127**
Haseler & Holmes **195**, *216, 308*
Haseler & Milner **35, 202**
Haseler Brothers **128**, *152, 193*
Haseler, Arnold **35, 202**
Haseler, Edward John **413**
Haseler, Frank **455**
Haseler, G C & Co *298*
Haseler, H & P **206**
Haseler, Henry **206**
Haseler, Herbert **35, 202**
Haseler, John **65, 195**
Haseler, Noble **128**, *185*, **413**
Haseler, Percy **206**
Haseler, W H Ltd **455**
Haseler, William Hair *114*, **455**
Haseler, Will Rabone **65**
Hawkford, Charles Singleby **208**
Hawkford, Francis Charles **208**
Hawkings, Joseph & Son **258**
Hawkins, F H **88**
Hawkins, George Ernest **166**
Hawkins, Joseph **61, 253, 255**
Hawksworth, Eyre & Co Ltd **191**
Hawley, A E H *173*
Hawley, Cecil F **236**
Hawley, J *108*
Hawley, J & Son *108*
Hayes & Finch Ltd **192**

Hayes Brothers **184**
Hayes, Harry **184**
Hayes, John **223, 253**
Hayes, Ridley **173, 325, 352, 353**
Hayes, Tom **411**
Hayes, William **184**
Haylett, Henry **196**
Hayman & Co **189**
Hayman, Harold Lachman **189**
Hayman, Harry Lewes **189**
Hayne & Co **188, 388**
Hayne, Samuel & Co **188, 388**
Hayne, Sam Holditch Thos **188, 388**
Haynes, Edward Albert **118**
Haysty, Eric John **127**
Hayward, H A **258**
Hayward(wood), J *302, 314, 334, 362, 447*
Hayward(wood), Jos **255, 256, 258**
Hayward, Joseph & Son **258**
Hayward, Percy C **258**
Haywood ? *375*
Haywood, J (Hayward?) *31, 49, 60, 94, 136, 148, 251, 280*
Hazell, Jonathan *128*, **255**
Hazlewood, Geo' Henry **196**
Hazley, Thos Augustine **253**
Heal, Monica **315**
Heales, James **256**
Heaps, Louis **206**
Heaps, Rosenberg & Co **206**
Heasman & Co **38**
Heasman, Alfred John **206, 207**
Heath, Charles **85**
Heath, George & Co **170**
Heath, William **451**
Heaven, Chas Geo **85**, *94*, **150, 314**
Heaven, William Peter **386**
Hector & Watson **212, 213**
Hector, R L **358**
Hector, William **212**
Heeley, Chas Norman **94**
Heinzelmann, Leopold **301**
Hellwig, Marianne **314**
Helsby, James *254*
Helsby, John **254, 255**
Helsby, Margaret **254**
Helsby, Thomas *254*, **410, 411, 412**
Helsby, Thomas & Co **413**
Helsby, Thomas & John **413**
Helsby, Thomas & Son(s) **414**
Helsby, William **451**
Hemming & Hazlewood *99, 155*, **196**, *282*
Hemming, James **254**
Hemming, William **451**
Hemmingway & Glover **193**
Hemmingway, John **254**
Henderson, Dora F S **318**
Henderson, Herbert **195**
Henderson, M M Ltd **318**
Henderson, W Gordon **318**
Henry, Richard Leowe **358**
Hepburn & Wilcox **213, 214**
Hepburn, M G **213, 214**
Herron, George **74**
Hewett, Reginald Walter & Co **373**
Hewitt, John **255**
Hewitt, Joseph **223**
Hewitt, William **62, 452**
Hewitt, Thomas Peter *31, 33, 55, 75, 251, 274, 369, 384, 408, 410*, **419**, *443, 473*
Hewlett, A *35, 248*, **380**
Hewlett, A Ltd **35**
Hewlett, Arthur **35**, *248*
Hewson, F of London *243, 244*
Heywood, Oliver **328**
Heywood, William **450**
Hibberd, George Henry **170**
Hickman, Edward **126, 390**
Hickman, William *123*, **448**
Higgison, Alfred **35**
Higgs Brothers **197**
Higgs, Fred **197**
Higgs, George **197**
Higgins, S **388**
Highland, Alfred **35**
Highland, Frederick **146**
Highman & Co **189**
Highman, Charles **189**
Highman, Henry **189**
Hildyard & Shindler **208**
Hildyard, William Arthur **208**
Hiley, Joseph **256**
Hill Brothers (Wholesale) Ltd **183**
Hill, Arthur **35, 193**
Hill, Charles **86**
Hill, Charles J **86, 485**
Hill, Harry **180**
Hill, Rowland **353**
Hill, Samuel **388**
Hill, Stanley George **489**
Hill, Thomas **411**
Hill, Thomas & Co **353, 411**
Hillary, Vera **430**
Hillcox, Gordon **169**
Hilliard & Thompson *124*, **211**
Hilling, Arthur William **29**
Hilling, Julian Oliver **29**
Hilton, Philip **335**
Hilton, Robert **296, 352**
Hinds Ltd **201**
Hinds, T N **201**
Hinds, W **201**
Hinds, W Ltd **201**
Hinds, William **201**
Hines, Richard **458**
Hinks, John **61**
Hirschfeld, Alex **414**
Hirschfeld, Tobias **411, 414**
Hirschfeld, T & Son **414**
Hirst Brothers & Co Ltd **184, 185, 186, 305**, *435, 438*
Hirst, Alfred **184, 185**
Hiscocks, F **146**
Hitchin, C *436*
Hobson, Mrs Annie **35**
Hobson, George F **196, 197**
Hobson, Henry & Son **196, 197**
Hobson, Henry Stanley **196, 197**
Hodel, Joseph A **254**
Hodges, John J **177**
Hodgetts, Chas Victor **163**
Hodgetts, G & C **163**
Hodgetts, George Henry **163**
Hodgson, Henry Stockdale **209**
Hodson, Philip **365**
Hoffnung, S & Co **205**
Holden, Charles Arthur **212**
Holden, George **169**
Holden, Hyla George **169**
Holder, Samuel **388**
Holland, Arthur Leslie **42**
Holland, Marc Alfred **307**
Holland, Hugh **486**
Holland, Wm Charles **100**
Hollander, David & Son **112**
Hollander, Elias Pinkus **112**
Hollick, John Henry **454**
Hollins & Jacques *41, 152*, **197**, *467*
Hollins, Henry **197**
Hollings, John **253**
Hollis & Newman *124*, **204**, *299, 346*
Hollis, Frederick **146**
Hollis, John William **288**
Hollis, William Edward **204**
Holman, Archibald Stephen **49**
Holmes, C W *348*
Holmes, Donald Francis **146**
Holmes, Harold **195**
Holmes, Helen **195**
Holmes, Howard **460**
Holmes, W F **444**
Holmes, Willm Fred **163, 195, 444**
Holmes, William J *240*, **461**
Holmes, William J Ltd **460**
Holt, Lawrence C Whalley **300**
Hooper, Charles John **146**
Hooper, Edwin **126**
Hooper, Isabel Florence **222**
Hope, Edward **270**
Hope, Rose **388**
Hope, Samuel *106, 149, 201, 206, 336*, **388**, *409, 427*
Hope, Samuel Henry **388**
Hopkinson, Dorothy Irene **113**
Hopkinson, John Hubert **257**
Hopwood, Arthur **34**
Hopwood, Peter **205, 489**
Horne, R S **370, 371**
Horner, Bertram **62**
Horner, Charles *22, 28, 38*, **75, 86**, *125, 182, 185, 187, 192, 211, 215, 217, 241, 257, 284, 309, 310, 339, 364, 383, 415, 417, 437, 455, 458*
Horner, Charles Ltd *82, 84*, **85, 86, 87**, *178, 185, 258, 284, 315, 321, 340*
Horner, Charles Henry **86**
Horner, Colin Stephen **85, 86, 87**
Horner, E W Thadaway **215**
Hort, N **325**
Horton & Allday *170*, **182, 183**, *211*
Horton & Co **126**
Horton & Jolliffe **197**
Horton Brothers **186**
Horton, C A *20*
Horton, Chas Arthur **73**
Horton, E *193*
Horton, Edwin **126**
Horton, Frederick Hart **197**
Horton, J *73*
Horton, J & Son **71, 258, 259**
Horton, James **186**
Horton, J H *197*
Horton, John **186, 255**, *311*
Horton, Joshua & Son **258**
Horton, J V **285**
Horton, J V & Son *285*
Horwitz, Arthur Julius **38**
Houel & Co **188, 301**
Houel, Louis **188, 301**, *422*
Hough, Richard **163**
Houghton, Fred George **145**
Houlston, J *227*
Houlston, J &H *362*, **442**
Houlston, William Ernest *284*, **442**
Hovenden, Albert **353**
Hovenden, Charles Wm **353**
Hovenden, R & Son Ltd **353**
Hovenden, R & Sons **353**
Hovenden, Robert **353**
Howard & Baker *452*
Howard & Walsh Ltd **217, 218**
Howard, Hannah **196**
Howard, S **108**
Howard, William **453**
Howell, Henry & Co **255**
Howell, Jonathan **255**
Howell, Thomas **205, 490**
Howes, Samuel Johnson **388**
Howitt, Dudley Russell **115**
Howitt, Harry **196**
Howitt, Harry Joseph **199**
Hoyle, Frederick William **158**
Hubbert, Henry James **237**
Huber, William James **460**
Hufton, G L **309**
Hugh, Edward **126**
Hughes & Son **207**
Hughes & Young **218**
Hughes, Charles **411**
Hughes, Herbert **218**
Hughes, Robert Llewellyn **207**
Hughes, T E *322*
Hughes, Thomas Edgar **408**
Hughes, Thomas Edward **408**
Hughes, William **448, 452, 453**
Hulbert, Henry James **65**
Hull, Henry **195**
Hull, Thomas **412**
Hull, William **451**
Hume, James Cookson **301**
Humphreys, Alfred Wm **54**
Humphries, Benjamin **62**
Humpidge, Chauncey Ltd **88**
Hundy & Co **36**
Hundy, A & Co **35**
Hundy, Albert **35, 36**
Hunt, E M **460**
Hunt, Frank **146**
Hunt, George Edward **170**
Hunt, George J **171**
Hunt, John Price **272**
Hunt, Percy George **455**
Hunt, W H **455**
Huntingdon, H M **195, 315**
Huntingdon, Mary **315**
Huntingdon, S **315, 388**
Huntley, H & Sons **196**, *393*
Huntriss, Dorothy **112**
Hussey, H **383**
Hutchense & Cooper **186**
Hutchfield, I M **225**
Hutchings, John Hanmer **257**
Hutchinson, E J **369**
Hutchinson, F & Co **147, 460**
Hutchinson, Francis William **460**
Hutchinson, Frederick **147**
Hutchinson, George E **369**
Hutchinson, William **451**
Hutchinson, William John **460**
Hutchinson, W L **369**
Hutt, William **448**
Hutton, Herbert **476**
Hutton, Robert **476**
Hutton, Robert Salmon **476**
Hutton, William & Son Ltd **476**
Huxley & Sidebotham **207**
Huxley, George **207**
Hyams, Arthur **209**
Hyatt, William **451**
Hyde, Henry & Son *100*, **208**
Hyde (Newton &) **325**

Illiffe, Charles G **85**
Illinois Watch Case Co Ltd **230**
Imbrey, William Thomas **477**
Imperial Tobacco Co *52, 92, 130, 140, 191, 196, 207, 209, 355, 391, 392, 450*
Inge, Bernard **64**
International Watch Co **144**
Ireland, Arthur George **37, 389**
Irwin Brothers **220**
Irwin, Albert **220**
Irwin, Ebenezar **127**
Irwin, Chas **325**
Irwin, Leonard **220**
Isaac & Co **220**
Isaac, Louis **220**
Isaacs, Arthur Danziger **112, 113**
Isaacs, J W **177**
Isherwood, A **36**
Isherwood, Alfred **36, 37**, *81*
Isherwood, Edmund **197**
Isherwood, I & Partners **37**
Izon, John **260**

Jackson & Hickman **390**
Jackson & Sons *111, 114*
Jackson Brothers *41, 231*, **238**
Jackson, A *100, 397*
Jackson, Albert **37**
Jackson, Arthur **38**
Jackson, D F Ltd **112**
Jackson, Edward **127**
Jackson, Edwin **311**
Jackson, Frank Clarabut **311**
Jackson, G H **170**
Jackson, H & Sons *200*
Jackson, Henry **414**
Jackson, Henry Philip **200**
Jackson, James **260**
Jackson, James Arthur **233**
Jackson, James & Son **261**
Jackson, Joseph *179*, **261**
Jackson, Joseph Marshall **269**, *297*
Jackson, J W **112**
Jackson, L & Co **88, 171, 302**
Jackson, Leonard George **88, 171**
Jackson, Leslie Edwin **311**
Jackson, Montague Leonard **317**
Jackson, P **238**
Jackson, P F Ltd *273*, **334**, *335*
Jackson, Percy Freder'k **334, 335, 441**
Jackson, Samuel **390**, *402*
Jackson, Walter **112**
Jackson, William **430, 459**
Jacob, Louis **301**
Jacob, Samuel **299**
Jacobinsky, Mark **315**
Jacobs Brothers **260**
Jacobs, Daniel **113, 204**
Jacobs, E & Co **129**
Jacobs, Edward Lewis **128, 129**
Jacobs, E & Son **128, 129**
Jacobs, J L **20**
Jacobs, John Gibborn **252**
Jacobs, Joshua **260**
Jacobs, Joshua Michael **269**
Jacobs, J M & Co **269**
Jacobs, Lewis Henry **129**

Jacobs, Richard Alfred **200**
Jacobs, Samuel James **200**
Jacobson, A & Co **38**
Jacobson, Aaron Harry **38**
Jacobson, Joseph **260**
Jacobson, Julius **38**
Jacques, Frederick **197**
James & Co **240**
James Brothers **238**
James, George **238**
James, Howard **197**
James, John **260**
Jardalla, Josephine Georgina **251**
Jay Brothers **235**
Jay, Arthur Wolf **235**
Jay, David Fack **235**
Jay, James **260**
Jay, James Charles **261, 276**
Jay, Richard Attenborough & Co **260**
Jay, Rich Attenborough & Co Ltd **276**
Jays **374**
Jays, Robert William **374**
Jee, William **459**
Jeffries & Smith *213*, **278**
Jellinek, Sigmund Edmund **386**
Jenkes, Henry **221**
Jenkins, Albert Ernest *31, 284*
Jenner, A W & Co **54**
Jenner, Chas F **105**
Jensen, Georg **171**
Jeremiah, Duncan Eric **111**
Jessup, Matthew John **316**
Jinks, Edward & Co **127**
Joel, Joe **260**
John, Charles **157**
John, Kathleen May **295**
Johnson & Co **37**
Johnson & White **322**
Johnson & Yates **290**
Johnson, Walker & Tolhurst **477**
Johnson, Walker & Tolhurst Ltd **290, 480**
Johnson, Alfred **37**
Johnson, Charles **290**
Johnson, Edward & Son **128, 129**
Johnson, James **224, 260**
Johnson, J J *389*
Johnson, P **136**
Johnson, T **147**
Johnson, William Henry **459, 463**
Johnson, W & Son Ltd **463**
Johnson, W C **463**
Johnston, J *326*
Johnston, Will Harold & Sons **461**
Johnston, William Jackson **461**
Johnstone, George Harry **486**
Johnstone, George Hope **486**
Johnstone, G H & Co *329, 378*
Jolly, Thomas **414**
Jonas Brothers **238**
Jonas, Isaac **238**
Jones & Abbott **37, 458**
Jones & Crompton *196*, **240**
Jones & Griffiths **90**
Jones & Hazley **253**
Jones & Jackson **261**
Jones & Painter **272**
Jones & Reeves **227**
Jones & Stubbs **279**
Jones & Walley **286, 459**
Jones, Albert Edward **31**, *147*
Jones, Arthur Percy **347**
Jones, Christopher **88, 89, 90**
Jones, David **418**
Jones, Edward **127**
Jones, Edward Cecil **346, 347**
Jones, E S **240**, *243*
Jones, Francis Robert **398**
Jones, Frederick William **82**
Jones, George **90**
Jones, Grahame **170**
Jones, Harry **151**
Jones, Henry Joseph **253**
Jones, Hugh Edward **191, 279**
Jones, John **224, 260**
Jones, Joseph **261**
Jones, Owen **329**
Jones, Percy John **336**
Jones, R *149, 239, 322, 334, 347, 412*
Jones, R A & Sons **347**
Jones, R A & Sons Ltd **346, 347**
Jones, R & Co **354**
Jones, Reuben **355**
Jones, Richard **355**
Jones, Robert **354, 355**
Jones, Robert Arthur **347**
Jones, Robert & Co **355**
Jones, Robert Henry **353**
Jones, R & Son **354**
Jones, Sidney Herbert **89**
Jones, Thomas **414**
Jones, Wilfred Hird **82**
Jones, William **458, 459**
Jones, William Edward **268**
Jones, William Stewart **475**
Jordan, Reuben **355**
Joseph Brothers **236**
Joseph, Barnett Henry **62**
Joseph, B H & Co **62, 63, 64**, *74, 310, 332, 427, 459*
Joseph, B H & Son *140*
Joseph, George Lionel **63, 340**
Joseph, Joseph **63, 262**
Joseph, Joseph & Sons **262**
Joseph, Leslie Henry **63**
Joseph, Lyon Joseph **302**
Joseph, Percy Barnett **63**
Jowett, Sidney Hill **389**
Junghans Brothers Ltd **239**
Junior Army & Navy Stores **234**

Kalken, Charles Van **102**
Katz, Oscar **40**
Kaufman, H **200**
Kaufman, H & Co **200**
Kaufman, Henry **200**
Kay & Co **293**
Kay & Co Ltd **293, 294, 464**
Kay Brothers **293**
Kay, Ernest **293**
Kay, Frederick **149**
Kay, M **321**
Kay, Teresa **321**
Kay, Willm Kilbourne **293, 294, 464**
Kayman, Gerrard *326*
Kayman, N Ltd **326**
Kean, Annie Macfarlane **40**
Kearton, Janet **487**
Keegan, Mary **316**
Kelly, James Joseph **294**
Kelly, John Derek **243, 262**
Kelly, William **463**
Kemp Brothers **292, 296**
Kemp, Arthur Sidney **292**
Kemp, Charles Milford **292**
Kemp, Charles Wilson **292, 296**
Kemp, Herbert Cunliffe **292**
Kemp, R W **480**
Kemp, W W & Son Ltd **480**
Kendal & Dent **294**
Kendal, James Francis **294**
Kennedy, James **357**
Kennedy, Richard **357**
Kenning, Edwin **129, 130**
Kenning, George **171**
Kent, Alfred **40**
Kent, Grendon **197, 198**
Kent, Harriet **200**
Kerby, Benjamin **64, 65**
Kerby, Edward **130**
Kerby, Herbert **200**
Kernsley, D **415**
Kernsley, Walter **415**
Kerr & Phillips **296**
Kerridge, Arthur Andrew **20**
Kershaw, Fred Francis **89**
Kershaw, Joseph Crabb **89**
Keswick School of Industrial Arts **296**
Ketterer, Bernadine **408**
Ketterer, T E & Co Ltd **408**
Ketterer, Thomas Edward **408**
Keyzor, Baron Isaac **64**
Keyzor, B J & Co **64**
Khun & Co, J N **270**
Khun, J N **270**
Kibble, Charles William **357**
Kibble, Constance Winifred **104**
Kilshaw, Richard **357**
Kind, John **224**
King & Son **262**
King & Sons **294**
King, Henry William **215, 262**
King, Henry W & Son **215**
King, John Percy **262, 294**
Kinnear Ltd **295**
Kinnear & Co **293**
Kinnear Brothers *356*
Kinnear, Charles Maxwell **293, 295**
Kinsey Brothers & Patrick *44, 75, 105, 227, 228*, **292, 293**, *334, 465*
Kinsey Brothers & Patrick Ltd **199**, *298, 335, 404, 423, 442*
Kinsey, John Albert **293**
Kinsey, William Allen **292**
Kippax Brothers **292**
Kippax Brothers Ltd **292**
Kippax, Luke **292**
Kirby, Charles Thomas **101**
Kirby, William Isaac **224**
Kirk, James J **261**
Kirk, John Pattison **318**
Kirk, Jeremiah **262**
Kirk, Joseph **262**
Kirkcaldy, Joan **350**
Kirkes, Daniel **113**
Kirkham, Charles **90**
Kirkley, Isaac **26**
Kirkman & Stuart **130**
Kirkman, Edward **129, 130**
Kirkman, Edward & Co **130**
Kirkman, Richard **357**
Kirkness, S Raleigh **241**
Kirner Brothers **293**
Kirner, Anthony **293**
Kirner, Anthony Leonard **293**
Kirwan & Bolding **292**
Kirwan & Co **288**
Kirwan & Co Ltd **295**
Kirwan, J W **288**
Kirwan, J W & Co **288**
Kitson, Frank **148**
Kitson, Geoffrey Knowles **150**
Kleane, M & Co **316**
Kleane, Simeon **172, 316**
Knight, J *122*
Knight, Joseph **262**
Knight, Kenneth Ltd **295**
Knight, W G & Co **287, 446**
Knight, William **467**
Knight, William George **446**
Kosciukiewicz, M **321**
Kosciukiewicz, Teresa **321**
Koppenhagen Brothers **262**
Koppenhagen, Jacob **262**
Korn, Elias **130**
Krauth, F T **155**
Krumm, Maurice **316**
Kuhn, J N **270**
Kuhn, J N & Co **270**
Kuit, A **391**
Kuit, Aaron **40**
Kuit, Morris **391**
Kuit, Solomon **391**
Kunderd, Fritz **148, 149**
Kunderd, Herbert Fritz **148, 149**
Kyle, Hugh **200**

Lack, Tom William **428**
Lacy, Charles **90**
Lacy-Hulbert, Denise **113**
Lainas, Niobe George **325**
Laithwait, Robert **328**
Laithwait, William **464, 465**
Lake, George Henry **429**
Lake, U **429**
Lakeland Rural Industries **304**
Lakin, William W **465**
Lamb & Co **299**
Lamb, Fred **130**
Lamb, John Edward **247**
Lambin, Henri **200**
Lames & Co **299**
Lampkin, David **113**
Lancashire Watch Co *31, 55, 140, 248, 251, 464*
Lancashire Watch Co Ltd **419**
Lancaster, R F **140**
Lancaster, Ruth **464**
Lancaster, William **464**
Lancasters **464**
Lancelott, G E **172**
Lancelott, G E Ltd **172**
Landeck, Boaz Moses **66**
Landeck, Samuel Boyce (Boaz) **377**
Landenberger & Co **90**
Landenberger, Christian Martin **90**
Landon, Frank Fincher **149**
Landon, Harold Edwin **191**
Lander, Chas Herbert **88**
Landless, Alfred Howarth *36, 405*
Lane, George **172**
Lang Co Ltd **401**
Langford, Francis James **369, 403**
Langford, J Deverill **243**
Langford, Percival Vincent Stan **370**
Langlands, John **224**
Langley & Co **299**
Langley, William **299**
Langman, John Lawrence **309**
Langridge, Alfred **131**
Langridge, E & Co *20*, **131**, *157, 203, 243, 318, 359*
Langridge, Edward **131**
Langridge, Frederick John **131**
Lascelles, Alfred James **348**
Last & Gregory Ltd **301**
Last & Smith **304**
Last, M **301**
Last, W N & Co **469**
Last, William Nelson **304**
Lataiche, Constant Francis **90**
Latham & Morton **416**
Latham, John Francis **249**
Latham, Thomas **416**
Latimer & Sons **305**
Latimer, George Brown **305**
Latimer, Sydney **391**
Latten, Joseph **264**
Lawrence & Lingard **302**
Lawrence, Arthur Jas **39**
Lawrence, Henry **200**
Lawrence, James **263**
Lawrence, Percy **337**
Lawson & Co Ltd **299**
Lawson & Ward **201, 305, 306**
Lawson, Ward & Gammage *43, 58, 65, 69, 74, 138, 170, 250*, **306**, *350, 382, 400*
Lawson, Ward & Gammage Ltd **250, 251**
Lawson, Charles Handley **413**
Lawson, Ernest Fenton **189**
Lawson, Fenton Bowman **416**
Lawson, George Duncan **41**
Lawson, Hy **201, 250, 251, 305, 306**
Lawson, Son & Ward **305**
Lawson, T & Son **416**
Lawson, T H & Co **416**
Lawson, Thomas B **299**
Lawton, Alfred **41**
Laycock, Benjamin **293**
Layfield, Richard Cha **349**
Lazams, John **263**
Lazarus, J **160**
Lea, R J **356**
Lea, Walter Ernest **442**
Leadbeater, Edith **300**
Leapman, Isadore **224**
Leary, James **318**
Leather & Hume **301**
Leather, W A *29*
Leather, W H *352, 445*
Leather, W H & Son *347*
Leather, Will Henry *222, 227, 301*
Leatherbarrow & Hume **301**
Leatherbarrow, William George **301**
Leatlick, W H *377*
LeBas, Samuel **392**
Lecomber, J & E **263**
Lecomber, John *153*, **263**, *281*
Lecte, William Herbert **370**
Lecte, William Septimus **370**
Lederman, A M **395**
Lee, Agnes **42**
Lee, Edward **486**
Lee, Edwin **130**
Lee, Herbert **65**
Lee, Matthew **317**
Lee, Nathaniel **326**
Lee, Nicholson **326**
Leece, John Andrew jnr **233**
Leece, John Arthur **233**

Lees, Frank **149**
Lees, H & Co **201**
Lees, H & Son **201**
Lees, Herbert **201**
Lees, J **325**
Leeson, Ernest **90**, **172**
Leeson, George K **172**, *246*, *251*, *362*
Leeson, G K *73*, *393*
Leete, Mason **317**
Leete, Mason & Co **317**
Lehrer, Stuart **392**
Lennie, Thomas **415**
Lennon, Thomas Henry **415**
Leonard, Patrick **336**
Leonardt Ltd **106**
Leopold Ltd **302**
Leslie & Co **299**
Leton, Joseph **264**
Lester & Damsell **300**
Lester, Henry James **300**
Leonardt, O **105**, **300**
Leonardt, O & Co **300**
Leslie, George **482**
Letowsky, Joseph **263**
Levenberg, Moses **316**
Levetus, Edward Moses **132**
Levetus, Hymen **65**
Levi & Salaman *243*, *244*
Levi & Salaman Ltd **304**
Levi, Charles M **395**
Levi, Clive Joseph **304**
Levi, Cloe J **59**
Levi, Emanuel Henry **23**
Levi, Olive Joseph **191**
Levi, Phineas Harris **304**
Levi, Samuel M **395**
Levy, Louis J & Co **302**
Levy, Louis Jules **302**
Levy, Morris Lawrence **317**
Levy, Ralph **431**
Levy, Samuel David **385**
Levy, Sidney **385**
Levy, Victor **431**
Levy, Victor & Co **431**
Lewis Brothers **297**, **298**
Lewis, Alfred **41**
Lewis, D'Arcy Eville **289**
Lewis, Edward **19**, **131**, **297**
Lewis, Frank **297**
Lewis, Frederick Eric **297**
Lewis, Philip **337**
Lewis, William **464**, **465**
Lichtblan, Rudolf **357**
Liebisch, Richard **357**
Lihman, Hehre **483**
Lilley, E A *130*
Lilley, Edmund **299**
Lilley, Edward *54*, **130**
Lillie, Henry **200**
Lillman & Co **299**
Linday, M **277**
Lindop, William **464**
Line, Arthur James **27**, **90**
Lines, Bunn & Mason *243*
Lingard, Edward **302**
Lingard, Joseph William **302**
Lingley, John I **224**
Lingley, John II **224**
Lingley, Joseph I **224**
Lingley, Joseph II **224**
Linnett, Edw Will *89*, **131**, **138**, *375*
Linsley, William **464**
Lister, Charles & Son **91**
Lister, Samuel **91**
Lister, William & Sons Ltd **466**
Litherland, Davis & Co **300**
Litherland, H *73*, **102**, *464*
Litherland, Henry Raymond **329**
Litherland, Herbert **102**
Littlewood, Marian **317**
Livingstone, Ferdinand **299**
Livingstone, Frederick **299**
Lloyd, Agnes *50*
Lloyd, David **113**
Lloyd, Francis William **60**
Lloyd, James **62**, **264**
Lloyd, James Ossian **158**
Lloyd, R N F **66**
Loach Brothers *59*, *82*, **298**, *417*
Loach, Joseph **298**
Loake, Charles **37**
Lobel, Alfred **42**
Locke, W & Co **465**
Locke, William & Co **465**
Loe, E & Co **131**
Loe, Ernest **131**
Loebl, David **113**
Loecker, Thomas D **329**
Loeker, Thomas M de **407**
Loewenstark, Abraham David **30**
Loewenstark, Marcus David **312**
Lofthouse, Arthur **41**
Lofthouse, Benjamin **65**
Loftus, Asher *54*
London Assay Office *171*
London Refining & Metallurgical Works **305**
London Watch Case Co **126**
Long, John & Co **264**
Long, John **264**
Longfield, Arthur Alabaster **51**
Longines Watch Co **21**
Longworth, Margaret **317**
Lorton, Thomas **95**, **415**, **465**
Lotheim, Moritz **320**
Lotheim, M & S **320**
Lotheim, Simon **320**
Lourenco, Jose Hermano de Netto **257**
Lovekin, Alfred **41**, **42**
Loveridge, Henry **465**
Lowden, John Frederick **249**
Lowe & Sons *120*, **142**, **263**, **265**
Lowe, Adrian **41**
Lowe, Alfred **45**
Lowe, Francis & Sons **149**
Lowe, Francis Sydney **149**
Lowe, George **172**
Lowe, George Bennett **265**
Lowe, George Cliff **163**
Lowe, George I **172**
Lowe, George I & II **172**
Lowe, G F **142**
Lowe, G F Mrs **168**
Lowe, George Frederick **168**
Lowe, Harold Ernest **149**
Lowe, Hugh Cawley **188**
Lowe, J Cecil **142**
Lowe, John **263**
Lowe, John & Thomas **225**, **229**
Lowe, John Ffoulkes **265**
Lowe, Margaret Joyce **265**
Lowe, Robert **358**
Lowe, Thomas **149**
Lucas & Co **299**
Lucas Brothers Ltd *44*, *135*, *188*, *196*, **298**
Lucas, B *400*
Lucas, B junior *400*
Lucas, Bertram Charles **91**
Lucas, Bertram Charles Busby **91**
Lucas, C *428*, *471*
Lucas, Charles **90**, **91**, *174*
Lucas, Charles & Co **91**, *243*
Lucas, Charles & Son **91**
Lucas, Charles Walter **91**
Lucas, John Goodwin **194**
Lucas, Norman **91**
Lucas, Richard **358**
Lucas, William **464**
Lucking, James **264**
Lucking, James & Co **264**
Lugg, A G & Co **33**
Lugg, Albert George **33**
Lugg, George Luke **33**
Lunn, J H **116**, **117**
Luxenberg, Victor **430**, **431**
Lyddiatt, Joseph **263**, **264**
Lyde, Harry **177**, **178**
Lyne, Frederick **149**
Lynglay, John **224**
Lynn & Aarons **297**
Lynn, Haggman **297**
Lyon, Edward **41**, **131**, **375**
Lyon, Edward & Co **131**
Lyon, Solomon **392**
Lyons, Claude Octavius Asher **432**
Lyons, S *313*
Lyons, Samuel **91**, **391**, **391**
Lyster, Charles & Son *28*, *76*, **91**, *198*, *272*, *362*
Lyster, Samuel **91**
Maas, Charles **92**
Maas, Charles & Co **92**, **93**
Maas, Charles Leopold **92**, **93**
Maas, Marcus **92**, **93**
MacCame, D **48**
MacConnell, Arthur John **188**, **189**
MacConnell, Robert Raynor **337**, **338**
MacDonald, Archibald William **54**
MacDonald, Catherine **93**
MacDonald, Charles Cumming **93**
MacDonald, Greta Margaret **173**
MacDonall, William Robertson **310**
MacDougall, Margaret White **322**
MacDowell, Mary Eveline **312**
MacGeoch, James Paul **272**
MacInerny, Thomas **416**
MacInnes, James **110**
MacKay & Chisholme **310**
MacKinder, Stanley D **393**
MacKinnon, Alice **299**
MacKenzie, Alfred Russell **100**
MacKenzie, Henry Arthur **394**
MacKenzie, John Alfred **234**, *259*
MacKenzie, Robert **132**
MacLaren, John **188**
MacLean, Dorothy **114**
MacLeod, Jean Agnes Gordon **38**
MacWilliam, James **384**
Maddock, Edward I **132**
Maddock, Edward II **131**
Maddock, Thomas **307**, **417**
Maddock, Walter Thorpe **318**
Maddock, William **466**, **467**
Magen Brothers **309**
Magen, Abraham Emanuel **31**, **309**
Magen, Pinkus **309**, **337**
Maginnis, A Gordon **318**
Maitland, Gordon & Co Ltd **173**
Makin, George **173**
Makin, George & Son **173**
Makin, Joseph **173**
Makins, William **384**
Makinson, Kathleen Irene **295**
Male & Jones **316**
Male, Frederick **316**
Mander, E & Son **132**, *244*
Mander, H & Co **204**
Mander, Henry **204**
Mander, Louis **202**
Mander, Lucy **303**
Mander, Richard **489**
Mander, Richard & Son **489**
Manger, John **267**
Manison, Bayliss & Co Ltd **309**
Manison, C & W **104**
Manison, Harry **203**
Manison, James **54**
Manison, Philip Henry **309**
Manison, Walter **104**
Manison, W E **54**
Mannox, Frank H **147**
Mannox, Thos Edward **408**
Mansell, George James **173**
Mansell, H *199*, **202**, *278*, *345*, *357*
Mansfield, Alfred **44**
Mansfield, Ethel Lilian **131**
Manson, John Richard **119**
Mantle, Frederick **266**, **267**
Mantle, John **267**
Mantle, J & Sons **267**
Mantle, J Stafford **267**
Mantle, John M **30**
Manton & Mole **317**
Manton, W *28*, *76*, *311*, *392*
Manton, Walter Louis **466**
Manton, William *445*, **467**
Manton, W R *357*
Mappin & Webb **318**
Mappin & Webb Ltd **318**, **321**, **322**
Mappin & Webb (1908) Ltd **318**
Mappin Brothers **309**
Mappin, Herbert Joseph **318**
Mappin, John Newton **318**
Mappin, Stanley Arthur **318**
Mappin, Walter Joseph **318**
March, T H & Co **413**
March, Thomas Harold **413**
Marcius, Albert **44**
Margrave, Bessie **66**
Margulis, William *121*
Marion & Co **311**, **318**
Marion & Co Ltd **311**
Marion, Leon **318**
Marks, Walter Henry **310**
Marlow & Co **311**
Marlow & Vaughton *136*, *204*, *216*, **321**
Marlow, Charles **92**
Marlow, Charles J H **89**
Marlow, James **268**, **321**
Marples & Beasley **307**
Marples & Co **311**
Marples, Edward Osborne **133**, **307**
Marples, Hadyn *366*
Marples, Robert Moffat **359**
Marran, N L **146**
Marran, W L **146**
Marrison, James **349**
Marsden, G **474**
Marsh & Co **311**
Marsh, E A Ltd **118**
Marsh, Edwin Alfred **118**
Marsh, Phyllis **337**
Marsh, Richard Charles **311**
Marsh, Robert **359**
Marsh, Thomas **417**
Marshall, George Robert **203**
Marshall, Gibson **66**
Marshall, H **203**
Marshall, Henry **203**
Marshall, John **266**
Marshall, Robert **359**
Marshall, Walter **417**
Marshall, Walter Henry **417**
Marson & Moseley **318**
Marson, F *28*, *76*, *197*, *198*, *346*
Marson, F & Co **151**
Marson, Frederick **150**, **151**, *199*
Marston & Bayliss *173*, **308**
Marston, Alfred **43**, **308**
Marston, Walter Starkey **475**
Martin Hall & Co *311*
Martin Hall & Co Ltd **359**, **350**
Martin, Abraham **43**
Martin, Alfred **44**
Martin, Ethel S **135**
Martin, F *334*
Martin, John **266**
Martin, Richard **359**
Martin, Thomas William **428**
Martinet, Nicholas **326**
Martin's Ltd **317**
Maryon, Herbert **203**
Mascall, Alfred George **33**
Mason, Alexander **43**
Mason, Arthur Joseph **43**
Mason, Claud **93**
Mason, George Hammond **170**
Mason, Howard Arthur **183**
Mason, James **267**
Mason, Jeremiah William **307**
Mason, J W & Co **307**
Mason, William John **461**
Massingham, F **310**, *455*
Massingham, William Alfred **310**, *311*, **329**, **424**, *455*
Masters, Julia M **92**
Masters, J N **270**
Mathey & Fils *375*
Mathews, Jessie **266**
Matthews & George **314**
Matthews, Henry **203**, **314**
Matthews, W **113**
Matthews, Walter Ernest **446**
Matthews, Walter George **446**
Matthews, W G *65*, *288*, **446**, **447**, *480*
Matthews, William **466**, **490**
Mattocks & Whitehead **321**
Mattocks, Henry & Co **202**
Max Brothers **310**
Maxfield & Son Ltd **320**
Maxfield, Alfred Ernest **359**
May, William Henry **456**
Mayell Brothers *227*, *297*, *299*, *331*, *378*, *435*, **464**
Mayell, N J **338**
Mayell, William **466**
Mayell, William James *337*
Mayell, William John **337**
Mayer -- *265*
Mayer Brothers *127*
Mayer, Joseph **265**, **266**, **307**

Mayer, Simon **394**
Mayers & Harrison Ltd **314**
Mayers, A **314**
Mayers, L **314**
Mayers, R **67**
McClelland & Duffus **310**
McClelland Brothers & Co **310**
McClelland, Hugh **310**
McClelland, John **310**
McCormack, John **266**, **411**
McGregor & Gardner **310**
McKnight, Emma **269**
McKnight, J *89*, *98*, **269**
McKnight, James **269**
McLardy, Samuel & Co **393**, **394**
McLaren, George **329**
Meak, Thomas **417**
Medley, Albert **151**
Meek, Irene **225**
Melhuish, Harry Laxton **201**
Melhuish, H L **201**
Mendel, William **348**
Mendelson, Solomon **393**
Mercer, K J **92**
Mercer, William **466**, **467**
Merle, Edgar L *84*, *92*, *157*, *183*
Merrey, H E **473**
Merrick, H **140**
Merrick, Richard George **352**
Merson, Thomas & Sons **414**
Merton, Harold M **204**
Metcalf, Augustine **43**
Metcalfe, Frederick **150**
Metherell, William **286**
Meyer Brothers *118*, **310**
Meyer, Arthur **43**
Meyer, Bertha **315**
Meyer, Henry **202**
Meyer, Henry Edward **202**, **203**
Meyer, J L Sons & Co **202**
Meyer, M H Ltd **315**
Meyer, Theodore **315**
Meyers, E & Co **311**
Meza, Nathaniel de **23**
Michael, C & Co *65*, **93**
Michael, Charles **93**
Michaels, Abraham **43**
Middleton, Charles Edw **82**
Middleton, John Richmond **181**
Middleton, Jn William Richmond **181**
Midland Chain & Mesh Co **310**
Mihill, Alfred **43**
Mikimoto, Kokichi **295**
Miles, Horace Alexander **276**
Millbourne, Robert **415**
Miller Brothers **309**
Miller Brothers London Ltd **309**
Miller, Alan Cecil **485**
Miller, Alfred William **456**
Miller, Ann **43**
Miller, Charles Dew **309**
Miller, E Irwin **439**
Miller, J **225**
Miller, John **266**
Miller, L R **456**
Miller, Richard William Bentley **309**
Miller, W C **309**
Miller, William Henry **456**
Millers (Jewellers) Ltd **456**
Millington, Ernest **131**
Mills & Gilpin *302*
Mills & Reynolds **319**
Mills, Edward John Sanders **287**
Mills, Francis **150**
Mills, Thomas **417**
Mills, W *41*, *45*, *157*, *287*, *315*, *289*, *400*, *444* ,*467*
Mills, William **466**
Milne, Ernest **369**
Mindel, Harry **202**
Minshall & Latimer *261*, *309*, **317**
Mitchell, Allan Thomas Smith **50**
Mitchell, Bosley & Co Ltd **308**
Mitchell, George Henry **488**
Mitchell, James **292**
Mitchell, S **145**
Mitchell, Thomas *381*
Mitcher, Mr **486**
Mocatta, B **302**
Mojon & Montandon **132**
Mold, John Kirby **295**
Mole, James Henry **317**
Mole, Wilfred Bernard **317**
Molyneux, Peter **337**
Monk, William **440**
Montal Watch Fittings Ltd **322**
Mooder, Andrew **43**
Moodie, Andrew **167**
Moore Brothers *41*, **308**
Moore Brothers & Co **309**
Moore Bros & Co (Jewellers) Ltd **309**
Moore, A *150*, *263*, *400*, *442*
Moore, Albert **42**
Moore, Alfred **43**
Moore, Alice Emma **43**
Moore, Arthur Charles **309**
Moore, Edward **308**
Moore, Frank **266**
Moore, J *87*
Moore, James **309**
Moore, J E **266**
Moore, John **266**
Moore, Joseph *154*, **266**, **267**
Mordan, F & Co **151**
Mordan, S & Co *241*,*270*, *350*, **394**, **395**
Mordan, Sampson & Co Ltd **395**
More, J W **295**
Moreland, Thomas **167**
Moreton, H *153*, *362*
Moreton, Henry **203**
Morgan, Bonner **66**
Morgan, Ethel **327**
Morrall, Thomas **417**
Morris, J *150*
Morris, James **240**
Morris, John Barrymore **238**
Morris, Lionel E **126**
Morrison, Edward **132**
Morrow, Richard **359**
Morrow, Thomas **417**
Morser, Harry **202**, **203**
Mortimer, John **267**
Morton & James **316**
Morton, Alfred J **348**, *434*
Morton, Ernest **416**
Morton, Joseph **225**
Mosley, Robert Frederick **29**
Moss, Florence Annie **413**
Moss, Frank **237**, **348**
Moss, Joan Barrington **238**
Moss, Lawrence **377**
Moss, Phyllis Joan **266**
Moss, W Henry **114**
Mott, C C **416**
Mott, Charles Arthur **416**
Mott, Thomas L Ltd **416**
Mott, Thomas Lynton **416**
Mottram, H **117**
Mottram, Sydney Will Royle **393**
Moule, Frederick **150**, **151**
Mozon & Co Ltd **311**
Muir & Son **320**
Muir, Henry **320**
Muir, James B **320**
Muir, John MacGregor **320**
Muir, R E **434**
Muir, T Mrs **434**
Muir, W A **434**
Muir, William M Ltd **434**
Mulholland, Jean Barbara **238**
Mulholland, Thomas Patrick Cunningham *238*, **419**
Mulland, Charles **321**
Muller, B & Son **66**
Muller, Berthold **66**
Muller, Berthold H **64**
Munos Ltd **317**
Munsey & Co **311**
Munsey & Co Ltd **311**
Murphy, Elizabeth **303**
Murray, John Charles **241**
Murray, Robert *103*
Murrell(Murrle), Ernest **308**
Murrle, Bennett & Co **308**, **309**
Murrle, Ernest **308**, **309**
Musker, H **383**
Mutton, William **19**
Myatt & Pullingne *34*, *243*
Myatt, George T **177**
Myatt, William James **462**
Myatt, William James & Co *67*, *68*, *244*, *280*, *286*, *385*, **462**, *471*
Myell Brothers *48*
Myer Brothers **81**, *236*, *447*
Myers Brothers **322**
Myers, Isaac **322**
Myers, John & Co Ltd **268**
Myers, Joseph **266**, **269**
Myers, Joseph & Son **269**
Myers, Reginald **269**
Myers, Walter & George **173**, **447**
Myerstone, Woolf **466**

Nalty, Edward Thomas **178**
Nalty, Herbert **178**
Nalty, Thomas Edward **178**
Napper & Davenport *245*
Narborough, Frederick **151**
Nathan & Davis **324**
Nathan & Hayes *115*, **173**, **174**, *301*, **325**, **352**, *374*
Nathan Brothers *270*, *297*, *298*, **323**
Nathan, Alfred Jerrold **39**
Nathan, Benjamin **67**
Nathan, Elias **132**
Nathan, Fanny **67**
Nathan, Frederick **323**
Nathan, G & G **169**
Nathan, George **173**, **174**, **325**, **352**
Nathan, Gordon Ellis **169**
Nathan, H & Co **204**
Nathan, Leonard **323**
Nathan, Reuben **323**
Nathan, Maurice **323**
Nathan, Walter **468**
Nathan, Walter & Brothers **468**
Naul, William **468**
Nayler Brothers **323**
Naylor, Robert Norman **360**
Neal, George **469**
Neal, George Arthur **469**
Neal, William **468**
Neal, W & G **469**
Neale & Freeman **324**
Neale, Arthur **468**, **469**
Neale, Harold 469
Neale, Harold Auguste **373**
Neale, James **270**, *473*
Neale, James **324**
Neale, Lewis Edwin *136*, *226*, *315*, *320*, *411*
Neale, Richard **360**
Neale, William *94*, **468**, **469**
Neale, William junior **469**
Neale, W & Son *449*
Neale, W & Sons *28*, *34*, *73*, *76*, *374*, *385*, *435*, *474*
Neale, Will & Son *29*, *42*, *329*, *370*
Neale, Will & Son Ltd *384*, **468**, **469**
Needham, Edward **133**
Needham, Edward & Co **133**
Needham, Robert **468**
Needham, Walter **467**, **468**
Neill, Sharman Dermott **115**, **116**
Neill, Sharman D Ltd **116**, **117**
Nelson, Ernest **369**
Nettleton, George Will' *172*, **180**, *261*
Netto Lourenco, Jose Hermano de **257**
Nevill, Charles **94**
Nevill, R *236*, *336*, **360**
Nevill, Richard *58*, *153*, *273*
Nevill, Richard Arthur **360**
Nevill, Walter Austin **360**
Neville, Frank **151**
Newbold, Alfred William **45**, *46*
Newbold, J G *39*, *54*, *55*, *113*, *200*, *202*, *210*, *297*, *329*, *394*, *396*, *406*, *407*, *477*
Newbold, James Geo *154*, **252**, *301*
Newbolt, Francis Geo **215**, **216**, **217**
Newcastle Handicrafts Co **325**
Newman, Arthur **204**
Newman, Benjamin **299**
Newman, James Thomas **283**
Newman, W H Ltd *393*, **457**
Newman, William Henry **457**
Newmark & Abrahams **323**
Newmark, Elizabeth **303**
Newmark, Louis **303**
Newmark, Louis Ltd **204**, **303**
Newsome, Isaac Jabez Theo **224**, **443**
Newsome, J **224**, **270**
Newton & Hyde **325**
Newton, A F **380**, **381**
Newton, Thomas **418**
Nicholas & Foye *189*, **324**, *350*
Nicholas & Hardy **325**
Nicholet, Charles **94**
Nicholls, Henry **204**
Nicholls, Henry J **199**
Nicholson, Charles Stanley **101**
Nicholson, Cuthbert Laws **91**
Nicholson, Richard Lavoisier **360**
Nicholson, Walter W 481
Nicol, Andrew **45**
Nieviaski, Samuel **396**
Nightingale, Edward **132**
Nightingale, Frank **418**
Nightingale, T *78*, *111*
Nightingale, Thomas *311*, **418**
Nightingale, T & Son **418**
Nimerzowsky, Barnett **398**
Nind-Wind, Percy **338**
Nix, Gerald Patrick **175**
Nixon & Son **247**
Nixon, T C **184**
Noble, A & Son **45**
Noble, Arthur jnr & snr **45**
Noblett, Lilian Dorning **317**
Nock & Sanders **327**
Nock, Henry B **327**
Noel, Alfred **45**, *126*, *136*
Noon, George Hewitt **170**
Noonan, Raymond Thornton **372**
Norris, Henry John **199**
Norris, Peter **338**
Norris, William **189**
North, Augusta **45**
Northern Goldsmiths Co **324**, **325**
Northern Goldsmiths & Silversmiths Co **324**
Norton, John Abraham **234**
Norton, William **468**
Noscoe, Robin John **356**
Notton, Sebastian **396**

Oakley, Edward James **128**, *189*
O'Boyle, Michael **319**
O'Boyle, Rose **319**
O'Donnell, Silvester Joseph **390**
Ogden, Frank **151**
O'Keefe, John **226**, **271**
Okell & Owen **329**
Okell, George **329**
Old, Ernest **378**
Old, F A **152**
Old, F A & Son **152**
Old, T **152**
Old, W E *378*
Oldridge, Sidney Thomas **180**, **181**
Oliver, Albert Thomas **50**, *356*
Oliver, James **270**
Oliver, Richard **361**
Oliver, Richard James **356**
Oliver, S W **320**
Oliver, William **469**
Ollivant & Botsford **329**
Ollivant & Botsford Ltd **328**
Ollivant & France **328**
Ollivant, John **225**
Ollivant, Thomas II **418**
Olney, Amsden & Sons **328**
Olney, Henry Thomas **328**
Oppenheimer, Seckel & Co **396**
Oppenheimer, Sina **396**
Orchard, Edward Steadman **396**
Orchard, Henry Pitman **206**
Orchard, Ruby **489**
Oritch, Alexander Hippolyte **484**
Orlik, Alfred **297**
Orlik, L & A **297**
Orlik, Louis **297**, **303**
Osborn, Thomas Edward *312*, **425**
Osborn, Thos Sam *136*, *146*, *151*, **425**
Osborn, T S *39*, *332*, *417*, **425**, *473*
Osborn, W Ltd **469**
Osborn, William **469**
Osborne & Bailey **328**
Osborne & Co **328**
Osborne, William T **477**
Oulton, George **351**
Outhwaite & Litherland **329**

Outhwaite, Thomas Oscar **329**
Outhwaite, Thomas Reynolds **329**
Over, Robert **361**
Over, Thomas **418**
Overan, James **270**
Owen & Robinson Ltd **329**
Owen, Richard Robert **329**
Owen, William **470**

Packer, Charles & Co Ltd **324, 325**
Packwood & Harris **335**
Packwood, David **335**
Padgett, C & W **104**
Padgett, Charles Willm **104**
Padgett, Walter John **104**
Page, E *217*
Page, Edwin *111*, **133**
Page, Peach M **338**
Pairman, John & Sons **273**
Pairman, Will, Watson **273**
Pallis, Andrea Pandea **45, 46**
Palmer, Albert E **205**
Pannett, T D & Son Ltd **418**
Parfitt, Walter **471**
Parke, Alfred **46**
Parke (s), R *22, 140, 216, 334*
Parke (s), R & Co *82*, **361**, *458*
Parker, Brian H *125*
Parker, Eustace George **125**
Parker, Eustace George Ltd **125**
Parker, Henry **67**
Parker, Oliver Llewellyn **303**
Parker, Richard *136, 169, 283, 288*
Parker, Richmond **361**
Parker, William **470**
Parkes, Francis Joseph **148**
Parkes, James G **465**
Parkes, James Gouldberg **465**
Parkes, R & Co (see also Parke) *28, 53, 78, 148, 180, 241, 416*
Parkin, Arthur **347**
Parkin, George **347**
Parkin, R A & Son **347**
Parkinson, Robert **361**
Parry, Gwen Enid **166**
Parry, William **470**
Pars, Ernest Henry **126**
Parsonage, John **271**
Parsons Ltd *95*
Parsons The Jewellers Ltd **336**
Parsons, Cyril G **336**
Parsons, F C *324*
Parsons, F C Ltd **142**
Parsons, L D **336**
Partington, Richard **361**
Partington, Richard Scott **371**
Pass, John **271**
Paterson, James **272**
Paterson, John & Son **272**
Patrick, C *334*
Patrick, Clarence **199**
Patrick, Harold J **199**
Patrick, Joseph Benjamin **293**
Patrick, Roy William **374**
Patrick, W B **199**
Pattenden, Richard *202*, **361**
Patterson, W E **442**
Patterson, W E & Co **442**
Paul, Joseph **487**
Payne, Arthur William **54, 55**
Payne, Ernest Walter **133, 138**
Payton, Francis William **152, 158**
Payton, Henry **339, 340**
Payton Pepper Ltd **339**
Payton Pepper & Co *67, 299*
Payton Pepper & Son Ltd *78, 116, 299*
Payton Pepper & Sons Ltd **339, 340**, *350*
Payton-Smith, B **278**
Peach Brothers **332**
Peach, Aubrey Charles **95**
Peach, C & Sons **95**, *342, 453*
Peach, Charles **94,95**
Peach, Chas & Son **95**, *311, 314, 368*
Peach, Charles & Sons Ltd *175*
Peach, Ernest William **332**
Peach, Frederick William **332**
Peacock, Mansfield & Britton **44**
Pearce & Co **342**
Pearce & Son **342**
Pearce & Sons Ltd **334**
Pearce & Thompson **342**
Pearce, Arthur **334**
Pearce, John **334, 342**
Pearce, John junior **334**
Pearce, T Arthur **342**
Pearce, William **342, 471**
Pearce, William Henry **457**
Pearsall, Samuel Ernest **98**
Pearse, Elford **476**
Pearson, A J & Sons Ltd **342**
Pearson, Albert Edward **158**
Pearson, Alfred E **342**
Pearson, F W & Co **158**
Pearson, H Ltd **206**
Peat, Duncan Dalziel **110**
Pedlingham, Bernard Albert **397**
Peel, Alfred **46**
Peers & Clarke **332**
Pellow, Will John *178, 216, 294, 299*
Pellow, W J Ltd *24, 81, 83, 84, 170, 183, 253, 258, 307, 365, 391*, **462, 463**
Pelsin, M G **238**
Pemberton, Benjamin I **69**
Pemberton, Peter **19, 333, 338, 339**
Pemberton, Thomas **333**
Pemberton, William **470**
Pembridge, R M **75**
Pembroke & Dickins **333**
Pendlebury, Arthur Percy **283**
Pendlebury, James Thomas **283**
Pendlebury, Jonathan **283**
Pendlebury, J T Ltd **283**
Pendleton, Ernest Thos **58, 342**
Pendleton, Lewis Willm **342**
Pendleton & Sons **341**
Pendleton, W & Sons **342**, *471*
Penlington & Hutton *26*, **335, 336**
Pennington, Arthur Willmore **54, 55**
Pennington, John **271**
Pennington, Thomas **418**
Pennington, William **470**
Pennlington, Joseph **271**
Pepper, A J **39, 211**
Pepper, A J Ltd **39**
Pepper, Payton & Co **339**
Perkin, John Marsden **328**
Perkins, Frank Trevor **155**
Perkins, G & Sons *28, 76*
Perkins, Henry *23, 188, 189*, **205**, *421*
Perkins, J M *328*
Perkins, William Burnett **436**
Perks, Charles John **89**
Perks, Edgar **341**
Perks, Marks **319**
Perks, Thomas & Co *416*
Perks, Thos & Son *331, 332*
Perks, Thos & Sons **341**, *416*
Permanent Enamel Co **333**
Perreau, Montague John Lt Col **269**
Perrin Watch Co Ltd **343**
Perry & Co **333**
Perry & Co Ltd **333**
Perry, Annie Louise **95**
Perry, C & Co *75, 95*
Perry, Bernard Leslie **68**
Perry, Christopher **95**, *374*
Perry, Harry Thomas **470**
Perry, W A Ltd **434**
Perry, William Arthur **95**
Peskin, Jacob **271**
Peters, G *188, 396*
Peters, George Albert **174**
Peters, James W **230, 289**
Peters, William Henry **470**
Petitpierre, Fritz **152**
Petterton, J P **185**
Pettinger, Albert Thomas **324**
Phelps Brothers **343**
Phelps, Alfred James **39**
Phelps, Benjamin *447*
Phelps, James **316**
Phelps, Stephen *57, 216*, **338**, *339*, **397**
Phillip, E Dixon **122**
Phillip, John **122**
Phillip, William Edmund **122**
Phillips & Mayell Ltd *215, 217*, **337, 338**
Phillips, Archibald **337, 368**
Phillips, Benjamin Samuel **152**
Phillips, C H **187**
Phillips, Francis **399**
Phillips, Joel **273**
Phillips, Percy **344**
Phillips, P S & Co Ltd **342**
Phillips, P & W *344*
Phillips, Samuel Henry **152, 205**
Phillips, Sir George Faudel **152**
Phillips, T *320*
Phillips, Wilfred **344**
Pickering & Briault **331**
Pickering, A & Co **46**, *386*
Pickering, Arthur **46**
Pickering, Fred **93**
Pickering, G E **328**
Pickering, Geo William **93, 331**
Pickering, Herbert Burton **469**
Pickett, D Mrs **273**
Pickett, G Miss **273**
Pickett, R E **273**
Pierce & Co *260*
Pierce, William Henry **457**
Pierrepoint, Thomas **418**
Pigot, John A **164**
Pike, R J *40, 75, 89, 112, 144, 199, 207, 234, 255, 351, 353*, **356, 357**, *443, 479*
Pillar, W J *76*
Pinces, Isaac **390**
Pinces, Saul **390**
Pinson, Lillian Mary **303**
Pipe, J Wil$^{m}$ **230**
Piper, William **311**
Pithey, Harold Vyvyan **212, 486, 487**
Pithey, H V & Co **212**, *385*, **486, 487**
Pitt, Oliver William **396**
Pitt, Samuel **396, 397**
Pitt, William **396**
Plant, Arthur Thomas **470**
Plant, Henry Griffin **170**
Plat, A G du **64**
Platinum Watch Case Co Ltd **344**
Platnauer & Co *265*
Platnauer Brothers **331**
Platnauer, Albert **45, 46**
Platnauer, G **174**
Platnauer, Gertrude **174**
Platnauer, Percy L **45**
Platnauer, Septimus Louis **174**
Player, William John **100**
Pleasance & Harper **336**
Pleasance & Harper Ltd **336**
Plimmer, Ernest Edward **350**
Plimpton, J C & Co **241**
Plimpton, John **241**
Plower, Johan Milton **269**
Plumb & Rigby **341**
Plumb, James **271, 341**
Plumb, John **271**
Plucknett, Chas John **89**
Plucknett, C J & Co *313*
Podolsky **27**
Pollard, George **174**
Pool, John Edward **247**
Pool, John Edwin **247**
Poole, Alfred Walter **152**
Poole, Maurice **319**
Poole, Thomas Gibson **410**
Poorten, William **470**
Pope & Phelps *48, 81, 259, 267, 302, 310, 357*, **338**, *475*
Pope, H *282*
Pope, Henry **204, 338**
Popham, B F **383**
Popley, W D **387**
Porter, Henry **439**
Porter, Nathaniel **439**
Portlock(Purlock), Henry **321, 322**
Posener, Adolph **46**
Posener, Adolph & Co **46**
Posnett, Doris Mary **114**
Poston, John **271**
Postons, J *157*
Pothecary, Isaac **226**
Potter, Charles Edward Farquar **82**
Potter, John Henry **257**
Pott Chapel **332**
Pott Shrigley **332**
Pound, John **272**
Pound, John & Co **272**
Pound, John Lulham **272**
Pound, Percy Herbert **272**
Powell, C & Co **95**
Powell, Charles **95**
Powell, Chas Henry **88**
Powell, Edward **133**
Powell, F **182**
Powell, Owen **329**
Power Brothers **133, 338**
Power, Edward **133**
Power, John **133**
Power, T & Son **338**
Powers, George **114, 115**
Powers, Thomas & Co **419**
Poyser & Privett **338**
Poyser & Rowland **341**
Poyser, Arthur **341**
Poyser, Arthur Wellesley **46, 338**
Pratt, Charles Harry **189**
Preedy, J & Co **272**
Preedy, John **272**
Prescott, J Mulleneux **319**
Prescott, Margaret **319**
Preston, Edward Carter **333**
Preston Ltd **337**
Preston, James **272**
Preston, Robert **361**
Price & Williams **344**
Price, James **344**
Price, Nancy Jones **325**
Price, Rimmel & Co **341**
Priestland, William **471**
Prime, Thomas & Son **419**
Prince, John **271**
Prince, Nathaniel Greenside **325**
Pringle, Edwin **363, 364, 365**
Pringle, James **363, 364, 365**
Pringle, R & Son *34*
Pringle, Robert **362, 363, 364, 365**
Pringle, Robert junior **362, 363**
Pringle, Robert & Co **362**
Pringle, Robert & Son **362, 364**
Pringle, Robert & Sons **362, 363**
Pringle, Robert & Sons (London) Ltd **362, 363, 365**
Pringle, W E **365**
Pringle, William **362, 363, 364, 365**
Pritchard, Henry **205**
Pritchard, Leonard **109**
Pritchard, Thomas **418**
Privett, Benjamin Alfred **338**
Proctor, John **271**
Proffitt, James Henry **257**
Promoli, Frederick William **158**
Pronczuk, Josef **272**
Pryatt, Sidney **396**
Pryde, John A **164**
Pugh, William **471**
Pulford, Alexander **484**
Pulley, James **395**
Pullinger, John S **280**
Purdon **343**
Purlock (Portlock), Henry **318, 321**
Purser, Cyril Robarts **273**
Purser, John & Sons **273**
Purser, J & Sons Ltd **273**
Pyke, Robert **361**
Pyke, R K see Pike

Quick, John Friar **222**
Quilley, Albert Stanley **345**
Quilley, Chas William **345**
Quilley, David **345, 365**
Quilley, David Henry **345**
Quilley Sons & Curtois **345**
Quilliam & Cooper **345**
Quilliam, Samuel *249*, **397**
Quilliam, Samuel & Son **345**

Rabone, Frank **27, 28, 36, 37, 444**
Rabone, Walter Hayes **27, 28, 36, 37**
Rabone, W H & F **36**, *63, 126, 204, 413*, **444**
Radcliffe & Pollard & Co *74*
Radges, Charles **96**
Radges, Joseph **275**
Randle, David **115**
Randle, James *112*, **274**
Randles, William **472, 473**
Rankin Brothers **348**
Rankin, William Cunningham **135**

Raphael, Nathaniel **467**
Rasburn, Wallace **471**
Ratcliff, Alexander Henry **36**, *290*
Rathausky, Leo **303**
Rathbone, Richard Llewelyn **358, 359**
Rattray & Co **350**
Raymond, J *400*
Rayner, A P **68**
Rayner, Horace Agencies Ltd **347**
Rayner, W A **68**
Raynor, H G **304, 347**
Raynor, Louis Ltd **304**
Read, Alfred Henry **36**
Read, Charles **96, 97**
Read, Samuel William **402**
Read, William **471**
Reader, George **175**, *459*
Reading & Lea **358**
Reading, N & Co **323**
Reading, Nathanel C **323, 324**
Reading, N C & Co **324**
Reading, Walter Francis **444**
Readman, David **115**
Reddish, Elizabeth **134**
Reddrop, William Harris **457**
Redfern, William **471**
Redgrove, William Raynsford **473**
Redman, Phillip Henry **68**
Redman, Richard **367**
Redmond, Richard **366**
Reed, George **175**
Reed, W & Co **472**
Reed, William **472**
Reed Williams, W Ltd **473**
Reeder, Madge **319**
Reeves & Herzberg *73*
Reeves, Charles **95, 96**
Reeves, H *259*
Reeves, Thomas **420**
Reeves, W *313*
Reeves, Walter **417**
Reeves, William **472**
Regal Watch Case Co **351, 373**
Reichenberg & Co **350**
Reichenberg, James **350**
Reid & Son **403**
Reid & Sons **369**
Reid, Christian Leopold **370, 403**
Reid, James **93**
Reid, Robert & Co **368**
Reid, Robert James **368**
Reid, Thomas Arthur **369, 403**
Reid, T B **121**
Reid, Walter Cecil **369**
Relf & Co **350**
Relf, Walter Richard **350**
Remfrey, Davies & Co *188, 189*
Rendell, Arthur George **34**
Restall, Norman **420**
Restall, Thomas *420*
Retchford, George Alfred *159*
Revell & Co **350**
Revell, A & Co *375*
Revell, Alfred Charles **350**
Revell, C & Co **97**
Revell, Charles **96, 97**
Revell, Charles Thomas **366**
Revell, C T & Co **366**
Rex, Arthur **47**
Reynolds & Westwood *244*, **372**
Reynolds, E **373**
Reynolds, Frank **472, 473**
Reynolds, Margaret **319**
Reynolds, Samuel John **372, 473**
Reynolds, William Bainbridge Ltd **436**
Rhodes, Anthony Joseph **234**
Rholeder, R *99*
Rice, James William **177**
Richard & Quilley **365**
Richard, A W **55**
Richard, Arthur William **365**
Richarde, Henry Chas **206**
Richards & Walsh **372**
Richards, George A **60**, *299*
Richards, Harry W E **187**
Richards, James **226**
Richards, John **226**, *233*, *419*
Richards, Joshua **274**
Richards, S **431**
Richardson, Chas James **89**
Richardson, James **275**
Richardson, James Francis **275**
Richardson, John jnr **487**
Richardson, Joseph John **211**
Richardson, R *71*
Richardson, Richard (Sheffield) **367**
Richardson, Rich I **354, 365**
Richardson, Richard II **366, 367**
Richardson, Richard III **368**
Richardson, Richard IV **366, 367, 368**
Richardson, William **354**
Richardson, William I **472**
Richardson, William II **367**
Richmond, Alfred Albert **47**
Richmond, W **472**
Richter & Gluck **319**
Riddle, J C **448**
Ridge, Jonathan **353**
Ridge, Joseph **274, 275**
Ridley, Brothers & Merton **348**
Ries, B H Ltd **64**
Rigby & Wilson **372**
Rigby, Henry **64**
Rigby, William **206, 341, 471**
Riheiro, Emmanuel **133**
Rimmel, Ralph **341**
Rink & Dalby *46, 249*, **350**
Rink, Arthur B **350**
Ritche, Alex **47**
Rixon, H *483*
Roberts & Belk Ltd *325*, **347**, *387*
Roberts, Charles **96**
Roberts, Dorothy *119*
Roberts, Evan **134**
Roberts, Frederick Gerrard **145**
Roberts, George **175**, *263*
Roberts, James **274**
Roberts, Philip William **344**
Roberts, Richard Pryce **365**
Roberts, T A *426*
Robertson, J B *63*
Robertson, John Bayton **238**
Robin, Charles **97**
Robinson & Co **350**
Robinson & Co Ltd **350**
Robinson & McKewan **359**
Robinson Brothers **348**
Robinson, Albert Edward **366**
Robinson, Alfred Ernest **370**
Robinson, Bernard **68**
Robinson, C *288, 455*
Robinson, E J *100*
Robinson, George **175**
Robinson, James Valentine **285**
Robinson, John Bayton **238**
Robinson, Joseph **274**
Robinson, Smith & Co **370**
Robinson, Thomas **361, 490**
Robinson, William **359**
Roden Brothers & Co **348**
Roden, Alfred George **348**
Roden, A & Son **47**
Roden, R C *174*
Rodime Manufacturing Co **359**
Roek & Dreyfus *270*, **351**
Roek, Charles **351**
Roek, Edward **351**
Rogers, Arthur **320**
Rogers, Arthur Guinness **33**
Rohleder, Robert **366**
Rolason Brothers **348, 349**
Rolason, John William **348, 349**
Rolason, Joseph Gilbert **348, 349**
Rollason, Albert Henry *36*
Rolex Watch Company **441**
Rome Watch Co **373**
Rooker, E J & Co **128**
Rooker, Elizabeth Jane **128**
Rooker, James **275**, *378*
Roost, H F **483**
Rose, Arthur Brian **391**
Rose, Benjamin **68**
Rose, Charles Edgar **82**
Rose, Gertrude Hercurla **391**
Rose, Henry **206**
Rose, Julian Stephen **391**
Rose, S J & Son **391**
Rose, Stephen J **390**
Rosen & Alexander **346**
Rosen, Simon **346**
Rosenberg, Louis **208**
Rosenberger, Edward **301**
Rosenthal & Co **227**
Rosenthal, Aronson & Co **346, 397**
Rosenthal, Bianca **342**
Rosenthal, Harold **342**
Rosenthal, Isidor **342**
Rosenthal, Israel **227**
Rosenthal, Joseph **274, 276**
Rosenweig, Nathan **306**
Roskell, William **471, 472**
Ross, Charles William **104**
Ross, Frederick James **148**
Ross, George Malcolm **148**
Ross, Herbert Frederick **148**
Ross, John **275**
Ross, J & Son **148**
Rossiter, George **175**
Rosson, William Henry *216, 218*, **457**
Roth, Isobell **226**
Rotherham & Son **368**
Rotherham & Sons **274, 369, 370**
Rotherham & Sons Ltd **369**
Rotherham & Sons (Coventry) Ltd **369**
Rotherham, Ewan **368, 369**
Rotherham, Hugh **368, 369**
Rotherham, John & Sons **274**
Rotherham, Kevitt **368, 369**
Rotherham, Richard Kevitt **357**
Rothery, Arthur William **55**
Rothschild, Frank Saul **154**
Rothschild, J **487**
Rothwell, Thomas Henry **413**
Round, John & Son Ltd **274**
Rowan, Frederick Charles **142**
Rowbotham, Charles **96, 97**
Rowbotham, Frederick Geo **145**
Rowbotham, G & Son **145**
Rowe, Henry **73**
Rowe, T C **353**
Rowell, Frederick Arthur **140**
Rowland & Kibble *433*
Rowland(s), A T & Son **369**
Rowland, Edward **134**
Rowland, Edward Daniel **134**
Rowland, John Henry *207*, **257, 258, 341, 357**, *390*
Rowlands, Geo' Thomas **177**
Rowlinson, Mary Howarth **488**
Rowles, Daniel **428**
Rudell Brothers **348**
Rudell, Leon Wilfred **348**
Ruden, Dorothy *359*
Ruden, George *359*
Rudge, E J *234, 413, 447, 468*
Rudge, Edwin Jas **128**, *248, 287, 335*
Rue, Thomas de la **407**
Rushbridges **142**
Rushworth & Co **350**
Rushworth, James **350**
Rushworth, Mary *326*
Rushworth, Nich **324, 325, 326, 350**
Rushworth, Nicholas & Co **326**, *413*
Russell Ltd **358**
Russell's Ltd **359, 421**
Russell & Co *444*
Russell, A & Co *44, 46, 297*
Russell, Alfred **420**
Russell, Bernard Alfred **256, 372, 421**
Russell, Fenton & Co Ltd **152**
Russell, Herbert George **194**
Russell, James Williamson **439**
Russell, Margaret Fulton **473**
Russell, Stanley **358**
Russell, Thomas **419, 420**
Russell, Tho & Son **372, 419, 420, 421**
Russell, Thomas Townsend **256, 372, 420, 421**
Russell, Walter **358**
Russell, William **472, 473**
Russell, William Barnes **435, 437**
Ryf & Marchands Ltd **366**
Ryf, M **343, 366**
Ryf, R **366**
Ryley, William **472**
Ryley, William Taylor **478**
Rymell, Frederick **152**

Sackville, W P **466**
Sacov, Benjamin **69**
Saddleton, William **459**
Salaman, Joseph Wolff **304**
Salaman, Levi **304**
Salaman, Lewis Henry **304**
Salisbury, Edward **134**
Salisbury, Thomas **423**
Salmon & Gluckstein **388**
Salmon & Gluckstein Ltd *52*
Salmon, Barnett **388**
Salmon, John Buxton **238, 399**
Sampson, Pauline Alwyne **341**
Samuel & Rogers **33, 34, 47,** *86, 96, 97, 224, 256,261,275,292,* **320,** *345, 385, 387,* **398**, *402, 419, 426*
Samuel, Edgar **207, 208**
Samuel, H **208**
Samuel, H Ltd **151, 208**
Samuel, Harriet **207, 208, 209**
Samuel, Jacob Lewis **227**
Samuel, Joseph Lewis **225, 265**
Samuel, Lewis & Co **304**
Samuel, Mary **320, 398**
Samuel, Mary Smith **319**
Samuel, Ralph **369, 370**
Samuel, Selim **398**
Samuel, Sylvester Lewis **393**
Samuel, T H Harvey **348**
Sanders & Co **286**
Sanders & Co Ltd **382, 383**
Sanders & MacKenzie **394**
Sanders, Alfred H **327**
Sanders, Ernest Wilfred **139, 176, 394**
Sanders, E W & Co **139**
Sanders, Lawrence **100**
Sanders, Sampson **397**
Sanders, Sidney **286, 289**
Sanford, Robert **375**
Sapiro, Harry **208**
Satchwell, John & Co Ltd **280**
Saunders & Shepherd *47*, **100**, *242, 416*
Saunders & Shepherd Co Ltd **100**
Saunders & Shepherd Ltd **100**
Saunders Brothers **379**
Saunders Brothers & Co **377, 378**
Saunders, Charles **99**
Saunders, Cornelius Desmormeaux **100**
Saunders, C P **100**
Saunders, John **377, 463**
Saunders, John Cooper **100**
Saunders, S & Co **400**
Saunders, Sidney **400**
Saunders, Walter James **377, 463**
Saunders, W & J **463**
Savage, Ethel Irene **127**
Saynor, John William **400**
Saynor, Scotland & Toft **400**
Scains, Eric Stanley **135**
Scales Brothers **376**
Scasebrick, John **227**
Schaefer, C **98**
Scherner, Gladys **176**
Schindler & Co **113**
Schlesinger, B **380, 381**
Schlesinger, S B & Co Ltd **380, 381**
Schneader, Alexander **48**
Schoder, Max **319**
Scholes, Ralph **368**
Schonberg, S Co *398*
Schonberg, S Ltd **398**
Schonberg, Solomon **398**
Schroepfer, P A **445**
Scheund, Leon & Co **305**
Schuler, Will Christian **440**
Schwarck, Theodore **389, 390**
Schwersee, Solomon Henry **389**
Schuler, Jacob Otto **270, 271**
Schulze, Susie Mathilde Charlotte **489**
Scotland, James **400**
Scott, Adolph **48, 49**
Scott, Adolph Ltd **48, 49**
Scott, D W **276**
Scott, Edward John **128**
Scott, John **257**
Scott, Thomas Alfred **191**
Scott, Walter William **276**
Seal, Mr **295**
Seckel, Louis **396**
Sedgwick, William **271**
Seeland, Frederick Francis *22*, **144**
Segal, Borris **375, 376**
Segal, Robinson **375, 376**
Segal, Ruben **368**
Segal, S & Co **400**

Segal, Solomon **400**
Selfe, Charles G **234**
Selfridge & Co **383**
Selfridge & Co Ltd *383*, **384**
Selfridge, Harry Gordon **383**, **384**
Semple, Raymond Peter **365**
Sermon, Rowland **101**
Sewell, John **98**
Sewell, John A **98**
Sewill, Joseph **278**, **279**
Sexton & Wickes **476**
Sexton, William *36*, *290*, *385*, *483*
Seymour, Charles Appleton **98**
Seyworth, J **280**
Shapland, Charles William **485**
Sharman D Neill Ltd **116**
Sharman, W *204*, *264*
Sharp, Paul **342**
Sharp, Paul & Co **342**
Sharpe & Green **387**
Sharpe, Joseph *70*, *153*, *224*, *270*, *275*, **278**, **279**, *414*, *472*
Sharples, Annie **48**
Shaw, Alfred Henry **48**
Shaw, William Thomas **407**
Sheald, George **210**
Sheen, Harry **209**
Sheen, Harry Leonard **207**
Sheffield Goldsmiths Co **387**
Sheldon Brothers **378**
Sheldon, Chas Thomas **378**
Sheldon, Henry **134**
Sheldon, William Samuel **378**
Shelland, John **350**
Shenton, George **48**
Shepherd, Francis **99**
Shepherd, James Francis Hollings **100**
Shepley, Thomas **292**
Sherrett, D & Co *228*
Sherwood, George **281**
Sherwood , John & Sons **281**
Sherwood, Wilfred **281**
Sherwood, William **281**
Shibko, Marks Barnett **310**
Shields, Robert **388**
Shindler, Joshua **208**
Shipton & Co Ltd **382**
Shipton, A G **382**
Shipton, F W **158**
Shipton, Sydney John **391**
Shoeps Brothers **379**
Shoeps, Henry **379**
Shoeps, Jacob **379**
Shoeratts, H **207**
Short, Martin **257**
Shure, Julius Louis **265**
Sibray Hall Co *348*
Sidebotham, Jessie **280**
Sigalov, Lewis **305**
Silber & Fleming **44**
Silver, Lewis **483**
Silvers, James Henry **258**
Silverston & Co **227**
Silverston, Isaac **227**
Silverston, Isaac & Co **227**
Silverston, John **279**
Simm, Alfred **47**
Simmons & Venour **401**
Simmons, Bernard Rintel **68**, **401**
Simmons, E & R **134**
Simmons, Ernest **134**
Simmons, Frederick **42**
Simmons, Isaac **227**
Simon & Strauss **210**
Simon, Vuillard & Strauss **210**
Simon, Henry **210**
Simon, Sigfried **310**, **398**
Simpson, Benzie **376**
Simpson, Ernest **134**
Simpson, Frederick **154**
Simpson, John **278**
Simpson, S I & Son **390**
Simpson, Samuel Isidore **390**
Sinauer, B **205**
Sinclair, Arthur C C **276**
Singleton & Cole **180**
Skelton, Percy John **415**
Skelton, Thomas James **414**, **415**
Skelton, T J *33*, *47*, *52*, *72*, *91*, *92*, *176*, *197*, *201*, *205*, *239*, *257*, *260*, *296*, *300*, *324*, *327*, *332*, *342*, *343*, *359*, **415**, *416*
Skelton, William James **176**, **463**
Skidmore, William **474**
Skinner, John **278**
Slade, Albert **149**
Slater, G R **448**, **449**
Slide, John G & Co *209*, **280**, *467*
Slide, John George **280**
Slingsby, Henry **210**
Slingsby, H & Son **210**
Sloan, James **358**, **421**
Slone, Patricia Dorothy **333**
Slyomovier, H **393**
Small, William Bromley **437**
Smalley, Thomas **423**
Smallwood, Charles **98**
Smallwood, C Ltd **101**
Smallwood, George *136*, *176*
Smallwood, G W **116**
Smart, Bertram Thomas **371**
Smart, Charles Edward **371**
Smart, R *137*
Smart, Richard **369**, **371**
Smart, R & Son **371**
Smawley Brothers **378**
Smawley, George Alfred **378**
Smawley, Gordon Ernest **378**
Smets, H S *435*
Smith & Bartlam **377**
Smith & Co *150*
Smith & Ewen (Aeroparts) Ltd *380*, **385**
Smith, Ewen & Stylic Ltd *24*, *59*, *83*, *187*, *188*, *208*, *256*, *369*, *384*, **385**, *401*, *486*, *466*, *483*
Smith & Pepper *126*, **396**, **397**
Smith & Pepper Ltd *83*, *84*
Smith & Salaman **399**
Smith & Stephenson **399**
Smith Brothers **376**, **378**
Smith, Ann **475**
Smith, Alfred John **40**, **304**
Smith, Arthur John **39**, *124*
Smith, Arthur Johnson **39**, **40**
Smith, C P **280**
Smith, Cyril Thomas **323**
Smith, E *78*
Smith, E C **42**
Smith, Edgar Harold **126**
Smith, Edward **134**
Smith, Edward Ernest **377**
Smith, Frederick Chas **142**
Smith, Frederick Hinde **378**
Smith, George **176**, **177**
Smith, George Alfred **399**
Smith, Harry Hinde **378**
Smith, Herbert **333**
Smith, J *216*
Smith, James Arkman **239**
Smith, J Martin **333**
Smith, John **280**, *339*
Smith, John Frank **189**
Smith, John William **289**
Smith, Joseph **71**
Smith, Joseph & Son Ltd *112*, **280**
Smith, Joseph & Sons *280*
Smith, Joseph & Sons (Birmingham) Ltd *24*, **278**, **279**, *315*
Smith, Josiah Timmis **191**
Smith, L **126**
Smith, L & Co *245*
Smith, Leonard **54**
Smith, Lionel **305**
Smith, Lionel & Co *62*, *113*, **305**, **407**
Smith, Lionel & Co Ltd **305**
Smith, Louis **399**
Smith, M P *160*
Smith, Norman **326**
Smith, Phyllis **323**
Smith, Phyllis Kerrison **336**
Smith, Salaman & Co *390*
Smith, Salmon & Co **399**
Smith, Samuel **399**
Smith, Samuel Walton **402**
Smith, S & Son **399**
Smith, Sidney **278**, **280**
Smith, S P **278**
Smith, T C *59*, *62*, *152*, *184*
Smith, Thomas **385**, **423**
Smith, Vincent C *470*
Smith, Walter F **351**, **385**, **395**, **444**
Smith, Willm **188**, **189**, **473**, **474**, **475**
Smith, William Albert **434**
Smith, William George **378**
Smithies, James **278**
Smollens & Mitchell **393**
Smollens, William **393**
Smylie, Hugh **116**
Snell, S & Co **399**
Snook, George **176**
Snook, George & Co **176**
Soloman, Charles **28**, **76**, **77**
Soloman, Chas Edward **82**, *112*, *114*
Solomon, Alfred **223**
Solomon, Lewis **131**
Solomon, M **319**
Sorley, R & W **371**, **374**
Sorley, William **371**, **374**
Sothers & Orchard **396**
Sothers, William George **396**
Souvenir Manufacturing Co Ltd **394**
Sovereign Supply Stores **400**
Spalding, William **418**
Sparrow, William Henry **457**
Speculand, David **115**
Speak, E & N *236*
Speakman, Arthur Polycarp **422**, **423**
Spelman, Rich'd Whately Raynold **368**
Spence, Margaret Clara **311**
Spenceland Brothers Ltd **377**
Spenceland, J H **377**
Spencer & Co **369**
Spencer, A H **173**
Spencer, Willm Jos *76*, *207*, *317*, **463**
Spicer, Gilbert Harry **343**
Spicer, P & Son *343*
Spicer, Peter **343**
Spicer, William Sydney **343**
Spiers, D & L **113**, *169*, **203**, *245*, *350*, *447*, *450*
Spiers, Henry **370**
Spiers, Henry Charles **189**
Spiers, Isaac **280**
Spiers, John **280**
Spiers, John & Co **280**
Spiers, Lionel **51**, **149**, **203**
Spiers, R & Co **370**
Spikins, William Charles **440**
Spink & Son **225**, **226**
Spink, Chas Frederick **225**, **226**
Spink, John Marshall **225**, **226**
Spink, Samuel Martin **225**, **226**
Spiro, Henry **208**
Spiro, Maurice **320**, **350**
Sproston, G H **463**
Spurrier, John Walter **289**
Squire, Stanley Brimsmead **89**
Stacey, G **176**
Stainsby & Coupland *203*, *216*, *275*, *318*, **371**
Stainsby, Richard **371**
Stainton Brothers *184*, *293*, *461*
Stallard, W E **442**
Stanger, Hermann **261**
Stanger, J J **261**
Stanley (Fancy Goods) Ltd **392**
Stapleton, Benjamin **70**
Stauffer, Son & Co **94**
Stebbings, Robert **370**
Steel, Wilfred **476**
Steele & Dolphin *363*, **384**
Steele, Elliot **384**
Steele, William **374**
Steely, William Henry **16**
Stein, Barnett **49**
Steiner, Leon **70**, **304**
Steines, G W **383**
Steingold, Nathan **327**
Steinhart & Co **383**
Steinhart, Siefried Emil **383**
Stell, J H & Co **259**
Stell, John Henry **259**
Stephens & Myddleton *108*
Stephenson & Son **399**
Stephenson, Gordon **399**
Stephenson, H G **399**
Stephenson, H M **399**
Stephenson, V G **399**
Stevens, W A *264*
Stevens, Will'm Edward **443**
Stevenson, William Lennie **490**
Stewart, Amy Eleanor **32**
Stewart, Edna Mrs **134**
Stewart, Harold David **190**
Stewart, Henry J **208**, **209**
Stewart, Kenneth **296**
Stewart, Tom **422**, **423**
Steyerman, Max **319**
Stiffin, W G *396*
Stillwell, E Digby **135**
Stillwell, Edward Willm **139**
Stillwell, Edward & Son **139**
Stillwell, Edward & Son Ltd **135**
Stirk, C **57**
Stockwell & Co Ltd **177**
Stockwell, George **177**
Stoker, H *294*
Stokes & Ireland *25*, *29*, **37**, *110*, *116*, *135*, *148*, *185*, *210*, *225*, *285*, *289*, *295*, *309*, *313*, *334*, *342*, *374*, *376*, **389**, **390**, *442*, *474*, *483*, *489*
Stokes & Ireland Ltd *214*, *410*, *483*
Stokes, Henry **209**
Stokes, William Henry **389**
Stoll, George Arnold **16**
Stollsteimer, Max **319**
Stone Brothers (Jewellers) Ltd **377**
Stone, A *377*
Stone, Frank *444*
Stone, Frederick **155**
Stone, John **278**
Stone, Robert Edgar **351**
Strauss, Maurice **210**
Struminger, Morris **209**
Stovell, John **289**
Stovell, J & W **289**
Stovell, William **289**
Stuart & Kirkman **130**
Stuart, H **279**
Stuart, H & Co **279**
Stuart, Henry **209**
Stuart, John **209**, **279**
Stubbs, Frank **248**, **249**
Stubbs, J F & F **248**, **249**
Stubbs, James Frederick **248**, **249**, **279**
Stubbs, Lillian Molyneux **303**
Styles, Joseph Gray **252**
Stylic Manufacturing Co *72*, *338*, *457*
Stylic Manufacturing Co Ltd **395**
Stylic Watch Case Co Ltd *53*, *375*, **444**
Subenberg, Hyman **207**
Suckling Ltd **60**, **392**
Suckling, Joseph **392**
Suckling, William **392**
Sudlow, John **280**
Summers, Isaac **227**
Summers, Oliver Ellington **328**
Sumner, Evelyn **134**
Sumner, Peggy **341**
Sussex Goldsmiths & Silversmiths Co Ltd **387**
Suter, George Alfred **176**
Sutherland Brown & Co **377**
Sutherland, David Preston **377**
Sutherland, James **377**
Sutherland, James Mackintosh **28**
Sutter, I E *379*
Sutter, John **280**
Sutters, J E *321*, *322*
Sutton, G W **463**
Sutton, Joseph Edward **247**
Sutton, Robert **368**
Sutton, T E *414*
Sutton, William Josiah **463**
Sutton, W J Ltd **463**
Swain, Herbert J **68**
Swallow, Law **305**
Swan & Edgar Ltd **385**
Swan Brothers **379**
Swan(n), James **278**
Swan, Sydney Bartlett **379**
Swann, Walter **473**
Swansbrook, William **474**
Swiss Agency **375**
Sydenham Brothers **378**
Sydenham Brothers Ltd **378**
Sydenham, Albert **48**, **49**
Sydenham, George **378**
Sydenham, Robert **378**
Sydenham, William **378**
Sydnercombe, H C **317**
Sydney & Co **382**, **383**
Sydney Brothers *243*, *383*
Symelman, Louis **304**
Symonds, H **394**

Symonds, Harry Lambert **395**
Synyer & Beddoes *318*, **376**
Synyer, Harry **376**

Tabberner, George Turner **177**
Talbot, J R **277**
Talbot, J R Ltd **277**
Tandy & Rudge *61*, *81*
Tandy & Son **423**, **458**
Tandy, George **423**
Tandy, Harry George **423**, **424**, **458**
Tandy, Henry George **423**, **424**
Tandy, Ronald Hickman **424**
Tandy, W H & Sons *62*, *122*, *172*, *315*, **422**, **423**, **424**, *467*, *480*
Tandy, William **423**
Tandy, William Harry **423**, **424**
Tandy, William Steward **423**, **424**, **458**
Tanner, C E **180**
Tanner, E **180**
Tanner, J A **180**
Tarleton, Henry **210**
Tarleton, Richard **371**
Tate, Broadhurst & Lees **201**
Tate, George Arthur **159**
Tate, William Alfred **476**, **477**
Tatler, Edward **135**
Tattershall, Henry *180*, **211**
Taylor & Hancock *293*, **412**
Taylor Brothers **405**
Taylor -- **403**
Taylor, Alfred Richard **47**
Taylor, A & Son *50*
Taylor, Alfred William **55**
Taylor, Andrew & Son **50**
Taylor, Beatrice **71**
Taylor, Charles **50**, **101**, **142**
Taylor, David **117**
Taylor, Dora Margaret **114**
Taylor, Fred **142**, **154**
Taylor, George **177**
Taylor, George & Co **177**
Taylor, Harry Langley **259**
Taylor, Herbert Henry **90**
Taylor, J *197*, **227**
Taylor, James **281**
Taylor, J & H *66*, **259**
Taylor, John **227**, **281**
Taylor, John Oliver **259**
Taylor, Joseph **281**
Taylor, Joseph Hayes **259**
Taylor, Montgomery **405**
Taylor, Roland James **257**
Taylor, Ruth **371**
Taylor, Thomas Arthur **405**
Taylor, T M **417**
Taylor, T M & Son **417**
Taylor, Walter Howard Gamlies **455**, **460**
Taylor, William Henry **457**
Taylor, William Thomas Price **341**
Tayson, Henry Alfred **183**
Tayton, J *209*, *286*
Tayton, John Gaskin & Sons **281**
Telfer, John & Sons **284**
Telford & Speakman **422**
Telford, James **421**, **422**
Templer, James Walter **289**, **290**
Templer, J W & Co **290**
Templeton, Frank **155**
Tennant, F *145*, **155**
Tennant, F Ltd **155**
Tennant, Sheila **400**
Terry, Frank Urquart **444**
Terry, H & Co **211**
Terry, W & F **444**
Terry, William **444**
Tetter, Joseph **227**
Themans & Co **320**, *321*
Themans, Henry **320**, **321**
Themans, Marcus **320**, **321**
Thomas & Marshall **417**
Thomas, Francis John Horace **211**
Thomas, Henry Sidney **210**
Thomas, Horace **417**
Thomas, Joseph **211**
Thomas, Lewis **305**
Thomas, S W **343**, **366**
Thomason & Haseler Bros *371*, **413**
Thomason, J *115*
Thomason, John & Nephews **211**
Thomason, Will' Edwin **211**
Thompson & Brook **404**
Thompson, Albert **67**, **68**
Thompson, Alfred **431**
Thompson, Arthur James **71**
Thompson, Doris May **114**
Thompson, Henry **211**
Thompson, Henry Graham **284**
Thompson, J & Son **284**
Thompson, John jnr **284**
Thompson, John snr **284**
Thompson, Richd Edwin **351**
Thompson, Walter Horace **457**
Thorne, Alfred Albert **405**
Thorne, Herbert Fred **328**
Thornley, George William **474**
Thorneywork, A & F **32**
Thorneywork, Arthur **32**, **50**
Thorneywork, Fred **32**
Thorneywork, W **476**
Thorneywork, William **476**
Thornley, Edith **136**
Thornton, James **282**, **488**
Thorpe & Clark **405**
Thyne, Christian **101**
Tickell, Walter **477**
Tidy & Blanchard **404**
Tidy, George **404**
Tierney, J M Ltd **270**
Tierney, James Michael **270**
Tillinghast, Stephen **400**
Timmins, Albert **50**
Tindley, W H Ltd **57**
Tinings, F C **123**
Tiptaft, Hilda **327**
Tiptaft, James Walter **290**
Tiptaft, Norman **327**
Tiptaft, Norman Ltd **327**
Titterington, Doris **117**
Tobias, Morris **410**
Tobias, Myer I **315**
Tobin, John O'Hara **271**
Todd, Joseph Fergus **249**
Todd, Richard **130**
Toft, William **400**
Toghill, William Thomas **406**
Toghill, W T & Co **406**
Tolhurst, Brownfield **290**
Tolhurst, George **290**
Tolhurst, Walter Crellin **477**
Tolman, Thomas C *263*, **407**
Tomlin, Agnes **484**
Tompkins & Jackson **414**
Tompkins, S **295**
Tompkins, Tom **414**
Tongue & Walker **427**
Tongue, A H *20*, *47*, *59*, *117*, *118*, *122*, *185*, *188*, *202*, *209*, *236*, *237*, *313*, *353*, *388*, *396*, *400*, *488*, *433*
Tongue, Arthur Charles **427**
Tongue, Frank **130**
Tongue, H *205*
Tongue, Henry **211**
Toole, Walter **477**
Towns, Joseph **281**
Tozer, A H **415**
Tozer, Edward **415**
Tozer, H **415**
Tozer, Kernsley & Fisher Ltd **415**
Trahern, Alfred Wickes **155**
Trahern, Frederick **54**, **155**
Trahern, Fred Thos *314*, 355, 403, *485*
Trahern, F T & Sons **155**
Trahern, Frederick William **155**
Trahern, Thomas **425**
Travers Kessel & Co **415**
Travers, Arthur A **415**
Travers, G W **427**
Travis, Wilson & Co Ltd **427**
Tree, Stephen **400**
Trevine & Gilpin *197*
Trevitt, Alfred Wallace **422**
Trevitt, Charles James **421**, **442**
Trevitt, E J & Sons *76*, *90*, *125*, **421**, **422**
Trevitt, Enoch James **129**, **421**, **422**
Trevitt, K L **422**
Tropp, Harry **229**
Tropp, I & Son **229**
Tropp, Isaac **229**
Troup & Ford **409**
Troup, Fred' William **282**, **284**
Troup, J & Sons **284**
Troup, John & Sons **282**, **283**, **284**
Truman, Edward **136**
Tucker, Will'm Edward **215**, **216**, **217**
Tudor-Thomas, Neville James **327**
Turnbull Brothers **405**
Turnbull, Joseph Edward **405**
Turnbull, W F **405**
Turnbull, William Foster **405**
Turner & Somers **423**
Turner Brothers **405**
Turner, C E *100*, *242*, *244*
Turner, Charles Edward **405**
Turner, Charles Edwin **82**
Turner, Dollie **117**
Turner, Frank **155**
Turner, Frederick Russell **477**
Turner, Harold **477**
Turner, Harold Stewart **423**
Turner, Henry **242**
Turner, Richard **371**
Turner, S W **405**
Turner, W *243*
Turner, William **477**
Turner, William & Co **477**
Turner, William Glacier **477**
Turton, Emily Irene **127**
Turton, Frederick W **158**
Turton, F W & Co *244*
Turton, F W Ltd *243*
Turton, George Frederick **168**
Turton, William **477**
Tushingham, Thomas **425**
Tweedale, Thomas **425**
Twemlow, John **228**, **281**
Twemlow, William **477**
Twine & Gilpin *78*, *147*, *169*, *284*, *284*, **409**, **444**
Twine, W F *94*, *216*, *375*, **409**, **444**
Twiss, Joan **281**
Twist, Theodor **202**
Tyldesley, Frank **155**
Tyrer, Francis Robert **155**
Tyrrell, Henry Edgar **292**
Tyson, Robert J **292**

Ullman, Louis **393**
Ullman, S & L **393**
Underwood, Harold Archer **183**
Unite, George **178**
Unite, George & Sons **177**, *214*
Unite, William **478**
Upcott, Wm George **321**
Upton, William J **78**
Usher Ltd **401**
Usher Manufacturing Co **101**
Usher, Charles **101**
Usher, Frank Edward **401**
Usher, G E **401**
Usher, Gustavus William **401**
Usher, James & Sons **284**
Usher, James Ward **284**
Usher, John Mark **401**
Usher, Reuben **101**
Usher, Reuben Percival **101**
Usher, S *268*, *280*, *294*, *446*
Usher, Samuel **400**, **401**
Usher, Samuel Ltd **401**
Usher, S Ltd *84*, *336*
Usherwood, C J **453**
Ustonson, C B **259**

Vale Brothers & Sermon **101**, *260*, **430**
Vale, Howlette & Carr **430**
Vale & Company **430**
Vale & Howlette **430**
Vale & Rotherham **431**
Vale & Simmons *276*
Vale & Sons *81*
Vale, Charles **101**, *309*, **430**
Vale, Henry **101**
Vale, Thomas Henry **478**
Vale, W & Sons *76*, *178*, *244*, **478**
Vale, William & Son **478**
Van Andelest Fiolet **407**
Vander, Alfred **212**
Vander, C J **212**
Vander, Henry **212**
Vann, James **111**
Vann, J R **112**
Vaughton, Edward *22*, *44*, *49*, *100*, **136**, *152*, *175*, *275*, *276*, *292*, *334*, *346*, *370*, *443*, *467*
Vaughton, Ernest Vernon **321**
Veitch, Henry Newton **487**
Venour, Frederick jnr **156**
Venour, Henry Edward **191**, **401**
Venour, Frederick & Son **156**
Vernon, Alfred **50**
Vernon, L A **273**
Vertex Watch Co **432**
Vicars, Isaac **229**
Vicars, John **229**
Vickers, Isaac **229**
Vickers, Peter Julian **336**
Vickery, John Collard **241**, **242**
Vigers, Herbert **302**
Villiers & Jackson *61*, *169*, *183*, *282*, *309*, **430**
Vince, William Henry **457**
Vincent, John **285**
Vine & Thompson **431**
Vine, George Henry Weston **431**
Viner, A **136**
Viners Ltd **136**
Vollhardt, Chas John **385**
Vose, Henry **212**

Wacaron, L A **170**
Wachenheimer, E G **322**
Wachenheimer, M **222**
Wachenheimer, M & Co Ltd **322**
Waddington, Robert **372**
Wade, B **72**, *152*, *179*, *234*, *239*, *248*, *256*, *303*, *357*, *421*, *442*, *456*, *470*, *477*
Wade, Benjamin **72**
Wade, Benjamin Ltd **72**
Wade, C *423*
Wade, Edwin **72**
Wade, Eliza **72**
Wade, Herbert **72**
Wade, Margaret **72**
Wade, R *356*
Wade, Samuel **401**
Wagstaff, Frederick **156**
Wain, Archibald Leslie **299**
Wainwright, Harry **213**
Waite, Frederick **318**
Waithman, Edward **137**
Wake, Philip Kenyon **359**
Wakefield, George Frederick **168**
Wakefield, Richard John *22*, *32*, *117*, *222*, **357**, *425*, *427*
Wakefield, Ralph **372**
Wakely & Walker **479**
Wakely, James **287**
Waldren & Cheshire **438**
Waldren, George **438**, **439**
Wales & McCullock **189**
Wales, Henry Charles **189**
Walker & Hall **448**, **449**, **450**
Walker & Hall Ltd **448**, **449**
Walker, Amelia **102**
Walker, Arthur James **40**
Walker, C **102**, *201*, *207*, *442*, *464*
Walker, Charles **103**
Walker, Chas Burton **103**
Walker, Christopher **102**, **103**
Walker, Edwin James **129**
Walker, Ernest Alfred **290**, **477**
Walker, George Arthur **427**
Walker, George Fred'ick **168**
Walker, George I **179**
Walker, George II **179**
Walker, Guy **290**
Walker, Henry **213**
Walker, Jas *103*, *261*, **285**, **286**, **289**, *332*
Walker, John **230**, **285**
Walker, James Ltd **242**
Walker, Ralph **372**, **373**
Walker, Ralph Stanley **390**
Walker, Sydney **440**
Walker, Thomas **425**, **426**
Walker, W *21*, *33*, *41*, *46*, *48*, *59*, *89*, *152*, *189*, *200*, *205*, *207*, *219*, *269*, *235*, *292*, *297*, *301*, *306*, *341*, *355*, *386*, *396*, *399*, *406*, *407*, *413*, *463*, *472*
Walker, Walter Crellin **480**

Walker, William **478**, **479**
Walker, William P **214**
Walker-Litherland, C Ltd **103**, *180*
Wall, Arthur **51**, **53**
Wall, J **458**
Wallace, J Wilson **241**
Wallbridge & Co **439**
Wallbridge, Walter **479**
Wallen, Thomas **426**
Waller, Charles **105**
Waller, Charles & Son **105**
Waller, Frederick John **105**
Walley & Jones **286**, **459**
Walley, Joseph **229**, **230**, **286**
Walley, Ralph **373**
Wallis, Brian Mills **213**
Wallis, Frances Mary **151**
Wallis, Frederick **190**, **191**
Wallis, Hugh **213**
Wallis, Raymond Marriage **360**
Wallis, William Bernard **438**
Walmsby, Ethel Joan **129**
Walsh, Francis Charles John **142**
Walsh, Harold Augustus **183**
Walsh, Thomas **217**, **218**
Walter, Amy Coral **30**
Walter, Carl **103**
Walter, Harold **215**
Walter, Harold & Co **215**
Walter, William Harrison **458**
Walters, F & Co **158**
Walters, Peter **343**, **344**
Waltham Watch Co **144**
Walton & Co **167**
Walton, Bertram **72**
Wal*/ton, G E & Co Ltd *199*
Walton, G E Ltd *43*, *74*, *126*
Walton, George Edwin **167**
Walton, Joseph **286**
Walton, Walter Discombe **182**
Waplington, John Alfred Charles **233**
Warburton, Cynthia Hazel **88**
Ward & Francis **443**
Ward Brothers *147*, *362*, *363*, **437**
Ward Brothers (Birmingham) Ltd **122**, *295*, **437**
Ward, A & Son **55**
Ward, Albert E **50**
Ward, Alfred **52**, **103**, **443**
Ward, Alice Audrey **20**
Ward, Arthur Vincent **50**
Ward, B *306*
Ward, Charles Augusta (us) **437**
Ward, Charles John **357**
Ward, Edgar Ernest **122**
Ward, Frederick Walter **156**, **475**
Ward, G **179**
Ward, George **179**
Ward, G G **437**
Ward, J **55**
Ward, John **201**, *298*, *304*
Ward, John Barron **305**, **306**
Ward, John Horace **259**
Ward, L **437**
Ward, Leonard **299**
Ward, Richard Joseph **357**
Ward, S & Son *383*
Ward, Samuel & Son **401**
Ward, Samuel Herbert **475**
Ward, Samuel Robert **437**, **475**
Ward, S R & Son *289*, *390*
Ward, S R & Sons **475**
Ward, Thomas Walton **357**
Ward, William Goodman **194**
Warden & Aitken **433**
Warden, Florence **157**
Warmingshaw, Richard *373*
Warmsley & Son **474**
Warmsley, M L **474**
Warren, Anthony Arthur **21**
Warrington, John **285**
Warstone Manufacturing Co **467**
Wartski, C H **88**
Wartski, Henry **88**
Washington, Richard **372**
Wasserberg, Isidor **229**
Wasty, L P **138**
Watches Ltd **466**
Waterfall & Gravenor **55**
Waterfall, Albert **52**, **55**
Waters, Mark **297**
Waterson, Allan **180**
Waterson, George & Son Ltd **180**
Wathew, John F **222**
Watkins, D T **161**
Watkins, R H **161**
Watson, Charles **54**
Watson, Chas Edward **82**
Watson, Edith **137**
Watson, James Taylor Niven **212**, **213**
Watson, J W **290**
Watson, Stanley **304**
Watson, Thomas Jones **415**
Watts & Rumball Ltd **121**
Watts, Albert John **40**
Watts, Arthur **51**, **434**
Watts, George **179**
Watts, George & Co **179**
Watts, James Daniel **37**
Watts, William **478**
Wayell, Horatio **213**
Wayne Hart Co **448**
Weale, Charles **102**
Webb, John Christopher **342**
Webb, Frederick & Walter **158**
Webb, Thomas **426**
Webb, Vera **432**
Webster, Henry Conyers **486**
Wedge, Ernest William **306**
Weddell, Andrew **52**
Weedon, A F **174**
Weetman, J E *93*, **247**
Weill & Harburg **451**
Weill, Louis **306**, **451**
Weinberg, Israel Victor **229**
Weiner, Ferdinand **156**
Weir, George T **117**
Weir, J & Sons **289**
Weir, James Arthur **289**
Weir, John Hunt **289**
Weir, T F **116**, **117**
Weiss, Fritz **56**
Weiss, Ignatz **229**
Weiss, Leopold **306**
Welch & Banks **435**
Welch, Frederick Albert **142**, **143**
Welch, Frederick Charles **143**
Wellby, David & John **117**
Wells, Arthur **259**
Wells, Charles **103**
Wells, Edward Charles Victor **33**
Wells, Henry **212**, **214**
Wells, George *119*
Welsford, G T C **413**
Welsh, F A **140**
Welsh (Liverpool), F A **140**
Welshman, Robert **373**
Welton, Thomas Abercrombie **215**, **216**, **217**
Wengold Brothers **437**
Wengold, B M **437**
Wengold, S H **437**
West, Annie Ethel **32**
West, Ann Mavis **45**
West, Cecil L'Estrange **474**
West, Langley Archer **474**
West, Lincoln **474**
West & Son **474**
Westman, John Eli **247**
Weston, Dorothy **117**
Weston, Joseph **71**
Weston, Robert **481**
Weston, W *78*, *212*
Weston, W & Son *79*, **481**
Weston, W & Son Ltd **481**
Weston, W & Sons *456*
Weston, W H **458**
Weston, William **78**, **79**, **479**
Westwood & Sons *243*
Westwood, Alfred Henry **86**, **105**
Westwood, Arthur Hamil **212**
Westwood, C & Son **105**
Westwood, Charles **86**
Westwood, Charles William *65*
Westwood, Francis Herbert **86**, **105**
Westwood, George Frederick **372**
Westwood, William Walker **105**
Wetherell, William **382**, **400**
Wettenberg, E *386*
Wheatley, Amos **51**
Wheeler, Frank Clark **287**
Wheeler, James **285**
Wheeler, Thomas **426**, **427**
Wheldon, John Potter **273**
Whelpdale, Arthur **100**
Whilter, J *213*
Whirrett, George **178**
Whitacker, E *186*
White & Co **439**
White & Hawkins **88**, **451**
White & Reynolds **472**
White, C H **88**
White, Charles **429**
White, Cuthbert George **473**
White, Ebenezar **137**
White, George **179**
White, James Henry **473**
White, James Thomas **284**
White, Joseph **285**
White, Matthew Will'm **322**
White, Redgrove & Whyte **473**
White, Samuel Hillyard **389**
White, William A **472**
White, William Alfred **472**
Whitehouse & Cox *439*
Whitehouse, A E B **138**
Whitehouse, Albert **61**, **138**, **139**
Whitehouse, Bernard **71**
Whitehouse, Cedric Harold **104**
Whitehouse, Cox & Co Ltd **439**
Whitehouse, E *44*, *47*, *58*, *284*, *310*
Whitehouse, E & Son *72*, *84*, *105*, *112*, **138**, *206*, *223*, *228*, *284*, *390*, *411*, *415*, *454*
Whitehouse, E & Son Ltd **138**
Whitehouse, Edwin **61**, **137**, **139**
Whitehouse, Edwin & Sons *83*, **139**
Whitehouse, Eric **72**
Whitehouse, Frank **138**
Whitehouse, George Lowe **179**
Whitehouse, R H **138**
Whiteman, William Philip **471**
Whitfield, George & Co **180**
Whittaker & Son **475**
Whittaker, Ethel **137**
Whittaker, John Thomas **475**
Whittaker, Rich Healey **353**
Whittaker, Thomas **475**
Whitten, Joseph **285**
Whittem, Christopher & Co **103**
Wick, Frederick **157**
Wickes & Trahern **54**
Wickes, Alfred **51**, **54**
Wickes, Thomas **476**
Wickes, William **478**, **479**
Wickhorn, A M **373**
Widdowson, John **229**
Widdup, Kenneth Noel **295**
Widmer, C & Co *109*
Widmer, C & Sons *44*, **105**, *203*
Widmer, Gabriel **285**
Widmer, James **178**
Widowson, James **229**
Wigley & Hall *22*, *49*, *79*, **90**, **448**, **451**, *486*
Wigley, Alfred **52**
Wigley, Charles John **90**, **448**, **451**
Wigley, Charles John & Son **90**
Wigley, Ernest **52**
Wigley, Leslie **90**
Wigley, Thomas John Howell **469**
Wilcox, A *43*, **51**, *135*, *441*, *459*
Wilcox, Alfred **50**, **52**, *238*
Wilcox, H **272**
Wilcox, Harold Wright **322**
Wilcox, Matthew & Son **322**
Wilday, E *272*
Wilday, Edward **137**
Wilday, Frank **156**
Wilday, Joseph Samuel **281**
Wilde, Frank Howard **147**
Wilde, Jane Mrs **488**
Wilde, Myra **321**
Wilkes, Charles **103**
Wilkins, Frederick **156**, **157**
Wilkins, Harry **311**, **359**
Wilkins, Harry Josiah *288*
Wilkins, Henry **360**
Wilkins, Richard Samuel **371**
Wilkinson, Arthur **485**
Wilkinson, Grace Monica **173**
Wilkinson, S F **478**
Wilkinson, Stanley Frank **480**
Wilkinson, W **480**
Wilkinson, William **478**
Wilkinson, William Ltd **478**
Willey, William **333**
Williams Ltd **479**
Williams & Franks *199*
Williams (Bham) Ltd **436**
Williams, Daniel Richard **115**
Williams, Edith Lilian **131**
Williams, George Henry *77*, **179**
Williams, R *353*
Williams, Richard Owen **329**, **330**
Williams, R Owen **329**, **330**
Williams, R Owen Ltd **330**
Williams, Robert Owen **372**, **421**
Williams, Samuel **344**
Williams, Samuel Roger **398**
Williams, Sidney **253**
Williams, S R & Co *343*, *379*, **398**
Williams, W Reed **473**
Williams, W Reed Ltd **473**
Williams, W Reed (1908) Ltd **473**
Williams, William **479**
Williamson & Co **439**
Williamson, Alfred **216**
Williamson, Charles Herbert **215**, **216**, **217**
Williamson, H & Co *294*
Williamson, H Ltd **215**, **216**, **217**, **457**
Williamson, Henry **212**, **213**, **214**, **215**, **216**, **217**, *249*
Williamson, Henry Ltd **215**, **216**, **217**, **457**
Williamson, Thomas **425**
Willin, Thomas Willis **428**
Willington, Dorothy **117**
Willis, Thomas & Co **427**
Wilmot Manufacturing Co **467**
Wilmot, Edward D & Son **122**
Wilmot, H E **458**
Wilmot, John Paul **467**
Wilmot, W H Ltd **458**
Wilsdorf & Davis **441**
Wilsdorf, W **441**
Wilson Brothers **437**, *477*
Wilson, A *135*
Wilson, A W *272*
Wilson, Norman F **295**
Wilson, Richard William **399**
Wilson, Robert **35**, **36**
Wilson, Thomas **427**
Wilson, Thomas William **437**
Wilson, William Rex **473**
Wincer & Plant **470**
Wincer, Walter Thomas **470**
Windle, James H **260**
Windridge, J *220*
Windridge, James **286**
Winegarten **401**
Winegarten, Simon **401**
Wing, George **179**
Wingate, W & Johnson Ltd **480**
Wingrove, W & Co Ltd **480**
Winterbottom, J **312**
Winwood & Asprey **433**
Winwood, Frederick **433**
Wise & Howard **452**
Wise, Hayam George **452**
Withecomb, Thos Robert **421**
Witten Patent Pipe Co Ltd **440**
Wittenberg & Bateson *371*, **435**
Wittenberg, Max Ehrigott Aaron **321**, **435**, **439**, **440**
Wittenberg, M E & Co *356*
Wittenburg & Co **439**, **440**
Witting, Arthur **51**
Woef, Herbert **192**
Woffenden & Turner **477**
Wolfe Brothers **437**
Wolffe Brothers **435**, **470**
Wood Brothers **437**
Wood, Albert **52**
Wood, Edward Albert **118**
Wood, Henry **214**, **437**
Wood, John James **262**
Wood, Montague **302**
Woodcock, Ernest **136**, **310**
Woodhouse, James **286**
Woodman & Son *366*
Woodman, John **286**
Woodroffe, Fredrick Arthur **140**

Woodroffe, Joseph **286**
Woods, W H J Ltd **456**
Woodward, James **317**
Woodward, Joseph **286**
Woodward, Thos Hall **414**
Woodwood, Horace Co *242*
Wood Workers Co, The **428**
Wooley, Harold **434**
Wooley, John **285**
Wooley, W A **434**
Wooley, Walter Albert **434**, **435**
Woolf, Morris **321**
Woolfield, Thomas **425**, **426**
Woolfson, Philip **118**, **343**
Woolley, Harold Victor **212**
Woolley, Thomas **426**
Woolnough, Thomas **426**
Woolston, Harold E **315**
Woosnam, Catherine Evelyn **82**
Wootton, Samuel George **286**
Wordley, James **285**
Workall, J H *362*
World Watch Co Ltd **480**
Worrall, Edgar **29**
Worrall, Herbert O **422**
Worrall, William **29**
Wortley, A J **40**
Wrench, John **285**
Wrench, William **479**
Wrenerberger & Parry **470**
Wrenerberger, Ferdinand **470**
Wright & Griffiths **445**
Wright & Hadgkiss *412*, **452**, **456**, *460*
Wright & Hadgkiss Ltd **346**
Wright & Perry *238*, *288*, *316*
Wright, Annie **51**
Wright, Arthur **50**, **51**, **52**
Wright, Ernest Robert **137**
Wright, E W **311**
Wright, F *89*, *104*, **156**, *266*
Wright, Francis Harry **445**
Wright, Frederick **156**
Wright, George Fred'ick **168**
Wright, Harold Coleman **470**
Wright, Henry Robert **452**, **456**
Wright, Joan Mrs **285**
Wright, Joseph **421**
Wright, Lott John **302**
Wright, Maurice **321**
Wright, Noah **327**
Wright, R & R **372**
Wright, Thomas Weston **425**
Wright, W Ltd **480**
Wrighton, Charles **94**
Wrighton, Charles Morris *24*, **93**, **94**, *111*, *299*
Wrighton, C M Ltd **94**
Wrighton, Ernest **137**, **138**
Wrighton, Frank **94**
Wyatt, Barbara Margaret **67**
Wyatt, W J *212*
Wyatt, Lewis **305**
Wyke, John & Green, Thomas **230**
Wynn, J H *118*, *249*, *280*, *312*, *319*, *343*, *376*, *389*, *428*
Wynn, J H Ltd *428*
Wynn, John Henry *136*, *241*, **259**, **260**
Wynn, William **156**, **479**
Wythe, Richard **372**

Yale, James **291**
Yandell, William **481**
Yardley & Buckland *209*, **374**
Yardley, Alfred **55**
Yardley, Henry **218**
Yardley, John **291**
Yardley, Joseph **291**
Yardley, Richard **374**
Yardley, William Henry **458**
Yateman, William **481**
Yates, Edward Dootson **291**
Yates, James **291**
Yates, James & Son **291**
Yates, Thomas **290**
Yeomans, Charles H **402**
Yeomans, Frederick S **402**
Yeomans, George W **402**
Yeomans, Samuel **402**
Yeomans, Thos Edward **482**
Yerburg, Sydney Percy **481**
Yerburg, Walter Henry **481**
Yerburg, W H & Son **481**
Yewdall, Albert **55**
Yorke-Radleigh, James Richard **278**
Yorkshire Stick Co, The **482**
Young, Frederick **158**
Young, G H **218**
Young, Oliver **330**
Young, William Henry **458**

Zehetmayr, Ferdinand **60**
Zenith Watch Co (Great Britain) **483**
Zeving, J *291*
Zeving, Samuel *291*
Zimmerman, A & J *245*
Zimmerman, L W **306**
Zinkin, Abraham **483**
Zoltsberg, Zisman **483**
Zyto, Sigmund **402**